June 26–30, 2017
Cambridge, MA, USA

Association for Computing Machinery

Advancing Computing as a Science & Profession

EC'17

Proceedings of the 2017 ACM Conference on Economics and Computation

Sponsored by:

ACM SIGecom

Supported by:

Facebook, Google, Microsoft, MIT, and MIT CSAIL

Association for
Computing Machinery

Advancing Computing as a Science & Profession

The Association for Computing Machinery
2 Penn Plaza, Suite 701
New York, New York 10121-0701

ISBN: 978-1-4503-4527-9 (Digital)

ISBN: 978-1-4503-5599-5 (Print)

Additional copies may be ordered prepaid from:

ACM Order Department
PO Box 30777
New York, NY 10087-0777, USA

Phone: 1-800-342-6626 (USA and Canada)
+1-212-626-0500 (Global)
Fax: +1-212-944-1318
E-mail: acmhelp@acm.org
Hours of Operation: 8:30 am – 4:30 pm ET

EC 2017 Foreword

The papers in these Proceedings were presented at the Eighteenth ACM Conference on Economics and Computation (EC'17), held between June 26 and 30, 2017, at MIT in Cambridge, Massachusetts, USA. Since 1999 the ACM Special Interest Group on Electronic Commerce (SIGecom) has sponsored EC, the leading scientific conference on advances in theory, systems, and applications at the interface of economics and computation, including applications to electronic commerce.

The program committee has selected 75 papers from among 257 submissions that were received by February 13, 2017. Paper submissions were invited in the following three non-exclusive focus areas:

- TF: Theory and Foundations
- AI: Artificial Intelligence and Applied Game Theory
- EEA: Experimental, Empirical, and Applications

The call for papers attracted 257 distinct submissions. Each paper was reviewed by at least three program committee members and two senior program committee members on the basis of significance, scientific novelty, technical quality, readability, and relevance to the conference. Following the tradition of recent iterations of the conference, the authors were asked to align their submission with one or two of the tracks. The next table summarizes the number of submissions and the number of accepted papers for each possible combination of tracks.

Tracks	Submissions	Accepted
TF	161	52
AI	34	9
TF+AI	26	7
EEA	18	4
TF+EEA	15	2
AI+EEA	3	1
Total	**257**	**75**

Out of the 75 accepted papers, 35 papers are published in these Proceedings. For the remaining 40 papers, at the authors' request, only abstracts are included along with pointers to full working papers that the authors guarantee to be reliable for at least two years. This option accommodates the practices of fields outside of computer science in which conference publishing can preclude journal publishing. We expect that many of the papers in these Proceedings will appear in a more polished and complete form in scientific journals in the future.

Papers were presented in two parallel sessions, with the exception of a plenary session with talks for the following award-winners:

- *SIGecom Best Paper Award: Combinatorial Cost Sharing,* by Shahar Dobzinski and Shahar Ovadia
- *SIGecom Doctoral Dissertation Award,* by Peng Shi

A separate *SIGecom Best Paper with a Student Lead Author Award* was not given as the *SIGecom Best Paper Award* was given to a paper that has a student lead author.

To emphasize commonalities among the problems studied at EC, and to facilitate interchange at the conference, sessions were organized by topic rather than by focus area, and no indication of a paper's focus area(s) was given at the conference or appears in these proceedings.

EC'17 featured the following invited plenary talks:

- *Graphons: A Nonparametric Method to Model, Estimate, and Design Algorithms for Massive Networks*, by Jennifer Chayes (Microsoft Research)
- *Fair Algorithms for Machine Learning*, by Michael Kearns (University of Pennsylvania)
- *ACM SIGecom Test of Time Award: Truth Revelation in Approximately Efficient Combinatorial Auctions*, by Daniel Lehmann, Liadan Ita O'Callaghan and Yoav Shoham (ACM EC 1999, Journal of the ACM 2002)

In addition to the main technical program, EC'17 also featured four workshops:

- *The 3rd Workshop on Algorithmic Game Theory and Data Science.* Organizers: Jean Honorio, Denis Nekipelov, Renato Paes Leme, Yaron Singer, Vasilis Syrgkanis, and Elie Tamer
- *Workshop on Mechanism Design for Social Good.* Organizers: Rediet Abebe and Kira Goldner
- *The 12th Workshop on the Economics of Networks, Systems and Computation (NetEcon).* PC Chairs: Vincent Conitzer and Roche Guerin
- *Forecasting Workshop.* Organizers: Rafael Frongillo, David Rothschild, and Bo Waggoner

five tutorials:

- *Advances in Game Theory for Security and Privacy*, presented by Bo An, Fei Fang, and Yevgeniy Vorobeychik
- *An information Theoretical View of Information Elicitation Mechanisms*, presented by Yuqing Kong and Grant Schoenebeck
- *Bargaining, Trading, and Coordination in Networks: Theory and Challenges*, presented by Benjamin Golub
- *Incentivizing and Coordinating Exploration*, presented by Robert Kleinberg and Aleksandrs Slivkins
- *Pricing in Combinatorial Markets: Equilibria and Prophet Inequalities*, presented by Michal Feldman and Brendan Lucier

as well as a poster session in which 30 posters were presented.

We thank the Workshop Chairs, Shuchi Chawla and Jenn Wortman Vaughan, and Tutorial Chairs, Edith Elkind and Katrina Ligett, for putting together the workshop and tutorial programs. We also thank the Posters Session Chair Yannai Gonczarowski for organizing the poster session.

We hope that you find this conference program interesting and thought provoking and that the conference provides you with a valuable opportunity to share ideas with other researchers from institutions around the world.

We are very grateful to the SIGecom chair Kevin Leyton-Brown, for all his help in organizing the conference. We thank Brendan Lucier for serving as the Local Arrangements Chair and the Treasurer of the conference. We thank Rebecca Yadegar for providing administrative support. We thank Anne-Marie King for the conference website maintenance. We are grateful to Thomas Preuss and David Shield for their constant support with the confmaster software and the review process. We thank Simina Brânzei for her help with the review system testing and Yannai Gonczarowski for his extensive help with the review process automation. We thank Lisa Tolles for her professional work in the production of the conference proceedings. We are very grateful to MIT and CSAIL for hosting the conference and to Microsoft for hosting the conference dinner. We are also very grateful to our sponsors: Facebook, Google, Microsoft Research, and SIGecom.

We owe big thanks to a large number of members of the community (listed on a separate page) who assisted the committee in assessing the merits of the submissions. Last, but not least, we wish to thank the Program Committee and the Senior Program Committee members for their wisdom and devotion and for their hard work throughout the process.

Moshe Babaioff
EC'17 Program Chair
Microsoft Research, Israel

Hervé Moulin
EC'17 Program Chair
University of Glasgow, UK

Constantinos Daskalakis
EC'17 General Chair
MIT, USA

Table of Contents

Session 2b: Predictions and Queries

Session 3a: Dynamic Revenue Maximization 1

Session 3b: Economic Equilibrium

Session 4a: Matching 2

Session 4b: Voting

Session 5a: Static Revenue Maximization 2

Session 5b: Information Games

Session 7b: Experiments

Session 8a: Mechanism Design – General

Session 8b: Decision Making and Learning

Session 9a: Auctions – Equilibrium

EC 2017 Conference Organization

General Chair: Constantinos Daskalakis, Massachusetts Institute of Technology, USA

Program Chairs: Moshe Babaioff, Microsoft Research, Israel
Hervé Moulin, University of Glasgow, UK

Workshop Chairs: Shuchi Chawla, University of Wisconsin-Madison, USA
Jenn Wortman Vaughan, Microsoft Research, USA

Tutorial Chairs: Edith Elkind, University of Oxford, UK
Katrina Ligett, Caltech and Hebrew University, USA & Israel

Local Arrangement Chair: Brendan Lucier, Microsoft Research, USA

Poster Session Chair: Yannai A. Gonczarowski, Hebrew University of Jerusalem and Microsoft Research, Israel

SIGecom Executive Committee: Kevin Leyton-Brown, University of British Columbia, Canada
Michal Feldman, Tel Aviv University, Israel
Jennifer Wortman Vaughan, Microsoft Research, USA

Webmasters: Constantinos Daskalakis, Massachusetts Institute of Technology, USA
Ann Marie King, Harvard University, USA
Brendan Lucier, Microsoft, USA

Senior Program Committees

Theory & Foundations SPC:
Maria-Florina Balcan, Carnegie Mellon University, USA
Liad Blumrosen, Hebrew University, Israel
Shuchi Chawla, University of Wisconsin-Madison, USA
Avinatan Hassidim, Bar-Ilan University, Israel
Nicole Immorlica, Microsoft Research, USA
Anna Karlin, University of Washington, USA
David Kempe, University of Southern California, USA
Robert Kleinberg, Cornell University, USA
Fuhito Kojima, Stanford University, USA
Scott Kominers, Harvard University, USA
Stefano Leonardi, Sapienza University of Rome, Italy
Katrina Ligett, Caltech and Hebrew University, USA & Israel
Yishay Mansour, Tel Aviv University, Israel
Vahab Mirrokni, Google Research, USA
Noam Nisan, Hebrew University, Israel
Tim Roughgarden, Stanford University, USA
Ilya Segal, Stanford University, USA
Uzi Segal, Boston College, USA
Aleksandrs Slivkins, Microsoft Research, USA
Eva Tardos, Cornell University, USA
Bernhard von Stengel, London School of Economics, UK
Matt Weinberg, Princeton University, USA
Glen Weyl, Microsoft Research, USA

Artificial Intelligence and Applied Game Theory SPC:
Felix Brandt, Technical University of Munich, Germany
Vincent Conitzer, Duke University, USA
Gabrielle Demange , Paris School of Economics, France
David Easley, Cornell University, USA
Federico Echenique, California Institute of Technology, USA
Edith Elkind, University of Oxford, UK
Ian Kash, Microsoft Research, USA
David Pennock, Microsoft Research, USA
Ariel Procaccia, Carnegie Mellon University, USA

Experimental, Empirical and Applications SPC: Eric Budish, University of Chicago, USA
Larry Blume, Cornell University, USA
Denis Nekipelov, University of Virginia, USA
Vasilis Syrgkanis, Microsoft Research, USA
Siddharth Suri, Microsoft Research, USA
John Wooders, New York University Abu Dhabi, UAE
Georgios Zervas, Boston University, USA

Program Committee: Saeed Alaei, Google, USA
Ashton Anderson, Microsoft Research, USA
Elliot Anshelevich, RPI, USA
Nick Arnosti, Columbia University, USA
Itai Ashlagi, Stanford University, USA
Yossi Azar, Tel Aviv University, Israel
Eduardo Azevedo, Wharton, USA
Haris Aziz, Data61 and UNSW, Australia
Yakov Babichenko, Technion, Israel
Matthew Backus, Columbia University, USA
Ashwinkumar Badanidiyuru, Google, USA
Sid Banerjee, Cornell University, USA
Siddharth Barman, IISc, India
Umang Bhaskar, Tata Institute of Fundamental Research, India
Peter Biro, Institute of Economics, Hungarian Academy of Sciences, Hungary
Francis Bloch, Paris School of Economics, France
Aaron Bodoh-Creed, University of California, Berkeley, USA
Gary Bolton, University of Texas at Dallas, USA
Simina Branzei, Hebrew University of Jerusalem, Israel
Benjamin Brooks, University of Chicago, USA
Ceren Budak, University of Michigan, USA
Yang Cai, McGill University, Canada
Ioannis Caragiannis, University of Patras, Greece
Ruggiero Cavallo, Yahoo Research, USA
Jing Chen, Stony Brook University, USA
Giorgos Christodoulou, University of Liverpool, USA
Richard Cole, NYU, USA
Rachel Cummings, California Institute of Technology, USA
Bart de Keijzer, CWI Amsterdam, Netherlands
Tommaso Denti, Princeton, USA

Program Committee (continued):

Nikhil R Devanur, Microsoft Research, USA
John P. Dickerson, University of Maryland, USA
Shahar Dobzinski, Weizmann, Israel
Laura Doval, Cowles Foundation for Research in Economics and CalTech, USA
Paul Duetting, London School of Economics, UK
Umut Dur, NCSU, USA
Piotr Dworczak, Stanford Graduate School of Business, USA
Dean Eckles, Massachusetts Institute of Technology, USA
Piotr Faliszewski, AGH University, Poland
Fei Fang, Harvard University, USA
Michal Feldman, Tel-Aviv University & Microsoft Research, USA
Amos Fiat, Tel Aviv University, Israel
Felix Fischer, University of Glasgow, UK
Michele Flammini, University of L'Aquila and Gran Sasso Science Institute, Italy
Tamas Fleiner, Budapest University of Technology and Economics & Eotvos Lorand, University, Hungary
Rafael Frongillo, University of Colorado Boulder, USA
Hu Fu, University of British Columbia, Canada
Martin Gairing, University of Liverpool, UK
Vasilis Gkatzelis, Drexel University, USA
Ashish Goel, Stanford University, USA
Renato Gomes, Toulouse School of Economics and CNRS, France
Yannai A. Gonczarowski, Hebrew University of Jerusalem & Microsoft Research, Israel
Simon Grant, Australian National University, Australia
Nick Gravin, Shanghai University of Finance and Economics and Massachusetts Institute of Technology, China & USA
Ben Greiner, Wirtschaftsuniversitaet Wien, Austria
Mingyu Guo, University of Adelaide, Australia
Nima Haghpanah, Penn State University, USA
Jason Hartline, Northwestern University, USA
John W Hatfield, University of Texas at Austin, USA
Chien-Ju Ho, Cornell University, USA
Martin Hoefer, Goethe-University, Germany
John Horton, NYU, USA
Zhiyi Huang, The University of Hong Kong, Hong Kong
Patrick Hummel, Google, USA

Program Committee (continued):

Krishnamurthy Iyer, Cornell University, USA
Sergei Izmalkov, NES, Russia
Albert Xin Jiang, Trinity University, USA
Ramesh Johari, Stanford University, USA
Yash Kanoria, Columbia Business School, USA
Thomas Kesselheim, Max-Planck-Institut fuer Informatik, Germany
Nicolas Lambert, Stanford University, USA
Laurent Lamy, CIRED - ENPC and Ecole Nationale des Ponts et Chaussees, France
Jerome Lang, CNRS, France
Brad Larsen, Stanford University, USA
Kate Larson, University of Waterloo, Canada
Ron Lavi, Technion, Israel
SangMok Lee, University of Pennsylvania, Economics, USA
Annie Liang, Microsoft Research New England, USA
Ben Lubin, Boston University, USA
Brendan Lucier, Microsoft, USA
Troels B. Lund, IT University of Copenhagen, Denmark
Mohammad Mahdian, Google, USA
Azarakhsh Malekian, University of Toronto, USA
Andrew Mao, Microsoft Research NYC, USA
Evangelos Markakis, Athens University of Economics and Business, Greece
Ruta Mehta, University of Illinois at Urbana-Champaign, USA
Reshef Meir, Technion, Israel Institute of Technology, Israel
Claudio Mezzetti, University of Queensland & University of Warwick, Australia and UK
Joshua Mollner, Northwestern Kellogg School of Management, USA
Jamie Morgenstern, Carnegie Mellon University & University of Pennsylvania, USA
Thayer Morrill, North Carolina State University, USA
Hamid Nazerzadeh, USC Marshall School of Business, USA
Thanh Nguyen, Purdue, USA
Evdokia Nikolova, UT Austin, USA
Sigal Oren, Ben-Gurion University of the Negev, Israel
Renato Paes Leme, Google Research, USA
Alexander Peysakhovich, Facebook, USA
Georgios Piliouras, Singapore University of Technology & Design, Singapore

Program Committee (continued):

Marek Pycia, University of California, Los Angeles, USA
Justin Rao, Microsoft Research, USA
Assaf Romm, Hebrew University, Israel
Aaron Roth, University of Pennsylvania, USA
Aviad Rubinstein, University of California, Berkeley, USA
Daniela Saban, Stanford University, USA
Kato Saito, Caltech, USA
Rahul Savani, University of Liverpool, UK
Guido Schaefer, CWI and VU University Amsterdam, Netherlands
Grant R Schoenebeck, University of Michigan, USA
Jay Sethuraman, Columbia University, USA
Sven Seuken, University of Zurich, Switzerland
Nisarg Shah, Harvard University and University of Toronto, USA & Canada
Peng Shi, Microsoft Research, USA
Yaron Singer, Harvard University, USA
Balasubramanian Sivan, Google Research, USA
Rann Smorodinsky, Technion, Israel
Chaitanya Swamy, University of Waterloo, Canada
Steven Tadelis, University of California, Berkeley, USA
Inbal Talgam-Cohen, Hebrew University, USA
Pingzhong Tang, IIIS, Tsinghua University, China
Peter Troyan, University of Virginia, USA
Christos Tzamos, Massachusetts Institute of Technology, USA
Matt Van Essen, University of Alabama, USA
Shai Vardi, California Institute of Technology, USA
Adrian Vetta, McGill University, Canada
Zihe Wang, Shanghai University of Finance and Economics, China
Michael Wellman, University of Michigan, USA
Alexander Westkamp, University of Cologne, Germany
Chris Wilkens, Yahoo, USA
James R. Wright, Microsoft Research, USA
Lirong Xia, RPI, USA
Andy Zapechelnyuk, University of Glasgow, UK
Yair Zick, National University of Singapore, Singapore

Additional reviewers: Lia Bozarth, University of Michigan, USA
Gianluca Brero, University of Zurich, Switzerland
Erik Brinkman, University of Michigan, USA
Niv Buchbinder, Tel Aviv University, Israel
Hau Chan, Trinity University, USA
Frank Cheng, University of Michigan, USA
Ashish Chiplunkar, Tel Aviv University, Israel
Gal Cohensius, Technion, Israel
Riccardo Colini-Baldeschi, LUISS, Italy
Agnes Cseh, Hungarian Academy of Sciences, Hungary
Argyrios Deligkas, Technion, Israel
Ludwig Dierks, University of Zurich, Switzerland
Alon Eden, Tel Aviv University
Tomer Ezra, Tel Aviv University
Ark Fangzhou Zhang, University of Michigan, USA
Rupert Freeman, Duke University, USA
Ophir Friedler, Tel Aviv University, Israel
Jiayang Gao, Cornell University, USA
Negin Golrezaei, University of Southern California, USA
Ben Golub, Harvard University, USA
Artur Gorokh, Cornell University, USA
Ronald de Haan, TU Vienna, Australia
Nika Haghtalab, Carnegie Mellon University, USA
Hoda Heidari, University of Pennsylvania, USA
Zsuzsanna Jankó, Corvinus University of Budapest, Hungary
Hossein Karkeabadi, Stanford University, USA
Pieter Kleer, Centrum Wiskunde & Informatica (CWI), Amsterdam, The Netherlands
Yuqing Kong, University of Michigan, USA
Christian Kroer, Carnegie Mellon University, USA
Gunjan Kumar, Tata Institute of Fundamental Research, India
Edward Lee, UNSW, Australia
Omer Lev, University of Toronto, Canada
Bo Li, Stony Brook University, USA
Yingkai Li, Stony Brook University, USA
Guang Li, Queen's University, Canada
David Lingenbrink, Cornell University, USA
Yang Liu, Harvard University, USA

Additional reviewers (continued):

Ali Makhdoumi, Massachusetts Institute of Technology, USA
Pasin Manurangsi, University of California, Berkeley, USA
Barnabé Monnot, Singapore University of Technology & Design, Singapore
DMassachusetts Institute of Technologyry Moor, University of Zurich, Switzerland
Paresh Nakhe, Goethe University Frankfurt, Germany
Thanh Nguyen, University of Michigan, USA
Ioannis Panageas, Singapore University of Technology & Design, Singapore
Valentin Robu, Heriot Watt University, UK
Steffen Schuldenzucker, University of Zurich, Switzerland
Shreyas Sekar, Rensselaer Polytechnic Institute, USA
Megan Shearer, University of Michigan, USA
Yangguang Shi, Technion, Israel
Milad Siami, Massachusetts Institute of Technology, USA
Alkmini Sgouritsa, University of Liverpool, UK
Jakub Sliwinski, National University of Singapore
Biaoshuai Tao, University of Michigan, USA
Bo Tang, University of Oxford, UK
Alexandros Voudouris, University of Patras, Greece
Xintong Wang, University of Michigan, USA
Mason Wright, University of Michigan, USA
Steven Wu, University of Pennsylvania, USA
Fang-Yi Yu, University of Michigan, USA
Heng Zhang, University of Southern California, USA
Song Zuo, Tsinghua University, China

EC 2017 Sponsors & Supporters

Sponsor: ACM SIGecom

Supporters: facebook

Google

Microsoft

Massachusetts Institute of Technology

MIT CSAIL

Fair Algorithms for Machine Learning

MICHAEL KEARNS, University of Pennsylvania

The widespread use of machine learning to make consequential decisions about individual citizens (such as those involving credit, employment, insurance, and education) has been accompanied by rising alarm over instances of bias or discrimination in the algorithms and models used. While legal, regulatory and watchdog challenges to discriminatory algorithms will play an important role, it is also crucial to examine and quantify the extent to which social norms such as fairness can be "endogenized" into the learning process itself. Can we develop a rigorous and useful science of *fair* machine learning?

The early answer appears to be positive, although we also know it will not be simple, and that there will not be a single "right" definition of fairness for learning. Much research to date has also focused on making the final *output* of a learning algorithm fair --- for instance, by ensuring that a learned classifier has approximately equal false positive or false negative rates across two subpopulations. Less attention has been paid to making the algorithms themselves fair, including during the training process.

I will survey these developments, with special attention on recent work on defining and designing fair learning algorithms for sequential decision-making, reinforcement learning, cross-population ranking, and other problems. Of particular interest is the effort to quantify the informational, computational and other costs of fairness compared to the classical non-fair settings.

BIOGRAPHY

Michael Kearns is Professor and National Center Chair in the Department of Computer and Information Sciences at the University of Pennsylvania, with secondary appointments in Penn's Economics department, and in Statistics, and Operations, Information and Decisions of the Wharton School. Kearns is the Founding Director of Penn's Warren Center for Network and Data Sciences, as well as the Penn Program in Networked and Social Systems Engineering. His research includes topics in machine learning, algorithmic game theory, computational social science, and quantitative finance and algorithmic trading. Kearns spent a decade at AT&T Bell Labs, where he was head of the AI department, which conducted a range of systems and foundational AI and machine learning research. He has consulted extensively in the technology and finance industries, and is currently Chief Scientist of MANA Partners, a New York trading and technology company. He studied math and computer science at UC Berkeley, and completed his Ph.D. in computer science at Harvard University in 1989. He is an elected Fellow of the American Academy of Arts and Sciences, the Association for Computing Machinery, the Association for the Advancement of Artificial Intelligence, and the Society for the Advancement of Economic Theory.

EC'17, June 26–30, 2017, Cambridge, MA, USA.
 ACM ISBN 978-1-4503-4527-9/17/06.
DOI: http://dx.doi.org/10.1145/3033274.3084096

Dominant-Strategy versus Bayesian Multi-item Auctions: Maximum Revenue Determination and Comparison

ANDREW CHI-CHIH YAO, Tsinghua University

We address two related unanswered questions in maximum revenue multi-item auctions. Is dominant-strategy implementation equivalent to the semantically less stringent Bayesian one (as in the case of Myerson's 1-item auction)? Can one find explicit solutions for non-trivial families of multi-item auctions (as in the 1-item case)? In this paper, we present such natural families whose explicit solutions exhibit a revenue gap between the two implementations. More precisely, consider the k-item n-buyer maximum revenue auction where $k, n > 1$ with additive valuation in the independent setting (i.e., the buyers i have independent private distributions F_{ij} on items j). We derive exact formulas for the maximum revenue when $k = 2$ and F_{ij} are any IID distributions on support of size 2, for both the dominant-strategy (DIC) and the Bayesian (BIC) implementations. The formulas lead to the simple characterization that, the two models have identical maximum revenue if and only if selling-separately is optimal for the distribution. Our results also give the first demonstration, in this setting, of revenue gaps between the two models. For instance, if $k = n = 2$ and $Pr\{X_F = 1\} = Pr\{X_F = 2\} = \frac{1}{2}$, then the maximum revenue in the Bayesian implementation exceeds that in the dominant-strategy by exactly 2%; the same gap exists for the continuous uniform distribution X_F over $[a, a + 1] \cup [2a, 2a + 1]$ for all large a.

Additional Key Words and Phrases: maximum revenue; multi-item auction; dominant strategy; Bayesian implementation

1 INTRODUCTION

We consider the k-item n-buyer maximum revenue auction with additive[1] valuation in the independent setting (i.e., the buyers i have independent private distributions F_i^j over the range $[0, \infty)$ on items j). How should the optimal mechanisms be designed?

Myersons's classical paper [24] elegantly solved the problem for the single item case. For multiple items ($k > 1$), the problem is much more complex with an extensive literature (see *Related Work* below). Much progress has been made, but many interesting questions remain open. In this paper we focus on two such questions that arise naturally.

Firstly, there are two standard models of mechanism design for auctions, known respectively as *dominant-strategy incentive-compatible* (DIC) and *Bayesian incentive-compatible* (BIC) mechanisms. Formally, the BIC constraints look much weaker than the DIC constraints. It is thus a remarkable feature of Myersons's theory that exactly the same maximum revenue is achieved by the BIC mechanisms and the DIC mechanisms for single-item auctions. Can this equivalence hold for $k > 1$?

Q1. For $k > 1$, can Bayesian incentive-compatible (BIC) mechanisms ever produce strictly more revenue than the dominant-strategy incentive-compatible (DIC) mechanisms?

[1]Namely, for each buyer i, the valuation of a set S of items is the sum of valuations for all the items in S.

Author's email address: andrewcyao@tsinghua.edu.cn .

EC'17, June 26–30, 2017, Cambridge, Massachusetts, USA. © 2017 ACM ISBN 978-1-4503-4527-9/17/06...$15.00.
DOI: http://dx.doi.org/10.1145/3033274.3085120

(A substantial literature exists on the above DIC versus BIC question: see *Related Work* below). For our second question, note that Myerson's characterization of optimal mechanisms for $k = 1$ leads to explicit formulas for the maximum revenue. For $k > 1$, in the single buyer ($n = 1$) case, there is a rich collection of sophisticated results (e.g., [14–19, 23, 25, 28]), where explicit expressions for optimal revenue are obtained for certain discrete and continuous distributions. However, for $k > 1$ and $n > 1$, there do not seem to be any interesting results of this kind in the literature. Thus we pose the following question:

Q2. For $k > 1$ and $n > 1$, can we obtain explicit expressions of the optimal revenue for interesting families of distributions?

In this paper we address questions Q1 and Q2. In the direction of Q2, we derive exact formulas for the maximum revenue for both DIC and BIC implementations for $k = 2$ and any $n > 1$, where the 2n distributions F_i^j are IID with a common F of support size 2. As a by-product, these formulas give an answer to Q1, showing the BIC optimal revenue expression to be strictly greater than that of DIC for a broad range of parameters. In fact the formulas lead to the simple characterization that, the two implementations have identical maximum revenue if and only if selling-separately is optimal for the distribution. For instance, if $k = n = 2$ and $Pr\{X_F = 1\} = Pr\{X_F = 2\} = \frac{1}{2}$, then the maximum revenue in the Bayesian implementation exceeds that in the dominant-strategy by exactly 2%. A natural extension to the continuous case shows that the same 2% gap holds for the uniform distribution over $[a, a+1] \cup [2a, 2a+1]$ as $a \rightarrow \infty$. We also remark that our result complements a theorem in [30] that the BIC maximum revenue is always upper bounded by a constant factor of the DIC maximum revenue.

Beyond providing an answer to Q1 and Q2, our techniques may have several other contributions. Firstly, it is demonstrated in a natural context how to turn a DIC mechanism into a BIC mechanism with increased revenue (see a specific example in Section 3.3). Secondly, our proposed optimal mechanisms, while applicable to arbitrary n buyers, have simple descriptions. Each mechanism employs only a pure hierarchical allocation rule. Such simple designs may lend these mechanisms to other applications. Finally, the problem of finding explicit exact solutions to multi-item auctions is an interesting open area. Economic concepts and interpretations often value precision over constant approximations. A collection of exactly solvable auction problems could be valuable for other econometrics explorations.

The main results of this paper will be stated in Section 3 with proofs given in Sections 4 and 5. Formal descriptions of our mechanisms and formulas will be illustrated through concrete examples (see Example 1 in Section 3.1 and 3.3) to help the understanding.

Related Work

Regarding Q1, when the independence condition on the distributions F_i^j is dropped, then the answer is known. [9] showed BIC can generate unbounded more revenue than DIC, when F_i^j are *correlated across buyers* even for $k = 1$. Recently, [29] showed in some instance with $k > 1$, BIC can generate strictly more revenue than DIC, when F_i^j are *correlated across items*. There are other examples (e.g. [13, 23]) where DIC and BIC are shown to be inequivalent in revenue (and other attributes), but their models are farther away from our model under consideration here.

We note that much progress has been made on the computational aspects of multi-item auctions. The intrinsic complexity of computing the optimal revenue has been investigated (e.g. [8, 10]; efficient algorithms have been found in a variety of circumstances (e.g. [4, 5, 11]); furthermore, simple approximation mechanisms have been extensively studied in various environments (e.g. [1, 6, 7, 12, 18, 21, 22, 26, 27, 30]).

2 PRELIMINARIES

2.1 Basic Concepts

Let $\mathcal{F}$ be a multi-dimensional distribution on $[0, \infty)^{nk}$. Consider the k-item n-buyer auction problem where the valuation $n \times k$ matrix $t = (t_i^j)$ is drawn from $\mathcal{F}$. Each buyer i has $t_i \equiv (t_i^1, t_i^2, \cdots, t_i^k)$ as his valuations of the k items. We also refer to t_i as buyer i's *type*, and t as the *type profile* of the buyers (or *profile* for short). For convenience, let t_{-i} denote the valuations of all buyers except buyer i; that is, $t_{-i} = (t_{i'} \mid i' \neq i)$. Note that t^j, the j-th column of the matrix t, contains the valuations of all the buyers on item j.

A *mechanism* M specifies an *allocation* $q(t) = (q_i^j(t)) \in [0, \infty)^{nk}$, where $q_i^j(t)$ denotes the probability that item j is allocated to buyer i when $t = (t_i^j)$ is reported as the type profile to M by the buyers. We require that $\sum_{i=1}^n q_i^j(t) \leq 1$ for all j, so that the total probability of allocating item j is at most 1. M also specifies a *payment* $s_i(t) \in (-\infty, \infty)$ for buyer i.

The *utility* $u_i(t)$ for buyer i is defined to be $t_i \cdot q_i(t) - s_i(t)$, where $t_i \cdot q_i(t)$ stands for the inner product $\sum_{j=1}^k t_i^j q_i^j(t)$. Let $u_i(t_i \leftarrow t_i', t_{-i}) = t_i \cdot q_i(t_i', t_{-i}) - s_i(t_i', t_{-i})$, i.e. the utility buyer i would obtain if he has type t_i but reports to the seller as t_i'. The *expected allocation* $\bar{q}_i(t_i)$ for buyer i is defined to be $E_{t_{-i}}(q(t_i, t_{-i}))$. The *expected utility* $\bar{u}_i(t_i)$ for buyer i is defined to be $E_{t_{-i}}(u(t_i, t_{-i}))$. Also let $\bar{u}_i(t_i \leftarrow t_i') = E_{t_{-i}}(\bar{u}_i(t_i \leftarrow t_i', t_{-i}))$.

The following formulas are well known:

$$\textit{Transfer Equations: } u_i(t_i \leftarrow t_i', t_{-i}) = u_i(t_i', t_{-i}) + (t_i - t_i') \cdot q_i(t_i', t_{-i}) \text{ for all } t_i, t_i', t_{-i}.$$

$$\textit{Averaged Form: } \bar{u}_i(t_i \leftarrow t_i') = \bar{u}_i(t_i') + (t_i - t_i') \cdot \bar{q}_i(t_i') \text{ for all } t_i, t_i'.$$

Two kinds of mechanisms have been widely studied, referred to as *Dominant-strategy* and *Bayesian* implementations as specified below.

Dominant-strategy: *IR* conditions: $u_i(t) \geq 0$ for all i and t.
DIC conditions: $u_i(t_i, t_{-i}) \geq u_i(t_i \leftarrow t_i', t_{-i})$ for all t_i, t_i' and t_{-i}, or equivalently,
DIC conditions (alternate): $u_i(t_i, t_{-i}) - u_i(t_i', t_{-i}) \geq (t_i - t_i') \cdot q_i(t_i', t_{-i})$ for all t_i, t_i' and t_{-i}.
A mechanism is called *individually rational (IR)/dominant-strategy incentive compatible (DIC)*, if it satisfies the IR conditions/the DIC conditions, respectively.

Bayesian: *BIR* conditions: $\bar{u}_i(t_i) \geq 0$ for all i and t_i.
BIC conditions: $\bar{u}_i(t_i) \geq \bar{u}_i(t_i \leftarrow t_i')$ for all t_i, t_i', or equivalently,
BIC conditions (alternate): $\bar{u}_i(t_i) - \bar{u}_i(t_i') \geq (t_i - t_i') \cdot \bar{q}_i(t_i')$ for all t_i, t_i'.
A mechanism is called *Bayesian individually rational (BIR)/Bayesian incentive compatible (BIC)*, if it satisfies the BIR conditions/the BIC conditions, respectively.

Let $s(x) = \sum_{i=1}^n s_i(x)$ be the total payments received by the seller. For any mechanism M on $\mathcal{F}$, let $M(\mathcal{F}) = E_{x\sim\mathcal{F}}(s(x))$ be the (expected) revenue received by the seller from all buyers. The *optimal* revenue is defined as $REV_D(\mathcal{F}) = \sup_M M(\mathcal{F})$ when M ranges over all the IR-DIC mechanisms. Similarly, in the Bayesian model, the optimal revenue is defined as $REV_B(\mathcal{F}) = \sup_M M(\mathcal{F})$ where M ranges over all the BIR-BIC mechanisms. As a benchmark for comparison, let $SREV(\mathcal{F})$ stand for the revenue yielded when each item is sold separately by using the optimal mechanism of [24].

2.2 Hierarchy Allocation

The optimal BIC and DIC mechanisms proposed in this paper for n-buyer 2-item auctions will be described using the formalism of *hierarchy allocations*. The concept of hierarchy allocation was first raised in [2, 3] for one item, and later for multi-items in [4]. Here we only need the concept as a convenient language to succinctly present our mechanisms.

Consider an n-buyer 1-item auction. A *hierarchy allocation scheme* H is specified by a mapping $Rank : T \to \mathcal{R} \cup \{\infty\}$. Given a type $t \in (t_1, t_2, \ldots, t_n)$, scheme H allocates the item uniformly among the set of buyers i with the smallest ranking. If $Rank(t_i) = \infty$ for all i, then no allocation will be made to any buyer. For convenience, we use the notation $H = [\tau_{11}, \ldots, \tau_{1a_1}; \tau_{21}, \ldots, \tau_{2a_2}; \ldots; \tau_{\ell 1}, \ldots, \tau_{\ell a_\ell}]$ with the understanding $Rank(\tau_{dm}) = d$ for all $1 \le d \le \ell$, $1 \le m \le a_d$, and $Rank(t) = \infty$ for any type t not listed among τ_{dm}.

In an n-buyer k-item auction, a *hierarchy mechanism* M uses a *hierarchy allocation function* specified by a k-tuple $\mathcal{H} = (H^1, H^2, \cdots, H^k)$, where each H^j is a hierarchy allocation scheme to be used for item j; also a utility function $u_i(t)$ for each buyer i needs to be specified for M. Note that the payment for buyer i is determined by $s_i(t) = \sum_j q_i^j(t) t_i^j - u_i(t)$.

3 MAIN RESULTS

In this paper, we solve for $REV_D(\mathcal{F})$ and $REV_B(\mathcal{F})$ in the n-buyer, 2-item case when $\mathcal{F}$ consists of 2n IID's of a common F with support size 2. Any such $\mathcal{F}$ can be specified by a 4-tuple $\delta = (n, p, a, b)$ where $n \ge 2$ is an integer, $0 < p < 1$, and $0 \le a < b$. Let $\mathcal{F}_\delta$ denote the valuation distribution for the n-buyer 2-item auction, where the distributions F_i^j for buyer i and item j are independent and identical (IID) copies of random variables X defined by $Pr\{X = a\} = p$ and $Pr\{X = b\} = 1 - p$. Assuming additive valuation on items for each buyer, we are interested in determining $REV_D(\mathcal{F}_\delta)$ and $REV_B(\mathcal{F}_\delta)$, the maximum revenue achievable under IR-DIC and BIR-BIC, respectively, for distribution $\mathcal{F}_\delta$. We find two benchmarks relevant, $SREV(\mathcal{F}_\delta)$ and $s_b = 2(1 - p^n)b$: the former is the revenue obtained by selling separately each item using Myerson's optimal mechanism; the latter is the revenue by selling separately each item at price b.

Fact 1. $SREV(\mathcal{F}_\delta) = 2 \cdot \max\{(1 - p^n)b,\ p^{n-1}a + (1 - p^{n-1})b\}$.

It suffices to show that, for 1-item auction with n buyers and IID distributions $\mathcal{F}_\delta$, the maximum revenue possible is equal to $\max\{(1 - p^n)b,\ p^{n-1}a + (1 - p^{n-1})b\}$. According to Myerson's optimal auction theory, the revenue maximization problem in this setting reduces to the welfare maximization problem where the valuation is replaced by a modified valuation (dependent on the distribution), called the *ironed virtual valuation* ϕ. It is easy to show that for the distribution $\mathcal{F}_\delta$, $\phi(a) = (a - (1 - p)b)/p$ and $\phi(b) = b$. The maximum welfare achievable is given by $p^n \max\{\phi(a), 0\} + (1 - p^n)\phi(b)$, which is exactly $\max\{(1 - p^n)b,\ p^{n-1}a + (1 - p^{n-1})b\}$. This proves Fact 1.

3.1 The Main Theorem

For any real-valued function G, we use G_+ to denote the nonnegative function defined as $G_+ = \max\{G, 0\}$. The functions $r_D(\delta)$ and $r_B(\delta)$ below will be used to express revenues.

Definition 3.1. Let $p_0 = p^{2n}$, $p_1 = 2np^{2n-1}(1 - p)$, and $p_2 = 2p^n \left(1 - p^n - np^{n-1}(1 - p)\right)$. Define

$$r_D(\delta) = 2(1 - p^n)b + p_0\left[2a - \frac{1 - p^2}{p^2}(b - a)\right]_+ + p_1\left[a - \frac{1 - p}{2p}(b - a)\right]_+ + p_2\left[a - \frac{1 - p}{p}(b - a)\right]_+$$

$$r_B(\delta) = 2(1 - p^n)b + p_0\left[2a - \frac{1 - p^2}{p^2}(b - a)\right]_+ + (p_1 + p_2)\left[a - \frac{1 - p}{2p}(b - a)\right]_+$$

Theorem 3.2 (**Main Theorem**). *$REV_B(\mathcal{F}_\delta) = r_B(\delta)$ and $REV_D(\mathcal{F}_\delta) = r_D(\delta)$.*

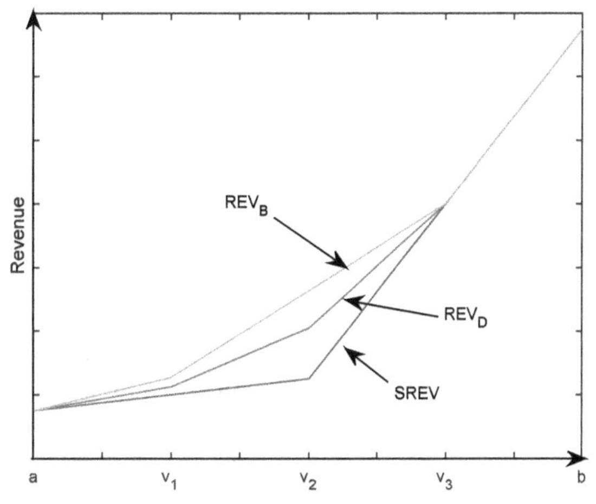

Fig. 1. REV_B, REV_D, and $SREV$ as functions of b

COROLLARY 3.3.

$$(a)\ REV_B(\mathcal{F}_\delta) = REV_D(\mathcal{F}_\delta) = SREV(\mathcal{F}_\delta)\ \text{ if } b \geq a(1+p)/(1-p),$$
$$REV_B(\mathcal{F}_\delta) > REV_D(\mathcal{F}_\delta) > SREV(\mathcal{F}_\delta)\ \text{ otherwise.}$$
$$(b)\ REV_D(\mathcal{F}_\delta) = REV_B(\mathcal{F}_\delta)\ \text{ if and only if Selling-Separately is optimal.}$$

Remark 1. For fixed n, p, a, the functions $r_B(\delta)$, $r_D(\delta)$ and $SREV(\mathcal{F}_\delta)$ are each continuous, piecewise-linear functions in b as shown in Figure 1. Breakpoints of linearity occur at $v_1 = \frac{1+p^2}{1-p^2}a$, $v_2 = \frac{1}{1-p}a$, and $v_3 = \frac{1+p}{1-p}a$ along the b-axis. The last two additive terms of $r_B(\delta)$ are 0 when $b \geq v_1$, and $b \geq v_3$, respectively. Similarly, the last three additive terms of $r_D(\delta)$ are 0 when $b \geq v_1$, $b \geq v_3$, and $b \geq v_2$, respectively.

Remark 2. The formula for $r_D(\delta)$ can be interpreted as follows (and likewise for $r_B(\delta)$). The first term $2(1-p^n)b$ is equal to s_b. The three additive terms represent the extra revenue, beyond selling-separately at b, that can be gleaned from three specific subsets of profiles. (These subsets are defined as S_0, S_1, S_2 in Definition 5 later, with non-zero probability of occurrence p_0, p_1, p_2, respectively.)

Corollary 3.3 can be derived as follows. When $b \geq v_3 = \frac{1+p}{1-p}a$, all terms in square brackets in Definition 1 are 0, hence $r_D(\delta) = r_B(\delta) = 2(1-p^n)b = s_b$. As by definition $s_b \leq SREV(\mathcal{F}_\delta) \leq r_D(\delta)$, we conclude $r_D(\delta) = r_B(\delta) = SREV(\mathcal{F}_\delta)$ in this case. When $b < v_3$, we have $a - \frac{1-p}{2p}(b-a) > 0$, implying

$$r_B(\delta) - r_D(\delta) = p_2\left(\left[a - \frac{1-p}{2p}(b-a)\right]_+ - \left[a - \frac{1-p}{p}(b-a)\right]_+\right) > 0.$$

To compare $r_D(\delta)$ with $SREV(\mathcal{F}_\delta)$ when $b < v_3$, notice that the two continuous piecewise-linear functions are equal when $b = a$ and $b = v_3$. It is easy to check from their formulas that, $r_D(\delta)$ strictly dominates $SREV(\mathcal{F}_\delta)$ at both breakpoints v_1 and v_2 interior to $[a, v_3]$. We conclude that $r_D(\delta) > SREV(\mathcal{F}_\delta)$ over the entire interval (a, v_3). Corollary 3.3(a) follows. Corollary 3.3(b) follows immediately from (a). □

Example 1. As an illustration, consider the case $\delta = (n, p, a, b)$ with $n = 2$, $p = \frac{1}{2}$, $a = 1$, $b = 2$. The formulas in the Main Theorem tell us $REV_D(\mathcal{F}_\delta) = \frac{1}{8}(3 + 11b)$ for $b \in [2, 3)$, and $REV_B(\mathcal{F}_\delta) = \frac{1}{16}(9 + 21b)$ for $b \in [\frac{5}{3}, 3)$. Thus for $b = 2$ we have $REV_D(\mathcal{F}_\delta) = 25/8 = 3.125$ and $REV_B(\mathcal{F}_\delta) = 51/16 = 3.1875$, with a gap of 2%. Note that grand bundling yields only revenue 45/16, while selling separately yields revenue 3, both strictly less than 3.125.

Open Questions: It is an interesting open question to determine whether the 2% gap in Example 1 is the largest gap between DIC and BIC revenue for the family of distributions considered in our model. It would also be interesting to extend our results to more general models, say, where the two items have distinct IID distributions.

3.2 Optimal Mechanisms

The optimal revenue $r_D(\delta)$ and $r_B(\delta)$ stated in the Main Theorem can be realized, respectively, by the IR-DIC mechanism $M_{D,\delta}$ and the IR-BIC mechanism $M_{B,\delta}$ defined below. First, we name the characteristic functions for the three intervals where the individual terms of $r_D(\delta)$, $r_B(\delta)$ are non-zero.

Definition 3.4. Define

$$\begin{cases} \alpha_{p,a,b} = 1 & \text{if } b < v_1, \quad \text{and 0 otherwise.} \\ \beta_{p,a,b} = 1 & \text{if } b < v_3, \quad \text{and 0 otherwise.} \\ \gamma_{p,a,b} = 1 & \text{if } b < v_2, \quad \text{and 0 otherwise.} \end{cases}$$

The subscripts in $\alpha_{p,a,b}$, $\gamma_{p,a,b}$, $\beta_{p,a,b}$ can be dropped when p, a, b are clear from the context. Note that, if desired, the formulas for $r_D(\delta)$ and $r_B(\delta)$ can be written using α, β, γ as multipliers in place of the notation $G_+ \equiv \max\{G, 0\}$.

Definition 3.5. In what follows, the term *profile* refers to a profile in the support of $\mathcal{F}_\delta$, a *type* refers to a type in $\{a, b\} \times \{a, b\}$. For any profile t and $j \in \{1, 2\}$, we say t^j is *cheap* if $t_i^j = a$ for all $1 \le i \le n$ (we also say item j is cheap); otherwise t^j is *non-cheap*. Call a profile t *1-cheap* if t has exactly 1 cheap item. We use $I(t)$ to denote the subset of buyers i with $t_i \neq (a, a)$, that is, only excluding those who value both items at a. Note that, if t is 1-cheap, then $|I(t)|$ is equal to the number of b's in t (and all appearing in the same column).

We now define mechanism $M_{D,\delta}$ and $M_{B,\delta}$ below, using the language of hierarchy mechanism. First divide the range (a, ∞) of b into 4 subintervals: $I_1 = (a, v_1)$, $I_2 = [v_1, v_2)$, $I_3 = [v_2, v_3)$ and $I_4 = [v_3, \infty)$.

ALGORITHM 1: Mechanism $M_{D,\delta}$

Case 1. $b \in I_1$. Use the hierarchy allocation function (H^1, H^2) where $H^1 = [(b, b); (b, a); (a, b); (a, a)]$ and $H^2 = [(b, b); (a, b); (b, a); (a, a)]$;
Case 2. $b \in I_2$. Use the hierarchy allocation function (H^1, H^2) where $H^1 = [(b, b); (b, a); (a, b)]$ and $H^2 = [(b, b); (a, b); (b, a)]$;
Case 3. $b \in I_3$. If $t = (t_i, t_{-i})$ with t_{-i} being the lowest profile $(a, a)^{n-1}$, then offer items 1 and 2 to buyer i as a bundle at price $a + b$. Otherwise, use the hierarchy allocation function (H^1, H^2) where $H^1 = [(b, b); (b, a)]$, $H^2 = [(b, b); (a, b)]$;
Case 4. $b \in I_4$. Use the hierarchy allocation function (H^1, H^2) where $H^1 = [(b, b); (b, a)]$, $H^2 = [(b, b); (a, b)]$;

The payment of $M(\mathcal{F}_\delta)$ is determined by the following utility function: for $1 \le i \le n$, $t = (t_i, t_{-i})$,

$$u_i(t_i, t_{-i}) = \begin{cases} (b-a)\frac{\alpha}{n} & \text{if } t_i = (b,a) \text{ or } (a,b), \text{ and } t_{-i} = (a,a)^{n-1} \\ (b-a)(\frac{\alpha}{n} + \beta) & \text{if } t_i = (b,b), \text{ and } t_{-i} = (a,a)^{n-1} \\ (b-a)\frac{\gamma}{1+|I(t_{-i})|} & \text{if } t_i = (b,b),\ t_{-i} \text{ is 1-cheap} \\ 0 & \text{otherwise.} \end{cases} \tag{1}$$

Remark 3. Strictly speaking, $M_{D,\delta}$ in Case 3 is not a hierarchy mechanism. We abuse the term slightly for convenience. Observe that, when $b \in I_4$, $M_{D,\delta}$ can be described as selling each item separately at price b with a particular tie-breaking rule as dictated by the Case 4 allocation function (H^1, H^2). When $b \in I_3$, $M_{D,\delta}$ can be described as follows: if $t = (t_i, t_{-i})$ with $t_{-i} = (a,a)^{n-1}$, then offer items 1 and 2 to buyer i as a bundle at price $a + b$; otherwise sell each item separately at price b with a particular tie-breaking rule as dictated by the Case 3 allocation function (H^1, H^2).

ALGORITHM 2: Mechanism $M_{B,\delta}$

Case 1. $b \in I_1$: Use the hierarchy allocation function as defined in Case 1 of $M_{D,\delta}$;
Case 2. $b \in I_2 \cup I_3$: Use the hierarchy allocation function as defined in Case 2 of $M_{D,\delta}$;
Case 3. $b \in I_4$: Define $M_{B,\delta} = M_{D,\delta}$;

In both Case 1 and 2, the payment is defined by the same utility function $u_i(t_i, t_{-i})$ as in $M_{D,\delta}$ with only one *exception*: if $t_i = (b,b)$ and t_{-i} is 1-cheap, then let

$$u_i(t_i, t_{-i}) = \frac{1}{2}(b-a)\frac{\beta}{1 + |I(t_{-i})|}.$$

Remark 4. In fact, $M_{B,\delta}(\mathcal{F}_\delta)$ is an IR-BIC mechanisms (not just BIR-BIC), as will be shown later.

3.3 Example 1 Revisited

As an illustration, let us apply mechanisms $M_{D,\delta}$ and $M_{B,\delta}$ to the distribution $\delta = (n, p, a, b)$ in Example 1 where $n = 2$, $p = 1/2$, $a = 1$ and $b \in [2,3)$. Since both mechanisms are designed to be fully symmetric with respect to the swapping of items 1 and 2, and to the swapping of buyers 1 and 2, we only need to specify enough details up to these symmetries. This δ falls under Case 3 of mechanism $M_{D,\delta}$ and Case 2 of $M_{B,\delta}$, respectively.

ALGORITHM 3: Mechanism $M_{B,\delta}$ for Example 1

Case 1. If $t_2 = (1,1)$, then buyer 1 is offered both items as a bundle at price $1 + b$;
Case 2. If $t_2 = (1,b)$: ;
if $t_1 = (1,b)$, then each buyer is offered 50% of both items as a bundle at price $\frac{1}{2}(1+b)$;
if $t_1 = (b,1)$, then each buyer gets his most-valued item at price b;
if $t_1 = (b,b)$, then buyer 1 gets both items as a bundle at price $2b - \frac{1}{4}(b-1)$;
Case 3. If $t_1 = t_2 = (b,b)$, then each buyer gets 50% of both items as a bundle at price b;

Question: What is the difference between the allocations by $M_{D,\delta}$ and $M_{B,\delta}$ in Example 1, and how does $M_{B,\delta}$ manage to outperform $M_{D,\delta}$?
Ans. The two mechanisms differ only in the way they handle the following two sets of profiles:
(A) Assume $t_1 = t_2 = (1,b)$ or $t_1 = t_2 = (b,1)$. Here $M_{B,\delta}$ offers each buyer 50% of both items as a bundle at price $\frac{1}{2}(1+b)$, while $M_{D,\delta}$ offers each buyer 50% of item 2 at price $\frac{b}{2}$;

ALGORITHM 4: Mechanism $M_{D,\delta}$ for Example 1

If any buyer i submits the bid $t_i = (1,1)$, then the other buyer is offered items 1 and 2 as a bundle at price $1+b$; otherwise, the items are sold separately at price b each (with a particular tie-breaking rule specified by the hierarchy allocation function (H^1, H^2) where $H^1 = [(b,b);(b,a)]$, $H^2 = [(b,b);(a,b)]$);

(B) Assume i has type (b,b) and the other buyer has type $(1,b)$ or $(b,1)$. Here $M_{B,\delta}$ offers buyer i both items as a bundle at price $2b - \frac{1}{4}(b-1)$, while $M_{D,\delta}$ offers buyer i both items as a bundle at price $2b$.

Mechanism $M_{B,\delta}$ gets more payment than $M_{D,\delta}$ in situation A and gets less in situation B, but gains an overall improvement of $\frac{1}{16}(3-b)$ over $M_{B,\delta}$. It is key to observe that mechanism $M_{B,\delta}$ *violates* the DIC constraint $u_1((b,b),(1,b)) \geq u_1((1,b),(1,b)) + (b-1)q_1^1((1,b),(1,b))$.

3.4 Application to Continuous Distributions

The results in the Main Theorem have implications on the maximum revenue for continuous distributions if the latter can be well approximated by $\mathcal{F}_\delta$. As an application, let $\lambda > 1$, $a > \frac{1}{\lambda-1}$, and let $\mathcal{F} = (F_i^j \mid 1 \leq i \leq n, 1 \leq j \leq 2)$ be a distribution where $F_i^j = F$ are IID distributions with $support(X_F) = [a, a+1] \cup [\lambda a, \lambda a + 1]$; let $p = Pr\{X_F \leq a+1\}$. We can regard F_δ, where $\delta = (n, p, 1, \lambda)$, as a normalized discrete approximation of $\mathcal{F}$.

Corollary 3.6. *Let $\delta = (n,p,1,\lambda)$. There exists a constant C_δ such that*

$$|REV_Z(\mathcal{F}) - r_Z(\delta) \cdot a| < C_\delta \quad \text{for } Z \in \{D, B\}.$$

Corollary 3.6 is proved by an extension of our proof of the Main Theorem to the continuous setting (details omitted here).

Remark 5. There are general high-precision approximation theorems in the literature (e.g. see[6, 11, 20, 27]) connecting continuous and discrete distributions for the BIC maximum revenue auction. Our derivation of Corollary 3.6 does not rely on such general theorems.

We consider an illustrative example of Corollary 3.6 where $n = 2$. Let $\mathcal{G}_a = (F_i^j \mid i,j \in \{1,2\})$, where $F_i^j = F$ are IID distributions with X_F uniformly distributed over $[a, a+1] \cup [2a, 2a+1]$. According to Corollary 3.6, we have $\frac{1}{a}\lim_{a\to\infty} REV_Z(\mathcal{G}_a) = r_Z(\delta)$ for $Z \in \{D, B\}$ where $\delta = (2, \frac{1}{2}, 1, 2)$. More precise bounds for this example are given below. Note that from Definition 1, one has $r_D(\delta) = \frac{25}{8}$ and $r_B(\delta) = \frac{51}{16}$, with a 2% difference.

Corollary 3.7. *For $a \geq 20$, the BIC maximum revenue for $\mathcal{G}_a$ strictly exceeds its DIC maximum revenue. In fact, we have for $a \geq 6$,*

$$\frac{25}{8}a \leq REV_D(\mathcal{G}_a) < \frac{25}{8}a + \frac{5}{4}$$
$$\frac{51}{16}a \leq REV_B(\mathcal{G}_a) < \frac{51}{16}a + \frac{3}{2}.$$

4 DIC MAXIMUM REVENUE

In this section we give a proof outline of the Main Theorem for the dominant strategy implementation:

Theorem 4.1. *Any IR-DIC mechanisms M must satisfy $M(\mathcal{F}_\delta) \leq r_D(\delta)$.*

Theorem 4.2. *$M_{D,\delta}$ is IR-DIC, and $M_{D,\delta}(\mathcal{F}_\delta) = r_D(\delta)$.*

We begin with a general discussion applicable to any mechanism. Let M be a mechanism with allocation q_i^j and utility u_i. We separate out the allocation of cheap items from non-cheap items. Thus, define $q'^j_i(t) = q_i^j(t)\eta^j(t)$ where $\eta^j(t) = 1$ if item j is cheap, and $\eta^j(t) = 0$ if j is non-cheap. Note that the welfare of the buyers from the allocation of cheap items is $a \cdot \sum_{i,j,t} Pr\{t\}q'^j_i(t)$, while the welfare from the non-cheap items is $\sum_{i,j,t} Pr\{t\}(1-\eta^j(t))q_i^j(t)t_i^j$ which is at most $2(1-p^n)b$ (the revenue obtained by selling-separately at price b). By definition of utility, it is clear that the revenue $M(\mathcal{F}_\delta)$ equals the total welfare minus utility of the buyers. This leads to the following formula:

Basic Formula. For any mechanism M, we have

$$M(\mathcal{F}_\delta) \leq 2(1-p^n)b + Qa - U,$$

where $Q = \sum_{i,j,t} Pr\{t\}q'^j_i(t)$ and $U = \sum_{i,t} Pr\{t\}u_i(t)$.

Definition 4.3. For any set S of profiles, let $Q(S) = \sum_{t\in S} Pr\{t\} \sum_{i,j} q'^j_i(t)$ and $U(S) = \sum_{t\in S} Pr\{t\} \sum_i u_i(t)$.

To make use of the Basic Formula, we partition the profiles that can possibly contribute to the Q term into three subsets S_0, S_1, S_2, and then use the IR-DIC Conditions to show that the U term (utility obtained by buyers) is greater than a certain linear combination of $Q(S_0)$, $Q(S_1)$, $Q(S_2)$. The Basic Formula then yields $r_D(\delta)$ as an upper bound to $M(\mathcal{F}_\delta)$.

Definition 4.4. Let $S_0 = \{(a,a)^n\}$ be the set containing a single element, namely, the lowest profile. Let S_1 be the set of 1-cheap profiles t satisfying $|I(t)| = 1$. Let S_2 be the set of 1-cheap profiles t satisfying $|I(t)| \geq 2$.

Fact 2. $q'^j_i(t) = 0$ for all $t \notin S_0 \cup S_1 \cup S_2$.

Recall that $p_0 = p^{2n}$, $p_1 = 2np^{2n-1}(1-p)$, $p_2 = 2p^n(1-p^n-np^{n-1}(1-p))$. They have the following interpretation as can be easily verified.

Fact 3. $Pr\{t \in S_\ell\} = p_\ell$ for $\ell \in \{0,1,2\}$, where t is distributed according to $\mathcal{F}_\delta$.

Lemma 4.5.

$$Q(S_0) \leq 2p_0, Q(S_1) \leq p_1, Q(S_2) \leq p_2. \tag{2}$$

Proof. Any profile in S_1 or S_2 has exactly one cheap item, and the (only) profile in S_0 has two cheap items. Lemma 4.5 then follows from Fact 3. □

Lemma 4.6.

$$M(\mathcal{F}_\delta) \leq 2b(1-p^n) + a \sum_{0\leq\ell\leq 2} Q(S_\ell) - U. \tag{3}$$

Proof. It follows from Fact 2 that $Q = Q(S_0) + Q(S_1) + Q(S_2)$. Lemma 4.6 then follows from the Basic Formula. □

Lemmas 4.5 and 4.6 set the stage. We are ready to invoke the incentive compatibility requirements to prove Theorem 4.1. This setting is also useful in the next section when we prove the BIC part of the Main Theorem.

4.1 Upper Bound to DIC Revenue

We prove Theorem 4.1 in this subsection. The key is to prove the following proposition.
Proposition 1. Any IR-DIC mechanism M must satisfy the following inequality:

$$U \geq (b-a)\left(\frac{1-p^2}{2p^2}Q(S_0) + \frac{1-p}{2p}Q(S_1) + \frac{1-p}{p}Q(S_2)\right). \tag{4}$$

We first show that Theorem 4.1 follows from Proposition 1. It follows from Lemma 4.6 and Proposition 1 that, for any IR-DIC mechanism M, we have

$$\begin{aligned} M(\mathcal{F}_\delta) \leq 2(1-p^n)b &+ Q(S_0)\left[a - \frac{1-p^2}{2p^2}(b-a)\right]_+ \\ &+ Q(S_1)\left[a - \frac{1-p}{2p}(b-a)\right]_+ \\ &+ Q(S_2)\left[a - \frac{1-p}{p}(b-a)\right]_+. \end{aligned}$$

With no negative terms, the above expression together with Lemma 4.5 immediately yield Theorem 4.1. Thus to establish Theorem 4.1, it suffices to prove Proposition 1.

Definition 4.7. For any $1 \leq i, i' \leq n$,
let $\tau_{i,i'}$ be the profile t such that $t_i^1 = t_{i'}^2 = b$ and all other $t_\ell^j = a$;
let $\tau_{i,0}$ be the profile t with $t_i^1 = b$ and all other $t_\ell^j = a$;
let $\tau_{0,i'}$ be the profile t with $t_{i'}^2 = b$ and all other $t_\ell^j = a$;
let $\tau_{0,0} = (a,a)^n$.

Fact 4. $S_0 = \{\tau_{0,0}\}$, $S_1 = \{\tau_{i,0}, \tau_{0,i} \mid 1 \leq i \leq n\}$.

Definition 4.8. For any $t \in S_2$ and $1 \leq i \leq n$, define $\tau_{t,i}$ as follows: let item j ($j \in \{1,2\}$) be the cheap item for t; define $\tau_{t,i} = t'$ where $t'^j_i = b$ and $t'^{j'}_{i'} = t^{j'}_{i'}$ for all other $(i', j') \neq (i, j)$.

Definition 4.9. Let $S_1' = \{\tau_{i,i'} \mid 1 \leq i, i' \leq n\}$. Let $S_2' = \{\tau_{t,i} \mid t \in S_2, 1 \leq i \leq n\}$.

Fact 5. S_1', S_2' are disjoint sets of profiles containing no cheap items.
From Fact 5 and the IR Conditions, we have

$$U \geq U(S_1) + U(S_1') + U(S_2'). \tag{5}$$

We now utilize the DIC-conditions to establish the following lemma relating the U and Q values on different types.

Lemma 4.10.

$$U(S_1) \geq \frac{1-p}{p}((b-a)Q(S_0) + 2U(S_0)), \tag{6}$$

$$U(S_1') \geq \frac{1-p}{2p}((b-a)Q(S_1) + U(S_1)), \tag{7}$$

$$U(S_2') \geq \frac{1-p}{p}((b-a)Q(S_2) + U(S_2)). \tag{8}$$

Proof. The DIC-conditions require that, for all t_i, t_i', t_{-i},

$$u_i(t_i, t_{-i}) \geq u_i(t_i', t_{-i}) + \sum_j (t_i^j - t'^j_i) q_i^j(t_i', t_{-i}).$$

We only need a subset of these conditions where $t_i > t'_i$. In such cases, we can use q'^j_i instead of q^j_i and write

DIC-Conditions: For all $t_i > t'_i$ and any t_{-i},

$$u_i(t_i, t_{-i}) \geq u_i(t'_i, t_{-i}) + \sum_j (t^j_i - t'^j_i) q'^j_i(t'_i, t_{-i}). \tag{9}$$

To prove Eq. 6, consider $t_i \in \{(b,a),(a,b)\}$, $t'_i = (a,a)$. We have

$$\begin{aligned} u_i(\tau_{i,0}) = u_i((b,a),(a,a)^{n-1}) &\geq u_i(\tau_{0,0}) + (b-a)q'^1_i(\tau_{0,0}), \\ \text{and} \quad u_i(\tau_{0,i}) &\geq u_i(\tau_{0,0}) + (b-a)q'^2_i(\tau_{0,0}). \end{aligned} \tag{10}$$

By Fact 4 we have

$$\begin{aligned} U(S_1) &= \sum_{t \in S_1} Pr\{t\} \sum_{i'} u_{i'}(t) \\ &= p^{2n-1}(1-p) \sum_i \Big(\sum_{i'} u_{i'}(\tau_{i,0}) + \sum_{i'} u_{i'}(\tau_{0,i}) \Big). \end{aligned}$$

Using Eq. 10 and the IR Conditions $u_{i'}(t) \geq 0$, we obtain

$$\begin{aligned} U(S_1) &\geq p^{2n-1}(1-p)\Big(\sum_i u_i(\tau_{i,0}) + \sum_i u_i(\tau_{0,i}) \Big) \\ &\geq p^{2n-1}(1-p) \sum_i \big(2u_i(\tau_{0,0}) + (b-a)q'^1_i(\tau_{0,0}) + (b-a)q'^2_i(\tau_{0,0}) \big) \\ &= \frac{1-p}{p} Pr\{\tau_{0,0}\} \Big(2\sum_i u_i(\tau_{0,0}) + (b-a) \sum_j \sum_i q'^j_i(\tau_{0,0}) \Big) \\ &= \frac{1-p}{p} (2U(S_0) + (b-a)Q(S_0)). \end{aligned}$$

This proves Eq. 6, the first inequality in the Lemma.

We now prove Eq. 7. Write $S_1 = S^L_1 \cup S^R_1$ where $S^L_1 = \{\tau_{0,i} | \, 1 \leq i \leq n\}$ and $S^R_1 = \{\tau_{i,0} | \, 1 \leq i \leq n\}$. It suffices to prove for $x \in \{L, R\}$,

$$U(S'_1) \geq \frac{1-p}{p}((b-a)Q(S^x_1) + U(S^x_1)). \tag{11}$$

We prove Eq. 11 for $x = L$; the case for $x = R$ is similar.

$$\begin{aligned} (b-a)Q(S^L_1) + U(S^L_1) &= \sum_{t \in S^L_1} Pr\{t\} \Big((b-a) \sum_j \sum_i q'^j_i(t) + \sum_i u_i(t) \Big) \\ &= \sum_{t \in S^L_1} p^{2n-1}(1-p) \sum_i \big((b-a)q'^1_i(t) + u_i(t) \big) \\ &= p^{2n-1}(1-p) \sum_{i'} \sum_i \big((b-a)q'^1_i(\tau_{0,i'}) + u_i(\tau_{0,i'}) \big). \end{aligned} \tag{12}$$

Now consider the DIC-Conditions (Eq. 9) for $(t_i, t_{-i}) = \tau_{i,i'}$ and $(t'_i, t_{-i}) = \tau_{0,i'}$, which gives

$$u_i(\tau_{i,i'}) \geq u_i(\tau_{0,i'}) + (b-a)q'^1_i(\tau_{0,i'}). \tag{13}$$

From Eqs. 12 and 13, we obtain

$$\begin{aligned}(b-a)Q(S_1^L)+U(S_1^L) &\leq p^{2n-1}(1-p)\sum_i\sum_{i'}u_i(\tau_{i,i'})\\ &\leq \frac{p}{1-p}\sum_i\sum_{i'}Pr\{\tau_{i,i'}\}\sum_{i''}u_{i''}(\tau_{i,i'})\\ &= \frac{p}{1-p}\sum_{t\in S_1'}Pr\{t\}\sum_i u_i(t)\\ &= \frac{p}{1-p}U(S_1').\end{aligned}$$

This proves Eq. 11, thus completing the proof of Eq. 7.

We now prove Eq. 8, the third inequality of Lemma 4.10. By definition

$$(b-a)Q(S_2)+U(S_2)=\sum_{t\in S_2}Pr\{t\}((b-a)\sum_{i,j}q'^j_i(t)+\sum_i u_i(t)). \tag{14}$$

Now observe that the DIC-Condition Eq. 9 for $\tau_{t,i}\in S_2'$ and $t\in S_2$ implies[2]

$$u_i(\tau_{t,i})\geq u_i(t)+(b-a)\sum_j q'^j_i(t) \tag{15}$$

From Eq. 14 and 15, we obtain

$$\begin{aligned}(b-a)Q(S_2)+U(S_2) &\leq \sum_{t\in S_2}Pr\{t\}\sum_i u_i(\tau_{t,i})\\ &= \frac{p}{1-p}\sum_{t\in S_2}\sum_i Pr\{\tau_{t,i}\}u_i(\tau_{t,i})\\ &\leq \frac{p}{1-p}\sum_{t\in S_2'}Pr\{t\}\sum_{i''}u_i(t)\\ &= \frac{p}{1-p}U(S_2').\end{aligned}$$

This proves Eq. 8. We have completed the proof of the Lemma 4.10. □

Proposition 1 can be straightforwardly derived from Lemma 4.10, Eq. 5, and the IR conditions $U(S_0), U(S_2)\geq 0$. This completes the proof of Proposition 1 and hence Theorem 4.1.

4.2 Realizing DIC Revenue

We turn to the proof of Theorem 4.2. We need to prove two statements.
Statement 1. $M_{D,\delta}$ is IR and DIC;
Statement 2. $M_{D,\delta}(\mathcal{F}_\delta)=r_D(\delta)$.

The proof of Statement 1 is straightforward by case analysis, and is omitted here (see the Appendix of arXiv: 1607.03685). For the rest of this subsection, we prove Statement 2. Here is the top level view of the proof. To show that the upper bound on revenue from Theorem 4.1 can be achieved, we demonstrate that several critical inequalities involved in the upper bound proof can be replaced by equalities. First, for mechanism $M_{D,\delta}$, it can be verified that Eqs. 3, 4 now are equalities, while

[2]If j is the cheap item in t, then $u_i(\tau_{t,i})\geq u_i(t)+(b-a)q'^j_i(t)$. However, $q'^j_i(t)=\sum_{j'}q'^{j'}_i(t)$ in this case, since $q'^{j'}_i(t)=0$ for $j'\neq j$.

Eq. 2 is replaced by $Q(S_0) = 2\alpha p_0, Q(S_1) = \beta p_1, Q(S_2) = \gamma p_2$. Combining these equalities gives us $M_{D,\delta}(\mathcal{F}_\delta) = r_D(\delta)$. We now give the details.

Fact 6. $u_i(t) = 0$ for all $t \notin S_1 \cup S_1' \cup S_2'$ and all i. Thus, $U = U(S_1) + U(S_1') + U(S_2')$.

Proof. From Eq. 1, we know that $u_i(t) \neq 0$ may occur only when $t = (t_i, t_{-i})$ and one of the following is valid: (a) $t_{-i} = (a,a)^{n-1}$ and $t_i \neq (a,a)$; (b) t_{-i} is 1-cheap and $t_i = (b,b)$. In case (a) we have $t \in S_1 \cup S_1'$, and in case (b) we have $t \in S_2'$. □

Fact 7.

$$\sum_{i,j} q'^j_i(t) = \begin{cases} 2\alpha & \text{if } t \in S_0 \\ \beta & \text{if } t \in S_1 \\ \gamma & \text{if } t \in S_2 \end{cases} \tag{16}$$

Proof. For the (only) profile t in S_0, the allocation function of $M_{D,\delta}$ specifies $\sum_{i,j} q'^j_i(t) = 2$ if $b < v_1$, and 0 otherwise. Similarly, for any profile $t \in S_1$, $\sum_{i,j} q'^j_i(t) = 1$ if $b < v_3$, and 0 otherwise; and for any profile $t \in S_2$, $\sum_{i,j} q'^j_i(t) = 1$ if $b < v_2$, and 0 otherwise. This is exactly the assertion of Fact 7. □

Lemma 4.11.

$$Q(S_0) = 2p_0\alpha, Q(S_1) = p_1\beta, Q(S_2) = p_2\gamma. \tag{17}$$

Proof. Follows immediately from Fact 3 and 7. □

Lemma 4.12.

$$M_{D,\delta}(\mathcal{F}_\delta) = 2(1-p^n)b + a\sum_{0\le \ell \le 2} Q(S_\ell) - (U(S_1) + U(S_1') + U(S_2')).$$

Proof. As under $M_{D,\delta}$ all the non-cheap items are allocated in full, the Basic Formula achieves equality, i.e. $M_{D,\delta}(\mathcal{F}_\delta) = 2(1-p^n)b + Qa - U$. Also from Fact 2 we have $Q = Q(S_0) + Q(S_1) + Q(S_2)$, and from Fact 6 we have $U = U(S_1) + U(S_1') + U(S_2')$. Lemma 4.12 follows. □

Lemma 4.13.

$$U(S_1) = (b-a)\frac{1-p}{p}Q(S_0), \tag{18}$$

$$U(S_1') = (b-a)\frac{1}{2}((\frac{1-p}{p})^2 Q(S_0) + (\frac{1-p}{p})Q(S_1)), \tag{19}$$

$$U(S_2') = (b-a)\frac{1-p}{p}Q(S_2). \tag{20}$$

Proof. Eq. 18 can easily be derived from Eq. 1, Lemma 4.11, and Fact 3. We omit the proof here.

To prove Eq. 19, note that for any $\tau_{i,i'} \in S_1'$, Eq. 1 implies $\sum_{i''} u_{i''}(\tau_{i,i'}) = (\frac{\alpha}{n} + \beta)(b-a)$ if $i = i'$, and 0 otherwise. Thus we have

$$\begin{aligned} U(S_1') &= \sum_{t \in S_1'} Pr\{t\} \sum_{i''} u_{i''}(t) \\ &= \sum_{i,i'} Pr\{\tau_{i,i'}\} \sum_{i''} u_{i''}(\tau_{i,i'}) \\ &= \sum_{i} Pr\{\tau_{i,i}\}(\frac{\alpha}{n} + \beta)(b-a) \\ &= p^{2n-2}(1-p)^2(\alpha + n\beta)(b-a). \end{aligned}$$

Making use of Lemma 4.11 and Fact 3, we obtain Eq. 19.

To prove Eq. 20, note that for any $t \in S_2, 1 \le i, i' \le n$ we have from Eq. 1

$$u_{i'}(\tau_{t,i}) = \begin{cases} \frac{\gamma}{|I(t)|}(b-a) & \text{if } i' = i \in I(t) \\ 0 & \text{otherwise.} \end{cases} \tag{21}$$

It follows that

$$\begin{aligned} U(S_2') &= \sum_{t' \in S_2'} Pr\{t'\} \sum_{i'} u_{i'}(t') \\ &= \sum_{t \in S_2} \sum_{i} \frac{1-p}{p} Pr\{t\} \sum_{i'} u_{i'}(\tau_{t,i}) \\ &= \frac{1-p}{p} \sum_{t \in S_2} Pr\{t\} \sum_{i \in I(t)} \frac{\gamma}{|I(t)|}(b-a) \\ &= \frac{1-p}{p} \gamma(b-a) \sum_{t \in S_2} Pr\{t\} \\ &= (b-a)\frac{1-p}{p} Q(S_2), \end{aligned} \tag{22}$$

where we used Lemma 4.11 and Fact 3 in the last step. This proves Eq. 20. We have finished the proof of Lemma 4.13. □

Using Lemmas 4.11-4.13 and simplifying the above equation, we obtain

$$M_{D,\delta}(\mathcal{F}_\delta) = r_D(\delta).$$

This proves Statement 2, and completes the proof of Theorem 4.2.

5 BIC MAXIMUM REVENUE

In this section we give a proof of the Main Theorem for the Bayesian implementation:

Theorem 5.1. *Any BIR-BIC mechanisms M must satisfy $M(\mathcal{F}_\delta) \le r_B(\delta)$.*

Theorem 5.2. *$M_{B,\delta}$ is IR-BIC, and $M_{B,\delta}(\mathcal{F}_\delta) = r_B(\delta)$.*

The proofs of Theorem 5.1 and 5.2 follow the same top-level outline as the proofs of Theorem 4.1 and 4.2. Lemma 4.5 and 4.6 proved in Section 4 are valid for any mechanism M, and will also be the starting point for the BIC proof.

5.1 Upper Bound to BIC Revenue

We prove Theorem 5.1 in this subsection. The key is to prove the following proposition.

Proposition 2. Any BIR-BIC mechanism M must satisfy the following inequality:

$$U \ge (b-a)\Big(\frac{1-p^2}{2p^2} Q(S_0) + \frac{1-p}{2p}(Q(S_1) + Q(S_2))\Big).$$

Theorem 5.1 can be derived from Lemma 4.5, 4.6 and Proposition 2 in exactly the same way as Theorem 4.1's derivation from Lemma 4.5, 4.6 and Proposition 1, and will not be repeated here. It remains to prove Proposition 2.

We use a subset of the BIR-BIC Conditions in our proof; these conditions are listed below for easy reference.

(a) BIR Condition: For each i,

$$\bar{u}_i(t_i) \geq 0 \text{ where } t_i = (a, a). \tag{23}$$

(b) BIC Condition: For each i,

$$\bar{u}_i(b, a) \geq \bar{u}_i(a, a) + (b - a)\bar{q'}^1_i(a, a). \tag{24}$$

$$\bar{u}_i(a, b) \geq \bar{u}_i(a, a) + (b - a)\bar{q'}^2_i(a, a). \tag{25}$$

$$\bar{u}_i(b, b) \geq \bar{u}_i(a, b) + (b - a)\bar{q'}^1_i(a, b). \tag{26}$$

$$\bar{u}_i(b, b) \geq \bar{u}_i(b, a) + (b - a)\bar{q'}^2_i(b, a). \tag{27}$$

The plan is to use Eqs. 23-27 to obtain a lower bound on U in terms of $Q(S_0)$, $Q(S_1)$ and $Q(S_2)$.

Lemma 5.3. *For each i,*

$$\bar{u}_i(b, a) + \bar{u}_i(a, b) \geq (b - a) \sum_j \bar{q'}^j_i(a, a).$$

Proof. Immediate from Eqs. 23-25. □

Lemma 5.4. *For each i,*

$$\begin{aligned}\bar{u}_i(b, b) \geq &\frac{1}{2}(b - a) \sum_j \bar{q'}^j_i(a, a) \\ &+ \frac{1}{2}(b - a) \sum_j \left(\bar{q'}^j_i(a, b) + \bar{q'}^j_i(b, a)\right).\end{aligned}$$

Proof. Adding up Eqs. 26 and 27, we obtain

$$\begin{aligned}\bar{u}_i(b, b) \geq &\frac{1}{2}\left(\bar{u}_i(b, a) + \bar{u}_i(b, a)\right) \\ &+ \frac{1}{2}(b - a) \sum_j \left(\bar{q'}^j_i(a, b) + \bar{q'}^j_i(b, a)\right),\end{aligned} \tag{28}$$

where we have used the fact that $q'^2_i((a, b), t_{-i}) = q'^1_i((b, a), t_{-i}) = 0$ for all t_{-i}. Lemma 5.4 now follows by using Lemma 5.3 on Eq. 28. □

We now express U as a convex combination of the left-hand sides of Eq 23, Lemmas 5.3 and 5.4, and obtain a lower bound in terms of $Q(S_\ell)$:

$$\begin{aligned}U &= \sum_i \sum_t Pr\{t\} u_i(t) \\ &= p^2 \sum_i \bar{u}_i(a, a) \\ &+ p(1 - p) \sum_i \left(\bar{u}_i(b, a) + \bar{u}_i(a, b)\right) \\ &+ (1 - p)^2 \sum_i \bar{u}_i(b, b) \\ &\geq C_1 + C_2,\end{aligned} \tag{29}$$

where

$$C_1 = (b-a)\big(p(1-p) + \frac{1}{2}(1-p)^2\big)\Big[\sum_i \sum_{t_{-i}} Pr\{t_{-i}\} \sum_j q'^j_i((a,a),t_{-i})\Big]$$

$$= (b-a)\frac{1-p^2}{2} \sum_i \sum_{t_{-i}} Pr\{t_{-i}\} \sum_j q'^j_i((a,a),t_{-i}), \tag{30}$$

$$\text{and} \quad C_2 = \frac{1}{2}(b-a)(1-p)^2 \sum_i \sum_{t_{-i}} Pr\{t_{-i}\} \sum_j \big(q'^j_i((a,b),t_{-i}) + q'^j_i((b,a),t_{-i})\big). \tag{31}$$

Separating out the $t_{-i} = (a,a)^{n-1}$ term in Eq. 30, we obtain

$$\begin{aligned} C_1 &= (b-a)\frac{1-p^2}{2}\Big[\sum_i p^{2n-2} \sum_j q'^j_i(\tau_{00}) \\ &\quad + \sum_i \sum_{t_{-i} \neq (a,a)^{n-1}} Pr\{t_{-i}\} \sum_j q'^j_i((a,a),t_{-i})\Big] \\ &\geq (b-a)\frac{1-p^2}{2p^2} Pr\{\tau_{00}\} \sum_{i,j} q'^j_i(\tau_{00}) \\ &\quad + (b-a)\frac{1-p}{2p} \sum_{\substack{t,i,t_i=(a,a) \\ t_{-i}\neq(a,a)^{n-1}}} Pr\{t\} \sum_j q'^j_i(t), \\ C_2 &= (b-a)\frac{1-p}{2p} \sum_{\substack{t,\ i \\ t_i \in \{(a,b),(b,a)\}}} Pr\{t\} \sum_j q'^j_i(t). \end{aligned}$$

It follows that

$$\begin{aligned} C_1 + C_2 &\geq (b-a)\frac{1-p^2}{2p^2} Q(S_0) \\ &\quad + (b-a)\frac{1-p}{2p} \sum_{t \neq \tau_{00}} \sum_{i, t_i \neq (b,b)} Pr\{t\} \sum_j q'^j_i(t). \end{aligned}$$

Now, noting that $\sum_j q'^j_i(t) = 0$ if $t_i = (b,b)$, we have

$$\begin{aligned} \sum_{t \neq \tau_{00}} \sum_{i, t_i \neq (b,b)} Pr\{t\} \sum_j q'^j_i(t) &= \sum_{t \neq \tau_{00}} Pr\{t\} \sum_i \sum_j q'^j_i(t) \\ &= \sum_{t \in S_1 \cup S_2} Pr\{t\} \sum_i \sum_j q'^j_i(t) \\ &= Q(S_1) + Q(S_2) \end{aligned} \tag{32}$$

where we have used Fact 2.

It follows from Eqs. 30-32 that

$$U \geq (b-a)\frac{1-p^2}{2p^2} Q(S_0) + (b-a)\frac{1-p}{2p}(Q(S_1) + Q(S_2)).$$

This proves Proposition 2, and completes the proof of Theorem 5.1.

5.2 Realizing BIC Revenue

To prove Theorem 5.2, it suffices to prove the following two statements.
Statement 3. $M_{B,\delta}$ is IR and BIC.
Statement 4. $M_{B,\delta}(\mathcal{F}_\delta) = r_B(\delta)$.

The proof of Statement 3 is straightforward, and is omitted here (see the Appendix of arXiv: 1607.03685). The rest of this subsection is devoted to the proof of Statement 4. The statement is clearly true if $b \geq v_3$ (i.e. *Case 3* in the definition of $M_{B,\delta}$), since in this case by definition $r_B(\delta) = r_D(\delta)$, $M_B(\mathcal{F}_\delta) = M_D(\mathcal{F}_\delta)$, and Theorem 4.2 has established $M_D(\mathcal{F}_\delta) = r_D(\delta)$. Thus we can assume $b \in (a, v_3)$ (i.e. Case 1 or 2). Note that in this situation $\beta = 1$ and $\alpha \in \{0, 1\}$.

The proof follows essentially the same outline as the proof of Statement 2 in Section 4.2. Fact 2, 3, 6 remain true; Fact 7, Lemmas 4.11, 4.12 are modified to the following.
Fact 8.

$$\sum_{i,j} q'^j_i(t) = \begin{cases} 2\alpha & \text{if } t \in S_0 \\ \beta & \text{if } t \in S_1 \cup S_2. \end{cases}$$

Lemma 5.5. $Q(S_0) = 2p_0\alpha, Q(S_1) = p_1\beta,$ *and* $Q(S_2) = p_2\beta$.

Lemma 5.6. $M_{B,\delta}(\mathcal{F}_\delta) = 2b(1-p^n) + a\sum_{0\leq\ell\leq2} Q(S_\ell) - (U(S_1) + U(S_1') + U(S_2'))$.

The two lemmas above are straightforward to prove. Finally, Lemma 4.13 is modified to the following:

Lemma 5.7.

$$U(S_1) = (b-a)\frac{1-p}{p}Q(S_0), \tag{33}$$

$$U(S_1') = (b-a)\frac{1}{2}((\frac{1-p}{p})^2 Q(S_0) + (\frac{1-p}{p})Q(S_1)), \tag{34}$$

$$U(S_2') = (b-a)\frac{1-p}{2p}Q(S_2). \tag{35}$$

The proof of Eqs. 33-34 is exactly the same as in the proof of Eqs. 18-19 in Lemma 4.13. The proof of Eq. 35 is also similar to the proof of Eq. 20 in Lemma 4.13. We omit the details here. Use Lemmas 5.5-5.7 and simplify, we obtain

$$M_{B,\delta}(\mathcal{F}_\delta) = r_B(\delta).$$

This proves Statement 4, and completes the proof of Theorem 5.2.

REFERENCES

[1] M. Babaioff, N. Immorlica, B. Lucier, and S. M. Weinberg. 2014. A simple and aproximately optimal mechanism for an additive buyer. *Proceedings of the 55th Annual IEEE Symposium on Foundations of Computer Science(FOCS)* (2014).

[2] K. C. Border. 1991. Implementations of reduced form auctions: a geometric approach. *Econometrica* 59, 4 (1991), 1175–1187.

[3] K. C. Border. 2007. Reduced form revisited. *Economic Theory* 31 (2007), 167–181.

[4] Y. Cai, C. Daskalakis, and S. M. Weinberg. 2012. An algorithmic characterization of multi-dimensional mechanisms. *Proceedings of the 44th Annual ACM Symposium on Theory of Computing (STOC)* (2012), 459–478.

[5] Y. Cai, C. Daskalakis, and S. M. Weinberg. 2013. Reducing revenue to welfare maximization: approximation algorithms and other generalizations. *Proceedings of the 24th ACM-SIAM Symposium on Discrete Algorithms (SODA)* (2013), 578–595.

[6] Y. Cai, N. R. Devanur, and S. M. Weinberg. 2016. A duality based unified approach to Bayesian mechanism design. *Proceedings of the 52th Annual ACM Symposium on Theory of Computing (STOC)* (2016).

[7] S. Chawla, J. D. Hartline, D. L. Malec, and B. Sivan. 2010. Multi-parameter mechanism design and sequential posted pricing. *Proceedings of the 42th Annual ACM Symposium on Theory of Computing (STOC)* (2010), 311–320.

[8] X. Chen, I. Diakonikolas, D. Paparas, X. Sun, and M. Yannakakis. 2014. The complexity of optimal multidimensional pricing. *Proceedings of the 25th Annual ACM-SIAM Symposium on Discrete Algorithms (SODA)* (2014).

[9] J. Cremer and R. P. McLean. 1988. Full extraction of the surplus in Bayesian and dominant-strategy auction. *Econometrica* 56 (1988), 1247–1257.

[10] C. Daskalakis, A. Deckelbaum, and C. Tzamos. 2014. The complexity of optimal mechanism design. *Proceedings of the 25th Annual ACM-SIAM Symposium on Discrete Algorithms (SODA)* (2014).

[11] C. Daskalakis and S. M. Weinberg. 2012. Symmetries and optimal multi-dimensional mechanism design. *Proceedings of the 13th ACM Conference on Electronic Commerce* (2012), 370–387.

[12] M. Feldman, N. Gravin, and B. Lucier. 2015. Combinatorial auctions via posted price. *Proceedings of the 26th ACM-SIAM Symposium on Discrete Algorithms (SODA)* (2015), 123–135.

[13] A. Gershkov, J. K. Goeree, A. Kushnir, B. Moldovanu, and X. Shi. 2013. On the equivalence of Bayesian and dominant-strategy implementation. *Econometrica* 81 (2013), 197–220.

[14] Y. Giannakopoulos. 2014. Bounding the optimal revenue of selling multiple goods. *arxiv report 1404.2832* (2014), 259–276.

[15] Y. Giannakopoulos. 2014. A note on selling optimally two uniformly distributed goods. *arxiv report 1409.6925* (2014).

[16] Y. Giannakopoulos and E. Koutsoupias. 2014. Duality and optimality of auctions for uniform distributions. *Proceedings of the 15th ACM Conference on Electronic Commerce* (2014), 259–276.

[17] Y. Giannakopoulos and E. Koutsoupias. 2015. Selling two goods optimally. *Proceedings of ICALP'15* (2015), 650–662.

[18] S. Hart and N. Nisan. 2012. Approximate revenue maximization with multiple items. *Proceedings of the 13th ACM Conference on Electric Commerce (EC)* (2012), 656.

[19] S. Hart and P. Reny. 2015. Maximizing revenue with multiple goods: Nonmonotonicity and other observations. *Theoretical Economics* 10 (2015), 893–992.

[20] J. D. Hartline, R. Kleinberg, and A. Malekian. 2011. Bayesian incentive compatability via matchings. *Proceedings of the 22th ACM-SIAM Symposium on Discrete Algorithms (SODA)* (2011), 734–747.

[21] J. D. Hartline and T. Roughgarden. 2009. Simple mechanisms for a subadditive buyer and applications to revenue monotonicity. *Proceedings of the 10th ACM Conference on Electronic Commerce* (2009).

[22] X. Li and A. C. Yao. 2013. On revenue maximization for selling multiple independently distributed items. *Proceedings of the National Academy of Sciences USA* 110, 28 (2013), 11232–11237.

[23] A. M. Manelli and D. R. Vincent. 2006. Bundling as an optimal selling mechanism for a multiple-good monopolist. *Journal of Economic Theory* 127, 1 (2006), 1–35.

[24] R. B. Myerson. 1981. Optimal auction design. *Mathematics of Operations Research* 6, 1 (1981), 58–73.

[25] G. Pavlov. 2011. Optimal mechanism for selling two goods. *The BE Journal of Theoretical Economics* 11 (2011).

[26] A. Ronen. 2001. On approximating optimal auctions. *Proceedings of the 3rd ACM Conference on Electric Commerce (EC)* (2001), 11–17.

[27] A. Rubinstein and S. M. Weinberg. 2015. Simple mechanisms for a subadditive buyer and applications to revenue monotonicity. *Proceedings of the 16th ACM Conference on Electronic Commerce* (2015), 377–394.

[28] Z. Wang and P. Tang. 2014. Optimal mechanisms with simple menus. *Proceedings of the 15th ACM Conference on Electronic Commerce* (2014), 227–240.

[29] Z. Wang and P. Tang. 2016. Ironing the border: optimal auctions for negatively correlated items. *Proceedings of the 17th ACM Conference on Electronic Commerce* (2016).

[30] A. C. Yao. 2015. An n-to-1 bidder reduction for multi-item auctions and its applications. *Proceedings of the 25th ACM-SIAM Symposium on Discrete Algorithms (SODA)* (2015), 92–109.

Deferred-Acceptance Auctions for Multiple Levels of Service

VASILIS GKATZELIS, Drexel University
EVANGELOS MARKAKIS, Athens University of Economics & Business
TIM ROUGHGARDEN, Stanford University

Deferred-acceptance (DA) auctions are mechanisms that are based on backward-greedy algorithms and possess a number of remarkable incentive properties, including implementation as an obviously-strategyproof ascending auction. All existing work on DA auctions considers only binary single-parameter problems, where each bidder either "wins" or "loses." This paper generalizes the DA auction framework to non-binary settings, and applies this generalized framework to obtain approximately welfare-maximizing DA auctions for a number of basic mechanism design problems: multiunit auctions, problems with polymatroid constraints or multiple knapsack constraints, and the problem of scheduling jobs to minimize their total weighted completion time. Our results require the design of novel backward-greedy algorithms with good approximation guarantees.

CCS Concepts: • **Theory of computation → Approximation algorithms analysis**; **Algorithmic game theory and mechanism design**;

Additional Key Words and Phrases: deferred-acceptance auctions; mechanism design; social welfare; approximation algorithms; scheduling

1 INTRODUCTION

The work of Milgrom and Segal [33] recently proposed the framework of *Deferred-Acceptance (DA) Auctions*, a family of single-parameter mechanisms with a number of remarkable incentive properties. In fact, the reverse auction part of the very recently concluded FCC Incentive Auction for reallocating spectrum was a DA auction [14]. DA auctions can be thought of as running an adaptive backward greedy algorithm for deciding the set of accepted bidders. The mechanism maintains a score for each active bidder (which can change from round to round), and rejects in each round the bidder with the lowest score, stopping when the still-active bidders constitute a feasible solution. This contrasts with standard (forward) greedy algorithms, which begin with the empty set and iteratively add the bidder with the highest score (subject to feasibility constraints).

DA auctions are appealing in practice for a number of reasons. First, DA auctions can be implemented as ascending clock auctions (or descending auctions if applied to procurement auctions), which has several desirable consequences. Truthful bidding is a dominant strategy, even in the sense of *obvious strategyproofness* formalized by Li [28]; see the discussion in Section 3. In contrast, a sealed-bid Vickrey auction, for example, is not obviously strategyproof in this sense. This is important for the participation and behavior of non-expert users, who may not fully understand the computations involved in setting the clock prices. Furthermore, every DA auction satisfies

This work is supported by the National Science Foundation, under grants CCF-1216073, CCF-1161813, CCF-1408635, and CCF-1524062. Part of this work took place while the authors were visiting the Simons Institute for the Theory of Computing.

EC'17, June 26–30, 2017, Cambridge, Massachusetts, USA. © 2017 ACM. ISBN 978-1-4503-4527-9/17/06...$15.00.
DOI: http://dx.doi.org/10.1145/3033274.3085142

weak group-strategyproofness (WGSP). That is, no coalition of bidders can collectively submit false bids in a way that makes every bidder of the coalition strictly better off. We refer the reader to [34] for further advantages and motivation behind DA auctions.

Unfortunately, DA auctions do not always achieve a good approximation to the social welfare. Backward greedy algorithms can be inferior to forward greedy algorithms, and the former need not even produce an inclusion-maximal solution. Driven by this concern, Dütting et al. [11] subsequently explored the power and limitations of DA auctions from an approximation algorithms viewpoint (see also related work below). Their main results concern knapsack auctions and combinatorial auctions with single-minded bidders. For example, in the latter setting, novel DA auctions can nearly match the performance of arbitrary truthful and computationally efficient mechanisms.

All work thus far on DA auctions has concerned *binary* problems, i.e., settings where each bidder either "wins" or "loses." In many scenarios, however, a bidder receives some "level of service" rather than a binary decision. Think, for example, of an air ticket purchase. Depending on the buyer's willingness to pay, the available choices may include basic economy class, economy class with a more comfortable seat and more leg room, economy class with extra bag allowance, or business class. In a multi-unit auction with non-unit demand bidders, the level of service corresponds to the number of items awarded. In a cloud computing setting, levels of service could correspond to possible completion times of a user's task. The goal of this paper is to generalize the DA auction framework to non-binary settings, and apply this generalized framework to a number of basic mechanism design problems.

Our results: The first contribution of this paper is to extend the DA auction framework to non-binary settings, where each bidder receives some level of service, subject to feasibility constraints (Definitions 3.1 and 7.1). We consider bidders with downward-sloping valuations, meaning that a bidder's marginal value for upgrading to the next level of service is non-increasing in the level. The key idea in the generalization is to complement the usual DA auction scoring function with a *clinching function* that specifies the level of service that each bidder has clinched as the auction progresses. Just like in a DA auction, at each stage, a generalized DA auction decides which bidder to remove from the set of active bidders. The difference is that upon removal, the clinching function also determines the level of service received by the bidder who leaves the auction. We show that, provided the clinching functions are monotone, these generalized DA auctions possess the key incentive guarantees of binary DA auctions, including an obviously strategyproof ascending implementation and weak group-strategyproofness.

We demonstrate the usefulness of this framework by designing new DA auctions for four different problems.

(i) Allocation problems where the service levels of the bidders must obey a polymatroid constraint and where bidders have linear valuations. Here, we show that the VCG mechanism can be implemented in our generalized DA framework (Proposition 4.1).

(ii) Job scheduling for minimizing the total weighted completion time. Here, we give a novel generalized DA scheduling auction that achieves a $2(1+\sqrt{2})$-approximation of the optimal social welfare (Section 5). A priori, it is not obvious that a constant factor approximation can be achieved by any backward greedy algorithm.

(iii) Knapsack auctions with multiple knapsacks available, where the set of bidders assigned to the same level need to satisfy a knapsack constraint, and bidders have linear valuations. Even in the binary setting with one knapsack, no DA auction can achieve an approximation ratio better than $O(\log m)$, where m is the size of the knapsack. We show that even with multiple knapsacks, there is a DA auction achieving a $O(\log m)$-approximation of the optimal social welfare (Theorem 6.1).

(iv) Multi-unit auctions where bidders have general downward-sloping valuations. Even with two bidders and two units, the VCG mechanism cannot be implemented as a generalized DA auction, and neither can any weakly group-strategyproof mechanism (Proposition 7.3). We give a novel DA multiunit auction that achieves an $O(\log n)$-approximation to the social welfare, where n is the number of agents (Theorem 7.6).

For settings (ii)–(iv), we are not aware of any existing weakly group-strategyproof mechanisms (DA or otherwise) with non-trivial approximation guarantees.

Related Work. Milgrom and Segal [33] initiated the study of procurement DA auctions, motivated by FCC auctions for reallocating spectrum. In a procurement auction it is the bidders who own the resources that the auctioneer wishes to buy. As discussed in their work, the properties that they established, such as group-strategyproofness and implementability as a clock auction, can be easily shown to hold also for the more common type of selling auctions, which is the focus of our work. In a recent version of their paper, Milgrom and Segal [34] analyze the social welfare that can be attained by DA auctions in a procurement setting with near matroid structure. They show that in this setting a DA auction attains near optimal performance, generalizing well-known results in combinatorial optimization which show that forward and backward greedy algorithms are optimal on matroids [see, e.g., 26].

Following up on the work of [33], Dütting et al. [11] explored the power and limitations of DA auctions from an approximation algorithms viewpoint. They provided both positive and negative results for knapsack auctions and auctions with single-minded bidders. On the positive side, for single-minded bidders, it was shown that we can have almost matching approximation results by DA auctions as the existing ones in the literature, hence providing stronger incentive guarantees to the known approximations. In particular, an $O(d)$-approximation was obtained via a DA auction, when the size of each requested bundle is at most d, matching the known d-approximation of [27], which is obtained by a forward greedy algorithm. A different DA auction was also shown to achieve a $\sqrt{m \log m}$-approximation, almost matching the known $\sqrt{m}$-approximation of [27], where m is the number of available items. On the negative side, for knapsack auctions, it was shown that no DA auction can achieve an approximation that is sublogarithmic in m, establishing a separation with the constant factor approximations that are known if we only want strategyproof mechanisms.

There have been several other works that have already appeared regarding the applicability of the DA auctions framework. In the procurement setting, the performance of DA auctions has been further studied by Kim [25], for spectrum and bandwidth reallocation problems. Nguyen and Sandholm [37] provide an experimental evaluation of the performance of various DA heuristics for the actual interference constraints of the upcoming FCC auction. The DA framework has also been extended to double auctions by Dütting et al. [12] and to multilateral markets by Blumrosen and Zohar [7]. The application to double auctions is explored further by Marx and Loertscher [29]. These works also point out the advantages of the DA framework in obtaining budget balance for double auctions. In a similar spirit, Ensthaler and Giebe [13] and Jarman and Meisner [20] point out the advantages of the DA auctions in the design of budget-constrained procurement auctions.

Group-strategyproof mechanisms have been studied extensively prior to the DA auctions framework, among others, in the context of cost-sharing mechanisms [10, 18, 19, 21, 22, 30, 35]. This line of work has also analyzed the economic efficiency that can be achieved with these mechanisms. As has been observed, often the stronger incentive properties come at a significant cost in terms of economic efficiency [see, e.g., 39]. Finally, the stronger notion of "obvious strategyproofness" has been recently introduced by [28].

There is an extensive literature on ascending auctions for both single-parameter and multi-parameter settings pre-dating the DA framework. For single-parameter settings, an ascending auction based on the backward greedy algorithm for matroids is described in Bikhchandani et al. [4]. Babaioff et al. [3] provide a procedure converting any algorithm to a dominant-strategy ascending auction (with some loss in the approximation factor). For multi-parameter settings, Ausubel [1] describes an ascending auction for identical items and bidders with decreasing marginal values. Ascending auctions for non-identical items and bidders with gross substitute preferences appear in [2, 17, 24, 31]. For a comprehensive study of the computational and informational aspects of iterative auctions see [5, 6].

2 PRELIMINARIES

We focus on problems where some type of service needs to be assigned to each of n agents in a set N. This service can be offered at different quality levels (including no service at all) but, due to scarcity or cost of this service, there are restrictions in the levels that can be allocated. We represent the levels of service as rational numbers, hence, the feasible service allocation outcomes are defined by a set system $\mathcal{I} \subseteq \mathbb{Q}^N$.[1] We assume that $\mathcal{I}$ is non-empty and *downward closed*, meaning that if $T \in \mathcal{I}$ and $T' \subseteq T$, then $T' \in \mathcal{I}$. Note that the binary setting, to which previous work on DA auctions was restricted, corresponds to the special case where $\mathcal{I} \subseteq \{0,1\}^N$.

We assume that each bidder has a private valuation function such that $v_i(\ell)$ is the value of bidder i for obtaining the level of service ℓ. Although all of our mechanisms can be implemented as ascending auctions, our presentation focuses on direct-revelation mechanisms in the form $\mathcal{M} = (f, p)$, which consist of an outcome rule f and a payment rule p. In our setting, given a vector of bids $\mathbf{b} = (b_i)_{i \in N}$, where b_i denotes the bid reported by bidder i (coming either from a single-parameter or multi-parameter domain, depending on the form of the function $v_i(\cdot)$), the outcome rule f computes a feasible solution, i.e., a set of $\mathcal{I}$, so that every bidder is assigned a level of service. On the same input, the payment rule p computes payments $\mathbf{p} = (p_i(\mathbf{b}))_{i \in N} \in \mathbb{R}^n$ where $p_i(\mathbf{b})$ denotes the payment of bidder i.

Given a mechanism $\mathcal{M} = (f, p)$, and a bid vector $\mathbf{b}$, let $\ell_i = f_i(\mathbf{b})$ be the level of service assigned to bidder i by the mechanism. We assume that the bidders have quasi-linear utilities and hence bidder i's utility equals $u_i^{\mathcal{M}}(\mathbf{b}) = v_i(\ell_i) - p_i(\mathbf{b})$. Since bidders can be strategic in reporting their bids to the mechanism, towards maximizing their own utility, we aim for mechanisms that provide incentive guarantees. We say that a mechanism $\mathcal{M}$ is *strategyproof* or *incentive compatible* if for any bidder i, for any bid vector $\mathbf{b}_{-i} = (b_j)_{j \neq i}$, and any bid $\bar{b}_i$ of bidder i

$$u_i^{\mathcal{M}}(v_i, \mathbf{b}_{-i}) \geq u_i^{\mathcal{M}}(\bar{b}_i, \mathbf{b}_{-i}).$$

We are interested in an even stronger form of resistance to manipulation, namely resistance against coalitions of bidders. Given a subset of bidders $S \subseteq N$, and a bidding vector $\mathbf{b}$, we denote by $\mathbf{b}_S$, the vector containing only the bids of S, and by $\mathbf{b}_{-S}$ the bids of the remaining bidders. We say that a mechanism $\mathcal{M}$ is *weakly group-strategyproof* (WGSP) if for any coalition $S \subseteq N$, for any vector $\mathbf{b}_{-S} = (b_j)_{j \notin S}$, and for any vector $\bar{\mathbf{b}}_S = (\bar{b}_j)_{j \in S}$ of the bidders in S, it holds that

$$u_i^{\mathcal{M}}(\mathbf{v}_S, \mathbf{b}_{-S}) \geq u_i^{\mathcal{M}}(\bar{\mathbf{b}}_S, \mathbf{b}_{-S}) \text{ for some } i \in S.$$

Hence, there is no coalition that can make all its members strictly better off by deviating from the truth.[2]

[1] In our exposition, we do not need to impose a priori an upper bound on the maximum possible level of service.

[2] There is an even stronger form of group-strategyproofness, requiring that there is no coalitional deviation where some members are better off and the rest are not worse off, but DA auctions do not usually guarantee this property.

Apart from the incentive issues, one of the main objectives we try to optimize in mechanism design is the *social welfare*. If $T = (\ell_1, \ldots, \ell_n) \in \mathcal{I}$ is a feasible solution, the generated social welfare is $SW(T) = \sum_i v_i(\ell_i)$. A mechanism $\mathcal{M}$ with an allocation rule f achieves an approximation ratio of ρ if

$$\max_{\mathbf{v}} \frac{SW(OPT(\mathbf{v}))}{SW(f(\mathbf{v}))} \leq \rho,$$

where $OPT(\mathbf{v}) = \arg\max_{T \in \mathcal{I}} \{SW(T)\}$ denotes a welfare-maximizing outcome.

3 GENERALIZED SINGLE-PARAMETER DEFERRED-ACCEPTANCE AUCTIONS

We begin by proposing a generalization of the DA auctions framework of [34] that captures non-binary single-parameter settings. We assume that each bidder can receive one of multiple levels of service, and for now, that her value for level $\ell \in \mathbb{Q}$ equals to $v_i \cdot \ell$. This linearity assumption is common in many applications, including sponsored search advertising and job scheduling. Section 7 generalizes the framework to the multi-parameter setting of downward-sloping valuations.

We define a generalized DA auction by combining a scoring function with a provisional allocation function, which we will refer to as the *clinching function*. Clinching functions are the key innovation of our generalized framework. The auction begins with all bidders being active, it operates in a sequence of stages, and after each stage it finalizes the level of service of some active bidder. This process continues, until the level of service for every bidder has been finalized. Prices are then set using Myerson's Lemma, to enforce truthfulness (see below).

Definition 3.1. A DA auction operates in discrete stages $t \geq 1$. We denote by $A_t \subseteq N$ the set of currently active bidders in the beginning of each stage t; initially, $A_1 = N$, and $A_{t+1} \subset A_t$, for every $t \geq 1$. The DA auction is fully defined by two collections of functions:

- The **scoring functions** $\sigma_i^{A_t}(b_i, \mathbf{b}_{N \setminus A_t})$, that are non-decreasing in their first argument.
- The **clinching functions** $g_i^{A_t}(\mathbf{b}_{N \setminus A_t})$, which are non-increasing w.r.t. the set of active bidders, i.e.: $g_i^{A_{t+1}}(\mathbf{b}_{N \setminus A_{t+1}}) \geq g_i^{A_t}(\mathbf{b}_{N \setminus A_t})$.

At each stage t, if $A_t \neq \emptyset$, then the level of service of some active bidder $i \in \arg\min_{i \in A_t} \{\sigma_i^{A_t}(b_i, \mathbf{b}_{N \setminus A_t})\}$ is finalized, possibly with the use of some tie-breaking rule. That is, a bidder i with the lowest score stops being active, we set $A_{t+1} = A_t \setminus \{i\}$, and her level of service is finalized at level $g_i^{A_t}(\mathbf{b}_{N \setminus A_t})$. When we reach $A_t = \emptyset$, then the auction terminates and the payment of each bidder is determined by Myerson's lemma (see Equation (1)).

The scoring and clinching functions generally change throughout the stages. These functions can depend on the bids of non-active bidders, $\mathbf{b}_{N \setminus A_t}$, and on the set of active bidders, A_t, though not the actual bids of active bidders, for incentive reasons.

For a given bid vector $\mathbf{b} = (b_i)_{i \in N} \in \mathbb{R}_+^n$, the DA auction implies an outcome rule f, which defines the level of service $f_i(\mathbf{b})$ of each bidder i. If this outcome rule always outputs a feasible solution (a set of $\mathcal{I}$), then we say that the DA auction is *feasible*. The following lemma shows that the allocation rule $f_i(\mathbf{b})$ implied by a DA auction is always monotone w.r.t. the bid b_i of bidder i. The proof of the lemma is deferred to the full version of the paper.

Lemma 3.2. *Any generalized DA auction yields a monotone allocation rule, i.e., for any bid vector* $\mathbf{b}$, *and any* $b_i' < b_i$, *we have* $f_i(b_i', \mathbf{b}_{-i}) \leq f_i(\mathbf{b})$.

Next we derive payments according to Myerson's lemma [36], given the monotone allocation function $f(b_i, \mathbf{b}_{-i})$, which are appropriate summations of threshold values for each level of service. Formally, suppose that under $(b_i, \mathbf{b}_{-i})$, bidder i receives level of service i_ℓ. Let $L_i = \{i_1, i_2, ..., i_\ell\}$

with $i_1 < i_2 < \cdots < i_\ell$, be the levels of service that are attainable, as we let the bid of i increase from 0 to b_i, keeping $\mathbf{b}_{-i}$ fixed. The monotonicity of the levels we encounter is ensured by the monotonicity of the allocation rule $f_i(\cdot)$. For each $i_j \in L_i$, let z_j be the following threshold value:

$$z_j(\mathbf{b}_{-i}) = \inf_{b'_i \geq 0} \{b'_i : f_i(b'_i, \mathbf{b}_{-i}) \geq i_j\}.$$

Then, the payment of bidder i comes from the following formula:

$$p_i(\mathbf{b}) = \sum_{j=1}^{\ell} z_j(\mathbf{b}_{-i}) \cdot (i_j - i_{j-1}), \tag{1}$$

where for $j = 1$, we set $i_0 = 0$.

We next show that the mechanism induced by such an allocation rule and corresponding payment rule is weakly group-strategyproof.

Theorem 3.3. *Every generalized DA auction is weakly group strategy-proof.*

Proof. Assume there exists a coalition of bidders $K \subseteq N$ that can coordinate in misreporting their values in a way that strictly improves the utility of every $i \in K$. We show that this assumption leads to a contradiction.

Let v_i denote the true value of each bidder i and v'_i be the value reported by $i \in K$. Also, let $\alpha \in K$ be the bidder of the coalition who would be finalized first (at stage t_α) according to the true values, and let $\beta \in K$ be the bidder of the coalition who is finalized first (at stage t_β) after the deviation.

First, we show that $t_\beta > t_\alpha$. Aiming for a contradiction assume that, after the deviation, bidder β is finalized at stage $t_\beta \leq t_\alpha$, and this deviation strictly increases her utility. According to the definition of the generalized DA auctions, the sequence of bidders finalized during the first $t_\beta - 1$ stages under the deviation is identical to the corresponding sequence of bidders finalized prior to the deviation. To verify this fact, note that the scores of these bidders are not affected by the deviation, since all the bidders in K remain active during the first $t_\beta - 1$ stages (recall that the scores at a stage t maybe affected by the bids of $N \setminus A_t$ and not by active bidders). Hence, both in the original profile as well as in the deviation, the level of service that has been clinched by bidder β by stage t_β, and the total payment for this level is the same. Since we have assumed $t_\beta \leq t_\alpha$, bidder β was receiving a weakly higher level of service prior to the deviation. Moreover, the cost for any additional levels of service compared to the level she receives under the deviation, was at most v_β. Hence, overall the utility of β cannot have increased with the deviation, leading to a contradiction.

Therefore, there exists some bidder $i \notin K$ who is rejected at stage t_α after the deviation, and was finalized at some stage $t_i > t_\alpha$ prior to the deviation. Since bidder α was finalized before bidder i prior to the deviation, and using the fact that both of these bidders' scores are the same before and after the deviation, we infer that $v'_\alpha > v_\alpha$. Also, if ℓ_α and ℓ'_α is the level of service that α receives before and after the deviation, this means that $\ell'_\alpha > \ell_\alpha$ (otherwise the utility of α would be the same after the deviation) and the threshold price of any level higher than ℓ_α is at least v_α (since α would be rejected at stage t_α if she did not strictly increase her bid). Then, according to Equation 1, the additional payment of α, for the additional $\ell'_\alpha - \ell_\alpha$ levels of service is at least

$$\sum_{j=\ell_\alpha+1}^{\ell'_\alpha} v_\alpha \cdot (i_j - i_{j-1}) \geq (\ell'_\alpha - \ell_\alpha) v_\alpha.$$

Note that the payment of α for the first ℓ_α levels is the same as before since $t_\beta > t_\alpha$. Hence, since the value of α for these additional levels of service is $(\ell'_\alpha - \ell_\alpha)v_\alpha$, this means that bidder α could not have strictly increased her utility upon deviating. □

Apart from group-strategy-proofness, the DA framework also guarantees several other important properties that are desirable for practical purposes. In particular, [34] showed that a (binary) DA auction can be implemented by an ascending clock auction. This means that we can think of the auction as running in a sequence of periods, and offering an ascending sequence of prices to every bidder. Our generalization can also be implemented as such an ascending auction. As a result, it obvious for the bidders to verify that truth-telling is their optimal strategy, even if they are not aware of how the clock prices are set. This is in contrast, e.g., to the VCG mechanism, where it is not at all clear a priori why a bidder should behave truthfully. This distinction is formalized under the notion of *obvious strategy-proofness* in [28].

The following two propositions summarize the fact that such properties carry over to the setting of generalized DA auctions as well, which further justifies their appeal. The proof of the propositions as well as a discussion regarding clock auctions can be found in the full version of the paper.

Proposition 3.4. *Every generalized DA auction, can be implemented as an ascending clock auction.*

We henceforth refer to the class of ascending clock auctions derived from generalized DA auctions according to Proposition 3.4 as *generalized DA ascending auctions.*

Proposition 3.5. *Every generalized DA ascending auction is obviously strategyproof.*

4 WARM-UP: POLYMATROID CONSTRAINTS

We begin our study of generalized DA auctions by considering settings where the set of feasible outcomes is defined by a polymatroid constraint (defined below).

For instance, consider a multiunit auction with k identical copies of the same good, and additive bidders, so that bidder i's value for acquiring ℓ_i units of the good (a level of service ℓ_i) is $\ell_i \cdot v_i$. The constraint in this case is that $\sum_i \ell_i \leq k$, i.e., the number of units to be allocated is at most k. For another example, consider the keyword sponsored search auctions, where the sellers are competing for a sequence of $q < n$ advertising slots, and each slot j has a click-through rate r_j. If bidder i's value for a click is v_i, then its value for slot j is $r_j \cdot v_i$, and we say that i receives a level of service of $\ell_i = r_j$. This time, the constraint is that the outcome $(\ell_1, \ell_2, ..., \ell_n)$ needs to correspond to a matching of bidders to slots, with $\ell_i = 0$ for any bidder who is not matched to a slot. For more motivating examples see also [4].

More generally, in this section we consider problems, where the set of feasible outcomes is defined via a given submodular function $h : 2^n \longrightarrow \mathbb{R}_+$, as follows:

$$P_h = \left\{ \ell \in \mathbb{N}^n \mid \sum_{i \in S} \ell_i \leq h(S) \; \forall S \subseteq N \right\}.$$

In the first setting provided above, i.e., the multiunit auction with k available units, the polymatroid constraint is defined by the constant (submodular) function h, with $h(S) = k$ for every $S \subseteq N$. In the second setting, if we assume that $r_1 \geq r_2 \geq \cdots \geq r_q$, the polymatroid constraint is defined by $h(S) = \sum_{j=1}^{|S|} r_j$. This implies that any single bidder i gets $\ell_i \leq r_1$, any two bidders i, i' get $\ell_i + \ell_{i'} \leq r_1 + r_2$, and so on.

As a first application of our framework, we show that, in fact, there is a simple generalized DA auction that achieves the optimal social welfare in any problem instance involving polymatroid constraints. Given the submodular function h of the polymatroid constraint, the scoring and clinching functions of this auction are as follows:

- The polymatroid auction scoring function is $\sigma_i^{A_t}(b_i, \mathbf{b}_{N \setminus A_t}) = b_i$.
- The polymatroid auction clinching function is $g_i^{A_t}(b_{N \setminus A_t}) = h(A_t) - h(A_t \setminus \{i\})$.

Note that this DA auction has a very simple scoring function, which is not adaptive. In particular, at every stage, the bidder who is finalized by this DA auction is the one with the smallest bid, among the ones that are still active. What is more interesting is the clinching function, according to which, at each stage t each bidder $i \in A_t$ has clinched a level of service equal to her marginal contribution to the value of $h(A_t)$. Since h is submodular, this marginal contribution weakly increases as A_t shrinks, so this is a valid clinching function.

For a concrete example of how this auction works, we consider the two settings described above. In the multiunit setting, this auction would keep finalizing the lower valued bidders without letting them clinch any item, until only the highest bidder is active, at which point this bidder clinches all k units. For each one of these units, the price is equal to the second highest bid. In the keyword sponsored search setting, during the first $n-q$ stages, the $n-q$ lowest bidders are finalized without clinching any slots. Then, at stage $n-q+1$ *every* active bidder clinches a level of service of r_q, which is the click through rate of the worst slot, q, and the lowest value bidder $i \in A_{n-q+1}$ is finalized at $\ell_i = r_q$, i.e., it is assigned to that slot. Note that, after stage $n-q+1$, every active bidder is guaranteed a level of service of at least r_q, and the price that the top q bidders pay for clinching this level of service is $b_{q+1}r_q$, i.e., r_q times the $(q+1)$-th highest bid. As the auction moves on, more bidders get finalized, and the price that they pay for the additional levels of service that they clinch weakly increases over time.

To verify that this auction always yields the maximum social welfare, note that its outcome is exactly the same as the one that would arise if we instead used the following forward greedy algorithm. First, give the highest bidder, i, the highest level of service possible, i.e., $h(\{i\})$. Then, give the second highest bidder the highest level possible, given the existing assignment to i, i.e., i' gets $h(\{i,i'\}) - h(\{i\})$, and so on. This greedy algorithm is known to be optimal in polymatroid settings [15].

In fact, the auction presented above is exactly what the ascending auction of [4] reduces to if the valuations of the bidders are additive, and what the ascending auction of [16] reduces to if we remove the budget constraints. Furthermore, the allocation and the payments of this auction is the same as that of the VCG auction. Since these auctions lie within the generalized DA framework, all of the incentive guarantees of the previous section (Theorem 3.3–Proposition 3.5) apply.

Proposition 4.1. *When the set of feasible allocations is defined by a polymatroid constraint, the VCG mechanism is a generalized DA auction.*

In contrast to Proposition 4.1, in Section 7 we show that the VCG mechanism is not generally a DA auction when bidders have downward-sloping valuations.

5 SCHEDULING CONSTRAINTS

To exhibit the strength of our generalization and the diversity of settings that it applies to, we now consider a well-studied non-binary problem of job scheduling.

Given a set of m identical machines and a set N of n jobs, each of which needs processing time p_i on any one of the machines, a *schedule* is an assignment of each job to a machine. Furthermore, for each machine j, the schedule defines which one of its assigned jobs the machine will process at any given time. As a result, if a schedule x assigns the jobs of bidders 1, 2, and 3 on the same machine, to be processed in that order with no idle time, the *completion times* of the jobs will be $c_1(x) = p_1$, $c_2(x) = p_1 + p_2$, and $c_3(x) = p_1 + p_2 + p_3$ respectively. Depending on its urgency, or importance, each job i also has a weight v_i, and the objective of this scheduling problem is to compute a schedule x that minimizes the weighted completion time $\sum_{i \in N} v_i c_i(x)$.

This problem has received considerable attention (see [9] for a survey of relevant results) and it is known to be NP-hard [8]. But, the following simple greedy algorithm achieves a $(1+\sqrt{2})/2 \approx 1.207$-approximation for this problem [23, 40]: order the jobs in non-increasing order of their v_i/p_i ratio and schedule them, in that order, on the first available machine.

In this section, rather than assuming that the scheduler knows the weight v_i of each job, we consider the harder problem where this information is private to agent i, who owns this job. The completion time c_i of job i then corresponds to the delay that user i suffers, and the weight v_i corresponds to the value of agent i for improving the completion time of her job by a unit of time. Every agent is guaranteed completion by some deadline d (defined later on) but, depending on its value, v_i, the agent may be willing to pay in order to improve its completion time, i.e., to get a higher level of service. Our goal is to design a DA auction that elicits bids b_i corresponding to the private values v_i and outputs a schedule x, aiming to minimize the social cost, i.e., $\sum_i b_i c_i(x)$. As we have shown, every DA auction can be implemented as an ascending auction. But, what would an ascending auction for job scheduling look like?

Ascending Job Scheduling Auctions. In an ascending auction for job scheduling, as the prices increase, the bidders who remain active should be guaranteed outcomes of increasingly high quality, i.e., a lower completion time. This means that rather than scheduling the jobs in a bottom-up fashion, starting from lower completion times and moving toward higher ones, like all known list-processing algorithms do, an ascending auction schedules jobs top-to-bottom. In particular, a DA ascending auction uses a clinching function to "promise" increasingly better completion times to the active bidders and to decide their actual completion time when they are finalized. But, a clinching decision is irreversible, and it cannot depend on the bids of jobs in A_t, i.e., the ones still competing for lower completion times. Therefore, a generalized DA auction needs to ensure that, *no matter the values of the active jobs* to be finalized later on, there exists a *feasible* way of scheduling them that *respects the clinching promises* and yields a *good approximation factor.* This introduces a novel and non-trivial trade-off for the designer: on one hand, the designer wants to allow the jobs to clinch low completion times, aiming for a good approximation factor but, on the other hand, if the promised completion times are too low, this may lead to an infeasible schedule.

Aiming for a good approximation, we design a *backward* greedy algorithm whose social cost is within a constant factor of the greedy algorithm described above. In fact, we ensure that our DA auction assigns to every job a completion time within a constant factor of its completion time in the forward greedy schedule. The most natural way to achieve that would be to let our DA auction use the same scoring function, i.e., to finalize bids in increasing order of their b_i/p_i ratio. But, how can we ensure that the completion time of the job i with the worst ratio, the one finalized first, is within a constant of its completion time in the greedy schedule?

Note that the clinching function needs to be oblivious to the values of the active bids and, depending on what these values are, the completion time of job i in the forward greedy outcome may vary significantly. For a concrete example, consider the case when, apart from the job i with the smallest value over size ratio, A_t also comprises two sets of jobs X and Y, where X contains m jobs of size 1 and Y contains $m-1$ jobs of size m. If the jobs in Y have higher ratios than those in X, the completion time of job i in the forward greedy outcome would be $m+1$. On the other hand, if the jobs in X have higher ratios than those in Y, the completion time of job i in the forward greedy outcome would be 2! But, we cannot finalize i with a constant completion time for any m, as this would quickly lead to feasibility issues, since the average load per machine is not constant.

5.1 Deferred-Acceptance Scheduling Auction

In this section, we provide a DA auction that determines a feasible schedule of the tasks and achieves a $2(1+\sqrt{2}) \approx 4.83$-approximation. At each stage t, our auction will be leveraging two parameters that depend on A_t but not on the values of the bidders in it: a) $M_t = \frac{1}{m}\sum_{i\in A_t} p_i$, i.e., the value of the fractional makespan for the jobs in A_t, and b) $\overline{p}_t = \max_{i\in A_t}\{p_i\}$, i.e., the maximum processing time among the jobs in A_t. Our auction guarantees to every bidder a completion time by the deadline $d = M_1 + 2\overline{p}_1$, and depending on their bids and processing times, some jobs get the opportunity to pay for improved completion times. These improvements of the completion time, beyond the initial deadline, are captured by the clinching function, which decides what the completion time of a job will be when it is finalized.

Scoring function. As long as $\overline{p}_t \leq M_t/2$, our DA scheduling auction uses a scoring function based on the greedy algorithm ratio, i.e., $\sigma_i(b_i) = b_i/p_i$. But, when there exist jobs whose processing time is higher than $M_t/2$, the auction finalizes them first in a largest job first fashion. Formally,

$$\sigma_i^{A_t}(b_i) = \begin{cases} b_i/p_i, & \text{if } \overline{p}_t < M_t/2 \text{ or } p_i \neq \overline{p}_t \\ 0, & \text{if } \overline{p}_t \geq M_t/2 \text{ and } p_i = \overline{p}_t. \end{cases}$$

Clinching function. For each machine j, we denote by $E_j(t)$ the minimum starting time among all the tasks scheduled on machine j prior to stage t, and let $E_{\max}(t) = \max_j\{E_j(t)\}$. For $t = 1$, we set $E_j(1) = d$ for every $j \in [m]$. The clinching function is defined as:

$$g_i^{A_t}(\mathbf{b}_{N\setminus A_t}) = M_1 + 2\overline{p}_1 - \min\left\{M_t + 2\overline{p}_t\,,\ E_{\max}(t)\right\}.$$

In more detail, at each stage t, this clinching function defines how much earlier than the deadline $(M_1 + 2\overline{p}_1)$ job i is guaranteed to terminate (recall that we want the clinching function to be nonincreasing w.r.t. A_t, hence we take the difference between the deadline and the completion time). In other words, at stage t, every job is guaranteed to complete no later than $\min\left\{M_t + 2\overline{p}_t\,,\ E_{\max}(t)\right\}$. The job i finalized at stage t is the one with minimum score $\sigma_i^{A_t}(b_i)$, and it is scheduled on some machine $j \in \arg\max_j\{E_j(t)\}$. If no other jobs have been scheduled to be processed on this machine in the time interval $[0, M_t+2\overline{p}_t]$, then job i is scheduled so that its completion time is $c_i(x) = M_t+2\overline{p}_t$. If, on the other hand, every machine is has scheduled a job in that interval, then job i is scheduled so that its completion time is exactly $E_{\max}(t) = E_{j(t)}(t)$, i.e., right before the previously scheduled tasks on the machine.

The following theorem, whose proof is deferred to the full version of the paper, shows that the completion times defined above yield a 4.83-approximation of the optimal social cost ($\sum_i b_i c_i(x)$).

Theorem 5.1. *The DA scheduling auction yields a* $2(1+\sqrt{2}) \approx 4.83$ *approximation.*

What is more demanding, is that we also need to verify that the DA auction always yields a feasible schedule. That is, we need to ensure that there exists a schedule where all the jobs can be processed by the completion times that they have clinched.

To do this, we first define some appropriate quantities for every stage t, that will guide us in the analysis. Let $\text{Goal}(t) = M_t+2\overline{p}_t$, and for every processor $j \in [m]$, let $\delta_j(t) = \max\{0, \text{Goal}(t)-E_j(t)\}$. Hence, δ_j is the difference between the Goal function and the time at which j starts processing the jobs currently assigned to it. For technical convenience, we set this to 0 when $E_j(t)$ exceeds $\text{Goal}(t)$. The rest of the analysis focuses on arguing about the behavior of the vector $(\delta_j(\cdot))_{j\in[m]}$ over time, with respect to the following features:

$$\text{Max}(t) = \max_{j\in[m]} \delta_j(t), \qquad \text{Min}(t) = \min_{j\in[m]} \delta_j(t), \qquad \text{Avg}(t) = \frac{1}{m}\sum_{j\in[m]} \delta_j(t)$$

For an illustration of these quantities, see Figure 1. We can think of $\text{GOAL}(t)$ as the updated deadline at stage t, which keeps decreasing between successive stages. The initial deadline was $\text{GOAL}(1) = d = M_1 + 2\overline{p}_1$, and it is easy to see that $\text{GOAL}(t+1) \leq \text{GOAL}(t)$. Our proof examines the area below the dashed line at time $\text{GOAL}(t)$ to argue about the existence of a feasible schedule.

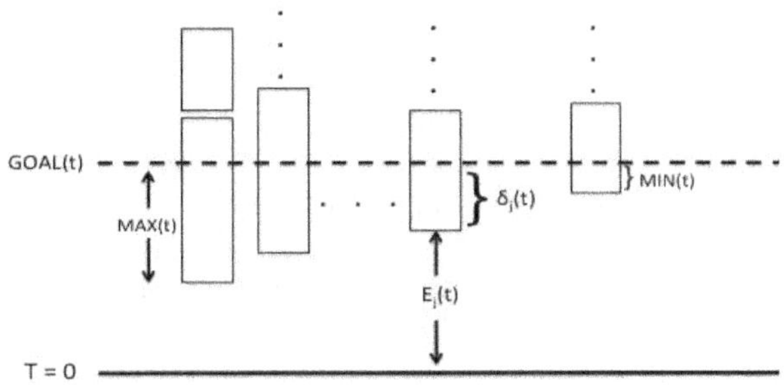

Fig. 1. An illustration of the relevant quantities at a stage t.

To proceed, we prove the following important lemma, which is critical in verifying that our DA auction always yields a feasible schedule. A rough intuition behind the proof is that, whenever, after stage t, $\text{GOAL}(t)$ drops to $\text{GOAL}(t+1)$ it causes either $\text{MAX}(t) - \text{MIN}(t)$ or $\text{AVG}(t)$ to drop (or it causes an aggregate drop) by enough time so as to maintain that Inequality (2) remains true.

LEMMA 5.2. *For every stage t of the auction we have*

$$\text{MAX}(t) - \text{MIN}(t) + \text{AVG}(t) \leq 2\overline{p}_t. \tag{2}$$

PROOF. The proof is by induction on t. For $t = 1$ this is straightforward to verify, since $E_j(1) = d$ for every $j \in [m]$. Hence, we now assume that Inequality (2) holds for every stage up to t, and our goal is to show that it then remains true at stage $t+1$. We distinguish three possible cases: a) $\text{MIN}(t) > 0$ and $\text{MIN}(t+1) > 0$, b) $\text{MIN}(t) > 0$ and $\text{MIN}(t+1) = 0$, and c) $\text{MIN}(t) = 0$. In the analysis that follows, we will refer to a job as being *tight*, if it is scheduled without leaving any idle time, till the next job. I.e., for a job scheduled on machine j at stage t, tightness means that its completion time is $E_j(t)$ (thus all machines are busy at time $M_t + 2\overline{p}_t$).

a) If $\text{MIN}(t) > 0$ and $\text{MIN}(t+1) > 0$, let t' be the last stage before t when $\text{MIN}(t') = 0$ (the existence of such a stage is clearly guaranteed, e.g., $t' = 1$). All the machines are always busy in the time interval between $\text{GOAL}(t')$ and $\text{GOAL}(t+1)$ (by definition of t' and since $\text{MIN}(t+1) > 0$). Therefore

$$\text{AVG}(t+1) = \text{AVG}(t') - 2(\overline{p}_{t'} - \overline{p}_{t+1}). \tag{3}$$

- If $\text{MAX}(t') \geq \overline{p}_{t'}$, then $\text{MAX}(t+1) - \text{MIN}(t+1) \leq \text{MAX}(t')$. This is true because all jobs scheduled between t' and $t+1$ are tight, and their size is no more than $\overline{p}_{t'} \leq \text{MAX}(t')$. Hence, the gap between $\text{MAX}(t)$ and $\text{MIN}(t)$ will not increase when we go to stage $t+1$. Using Inequality (3), this implies that

$$\begin{aligned}
\text{MAX}(t+1) - \text{MIN}(t+1) + \text{AVG}(t+1) &\leq \text{MAX}(t') + \text{AVG}(t') - 2(\overline{p}_{t'} - \overline{p}_{t+1}) \\
&= \text{MAX}(t') - \text{MIN}(t') + \text{AVG}(t') - 2(\overline{p}_{t'} - \overline{p}_{t+1}) \\
&\leq 2\overline{p}_{t'} - 2(\overline{p}_{t'} - \overline{p}_{t+1}) \\
&= 2\overline{p}_{t+1}
\end{aligned}$$

The last inequality above is true by the induction hypothesis applied to t'.

- If $\text{Max}(t') < \overline{p}_{t'}$, then $\text{Max}(t+1) - \text{Min}(t+1) \leq \overline{p}_{t'}$. This is true because all jobs scheduled between t' and $t+1$ are tight, and their size is no more than $\overline{p}_{t'} \leq \text{Max}(t')$. Hence, the gap between $\text{Max}(t+1)$ and $\text{Min}(t+1)$ may increase, but not beyond $\overline{p}_{t'}$. Also, since $\text{Max}(t') < \overline{p}_{t'}$ we also have $\text{Avg}(t') < \overline{p}_{t'}$. Using Inequality (3), this implies that

$$\begin{aligned}\text{Max}(t+1) - \text{Min}(t+1) + \text{Avg}(t+1) &\leq \overline{p}_{t'} + \text{Avg}(t') - 2(\overline{p}_{t'} - \overline{p}_{t+1}) \\ &\leq 2\overline{p}_{t'} - 2(\overline{p}_{t'} - \overline{p}_{t+1}) \\ &= 2\overline{p}_{t+1}\end{aligned}$$

b) $\text{Min}(t) > 0$ and $\text{Min}(t+1) = 0$. This case is more lengthy and complicated to analyze, yet it is similar in spirit with Case (a) and and we omit it from this version.

c) If $\text{Min}(t) = 0$, then $\text{Max}(t) + \text{Avg}(t) \leq 2\overline{p}_t$, and we consider two possible cases:

- If the job scheduled at stage t is not the one with the earliest starting time at stage $t+1$ (i.e., if it does not affect $\text{Max}(t+1)$), then $\text{Max}(t+1) \leq \text{Max}(t) - 2(\overline{p}_t - \overline{p}_{t+1}) - p_t/m$. Combined with the fact that $\text{Avg}(t+1) \leq \text{Avg}(t) + p_t/m$, we get that

$$\begin{aligned}\text{Max}(t+1) - \text{Min}(t+1) + \text{Avg}(t+1) &\leq \text{Max}(t+1) + \text{Avg}(t+1) \\ &\leq \text{Max}(t) - 2(\overline{p}_t - \overline{p}_{t+1}) + \text{Avg}(t) \\ &\leq 2\overline{p}_t - 2(\overline{p}_t - \overline{p}_{t+1}) \\ &= 2\overline{p}_{t+1}\end{aligned}$$

- If the job scheduled at stage t is the one with the earliest starting time at stage $t+1$ (i.e., if it defines $\text{Max}(t+1)$), then $\text{Max}(t+1) \leq \overline{p}_t - 2(\overline{p}_t - \overline{p}_{t+1}) - p_t/m$. Since $\text{Avg}(t+1) \leq \text{Max}(t+1)$ we get

$$\begin{aligned}\text{Max}(t+1) - \text{Min}(t+1) + \text{Avg}(t+1) &\leq \text{Max}(t+1) + \text{Avg}(t+1) \\ &\leq 2\text{Max}(t+1) \\ &\leq 2(\overline{p}_t - 2(\overline{p}_t - \overline{p}_{t+1}) - p_t/m) \\ &\leq 2\overline{p}_{t+1}\end{aligned}$$

□

Note that the guarantee provided in the previous lemma is actually tight. This can be verified even with an instance with just two machines, in which the jobs have processing times (listed in order of being finalized): $1, 1/2, 1, 3/4, 1, 7/8, 1, 15/16, \ldots, 1, (2^k - 1)/2^k$. This instance also shows that our clinching function is essential tight. Using Lemma 5.2, we can now prove feasibility.

Theorem 5.3. *The DA scheduling auction is always feasible.*

Proof. Assume that at some stage t there exists a job that cannot fit in any machine, i.e., $max_j\{E_j(t)\} < \overline{p}_t$. Let t' be the last stage before t when $\text{Min}(t') = 0$. Given the result of Lemma 5.2, at stage t' we have $\text{Max}(t') + \text{Avg}(t') \leq 2\overline{p}_{t'}$, and hence $\text{Avg}(t') \leq (\text{Max}(t') + \text{Avg}(t'))/2 \leq \overline{p}_{t'}$. Since all subsequently scheduled jobs are tight, if P is the total processing time of the jobs scheduled from t' to t, the average busy time below $\text{Goal}(t')$ increased by P/m, and the drop from $\text{Goal}(t')$ to $\text{Goal}(t)$ is exactly $P/m + 2(\overline{p}_{t'} - \overline{p}_t)$. As a result,

$$\text{Avg}(t) \leq \text{Avg}(t') - 2(\overline{p}_{t'} - \overline{p}_t) \leq \overline{p}_{t'} - 2(\overline{p}_{t'} - \overline{p}_t) \leq 2\overline{p}_t - \overline{p}_{t'} \leq \overline{p}_t.$$

But, this means that $\max_j\{E_j(t)\} \geq \text{Goal}(t) - \overline{p}_t \geq \overline{p}_t$, which contradicts our assumption that $max_j\{E_j(t)\} < \overline{p}_t$. □

6 MULTIPLE KNAPSACK CONSTRAINTS

As a third application of the generalized DA auctions framework, we also study settings where the set of feasible solutions is defined via multiple knapsack constraints though, due to space constraints, most of this section is deferred to the full version of the paper.

There are multiple motivating examples for knapsack constraints: in FCC auctions there are different bands (VHF, UHF) each with its own capacity constraints, and with a different value. Similarly, the economy, business, and first class seats in an airplane correspond to three different knapsack constraints, each with a different value. As a final example, consider cross country moving trucks that are scheduled to move property or products from a source to a destination. Each truck has a capacity constraint and the earlier the arrival date the higher the value.

Formally, in this section we assume that each possible level of service ℓ has a capacity of m "slots", and we let s_i be the "size" of each bidder i, i.e., the number of slots that the bidder needs to occupy, if assigned level ℓ. The presence of multiple knapsack constraints then imply that an outcome is feasible if the total size of the set of bidders $N_\ell \subseteq N$ finalized at a level of service ℓ is at most m, i.e., $\sum_{i \in N_\ell} s_i \leq m$ for every possible level of service ℓ.

Dütting et al. [11] showed that, even in the binary setting, if the set of bidders that can be simultaneously accepted is defined by a single knapsack constraint of size m, then no DA auction can achieve an approximation better than $O(\log m)$. The following theorem provides a matching positive result: a generalized DA auction that achieves the optimal logarithmic approximation.

Theorem 6.1. *There exists a multiple knapsack DA auction achieving a $O(\log m)$ approximation for an arbitrary number of knapsacks.*

Just like in the previous section, the DA auction that we propose manages to strike a balance between allowing the bidders to clinch higher levels of service as quickly as possible, yet ensuring that these "promises" will not eventually violate any knapsack constraints.

7 MULTI-PARAMETER DEFERRED-ACCEPTANCE AUCTIONS

This section further generalizes DA auctions to a multi-parameter setting: bidders with downward-sloping (a.k.a. submodular) valuations in the level of service awarded. For notational simplicity, we assume that the possible levels of service are represented by a set $L = \{1, 2, \ldots, k\}$ and that each bidder i reports her marginal value for each additional level, as $b_i(1) = v_i(1)$, $b_i(2) = v_i(2) - v_i(1)$, up to $b_i(k) = v_i(k) - v_i(k-1)$ with $b_i(1) \geq b_i(2) \cdots \geq b_i(k)$. Hence, $b_i(j)$ is the added value for the bidder if she jumps from level of service $j-1$ to j.

Just like the generalized DA auction framework that we defined in Section 3, the multi-parameter framework that we propose here also uses a collection of scoring functions and clinching functions for each bidder. The important difference is that the agents now report a sequence of bids that correspond to their marginal valuations for the different levels of service. Given these marginal bids for each bidder i, at each stage t, the multi-parameter DA auction computes the score of each active bidder using her bid corresponding to the next level of service that i is considered for clinching. That is, if $g_i^{A_t}(\mathbf{b}_{N \setminus A_t})$ is the level of service that i has clinched by stage t, which we henceforth denote by just g_{it}, her score is computed based on her marginal value for clinching one more level of service, i.e, based on $b_i(g_{it} + 1)$.

Definition 7.1. A multi-parameter DA auction operates in stages $t \geq 1$. In each stage t a set of bidders $A_t \subseteq N$ is active; initially, $A_1 = N$, and $A_{t+1} \subset A_t$, for every $t \geq 1$. Just as in the single-parameter case, the DA auction is fully defined by two collections of functions:

- The **scoring functions** $\sigma_i^{A_t}(\,\cdot\,, \mathbf{b}_{N \setminus A_t})$ that are non-decreasing in their first argument.

- The **clinching functions** $g_i^{A_t}(\mathbf{b}_{N\setminus A_t})$, that are non-decreasing w.r.t. the set of active bidders, i.e., if for every $t \geq 1$, $g_i^{A_{t+1}}(\mathbf{b}_{N\setminus A_{t+1}}) \geq g_i^{A_t}(\mathbf{b}_{N\setminus A_t})$.

At each stage t, if $A_t \neq \emptyset$, the score of bidder $i \in A_t$ is computed as:

$$\sigma_i^{A_t}(b_i(g_{it}+1), \mathbf{b}_{N\setminus A_t}),$$

i.e., the score is a function of the bidder's marginal value for receiving a level increase, given the level that she has already clinched. The bidder with the smallest score is finalized at level $g_{it} = g_i^{A_t}(\mathbf{b}_{N\setminus A_t})$ and she is removed from the set of active bidders ($A_{t+1} = A_t \setminus \{i\}$).

All the incentive guarantees for single-parameter DA auctions carry over to the present setting. The proof of these properties follows essentially the same arguments as in Theorem 3.3 and Propositions 3.4 and 3.5. These properties are summarized below.

Proposition 7.2. *Every multi-parameter DA auction is weakly group-strategyproof, and has an equivalent clock auction implementation that is obviously strategyproof.*

7.1 Multiunit Auctions with Decreasing Marginal Values

To demonstrate an application of multi-parameter DA auctions, we consider the setting of multiunit auctions with submodular bidders. Multi-unit auctions are being deployed in practice in a wide range of applications, and more recently they have also been used by various online brokers (for more, see e.g., [32, 38]). Such auctions are defined by a collection of m identical units of some good that need to be allocated among n agents. The level of service in this setting corresponds to the number of units that each agent receives, and the value of an agent for a bundle of items is a submodular function of the bundle's size. Hence the valuation function here is fully described by a nonincreasing vector of marginal values, for bundles up to size m.

Ascending Multiunit Auctions. There is a well-known ascending multiunit auction, the "clinching auction" of Ausubel [1]. Given an ascending price per unit, the bidders in this auction respond by reporting the number of units that they would be interested in acquiring at the current price, i.e., the number of their marginal valuations that are at least as high as the price. As the price increases, the number of items that the bidders request drops, and a bidder clinches a unit at the point where, even if he were to leave the auction, the total demand of the other bidders would leave that unit unallocated. This auction is known to be strategy-proof and in fact implements the VCG mechanism. However it is also known to be susceptible to demand reduction in group deviations, and hence is not weakly group-strategyproof.

For a simple example, consider an instance involving two units and two bidders: bidder a has marginal values $(1, 1)$, while bidder b has marginal values $(0.6, 0.6)$. If we were to run the clinching auction of [1] in this instance, after the price would exceed 0.6, bidder b would leave the auction and bidder a would clinch both units at that price for a utility of $2 - 1.2 = 0.8$. If, on the other hand, both agents reduced their demand by claiming that they have no value for a second item, they would get one unit each for a price of 0! The equivalence of Ausubel's auction with the VCG mechanism implies the following contrast to Proposition 4.1.

Observation 1. *In the setting of multiunit auctions with downward-sloping valuations, the VCG mechanism is not a DA auction.*

We next define a DA auction for multiunit auctions. But before that, we first establish that some loss in social welfare will be unavoidable, even if we only insist on a weakly group-strategyproof mechanism. In particular, we have the following impossibility result, the proof of which is omitted.

Proposition 7.3. *Even for 2 players and 2 units, no weakly group-strategyproof mechanism can guarantee an approximation factor to the social welfare, that is better than* $\sqrt{2}$.

The DA auction that we propose in the next subsection provides an $O(\log n)$-approximation. Whether there exists a DA (or at least a weakly group-strategyproof) auction with a better approximation factor remains an interesting open problem.

7.2 Deferred-Acceptance Multiunit Auction with Decreasing Marginal Valuations

Without loss of generality, assume that $n = 2^\kappa$ for some $\kappa \in \mathbb{N}_+$, and also $m \geq n \log n$.[3] Let $\lambda = \lfloor m/(n \log n) \rfloor$, i.e., $\lambda \geq 1$. In order to achieve the logarithmic approximation, we restrict the distribution of units to agents so that it obeys a very particular structure:

- The total units that each bidder may be allocated is exactly $\lambda\, 2^r$, for some $r \in \{0, 1, \ldots, \kappa\}$. In particular, we restrict each bidder to clinching the units in blocks of gradually increasing size: λ, λ, 2λ, 4λ, and so on, up to $\lambda\, 2^{\kappa-1}$.
- The number of agents that receive at least $\lambda\, 2^r$ units is at most $n/2^r$.

In this restricted setting, instead of providing m possible levels of service to each bidder (the number of units they can receive), the levels of service are $\kappa + 1$ (the number of unit blocks they can receive). Hence, rather than reporting all of their m marginal valuations, the agents report only their *average* marginal value for receiving exactly $\lambda\, 2^r$ units of the good, for $r \in \{0, 1, \ldots, \kappa\}$, i.e., their average marginal value for each one of the $\kappa + 1$ blocks. That is, the agents report a bid vector of size $\kappa + 1$ containing weakly decreasing marginal values. For instance, if $n = 4$ and $m = 8$, then $\kappa = 2$ and $\lambda = 1$. If the marginal valuations of an agent for the units are $[8, 7, 6, 4, 4, 3, 2, 1]$, then her average marginal valuations for the blocks of units would be $[8, 7, \text{avg}(6, 4)] = [8, 7, 5]$. Our auction does not assign more than $\lambda m/\kappa$ units to any agent, so the remaining marginal values are disregarded.

Definition 7.4. The DA multiunit auction receives $\kappa + 1$ marginal bids from each bidder, corresponding to their average marginal values for each block. At every stage the scoring function of every bidder is the identify function, i.e., $\sigma_i^{A_t}(b_i(g_{it} + 1)) = b_i(g_{it} + 1)$. The clinching function is $g_i^{A_t}(\cdot) = \left\lfloor \frac{n}{|A_t|} \right\rfloor$, which means that initially (when $n = |A_t|$), every bidder has clinched the first block, which contains $\lambda\, 2^0 = \lambda$ units. Then, after the $n/2$ agents with the smallest score are finalized, bidders that remain active clinch an additional block of $\lambda\, 2^1 = 2\lambda$ units. Every time the set of active bidders is halved, those that remain active clinch another block, until they are all finalized.

For the analysis of the auction, it is convenient to also describe it as an ascending auction. Similarly to the Ausubel clinching auction, the blocks of units are clinched when the demand of the competitors drops below a specific threshold but, unlike the clinching auction, ours is a DA auction, so it is weakly group-strategyproof. The ascending auction implementation of our DA auction uses a price per unit p, which happens to be the same for every bidder, and is initially set to $p = 0$. The auction begins by assigning λ units to each bidder at a price of $p = 0$. Then, the agents compete for an additional block of λ units. The auction offers an average price p per unit for this block, and p is gradually increased until exactly $n/2$ agents are still willing to pay this amount per unit of the block. The bidders who do not receive these extra λ units are finalized, and they hence receive just the first block of λ units for a price of 0. The $n/2$ bidders that remain active clinch each unit of the second block for a "threshold price" p and they then compete for the third block, which contains 2λ more units. A third block can be allocated to at most $n/4$ bidders among them. Note

[3]If n is not a power of 2 and/or does not satisfy $m \geq n \log n$, we can reject the bidders with the lowest first marginal value until the new number of players n' is the largest power of 2 with $m \geq n' \log n'$. As we show in the full version of the paper, this does not affect the order of magnitude of the approximation guarantee that we establish.

that the price for each unit in this block remains equal to p, i.e., the one used for the previous block, so some of the active bidders might not be willing to pay this amount. If the number of bidders willing to pay p for each unit of the third block is not more than $n/4$, then all these bidders clinch this block for the existing price p per unit. Otherwise, p is increased further, until exactly $n/4$ of these bidders remain interested. We repeat this process by gradually doubling the size of the block, and halving the number of bidders that can receive one, until two agents compete for the single remaining block of $n\lambda/2$ units.

Example 7.5. Consider a problem instance with $n = 4$ and $m = 8$, which implies that $\kappa = 2$ and $\lambda = 1$. Assume that the bid vectors of the four agents $\{A, B, C, D\}$ are $[7, 6, 6]$, $[6, 5, 5]$, $[8, 4, 4]$, and $[5, 4, 3]$. Every agent is assigned one unit at a price $p = 0$ (this means that we disregard the first parameter of the bid vector, but we will use it when m is smaller). Then, the agents compete for an additional unit that only two of them can win. The price is increased to $p = 4 + \epsilon$, at which point agents C and D drop out (since their average marginal value for a second unit is 4) and agents A and B clinch one unit each for this price. Finally, the remaining two active agents compete for a single block of two units. The price is increased to $p = 5 + \epsilon$ and agent B drops out as well, so A clinches the block of two units for this price.

Approximation Guarantee. We now prove that the DA auction that we propose above guarantees a logarithmic approximation factor w.r.t. the social welfare. Note that, although our auction is restricted to allocations that bundle units into groups and does not need the whole marginal valuation vector, the approximation guarantee is comparing the outcome with the optimal allocation that uses all this information.

THEOREM 7.6. *For bidders with submodular valuations, the DA multiunit auction that we propose guarantees an approximation factor of $O(\log n)$.*

Benchmark. To prove the approximation guarantee, we use a different allocation as a benchmark. In particular, let $\overline{x}$ be the social welfare maximizing allocation with the same bidders if the number of units were $m/(2\kappa)$ instead of m. This allocation finds, among the mn marginal values, the $m/(2\kappa)$ highest ones, and it allocates the corresponding number of units to each agent. Since the values of the agents exhibit decreasing marginal valuations for additional units, this implies that the social welfare in $\overline{x}$ is a 2κ-approximation of the social welfare maximizing allocation x^* with m units:

$$\sum_{i \in N} v_i(x^*) \leq 2\kappa \sum_{i \in N} v_i(\overline{x}).$$

We now show that our auction provides each agent with at least half the value that she would receive in $\overline{x}$. This implies that the allocation x that our auction computes guarantees:

$$\sum_{i \in N} v_i(x^*) \leq 2\kappa \sum_{i \in N} v_i(\overline{x}) \leq 4\kappa \sum_{i \in N} v_i(x) = 4 \log n \sum_{i \in N} v_i(x).$$

We begin with the following lemma, which shows that for any value that the unit price p takes during our auction, there exist at least $m/(2\kappa)$ marginal values that are at least as high.

LEMMA 7.7. *Let $p_{\max}$ be the highest price that our ascending auction reaches. Then, among the mn marginal values of the agents, there exist at least $m/(2\kappa)$ ones whose value is at least $p_{\max}$.*

PROOF. Let $r > 1$ be the round when the price is increased for the last time, thus reaching the value of $p_{\max}$. According to the definition of our mechanism, at that point, there are exactly $n/2^r$ agents who are willing to pay this price per unit for an additional block of $\lambda\, 2^{r-1}$ units[4]; they have

[4] The fact that the price was increased during round r means that the agents willing to pay the initial price were more, and the price increase brings them down to exactly $n/2^r$.

already clinched a total of $\lambda\, 2^{r-1}$ units in previous rounds. Since the average marginal value of these agents for the additional block is at least $p_{\max}$, this means that the marginal value of *every unit* within the blocks that these agents clinched during previous rounds is also at least $p_{\max}$. Therefore, the number of marginal values in the agents' bid vectors which are at least $p_{\max}$, is at least

$$\frac{n}{2^r}\left(\lambda\, 2^{r-1}\right) = \frac{n\lambda}{2} = \frac{nm/(\kappa n)}{2} = \frac{m}{2\kappa}$$

□

Using the lemma above we continue by showing that our auction provides every agent with a value at least half as much as the value that the agent would receive in $\overline{x}$.

Lemma 7.8. *Let x be the allocation computed by our auction. For every agent $i \in N$, $v_i(x) \geq v_i(\overline{x})/2$.*

Proof. To prove this lemma we show that our auction allocates to each agent at least half the number of units that the agent receives in $\overline{x}$. Since the valuations are concave this implies that the agent receives half the value as well.

Assume that there exists some agent i who is rejected during round $r > 1$ by our auction and hence receives exactly $\lambda\, 2^{r-1}$ units, while the same agent receives more than $\lambda\, 2^r$ in $\overline{x}$. Let p be the price per unit at the time when this agent was rejected by our auction. The fact that the agent is rejected means that the average marginal value of that user for an additional block of $\lambda\, 2^{r-1}$ units is less than p. This implies that the lowest marginal value over all these units, which is the last, is less than p. Therefore, the agent's marginal value for a $(\lambda\, 2^r + 1)$-th unit is less than p. Given Lemma 7.7 though, there exist at least $m/(2\kappa)$ units with marginal values at least $p_{\max} \geq p$, which means that the $(\lambda\, 2^r + 1)$-th unit of that agent cannot be one of the $m/(2\kappa)$ highest value marginals and thus part of the assignment $\overline{x}$, leading to a contradiction. □

Finally, we conclude by exhibiting that our auction is feasible, i.e., the number of units it allocates does not exceed the number of available units. The proof of the following lemma is omitted.

Lemma 7.9. *For $n \geq 4$, the DA multiunit auction is feasible, i.e., it always assigns at most m units.*

REFERENCES

[1] L. Ausubel. 2004. An Efficient Ascending-bid Auction for Multiple Objects. *American Economic Review* 94 (2004), 1452–1475.

[2] L. Ausubel. 2006. An Efficient Dynamic Auction for Heterogeneous Commodities. *American Economic Review* 96 (2006), 602–629. Issue 3.

[3] M. Babaioff, R. Lavi, and E. Pavlov. 2009. Single-value Combinatorial Auctions and Algorithmic Implementation in Undominated Strategies. *J. ACM* 56, 1, Article 4 (2009), 4:1–4:32 pages.

[4] S. Bikhchandani, S. de Vries, S. J. Schummer, and R. V. Vohra. 2011. An Ascending Vickrey Auction for Selling Bases of a Matroid. *Operations Research* 59 (2011), 400–413. Issue 2.

[5] L. Blumrosen and N. Nisan. 2009. On the Computational Power of Demand Queries. *SIAM J. Comput.* 39, 4 (2009), 1372–1391.

[6] L. Blumrosen and N. Nisan. 2010. Informational limitations of ascending combinatorial auctions. *Journal of Economic Theory* 145, 3 (2010), 1203–1223.

[7] L. Blumrosen and O. Zohar. 2015. Multilateral Deferred-Acceptance Mechanisms. In *Proceedings of the 11th Conference on Web and Internet Economics.* 173–186.

[8] P. Brucker. 2004. *Scheduling algorithms (4. ed.).* Springer.

[9] C. Chekuri and S. Khanna. 2004. Approximation Algorithms for Minimizing AverageWeighted Completion Time. In *Handbook of Scheduling - Algorithms, Models, and Performance Analysis.*

[10] N. R. Devanur, M. Mihail, and V. V. Vazirani. 2005. Strategyproof cost-sharing mechanisms for set cover and facility location games. *Decision Support Systems* 39 (2005), 11–22.

[11] P. Dütting, V. Gkatzelis, and T. Roughgarden. 2014. The performance of deferred-acceptance auctions. In *ACM Conference on Economics and Computation, EC '14, Stanford , CA, USA, June 8-12, 2014.* 187–204.

[12] P. Dütting, T. Roughgarden, and I. Talgam-Cohen. 2014. Modularity and greed in double auctions. In *Proceedings of the 15th ACM Conference on Economics and Computation.* 241–258.

[13] L. Ensthaler and T. Giebe. 2015. A Dynamic Auction for Multi-object Procurement under a Hard Budget Constraint. *Research Policy* 143 (2015), 179–189.

[14] FCC. 2017. Broadcast Incentive Auction. https://www.fcc.gov/about-fcc/fcc-initiatives/incentive-auctions. (2017).

[15] S. Fujishige. 1980. Lexicographically Optimal Base of a Polymatroid with respect to a Weight Vector. *Mathematics of Operations Research* 5 (1980), 186–196. Issue 2.

[16] G. Goel, V.S. Mirrokni, and R. Paes Leme. 2015. Polyhedral Clinching Auctions and the AdWords Polytope. *J. ACM* 62, 3 (2015), 18:1–18:27.

[17] F. Gul and E. Stacchetti. 2000. The English Auction with Differentiated Commodities. *Journal of Economic Theory* 92 (2000), 66–95. Issue 1.

[18] N. Immorlica, M. Mahdian, and V. S. Mirrokni. 2008. Limitations of cross-monotonic cost-sharing schemes. *ACM Transactions on Algorithms* 4, 2 (2008).

[19] N. Immorlica and E. Pountourakis. 2012. On Budget-Balanced Group-Strategyproof Cost-Sharing Mechanisms. In *Proceedings of the 8th Workshop on Internet and Network Economics.* 244–255.

[20] F. Jarman and V. Meisner. 2015. Ex-post Optimal Knapsack Procurement. In *SSRN Working Paper No. 2548543.*

[21] R. Juarez. 2013. Group strategyproof cost sharing: The role of indifferences. *Games and Economic Behavior* 82, C (2013), 218–239.

[22] R. Juarez. 2013. Optimal Group Strategyproof Cost Sharing. In *Working paper.* Available from: http://www2.hawaii.edu/~rubenj/optimalgsp.pdf. Last accessed: May 8, 2017.

[23] T. Kawaguchi and S. Kyan. 1986. Worst Case Bound of an LRF Schedule for the Mean Weighted Flow-time Problem. *SIAM J. Comput.* 15, 4 (Nov. 1986), 1119–1129.

[24] A. Kelso and V. Crawford. 1982. Job Matching, Coalition Formation, and Gross Substitutes. *Econometrica* 50 (1982), 1483–1504. Issue 6.

[25] A. Kim. 2015. Welfare Maximization with Deferred Acceptance Auctions in Reallocation Problems. In *Proceedings of the 23rd Annual Symposium on Algorithms.* 804–815.

[26] B. Korte and J. Vygen. 2007. *Combinatorial Optimization: Theory and Algorithms.* Springer Verlag, Berlin Heidelberg, Germany.

[27] D. Lehmann, L. I. O'Callaghan, and Y. Shoham. 2002. Truth Revelation in Approximately Efficient Combinatorial Auctions. *J. ACM* 49 (2002), 577–602. Issue 5.

[28] S. Li. 2015. Obviously Strategy-Proof Mechanisms. In *SSRN Working Paper No. 2560028.*

[29] L. M. Marx and S. Loertscher. 2015. Prior-free Bayesian optimal Double-Clock Auctions. In *Working paper.* Available from: https://faculty.fuqua.duke.edu/~marx/bio/papers/PriorFree.pdf. Last accessed: May 8, 2017.

[30] A. Mehta, T. Roughgarden, and M. Sundararajan. 2009. Beyond Moulin mechanisms. *Games and Economic Behavior* 67, 1 (2009), 125–155.

[31] P. Milgrom. 2000. Putting Auction Theory to Work: The Simultaneous Ascending Auction. *Journal of Political Economy* 108 (2000), 245–272. Issue 2.

[32] P. Milgrom. 2004. *Putting Auction Theory to Work.* Cambridge University Press.

[33] P. Milgrom and I. Segal. 2014. Deferred-acceptance auctions and radio spectrum reallocation. In *ACM Conference on Economics and Computation, EC '14, Stanford , CA, USA, June 8-12, 2014.* 185–186.

[34] P. Milgrom and I. Segal. 2015. Deferred-Acceptance Auctions and Radio Spectrum Reallocation. In *Working paper.* Available from: http://web.stanford.edu/~isegal/heuristic.pdf. Last accessed: May 8, 2017.

[35] H. Moulin. 1999. Incremental cost sharing: Characterization by coalition strategy-proofness. *Social Choice and Welfare* 16, 2 (1999), 279–320.

[36] R. Myerson. 1981. Optimal Auction Design. *Mathematics of Operations Research* 6, 1 (1981), 58–73.

[37] T. Nguyen and T. Sandholm. 2014. Optimizing prices in descending clock auctions. In *Proceedings of the 15th ACM Conference on Economics and Computation.* 93–110.

[38] A. Ockenfels, D. H. Reiley, and A. Sadrieh. 2006. *Economics and Information Systems.* Handbooks in Information Systems, Vol. 1. Elsevier, Chapter 12. Online Auctions, 571–628.

[39] T. Roughgarden and M. Sundararajan. 2009. Quantifying inefficiency in cost-sharing mechanisms. *Journal of the ACM* 56, 4 (2009).

[40] U. Schwiegelshohn. 2011. An alternative proof of the Kawaguchi-Kyan bound for the Largest-Ratio-First rule. *Operations Research Letters* 39, 4 (2011), 255 - 259.

The Optimal Mechanism for Selling to a Budget-Constrained Buyer: The General Case

NIKHIL R. DEVANUR, Microsoft Research
S. MATTHEW WEINBERG, Princeton University

We consider a revenue-maximizing seller with a single item facing a single buyer with a private budget. The (value, budget) pair is drawn from an *arbitrary* and possibly correlated distribution. We characterize the optimal mechanism in such cases, and quantify the amount of price discrimination that might be present. For example, there could be up to $3 \cdot 2^{k-1} - 1$ distinct non-trivial menu options in the optimal mechanism for such a buyer with k distinct possible budgets (compared to k if the marginal distribution of values conditioned on each budget has decreasing marginal revenue [CG00], or 2 if there is an arbitrary distribution and one possible budget [CMM11]).

Our approach makes use of the duality framework of [CDW16], and duality techniques related to the "FedEx Problem" of [FGKK16]. In contrast to [FGKK16] and other prior work, we characterize the optimal primal/dual without nailing down an explicit closed form.

CCS Concepts: •**Theory of computation → Algorithmic mechanism design;**

Additional Key Words and Phrases: Revenue maximization; budgets

The theory of optimal auction often equates willingness to pay with the ability to pay. While this leads to clean formulations and elegant solutions, there are many instances where this assumption is violated (see [CG00] for more discussion). In this paper we consider selling a single item to a single bidder, who has a quasi-linear utility function as well as a hard upper bound on her payment. In other words, if the buyer obtains the item and pays p, then her utility is $v - p$, as long as $p < b$, for some two numbers v and b. We call v her valuation and b her budget, and both of them are private information. We consider the problem in the Bayesian setting, where there is a joint probability distribution over types (v, b), which is known to the seller. In such settings, it is known that the optimal mechanism necessitates selling *lotteries* (e.g. awarding the item with probability in $(0, 1)$).

We study the optimal *conditional* mechanism, where the seller prevents the buyer from exaggerating her budget (but not under-reporting her budget). This can be enforced, for example, by requiring a cash bond or by requiring the buyer to pay her full budget with some small probability.

The core of the matter is how to use the budget constraints to do price discrimination. Buyers can feasibly report a lower budget, so the ones with higher budgets extract higher information rents. The economic intuition gained from previous work on this subject is restricted to cases where the budget is fixed/known ([LR96, CMM11]), or the marginal distribution of values conditioned on each

The full version can be found at www.cs.princeton.edu/~smattw/EC17Budgets.pdf.

Work done in part while the authors were visiting the Simons Institute for the Theory of Computing.

Author emails: nikdev@microsoft.com, smweinberg@princeton.edu.

EC'17, June 26–30, 2017, Cambridge, MA, USA.

 ACM ISBN 978-1-4503-4527-9/17/06
http://dx.doi.org/10.1145/3033274.3085132

possible budget satisfies *declining marginal revenues* (DMR) [CG00].[1] In all cases previously studied, the number of non-trivial menu items is shown to be at most the number of distinct budgets.

Our main contribution in this paper is to characterize the optimal mechanism in the private budget setting without any assumption on the distributions. The main economic intuition gained from our results is a quantitative understanding of the degree of price discrimination that might arise in the general case. For example:

> If the buyer's value is drawn from an arbitrary distribution and there are possible budgets $b_1 < \ldots < b_k$, private to the buyer, the optimal mechanism has the following format: the menu offered to buyers with budget b_1 has at most two non-trivial options. There is a cuttoff budget b_i, below which the budget binds and above which the menu contains an option to receive the item with probability 1. Every option on the menu presented to a buyer with budget b_{j-1} *splits* into at most two options to be included on the menu presented to a buyer with budget b_j. In addition, there is at most one additional option at the top (i.e. higher allocation probability than all other options). If $j < i$, the additional option offers the item at probability $q < 1$ at price $b_j q$. If $j \geq i$, the additional option offers the item at probability 1 ($\leq 3 \cdot 2^{k-1} - 1$ non-trivial menu options in total).

A key aspect of our approach is the idea of Lagrangifying only the incentive/budget constraints, as in the duality framework of [CDW16]. A particularly nice property of this is that the duals give a virtual valuation for each type. The optimal mechanism is then such that all the types with positive virtual values are allocated with probability 1, and all the types with negative virtual values are not allocated at all. For the types with a zero virtual value the allocation probability is typically in $(0, 1)$; and we need to use additional structure of the dual to pin down these probabilities (specifically, complementary slackness). The optimal dual is such that the sign of the virtual value is monotone in the buyer's value.

We emphasize one key technical departure from previous works. In prior works, an explicit optimal dual solution and explicit optimal primal solution are proposed, and then complementary slackness is proved. In our setting, this would be a complete nightmare - mostly due to the multiple budget constraints, so instead we characterize the optimal dual solution without nailing down a closed form. A little more specifically, we provide three elementary operations on a candidate dual solution that can only *improve* the candidate's quality. We can then conclude that there exists an optimal dual such that no more of these operations are possible, thereby characterizing what optimal duals might look like. This structure turns out to be enough to show that there exists an optimal primal solution of the desired form which satisfies complementary slackness. All this is done without excessive algebraic calculation to nail down a closed form.

REFERENCES

[CDW16] Yang Cai, Nikhil R Devanur, and S Matthew Weinberg. A duality based unified approach to bayesian mechanism design. In *Proceedings of the 48th Annual ACM SIGACT Symposium on Theory of Computing*, pages 926–939. ACM, 2016.

[CG00] Yeon-Koo Che and Ian Gale. The optimal mechanism for selling to a budget-constrained buyer. *Journal of Economic theory*, 92(2):198–233, 2000.

[CMM11] Shuchi Chawla, David L. Malec, and Azarakhsh Malekian. Bayesian mechanism design for budget-constrained agents. In *ACM Conference on Electronic Commerce*, pages 253–262, 2011.

[FGKK16] Amos Fiat, Kira Goldner, Anna R Karlin, and Elias Koutsoupias. The fedex problem. In *Proceedings of the 2016 ACM Conference on Economics and Computation*, pages 21–22. ACM, 2016.

[LR96] Jean-Jacques Laffont and Jacques Robert. Optimal auction with financially constrained buyers. *Economics Letters*, 52(2):181–186, 1996.

[1] A one-dimensional distribution with CDF F and density f satisfies DMR if $v(1 - F(v))$ is concave.

Optimal Multi-Unit Mechanisms with Private Demands

NIKHIL R. DEVANUR, Microsoft Research
NIMA HAGHPANAH, Penn State University
CHRISTOS-ALEXANDROS PSOMAS, UC Berkeley

We study a pricing problem that is motivated by the following examples. A cloud computing platform such as Amazon EC2 sells virtual machines to clients, each of who needs a different number of virtual machine hours. Similarly, cloud storage providers such as Dropbox have customers that require different amounts of storage. Software companies such as Microsoft sell software subscriptions that can have different levels of service. The levels could be the number of different documents you are allowed to create, or the number of hours you are allowed to use the software. Companies like Google and Microsoft sell API calls to artificial intelligence software such as face recognition, to other software developers. Video and mobile games are increasingly designed in such a way that one can pay for better access to certain features. Spotify and iTunes sell music subscription, and different people listen to different number of songs in a month. Cellphone service providers like AT&T and Verizon offer cellular phone call minutes and data. People have widely varying amounts of data consumption.

Pricing is an important component in all these examples. The aim of this paper is to understand how to price such goods, for a monopolist seller who aims to maximize her revenue. The following common features (to a first degree of approximation) of these examples are crucial for our model.

- The marginal cost of offering a higher level of service is essentially a constant.
- The valuations for the different levels of service are roughly linear, subject to a cap.

Based on this, we consider the following problem. There is a single good with multiple units of it for sale. Equivalently, there is a single service with various levels of service. The marginal cost to the seller for procuring another unit of the good is a constant. There is a population of buyers, each of who has a *linear* valuation for consuming a number of units of the good, subject to a *cap* (which we refer to as *demand*). The type/private information of a buyer is determined by the per-unit valuation and the demand. Buyers try to maximize their utility which is quasi linear, i.e., the valuation minus their payment. The question is what is the revenue maximizing pricing scheme.

Additional Key Words and Phrases: Revenue Maximization; Multidimensional Auctions

The standard approach in mechanism design [5] is Bayesian: assume that the types are drawn from a given distribution and find/characterize the incentive compatible (IC) mechanism that maximizes the expected revenue when the buyer types are drawn from this distribution. The optimization is over randomized mechanisms, which in our case corresponds to pricing lotteries.

It appears that the optimal mechanism is usually randomized for small examples with discrete support. This phenomenon is quite common. While Myerson [5] showed that the optimal mechanism for single dimensional types is deterministic under quite a general assumption about the prior distribution called regularity, even slight multi dimensional generalizations end up in randomized mechanisms as optimal [3]. However, practical considerations force a seller to stick to deterministic

The full version of this paper can be found in [2].

This work is supported by the NSF, under grants CCF1408635, CCF0964033, Templeton Foundation grant 3966.

EC'17, June 26–30, 2017, Cambridge, MA, USA.

ACM ISBN 978-1-4503-4527-9/17/06
http://dx.doi.org/10.1145/3033274.3085122

mechanisms for the most part. Moreover, the optimal randomized mechanism sometimes doesn't even have a finite description [1]. Hence it is important to understand the structure of the optimal deterministic mechanism. In this paper we offer two insights in this regard.

Our first contribution is to identify a natural condition that guarantees that the optimal (randomized) mechanism is deterministic. The condition we need is called *decreasing marginal revenue* (DMR). Regularity requires that the *virtual value function* is monotone, or equivalently, that the revenue function is concave in the *quantile* space. DMR requires that *in the value space*, the marginal revenue is decreasing or equivalently that revenue function is concave. In other words, a probability distribution with CDF F is DMR, if the function $v(1 - F(v))$, the expected revenue of posting a price v, is concave. The condition we need for the optimal pricing to be deterministic is that the marginal distributions for v, conditioned on a given demand, are all DMR.

Our first result implies that the optimal pricing scheme is a price vector, which offers each number of units for a given price. **Our second contribution is to show that the revenue as a function of the price vector is concave**, under the same assumption of DMR. This implies that the optimal prices can be found efficiently using the ellipsoid or other cutting plane methods [4]. Note that DMR is a condition on the marginal distributions of values, and does not immediately imply concavity as a function of the vector of prices.

As a corollary, we obtain that under the DMR assumption, there is an efficient *dynamic pricing* scheme, defined as follows. Consider a repeated setting where in each round $\tau \in \{1, 2, \ldots, T\}$, the seller posts a price vector $\mathbf{p}^{\tau}$, a buyer is drawn from a fixed distribution, and buys her utility maximizing bundle. The seller does not know the distribution of buyer types, and has to only use the purchase information in previous rounds to set the price. The goal is to approach the optimal revenue as T goes to infinity. Given that the distribution satisfies the DMR assumption, our result on the concavity of the revenue curve implies that the average revenue per round converges to the optimal revenue at the rate of $\frac{poly(n)}{\sqrt{T}}$, where n is the number of units. These bounds are quite strong, since the best known bounds for the dynamic pricing problem in general scale *exponentially* in n. The concavity of the revenue function is an assumption often made to escape this curse of dimensionality [6]; we show that this assumption can be weakened, from the concavity of the multidimensional function to that of the 1 dimensional revenue functions for each d.

REFERENCES

[1] Constantinos Daskalakis, Alan Deckelbaum, and Christos Tzamos. 2013. Mechanism Design via Optimal Transport. In *Proceedings of the Fourteenth ACM Conference on Economics and Computation (EC)*.

[2] Nikhil R Devanur, Nima Haghpanah, and Christos-Alexandros Psomas. 2017. Optimal Multi-Unit Mechanisms with Private Demands. *arXiv preprint arXiv:1704.05027* (2017).

[3] Sergiu Hart and Philip J Reny. 2015. Maximal revenue with multiple goods: Nonmonotonicity and other observations. *Theoretical Economics* 10, 3 (2015), 893–922.

[4] Leonid G Khachiyan. 1980. Polynomial algorithms in linear programming. *U. S. S. R. Comput. Math. and Math. Phys.* 20, 1 (1980), 53–72.

[5] Roger B. Myerson. 1981. Optimal Auction Design. *Mathematics of Operations Research* 6, 1 (1981), 58–73.

[6] Kalyan T Talluri and Garrett J Van Ryzin. 2006. *The theory and practice of revenue management.* Vol. 68. Springer Science & Business Media.

The Double Clinching Auction for Wagering

RUPERT FREEMAN, Duke University[1]
DAVID M. PENNOCK, Microsoft Research
JENNIFER WORTMAN VAUGHAN, Microsoft Research

We develop the first incentive compatible and near-Pareto-optimal wagering mechanism. Wagering mechanisms can be used to elicit predictions from agents who reveal their beliefs by placing bets. Lambert et al. [20, 21] introduced weighted score wagering mechanisms, a class of budget-balanced wagering mechanisms under which agents with immutable beliefs truthfully report their predictions. However, we demonstrate that these and other existing incentive compatible wagering mechanisms are not Pareto optimal: agents have significant budget left over even when additional trade would be mutually beneficial. Motivated by this observation, we design a new wagering mechanism, the *double clinching auction*, a two-sided version of the adaptive clinching auction [9]. We show that no wagering mechanism can simultaneously satisfy weak budget balance, individual rationality, weak incentive compatibility, and Pareto optimality. However, we prove that the double clinching auction attains the first three and show in a series of simulations using real contest data that it comes much closer to Pareto optimality than previously known incentive compatible wagering mechanisms, in some cases almost matching the efficiency of the Pareto optimal (but not incentive compatible) parimutuel consensus mechanism. When the goal of wagering is to crowdsource probabilities, Pareto optimality drives participation and incentive compatibility drives accuracy, making the double clinching auction an attractive and practical choice. Our mechanism may be of independent interest as the first two-sided version of the adaptive clinching auction.

1 INTRODUCTION

Wagering mechanisms allow a principal to elicit the beliefs of a group of agents without paying them directly or taking on any risk. Each agent specifies a *belief*, her own subjective estimate of the likelihood of a future event, such as the Democratic nominee winning the 2020 U.S. Presidential election. She also specifies a monetary budget or *wager*, the maximum amount that she is willing to lose. These wagers are then collected by the principal and, after the truth is revealed, redistributed to agents in such a way that agents with more accurate predictions are more highly rewarded. Meanwhile, since agents directly report their beliefs, the principal is able to leverage the wisdom of crowds to obtain an accurate consensus forecast for the event, for example by computing an average [16], a budget-weighted average [3], a supra-Bayesian inference [22], or another aggregate measure of the forecasts [13].

Lambert et al. [20, 21] introduced the class of *weighted-score wagering mechanisms* (WSWMs), the unique wagering mechanisms to simultaneously satisfy a set of desirable properties including strict budget balance and incentive compatibility. Incentive compatibility is achieved through the use of *strictly proper scoring rules*, reward functions designed to incentivize truthful reports from risk-neutral agents. In particular, each agent's payoff under a WSWM is proportional to the

[1]Work conducted in part while R. Freeman was an intern at Microsoft Research. He is also thankful for support from NSF under award IIS-1527434 and ARO under grant W911NF-12-1-0550.

EC'17, June 26–30, 2017, Cambridge, Massachusetts, USA. ACM ISBN 978-1-4503-4527-9/17/06...$15.00.

DOI: http://dx.doi.org/10.1145/3033274.3085118

difference between her own score and the budget-weighted score of the other agents. Chen et al. [6] later proposed the class of *no-arbitrage wagering mechanisms* (NAWMs), which are incentive compatible but only weakly budget balanced, allowing the principal to profit off of disagreement among agents. Under an NAWM, an agent's payoff is proportional to her score minus the score of the budget-weighted average belief. To our knowledge, these mechanisms and their derivatives (such as the randomized, private WSWM of Cummings et al. [8]) are the only known incentive compatible wagering mechanisms.

As an artifact of their use of proper scoring rules, these mechanisms have one undesirable property: In general, it is not possible for any agent to lose her full wager, even if all other agents are perfectly informed. In other words, the mechanisms are not *Pareto optimal*, in the sense that agents have significant budget left over even when additional trade would be mutually beneficial. This is a serious concern in practice since agents typically gravitate to venues where they have the opportunity for large gains. If these mechanisms yield badly suboptimal allocations, agents may question the rules or simply go elsewhere. Indeed, all widely deployed wagering mechanisms, including parimutuels, bookmakers, and double auctions, feature Pareto optimality. Additionally, wagers effectively lose their meaning as budgets. This has a surprising implication on the quality of reports. Because an agent can never lose her full wager, she may be able to artificially inflate her reported budget risk-free. It turns out that when agents misreport their budgets, they can also have incentive to misreport their beliefs. (See Example 3.3.)

Motivated by this observation, we ask whether it is possible to design an incentive compatible wagering mechanism that achieves Pareto optimality without sacrificing other key properties. Unfortunately, the answer is no. We prove that no weakly incentive compatible wagering mechanism can achieve Pareto optimality along with individual rationality (meaning agents have incentive to participate) and weak budget balance. If the principal cannot force agents to participate and does not wish to subsidize the market, he must compromise on Pareto optimality. Given that, we seek an incentive compatible mechanism that is near-Pareto-optimal in practice.

Our mechanism is inspired by the observation that the output of a wagering mechanism has a natural interpretation as an allocation of securities. An agent who wins ρ_1 dollars if the Democrat is elected and loses ρ_0 dollars otherwise can equivalently be viewed as paying ρ_0 dollars up front for $\rho_0 + \rho_1$ shares of an Arrow-Debreu security worth \$1 if and only if the Democrat is elected. Thus wagering mechanisms can be viewed as allocating items (the securities) to agents, and it is natural to ask whether techniques from the auctions literature can be used. The *clinching auction* [2] produces VCG allocations and payments for multiple identical items, but VCG-style approaches cannot be applied when agents have budgets. Instead, we build on the *adaptive clinching auction* [4, 9], an extension of the clinching auction that incorporates budget constraints.

Our mechanism, the *double clinching auction* (DCA), is a two-sided version of the adaptive clinching auction. It elicits truthful reports by selling a variable number of securities to the agents via two simultaneous instances of the adaptive clinching auction, one which sells securities that pay off \$1 only if the event of interest happens (yes securities), and one which sells securities that pay off \$1 only if it does not (no securities). The principal can always sell a pair of yes and no securities for \$1 or more without risk, since he will owe exactly \$1 to the agents regardless of the outcome. Our key technical contribution is determining the number of security pairs that the principal can sell via adaptive clinching auctions in such a way that he never loses money, without incentivizing agents to misreport their beliefs.

We also show that under the double clinching auction, each agent has at least some risk of losing her entire budget, making the budget declaration risky to inflate and restoring the semantics of the wager as the largest acceptable worst-case loss.

To evaluate the efficiency of the DCA, we run a series of simulations using thousands of probability judgments about hundreds of events, collected from an online forecasting contest called ProbabilitySports [12]. We compare the performance of the DCA with WSWMs, NAWMs, and the *parimutuel consensus mechanism* [11], which is Pareto optimal but not incentive compatible. Our simulations show that the DCA is indeed significantly closer to Pareto optimal than the other incentive compatible mechanisms, sometimes approaching the efficiency of the parimutuel consensus mechanism, which was specifically designed to maximize trade. Given the results, we are optimistic that the DCA can serve as a practical wagering mechanism that both satisfies agent demand and encourages honest revelations.

We follow previous authors [6, 17, 19, 21], assuming that agents have *immutable beliefs* that do not update during wagering. Our agents "agree to disagree", unlike Bayesian agents. While immutable beliefs and perfect Bayesian reasoning are both idealizations, the former is arguably closer to reality. In practice, overconfident opponents, each expecting to gain, trade all the time [10, 18], contradicting the no-trade theorems implied in the Bayesian setting. Other authors have explored incentive properties of wagering mechanisms with Bayesian [20] or boundedly rational [23] agents.

2 WAGERING MECHANISMS

Let X be a binary random variable or *event* with value or *outcome* in $\{0, 1\}$. For example, imagine $X = 1$ is the outcome that the Democratic nominee wins the 2020 U.S. Presidential election and $X = 0$ is the outcome that he or she loses. We consider a setting in which a principal is interested in eliciting the beliefs of a set of agents $\mathcal{N} = \{1, \cdots, N\}$ about the likelihood that $X = 1$. Following the line of work initiated by Lambert et al. [21], we assume that each agent $i \in \{1, \cdots, N\}$ has a private, subjective, immutable belief p_i about the probability that $X = 1$, and that agents are risk neutral up to some budget limitation. That is, each agent budgets for the largest loss that she is willing to tolerate, then maximizes her expected wealth subject to the budget constraint.

The principal operates a *wagering mechanism* in which each agent i submits a report $\hat{p}_i \in [0, 1]$, capturing her subjective belief about the likelihood that $X = 1$, and a wager $w_i \geq 0$, representing the maximum amount that she is prepared to lose. After observing the realized value of X, denoted x, the principal redistributes the agents' wagers, rewarding agents based on their wagers and the accuracy of their reports. We denote by $\Pi_i(\hat{\mathbf{p}}, \mathbf{w}, x)$ the net payoff to agent i under reports $\hat{\mathbf{p}}$ and wagers $\mathbf{w}$ when $X = x$. For a wagering mechanism to be valid, it must be the case that no agent can lose more than her wager (i.e., for all i, $\hat{\mathbf{p}}$, $\mathbf{w}$, and x, we have $\Pi_i(\hat{\mathbf{p}}, \mathbf{w}, x) \geq -w_i$) and an agent can choose not to participate by wagering 0 (i.e., $\Pi_i(\hat{\mathbf{p}}, \mathbf{w}, x) = 0$ whenever $w_i = 0$). We denote by $\hat{\mathbf{p}}_{-\mathbf{i}}$ the predictions of all agents other than i and by $\mathbf{w}_{-\mathbf{i}}$ the wagers of all agents other than i.

2.1 Examples of Wagering Mechanisms and Connections to Proper Scoring Rules

There is a close connection between wagering mechanisms and *proper scoring rules* used to elicit truthful predictions from individual agents [14, 25]. A scoring rule s maps a prediction $p \in [0, 1]$ and an outcome $x \in \{0, 1\}$ to a score or reward in $\mathbb{R} \cup \{-\infty\}$. We say s is *proper* if for all $p, q \in [0, 1]$, $ps(p, 1) + (1-p)s(p, 0) \geq ps(q, 1) + (1-p)s(q, 0)$, and *strictly proper* if this inequality is strict whenever $p \neq q$. An agent who is rewarded for her prediction using a proper scoring rule therefore maximizes her expected reward by reporting her true belief, uniquely if the scoring rule is strictly proper. A common example of a strictly proper scoring rule is the Brier score [5], $s(p, x) = 1 - (x - p)^2$.

For a wagering mechanism to elicit truthful reports about the likelihood of X, it must be the case that, fixing the wagers $\mathbf{w}$ and reports $\hat{\mathbf{p}}_{-\mathbf{i}}$ of other agents, agent i's payoff Π_i is a proper scoring rule. Building on this idea, Lambert et al. [20, 21] introduced the class of *weighted score wagering mechanisms (WSWMs).* A WSWM has a payoff function of the form

$$\Pi_i(\hat{\mathbf{p}}, \mathbf{w}, x) = w_i \left(s(\hat{p}_i, x) - \frac{\sum_{j \in \mathcal{N}} w_j s(\hat{p}_j, x)}{\sum_{j \in \mathcal{N}} w_j} \right) \tag{1}$$

where s is any strictly proper scoring rule bounded in $[0, 1]$. WSWMs are the unique wagering mechanisms to simultaneously satisfy a set of desirable axioms that includes strict budget balance (the principal neither makes nor loses money), individual rationality (all agents have incentive to participate), strict incentive compatibility (agents have incentive to truthfully reveal their beliefs about X), anonymity (all agents are treated the same), sybilproofness (agents cannot profit by creating false identities), and a normality property (loosely, if agent i changes her report to improve her own expected payoff, the expected payoffs of other agents can't increase).

Chen et al. [6] pointed out that under a WSWM, it can be possible for an agent to risklessly profit: there exist reports $\hat{\mathbf{p}}$ and wagers $\mathbf{w}$ such that for some agent i, both $\Pi_i(\hat{\mathbf{p}}, \mathbf{w}, 1)$ and $\Pi_i(\hat{\mathbf{p}}, \mathbf{w}, 0)$ are positive. They proposed an alternative class of incentive compatible mechanisms called *no-arbitrage wagering mechanisms (NAWMs)*, in which this extra profit is instead collected by the principal. The payoff to each agent is proportional to the difference between the score of his own prediction and the score of a type of weighted average of the other agents' predictions. We will return to these mechanisms later in the paper.

2.2 Security Interpretation of Wagering Mechanisms

The output of a wagering mechanism has a natural interpretation as an allocation of Arrow-Debreu securities with payoffs that are contingent on the realization of X. We define a yes security to be a contract worth \$1 in the outcome $X = 1$ and \$0 if $X = 0$. Similarly, a no security is worth \$0 if $X = 1$ and \$1 if $X = 0$. A risk neutral agent with belief p about the likelihood that $X = 1$ would be willing to buy a yes security at any price up to p or a no security at any price up to $1 - p$. Since such trades reveal information about agents' beliefs, securities of this form are often considered in the context of prediction markets.

Suppose a wagering mechanism would yield a net payoff to agent i of $\rho_1 = \Pi_i(\hat{\mathbf{p}}, \mathbf{w}, 1)$ when $X = 1$ and $\rho_0 = \Pi_i(\hat{\mathbf{p}}, \mathbf{w}, 0)$ when $X = 0$. This is equivalent to the payoff that i would receive if she were sold $y_i = \max\{\rho_1 - \rho_0, 0\}$ yes securities and $n_i = \max\{\rho_0 - \rho_1, 0\}$ no securities for a total cost of $\pi_i = \max\{-\rho_0, -\rho_1\}$. For example, if $\rho_0 < \rho_1$, then agent i's participation in the wagering mechanism is equivalent to agent i paying the principal $\pi_i = -\rho_0$ before X is realized and then receiving $y_i = \rho_1 - \rho_0$ from the principal in the outcome $X = 1$.

Therefore, the output of a wagering mechanism can be completely specified by a triple $(\mathbf{y}, \mathbf{n}, \boldsymbol{\pi})$, where for each agent i, $y_i \geq 0$ is the number of yes securities allocated to i, $n_i \geq 0$ is the number of no securities allocated to i, and π_i is the cost paid by i for these securities. To be a valid output, we require that for all i, either $y_i = 0$ or $n_i = 0$ (or both), and $\pi_i \leq w_i$. This requirement is without loss of generality since any (fraction of a) pair of yes and no securities can be precisely converted into (a fraction of) \$1. We rely on the securities-based interpretation of wagering mechanisms for the remainder of this paper.[1]

2.3 Properties of Wagering Mechanisms

Lambert et al. [21] introduced several desirable properties for wagering mechanisms. We focus on three of these properties in our analysis: individual rationality, incentive compatibility, and budget balance. The definitions from Lambert et al. [21] are easily translated into our security-based

[1]Note that in the case of WSWMs, the observation of Chen et al. [6] implies that it is possible to have $\pi_i < 0$ for some i, meaning that i is allocated securities and actually *receives* money from the principal.

representation. First, individual rationality requires that agents participate willingly; agents have nothing to lose (in expectation) by participating.

Definition 2.1. A wagering mechanism is *individually rational* if, for any player i and any subjective probability p_i, there exists a report $\hat{p}_i$ such that for all $\hat{\mathbf{p}}_{-\mathbf{i}}, \mathbf{w}$,

$$p_i y_i(\hat{\mathbf{p}}, \mathbf{w}) + (1 - p_i) n_i(\hat{\mathbf{p}}, \mathbf{w}) \geq \pi_i(\hat{\mathbf{p}}, \mathbf{w}).$$

Incentive compatibility requires that each agent maximizes her expected payoff by reporting truthfully, regardless of the reports and wagers of other agents.

Definition 2.2. A wagering mechanism is *weakly incentive compatible* if, for every agent i with belief p_i and all reports $\hat{\mathbf{p}}$ and wagers $\mathbf{w}$,

$$\begin{aligned} p_i y_i((p_i, \hat{\mathbf{p}}_{-i}), \mathbf{w}) + (1 - p_i) n_i((p_i, \hat{\mathbf{p}}_{-i}), \mathbf{w}) - \pi_i((p_i, \hat{\mathbf{p}}_{-i}), \mathbf{w}) \\ \geq p_i y_i(\hat{\mathbf{p}}, \mathbf{w}) + (1 - p_i) n_i(\hat{\mathbf{p}}, \mathbf{w}) - \pi_i(\hat{\mathbf{p}}, \mathbf{w}). \end{aligned}$$

The mechanism satisfies *strict incentive compatibility* if the inequality is strict whenever $p_i \neq \hat{p}_i$.

Finally, a wagering mechanism is budget balanced if the principal never loses.

Definition 2.3. A wagering mechanism is *weakly budget balanced* if, for all $\hat{\mathbf{p}}$ and $\mathbf{w}$,

$$\sum_{i \in N} y_i(\hat{\mathbf{p}}, \mathbf{w}) \leq \sum_{i \in N} \pi_i(\hat{\mathbf{p}}, \mathbf{w}) \quad \text{and} \quad \sum_{i \in N} n_i(\hat{\mathbf{p}}, \mathbf{w}) \leq \sum_{i \in N} \pi_i(\hat{\mathbf{p}}, \mathbf{w}).$$

The mechanism is *strictly budget balanced* if the inequalities hold with equality for all $\hat{\mathbf{p}}$ and $\mathbf{w}$.

3 A TRADEOFF BETWEEN EFFICIENCY AND INCENTIVE COMPATIBILITY

Our goal is to design a wagering mechanism not to maximize profit but to maximize the amount of useful and credible information gathered. In this context, both incentive compatibility and Pareto optimality are important. The former literally keeps agents honest, steering them to report their true best estimates and reassuring the principal that probabilities are not tainted by irrelevant strategic play. The latter keeps agents happy, earning them as much utility as possible without inexplicably leaving dollars on the table. Pareto optimality is standard in prediction markets, parimutuel markets, betting exchanges, and financial exchanges. A badly suboptimal allocation may confuse agents, discourage them from playing, or encourage them to inflate their budgets, as we shall see below, which may cause their probability reports to become untruthful too.

3.1 Inefficient Allocations and Budget Inflation

In this section, we consider the undesirable effects of Pareto inefficiency. We start with an example.

Example 3.1. There are $N = 4$ agents with reported beliefs $\hat{\mathbf{p}} = (0.1, 0.2, 0.5, 0.7)$ and wagers $\mathbf{w} = (1, 1, 1, 1)$. Under the Brier scoring rule WSWM, the outcome is $(\mathbf{y} = (0, 0, 0.25, 0.65), \mathbf{n} = (0.55, 0.35, 0, 0), \boldsymbol{\pi} = (0.36, 0.19, 0.05, 0.29))$.

Observe that in Example 3.1, no agent stands to lose her full wager, regardless of the outcome. Indeed, the closest is agent 1, who risks losing 36% of her wager in the worst case. The *total risk*—the sum of all the agents' worst-case losses—is less than 25% of the total wagers. Thus WSWM is facilitating much less trade than if the agents were left to trade amongst themselves. Further, consider the 0.9 yes and 0.9 no securities allocated in Example 3.1. Thinking of these securities as any other commodity, we see that their allocation is not efficient. Some yes securities are allocated to agent 3 even though agent 4 has both a higher valuation and leftover budget.

The example above is in no way an edge case or specially manufactured; we will see in Section 6 that, if anything, it shows higher-than-average efficiency compared to our real-data simulations. Indeed, the following observation, which was originally made by Lambert et al. [21], shows that under a WSWM, agents who report any uncertainty will never lose their entire wager.

PROPOSITION 3.2 (LAMBERT ET AL. 21). *For any weighted score wagering mechanism, for any $i \in \mathcal{N}$ and any reports $\hat{\mathbf{p}}$ and $\mathbf{w}$, if $\hat{p}_i \in (0,1)$ and $w_i > 0$, then $\pi_i(\hat{\mathbf{p}}, \mathbf{w}) < w_i$.*

This observation has an important implication that goes beyond the desire to facilitate as much trade as possible. Because an agent who reports her true budget w_i can never lose it all, she may be able to report a higher budget w_i' such that her maximum loss is still bounded by w_i. It turns out that when agents misreport their budgets, they may also have incentive to misreport their beliefs.

Example 3.3. In Example 3.1, agent 4 derives utility $0.65 \cdot 0.7 - 0.29 = 0.17$ for being allocated 0.65 yes securities at a cost of 0.29, since she values each yes security at 0.7. However, since this does not exhaust her budget, she could inflate her budget to $w_4' = 2.04$ and instead be allocated 1.05 yes securities at a cost of 0.47, deriving utility 0.26. This budget inflation is completely safe in the sense that she never loses more than her budget, regardless of the reports and wagers of the other agents, (even if all other agents have arbitrarily large budgets and perfectly predict the outcome).

However, if agent 4 lowers her probability report to $\hat{p}_4 = 0.6$, she is able to inflate her budget even further. Intuitively, this is because 0.6 is a more moderate report than 0.7, so that even if $X = 0$, her loss will be lower. Agent 4 can safely report $w_4' = 2.78$ along with $\hat{p}_4 = 0.6$ without any risk of spending more than her budget, regardless of the reports and wagers of the other agents. She is then allocated 0.96 yes securities at a cost of 0.38. Her expected utility is now $0.96 \cdot 0.7 - 0.38 = 0.30$, which is higher than she could safely obtain by truthfully reporting $\hat{p}_i = 0.7$.

3.2 Pareto Optimality

In this section, we define a natural notion of Pareto optimality for wagering mechanisms. For a fixed number of securities, a Pareto optimal allocation is, as usual, any locally optimal allocation that cannot be improved for one agent without harming others. However, the number of pairs of securities is not fixed: the principal or the agents can always manufacture more yes-no pairs at the cost of \$1. Given this, we need a slightly expanded definition of Pareto optimality.

We say that a wagering mechanism is *Pareto optimal* if, treating agents' reports and wagers as their true beliefs and budgets, after all yes and no securities have been allocated and payments for these securities collected by the principal, there is no side bet that agents could make that would strictly benefit one without harming another, even if agents are allowed to create their own securities. We first define the notion of a profitable side bet.

Definition 3.4. Given reports $\hat{\mathbf{p}}$, wagers $\mathbf{w}$, allocations $\mathbf{y}$ and $\mathbf{n}$ of yes and no securities, and payments $\boldsymbol{\pi}$, a triple $(\Delta\mathbf{y}, \Delta\mathbf{n}, \Delta\boldsymbol{\pi})$ is a *profitable side bet* if the following three conditions hold:

(1) $\sum_{i \in \mathcal{N}} \Delta y_i = \sum_{i \in \mathcal{N}} \Delta n_i = \sum_{i \in \mathcal{N}} \Delta \pi_i = 0$.
(2) For all $i \in \mathcal{N}$, $\min\{y_i + \Delta y_i, n_i + \Delta n_i\} - (\pi_i + \Delta \pi_i) \geq -w_i$.
(3) For all $i \in \mathcal{N}$, $\hat{p}_i \Delta y_i + (1 - \hat{p}_i) \Delta n_i \geq \Delta \pi_i$, with strict inequality for at least one i.

Let's examine this definition. The first condition ensures that $(\Delta\mathbf{y}, \Delta\mathbf{n}, \Delta\boldsymbol{\pi})$ is a valid exchange among the agents, that is, all cash or securities given to one agent must come from other agents. The second condition ensures that no agent's budget is violated. The third guarantees that the exchange is profitable for at least one agent without harming any other agent (assuming truthful reports). We can now formally define Pareto optimality.

Definition 3.5. A wagering mechanism is *Pareto optimal* if for all reports $\hat{\mathbf{p}}$ and wagers $\mathbf{w}$, the mechanism's output $(\mathbf{y}(\hat{\mathbf{p}}, \mathbf{w}), \mathbf{n}(\hat{\mathbf{p}}, \mathbf{w}), \boldsymbol{\pi}(\hat{\mathbf{p}}, \mathbf{w}))$ is such that there exists no profitable side bet.

This definition is difficult to work with directly. We show that there is an intuitive equivalent characterization of Pareto optimality in terms of allocations and costs: A mechanism is Pareto optimal if and only if there is some threshold price such that all agents with beliefs above the threshold spend their entire budget on yes securities while all agents with beliefs below the threshold spend their entire budget on no securities. This is formalized in the following theorem.

THEOREM 3.6. *A wagering mechanism is Pareto optimal if and only if for all reports* $\hat{\mathbf{p}}$ *and* $\mathbf{w}$, *there exists an agent* $j \in \mathcal{N}$ *such that*

$$\forall i : \hat{p}_i < \hat{p}_j, \quad \pi_i(\hat{\mathbf{p}}, \mathbf{w}) = w_i \quad \text{and} \quad y_i(\hat{\mathbf{p}}, \mathbf{w}) = 0,$$
$$\forall i : \hat{p}_i > \hat{p}_j, \quad \pi_i(\hat{\mathbf{p}}, \mathbf{w}) = w_i \quad \text{and} \quad n_i(\hat{\mathbf{p}}, \mathbf{w}) = 0.$$

The first step of the proof, which appears in the appendix,[2] is to show that any time a profitable side bet exists, there is a profitable side bet with $\Delta\pi_i = 0$ for all agents i. This is because \$1 in cash is equivalent to a pair of yes and no securities. Thus we can limit attention to side bets that only involve the exchange of securities. The second step shows that, any time a profitable side bet exists, there exists a profitable side bet involving only two agents. The final step is to show that there is no profitable side bet between two agents if and only if the conditions in Theorem 3.6 hold.

Eisenberg and Gale [11] defined and analyzed the *parimutuel consensus mechanism* (PCM), a natural Pareto-optimal wagering mechanism. The outcome of the PCM is defined by a price p, such that all agents with $\hat{p}_i > p$ exhaust their entire wager buying yes securities at price p, and all agents with $\hat{p}_i < p$ exhaust their entire wager buying no securities at price $1 - p$. Any imbalance in demand for yes and no securities at price p is bridged by agents with report exactly p, who may buy either yes or no securities at the discretion of the mechanism. We can think of the PCM as a parimutuel mechanism with a proxy agent that switches agents' bets to the outcome most favorable to them, given the price. The PCM satisfies budget balance and individual rationality. However, the PCM does not satisfy incentive compatibility. An agent may affect the price p in a way that is favorable to them, as illustrated by the following example.

Example 3.7. Let $N = 2$, with $\mathbf{p} = (0.5, 0.75)$ and $\mathbf{w} = (1, 1)$. The outcome of the PCM with truthful reports is $(\mathbf{y} = (0, 2), \mathbf{n} = (2, 0), \boldsymbol{\pi} = (1, 1))$. Note that the price p is 0.5, so agent 1 achieves 0 utility. If agent 1 misreports $\hat{p}_1 = 2/3$, then the outcome becomes $(\mathbf{y} = (0, 1.5), \mathbf{n} = (1.5, 0), \boldsymbol{\pi} = (0.5, 1))$. Now, the price p is $2/3$, so agent 1 gets no securities at a price of $1/3$, gaining positive utility.

3.3 An Impossibility Result

We have shown that WSWM fails to produce Pareto optimal allocations and PCM fails to achieve incentive compatibility. In this section, we show that the tradeoff is unavoidable: no incentive compatible wagering mechanism can achieve Pareto optimality along with two other core properties.

The proof extends the intuition that for any two agents i and j with differing reports $\hat{p}_i < \hat{p}_j$, they must trade according to some intermediate price $p \in [\hat{p}_i, \hat{p}_j]$. It is therefore always in the interests of at least one of the agents to misreport her belief closer to that of the other agent, forcing the price further from her own true belief and thus achieving a higher payoff in expectation.

THEOREM 3.8. *No wagering mechanism simultaneously satisfies individual rationality, weak incentive compatibility, weak budget balance, and Pareto optimality. This holds even if the number of agents*

[2] An appendix containing all omitted proofs can be found in the full version of the paper on the authors' websites.

is arbitrarily large and all agents wager the same amount of money. Any three of the four properties are simultaneously attainable.

Individual rationality is hard to imagine giving up: We cannot force agents to participate. Weak incentive compatibility is key to ensuring the credibility of agents' reports. Although untruthful mechanisms like parimutuel wagering flourish in practice and do display an ability to aggregate useful information [1, 24], our goal is to create a mechanism that simplifies reasoning for the agents and principal and that offers some modicum of assurance that the reports the principal is seeing are accurate to the best abilities of the agents. Some wagering mechanisms, in particular automated market maker algorithms for prediction markets [7], do give up budget balance, subsidizing trade as a reward for information. However, most mechanisms seek profits if anything, not losses. When a subsidy is not possible or desired, we must relax Pareto optimality. In the remainder of this paper, we present and analyze our *double clinching auction* wagering mechanism which maintains individual rationality, weak incentive compatibility, and weak budget balance, while coming close to Pareto optimality in practice.

4 THE ADAPTIVE CLINCHING AUCTION

Since wagering mechanisms can be interpreted as allocating items (securities) to agents, it is natural to ask whether techniques from the auctions literature might be useful. Ausubel's clinching auction [2] produces VCG allocations and payments in the setting in which there are multiple identical items and each agent has a fixed valuation per item. However, VCG-style approaches cannot be applied in our setting since agents have budgets. Instead, we build on the *adaptive clinching auction* of Dobzinski et al. [9], which extends Ausubel's auction to handle budget constraints.

In this section, we review the adaptive clinching auction and state some known results that are used in our analysis. Many details are necessarily omitted. For a full description, we point the reader to Dobzinski et al. [9] and, for the divisible-items version, Bhattacharya et al. [4]. In describing the auction, we use notation that parallels that of the wagering mechanism setting, but the general description in this section is for arbitrary items.

Suppose that there are m identical, indivisible items for sale to a set of agents $\mathcal{N}$. Each agent i has a private value p_i for each item and a budget w_i, which we assume is known to the auctioneer.

The adaptive clinching auction is an ascending price auction. Each agent $i \in \mathcal{N}$ reports a bid $\hat{p}_i$. The price p per item starts at 0 and grows over time. Items are allocated as the price increases. As this happens, the auctioneer keeps track of the number of items $q_i(p)$ that have been allocated to each agent i at prices less than p along with the total cost $c_i(p)$ of those items and the agent's remaining budget $B_i(p) = w_i - c_i(p)$. Define the demand of agent i at price p to be

$$D_i(p) = \begin{cases} \infty & p = 0, \\ \left\lfloor \frac{B_i(p)}{p} \right\rfloor & 0 < p < \hat{p}_i, \\ 0 & p \geq \hat{p}_i \text{ and } p > 0. \end{cases} \tag{2}$$

The adaptive clinching auction allocates items to agent i at price p if the total demand of the other agents falls below the total supply. In particular, let $q(p) = m - \sum_{i \in \mathcal{N}} q_i(p)$ be the total number of items yet to be allocated. At any point, if $D_{-i}(p) = \sum_{j \neq i} D_j(p) < q(p)$, then $q(p) - D_{-i}(p)$ items are allocated to (or "clinched by") agent i at a price of p per item, and the relevant variables are updated accordingly.

The auction ends when the total demand no longer exceeds the total supply, that is, when $\sum_{i \in \mathcal{N}} D_i(p) \leq q(p)$. At this point, the price stops ascending and all agents with $D_i(p) > 0$ are allocated their full demand at a per-item price of p. If the total demand at price p is strictly less than the supply (i.e., $\sum_{i \in \mathcal{N}} D_i(p) < q(p)$), then the remaining $q(p) - \sum_{i \in \mathcal{N}} D_i(p)$ items are allocated to agents i with $\hat{p}_i = p$. (We will see below that this is always possible to do.) A worked example is contained in the appendix.

The adaptive clinching auction can be extended to handle divisible items. While this extension is more complicated to write down, conceptually we simply view the auction as a continuous-time process. Bhattacharya et al. [4] give a formal description. We omit the details, but summarize the properties of the auction that we use to derive our results.[3]

First, agents have incentive to participate in the auction and to bid truthfully.

Lemma 4.1 (Dobzinski et al. [9]). *The adaptive clinching auction for divisible items is individually rational. When budgets are known to the auctioneer, it is also incentive compatible: Every agent i maximizes expected utility by reporting $\hat{p}_i = p_i$.*

While Dobzinski et al. [9] only state incentive compatibility for the case of indivisible items, their proof carries through for the continuous version, and this fact is used heavily by Bhattacharya et al. [4]. It follows from the observation that the report $\hat{p}_i$ only determines the price at which agent i drops out of the auction. While the price is below p_i, agent i can clinch (portions of) items at a per-item price below her value, thus deriving positive utility. After the price rises above p_i, any items she would clinch would cost more than her value, so she would derive negative utility. Thus, it is optimal to drop out of the auction exactly when the price reaches p_i.

We additionally use the fact that no agent is charged more than her budget.

Lemma 4.2 (Bhattacharya et al. [4], Dobzinski et al. [9]). *The adaptive clinching auction for divisible items never charges an agent more than her budget.*

We also rely heavily on the following facts, which together imply that no agent (or the auctioneer) can be made better off without harming another agent.

Lemma 4.3 (Bhattacharya et al. [4], Dobzinski et al. [9]). *The adaptive clinching auction for divisible items always allocates all m items.*

Lemma 4.4 (Bhattacharya et al. [4], Dobzinski et al. [9]). *If an agent receives a non-zero allocation of items from the adaptive clinching auction for divisible items, then any player with a higher bid exhausts her entire budget.*

Finally, the utility of each agent is (weakly) increasing in the number of items sold.

Lemma 4.5 (Goel et al. [15]). *Fixing $\hat{\mathbf{p}}$ and $\mathbf{w}$, if $\hat{p}_i = p_i$ then i receives weakly greater expected utility from the adaptive clinching auction for divisible items when the number of items m increases.*

5 THE DOUBLE CLINCHING AUCTION

In this section, we present the double clinching auction. Motivated by the observation that existing incentive compatible wagering mechanisms do not even allocate securities efficiently, we turn to the adaptive clinching auction as a way to efficiently allocate any fixed number of securities. The principal runs two instances of the adaptive clinching auction for divisible items, deriving the agents' bids from their reports. The first instance, which we refer to as the yes auction, sells some number m^* of yes securities to the agents, fixing the bid of each agent i to equal her report $\hat{p}_i$. The second instance, which we refer to as the no auction, sells m^* no securities, fixing the bid of agent i to $1 - \hat{p}_i$. If m^* is chosen such that the payment collected for each pair of yes and no securities is at least \$1, then the principal never loses money, that is, the mechanism is weakly

[3] Both Dobzinski et al. [9] and Bhattacharya et al. [4] describe the divisible-items version in terms of a *single* divisible item. For our purposes, it is more convenient to view it as an auction over some number m of divisible items. This is equivalent and simply requires a rescaling of agent values.

budget balanced. While many values of m^* balance the budget, we define one particular value of m^*, carefully selected to ensure that agents cannot profit by misreporting their beliefs.

The primary technical contribution of this section is the derivation of m^* and the proof that the resulting auction is indeed (weakly) incentive compatible.

5.1 Definition of the Double Clinching Auction

To formally define the double clinching auction, we first describe the selection of m^*, the number of securities to be sold in each of the two instances of the adaptive clinching auction. We start by defining a pair of demand functions. These are similar to Equation (2), but do not take into account items that may have been allocated. Let D_i^y be the demand of agent i for (arbitrarily divisible) yes securities at price p assuming a per-item value of $\hat{p}_i$, and D_i^n her demand for no securities at price p assuming a per-item value of $1 - \hat{p}_i$, that is,

$$D_i^y(p) = \begin{cases} \infty & p = 0, \\ \frac{w_i}{p} & 0 < p < \hat{p}_i, \\ 0 & p \geq \hat{p}_i \text{ and } p > 0, \end{cases} \qquad \text{and} \qquad D_i^n(p) = \begin{cases} \infty & p = 0, \\ \frac{w_i}{p} & 0 < p < 1 - \hat{p}_i, \\ 0 & p \geq \hat{p}_i \text{ and } p > 0. \end{cases}$$

Let $D^y(p) = \sum_{i \in N} D_i^y(p)$ be the total demand of all agents for yes securities at price p, and $D_{-i}^y(p) = \sum_{j \neq i} D_j^y(p)$ be the total excluding agent i. Define $D^n(p)$ and $D_{-i}^n(p)$ similarly.

The double clinching auction allocates securities only when there are 4 or more agents with positive wagers. (Agents with wagers of zero can simply be dropped since this is equivalent to not participating.) If there are fewer than 4, then no trade occurs. For the remainder of this section, assume that there are $N \geq 4$ agents who submit reports $\hat{p}_1 \leq \hat{p}_2 \leq \ldots \leq \hat{p}_N$ and wagers $\mathbf{w} > \mathbf{0}$.

Fixing the number of securities m, define the *lowest clinching prices* as

$$c_y(m) = \begin{cases} \inf\{p : \min_{i \in N} D_{-i}^y(p) < m\} & m > 0, \\ \hat{p}_{N-1} & m = 0, \end{cases}$$

and

$$c_n(m) = \begin{cases} \inf\{p : \min_{i \in N} D_{-i}^n(p) < m\} & m > 0, \\ 1 - \hat{p}_2 & m = 0. \end{cases}$$

Here $c_y(m)$ can be thought of as the price at which the first (possibly infinitesimal) fraction of a security would be clinched in an adaptive clinching auction for m yes securities, and similarly, $c_n(m)$ the price at which the first fraction of a security would be clinched in an auction for m no securities. The $m = 0$ case is simply a technical definition that is required in our proofs. Both $c_y(m)$ and $c_n(m)$ are well-defined since they each take the infimum of a non-empty set that is bounded below by 0 since $D_{-i}^y(0) = D_{-i}^n(0) = \infty$ for all agents i. It is easy to see that for all m, $c_y(m) \in (0, \hat{p}_{N-1}]$ and $c_n(m) \in (0, 1 - \hat{p}_2]$. The following lemma gives additional useful properties of these functions. To show continuity, it is sufficient to show that the functions are surjective (onto), since a surjective, monotonic function is continuous.

Lemma 5.1. *Fixing reports* $\hat{\mathbf{p}}$ *and wagers* $\mathbf{w}$, c_y *and* c_n *are continuous and weakly decreasing.*

Let $M = \{m : c_y(m) + c_n(m) > 1\}$. For any $m \in M$, auctioning off m yes and m no securities via two adaptive clinching auctions is guaranteed to collect more than m dollars total, or more than \$1 for each pair, guaranteeing no loss for the principal. We set m^* to be the largest m in M: the most pairs of securities such that every pair, even every fraction of a pair, costs more than \$1 per share (i.e., every ϵ shares cost more than \$$\epsilon$). Formally, the number of pairs of securities auctioned is

$$m^* = \begin{cases} \sup M & \hat{p}_2 < \hat{p}_{N-1}, \\ 0 & \hat{p}_2 = \hat{p}_{N-1}. \end{cases} \tag{3}$$

The following lemma guarantees that m^* is well-defined. This is clearly the case when $\hat{p}_2 = \hat{p}_{N-1}$. To show that m^* is well-defined when $\hat{p}_2 < \hat{p}_{N-1}$, it is sufficient to show that the set M is non-empty and bounded above, which implies the existence of a unique least upper bound. To show that $m^* > 0$ when $\hat{p}_{N-1} > \hat{p}_2$, we argue that $c_y(0) + c_n(0) > 1$, which implies there must exist some $m' > 0$ such that $c_y(m') + c_n(m') > 1$. This in turn implies that $m' \in M$ and therefore, $m^* = \sup M \geq m' > 0$.

Lemma 5.2. *For any* $\hat{\mathbf{p}}$ *and* $\mathbf{w}$*,* m^* *is well-defined. Furthermore,* $m^* > 0$ *when* $\hat{p}_{N-1} > \hat{p}_2$*.*

With these definitions in place, we can formally define the double clinching auction; see Algorithm 1. The principal first sets m^* according to Equation 3. He then runs an auction for m^* yes securities (the yes auction) and an auction for m^* no securities (the no auction). A worked example of the double clinching auction on the reports from Example 3.1 is given in the appendix.

We have already shown that this procedure is well defined. However, to show that the double clinching auction is a valid wagering mechanism, we must also show that no agent ever loses more than her wager; that is, for any $\hat{\mathbf{p}}$ and $\mathbf{w}$, the double clinching auction produces output $(\mathbf{y}, \mathbf{n}, \boldsymbol{\pi})$ such that for all $i \in \mathcal{N}$, $\min\{y_i, n_i\} = 0$ and $\pi_i \leq w_i$. We show this in the following theorem.

Algorithm 1: The Double Clinching Auction. Here *ClinchingAuction*$(m, \hat{\mathbf{p}}, \mathbf{w})$ denotes the allocation and payments produced by an adaptive clinching auction for m arbitrarily divisible items on bids $\hat{\mathbf{p}}$ and budgets $\mathbf{w}$.

```
Input: reports p̂ and wagers w > 0 of N agents
if N < 4 or p̂_2 = p̂_{N-1} then
   Set (y, n, π) = (0, 0, 0)
else
   Set m* as in Equation 3
   Let (y, π_y) = ClinchingAuction(m*, p̂, w)
   Let (n, π_n) = ClinchingAuction(m*, 1 − p̂, w)
   Let π = π_y + π_n
end if
Output (y, n, π)
```

Theorem 5.3. *The double clinching auction is a valid wagering mechanism.*

From Lemma 4.2, we know that no agent can lose more than her wager in either the yes auction or the no auction alone. It is therefore sufficient to show that no agent is ever allocated a positive number of securities in both auctions. This follows immediately from the following lemma, taking p to be the report $\hat{p}_i$ of any agent, and the definition of the clinching auction.

Lemma 5.4. *Fixing any reports* $\hat{\mathbf{p}}$ *and wagers* $\mathbf{w}$*, for any* $p \in [0, 1]$*, either* $\min_{i \in \mathcal{N}} D^y_{-i}(p) \geq m^*$*,* $\min_{i \in \mathcal{N}} D^n_{-i}(1-p) \geq m^*$*, or both.*

Proof. If $m^* = 0$ then this claim is trivially true, since for all p, $\min_{i \in \mathcal{N}} D^y_{-i}(p) \geq 0$ and $\min_{i \in \mathcal{N}} D^n_{-i}(p) \geq 0$. So suppose that $m^* > 0$. Suppose that $\min_{i \in \mathcal{N}} D^y_{-i}(p) < m^*$ and $\min_{i \in \mathcal{N}} D^n_{-i}(1-p) < m^*$. Then there exists an $m' < m^*$ such that $\min_{i \in \mathcal{N}} D^y_{-i}(p) < m'$ and $\min_{i \in \mathcal{N}} D^n_{-i}(1-p) < m'$.

Therefore, when m' securities are sold, clinching in the yes auction begins at (or before) p, and clinching in the no auction begins at (or before) $1 - p$. That is, $c_y(m') \leq p$ and $c_n(m') \leq 1 - p$. So $c_y(m') + c_n(m') \leq p + 1 - p = 1$. This implies that m' is a lower upper bound on the set $\{m : c_y(m) + c_n(m) > 1\}$ than m^* is, violating the definition of m^*. □

5.2 Properties of the Double Clinching Auction

In this section, we discuss some desirable properties of the double clinching auction. We first observe that the double clinching auction is weakly budget balanced and individually rational.

Proposition 5.5. *The double clinching auction is weakly budget balanced and individually rational.*

The proof of individual rationality invokes the incentive compatibility and individual rationality of the clinching mechanism. The proof of budget balance uses the fact that all m^* yes and no security pairs are allocated by the yes and no clinching auctions and the following lemma, which implies that each pair sells for more than \$1. The proof relies on the continuity and monotonicity of the functions c_y and c_n.

Lemma 5.6. *For any reports* $\hat{\mathbf{p}}$ *and wagers* $\mathbf{w}$, $c_y(m^*) + c_n(m^*) = 1$.

Finally we state our main theoretical result: incentive compatibility of the double clinching auction. The proof is significantly more involved and we develop it in the next subsection.

Theorem 5.7. *The double clinching auction is weakly incentive compatible.*

5.3 Proof of Incentive Compatibility

In this section, we prove Theorem 5.7, beginning with some useful lemmas. The first states that an agent cannot benefit from misreporting her belief unless it increases the number of securities.

Lemma 5.8. *For any* $i \in \mathcal{N}$, *fix the wagers* $\mathbf{w}$ *of all agents and reports* $\hat{\mathbf{p}}_{-i}$ *of all agents but i, and let* $\hat{p}_i = p_i$. *Agent i cannot increase her expected utility under the double clinching auction by reporting any* $\hat{p}_i' \neq p_i$ *unless this report increases the value of* m^*.

Proof. Let m^* denote the number of security pairs allocated by the double clinching auction when i reports $\hat{p}_i = p_i$, and $\hat{m}^*$ the number when i reports $\hat{p}_i'$.

First, observe that agent i cannot benefit from any misreport for which $m^* = \hat{m}^*$. This follows immediately from the incentive compatibility of the adaptive clinching auction (Lemma 4.1). Agent i maximizes the utility she gains from both the yes and no auctions individually when her bids in these auctions are truthful. Fixing m^*, the yes and no auctions are run independently, so agent i maximizes her total utility by reporting her true belief. Next, suppose that $\hat{m}^* < m^*$. Agent i's utility for bidding untruthfully for $\hat{m}^*$ securities is weakly less than her utility for bidding truthfully for $\hat{m}^*$ securities, by incentive compatibility of the adaptive clinching auction, which is weakly less than her utility for bidding truthfully for m^* securities, by Lemma 4.5. Thus she would weakly prefer to bid truthfully than to make any misreport that reduces m^*. □

Lemma 5.9 follows because, when any agent increases her report, the demand for yes (respectively, no) securities at a fixed price does not decrease (respectively, increase).

Lemma 5.9. *For any* $i \in \mathcal{N}$, *fix the wagers* $\mathbf{w}$ *of all agents and reports* $\hat{\mathbf{p}}_{-i}$ *of all agents but i. For any fixed m, as i's report* $\hat{p}_i$ *increases, the lowest clinching price* $c_y(m)$ *weakly increases, while the lowest clinching price* $c_n(m)$ *weakly decreases.*

The proof of Lemma 5.10 uses the fact that as the price moves from any value p to a sufficiently close higher value p', no new agent will drop out of the auction, and so demand functions only change by a very small amount.

Lemma 5.10. *For any reports* $\hat{\mathbf{p}}$ *and wagers* $\mathbf{w}$, *and any* m, $\min_{i \in N} D^y_{-i}(c_y(m)) \leq m$ *and* $\min_{i \in N} D^n_{-i}(c_n(m)) \leq m$.

We are now ready to complete the proof of Theorem 5.7. We start by observing that no agent can be allocated both yes *and* no securities. We treat two cases. If an agent's misreport does not change the type of security that she is allocated, then it cannot increase the number of securities sold, and so by Lemma 5.8, cannot be profitable. If her misreport does change the type of security that she is allocated, she may be able to increase the number of securities auctioned. However, in this case, the amount she pays would be higher than her value for the securities she gets.

Proof of Theorem 5.7. Consider an agent i with belief p_i and let $\hat{\mathbf{p}}_{-i}$ denote the reports of all agents other than i. Let m^* be the number of pairs of securities auctioned if i truthfully reports p_i. Denote by $\hat{c}_y$ and $\hat{c}_n$ the lowest clinching price functions if i misreports $\hat{p}_i \neq p_i$, and by $\hat{D}$ the demand functions in the misreported instance. Let $\hat{m}^*$ denote the number of pairs of securities auctioned in the misreported instance.

Noting that $\hat{p}_i \neq p_i$, we can break the analysis into four cases:

(1) $p_i < c_y(m^*)$ and $\hat{p}_i \leq c_y(m^*)$ (3) $p_i \leq c_y(m^*)$ and $\hat{p}_i > c_y(m^*)$

(2) $p_i > c_y(m^*)$ and $\hat{p}_i \geq c_y(m^*)$ (4) $p_i \geq c_y(m^*)$ and $\hat{p}_i < c_y(m^*)$

Case 1 and Case 2 are symmetric, since in Case 2 $1 - p_i < c_n(m^*)$ and $1 - \hat{p}_i \leq c_n(m^*)$, which is equivalent to Case 1 reversing the outcomes yes and no. Similarly, Case 3 and Case 4 are symmetric. Therefore, it is sufficient to show that i does not benefit from misreporting in Cases 1 or 3.

Case 1: $p_i < c_y(m^*)$ and $\hat{p}_i \leq c_y(m^*)$. To show that i can not benefit from this misreport, we prove that she does not change the clinching prices $c_y(m^*)$ and $c_n(m^*)$. We will show that if $\hat{p}_i < c_y(m^*)$ then this is true because the global demand can only change at prices between p_i and $\hat{p}_i$, and this interval does not contain $c_y(m^*)$. When $\hat{p}_i = c_y(m^*)$, some more care is necessary.

If $m^* = 0$ then $c_y(m^*) = p_{N-1}$. Further, we know that $p_{N-1} = p_2$, or else it would be the case that $m^* > 0$, by Lemma 5.2. And, since we have assumed that $p_i < c_y(m^*)$, we know that i's report is the lowest of all agents. Since $\hat{p}_i \leq c_y(m^*) = p_{N-1} = p_2$, $\hat{p}_i$ is still the (equal) lowest report, and therefore both the second highest and second lowest reports are unchanged. In particular, $\hat{p}_2 = \hat{p}_{N-1}$, so $\hat{m}^* = 0$. By Lemma 5.8, this misreport does not benefit i.

Now suppose that $m^* > 0$. We first show that $c_y(m^*) = \hat{c}_y(m^*)$ and $c_n(m^*) = \hat{c}_n(m^*)$. If $\hat{p}_i < c_y(m^*)$ then the demand locally around $c_y(m^*)$ and $c_n(m^*)$ is unchanged. Therefore, since $c_y(m^*)$ and $c_n(m^*)$ are the prices at which demand drops below m^*, these quantities remain unchanged in the misreported instance. If $\hat{p}_i = c_y(m^*)$ then, by Lemma 5.9, $c_y(m^*) \leq \hat{c}_y(m^*)$, since $p_i < \hat{p}_i = c_y(m^*)$. However, for all $p > c_y(m^*)$, the demand in the misreported instance is exactly the same as that in the truthful instance, and therefore $\min_i \hat{D}^y_{-i}(p) < m^*$ for all $p > c_y(m^*)$, which implies that $\hat{c}_y(m^*) \leq c_y(m^*)$. This, together with the earlier statement that $\hat{c}_y(m^*) \geq c_y(m^*)$, gives us $c_y(m^*) = \hat{c}_y(m^*)$. By similar reasoning, $c_n(m^*) = \hat{c}_n(m^*)$.

Therefore $\hat{c}_y(m^*) + \hat{c}_n(m^*) = c_y(m^*) + c_n(m^*) = 1$. Since $\hat{c}_y$ and $\hat{c}_n$ are decreasing functions, m^* is an upper bound on the set $M = \{m : \hat{c}_y(m) + \hat{c}_n(m) > 1\}$. Since the double clinching auction sells a number of securities equal to the least upper bound of M, it therefore sells at most m^* securities in the misreported instance. By Corollary 5.8, agent i does not profit from this misreport.

Case 3: $p_i \leq c_y(m^*)$ and $\hat{p}_i > c_y(m^*)$. In this case, i's misreport can increase the number of securities sold. However, we show that to do so, i must be allocated some yes securities. But since i's misreport is higher than her true value, it must also be the case that the price for yes securities is higher in the misreported instance than the truthful instance. Because all yes securities are sold at a price higher than i's valuation in the truthful instance, it must still be the case in the misreported instance. Therefore i does not get any positive utility from the securities she is allocated.

There are two possibilities. First is that $\hat{c}_y(m^*) + \hat{c}_n(m^*) \leq 1$, in which case we need to sell (weakly) fewer securities in the misreported instance than the truthful instance. That is, $\hat{m}^* \leq m^*$. By Lemma 5.8, the misreport can not be profitable for i in this case.

Second is that $\hat{c}_y(m^*) + \hat{c}_n(m^*) > 1$. In this case it may be possible to sell more securities, so assume that $\hat{m}^* > m^*$ (otherwise i's misreport is not profitable, by Lemma 5.8). By Lemma 5.10, $\min_j \hat{D}^y_{-j}(\hat{c}_y(m^*)) \leq m^* < \hat{m}^*$. So, by Lemma 5.4,

$$\min_j \hat{D}^n_{-j}(1 - \hat{c}_y(m^*)) \geq \hat{m}^*. \tag{4}$$

In what remains of the proof, we show that holding the number of securities the same as in the truthful instance, i's misreport cannot result in the clinching price rising all the way *above* $\hat{p}_i$. We can then use the fact that the clinching price decreases as we sell more securities to deduce that $\hat{p}_i \geq \hat{c}_y(\hat{m}^*)$, which (after addressing some details) says that i is allocated yes securities, and not no securities. By lower bounding the price of the yes securities by i's true valuation p_i, this says that i can not derive positive utility from this misreport. We now prove this formally.

We first show that $\hat{p}_i \geq \hat{c}_y(m^*)$. In the case that $m^* = 0$, this is true because $\hat{p}_i > c_y(m^*) = p_{N-1}$, so therefore $\hat{p}_i$ is one of the two highest reports in the misreported instance. And, since $m^* = 0$, it follows that $\hat{c}_y(m^*) = \hat{p}_{N-1} \leq \hat{p}_i$.

For the case that $m^* > 0$, note that the demand is unchanged from the truthful instance at all prices greater than or equal to $\hat{p}_i$. Therefore for all $p \geq \hat{p}_i$, we have that $\min_j \hat{D}^y_{-j}(p) = \min_j D^y_{-j}(p) < m^*$, where the inequality holds because $p \geq \hat{p}_i > c_y(m^*)$. In particular, $\min_j \hat{D}^y_{-j}(\hat{p}_i) < m^*$, which implies that $\hat{p}_i \geq \hat{c}_y(m^*)$.

From $\hat{p}_i \geq \hat{c}_y(m^*)$, we have that $1 - \hat{p}_i \leq 1 - \hat{c}_y(m^*)$, which implies that $\hat{D}^n_{-i}(1 - \hat{p}_i) \geq \hat{D}^n_{-i}(1 - \hat{c}_y(m^*))$. Combining this with Equation 4, $\hat{D}^n_{-i}(1 - \hat{p}_i) \geq \hat{D}^n_{-i}(1 - \hat{c}_y(m^*)) \geq \min_j \hat{D}^n_{-j}(1 - \hat{c}_y(m^*)) \geq \hat{m}^*$, which implies that i does not receive no securities in the misreported instance. There are two possibilities remaining. If i also does not receive yes securities, then agent i achieves zero overall payoff after misreporting, which is no better than her payoff from reporting truthfully. Otherwise, the average price paid per yes security is at least $\hat{c}_y(\hat{m}^*) = 1 - \hat{c}_n(\hat{m}^*) \geq 1 - \hat{c}_n(m^*) \geq 1 - c_n(m^*) = c_y(m^*) \geq p_i$, where the first inequality follows from the fact that $\hat{c}_n$ is decreasing and $\hat{m}^* > m^*$, and the second inequality follows from Lemma 5.9, because $\hat{p}_i > p_i$. Therefore i is paying a price for the securities equal to or greater than they are worth to her, so she obtains non-positive expected payoff, which is no better than her (non-negative) truthful payoff. □

5.4 Beyond Weak Incentive Compatibility

Theorem 5.7 proves weak incentive compatibility. Taken at face value, weak incentive compatibility is, well, extremely weak. Indeed, simply paying each agent a constant amount regardless of her report satisfies weak incentive compatibility.

We show that the double clinching auction actually satisfies a stronger property: If agent i makes any misreport $\hat{p}_i \neq p_i$, then, for some set of reports $\hat{\mathbf{p}}_{-i}$ of the other agents, agent i obtains strictly lower expected utility than she would by reporting truthfully. If agent i is sufficiently uncertain about other agents, she is strictly better off reporting her true belief.

Theorem 5.11. *Fix any set of agents $\mathcal{N}$ with $N \geq 4$ and any wagers $\mathbf{w}$. For any agent i with belief p_i and any report $\hat{p}_i \neq p_i$, there exist reports $\hat{\mathbf{p}}_{-i}$ of the other agents such that under the double* *clinching auction*

$$p_i y_i((p_i, \hat{\mathbf{p}}_{-i}), \mathbf{w}) + (1 - p_i) n_i((p_i, \hat{\mathbf{p}}_{-i}), \mathbf{w}) - \pi_i((p_i, \hat{\mathbf{p}}_{-i}), \mathbf{w}) > p_i y_i(\hat{\mathbf{p}}, \mathbf{w}) + (1 - p_i) n_i(\hat{\mathbf{p}}, \mathbf{w}) - \pi_i(\hat{\mathbf{p}}, \mathbf{w}).$$

5.5 Budget Inflation Under the Double Clinching Auction

As discussed in Section 3, even a wagering mechanism that satisfies incentive compatibility may give an agent incentive to misreport her belief if she can safely inflate her budget. Since the double clinching auction is not Pareto optimal, a bidder with complete knowledge of the reports and wagers of other agents could have incentive to inflate her budget. Further, there exist examples analogous to Example 3.3 where the potential for an agent to inflate her budget may also affect her incentive to report truthfully.

However, in reality agents operate with only limited knowledge about the reports of other agents. While the budget misreport in Example 3.3 was safe in the sense that the budget inflation could not lead to the misreporting agent overspending her true budget, we can show that completely safe manipulations are not possible under the double clinching auction. An agent cannot inflate her wager without at least some risk of losing more than her true budget. This is in stark contrast to Proposition 3.2 for the WSWM.

THEOREM 5.12. *Fix any set of agents $\mathcal{N}$ with $N \geq 4$. For any agent i with report $\hat{p}_i$ and wager w_i, there exist reports $\hat{\mathbf{p}}_{-i}$ and wagers $\mathbf{w}_{-i}$ of the other agents such that $\pi_i = w_i$ under the double clinching auction.*

6 SIMULATIONS

For a fixed number of yes securities, the adaptive clinching auction is efficient, so we had reason to suspect that the double clinching auction, selling m^* yes and no securities, would be near efficient. In this section, in a series of simulations based on real probability reports, we show that indeed the DCA is much more efficient than the WSWM or the NAWM, in some cases coming remarkably close to Pareto optimality.

We compare the performance of the double clinching auction to the parimutuel consensus mechanism (PCM), the Brier scoring rule version of the weighted score wagering mechanism (WSWM), and the Brier-score no-arbitrage wagering mechanism (NAWM). The PCM is known to be Pareto optimal, serving as the gold standard with respect to the amount of trade generated, though is not incentive compatible. WSWMs and NAWMs provide a natural comparison as the only other known, non-trivial wagering mechanisms that are individually rational, incentive compatible, and budget balanced. We chose the Brier scoring rule since it is commonly used in practice.

We tested each wagering mechanism on a data set consisting of probability reports collected from an online prediction contest called ProbabilitySports [12].[4,5] The data set consists of probabilistic predictions about the outcomes of 1643 U.S. National Football League games between the start of the 2000 preseason and the end of the 2004 season. For each match, between 64 and 1574 people reported their subjective probability of the home team winning the game. After each game, they earned points in the contest according to a Brier scoring rule.

The ProbabilitySports users provided probabilities but not wager amounts. We simulate wagers in two ways. First, we generate uniform wagers: we fix all wagers at 1, modeling a scenario where

---

[4]We thank Brian Galebach for providing us with this data.

[5]We also conducted simulations with random probability reports, generated both uniformly at random and according to a beta distribution. The results, and in particular the relative performance of the mechanisms, are very similar to those obtained using the ProbabilitySports data set.

agents are equal or cannot vary the default wager amount. Second, we generate wagers according to a Pareto distribution, reflecting the typical distribution of wealth in a population. We used a Pareto distribution with shape parameter 1.16 and scale parameter 1, which is often described as "20% of the population has 80% of the wealth." Each random set of wagers was scaled so that the average wager for any single match is exactly 1, allowing a comparison to the uniform wager case.

6.1 Notes on Implementation

A perfectly faithful implementation of the double clinching auction, as defined in Section 5, would require running an adaptive clinching auction for arbitrarily divisible goods with continuously increasing price function and allocations. In practice, it is necessary to discretize the price increases, thus computing allocations and prices that approximately match the double clinching auction.

One might be concerned that this discretization could adversely affect the nice properties of the double clinching auction. In particular, it might now be possible for an agent to profit by misreporting her probability. To check whether this was the case, we empirically tested incentive compatibility on the 1643 matches from the ProbabilitySports data set. For each match, we chose a random agent i and ran the double clinching auction 101 times to calculate the expected payoff i would receive reporting each value in the set $\{0, 0.01, 0.02, \ldots, 0.99, 1\}$. We found a single profitable misreport for only a single one of these matches, with the misreporting agent able to increase her expected utility from 5.1611 to 5.1612. This suggests that the mechanism retains (at least approximate) incentive compatibility when discretized.

6.2 Results

The results are summarized in Table 1. The top table shows various statistics averaged across all 1643 matches, with wagers for each match drawn from a Pareto distribution. The Risk/Wagers column reports the total risk, summed across all agents, divided by the total wager, summed across all agents, or $\sum_{i \in N} \pi_i / \sum_{i \in N} w_i$. A value of 1 means that every agent risks losing her entire wager for one outcome; a value of 0 means that no trade occurs. The %Full Stakes column reports the percentage of agents that risk losing their entire wager under one outcome (i.e., $\pi_i = w_i$). The #Securities column gives the total number of pairs of securities sold to the agents, or $\sum_{i \in N} y_i = \sum_{i \in N} n_i$. The Principal Profit column shows the principal's net profit. Finally, the Agent Utility column gives the sum of the agents' expected utilities, assuming immutable beliefs and truthful reports.

As expected, the PCM facilitates the most trade, in terms of both the risk:budget ratio and the number of securities sold. However, there is a notably large gap in these metrics between the double clinching auction and the NAWM and WSWM, with the double clinching auction selling almost five times as many securities as the NAWM and WSWM. Additionally, under the double clinching auction, over 80% of agents risk their entire wagers, compared with no agents under NAWM and WSWM. This is further evidence that falsely inflating a wager amount under the double clinching auction, while possibly beneficial in theory, would be extremely risky in practice, with a high chance of the manipulating agent losing more than her true budget.

We note that, while our objective is not to make a profit for the principal, the double clinching auction does yield a reasonable profit without sacrificing agent welfare.

The bottom table reports the same metrics when the agents' wagers are equal. While the three other mechanisms exhibit very similar performance in this case, the double clinching auction displays a marked increase in the amount of trade facilitated, under all metrics, and a drop in profit. For the objective of maximizing trade, this is a particularly compelling argument to use the double clinching auction in cases when equal wagers are natural.

Note that all matches in the ProbabilitySports data set have a relatively large number of agents participating. However, in many cases we are interested in instances with smaller numbers of agents.

	Risk/Wagers	%Full Stakes	#Securities	Principal Profit	Agent Utility
PCM	0.94	97.2	601.1	0	200.1
DCA	0.80	82.6	489.3	28.4	152.1
NAWM	0.20	0	98.4	25.8	27.9
WSWM	0.16	0	101.2	0	53.7

	Risk/Wagers	%Full Stakes	#Securities	Principal Profit	Agent Utility
PCM	0.97	96.9	618.5	0	208.1
DCA	0.97	96.4	616.4	1.3	206.3
NAWM	0.21	0	102.5	28.7	28.8
WSWM	0.17	0	105.7	0	57.4

Table 1. Evaluation of wagering mechanisms using reports from the ProbabilitySports data set. The top table was generated using Pareto distribution wagers, the bottom with uniform wagers.

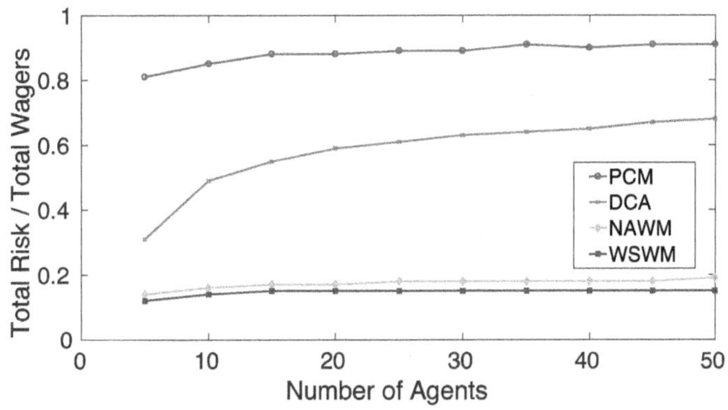

Fig. 1. The risk:budget ratio for each of the four wagering mechanisms, plotted as a function of N.

To investigate this behavior, we generated smaller instances by subsampling reports from the full set of reports for each match. Figure 1 plots the ratio of total risk to total budget, $(\sum_{i\in N}\pi_i)/(\sum_{i\in N} w_i)$, for the four mechanisms for values of N ranging from 5 to 50, with wagers randomly drawn from a Pareto distribution. We see that while the PCM, NAWM, and WSWM exhibit only minimal change as N increases, the double clinching auction facilitates more trade for larger values of N. However, even for $N = 5$, the double clinching auction facilitates approximately twice the trade as the WSWM and the NAWM, suggesting that the double clinching auction is the best truthful mechanism when maximizing trade is a primary objective.

7 CONCLUSION

We have defined and analyzed the double clinching auction, proving that it simultaneously satisfies incentive compatibility, budget balance, and individual rationality. While we showed that no wagering mechanism can simultaneously achieve these three properties along with Pareto optimality, our simulations suggest that the DCA comes close to Pareto optimality in practice, making it the first known incentive compatible wagering mechanism to do so.

It would be valuable, but apparently non-trivial, to extend the DCA to settings with non-binary outcomes. The DCA crucially exploits the fact that agents can be ordered by their reports in one dimension, allowing us to guarantee that no agent is allocated both yes and no securities. With larger outcome spaces, this property no longer holds, and designing a mechanism in which the principal auctions off three or more types of securities would require novel techniques.

Even in the binary-outcome setting, a number of interesting problems remain. While our simulations suggest that the DCA comes close to achieving Pareto optimality, we have not established any formal approximation guarantee. An additional particularly compelling question is whether our choice of m^* is the largest number of securities that can be sold via a pair of adaptive clinching auctions while satisfying incentive compatibility and budget balance.

REFERENCES

[1] Mukhtar M. Ali. 1977. Probability and utility estimates for racetrack bettors. *J. Political Economy* 85, 4 (1977), 803–816.
[2] Lawrence M Ausubel. 2004. An efficient ascending-bid auction for multiple objects. *The American Economic Review* 94, 5 (2004), 1452–1475.
[3] Alina Beygelzimer, John Langford, and David M. Pennock. 2012. Learning performance of prediction markets with Kelly bettors. In *International Conference on Autonomous Agents and Multiagent Systems (AAMAS)*.
[4] Sayan Bhattacharya, Vincent Conitzer, Kamesh Munagala, and Lirong Xia. 2010. Incentive compatible budget elicitation in multi-unit auctions. In *ACM-SIAM Symposium on Discrete Algorithms (SODA)*.
[5] Glenn W. Brier. 1950. Verification of forecasts expressed in terms of probability. *Monthly Weather Review* 78, 1 (1950), 1–3.
[6] Yiling Chen, Nikhil R. Devanur, David M. Pennock, and Jennifer Wortman Vaughan. 2014. Removing arbitrage from wagering mechanisms. In *ACM Conference on Economics and Computation (EC)*.
[7] Yiling Chen and David M. Pennock. 2007. A utility framework for bounded-loss market makers. In *Conference on Uncertainty in Artificial Intelligence (UAI)*.
[8] Rachel Cummings, David M. Pennock, and Jennifer Wortman Vaughan. 2016. The possibilities and limitations of private prediction markets. In *ACM Conference on Economics and Computation (EC)*.
[9] Shahar Dobzinski, Ron Lavi, and Noam Nisan. 2012. Multi-unit auctions with budget limits. *Games and Economic Behavior* 74, 2 (2012), 486–503.
[10] Pradeep Dubey, John Geanakoplos, and Martin Shubik. 1987. The revelation of information in strategic market games: A critique of rational expectations equilibrium. *Journal of Mathematical Economics* 16 (1987), 3105–3137.
[11] Edmund Eisenberg and David Gale. 1959. Consensus of subjective probabilities: The pari-mutuel method. *The Annals of Mathematical Statistics* 30, 1 (1959), 165–168.
[12] Brian Galebach. 2017. ProbabilitySports. http://probabilitysports.com/. (2017).
[13] Christian Genest and James V. Zidek. 1986. Combining probability distributions: A critique and an annotated bibliography. *Statist. Sci.* 1, 1 (1986), 114–148.
[14] Tilmann Gneiting and Adrian E. Raftery. 2007. Strictly proper scoring rules, prediction, and estimation. *J. Amer. Statist. Assoc.* 102, 477 (2007), 359–378.
[15] Gagan Goel, Vahab Mirrokni, and Renato Paes Leme. 2015. Clinching auctions with online supply. *Games and Economic Behavior* (2015).
[16] Robert A. Jacobs. 1995. Methods for combining experts' probability assessments. *Neural Computation* 7, 5 (1995), 867–888.
[17] David J. Johnstone. 2007. The Parimutuel Kelly Probability Scoring Rule. *Decision Analysis* 4, 2 (2007), 66–75.
[18] James Jordan and R. Radner. 1979. The nonexistence of Rational expectations equilibrium: A robust example. (1979). Working paper, Department of Economics, University of Minnesota.
[19] D. Marc Kilgour and Yigal Gerchak. 2004. Elicitation of Probabilities Using Competitive Scoring Rules. *Decision Analysis* 1, 2 (2004), 108–113.
[20] Nicolas S. Lambert, John Langford, Jennifer Wortman Vaughan, Yiling Chen, Daniel Reeves, Yoav Shoham, and David M. Pennock. 2015. An axiomatic characterization of wagering mechanisms. *Journal of Economic Theory* 156 (2015), 389–416.
[21] Nicolas S. Lambert, John Langford, Jennifer Wortman, Yiling Chen, Daniel Reeves, Yoav Shoham, and David M. Pennock. 2008. Self-financed wagering mechanisms for forecasting. In *ACM Conference on Electronic Commerce (EC)*.
[22] Peter A. Morris. 1977. Combining expert judgments: A Bayesian approach. *Management Science* 23, 7 (1977), 679–693.
[23] David M. Pennock, Vasilis Syrgkanis, and Jennifer Wortman Vaughan. 2016. Bounded rationality in wagering mechanisms. In *Conference on Uncertainty in Artificial Intelligence (UAI)*.
[24] Charles R. Plott, Jorgen Wit, and Winston C. Yang. 1997. *Parimutuel betting markets as information aggregation devices: Experimental results.* Technical Report Social Science Working Paper 986. California Institute of Technology.
[25] Leonard J. Savage. 1971. Elicitation of personal probabilities and expectations. *J. Amer. Statist. Assoc.* 66, 336 (1971), 783–801.

Forecast Aggregation

ITAI ARIELI, Technion, Industrial Engineering and Management, Haifa, Israel.
YAKOV BABICHENKO, Technion, Industrial Engineering and Management, Haifa, Israel.
RANN SMORODINSKY, Technion, Industrial Engineering and Management, Haifa, Israel.

Just the other day we were planning our weekend activities and looked at the forecast for the weather in Tel-Aviv on Friday, January 27. In particular what interested us was the probability for rain (precipitation). Accuweather's precipitation forecast was 77% while Yahoo! had a forecast of 60% and the Weather Channel was at 90% (all three screenshots are provided in the appendix). It was unclear to us how to aggregate these conflicting forecasts although we knew all three were reputable sources and were using sound weather models and reliable data.

Our dilemma was not unique. In fact many of us face such conflicting sources of advice from experts on a daily basis. Forecasts from reliable pollsters on the outcome of the presidential elections, medical prognosis from trusted physicians, investment advice from experienced financial pundits and more. This challenge is in fact the crux of the working of many governing bodies. In the political arena we often see ministers and legislators that are chosen electives and must decide on critical issues and policies with any subject matter expertise. Such public electives dictate health care policies, decide on military development and deployment, financial regulation and so on without prior medical / military / financial background. To do so they reach out to experts advices whose information they should aggregate.

We consider a model with three agents. There are two experts who provide a forecast about the probability over some given future event. The experts agree on the prior probability, both receive some common information, however, one of them is better informed and has access to additional private information[1]. Both agents form posterior forecasts vis-a-vis Bayes rule. The two forecasts are shared with the third player, the *policy maker* (PM), who now aggregates them to form his own subjective forecast. Unfortunately, the identity of the better informed expert is not known to the PM.

We assume that the PM is ignorant in the subject matter and hence has no knowledge of the prior distribution nor the information available to the experts. In particular he has no idea which expert is better informed. On the other hand the experts are familiar with the Bayesian framework and PM knows that the experts are Bayesian. In this framework we propose an optimal forecast aggregation scheme for the non-Bayesian PM. To do so we first must discuss how to evaluate an aggregation scheme.

The PM, being accountable to the public, is evaluated by the public whose objective is that the PM will provide his most accurate forecast. Namely, we assume the public resorts to *proper scoring rules*, natural and

[1]This natural order of information structures is called *Blackwell ordering.*

Full paper version is available at SSRN: https://papers.ssrn.com/sol3/ papers.cfm?abstract_id=2934104.
We thank Sergiu Hart for useful discussion and comments, and in particular, for pointing out the connection of our result to the notion of precision. I. Arieli acknowledges the support of the Israeli Science Foundation, grant number 2018889 and The German-Israeli Foundation for Scientific Research and Development, grant number 2022309. Y. Babichenko acknowledges the support of the Israeli Science Foundation, grant number 2021296. R. Smorodinsky acknowledges the supported by Technion VPR grants, the Bernard M. Gordon Center for Systems Engineering at the Technion, and the TASP Center at the Technion.
Author's addresses: I. Arieli, Industrial Engineering and Management, Technion Israel Institute of Technology, iarieli@tx.technion.ac.il; Y. Babichenko, Industrial Engineering and Management, Technion Israel Institute of Technology, yakovbab@tx.technion.ac.il; R. Smorodinsky, Industrial Engineering and Management, Technion Israel Institute of Technology, rann@ie.technion.ac.il.

ACM ISBN 978-1-4503-4527-9/17/06. DOI: http://dx.doi.org/10.1145/3033274.3084090

prevalent family of measures of forecast accuracy that motivate a Bayesian forecaster to be truthful about his forecast. The specific rule we consider is the square loss function. However, as the PM is not Bayesian he cannot use the prior to aggregate the two forecasts and must follow an alternative aggregation scheme. For a given aggregation scheme we adopt the notion of *regret*, and say that the PM can guarantee a regret of α if his expected score is no more than α higher than that of the better informed expert, *for any information structure accessible to the experts.* With this in mind, we ask what is the lowest regret the PM can guarantee.

In this paper we provide a closed form formula for aggregating forecasts that minimizes regret with respect to the better informed expert (whose identity is anonymous). Our main result makes use of the notion of *precision* in statistics. The precision of a random variable is the reciprocal of its variance. For a Bernoulli random variable with parameter x let us denote the precision by $\phi(x) = \frac{1}{x(1-x)}$. We characterize the PM's optimal aggregation policy which is the following function we deem as the *precision scheme*:

$$f(x_1, x_2) = \begin{cases} \frac{\sqrt{\phi(x_1)}}{\sqrt{\phi(x_1)}+\sqrt{\phi(x_2)}} x_1 + \frac{\sqrt{\phi(x_2)}}{\sqrt{\phi(x_1)}+\sqrt{\phi(x_2)}} x_2 & \text{if } |x_1 - x_2| \geq 0.4 \\ \frac{\phi(x_1)}{\phi(x_1)+\phi(x_2)} x_1 + \frac{\phi(x_2)}{\phi(x_1)+\phi(x_2)} x_2 & \text{if } |x_1 - x_2| < 0.4. \end{cases}$$

Our main theorem states the following:

Main Theorem (informal). The precision scheme guarantees a regret of no more than $\frac{1}{8}(5\sqrt{5}-11) \approx 0.0225425$. Moreover, $\frac{1}{8}(5\sqrt{5}-11)$ is the *optimal* regret the PM can guarantee. Namely, there exist an information structure, where one agent is better informed than the other, such that the utility of the more informed expert exceeds that of the PM by at least $\frac{1}{8}(5\sqrt{5} - 11)$ for every aggregation scheme.

To appreciate how well this scheme performs let's compare it with a few 'naive' approaches to the problem:

- The standard average, with equal weights, yields a regret that is as high as $\frac{1}{16} = 0.0625$, almost a three fold higher than the precision work.
- Choosing randomly one of the two experts with equal probability results in a regret as high as $\frac{1}{8}$.
- If the PM Chooses to adopt the forecast with minimal uncertainty, as measured by entropy (in other words the more extreme forecast), and ignores the other, then his regret is as high as 4 times the regret bounds from the optimal precision scheme.

Machine-Learning Aided Peer Prediction

YANG LIU, Harvard University
YILING CHEN, Harvard University

Information Elicitation without Verification (IEWV) is a classic problem where a principal wants to truthfully elicit high-quality answers of some tasks from strategic agents despite that she cannot evaluate the quality of agents' contributions. The established solution to this problem is a class of peer prediction mechanisms, where each agent is rewarded based on how his answers compare with those of his peer agents. These peer prediction mechanisms are designed by exploring the stochastic correlation of agents' answers. The prior distribution of agents' true answers is often assumed to be known to the principal or at least to the agents.

In this paper, we consider the problem of IEWV for heterogeneous binary signal tasks, where the answer distributions for different tasks are different and unknown a priori. A concrete setting is eliciting labels for training data. Here, data points are represented by their feature vectors $\mathbf{x}$'s and the principal wants to obtain corresponding binary labels y's from strategic agents. We design peer prediction mechanisms that leverage not only the stochastic correlation of agents' labels for the same feature vector $\mathbf{x}$ but also the (learned) correlation between feature vectors $\mathbf{x}$'s and the ground-truth labels y's. In our mechanism, each agent is rewarded by how his answer compares with a reference answer generated by a classification algorithm specialized for dealing with noisy data. Every agent truthfully reporting and exerting high effort form a Bayesian Nash Equilibrium. Some benefits of this approach include: (1) we do not need to always re-assign each task to multiple workers to obtain redundant answers. (2) A class of surrogate loss functions for binary classification can help us design new reward functions for peer prediction. (3) Symmetric uninformative reporting strategy (pure or mixed) is not an equilibrium strategy. (4) The principal does not need to know the joint distribution of workers' information a priori. We hope this work can point to a new and promising direction of information elicitation via more intelligent algorithms.

CCS Concepts: •**Information systems → Incentive schemes;** •**Theory of computation → Algorithmic mechanism design;** •**Computing methodologies →** *Supervised learning by classification;*

1 INTRODUCTION

Information Elicitation without Verification (IEWV) [25] is a classic problem where a principal wants to truthfully elicit high-quality answers of some tasks from strategic agents despite that she cannot evaluate the quality of agents' contributions. The lack of verification is either due to the subjective nature of the answers or because verifying answers is too costly to be practical. For example, a principal may be interested in knowing whether people find each of a set of restaurants as a desirable place for Valentine's Day dinner. Or the principal may want to find out whether each of a set of websites contains adult content.

A class of mechanisms, collectively called *peer prediction* [4, 5, 13, 15, 17, 22], has been proposed for the IEWV problem. The high-level idea of these peer prediction mechanisms is to take advantage

This work is supported by the National Science Foundation under grant CCF-1301976. Authors' emails: Yang Liu yangl@seas.harvard.edu, Yiling Chen yiling@seas.harvard.edu.

EC'17, June 26–30, 2017, Cambridge, MA, USA. ACM ISBN 978-1-4503-4527-9/17/06...$15.00.

DOI: http://dx.doi.org/10.1145/3033274.3085126

of the stochastic correlation of agents' answers for the same (or sometimes different) tasks and reward an agent based on how his answers compare with those of some peer agents. The reward functions of peer prediction mechanisms are designed in a way such that all agents truthfully reporting their answers (or exerting effort to obtain high-quality answers and then truthfully reporting them) forms a Bayesian Nash equilibrium (BNE). This is quite marvelous to achieve given the lack of direct verification.

One major benefit of being able to elicit high-quality information from strategic agents without direct verification is that it can serve as a way to collect training samples for machine learning. In fact, getting training data from crowd workers (e.g., to label images and to collect personal data for social studies) has become a popular practice for machine learning [12, 21]. For instance, the above-mentioned principal may want to train a classifier on elicited data to help her predict whether a new restaurant is Valentine's Day friendly or whether a new website contains adult content. Because people are error-prone and/or strategic, techniques on learning from crowd-generated training samples have been developed to innovatively handle the noise of the training data [2, 12, 16, 20].

The above brief overview of the current status quo of solutions to the IEWV problem and how crowd-generated data are used to train machine learning algorithms reveals one interesting observation. We can view the tasks (e.g. restaurants and websites) that a principal wants to elicit information about as feature vectors $\mathbf{x}$'s and the desirable information about these tasks as their corresponding labels y's. Then, the reward functions of existing peer prediction mechanisms are designed by leveraging the correlations of y's, because such correlation gives a way to accurately predict the true label for a particular feature vector and the prediction can be used as a benchmark to evaluate the elicited label for the feature vector, while machine learning algorithms trained on the elicited data aims to learn the correlation between $\mathbf{x}$'s and y's. Since the learned structural relationship between $\mathbf{x}$'s and y's can also offer a good prediction on the true label of any given feature vector, this suggests that we may take advantage of the correlation between $\mathbf{x}$'s and y's, in addition to the correlation of y's, to design peer prediction mechanisms that are possibly more efficient at eliciting information from strategic agents for heterogeneous tasks for IEWV and may have better incentive properties. This is the approach that we take in this paper.

More specifically, we design peer prediction mechanisms for eliciting binary labels from strategic agents for a set of heterogeneous tasks. Agents observe labels of tasks with errors (i.e. agents' observed labels sometimes are different from the true labels) and they can strategically decide whether to truthfully reveal their observed labels or not. The exact error rates are unknown to the principal. Our mechanism trains a classifier using the collected data, this classifier can generate a prediction on the label of a given feature vector and this prediction is then used as a machine-generated reference report in a scoring function to evaluate a reported label for this feature vector. We find that if the structural relationship between $\mathbf{x}$'s and the corresponding true y's is "learnable" in the sense that there exists a concept class $\mathcal{F}$ with bounded VC-dimension such that the optimal classifier $f^* \in \mathcal{F}$ has performance that is better than random guessing, which is a rather weak requirement for classification problems, then we can use the above described approach to design a peer prediction mechanism such that all agents truthfully reporting their observed labels is a BNE. In an effort sensitive model where agents can incur a costly effort to reduce the error of their observed labels, this result generalizes to induce a BNE where all agents exert the effort and then truthfully report their observed labels.

The advantages of this machine-learning inspired approach and our designed mechanism include: (1) Our mechanism is more "efficient" in the sense that we do not need to assign every task to multiple agents to obtain redundant labels, while almost all existing peer prediction mechanisms depend on such redundant assignments. (2) Our mechanisms have better incentive properties.

Everyone always reporting the same label or the same distribution of labels independent of the observed label or everyone always reporting a fixed permutation of observed labels is not an equilibrium in our mechanism, while these are equilibria in existing peer prediction mechanisms. (3) Our mechanism allows the principal and the agents to have less knowledge about agents' observations. The principal and the agents do not need to know the error rates of the agent observations a priori and hence do not know the prior distribution of agents' labels. Many peer prediction mechanisms require that the principal knows the joint distribution of agents' labels to operate the mechanisms [9, 10, 15]. Most peer prediction mechanisms require agents know this joint distribution for the equilibrium results to hold [4, 9, 10, 15, 22]. (4) Our mechanism is especially suitable for heterogeneous tasks, while existing multi-task peer prediction mechanisms [4, 13, 22] have been designed for homogeneous tasks, with the exception of [14]. (5) A class of surrogate loss functions for binary classification can help us design reward functions for peer prediction.

At the technical level, our approach is built upon a set of machine learning techniques, often referred as learning with "noisy data" [16]. This set of techniques helps to learn a classifier, using training data with *known* error, that converges to the optimal classifier as if it is trained on data without error. It offers a way to counter the noise of the data to generate a good prediction on the true label of a feature vector. Our setting has additional challenges in that the error of agents' observations is unknown and the reported labels are a result of agents' strategic decisions.

The rest of the work is organized as follows. We survey related work in the rest of this section. Our problem is formulated in Section 2. Section 3 introduces our approach, and reviews preliminaries on machine learning techniques that we build our results on. Our main results are discussed in Section 4. Then we discuss how we overcome the challenge of not knowing the errors of agents' observations in Section 5. In Section 6, we show how our mechanism can be adapted so that uninformative strategies do not form an equilibrium. A simple output agreement type of mechanism is then presented in Section 7. We show the extension of our results to effort-sensitive workers in Section 8. Section 9 concludes the paper. Full version with appendix of this paper can be found on arXiv and the authors' websites.

1.1 Related work

Our work is an addition to an already large literature on *peer prediction* [4, 9, 10, 15, 17, 18, 27, 28]. The term *peer prediction* was coined up by Miller et al. [2005] who showed that any *strictly proper scoring rule* [7] for truthfully eliciting information about events with (future observable) ground truth can be turned into a scoring function for truthfully eliciting information for the IEWV problem if the principal knows the joint distribution of private signals and this distribution is common knowledge to all agents. The mechanism of Miller et al. [2005] has truthful reporting as a BNE. But it also has uninformative BNEs where all agents play a strategy that is independent of their observed signal. Moreover, agents receive higher payoff at the uninformative BNEs than at the truthful BNE. One year prior to the publication of Miller et al. [2005], Prelec [2004] proposed *Bayesian Truth Serum* (BTS), an elegant mechanism for IEVW that achieves truthful reporting as a BNE for a large enough population of agents by asking each agent to report not only his observed signal but also a prediction on the distribution of others' reports. While BTS still requires agents to know the joint distribution of private signals for the truthful BNE to hold, the principal in BTS doesn't need to know this distribution to operate the mechanism. BTS also admits uninformative equilibria. A sequence of follow up work has been done to relax the assumptions made by these mechanisms [18, 27, 28] and to make the truthful reporting equilibrium more focal [10]. More recently, Witkowski et al. [2013] and Dasgupta and Ghosh [2013] formally studied an effort sensitive model for eliciting binary signals for IEWV. In particular, Dasgupta and Ghosh [2013] proposed a multi-task peer prediction mechanism that ensures a desirable BNE where every agent first exerts maximum effort to obtain a high-quality signal and then truthfully reports it. Moreover, among all BNEs, this equilibrium gives the highest payoff to all agents. Shnayder et al. [2016] and Kong and Schoenebeck [2016] then extended the results to non-binary signal elicitation. However, in all existing mechanisms, there exists BNEs where agents play an uninformative reporting strategy, although such equilibrium leads to lower agent payoff than the truthful equilibrium in the recent mechanisms of Dasgupta and Ghosh [2013], Shnayder et al. [2016] and Kong and Schoenebeck [2016]. Furthermore, agents reporting a fixed permutation of signals is also a BNE in existing mechanisms and this equilibrium offers the same payoff to agents as the truthful equilibrium. Our mechanism in this paper removes both the uninformative equilibria and the permutation equilibrium.

Our mechanism uses a "machine" prediction as a reference answer. This has some resemblance to the notion of creating a reference answer from a model's output. Several studies focused on using models that aggregate answers from different agents [6, 11, 19]. These studies didn't consider a machine learning setting like us, and didn't establish equilibrium behavior.

From a different angle, our work fits into the notion of *learning with strategic data sources*, which concerns machine learning systems when either their training data or incoming test data or both come from strategic agents. For example, several recent results have focused on optimally training regression models via incentivizing high-quality training data, when they are collected from strategic agents who are either effort sensitive [2] or privacy sensitive [3, 8]. Our work focuses on classification problems.

In machine learning, how to learn appropriately with non-strategic, yet biased data has received quite a bit of attention in recently [16, 20]. We demonstrate yet another novel application of these methods for information elicitation. In some sense, our work completes this line of research by demonstrating that a method for learning from noisy training data can also be made Bayesian incentive compatible for eliciting the training data.

2 PROBLEM FORMULATION

A principal has a set of data $\{\mathbf{x}_i\}_{i=1}^N$, where each $x_i \in \mathbb{R}^M$ can be viewed as an M-dimensional feature vector. The space of x_i's is $\mathcal{X}$. This set of data has corresponding (binary) labels, $\{\mathbf{y}_i\}_{i=1}^N$ where $y_i \in \{-1, +1\}$, that are unknown to the principal. $\{(\mathbf{x}_i, y_i)\}_{i=1}^N$ are drawn i.i.d. according to an unknown joint distribution $\mathcal{D}$. The prior probabilities for the $+1$ and the -1 labels are $\mathcal{P}_+$ and $\mathcal{P}_-$ respectively. The principal knows $\mathcal{P}_+$ and $\mathcal{P}_-$. She can ask a set of agents (e.g. crowd workers) to label the data. Without knowing the true labels, she cannot directly verify the elicited labels. The principal would like to design reward mechanisms so that she can obtain high-quality labels from the agents.

2.1 Agent model

The principal recruits $T \geq N$ agents (workers). Each worker i is assigned exactly one data point, denoted $\mathbf{x}_i$ (with a bit abuse of notation), and is asked to report a label $\hat{y}_i$. Each data point is assigned to one worker and sometimes more.[1] The re-assigned tasks are randomly selected, and if selected the task will be re-assigned once (so assigned twice in all, for details please refer to Section 5). Denote $\mathcal{U}$ as the set that contains each independent task exactly once, so $|\mathcal{U}| = N$. We consider two worker observation models in this paper: an *effort insensitive* model where each worker exogenous observes a label with noise and an *effort sensitive* model where a worker can choose to exert costly effort to improve the accuracy of his observation. We introduce the effort

[1]Note with redundant assignments, we may have $\mathbf{x}_i = \mathbf{x}_j$, $i \neq j$, $i, j = 1, \ldots, T$.

insensitive model below. Our analysis in the next few sections will focus on this model. Then, we will introduce the effort sensitive model and extend our main results to it in Section 8.

Effort insensitive worker observation model: Each worker observes a signal (which is the worker's observed label) once a task is assigned. Denote worker i's observation for data x_i as $\tilde{y}_i$. Worker observations are *conditionally independent* (on y_i) and follow a two-coin flipping-error model: $\Pr(\tilde{y}_i = -1|y_i = +1) = p_+$ and $\Pr(\tilde{y}_i = +1|y_i = -1) = p_-$, where p_+ and p_- satisfy:

(i) $p_+ + p_- < 1$, that is, the sum of the error rates for the two classes is less than 1.

This assumption requires that a worker's observation is informative with respect to the true label in the sense that the probability for the worker to observe label s is higher when the true label is s than when the true label is $-s$, i.e. $\Pr(\tilde{y}_i = s|y_i = s) > \Pr(\tilde{y}_i = s|y_i = -s), \forall s \in \{-1, +1\}$. It is a necessary and sufficient condition so that Bayesian updating increases one's belief that the observed label is the true label. This is formally stated in Lemma 2.1.

Lemma 2.1. $\Pr(y_i = s|\tilde{y}_i = s) > \mathcal{P}_s, \forall s \in \{-1, +1\}$, *if and only if* $p_+ + p_- < 1$.

Similar assumptions are made for agent belief models in the peer prediction literature [4, 22].

(ii) $p_-, p_+ \geq \kappa > 0$ where $0 < \kappa < 1/2$. That is, workers do not have perfect information.

We assume that the error models are common knowledge to both the workers and the principal. The prior on true labels, $\mathcal{P}_+$ and $\mathcal{P}_-$, are common knowledge too. But the principal and the workers do not necessarily know the values of p_+ and p_-. Most of our discussion in this paper focuses on homogeneous workers that have the same p_+ and p_-, but we discuss the possibility of extending to the case with heterogeneous workers in the Appendix.

After observing the signals, each worker i decides on which label to report. A pure reporting strategy of an agent is a mapping from the agent's observation to a report: $r_i(\tilde{y}_i) : \{-1, +1\} \to \{-1, +1\}$. In the case of mix strategies, the mapping is to a distribution on the two possible reports $\{-1, +1\}$. For example, a truthful reporting strategy corresponds to the case that an agent truthfully reports his observation, and an uninformative strategy, pure or mixed, has the same report distribution for all signals. We then define $\hat{p}_{i,+} := \Pr(\hat{y}_i = -1|y_i = +1, r_i(\tilde{y}_i)) = \sum_{s \in \{-1,+1\}} \Pr(\tilde{y}_i = s|y_i = +1) \Pr(r_i(\tilde{y}_i) = -1|\tilde{y}_i = s)$ and $\hat{p}_{i,-} := \Pr(\hat{y}_i = +1|y_i = -1, r_i(\tilde{y}_i)) = \sum_{s \in \{-1,+1\}} \Pr(\tilde{y}_i = s|y_i = -1) \Pr(r_i(\tilde{y}_i) = +1|\tilde{y}_i = s)$ as the flipping error rates of agent i's report when he plays strategy $r_i(\tilde{y}_i)$. Workers can be incentivized via payment, and they would like to maximize their expected payment.

2.2 The principal's design objective

The principal wants to design a reward mechanism $\mathcal{M}$ to incentivize agents to contribute high-quality labels. Under the effort insensitive model, this means that the principal would like the agents to truthfully report their observed labels. Under the effort sensitive model, the principal wants agents to exert effort to obtain more accurate labels and then truthfully report them. Since the principal cannot directly verify the contributed labels, the mechanism can only reward agents based on the data and the reported labels collected from the T agents, i.e. $\{\mathbf{x}_i, \hat{y}_i\}_{i=1}^T$. The principal would like to achieve the above high-quality elicitation at a Bayesian Nash equilibrium (BNE) and ideally remove other BNE where the elicited labels are of lower quality. In this paper, we focus on symmetric BNEs where agents' strategies $r_i(\tilde{y}_i)$ are the same.

3 OUR APPROACH

In this section we first describe our approach toward designing the principal's mechanism. Then, we briefly introduce a set of machine learning techniques, learning with "noisy data" (when the rates of flipping errors are known), that our approach is built upon.

3.1 Design of scoring function and reference answer using Machine Learning

In designing a mechanism $\mathcal{M}$, the principal needs to choose a scoring function $S((\mathbf{x}_i, \hat{y}_i), \{(\mathbf{x}_j, \hat{y}_j)\}_{j \neq i})$ to determine the reward for agent i. Let $\mathcal{K}_{-i}$ denotes $\{(\mathbf{x}_j, \hat{y}_j)\}_{j \neq i}$. In this paper, we consider a smaller design space where the mechanism's scoring function for each agent i is of the form:

$$S(\hat{y}_i, f^{\mathcal{A}}_{\mathcal{K}_{-i}}(\mathbf{x}_i)) : \mathbb{R}^2 \to \mathbb{R}. \tag{1}$$

where $f^{\mathcal{A}}_{\mathcal{K}_{-i}}(\cdot) : \mathbb{R}^M \to \mathbb{R}$ is a function obtained by training algorithm $\mathcal{A}$ on dataset $\mathcal{K}_{-i}$, that is, $f^{\mathcal{A}}_{\mathcal{K}_{-i}}(\cdot) = \mathcal{A}(\mathcal{K}_{-i})$. $\mathcal{F}$ is the concept class that algorithm $\mathcal{A}$ maps into and hence $f^{\mathcal{A}}_{\mathcal{K}_{-i}}(\cdot) \in \mathcal{F}$. In other words, we consider mechanisms that reward a worker based on how his reported label compares to that of a prediction of a learning algorithm, where the algorithm is trained on the data and the reported labels of other agents. Hence, a mechanism $\mathcal{M}$ in this paper is a tuple $(S, \mathcal{A})$.

As mentioned earlier, the principal would like to obtain high-quality labels at a BNE. Denote $\mathcal{P}(\{(\mathbf{x}_j, \tilde{y}_j)\}_{j=1}^T | (\mathbf{x}_i, \tilde{y}_i))$ as agent i's belief about the realized labels of all agents after agent i has observed his own label. Then a mechanism $\mathcal{M} = (S, \mathcal{A})$ induces a (strictly) truthful BNE if

$$\mathbb{E}_{\mathcal{P}(\{(\mathbf{x}_j, \tilde{y}_j)\}_{j=1}^T | (\mathbf{x}_i, \tilde{y}_i))}[S(\tilde{y}_i, f^{\mathcal{A}}_{\mathcal{K}_{-i}}(\mathbf{x}_i))] > \mathbb{E}_{\mathcal{P}(\{(\mathbf{x}_j, \tilde{y}_j)\}_{j=1}^T | (\mathbf{x}_i, \tilde{y}_i))}[S(\hat{y}_i, f^{\mathcal{A}}_{\mathcal{K}_{-i}}(\mathbf{x}_i))] \tag{2}$$

for all i, $\tilde{y}_i$ and $\hat{y}_i \neq \tilde{y}_i$.

In the rest of the paper, we'll write $S(\hat{y}_i, f^{\mathcal{A}}_{\mathcal{K}_{-i}}(\mathbf{x}_i))$ as $S(\hat{y}_i, f(\mathbf{x}_i))$ for notation simplicity, but a reader should understand the dependency of f on algorithm $\mathcal{A}$ and training dataset $\mathcal{K}_{-i}$.

The scoring function (1) resembles those designed in the peer prediction literature for the IEWV problem in the sense that it scores an agent's report against a benchmark that is based on other agents' reports. But it has some fundamental differences. Existing peer prediction mechanisms use scoring functions that are completely defined over agents' reports: $S(\hat{y}_i, \{\hat{y}_j\}_{j \neq i}) : \mathbb{R}^T \to \mathbb{R}$. The second argument of the scoring function for many peer prediction mechanisms is simply the report from a random peer agent for the *same* task. In some more recent mechanisms, this second argument includes agents' reports on other tasks but still needs to contain reports from peer agent for the same tasks [4, 22]. In contrast, the scoring function in (1) incorporates the feature vectors $\mathbf{x}_i$'s. It doesn't require that we have to have redundant reports for the same task (except for a small number of selected re-assigned tasks). Instead, we seek to learn a machine predictor f from a heterogeneous set of data to generate the second argument in the scoring function S.

Our approach toward designing a mechanism to induce a truth-telling BNE takes two-steps. First, assuming agents reports truthfully, we focus on designing an algorithm $\mathcal{A}$ such that, although it is trained on data with flipping errors, it outputs a function f that converges to the optimal classifier $f^* \in \mathcal{F}$ as if it is trained on data without flipping errors. The algorithm $\mathcal{A}$ "counters" the noise in the reported data. This guarantees that if everyone else report truthfully, the reference report $f(\mathbf{x}_i)$ for agent i is an accurate prediction of the true label y_i when the number of data is large. Second, we design the scoring function S such that truth-telling is the best action for agent i if the agent knows that his reference report is an accurate prediction of the true label y_i. Now, the agent's observed label has noise as a result of the flipping errors, but the reference report does not in expectation. When designing the scoring function, we engage a similar "counter-noise" technique as the machine learning algorithm does in the previous step. These two steps together ensure that truth-telling is a BNE in the resultant mechanism $(S, \mathcal{A})$.

At the technical level, our approach is built on a set of machine learning techniques, often referred as learning with "noisy data" [16]. If flipping errors $\hat{p}_+$ and $\hat{p}_-$ of training data are *known* to the principal, this set of techniques can learn an f that converges to the optimal classifier f^* in classification risk from the noisy training data. In our setting, however, the principal does not know the flipping-error rates in the reported data due to lack of knowledge of both p_+ and p_- and agents' strategies. This poses additional challenge of finding such an f. We will defer the details on learning the flipping-error rates to Section 5.

3.2 Learning with noisy labels

We now introduce the techniques for learning with noisy lables, which our mechanisms will build upon. Though there are clear differences between different methods for learning with noisy labels, the basic idea tends to build on finding surrogate loss functions that can compensate the bias in training data, when evaluating a function $f \in \mathcal{F}$. We briefly survey a particular algorithm and its results from Natarajan et al. [2013], in hope of delivering the idea on how learning can be done in face of biased data.

Preliminaries: Denote the 0-1 loss of f as $R_{\mathcal{D}}(f) = \mathbb{E}_{(\mathbf{x},y)\sim\mathcal{D}}[\mathbb{1}(f(\mathbf{x}) \neq y)]$, and a general l loss as $R_{l,\mathcal{D}}(f) = \mathbb{E}_{(\mathbf{x},y)\sim\mathcal{D}}[l(f(\mathbf{x}),y)]$. Denote the minimum risk over the concept class as $R^* := \min_{f\in\mathcal{F}} R_{\mathcal{D}}(f)$ and $R^*_l := \min_{f\in\mathcal{F}} R_{l,\mathcal{D}}(f)$ respectively. We further denote $f^* := \text{argmin}_{f\in\mathcal{F}} R_{\mathcal{D}}(f)$ and $f^*_l := \text{argmin}_{f\in\mathcal{F}} R_{l,\mathcal{D}}(f)$.

The setup of Natarajan et al. [2013] assumes that the flipping-errors of the reports are the same across all agents, that is $\hat{p}_+ := \hat{p}_{1,+} = \ldots = \hat{p}_{N,+}$ and $\hat{p}_- := \hat{p}_{1,-} = \ldots = \hat{p}_{N,-}$, and $\hat{p}_+ + \hat{p}_- < 1$. Furthermore, the principal *knows* the values of $\hat{p}_+$ and $\hat{p}_-$. (This can be viewed as a special case of our setting where the principal knows p_+ and p_- and every agent truthfully reports his observed signal.) Suppose the principal has collected N i.i.d. training samples $\{(\mathbf{x}_j, \hat{y}_j)\}_{j=1}^N$, indexed from 1 to N. The naive approach of directly minimizing empirical 0-1 loss over reported data not only is technically difficult but also would give a biased classifier that may not converge to the optimal classifier. Natarajan et al. [2013] tackle this problem by first finding a convex and *classification-calibrated* (CC) loss function $l(t,y)$ (with prediction t and label y as the inputs), where CC is defined as follows:

Definition 3.1 (Classification-Calibrated (CC)). l is CC if $\exists$ a convex, invertible, nondecreasing transformation ϕ_l with $\phi_l(0) = 0$ s.t. $\phi_l(R_{\mathcal{D}}(\tilde{f}) - R^*) \leq R_{l,\mathcal{D}}(\tilde{f}) - \min_f R_{l,\mathcal{D}}(f)$.

The introduce of a convex loss function l helps to remove the computational challenge in minimizing 0-1 loss directly. Classification-calibration helps us control the 0-1 loss via controlling the l-loss, i.e., if we find a classifier that converges to the optimal one in l-loss, its 0-1 loss also converges. It is generally possible to assume the existence of such an l [1, 16]. Particularly it is shown in by Bartlett et al. [2006] that, if the loss function can be written as $l(t,y) = \psi(yt)$ where ψ is convex and differentiable at 0 with $\psi'(0) < 0$, then l is classification-calibrated. Following above assumptions, we assume such an l exists for now.

Natarajan et al. [2013] then further define an *"un-biased" surrogate loss functions* over l to help "remove" noise, when $\hat{p}_+ + \hat{p}_- < 1$:

$$\varphi(t,y) := \frac{(1-\hat{p}_{\text{sgn}(-y)})l(t,y) - \hat{p}_{\text{sgn}(y)}l(t,-y)}{1-\hat{p}_+ - \hat{p}_-}, \tag{3}$$

where sgn$(\cdot)$ is a sign function that sgn$(+1) = +$, sgn$(-1) = -$. The surrogate loss φ is defined such that when a prediction is evaluated against a noisy label using this surrogate loss function, the prediction is as if evaluated against the ground-truth label using l in expectation. Hence the loss of the prediction is "unbiased" in expectation. This is formally stated in Lemma 3.2 below.

Lemma 3.2 (Lemma 1 [16]). *$\forall$ prediction t, $\mathbb{E}_{\tilde{y}}[\varphi(t,\tilde{y})] = l(t,y)$, where $\tilde{y}$ is the report from non-strategic workers with known flipping errors, and y is the ground-truth label.*

Natarajan et al. [2013] proceeds to find a classifier via minimizing the empirical risk w.r.t. $\varphi(\cdot)$:

$$\tilde{f}^*_\varphi = \text{argmin}_{f\in\mathcal{F}} \hat{R}_\varphi(f) := \frac{1}{N}\sum_{j=1}^{N} \varphi(f(\mathbf{x}_j), \tilde{y}_j). \quad (4)$$

The performance guarantee for $\tilde{f}^*_\varphi$ is given by the following lemma.

Lemma 3.3 (Theorem 3 [16]). *With probability at least $1-\delta$,*

$$R_{l,\mathcal{D}}(\tilde{f}^*_\varphi) \le \min_{f\in\mathcal{F}} R_{l,\mathcal{D}}(f) + 4L_p\mathfrak{R}(\mathcal{F}) + \sqrt{\frac{\log 1/\delta}{2N}}, \quad (5)$$

where $L_p \le 2L/(1-\hat{p}_+ - \hat{p}_-)$. $\mathfrak{R}(\mathcal{F})$ is the Rademacher complexity of function class $\mathcal{F}$.

Sine the VC dimension of the concept class $\mathcal{F}$ is finite [23], we have a converging $\mathfrak{R}(\mathcal{F}) = O\left(\sqrt{\log \texttt{VCDim}(\mathcal{F})/N}\right)$. Also as l is classification calibrated, this lemma guarantees that the 0-1 risk of $\tilde{f}^*_\varphi$ converges to that of R^*. It also implies that the smaller $\hat{p}_+, \hat{p}_-$ are, the faster the error convergence is.

Other successful examples in defining surrogate loss functions for dealing with biased training data include *label dependent cost surrogate loss* [16, 20]. The idea is to scale up the loss function differently for different labels; e.g., the following one was also studied by Natarajan et al. [2013]:

$$\varphi(t,y) := (1-\alpha)\mathbb{1}(y=+1)\cdot l(t,y) + \alpha\mathbb{1}(y=-1)\cdot l(t,y),\ \alpha = \frac{1-\hat{p}_+ + \hat{p}_-}{2}. \quad (6)$$

4 MECHANISM AND RESULTS FOR ELICITING TRUTHFUL REPORTS

In this section, we will establish that a class of surrogate loss functions can both serve to train a classifier to provide an accurate reference answer and be used as peer prediction scoring functions for eliciting truthful reports. Then we show that our mechanism no longer admit the undesirable permutation equilibrium.

To better deliver the intuition of our mechanism, we will present our mechanism and results assuming everything is "learnable" in this section. Particularly we will assume that the principal can estimate the flipping error rates of the reported data and the optimal classifier to arbitrary accuracy. While this is obviously too strong to assume without investigation, this assumption allows us to focus on establishing the equilibrium results of our mechanism, given that we have access to such accurate estimates. Later in Section 5, we will show how to obtain such accurate estimates from the reported data if agents are playing some symmetric strategies.

4.1 When a distribution is elicitable via Machine Learning?

While we seek to use machine learning (ML) to help data elicitation, asking ML methods to help eliciting arbitrarily distributed data is likely over demanding. After all, we are hoping that the learned structural relationship between $\mathbf{x}$ and y can provide a good prediction of y for any given $\mathbf{x}$ and this prediction is then used as a reference answer for scoring a reported label for this $\mathbf{x}$. If the structural relationship cannot be learned, we shouldn't hope that this approach can help us to achieve better elicitation. We formalize this idea as *ML elicitability*:

Definition 4.1 (ML elicitability). $(\mathbf{x}, y) \sim \mathcal{D}$ is *ML elicitable*, if there exists a mechanism $\mathcal{M} = (S, \mathcal{A})$ that satisfies Eqn. (2), that is, $\mathcal{M}$ induces a (strictly) truthful BNE for workers who have been assigned tasks drawn from $\mathcal{D}$.

ML elicitability intends to capture when the structural relationship between $\mathbf{x}$ and y is "learnable" so that a machine prediction can be used in peer prediction scoring to induce the truthful reporting BNE. Classic peer prediction has an analogous concept: most existing peer prediction mechanisms admit the truthful BNE only when signals of agents are *stochastic relevant* [15, 29], a condition that essentially captures when the correlation of agents' signals are strong enough so that peer reports can be used in scoring to induce the truthful reporting BNE.

We now introduce a set of *ML elicitability conditions.* We will design mechanisms in Section 4.2 that induce the truthful reporting BNE when these conditions are satisfied.

ML elicitability conditions:

(1) There exists a concept class $\mathcal{F}$, with each decision function $f \in \mathcal{F}$ mapping a feature vector $\mathbf{x} \in \mathcal{X}$ to a prediction on label y (i.e. $f : \mathcal{X} \rightarrow \{-1, +1\}$), that has a bounded Vapnik-Chervonenkis (VC) dimension [23], $\texttt{VCDim}(\mathcal{F}) < \infty$.
(2) Denote $f^* := \min_{f \in \mathcal{F}} \mathbb{E}_{(\mathbf{x},y)\sim\mathcal{D}}[\mathbb{1}(f(\mathbf{x}) \neq y)]$. Then $\mathbb{E}_{(\mathbf{x},y)\sim\mathcal{D}}[\mathbb{1}(f^*(\mathbf{x}) \neq y)] < 0.5$.
(3) $\mathbb{E}_{(\mathbf{x},y)\sim\mathcal{D}|y}[\mathbb{1}(f^*(\mathbf{x}) \neq y)] \leq 0.5$ for $y \in \{-1, +1\}$.

From a learning perspective, these ML elicitability conditions are rather weak learnability conditions. All they require is that there exists a f^* that comes from a concept class with bounded VC dimension (learnable in finite samples), and it can separate the data from one class to another with its 0-1 prediction performance being strictly better than random guess. Condition (3) states that the optimal classifier f^* does not perform worse than random guess on both classes' conditional distributions. Throughout this paper, we assume for the data distribution of interest, the principal is aware of such an $\mathcal{F}$ (but not f^*). Denote its VC dimension as $d := \texttt{VCDim}(\mathcal{F})$.

4.2 Main Mechanism

With the above preparation, we now construct a mechanism that induces the truthful BNE when the ML elicitability conditions are satisfied.

MECHANISM 1: ML Prediction (MLP)

For each worker i:

1. Assign tasks, and estimate flipping errors $\tilde{p}_{-i,+}, \tilde{p}_{-i,-}$ based on reported data from workers $j \neq i$ (Mechanism 2).
   - When returned solution satisfies $\tilde{p}_{-i,+} + \tilde{p}_{-i,-} \neq 1$, continue.
   - Otherwise trigger exception handler (Mechanism 4), and stop.
2. Define $\tilde{\varphi}(\cdot)$ using $(\tilde{p}_{-i,+}, \tilde{p}_{-i,-})$. Train a classifier $\tilde{f}^*_{\tilde{\varphi},-i}$:
   $\tilde{f}^*_{\tilde{\varphi},-i} = \text{argmin}_{f \in \mathcal{F}} \frac{1}{N-1} \sum_{j \in \mathcal{U}\setminus\{i\}} \tilde{\varphi}(f(\mathbf{x}_j), \hat{y}_j)$.
3. If $\tilde{p}_{-i,+} + \tilde{p}_{-i,-} > 1$, flip them: $\tilde{p}_{-i,+} := 1 - \tilde{p}_{-i,+}, \tilde{p}_{-i,-} := 1 - \tilde{p}_{-i,-}$. Define $\tilde{\varphi}_{\text{unbias}}(\cdot)$ using $(\tilde{p}_{-i,+}, \tilde{p}_{-i,-})$.
4. Score each worker i using $S(\hat{y}_i, \tilde{f}^*_{\tilde{\varphi},-i}) := -\tilde{\varphi}_{\text{unbias}}(\tilde{f}^*_{\tilde{\varphi},-i}, \hat{y}_i)$ (or any affine transformation of it).

The basic recipes of the mechanism are as follows. First, for each agent i, assuming that other agents play a symmetric strategy, the principal estimates the flipping-error rates of other agents' reports (denote the estimates as $\tilde{p}_{-i,+}$ and $\tilde{p}_{-i,-}$). Then, an estimated surrogate loss function $\tilde{\varphi}(\cdot)$ (any surrogate loss function that can learn from noisy data, e.g., the ones in Eqn.(3) and (6)) defined using $\tilde{p}_{-i,+}$ and $\tilde{p}_{-i,-}$ allows the principal to train a classifier $\tilde{f}^*_{\tilde{\varphi},-i}$, with its prediction performance converging to the optimal one. Then we use this classifier to make prediction on worker i's assigned data, to serve as a "machine prediction" instead of "peer prediction". Finally, we construct a reward function for each agent i using surrogate loss function $\tilde{\varphi}_{\text{unbias}}$:

$$\tilde{\varphi}_{\text{unbias}}(t,y) := \frac{(1-\tilde{p}_{-i,\text{sgn}(-y)})l(t,y) - \tilde{p}_{-i,\text{sgn}(y)}l(t,-y)}{1-\tilde{p}_{-i,+}-\tilde{p}_{-i,-}},$$

as defined in Eqn. (3), with $(\hat{y}_i, \tilde{f}^*_{\tilde{\varphi}}(\mathbf{x}_i))$ being its inputs.

When $\tilde{p}_{-i,+} + \tilde{p}_{-i,-} = 1$, the assumptions made in existing learning with noisy data methods will be violated, in that both the surrogate loss function and its training steps are not well defined. We handle this exception case in Section 6.

We'd like to focus on the equilibrium analysis of our proposed mechanism in this section, thus for now, we assume that the principal can accurately learn the error rates in the reported data if the reported data are generated from either a symmetric truthful reporting strategy or a symmetric permutation strategy, and hence the principal can approximate the surrogate loss functions defined using these error rates and the optimal classifier well.

Assumption 1 (Informal). *When either all agents $j \neq i$ play the truthful reporting strategy or they all play a permutation strategy, the principal can obtain arbitrarily accurate estimates $\tilde{p}_{-i,+}, \tilde{p}_{-i,-}, \tilde{\varphi}$, and $\tilde{f}^*_{\tilde{\varphi},-i}$. That is, there exist positive constants $\epsilon, \epsilon_1, \delta_1, \epsilon_2$, and δ_2 s.t.*

(1) $|\tilde{p}_{-i,+} - \hat{p}_{-i,+}| \leq \epsilon$, $|\tilde{p}_{-i,-} - \hat{p}_{-i,-}| \leq \epsilon$.
(2) *For the surrogate loss function defined using $\tilde{p}_{-i,+}, \tilde{p}_{-i,-1}$, with probability at least $1-\delta_1$, $|\tilde{\varphi}(t,y) - \varphi(t,y)| \leq \epsilon_1, \forall t, y$.*
(3) *With probability at least $1-\delta_2$, $R_{\mathcal{D}}(\tilde{f}^*_{\tilde{\varphi},-i}) - R^* \leq \epsilon_2$.*

All terms $\epsilon, \epsilon_1, \delta_1, \epsilon_2$, and δ_2 can be made arbitrarily small with increasing number of samples N.

This assumption is made entirely for the sake of presentation. Particularly, Assumption 1 will be used in place of Steps 1 and 2 of Mechanism 1. Later in Section 5, we will show how to estimate the error rates of the reported data to satisfy this assumption.

Assuming workers have perfect knowledge of the mechanism, and know that ML elicitability conditions are satisfied. Our next theorem shows that $S(\cdot) := -\tilde{\varphi}_{\text{unbias}}(\cdot)$, along with the Assumption 1 induces strictly truthful BNE.

Theorem 4.2. *Suppose that ML elicitability conditions are satisfied. Under Assumption 1, when the error terms in Assumption 1 approach 0 (small enough, decreasing as functions of N), (*`MLP`*) induces strictly truthful BNE for all workers.*

Intuition: Proving above theorem hinges on the following facts: first when agents truthfully report, we know their score is going to converge to $-\mathbb{E}[l(f^*(\mathbf{x}), y)]$, negative of the minimum l-loss, due to the fact that the surrogate loss function calibrates the noise in agent's report. Then we show that deviating to other strategies will introduce $l(f^*(\mathbf{x}), -y)$ term into the expected score. This leads to higher surrogate loss, due to the fact that $l(f^*(\mathbf{x}), -y) = l(-f^*(\mathbf{x}), y)$ and informativeness of f^* w.r.t. the ground-truth label y. For easiness of presentation we will omit the unbias subscript in φ, and when we use φ we meant the un-bias surrogate loss function defined in Eqn. (3). Also we will short hand $f^*(\mathbf{x})$ as f^*.

Proof. (Sketch) Consider agent i. Denote the reporting strategy as follows: $\hat{y}_i = \tilde{y}_i \cdot (-1)^{r(\tilde{y}_i)}, r(\tilde{y}_i) \in \{0,1\}$, i.e., based on the observation $\tilde{y}_i$, the agent can decide whether to truthfully report $(r(\tilde{y}_i) = 0)$, or revert the answer $(r(\tilde{y}_i) = 1)$. All together the agent has four possible pure strategies: $\{-1,+1\} \times \{0,1\}$. It is straightforward to argue that any other strategy can be written as a linear combination of the four, i.e., these four strategies form the basis of the strategy space. Therefore we only need to check that truth telling is strictly proper among the four strategies. [2] First note

$$\mathbb{E}[S(\tilde{y}_i(-1)^{\tilde{y}_i}, \tilde{f}_{\tilde{\varphi},-i}(\mathbf{x}_i))] \rightarrow -\mathbb{E}[p_{\text{sgn}(y_i)}\varphi(f^*(\mathbf{x}_i), y_i(-1)^{r(y_i)}) + (1-p_{\text{sgn}(y_i)})\varphi(f^*(\mathbf{x}_i), y_i(-1)^{r(-y_i)}].$$

The above convergence is due to Assumption 1, as well as the fact that we consider the case agents $j \neq i$ are truthfully reporting, so that $\hat{p}_{-i,+} = p_+, \hat{p}_{-i,-} = p_-$. We will then reason with this clean case with (φ, f^*), as we can always bring down the approximation error via increasing N.

By truthfully reporting $r(\tilde{y}_i) \equiv 0$, agent i's expected utility is:

$$\mathbb{E}_{(\mathbf{x},y)\sim\mathcal{D}}[S(\tilde{y}_i, \tilde{f}_{\tilde{\varphi},-i}(\mathbf{x}_i))] \rightarrow -\mathbb{E}[l(f^*(\mathbf{x}), y)].$$

Then we first prove the following fact: $R_{l,\mathcal{D}}(f^*) - R_{l,\mathcal{D}}(-f^*) < 0$, which is essentially saying f^* performs strictly better than $-f^*$ in l-loss. This will help us prove non-profitability for the case that $r(\tilde{y}_i) \equiv 1$, that is the agent always reverts the answer. In this case we have (replacing $(\mathbf{x}_i, y_i)$ pair with $(\mathbf{x}, y)$ in notation)

$$\mathbb{E}[\varphi(f^*, -\tilde{y}_i)] = \mathbb{E}[p_{\text{sgn}(y)}\varphi(f^*, y) + (1-p_{\text{sgn}(y)})\varphi(f^*, y)], \tag{7}$$

and we prove that conditional on each label $y \in \{-1, +\}$

$$\mathbb{E}_{\cdot|y=+1}[p_{\text{sgn}(y)}\varphi(f^*, y) + (1-p_{\text{sgn}(y)})\varphi(f^*, -y)] \geq \mathbb{E}_{\cdot|y=+1} l(f^*, +1), \tag{8}$$

$$\mathbb{E}_{\cdot|y=-1}[p_{\text{sgn}(y)}\varphi(f^*, y) + (1-p_{\text{sgn}(y)})\varphi(f^*, -y)] \geq \mathbb{E}_{\cdot|y=-1} l(f^*, -1), \tag{9}$$

and thus $\mathbb{E}[\varphi(f^*, -\tilde{y})] \geq \mathbb{E}[l(f^*, y)]$. Yet the two inequalities in Eqn. (8) and (9) cannot hold simultaneously, as otherwise we will have $\mathbb{E}[l(f^*, y)] = \mathbb{E}[l(-f^*, y)]$, contradicting the fact $R_{l,\mathcal{D}}(f^*) - R_{l,\mathcal{D}}(-f^*) < 0$. Thus we have proved that reverting is strictly dominated by truthfully reporting.

Consider the case that agents only revert one observation: denote $\alpha_+ := \frac{1-p_-}{1-p_+-p_-}, \alpha_- := \frac{1-p_+}{1-p_+-p_-}$.

- When $r(+1) = 1, r(-1) = 0$: $\mathbb{E}[\varphi(f^*, \tilde{y}_i \cdot (-1)^{r(\tilde{y}_i)})] = \alpha_-\mathbb{E}[l(f^*, -1)] + (1-\alpha_-)\mathbb{E}[l(f^*, +1)]$
- When $r(+1) = 0, r(-1) = 1$: $\mathbb{E}[\varphi(f^*, \tilde{y}_i \cdot (-1)^{r(\tilde{y}_i)})] = \alpha_+\mathbb{E}[l(f^*, +1)] + (1-\alpha_+)\mathbb{E}[l(f^*, -1)]$

We will then prove that

$$\begin{aligned}\mathbb{E}[\varphi(f^*, -\tilde{y}_i)] > \max\{&\alpha_-\mathbb{E}[l(f^*, -1)] + (1-\alpha_-)\mathbb{E}[l(f^*, +1)],\\ &\alpha_+\mathbb{E}[l(f^*, +1)] + (1-\alpha_+)\mathbb{E}[l(f^*, -1)]\}.\end{aligned} \tag{10}$$

Since the sum of the expected surrogate loss for cases of reporting $\tilde{y}, -\tilde{y}$ is the same as the sum for the other two reporting strategies that only revert "half" of the observations, we have

$$\begin{aligned}&\mathbb{E}[\varphi(f^*, -\tilde{y}_i)] + \mathbb{E}[\varphi(f^*, \tilde{y}_i)] = (\alpha_+\mathbb{E}[l(f^*, +1)]\\ &+ (1-\alpha_+)\mathbb{E}[l(f^*, -1)]) + (\alpha_-\mathbb{E}[l(f^*, -1)] + (1-\alpha_-)\mathbb{E}[l(f^*, +1)]).\end{aligned} \tag{11}$$

Since $\mathbb{E}[\varphi(f^*, -\tilde{y}_i)] > \mathbb{E}[\varphi(f^*, \tilde{y}_i)]$ and the fact that Eqn.(10) holds, we must have both terms on the RHS of Eqn. (11) being larger than $\mathbb{E}[\varphi(f^*, \tilde{y}_i)]$ – so their negatives (reward) are smaller than truthful reporting. □

We can also similarly show that, (MLP) doesn't admit a permutation equilibrium.

THEOREM 4.3. *Suppose that ML elicitability conditions are satisfied. Under Assumption 1, when the error terms in Assumption 1 approach 0 (small enough, decreasing as functions of N), everyone playing a fixed permutation strategy is not a BNE in (*`MLP`*).*

[2] Similar argument can be found in [4]. For completeness we give details in the full version.

Almost all existing peer prediction mechanisms[4, 13, 22, 26] have a permutation BNE. Intuitively, when workers reach an agreement on permuting their reports according to a fixed order, it's difficult for the the principal to tell the day from night. While Assumption 1 assumes this difficulty away, in Section 5, we'll show that we can still correctly estimate the error rates of the reported data (hence can tell the day from night) even if agents all permute their reports. It may be noticed that in this case $\tilde{p}_{-i,+} + \tilde{p}_{-i,-} > 1$, which violates the assumption for surrogate loss function based learning we introduced in Section 3.2. However we will show that plugging this pair of true error rates into the surrogate loss functions will help revert the surrogate loss function back to the one as if workers are truthfully reporting (Eqn. 16). So in training, it is as if we are reverting the label back. Thus the learning part will still go through.

In practice, how to select the number of samples so to make the error terms in Assumption 1 small enough depends on how faster the trained classifier converges, which can be quantified using our analysis in Section 5. Often the large enough quantity is a function of the following parameters: $(d, 1/2 - R^*, \delta_p, \Delta)$, which control the difficulties of learning.

It may be noticed that in order to run Mechanism 1, we need to train a classifier for each worker to provide a reference answer, which raises computational concerns. Practically we only need to train two classifiers. Consider separating the group of workers into two groups with equal sizes, completely randomly and uniformly; let's call these two groups as G_A and G_B. Each of the group has size $|G_A|, |G_B| \geq \lfloor N/2 \rfloor$. Then train classifiers $\tilde{f}^*_{\tilde{\varphi},-G_A}, \tilde{f}^*_{\tilde{\varphi},-G_B}$ using data from group G_B and G_A respectively. For worker i in group G_A, reward him using $S(\hat{y}_i, \tilde{f}^*_{\tilde{\varphi},-G_A}(\mathbf{x}_i))$. Similarly we will reward a worker from group G_B using $\tilde{f}^*_{\tilde{\varphi},-G_B}$. This significantly reduces the effort for re-training.

5 LEARNABILITY OF ERROR RATES, AND SURROGATE LOSS FUNCTIONS

In our setting, the principle doesn't know the flipping-error rates in agents' reported data. In this section we discuss the challenges for the learning due to unknown flipping errors and how we address them. We note that many, if not all, of the surrogate loss function based methods that we are aware of for solving the learning with noisy labels problem, e.g. the ones defined in Eqn.(3) and (6), require the knowledge of the error rates of the noisy input data. In practice, however, this is hardly the case. In this section, we discuss the concept of learnability of $\hat{p}_{-i,+}, \hat{p}_{-i,-}$ for each agent i, and further the surrogate loss. We'll show that our learning process satisfies Assumption 1 when all other agents play either the truthful or a permutation strategy.

We assume that the principal knows the lower bounds of the following quantities: $\Delta := 1/2 - R^*$ and $\delta_p := 1 - (p_+ + p_-)$. The principal would need such knowledge to decide the number of training samples N to be elicited such that the learning of the error rates converges.

First we demonstrate how to estimate $\hat{p}_{-i,+}, \hat{p}_{-i,-}$, and prove a couple of consistency results under noisy labels. Assuming agents play a symmetric strategy, our method starts with estimating the following two quantities that can be computed from the collected/reported data directly:

(i) Matching probability: this is the probability when a task is assigned to two different workers, the chance of the outputs match each other. Denote this quantity as q. In order to evaluate the matching on the same task, we need to re-assign the tasks. First we separate the tasks into two sets: we will randomly select K (to ensure enough samples for an accurate estimation) tasks to re-assign to one more worker [3]. Denote the set of re-assigned tasks as $\mathcal{U}^r$. Suppose $T = K + N$. Estimate for

[3]When N is large enough, taking $K = O(\log N)$ often suffices. Also note, if the principal knows p_+ and p_-, we don't even need to obtain redundant labels.

worker $j \neq i$:

$$\tilde{q}_{-i} := \frac{1}{|\mathcal{U}^r \backslash \{i\}|} \sum_{n \in \mathcal{U}^r \backslash \{i\}} \mathbb{1}(\text{there is a match on task } n). \tag{12}$$

(ii) Fraction of +1/-1 labels that we observe from workers' contribution P_+, P_-; denote $\tilde{P}_+^{-i}, \tilde{P}_-^{-i}$ as the corresponding estimations for workers $j \neq i$:

$$\tilde{P}_-^{-i} := \frac{1}{|\mathcal{U} \backslash \{i\}|} \sum_{n \in \mathcal{U} \backslash \{i\}} \mathbb{1}(\text{task } n \text{ has label -1}). \tag{13}$$

MECHANISM 2: Estimation of $\hat{p}_+, \hat{p}_-$

1. Assign data; randomly select K of the tasks to re-assign once; estimate $\tilde{q}_{-i}, \tilde{P}_-^{-i}$ as in Eqn. (12) and (13).
2. Solve the following set of equations.

$$\text{(I)}: \mathcal{P}_+[\tilde{p}_{-i,+}^2 + (1-\tilde{p}_{-i,+})^2] + \mathcal{P}_-[\tilde{p}_{-i,-}^2 + (1-\tilde{p}_{-i,-})^2] = \tilde{q}_{-i},$$

$$\text{(II)}: \mathcal{P}_+\tilde{p}_{-i,+} + \mathcal{P}_-(1-\tilde{p}_{-i,-}) = \tilde{P}_-^{-i}.$$

Denote the solution(s) as $\tilde{p}_{-i,+}, \tilde{p}_{-i,-}$.

3. When there are more than one solution, call Mechanism 3.
4. Return the selected root, or no solution to Mechanism 1.

We propose Mechanism 2 for learning $\tilde{p}_{-i,+}, \tilde{p}_{-i,-}$. The set of equations set up in Mechanism 2 aims to estimate the error rates in agents' reported data when agents play a symmetric strategy. When workers are arbitrarily reporting, the solution for the system of equations in Mechanism 2 leads to meaningless numbers, or simply there does not exist a solution. When workers are reporting according to symmetric strategies[4], the first equation characterizes the probability of observing a matching signal, while the second one characterizes the fraction of observed negative samples. Note that the second equation is also equivalent with $\mathcal{P}_+(1-\tilde{p}_{-i,-}) + \mathcal{P}_-\tilde{p}_{-i,-} = \tilde{P}_+^{-i}$, i.e., the equation for probability of observing a positive signal. Readers may also notice that there may exist more than one pair of solutions from the system of equations we have formed ((I) & (II)), due to its quadratic form. Nevertheless the following result holds, which will help remove this ambiguity.

LEMMA 5.1. *When there are two pairs of solutions from Mechanism 2, only one pair of them satisfies that* $\tilde{p}_{-i,+} + \tilde{p}_{-i,-} < 1$.

When agents are truthfully reporting, the above estimation algorithm is ready to give us the right flipping error rate if we choose the pair s.t. $\tilde{p}_{-i,+} + \tilde{p}_{-i,-} < 1$ after step 2 and terminate without going into step 3. But this won't give us the right solution if agents play a permutation strategy. Mechanism 3 makes the estimation robust to permutation strategies.

MECHANISM 3: Root selection

When $P_+ - P_- > 0$, return the solution $\tilde{p}_{-i,+}, \tilde{p}_{-i,-}$ s.t.,

$$\{\tilde{p}_{-i,+}, \tilde{p}_{-i,-}\} := \text{argmax}_{\{\tilde{p}_{-i,+}, \tilde{p}_{-i,-}\}} \tilde{p}_{-i,-}/\tilde{p}_{-i,+}, \tag{14}$$

When $P_+ - P_- < 0$, return the solution $\tilde{p}_{-i,+}, \tilde{p}_{-i,-}$ s.t.,

$$\{\tilde{p}_{-i,+}, \tilde{p}_{-i,-}\} := \text{argmax}_{\{\tilde{p}_{-i,+}, \tilde{p}_{-i,-}\}} \tilde{p}_{-i,+}/\tilde{p}_{-i,-}. \tag{15}$$

The basic implication of Mechanism 3 is that when there is ambiguity in root selection, we select the solution with $\tilde{p}_{-i,-}, \tilde{p}_{-i,+}$ being further away from each other in ratio. Note (1) our solution does not cover the case $P_+ = P_-$. (2) In the above selection, when agents truthfully report, the solution

[4]The estimation approach in the current form works only for symmetric strategies.

satisfying $\tilde{p}_{-i,+} + \tilde{p}_{-i,-} < 1$ will be selected (see proof in our full version). (3) When agents report a permutation of their signals, the solution captures the actual flipping error rates in the reports, i.e. $\tilde{p}_{-i,+}$ approaches to $1 - p_+$ and $\tilde{p}_{-i,-}$ approaches to $1 - p_-$.

We thus have the following consistency results in estimating the error rates in the reported data using Mechanism 2.

Lemma 5.2. *When agents $j \neq i$ are either all truthfully reporting or all reporting permuted signals, and when K,N are large enough, w.p. $\geq 1 - \delta_1(K,N), 1 - \delta_2(K,N)$ respectively: $|\tilde{p}_{-i,+} - \hat{p}_{-i,+}| \leq \epsilon_1(K,N)$, $|\tilde{p}_{-i,-} - \hat{p}_{-i,-}| \leq \epsilon_2(K,N)$. $\delta_1(\cdot), \delta_2(\cdot), \epsilon_1(\cdot), \epsilon_2(\cdot)$ are diminishing in K,N uniformly, s.t. $\forall \gamma > 0$, there exists K,N such that $0 \leq \delta_1(K,N), \delta_2(K,N), \epsilon_1(K,N), \epsilon_2(K,N) \leq \gamma$.*

This can be established based on our estimation of $\tilde{q}_{-i}, \tilde{P}_-^{-i}$, followed by perturbation analysis on solving the quadratic equations in Mechanism 2.

Denote by $\tilde{\varphi}(,)$ the noisy surrogate loss function defined using estimated $(\tilde{p}_{-i,+}, \tilde{p}_{-i,-})$s. With above consistency results, we define "learnable surrogate loss function":

Definition 5.3 (Learnable surrogate loss function). A surrogate loss function $\varphi(,)$ is learnable in $\hat{p}_{-i,+}, \hat{p}_{-i,-}$, if for any $\delta, \epsilon > 0$, there exists a (K,N) pair such that with probability at least $1 - \delta$, we have $|\tilde{\varphi}(t,y) - \varphi(t,y)| \leq \epsilon, \forall t, y$.

For example, consider the un-biased surrogate loss function proposed in [16]. Recall in this case we will have

$$\tilde{\varphi}(t,y) := \frac{(1 - \tilde{p}_{-i,\text{sgn}(-y)})l(t,y) - \tilde{p}_{-i,\text{sgn}(y)}l(t,-y)}{1 - \tilde{p}_{-i,+} - \tilde{p}_{-i,-}}.$$

Using Lemma 5.2, we prove the following (following notations in Lemma 5.2)

Lemma 5.4. *When agents $j \neq i$ are either all truthfully reporting or all reporting permuted signals, and when K,N are large enough s.t. $\epsilon_1(K,N) + \epsilon_2(K,N) \leq \delta_p/2.$, with probability at least $1 - \delta_1(K,N) - \delta_2(K,N)$, $|\tilde{\varphi}(t,y) - \varphi(t,y)| \leq \epsilon^{est}(K,N)$, where $\epsilon^{est}(K,N) := 2l^*(4 + \delta_p)\delta_p^{-2}(\epsilon_1(K,N) + \epsilon_2(K,N))$.*

So the φ is indeed learnable for this case. This claim is generally not uncommon for the others, but the analysis is rather ad-hoc. In this paper we focus on surrogate loss functions that are learnable.

With the same set of training data $\{\mathbf{x}_i, \hat{y}_i\}_{i=1}^N$ as we assumed in Section 3.2, denote $\tilde{f}_{\tilde{\varphi}}^* = \text{argmin}_{f \in \mathcal{F}} \hat{R}_{\tilde{\varphi}}(f)$ as the optimal classifier trained using the learned surrogate loss function. Denote the distribution over $(\mathbf{x}, \tilde{y})$ (workers' observed labels) as $\mathcal{D}_\rho$.

When agents truthfully report such that $\hat{p}_+ + \hat{p}_- < 1$, using sample complexity bound, we can prove that with probability at least $1 - \delta$, $\max_{f \in \mathcal{F}} |R_{\varphi,\mathcal{D}_\rho}(f) - \hat{R}_\varphi(f)| \leq \epsilon(\Re(\mathcal{F}), N, \delta, p_+, p_-)$ (proved in [16]), where $\epsilon(\cdot) \to 0$ as N increases. Suppose $R_{l,\mathcal{D}}(f) = c_A R_{\varphi,\mathcal{D}_\rho}(f) + c_B$ for some constants (c_A, c_B): using the surrogate loss function defined in Eqn.(3) we have $c_A = 1$, while for Eqn. (6) we have $c_A = \frac{1 - \hat{p}_+ - \hat{p}_-}{2}$. We assert that this is also true when agents' permute their signal s.t. $\hat{p}_+ = 1 - p_+$, $\hat{p}_- = 1 - p_-$ and $\hat{p}_+ + \hat{p}_- > 1$. Consider the following fact

$$\frac{(1 - \hat{p}_{\text{sgn}(-y)})l(t,y) - \hat{p}_{\text{sgn}(y)}l(t,-y)}{1 - \hat{p}_+ - \hat{p}_-} = \frac{p_{\text{sgn}(-y)}l(t,y) - (1 - p_{\text{sgn}(y)})l(t,-y)}{p_+ + p_- - 1} = \varphi(t,-y), \tag{16}$$

where $\varphi(t,-y)$ denotes the surrogate loss defined over the error rates p_+, p_- when workers truthfully report. So in training, it is as if we are reverting the label back. Therefore the trained classifier will be converging to the optimal one, instead of its opposite.

The following lemma shows that the estimation error in surrogate loss function wouldn't affect the learning results by much (δ, ϵ as in Definition 5.3).

LEMMA 5.5. *W.p.* $\geq 1 - 2\delta$ $R_{l,\mathcal{D}}(\tilde{f}^*_{\tilde{\varphi}}) \leq \min_{f \in \mathcal{F}} R_{l,\mathcal{D}}(f) + 2c_A^{-1} \cdot (\epsilon(\Re(\mathcal{F}), N, \delta, p_+, p_-) + \epsilon)$.

Above lemma, along with the classification calibration property of l, let us know that training with $\tilde{\varphi}(\cdot)$, despite the noise, will let us converge to the optimal classifier f^*:

LEMMA 5.6. *For any* $(\epsilon,\delta) > 0$ *pair, there exists large enough* K, N *such that with probability at least* $1 - \delta$, $R_{\mathcal{D}}(\tilde{f}^*_{\tilde{\varphi}}) - R^* \leq \epsilon$.

6 UNINFORMATIVE STRATEGIES

We show the above mechanism can help eliminate undesirable uninformative equilibria that exist in peer prediction literature. Though we are not really comparing two agents' outputs (may it be simple output agreement, or more sophisticated ones) for sending payment, it is possible that workers reporting the same labels leads to trivial reference answers that favor collusion. We show that with the call to Mechanism 4, agents reporting a symmetric uninformative strategy is not a BNE in our mechanism.

THEOREM 6.1. *In Mechanism 1, (1) reporting symmetric uninformative pure signal is not an equilibrium. (2) Reporting symmetric uninformative mixed signal with randomization probability* $p \neq 1/2$ *is also not an equilibrium.*

We first observe that when agents report according to uninformative strategies, we will have $\tilde{p}_{-i,+} + \tilde{p}_{-i,-} = 1$. Thus Mechanism 1 will trigger a call to Mechanism 4. When the de-bias technique cannot be applied, we will randomly select another worker's report as a reference answer, and plug it into the scoring function, which creates a penalty for agreement. When there doesn't exist solution for $\tilde{p}_{-i,+}, \tilde{p}_{-i,-}$, we will score agent a sufficiently small value to ensure that truth-telling returns higher payment. Knowing only bounds on p_+, p_- would allow us the estimate a lower bound for $\min -\varphi_{\text{unbias}}(\cdot)$. In practice, after we shift the score in Mechanism 1 to be positive (use affine transformation, for individual rationality), the payment for this case can be set to 0.

MECHANISM 4: Exception handler

When $\tilde{p}_{-i,+} + \tilde{p}_{-i,-} = 1$:

1. Set $\tilde{p}_{-i,+} := \min\{1, \tilde{p}_{-i,+} + \kappa\}$, $\tilde{p}_{-i,-} := \min\{1, \tilde{p}_{-i,-} + \kappa\}$.
2. Randomly select another agent's report $\hat{y}_j$, $j \neq i$.
3. Score each worker i: $-\tilde{\varphi}_{\text{unbias}}(\hat{y}_i, \hat{y}_j)$.

When there doesn't exist solution for $\tilde{p}_{-i,+}, \tilde{p}_{-i,-}$: Score agent a sufficiently small value that is less than $\min -\varphi_{\text{unbias}}(\cdot)$ (the minimum value of $-\varphi_{\text{unbias}}(\cdot)$).

PROOF. W.l.o.g., we consider the case workers contribute uninformative signals by always reporting label -1. Consider worker i. According to our estimation Eqn.(12) and (13), we have $\tilde{q}_{-i} = 1$ (always match), $\tilde{P}_-^{-i} = 1$. Plug back in Mechanism 2:

$$\text{(I)}: \mathcal{P}_+(\tilde{p}^2_{-i,+} + (1-\tilde{p}_{-i,+})^2] + \mathcal{P}_-(\tilde{p}^2_{-i,-} + (1-\tilde{p}_{-i,-})^2] = 1, \ \text{(II)}: \mathcal{P}_+\tilde{p}_{-i,+} + \mathcal{P}_-(1-\tilde{p}_{-i,-}) = 1 \, .$$

Since $\mathcal{P}_+\tilde{p}_{-i,+} \leq \mathcal{P}_+$, $\mathcal{P}_-(1-\tilde{p}_{-i,-}) \leq \mathcal{P}_-$, and $\mathcal{P}_+ + \mathcal{P}_- = 1$, we know the only possible case that equation (II) holds is when both of the equalities hold. So we are led to the solution that $\tilde{p}_{-i,+} = 1, \tilde{p}_{-i,-} = 0$. Not hard to validate the above solution also satisfies Equation (1). According to Mechanism 4, we reset $\tilde{p}_{-i,-} := \kappa > 0$. Then the scoring function for agent i becomes:[5]

$$-\tilde{\varphi}(\hat{y}_i, y = -1) := -\frac{(1-\tilde{p}_{-i,+})l(\hat{y}_i, -1) - \tilde{p}_{-i,-}l(\hat{y}_i, +1)}{1 - \tilde{p}_{-i,+} - \tilde{p}_{-i,-}} = -l(\hat{y}_i, +1)$$

[5]For simplicity of presentation, we drop the subscript and use φ to denote φ_{unbias}.

So to maximize the score it is profitable for agent i to report $\hat{y}_i = +1 \Rightarrow$ workers contributing the same uninformative signal is not an equilibrium. □

The case with mixed uninformative strategy can be argued in a similar flavor (see full version).

7 A SIMPLE MACHINE OUTPUT AGREEMENT MECHANISM

We have established the fact that a class of surrogate loss functions, combined with the classifier trained with it, can serve as a peer prediction scoring function that induces strictly truthful BNE. Likely there exist many other scoring functions that can also incorporate the machine prediction in peer prediction scoring. Probably the most intuitive mechanism under a peer prediction setting is the Output Agreement (OA) [24] mechanism. However, (OA) does not induce a truthful BNE if some agents know that they have received a minority signal. Yet in our mechanism, each agent's signal will be scored by an "informative" prediction given by the trained classifier, thus a truthful BNE will be induced. In this section we demonstrate the existence of a very simple Machine OA (MOA) mechanism that induces truthful BNE when ML elicitability conditions are satisfied.

MECHANISM 5: Machine Output Agreement (MOA)

For each worker i:

1. Train a classifier $\tilde{f}^*_{\tilde{\varphi},-i}$ as similarly done in Mechanism 1.
2. Pay worker i: $C_p \cdot \mathbb{1}(\tilde{f}^*_{\tilde{\varphi},-i}(\mathbf{x}_i) = \hat{y}_i)$, for some $C_p > 0$.

The idea is simply to check whether agent's report matches the classifier prediction. Denote by $\delta_R := 1 - R_{\mathcal{D}|y=+1}(f^*) - R_{\mathcal{D}|y=+1}(f^*)$ (which we will prove to be positive later) and assume workers have perfect knowledge of the mechanism. We have the following results (where we use *Const(·)* to denote a constant that depends only on its inputs):

Theorem 7.1. *With (MOA), when $K \geq Const1(\delta_p, \delta_R, \Delta, N)$, $N \geq Const2(\delta_p, \delta_R, \Delta)$, and C_p is set appropriately, every worker truthfully reporting is a BNE.*

For concise presentation, we only provide some intuitive reasoning on why the mechanism works and how we obtain the results: first we show that $R_{\mathcal{D}|y=+1}(f^*) + R_{\mathcal{D}|y=+1}(f^*) < 1$. The implication of this result is not unlike the $p_+ + p_- < 1$ one, in that the optimal classifier's prediction is informative under Bayesian updates. Particularly similar to Lemma 2.1, we can show this condition is equivalent with $\Pr(y_i = s|f^*(\mathbf{x}_i) = s|) > \mathcal{P}_s$, $\forall s \in \{+1, -1\}$. So in short, f^* is "informative" in a posterior way. When the number of training samples is large enough, the trained classifier $\tilde{f}^*_{\tilde{\varphi},-i}$ is also going to be informative. As $\hat{y}_i$ is compared to an informative answer, worker i is better off truth telling, due to Bayesian informativeness of his own observation proved in Lemma 2.1.

8 EFFORT SENSITIVE WORKERS

We extend our model and results to the case when workers are effort sensitive: once given a task, each worker i can choose to exert effort $e_i = 1$ to improve the quality of his label, or he can shirk from doing so ($e_i = 0$). Exerting effort incurs cost $c > 0$, and this is common knowledge to all workers and the principal. After making decision on effort exertion, each worker observes a signal (label) $\tilde{y}_i$. We assume that different effort levels lead to different flipping-error rates:

$$\Pr(\tilde{y}_i = -1|y_i = +1, e_i) = p_+(e_i),\ \Pr(\tilde{y}_i = +1|y_i = -1, e_i) = p_-(e_i).$$

Not exerting effort leads to an uniform random observation, while exerting effort returns an informative observation with less error: that is, we assume $p_+(0) = p_-(0) = 1/2$ and $p_+(1) + p_-(1) < 1$. Workers would like to maximize their net payment (i.e. payment minus cost of effort). A worker's strategy now has two components: an effort exertion decision and a reporting decision.

The principal's goal is to design a mechanism $\mathcal{M} = (S, \mathcal{A})$ to induce a strict BNE where every worker exerts effort and truthfully reports his observed signal. Denote $\mathcal{P}(\{(\mathbf{x}_j, \tilde{y}_j)\}_{j=1}^T | \{e_j\}_{j=1}^T)$ as an agent's belief about the realized labels of all agents when effort levels e_j's are selected. Then a mechanism $\mathcal{M}$ induces such a BNE if for $\mathcal{K}_{-i} = \{(\mathbf{x}_j, \tilde{y}_j)\}_{j \neq i}$,

$$\mathbb{E}_{\mathcal{P}(\{(\mathbf{x}_j,\tilde{y}_j)\}_{j=1}^T | \{e_j=1\}_{j=1}^T)}[S(\tilde{y}_i, f^{\mathcal{A}}_{\mathcal{K}_{-i}}(\mathbf{x}_i))] > \mathbb{E}_{\mathcal{P}(\{(\mathbf{x}_j,\tilde{y}_j)\}_{j=1}^T | \{e_i, \{e_j=1\}_{j\neq i}\})}[S(\hat{y}_i, f^{\mathcal{A}}_{\mathcal{K}_{-i}}(\mathbf{x}_i))],$$

for all i, either that $e_i \neq 1$ or $\hat{y}_i \neq \tilde{y}_i$, or both.

We show that we can again design mechanisms using surrogate loss functions to incentivize both effort and truth-telling. The truth telling part can be similarly established as for the effort insensitive case, but a slightly different argument is needed for eliciting effort.

Theorem 8.1. *When K, N are large enough, $S(\hat{y}_i, \tilde{f}_{\tilde{\varphi},-i}(\mathbf{x}_i)) = -a \cdot \tilde{\varphi}_{unbias}(\tilde{f}_{\tilde{\varphi},-i}(\mathbf{x}_i), \hat{y}_i)$, along with the algorithm detailed in (*MLP*), induce a strict BNE for workers to exert effort and report truthfully, with an appropriately selected scaling factor $a > 0$.*

Proof. (Sketch) Again for easiness of presentation we will omit the unbias subscript in φ. According to Theorem 4.2, we know if all other workers exert effort and report truthfully, if worker i decides to exert effort, he will report truthfully. The only case we need to consider is when agent i chooses not to exert effort. When agent i sets $e_i = 0$, the negative of his expected utility is [6] $\mathbb{E}[\varphi(f^*, \hat{y}_i)|e_i = 0] = \frac{1}{2}(\mathbb{E}[\varphi(f^*, y_i)] + \mathbb{E}[\varphi(f^*, y_i)])$, regardless of his reporting strategy. We show the difference between above and the case with exerting effort and truthfully reporting is negative, which can be proved via using the fact that $-\mathbb{E}[\varphi(f^*, \tilde{y}_i)|e_i = 1] > -\mathbb{E}[\varphi(f^*, -\tilde{y}_i)|e_i = 1]$ (truth telling is better than reverting):

$$\mathbb{E}[\varphi(f^*, \tilde{y}_i)|e_i = 1] - \mathbb{E}[\varphi(f^*, \hat{y}_i)|e_i = 0] = \mathbb{E}[(p_{\text{sgn}(y_i)} - 1/2)\varphi(f^*, -y_i) + (1/2 - p_{\text{sgn}(y_i)})\varphi(f^*, y_i)] > 0.$$

Scaling up $(-a \cdot \varphi(f^*, \hat{y}_i))$ will cover cost c so to make it incentive compatible to exert effort. □

9 DISCUSSIONS AND CONCLUSION

We have introduced a new approach that connects information elicitation without verification with machine learning. We now summarize the practical advantages of this approach. First our mechanism does not heavily rely on obtaining redundant labels by assigning a task to multiple workers. Hence, we can save learning budget to more efficiently train a classifier as the performance of classifiers ties closely to the number of unique training data. Second, we remove the requirement of knowing the joint distribution of workers' signals; rather such statistics is learned through workers' reports (via learning workers' error rates). Third, our mechanism can easily handle (and are specialized for) heterogeneous tasks. Finally, our mechanism no long have the undesirable uninformative and permutation equilibria that most other peer prediction mechanisms have.

Our mechanism is also robust when a small number of agents deviate from the equilibrium: this can be established by using the robustness of the training procedure. When a sublinear (in N) $N^\theta, 0 < \theta < 1$ number of agents deviate, this will create a $O(N^\theta/N) = O(N^{\theta-1})$ bias in the learned surrogate loss function, as well as in the empirical loss defined over training data. According to Lemma 5.5, the resultant classifier will still converge to the optimal one, with this additional converging error (in N). Also agent's report will be evaluated against an accurate scoring function.

REFERENCES

[1] Peter L Bartlett, Michael I Jordan, and Jon D McAuliffe. 2006. Convexity, Classification, and Risk Bounds. *J. Amer. Statist. Assoc.* 101, 473 (2006), 138–156.

[6] Again for simplicity we will evaluate the noise free scoring function, along with f^*, due to convergence.

[2] Yang Cai, Constantinos Daskalakis, and Christos H Papadimitriou. 2015. Optimum Statistical Estimation with Strategic Data Sources. In *COLT*.

[3] Rachel Cummings, Stratis Ioannidis, and Katrina Ligett. 2015. Truthful Linear Regression. In *Proceedings of The 28th Conference on Learning Theory, COLT 2015, Paris, France, July 3-6, 2015.* 448–483.

[4] Anirban Dasgupta and Arpita Ghosh. 2013. Crowdsourced Judgement Elicitation with Endogenous Proficiency. In *Proceedings of the 22nd international conference on World Wide Web.* 319–330.

[5] Boi Faltings, Radu Jurca, Pearl Pu, and Bao Duy Tran. 2014. Incentives to Counter Bias in Human Computation. In *Second AAAI Conference on Human Computation and Crowdsourcing.*

[6] Boi Faltings, Jason Jingshi Li, and Radu Jurca. 2014. Incentive mechanisms for community sensing. *IEEE Trans. Comput.* 63, 1 (2014), 115–128.

[7] Tilmann Gneiting and Adrian E. Raftery. 2007. Strictly Proper Scoring Rules, Prediction, and Estimation. *J. Amer. Statist. Assoc.* 102, 477 (2007), 359–378.

[8] Stratis Ioannidis and Patrick Loiseau. 2013. Linear Regression as a Non-cooperative Game. In *International Conference on Web and Internet Economics.* Springer, 277–290.

[9] Radu Jurca and Boi Faltings. 2006. Minimum Payments that Reward Honest Reputation Feedback. In *Proceedings of the 7th ACM conference on Electronic commerce (EC '06).* ACM, 190–199.

[10] Radu Jurca, Boi Faltings, and others. 2009. Mechanisms for Making Crowds Truthful. *Journal of Artificial Intelligence Research* 34, 1 (2009), 209.

[11] Ece Kamar and Eric Horvitz. 2012. Incentives for Truthful Reporting in Crowdsourcing. In *Proceedings of the 11th international conference on autonomous agents and multiagent systems-volume 3.* International Foundation for Autonomous Agents and Multiagent Systems, 1329–1330.

[12] David R Karger, Sewoong Oh, and Devavrat Shah. 2011. Iterative Learning for Reliable Crowdsourcing Systems. In *Advances in neural information processing systems.* 1953–1961.

[13] Yuqing Kong and Grant Schoenebeck. 2016. A Framework For Designing Information Elicitation Mechanisms That Reward Truth-telling. *arXiv preprint arXiv:1605.01021* (2016).

[14] Debmalya Mandal, Matthew Leifer, David C. Parkes, Galen Pickard, and Victor Shnayder. 2016. Peer Prediction with Heterogeneous Tasks. In *Proc. of the NIPS Workshop on Crowdsourcing and Machine Learning.* https://arxiv.org/abs/1612.00928

[15] Nolan Miller, Paul Resnick, and Richard Zeckhauser. 2005. Eliciting Informative Feedback: The Peer-Prediction Method. *Management Science* 51, 9 (2005), 1359 –1373.

[16] Nagarajan Natarajan, Inderjit S Dhillon, Pradeep K Ravikumar, and Ambuj Tewari. 2013. Learning with Noisy Labels. In *Advances in neural information processing systems.* 1196–1204.

[17] Dražen Prelec. 2004. A Bayesian Truth Serum for Subjective Data. *Science* 306, 5695 (2004), 462–466.

[18] Goran Radanovic and B. Faltings. 2013. A Robust Bayesian Truth Serum for Non-Binary Signals. In *Proceedings of the 27th AAAI Conference on Artificial Intelligence (AAAI '13).*

[19] Goran Radanovic, Boi Faltings, and Radu Jurca. 2016. Incentives for Effort in Crowdsourcing using the Peer Truth Serum. *ACM Transactions on Intelligent Systems and Technology (TIST)* 7, 4 (2016), 48.

[20] Clayton Scott. 2015. A Rate of Convergence for Mixture Proportion Estimation, with Application to Learning from Noisy Labels.. In *AISTATS.*

[21] Victor S Sheng, Foster Provost, and Panagiotis G Ipeirotis. 2008. Get another Label? Improving Data Quality and Data Mining using Multiple, Noisy Labelers. In *Proceedings of the 14th ACM SIGKDD international conference on Knowledge discovery and data mining.* ACM, 614–622.

[22] Victor Shnayder, Arpit Agarwal, Rafael Frongillo, and David C. Parkes. 2016. Informed Truthfulness in Multi-Task Peer Prediction. *ACM EC* (March 2016). arXiv:cs.GT/1603.03151

[23] Vladimir Vapnik. 2013. *The Nature of Statistical Learning Theory.* Springer Science & Business Media.

[24] Luis von Ahn and Laura Dabbish. 2004. Labeling images with a computer game. In *Proceedings of the SIGCHI conference on human factors in computing systems (CHI '04).* ACM, 319–326.

[25] Bo Waggoner and Yiling Chen. 2014. Output Agreement Mechanisms and Common Knowledge. In *Proceedings of the 2nd AAAI Conference on Human Computation and Crowdsourcing (HCOMP'14).*

[26] Jens Witkowski, Yoram Bachrach, Peter Key, and David C. Parkes. 2013. Dwelling on the Negative: Incentivizing Effort in Peer Prediction. In *Proceedings of the 1st AAAI Conference on Human Computation and Crowdsourcing (HCOMP'13).*

[27] Jens Witkowski and David Parkes. 2012. A Robust Bayesian Truth Serum for Small Populations. In *Proceedings of the 26th AAAI Conference on Artificial Intelligence (AAAI '12).*

[28] Jens Witkowski and David C. Parkes. 2012. Peer Prediction without a Common Prior. In *Proceedings of the 13th ACM Conference on Electronic Commerce (EC '12).* ACM, 964–981.

[29] Peter Zhang and Yiling Chen. 2014. Elicitability and Knowledge-free Elicitation with Peer Prediction. In *Proceedings of the 2014 International Conference on Autonomous Agents and Multi-agent Systems (AAMAS '14).* 245–252.

Peer Prediction with Heterogeneous Users

ARPIT AGARWAL, University of Pennsylvania
DEBMALYA MANDAL, Harvard University
DAVID C. PARKES, Harvard University
NISARG SHAH, Harvard University

Peer prediction mechanisms incentivize agents to truthfully report their signals, in the absence of a verification mechanism, by comparing their reports with those of their peers. Prior work in this area is essentially restricted to the case of homogeneous agents, whose signal distributions are identical. This is limiting in many domains, where we would expect agents to differ in taste, judgment and reliability. Although the Correlated Agreement (CA) mechanism [30] can be extended to handle heterogeneous agents, the new challenge is with the efficient estimation of agent signal types. We solve this problem by clustering agents based on their reporting behavior, proposing a mechanism that works with clusters of agents and designing algorithms that learn such a clustering. In this way, we also connect peer prediction with the Dawid and Skene [5] literature on latent types. We retain the robustness against coordinated misreports of the CA mechanism, achieving an approximate incentive guarantee of ε-informed truthfulness. We show on real data that this incentive approximation is reasonable in practice, and even with a small number of clusters.

CCS Concepts: •**Theory of computation** → **Algorithmic game theory and mechanism design;**

Additional Key Words and Phrases: Peer Prediction; Information Elicitation; Clustering; Tensor Decompsition

1 INTRODUCTION

Peer prediction is the problem of information elicitation without verification. Peer prediction mechanisms incentivize users to provide honest reports when the reports cannot be verified, either because there is no objective ground truth or because it is costly to acquire the ground truth. Peer prediction mechanisms leverage correlation in the reports of peers in order to score contributions. In recent years, peer prediction has been studied in several domains, including peer assessment in massively open online courses (MOOCs) [Gao et al., 2016, Shnayder and Parkes, 2016], feedback on the local places in a city [Mandal et al., 2016], and in the context of collaborative sensing platforms [Radanovic and Faltings, 2015a].

The simplest peer prediction mechanism is *output agreement*, which pairs up two users and rewards them in the event that their reports agree (the ESP game [von Ahn and Dabbish, 2004] can be interpreted this way). However, output agreement is not incentive aligned for reports of *a priori* unlikely signals. As a result, there has been a lot of attention in recent years to finding methods that work more generally, as well as providing robustness to coordinated misreports.

We thank Adish Singla and Dengyong Zhou for providing us the Stanford Dogs (Dogs) and the Waterbird dataset (WB). We also acknowledge the useful feedback from anonymous reviewers.
This work is supported in part by Google, the SEAS TomKat fund, and NSF grant CCF-1301976.
Authors' email addresses: Arpit Agarwal: aarpit@seas.upenn.edu; Debmalya Mandal: dmandal@g.harvard.edu; David C. Parkes: parkes@eecs.harvard.edu; Nisarg Shah: nisarg@g.harvard.edu.

EC'17, June 26–30, 2017, Cambridge, MA, USA. © 2017 Association for Computing Machinery.
ACM ISBN 978-1-4503-4527-9/17/06...$15.00. DOI: http://dx.doi.org/10.1145/3033274.3085127

All existing, general methods are essentially restricted to settings with homogeneous participants, whose signal distributions are identical. This is a poor fit with many suggested applications of peer prediction. Consider for example, the problem of peer assessment in MOOCs. DeBoer et al. [2013] and Wilkowski et al. [2014] observe that students differ based on their geographical locations, educational backgrounds, and level of commitment, and indeed the heterogeneity of assessment is clear from a study of Coursera data [Kulkarni et al., 2015]. A similar problem occurs in determining whether a news headline is offensive or not. Depending on which social community a user belongs to, we should expect to get different opinions [Zafar et al., 2016]. In feedback about places such as restaurants or in responses to marketing surveys, user responses will vary because of idiosyncratic differences in taste.

One obstacle behind designing peer prediction mechanisms for heterogeneous agents is an impossibility result. No mechanism can provide strict incentive for truth-telling to a population of heterogeneous agents without knowledge of their signal distributions [Radanovic and Faltings, 2015c]. This negative result holds for minimal mechanisms, which only elicit signals and not beliefs from agents. One way to alleviate this problem, without going to non-minimal mechanisms, is to use the reports from agents across multiple tasks to estimate the signal distribution of an agent. This is our goal: to use minimal peer prediction mechanisms with heterogeneous agents, while using reports from agents for both learning and scoring. We also want to provide robustness against coordinated misreports.

As a starting point, we consider the *correlated agreement* (CA) mechanism proposed in Shnayder et al. [2016]. If the agents are homogeneous and the designer has knowledge of their joint signal distribution, then the CA mechanism is *informed truthful*, i.e. no (even coordinated) strategy profile provides more expected payment than truth-telling and the expected payment under an uninformed strategy (where an agent's report is independent of signal) is strictly less than the expected payment under truth-telling. These two properties remove the incentive for coordinated deviations and promote effort in acquiring and reporting signals, respectively. In a detail-free variation, where the designer learns the signal distribution from reports, approximate incentive alignment is provided (still maintaining the second property as a strict guarantee.) The detail-free CA mechanism can be extended to handle agent heterogeneity, but a naive approach would require learning the joint signal distributions between every pair of agents, and the total number of reports that need to be collected would be prohibitive for many settings.

Our contributions: We design the first minimal and detail-free mechanism for peer prediction with heterogeneous agents, and establish that the sample complexity is linear in the number of agents, while providing an incentive guarantee of approximate informed truthfulness. first inAs with the CA mechanism, this is a multi-task mechanism in that each agent makes reports across multiple tasks. Since our mechanism has a learning component, the task assignments to agents should be such that both the goals of incentive alignment and learning are simultaneously achieved. We consider two assignment schemes under which these goals can be achieved and analyze the sample complexity of our methods for these schemes.

The new mechanism clusters the agents based on their reported behavior and learns the pairwise correlations between these clusters. The clustering introduces one component of the incentive approximation, and could be problematic in the absence of a good clustering such that agents within a cluster behave similarly. Using eight real-world datasets, which contain reports of users on crowdsourcing platforms for multiple labeling tasks, we show that the clustering error is small in practice even when using a relatively small number of clusters. The additional approximation that results from needing to learn the pairwise correlations between clusters can be made arbitrarily small using a sufficient number of signal reports.

Another contribution is to connect, we think for the first time, the peer prediction literature with the extensive and influential literature on latent, confusion matrix models of label aggregation [Dawid and Skene, 1979b]. The Dawid-Skene model assumes that signals are generated independently, conditional on a latent attribute of a task and according to an agent's confusion matrix. We estimate the cluster average confusion matrices using recent developments in tensor decomposition algorithms [Anandkumar et al., 2014, Zhang et al., 2016]. These matrices are used to design reward schemes and achieve approximate informed truthfulness.

In effect, the mechanism learns how to translate one agent's signal reports so that they map onto the signal reports of other agents. For example, in the context of a MOOC, an agent in an "extremal" cluster that only uses the 'A' and 'E' grades may be scored positively when her 'A' report is matched with a 'B' report from another agent assigned to the same essay and a member of the "accurate" cluster. Similarly, an agent in the "contrarian" cluster may be scored positively when her 'E' report is matched with an 'A' report from another agent in the "accurate" cluster and assigned to the same essay. In practice, our mechanism would be trained on the data collected during a semester of peer assessment reports, with students then clustered, cluster-pairwise signal distributions estimated, and scores eventually assigned (this scoring done retrospectively).

1.1 Related Work

We focus our discussion on related work about minimal mechanisms, but remark that we are aware of no, non-minimal mechanisms (following from [Prelec, 2004]) that handle agent heterogeneity. Miller et al. [2005] introduced the peer prediction problem, and proposed an incentive-aligned mechanism for a single-task setting. However their mechanism requires knowledge of the joint signal distribution and is vulnerable to coordinated misreports. In regard to coordinated misreports, Jurca et al. [2009] show how to eliminate uninformative, pure-strategy equilibria through a three-peer mechanism, and Kong et al. [2016] provide a method to design robust, single-task, binary signal mechanisms (but need knowledge of the joint signal distribution). Frongillo and Witkowski [2017] provide a characterization of minimal (single task) peer prediction mechanisms.

Witkowski and Parkes [2013] introduced the combination of learning and peer prediction, coupling the estimation of the signal prior together with the shadowing mechanism. Some results make use of reports from a large population. Radanovic and Faltings [2015b], for example, establish robust incentive properties in a large-market limit where both the number of tasks and the number of agents assigned to each task grow without bound. Radanovic et al. [2016] provide complementary theoretical results, giving a mechanism in which truthfulness is the equilibrium with highest payoff in the asymptote of a large population and with a structural property on the signal distribution.

Dasgupta and Ghosh [2013] show that robustness to coordinated misreports can be achieved for binary signals in a small population by using a multi-task mechanism. The idea is to reward agents if they provide the same signal on the same task, but punish them if one agent's report on one task is the same as another's on another task. The correlated agreement (CA) mechanism [Shnayder et al., 2016] generalizes this mechanism to handle multiple signals, and uses reports to estimate the correlation structure on pairs of signals without compromising incentives. In related work, Kong and Schoenebeck [2016] show that many peer prediction mechanisms can be derived within a single information-theoretic framework. Their results use different technical tools than Shnayder et al. [2016], and also include a different multi-signal generalization of the Dasgupta-Ghosh mechanism that provides robustness against coordinated misreports in the limit of a large number of tasks. Shnayder et al. [2016] adopt replicator dynamics as a model of population learning in peer prediction, and confirm that these multi-task mechanisms (including Kamble et al. [2015]) are successful at avoiding uninformed equilibria.

There are very few results on handling agent heterogeneity in peer prediction. For binary signals, the method of Dasgupta and Ghosh [2013] is likely to be an effective solution because their assumption on correlation structure will tend to hold for most reasonable models of heterogeneity. But it will break down for more than binary signals, as explained by Shnayder et al. [2016]. Moreover, although the CA mechanism can in principle be extended to handle heterogeneity, it is not clear how the required statistical information about signal distributions can be efficiently learned and coupled with an analysis of approximate incentives. For a setting with binary signals and where each task has one of a fixed number of latent types, Kamble et al. [2015] design a mechanism that provides strict incentive compatibility for a suitably large number of heterogeneous agents, and when the number of tasks grows without bound (while allowing each agent to only provide reports on a bounded number of tasks). Their result is restricted to binary signals, and requires a strong regularity assumption on the generative model of signals. Finally, we consider only binary effort of a user, i.e. the agent either invests effort and receives a signal or does not invest effort and receives an uninformed signal. Other work that has considered the importance of motivating effort in the context of peer prediction includes Liu and Chen [2016] and Witkowski et al. [2013].[1] See Mandal et al. [2016] for a setting with heterogeneous tasks but homogeneous agents.

2 MODEL

Let notation $[t]$ denote $\{1, \ldots, t\}$ for $t \in \mathbb{N}$. We consider a population of agents $P = [\ell]$, and use indices such as p and q to refer to agents from this population. There is a set of tasks $M = [m]$. When an agent performs a task, she receives a signal from $N = [n]$. As mentioned before, we assume that the effort of an agent is binary. We also assume that the tasks are *ex ante* identical, that is, the signals of an agent for different tasks are sampled i.i.d. We use S_p to denote the random variable for the signal of agent p for a task.

We work in the setting where the agents are heterogeneous, i.e., the distribution of signals can be different for different agents. We say they vary by *signal type*. Let $D_{p,q}(i,j)$ denote the joint probability that agent p receives signal i while agent q receives signal j on a random task. Let $D_p(i)$ and $D_q(j)$ denote the corresponding marginal probabilities. We define the *Delta matrix* $\Delta_{p,q}$ between agents p and q as

$$\Delta_{p,q}(i,j) = D_{p,q}(i,j) - D_p(i) \cdot D_q(j), \ \forall i,j \in [n]. \tag{1}$$

Shnayder et al. [2016] show that it is without loss of generality for the class of mechanisms we study in this paper to assume that an agent's strategy is uniform across different tasks. Given this, let R_p denote the random variable for the report of agent p for a task. The strategy of agent p, denoted F^p, defines the distribution on reports for each possible signal i, with $F^p_{ir} = \Pr(R_p = r | S_p = i)$. The collection of agent strategies, denoted $\{F^p\}_{p \in P}$, is the *strategy profile*. A strategy of agent p is *informed* if there exist distinct $i,j \in [n]$ and $r \in [n]$ such that $F^p_{ir} \neq F^p_{jr}$, i.e., if not all rows of F^p are identical. We say that a strategy is *uninformed* otherwise.

2.1 Multi-Task Peer Prediction

We consider *multi-task peer prediction* mechanisms. In particular, we adapt the *correlated agreement* (CA) mechanism [Shnayder et al., 2016] to our setting with heterogeneous agents. For every pair of agents $p, q \in P$, we define a *scoring matrix* $S_{p,q} : [n] \times [n] \rightarrow \mathbb{R}$ as a means of scoring agent

[1] Cai et al. [2015] work in a different model, showing how to achieve optimal statistical estimation from data provided by rational agents. These authors focus on the cost of effort, and do not consider misreports (and their mechanism is vulnerable to coordinated misreports).

reports.[2] We randomly divide (without the knowledge of an agent) the set of tasks performed by each agent into nonempty sets of *bonus tasks* and *penalty tasks*. For agent p, we denote the set of her bonus tasks by M_1^p and the set of her penalty tasks by M_2^p.

To calculate the payment to an agent p for a bonus task $t \in M_1^p$, we do the following:

(1) Randomly select an agent $q \in P \setminus \{p\}$ such that $t \in M_1^q$, and the set $M_2^p \cup M_2^q$ has at least 2 distinct tasks, and call q the *peer* of p.
(2) Pick tasks $t' \in M_2^p$ and $t'' \in M_2^q$ randomly such that $t' \neq t''$ (t' and t'' are the penalty tasks for agents p and q respectively)
(3) Let the reports of agent p on tasks t and t' be r_p^t and $r_p^{t'}$, respectively and the reports of agent q on tasks t and t'' be r_q^t and $r_q^{t''}$ respectively.
(4) The payment of agent p for task t is then $S_{p,q}(r_p^t, r_q^t) - S_{p,q}(r_p^{t'}, r_q^{t''})$.

The total payment to an agent is the sum of payments for the agent's bonus tasks. We assume that from an agent's perspective, every other agent is equally likely to be her peer. This requires agents not to know each other's task assignments. In Section 4 we give two task assignment schemes such that from an agent's perspective all peers are equally likely.

The expected payment to agent p for any bonus task performed by her— equal across all bonus tasks as the tasks are *ex ante* identical —is given by

$$u_p(F^p, \{F^q\}_{q \neq p}) = \frac{1}{\ell - 1} \sum_{q \neq p} \sum_{i,j} \Delta_{p,q}(i,j) \sum_{r_p, r_q} S_{p,q}(r_p, r_q) \cdot F^p_{ir_p} \cdot F^q_{jr_q}. \tag{2}$$

Using the fact that there exist optimal solutions to linear functions that are are extremal, it is easy to show that there always exists an optimal strategy for agent p that is deterministic (see also Shnayder et al. [2016]).

Lemma 2.1. *For every player p, and any strategies of others, there always exists an optimal strategy F^p maximizing u_p that is deterministic.*

Hereafter, we assume without loss of generality that agent strategies are deterministic. For a deterministic strategy F^p of agent p, we will slightly abuse notation and write F_i^p to denote the signal reported by agent p when she observes signal i. For a deterministic strategy profile $\{F^q\}_{q \in P}$, the expected payment to agent p is

$$u_p(F^p, \{F^q\}_{q \neq p}) = \frac{1}{\ell - 1} \sum_{q \neq p} \sum_{i,j} \Delta_{p,q}(i,j) \cdot S_{p,q}(F_i^p, F_j^q). \tag{3}$$

2.2 Informed Truthfulness

Following Shnayder et al. [2016], we define the notion of approximate informed truthfulness for a multi-task peer prediction mechanism.

Definition 2.2. (ε-informed truthfulness) We say that a multi-task peer prediction mechanism is ε-informed truthful, for some $\varepsilon \geqslant 0$, if and only if for every strategy profile $\{F^q\}_{q \in P}$ and every agent $p \in P$, we have $u_p(\mathbb{I}, \{\mathbb{I}\}_{q \neq p}) \geqslant u_p(F^p, \{F^q\}_{q \neq p}) - \varepsilon$, where $\mathbb{I}$ is the truthful strategy, and $u_p(\mathbb{I}, \{\mathbb{I}\}_{q \neq p}) > u_p(F_0^p, \{F^q\}_{q \neq p})$ where F_0^p is an uninformed strategy.

An ε-informed truthful mechanism ensures that every agent prefers (up to ε) the truthful strategy profile over any other strategy profile, and strictly prefers the truthful strategy profile over any uninformed strategy. For a small ε, this is responsive to the main concerns about incentives in peer

[2]Multi-task peer prediction mechanisms for homogeneous agents need a single Delta and a single scoring matrix.

prediction: a minimal opportunity for coordinated manipulations, and a strict incentive to invest effort in collecting and reporting an informative signal.[3]

2.3 Agent Clustering

While the natural extension of the detail-free CA mechanism to our setting with heterogeneous agents preserves informed truthfulness, it would require learning the Delta matrix between every pair of agents. In order to learn this from data without additional assumptions, we would require $\Omega(\ell^2)$ samples, which will often be impractical. Rather, the number of reports in a practical mechanism should scale closer to linearly in the number of agents.

In response, we will assume that agents can be (approximately) clustered into a bounded number K of agent signal types, with all agents of the same type having nearly identical signal distributions. Let $G_1, \dots, G_K$ denote a partitioning of agents into K clusters. With a slight abuse of notation, we also use $G(p)$ to denote the cluster to which agent p belongs.

Definition 2.3. We say that clustering $G_1, \dots, G_K$ is ε_1*-accurate*, for some $\varepsilon_1 \geqslant 0$, if for every pair of agents $p, q \in P$,

$$\|\Delta_{p,q} - \Delta_{G(p),G(q)}\|_1 \leqslant \varepsilon_1, \tag{4}$$

where $\Delta_{G(p),G(q)}$ is the *cluster Delta matrix* between clusters $G(p)$ and $G(q)$, defined as the average of the Delta matrices between agents in $G(p)$ and agents in $G(q)$:

$$\Delta_{G_s,G_t} = \frac{1}{|G_s| \times |G_t|} \sum_{p \in G_s, q \in G_t} \Delta_{p,q}.$$

Our mechanism will use $\Delta_{G(p),G(q)}$ in place of $\Delta_{p,q}$ to define the scoring matrix $S_{p,q}$. Thus, the accuracy of the clustering will translate directly to the incentive guarantee of the mechanism and we seek a clustering that is as accurate as possible. For the incentive properties to hold, we will need high between-cluster similarity between agents (i.e., two agents in cluster 1 interact with agents in other clusters in a similar way).

There is an inverse relationship between the number of clusters, K, and the cluster accuracy, ε_1. On the one extreme, we can let every agent be a separate cluster ($K = \ell$), which results in $\varepsilon_1 = 0$. On the other hand, a small number of clusters is essential for reasonable sample complexity, as we will need to learn K^2 cluster Delta matrices. In Section 4, we give a learning algorithm that can learn all the pairwise cluster Delta matrices with $\tilde{O}(K)$ samples given a clustering of the agents. In Section 5, we show using real-world data that a reasonably small clustering error can be achieved with relatively few clusters.

3 CORRELATED AGREEMENT FOR CLUSTERED, HETEROGENEOUS AGENTS

In this section we define mechanism CAHU, presented as Algorithm 1, which takes as input a clustering as well as estimates of the cluster Delta matrices. Specifically, CAHU takes as input a clustering $G_1, \dots, G_K$, together with estimates of cluster Delta matrices $\{\overline{\Delta}_{G_s,G_t}\}_{s,t\in[K]}$.

Definition 3.1. We say that a clustering $\{G_s\}_{s\in[K]}$ and the estimates $\{\overline{\Delta}_{G_s,G_t}\}_{s,t\in[K]}$ are $(\varepsilon_1, \varepsilon_2)$-accurate if

- $\|\Delta_{p,q} - \Delta_{G(p),G(q)}\|_1 \leqslant \varepsilon_1$ for all agents $p, q \in P$, i.e., the clustering is ε_1-accurate, and
- $\|\Delta_{G_s,G_t} - \overline{\Delta}_{G_s,G_t}\|_1 \leqslant \varepsilon_2$ for all clusters $s, t \in [K]$, i.e., the cluster Delta matrix estimates are ε_2-accurate.

[3] We do not model the cost of effort explicitly in this paper, but a binary cost model (effort → signal, no-effort → no signal) can be handled in a straightforward way. See Shnayder et al. [2016].

When we have a clustering and estimates of the delta matrices which are $(\varepsilon_1, \varepsilon_2)$-accurate, we prove that the CAHU mechanism is $(\varepsilon_1 + \varepsilon_2)$-informed truthful. In Section 4, we present algorithms that can learn an ε_1-accurate clustering and ε_2-accurate estimates of cluster Delta matrices.

Throughout the rest of this section, we will use ε_1 to denote the clustering error and ε_2 to denote the learning error. We remark that the clustering error ε_1 is determined by the level of similarity present in agent signal-report behavior, as well as the number of clusters K used, whereas the learning error ε_2 depends on how many samples the learning algorithm sees.

Algorithm 1 Mechanism CAHU

Let $\text{Sign}(x) = 1$ if $x > 0$, and 0 otherwise.

Input:

A clustering $G_1, \ldots, G_K$ such that $\|\Delta_{p,q} - \Delta_{G(p),G(q)}\|_1 \leqslant \varepsilon_1$ for all $p, q \in P$;
estimates $\{\overline{\Delta}_{G_s,G_t}\}_{s,t\in[K]}$ such that $\|\overline{\Delta}_{G_s,G_t} - \Delta_{G_s,G_t}\|_1 \leqslant \varepsilon_2$ for all $s, t \in [K]$; and
for each agent $p \in P$, her bonus tasks M_1^p, penalty tasks M_2^p, and responses $\{r_b^p\}_{b\in M_1^p \cup M_2^p}$.

Method:

```
for every agent p ∈ P do
    for every task b ∈ M_1^p do                                          ▷ Reward response r_b^p
        q ← uniformly at random conditioned on b ∈ M_1^q ∪ M_2^q and (either |M_2^q| ⩾ 2, |M_2^p| ⩾ 2
    or M_2^q ≠ M_2^p)                                                     ▷ Peer agent
        Pick tasks b' ∈ M_2^p and b'' ∈ M_2^q randomly such that b' ≠ b''  ▷ Penalty tasks
        S_{G(p),G(q)} ← Sign(Δ̄_{G(p),G(q)})
        Reward to agent p for task b is S_{G(p),G(q)}(r_b^p, r_b^q) − S_{G(p),G(q)}(r_{b'}^p, r_{b''}^q)
    end for
end for
```

3.1 Analysis of CAHU

Because mechanism CAHU uses scoring matrix $S_{G(p),G(q)}$ to reward agent p given peer agent q in place of a separate scoring matrix $S_{p,q}$ for every pair of agents (p, q), the payoff equation (3) transforms to

$$u_p(F^p, \{F^q\}_{q\neq p}) = \frac{1}{\ell - 1} \sum_{q\in P\setminus\{p\}} \sum_{i,j} \Delta_{p,q}(i,j) \cdot S_{G(p),G(q)}(F_i^p, F_j^q). \tag{5}$$

Next, we prove a sequence of results that show that mechanism CAHU is $(\varepsilon_1 + \varepsilon_2)$-informed truthful when the clustering is ε_1-accurate and the cluster Delta matrix estimates are ε_2-accurate. We first show that the mechanism would be (exactly) informed truthful if it used the Delta matrices between agents instead of using estimates of cluster Delta matrices. In the following we use $u_p^*(\cdot)$ (resp. $u_p(\cdot)$) to denote the utility of agent p under the CA (resp. CAHU) mechanism.

Lemma 3.2. *For a strategy profile $\{F^q\}_{q\in P}$ and an agent $p \in P$, define*

$$u_p^*(F^p, \{F^q\}_{q\neq p}) = \frac{1}{\ell - 1} \sum_{q\in P\setminus\{p\}} \sum_{i,j} \Delta_{p,q}(i,j) \cdot S_{p,q}(F_i^p, F_j^q),$$

where $S_{p,q}(i,j) = \text{Sign}(\Delta_{p,q}(i,j))$ for all $i, j \in [n]$. Then, $u_p^*(\mathbb{I}, \{\mathbb{I}\}_{q\neq p}) \geqslant u_p^*(F^p, \{F^q\}_{q\neq p})$. Moreover, for any uninformed strategy $F^p = r$, $u_p^*(\mathbb{I}, \{\mathbb{I}\}_{q\neq p}) > u_p^*(r, \{F^q\}_{q\neq p})$.

The proof of all theorems and lemmas appear in the full version of the paper.[4] We now use this result to prove one of our main theorems, which is the desired informed truthfulness guarantee about mechanism CAHU.

THEOREM 3.3. *With $(\varepsilon_1, \varepsilon_2)$-accurate clustering and learning, mechanism CAHU is $(\varepsilon_1+\varepsilon_2)$-informed truthful if* $\min_p u_p^*(\mathbb{I}, \{\mathbb{I}\}_{q\neq p}) > \varepsilon_1$. *In particular,*

(1) *For every profile* $\{F^q\}_{q\in P}$ *and agent* $p \in P$, *we have* $u_p(\mathbb{I}, \{\mathbb{I}\}_{q\neq p}) \geqslant u_p(F^p, \{F^q\}_{q\neq p}) - \varepsilon_1 - \varepsilon_2$.
(2) *For any uninformed strategy* F_0^p, $u_p(F_0^p, \{F^q\}_{q\neq p}) < u_p(\mathbb{I}, \{\mathbb{I}\}_{q\neq p})$.

The CAHU mechanism always ensures that there is no strategy profile which gives an expected utility more than $\varepsilon_1 + \varepsilon_2$ above truthful reporting. The condition $\min_p u_p^*(\mathbb{I}, \{\mathbb{I}\}_{q\neq p}) > \varepsilon_1$ is required to ensure that any uninformed strategy gives strictly less than the truth-telling equilibrium. This is important to promote effort in collecting and reporting an informative signal. Writing it out, this condition requires that for each agent p the following holds :

$$\frac{1}{\ell-1}\sum_{q\neq p}\sum_{i,j:\Delta_{p,q}(i,j)>0}\Delta_{p,q}(i,j) > \varepsilon_1. \tag{6}$$

In particular, a sufficient condition for this property is that for every pair of agents the expected reward on a bonus task in the CA mechanism when making truthful reports is at least ε_1, i.e. for every pair of agents p and q,

$$\sum_{i,j:\Delta_{p,q}(i,j)>0}\Delta_{p,q}(i,j) > \varepsilon_1. \tag{7}$$

In turn, as pointed out in Shnayder et al. [2016], the LHS in (7) quantity can be interpreted as a measure of how much positive correlation there is in the joint distribution on signals between a pair of agents. Note that it is not important that this is same-signal correlation. For example, this quantity would be large between an accurate and an always-wrong agent in a binary-signal domain, since the positive correlation would be between one agent's report and the flipped report from the other agent.

The incentive properties of the mechanism are retained when used together with learning the cluster structure and cluster Delta matrices. This follows because the agents can do no better than have the mechanism be designed with the correct scoring matrices (see Shnayder et al. [2016]).

4 LEARNING THE AGENT SIGNAL TYPES

In this section, we provide algorithms for learning a clustering of agent signal types from reports, and further, for learning the cluster pairwise Δ matrices. The estimates of the Δ matrices can then be used to give an approximate-informed truthful mechanism. Along the way, we couple our methods with the latent "confusion matrix" methods of Dawid and Skene [1979b].

Recall that m is the total number of tasks about which reports are collected. Reports on m_1 of these tasks will also be used for clustering, and reports on a further m_2 of these tasks will be used for learning the cluster pairwise Δ matrices. We consider two different schemes for assigning agents to tasks for the purpose of clustering and learning (see Figures 1 and 2):

(1) **Fixed Task Assignment**: Each agent is assigned to the same, random subset of tasks of size $m_1 + m_2$ of the given m tasks.
(2) **Uniform Task Assignment**: For clustering, we select two agents r_1 and r_2, uniformly at random, to be *reference agents*. These agents are assigned to a subset of tasks of size

[4] The full version is available on the authors' website.

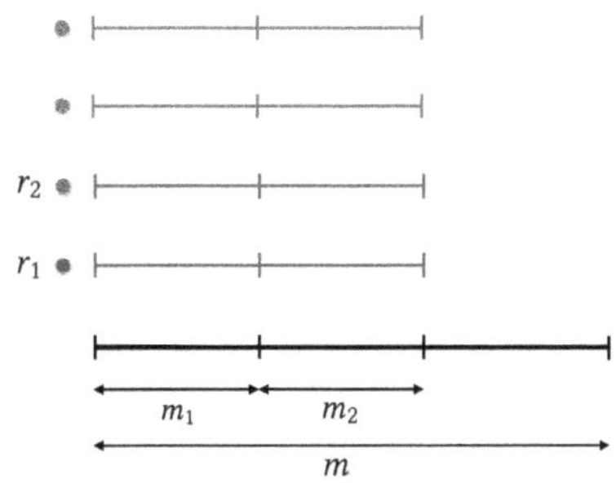

Fig. 1. Fixed Task Assignment

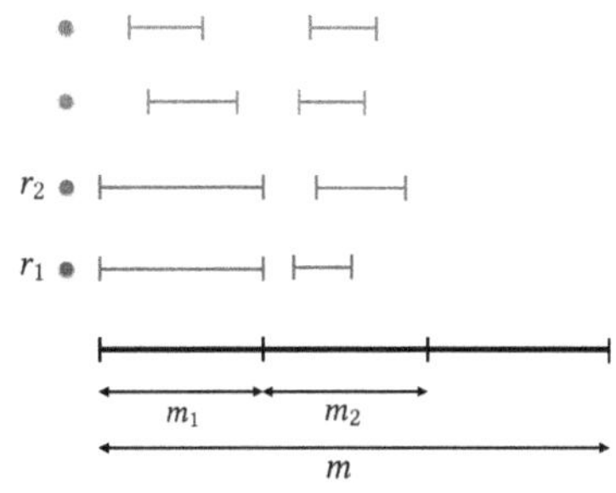

Fig. 2. Uniform Task Assignment

Table 1. Sample complexity for the CAHU mechanism. The rows indicate the assignment scheme and the columns indicate the modeling assumption. Here ℓ is the number of agents, n is the number of signals, ε' is a parameter that controls learning accuracy ‡ , γ is a clustering parameter, K is the number of clusters, and m_1 (resp. m_2) is the size of the set of tasks from which the tasks used for clustering (resp. learning) are sampled.

	No Assumption	Dawid-Skene
Fixed Assignment	Clustering: $\tilde{O}\left(\frac{\ell n^2}{\gamma^2}\right)$ Learning: $\tilde{O}\left(\frac{Kn^2}{(\varepsilon')^2}\right)$	Clustering: $\tilde{O}\left(\frac{\ell n^2}{\gamma^2}\right)$ Learning: $\tilde{O}\left(\frac{\ell n^7}{(\varepsilon')^2}\right)$
Uniform Assignment	Clustering: $\tilde{O}\left(\frac{\ell n^2}{\gamma^2} + m_1\right)$ Learning: $\tilde{O}\left(Km_2^{7/8}\sqrt{\frac{n^2}{(\varepsilon')^2}}\right)$	Clustering: $\tilde{O}\left(\frac{\ell n^2}{\gamma^2} + m_1\right)$ Learning: $\tilde{O}\left(\frac{Kn^7}{(\varepsilon')^2}\right)^\dagger$

$m_1(< m)$. For all other agents, we then assign a required number of tasks, s_1, uniformly at random from the set of m_1 tasks. For learning the cluster pairwise Δ-matrices, we also assign one agent from each cluster to some subset of tasks of size s_2, selected uniformly at random from a second set of $m_2(< m - m_1)$ tasks.

For each assignment scheme, the analysis establishes that there are enough agents who have done a sufficient number of joint tasks. Table 1 summarizes the sample complexity results, stating them under two different assumptions about the way in which signals are generated.

4.1 Clustering

We proceed by presenting and analyzing a simple clustering algorithm.

Definition 4.1. A clustering $G_1, \ldots, G_K$ is ε-good if for some $\gamma > 0$

$$G(q) = G(r) \Rightarrow \|\Delta_{pq} - \Delta_{pr}\|_1 \leqslant \varepsilon - 4\gamma \;\forall p \in [\ell] \setminus \{q, r\} \tag{8}$$

$$G(q) \neq G(r) \Rightarrow \|\Delta_{pq} - \Delta_{pr}\|_1 > \varepsilon \;\forall p \in [\ell] \setminus \{q, r\} \tag{9}$$

We first show that an ε-good clustering, if exists, must be unique.

THEOREM 4.2. *Suppose there exist two clustering $\{G_j\}_{j\in[K]}$ and $\{T_i\}_{i\in[K']}$ that are ε-good. Then $K' = K$ and $G_j = T_{\pi(j)}$ for some permutation π over $[K]$.*

† For an arbitrary m_2, this bound is Km_2 as long as m_2 is $\Omega\left(n^7/(\varepsilon')^2\right)$

‡ In the no assumption approach (resp. Dawid-Skene Model), ε' is the error in the estimation of the joint probability distribution (resp. aggregate confusion matrix).

Algorithm 2 Clustering

Input: ε, γ such that there exists an ε-good clustering with parameter γ.
Output: A clustering $\{\hat{G}_t\}_{t=1}^{\hat{K}}$

$\hat{G} \leftarrow \emptyset, \hat{K} \leftarrow 0$ ▷ $\hat{G}$ is the list of clusters, $\hat{K} = |\hat{G}|$
Make a new cluster $\hat{G}_1$ and add agent 1
Add $\hat{G}_1$ to $\hat{G}$, $\hat{K} \leftarrow \hat{K} + 1$
for $i = 2, \ldots, \ell$ **do**
  for $t \in [\hat{K}]$ **do**
    Pick an arbitrary agent $q_t \in \hat{G}_t$
    Pick $p_t \in [l] \setminus \{i, q_t\}$ **(Fixed)** or $p_t \in \{r_1, r_2\} \setminus \{i, q_t\}$ **(Uniform)**, such that p_t has at least $\Omega(\frac{n^2 \log(K\ell/\delta)}{\gamma^2})$ tasks in common with both q_t and i
    Let $\bar{\Delta}_{p_t,q_t}$ be the empirical Delta matrix from reports of agents p_t and q_t
    Let $\bar{\Delta}_{p_t,i}$ be the empirical Delta matrix from reports of agents p_t and i
  end for
  if $\exists t \in [\hat{K}] : \|\bar{\Delta}_{p_t,q_t} - \bar{\Delta}_{p_t,i}\|_1 \leqslant \varepsilon - 2\gamma$ **then**
    add i to $\hat{G}_t$ (with ties broken arbitrarily for t)
  else
    Make a new cluster $\hat{G}_{\hat{K}+1}$ and add agent i to it
    Add $\hat{G}_{\hat{K}+1}$ to $\hat{G}$, $\hat{K} \leftarrow \hat{K} + 1$
  end if
end for

Since there is a unique ε-good clustering (up to a permutation), we will refer to this clustering as the *correct clustering*. The assumption that there exists an ε-good clustering is stronger than Equation (4) introduced earlier.

In particular, identifying the correct clustering requires need eq. (9), i.e. the Δ-matrices of two agents belonging to two different clusters are different with respect to every other agent. So, we need low inter-cluster similarities in addition to high intra-cluster similarities. The pseudo-code for the clustering algorithm is presented in Algorithm 2. This algorithm iterates over the agents, and forms clusters in a greedy manner. First, we prove that as long as we can find an agent p_t that has $\Omega(\frac{n^2 \log(\ell/\delta)}{\gamma^2})$ tasks in common with both q_t and i, then the clustering produced by Algorithm 2 is correct with probability at least $1 - \delta$.

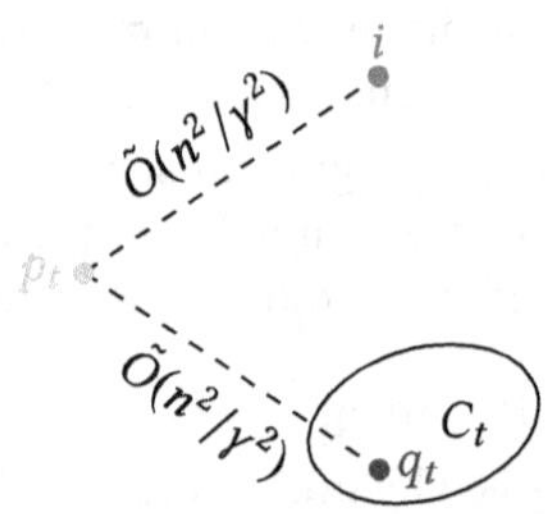

Fig. 3. Algorithm 2 checks whether i and q_t are in the same cluster by estimating Δ_{p_t,q_t} and $\Delta_{p_t,i}$.

Theorem 4.3. *If for all $i \in P$ and $q_t \in G(i)$, there exists p_t which has $\Omega(\frac{n^2 \log(\ell/\delta)}{\gamma^2})$ tasks in common with both q_t and i, then Algorithm 2 recovers the correct clustering i.e. $\hat{G}_t = G_t$ for $t = 1, \ldots, K$ with probability at least $1 - \delta$.*

Next we show how the assumption in regard to task overlap is satisfied under each assignment scheme, and characterize the sample complexity of learning the clusterings under each scheme. In the fixed assignment scheme, all the agents are assigned to the same set of $m_1 = \Omega(\frac{n^2}{\gamma^2} \log(K\ell/\delta))$

tasks. Thus, for each agent pair q_t and i, any other agent in the population can act as p_t. The total number of tasks performed is $O\left(\frac{\ell n^2}{\gamma^2}\log(K\ell/\delta)\right)$.

In the uniform assignment scheme, we select two agents r_1 and r_2 uniformly at random to be reference agents, and assign these agents to each of $m_1 = \Omega(\frac{n^2}{\gamma^2}\log(K\ell/\delta))$ tasks. For all other agents we then assign $s_1 = \Omega(\frac{n^2}{\gamma^2}\log(K\ell/\delta))$ tasks uniformly at random from this set of m_1 tasks. If $m_1 = s_1$, then the uniform task assignment is the same as fixed task assignment. However, in applications, for example [Karger et al., 2011], where one wants the task assignments to be more uniform across tasks, it will make sense to use a larger value of m_1. The reference agent r_1 can act as p_t for all agent pairs q_t and i other than r_1. Similarly, reference r_2 can act as p_t for all agent pairs q_t and i other than r_2. If $q_t = r_1$ and $i = r_2$ or $q_t = r_2$ and $i = r_1$, then any other agent can act as p_t. The total number of tasks performed is $\Omega(\frac{\ell n^2}{\gamma^2}\log(K\ell/\delta) + m_1)$, which is sufficient for the high probability result.

4.2 Learning the Cluster Pairwise Δ Matrices

We proceed now under the assumption that the agents are clustered into K groups, $G_1, \ldots, G_K$. Our goal is to estimate the cluster-pairwise delta matrices Δ_{G_s,G_t} as required by Algorithm 1. We estimate the Δ_{G_s,G_t} under two different settings: when we have no model of the signal distribution, and in the Dawid-Skene latent attribute model.

Algorithm 3 Learning-Δ-No-Assumption

for $t = 1, \ldots, K$ **do**
  Chose agent $q_t \in G_t$ arbitrarily.
end for
for each pair of clusters G_s, G_t **do**
  Let q_s and q_t be the chosen agents for G_s and G_t, respectively.
  Let $\bar{D}_{q_s,q_t}$ be the empirical estimate of D_{q_s,q_t} such that $\|\bar{D}_{q_s,q_t} - D_{q_s,q_t}\|_1 \leqslant \varepsilon'$ with probability at least $1 - \delta/K^2$
  Let $\bar{\Delta}_{q_s,q_t}$ be the empirical Delta matrix computed using $\bar{D}_{q_s,q_t}$
  Set $\bar{\Delta}_{G_s,G_t} = \bar{\Delta}_{q_s,q_t}$
end for

4.2.1 *Learning the Δ-Matrices with No Assumption.*

We first characterize the sample complexity of learning the Δ-matrices in the absence of any modeling assumptions. In order to estimate $\bar{\Delta}_{G_s,G_t}$, Algorithm 3 first picks agent q_s from cluster G_s, estimates $\bar{\Delta}_{q_s,q_t}$ and use this estimate in place of $\bar{\Delta}_{G_s,G_t}$. For the fixed assignment scheme, we assign the agents q_s to the same set of tasks of size $O\left(\frac{n^2}{(\varepsilon')^2}\log(K/\delta)\right)$. For the uniform assignment scheme, we assign the agents to subsets of tasks of an appropriate size among the pool of m_2 tasks.

Theorem 4.4. *Given an ε-good clustering $\{G_s\}_{s=1}^K$, if the number of shared tasks between any pair of agents q_s, q_t is $O\left(\frac{n^2}{(\varepsilon')^2}\log(K/\delta)\right)$, then algorithm 3 guarantees that for all s, t, $\|\bar{\Delta}_{G_s,G_t} - \Delta_{G_s,G_t}\|_1 \leqslant 3\varepsilon' + 2\varepsilon$ with probability at least $1 - \delta$. The total number of samples collected by the algorithm is $O\left(\frac{Kn^2}{(\varepsilon')^2}\log(K/\delta)\right)$ $\left(\text{resp. } O\left(Km_2^{7/8}\sqrt{\frac{n^2}{(\varepsilon')^2}\log(K/\delta)}\right) \text{ w.h.p.}\right)$ under the fixed (resp. uniform) assignment scheme.*

4.2.2 ***Learning the Δ-matrices Under the Dawid-Skene Model.*** In this section, we assume that the agents receive signals according to the Dawid and Skene [1979a] model. In this model, each task has a latent attribute and each agent has a confusion matrix to parameterize its signal distribution conditioned on this latent value. More formally:

- Let $\{\pi_k\}_{k=1}^n$ denote the prior probability over n latent values.
- Agent p has *confusion matrix* $C^p \in \mathbb{R}^{n \times n}$, such that $C^p_{ij} = D_p(S_p = j | T = i)$ where T is the latent value. Given this, the joint signal distribution for a pair of agents p and q is

$$D_{p,q}(S_p = i, S_q = j) = \sum_{k=1}^{n} \pi_k C^p_{ki} C^q_{kj}, \tag{10}$$

and the marginal signal distribution for agent p is

$$D_p(S_p = i) = \sum_{k=1}^{n} \pi_k C^p_{ki}. \tag{11}$$

For cluster G_t, we write $C^t = \frac{1}{|G_t|} \sum_{p \in G_t} C^p$ to denote the aggregate confusion matrix of G_t. As before, we assume that we are given an ε-good clustering, $G_1, \ldots, G_K$, of the agents. Our goal is to provide an estimate of the Δ_{G_s,G_t}-matrices.

Lemma 4.5 proves that in order to estimate Δ_{G_s,G_t} within an L1 distance of ε', it is enough to estimate the aggregate confusion matrices within an L1 distance of $\varepsilon'/4$. So in order to learn the pairwise delta matrices between clusters, we first ensure that for each cluster G_t, we have $\|\bar{C}^t - C^t\|_1 \leqslant \varepsilon'/4$ with probability at least $1 - \delta/K$, and then use the following formula to compute the delta matrices:

$$\Delta_{G_s,G_t}(i,j) = \sum_{k=1}^{n} \pi_k \bar{C}^s_{ki} \bar{C}^t_{kj} - \sum_{k=1}^{n} \pi_k \bar{C}^s_{ki} \sum_{k=1}^{n} \pi_k \bar{C}^t_{kj} \tag{12}$$

Lemma 4.5. *Forall G_a, G_b, $\|\bar{C}^a - C^a\|_1 \leqslant \varepsilon'/4$ and $\|\bar{C}^b - C^b\|_1 \leqslant \varepsilon'/4 \Rightarrow \|\bar{\Delta}_{G_a,G_b} - \Delta_{G_a,G_b}\| \leqslant \varepsilon'$.*

We turn now to estimating the aggregate confusion matrix of each cluster. Let us assume for now that the agents are assigned to the tasks according to the uniform assignment scheme, i.e. agent p belonging to cluster G_a is assigned to a subset of B_a tasks selected uniformly at random from a pool of m_2 tasks. For cluster G_a, we choose $B_a = \frac{m_2}{|G_a|} \ln(\frac{m_2 K}{\beta})$. This implies:

(1) For each $j \in [m_2]$, Pr [agent $p \in G_a$ completes task j] $= \frac{\log(m_2 K/\beta)}{|G_a|}$, i.e. each agent p in G_a is equally likely to complete every task j.
(2) Pr [task j is unlabeled by G_a] $= \left(1 - \frac{\log(m_2 K/\beta)}{|G_a|}\right)^{|G_a|} \leqslant \frac{\beta}{m_2 K}$. Taking a union bound over the m_2 tasks and K clusters, we get the probability that any task is unlabeled is at most β. Now if we choose $\beta = 1/\text{poly}(m_2)$, we observe that with probability at least $1 - 1/\text{poly}(m_2)$, each task j is labeled by some agent in each cluster when $B_a = \tilde{O}(\frac{m_2}{|G_a|})$.

Left to do is to provide an algorithm and sample complexity for learning the aggregate confusion matrices. For this, we will use n dimensional unit vectors to denote the reports of the agents (recall that there are n possible signals). In particular agent p's report on task j, $r_{pj} \in \{0,1\}^n$. If p's report on task j is c, then the c-th coordinate of r_{pj} is 1 and all the other coordinates are 0. The expected value of agent p's report on jth task is $\mathrm{E}\left[r_{pj}\right] = \sum_{k=1}^{n} \pi_k C^p_k$ The aggregated report for a cluster G_t is given as $R_{tj} = \frac{1}{|G_t|} \sum_{p \in G_t} r_{pj}$.

Suppose we want to estimate the aggregate confusion matrix C^1 of some cluster G_1. To do so, we first pick three clusters G_1, G_2 and G_3 and write down the corresponding cross moments. Let

(a, b, c) be a permutation of the set $\{1, 2, 3\}$. We have:

$$M_1 = E[R_{aj}] = \sum_k \pi_k C_k^a \tag{13}$$

$$M_2 = E[R_{aj} \otimes R_{bj}] = \sum_k \pi_k C_k^a \otimes C_k^b \tag{14}$$

$$M_3 = E[R_{aj} \otimes R_{bj} \otimes R_{cj}] = \sum_k \pi_k C_k^a \otimes C_k^b \otimes C_k^c \tag{15}$$

The cross moments are asymmetric, however using Theorem 3.6 of Anandkumar et al. [2014], we can write the cross-moments in a symmetric form.

Lemma 4.6. *Assume that the vectors $\{C_1^t, \dots, C_n^t\}$ are linearly independent for each $t \in \{1, 2, 3\}$. For any permutation (a, b, c) of the set $\{1, 2, 3\}$ define*

$$R'_{aj} = \mathrm{E}\left[R_{cj} \otimes R_{bj}\right] \left(\mathrm{E}\left[R_{aj} \otimes R_{bj}\right]\right)^{-1} R_{aj}$$

$$R'_{bj} = \mathrm{E}\left[R_{cj} \otimes R_{aj}\right] \left(\mathrm{E}\left[R_{bj} \otimes R_{aj}\right]\right)^{-1} R_{bj}$$

$$M_2 = \mathrm{E}\left[R'_{aj} \otimes R'_{bj}\right] \text{ and } M_3 = \mathrm{E}\left[R'_{aj} \otimes R'_{bj} \otimes R_{cj}\right]$$

$$\text{Then } M_2 = \sum_{k=1}^{n} \pi_k C_k^c \otimes C_k^c \text{ and } M_3 = \sum_{k=1}^{n} \pi_k C_k^c \otimes C_k^c \otimes C_k^c$$

We cannot compute the moments exactly, but rather estimate the moments from samples observed from different tasks. Furthermore, for a given task j, instead of exactly computing the aggregate label R_{gj}, we select one agent p uniformly at random from G_g and use agent p's report on task j as a proxy for R_{gj}. We will denote the corresponding report as $\tilde{R}_{gj}$. The next lemma proves that the cross-moments of $\{\tilde{R}_{gj}\}_{g=1}^K$ and $\{R_{gj}\}_{g=1}^K$ are the same.

Lemma 4.7. (1) *For any group G_a, $\mathrm{E}\left[\tilde{R}_{aj}\right] = \mathrm{E}\left[R_{aj}\right]$*
(2) *For any pair of groups G_a and G_b, $\mathrm{E}\left[\tilde{R}_{aj} \otimes \tilde{R}_{bj}\right] = \mathrm{E}\left[R_{aj} \otimes R_{bj}\right]$*
(3) *For any three groups G_a, G_b and G_c, $\mathrm{E}\left[\tilde{R}_{aj} \otimes \tilde{R}_{bj} \otimes \tilde{R}_{cj}\right] = \mathrm{E}\left[R_{aj} \otimes R_{bj} \otimes R_{cj}\right]$*

The next set of equations show how to approximate the moments M_2 and M_3:

$$\hat{R}'_{aj} = \left(\frac{1}{m_2}\sum_{j'=1}^{m_2} \tilde{R}_{cj'} \otimes \tilde{R}_{bj'}\right)\left(\frac{1}{m_2}\sum_{j'=1}^{m_2} \tilde{R}_{aj'} \otimes \tilde{R}_{bj'}\right)^{-1} \tilde{R}_{aj} \tag{16}$$

$$\hat{R}'_{bj} = \left(\frac{1}{m_2}\sum_{j'=1}^{m_2} \tilde{R}_{cj'} \otimes \tilde{R}_{aj'}\right)\left(\frac{1}{m_2}\sum_{j'=1}^{m_2} \tilde{R}_{bj'} \otimes \tilde{R}_{aj'}\right)^{-1} \tilde{R}_{bj} \tag{17}$$

$$\hat{M}_2 = \frac{1}{m_2}\sum_{j'=1}^{m_2} \hat{R}'_{aj'} \otimes \hat{R}'_{bj'} \text{ and } \hat{M}_3 = \frac{1}{m_2}\sum_{j'=1}^{m_2} \hat{R}'_{aj'} \otimes \hat{R}'_{bj'} \otimes \tilde{R}_{cj'} \tag{18}$$

We use the tensor decomposition algorithm (4) on $\hat{M}_2$ and $\hat{M}_3$ to recover the aggregate confusion matrix $\bar{C}^c$ and $\bar{\Pi}$, where $\bar{\Pi}$ is a diagonal matrix whose k-th component is $\bar{\pi}_k$, an estimate of π_k. In order to analyze the sample complexity of Algorithm 4, we need to make some mild assumptions about the problem instance. For any two clusters G_a and G_b, define $S_{ab} = \mathrm{E}\left[R_{aj} \otimes R_{bj}\right] = \sum_{k=1}^{n} \pi_k C_k^a \otimes C_k^b$. We make the following assumptions:

Algorithm 4 Estimating Aggregate Confusion Matrix

Input: K clusters of agents $G_1, G_2, \ldots, G_K$ and the reports $\tilde{R}_{gj} \in \{0,1\}^n$ for $j \in [m]$ and $g \in [K]$
Output: Estimate of the aggregate confusion matrices $\bar{C}^g$ for all $g \in [K]$

```
Partition the K clusters into groups of three
for Each group of three clusters {g_a, g_b, g_c} do
    for (a, b, c) ∈ {(g_b, g_c, g_a), (g_c, g_a, g_b), (g_a, g_b, g_c)} do
        Compute the second and the third order moments M̂_2 ∈ R^{n×n}, M̂_3 ∈ R^{n×n×n}.    ▷ Compute C̄^g and Π̄ by tensor decomposition
        Compute whitening matrix Q̂ ∈ R^{n×n} such that Q̂^T M̂_2 Q̂ = I
        Compute eigenvalue-eigenvector pairs (α̂_k, v̂_k)_{k=1}^n of the whitened tensor M̂_3(Q̂, Q̂, Q̂) by using the robust tensor power method
        Compute ŵ_k = α̂_k^{-2} and μ̂_k = (Q̂^T)^{-1} α̂ v̂_k
        For k = 1, ..., n set the k-th column of C̄^c by some μ̂_k whose k-th coordinate has the greatest component, then set the k-th diagonal entry of Π̄ by ŵ_k
    end for
end for
```

(1) There exists $\sigma_L > 0$ such that $\sigma_n(S_{ab}) \geqslant \sigma_L$ for each pair of clusters a and b, where $\sigma_n(M)$ is the n-th smallest eigenvalue of M.
(2) $\kappa = \min_{t \in [k]} \min_{s \in [n]} \min_{r \neq s} \left\{ C^t_{rr} - C^t_{rs} \right\} > 0$

The first assumption implies that the matrices S_{ab} are non-singular. The second assumption implies that within a group, the probability of assigning the correct label is always higher than the probability of assigning any incorrect label. The following theorem gives the number of tasks each agent needs to complete to get an ε'-estimate of the aggregate confusion matrices.

Theorem 4.8. *For any $\varepsilon' \leqslant \min\left\{\frac{31}{\sigma_L^2}, \frac{\kappa}{2}\right\} n^2$ and $\delta > 0$, if the size of the universe of shared tasks m_2 is at least $O\left(\frac{n^7}{(\varepsilon')^2 \sigma_L^{11}} \log\left(\frac{nK}{\delta}\right)\right)$, then we have $\|\bar{C}^t - C^t\|_1 \leqslant \varepsilon'$ for each cluster G_t. The total number of samples collected by Algorithm 4 is $\tilde{O}(Km_2)$ under the uniform assignment scheme.*

Discussion. If the algorithm chooses $m_2 = \tilde{O}\left(\frac{n^7}{(\varepsilon')^2 \sigma_L^{11}}\right)$, then the total number of samples collected under the uniform assignment scheme is at most $\tilde{O}\left(\frac{n^7}{(\varepsilon')^2 \sigma_L^{11}}\right)$. So far we have analyzed the Dawid-Skene model under the uniform assignment scheme. When the assignment scheme is fixed, the moments of R_{aj} and $\tilde{R}_{aj}$ need not be the same. In this case we will have to run Algorithm 4 with respect to the actual aggregate labels $\{R_{gj}\}_{g=1}^K$. This requires collecting samples from every member of a cluster, leading to a sample complexity of $O\left(\frac{\ell n^7}{(\varepsilon')^2 \sigma_L^{11}} \log\left(\frac{nK}{\delta}\right)\right)$

In order to estimate the confusion matrices, Zhang et al. [2016] require each agent to provide at least $O\left(n^5 \log((\ell + n)/\delta)/(\varepsilon')^2\right)$ samples. Our algorithm requires $O\left(n^7 \log(nK/\delta)/(\varepsilon')^2\right)$ samples from each cluster. The increase of n^2 in the sample complexity comes about because we are estimating the aggregate confusion matrices in L1 norm instead of the infinity norm. Moreover when the number of clusters is small ($K << \ell$), the number of samples required from each cluster does not grow with ℓ. This improvement is due to the fact that, unlike Zhang et al. [2016], we do not have to recover individual confusion matrices from the aggregate confusion matrices.

Note that the Dawid and Skene [1979b] based approach, for the uniform assignment scheme, does not require all agents to provide reports on the same set of shared tasks. Rather, we need that for each group of three clusters (as partitioned by Algorithm 4 on line 1) and each task, there exists one agent from the three clusters who completes the same task. In particular the reports for different tasks can be acquired from different agents within the same cluster. The assignment scheme makes sure that this property holds with high probability.

We now briefly compare the learning algorithms under the no-assumptions and model-based approach. When it is difficult to assign agents to the same tasks, and when the number of signals is small (which is often true in practice), the Dawid-Skene method has a strong advantage. Another advantage of the Dawid-Skene method is that the learning error ε' can be made arbitrarily small since each aggregate confusion matrix can be learned with arbitrary accuracy, whereas the true learning error of the no-assumption approach is at least 2ε (see Theorem 4.4), and depends on the problem instance.

5 CLUSTERING EXPERIMENTS

In this section, we study the clustering error on eight real-world, crowdsourcing datasets. Six of these datasets are from the *SQUARE* benchmark [Sheshadri and Lease, 2013], selected to ensure a sufficient density of worker labels across different latent attributes as well as the availability of latent attributes for sufficiently many tasks. In addition, we also use the Stanford *Dogs* dataset [Khosla et al., 2011] and the *Expressions* dataset [Mozafari et al., 2012, 2014]. Below, we briefly describe the format of task, the number of agents ℓ, and the number of signals n for each dataset.[5] The description of the dataset is available in the full version of the paper.

Recall that the maximum incentive an agent has to use a non-truthful strategy in the CAHU mechanism can be upper-bounded in terms of two sources of error:

- The clustering error. This represents how "clusterable" the agents are. From theory, we have the upper bound $\varepsilon_1 = \max_{p,q\in[\ell]} ||\Delta_{p,q} - \Delta_{G(p),G(q)}||_1$.
- The learning error. This represents how accurate our estimates for the cluster Delta matrices are. From theory, we have the upper bound $\varepsilon_2 = \max_{i,j\in[K]} ||\Delta_{G_i,G_j} - \overline{\Delta}_{G_i,G_j}||_1$.

Based on this, the CAHU mechanism is $(\varepsilon_1 + \varepsilon_2)$-informed truthful (Theorem 3.3) where ε_1 is the clustering error and ε_2 is the learning error. Even with the best clustering, the clustering error ε_1 cannot be made arbitrarily small because it depends on how close the signal distributions of the agents are as well as the number of clusters. In contrast, the learning error ε_2 of the no-assumption approach is $3\varepsilon' + 2\varepsilon$, (theorem 4.4) where the error due to ε' can indeed be made arbitrarily small by simply acquiring more data about agents' behavior. Similarly, the learning error ε_2 in the Dawid-Skene approach can be made arbitrarily small by acquiring more agent reports (theorem 4.8). Hence the total error is dominated by the clustering error ε_1.

For this reason, we focus on the clustering error, and show that it can be small even with a relatively small number of clusters. Rather than the use the weak bound $\max_{p,q\in[\ell]} ||\Delta_{p,q} - \Delta_{G(p),G(q)}||_1$ on the clustering error (which is nevertheless helpful for our theoretical results), we use the following tighter bound from the proof of Theorem 3.3.

$$|u_p^*(\mathbb{I}, \{\mathbb{I}\}_{q\neq p}) - u_p(\mathbb{I}, \{\mathbb{I}\}_{q\neq p})| = \left|\frac{1}{(\ell-1)} \sum_{q\in P\setminus\{p\}} \sum_{i,j} \Delta_{p,q}(i,j)(\mathrm{Sign}(\Delta_{p,q})_{i,j} - \mathrm{Sign}(\overline{\Delta}_{G(p),G(q)})_{i,j})\right| \tag{19}$$

[5] We filter each dataset to remove tasks for which the latent attribute is unknown, and remove workers who only perform such tasks. ℓ is the number of agents that remain after filtering.

The datasets specify the latent value of each task. Because of this, we can adopt the Dawid-Skene model, and estimate the confusion matrices from the frequency which with each agent p reports each label j in the case of each latent attribute i.

Typical clustering algorithms take a distance metric over the space of data points and attempt to minimize the maximum cluster diameter, which is the maximum distance between any two points within a cluster. In contrast, our objective (the tighter bound on the incentive in Equation (19)) is a complex function of the underlying confusion matrices. We therefore compare two approaches:

1) We cluster the confusion matrices using the standard k-means++ algorithm with the $L2$ norm distance (available in Matlab), and hope that resulting clustering leads to a small incentive bound.[6]
2) In the following lemma, we derive a distance metric between confusion matrices for which the maximum cluster diameter is provably an upper bound on the incentive, and use k-means++ with this metric (implemented in Matlab).[7] Note that computing this metric requires knowledge of the prior over the latent attribute.

Lemma 5.1. *For all agents p, q, r, we have* $\|\Delta_{p,q} - \Delta_{p,r}\|_1 \leqslant 2 \cdot \sum_k \pi_k \sum_j |C^q_{kj} - C^r_{kj}|$.

Lemma 5.2. *For every pair of agents p, q, we have*

$$\|\Delta_{p,q} - \Delta_{G(p),G(q)}\|_1 \leqslant 2 \cdot \max_{a,b,c \in P: G(a)=G(b)} \|\Delta_{a,c} - \Delta_{b,c}\|_1.$$

Note that $\sum_k \pi_k \sum_j |C^q_{kj} - C^r_{kj}| \leqslant \|C^q - C^r\|_1$ because $\sum_j \left|C^q_{lj} - C^r_{lj}\right| \leqslant \|C^q - C^r\|_1$. Lemma 5.1, along with Lemma 5.2, shows that the incentive is upper bounded by four times the maximum cluster diameter under our metric. For each dataset, we vary the number of clusters K from 5% to 15% of the number of agents in the dataset. We repeat the experiment 20 times, and select the clustering that produces the smallest incentive bound. Figures 4 and 5 show the incentive bound achieved using the standard $L2$ metric and using our custom metric, respectively. We see that the incentive bound is small compared to the maximum payment of 1 by CAHU, even with the number of clusters K as small as 15% of the number of workers. The number of agents does not seem to affect this bound as long as the number of clusters is small relative to the number of agents. Using our custom metric leads to a clustering with a noticeably better incentive bound.

6 CONCLUSION

We have provided the first, general solution to the problem of peer prediction with heterogeneous agents. This is a compelling research direction, where new theory and algorithms can help to guide practice. In particular, heterogeneity is likely to be quite ubiquitous because of differences in taste, context, judgment, and reliability across users. Beyond testing these methods in a real-world application such as marketing surveys, there remain interesting directions for ongoing research. For example, is it possible to solve this problem with similar sample complexity but without a clustering approach, and to couple methods of peer prediction with optimal methods for inference in crowdsourced classification [Ok et al., 2016], and with methods for task assignment in budgeted

[6]We use $L2$ norm rather than $L1$ norm because the standard k-means++ implementation uses as the centroid of a cluster the confusion matrix that minimizes the sum of distances from the confusion matrices of the agents in the cluster. For $L2$ norm, this amounts to averaging over the confusion matrices, which is precisely what we want. For $L1$ norm, this amounts to taking a pointwise median, which does not even result in a valid confusion matrix. Perhaps for this reason, we observe that using the $L1$ norm performs worse.

[7]For computing the centroid of a cluster, we still average over the confusion matrices of the agents in the cluster. Also, since the algorithm is no longer guaranteed to converge (indeed, we observe cycles), we restart the algorithm when a cycle is detected, at most 10 times.

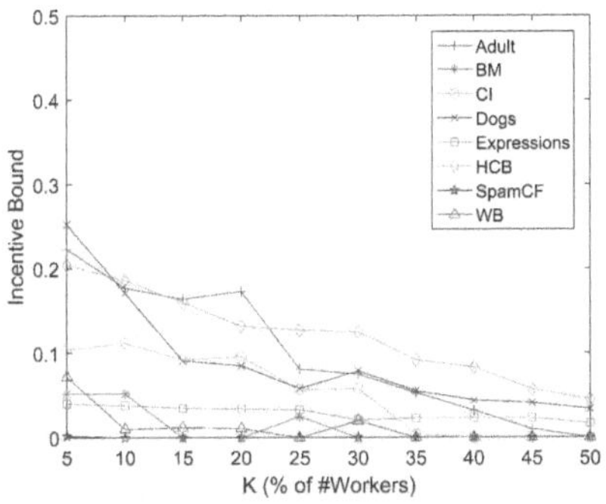

Fig. 4. Incentive bound on each of the 8 different data sets when using k-means++ with the $L2$ norm

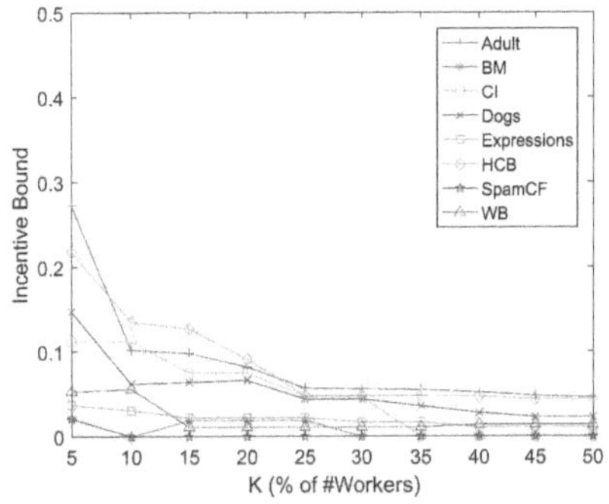

Fig. 5. Incentive bound on each of the 8 different data sets when using k-means++ with our custom metric

settings [Karger et al., 2014]? This should include attention to adaptive assignment schemes [Khetan and Oh, 2016] that leverage generalized Dawid-Skene models [Zhou et al., 2015], and could connect with recent progress on task heterogeneity within peer prediction [Mandal et al., 2016].

REFERENCES

Animashree Anandkumar, Rong Ge, Daniel J Hsu, Sham M Kakade, and Matus Telgarsky. 2014. Tensor Decompositions for Learning Latent Variable Models. *Journal of Machine Learning Research* 15, 1 (2014), 2773–2832.

Yang Cai, Constantinos Daskalakis, and Christos Papadimitriou. 2015. Optimum Statistical Estimation with Strategic Data Sources. In *Proceedings of The 28th Conference on Learning Theory*. 280–296.

Anirban Dasgupta and Arpita Ghosh. 2013. Crowdsourced Judgement Elicitation with Endogenous Proficiency. In *Proceedings of the 22nd international conference on World Wide Web*. ACM, 319–330.

Alexander Philip Dawid and Allan M Skene. 1979a. Maximum Likelihood Estimation of Observer Error-Rates Using the EM Algorithm. *Applied statistics* (1979), 20–28.

Philip A Dawid and Allan M Skene. 1979b. Maximum Likelihood Estimation of Observer Error-Rates Using the EM Algorithm. *Applied statistics* 28 (1979), 20–28.

Jennifer DeBoer, Glenda S Stump, Daniel Seaton, and Lori Breslow. 2013. Diversity in MOOC Students' Backgrounds and Behaviors in Relationship to Performance in 6.002 x. In *Proceedings of the Sixth Learning International Networks Consortium Conference*, Vol. 4.

Rafael Frongillo and Jens Witkowski. 2017. A Geometric Perspective on Minimal Peer Prediction. *ACM Transactions on Economics and Computation (TEAC)* (2017).

Alice Gao, James R Wright, and Kevin Leyton-Brown. 2016. Incentivizing Evaluation via Limited Access to Ground Truth: Peer-Prediction Makes Things Worse. *EC 2016 Workshop on Algorithmic Game Theory and Data Science* (2016).

Radu Jurca, Boi Faltings, et al. 2009. Mechanisms for Making Crowds Truthful. *Journal of Artificial Intelligence Research* 34, 1 (2009), 209.

Vijay Kamble, David Marn, Nihar Shah, Abhay Parekh, and Kannan Ramachandran. 2015. Truth Serums for Massively Crowdsourced Evaluation Tasks. *The 5th Workshop on Social Computing and User-Generated Content* (2015).

David R. Karger, Sewoong Oh, and Devavrat Shah. 2011. Budget-Optimal Task Allocation for Reliable Crowdsourcing Systems. *CoRR* abs/1110.3564 (2011). http://arxiv.org/abs/1110.3564

David R. Karger, Sewoong Oh, and Devavrat Shah. 2014. Budget-Optimal Task Allocation for Reliable Crowdsourcing Systems. *Operations Research* 62, 1 (2014), 1–24. https://doi.org/10.1287/opre.2013.1235

Ashish Khetan and Sewoong Oh. 2016. Achieving budget-optimality with adaptive schemes in crowdsourcing. In *Annual Conference on Neural Information Processing Systems*. 4844–4852.

Aditya Khosla, Nityananda Jayadevaprakash, Bangpeng Yao, and Li Fei-Fei. 2011. Novel Dataset for Fine-Grained Image Categorization. In *First CVPR Workshop on Fine-Grained Visual Categorization*.

Yuqing Kong, Katrina Ligett, and Grant Schoenebeck. 2016. Putting Peer Prediction Under the Micro (economic) scope and Making Truth-telling Focal. In *International Conference on Web and Internet Economics*. Springer, 251–264.

Yuqing Kong and Grant Schoenebeck. 2016. A Framework For Designing Information Elicitation Mechanism That Rewards Truth-telling. (2016). http://arxiv.org/abs/1605.01021

Chinmay Kulkarni, Koh Pang Wei, Huy Le, Daniel Chia, Kathryn Papadopoulos, Justin Cheng, Daphne Koller, and Scott R Klemmer. 2015. Peer and Self Assessment in Massive Online Classes. In *Design thinking research*. Springer, 131–168.

Yang Liu and Yiling Chen. 2016. Sequential Peer Prediction: Learning to Elicit Effort using Posted Prices. *arXiv preprint arXiv:1611.09219* (2016).

Debmalya Mandal, Matthew Leifer, David C Parkes, Galen Pickard, and Victor Shnayder. 2016. Peer Prediction with Heterogeneous Tasks. *NIPS 2016 Workshop on Crowdsourcing and Machine Learning* (2016).

Nolan Miller, Paul Resnick, and Richard Zeckhauser. 2005. Eliciting informative feedback: The peer-prediction method. *Management Science* 51 (2005), 1359–1373.

Barzan Mozafari, Purnamrita Sarkar, Michael J. Franklin, Michael I. Jordan, and Samuel Madden. 2012. Active Learning for Crowd-Sourced Databases. *CoRR* abs/1209.3686 (2012).

Barzan Mozafari, Purnamrita Sarkar, Michael J. Franklin, Michael I. Jordan, and Samuel Madden. 2014. Scaling Up Crowd-Sourcing to Very Large Datasets: A Case for Active Learning. *PVLDB* 8, 2 (2014), 125–136.

Jungseul Ok, Sewoong Oh, Jinwoo Shin, and Yung Yi. 2016. Optimality of Belief Propagation for Crowdsourced Classification. In *Proc. 33nd Int. Conf. on Machine Learning (ICML)*. 535–544.

Drazen Prelec. 2004. A Bayesian Truth Serum For Subjective Data. *Science* 306, 5695 (2004), 462.

Goran Radanovic and Boi Faltings. 2015a. Incentive Schemes for Participatory Sensing. In *Proc. Int. Conf. on Autonomous Agents and Multiagent Systems, AAMAS*. 1081–1089.

Goran Radanovic and Boi Faltings. 2015b. Incentive Schemes for Participatory Sensing. In *AAMAS 2015*.

Goran Radanovic and Boi Faltings. 2015c. Incentives for Subjective Evaluations with Private Beliefs. In *Proc. 29th AAAI Conf. on Art. Intell. (AAAI'15)*. 1014–1020.

Goran Radanovic, Boi Faltings, and Radu Jurca. 2016. Incentives for effort in crowdsourcing using the peer truth serum. *ACM Transactions on Intelligent Systems and Technology (TIST)* 7, 4 (2016), 48.

Aashish Sheshadri and Matthew Lease. 2013. SQUARE: A Benchmark for Research on Computing Crowd Consensus. In *Proc. 1st AAAI Conf. on Human Computation (HCOMP)*. 156–164.

Victor Shnayder, Arpit Agarwal, Rafael Frongillo, and David C Parkes. 2016. Informed Truthfulness in Multi-Task Peer Prediction. In *Proceedings of the 2016 ACM Conference on Economics and Computation*. ACM, 179–196.

Victor Shnayder, Rafael Frongillo, and David C. Parkes. 2016. Measuring Performance Of Peer Prediction Mechanisms Using Replicator Dynamics. In *Proc. 25th Int. Joint Conf. on Art. Intell. (IJCAI'16)*. 2611–2617.

Victor Shnayder and David C Parkes. 2016. Practical Peer Prediction for Peer Assessment. In *Fourth AAAI Conference on Human Computation and Crowdsourcing*.

Luis von Ahn and Laura Dabbish. 2004. Labeling Images with a Computer Game. In *Proc. SIGCHI Conf. on Human Factors in Computing Systems (CHI'04)*. 319–326.

Julia Wilkowski, Amit Deutsch, and Daniel M Russell. 2014. Student Skill and Goal Achievement in the Mapping with Google MOOC. In *Proceedings of the first ACM conference on Learning@ scale conference*. ACM, 3–10.

Jens Witkowski, Yoram Bachrach, Peter Key, and David Parkes. 2013. Dwelling on the negative: Incentivizing effort in peer prediction. In *First AAAI Conference on Human Computation and Crowdsourcing*.

Jens Witkowski and David C Parkes. 2013. Learning the Prior in Minimal Peer Prediction. In *Proceedings of the 3rd Workshop on Social Computing and User Generated Content at the ACM Conference on Electronic Commerce*. 14.

Muhammad Bilal Zafar, Krishna P Gummadi, and Cristian Danescu-Niculescu-Mizil. 2016. Message Impartiality in Social Media Discussions. In *ICWSM*. 466–475.

Yuchen Zhang, Xi Chen, Dengyong Zhou, and Michael I Jordan. 2016. Spectral Methods Meet EM: A Provably Optimal Algorithm for Crowdsourcing. *Journal of Machine Learning Research* 17, 102 (2016), 1–44.

Dengyong Zhou, Qiang Liu, John C. Platt, Christopher Meek, and Nihar B. Shah. 2015. Regularized Minimax Conditional Entropy for Crowdsourcing. *CoRR* abs/1503.07240 (2015). http://arxiv.org/abs/1503.07240

The Stochastic Matching Problem: Beating Half with a Non-Adaptive Algorithm

SEPEHR ASSADI, University of Pennsylvania
SANJEEV KHANNA, University of Pennsylvania
YANG LI, University of Pennsylvania

In the *stochastic matching* problem, we are given a general (not necessarily bipartite) graph $G(V, E)$, where each edge in E is *realized* with some constant probability $p > 0$ and the goal is to compute a *bounded-degree* (bounded by a function depending only on p) subgraph H of G such that the expected maximum matching size in H is close to the expected maximum matching size in G. The algorithms in this setting are considered *non-adaptive* as they have to choose the subgraph H without knowing any information about the set of realized edges in G. Originally motivated by an application to *kidney exchange*, the stochastic matching problem and its variants have received significant attention in recent years.

The state-of-the-art non-adaptive algorithms for stochastic matching achieve an approximation ratio of $\frac{1}{2} - \varepsilon$ for any $\varepsilon > 0$, naturally raising the question that if $1/2$ is the limit of what can be achieved with a non-adaptive algorithm. In this work, we resolve this question by presenting the first algorithm for stochastic matching with an approximation guarantee that is strictly better than $1/2$: the algorithm computes a subgraph H of G with the maximum degree $O\left(\frac{\log(1/p)}{p}\right)$ such that the ratio of expected size of a maximum matching in realizations of H and G is at least $1/2 + \delta_0$ for some absolute constant $\delta_0 > 0$. The degree bound on H achieved by our algorithm is essentially the best possible (up to an $O(\log(1/p))$ factor) for any *constant factor* approximation algorithm, since an $\Omega(\frac{1}{p})$ degree in H is necessary for a vertex to acquire at least one incident edge in a realization.

Our result makes progress towards answering an open problem of Blum *et al.* (EC 2015) regarding the possibility of achieving a $(1 - \varepsilon)$-approximation for the stochastic matching problem using non-adaptive algorithms. From the technical point of view, a key ingredient of our algorithm is a structural result showing that a graph whose expected maximum matching size is OPT always contains a b-matching of size (essentially) $b \cdot \text{OPT}$, for $b = \frac{1}{p}$.

CCS Concepts: • **Theory of computation → Design and analysis of algorithms**;

Additional Key Words and Phrases: stochastic matching, kidney exchange

1 INTRODUCTION

We study the problem of finding a maximum matching in presence of *uncertainty* in the input graph. Specifically, we consider the *stochastic* setting where for an input graph $G(V, E)$ and a parameter $p > 0$, each edge in E is realized *independently* w.p.[1] p. We call the graph obtained from this stochastic process (which should be viewed as a random variable) a *realization* of $G(V, E)$,

[1]Throughout, we use *w.p.*, *w.h.p*, and *prob.* to abbreviate "with probability", "with high probability", and "probability", respectively.

A full version of this paper is available as an online preprint at [7].

EC'17, June 26–30, 2017, Cambridge, Massachusetts, USA. ©2017 ACM. ISBN 978-1-4503-4527-9/17/06...$15.00
DOI: https://doi.org/10.1145/3033274.3085146

denoted by $G_p(V, E_p)$. The *stochastic matching* problem can now be defined as follows. Given a general (not necessarily bipartite) graph $G(V, E)$ and an edge realization probability $p > 0$, compute a subgraph H of G such that:

(i) The expected maximum matching size in a realization of H is close to the expected maximum matching size in a realization of G.
(ii) The degree of each vertex in H is bounded by some function that only depends on p, independent of the size of G.

In other words, the stochastic matching problem asks if every graph G contains a subgraph H of *bounded degree* (depending only on the realization probability p) such that the expected matching size in realizations of G and H are close.

Kidney exchange. A canonical and arguably the most important application of the stochastic matching problem appears in *kidney exchange*, where patients waiting for kidney transplant can *swap* their incompatible donors to each get a compatible donor. The goal is to identify a maximum set of patient-donor pairs to perform such a swap (i.e., finds a maximum matching). However, through medical records of patients and donors, one can only filter out the patient-donor pairs where donation is *impossible*, and more costly and time consuming tests must be performed before a transplant can be performed.

The stochastic setting captures the essence of the need of extra tests for kidney exchange: an algorithm selects a set of patient-donor pairs to perform the extra tests (i.e., computes a subgraph H), while making sure that there is a large matching among the pairs that pass the extra tests. The objective that the subgraph H has small degree captures the essence of minimizing the number of (costly and time consuming) tests that each patient needs to go through. The kidney exchange problem has been extensively studied in the literature, particularly under stochastic settings (see, e.g., [2–4, 8, 16–18, 25, 30]). We remark that the the stochastic matching problem captures the simplest form of the kidney exchange, referred to as *pairwise exchange*. Modern kidney exchange programs regularly employ swaps between three or patient-donor pairs and this setting has also been studied previously in the literature; we refer the interested reader to [10] for more details.

Previous work. Our results are directly related to the results in [10] and [6] which we describe in detail below. Blum *et al.* [10] introduced the (variant of) stochastic matching problem and proposed a $(\frac{1}{2} - \varepsilon)$-approximation algorithm (for any $\varepsilon > 0$) which requires the subgraph H to have maximum degree of $\frac{\log(1/\varepsilon)}{p^{\Theta(1/\varepsilon)}}$. The algorithm of Blum *et al.* [10] works as follows: Pick a maximum matching M_i in G and remove the edges in M_i; repeat for $R := \frac{\log(1/\varepsilon)}{p^{\Theta(1/\varepsilon)}}$ times. In order to analyze this algorithm, the authors showed that, for any $i \in [R]$, if the size of the maximum matching among the realized edges in $M_1, \ldots, M_i$ is less than $\text{OPT}/2$, the matching M_{i+1} contains many augmenting paths of M of length $O(\frac{1}{\varepsilon})$; since each such augmenting path is realized w.p. $p^{O(\frac{1}{\varepsilon})}$, one needs to repeat this augmentation process for $\frac{1}{p^{O(\frac{1}{\varepsilon})}}$ time (as is roughly the value of R) to increase the matching size to $(\frac{1}{2} - \varepsilon) \cdot \text{OPT}$.

In a recent work [6], we showed that in order to obtain a $(\frac{1}{2}-\varepsilon)$-approximation algorithm, one only needs a subgraph H with max-degree of $O(\frac{\log(1/\varepsilon p)}{\varepsilon p})$, significantly smaller than the bounds in [10]. Interestingly, the algorithm of [6] and the one in [10] are essentially identical (modulo an extra sparsification part required in [6]) and the main difference is in the analysis. In [6], we completely bypassed the need for using augmenting paths in the analysis and instead, took advantage of structural properties of matchings in a global manner (by using *Tutte-Berge formula*; see, e.g., [24]). In particular, we showed that repeatedly picking $O(\frac{\log(1/\varepsilon p)}{\varepsilon p})$ maximum matchings (as described before) suffices to ensure that, among the chosen edges, a matching of size (essentially) equal to the size of the last chosen matching would be realized (with high probability). Having this, one can show that running the aforementioned algorithm even for $R := O(\frac{\log(1/\varepsilon p)}{\varepsilon p})$ suffices to obtain a $(\frac{1}{2} - \varepsilon)$-approximation.

Adaptive algorithms for stochastic matching have also been studied by [6, 10]. In an adaptive algorithm, instead of a single graph H, one is allowed to pick a *small* number of bounded-degree graphs $H_1, \ldots, H_k$ where the choice of each H_i can be made after *probing* the edges in $H_1, H_2, \ldots, H_{i-1}$ to see if they are realized or not. A $(1-\varepsilon)$-approximation adaptive algorithm for this problem was first proposed in [10] and further refined in [6].

Beating the half approximation. This state-of-the-art highlights the following natural question:

> *Is half-approximation the limit for non-adaptive algorithms or is there a non-adaptive algorithm that achieves approximation guarantee of strictly better than half?*

It is worth mentioning that in many variations, obtaining half approximation for the maximum matching problem is typically a relatively easy task (usually via a greedy approach), while beating half approximation turns out to be difficult. Some notable examples include, randomized greedy matching [5, 13, 19, 28], online stochastic matching [22, 26, 27], and semi-streaming matching [20, 23].

1.1 Our Contributions

We resolve the aforementioned question of obtaining an algorithm for stochastic matching with an approximation guarantee of *strictly* better than half. Formally,

Theorem 1.1. *There exists an algorithm that given any graph $G(V,E)$ and any parameter $p > 0$, computes a subgraph $H(V,Q)$ of G with a maximum degree of $O\left(\frac{\log(1/p)}{p}\right)$ such that the ratio of the expected maximum matching size of a realization of H to a realization of G is at least:*

(i) 0.52 *when* $p \leq p_0$ *for an* absolute *constant* $p_0 > 0$.
(ii) $0.5 + \delta_0$ *for any* $0 < p < 1$, *where* $\delta_0 > 0$ *is an* absolute *constant.*

Our result in Theorem 1.1 makes progress towards an open problem posed by Blum *et al.* [10] regarding the possibility of having a non-adaptive $(1-\varepsilon)$-approximation algorithm for stochastic matching. We further remark that the assumption in Part (i) of Theorem 1.1 is standard in the stochastic matching literature and is referred as the case of *vanishing probabilities*, see, e.g. [26, 27].

It is worth mentioning the max-degree on H achieved in Theorem 1.1 is essentially the best possible (up to an $O(\log\frac{1}{p})$ factor) for any *constant factor* approximation algorithm: suppose G is a complete graph; in this case the expected matching size in G is $n - o(n)$ by standard results on random graphs (see, e.g., [12], Chapter 7); however, if max-degree of H is $o(\frac{1}{p})$, then the expected number of realized edges in H is $o(n)$, implying that the expected matching size in H is $o(n)$.

Our approach to proving Theorem 1.1 can be divided into two parts. In the first part, we prove a structural result showing that if a realization of G has expected maximum matching size OPT, then G itself should contain essentially $\frac{1}{p}$ edge-disjoint matchings of size OPT each. This result, established through a characterization of b-matching size in general graphs (see Section 3), sheds more light into the structure of a graph in terms of its expected maximum matching size, which may be of independent interest.

In the second part, we combine the aforementioned structural result with the $(\frac{1}{2}-\varepsilon)$-approximation algorithm of [6] to obtain a matching of size strictly larger than OPT/2. In order to do this, we first find a collection of $\frac{1}{p}$ edge-disjoint matchings of size at least OPT, remove them from the graph, and then run the algorithm of [6] on the remaining edges. We show that the edges in this collection of edge-disjoint matchings must form many *length-three augmenting paths* of the matching computed by the algorithm of [6], hence leading to a matching of size strictly larger than OPT/2. The analysis is separated into two steps: we first formulate the increment in the matching size (through these augmenting paths) via a (non-linear) minimization program, and then analyze the optimal solution of this minimization program and hence lower bound the increment in the matching size obtained from the augmenting paths.

Other related work. Multiple variants of stochastic matching have been considered in the literature. Blum *et al.* [11] studied a similar setting where one can only probe *two* edges incident on any vertex and the goal is to find the optimal set of edges to query. Another well studied setting is the *query-commit* model, whereby an algorithm probes one edge at a time and if an edge e is probed and realized, then the algorithm must take e as part of the matching it outputs [1, 9, 14, 15, 21]. We refer the reader to [10] for a detailed description of the related work.

2 TECHNICAL OVERVIEW

In this section, we give a more detailed overview of the main ideas used in our algorithm for stochastic matching. For clarity of exposition, throughout this section, we assume p is a sufficiently small constant (corresponding to Part (i) of Theorem 1.1) and the expected maximum matching size in G (i.e., OPT) is $n - o(n)$, or in other words, a realization of G, G_p, has a near perfect matching in expectation.

Our starting point is the following observation: In order for G_p to have a (near) perfect matching in expectation, the input graph G must have many (roughly $1/p$) edge-disjoint (near) perfect matchings. To gain some intuition why this is true, suppose for the moment that the input graph is a bipartite graph $G(L, R, E)$. Then, by *Hall's Marriage Theorem*, we know that in order for G_p to have a matching of size $n - o(n)$, for any two subsets $X \subseteq L$ and $Y \subseteq R$, with $|X| - |Y| \geq o(n)$, at least one edge from X to $\bar{Y}$ should realize in G_p. However, this requirement implies that in G, there should be $1/p$ edges from X to $\bar{Y}$ so that at least one of these edges appears in G_p. One can then show that a bipartite graph G with such a structure has $1/p$ edge-disjoint matchings of size at least $n - o(n)$.

In general, we need to handle graphs that are not necessarily bipartite. In order to adapt the previous strategy, we slightly relax our requirement of having $1/p$ edge-disjoint matchings to having one (simple) b-matching[2] of size nb for the parameter $b = \frac{1}{p}$. We show that,

> **b-Matching Lemma.** Any graph G where G_p has a matching of size $n - o(n)$ in expectation, has a $\frac{1}{p}$-matching of size (essentially) $\frac{n}{p}$.

Next, we combine the fact that a large $\frac{1}{p}$-matching, denoted by B, always exists in G, with the $(\frac{1}{2} - \varepsilon)$-approximation algorithm of [6] to obtain a strictly better than $\frac{1}{2}$-approximation algorithm.

To continue, we briefly describe the algorithm of [6], which we refer to as MatchingCover. MatchingCover works by picking a maximum matching M_i in G and removing the edges of M_i for $R := \Theta\left(\frac{\log(1/p)}{p}\right)$ times[3]. This collection of matchings, denoted by E_{MC}, is referred to as a *matching cover* of the original graph G. The main property of this matching cover, proved in [6], is that the set of realized edges in E_{MC} has a matching of size (essentially) $|M_R|$; note that M_R is the smallest size matchings among the matchings in E_{MC}.

We are now ready to define our main algorithm: Pick a maximum $\frac{1}{p}$-matching B from G; run MatchingCover over the edges $E \setminus B$ and obtain a matching cover E_{MC}; return $H(V, B \cup E_{MC})$. If $|M_R| < (\frac{1}{2} - \delta_0)n$, using the fact that E_{MC} is obtained by repeatedly picking maximum matchings,

[2] Recall that a (simple) b-matching is simply a graph with degree of each vertex bounded by b. See Section 3 for more details.
[3] We remark that this algorithm has an extra *sparsification* step which is needed to handle the case where OPT $= o(n)$. However, since in this section we assume OPT $= n - o(n)$, this extra step is not required.

one can show that any matching M of size $n - o(n)$ in G has more than $(\frac{1}{2} + \delta_0)n - o(n)$ edges in $B \cup E_{MC}$. This also implies that the expected matching size in H is at least $(\frac{1}{2} + \delta_0)n - o(n)$. The more difficult case, which is where we concentrate bulk of our technical effort, is when $|M_R| \geq (\frac{1}{2} - \delta_0)n$. For simplicity, assume $|M_R| = n/2$ from here on.

As stated above, if $|M_R| = n/2$, then in almost every realization of the edges in E_{MC}, there exists a matching M of size at least $n/2$. Our strategy is to *augment* the matching M using the (realized) edges in B, so that the matching size becomes $(\frac{1}{2} + \delta_0)n$. It is important to note that the set of edges in E_{MC} and B are disjoint, and hence whether edges in E_{MC} and B are realized are independent of each other.

Let U be the set of vertices matched by M. There are two cases here to consider:

- **Case 1.** Nearly all edges in B are incident on vertices in U.
- **Case 2.** An ε-fraction of edges in B are not incident on U (for some constant $\varepsilon > 0$).

The second case is relatively easy to handle: we show that a realization of a $\frac{1}{p}$-matching with N/p edges has a matching of size at least $N/3$ in expectation. This implies that B_p has a matching M' of size $\varepsilon \cdot \frac{n}{3} = \Theta(\varepsilon) \cdot n$ which is not incident on U. Consequently, $B \cup E_{MC}$ has a matching of size $\frac{n}{2} + \Theta(\varepsilon) \cdot n$ in expectation. The more challenging task is to tackle the first case. To convey the main idea, we make a series of simplifying assumptions here: (*i*) all edges in B are incident on U, (*ii*) each edge in B is incident on exactly one vertex in U, and (*iii*) every vertex in U is incident on exactly $\frac{1}{p}$ edges of B.

Our goal is to identify a large collection of length-three augmenting paths for the matching M using the edges of B. To achieve this, we consider the event that an edge (u, v) in M has a length-three augmenting path $a - u - v - b$ where u (resp. v) is the only neighbor of a (resp. b). We say such an edge (u, v) is *successful*. Since the length-three augmenting that certifies successful edges are vertex-disjoint by definition, they can all (simultaneously) augment M. Consequently, it suffices to lower bound the expected number of successful edges, or, equivalently, to lower bound the prob. that each edge is successful.

Let us further assume for the moment that G is a bipartite graph. In this case, u and v do not share a common neighbor and we can consider the neighborhood of u and v separately. The prob. that u has a neighbor w where u is the only neighbor of w (we say u is successful in this case) is not difficult to bound: enumerate all $1/p$ neighbors w of u and account for the the prob. that the edge (u, w) is realized and the prob. that no other edge incident on w is realized. A similar argument can be made for v. Now, the prob. that (u, v) is successful is simply the product of the prob. that u is successful and the prob. that v is successful.

However, in general (non-bipartite) graphs, u and v might have common neighbors which results in prob. of u being successful *not independent* of prob. of v being successful. Handling this case requires a more careful argument and analysis. Moreover, recall that in the above discussion, we made rather strong simplifying assumptions about how the edges in B are distributed across the vertices of U. In order to further remove these assumptions, in the actual analysis, we cast the probability of each edge (u, v) being successful as a function of the degrees of the vertices u and v, and formulate a (non-linear) minimization program to capture the minimum number of possible successful edges. Finally, we analyze the optimal solution of this minimization program, which allows us to achieve the target lower bound on the expected increment in the matching size.

3 PRELIMINARIES

Notation. For a graph $G(V, E)$, n denotes the number of vertices in G. For any $U \subseteq V$, we use $G[U]$ to denote the subgraph of G induced only on vertices in U, and use $E[U]$ to denote the set of edges in $G[U]$, i.e., the set of edges with both end points in U. For any two subsets U, W of V, we further use $E[U, W]$ to denote the set of edges with one end point in U and another in W. For any $X \subseteq E$, we use $V(X)$ to denote the set of vertices incident on X. Finally, we use $\mu(E)$ to denote the maximum matching size among a set of edge E.

When sampling from a set of edges X (resp. a graph H) where each edge in X (resp. H) is sampled w.p. p, we use X_p (resp. H_p) to denote the random variable for the set of sampled edges. We use $\textsc{opt}(G)$ (or shortly $\textsc{opt}$ if the graph G is clear from the context) to denote the *expected* maximum matching size of a realization of G (i.e., $G_p(V, E_p)$)[4]. For any algorithm for the stochastic matching problem, we use $\textsc{alg}$ to denote the expected matching size in a realization of H, where H is the subgraph computed by the algorithm.

b-matchings. For any graph $G(V, E)$ and any integer $b \geq 1$, a subset $M \subseteq E$ is called a *simple b-matching*, iff the number of edges M that are incident on each vertex is at most b. Throughout, we drop the word 'simple', and refer to M as a b-matching.

We use the following characterization of the maximum b-matching size in general graphs (see [29], Volume A, Chapter 33).

THEOREM 3.1. *Let $G(V, E)$ be a graph and $b \geq 1$ be any integer. The maximum size of a b-matching is equal to the minimum value of*

$$b \cdot |U| + |E[W]| + \sum_K \left\lfloor \frac{1}{2}\Big(b \cdot |K| + |E[K, W]|\Big) \right\rfloor$$

taken over all disjoint subsets U, W of V, where K ranges over all connected components in the graph $G[V - U - W]$.

Useful inequalities. We also use the following simple inequalities (see [7] for the proofs).

PROPOSITION 3.2. *Let $f(x) := \frac{1-e^{-x}}{x}$. Then, for any c, and any $x \in [0, c]$, $e^{-x} \leq 1 - f(c) \cdot x$.*

PROPOSITION 3.3. *For any $x \in (0, 0.43]$, $(1-x)^{\frac{1}{x}} \geq \frac{1-x}{e}$.*

3.1 MatchingCover Algorithm

We use the $(0.5 - \varepsilon)$-approximation algorithm of [6] (Algorithm 3) as a sub-routine. For simplicity, throughout the paper, we refer to this algorithm as MatchingCover. In the following lemma, we summarize the properties of MatchingCover that we use in this paper. The proof of this lemma immediately follows from Lemma 3.9 and Lemma 5.2 in [6].

LEMMA 3.4 ([6]). *For any graph $G(V, E)$, and any input parameter $\varepsilon > 0$, MatchingCover(G, ε) outputs a collection of R matchings $M_1, M_2, \ldots, M_R$ (denote $E_{MC} = M_1 \cup M_2 \cup \ldots \cup M_R$), such that, w.p. $1 - o(1)$:*

1. *The size of a maximum matching among realized edges in E_{MC} is at least $(1-\varepsilon)\,|M_R|$.*
2. *$|M_1| \geq \ldots \geq |M_R| \geq (1-\varepsilon) \cdot \mu(E \setminus E_{MC})$.*
3. *$R = \Theta(\frac{\log 1/(\varepsilon p)}{\varepsilon p})$.*

We can also prove the following simple claim based on the second property of the MatchingCover in Lemma 3.4. Roughly speaking, this claim states that if the MatchingCover is not able to extract any further large matching (of size essentially $\textsc{opt}/2$) from G, then the set of extracted edges already provides a matching of size $\textsc{opt}/2$ in any realization. We defer the proof of this claim to the full version of the paper [7]; we also note that a similar result is proven in [6] (see Lemma 5.3).

[4] We assume $\textsc{opt} = \omega(1)$ to obtain the desired concentration bounds (for example in Lemma 3.4).

Claim 3.5. *Fix $0 < \varepsilon < \delta < 1$. Let $G(V, E)$ be a graph, X be any arbitrary subset of E, and $(M_1, \ldots, M_R) = MatchingCover(G(V, E \setminus X), \varepsilon)$. Define $E_{MC} = M_1 \cup \ldots \cup M_R$. If $|M_R| \leq \left(\frac{1}{2} - \delta\right)$ OPT, then the expected maximum matching size in a realization of $G(V, X \cup E_{MC})$ is at least $\left(\frac{1}{2} + \delta - \varepsilon\right)$ OPT.*

4 *B*-MATCHING LEMMA

Here, we develop one of the main ingredients of our algorithm, namely, any input graph G contains a b-matching of size almost $b \cdot \text{OPT}(G)$ for $b = 1/p$. Intuitively, if the expected matching size in G is OPT, then since only p fraction of edges are realized in expectation, one may hope to find up to $1/p$ edge-disjoint matchings of size OPT in G. The following lemma formalizes this intuition by using b-matchings (for $b = 1/p$) instead of a collection of edge-disjoint matchings.

Lemma 4.1 (b-matching lemma). *Let $b = \left\lfloor \frac{1}{p} \right\rfloor$; any graph $G(V, E)$ has a b-matching of size at least $(b-1) \cdot \text{OPT}(G)$.*

Proof. Suppose by contradiction that the maximum b-matching B in G is of size less than $(b-1) \cdot \text{OPT}$. Consequently, by Theorem 3.1, there exist disjoint subsets U, W of V such that,

$$b \cdot |U| + |E[W]| + \sum_K \left\lfloor \frac{1}{2}\left(b \cdot |K| + |E[K, W]|\right) \right\rfloor < (b-1) \cdot \text{OPT} \tag{1}$$

where K ranges over all connected components in the graph $G[V - U - W]$. Let c be the number of connected components in $G[V - U - W]$. We first note that $c < 2\text{OPT}$; otherwise,

$$\sum_K \left\lfloor \frac{1}{2}\left(b \cdot |K| + |E[K, W]|\right) \right\rfloor \geq \sum_K \left\lfloor \frac{b}{2} \right\rfloor \geq c \cdot \left(\frac{b-1}{2}\right) \geq (b-1) \cdot \text{OPT}$$

and hence the LHS in Eq (1) would be more than $(b-1) \cdot \text{OPT}$, i.e., the RHS; a contradiction.

Additionally, we have $|U| + |W| + \sum_K |K| = n$. Hence, by multiplying each side in Eq (1) by 2 and plugging in this bound, we have,

$$\begin{aligned} 2b \cdot \text{OPT} - 2\text{OPT} &> nb - b\,|W| + b\,|U| + 2\,|E[W]| + \sum_K \left(|E[K, W]| - 1\right) \\ &\geq nb - b\,|W| + b\,|U| + 2\,|E[W]| + \sum_K |E[K, W]| - 2\text{OPT} \end{aligned}$$

Let $T := V \setminus (U \cup W)$, i.e., the set of vertices in connected components K. Using this notation, we can write the above equation simply as,

$$b \cdot |W| - b \cdot |U| - 2\,|E[W]| - |E[T, W]| > b \cdot (n - 2\text{OPT}) \tag{2}$$

Now consider the partition T, U, W in a *realized* graph $G(V, E_p)$. Let $E_p[W]$ and $E_p[T, W]$ denote, respectively, the set of edges in $E[W]$ and $E[T, W]$ after sampling the edges w.p. p. For any matching M in G_p, define $x(M)$ to be the number of *unmatched* vertices (by M) in W. Finally, define $x^\star := \min_M x(M)$, where the minimum is taken over all matchings in G_p. Clearly, $x^\star$ is a random variable depending on the choice of edges in G_p. We have the following simple claim.

Claim 4.2. *For any realization G_p, $x^\star \geq |W| - |U| - 2\left|E_p[W]\right| - \left|E_p[T, W]\right|$.*

Proof. Consider the set of vertices in W. At most $|U|$ vertices of W can be matched to vertices in U. Additionally, any edge in $E_p[W]$ can further reduce the number of unmatched vertices in W by at most 2. Finally, any edge in $E_p[T, W]$ can reduce the number of remaining unmatched vertices in W by at most 1. □

Using the fact that $\mathbb{E}[x^\star] \leq n - 2\text{OPT}$, we have,

$$\begin{aligned} b \cdot (n - 2\text{OPT}) &\geq b \cdot \mathbb{E}[x^\star] \\ &\geq b \cdot |W| - b \cdot |U| - b \cdot \mathbb{E}\Big[2\left|E_p[W]\right| + \left|E_p[T, W]\right|\Big] && \text{(by Claim 4.2)} \\ &= b \cdot |W| - b \cdot |U| - pb \cdot (2\,|E[W]| + |E[T, W]|) \\ &\geq b \cdot |W| - b \cdot |U| - 2\,|E[W]| - |E[T, W]| && \text{(since } pb = p\left\lfloor \tfrac{1}{p} \right\rfloor \leq 1) \\ &> b \cdot (n - 2\text{OPT}) && \text{(by Eq (2))} \end{aligned}$$

a contradiction. □

We can further show that the bound established in Lemma 4.1 is essentially tight (see the full version of the paper [7]).

Claim 4.3. *For any constant $0 < p < 1$, there exist bipartite graphs G where G_p has a matching of size $n - o(n)$ in expectation, but for any $b \geq \frac{2}{p}$, there is no b-matching in G with (at least) $b \cdot 0.99n$ edges; here n is the number of vertices on each side of G.*

Finally, we establish the following auxiliary lemma. The proof is deferred to the full version [7].

Lemma 4.4. *Let B be a $\left\lfloor \frac{1}{p} \right\rfloor$-matching with $\left(\left\lfloor \frac{1}{p} \right\rfloor \cdot N\right)$ edges; then, $\mathbb{E}\left[\mu(B_p)\right] \geq (1 - 3p) \cdot \frac{N}{3}$.*

5 MAIN ALGORITHM AND ANALYSIS

We provide our main algorithm for the stochastic matching problem (when p is sufficiently small) in this section and prove Part (i) of Theorem 1.1. We assume throughout this section that the edge realization probability $p \leq p_0$ for some sufficiently small constant p_0. In this case, $\left\lfloor \frac{1}{p} \right\rfloor - 1 \geq (1 - O(p_0)) \cdot \frac{1}{p}$ and we use this inequality frequently in the proof. Indeed, throughout this section, one should view p_0 as a negligible constant and hence the term $(1 - O(p_0))$ can essentially be ignored.

Let $\delta_0 = 0.02$, and $\varepsilon_0 = 0.02001$. Our algorithm is stated as Algorithm 1 below:

ALGORITHM 1: A 0.52-Approximation Algorithm for Stochastic Matching

---

Input: A graph $G(V, E)$ and an edge realization probability $p \leq p_0$.
Output: A subgraph $H(V, Q)$ of $G(V, E)$.

(1) Let B be a maximum $\left\lfloor \frac{1}{p} \right\rfloor$-matching in G.
(2) Let $(M_1, M_2, \ldots, M_R) :=$ MatchingCover$(G(V, E \setminus B), \varepsilon_1)$
for $\varepsilon_1 = (\varepsilon_0 - \delta_0)/2$, and $E_{MC} = M_1 \cup \ldots \cup M_R$.
(3) Return $H(V, Q)$ where $Q := B \cup E_{MC}$.

Each vertex in H has degree $O\left(\frac{\log(1/p)}{p}\right)$ – this follows immediately from Lemma 3.4. In what follows, we prove that H has a matching of size at least $(0.5 + \delta_0) \cdot \text{OPT} = 0.52 \cdot \text{OPT}$ in expectation, which will complete the proof of Part (i) of Theorem 1.1.

First notice that if $|M_R| < (\frac{1}{2} - \frac{\varepsilon_0 + \delta_0}{2})\text{OPT}$ where M_R is the smallest matching in the matching cover E_{MC} found by Algorithm 1, then by Claim 3.5, the expected matching size in Q is at least $(\frac{1}{2} + \frac{\varepsilon_0 + \delta_0}{2} - \frac{\varepsilon_0 - \delta_0}{2})\text{OPT} = (\frac{1}{2} + \delta_0) \cdot \text{OPT}$. Therefore, from now on we focus on the case that $|M_R| \geq (\frac{1}{2} - \frac{\varepsilon_0 + \delta_0}{2})\text{OPT}$.

In this case, by Lemma 3.4, w.p. $1 - o(1)$, there exists a matching M among the realized edges in E_{MC} with size at least

$$\left(1 - \frac{\varepsilon_0 - \delta_0}{2}\right)\left(\frac{1}{2} - \frac{\varepsilon_0 + \delta_0}{2}\right)\text{OPT} \geq \left(\frac{1}{2} - \frac{\varepsilon_0 + \delta_0}{2} - \frac{\varepsilon_0 - \delta_0}{4}\right)\text{OPT}$$
$$= \left(\frac{1}{2} - \frac{3\varepsilon_0}{4} - \frac{\delta_0}{4}\right)\text{OPT} \geq \left(\frac{1}{2} - \varepsilon_0\right)\text{OPT}$$

In the following, we assume this event happens[5] and prove that the set of edges realized in the $\lfloor \frac{1}{p} \rfloor$-matching B can be used to augment the matching M to create a matching of size $(\frac{1}{2} + \delta_0) \cdot \text{OPT}$ in expectation. To simplify the analysis, we assume w.l.o.g. that $|M| = (\frac{1}{2} - \varepsilon_0)\text{OPT}$ (i.e., we only keep $(\frac{1}{2} - \varepsilon_0)\text{OPT}$ edges of M and remove any additional edges if there is any). By the b-matching lemma (Lemma 4.1), $|B| \geq \left(\lfloor \frac{1}{p} \rfloor - 1\right)\text{OPT} \geq (1 - O(p_0)) \cdot \frac{\text{OPT}}{p}$, and hence, to prove Part (1) of Theorem 1.1, it suffices to prove the following statement.

Lemma 5.1. *Let M be a matching of size $\left(\frac{1}{2} - \varepsilon_0\right)\text{OPT}$, and B be a $\lfloor \frac{1}{p} \rfloor$-matching of size at least $(1 - O(p_0)) \cdot \frac{\text{OPT}}{p}$; then the expected maximum matching size in $M \cup B_{\overline{M}}$ is at least $(\frac{1}{2} + \delta_0)\text{OPT}$.*

Proof. Let B_M be the set of edges in B that are incident on the vertices in the matching M, and let $B_{\overline{M}} = B \setminus B_M$. Let $s_{\overline{M}}$ be the random variable denoting the maximum matching size of a realization of $B_{\overline{M}}$. By Lemma 4.4,

$$\mathbb{E}[s_{\overline{M}}] \geq \frac{\left|B_{\overline{M}}\right|}{\lfloor \frac{1}{p} \rfloor} \cdot \frac{1-3p}{3} \geq p\left|B_{\overline{M}}\right| \cdot \frac{1-3p}{3} \tag{3}$$

Therefore, if $\left|B_{\overline{M}}\right| \geq 6\varepsilon_0 \cdot \frac{\text{OPT}}{p}$, then

$$\mathbb{E}[s_{\overline{M}}] \geq 6\varepsilon_0 \cdot \text{OPT} \cdot \frac{1-3p}{3} = 2\varepsilon_0(1-3p) \cdot \text{OPT} \geq (\varepsilon_0 + \delta_0) \cdot \text{OPT} \qquad (\text{assuming } p_0 \leq \tfrac{\varepsilon_0 - \delta_0}{6\varepsilon_0})$$

and since no edge in $B_{\overline{M}}$ is incident on the vertices in M, the expected matching size in $M \cup B_p$ is at least

$$\left(\frac{1}{2} - \varepsilon_0\right)\text{OPT} + (\varepsilon_0 + \delta_0)\text{OPT} = \left(\frac{1}{2} + \delta_0\right)\text{OPT}$$

as asserted by Lemma 5.1. In the following, we assume $\left|B_{\overline{M}}\right| \leq 6\varepsilon_0 \cdot \frac{\text{OPT}}{p}$. Furthermore, we fix a realization of $B_{\overline{M}}$ and fix a maximum matching M' in the realization of $B_{\overline{M}}$ (whose size is $s_{\overline{M}}$ by definition). In other words, we will lower bound the expected maximum matching size in $M \cup B_p$ conditioned on *any* realization of $B_{\overline{M}}$. The lower bound we obtain would be a linear function of $s_{\overline{M}}$, and by linearity of expectation, we can simply replace $s_{\overline{M}}$ with $\mathbb{E}[s_{\overline{M}}]$, use Eq (3) to lower bound $\mathbb{E}[s_{\overline{M}}]$, and obtain the desired lower bound of $(1/2+\delta_0)\text{OPT}$ on the expected maximum matching size.

Denote by M^+ the matching $M \cup M'$ (since the matchings M and M' are vertex-disjoint, $M \cup M'$ is indeed a valid matching of size $|M| + s_{\overline{M}}$). We can focus the realizations of $B_{\overline{M}}$ where $s_{\overline{M}} \leq 2\varepsilon_0 \cdot \text{OPT}$ since otherwise the matching M^+ already have size $(1/2 + \varepsilon_0) \cdot \text{OPT} > (1/2 + \delta_0) \cdot \text{OPT}$. Therefore, we have $s_{\overline{M}} \leq 2\varepsilon_0 \cdot \text{OPT} = O(\text{OPT})$ and $|M^+| = O(\text{OPT})$, which will be useful in simplifying the presentation.

Now consider the edges in B_M. We further denote by C the set of edges in B_M that are incident on *exactly* one vertex in M^+. In the following, we first show that $|C|$ must be large (Claim 5.2) and then show that many edges in C can be used to augment the matching M^+, which leads to an

[5]This assumption can be removed while losing a negligible factor of $o(1)$ in the size of final matching.

increment on the matching size as a function of $|C|$ (Lemma 5.3 and Lemma 5.4). Combining these two statements completes the proof of Lemma 5.1.

CLAIM 5.2. $|C| \geq 2|B_M| - \frac{2|M^+|}{p}$.

PROOF. Let x denote the number of edges in B_M that have degree 2 to $V(M^+)$ (i.e., are incident on two vertices in M^+). By definition, every edge in B_M is incident on M, and hence every edge in B_M is also incident on $M^+ (= M \cup M')$. Consequently, there are $|B_M| - x$ edges in B_M that have degree 1 to $V(M^+)$ (i.e. belongs to C). Therefore, the total degrees of all vertices $V(M^+)$ provided by B_M is at least: $2 \cdot x + 1 \cdot (|B_M| - x) = x + |B_M|$.

On the other hand, since $|V(M^+)| = 2|M^+|$ and B (hence B_M) is a $\left\lfloor \frac{1}{p} \right\rfloor$-matching, the total degree of the vertices $V(M^+)$ provided by B_M is at most $\frac{2|M^+|}{p}$. Therefore, $x + |B_M| \leq \frac{2|M^+|}{p}$, which implies $x \leq \frac{2|M^+|}{p} - |B_M|$. Therefore, the number of edges in B_M incident on exactly one vertex in $V(M^+)$ (i.e., $|C|$) is at least

$$|B_M| - \left(\frac{2|M^+|}{p} - |B_M|\right) = 2|B_M| - \frac{2|M^+|}{p}$$

completing the proof. □

The following two lemmas are dedicated to showing that the edges in a realization of C, C_p, form many vertex-disjoint length-three augmenting paths for the matching M^+ in expectation, which is a lower bound on the expected increment on the matching size. We first define some notation. Let $W := V \setminus V(M^+)$, i.e., W is the set of vertices *not* matched by M^+. Denote the edges in M^+ by $\{(u_i, v_i) \mid i \in [|M^+|]\}$, and denote by $d(u_i)$ (resp. $d(v_i)$) the number of edges in C incident on u_i (resp. v_i). Since, by definition, the edges in C are only incident on one vertex in $V(M^+)$, $d(u_i)$ (resp. $d(v_i)$) is also the number of edges in C between u_i (resp. v_i) and W. In the following, whenever we say "neighbors" or "degrees", they are only w.r.t. the edges C. Let $f(x)$ be the function defined in Proposition 3.2.

LEMMA 5.3. *For any edge $(u_i, v_i) \in M$, w.p. at least*

$$(1 - O(p_0))\frac{f(1/e) \cdot p}{e^2}\left(1 - e^{-p \cdot d(v_i)}\right) \cdot \max\{d(u_i) - 1, 0\},$$

there exists a length-three augmenting path $a_i - u_i - v_i - b_i$ in the realization C_p of C, such that a_i, b_i have no neighbors other than u_i and v_i.

Note that we can use all edges (u_i, v_i) in M^+ with such an augmenting path $a_i - u_i - v_i - b_i$ to (simultaneously) augment M^+ since these augmenting paths are vertex-disjoint (a_i and b_i are only neighbors of u_i and v_i). Therefore, the expected number of edges in M^+ that has such an augmenting path is a lower bound on the expected increment on the matching size.

PROOF OF LEMMA 5.3. We consider three disjoint subsets of edges in C one by one: (i) the edges between v_i and W, (ii) the edges incident on a specific vertex w in W (excluding the edge (v_i, w)), and (iii) the edges incident on neighbors of u_i other than w (excluding the edges incident on v_i).

First, consider the edges between v_i and W. The prob. that none of these $d(v_i)$ edges are realized is at most

$$(1 - p)^{d(v_i)} \leq e^{-p \cdot d(v_i)}$$

Therefore, w.p. at least $1 - e^{-p \cdot d(v_i)}$, at least one edge between v_i and W is realized. We condition on this event and fix any such edge, denoted by (v_i, b_i).

Second, consider the edges incident on b_i (excluding the edge (v_i, b_i)). There are at most $1/p$ such edges, and the prob. that none of them is realized is at least

$$(1-p)^{1/p} \geq \frac{1-p}{e} \geq \frac{1-p_0}{e} \qquad (p \leq p_0 \leq 0.43)$$

where the first inequality is by Proposition 3.3. In the following, we further condition on no other edges incident on w is realized.

Third, consider all neighbors of u_i other than b_i (there are at least $\max\{d(u_i)-1, 0\}$ such neighbors) and the edges incident on these neighbors (excluding the edges incident on v_i). For each one of these neighbors w of u_i, the prob. that the edge (u_i, w) is realized (w.p. p) and w does not have any neighbor other than u_i (and possibly v_i) (w.p. at least $\frac{1-p_0}{e}$ by Proposition 3.3) is at least $p \cdot \frac{1-p_0}{e}$. Therefore, the prob. that at least one neighbor of u_i satisfies these two properties is at least

$$\begin{aligned} 1-\left(1-p\cdot\frac{1-p_0}{e}\right)^{\max\{d(u_i)-1,0\}} &\geq 1-e^{-(1-p_0)\cdot p\cdot\max\{d(u_i)-1,0\}/e} \\ &\geq f(\frac{1}{e})\cdot(1-p_0)\cdot p\cdot\max\{d(u_i)-1,0\}/e \end{aligned}$$

where $f(x) = \frac{1-e^{-x}}{x}$ and the second inequality is by Proposition 3.2, using the fact that

$$\frac{(1-p_0)\cdot p\max\{d(u_i)-1,0\}}{e} \leq \frac{1}{e} \qquad (\text{since } d(u_i) \leq \tfrac{1}{p})$$

Putting the three steps together, the prob. that there is an augmenting path $a_i - u_i - v_i - b_i$ where a_i and b_i has no neighbors other than u_i and v_i is at least

$$\begin{aligned} &\left(1-e^{-p\cdot d(v_i)}\right)\cdot\frac{1-p_0}{e}\cdot\frac{f(\frac{1}{e})\cdot(1-p_0)\cdot p\cdot\max\{d(u_i)-1,0\}}{e} \\ &= (1-O(p_0))\cdot f(\frac{1}{e})\cdot\frac{p}{e^2}\left(1-e^{-p\cdot d(v_i)}\right)\cdot\max\{d(u_i)-1,0\} \end{aligned}$$

□

As we pointed out after the statement of Lemma 5.3, we need to lower bound the expected number of edges in M^+ that has such an augmenting path, which, by Lemma 5.3, is lower bounded by the function F defined below. For the two vectors $d_u := (d(u_1), \ldots, d(u_{|M^+|}))$ and $d_v := (d(v_1), \ldots, d(v_{|M^+|}))$,

$$F(d_u, d_v) := \sum_{i\in[|M^+|]} (1-O(p_0))\cdot f(\frac{1}{e})\cdot\frac{p}{e^2}\left(1-e^{-p\cdot d(v_i)}\right)\cdot\max\{d(u_i)-1,0\}$$

The goal now is to find the smallest value of $F(d_u, d_v)$, with the constraint on the vectors d_u and d_v formulated in the following (non-linear) minimization program (referred to as MP-(4)).

$$\begin{aligned} \text{minimize} \quad & F(d_u, d_v) \\ \text{subject to} \quad & \textstyle\sum_{i\in[|M^+|]} d(u_i) + d(v_i) = |C| \\ & d(u_i), d(v_i) \in \left[\left\lfloor\tfrac{1}{p}\right\rfloor\right] \quad i = 1, \ldots, |M^+| \end{aligned} \tag{4}$$

The constraint on each individual $d(u_i)$ and $d(v_i)$ is because C is a $\left\lfloor\frac{1}{p}\right\rfloor$-matching. The following lemma lower bounds the value of the objective function in MP-(4).

Lemma 5.4. *Let $F^\star$ denote the optimal value of* MP-(4)*; then,*

$$F^\star \geq (p \cdot |C| - |M^+|) \cdot \eta - O(p_0) \cdot \text{OPT}$$

where $\eta := f(\frac{1}{e}) \cdot \frac{1}{e^2}\left(1 - e^{-1}\right) > 0.07157$.

The proof of the Lemma 5.4 is technical, and we defer it to Section 5.1. By Lemma 5.4 and Claim 5.2 (the lower bound on $|C|$) the expected increment (over M^+) of the matching size is at least

$$\begin{aligned}
F^\star &\geq (p \cdot |C| - |M^+|) \cdot \eta - O(p_0) \cdot \text{OPT} \\
&\geq (p \cdot (2\,|B_M| - 2\,|M^+|\,/p) - |M^+|) \cdot \eta - O(p_0) \cdot \text{OPT} && \text{(By Claim 5.2)} \\
&= (2p\,|B_M| - 3\,|M^+|) \cdot \eta - O(p_0) \cdot \text{OPT} \\
&= \left(2p(|B| - \left|B_{\overline{M}}\right|) - 3(|M| + s_{\overline{M}})\right) \cdot \eta - O(p_0) \cdot \text{OPT} \\
&= \left(2p\,|B| - 3\,|M| - 2p\left|B_{\overline{M}}\right| - 3s_{\overline{M}}\right) \cdot \eta - O(p_0) \cdot \text{OPT} \\
&= \left(2p(1 - O(p_0))\frac{\text{OPT}}{p} - 3\left(\frac{1}{2} - \varepsilon_0\right)\text{OPT} - 2p\left|B_{\overline{M}}\right| - 3s_{\overline{M}}\right) \cdot \eta - O(p_0)\text{OPT} \\
&= \left(\left(\frac{1}{2} + 3\varepsilon_0\right)\text{OPT} - 2p\left|B_{\overline{M}}\right| - 3s_{\overline{M}}\right) \cdot \eta - O(p_0) \cdot \text{OPT}
\end{aligned}$$

Since the original matching M^+ is of size $(1/2 - \varepsilon_0) \cdot \text{OPT} + s_{\overline{M}}$, the expected matching size in $M \cup B_p$, i.e., $\mu(M \cup B_p)$, is

$$\begin{aligned}
\mathbb{E}[\mu(M \cup B_p)] &= \sum_{s_{\overline{M}}} \Pr\left(s_{\overline{M}}\right) \mathbb{E}[\mu(M \cup B_p) \mid s_{\overline{M}}] && (\mathbb{E}[X] = \textstyle\sum_Y \Pr(Y)\,\mathbb{E}[X \mid Y]) \\
&\geq \sum_{s_{\overline{M}}} \Pr\left(s_{\overline{M}}\right)(|M^+| + F^\star) \\
&\geq \left(\frac{1}{2} - \varepsilon_0\right) \cdot \text{OPT} + \mathbb{E}[s_{\overline{M}}] + \left(\left(\frac{1}{2} + 3\varepsilon_0\right)\text{OPT} - 2p\left|B_{\overline{M}}\right| - 3\mathbb{E}[s_{\overline{M}}]\right) \cdot \eta - O(p_0) \cdot \text{OPT} \\
&\geq \left(\frac{1}{2} + \frac{\eta}{2} - \varepsilon_0 + 3\eta\varepsilon_0\right) \cdot \text{OPT} + (1 - 3\eta)\mathbb{E}[s_{\overline{M}}] - 2p\eta\left|B_{\overline{M}}\right| - O(p_0) \cdot \text{OPT} \\
&\geq \left(\frac{1}{2} + \frac{\eta}{2} - \varepsilon_0 + 3\eta\varepsilon_0\right) \cdot \text{OPT} + (1 - 3\eta)(1 - O(p_0))\frac{p\left|B_{\overline{M}}\right|}{3} - 2p\eta\left|B_{\overline{M}}\right| - O(p_0) \cdot \text{OPT} \\
& && \text{(By Equation 3)} \\
&\geq \left(\frac{1}{2} + \frac{\eta}{2} - \varepsilon_0 + 3\eta\varepsilon_0\right) \cdot \text{OPT} + \left(\frac{1}{3} - 3\eta\right)p\left|B_{\overline{M}}\right| - O(p_0) \cdot \text{OPT}
\end{aligned}$$

Since $\eta \approx 0.07157$, $\frac{1}{3} - 3\eta > 0$, and we have

$$\begin{aligned}
&\left(\frac{1}{2} + \frac{\eta}{2} - \varepsilon_0 + 3\eta\varepsilon_0\right) \cdot \text{OPT} + \left(\frac{1}{3} - 3\eta\right)p\left|B_{\overline{M}}\right| - O(p_0) \cdot \text{OPT} \\
&\geq \left(\frac{1}{2} + \frac{\eta}{2} - \varepsilon_0 + 3\eta\varepsilon_0\right) \cdot \text{OPT} - O(p_0) \cdot \text{OPT} \\
&> 0.52 \cdot \text{OPT} && (\varepsilon_0 = 0.02001,\ \eta > 0.07157, \text{ and } p_0 \text{ is sufficiently small.}) \\
&= (1/2 + \delta_0) \cdot \text{OPT}
\end{aligned}$$

completing the proof of Lemma 5.1.

5.1 Lower Bounding the Value of MP-(4)

In this section, we prove Lemma 5.4, i.e., the following inequality,

$$F^\star \ (= \min F(d_u, d_v)) \geq (p \cdot |C| - |M^+|) \cdot \eta - O(p_0)\text{OPT}$$

where $\eta := f(\frac{1}{e}) \cdot \frac{1}{e^2}\left(1 - e^{-1}\right)$.

Recall that

$$\begin{aligned} F(d_u, d_v) &= \sum_i (1 - O(p_0)) \cdot f(\frac{1}{e}) \cdot \frac{p}{e^2}\left(1 - e^{-p \cdot d(v_i)}\right) \cdot \max\{d(u_i) - 1, 0\} \\ &= (1 - O(p_0)) \cdot f(\frac{1}{e}) \cdot \frac{p}{e^2} \sum_i \left(1 - e^{-p \cdot d(v_i)}\right) \cdot \max\{d(u_i) - 1, 0\} \end{aligned}$$

Since the term $(1 - O(p_0)) \cdot f(\frac{1}{e}) \cdot \frac{p}{e^2}$ is independent of d_u and d_v,

$$\arg\min_{d_u, d_v} F = \arg\min_{d_u, d_v} \sum_i \left(1 - e^{-p \cdot d(v_i)}\right) \cdot \max\{d(u_i) - 1, 0\}$$

Define $d(V) := \sum_i d(v_i)$ and $d(U) := \sum_i d(u_i)$; then, $d(V) + d(U) = |C|$. We need to prove that for any choice of $d(V)$ and $d(U)$, the lemma statement holds. First of all, we can assume $d(U) \geq |M^+|$: otherwise, since $d(V) \leq \left\lfloor \frac{1}{p} \right\rfloor |M^+|$, we will have

$$|C| = d(V) + d(U) \leq \left\lfloor \frac{1}{p} \right\rfloor |M^+| + |M^+| \leq \left(\frac{1}{p} + 1\right) |M^+|$$

Therefore, for the target lower bound on $F^\star$

$$\begin{aligned} &(p \cdot |C| - |M^+|) \cdot \eta - O(p_0)\text{OPT} \\ \leq &\left(p\left(\frac{1}{p} + 1\right)|M^+| - |M^+|\right) \cdot \eta - O(p_0)\text{OPT} \\ \leq &p_0 \eta \, |M^+| - O(p_0)\text{OPT} \end{aligned}$$

which can be made negative by choosing the constant hidden in $O(p_0)$ to be 1, proving Lemma 5.4.

We further assume $d(U) - |M^+|$ is an integer multiple of $\left\lfloor \frac{1}{p} \right\rfloor - 1$ and $d(V)$ is an integer multiple of $\left\lfloor \frac{1}{p} \right\rfloor$. This can be achieved by removing at most $1/p$ edges from $d(U)$ and $d(V)$ respectively. Since F is monotonically increasing with any $d(u_i)$ or $d(v_i)$, removing edges from $d(U)$ and $d(V)$ can only make $F^\star$ even smaller. Therefore, if we show that after removing these edges, the target lower bound on $F^\star$ holds, then it definitely holds for the original $d(U)$ and $d(V)$. In the following, we fix any $d(U)$ and $d(V)$ where $d(U) - |M^+|$ is an integer multiple of $\left\lfloor \frac{1}{p} \right\rfloor - 1$, $d(V)$ is an integer multiple of $\left\lfloor \frac{1}{p} \right\rfloor$, and $d(V) + d(U) \geq |C| - \frac{2}{p}$. We prove the following key property of $F(d_u, d_v)$.

Lemma 5.5. *There exists d_u and d_v that minimizes $F(d_u, d_v)$ where any entry in d_u is either* 1 *or* $\left\lfloor \frac{1}{p} \right\rfloor$ *and any entry in d_v is either* 0 *or* $\left\lfloor \frac{1}{p} \right\rfloor$.

We first show why Lemma 5.5 implies the target lower bound on $F^\star$, and then prove Lemma 5.5. Fix $d^\star(u_i)$ and $d^\star(v_i)$ that satisfy the property in Lemma 5.5. Since every entry in $d_u^\star$ is either 1 or $\left\lfloor \frac{1}{p} \right\rfloor$, the number of 1's in $d_u^\star$ is $x := |M^+| - (d(U) - |M^+|)/(\left\lfloor \frac{1}{p} \right\rfloor - 1)$. Similarly, the number of 0's in $d_v^\star$ is $y := |M^+| - d(V)/\left\lfloor \frac{1}{p} \right\rfloor$. Therefore, the number of edges in M^+ where $d^\star(v_i) = d^\star(u_i) = \left\lfloor \frac{1}{p} \right\rfloor$

is at least

$$
\begin{aligned}
|M^+| - x - y = & |M^+| - \left(|M^+| - \frac{d(U) - |M^+|}{\lfloor \frac{1}{p} \rfloor - 1} \right) - \left(|M^+| - \frac{d(V)}{\lfloor \frac{1}{p} \rfloor} \right) \\
= & \frac{d(U) - |M^+|}{\lfloor \frac{1}{p} \rfloor - 1} - |M^+| + \frac{d(V)}{\lfloor \frac{1}{p} \rfloor} \\
\geq & \frac{d(U) - |M^+|}{\frac{1}{p}} - |M^+| + d(V)p \qquad (\lfloor \tfrac{1}{p} \rfloor - 1 \leq \lfloor \tfrac{1}{p} \rfloor \leq \tfrac{1}{p}) \\
= & p \cdot d(U) + p \cdot d(V) - (1+p)\,|M^+| \\
\geq & p \left(|C| - \frac{2}{p} \right) - (1+p)\,|M^+| \qquad (d(V) + d(U) \geq |C| - \tfrac{2}{p}.) \\
= & p\,|C| - |M^+| - O(p_0)\textsc{opt} \qquad (|M^+| = O(\textsc{opt}))
\end{aligned}
$$

And just focusing on these $p\,|C| - |M^+| - O(p_0)\textsc{opt}$ edges, we have

$$
\begin{aligned}
F^\star \geq & (p\,|C| - |M^+| - O(p_0)\textsc{opt}) \cdot (1 - O(p_0)) \cdot f(\frac{1}{e}) \cdot \frac{p}{e^2} \left(1 - e^{-1}\right) \cdot (\left\lfloor \frac{1}{p} \right\rfloor - 1) \\
\geq & (p\,|C| - |M^+| - O(p_0)\textsc{opt}) \cdot (1 - O(p_0)) \cdot f(\frac{1}{e}) \cdot \frac{p}{e^2} \left(1 - e^{-1}\right) \cdot \frac{1}{p} \quad (\lfloor \tfrac{1}{p} \rfloor - 1 \geq (1 - O(p_0))\tfrac{1}{p}) \\
\geq & (p\,|C| - |M^+| - O(p_0)\textsc{opt}) \cdot (1 - O(p_0)) \cdot \eta \\
\geq & (p\,|C| - |M^+|) \cdot \eta - O(p_0)\textsc{opt} \qquad (|M^+| = O(\textsc{opt}), p\,|C| \leq p\,|B_M| = O(\textsc{opt}))
\end{aligned}
$$

which proves Lemma 5.4. We now prove Lemma 5.5 which will complete the proof.

Proof of Lemma 5.5. Fix any allocation $d_u^\star$ and $d_v^\star$ that minimizes $F(d_u, d_v)$. We will show that first, there exists a sequence of locally reallocating the values (i.e., degrees) in $d_u^\star$ without changing the value of $F(d_u, d_v)$ such that at the end, every entry in $d_u^\star$ is either 1 or $\lfloor \frac{1}{p} \rfloor$. After changing the vector $d_u^\star$, we then show that there exists a sequence of locally reallocating the values in $d_v^\star$ without changing the value of $F(d_u, d_v)$ such that at the end, every entry in $d_v^\star$ is either 0 or $\lfloor \frac{1}{p} \rfloor$.

We first explain how to change $d_u^\star$. To simplify the presentation, we define $q_i = 1 - e^{-p \cdot d^\star(v_i)}$ and the target expression becomes

$$\sum_i \left(1 - e^{-p \cdot d^\star(v_i)}\right) \cdot \max\left\{d^\star(u_i) - 1, 0\right\} = \sum_i q_i \cdot \max\left\{d^\star(u_i) - 1, 0\right\} \tag{5}$$

Recall that $d^\star(u_i)$ satisfies $d^\star(u_i) \in \left[\lfloor \frac{1}{p} \rfloor\right]$ (in MP-(4)) (and hence $q_i \geq 0$) and $\sum_i d^\star(u_i) = d(U)$. First of all, if there exists some i_1 where $d^\star(u_{i_1}) = 0$, then since $d(U) \geq |M^+|$, there must exist an index i_2 where $d^\star(u_{i_2}) \geq 2$. Then, we can shift one degree from $d^\star(u_{i_2})$ to $d^\star(u_{i_1})$ and after the shift, (a) $\max\{d^\star(u_{i_1}) - 1, 0\}$ remains 0 and hence $q_{i_1} \max\{d^\star(u_i) - 1, 0\}$ remains 0, and (b) $\max\{d^\star(u_{i_2}) - 1, 0\}$ decreases and hence $q_{i_1} \max\{d^\star(u_{i_2}) - 1, 0\}$ does not increase. Therefore, $F(d_u, d_v)$ does not increase after the shift, and from now on, we have $d^\star(u_i) \geq 1$ for all $i \in [|M^+|]$. To proceed, we need the following property of $d^\star(u_i)$.

Claim 5.6. *For any pair of indices i_1, i_2 where $q_{i_1} > q_{i_2}$, either $d^\star(u_{i_2}) = \lfloor \frac{1}{p} \rfloor$ or $d^\star(u_{i_1}) \leq 1$.*

Proof. Suppose not. We have $d^\star(u_{i_2}) < \left\lfloor \frac{1}{p} \right\rfloor$ and $d^\star(u_{i_1}) > 1$, for some i_1 and i_2. We can shift one degree from $d^\star(u_{i_1})$ to $d^\star(u_{i_2})$ and still get a valid allocation. In the following, we show that this new allocation achieves a smaller value of F, which contradicts to the optimality of $d^\star(u_i)$.

Since shifting from $d^\star(u_{i_1})$ to $d^\star(u_{i_2})$ only changes the degrees for u_{i_1} and u_{i_2}, it suffices for us to prove that

$$\begin{aligned}\Delta :=&(q_{i_2} \max\left\{d^\star(u_{i_2}) - 1, 0\right\} + q_{i_1} \max\left\{d^\star(u_{i_1}) - 1, 0\right\}) \\ &- (q_{i_2} \max\left\{d^\star(u_{i_2}), 0\right\} + q_{i_1} \max\left\{d^\star(u_{i_1}) - 2, 0\right\}) > 0\end{aligned}$$

Since $d^\star(u_{i_1}) \geq 2$, $\max\{d^\star(u_{i_1}) - 1, 0\} = d^\star(u_{i_1}) - 1$, $\max\{d^\star(u_{i_1}) - 2, 0\} = d^\star(u_{i_1}) - 2$. In addition, since $d^\star(u_{i_2}) \geq 0$, $\max\{d^\star(u_{i_2}), 0\} = d^\star(u_{i_2})$. We have

$$\begin{aligned}\Delta =&(q_{i_2} \max\left\{d^\star(u_{i_2}) - 1, 0\right\} + q_{i_1}(d^\star(u_{i_1}) - 1)) - (q_{i_2} d^\star(u_{i_2}) + q_{i_1}(d^\star(u_{i_1}) - 2)) \\ =&q_{i_2}\left(\max\left\{d^\star(u_{i_2}) - 1, 0\right\} - d^\star(u_{i_2})\right) + q_{i_1} \\ \geq&q_{i_2}(d^\star(u_{i_2}) - 1 - d^\star(u_{i_2})) + q_{i_1} \\ =&q_{i_1} - q_{i_2}.\end{aligned}$$

Since we have $q_{i_1} > q_{i_2}$, the value of F decreases after the shifting according to Eq 5, a contradiction. □

We use Claim 5.6 to prove the correctness of the following sequence of reallocation of $d_u^\star$. Now, as long as there exists an index i_1, where $d^\star(u_{i_1}) \in (1, \left\lfloor \frac{1}{p} \right\rfloor)$, since $d(U) - |M^+|$ is an integer multiple of $(\left\lfloor \frac{1}{p} \right\rfloor - 1)$, there must exists some index i_2 where $d^\star(u_{i_2}) \in (1, \left\lfloor \frac{1}{p} \right\rfloor)$ (recall that $d^\star(u_i) \geq 1$), and we will shift the values between $d^\star(u_{i_1})$ and $d^\star(v_{i_2})$ such that one of them becomes either 1 or $\left\lfloor \frac{1}{p} \right\rfloor$ and both of them are still at least 1 (it is easy to see this is always possible). First of all, every step of this reallocation reduces the number of vertices with $d^\star(u_i) \in (1, \left\lfloor \frac{1}{p} \right\rfloor)$, and hence it will terminate. To see that this process never changes $F(d_u, d_v)$, (*a*) it cannot be that $q_{i_1} \neq q_{i_2}$, since otherwise the indices i_1 and i_2 will contradict Claim 5.6, and (*b*) if $q_{i_1} = q_{i_2}$, shifting the allocation between i_1 to i_2 will not change $F(d_u, d_v)$.

Therefore, we can focus on the case where the entries of $d^\star(u_i)$ are either 1 or $\left\lfloor \frac{1}{p} \right\rfloor$. We now consider $d^\star(v_i)$. Recall that $d(V) = \sum_i d(v_i)$ and $d(V)$ is an integer multiple of $\left\lfloor \frac{1}{p} \right\rfloor$. The target expression can be written as

$$\begin{aligned}&\sum_i \left(1 - e^{-p \cdot d^\star(v_i)}\right) \cdot \max\left\{d^\star(u_i) - 1, 0\right\} \\ =& \sum_{i:\ d^\star(u_i) = \left\lfloor \frac{1}{p} \right\rfloor} \left(1 - e^{-p \cdot d^\star(v_i)}\right)\left(\left\lfloor \frac{1}{p} \right\rfloor - 1\right) + \sum_{i:\ d^\star(u_i) = 1} \left(1 - e^{-p \cdot d^\star(v_i)}\right) \cdot 0 \\ =& \sum_{i:\ d^\star(u_i) = \left\lfloor \frac{1}{p} \right\rfloor} \left(1 - e^{-p \cdot d^\star(v_i)}\right)\end{aligned}$$

Since F is monotonically increasing when any $d(u_i)$ increases, for the indices i where $d^\star(u_i) = 1$, ideally, one should allocate as many degrees to $d^\star(v_i)$ as possible, i.e., $d^\star(v_i) = \left\lfloor \frac{1}{p} \right\rfloor$. However, it might be the case that $d(V)$ cannot supply $\left\lfloor \frac{1}{p} \right\rfloor$ degree for all i where $d^\star(u_i) = 1$. But in this case, we are done since reallocating between different $d^\star(v_i)$ where $d^\star(u_i) = 1$ does not change the F

(in fact, F is always 0), and we can shift them such that we have as many $d^\star(v_i) = \lfloor \frac{1}{p} \rfloor$ as possible and leave the rest equal to 0.

In the following, we assume $d(V)$ can supply $\lfloor \frac{1}{p} \rfloor$ degree for all i with $d^\star(u_i) = 1$, and hence $d^\star(v_i) = \lfloor \frac{1}{p} \rfloor$ whenever $d^\star(u_i) = 1$. It suffices to only focus on $d^\star(v_i)$ where $d^\star(u_i) = \lfloor \frac{1}{p} \rfloor$. We need the following property of $d^\star(v_i)$ to complete the argument.

Claim 5.7. *For any pair of indices i_1 and i_2 such that $d^\star(u_{i_1}) = d^\star(u_{i_2}) = \lfloor \frac{1}{p} \rfloor$, we have that either $\min\{d^\star(v_{i_1}), d^\star(v_{i_2})\} = 0$ or $\max\{d^\star(v_{i_1}), d^\star(v_{i_2})\} = \lfloor \frac{1}{p} \rfloor$.*

Proof. Suppose not. Then, for some i_1 and i_2, we have $\min\{d^\star(v_{i_1}), d^\star(v_{i_2})\} > 0$, and also $\max\{d^\star(v_{i_1}), d^\star(v_{i_2})\} < \lfloor \frac{1}{p} \rfloor$. Without lose of generality, assume $1 \leq d^\star(v_{i_1}) \leq d^\star(v_{i_2}) \leq \lfloor \frac{1}{p} \rfloor - 1$. Then, shifting one degree from $d^\star(v_{i_1})$ to $d^\star(v_{i_2})$ leads to a valid allocation, and we prove in the following that the new allocation decreases the objective function which contradicts the optimality of $d^\star_v$.

Since only the indices i_1 and i_2 are affected, it suffices for us to prove that

$$\Delta := \left(1 - e^{-p \cdot d^\star(v_{i_1})}\right) + \left(1 - e^{-p \cdot d^\star(v_{i_2})}\right) - \left(1 - e^{-p \cdot (d^\star(v_{i_1}) - 1)}\right) + \left(1 - e^{-p \cdot (d^\star(v_{i_2}) + 1)}\right) > 0$$

We have

$$\Delta \geq e^{-p \cdot d^\star(v_{i_1})}(e^p - 1) + e^{-p \cdot d^\star(v_{i_2})}(e^{-p} - 1)$$

Since $d^\star(v_{i_1}) \leq d^\star(v_{i_2})$, $e^{-p \cdot d^\star(v_{i_1})} \geq e^{-p \cdot d^\star(v_{i_2})}$. We further have

$$\begin{aligned} e^{-p \cdot d^\star(v_{i_1})}(e^p - 1) + e^{-p \cdot d^\star(v_{i_2})}(e^{-p} - 1) &\geq e^{-p \cdot d^\star(v_{i_2})}(e^p - 1) + e^{-p \cdot d^\star(v_{i_2})}(e^{-p} - 1) \\ &\geq e^{-p \cdot d^\star(v_{i_2})}(e^p - 1 + e^{-p} - 1) \\ &> e^{-p \cdot d^\star(v_{i_2})}(2\sqrt{e^p \cdot e^{-p}} - 2) = 0 \end{aligned}$$

where the strict inequality is true since the two terms can only be equal when $e^p = e^{-p}$ which does not happen for $p > 0$. □

Using Claim 5.7, we can now show that any $d^\star(v_i)$ where $d^\star(u_i) = \lfloor \frac{1}{p} \rfloor$, must be either 0 or $\lfloor \frac{1}{p} \rfloor$. Suppose not. If $d^\star(v_{i_1}) \in (0, \lfloor \frac{1}{p} \rfloor)$, then since $d(V)$ is an integer multiple of $\lfloor \frac{1}{p} \rfloor$, there must exists some other index i_2 where $d^\star(v_{i_2}) \in (0, \lfloor \frac{1}{p} \rfloor)$; hence, $0 < \min\{d^\star(v_{i_1}), d^\star(v_{i_2})\} < \max\{d^\star(v_{i_1}), d^\star(v_{i_2})\} < \lfloor \frac{1}{p} \rfloor$, a contradiction to Claim 5.7. □

□

6 AN ALGORITHM FOR LARGE VALUES OF P

In this section, we present Algorithm 2 with approximation ratio $\left(1/2 + \Theta(p^2)\right)$. Algorithm 2 is required to handle the case when p is not small enough for Algorithm 1 to perform well.

Let p_0 be any fixed constant independent of n, $\delta = \frac{p^2}{4}$, and $\varepsilon = \frac{p_0^2}{10^4}$. The new algorithm (i.e, Algorithm 2) is similar to Algorithm 1 with the only difference being that instead of a $\lfloor \frac{1}{p} \rfloor$-matching, here, we simply pick a single maximum matching in G. Our algorithm is stated as Algorithm 2.

The following lemma proves the approximation ratio of Algorithm 2. The proof is a simpler version of the proof for Algorithm 1 and is deferred to the full version of the paper [7].

Lemma 6.1. *For any constant $p_0 > 0$, any probability $p \geq p_0$, and any graph $G(V, E)$ the expected maximum matching size in the graph H computed by Algorithm 2 is at least $\left(\frac{1}{2} + \frac{p^2}{4} - \frac{p_0^2}{10^4}\right) \cdot \text{OPT}(G)$.*

ALGORITHM 2: A $\left(0.5 + \Theta(p^2)\right)$-Approximation Algorithm for Stochastic Matching

Input: A graph $G(V,E)$ and an edge realization probability $p_0 \leq p < 1$.
Output: A subgraph $H(V,Q)$ of $G(V,E)$.

(1) Let M be a maximum matching in G.
(2) Let $(M_1, M_2, \ldots, M_R) := \mathsf{MatchingCover}(G(V, E \setminus M), \varepsilon)$ (recall that $\varepsilon = \frac{p_0^2}{10^4}$), and $E_{MC} = M_1 \cup \ldots \cup M_R$.
(3) Return $H(V,Q)$ where $Q := M \cup E_{MC}$.

We now show how to combine Algorithm 1 and Algorithm 2 to prove Part (ii) of Theorem 1.1.

Proof of Theorem 1.1, Part (ii). Let p_0 be the constant such that Algorithm 1 achieves an approximation ratio of 0.52 for any $p \leq p_0$. The algorithm for Part (ii) is simply as follows. If the realization probability $p \leq p_0$, run Algorithm 1 and otherwise run Algorithm 2. By Lemma 6.1, the approximation ratio of this algorithm is $\min\left\{0.52, \frac{1}{2} + \frac{p^2}{4} - \frac{p_0^2}{10^4}\right\} = 0.5 + \delta_0$ for some absolute constant δ_0 (since p_0 is an absolute constant and $p \geq p_0$).

□

7 CONCLUDING REMARKS AND OPEN PROBLEMS

We presented the first non-adaptive algorithm for stochastic matching with an approximation ratio that is strictly better than half. In particular, we showed that any graph G has a subgraph H with maximum degree $O(\frac{\log(1/p)}{p})$ such that the ratio of expected size of a maximum matching in realizations of H and G is at least 0.52 when p is sufficiently small, i.e., case of vanishing probabilities, and $0.5 + \delta_0$ (for an absolute constant $\delta_0 > 0$) for any $p \in (0,1)$.

A main open problem is to determine the best approximation ratio achievable by a non-adaptive algorithm. In particular, can non-adaptive algorithms qualitatively match the performance of adaptive algorithms by achieving a $(1-\varepsilon)$-approximation for any $\varepsilon > 0$ using a subgraph with maximum degree $f(\varepsilon, p)$ for some function f? In the full version of the paper [7], we mention some potential directions towards resolving this problem.

ACKNOWLEDGMENTS

We thank the anonymous reviewers of EC 2017 for many insightful comments and suggestions. This work was supported in part by National Science Foundation grants CCF-1552909, CCF-1617851, and IIS-1447470.

REFERENCES

[1] Marek Adamczyk. 2011. Improved analysis of the greedy algorithm for stochastic matching. *Inf. Process. Lett.* 111, 15 (2011), 731–737.
[2] Mohammad Akbarpour, Shengwu Li, and Shayan Oveis Gharan. 2014. Dynamic matching market design. In *ACM Conference on Economics and Computation, EC '14, Stanford, CA, USA, June 8-12, 2014.* 355.
[3] Ross Anderson, Itai Ashlagi, David Gamarnik, and Yash Kanoria. 2015. A dynamic model of barter exchange. In *Proceedings of the Twenty-Sixth Annual ACM-SIAM Symposium on Discrete Algorithms, SODA 2015, San Diego, CA, USA, January 4-6, 2015.* 1925–1933.
[4] Ross Anderson, Itai Ashlagi, David Gamarnik, and Alvin E. Roth. 2015. Finding long chains in kidney exchange using the traveling salesman problem. *Proceedings of the National Academy of Sciences* 112, 3 (2015), 663–668.
[5] Jonathan Aronson, Martin E. Dyer, Alan M. Frieze, and Stephen Suen. 1995. Randomized Greedy Matching II. *Random Struct. Algorithms* 6, 1 (1995), 55–74.

[6] Sepehr Assadi, Sanjeev Khanna, and Yang Li. 2016. The Stochastic Matching Problem with (Very) Few Queries. *Proceedings of the 2016 ACM Conference on Economics and Computation, EC '16, Maastricht, The Netherlands, July 24-28, 2016* (2016), 43–60.

[7] Sepehr Assadi, Sanjeev Khanna, and Yang Li. 2017. The Stochastic Matching Problem: Beating Half with a Non-Adaptive Algorithm. *CoRR* abs/1705.02280 (2017).

[8] Pranjal Awasthi and Tuomas Sandholm. 2009. Online Stochastic Optimization in the Large: Application to Kidney Exchange. In *IJCAI 2009, Proceedings of the 21st International Joint Conference on Artificial Intelligence, 2009.* 405–411.

[9] Nikhil Bansal, Anupam Gupta, Jian Li, Julián Mestre, Viswanath Nagarajan, and Atri Rudra. 2012. When LP Is the Cure for Your Matching Woes: Improved Bounds for Stochastic Matchings. *Algorithmica* 63, 4 (2012), 733–762.

[10] Avrim Blum, John P. Dickerson, Nika Haghtalab, Ariel D. Procaccia, Tuomas Sandholm, and Ankit Sharma. 2015. Ignorance is Almost Bliss: Near-Optimal Stochastic Matching With Few Queries. In *Proceedings of the Sixteenth ACM Conference on Economics and Computation, EC '15, Portland, OR, USA, June 15-19, 2015.* 325–342.

[11] Avrim Blum, Anupam Gupta, Ariel D. Procaccia, and Ankit Sharma. 2013. Harnessing the power of two crossmatches. In *ACM Conference on Electronic Commerce, EC '13, Philadelphia, PA, USA, June 16-20, 2013.* 123–140.

[12] Béla Bollobás. 2001. *Random Graphs.* Number 73. Cambridge University Press.

[13] T.-H. Hubert Chan, Fei Chen, Xiaowei Wu, and Zhichao Zhao. 2014. Ranking on Arbitrary Graphs: Rematch via Continuous LP with Monotone and Boundary Condition Constraints. In *Proceedings of the Twenty-Fifth Annual ACM-SIAM Symposium on Discrete Algorithms, SODA 2014, Portland, Oregon, USA, January 5-7, 2014.* 1112–1122.

[14] Ning Chen, Nicole Immorlica, Anna R. Karlin, Mohammad Mahdian, and Atri Rudra. 2009. Approximating Matches Made in Heaven. In *Automata, Languages and Programming, 36th International Colloquium, ICALP 2009, Rhodes, Greece, July 5-12, 2009, Proceedings, Part I.* 266–278.

[15] Kevin P. Costello, Prasad Tetali, and Pushkar Tripathi. 2012. Stochastic Matching with Commitment. In *Automata, Languages, and Programming - 39th International Colloquium, ICALP 2012, Proceedings, Part I.* 822–833.

[16] John P. Dickerson, Ariel D. Procaccia, and Tuomas Sandholm. 2012. Dynamic Matching via Weighted Myopia with Application to Kidney Exchange. In *Proceedings of the Twenty-Sixth AAAI Conference on Artificial Intelligence.*

[17] John P. Dickerson, Ariel D. Procaccia, and Tuomas Sandholm. 2013. Failure-aware kidney exchange. In *ACM Conference on Electronic Commerce, EC '13.* 323–340.

[18] John P. Dickerson and Tuomas Sandholm. 2015. FutureMatch: Combining Human Value Judgments and Machine Learning to Match in Dynamic Environments. In *Proceedings of the Twenty-Ninth AAAI Conference on Artificial Intelligence, January 25-30, 2015, Austin, Texas, USA.* 622–628.

[19] Martin E. Dyer and Alan M. Frieze. 1991. Randomized Greedy Matching. *Random Struct. Algorithms* 2, 1 (1991), 29–46.

[20] Joan Feigenbaum, Sampath Kannan, Andrew McGregor, Siddharth Suri, and Jian Zhang. 2005. On graph problems in a semi-streaming model. *Theor. Comput. Sci.* 348, 2-3 (2005), 207–216. DOI: http://dx.doi.org/10.1016/j.tcs.2005.09.013

[21] Anupam Gupta and Viswanath Nagarajan. 2013. A Stochastic Probing Problem with Applications. In *Integer Programming and Combinatorial Optimization - 16th International Conference, IPCO 2013. Proceedings.* 205–216.

[22] Richard M. Karp, Umesh V. Vazirani, and Vijay V. Vazirani. 1990. An Optimal Algorithm for On-line Bipartite Matching. In *Proceedings of the 22nd Annual ACM Symposium on Theory of Computing, May 13-17, 1990, Baltimore, Maryland, USA.* 352–358. DOI: http://dx.doi.org/10.1145/100216.100262

[23] Christian Konrad, Frédéric Magniez, and Claire Mathieu. 2012. Maximum Matching in Semi-streaming with Few Passes. In *Approximation, Randomization, and Combinatorial Optimization. Algorithms and Techniques - 15th International Workshop, APPROX 2012, and 16th International Workshop, RANDOM 2012, Cambridge, MA, USA, August 15-17, 2012. Proceedings.* 231–242.

[24] L. Lovász and D. Plummer. 2009. *Matching Theory.* American Mathematical Soc. https://books.google.com/books?id=yW3WSVq8ygcC

[25] David F. Manlove and Gregg O'Malley. 2014. Paired and Altruistic Kidney Donation in the UK: Algorithms and Experimentation. *ACM Journal of Experimental Algorithmics* 19, 1 (2014).

[26] Aranyak Mehta and Debmalya Panigrahi. 2012. Online Matching with Stochastic Rewards. In *53rd Annual IEEE Symposium on Foundations of Computer Science, FOCS 2012, New Brunswick, NJ, USA, October 20-23, 2012.* 728–737.

[27] Aranyak Mehta, Bo Waggoner, and Morteza Zadimoghaddam. 2015. Online Stochastic Matching with Unequal Probabilities. In *Proceedings of the Twenty-Sixth Annual ACM-SIAM Symposium on Discrete Algorithms, SODA 2015, San Diego, CA, USA, January 4-6, 2015.* 1388–1404.

[28] Matthias Poloczek and Mario Szegedy. 2012. Randomized Greedy Algorithms for the Maximum Matching Problem with New Analysis. In *53rd Annual IEEE Symposium on Foundations of Computer Science, FOCS 2012, New Brunswick, NJ, USA, October 20-23, 2012.* 708–717.

[29] Alexander Schrijver. 2003. *Combinatorial optimization: polyhedra and efficiency.* Springer Science & Business Media.

[30] Utku Unver. 2010. Dynamic Kidney Exchange. *Review of Economic Studies* 77, 1 (2010), 372–414.

Facilitating the Search for Partners on Matching Platforms: Restricting Agent Actions

YASH KANORIA, Columbia Business School
DANIELA SABAN, Graduate School of Business, Stanford University

Two-sided matching platforms, such as those for labor, accommodation, dating, and taxi hailing, can control and optimize over many aspects of the search for partners. To understand how the search for partners should be designed, we consider a dynamic model of search by strategic agents with costly discovery of pair-specific match value. We find that in many settings, the platform can mitigate wasteful competition in partner search via restricting what agents can see/do. For medium-sized screening costs (relative to idiosyncratic variation in utilities), the platform should prevent one side of the market from exercising choice (similar to Instant Book on Airbnb), whereas for large screening costs, the platform should centrally determine matches (similar to taxi hailing marketplaces). Surprisingly, simple restrictions can improve social welfare even when screening costs are small, and agents on each side are ex-ante homogeneous. In asymmetric markets where agents on one side have a tendency to be more selective (due to smaller screening costs or greater market power), the platform should force the more selective side of the market to reach out first, by explicitly disallowing the less selective side from doing so. This allows the agents on the less selective side to exercise more choice in equilibrium. When agents are vertically differentiated, forcing one side of the market to propose results in a significant increase in welfare even in the limit of vanishing screening costs. Furthermore, a Pareto improvement in welfare is possible in this limit: the weakest agents can be helped without hurting other agents. In addition, in this setting the platform can further boost welfare by hiding quality information.

Additional Key Words and Phrases: matching markets, market design, search frictions, stationary equilibrium, sharing economy, platforms

A full version of this paper is available at http://web.stanford.edu/~dsaban/facilitating-search.pdf.

Authors' email addresses: Kanoria: ykanoria@columbia.edu; Saban: dsaban@stanford.edu.

Both authors acknowledge the support of the Simons Institute, Berkeley, CA. .

EC'17, June 26–30, 2017, Cambridge, MA, USA.

 ACM ISBN 978-1-4503-4527-9/17/06
DOI: http://dx.doi.org/10.1145/3033274.3084092

Matching while Learning

RAMESH JOHARI, Stanford University
VIJAY KAMBLE, Stanford University
YASH KANORIA, Columbia Business School

This paper considers a central operational challenge faced by platforms that serve as matchmakers between supply and demand. Such platforms face a fundamental *exploration-exploitation* trade-off: on the one hand, efficient operation involves making matches that generate the most value ("exploitation"); on the other hand, the platform must continuously learn about newly arriving participants, so that they can be efficiently matched ("exploration"). In this paper, we develop a structurally simple and nearly optimal approach to resolving this trade-off.

We consider a model with two groups of participants: *workers* and *jobs*. Time is discrete, and new workers and jobs arrive at the beginning of every time period. Each worker departs after performing a specified number of jobs. Every time a worker and job are matched, a (random) payoff is generated and observed by the platform, where the payoff distribution depends on the *type* of the worker and the job.

We consider the following learning challenge: in most platforms, more is known about one side of the platform than the other; accordingly, we assume job types are known, while the type of a new worker is unknown. The platform learns about workers' types through the payoffs obtained when they are matched to jobs. However, because the supply of jobs is limited, using jobs to learn can reduce immediate payoffs, as well as deplete the supply of jobs available to the rest of the marketplace. Thus the presence of capacity constraints presents a new challenge in the optimal resolution of the exploration vs. exploitation tradeoff.

Our main contribution in this paper is the development of a matching policy that is nearly payoff optimal. We find that the platform should estimate a *shadow price* for each job type, and use the payoffs adjusted by these prices, first, to determine its learning goals and then, for each worker, (i) to balance learning with payoffs during the "exploration phase", and (ii) to myopically match after it has achieved its learning goals during the "exploitation phase." We refer to our policy as *DEEM: Decentralized Explore-then-Exploit for Matching.*

Our main result shows that DEEM achieves essentially optimal regret as the number of jobs N performed by each worker during their lifetime grows, where regret is the loss in payoff relative to the maximum achievable with known worker types. In our setting, a lower bound on the regret is $C \log N/N(1 + o(1))$ for some $C \in [0, \infty)$ that is a function of system parameters. DEEM achieves this level of regret to leading order when $C > 0$, while it achieves a regret of $O(\log \log N/N)$ if $C = 0$. Our theory is complemented by implementation and simulation that demonstrate a natural and implementable heuristic that translates our work into practice. In particular, our simulations reveal substantial benefit from jointly managing capacity constraints and learning, as we do in DEEM.

We gratefully acknowledge support from the Simons Foundation, the National Science Foundation (NSF) via grant nos. CNS-1343253 and CNS-1544548, and the Army Research Office (ARO) via grant no. W911NF-14-1-0526. A draft of our paper can be found at https://arxiv.org/abs/1603.04549.

EC'17, June 26–30, 2017, Cambridge, MA, USA. ACM ISBN 978-1-4503-4527-9/17/06.

DOI: http://dx.doi.org/10.1145/3033274.3084095

Redesigning the Israeli Psychology Masters Match

AVINATAN HASSIDIM, Bar-Ilan University
ASSAF ROMM, Hebrew University of Jerusalem and Microsoft Research
RAN I. SHORRER, Penn State University

Prior to 2014, the admission to Master's and PhD programs in psychology in Israel was a mostly decentralized process. In 2013, in response to concerns about the existing procedure, we proposed to use a mechanism that is both *stable* and *strategy-proof* for applicants. The first part of this paper describes how we successfully centralized this market, and the critical role of recent advances in the theory of matching with contracts. In the second part of the paper we show empirically (using clearinghouse data) and theoretically that the regularity in preferences with respect to contractual terms leads to a large core. Our results stand in sharp contrast to findings of previous studies on two-sided matching markets without contracts [2, 10, 11, 13].

During the design of the Israeli Psychology Master's Match (IPMM), we met with the faculty of each of the participating programs and asked about the way they choose between applicants. We discovered that departments' choice functions cannot be summarized by a quota and a rank-ordered list (ROL) for each program. Some departments employ affirmative action through minority quotas. Others aim to equalize the number of advisees each faculty member receives. And finally, some departments are willing to admit a limited number of applicants with different contractual terms (e.g., funding). Since terms can alter preferences between programs, this last feature implies that in order to satisfy the aforementioned desiderata, the applicants' message space must be expressive enough to convey their preferences over program-terms pairs. This market is therefore a special case of the matching-with-contracts model [9].

In some cases departments' choice functions do not satisfy the substitutes condition [9], or even the unilateral substitutes condition [7]. Yet, after each meeting we were glad to realize that there was a way to accommodate these choice function while assuring the good properties of DA. Only after the first year of operation did we learn about the findings of Hatfield and Kominers [8], which explain why we were successful: the choice functions used by psychology departments have a substitutable completion that satisfies LoAD. This ensures that DA converges to a stable matching and that it is strategy-proof.

Our experience designing the IPMM provides a strong empirical validation to the practical relevance of recent advances in matching theory. The mechanism that we ended up implementing was indeed a variant of the applicant-proposing DA.[1] Programs report their choice functions using a special interface that offers an expressive enough "bidding language". Being able to accommodate departments' pre-existing choice functions was key for the implementation of our solution, as departments insisted on having the same flexibility they had under the previous process.

[1]Since 2015, application in couples has been supported through the Ashlagi et al. [1] extension.

A full version of this paper is available at http://ssrn.com/abstract=2964706.

Authors' email addresses: Hassidim: avinatanh@gmail.com; Romm: assaf.romm@mail.huji.ac.il; Shorrer: rshorrer@gmail.com.

This work is supported by ISF grants 1394/16 and 1780/16, and by a Falk Institute grant.

EC'17, June 26–30, 2017, Cambridge, MA, USA.
 ACM ISBN 978-1-4503-4527-9/17/06
http://dx.doi.org/10.1145/3033274.3085124

The data from the IPMM suggests that relatively many applicants receive different contracts under different stable matchings. A similar phenomenon is observed in data from the Hungarian college admissions process. This process is a one-sided matching-with-contracts market that is a governed by a variant of the applicant-proposing DA, where applicants rank study programs and financial terms. We find that a substantial fraction of the approximately 100,000 applicants who participate in this match every year were part of multiple stable matchings, and, moreover, that different stable matchings have a different number of assigned applicants.

We modify the models of Immorlica and Mahdian [10] and Kojima and Pathak [11] to capture the features of participants' preferences in the IPMM and the Hungarian market. In particular, we incorporate the fact that applicants like to be funded, but that for many applicants funding is of secondary importance relative to the program they will be assigned to. We find that the core is large, and that in the many-to-one version a the number of assigned applicants significantly varies between stable matchings.[2]

Additional Key Words and Phrases: matching with contracts; market design; substitutable preferences; deferred acceptance

REFERENCES

[1] Itai Ashlagi, Mark Braverman, and Avinatan Hassidim. 2014. Stability in large matching markets with complementarities. *Operations Research* 62, 4 (2014), 713–732.

[2] Itai Ashlagi, Yash Kanoria, and Jacob D Leshno. 2017. Unbalanced random matching markets: The stark effect of competition. *Journal of Political Economy* 125, 1 (2017), 69–98.

[3] Slava Bronfman, Noga Alon, Avinatan Hassidim, and Assaf Romm. 2015. Redesigning the Israeli Medical Internship Match. In *EC*. 753–754.

[4] Slava Bronfman, Avinatan Hassidim, Arnon Afek, Assaf Romm, Rony Shreberk, Ayal Hassidim, and Anda Massler. 2015. Assigning Israeli medical graduates to internships. *IJHPR* 4, 1 (2015), 6.

[5] Avinatan Hassidim, Marciano Déborah, Assaf Romm, and Ran I. Shorrer. 2017. The mechanism is truthful, why aren't you? *American Economic Review: Papers and Proceedings* 107, 5 (2017).

[6] Avinatan Hassidim, Assaf Romm, and Ran I. Shorrer. 2016. 'Strategic' Behavior in a Strategy-proof Environment. (2016). Working paper.

[7] John W. Hatfield and Fuhito Kojima. 2010. Substitutes and stability for matching with contracts. *Journal of Economic Theory* 145, 5 (2010), 1704–1723.

[8] John W. Hatfield and Scott D. Kominers. 2015. Hidden Substitutes. In *Proceedings of the 16th ACM Conference on Economics and Computation.* 37.

[9] John W. Hatfield and Paul R. Milgrom. 2005. Matching with contracts. *American Economic Review* 95, 4 (2005), 913–935.

[10] Nicole Immorlica and Mohammad Mahdian. 2005. Marriage, honesty, and stability. In *Proceedings of the sixteenth annual ACM-SIAM symposium on Discrete algorithms.* Society for Industrial and Applied Mathematics, 53–62.

[11] Fuhito Kojima and Parag A. Pathak. 2009. Incentives and Stability in Large Two-Sided Matching Markets. *American Economic Review* 99, 3 (2009), 608–27.

[12] Alvin E. Roth. 1986. On the Allocation of Residents to Rural Hospitals: A General Property of Two-Sided Matching Markets. *Econometrica* 54, 2 (1986), 425–427.

[13] Alvin E Roth and Elliott Peranson. 1999. The Redesign of the Matching Market for American Physicians: Some Engineering Aspects of Economic D. *American economic review* 89, 4 (1999), 748–782.

[14] Alvin E. Roth and Xiaolin Xing. 1997. Turnaround time and bottlenecks in market clearing: Decentralized matching in the market for clinical psychologists. *Journal of Political Economy* 105, 2 (1997), 284–329.

[15] Ran I. Shorrer and Sándor Sóvágó. 2017. Obvious mistakes in a strategically simple college-admissions environment. (2017). mimeo.

[2]In the one-to-one case the Rural Hospital Theorem holds [12].

A "Quantal Regret" Method for Structural Econometrics in Repeated Games

NOAM NISAN, Hebrew University and Microsoft Research
GALI NOTI, Hebrew University

We suggest[1] a general method for inferring players' values from their actions in repeated games. The method extends and improves upon the recent suggestion of (Nekipelov et al., EC 2015) and is based on the assumption that players are *more likely* to exhibit sequences of actions that have *lower regret.*

We evaluate this "quantal-regret" method on two different datasets from experiments of repeated games with controlled player values: those of (Selten and Chmura, AER 2008) on a variety of two-player 2x2 games and our own experiment on ad-auctions (Noti et al., WWW 2014). We find that the quantal-regret method is consistently and significantly more precise than either "classic" econometric methods that are based on Nash equilibria, or the "min-regret" method of (Nekipelov et al., EC 2015).

CCS Concepts: •**Theory of computation → Algorithmic game theory;** *Convergence and learning in games; Computational pricing and auctions;* •**Applied computing →** *Online auctions;* Psychology; Economics;

Additional Key Words and Phrases: Econometrics; Behavioral Economics; Cognitive Biases; Sponsored Search Auctions; Regret

[1]A full version of this paper is available at https://arxiv.org/abs/1702.04254.

This research is supported by ISF grant 1435/14 administered by the Israeli Academy of Sciences, by Israel-USA Bi-national Science Foundation (BSF) grant number 2014389, and by the Adams Fellowship Program of the Israel Academy of Sciences and Humanities.
Authors' email addresses: noam@cs.huji.ac.il and gali.noti@mail.huji.ac.il .

ACM ISBN 978-1-4503-4527-9/17/06. DOI: http://dx.doi.org/10.1145/3033274.3085111

The Theory is Predictive, but is it Complete? An Application to Human Perception of Randomness

JON KLEINBERG, Cornell University
ANNIE LIANG, Microsoft Research
SENDHIL MULLAINATHAN, Harvard University

Additional Key Words and Phrases: Prediction, randomness perception, theory completeness.

When we test theories, it is common to focus on what one might call *predictiveness*: how well do the theory's predictions match what we see in data? Evidence that a theory is predictive, however, provides little guidance towards whether there may exist alternative theories that are more predictive, and how much more predictive they might be. These questions point toward a second issue, distinct from predictiveness, which we call *completeness*: how close is the performance of a given theory to the best performance that is achievable in the domain?

Completeness is an important construct because it lets us ask how much room there is for improving the predictive performance of existing theories in any given domain. We would expect the best possible prediction performance to differ considerably across domains—for example, an accuracy of 55% is a stunning success for predicting stock movements based on past returns, but extremely weak for predicting movements of a planet based on physical measurements. This contrast reflects that variation in stock movements *conditioned on the features we know* is large, while planetary motions are well predicted by known features. To understand how much we can improve on the predictive performance of existing theories, we need to separate prediction error due to intrinsic noise (emerging from limitations of the feature set) from prediction error that reveals opportunities for a better model.

It is generally very difficult, however, to reason about the best predictive performance achievable in a domain. Here we identify a setting that simultaneously (i) contains complex structure and a rich line of published theories but (ii) is also tractable enough for us to establish a benchmark of optimal predictive accuracy. We use this benchmark to evaluate known theories in the domain, illustrating that testing theory completeness can be feasible for problems of scientific interest.

The domain we consider is human generation of random sequences, a problem with a long history in psychology and behavioral economics. Following a common approach [6], we ask human subjects to generate strings of (pseudo-)random coin flips. We then introduce the following natural prediction tasks: (1) *Continuation:* can we predict the kth flip in a string generated by a human subject, based

---

The complete paper can be found at **https://arxiv.org**.

Supported in part by a Simons Investigator Award, an ARO MURI grant, a Google Research Grant, and a Facebook Faculty Research Grant.

Author's addresses: J. Kleinberg, Computer Science Department, Cornell University; A. Liang, Microsoft Research New-England; S. Mullainathan, Department of Economics, Harvard University.

EC'17, June 26–30, 2017, Cambridge, MA, USA.

 ACM ISBN 978-1-4503-4527-9/17/06
http://dx.doi.org/10.1145/3033274.3084094

on the first $k-1$ flips? (2) *Classification:* given a set of n strings created by human participants, and n strings created by a Bernoulli process, can we identify which strings were human-generated?

A number of influential behavioral theories provide methods for estimating the probabilities of strings generated by a human source, and hence lead to predictions for these problems [4, 5]. Strikingly, though, despite the richness of the underlying behavioral questions, the Continuation and Classification problems are tasks where the benchmark of optimal prediction can be feasibly computed. Optimal predictions for this problem can be made via *table lookup*: enumerate all 2^k strings s of 0's and 1's, and learn their empirical proportions. We use table lookup to construct a benchmark for the best attainable level of prediction, and then compare its predictive accuracy with the accuracy achieved by principal behavioral models [4, 5].

We find that these behavioral models are *predictive*: they attain a mean-squared error of 0.249, which improves (to a statistically significant extent) on the error of 0.250 that we would obtain by random guessing. They are not, however, *complete*. Table lookup attains an error of 0.243; relative to this benchmark, the existing models attain 12% of the achievable gain over naive guessing.

Extending this basic result, we consider several further questions. First, do the limitations of existing theories relative to table lookup arise because (a) the existing theories miss crucial features of the problem, or because (b) they use the "right" features, but do not combine them effectively? We define interpretable features based on existing theories, and apply standard algorithms to combine them for prediction. These algorithms come close to the performance of table lookup, suggesting that the limitations of existing theories may be a consequence of (b) more than (a).

We also show that table lookup is robust to variations in the task: the table lookup predictor generalizes to "nearby" settings such as strings of different lengths, and over different alphabets.

Finally, we ask whether our methodology can also be used to evaluate theory completeness in real-life settings where human perception of randomness is believed to play a role. We focus on two such settings: sequential decisions by baseball umpires calling balls and strikes [2], where we ask how well an umpire's current call can be predicted from the past $k-1$ calls; and sequential choices by players in a rock-paper-scissors tournament [1], where we seek to predict a player's current choice from their past $k-1$. In both domains, table lookup achieves significant gains over naive guessing in predicting an individual's next decision. Moreover, a striking contrast emerges when we evaluate theory completeness: We show how use of table lookup as a benchmark reveals that the predictive model based on Rabin and Vayanos [5] differs significantly in its effectiveness relative to the optimum across these different domains.

Taken together, our results suggest that (1) there is significant structure in the problem of predicting human generation of randomness that existing models have yet to capture, and (2) our approach via the optimal predictive benchmark allows for evaluation of the completeness of theories in the given domain. As recently suggested also by [3], such an approach can be applied more generally in settings where this benchmark can be feasibly determined or approximated.

REFERENCES

[1] Dimitrios Batzilis, Sonia Jaffe, Steven Levitt, John A. List, and Jeff Picel. 2016. How Facebook Can Deepen our Understanding of Behavior in Strategic Settings: Evidence from a Million Rock-Paper-Scissors Games. (2016). W.P.

[2] Daniel Chen, Kelly Shue, and Tobias Moskowitz. 2016. Decision-Making under the Gambler's Fallacy: Evidence from Asylum Judges, Loan Officers, and Baseball Umpires. *Quarterly Journal of Economics* (2016).

[3] Alexander Peysakhovich and Jeffrey Naecker. 2017. Using Methods from Machine Learning to Evaluate Behavioral Models of Choice Under Risk and Ambiguity. *Journal of Economic Behavior and Organization* (2017).

[4] Matthew Rabin. 2002. Inference by Believers in the Law of Small Numbers. *The Quarterly Journal of Economics* (2002).

[5] Matthew Rabin and Dmitri Vayanos. 2010. The Gambler's and Hot-Hand Fallacies: Theory and Applications. *Review of Economic Studies* (2010).

[6] A. Rapaport and D. Budescu. 1997. Randomization in Individual Choice Behavior. *Psychological Review* (1997).

Comparison-Based Choices

JON KLEINBERG, Cornell University
SENDHIL MULLAINATHAN, Harvard University
JOHAN UGANDER, Stanford University

A broad range of on-line behaviors are mediated by interfaces in which people make choices among sets of options. A rich and growing line of work in the behavioral sciences indicate that human choices follow not only from the utility of alternatives, but also from the *choice set* in which alternatives are presented. In this work we study comparison-based choice functions, a simple but surprisingly rich class of functions capable of exhibiting so-called *choice-set effects*. Motivated by the challenge of predicting complex choices, we study the query complexity of these functions in a variety of settings. We consider settings that allow for active queries or passive observation of a stream of queries, and give analyses both at the granularity of individuals or populations that might exhibit heterogeneous choice behavior. Our main result is that any comparison-based choice function in one dimension can be inferred as efficiently as a basic maximum or minimum choice function across many query contexts, suggesting that choice-set effects need not entail any fundamental algorithmic barriers to inference. We also introduce a class of choice functions we call distance-comparison-based functions, and briefly discuss the analysis of such functions. The framework we outline provides intriguing connections between human choice behavior and a range of questions in the theory of sorting.

Additional Key Words and Phrases: Choice-set effects, sorting with noisy comparisons, sorting in one round.

1 INTRODUCTION

Modern information systems across a broad range of domains wrestle with increasingly expansive and heterogeneous corpora of data describing human decisions — from online marketplaces such as Amazon and AirBnB recording diverse purchasing behavior to search engines and recommendation systems that process continuous clickstreams, where clicks reflect choices.

Many of the decisions made in these on-line environments have a consistent structure: users are presented with a set of options — a list of recommended books, search results, flight options, or users to follow — and they select one or more items from the set. The ubiquity of this framework has led to an active line of research on the problem of learning ranking functions [1]. There are many formulations in the literature, but the essential core is to assume that a user has a ranking over alternatives that is hidden from us, and by observing their choices we would like to infer this ranking. This question can be asked at the level of individuals or at the level of populations containing heterogeneous but related rankings.

Choice-set effects. A central assumption in the work on rankings is that individuals start from an underlying total order on the possible alternatives. Roughly speaking, consider an inventory $Z = \{z_1, z_2, \ldots, z_n\}$ of possible choices, globally ordered so that a particular user prefers z_i to z_j

Authors' email addresses: kleinber@cs.cornell.edu; mullain@fas.harvard.edu; jugander@stanford.edu.

This work is supported in part by a Simons Investigator Award, an ARO MURI grant, a Google Research Grant, Facebook Faculty Research Grants, and a David Morgenthaler II Faculty Fellowship.

DOI: http://dx.doi.org/10.1145/3033274.3085134

for $i < j$. When the user is presented with a set of choices $S \subseteq Z$, they select the item in S that is ranked first according to this global order. There are many variations on this basic pattern – there may be noise in the selection, or options may be unobserved – but the total ordering is a crucial part of the structure.

A long line of work in behavioral science [9, 15, 22, 25, 28], however, indicates that people's empirical choices tend to deviate in significant ways from this picture. A person's choice will in fact typically depend not just on the total ordering on the full set of alternatives Z, which is often enormous and implicit, but also on the *choice set* S they are shown as part of the specific decision at hand. Notable examples of such choice-set effects include the compromise effect, similarity aversion, and the decoy effect (also known as asymmetric dominance), and have been observed in diverse contexts both offline and online; recent work in machine learning has highlighted the prevalence of choice-set effects [4, 19, 23, 33] and non-transitive comparisons [7, 8], particularly in online search, online ads, and online games.

A canonical example of a choice-set effect is the so-called *compromise effect* [24]: faced with the choice between a mediocre option for \$10, a good option for \$15, and an excellent option for \$20, people will tend to choose the good option for \$15; but faced instead with a choice between the same good option for \$15, the excellent option for \$20, and an outstanding option for \$25, people will be more likely to choose the excellent option for \$20. In other words, there is a tendency to favor the option that compromises between the two extremes in the set that is presented.

More generally, suppose that a set of products exhibit a trade-off between two factors – for example, price vs. quality, power vs. reliability, or aesthetics vs. fuel efficiency. There is a naturally defined one-dimensional set of products that are on the *Pareto frontier*: they are the options for which no other product is more desirable in both factors. Consider four products A, B, C, and D that are arranged in this order along the one-dimensional frontier (A is the least powerful but most reliable, and D as the most powerful but least reliable). In a wide variety of settings, B will be empirically chosen more often when it is presented as one of the three choices $S = \{A, B, C\}$ than when it is one of the three choices $S' = \{B, C, D\}$ – in other words, when it is the compromise option rather than an extreme option. By the same reasoning, C will be chosen more often when it is presented as part of S' than as part of S.

One can ask whether this is simply a representational issue, but in fact it is much deeper. The point is that in any model based on a total ordering on the alternatives Z, a user would prefer either B or C, and this would hold in *any* choice set S that contains both of them. But B and C are options in both the sets $S = \{A, B, C\}$ and $S' = \{B, C, D\}$, and the aggregate distribution of choices in favor of B versus C changes across these two sets. This suggests that the relative ordering of B and C in fact is not well-defined in isolation, but must be evaluated in the context of the choice set (S or S'). It matters what else is on offer.

Comparison-based choice functions. In this paper, we consider a set of basic algorithmic questions that arise when we seek to infer models of user choice in the presence of comparison-based choice-set effects. We focus on a basic formulation in which these effects arise, and show how our framework makes it possible to derive asymptotic bounds on query complexity and sample complexity in performing these types of inference. We set up the problem as follows.

(1) Embedding of alternatives. The full collection of alternatives is a set $U = \{u_1, \ldots, u_n\}$, and there is an embedding of U into a space of *attributes* X via a function $h : U \to X$. For most of our discussion we will take X to be the real line $\mathbb{R}^1$, so that $h(u_i)$ is a real number; thus most of the time we can think of the embedded points $\{h(u_1), \ldots, h(u_n)\}$ as representing a one-dimensional trade-off continuum as in the discussion above. We will assume that the embedding h is not known to us. Indeed, while we sometimes might know the crucial one-dimensional attribute of an item, such

as a price, the important attributes in many settings will not be explicitly presented to us: a user might have a mental ordering of clothing styles on a spectrum from "too dull" to "too ostentatious," or restaurants on a spectrum from "too bland" to "too exotic," or book or movie recommendations on a spectrum from "too much what I'm already reading" to "too far from my interests."

(2) Choice functions. We focus on an individual who is presented with a subset $S \subseteq U$ of a fixed size k and chooses one element from S. Throughout this discussion we will refer to subsets of U of size k as *k-sets* of U. We study k-sets, rather than subsets of arbitrary/varying size, both for conceptual clarity and also with the motivation that many of our motivating applications — online recommendations and search results — often present choices between a fixed number of options.

An individual's selections are represented using a *choice function* f: for each k-set $S \subseteq U$, we define $f(S) \in S$ as the individual's selection when presented with S. We say that f exhibits *choice-set effects* if the identity of the set S affects the relative choice between two elements: specifically, f exhibits choice-set effects if there exist k-sets S and T, and elements u_i and u_j, such that $u_i, u_j \in S \cap T$, and $f(S) = u_i$ while $f(T) = u_j$. If such choices can occur then a choice between u_i and u_j depends on whether they are presented in the context of S or T; one can view such a contextual effect as a violation of the independence of irrelevant alternatives ("IIA") [21].

We define choice functions here as deterministic for a given individual. Later in this work we study populations composed of a mixture of different choice functions, and our results there can be interpreted equivalently as applying to the choices of an individual making probabilistic decisions corresponding to a randomization over different choice functions. We can contrast such probabilistic choices (those expressible as mixtures), with random utility models (RUMs) [3, 17]: they lack some of the flexibility of RUMs; but discrete choice models such as RUMs on the other hand typically entail other restrictions, including assuming the independence of irrelevant alternatives. Identifying the expressive limits of random mixtures of choice functions for modeling probabilistic choice is an intriguing open challenge.

(3) Comparison-based functions. We focus here on comparison-based choice functions, which incorporate the ordinal structure inherent in preference learning, but which are still rich enough to exhibit choice-set effects. A choice function f on k-sets is *comparison-based* if the value $f(S)$ can be computed purely using comparisons on the ordering of the numbers $\{h(u_i) : u_i \in S\}$. It is not hard to see that for any comparison-based choice function f on k-sets, there is a number ℓ between 1 and k so that for all k-sets S, the value $f(S)$ is equal to the ℓth ranked element in S according to the embedding $h(\cdot)$. We can therefore characterize any comparison-based choice functions in one dimension as a *position-selecting choice function* for some position ℓ of k.

Thus, comparison-based choice functions represent different versions of the compromise effects discussed earlier: faced with a set S of k options ranked along a one-dimensional spectrum, an individual would choose the ℓth ranked option. For example, when $k = 3$ and $\ell = 2$, the individual always chooses the middle of three options, much like the sample instance with choices A, B, C, D discussed earlier. It is not hard to verify, using examples such as this one, that a comparison-based choice function exhibits choice-set effects if and only if $2 \leq \ell \leq k - 1$.

Choice functions over k-sets as we define them here are very general mathematical functions, capable of encoding an arbitrary choice for every k-set. Comparison-based functions in one dimension, however, are a structured subset of choice functions that provide a useful abstraction of many decision contexts. We are not aware of any prior inference work on general comparison-based functions, which is surprising given the central role of binary comparison in the fundamental problem of sorting. We focus on comparisons in one dimension. Comparison functions in higher dimensions can have a significantly more complex structure; extending our results to higher dimensions is beyond the scope of the present work.

A short-coming of comparison-based functions is that they lack the ability to grasp "similarity," an important aspect of choice-set effects such as similarity aversion and the decoy effect, and one that requires a notion of distance beyond ordinal comparison. As a step towards extending our framework to model such effects, we also study *distance-comparison-based choice functions* that model choices according to distance comparisons, possibly in high-dimensional latent spaces.

The present work: Asymptotic complexity of inference. There are many questions that one can consider for models of comparison-based choice functions; here we study a basic family of problems that are inherent in any inference procedure, and which form an interesting connection to fundamental questions in sorting.

The basic problem we study has the following structure: we observe a sequence of choices of the form $(S, f(S))$, and at the end of this sequence we must correctly report the value of $f(S)$ for all (or almost all) k-sets S. The question is how few observations $(S, f(S))$ we need in order to achieve various measures of success. We ask this question for different models of how the observations are generated. We first consider active queries, in which we can choose S and receive the value of $f(S)$; we investigate the potential for efficient inference both when a single individual is making choices with a fixed function f, and for population mixtures of different choice functions. As a second model we consider passive queries, a model whereby a stream of pairs $(S, f(S))$ is generated uniformly at random over possible k-sets S, without the control over S offered by the active query model.

For active queries, a natural baseline for understanding the problem formulation is the problem of sorting, which precisely consists of the case $k = 2$ and $\ell = 1$. A comparison-based sorting algorithm asks about a sequence of pairs $S = \{u_i, u_j\}$, and for each such pair it is told the identity of the preferred element. An efficient sorting algorithm given $O(n \log n)$ such queries can learn the sorted order of the elements, and thus can answer queries of the form $f(S)$ for arbitrary pairs after learning the sorted order.

We show that all comparison-based choice functions in one dimension exhibit the same $O(n \log n)$ active query complexity: for every ℓ and k, there is an algorithm that can ask about a sequence of $O(n \log n)$ k-sets S as queries, and from the values of $f(S)$ it is then prepared to correctly report $f(S)$ for all k-sets S. Roughly speaking, the algorithm works by first identifying a small set of elements that cannot be the answer to any query, and then it uses these elements as "anchors" on which to build sets that can simulate comparisons of pairs. Note that as the set size k grows, the $O(n \log n)$ queries form a smaller and smaller fraction of the set of all $\binom{n}{k}$ possible k-sets.

We then consider active queries for population mixtures, in which different people use different comparison-based choice functions on k-sets, and when we pose a query S, we get back the answer $f(S)$ for an individual selected uniformly at random from the population. We show that for a fixed but unknown vector of probabilities for each choice function under some natural non-degeneracy conditions we can determine $f(S)$ for each segment of the population after $O(n \log n)$ active queries. The algorithm here uses random sampling ideas combined with techniques for *sorting using noisy comparators* [10].

For passive queries, where an algorithm is presented with a stream of values $(f(S), S)$ for randomly selected sets S, the question is how long we need to observe values from the stream before being able to compute $f(S)$ for all (or almost all) k-sets S. We show that for comparison-based choice functions f that exhibit choice-set effects (with ℓ between 2 and $k-1$), we can do this after observing $o(n^k)$ values from the stream with high probability; for an arbitrary $\varepsilon > 0$ and $\delta > 0$, we can, with probability at least $1 - \delta$, determine $f(S)$ for at least a $1 - \varepsilon$ fraction of all k-sets S. Our analysis here builds on a sequence of combinatorial results on *sorting in one round*, culminating in an asymptotically tight analysis of that problem by Alon and Azar [2, 5].

Finally, we consider how our results for comparison-based functions apply to distance-comparison-based choice functions in which the geometry of the alternatives' embedding plays a consequential role. A range of earlier work have made use of the ambient space in different ways, including methods such as *conjoint analysis* [3, 12]. Here, we consider the effect of performing comparisons among the pairwise distances between alternatives. This consideration enables us to reason about elements that are either *central* or *outliers* in a comparison-based fashion, providing a plausible model for the choice-set effect commonly known as *similarity aversion.* This line of inquiry into metric embeddings also connects our results with recent research in the learning and crowdsourcing literature on learning stochastic triplet embeddings [30] and inferences using the crowd median algorithm [13].

2 ACTIVE QUERY COMPLEXITY

We will first focus on *active* query algorithms that may choose queries sequentially based on the results of previous queries, and our goal here is to develop algorithms that after performing a small number of queries can take an arbitrary k-set $S \subseteq U$ from a universe of n alternatives and correctly output $f(S)$.

We have previously noted that every comparison-based choice function over a one-dimensional ordering takes the form of a position-selecting choice function choosing the ℓth alternative of k for some ordering; we will denote this function by $q_{k,\ell}$. Our results in this section show that for any fixed $k \geq 2$ and any fixed but unknown $\ell \in \{1, ..., k\}$, we can in fact learn the output for any input using an efficient two-phase algorithm that performs only $O(n \log n)$ queries. This algorithm determines ℓ (up to a reflection we discuss below) by the time it terminates, but we also give a simple algorithm that recovers ℓ (up to the same reflection) more directly in just $O(1)$ queries (without learning the output for all inputs). Thus, we establish that learning the position ℓ of a comparison-based choice function does not require running a comprehensive recovery algorithm.

For recovering the choice function, we note that the orientation of the embedding is inconsequential. This symmetry is clear when considering the simplest example of $k = 2$, where f is either a max selector $q_{2,1}$ or a min selector $q_{2,2}$. In order to deduce $f(S)$ for every S we needn't know whether f is choosing the max or min, as we will simply learn an embedding aligned with our selector. More generally, we have no way or need to distinguish between $q_{k,\ell}$ over a given embedding and $q_{k,k-\ell+1}$ over the same embedding reversed, as they result in the exact same choices.

Recovering choice functions. The algorithm we propose consists of two phases. In the first phase, we use $O(n)$ queries to identify a set of "ineligible" alternatives. In the second phase, we use those ineligible alternatives to "anchor" the choice set down to a binary comparison between two eligible alternatives, allowing us to determine the ordering of the eligible alternatives in $O(n \log n)$ queries using comparison-based sorting.

Theorem 2.1. *Given a choice function f over k-sets S in a universe of n alternatives, there is an algorithm that recovers f after $O(n \log n)$ queries, meaning that after this set of queries it can output $f(S)$ for any S.*

We prove this theorem by describing the algorithm together with its analysis, divided into its two phases of operation. For the first phase, we identify the ineligible elements. In the second phase, we simulate pairwise comparisons.

Proof. We begin the first phase by observing that for a position selector $q_{k,\ell}$ making comparison-based choices over k-sets $S \subseteq U$ with $|U| = n$, there are $k - 1$ alternatives that will never be chosen. For max-selectors $q_{k,k}$ these are the $k - 1$ minimal alternatives, for min-selectors $q_{k,1}$ these are the $k - 1$ maximal alternatives, and for general $q_{k,\ell}$ these are the $\ell - 1$ maximal and $k - \ell$ minimal alternatives from the embedded order.

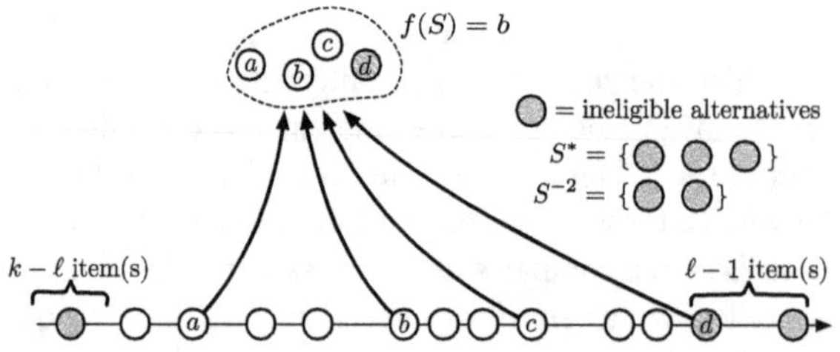

Fig. 1. For a given comparison-based choice function f over an unknown embedding, there are ineligible alternatives that will never be chosen, illustrated here for $k = 4$ and $\ell = 3$. The elements are embedded in a 1-dimensional space, where the $\ell - 1$ maximal and $k - \ell$ minimal elements can never be chosen.

To find these elements, we run a simple *discard algorithm*. Commencing with k arbitrary initial alternatives in a choice set S_1, we query the choice function f and learn the choice $f(S_1)$. We then construct our next choice set by discarding the previous choice and selecting a new arbitrary alternative $u \in U \setminus S_1$ to form $S_2 = (S_1 \setminus f(S_1)) \cup u$. We query for $f(S_2)$, and repeat this discard procedure for $n - k + 1$ queries. After the last query we will have exhausted U and learned that $S^* = S_{n-k+1} \setminus f(S_{n-k+1})$ are precisely the $k - 1$ alternatives in U that can never be selected by f. Having found the $k - 1$ ineligible alternatives S^*, we arbitrarily select $k - 2$ alternatives from S^* to form a set S^{-2}. See Figure 1 for an illustration of this procedure.

In the second phase of the algorithm we use the set S^{-2} constructed above as padding for a choice set construction with two open positions: notice that for any two alternatives u_i and u_j, a query for $f(\{u_i, u_j\} \cup S^{-2})$ will amount to binary comparison between u_i and u_j. If $\ell = 1$ or $\ell = k$, we know that this will be a max or a min selection, respectively. However, for intermediate values of ℓ we do not yet know whether such binary comparisons will be a max or a min selection, as it depends on what $k - 2$ elements from S^* were chosen to construct S^{-2}. There exists no basis for choosing S^{-2} from S^* in a non-arbitrary way, as we have no way of ever choosing any of the alternatives in S^{-2}. However, as noted earlier in the case of recovering choice functions for $k = 2$, we can simply assume that the comparator we have constructed is selecting the max of u_i and u_j, and then learn the order of the eligible alternatives from binary comparisons as oriented by that comparator. After $O(n \log n)$ padded comparison queries, we obtain a sorted order of the eligible alternatives.

To conclude this second phase, we perform a single additional query to determine ℓ, the position being selected, which is as yet unknown and unused. By querying for what we've come to suppose are the first k eligible elements, the chosen alternative will identify the ℓth position in the recovered embedding of the eligible alternatives. We again emphasize that we have no way of distinguishing between $q_{k,\ell}$ over a given embedding and $q_{k,k-\ell+1}$ over the same embedding reversed, but the direction of the ordering is nonessential, as the choices are identical for all choice sets. Having learned the embedded order of the eligible alternatives in U as well as the position ℓ being selected, we can now discern the choice $f(S)$ for any k-set $S \subseteq U$. □

As a further point, it is notable that no part of this algorithm depends on ℓ, as it is only learned at the end of the final query, meaning that the entire algorithm is in fact indifferent to whether an individual is selecting minima, maxima, or intermediate positions.

Lastly, we observe that the classic lower bound on sorting applies as a lower bound here as well, for fixed ℓ and k: there are $(n - k + 1)!/2$ possible permutations of how the eligible alternatives can be embedded (ignoring the $k - 1$ ineligible alternatives). Each query cements at most $k - 1$ relative orderings, at most reducing the number of feasible orderings by a factor of $k - 1$. We thus require at least $\log_k((n-k)!/2)$ queries to learn a choice function, yielding a lower bound of $\Omega(n \log n)$, as for sorting.

Type classification. It can be valuable to learn how a choice function makes comparisons without necessarily learning the ordering implicated in the comparisons. Here we establish that we can learn ℓ, up to the noted reflection equivalence, using $O(k)$ queries without learning the order of the alternatives.

PROPOSITION 2.2. *By querying for all k-set subsets of an arbitrary $(k+1)$-set, we can determine ℓ, up to reflection.*

PROOF. The algorithm performs $k+1$ queries for all the subsets of size k, where each of these subsets can be defined by what element is excluded. The $k+1$ alternatives have an unknown internal ordering, and we let u_i denote the ith alternative in order. From these queries, there can be only two possible elements selected as the output across the k different subsets: either the chosen alternative in the $(\ell+1)^{\text{th}}$ ordered position (when the excluded element is one of $u_1, \ldots, u_\ell$) or the chosen alternative in the ℓth ordered (when the excluded element is one of $u_{\ell+1}, \ldots, u_{k+1}$). Of these $k+1$ k-sets, the $(\ell+1)^{\text{th}}$ element will be chosen ℓ times, and the ℓth element will be chosen $k-\ell+1$ times.

Thus, for any k, in order to determine the position ℓ of a position-selecting choice function, one can simply take an arbitrary set of $k+1$ elements and query for all subsets of k. Then ℓ (up to reflection) is the frequency of the less frequent of the two response elements. □

3 POPULATION MIXTURES

The results in the previous section assumed that all queries were evaluated by the same deterministic choice function f, where $f(S)$ was consistently selecting the ℓth ordered alternative from within each k-set S. In this section, we show that we can recover choice functions in a more general setting, where the position ℓ chosen by f is drawn from a distribution over possible positions.

This setting covers two generalizations of our active query results. First, it describes situations where a single individual is being repeatedly queried, and may exhibit compromise effects for some queries, independently at random. Second, it describes situations where the queries are handled by a population of individuals that all base their choices on the same ordered embedding, but differ in what position within an ordering that their choice functions select for. We show that we can still recover choice functions in this setting using $O(n \log n)$ queries, almost surely.

Recalling one of our motivating examples from the introduction, this is a plausible reality: faced with a choice of restaurants ranging from "too bland" to "too exotic," some individuals will compromise, while some will optimize for one of the extremes. In online settings the choices being made often come from heterogeneous populations, and we wish to develop an algorithm that can still recover choices in these settings.

We define a *mixed choice function* as a comparison-based choice function on k-sets $S \subset U$ where the ℓth ordered element in S is selected independently at random with probability π_ℓ. A mixed choice function is then completely defined by an ordering of U and a probability distribution $(\pi_1, ..., \pi_k)$ over position-selecting choice functions with $\sum_{i=1}^{k} \pi_i = 1$. To avoid degeneracies, we require that $\pi_\ell > 0, \forall \ell$, and also require constant separation between the probabilities, $|\pi_\ell - \pi_{\ell'}| > \gamma, \forall \ell, \ell'$ with $\ell \neq \ell'$, for some constant $\gamma > 0$.

In its most basic instance, a mixed choice function over 2-sets is simply a noisy binary comparator over an ordering, with $(\pi_1, \pi_2) = (p, 1-p)$ for some probability p. In this case, results from the sorting literature contribute that as long as p is bounded away from $1/2$, the order can be recovered in $O(n \log n)$ queries almost surely [10]. Our contribution in this section is to generalize this result to arbitrary mixtures of comparison-based choice functions.

We begin by showing that for any $\epsilon > 0$, we can recover the mixture probabilities $(\pi_1, ..., \pi_k)$ of a mixed choice function with probability at least $1 - \epsilon$ in a number of queries that is $O(1)$ in n, the size of U. We then show that we can indeed recover any mixed choice function f using $O(n \log n)$ queries with probability at least $1 - \epsilon$.

Recovering mixture probabilities. We begin by showing that we can recover the mixture probabilities using a modified version of the algorithm we presented for recovering ℓ in an active query framework.

THEOREM 3.1. *Let f be a mixed comparison-based choice function over k-sets in a universe of n alternatives. Let $\pi = (\pi_1, ..., \pi_k)$ be the mixture distribution of f, and let $\pi_\ell > 0, \forall \ell$, and $|\pi_\ell - \pi_{\ell'}| > \gamma$, $\forall \ell, \ell'$ with $\ell' \neq \ell$, for some constant $\gamma > 0$.*

For any $\epsilon > 0$ and $\delta \in (0, \gamma/2)$ there exists a constant $C > 0$ such that an algorithm using C queries can recover π, meaning that it outputs a probability vector p for which

$$Pr(max_\ell |\hat{\pi}_\ell - \pi_\ell| \leq \delta) \geq 1 - \epsilon$$

holds for either $\hat{\pi} = (p_1, ..., p_k)$ or $\hat{\pi} = (p_k, ..., p_1)$.

PROOF. Our strategy is to study a single $(k+1)$-set S^+ closely, and by querying each k-set within S^+ sufficiently many times we can recover the mixture distribution with the required precision. We index the $k+1$ k-sets within S^+ as $S_1, ..., S_{k+1}$.

We define the random variables

$$X_{i,j}^u = \begin{cases} 1 \text{ if query } i \text{ of subset } S_j \text{ returns } u \in S_j \\ 0 \text{ otherwise,} \end{cases} \tag{1}$$

where $\mathbb{E}[X_{i,j}^u] = \pi_u^j$ for a vector of probabilities $\pi^j = (\pi_1^j, ..., \pi_k^j)$ that is an unknown permutation of $(\pi_1, ..., \pi_k)$.

We first show that for each subset we can recover the complete set of probabilities with the specified precision and correctly ordered by their relative frequency. In a second stage we will then align the permuted π^j vectors and thereby recover π itself (or π's reflection).

For each S_j, we consider the estimates $\hat{\pi}_u^j = \frac{1}{C} \sum_{i=1}^C X_{i,j}^u$, and we show that this is correct to within the requested error tolerance if we choose C large enough. Recalling that $\delta < \gamma/2$, a two-sided Chernoff bound tells us that:

$$\Pr\left(\left|\frac{1}{C}\sum_{i=1}^{C} X_{i,j}^u - \pi_u^j\right| \geq \delta_u^j \pi_u^j\right) \leq 2\exp\left(-\frac{(\delta_u^j)^2}{2+\delta_u^j} C\pi_u^j\right),$$

for which we can set $\delta_u^j = \delta/\pi_u^j$ and use $\pi_u^j \leq 1, \forall j, u$ to obtain

$$\Pr\left(|\hat{\pi}_u^j - \pi_u^j| \geq \delta\right) \leq 2\exp\left(-\frac{\delta^2}{2+\delta} C\right).$$

Let us define the bad events $\mathcal{E}_{j,u} = \{|\hat{\pi}_u^j - \pi_u^j| \geq \delta\}$, when we failed to recover π_u^j (the probability of selecting u from subset S_j) within the specified precision. By taking the Union Bound across the sets S_j and their alternatives u, we can set $C > \frac{2+\delta}{\delta^2} \log(\frac{\epsilon}{2k(k+1)})$ to obtain

$$\Pr\left(\max_{u,j} \left|\hat{\pi}_u^j - \pi_u^j\right| \leq \delta\right) \geq 1 - \sum_{j=1}^{k+1}\sum_{u=1}^{k} \Pr\left(\left|\hat{\pi}_u^j - \pi_u^j\right| \geq \delta\right) > 1 - \epsilon.$$

The remaining challenge is to determine what probability corresponds to what choice position, and we will show that recovering this correspondence is guaranteed if the bad events did not occur.

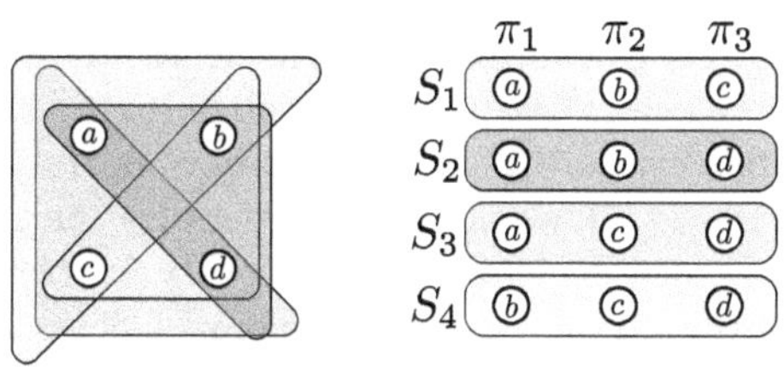

Fig. 2. A graphical sketch of the population alignment algorithm in Theorem 2, shown for $k = 3$. Left: a 4-set contains four 3-sets, S_1, S_2, S_3, S_4. Right: by querying for each 3-set sufficiently often, we can identify the frequencies π_1, π_2, π_3 with which each element occurs and then identify π_1 and π_3 by the fact that their frequencies corresponds to the same element in all but one of the 3-sets.

We recover the correspondence using an alignment procedure: since $\delta < \gamma/2$, inside each S_j we can order the elements from most frequently selected to least frequently selected. In this order the ith most frequent choice inside each vector $\hat{\pi}^j$ will correspond to the same underlying position selection for each S_j. The most frequently selected element from each S_j will have been selected by the ℓ-selector with the largest π_ℓ in π, and so on, for each selection frequency.

To discern what frequency corresponds to what ℓ, we look across the subsets $S_1, \dots, S_{k+1}$ and identify the two probabilities π_1 and π_k by the fact that they will be the only two frequencies that have selected some element u only once at that frequency, and another element v the remaining k times at that frequency. In other words, the alternatives selected at those frequencies will have the structure $\{u, v, \dots., v\}$ for some u and v, and these must be the frequencies π_1 and π_k. See Figure S1 for an illustration in the case of $k = 3$. We arbitrarily assign the more frequent of these two frequencies to be π_1, recalling that we're only looking to recover π up to reflection. The other frequency is assigned to be π_k.

Lastly, for each of these two end frequencies π_1 and π_k we take the "other" element v (that made up $k-1$ of the k choices at that frequency), and find what frequency corresponds to when each v was selected exactly twice, identifying the probabilities π_2 and π_{k-1}. Since $\pi_\ell > 0$ for all ℓ, we can continue this overlap procedure for all the frequencies, allowing us to identify the probability π_ℓ corresponding to each position ℓ. This alignment procedure fails only if one of the earlier bad events failed, and so we can return any one of the $\hat{\pi}^j$, which all had the necessary precision, and reorder it by our alignment procedure to produce our output p. □

A recovery algorithm for mixtures. We now show that in this setting where queries are handled by a mixed choice function—either representing a random individual or a random mixture of individuals—we can recover the choice function in $O(n \log n)$ queries with high probability, matching the asymptotic query complexity of the non-population case for any fixed error probability. We run our recovery algorithm against the mixture population, but for the purposes of recovering $f(S)$ for every S we assume that ℓ is then known.

Theorem 3.2. *Let f be a mixed comparison-based choice function over k-sets in a universe of n alternatives. Let $\pi = (\pi_1, ..., \pi_k)$ be the unknown mixture distribution of f, and let $\pi_\ell > 0, \forall \ell$, and $|\pi_\ell - \pi_{\ell'}| > \gamma, \forall \ell, \ell'$ with $\ell \neq \ell'$, for some constant $\gamma > 0$.*

Let $f_1, ..., f_k$ be pure versions of f, where $\pi_\ell = 1$ for f_ℓ, over the same ordered embedding. For any $\epsilon > 0$ there exists an algorithm using $O(n \log n)$ queries to f that with probability at least $1 - \epsilon$ can recover $f_\ell(S)$ for all ℓ, all S.

Our proof is constructive. The strategy for this algorithm is to first run our procedure from Theorem 2 for recovering π using a constant number of queries. We then focus on max-selectors, and run a modified discard algorithm (from Theorem 1) to identify the alternatives that are ineligible to the subpopulation of max-selectors. We use these ineligible alternatives for the max-selectors to create an anchored k-set that can furnish a noisy binary comparator. By employing results for sorting under noisy comparisons [10], we obtain the order over the alternatives that are eligible to a max-selector. If we only needed to recover $f_k(S)$ for every S, where f_k is the max-selector, we would be done. In order to also learn the order of the max-ineligible alternatives, we run a second sort using a query anchored with min-ineligible alternatives, thereby also recovering the order of the max-ineligible alternatives.

Proof. We begin by running the algorithm from Theorem 2 with a sufficiently large number of queries C_1 to obtain an estimate $\hat{\pi}$ of π, such that $\Pr(\max_\ell |\hat{\pi}_\ell - \pi_\ell| \le \gamma/2) > 1 - \epsilon/5$ where C_1 is a constant in n for every ϵ and γ. The usual caveats for reflection of the mixture vector apply, and we learn π for one of the orientations, arbitrarily chosen. We focus on our estimate of π_k, the probability that a query is answered by a max-selector.

We now initiate our standard discard algorithm, which we will use to find max-ineligible alternatives, starting with an arbitrary k-set $S \subset U$. In each discard step, we plan to identify the max element by posing enough queries to the population that the frequency with which we observe the maximum element is close enough to π_k. Let $\mathcal{E}_i$ be the bad event that discard round i incorrectly identified the max element in the set (π_k was not recovered with sufficient precision), and let $\mathcal{D}$ be the success event whereby no bad events occur and the discard algorithm terminates with the alternatives that are ineligible for the max-selectors. Using C_2 queries in each round i of the discard algorithm we can bound $\Pr[\mathcal{E}_i]$ using two-sided Chernoff bounds, followed by the Union Bound across the $n-2$ rounds of our discard algorithm to obtain:

$$\Pr[\mathcal{D}] \ge 1 - \sum_{i=1}^{n-2} \Pr[\mathcal{E}_i] \ge 1 - 2(n-2)\exp\left(-\frac{\gamma^2}{8+2\gamma} C_2\right).$$

Selecting $C_2 > \frac{8+2\gamma}{\gamma^2}\log(\frac{10}{\epsilon})\log(n) = C_2' \log(n)$, we obtain that $\Pr[\mathcal{D}] > 1 - \epsilon/5$ with $C_2' n \log n$ queries across all the rounds of this discard algorithm, where C_2' is constant in n.

Conditional on succeeding thus far, we can now create a padded k-set from the max-ineligible alternatives $S^*_{\max}$ that were never selected during our discard algorithm, forming a binary comparator for any u and v from a k-set of the form $\{u, v\} \cup S^{-2}_{\max}$ for any $(k-2)$-set $S^{-2}_{\max} \subset S^*_{\max}$. The max alternative will be selected with probability π_k, and the second most maximal alternative will be selected with probability π_{k-1}. Our goal is to hand this comparator off to the Feige et al. comparison-based query algorithm [10], but we note that the Feige et al. algorithm requires a binary comparator that returns each element with probabilities $\{p, 1-p\}$ for some $p > 1/2$. Our comparator, meanwhile, will "fail" with constant probability $\Delta = 1 - \pi_k - \pi_{k-1}$, in the sense that some alternative $u^* \in S^{-2}_{\max}$ will be selected that is not one of the elements u or v being subjected to the noisy binary comparison. If one of π_k or π_{k-1} exceed $1/2$ then we can apply the Feige et al. procedure as-is, as we can simply bundle any choice $u^* \in S^{-2}_{\max}$ as a choice of the less frequent of the two positions, producing the necessary binary comparator. If the selection probabilities π_k and π_{k-1} are both less than $1/2$, we can modify our comparator as follows.

For each step s that the Feige et al. algorithm performs a query, we repeat the query until we first see one of k or $k-1$. This means that the outcome space is not $\{k, k-1, \text{fail}\}$, but just $\{k, k-1\}$, one of which will have a fixed probability $p > 1/2$. Let C_s be a random variable that takes a value equal to the number of queries needed before first seeing k or $k-1$. Seeing as C_s is geometrically distributed, we have $\mathbb{E}[C_s] = 1/\Delta$, the inverse of the failure probability. But now the total number of queries being run throughout the Feige et al. algorithm is $\sum_{s=1}^{Dn\log n} C_s$, for a constant D large enough to control the Feige et al. error to at most $\epsilon/5$, and so in expectation it takes $\mathbb{E}[\sum_{s=1}^{Dn\log n} C_s] = (1/\Delta)Dn\log n$ queries. By Markov's inequality the probability that the number of queries exceeds its expectation by a multiplicative factor of $5/\epsilon$ is $\Pr(\sum_{s=1}^{Dn\log n} C_s \geq \frac{5D}{\epsilon\Delta} n\log n) \leq \epsilon/5$.

This modification of Feige et al. will then still only take $C_3 n\log n$ queries, for $C_3 = 5D/(\epsilon\Delta)$, to succeed in sorting the max-eligible alternatives, with two possible bad events: the failure of the Feige et al. algorithm, with probability at most $\epsilon/5$, and the number of queries exceeding the query budget, with probability at most $\epsilon/5$. This latter event is only a concern when both π_k and π_{k-1} are less than $1/2$.

If we only needed to recover the choices of a max-selector, we would be done. In order to recover all queries for any positions ℓ, however, we also need to know the order of the max-ineligible alternatives. To recover such choices, we switch our focus from the max-selector subpopulation to the min-selector subpopulation. As a final step we repeat the above procedure using an anchoring set $S^*_{\min}$ that contains the $k-2$ maximum alternatives of the ordering we just recovered. We then run the Feige et al. procedure to order the alternatives in $U_{\text{scrap}} = u_{n-k-2} \cup S^*_{\max}$. Here u_{n-k-2} is the last element of the order recovered above, included to orient the sort order with regard to the overall sorted order, and $S^*_{\max}$ was the set of max-ineligible alternatives that we are trying to order. Since $|U_{\text{scrap}}| = k-1$, we can drive this error probability below $1-\epsilon/5$ with a large constant C_4 that does not depend on n, thereby also recovering the order over the max-ineligible alternatives.

We have outlined five separate bad events that would make the algorithm fail. By taking the Union Bound over the five bad event probabilities, each controlled to have an error $\leq \epsilon/5$, the overall algorithm performs four sets of queries (where there are two bad events associated with the third set of queries) and succeeds with probability at least $1-\epsilon$ after $C_1 + C_2' n\log n + C_3 n\log n + C_4$ queries, asymptotically $O(n\log n)$ as specified. □

4 PASSIVE QUERY COMPLEXITY

We now shift our attention to *passive* query algorithms, algorithms that pose all their queries at once without the sequential benefit of previous responses. This framework is motivated by a common scenario in the study of large datasets of recorded choices from online marketplaces, ranking algorithms, and recommendation systems. These systems are teeming with choices being made over sets of alternatives, but often one cannot adaptively guide the queries towards our goal of recovering choice functions. What if we simply had a large corpus of choices by an individual over random subsets? Could we still recover the choice function? If so, how few queries would we need?

In this section we analyze a model for this process, in which we are not able to select queries but instead have to watch them passively. We focus on the output of a single f; handling population mixtures in a passive query model is an interesting open question.

Model of passive choice streams. We analyze the following process for generating and analyzing a stream of random queries that arrive over time. For each possible k-set S, we define a Poisson process of rate α: we draw a length of time t from an exponentially distributed random variable of rate α (with density $\alpha e^{-\alpha x}$), and after this time t elapses, we put the set S into the stream. We iterate this, repeatedly drawing a random length of time t and putting S into the stream when t is reached.

We run the process for each k-set S simultaneously, creating a merged stream of k-sets as they are selected and put into the stream. Now, suppose we observe the merged stream over the interval $[0, T]$. For any fixed k-set S, the probability that it appears in the interval is $1 - e^{-\alpha T}$, a quantity that we'll refer to as p_T. An algorithm is provided with the value $f(S)$ for each k-set that appears in the stream during $[0, T]$. After seeing these values it must correctly report the value of $f(S)$ for almost every k-set. We want an algorithm that can achieve this goal while keeping T as small as possible.

Our streaming model is arguably the simplest plausible model for generating collections of (choice set, choice) decisions that are independently drawn with replacement. Other seemingly simple models that query for a random set of k-sets without replacement exhibit an implausible slight dependence between decisions in the decision collection.

A recovery algorithm for passive streams. Our main result for this streaming model of passive queries is that for $2 \leq \ell \leq k-1$ there is an algorithm able to provide the desired performance guarantee for a choice of T with $p_T \to 0$, which is to say that the probability of seeing any fixed k-set S even once goes to zero. Equivalently, this result implies that we can recover $f(S)$ for almost every k-set after only seeing a tiny fraction of all possible k-sets.

Theorem 4.1. *Let f be a choice function over k-sets in a universe of n alternatives that selects the ℓth ordered position, with $k \geq 3$ and $2 \leq \ell \leq k-1$ known. For every $\varepsilon > 0$ and $\delta > 0$, there is a constant $\xi > 0$ and an algorithm that takes the stream over the interval $[0, T]$ with $p_T = \xi \log n \log\log n/n$ and with probability at least $1-\delta$ will recover the correct value of $f(S)$ for at least a $1-\varepsilon$ fraction of all k-sets.*

Proof. The algorithm operates in two phases similarly to the algorithm for active queries, in that it first identifies the set S^* of $k-1$ ineligible alternatives that cannot be selected in any query. Then it selects $k-2$ of these arbitrarily to form a set S^{-2} and analyzes sets of the form $\{u_i, u_j\} \cup S^{-2}$ to decide the relative ordering of pairs (u_i, u_j). The key difference from the case of active queries is that the algorithm needs to operate using only the k-sets that were handed to it initially at random, so it can't steer the queries to seek out the set S^*, or run an adaptive sorting algorithm on arbitrary pairs (u_i, u_j).

Because the algorithm has two phases, we split the time interval $[0, T]$ into two intervals $[0, T_1]$ and $(T_1, T_1 + T_2]$. Note that for a given k-set S, the Union Bound implies that $p_{T_1} + p_{T_2}$ is an upper bound on the probability seeing S during $[0, T]$, and hence $p_{T_1} + p_{T_2} \geq p_T$.

Given a time interval $[0, T]$ for generating the stream, for a sufficiently large constant b to be specified below, we choose T so that $p_T \geq b \log n/n + b \log n \log\log n/n$. We split $[0, T]$ into $[0, T_1]$ and $(T_1, T_1 + T_2]$ so that $p_{T_1} \geq b \log n/n$ and $p_{T_2} \geq b \log n \log\log n/n$.

Let $\mathcal{D}[a, b]$ denote the k-sets observed in the stream during the interval $[a, b]$. We will use $\mathcal{D}_1 = \mathcal{D}[0, T_1]$ for the first phase, and $\mathcal{D}_2 = \mathcal{D}(T_1, T_1 + T_2]$ for the second phase. Note that the contents of $\mathcal{D}_1$ and $\mathcal{D}_2$ are independent of each other, an important facet of the streaming model.

Phase 1: Finding ineligible elements. In the first phase, the algorithm will look at $\mathcal{D}_1$ and identify the set S^{**} of elements $v \in U$ for which v is not the output $f(S)$ for any $S \in \mathcal{D}_1$. Clearly $S^* \subseteq S^{**}$, since no element of S^* can be the answer to any $f(S)$. Now fix $v \notin S^*$; what is the probability that it belongs to S^{**}?

Every eligible alternative v will be the output $f(S)$ for some $S \in \mathcal{D}_1$ as long as there's a k-set in $\mathcal{D}_1$ containing exactly $\ell - 1$ elements above v and exactly $k - \ell$ element below v. Note that since $2 \leq \ell \leq k-1$, this means that there are a non-zero number of elements above and below v in this case. Let's call such a query a "revealing query" for v. Out of $\binom{n}{k}$ possible queries there are at least $n-2$ such revealing queries for v, since in the worst case there's only one way to choose $k-2$ alternatives above and $n-2$ ways to choose one alternatives below, or vice versa. Each revealing query for v is chosen with probability $p \geq b \log n/n$.

The probability that none of these $n-2$ revealing queries is chosen is then

$$(1-p)^{n-2} \leq (1 - b(\log n)/n)^{n-2} \leq (1 - b(\log n)/n)^{n/2} \leq e^{-(b/2)\log n} = n^{-b/2}.$$

Now taking the Union Bound over all $n-k$ eligible alternatives v says that the probability there exists a v for which no revealing query is chosen is bounded by $n \cdot n^{-b/2} \leq n^{-(b/2)+1}$. Let $\mathcal{E}_1$ denote the "bad event" that $S^* \neq S^{**}$, and let $\delta_0 \leq \delta/4$ be a constant. By choosing b large enough, we have $\Pr[\mathcal{E}_1] \leq n^{-(b/2)+1} \leq \delta_0$.

Phase 2: Simulating pairwise comparisons. In phase 2 we now use $k-2$ of the ineligible elements as anchors for performing pairwise comparisons. Recall that because we have split the stream over two disjoint time intervals, the algorithm's behavior now is independent of its success or failure at finding S^* in phase 1, so in our analysis we'll assume it has succeeded in finding S^*.

For this phase, we use p to denote p_{T_2}, where T_2 was chosen such that $p \geq b \log n \log\log n/n$. To begin, we fix an arbitrary set S^{-2} of $k-2$ elements from S^*, and let $U' = U \setminus S^{-2}$. Let G be the undirected graph on U' in which (u_i, u_j) is an edge if and only if $\{u_i, u_j\} \cup S^{-2}$ is a k-set in $\mathcal{D}_1$. Note that G is a uniform sample from the distribution $G_{n-k+2,p}$, the Erdős-Rényi random graph distribution. By a theorem of Alon and Azar [2], it follows that if we compare the pairs of elements (u_i, u_j) defined by the edges of G, then with probability at least $1-\delta_1$ we will be able to infer the relative order of at least a $1-\gamma$ fraction of pairs of elements of U', where γ and δ_1 depend on b. The remaining γ fraction of pairs are simply left with their choice uninferred. Let $\mathcal{E}_2$ denote the "bad event" that the Alon-Azar algorithm does not succeed, with $\Pr[\mathcal{E}_2] \leq \delta_1$. We choose b large enough that $\gamma \leq \varepsilon/2k^2$ and $\delta_1 \leq \delta/4$. Let H be a directed acyclic graph on U' in which u_i points to u_j if the Alon-Azar procedure has inferred that u_i is ranked ahead of u_j, and there is no edge between u_i and u_j otherwise.

Now we use the following procedure to answer queries of the form $f(S)$. If $S \not\subseteq U'$ then S contains an ineligible element and we answer arbitrarily. Otherwise, if $S \subseteq U'$, we look at all the pairwise comparisons of elements in S according to H. If these pairwise comparisons form a complete acyclic digraph then we choose the ℓth element in order; otherwise we answer arbitrarily.

For how many k-sets do we get the correct answer? Let P denote the set of node pairs in $U' \times U'$ for which there is no edge in H. If $\mathcal{E}_2$ does not happen, then $|P| \leq \gamma\binom{n-k+2}{2}$. The number of k-sets that involve a pair from P is thus at most

$$\sum_{(u_i,u_j)\in P} \binom{n-k}{k-2} \leq \gamma \binom{n-k+2}{2}\binom{n-k}{k-2} \leq \gamma k^2 \binom{n}{k}.$$

Meanwhile, the number of k-sets that involve an element outside U' is at most

$$(k-2)\binom{n-1}{k-1} \leq (k-2)\left(\frac{k}{n}\right)\binom{n}{k} \leq \gamma\binom{n}{k},$$

provided that n is large enough relative to k that $k(k-2)/n \leq \gamma$. But if a k-set S satisfies $S \subseteq U'$, and $S \times S$ contains no pair of P, then all pairwise comparisons inside S have been determined and thus we can report the correct value of $f(S)$. Hence if $\mathcal{E}_2$ does not occur, we report the correct value on all but at most $\gamma(1+k^2)\binom{n}{k} \leq \varepsilon\binom{n}{k}$ k-sets, as desired.

The full algorithm and its analysis. Now let's consider the full algorithm. It starts by identifying a set S^{**} of ineligible elements in phase 1. If S^{**} does not have $k-1$ elements, it terminates with no answer. Otherwise, it runs the second phase on the assumption that $S^* = S^{**}$.

If the event $\mathcal{E}_1 \cup \mathcal{E}_2$ does not occur, then $S^* = S^{**}$ and the output of phase 2 satisfies the performance guarantee of Theorem 4.1. With probability at least $1-(\delta_1+\delta_2) \geq 1-\delta/2$, this union $\mathcal{E}_1 \cup \mathcal{E}_2$ does not occur, in which case the full algorithm satisfies the performance guarantee. □

The above proof holds for all values of ℓ except for the two extremes of $\ell = 1$ and $\ell = k$, as stated. This distinction is intriguing since the two extreme values are the ones that don't exhibit choice-set effects: the individual making decisions is then selecting elements according to a fixed total ordering of U. The challenge with $\ell = 1$ and $\ell = k$ is actually that the notion of "ineligible" elements becomes more subtle: there are elements whose relative position in the embedding can be resolved, but only with a very large number of passive queries. Finding the right performance guarantee for this case is an interesting open question.

5 DISTANCE COMPARISON

All of our results thus far focus on recovering choice functions that are comparison-based functions over ordered alternatives. As noted in the introduction, this class of functions is surprisingly rich, with the ability to capture compromise effects in choices along any one-dimensional frontier, a choice-set effect that cannot be exhibited by functions that merely maximize over an ordering. The preceding sections develop a theory of inference for such comparison-based functions.

In this section we shift our focus to recovering choice functions defined by a different structural relationship, namely distance comparisons in a metric embedding. A choice function f on k-sets is *distance-comparison-based* if the value $f(S)$ can be computed purely using comparisons on the pairwise distances in a embedding h with metric $d(\cdot,\cdot)$, i.e. based on comparisons on the set of pairwise distances $\{d(h(u_i), h(u_j)) : u_i, u_j \in S\}$.

Distance comparisons form the basis of an additional important family of choice scenarios, namely choice queries answered with the "most medial" or the "most distinctive" alternative in a set, and in particular they model an important choice-set effect called *similarity aversion* [28]: given a choice between two dissimilar alternatives A and B and one of two alternatives A' and B' that are similar to A and B respectively, similarity aversion arises when $f(\{A, B, B'\}) = A$ but $f(\{A, B, A'\}) = B$. Essentially: given two similar alternatives and one dissimilar alternative, the dissimilar option is chosen.

It is important to note that similarity aversion cannot be modeled by a choice function that is strictly comparison-based: such a function can only evaluate ordinal comparisons, and when considering two elements A and B embedded in one dimension, a comparison-based function cannot resolve whether a third element A' positioned between A and B is closer to A or closer to B.

The remainder of the section has the following format. First we show how similarity aversion can be modeled using distance-comparison-based choice functions. Next, we present two observations that suggest some of the difficulties that must be overcome to learn such functions, a seemingly more difficult inference context than comparison-based functions. We then connect our observations to a broader literature on learning metric embeddings, albeit without resolving our inference questions.

Similarity aversion from distance comparisons. We now describe two choice functions of principle importance, and their capacity for being formulated as distance-comparison-based functions: the median choice function and the outlier choice function. We restrict our definitions to choices over k-sets where k is odd. The outlier choice function for triplets ($k = 3$) will serve as our model of similarity aversion.

The median choice function selects the element of a k-set S in $\mathbb{R}^m$ with metric $d(\cdot,\cdot)$ that minimizes the sum of distances to all other elements. In $m = 1$ dimension this choice is the traditional median element, and it can be selected according to the following distance-comparison procedure: repeatedly find the pair of alternatives $x, y \in S$ that are furthest apart and remove them from S. Since k is odd, after $(k-1)/2$ rounds there will be a single remaining element; return that element as the choice. Thus we see that the median choice function can be formulated as both a comparison-based function—in the earlier sections, $q_{(k-1)/2,k}$—or as a distance-comparison-based function.

For $m > 1$ dimensions and sets of size $k = 3$ it is easy to verify that the above distance-comparison procedure will still return the element that minimizes the sum of distances. For $m > 1$ and $k > 3$, however, it is an open question whether a distance-comparison-based function can return the element that minimizes the sum of distances. Observe that this question amounts to solving a version of the Fermat-Weber problem [32] with a very restricted functional toolkit, and may be quite difficult. We are not aware of any prior work on the capabilities of distance-comparison-based functions. Here we are principally interested in the special case of $k = 3$, allowing us to skirt this difficulty.

Building on the median choice function, the outlier choice function selects the element of a k-set S that is farthest (in $\mathbb{R}^m$ using $d(\cdot,\cdot)$) from the median element (the median element being

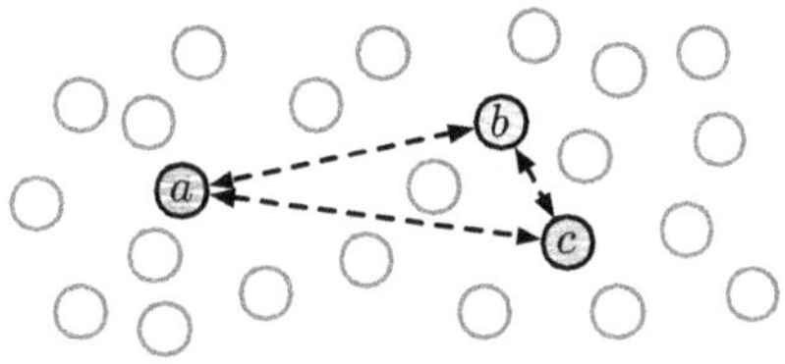

Fig. 3. A k-set $S = \{a, b, c\}$ of $k = 3$ alternatives embedded in 2 dimensions. In this setting we can think of distance comparison as a comparison-based choice between three pairwise distances $\{d(a,b), d(b,c), d(a,c)\}$. When a distance-comparison-based choice function f selects the *outlier* a, this choice is effectively a comparison-based choice of the shortest distance, $d(b,c)$. When f selects the *median element* b, this choice is effectively a comparison-based choice of the longest distance, $d(a,c)$.

the element that minimizes the sum of distances to all elements). The outlier choice function can clearly be written as a distance-comparison-based function whenever the median choice function can. For $k = 3$ elements it is precisely a model of similarity aversion on triplets.

As a general comment on the capabilities of distance-comparison-based functions, it is clear that they can make choices that ordinary comparison-based functions cannot, but it is important to highlight that the reverse is also true: the median choice function is the *only* position-selection function (in one dimension) that can be formulated as a distance-comparison-based function. A distance-comparison-based function cannot select a maximal or minimal element (or any off-center position), since it has no way of orienting a choice with regard to the direction of "more" (in any dimension). The sets of comparison-based functions and distance-comparison-based functions are therefore not neatly nested.

Distance comparison for triplets. In the particular case of $k = 3$, where choices are made over triplets $S = \{u, v, w\}$, we can think of a choice for an alternative $u \in S$ implicitly as a choice for the distance $d(v, w)$ between the two remaining alternatives in S. For a triplet $\{u, v, w\}$, the effective comparison-based query is over the set of distances $\{d(u, v), d(u, w), d(v, w)\}$, where a choice of a pairwise distance maps to a choice of the complementary alternative. See Figure 3 for an illustration. There are $N = \binom{n}{2}$ distances, and so it may seem as though it would be possible to learn the ordering in $O(N \log N)$ queries in the active query framework, with similar results carried over for other query frameworks. Reality is more complicated.

We now give two observations on the difficulties of carrying over comparison-based results to distance comparisons. The first observation asks: when are there enough queries to learn the relative ordering of all the distances? The second observation pertains to the restricted nature of the distance triplets that can be queried.

First, notice that each query for a 3-set furnishes 2 inequalities between distances. There are $\binom{n}{3}$ triplet queries for n elements, which means that querying for every possible 3-set would produce $2\binom{n}{3}$ inequalities. Meanwhile there are $\binom{n}{2}$ pairwise distances, meaning that there are $\binom{n}{2}!$ possible permutations of the distances, only one of which is the sorted order. A sufficient condition for inferring all choices is to know the sorted order of all the distances. Focusing on the outlier choice function (selecting the minimum distance that effectively returns the outlier element) in one does not need to know the relative order of the two largest distances. This tells us that it would take $\log_2(\binom{n}{2}!) - 1$ bisections of the set of permutations to identify the sorted order of all but the two largest distances.

We observe that $2\binom{n}{3} < \log_2(\binom{n}{2}!) - 1$ for $n \le 5$, which tells us that for $n \le 5$ elements we will learn the choice for every query before we can possibly know the sorted order of the relevant pairwise distances. This tells us that a generic procedure that seeks to learn all the pairwise distances will not always succeed.

While our earlier query complexity results focus on asymptotic complexity, the correctness of these algorithms holds for all n. The limiting observation presented here is specific to distance comparisons and does not apply to ordinary comparisons: in that context there are only $n!$ permutations rather than $\binom{n}{2}!$.

Second, observe that we cannot query for general triplets of distances $\{d(u,v), d(w,x), d(y,z)\}$, but are in fact restricted to queries in the special case of $w = u$, $y = x$, and $z = v$. It is unclear for what n it is possible to learn the relative ordering of all the distances from such restricted distance comparisons. While both of these initial observations are discouraging, an efficient inference algorithm for distance-comparison-based functions would contribute a useful tool for learning in the presence of similarity aversion and other choice-set effects, and we deem it important to present distance-comparison-based functions as significant objects of study.

As an additional open direction for future work, we briefly mention the choice-set effect known as the decoy effect (or asymmetric dominance). The decoy effect describes when the presence of a similar but inferior alternative increases the desirability of an option. The difference between similarity aversion and the decoy effect is that the former hinges on similarity while the latter incorporates both similarity and inferiority. As such, modeling the decoy effect requires a composition of both comparison and distance-comparison. We leave the study of this alluring general class of choice functions, which contains comparison-based and distance-comparison-based choice functions as special cases, as future work.

Relationship to metric embeddings. Beyond providing a model for similarity avoidance in the behavioral sciences, the ability to recover distance-comparison-based choice functions also speaks to a broad literature on learning metric embeddings of data from distance-comparison-based queries [20]. In that literature, the *stochastic triplet embedding* technique [30] has recently been introduced as a way to embed a generic dataset of elements through answers to choices of the form "Is A more similar to B or to C?". This question is effectively a comparison-based query requesting a choice from the set $\{d(A,B), d(A,C)\}$. As an extension of that work, the *crowd median algorithm* [13] tries to learn embeddings from triplet queries with the request "Out of three shown items pick one that appears to be different from the two others." The crowd median algorithm is employing precisely the outlier choice function for $k = 3$ described in this section.

Known work on the crowd median algorithm, however, leaves open the question of what embeddings it can learn. We observe that outside the behavioral modeling that drove our work, a slight modification of the crowd median algorithm to align with our results gives a method that can in fact learn embeddings efficiently. We define the *generalized crowd median algorithm*, which instead asks questions of the form "of these k pairs, which pair is least similar?". Under this more flexible query framework, the ordering on the distance could then be inferred by the algorithms developed in this work: for n elements, it would then be possible in an active query framework to learn the ordering of the $N = \binom{n}{2}$ distances in $O(N \log N)$ queries, for large n.

Our treatment of distance-comparison-based queries also speaks to a broad line or research in psychology on pair selection queries used to infer cognitive embeddings [14, 26, 27]. In these settings, sets of k elements (where k is often large) are presented to subjects with the question "which two elements are most similar?". Such queries generalize the crowd-median algorithm. Lastly, very recent work has developed learning results for binary clustering (a simple form of embedding) using so-called triangle queries of the form "which of these birds belong to the same species?" [31], with possible relevance to learning from distance-comparison-based choices.

6 DISCUSSION

The prevalence of choice-set effects in human decision-making highlights a need for a principled inference model that can support learning such effects. In this work we've proposed a framework aimed at helping with such an integration, focussing on comparison-based choices. A natural line of inquiry extending from choice-set effects quickly leads to rich issues related to the theory of sorting, including passive sorting ("sorting in one round") and sorting with noisy information.

There are clearly many directions for further work. We begin by mentioning a very concrete problem: while we studied passive queries and population mixtures, we did not attempt to combine these two aspects to infer a mixed collection of choice functions from a stream of passively observed queries. A challenge in trying to achieve such a combination can be seen in the technical ingredients that would need to be brought together; the mechanics of the Feige et al. procedure [10] and Alon-Azar procedure [2] are not obviously compatible. Even the basic question of binary sorting with passive queries in the presence of noisy information appears to be fairly open.

Many questions remain regarding how to capture relevant population-level heterogeneities in large-scale choice corpora. Our framework for comparisons generally assumed a universally agreed upon ordered embedding, and it is very reasonable to suggest generalizations to a dispersed distribution over possible embeddings. A long line of work has brought distributions over rankings into the literature on learning preferences [6, 11, 18], including through comparisons [16], and it would be natural to explore analogous distributional modeling for the embedding that underlies comparison-based choice functions. Analyzing mixtures of comparison-based choice functions as a model of probabilistic discrete choice [3] is another closely related open research direction.

One can also consider generalizing the embedding that defines the structure of the alternatives and the choice sets. For example, we could think about the alternatives as being embedded not just in one dimension (or a one-dimensional Pareto frontier) but in multiple dimensions, and an individual could execute a sequence of comparison-based rules to select an item from a choice set. Such a generalization could provide a way to incorporate a number of other well-documented choice-set effects [28], and could form intriguing potential connections to the *elimination by aspects* [29] model of discrete choice.

We find it encouraging that in the face of choice behavior much more complex than ordered preferences, we are able to fully match most of the known query complexity results from the theory of sorting from binary comparisons. Continued work to develop a more complete theory of inference for other increasingly rich classes of choice functions has the potential to lay a foundation for a much needed unified theory for learning choice-set effects.

REFERENCES

[1] Shivani Agarwal, Corinna Cortes, and Ralf Herbrich. 2005. *Learning to Rank (NIPS workshop).* MIT Press.
[2] Noga Alon and Yossi Azar. 1988. Sorting, approximate sorting, and searching in rounds. *SIAM J Discrete Math* 1, 3 (1988), 269–280.
[3] George Baltas and Peter Doyle. 2001. Random utility models in marketing research: a survey. *J Bus Res* 51, 2 (2001), 115–125.
[4] Austin Benson, Ravi Kumar, and Andrew Tomkins. 2016. On the relevance of irrelevant alternatives. In *WWW.* 963–973.
[5] Béla Bollobás and Moshe Rosenfeld. 1981. Sorting in one round. *Israel Journal of Mathematics* 38, 1-2 (1981), 154–160.
[6] Mark Braverman and Elchanan Mossel. 2009. Sorting from noisy information. *arXiv preprint arXiv:0910.1191* (2009).
[7] Shuo Chen and Thorsten Joachims. 2016. Modeling intransitivity in matchup and comparison data. In *Proceedings of the Ninth ACM International Conference on Web Search and Data Mining.* ACM, 227–236.

[8] Shuo Chen and Thorsten Joachims. 2016. Predicting matchups and preferences in context. In *Proceedings of the 22nd ACM SIGKDD International Conference on Knowledge Discovery and Data Mining*. ACM, 775–784.

[9] Federico Echenique, Sangmok Lee, and Matthew Shum. 2011. The Money Pump as a Measure of Revealed Preference Violations. *Journal of Political Economy* 119, 6 (2011), 1201–1223.

[10] Uriel Feige, Prabhakar Raghavan, David Peleg, and Eli Upfal. 1994. Computing with noisy information. *SIAM J. Computing* 23, 5 (1994), 1001–1018.

[11] Michael A Fligner and Joseph S Verducci. 1986. Distance based ranking models. *J Roy Statist Soc Ser B* (1986), 359–369.

[12] Paul E. Green, Abba M. Krieger, and Yoram Wind. 2001. Thirty Years of Conjoint Analysis: Reflections and Prospects. *Interface* 31 (2001).

[13] Hannes Heikinheimo and Antti Ukkonen. 2013. The Crowd-Median Algorithm. In *HCOMP*.

[14] Li-Jun Ji, Zhiyong Zhang, and Richard E Nisbett. 2004. Is it culture or is it language? Examination of language effects in cross-cultural research on categorization. *Journal of personality and social psychology* 87, 1 (2004), 57.

[15] Emir Kamenica. 2008. Contextual Inference in Markets: On the Informational Content of Product Lines. *American Economic Review* 98, 5 (2008), 2127–2149.

[16] Tyler Lu and Craig Boutilier. 2011. Learning Mallows models with pairwise preferences. In *ICML*. 145–152.

[17] R Duncan Luce. 1977. The choice axiom after twenty years. *Journal of Mathematical Psychology* 15, 3 (1977), 215–233.

[18] Colin L Mallows. 1957. Non-null ranking models. I. *Biometrika* (1957), 114–130.

[19] Stephen Ragain and Johan Ugander. 2016. Pairwise Choice Markov Chains. In *NIPS*. 3198–3206.

[20] Matthew Schultz and Thorsten Joachims. 2004. Learning a distance metric from relative comparisons. *NIPS* (2004), 41.

[21] Amartya Sen and Prasanta K Pattanaik. 1969. Necessary and sufficient conditions for rational choice under majority decision. *Journal of Economic Theory* 1, 2 (1969), 178–202.

[22] Eldar Shafir, Itamar Simonson, and Amos Tversky. 1993. Reason-based choice. *Cognition* 49 (1993), 11–36.

[23] Or Sheffet, Nina Mishra, and Samuel Ieong. 2012. Predicting Consumer Behavior in Commerce Search. In *ICML*.

[24] Itamar Simonson. 1989. Choice Based on Reasons: The Case of Attraction and Compromise Effects. *Journal of Consumer Research* 16 (1989), 158–174.

[25] Itamar Simonson and Amos Tversky. 1992. Choice in context: Tradeoff contrast and extremeness aversion. *Journal of Marketing Research* 29, 3 (1992), 281–295.

[26] Sandra S Smiley and Ann L Brown. 1979. Conceptual preference for thematic or taxonomic relations: A nonmonotonic age trend from preschool to old age. *Journal of Experimental Child Psychology* 28, 2 (1979), 249–257.

[27] Thomas Talhelm, Jonathan Haidt, Shigehiro Oishi, Xuemin Zhang, Felicity F Miao, and Shimin Chen. 2015. Liberals Think More Analytically (More "WEIRD") Than Conservatives. *Pers Soc Psychol Bull* 41, 2 (2015), 250–267.

[28] Jennifer S Trueblood, Scott D Brown, Andrew Heathcote, and Jerome R Busemeyer. 2013. Not just for consumers context effects are fundamental to decision making. *Psychological science* 24, 6 (2013), 901–908.

[29] Amos Tversky. 1972. Elimination by aspects: A theory of choice. *Psychological Review* 79, 4 (1972), 281–299.

[30] Laurens Van Der Maaten and Kilian Weinberger. 2012. Stochastic triplet embedding. In *MLSP*. 1–6.

[31] Ramya Korlakai Vinayak and Babak Hassibi. 2016. Crowdsourced Clustering: Querying Edges vs Triangles. In *NIPS*. 1316–1324.

[32] George O Wesolowsky. 1993. The Weber Problem: History and Perspectives. *Computers & Operations Research* (1993).

[33] Dawei Yin, Bin Cao, Jian-Tao Sun, and Brian D. Davison. 2014. Estimating ad group performance in sponsored search. In *WSDM*. 143–152.

Combinatorial Auctions Do Need Modest Interaction

SEPEHR ASSADI, University of Pennsylvania

We study the necessity of interaction for obtaining efficient allocations in combinatorial auctions with *subadditive bidders*. This problem was originally introduced by Dobzinski, Nisan, and Oren (STOC'14) as the following simple market scenario: m items are to be allocated among n bidders in a distributed setting where bidders valuations are private and hence *communication* is needed to obtain an efficient allocation. The communication happens in rounds: in each round, each bidder, *simultaneously* with others, broadcasts a message to all parties involved. At the end, the central planner computes an allocation solely based on the communicated messages. Dobzinski et al. showed that (at least some) interaction is necessary for obtaining any efficient allocation: no non-interactive (1-round) protocol with polynomial communication (in the number of items and bidders) can achieve approximation ratio better than $\Omega(m^{1/4})$, while for any $r \geq 1$, there exists r-round protocols that achieve $\widetilde{O}(r \cdot m^{1/r+1})$ approximation with polynomial communication; in particular, $O(\log m)$ rounds of interaction *suffice* to obtain an (almost) efficient allocation, i.e., a polylog(m)-approximation.

A natural question at this point is to identify the "right" level of interaction (i.e., number of rounds) *necessary* to obtain an efficient allocation. In this paper, we resolve this question by providing an almost tight *round-approximation* tradeoff for this problem: we show that for any $r \geq 1$, any r-round protocol that uses poly(m, n) bits of communication can only approximate the social welfare up to a factor of $\Omega(\frac{1}{r} \cdot m^{1/2r+1})$. This in particular implies that $\Omega(\frac{\log m}{\log\log m})$ rounds of interaction are *necessary* for obtaining any efficient allocation (i.e., a constant or even a polylog(m)-approximation) in these markets. Our work builds on the recent multi-party round-elimination technique of Alon, Nisan, Raz, and Weinstein (FOCS'15) – used to prove similar-in-spirit lower bounds for round-approximation tradeoff in unit-demand (matching) markets – and settles an open question posed initially by Dobzinski et al., and subsequently by Alon et al.

CCS Concepts: • **Theory of computation → Algorithmic mechanism design**; *Communication complexity*;

Additional Key Words and Phrases: combinatorial auctions, multi-party communication complexity, round-approximation tradeoff

1 INTRODUCTION

In a combinatorial auction, m items in M are to be allocated between n bidders (or players[1]) in N with valuation functions $v_i : 2^M \rightarrow \mathbb{R}_+$. The goal is to find a collection of disjoint bundles $A_1, \ldots, A_n$ of items in M (an *allocation*), that maximizes *social welfare* defined as the sum of bidder's valuations for the allocated bundles, i.e., $\sum_{i \in N} v_i(A_i)$. We study the tradeoff between the amount of interaction between the bidders and the efficiency of the allocation in combinatorial auctions.

In our model, each bidder $i \in N$ only knows the valuation function v_i and hence the bidders need to communicate to obtain an efficient allocation. Communication happens in rounds. In each

[1]Throughout the paper, we use the terms "bidder" and "player" interchangeably.

Supported in part by National Science Foundation grants CCF-1552909, CCF-1617851, and IIS-1447470.
A full version of this paper is available as an online preprint at [3].

EC'17, June 26–30, 2017, Cambridge, Massachusetts, USA. ©2017 ACM. ISBN 978-1-4503-4527-9/17/06...$15.00
DOI: https://doi.org/10.1145/3033274.3085121

round, each bidder i, *simultaneously* with others, broadcasts a message to all parties involved, based on the valuation function v_i and messages in previous rounds. In the last round, the central planner outputs the allocation solely based on the communicated messages. Notice that a "trivial solution" in this setting is for all players to communicate their entire input to the central planner who can then compute an efficient allocation; however, such a protocol is clearly infeasible in most settings as it has an enormous communication cost. As such, we are interested in protocols with significantly less communication cost, typically *exponentially smaller* than the input size.

This model was first introduced by Dobzinski, Nisan, and Oren [10] to address the following fundamental question in economics: *"To what extent is interaction between individuals required in order to efficiently allocate resources between themselves?"*. They considered this problem for two different classes of valuation functions: *unit-demand* valuations and *subadditive* valuations (see Section 2.1). For both settings, they showed that (at least some) interaction is necessary to obtain an efficient allocation: non-interactive (aka 1-round or simultaneous) protocols have enormous communication cost compared to interactive ones, while even allowing a modest amount of interaction allows for finding an (approximately) efficient allocation. We now elaborate more on these results.

For the case of matching markets with n unit-demand bidders and n items (and hence input-size of n bits per each player), Dobzinski et al. [10] proved a lower bound of $\Omega(\sqrt{n})$ on the approximation ratio of any simultaneous protocol that communicates $n^{o(1)}$ bits per each bidder. On the other hand, they showed that for any $r \geq 1$, there exists an r-round protocol that achieves an $O(n^{1/r+1})$ approximation by sending $O(\log n)$ bits per each bidder in each round. For the more general setting of combinatorial auctions with n subadditive bidders and m items (and hence input-size of $\exp(m)$ bits per each player), they showed that the best approximation ratio achievable by simultaneous protocols with $\text{poly}(m, n)$ communication is $\Omega(m^{1/4})$, while for any $r \geq 1$, there exists r-round protocols that achieve an approximation ratio of $\widetilde{O}(r \cdot m^{1/r+1})$. These results imply that in such markets, logarithmic rounds of interaction in the market size *suffice* to obtain an (almost) efficient allocation, i.e., a $\text{polylog}(m)$-approximation.

A natural question left open by [10] was to identify the amount of interaction *necessary* to obtain an efficient allocation in these markets. Recently, Alon, Nisan, Raz, and Weinstein [2] provided a partial answer to this question for matching markets: for any $r \geq 1$, any r-round protocol for unit-demand bidders in which each bidder sends at most $n^{o(1)}$ bits in each round can only achieve an $\Omega(n^{1/5^{r+1}})$ approximation [2]. This implies that at least $\Omega(\log \log n)$ rounds of interaction is necessary to achieve an efficient allocation in matching markets. Alon et al. [2] further conjectured that the "correct" lower bound for the convergence rate in this setting is $\Omega(\log n)$; in other words, $\Omega(\log n)$ rounds of interaction are necessary for achieving an efficient allocation.

Despite this progress for matching markets, the best known lower bounds for the more general setup of combinatorial auctions with subadditive bidders remained the aforementioned 1-round lower bound of [10], and a $(2 - \varepsilon)$-approximation (for every constant $\varepsilon > 0$) for any polynomial communication protocol with unrestricted number of rounds [11]. Indeed, obtaining better lower bounds for r-round protocols was posed as an open problem by Alon et al. [2] who also mentioned that: "from a communication complexity perspective, lower bounds in this setup are more compelling, since player valuations require exponentially many bits to encode, hence interaction has the potential to reduce the overall communication from exponential to polynomial.".

1.1 Our Results and Techniques

In this paper, we resolve the aforementioned open question of Dobzinski et al. [10] and Alon et al. [2] by proving an almost tight *round-approximation* tradeoff for polynomial communication protocols in subadditive combinatorial auctions.

Main Result. *For any $r \geq 1$, any r-round protocol (deterministic or randomized) for combinatorial auctions with* subadditive *bidders that uses polynomial communication can only achieve an approximation ratio of $\Omega(\frac{1}{r} \cdot m^{1/\Theta(r)})$ to the social welfare.*

We remark that this lower bound holds even when the bidders valuations are XOS functions, a strict subclass of subadditive valuations (see Section 2.1 for definition).

Our main result, combined with the upper bound result of [10], provides a near-complete understanding of the power of each additional round in improving the quality of the allocation in subadditive combinatorial auctions. Moreover, an immediate corollary of our result is that in these markets, $\Omega(\frac{\log m}{\log\log m})$ rounds of interaction are *necessary* to achieve any efficient allocation (i.e., constant or polylogarithmic approximation), which is *tight* up to an $O(\log\log m)$ factor. The qualitative message of this theoretical result is clear: *a modest amount of interaction between individuals in a market is crucial for obtaining an efficient allocation.*

Our first step in establishing this result is proving a new lower bound for simultaneous (1-round) protocols. We deviate from [10] by considering the problem of estimating the *value* of social welfare as opposed to finding the actual allocation; this problem can only be harder in terms of proving a lower bound as any protocol that can find an approximate allocation can also be used to estimate the value of social welfare with one additional round and $O(n)$ additional communication using a trivial reduction (see Section 2.2). As a result, the kind of combinatorial arguments used in [10] seem not sufficient for our purpose and we instead prove our lower bound using information-theoretic machinery and in particular a direct-sum style argument. This counterintuitive switch to establishing a lower bound for a seemingly harder problem however leads to a more modular proof that allows us to further carry out our results to multi-round protocols.

We establish our multi-round lower bound following the multi-party round-elimination technique of Alon et al. [2]. We create a recursive family of hard distributions $\mathcal{D}_1, \mathcal{D}_2, \ldots$ whereby for any $r \geq 1$, $\mathcal{D}_r$ is the hard input distribution for r-round protocols. Each instance in $\mathcal{D}_r$ is a careful combination of *exponentially many* sub-instances sampled from $\mathcal{D}_{r-1}$. One of these sub-instances is "special" in that to solve the original instance, the players also need to solve this special sub-instance completely. On the other hand, the players are not able to identify this special sub-instance *locally* and hence need to spend one round of interaction *only* for this purpose. In other words, we prove that the first round of protocol does not convey much information about the special instance beyond its identity. Using a further round-elimination argument, we inductively show that since solving the special instance is hard for $(r-1)$-round protocols, solving the original instance should be hard for r-round protocols as well.

Similar to [2], and unlike typical two-player round-elimination arguments (see, e.g. [22, 25]), eliminating a round in our round-elimination argument requires a reduction from "low dimensional" instances (with fewer players and items) to "high dimensional" instances. This reduction is delicate as the players need to "complete" their inputs in the higher dimensional instance by *independently* sampling the "missing part" *conditioned on the first message* of the protocol *without any further communication*, while this distribution is a *correlated* distribution.

Furthermore, in contrast to [2], our sub-instances in each distribution are *overlapping* (as otherwise exponentially many sub-instances cannot be embedded inside a single polynomially larger instance) and hence may interfere with each other, potentially diminishing the role of the special instance. We overcome this obstacle by embedding these sub-instances based on a family of *small-intersection sets* to limit the potential overlap between the sub-instances and prove that solving the special instance is crucial even in the presence of these overlaps. It is worth pointing out that this approach allows us to avoid the doubly-exponential rate of growth in the size of instances across different rounds in [2], resulting in exponentially better dependence on the parameter r in our lower bound compared to [2]. Finally, since our lower bound is for estimating the *value* of social welfare (as opposed to finding an allocation), we need a different embedding argument in our reduction than the one used in [2][2]. In particular, we now embed the low dimensional instance in *multiple* places of the high dimensional instance as opposed to only one.

1.2 Other Related Work

Communication complexity of combinatorial auctions has received quite a lot of attention in the literature. It is known that for *arbitrary valuations*, exponential amount of communication is needed to obtain an $\left(m^{1/2-\varepsilon}\right)$-approximate allocation (for every constant $\varepsilon > 0$) [24] (see also [23]), and this is also tight [1, 8, 19, 21]. For *subadditive valuations*, a constant factor approximation to the social welfare can be achieved in our model using only polynomial communication [11, 12, 14–16, 20, 26] (and polynomially many rounds of interaction); in particular, Feige [15] developed a 2-approximation polynomial communication protocol for this problem and Dobzinski, Nisan, and Schapira [11] proved that obtaining $(2-\varepsilon)$-approximation (for any constant $\varepsilon > 0$) requires exponential communication (regardless of the number of rounds). Moreover, Dutting and Kesselheim [14] designed an $O(\log m)$-approximation protocol with polynomial communication for subadditive combinatorial auctions in which each bidder needs to communicate exactly once; however, this protocol still requires n rounds of interaction in our model as the players need to communicate in a round-robin fashion making the message sent by a bidder crucially depending on the messages communicated earlier by the previous bidders.

Another line of relevant research considers the case where the valuation of the bidders are chosen *independently* from a commonly known distribution (see, e.g. [17, 18]) and aims to design "simple" and simultaneous protocols that achieve an efficient allocation. The main difference between this setting and ours is that we are interested in arbitrary distributions of inputs for the bidders which are not necessarily product distributions; as already shown by the strong impossibility results of [10], the aforementioned type of protocols cannot provably exist in our model when input distributions are correalted. Finally, we point out that "incompressability" results are also known for subadditive valuations: any polynomial-length encoding of subadditive valuations must lose $\Omega(\sqrt{m})$ in precision [5, 6].

We refer the interested reader to [10] for a comprehensive summary of related work and further discussion on the role of interaction in markets.

2 PRELIMINARIES

Notation. For any integer $a \geq 1$, we let $[a] := \{1, \ldots, a\}$. We say that a set $S \subseteq [n]$ with $|S| = s$ is a s-*subset* of $[n]$. For a k-dimensional tuple $X = (X_1, \ldots, X_k)$ and index $i \in [k]$, we define $X^{<i} := (X_1, \ldots, X_{i-1})$ and $X^{-i} := (X_1, \ldots, X_{i-1}, X_{i+1}, \ldots, X_k)$. We use capital letters to denote random variables. For a random variable A, $\text{supp}(A)$ denotes the support of A and $\text{dist}(A)$ denotes

[2]Our problem corresponds to the problem of estimating the *size* of a maximum matching as opposed to finding an *approximate* matching in the setting of [2]. To the best of our knowledge, no non-trivial lower bounds are known for the matching size estimation problem in the setting of [2]; see [4] for further details.

its distribution. We further define $|A| := \log |\text{supp}(A)|$. We write $A \perp B \mid C$ to denote that the random variables A and B are independent conditioned on C. We use "w.p." to mean "with probability".

Intersecting families. The following combinatorial construction plays a crucial role in our proofs.

Definition 2.1. A *(p, q, t, ℓ)-intersecting family $\mathcal{F}$* is a collection of p subsets of $[q]$ each of size t, such that for any two distinct sets $S, T \in \mathcal{F}$, $|S \cap T| \le \ell$.

We prove the existence of an exponentially large intersecting family with a small pair-wise intersection, using a probabilistic argument. The proof is deferred to the full version of the paper [3].

Lemma 2.2. *For any integer $r \ge 1$, any parameter $\varepsilon > 0$, and any integer $k \ge \left(2e^2 \cdot r^2\right)^{\frac{1}{\varepsilon}}$, there exists a (p, q, t, ℓ)-intersecting family with $p = \exp\left(\Theta(k^{2r-2+\varepsilon})\right)$, $q = k^{2r} + r \cdot k^{2r-1}$, $t = r \cdot k^{2r-1}$, and $\ell = k^{2r-2+\varepsilon}$.*

2.1 Combinatorial Auctions

We have a set N of n bidders, and a set M of m items. Each bidder $i \in N$ has a valuation function $v_i : 2^M \to \mathbb{R}_+$, which assigns a value to each *bundle* of items (we assume $v_i(\emptyset) = 0$ and $v_i(\cdot)$ is non-decreasing). The goal is to maximize the *social welfare* defined as $\max_{(A_1,\ldots,A_n)} \sum_{i \in N} v_i(A_i)$, where $(A_1, \ldots, A_n)$ ranges over all possible allocations of items in M to bidders in N such that bidder i receives the bundle A_i.

A valuation function $v(\cdot)$ is considered *subadditive* iff for any two bundles of items $S, T \subseteq M$, $v(S \cup T) \le v(S) + v(T)$. A valuation function is *additive* iff for any bundle $S \subseteq M$, $v(S) = \sum_{j \in S} v(\{j\})$. A valuation function is *XOS* iff there exists r additive valuation functions $a_1, \ldots, a_r$ such that for all bundles $S \subseteq M$, $v(S) = \max_r a_r(S)$. Each function a_j is called a *clause* of v and for any bundle S, any clause $a \in \arg\max_r a_r(S)$ is referred to as a *maximizing clause* of S. Finally, a valuation function is *unit-demand* iff for any $S \subseteq M$, $v(S) = \max_{j \in S} v(\{j\})$. It is easy to verify that both XOS and unit-demand functions are also subadditive.

Notice that in general, subadditive and XOS valuation functions require $\exp(m)$ many bits for representation, while unit-demand valuation functions can be represented with $O(m)$ numbers, i.e., by describing the value of each singleton set. As such, in subadditive combinatorial auctions, we are interested in protocols that can reduce the communication from exponential in m to polynomial, while in unit-demand auctions, we mainly seek protocols that reduce the communication from linear in m to logarithmic.

2.2 Communication Model

We use the (number-in-hand) multiparty communication model with shared blackboard: there are n players (corresponding to the bidders) receiving inputs $(x_1, \ldots, x_n)$, jointly distributed according to a prior distribution $\mathcal{D}$ on $\mathcal{X}_1 \times \ldots \times \mathcal{X}_n$. The communication proceeds in *rounds* whereby in each round r, the players *simultaneously* write a message on a *shared blackboard* visible to all parties. In a deterministic protocol, the message sent by any player i in each round can only depend on the private input of the player, i.e., x_i, plus the messages of all players in previous rounds, i.e., the content of the blackboard. In a randomized protocol, we further allow the players to have access to both public and private randomness and the message of players can depend on them as well.

For a protocol π, we use $\Pi = (\Pi_1, \ldots, \Pi_n)$ to denote the transcript of the message communicated by the players (i.e., the content of the blackboard). In addition to the n players, there exists also a $(n+1)$-th party called the *referee* which does not have any input, and is responsible for outputting the answer in the last round, solely based on content of the blackboard Π (plus the public randomness in case of randomized protocols). Finally, the *communication cost* of the protocol π, denoted by $\|\pi\|$, is the sum of worst-case length of the messages communicated by all players, i.e., $\|\pi\| = \sum_{i=1}^{n} |\Pi_i|$.

Approximation guarantee. We consider protocols that are required to estimate the *maximum value of social welfare* in any instance I of a combinatorial auction (denoted by $\mathsf{sw}(I)$). More formally, a δ-error α-approximation protocol needs to, for each input instance I sampled from $\mathcal{D}$, output a number in the range $[\frac{1}{\alpha} \cdot \mathsf{sw}(I), \mathsf{sw}(I)]$ w.p. at least $1 - \delta$, where the randomness is over the distribution $\mathcal{D}$ (and the randomness of protocol in case of randomized protocols).

This problem is provably easier than finding an approximate allocation in the interactive setting: any r-round protocol for finding an approximate allocation can be used to obtain an $(r + 1)$-round protocol for estimating the value of social welfare with $O(n)$ additional communication; simply compute the approximate allocation in the first r rounds and spend one additional round in which each player declares her value for the assigned bundle to the referee. It was shown very recently in [7] that this *loss of one round* in the reduction is unavoidable (see Section 3 for further details). However, this extra one round is essentially negligible for our purpose as we are interested in the asymptotic dependence of the approximation ratio and the number of rounds.

2.3 Tools from Information Theory

We briefly review some basic definitions and facts from information theory that are used in this paper. We refer the interested reader to the excellent text by Cover and Thomas [9] for an introduction to this field, and the proofs of the claims in this section (see Chapter 2).

In the following, we denote the *Shannon Entropy* of a random variable A by $\mathbb{H}(A)$ and the *mutual information* of two random variables A and B by $\mathbb{I}(A;B) = \mathbb{H}(A) - \mathbb{H}(A \mid B) = \mathbb{H}(B) - \mathbb{H}(B \mid A)$. The proof of the following basic properties of entropy and mutual information can be found in [9], Chapter 2.

FACT 2.3. *Let A, B, and C be three (possibly correlated) random variables.*

(1) $0 \leq \mathbb{H}(A) \leq |A|$, and $\mathbb{H}(A) = |A|$ iff A is uniformly distributed over its support.
(2) $\mathbb{I}(A;B \mid C) \geq 0$. The equality holds iff A and B are independent *conditioned on C.*
(3) $\mathbb{H}(A \mid B,C) \leq \mathbb{H}(A \mid B)$. The equality holds iff $A \perp C \mid B$.
*(4) $\mathbb{I}(A,B;C) = \mathbb{I}(A;C) + \mathbb{I}(B;C \mid A)$ (*chain rule of mutual information*).*
*(5) Suppose $f(A)$ is a deterministic function of A, then $\mathbb{I}(f(A);B \mid C) \leq \mathbb{I}(A;B \mid C)$ (*data processing inequality*).*

We also use the following two simple propositions. The proofs are standard (see [3]).

PROPOSITION 2.4. *For variables A, B, C, D, if $A \perp D \mid C$, then, $\mathbb{I}(A;B \mid C) \leq \mathbb{I}(A;B \mid C,D)$.*

PROPOSITION 2.5. *For variables A, B, C, D, if $A \perp D \mid B,C$, then, $\mathbb{I}(A;B \mid C) \geq \mathbb{I}(A;B \mid C,D)$.*

For two distributions μ and ν over the same probability space, the *Kullback-Leibler divergence* between μ and ν is defined as $\mathbb{D}(\mu \mid\mid \nu) := \mathbb{E}_{a\sim\mu}\left[\log \frac{\Pr_\mu(a)}{\Pr_\nu(a)}\right]$. We have,

FACT 2.6. *For random variables A, B, C,*

$$\mathbb{I}(A;B \mid C) = \mathop{\mathbb{E}}_{(b,c)\sim\text{dist}(B,C)}\left[\mathbb{D}(\text{dist}(A|C=c) \mid\mid \text{dist}(A|B=b,C=c))\right].$$

We denote the *total variation distance* between two distributions μ and ν over the same probability space Ω by $\|\mu - \nu\| = \frac{1}{2} \cdot \sum_{x\in\Omega} \left|\Pr_\mu(x) - \Pr_\nu(x)\right|$.

FACT 2.7 (PINSKER'S INEQUALITY). *For any two distributions μ and ν, $\|\mu - \nu\| \leq \sqrt{\frac{1}{2} \cdot \mathbb{D}(\mu \mid\mid \nu)}$.*

FACT 2.8. *Suppose μ and ν are two distributions for an event $\mathcal{E}$, then,* $\Pr_\mu(\mathcal{E}) \leq \Pr_\nu(\mathcal{E}) + \|\mu - \nu\|$.

3 WARM UP: A LOWER BOUND FOR SIMULTANEOUS PROTOCOLS

Our main lower bound result is based on analyzing a recursive family of distributions. As a warm up, we analyze the base case of this recursive construction in this section and prove a lower bound for 1-round (simultaneous) protocols. Formally,

THEOREM 3.1. *For any sufficiently small constant $\varepsilon > 0$, any simultaneous protocol (possibly randomized) for combinatorial auctions with subadditive (even XOS) bidders that can approximate the value of social welfare to a factor of $m^{\frac{1}{3}-\varepsilon}$ requires* $\exp\left(m^{\Omega(\varepsilon)}\right)$ *bits of communication.*

It is worth mentioning that the bound established in Theorem 3.1 on the approximation ratio of simultaneous protocols is *tight*. Previously, Dobzinski et al. [10] developed a simultaneous protocol that can approximate the social welfare up to an $\widetilde{O}(m^{1/3})$ factor using only polynomial communication. As such, Theorem 3.1 already makes a small contribution for simultaneous protocols. But more importantly, this theorem sets the stage for our main lower bound result in Section 4.

As pointed out earlier, Dobzinski et al. [10] have previously proved an $\Omega(m^{1/4})$ lower bound on the approximation ratio of the protocols that can find an approximate allocation. We should remark that this lower bound of [10] and our lower bound in Theorem 3.1 are *incomparable* in that neither imply (or strengthen) the other. The reason is that while the problem of estimating the social welfare is provably easier than the problem of finding an approximate allocation, the reduction requires one additional round of interaction and hence, in general, a simultaneous protocol for the problem of finding the allocation only implies a 2-round (and not a simultaneous) protocol for the social welfare estimation problem[3]. Interestingly, for $n = 2$ players, Braverman et al. [7] very recently showed that estimating the social welfare is indeed provably *harder* than finding an approximate allocation for *simultaneous* protocols. In the light of this result, it seems plausible that one can improve the protocol of [10] and obtain an $O(m^{1/4})$-approximation protocol for finding an approximate allocation (matching the lower bound of [10]); however, Theorem 3.1 suggests that such a protocol should necessarily be oblivious to the welfare of the allocation it provides.

3.1 A Hard Input Distribution for Simultaneous Protocols

In this section, we propose a hard input distribution $\mathcal{D}_1$ for simultaneous protocols and state several of its properties that are needed in proving the lower bound for this distribution. We start by providing an informal description of the distribution $\mathcal{D}_1$.

Let k be an integer and consider a set N of $n = k^2$ players and M of $m = k^3$ items. Each bidder $i \in N$, is given an exponentially large (in k) collection $\mathcal{F}_i$ of item-sets of size k each, such that for all $S \subseteq M$, $v_i(S) = \max_{T \in \mathcal{F}_i} |S \cap T|$ (recall that the input to player i is the valuation function $v_i(\cdot)$). Additionally, the sets in $\mathcal{F}_i$ are "barely overlapping", in the sense that for any two sets $S, T \in \mathcal{F}_i$, $|S \cap T| < k^{\varepsilon}$ (for any constant $\varepsilon > 0$).

This construction ensures that *locally* each player is confronted with exponentially many high value bundles (sets in $\mathcal{F}_i$) that look "exactly the same". However, these collections across different players are chosen in a correlated way such that except for a single "special bundle" $T_j \in \mathcal{F}_i$ (for each $i \in N$), the items in all other bundles are chosen (mostly) from a (relatively small) set of k^2 "shared" items across all players. The special bundles on the other hand consist of "unique" items.

[3]Note however that the $\widetilde{O}(m^{1/3})$-approximation protocol of [10] can already compute the welfare of the allocated allocation and hence does *not* need an additional round for estimating the social welfare, implying the tightness of the bounds in Theorem 3.1.

This imply that *globally* each player is assigned a special bundle and these special bundles are crucial to obtaining any $k^{1-\varepsilon}$-approximate allocation (recall that $k^{1-\varepsilon} = m^{\frac{1-\varepsilon}{3}}$).

We then use an additional randomization trick to ensure that any instance sampled from $\mathcal{D}_1$ either has a "large" social welfare (w.p., say, half) or a "small" one (with the remaining probability): we drop some of the bundles from the collection $\mathcal{F}_i$ of each player $i \in N$ randomly (in a correlated way), to create two sub-distributions whereby in one of them none of the special bundles are dropped and hence the social welfare is k^3, and in the other one all special bundles are dropped and hence the social welfare is at most $k^{2+\varepsilon}$ (k^2 for shared items plus k^ε intersection from any other bundle (in $\mathcal{F}_i$) for each of the k^2 players). This completes the description of our hard distribution. We now formally define $\mathcal{D}_1$.

Distribution $\mathcal{D}_1(N, M)$. A hard input distribution for simultaneous protocols.
Input: Collections N of $n = k^2$ players and M of $m = 2k^3$ items.
Output: A set of n valuation functions $(v_1, \ldots, v_n)$ for the players in N.

---

(1) Let $\mathcal{S} = \{S_1, \ldots, S_p\}$ be a (p, q, t, ℓ)-intersecting family with $p = \exp(\Theta(k^\varepsilon))$, $q = k^2 + k$, $t = k$, and $\ell = k^\varepsilon$ (guaranteed to exist by Lemma 2.2).
(2) Pick $j^\star \in [p]$ and $\theta \in \{0, 1\}$ independently and uniformly at random.
(3) For each player $i \in N$ independently,
   (a) Denote by $\mathcal{F}_i$ the *private collection* of player i (used below to define the valuation function v_i), initialized to be a copy of $\mathcal{S}$ on the universe $[q]$.
   (b) Let $x_i \in \{0, 1\}^p$ be a p-dimensional vector whereby $x_i(j^\star) = \theta$ and for any $j \neq j^\star$, $x_i(j)$ is chosen uniformly at random from $\{0, 1\}$.
   (c) For any $j \in [p]$, if $x_i(j) = 0$, remove the set S_j from $\mathcal{F}_i$, and otherwise keep S_j in $\mathcal{F}_i$.
(4) Pick a random permutation σ of M. For the i-th player in N, map the j-th item in $[q] \setminus S_{j^\star}$ to $\sigma(j)$. Moreover, map the j-th item in $S_{j^\star}$ to $\sigma(k^2 + (i-1) \cdot k + j)$. Under this mapping, the private collection $\mathcal{F}_i$ of player i consists of at most p sets of $t = k$ items from M.
(5) For all $i \in N$, define the valuation function of player i as $v_i(S) = \max_{T \in \mathcal{F}_i} |S \cap T|$.

We use $\mathcal{D}_1$ to denote the distribution $\mathcal{D}_1(N, M)$ whenever the sets N and M are clear from the context (or are irrelevant). We make several observations about the distribution $\mathcal{D}_1$.

Observation 3.2. *The valuation function of each bidder $i \in [n]$ in the distribution $\mathcal{D}_1$ is an XOS valuation (and hence is also subadditive) whereby each set $T \in \mathcal{F}_i$ defines a clause in which all items in T have value 1 and all other items have value 0.*

For any player $i \in N$, we define the *labeling function* ϕ_i as the function used to map the items in $[q]$ to M. Notice that ϕ_i is a function of σ and index $j^\star$.

Observation 3.3. *The input to player i can be uniquely identified by the pair (x_i, ϕ_i), as x_i defines the private collection $\mathcal{F}_i$ over the items $[q]$, and ϕ_i specifies the actual labeling of the items in M in the instance.*

We also point out a crucial property of this distribution: each player $i \in N$ is *oblivious* to which of the sets S_j (for $j \in [p]$), is the set $S_{j^\star}$. More formally,

Observation 3.4. *Conditioned on the input (x_i, ϕ_i) to player i, the index $j^\star \in [p]$ is chosen uniformly at random.*

Recall that for an instance $I \sim \mathcal{D}_1$, $\text{sw}(I)$ denotes the maximum value of social welfare, i.e., $\text{sw}(I) := \max_{(A_1,\dots,A_n)} \sum_{i \in N} v_i(A_i)$, where $(A_1, \dots, A_n)$ ranges over all possible allocation of items. The following lemma establishes a bound on the social welfare of any instance sampled from $\mathcal{D}_1$. The proof is deferred to the full version of the paper [3].

LEMMA 3.5. *For any $I \sim \mathcal{D}_1$, (i) if $\theta = 1$, then $\text{sw}(I) = k^3$, and (ii) if $\theta = 0$, then $\text{sw}(I) \leq 2k^{2+\varepsilon}$.*

3.2 The Lower Bound for Distribution $\mathcal{D}_1$

Let π be a public coin simultaneous protocol that can output a $\left(m^{\frac{1-\varepsilon}{3}}\right)$-approximation to the social welfare of any instance $I \sim \mathcal{D}_1$, w.p. of failure $\delta \leq 1/3$. In this section, we prove that the communication cost of the protocol π needs to be at least $\exp(k^{\Omega(\varepsilon)})$ bits. Note that by (the easy direction of) Yao's minimax principle [27], we only need to consider deterministic protocols on the distribution $\mathcal{D}_1$ to prove this result.

The intuition behind the proof is as follows. By Lemma 3.5, the social welfare in the given instance changes by a factor of $k^{1-\varepsilon}$ depending on the value of θ. This implies that any $k^{1-\varepsilon} = m^{\frac{1-\varepsilon}{3}}$ approximation algorithm for the social welfare can also determine the value of θ. Using this, we can argue that the message sent by the players needs to reveal $\Omega(1)$ bit of information about the parameter θ. Roughly speaking, this means that each of the n players is responsible for revealing $\Omega(1/n)$ bit about θ in average.

Furthermore, recall that the input to player $i \in N$ can be seen as a tuple (x_i, ϕ_i) (by Observation 3.3) and that $\theta = x_i(j^\star)$. Additionally, by Observation 3.4, given input (x_i, ϕ_i) to player i, the index $j^\star$ is chosen uniformly at random from $[p]$ and hence player i is oblivious to which index of x_i corresponds to the parameter θ. This essentially means that player i needs to reveal $\Omega(p/n)$ bits about the vector x_i to be able to reveal $\Omega(1/n)$ bit about $x_i(j^\star)$, hence forcing i to communicate $\Omega(p/n) = \exp\left(k^{\Omega(\varepsilon)}\right)$ bits also. To make the latter intuition precise, we argue that while the message sent by one player can, in principle, be used to infer information about the input of another player (as the input of the players are correlated), this extra information is limited to an "easy part", containing only $(\sigma, j^\star)$ that can even be assumed to be known to referee (but not players) beforehand. This allows us to "break" the information revealed to the referee to smaller pieces sent by each player, hence arguing that each player is indeed directly responsible for communicating the information about her input. We now formalize this intuition. We first need the following notation.

Notation. We use $\Pi = (\Pi_1, \dots, \Pi_n)$ to denote the random variable for the transcript of the messages communicated in π. For any player $i \in N$, and any $j \in [p]$, we use the random variable $X_{i,j} \in \{0, 1\}$ to denote the value of $x_i(j)$, i.e., $X_{i,j} = 1$ iff the set $S_j \in \mathcal{S}$ is included in the private collection $\mathcal{F}_i$. We further define X_i for $i \in N$ as the vector $X_i := (X_{i,1}, \dots, X_{i,p})$. We use Σ to denote the random variable for the permutation σ, J for the index $j^\star$, and Θ for the parameter θ. For each player $i \in N$, Φ_i denotes the random variable for the labeling function ϕ_i.

Recall that (Σ, J) is the "easy part" of the input: the part that we assume the referee (but not each individual player) knows beforehand. Assuming this knowledge can only strengthen our lower bound. We start by arguing that the protocol π needs to reveal $\Omega(1)$ bits of information about the value of parameter θ in the distribution. The proof is deferred to the full version of the paper [3].

CLAIM 3.6. $\mathbb{I}(\Theta ; \Pi \mid \Sigma, J) = \Omega(1)$.

We now show that the information revealed about Θ by the message Π is at most the sum of information revealed by each message Π_i for $i \in N$ individually. In other words, one does not gain an extra information by combining the messages of players (after conditioning on what is revealed by (Σ, J) already).

Claim 3.7. $\mathbb{I}(\Theta\,;\Pi \mid \Sigma, J) \leq \sum_{i\in N} \mathbb{I}(\Theta\,;\Pi_i \mid \Sigma, J)$.

Proof. We have,

$$\mathbb{I}(\Theta\,;\Pi \mid \Sigma, J) = \sum_{i\in N} \mathbb{I}(\Theta\,;\Pi_i \mid \Pi^{<i}, \Sigma, J) \leq \sum_{i\in N} \mathbb{I}(\Theta\,;\Pi_i \mid \Sigma, J)$$

where the equality is by chain rule (Fact 2.3-(4)), and the inequality follows from Proposition 2.5, as we show below that $\Pi_i \perp \Pi^{<i} \mid \Theta, \Sigma, J$, or equivalently $\mathbb{I}(\Pi_i\,;\Pi^{<i} \mid \Theta, \Sigma, J) = 0$ (by Fact 2.3-(2)).

As stated in Observation 3.3, the input of player $i \in N$ is uniquely determined by (x_i, ϕ_i) and hence Π_i is a deterministic function of variables X_i and Φ_i. Moreover, Φ_i is also uniquely determined by (Σ, J), hence, conditioned on (Σ, J), Π_i is only a function of X_i. On the other hand, conditioned on (Θ, Σ, J), X_i and $X^{<i}$ are chosen independently of each other in the distribution $\mathcal{D}_1$ (as $X_{i,j^\star} = \theta$ and the rest of X_i is chosen uniformly at random from $\{0, 1\}$). This implies that $\mathbb{I}(X_i\,;X^{<i} \mid \Theta, \Sigma, J) = 0$. As stated earlier, Π_i is a function of X_i and $\Pi^{<i}$ is a function of $X^{<i}$ alone (conditioned on (Θ, Σ, J)), hence, by data processing inequality (Fact 2.3-(5)), $\mathbb{I}(\Pi_i\,;\Pi^{<i} \mid \Theta, \Sigma, J) = 0$ as well. □

We now use a direct-sum style argument to prove that if a player $i \in N$ wants to communicate c bits about θ, she needs to communicate (essentially) $p \cdot c$ bits about her input.

Lemma 3.8. *For any $i \in N$, $\mathbb{I}(\Theta\,;\Pi_i \mid \Sigma, J) \leq |\Pi_i| / p$.*

Proof. We have,

$$\mathbb{I}(\Theta\,;\Pi_i \mid \Sigma, J) = \mathop{\mathbb{E}}_{j\in[p]} \left[\mathbb{I}(\Theta\,;\Pi_i \mid \Sigma, J = j)\right] = \mathop{\mathbb{E}}_{j\in[p]} \left[\mathbb{I}(X_{i,j}\,;\Pi_i \mid \Sigma, J = j)\right]$$

($\Theta = X_{i,j}$ conditioned on $J = j$)

$$= \frac{1}{p} \cdot \sum_{j\in[p]} \mathbb{I}(X_{i,j}\,;\Pi_i \mid \Sigma, J = j)$$

(the index $j^\star$ is chosen uniformly at random from $[p]$)

Define Σ^{-i} as the part of permutation Σ that does not affect the labeling function Φ_i of player i, i.e., the values of $\sigma(k^2 + 1) \ldots \sigma(k^2 + (i-1) \cdot k)$ and $\sigma(k^2 + i \cdot k + 1), \ldots, \sigma(k^3)$. With this notation, Σ can be written as a function of Φ_i, Σ^{-i}, and J (as J and Φ_i uniquely define the rest of Σ outside Σ^{-i}). Consequently, we can write,

$$\mathbb{I}(\Theta\,;\Pi_i \mid \Sigma, J) = \frac{1}{p} \cdot \sum_{j\in[p]} \mathbb{I}(X_{i,j}\,;\Pi_i \mid \Sigma^{-i}, \Phi_i, J = j)$$

Our goal is now to drop the conditioning on the event "$J = j$". To do so, notice that the distribution of (Σ^{-i}, Φ_i) is independent of the event $J = j$; this is immediate to see as Σ^{-i} is independent of Φ_i and $J = j$, and Φ_i is independent of $J = j$ by Observation 3.4. Moreover, $X_{i,j}$ is independent of all $(\Sigma^{-i}, \Phi_i, J = j)$ (as it is uniform over $\{0, 1\}$) and furthermore, Π_i is a function of Φ_i, X_i, which are independent of $J = j$. Consequently, we can drop the conditioning in the above information term and obtain that,

$$\mathbb{I}(\Theta\,;\Pi_i \mid \Sigma, J) = \frac{1}{p} \cdot \sum_{j\in[p]} \mathbb{I}(X_{i,j}\,;\Pi_i \mid \Sigma^{-i}, \Phi_i) \leq \frac{1}{p} \cdot \sum_{j\in[p]} \mathbb{I}(X_{i,j}\,;\Pi_i \mid X_i^{<j}, \Sigma^{-i}, \Phi_i)$$

(by Proposition 2.4 as $X_{i,j} \perp X_i^{<j} \mid \Sigma^{-i}, \Phi_i$)

$$= \frac{1}{p} \cdot \mathbb{I}(X_i\,;\Pi_i \mid \Sigma^{-i}, \Phi_i) \leq \frac{1}{p} \cdot \mathbb{H}(\Pi_i \mid \Sigma^{-i}, \Phi_i) \leq \frac{1}{p} \cdot \mathbb{H}(\Pi_i) \leq \frac{1}{p} \cdot |\Pi_i|$$

where the equality in the second line is by chain rule (Fact 2.3-(4)), and inequalities are by Fact 2.3-(1) and Fact 2.3-(3). □

We can now conclude the following lemma.

Lemma 3.9. *Communication cost of π is $\Omega(p)$.*

Proof. $\|\pi\| = \sum_{i \in N} |\Pi_i| \geq p \cdot \sum_{i \in N} \mathbb{I}(\Theta ; \Pi_i \mid \Sigma, J) \geq p \cdot \mathbb{I}(\Theta ; \Pi \mid \Sigma, J) = \Omega(p)$. where the last three equations are by, respectively, Lemma 3.8, Claim 3.7, and Claim 3.6. □

Theorem 3.1 now follows from Lemma 3.9 by re-parameterizing ε above by some $\Theta(\varepsilon)$ and noting that $p = \exp(\Theta(k^\varepsilon)) = \exp\left(m^{\Omega(\varepsilon)}\right)$ (as $m = k^3$).

4 MAIN RESULT: A LOWER BOUND FOR MULTI-ROUND PROTOCOLS

In this section, we establish our main result. Formally,

Theorem 4.1. *For any integer $1 \leq r \leq o\left(\frac{\log m}{\log\log m}\right)$, and any sufficiently small constant $\varepsilon > 0$, any r-round protocol (possibly randomized) for combinatorial auctions with subadditive (even XOS) bidders that can approximate the value of social welfare to a factor of $\left(\frac{1}{r} \cdot m^{\frac{1-\varepsilon}{2r+1}}\right)$ requires* $\exp\left(m^{\Omega(\frac{\varepsilon}{r})}\right)$ *bits of communication.*

We start by introducing the recursive family of hard input distributions that we use proving in Theorem 4.1 and then establish a lower bound for this distribution.

4.1 A Hard Input Distribution for r-Round Protocols

Our hard distribution $\mathcal{D}_r$ for r-round protocols is defined recursively with its base case ($r = 1$ case) being the distribution $\mathcal{D}_1$ introduced in Section 3.1. We first give an informal description of $\mathcal{D}_r$.

Let k be an integer and consider a set N of $n_r = k^{2r}$ players and a set M of $m_r = (r+1) \cdot k^{2r+1}$ items. The players are partitioned (arbitrary) between k^2 groups $N_1, \ldots, N_{k^2}$ each of size n_{r-1}. Fix a group N_g and for any player $i \in N_g$, we create an exponentially large (in k) collection C_i of item-sets of size m_{r-1} (over the universe M), such that the for any two sets $S, T \in C_i$, $|S \cap T| \leq k^{2r-2+\varepsilon}$ (for any constant $\varepsilon > 0$).

The *local* view of player $i \in N_g$ is as follows: over each set $S_j \in C_i$, we create an $(r-1)$-round instance of the problem, namely instance $I_{i,j}$, sampled from the distribution $\mathcal{D}_{r-1}$ with the set of players being N_g and the set of items being S_j, and then let the input of player i be the collective input of the i-th player in all these instances. In other words, player i finds herself "playing" in exponentially many "$(r-1)$-round instances" of $\mathcal{D}_{r-1}$.

On the *group level*, the input to players inside a group N_g are highly correlated: for each player $i \in N_g$, one of the instances, namely $I_{i,j^\star}$, is an "special instance" in the sense that *all* players in the group N_g has a "consistent" view of this instance, i.e., the collective view of players $1, \ldots, n_{r-1}$ in N_g on the instances $I_{1,j^\star}, \ldots, I_{n_{r-1},j^\star}$ forms a valid instance sampled from $\mathcal{D}_{r-1}$. However, for any other index $j \neq j^\star$, the collective view of players in N_g in the instances $I_{1,j^\star}, \ldots, I_{n_{r-1},j^\star}$ forms a "pseudo instance" that is *not* sampled from $\mathcal{D}_{r-1}$; these pseudo instances are created by sampling the input of each player *independently* according to $\mathcal{D}_{r-1}$. Note however that while the pseudo instances and the special instance of a player are fundamentally different, each player is oblivious to this difference, i.e., which instance is the special instance.

Finally, the input to players across the groups, i.e., the *global* input, is further correlated: the set of items in the special instances of players in a group N_g is a "unique" set of items (across all groups), while *all* other instances, across all groups, are constructed over a set of k^{2r} "shared" items. This correlation makes the special instance of a player i, in some sense, the *only important* instance: to obtain a large allocation, the players need to ultimately solve the problem for these special instances.

We now formally define distribution $\mathcal{D}_r$. In the following, for simplicity of exposition, we assume that the distribution $\mathcal{D}_r$, in addition to the valuation function of players, also outputs the *private collections* (defined similarly as in $\mathcal{D}_1$) of players that are used to define these functions[4].

Distribution $\mathcal{D}_r(N, M)$. A hard input distribution for r-round protocols (for $r \geq 2$).
Input: Collections N of $n_r = k^{2r}$ players and M of $m_r = (r+1) \cdot k^{2r+1}$ items.
Output: A set of n_r valuation functions $(v_1, \ldots, v_{n_r})$ for the players in N and n_r private collections $(\mathcal{F}_1, \ldots, \mathcal{F}_{n_r})$ used to define the valuation functions.

(1) Let $\mathcal{S}_r = \{S_1, \ldots, S_p\}$ be a (p_r, q_r, t_r, ℓ_r)-intersecting family with parameters $p_r = p = \exp(\Theta(k^\varepsilon))$, $q_r = k^{2r} + r \cdot k^{2r-1}$, $t_r = r \cdot k^{2r-1}$, and $\ell_r = k^{2r-2+\varepsilon}$ (guaranteed to exist by Lemma 2.2 as $k = m^{\Omega(1/r)} = \omega(r^{2/\varepsilon})$ by the assumption that $r = o\left(\frac{\log m}{\log\log m}\right)$).
(2) Arbitrary group the players into k^2 groups $\mathcal{N} = (N_1, \ldots, N_{k^2})$, whereby each group contains exactly $n_{r-1} = k^{2r-2}$ players.
(3) Pick an index $j^\star \in [p]$ uniformly at random and sample an instance $I_r^\star \sim \mathcal{D}_{r-1}([n_{r-1}], S_{j^\star})$.
(4) For each group $N_g \in \mathcal{N}$ independently,
  (a) Define $I_{N_g}^\star$ as $I_r^\star$ by mapping the players in $[n_{r-1}]$ to N_g.
  (b) For each player $i \in N_g$ *independently*, create p instances $I^{(i)} := (I_{i,1}, \ldots, I_{i,p})$ whereby for all $j \neq j^\star$, $I_{i,j} \sim \mathcal{D}_{r-1}(N_g, S_j)$, and $I_{i,j^\star} = I_{N_g}^\star$.
  (c) For a player $i \in N_g$ and index $j \in [p]$, let $\mathcal{F}_{i,j}$ be the set of *private collection* of that player in instance $I_{i,j}$ and let $\mathcal{F}_i = \bigcup_{j\in[p]} \mathcal{F}_{i,j}$.
(5) Pick a random permutation σ of M. For each $g \in [k^2]$ and group N_g, map the k^{2r} items in $[q_r] \setminus S_{j^\star}$ to $\sigma(1), \ldots, \sigma(k^{2r})$, and the t_r items in $S_{j^\star}$ to $\sigma((g-1) \cdot t_r + 1) \ldots \sigma(g \cdot t_r)$ (and for each player $i \in N_g$, update the item set of $\mathcal{F}_i$ and underlying instances $I_{i,1}, \ldots, I_{i,p}$ accordingly).
(6) For any player $i \in N$, define the valuation function of player i as $v_i(S) = \max_{T\in\mathcal{F}_i} |S \cap T|$ (note that these valuation functions are XOS valuation; see Observation 3.2).

We make several observations about the distribution $\mathcal{D}_r$. Recall that $\mathcal{F}_i$ denotes the private collection of player $i \in N$ that is used to define the valuation function v_i. By construction, the size of the sets inside each private collection is equal across any two distributions $\mathcal{D}_r$ and $\mathcal{D}_{r'}$ and hence is equal to k (by definition of distribution $\mathcal{D}_1$). A simple property of these sets is that,

Observation 4.2. *For any player $i \in N$, and any set $T \in \mathcal{F}_i$, the set T is chosen uniformly at random from all k-subsets of M.*

Fix any group $N_g \in \mathcal{N}$ and any player $i \in N_g$. The input to player i can be seen as the "view" of i in the p instances $I^{(i)} := (I_{i,1}, \ldots, I_{i,p})$, i.e., the input of the i-th player (in N_g) in $I_{i,j}$ (for all $j \in [p]$) and *not* the whole instance. However, in the following, we slightly abuse the notation and use $I_{i,j}$ to also denote the view of player i in the instance $I_{i,j}$. Moreover, we point out that $I_{i,j}$ is defined

[4]Strictly speaking, this is a redundant information as the valuation functions can uniquely determine the private collections; however, we include this redundant output for the ease of presentation.

over the set of items S_j; hence, the complete input to player i is the pair $(I^{(i)}, \phi_i)$ where ϕ_i is the labeling function to map the items in S_j to M (see also Observation 3.3).

For any player $i \in N$, we refer to the instance $I_{i,j^\star}$ of player i as the *special instance* of player i, and to all other instances $I_{i,j}$ for $j \neq j^\star$ as *fooling instances.*

Observation 4.3. *For any group $N_g \in \mathcal{N}$, the joint input of all players $i \in N_g$ in their special instances $I_{i,j^\star}$ form the instance $I^\star_{N_g}$ that is sampled from the distribution $\mathcal{D}_{r-1}$.*

On the other hand, the fooling instances of players $i \in N_g$ are sampled *independently* and hence the joint distribution of the players on their instances $I_{i,j}$ is *not* sampled from $\mathcal{D}_{r-1}$. Nevertheless, this difference is *not evident* to the player i.

Observation 4.4. *For any player $i \in N$, conditioned on the input $(I^{(i)}, \phi_i)$ given to the player i, the index $j^\star$ is chosen uniformly at random from $[p]$.*

Additionally,

Observation 4.5. *The distribution of collection of instances $\mathcal{I} := (I^{(1)}, \ldots, I^{(n_r)}) \sim \mathcal{D}_r \mid I^\star_r, \sigma, j^\star$ is a* product *distribution as instances in Line (4b) are sampled independently (except for instances $I_{i,j^\star} = I^\star_r$ which are already conditioned on above).*

Another important property of the special instances in distribution $\mathcal{D}_r$ is that,

Observation 4.6. *The special instances $I^\star_{N_1}, \ldots, I^\star_{N_{k^2}}$ are supported on disjoint set of items (according to the mapping σ).*

Notice that we can trace the special instances into a *unique* path $I^\star_r \to I^\star_{r-1} \to \ldots \to I^\star_2$, whereby $I^\star_2$ is sampled from the distribution $\mathcal{D}_1$. We use $\theta^\star$ to denote the parameter θ (in $\mathcal{D}_1$) in the instance $I^\star_2$ in this path. The following lemma proves a key relation between $\theta^\star$ and social welfare of the sampled instance. The proof is technical and is deferred to the full version of the paper [3].

Lemma 4.7. *For any instance $I \sim \mathcal{D}_r$:*

$$\Pr\left(\mathrm{sw}(I) \geq k^{2r+1} \mid \theta^\star = 1\right) = 1 \tag{1}$$

$$\Pr\left(\mathrm{sw}(I) \leq 2r \cdot k^{2r+2\varepsilon} \mid \theta^\star = 0\right) = 1 - r \cdot \exp\left(-\Omega(k^\varepsilon)\right) \tag{2}$$

4.2 The Lower Bound for Distribution $\mathcal{D}_r$

Let π be a r-round protocol that can output a $\left(\frac{1}{r} \cdot m_r^{\frac{1-2\varepsilon}{2r+1}}\right)$-approximation to the social welfare of any instance $I \sim \mathcal{D}_r$, w.p. of failure $\delta < 1/4$. In this section, we prove that the communication cost of the protocol π needs to be at least $\exp(\Omega(k^\varepsilon))$ bits. By (the easy direction of) Yao's minimax principle [27], it suffices to prove this lower bound for deterministic algorithms.

We start by providing a detailed overview of the proof. First, by Lemma 4.7 we can argue that the protocol π is also a $(\delta + o(1))$-error protocol for estimating the parameter $\theta^\star$, and hence we prove the lower bound for $\theta^\star$-estimation problem instead. Recall that in any instance $I_r \sim \mathcal{D}_r$, the value of $\theta^\star$ is equal to the value of $\theta^\star$ in the underlying special instance $I^\star_r$ in I_r, and that $I^\star_r$ is sampled from the distribution $\mathcal{D}_{r-1}$. Hence to "solve" the instance $I_r \sim \mathcal{D}_r$, the players need to be able to solve the instance $I^\star_r \sim \mathcal{D}_{r-1}$ as well. This suggests an inductive approach to prove the lower bound for the distribution $\mathcal{D}_r$.

Consider the first message $\Pi_1 = (\Pi_{1,1}, \ldots, \Pi_{1,n_r})$ of π. Recall that the input to any player $i \in N$ consists of p different instances (of $\mathcal{D}_{r-1}$), one of which being the instance $I^\star_r$. By Observation 4.4, each player i is oblivious to the identity of $I^\star_r$ and hence, intuitively, the message $\Pi_{1,i}$ cannot reveal more than $\approx |\Pi_{1,i}|/p$ bits of information about the instance $I_r^\star$. Considering the simultaneity of the protocol π, we can use a similar argument as in the previous section and prove that if $|\Pi_1| = o(p)$, then at most $o(1)$ bits of information is revealed about $I_r^\star$.

Now consider the second round of the protocol π. The task of players in each group $N_g \in \mathcal{N}$ is now to solve the instance $I_r^\star$ (on a separate set of players and items). As argued above, the first message of players can only reveal $o(1)$ bits of information about $I_r^\star$ and hence distribution of $I_r^\star$ is still "very close" to its original distribution $\mathcal{D}_{r-1}$, *even conditioned on the first message of players.* But $\mathcal{D}_{r-1}$ is assumed inductively to be a hard input distribution for $(r-1)$-round protocols and as π needs to solve $I_r^\star$ in $(r-1)$ rounds now, we may argue that it needs an exponential communication.

To make this intuition precise, we employ a *round-elimination* argument: Given any hard instance $I_{r-1} \sim \mathcal{D}_{r-1}$, we "embed" I_{r-1} in an r-round instance I_r sampled from $\mathcal{D}_r$ *conditioned on the first message* Π_1 of π with *no communication* between the players and then use π from the second round onwards to solve I_{r-1}. However, notice that as the number of players (and items) vary between I_r and I_{r-1}, we cannot directly apply π on I_{r-1}. Instead, the players first sample a message Π_1 (of π) according to the distribution $\mathcal{D}_r$ using public randomness. Next, each player $i \in [n_{r-1}]$ in the instance I_{r-1} mimics the role of k^2 different players (one "copy" in each group in $\mathcal{N}$ in I_r) by letting the input of each copy in the special instance (of I_r) be her input in I_{r-1} and then "completes" the rest of her input (i.e., her fooling instances in I_r) *independently* of other players to obtain an instance $I_r \sim \mathcal{D}_r \mid I_r^\star = I_{r-1}, \Pi_1$. Note that a-priori it is not clear that why such an embedding is possible since the first message Π_1 correlates the input of players in fooling instances, making independent sampling of these instances impossible. However, we show that by further conditioning on some "easy part" of the input in the first round, i.e., σ and $j^\star$ (by sampling these parts publicly also), the players can indeed implement this embedding *without any communication* and hence obtain a valid $(r-1)$-round protocol for I_{r-1}. We are now ready to present the formal proof. To continue, we need the following notation.

Notation. For any $j \in [r]$, we use $\Pi_j = (\Pi_{j,1}, \ldots, \Pi_{j,n_r})$ to denote the random variable for the transcript of the messages communicated in the round j of π. For any player $i \in N$, and any $j \in [p]$, we override the notation and use $I_{i,j}$ to also denote the random variable for the instance $I_{i,j}$ sampled in $\mathcal{D}_r$ (similarly for $I_r^\star$ and $I^{(i)}$). We further use Σ to denote the random variable for the permutation σ and J for the index $j^\star$. We start by the following simple claim.

Claim 4.8. *Protocol π can also determine the value of $\theta^\star$ w.p. $1 - \delta - o(1)$.*

Proof. By Lemma 4.7, the ratio of $\text{sw}(I)$ depending on the parameter $\theta^\star$ is (w.p. $1 - o(1)$):

$$\frac{k^{2r+1}}{2r \cdot k^{2r+2\varepsilon}} = \frac{k^{1-2\varepsilon}}{2r} = \frac{m_r^{\frac{1-2\varepsilon}{2r+1}}}{2r \cdot (r+1)^{\frac{1}{2r+1}}} > \frac{1}{r} \cdot m_r^{\frac{1-2\varepsilon}{2r+1}}$$

Hence, the δ-error $\left(\frac{1}{r} \cdot m_r^{\frac{1-2\varepsilon}{2r+1}}\right)$-approximation protocol π correctly determines the value of $\theta^\star$ w.p. $1 - \delta - o(1)$. □

We show that as long as the first message sent by the players is not too large, this message cannot reveal much information about the special instance $I_r^\star$ embedded in the distribution $\mathcal{D}_r$. This argument is a similar to the one in Section 3.2 and we defer it to the full version of the paper [3].

Lemma 4.9. *If $|\Pi_1| = o(p/r^4)$, then $\mathbb{I}(I_r^\star\,; \Pi_1 \mid \Sigma, J) = o(1/r^4)$.*

Recall that $I_r^\star$ is the special instance in distribution $\mathcal{D}_r$ which was sampled from distribution $\mathcal{D}_{r-1}$. We define ψ_r as the distribution of $I_r^\star$ conditioned on (Π_1, Σ, J), i.e., after seeing the first message of π and the easy part of the input (Σ, J). As a corollary of Lemma 4.9, we have that this further conditioning does not change the distribution of $I_r^\star$ by much.

Claim 4.10. *If* $|\Pi_r| = o(p/r^4)$, *then,* $\mathbb{E}_{(\Pi_1,\Sigma,J)}\left[\|\psi_r - \mathcal{D}_{r-1}\|\right] = o(1/r^2)$.

Proof. We have,

$$\begin{aligned}
\mathop{\mathbb{E}}_{(\Pi_1,\Sigma,J)}\left[\|\psi_r - \mathcal{D}_{r-1}\|\right] &= \mathop{\mathbb{E}}_{(\Pi_1,\Sigma,J)}\left[\|\psi_r - \text{dist}(I_r^\star \mid (\Sigma,J))\|\right] \qquad (\text{dist}(I_r^\star) = \mathcal{D}_{r-1} \text{ and } I_r^\star \perp \Sigma, J) \\
&\leq \mathop{\mathbb{E}}_{(\Pi_1,\Sigma,J)}\left[\sqrt{\frac{1}{2}\cdot \mathbb{D}(\psi_r \mid\mid \text{dist}(I_r^\star \mid (\Sigma,J)))}\right] \\
&\qquad\qquad (\text{by Pinsker's inequality (Fact 2.7)}) \\
&\leq \sqrt{\frac{1}{2}\cdot \mathop{\mathbb{E}}_{(\Pi_1,\Sigma,J)}\left[\mathbb{D}(\psi_r \mid\mid \text{dist}(I_r^\star \mid (\Sigma,J)))\right]} \\
&\qquad\qquad (\text{by concavity of } \sqrt{\cdot} \text{ and Jensen's inequality}) \\
&= \sqrt{\frac{1}{2}\cdot \mathbb{I}(I_r^\star ; \Pi_1 \mid \Sigma, J)} \qquad (\text{by Fact 2.6})
\end{aligned}$$

which is $o(1/r^2)$ by Lemma 4.9. □

We are now ready to state the main result of this section. Define the recursive function $e(r) := e(r-1) + o(1/r^2)$ (with $e(0) = 0$). Note that $e(r) = \sum_{i=1}^{r} o(1/i^2) = o(1)$. We have,

Lemma 4.11. *For any* $r \geq 1$, *any* r*-round protocol* π *for determining* $\theta^\star$ *on* $\mathcal{D}_r$ *with error probability at most* $\delta = 1/3 - e(r)$ *requires* $\Omega(p/r^4)$ *communication.*

Proof. We prove this lemma inductively. The base case for $r = 1$ follows from Lemma 3.9. Now suppose the result holds for all integers smaller than r and we aim to prove it for the case of r-round protocols. Let π be a δ-error protocol for estimating $\theta^\star$ with $\delta = 1/3 - e(r)$ and assume by contradiction that the communication cost of π is $o(p/r^4)$; we use π to design a randomized $(r-1)$-round protocol π' that has communication cost $o(p/r^4)$, and errs w.p. at most $1/3 - e(r-1)$ on $\mathcal{D}_{r-1}$, and then use averaging argument to fix its randomness to obtain a deterministic protocol that contradicts the induction hypothesis.

Protocol π'**:** An $(r-1)$-round protocol for solving instances of $\mathcal{D}_{r-1}$ using protocol π.
Input: An instance $I \sim \mathcal{D}_{r-1}$. **Output:** The value of $\theta^\star$ in I.

---

(1) Let $N = [n_r]$ and $M = [m_r]$.
(2) Using *public randomness*, the players sample $(\Pi_1, \sigma, j^\star) \sim \mathcal{D}_r(N, M)$, i.e., they sample from the joint distribution of the first message of π (denoted by Π_1), the permutation σ over M, and the index $j^\star \in [p]$.
(3) The players partition N into k^2 equal-size groups $\mathcal{N} = (N_1, \ldots, N_{k^2})$ (as is done in $\mathcal{D}_r$) and the i-th player (denoted by P_i) in I mimics the role of the i-th player in each group $N_g \in \mathcal{N}$ (denoted by $P_{i,g}$) individually, as follows:
  (a) P_i sets the input for $P_{i,g}$ (for $g \in [k^2]$) in the instance $I_{i,j^\star}$ (in $\mathcal{D}_r$) as the input of P_i in the input instance I mapped via σ to M (using the same procedure as in $\mathcal{D}_r$).

(b) P_i samples the input for $P_{i,g}$ (for $g \in [k^2]$) in all other instances $I_{i,j}$ (for $j \neq j^\star$), using *private randomness* from the distribution $I_{i,j} \sim \mathcal{D}_r \mid (I^\star = I, \Pi_1, \sigma, j^\star)$ (we prove this is indeed possible by Proposition 4.12 below).

(4) The players run the protocol π on the new sampled instance conditioned on the first message being Π_1, (i.e., run π from the second round assuming Π_1 is the content of blackboard after the first round) and output the same answer as π.

We start by arguing that π' is indeed a valid protocol; in particular, Line (3b) can be implemented without any communication. We first need some new notation. For any player $i \in N$, define $I_r^\star(i)$ as the input of player i in the instance $I_{i,j^\star} = I_r^\star$ (conditioned on Σ, J), and define $I_r^\star(-i)$ as the input of all other players in $I_r^\star$. To prove that π' is valid, it suffices to prove the following proposition.

Proposition 4.12. *The distribution* $\mathcal{I} := (I^{(1)}, \ldots, I^{(n)}) \sim (\mathcal{D}_r \mid I_r^\star, \Pi_1, \Sigma, J)$ *is a* product distribution *whereby each* $\mathcal{I}_i = I^{(i)}$ *is sampled from* $\mathcal{D}_r \mid I_r^\star(i), \Pi_1, \Sigma, J$.

Proof. For any $i \in N$, we prove that $\mathbb{I}(\mathcal{I}_i\,; \mathcal{I}^{-i}, I_r^\star(-i) \mid I_r^\star(i), \Pi_1, \Sigma, J) = 0$. By Fact 2.3-(2), this implies that $\mathcal{I}_i \perp (\mathcal{I}^{-i}, I_r^\star(-i)) \mid I_r^\star(i), \Pi_1, \Sigma, J$, hence proving the proposition. We have,

$$\begin{aligned}\mathbb{I}(\mathcal{I}_i\,; \mathcal{I}^{-i}, I_r^\star(-i) \mid I_r^\star(i), \Pi_1, \Sigma, J) &= \mathbb{I}(\mathcal{I}_i\,; \mathcal{I}^{-i}, I_r^\star(-i) \mid I_r^\star(i), \Pi_{1,i}, \Pi_1^{-i}, \Sigma, J) \quad (\text{as } \Pi_1 = \Pi_{1,i}, \Pi_1^{-i})\\ &\leq \mathbb{I}(\mathcal{I}_i\,; \mathcal{I}^{-i}, I_r^\star(-i) \mid I_r^\star(i), \Pi_{1,i}, \Sigma, J)\end{aligned}$$

since $\mathcal{I}_i \perp \Pi_1^{-i} \mid (\mathcal{I}^{-i}, I_r^\star = (I_r^\star(i), I_r^\star(-i)), \Pi_{1,i}, \Sigma, J)$ as Π_1^{-i} is a deterministic function of $\mathcal{I}^{-i}, I_r^\star, \Sigma, J$, and hence we can apply Proposition 2.5.

Furthermore,

$$\begin{aligned}\mathbb{I}(\mathcal{I}_i\,; \mathcal{I}^{-i}, I_r^\star(-i) \mid I_r^\star(i), \Pi_1, \Sigma, J) &\leq \mathbb{I}(\mathcal{I}_i\,; \mathcal{I}^{-i}, I_r^\star(-i) \mid I_r^\star(i), \Pi_{1,i}, \Sigma, J)\\ &\leq \mathbb{I}(\mathcal{I}_i\,; \mathcal{I}^{-i}, I_r^\star(-i) \mid I_r^\star(i), \Sigma, J)\end{aligned}$$

since $\left(\mathcal{I}^{-i}, I_r^\star(-i)\right) \perp \Pi_{1,i} \mid \mathcal{I}_i, I_r^\star(i), \Sigma, J)$ as $\Pi_{1,i}$ is a deterministic function of $I^{(i)} = (\mathcal{I}_i, I_r^\star(i)), \Sigma, J$ and hence we can again apply Proposition 2.5. Finally, $\mathbb{I}(\mathcal{I}_i\,; \mathcal{I}^{-i}, I_r^\star(-i) \mid I_r^\star(i), \Sigma, J) = 0$ by Observation 4.5 and Fact 2.3-(2), implying that $\mathbb{I}(\mathcal{I}_i\,; \mathcal{I}^{-i}, I_r^\star(-i) \mid I_r^\star(i), \Pi_1, \Sigma, J) = 0$ as well, proving the proposition. □

It is now easy to see that π' is indeed an $(r-1)$-round protocol: to sample from the distribution $\mathcal{D}_r \mid (I^\star = I, \Pi_1, \Sigma, J)$ in Line (3b), each player $i \in N$ needs to sample from the distribution $\mathcal{D}_r \mid (I_r^\star(i), \Pi_1, \Sigma, J)$ (by Proposition 4.12), and this is possible since $(I_r^\star(i), \Pi_1, \Sigma, J)$ are all known to i. Hence, the players do not need any communication for simulating the first round of protocol π. We now prove that.

Claim 4.13. π' *is a* δ'*-error protocol for* $\mathcal{D}_{r-1}$ *for* $\delta' = 1/3 - e(r-1)$.

Proof Sketch. Note that our goal is to calculate the probability that π' errs given an instance $I \sim \mathcal{D}_{r-1}$. For the sake of analysis, suppose that $I \sim \psi_r$ instead, i.e., is sampled from the distribution dist$(I_r^\star \mid \Pi_1, \Sigma, J)$ (according to distribution $\mathcal{D}_r$). In this case, one can see that the distribution of the r-round instance constructed by π' matches the distribution $\mathcal{D}_r$. Since π' outputs the same answer as π on this new sampled instance, and since $I = I_r^\star$ in the new instance, the probability that π' errs on ψ_r is equal to the probability that π errs on $\mathcal{D}_r$ which in turn is equal to $1/3 - e(r)$. Now notice that by Claim 4.10, the total variation distance between ψ_r and $\mathcal{D}_{r-1}$ is $o(1/r^2)$ and hence by Fact 2.8, $\Pr_{\mathcal{D}_{r-1}}(\pi' \text{ errs}) \leq \Pr_{\psi_r}(\pi' \text{ errs}) + o(1/r^2) = 1/3 - e(r-1)$. The complete proof can be found in the full version of the paper [3]. □

Lemma 4.11 now follows from Claim 4.13 by an averaging argument since we can fix the randomness in π' to obtain a deterministic protocol π'' that uses $o(p/r^4)$ bits of communication and errs w.p. at most $1/3 - e(r-1)$ on $\mathcal{D}_{r-1}$, a contradiction with the induction hypothesis. □

Theorem 4.1 now easily follows from Lemma 4.11.

Proof of Theorem 4.1. Let π be a $\left(\frac{1}{r} \cdot m^{\frac{1-2\varepsilon}{2r+1}}\right)$-approximation, $(1/4)$-error protocol for subadditive combinatorial auctions on the distribution $\mathcal{D}_r$. By Claim 4.8, π is also a $(1/4 + o(1))$-error protocol for $\theta^\star$ estimation on $\mathcal{D}_r$. Since $(1/4 + o(1)) < 1/3 - e(r)$, by Lemma 4.11, we have $\|\pi\| = \Omega(p/r^4) = \exp(\Theta(k^\varepsilon))/r^4 = \exp\left(m^{\Omega(\varepsilon/r)}\right)/r^4 = \exp\left(m^{\Omega(\varepsilon/r)}\right)$, as $k = m^{\Omega(1/r)}$ and $r = o(\frac{\log m}{\log\log m})$. Re-parametrizing ε by $\varepsilon/2$ in the lower bound argument finalizes the proof. □

5 CONCLUSION

In this paper, we studied the role of interaction in obtaining efficient allocations in subadditive combinatorial auctions. We showed that for any $r \geq 1$, any r-round protocol that uses polynomial communication can only achieve an $\Omega(\frac{1}{r} \cdot m^{1/2r+1})$ approximation to the social welfare. This settles an open question posed by [10] and [2] on the round-approximation tradeoff of polynomial communication protocols in subadditive combinatorial auctions.

An immediate corollary of our main result is that $\Omega(\frac{\log m}{\log\log m})$ rounds of interaction are necessary for obtaining an efficient allocation in subadditive combinatorial auctions. The qualitative message of this theoretical result is that *a modest amount of interaction between individuals in a market is crucial for obtaining an efficient allocation.* This further support the point of view of [10] on the necessity of interaction for economic efficiency.

An interesting direction for future research, also advocated by [10], is to consider the case where the bidders valuations are *submodular.* It is known that obtaining a better than $(1 - 1/2e)$-approximation to social welfare in submodular combinatorial auctions requires exponential communication [13] (regardless of the number of rounds of interaction). However, no better lower bounds are known for bounded-round protocols (even for simultaneous ones). Another interesting open problem is to close the gap between the $\Omega(\log\log n)$ lower bound of [2] and the $O(\log n)$ upper bound of [10] on the number of rounds necessary to achieve an efficient allocation in matching markets.

ACKNOWLEDGMENTS

I thank my advisor Sanjeev Khanna for many helpful advice and comments. I am also grateful to Jamie Morgenstern for helpful discussions in the earlier stages of this work and to Matthew Weinberg for bringing [7] to my attention. Finally, I would like to thank the anonymous reviewers of EC 2017 for many insightful comments and suggestions

REFERENCES

[1] Ron Aharoni, Paul Erdös, and Nathan Linial. 1988. Optima of dual integer linear programs. *Combinatorica* 8, 1 (1988), 13–20.

[2] Noga Alon, Noam Nisan, Ran Raz, and Omri Weinstein. 2015. Welfare Maximization with Limited Interaction. In *IEEE 56th Annual Symposium on Foundations of Computer Science, FOCS 2015, Berkeley, CA, USA, 17-20 October, 2015.* 1499–1512.

[3] Sepehr Assadi. 2017. Combinatorial Auctions Do Need Modest Interaction. *CoRR* abs/1705.01644 (2017).

[4] Sepehr Assadi, Sanjeev Khanna, and Yang Li. 2017. On Estimating Maximum Matching Size in Graph Streams. In *Proceedings of the Twenty-Eighth Annual ACM-SIAM Symposium on Discrete Algorithms, SODA 2017, Barcelona, Spain, Hotel Porta Fira, January 16-19.* 1723–1742.

[5] Ashwinkumar Badanidiyuru, Shahar Dobzinski, Hu Fu, Robert Kleinberg, Noam Nisan, and Tim Roughgarden. 2012. Sketching valuation functions. In *Proceedings of the Twenty-Third Annual ACM-SIAM Symposium on Discrete Algorithms, SODA 2012, Kyoto, Japan, January 17-19, 2012.* 1025–1035.

[6] Maria-Florina Balcan, Florin Constantin, Satoru Iwata, and Lei Wang. 2012. Learning Valuation Functions. In *COLT 2012 - The 25th Annual Conference on Learning Theory, June 25-27, 2012, Edinburgh, Scotland.* 4.1–4.24.

[7] Mark Braverman, Jieming Mao, and S Matthew Weinberg. 2017. On Simultaneous Two-player Combinatorial Auctions. *arXiv preprint arXiv:1704.03547* (2017).

[8] Patrick Briest, Piotr Krysta, and Berthold Vöcking. 2011. Approximation Techniques for Utilitarian Mechanism Design. *SIAM J. Comput.* 40, 6 (2011), 1587–1622.

[9] Thomas M. Cover and Joy A. Thomas. 2006. *Elements of information theory (2. ed.).* Wiley.

[10] Shahar Dobzinski, Noam Nisan, and Sigal Oren. 2014. Economic efficiency requires interaction. In *Symposium on Theory of Computing, STOC 2014, New York, NY, USA, May 31 - June 03, 2014.* 233–242.

[11] Shahar Dobzinski, Noam Nisan, and Michael Schapira. 2005. Approximation algorithms for combinatorial auctions with complement-free bidders. In *Proceedings of the 37th Annual ACM Symposium on Theory of Computing, Baltimore, MD, USA, May 22-24, 2005.* 610–618.

[12] Shahar Dobzinski and Michael Schapira. 2006. An improved approximation algorithm for combinatorial auctions with submodular bidders. In *Proceedings of the Seventeenth Annual ACM-SIAM Symposium on Discrete Algorithms, SODA 2006, Miami, Florida, USA, January 22-26, 2006.* 1064–1073.

[13] Shahar Dobzinski and Jan Vondrák. 2013. Communication Complexity of Combinatorial Auctions with Submodular Valuations. In *Proceedings of the Twenty-Fourth Annual ACM-SIAM Symposium on Discrete Algorithms, SODA 2013, New Orleans, Louisiana, USA, January 6-8, 2013.* 1205–1215.

[14] Paul Dütting and Thomas Kesselheim. 2017. Best-Response Dynamics in Combinatorial Auctions with Item Bidding. In *Proceedings of the Twenty-Eighth Annual ACM-SIAM Symposium on Discrete Algorithms, SODA 2017, Barcelona, Spain, Hotel Porta Fira, January 16-19.* 521–533.

[15] Uriel Feige. 2009. On Maximizing Welfare When Utility Functions Are Subadditive. *SIAM J. Comput.* 39, 1 (2009), 122–142.

[16] Uriel Feige and Jan Vondrák. 2006. Approximation algorithms for allocation problems: Improving the factor of 1 - 1/e. In *47th Annual IEEE Symposium on Foundations of Computer Science (FOCS 2006), 21-24 October 2006, Berkeley, California, USA, Proceedings.* 667–676.

[17] Michal Feldman, Hu Fu, Nick Gravin, and Brendan Lucier. 2013. Simultaneous auctions are (almost) efficient. In *Symposium on Theory of Computing Conference, STOC'13, Palo Alto, CA, USA, June 1-4, 2013.* 201–210.

[18] Michal Feldman, Nick Gravin, and Brendan Lucier. 2015. Combinatorial Auctions via Posted Prices. In *Proceedings of the Twenty-Sixth Annual ACM-SIAM Symposium on Discrete Algorithms, SODA 2015, San Diego, CA, USA, January 4-6, 2015.* 123–135.

[19] Ron Lavi and Chaitanya Swamy. 2011. Truthful and Near-Optimal Mechanism Design via Linear Programming. *J. ACM* 58, 6 (2011), 25:1–25:24.

[20] Benny Lehmann, Daniel J. Lehmann, and Noam Nisan. 2006. Combinatorial auctions with decreasing marginal utilities. *Games and Economic Behavior* 55, 2 (2006), 270–296.

[21] László Lovász. 1975. On the ratio of optimal integral and fractional covers. *Discrete mathematics* 13, 4 (1975), 383–390.

[22] Peter Bro Miltersen, Noam Nisan, Shmuel Safra, and Avi Wigderson. 1998. On Data Structures and Asymmetric Communication Complexity. *J. Comput. Syst. Sci.* 57, 1 (1998), 37–49.

[23] Noam Nisan. 2002. The Communication Complexity of Approximate Set Packing and Covering. In *Automata, Languages and Programming, 29th International Colloquium, ICALP 2002, Malaga, Spain, July 8-13, 2002, Proceedings.* 868–875.

[24] Noam Nisan and Ilya Segal. 2006. The communication requirements of efficient allocations and supporting prices. *J. Economic Theory* 129, 1 (2006), 192–224.

[25] Pranab Sen and Srinivasan Venkatesh. 2008. Lower bounds for predecessor searching in the cell probe model. *J. Comput. Syst. Sci.* 74, 3 (2008), 364–385.

[26] Jan Vondrák. 2008. Optimal approximation for the submodular welfare problem in the value oracle model. In *Proceedings of the 40th Annual ACM Symposium on Theory of Computing, Victoria, British Columbia, Canada, May 17-20, 2008.* 67–74.

[27] Andrew Chi-Chih Yao. 1979. Some Complexity Questions Related to Distributive Computing (Preliminary Report). In *Proceedings of the 11h Annual ACM Symposium on Theory of Computing, April 30 - May 2, 1979, Atlanta, Georgia, USA.* 209–213.

The Scope of Sequential Screening with Ex Post Participation Constraints

DIRK BERGEMANN, Yale University
FRANCISCO CASTRO, Columbia University
GABRIEL WEINTRAUB, Stanford University and AppNexus

In many markets, sellers are constrained to sell products in such a way that buyers obtain a non-negative net utility once they have realized their valuation. A leading example is the online display advertising market. In this setting, typical business constraints impose that publishers cannot use up-front fees and thus instead run a series of "waterfall auctions" that implicitly impose different priorities over participants. Commonly, higher-priority auctions have higher reserves. [1] Another example, is online shopping, in which shoppers have the chance to return the purchased item after delivery, usually at no or low cost.

Motivated by this, we study the sequential screening problem as described by Courty and Li [1] and in order to match our previous narrative we incorporate ex-post participation constraints. The goal of this work is to understand when the optimal selling mechanism is *static* (buyers are not screened ex-ante) or *dynamic* (buyers are screened ex-ante) and obtain a full characterization of such contracts.

Our model considers a seller who is selling one unit of an object, at no cost to the seller, to a buyer who has an outside option of zero. The sequence of events occurs in two periods. In the first, the buyer privately learns her type and the parties contract—we restrict our analysis to two types of buyers (low and high). The high type has a valuation distribution that dominates the low type one. The contract specifies allocation and payment functions. In the second period, the buyer privately learns her valuation, and allocations and transfers are realized. At this point, the buyer only accepts the contracting terms if her realized net utility is weakly larger than her outside option. This model aligns with our aforementioned examples. In the case of display advertising, the first period can be thought of as the time at which the buyer decide in which auction (priority/reserve) to participate in. The second period is when the auction is actually run.

One of our main contributions is to characterize when a static contract—that is, a contract that does not sequentially screen buyers—is optimal. We provide a necessary and sufficient condition

[1] See, for example, https://adexchanger.com/the-sell-sider/the-programmatic-waterfall-mystery.

A full version of this paper appears at: https://papers.ssrn.com/sol3/papers.cfm?abstract_id=2921459

Authors addresses: D. Bergemann, Department of Economics, Yale University, New Haven, CT 06520-8281. Email: dirk.bergemann@yale.edu. F. Castro, Graduate School of Business, Columbia University, Uris Hall, New York, NY 10027. Email: fcastro19@gsb.columbia.edu. G. Weintraub, Graduate School of Business, Stanford University 655 Knight Way, Stanford, CA 94305. Email: gweintra@stanford.edu.

EC'17, June 26–30, 2017, Cambridge, Massachusetts, USA. ACM ISBN 978-1-4503-4527-9/17/06.

 DOI: http://dx.doi.org/10.1145/3033274.3085102

for the optimality of the aforementioned contract. For further reference, we call this condition (NR). The characterization we provide is an average monotonicity condition around the optimal static threshold that encodes information about the similarity of the ex-ante types. For example, in the case of exponential valuations, the static contract is optimal if and only if the means of the distributions of the low and high type are appropriately close.

Our second main contribution characterizes the optimal mechanism when the condition mentioned above does not hold and a static contract is no longer optimal. Specifically, we prove that the optimal *dynamic* contract randomizes the low type and gives a deterministic allocation to the high type. Basically, randomization occurs to prevent the high type buyer from taking the low type's contract. To prove this, we first show that when (NR) is not satisfied, such a sequential screening contract with random allocations becomes feasible and yields an improvement in the seller's revenue compared to the static contract. Even though this contract yields an improvement over the static one, it does not need to be optimal. However, we are able to identify some regularity conditions that imply optimality.

More specifically, the optimal contract is characterized by an allocation probability $\chi \in (0, 1)$, and three thresholds θ_1, θ_2, and θ_3 with $\theta_1 \leq \theta_2 \leq \theta_3$. In this contract, the seller allocates the object to a low-type buyer with probability χ whenever her valuation is between θ_1 and θ_3, and asks for a payment of $\theta_1 \cdot \chi$. When the valuation of this type is above θ_3, the object is always allocated to her and the seller demands a payment of $\theta_3 - (\theta_3 - \theta_1) \cdot \chi$. The high-type buyer gets the object with certainty and only when her valuation is above θ_2, at which point the payment she has to make to the seller is θ_2. These parameters are set in such a way that the ex-ante incentive compatibility constraints are satisfied.

A salient feature of this type of contract is that it discriminates the low type in two dimensions. First, it can be proven that θ_1 is above the optimal threshold a seller would set if she was selling exclusively to low-type buyers. That is, the low type buyer is being allocated the object less often in the presence of high type buyers. An opposite result is true for high-type buyers, they are being allocated the object more often than if they were alone. Second, there is a range of values for which the object is sold to the low type with some probability, which further reduces the chances of a low type to receive the object compared to a case in which there are no high-type buyers. All these values and properties can be clearly expressed for the exponential distribution case.

REFERENCES

[1] Pascal Courty and Hao Li. 2000. Sequential Screening. *The Review of Economic Studies* 67, 4 (2000), 697–717.

Dynamic Mechanisms with Martingale Utilities

SANTIAGO BALSEIRO, Duke University - Decision Sciences
VAHAB MIRROKNI, Google Research
RENATO PAES LEME, Google Research

We study the dynamic mechanism design problem of a seller who repeatedly sells independent items to a buyer with private values. In this setting, the seller could potentially extract the entire buyer surplus by running efficient auctions and charging an upfront participation fee at the beginning of the horizon. In some markets, such as internet advertising, participation fees are not practical since buyers expect to inspect items before purchasing them. This motivates us to study the design of dynamic mechanisms under successively more stringent requirements that capture the implicit business constraints of these markets. We first consider a periodic individual rationality constraint, which limits the mechanism to charge at most the buyer's value in each period. While this prevents large upfront participation fees, the seller can still design mechanisms that spread a participation fee across the first few auctions. These mechanisms have the unappealing feature that they provide close-to-zero buyer utility in earlier auctions in exchange for higher utility in later auctions. To address this problem, we introduce a *martingale utility constraint*, which imposes the requirement that from the perspective of the buyer, the next item's expected utility is equal to the present one's. Our main result is providing a dynamic auction satisfying martingale utility and periodic individual rationality whose loss in profit with respect to first-best (full extraction of buyer surplus) is optimal up to polylogarithmic factors. The proposed mechanism is a dynamic two-tier auction with a hard floor and a soft floor that allocates the item whenever the buyer's bid is above the hard floor and charges the minimum of the bid and the soft floor.

Additional Key Words and Phrases: dynamic mechanism design; auction theory; stochastic processes

A full version of this paper is available at https://ssrn.com/abstract=2821261.

EC'17, June 26–30, 2017, Cambridge, MA, USA.

 ACM ISBN 978-1-4503-4527-9/17/06
http://dx.doi.org/10.1145/3033274.3084089

Repeated Sales with Multiple Strategic Buyers

NICOLE IMMORLICA, Microsoft Research
BRENDAN LUCIER, Microsoft Research
EMMANOUIL POUNTOURAKIS, University of Texas, Austin
SAMUEL TAGGART, Northwestern University

We study the repeated sale of non-durable goods to persistent, strategic buyers.[1] Each buyer has a value for obtaining a good each day, which is drawn from a known prior at the start of the game and does not change. Every day, the seller posts a price, and buyers decide whether or not to buy a good at that day's price. Crucially, the seller is unable to commit to a pricing policy. To predict the outcome of repeated sales in the absence of commitment, we study *Perfect Bayesian Equilibrium*: both the buyers and the seller are best-responding, no matter the history of play, and beliefs on buyers' values are derived from Bayesian updating.

This setting was first studied with a single buyer by **(author?)** [3]. They observed that there is an equilibrium with zero revenue for the seller. This extreme and counterintuitive equilibrium is driven by a self-fulfilling prophecy: the buyer never accepts any positive price out of fear that doing so will lead the seller to charge very high prices in the future; as a result, the seller infers that only a buyer with very high type would ever accept a positive price, so the seller would indeed charge very high prices in response. In revisiting this setting, **(author?)** [2] interpret this issue as an unpredictive pathology of the model. To begin our investigation, we offer a more nuanced view: there is a huge multiplicity of equilibria, but only the zero-revenue equilibrium survives several natural refinements that we propose, suggesting that this equilibrium is focal.

This negative result is unsatisfying, since the low-revenue equilibrium is not predictive of real-world outcomes. Why don't we see this behavior in practice? One simplifying assumption in the model is the presence of only a single buyer. This allows the seller to exploit the buyer's revealed preference in a very targetted way. In contrast, if the seller continues to sell by posting a single price, but that price will be faced by *multiple* buyers, then the opportunity for price-discrimination is diminished. We ask: does the presence of multiple buyers change the equilibrium structure?

We answer this question in the affirmative. We consider a single seller posting a single price to sell one item to n buyers with values drawn independently from an identical prior. We construct an equilibrium which in which the seller attains non-trivial revenue. In fact, we show that for a wide range of priors, the seller's revenue is a constant fraction of the optimal revenue even with commitment; i.e., of the Myerson revenue-optimal mechanism. Our equilibrium has two other notable properties. First, it survives the refinements that eliminated all but the zero-revenue equilibrium in the single-buyer case. Second, the seller's pricing policy has a natural explore-exploit structure, where the seller starts with low prices that gradually ascend to learn buyers' values, and in later rounds exploits the surviving high-valued buyers. The result resembles an ascending-price auction, implemented over time. This relates to the intuition from the Coase conjecture in the durable goods literature [1] which states that in the absence of commitment, one should expect the VCG outcome (which, for multiple buyers, yields non-trivial revenue for the seller). Our analysis of

[1]A full version of the paper can be found at http://www.samueltaggart.com/Repeated%20Sales.pdf

ACM ISBN 978-1-4503-4527-9/17/06. DOI: http://dx.doi.org/10.1145/3033274.3085130

the non-durable setting provides the further assurance, however, that the rate of learning outpaces the discount factor applied to future revenue.

We further explore this relationship to the Coase conjecture by considering a setting with unlimited supply of goods each round. The Coasian intuition would suggest that the seller makes no revenue in this case, since the VCG outcome gives each item away for a trivial price. However, we show that this intuition does not hold for our setting with non-durable goods. As in the single-item setting, when the seller is constrained to posting a single, *anonymous* price to all buyers, there exist equilibria for which the seller's revenue is within a constant factor of the Myerson optimal revenue. These equilibria have a similar explore-exploit structure to the single-item, multi-buyer equilibrium, and survive natural refinements. The high revenue is driven by the ability of the seller to implement supply restriction to increase competition between buyers.

Finally, we consider the importance of our restriction to anonymous prices. We show that if the seller is permitted to offer different prices to each agent then the Coasian intuition from the single-item setting binds once more: the seller is no longer able to extract nontrivial revenue from any equilibrium with sufficiently natural structure. In other words, the restriction of the seller to an anonymous price was crucial in deriving nontrivial revenue with unlimited supply. Intuitively, an anonymous price mitigates the ability of the seller to use the information an individual buyer leaks with each purchasing decision. Consequently, buyers are more willing to make nontrivial purchasing decisions, which in turn allows the seller to learn.

Additional Key Words and Phrases: repeated sales; perfect Bayesian equilibrium; revenue maximization; dynamic pricing; anonymous pricing

REFERENCES

[1] Coase, R. H. Durability and monopoly. *The Journal of Law and Economics 15*, 1 (1972), 143–149.

[2] Devanur, N. R., Peres, Y., and Sivan, B. Perfect bayesian equilibria in repeated sales. In *Proceedings of the Twenty-Sixth Annual ACM-SIAM Symposium on Discrete Algorithms, SODA 2015, San Diego, CA, USA, January 4-6, 2015* (2015), pp. 983–1002.

[3] Hart, O. D., and Tirole, J. Contract renegotiation and coasian dynamics. *The Review of Economic Studies 55*, 4 (1988), 509–540.

Posted Price Mechanisms for a Random Stream of Customers

JOSÉ CORREA, Universidad de Chile
PATRICIO FONCEA, Universidad de Chile
RUBEN HOEKSMA, Universidad de Chile
TIM OOSTERWIJK, Maastricht University
TJARK VREDEVELD, Maastricht University

Posted price mechanisms constitute a widely used way of selling items to strategic consumers. Although suboptimal, the attractiveness of these mechanisms comes from their simplicity and easy implementation. In this paper, we investigate the performance of posted price mechanisms when customers arrive in an unknown random order. We compare the expected revenue of these mechanisms to the expected revenue of the optimal auction in two different settings. Namely, the nonadaptive setting in which all offers are sent to the customers beforehand, and the adaptive setting in which an offer is made when a consumer arrives. For the nonadaptive case, we obtain a strategy achieving an expected revenue within at least a $1 - 1/e$ fraction of that of the optimal auction. We also show that this bound is tight, even if the customers have i.i.d. valuations for the item. For the adaptive case, we exhibit a posted price mechanism that achieves a factor 0.745 of the optimal revenue, when the customers have i.i.d. valuations for the item. Furthermore, we prove that our results extend to the prophet inequality setting and in particular our result for i.i.d. random valuations resolves a problem posed by Hill and Kertz [13].

Additional Key Words and Phrases: Posted prices; Prophet inequality; Mechanism design

1 INTRODUCTION

Posted price mechanisms constitute an attractive and widely applicable way of selling items to strategic consumers. In this context, consumers are faced with take-it-or-leave-it offers, and therefore strategic behaviour simply vanishes. This type of mechanism has been vastly studied, particularly in the marketing community [5]. In recent years, there has been a significant effort to understand the expected revenue of the outcome generated by different posted price mechanisms when compared to that of the optimal auction [2, 4, 6, 23]. In addition, several companies have started to apply *personalized pricing* to sell their products. Under this policy, companies set different prices for different consumers based on purchase history or other factors that may affect their willingness to pay. For example, the online data provider Lexis-Nexis sells to virtually every user at a different price [22]. In 2012, Orbitz online travel agency found that people who use Mac computers spent as much as 30% more on hotels, so it started to show them different, and sometimes costlier, travel options than those shown to Windows visitors [18]. Similarly, retailers and supermarket chains such as Safeway are

Authors' email addresses: José Correa: correa@uchile.cl; Patricio Foncea: patricio.foncea@ug.uchile.cl; Ruben Hoeksma: rhoeksma@dim.uchile.cl; Tim Oosterwijk: t.oosterwijk@maastrichtuniversity.nl; Tjark Vredeveld: t.vredeveld@maastrichtuniversity.nl.

This work was supported by The Millennium Nucleus Information and Coordination in Networks ICM/FIC RC130003.

EC17, June 26–30, 2017, Cambridge, MA, USA. Copyright 2017 ACM ISBN 978-1-4503-4527-9/17/06...$15.00
© 2017 ACM. ACM ISBN 978-1-4503-4527-9/17/06
http://dx.doi.org/10.1145/3033274.3085137

using data culled from billions of purchases to offer deals tailored to specific shoppers [15]. Choudhary et al. [7] further investigated this issue, providing more examples and developing a theoretical framework to analyze equilibria between firms that apply personalized pricing and those who do not.

In its simplest form, the problem we consider is described as follows. A monopolist sells a single item to a set of known potential buyers. The seller places no value on the item, while the buyers have independent, not necessarily identical, random valuations for the item. The main question is to design a mechanism maximizing the revenue of the seller. This question was answered in a seminal paper by Myerson [19], and the solution is, in some situations, a remarkably simple mechanism. However, in many situations it is hard to implement, and the mechanism of choice turns out to be a simple posted price mechanism. A common example of this practice is that of *direct mail campaigns*, in which the seller contacts its potential buyers directly and offers each one a certain price for the item. The item is then sold to the first consumer who accepts the offer [5, 8].

In this paper, we investigate the performance of posted price mechanisms to sell a single item to a given set of customers who arrive in a random unknown order. We consider two different models which share the property that each customer is offered the item at most once. Upon receiving an offer, a customer immediately decides whether to buy the item at that price or to pass and simply not buy. The *nonadaptive* model considers the situation in which all offers have to be made simultaneously, and customers respond in random order, akin to direct mail campaigns. The *adaptive* model considers a situation in which the seller may adapt the offer. Here, customers again arrive in random order. Whenever a customer arrives, she is offered the item at a price, which the seller may base on the customer he is offering to, as well as the customers who already rejected earlier offers.

Problem description. A seller has a single item to sell to a given set of customers $\mathcal{I}$. We assume that the seller has no value for keeping the item. Customers have independent random valuations for the item with customer $i \in \mathcal{I}$ valuing the item at v_i, drawn from distribution $F_i(\cdot)$. The customers arrive in (uniform) random order, and the goal of the seller is to maximize his expected revenue. To this end, we consider a nonadaptive and an adaptive scenario.

Nonadaptive: The seller sets prices $p_i \geq 0$ for all $i \in \mathcal{I}$, with the goal of maximizing his expected revenue, defined as

$$\sum_{i \in \mathcal{I}} p_i \mathbb{P}_{\sigma,v} \left[i = \operatorname*{argmin}_{j \in \mathcal{I}} \{\sigma(j) \mid v_j \geq p_j\} \right],$$

where the probability is taken over the arrival permutation σ and the customers' valuations v.

Adaptive: The seller offers each customer a price as she arrives. So, the seller sets functions $p_i : 2^{\mathcal{I}} \to \mathbb{R}$ for each customer i, such that, if S is the set of customers who already arrived and declined the offer, $p_i(S)$ is the price offered to customer i if she is next to arrive. For an arrival permutation σ, we denote $p_i(\sigma) = p_i(\{\sigma^{-1}(1), \dots, \sigma^{-1}(\sigma(i) - 1)\})$, and therefore we can write the seller's expected revenue as

$$\mathbb{E}_\sigma \left[\sum_{i \in \mathcal{I}} p_i(\sigma) \mathbb{P}_v \left[i = \operatorname*{argmin}_{j \in \mathcal{I}} \{\sigma(j) \mid v_j \geq p_j(\sigma) \right] \right],$$

where the expectation is taken over the arrival permutation σ, and the probability is taken over the customers' valuations v.

Our results. We present two posted price mechanisms: A nonadaptive posted price mechanism that guarantees an expected revenue within a factor $1 - 1/e$ of that of Myerson's optimal auction and an adaptive posted price mechanism for i.i.d. value distributions that has a guaranteed expected revenue of 0.745 of that of Myerson's optimal auction.[1]

[1]One may think here that the right benchmark should be the expectation of the maximum valuation. However, this cannot yield useful results. Consider a single customer whose valuation lies in $[1, +\infty)$ distributed according to $F(v) = 1 - 1/v$.

The factor achieved by our nonadaptive mechanism complements recent work of Alaei et al. [3] by showing that personalized pricing can increase the revenue from $1/e$ to $1-1/e$. On the other hand, the bound matches the well known result of Chawla et al. [6], who designed a *sequential* posted price mechanism with the same approximation guarantee. Although their mechanism is also nonadaptive in the sense that the selected prices are fixed a priori, it has the power to choose the arrival order of the customers. Thus, making it easier to extract revenue by offering to *good* customers first. Furthermore, this bound also matches the approximation guarantee obtained by Esfandiari et al. [10], who also consider the random arrival model, but in their mechanism the sequence of prices depends on the arrival order of customers, and it is therefore adaptive (according to the definition in this paper). Besides the natural application of our nonadaptive setting, it is interesting to note that one can achieve this approximation factor in the random arrival model without using adaptivity. Also, as opposed to previous results, we prove that the bound of $1-1/e$ is best possible for our setting.

THEOREM 1.1. *For any given set of potential customers $\mathcal{I}$, there exists a nonadaptive posted price mechanism that achieves an expected revenue of at least a $1-1/e$ fraction of that of Myerson's optimal auction on $\mathcal{I}$.*

In the case of monotone virtual valuations[2], the algorithm that achieves this result becomes remarkably simple.

INPUT: Customers $i \in \mathcal{I}$ with valuation distributed according to F_i.
ALGORITHM 1:

(1) Compute q_i = probability that optimal auction assigns to i.
(2) Discard customer i with probability $1 - \frac{2}{2+(e-2)q_i}$.
(3) Offer non-discarded customers price $F_i^{-1}(1-q_i)$.
(4) Item is allocated to a random customer accepting the offer.

The algorithm, while randomized, can be derandomized using standard techniques.

Algorithm 1 may seem counterintuitive since, in step (2), the higher the probability is that a customer wins the optimal auction, the higher the probability is that the algorithm discards her (though the probability of discarding any customer is at most $1-\frac{2}{e}$). The following example gives some intuition on why agents need to be discarded. Consider just two customers: customer 1 who has deterministic value equal to 1, and customer 2 who values the item at 100 with probability 1/10 and at 0 with probability 9/10. In this situation, the optimal mechanism assigns the item to customer 2 with probability 9/10 and the total expected revenue is 10+9/10. Now, if a nonadaptive algorithm makes offers to both customers the expected revenue is (1/10)(50.5)+(9/10)(1)=5.95, which is not within the claimed ratio of the optimal mechanism. Another somewhat surprising element of Algorithm 1 is that the probability of not assigning the item can be computed as $\prod_{i\in\mathcal{I}}(1-2q_i/(2+(e-2)q_i))) \geq 2/e$. Again, the previous example provides intuition to the fact that, if we shoot for an algorithm that assigns too frequently, we risk assigning the item for too low a price. This intuition does not hold in the adaptive case.

The cornerstone of our analysis is a basic result about Bernoulli random variables which may be of independent interest. The result states that if we are given a set of nonhomogeneous independent Bernoulli random variables with associated prizes, then there is a subset of variables so that the expected average prize of the successes is at least a factor $1-1/e$ of the expectation of the maximum prize over all random variables.

Clearly, if we charge price p the acceptance probability is $1/p$, for a total revenue of 1. On the other hand, the expectation of the valuation is actually $+\infty$. This example can easily be turned into one with finite expectation but arbitrarily large ratio between the optimal pricing and the expectation of the random variable.

[2]Recall that for a valuation distribution F, the virtual valuation is defined as $v - \frac{1-F(v)}{f(v)}$.

Lemma 1.2 (Bernoulli Selection Lemma). *Given a set $N = \{1, \ldots, n\}$ of independent Bernoulli random variables $X_1, \ldots, X_n$, where $X_i = 1$ with probability q_i and 0 otherwise, and associated prizes $b_1, \ldots, b_n$. The following inequalities hold:*

$$\frac{e}{e-1} \max_{S \subseteq N} \mathbb{E}\left[\frac{\sum_{i \in S} b_i X_i}{\sum_{i \in S} X_i}\right] \geq \max_{z_i \leq q_i} \left\{ \sum_{i \in N} b_i z_i \,\middle|\, \sum z_i \leq 1 \right\} \geq \mathbb{E}[\max_{i \in N} \{b_i X_i\}] .$$

Here, when evaluating the leftmost term, we define $0/0 = 0$.

To prove the lemma, we consider a continuous relaxation of the maximization problem, and then guess a solution in which each random variable is included in S with some instance-dependent probability. Then, we look for the worst possible instance by applying the first order optimality conditions of a nonlinear problem. These conditions reveal some structural insight on what a worst case instance looks like. Using this, we obtain the desired bound. Theorem 1.1 follows from Lemma 1.2 with fairly little extra work. The basic tool for this is a fundamental lemma by Chawla et al. [6, Lemma 4] that upper bounds the revenue of the optimal auction.

To complement our results, we provide instances that show that the bounds in Lemma 1.2 and Theorem 1.1 are tight. In particular, we show that even with *independent identically distributed* (*i.i.d.*) customer valuations the bound of Theorem 1.1 cannot be beaten. Therefore, adaptivity is necessary to go beyond $1 - 1/e$, even with i.i.d. distributions. For this setting we show the following.

Theorem 1.3. *For any given set of potential customers I whose values are independent and identically distributed, there exists an adaptive posted price mechanism that achieves an expected revenue of at least a $1/\beta > 0.745$ fraction of that of Myerson's optimal auction on I, where β is the unique value such that*

$$\int_0^1 \frac{1}{y(1 - \ln(y)) + (\beta - 1)} dy = 1 .$$

To achieve this result we use a quite natural idea: as less customers are left, the price should decrease. Besides this the key ingredient of our algorithm is to use random prices drawn from a well chosen distribution that mimics an expression we obtain for the revenue of an optimal auction. Again in the case of monotone virtual valuations our algorithms is as follows:

Input: Customers $i \in I$ with valuation i.i.d. according to F.

Algorithm 2:

(1) Partition the interval $[0, 1]$ into intervals $A_i = [a_{i-1}, a_i]$, s.t. $a_0 = 0$, $a_n = 1$.
(2) Sample q_i from A_i with an appropriately chosen distribution.
(3) When the i–th buyer comes, offer price $p_i = \max\{F^{-1}(1 - q_i), v^*\}$, where v^* is the reservation price of the optimal auction.

Like Algorithm 1, also Algorithm 2 can be derandomized using standard techniques.

We believe that the bound of Theorem 1.3 is tight. Although the best upper bound known for the i.i.d. case, due to Blumrosen and Holenstein [4], proves that no algorithm can achieve a fraction of at least 0.79, we believe that the family of instances provided by Hill and Kertz [13] in the context of prophet inequalities for i.i.d. random variables can be transformed into a tight family of instances for Theorem 1.3. We remark here that recent work of Dütting et al. [9] also studies the benefit of adaptivity in the i.i.d. case, but from a different perspective.

Due to space constraints many technical proofs have been omitted in this paper.

Prophet Inequalities. As it is common in the literature, we prove that our Theorems 1.1 and 1.3 also hold in the context of the vastly studied prophet inequalities [13, 14, 16, 17, 20, 21], whose study started in the sixties with the work of Gilbert and Mosteller [11].

In particular Theorem 1.1 becomes Corollary 2.2 and is related to recent work of Esfandiari et al. [10]. In this setting, known as *prophet secretary* or *full information secretary problem*, we are given n independent nonnegative random variables $X_1, \ldots, X_n$ that arrive in random order. Upon arrival of a random variable we see its value and may decide to keep it and finish or to drop it and continue. The goal is to design an algorithm that obtains a value within a large fraction of the expectation of the maximum of all X_i's. In Corollary 2.2 we use Lemma 1.2 to prove that, even nonadaptively, we may obtain a $1 - 1/e$ fraction, with an algorithm that sets a threshold for each random variable (independent of the arrival order) in advance and accepts the first random variable with value above the threshold. Moreover, this bound is also tight, which follows from the example in Section 2. In the case in which the probability of having two X_i's being the maximum is zero the algorithm is again quite simple:

(1) Compute q_i = probability that X_i is the maximum.
(2) Discard X_i with probability $1 - \frac{2}{2+(e-2)q_i}$.
(3) Set threshold $\tau_i = F_i^{-1}(1 - q_i)$.
(4) Keep first random variable whose realization is at least τ_i.

In the general situation we apply an arbitrary tie-breaking rule so that $\sum q_i = 1$.

Similarly in Corollary 4.7 (which follows from Theorem 1.3) we prove that a variant of Algorithm 2 gives a sequence of thresholds $\tau_1, \ldots, \tau_n$ such that, if we take the first of n i.i.d. random variables whose value is above the threshold, we obtain a value of at least a 0.745 fraction of the expectation of the maximum of the random variables. This result can be seen as a follow up on a result by Hill and Kertz [13] on the prophet inequality for i.i.d. random variables. They study the performance of the best stopping time when compared to a prophet that can extract the expectation of the maximum. The main result of Hill and Kertz is a recursive characterization of a_n, the best possible factor when faced with n random variables. More precisely, they prove that if $X_1, \ldots, X_n$ are i.i.d. nonnegative random variables and T_n denotes the set of stopping rules for $X_1, \ldots, X_n$ then

$$\mathbb{E}(\max\{X_1, \ldots, X_n\}) \leq a_n \sup\{\mathbb{E}(X_t) : t \in T_n\}.$$

Furthermore, Hill and Kertz find instances in which it is not possible to beat the factor a_n. They also prove that $a_n \leq e/(e-1)$, conjecture that the sequence is monotone, and leave open the existence and computation of its limit. The monotonicity together with the limit calculation would readily give a universal bound (valid for all n) on the performance of the best stopping rule. Shortly after, Samuel-Cahn [21] reports that Kertz proves existence of the limit a of the a_n sequence and conjectures that it equals 1.342 (obtained as the solution to $\int_0^1 (y - y\ln(y)) + a - 1)^{-1} dy = 1$). Finally, Kertz [14, Lemma 6.2] proves the latter conjecture (for which Saint-Mont [20] derives a simpler proof). However he is unable to prove that the sequence is monotone and therefore the best upper bound on the whole a_n sequence still stood at $e/(e-1) \approx 1.582$ [14, Lemma 3.4]. Very recently, and independently of our work, Abolhassani et al. [1] improved this upper bound to $1/0.738 \approx 1.355$. Our Corollary 4.7 closes this gap and implies that for all n, $a_n \leq a \approx 1.342$, and by the tight examples of Hill and Kertz [13] it turns out that this constant is best possible.

2 THE BERNOULLI SELECTION LEMMA

In this section we prove Lemma 1.2. Actually, we prove a slightly stronger version that will become clear at the end of the proof. We also provide a tight instance and discuss some generalizations.

The proof. The second inequality of Lemma 1.2 is trivial, as the expectation of the maximum is a sum over all values b_i weighed by the probability with which that value is the maximum. Since these probabilities sum to at most one, the inequality follows.

The proof for the first inequality has two main ingredients. First, we reformulate the left hand side in an appropriate way, and lower bound it by another function using KKT-conditions. Then, we show that this function is bounded from below by $1 - 1/e$.

As a warm up, we first show how to get a weaker result, that only gives us a factor of $\sqrt{e}$ instead of $\frac{e}{e-1}$, with more straightforward arguments.

Proof. We start the proof by rewriting the optimization problem:

$$\max_{S \subseteq N} \left\{ \mathbb{E}\left[\frac{\sum_{i \in S} b_i X_i}{\sum_{i \in S} X_i} \right] \right\} . \tag{P}$$

Instead of choosing a subset of N, we set for each $i \in N$ a value $\chi_i \in [0, 1]$, which represents the probability with which we actually choose i. Now, let $\pi_i = \chi_i q_i$ denote the probability of i being picked and having $X_i = 1$. So we can consider the following maximization problem, with decision variables π, as a relaxation of (P):

$$\max_{0 \le \pi_i \le q_i} \sum_{S \subseteq N} \left(\frac{b(S)}{|S|} \left(\prod_{i \in S} \pi_i \right) \left(\prod_{i \notin S} (1 - \pi_i) \right) \right) ,$$

where $b(S) = \sum_{i \in S} b_i$. Note that the previous objective is linear in each variable so that there is an extreme optimal solution [8]. Thus, the previous problem is in fact equivalent to (P). Now, by changing the order of the summations, we obtain

$$\max_{0 \le \pi_i \le q_i} \sum_{i \in N} b_i \pi_i \sum_{S \subseteq N \setminus \{i\}} \frac{1}{1 + |S|} \prod_{j \in S} \pi_j \prod_{j \in N \setminus (S \cup \{i\})} (1 - \pi_j) . \tag{1}$$

With (P) in this equivalent form, we now proceed to guess a feasible solution. To this end, consider an optimal solution z^* to

$$\max \left\{ \sum_{i \in N} b_i z_i \,\middle|\, \sum_{i \in N} z_i \le 1, z_i \le q_i \text{ for all } i \in N \right\} ,$$

and set $\pi_i = 2z_i^*/(2 + z_i^*)$. Note that $\pi_i \le q_i$, so that, substituting this in the objective of (1), we get

$$\sum_{i \in N} b_i z_i^* \prod_{j \in N} \frac{1}{1 + \frac{z_j^*}{2}} \sum_{S \subseteq N \setminus \{i\}} \frac{2^{|S|}}{1 + |S|} \prod_{j \in S} \frac{z_j^*}{2} \prod_{j \in N \setminus (S \cup \{i\})} \left(1 - \frac{z_j^*}{2} \right) . \tag{2}$$

It is easy to see that

$$\sum_{S \subseteq N \setminus \{i\}} \frac{2^{|S|}}{1 + |S|} \prod_{j \in S} \frac{z_j^*}{2} \prod_{j \in N \setminus (S \cup \{i\})} \left(1 - \frac{z_j^*}{2} \right) \ge 1 ,$$

since the left hand side corresponds to $\mathbb{E}[f(S)]$ over all $S \subseteq N \setminus \{i\}$ under probabilities $z_j^*/2$ for every element i and $f(S) = 2^{|S|}/(|S| + 1) \ge 1$. While for any values z_i such that $\sum_i z_i \le 1$, we have

$$\prod_{j=1}^{n} \frac{1}{1 + \frac{z_j}{2}} \ge e^{-\sum_{j=1}^{n} \frac{z_j}{2}} \ge \frac{1}{\sqrt{e}} ,$$

where the first inequality follows from $1 + x \le e^x$, concluding the proof. □

To obtain the improved factor $1 - 1/e$ we do the same as in the last proof, but make a subtle modification in the choice of π_i. We choose $\pi_i = \frac{2z_i^*}{2+(e-2)z_i^*}$,[3][4] such that $1 - \pi_i = \frac{2-(4-e)z_i^*}{2+(e-2)z_i^*}$. Note that this is a feasible choice of π_i for all $i \in N$, since for this choice $\pi_i \le z_i^* \le q_i$. We plug this back into (1), and obtain that (P) is lower bounded by

$$\sum_{i\in N} 2b_i z_i^* \left(\prod_{j\in N} \frac{1}{2+(e-2)z_j^*}\right) \sum_{S\subseteq N\setminus\{i\}} \frac{2^{|S|}}{1+|S|} \prod_{j\in S} z_j^* \prod_{j\in N\setminus(S\cup\{i\})} (2-(4-e)z_j^*). \tag{3}$$

We proceed to lower bound this quantity, where we use the following technical result.

Proposition 2.1. *Consider the problem* $\min_{x\in\mathbb{R}_+^M}\{f_M(x) : \sum_{i\in M} x_i \le a\}$, *where* $a \le 1$ *and*

$$f_M(x) = \left(\prod_{j\in M} \frac{1}{2+(e-2)x_j}\right) \sum_{S\subseteq M} \frac{2^{|S|}}{1+|S|} \prod_{j\in S} x_j \prod_{j\in M\setminus S} (2-(4-e)x_j).$$

An optimal solution satisfies that all nonzero variables have to be equal and $\sum_{i\in M} x_i = a$.

Using Proposition 2.1, we lower bound (3) as follows. Consider the term

$$\left(\prod_{j\in N\setminus\{i\}} \frac{1}{2+(e-2)z_j^*}\right) \sum_{S\subseteq N\setminus\{i\}} \frac{2^{|S|}}{1+|S|} \prod_{j\in S} z_j^* \prod_{j\in N\setminus(S\cup\{i\})} (2-(4-e)z_j^*).$$

Note that this is equal to $f_{N\setminus\{i\}}(z_{-i}^*)$.[5] So, Proposition 2.1 can be applied with $a = 1 - z_i^*$. Thus,

$$f_{N\setminus\{i\}}(z_{-i}^*) \ge f_{N\setminus\{i\}}(x^*),$$

with x^* the optimal solution to $\min_{x\in\mathbb{R}_+^{N\setminus\{i\}}}\{f_{N\setminus\{i\}}(x) : \sum_{j\in N\setminus\{i\}} x_j \le a\}$.

Proposition 2.1 states that $x_j^* = (1 - z_i^*)/k$, where $k \le n - 1$ is the number of nonzero variables in x^*. Conditioning on the cardinality of the set S, and using the Binomial Theorem, a straightforward but tedious calculation shows that

$$f_{N\setminus\{i\}}(x^*) = \frac{2k + (e-2)(1-z_i^*)}{2(k+1)(1-z_i^*)}\left(1 - \left(1 - \frac{2(1-z_i^*)}{2k+(e-2)(1-z_i^*)}\right)^{k+1}\right).$$

As this quantity only depends on k and z_i^*, we may define

$$\varphi_k(z_i^*) = \frac{2}{(2+(e-2)z_i^*)} f_{N\setminus\{i\}}(x^*),$$

to conclude that expression (3) (and in turn (P)) is lower bounded by

$$\sum_{i\in N} b_i z_i^* \varphi_{k(i)}(z_i^*).$$

where the index $k(i)$, denoting the number of nonzero variables in x^*, is always at least 1, yet may vary, depending on i.

The remainder of the proof establishes that $\varphi_{k(i)}(z_i^*) \ge 1 - \frac{1}{e}$. Indeed, we show that, for all $y \in [0, 1]$ and for all $n \ge 1$, we have that $\varphi_n(y) \ge 1 - \frac{1}{e}$. □

[3] Because of the choice of π_i, we actually prove the slightly stronger bound where we maximize over $z_i \le \frac{2q_i}{2-(e-2)q_i}$.

[4] The choice of π_i suggests that the random variables are not picked deterministically, but with probability less than 1, since $\pi_i < z_i^*$ if $z_i^* > 0$. However, as noted in the beginning of the proof, because of linearity of the objective in each variable, there is always an extreme optimal solution where the random variables are picked deterministically.

[5] x_{-i} denotes the vector x with coordinate i eliminated.

Tightness. We now provide a family of instances that show that the $1-1/e$ bound in the Bernoulli Selection Lemma is actually best possible. Consider n^2 independent identically distributed Bernoulli random variables with parameter $1/n$ and prizes $b_1 = n/(e-2)$ and $b_i = 1$ for $2 \le i \le n^2$. The expectation of the maximum prize is given by

$$\mathbb{E}\left[\max_{i\in N}\{b_i X_i\}\right] = \frac{1}{e-2} + \left(1-\frac{1}{n}\right)\left(1-\left(1-\frac{1}{n}\right)^{n^2-1}\right) \longrightarrow \frac{1}{e-2}+1\,.$$

In this particular setting, where the Bernoulli random variables are i.i.d., the best strategy is to sort by prize and take some subset with those of higher prize. This means to choose the first random variable and a subset of size $k-1$ of the rest for some $1 \le k \le n^2$. This yields an expected average value that can be upper bounded by

$$\left(1-\left(1-\frac{1}{n}\right)^{k}\right)\frac{\frac{n}{e-2}+k-1}{k} \le \left(1-\left(1-\frac{1}{n}\right)^{k}\right)\left(\frac{n}{k(e-2)}+1\right).$$

The above can be shown to converge, as $n \longrightarrow \infty$, to

$$\max_{0\le x\le n}\left(1-e^{-x}\right)\left(\frac{1}{x(e-2)}+1\right),$$

where $x = \frac{k}{n}$. Moreover, this expression is maximized at $x = 1$. This yields the value $(1-e^{-1})\left(\frac{1}{e-2}+1\right) = (1-1/e)\mathbb{E}[\max_{i\in N}\{b_i X_i\}]$.

Extension. The Bernoulli Selection Lemma can be used to prove a similar result for more general random variables. Suppose you can now choose one of n prizes whose values are random variables distributed according to n possibly different distributions. The prizes arrive in random order, and, upon arrival, we must decide whether we keep that prize, or we simply discard it and wait for the next. The goal is to maximize the expected value of the selected prize. Similar to the nonadaptive setting considered so far, we look for an acceptance criterion that is set beforehand, and only based on the distributions. This problem resembles the prophet inequality and also the prophet secretary problem [10].

Corollary 2.2. *Given n independent nonnegative random variables $X_1,\dots,X_n$ with $X_i \sim F_i$. There exist values $\tau_1,\dots,\tau_n$ such that*

$$\mathbb{E}\left[\frac{\sum_{i=1}^n X_i Y_i}{\sum_{i=1}^n Y_i}\right] \ge \left(1-\frac{1}{e}\right)\mathbb{E}\left[\max_{i=1,\dots,n} X_i\right],$$

where Y_i is a Bernoulli random variable that has value 1 if $X_i > \tau_i$.

In the context of the prophet inequality, note that the quantity on the left exactly corresponds to the expected value of the first X_i above τ_i, when the X_i's are ordered uniformly at random.

Proof. Assume first that the F_i are continuous for all i. Let $q_i = \mathbb{P}(X_i \ge X_j,\ \forall j = 1,\dots,n)$ be the probability that X_i is the largest and α_i be a value for which $1-F_i(\alpha_i) = q_i$. Consider $b_i = \mathbb{E}[X_i \mid X_i > \alpha_i]$ and the Bernoulli random variables $Z_1,\dots,Z_n$ where Z_i has parameter q_i. We apply the Bernoulli Selection Lemma to this instance, and thus let $S \subseteq \{1,\dots,n\}$ be a set for which the lemma holds. Now define $\tau_i = \alpha_i$ for $i \in S$ and $\tau_i = \infty$ otherwise, and note that for $i \notin S$, we have $Y_i = 0$ almost surely, and for $i \in S$, we have $\mathbb{P}(X_i > \alpha_i) = \mathbb{P}(Y_i = 1) = q_i$. It follows that

$$\begin{aligned}
\mathbb{E}\left[\frac{\sum_{i=1}^n X_i Y_i}{\sum_{i=1}^n Y_i}\right] &= \sum_{i\in S}\mathbb{E}\left[\frac{X_i Y_i}{\sum_{j\in S} Y_j}\right] \\
&= \sum_{i\in S}\mathbb{E}[X_i \mid Y_i = 1]\mathbb{E}\left[(1+\sum_{j\in S\setminus\{i\}} Y_j)^{-1}\middle| Y_i = 1\right]\mathbb{P}(Y_i = 1) \\
&= \sum_{i\in S}\mathbb{E}[X_i \mid X_i > \alpha_i]\mathbb{E}\left[\frac{Y_i}{\sum_{j\in S} Y_j}\right] \\
&= \mathbb{E}\left[\frac{\sum_{i\in S}\mathbb{E}[X_i|X_i>\alpha_i]Z_i}{\sum_{i\in S} Z_i}\right] \\
&\geq \tfrac{e-1}{e}\max_{z_i\leq q_i}\left\{\sum_{i=1}^n \mathbb{E}[X_i \mid X_i > \alpha_i]z_i \,\middle|\, \sum_{i=1}^n z_i \leq 1\right\} \\
&\geq \tfrac{e-1}{e}\sum_{i=1}^n \mathbb{E}[X_i \mid X_i > \alpha_i]q_i\,,
\end{aligned}$$

where the second to last inequality follows from the Bernoulli Selection Lemma, while the last holds since $\sum_{i=1}^n q_i = 1$. Now note that $\mathbb{E}\left[\max_{i=1,\dots,n} X_i\right] = \sum_{i=1}^n \mathbb{E}[X_i \mid X_i \geq X_j,\ \forall j = 1,\dots,n]q_i$. To finish the proof, it suffices to show that

$$\mathbb{E}[X_i \mid X_i > \alpha_i] \geq \mathbb{E}[X_i \mid X_i \geq X_j,\ \forall j = 1,\dots,n]\,.$$

Indeed, for $x > \alpha_i$, we have $\mathbb{P}(X_i > x \mid X_i > \alpha_i) = \int_x^\infty \frac{1}{q_i}dF_i(t)$, while, if $x \leq \alpha_i$, the previous probability equals 1. On the other hand,

$$\mathbb{P}(X_i > x \mid X_i \geq X_j\ \forall j = 1,\dots,n) = \int_x^\infty \frac{\prod_{j\neq i} F_j(t)}{q_i}dF_i(t)\,.$$

From this, it follows that $\mathbb{P}(X_i > x \mid X_i > \alpha_i) \geq \mathbb{P}(X_i > x \mid X_i \geq X_j,\ \forall j = 1,\dots,n)$ for all $x \geq 0$. Thus, $X_i \mid (X_i > \alpha_i)$ stochastically dominates $X_i \mid (X_i \geq X_j\ \forall j = 1,\dots,n)$, and the conclusion follows.

When some F_i are not continuous, it could be the case that there is no α_i such that $1 - F_i(\alpha_i) = q_i$ or that $\sum q_i > 1$. If the former happens, the result still holds provided α_i is chosen randomly. The latter case is solved by slightly perturbing the support of the random variables in a way that the probability that two or more are the maximum simultaniously is negligible. □

3 NONADAPTIVE POSTED PRICE MECHANISMS

In this section we prove our main result, namely, Theorem 1.1. Recall that we have a single item on sale, a set of customers $\mathcal{I}$, and for customer $i \in \mathcal{I}$ her valuation for the item is $v_i \sim F_i$. As is standard in the literature, we say that a distribution F_i is *regular* if the *virtual value function* $c_i(v) = v - (1 - F_i(v))/f_i(v)$ is nondecreasing, where f_i is the density of F_i.

Besides the Bernoulli Selection Lemma, key to our analysis is the by now classic result of Chawla et al. [6].

Lemma 3.1 ([6, Lemma 4]). *If all value distributions are regular, then the expected value of Myerson's optimal auction is bounded from above by*

$$\sum_{i\in\mathcal{I}} F_i^{-1}(1 - q_i^M)q_i^M\,,$$

where q_i^M is the probability that the optimal auction assigns the item to i.

Furthermore, for every i (with regular or nonregular value distribution) there exist two prices $\underline{p_i}$ and $\overline{p_i}$, with corresponding probabilities $\underline{q_i}$ and $\overline{q_i}$, and a number $0 \leq x_i \leq 1$, such that $x_i\underline{q_i} + (1-x_i)\overline{q_i} = q_i^M$, and the expected revenue of Myerson's optimal auction is bounded from above by

$$\sum_{i\in\mathcal{I}} x_i\underline{p_i}\,\underline{q_i} + (1 - x_i)\overline{p_i}\,\overline{q_i}\,.$$

Theorem 1.1. *For any given set of potential customers $\mathcal{I}$, there exists a nonadaptive posted price mechanism that achieves an expected revenue of at least a $1 - 1/e$ fraction of that of Myerson's optimal auction on $\mathcal{I}$.*

Proof. We prove the regular case first. Let q_i^M denote the probability with which Myerson's optimal auction assigns the item to customer $i \in \mathcal{I}$, and set $b_i = F_i^{-1}(1 - q_i^M)$. The expected revenue of a nonadaptive posted price mechanism, that chooses to sell only to customers in $S \subseteq \mathcal{I}$ while offering prices b_i, is given by

$$\begin{aligned}\sum_{i \in S} b_i \mathbb{P}[i = \operatorname{argmin}_{j \in S}\{\sigma(j) \mid v_j \geq b_j\}] &= \sum_{i \in S} b_i q_i^M \mathbb{P}[i = \operatorname{argmin}_{j \in S}\{\sigma(j) \mid v_j \geq b_j\} \mid v_i \geq b_i] \\ &= \sum_{i \in S} b_i q_i^M \sum_{R \subseteq S \setminus \{i\}} \frac{1}{1 + |R|} \prod_{j \in R} q_j^M \prod_{j \in S \setminus (R \cup \{i\})} (1 - q_j^M) \\ &= \sum_{i \in S} b_i q_i^M \mathbb{E}\left[\frac{1}{1 + \sum_{j \in S \setminus \{i\}} X_j}\right] = \mathbb{E}\left[\frac{\sum_{i \in S} b_i X_i}{\sum_{i \in S} X_i}\right],\end{aligned}$$

where $\{X_i\}_{i \in \mathcal{I}}$ are Bernoulli random variables with $X_i = 1$ with probability q_i^M. By the Bernoulli Selection Lemma we can choose the set $S \subseteq \mathcal{I}$ to be such that the latter is lower bounded by

$$\left(1 - \frac{1}{e}\right) \max_{z_i \leq q_i^M} \left\{\sum_{i \in \mathcal{I}} b_i z_i \,\middle|\, \sum z_i \leq 1\right\} \geq \left(1 - \frac{1}{e}\right) \sum_{i \in \mathcal{I}} F_i^{-1}(1 - q_i^M) q_i^M .$$

Therefore, Lemma 3.1 leads to the desired conclusion.

In the nonregular case, the posted price mechanism runs a lottery between two prices to get the desired bound.[6] First, for every bidder with positive probability of winning the optimal auction, set

$$b_i' = \frac{x_i \underline{p_i}\, \underline{q_i} + (1 - x_i) \overline{p_i}\, \overline{q_i}}{q_i^M},$$

where the variables are defined as in the lemma. Also consider the same Bernoulli random variables presented in the first part of the proof. The nonadaptive posted price mechanism sells only to a set S' of customers (to be defined). For every $i \in S'$, it offers a random price p_i equal to $\underline{p_i}$ with probability x_i, and $\overline{p}_i$ otherwise. This way, the a priori probability that v_i is above the price offered is exactly $x_i \underline{q_i} + (1 - x_i)\overline{q_i} = q_i^M$, while the expected revenue of the mechanism can be evaluated as

$$\begin{aligned}&\sum_{i \in S'} x_i \underline{p_i}\, \underline{q_i} \mathbb{P}[i = \operatorname{argmin}_{j \in S'}\{\sigma(j) \mid v_j \geq p_j\} \mid v_i \geq p_i,\, p_i = \underline{p_i}] \\ &\quad + (1 - x_i)\overline{p_i}\, \overline{q_i} \mathbb{P}[i = \operatorname{argmin}_{j \in S'}\{\sigma(j) \mid v_j \geq p_j\} \mid v_i \geq p_i,\, p_i = \overline{p_i}] \\ &= \sum_{i \in S'} (x_i \underline{p_i}\, \underline{q_i} + (1 - x_i)\overline{p_i}\, \overline{q_i}) \sum_{R \subseteq S' \setminus \{i\}} \frac{1}{1 + |R|} \prod_{j \in R} q_j^M \prod_{j \in S' \setminus (R \cup \{i\})} (1 - q_j^M) \\ &= \sum_{i \in S'} b_i' q_i^M \mathbb{E}\left[\frac{1}{1 + \sum_{j \in S' \setminus \{i\}} X_j}\right] = \mathbb{E}\left[\frac{\sum_{i \in S'} b_i' X_i}{\sum_{i \in S'} X_i}\right].\end{aligned}$$

By the same argument as before, Lemma 1.2 implies that there exists $S' \subseteq \mathcal{I}$ such that the latter is lower bounded by $(1 - 1/e) \sum_{i \in \mathcal{I}} b_i' q_i^M$. Lemma 3.1 implies the bound over the optimal auction. □

[6]This lottery can be derandomized using standard techniques, since each combination of prices offered to the customers is a deterministic mechanism in itself and the random mechanism is simply a lottery over, and thus a convex combination of, those deterministic mechanisms.

Tight instance with i.i.d. valuations. We construct a family of instances for Problem 1 with i.i.d. customer valuations, such that, for all $\varepsilon > 0$, there is an instance from this family for which no nonadaptive strategy can achieve an expected revenue within a factor $(1+\varepsilon)(1-1/e)$ of the optimal expected revenue. The idea is to mimic the instance that makes the Bernoulli Selection Lemma tight, but here we achieve this with i.i.d. valuations. Consider n^2 customers whose values are independent identically distributed according to

$$V = \begin{cases} \frac{n}{e-2} & \text{w.p. } \frac{1}{n^3}, \\ 1 & \text{w.p. } \frac{1}{n}, \\ 0 & \text{w.p. } 1 - \frac{1}{n} - \frac{1}{n^3}. \end{cases}$$

Then, it is easy to design an auction that achieves a revenue approaching $(e-1)/(e-2)$ as $n \to \infty$. Indeed, consider the auction that offers the item for price $n/(e-2)-c$ (with c a small value, say $c = 2$) to any bid above that price (and assigns the item at random if more than one such offer is received), and if no such bid is received, then it runs a lottery at price 1 among all the bids above that price. As there are many buyers of value 1, a potential large value customer will prefer to make a revenue of c rather than risking to lose the item in the lottery. Therefore the revenue the auction will generate will approach $1/(e-2)+1$ as $n \to \infty$. Of course, the revenue of the optimal auction is then at least this quantity. On the other hand, the best posted price mechanism offers a price of 1 to, say, customers $1, \ldots, k$ and $n/(e-2)$ to the rest of the customers, for some well chosen value of k which turns out to be roughly n. One can show that in the limit the revenue approaches $(\frac{1}{e-2}+1)(1-e^{-1})$.

4 ADAPTIVE POSTED PRICE MECHANISM

In the previous section we considered the setting in which the posted price only depends on the customer, not on the order. In this section we consider the setting in which the posted price may depend both on the customer and on the customers that arrived before her. We design an adaptive posted price mechanism that achieves an expected revenue of at least a 0.745 fraction of that of the optimal mechanism. In particular we prove the following.

Theorem 1.3. *For any given set of potential customers $\mathcal{I}$ whose values are independent and identically distributed, there exists an adaptive posted price mechanism that achieves an expected revenue of at least a $1/\beta > 0.745$ fraction of that of Myerson's optimal auction on $\mathcal{I}$, where β is the unique value such that*

$$\int_0^1 \frac{1}{y(1-\ln(y)) + (\beta - 1)} dy = 1\,.$$

We assume that the valuations of the customers are i.i.d. with cumulative distribution function $F(\cdot)$ and probability density function $f(\cdot)$. For our analysis the bound provided by Lemma 3.1 is not enough, so we derive an exact expression for the expected revenue of the optimal auction.

Expected value of Myerson's optimal auction for i.i.d. customers. Following Myerson [19], we define the *virtual valuation* as $c(v) = v - \frac{1-F(v)}{f(v)}$ and the *ironed virtual valuation* as $\bar{c}(v) = G'(F(v))$, where $G = \text{conv}(H)$[7] is the convexification of the negative revenue curve $H(q) = \int_0^q c(F^{-1}(\theta))d\theta$ as a function of the acceptance probability q. Also, let $\mathbb{E}(\text{MY}(n, F))$ be the expected revenue of the optimal auction over n customers with values drawn from distribution F.

The expected profit of the optimal auction equals its expected virtual surplus (see, e.g., [12]), i.e., the sum over all customers of the expected value of the maximum of $\bar{c}$ above zero. Note that $\bar{c}$ is

[7] $G(q) = \min\{\gamma H(q_1) + (1-\gamma)H(q_2) : \gamma q_1 + (1-\gamma)q_2 = q,\ \gamma, q_1, q_2 \in [0,1]\}$. Note that if $c(v)$ is monotone (also known as *regular*), then $G(q) = H(q)$.

an increasing function, and let v^* be the value at which $\bar{c}(v^*) = 0$ or zero, if no such value exists. Then, the latter can be evaluated as:

$$\mathbb{E}(\mathrm{MY}(n,F)) = \int_{v^*}^{\infty} nF(v)^{n-1}\bar{c}(v)f(v)dv.$$

Performing the change of variables $q = 1 - F(v)$ and $\alpha^* = 1 - F(v^*)$, we obtain

$$\begin{aligned}\mathbb{E}(\mathrm{MY}(n,F)) &= n\int_0^{\alpha^*} (1-q)^{n-1}\bar{c}(F^{-1}(1-q))dq \\ &= n\int_0^{\alpha^*} (1-q)^{n-1}G'(1-q)dq \\ &= -nG(1-q)(1-q)^{n-1}\Big|_0^{\alpha^*} - \int_0^{\alpha^*} n(n-1)(1-q)^{n-2}G(1-q)dq \\ &= nG(1) - nG(F(v^*))F(v^*)^{n-1} - n(n-1)\int_0^{\alpha^*} (1-q)^{n-2}G(1-q)dq\,.\end{aligned}$$

Since $\bar{c}(v^*) = 0$, we know that G attains a minimum at $F(v^*)$ and, therefore, equals $H(F(v^*))$ at that point. Now, observe that

$$H(q) = \int_0^q F^{-1}(\theta) - \frac{1-\theta}{f(F^{-1}(\theta))}d\theta = -(1-q)F^{-1}(q)\,.$$

Therefore, we can conclude that

$$\begin{aligned}\mathbb{E}(\mathrm{MY}(n,F)) &= -nH(F(v^*))F(v^*)^{n-1} - n(n-1)\int_0^{\alpha^*} (1-q)^{n-2}G(1-q)dq \\ &= nv^*(1-F(v^*))F(v^*)^{n-1} - n(n-1)\int_0^{\alpha^*} (1-q)^{n-2}G(1-q)dq\,.\end{aligned}$$

Now, let

$$\bar{G}(1-q) = \begin{cases} -G(1-q) & \text{if } 1-q > F(v^*)\,, \\ v^*(1-F(v^*)) & \text{otherwise}\,. \end{cases}$$

Then, we can write the expected revenue of the optimal mechanism as

$$\mathbb{E}(\mathrm{MY}(n,F)) = n(n-1)\int_0^1 (1-q)^{n-2}\bar{G}(1-q)dq\,. \tag{4}$$

We note that expression (4), although fairly natural to derive, appears to be new.

Adaptive posted price mechanism. In the adaptive setting, the price offered to a customer also depends on the set of customers that declined the offer. However, as the customers are i.i.d., an adaptive pricing mechanism only needs to know how many customers have received an offer and not exactly which customers. The intuition behind the mechanism is to start with a high price and decrease the price when the number of remaining customer decreases, such that the risk of not selling is mitigated. To describe the mechanism, we first restrict to monotone virtual valuations, and then describe how to deal with the general case.

We partition the interval $A = [0,1]$ into n intervals $A_i = [\varepsilon_{i-1}, \varepsilon_i]$, with $0 = \varepsilon_0 < \varepsilon_1 < \ldots < \varepsilon_{n-1} < \varepsilon_n = 1$. The pricing mechanism will thus choose a price for customer i such that the probability that this customer accepts the offer lies in A_i, making sure that no customer will ever receive an offer lower than the reservation price v^*. To implement this idea we use Expression (4) as a guide and construct the offer for customer i by drawing a q_i from the interval A_i according to probability density function $f_i(q) = \frac{\psi(q)}{\alpha_i}$,[8] where $\psi(q) = (n-1)(1-q)^{n-2}$ and α_i is a normalization parameter equal to $\alpha_i = \int_{q \in A_i} \psi(q)dq$. This q_i is meant to be the acceptance probability of customer i, so the price offered to her is $\max\{F^{-1}(1-q_i), v^*\}$.

Note that due to the assumption that the virtual valuations are monotone, we know that when offering a price $F^{-1}(1-q_i)$, the expected profit of customer i is $q_i F^{-1}(1-q_i) = -H(1-q_i) = \bar{G}(1-q_i)$. For nonmonotone virtual valuations, it might be the case that $q_i F^{-1}(1-q_i) = -H(1-q_i) < \bar{G}(1-q_i)$, and by offering a price $F^{-1}(1-q_i)$ we might not get the best revenue. To circumvent this problem, we can randomize between two acceptance probabilities q_{i1} and q_{i2} such that $G(1-q_i) = \gamma H(1-q_{i1}) + (1-\gamma)H(1-q_{i2})$ and $q_i = \gamma q_{i1} + (1-\gamma)q_{i2}$.

With the mechanism in place we now establish the approximation guarantee. To this end we prove that the expected revenue of the adaptive posted price mechanism with n customers whose valuations are drawn from F, $\mathbb{E}(\text{ADAP}(n, F))$, satisfies

$$\mathbb{E}(\text{ADAP}(n, F)) \geq \sum_{i=1}^{n} \rho_i \int_{\varepsilon_{i-1}}^{\varepsilon_i} (n-1)(1-q)^{n-2}\bar{G}(1-q)dq\,,$$

where $\rho_1 = \frac{1}{\alpha_1}$ and $\rho_{i+1} = \frac{\rho_i}{\alpha_{i+1}} \int_{\varepsilon_{i-1}}^{\varepsilon_i} \psi(q)(1-q)dq$ for $i = 1, \ldots, n-1$.

By choosing $\varepsilon_1, \ldots, \varepsilon_{n-1}$ in such a way that $\rho_1 = \rho_2 = \ldots = \rho_n$, we have $\mathbb{E}(\text{ADAP}(n, F)) \geq \frac{1}{n\alpha_1}\mathbb{E}(\text{MY}(n, F))$, and thus we wrap-up by proving that the term $1/(n\alpha_1)$ is bounded by 0.745. For the latter we set up a recursion whose solution determines α_1 and then approximate the recursion with an ordinary differential equation.

Relating the optimal auction and the adaptive posted price mechanism.

Lemma 4.1. *Let $\rho_1 = \frac{1}{\alpha_1}$ and $\rho_{i+1} = \frac{\rho_i}{\alpha_{i+1}} \int_{\varepsilon_{i-1}}^{\varepsilon_i} \psi(q)(1-q)dq$ for $i = 1, \ldots, n-1$. Then the expected value of the adaptive posted price mechanism that faces n customers with value distribution F, $\mathbb{E}(ADAP(n, F))$, satisfies*

$$\mathbb{E}(ADAP(n, F)) \geq \sum_{i=1}^{n} \rho_i \int_{\varepsilon_{i-1}}^{\varepsilon_i} (n-1)(1-q)^{n-2}\bar{G}(1-q)dq\,.$$

Proof. First, assume that the item is offered to customer i. Let q_i denote the drawn acceptance probability for customer i. The expected revenue obtained from selling the item to customer i is $\bar{G}(1-q_i)$. To see this, suppose that $q_i < 1 - F(v^*)$. Then, for monotone virtual valuations, the price offered to customer i is $F^{-1}(1-q_i)$, and thus the expected revenue is $q_i F^{-1}(1-q_i) = -G(1-q_i) = \bar{G}(1-q_i)$. On the other hand, if $q_i > 1 - F(v^*)$, the price offered to customer i is v^* which is accepted with probability $1 - F(v^*)$. Similar arguments hold when the virtual valuation is not monotone.

Now, for $j = 1, \ldots, n$, let q_j denote the drawn acceptance probability of customer j. Then, the probability that the item is offered to customer i is equal to $\Pi_{j=1}^{i-1} \max\{1-q_j, F(v^*)\}$. Hence, the

[8] Just as for the non-adaptive mechanism, this randomization can be derandomized using standard techniques, since each combination of set prices for the customers is in itself a deterministic mechanism and the random mechanism is simply a lottery over, and thus a convex combination of, those deterministic mechanisms.

expected value of our adaptive posted price mechanism is

$$\begin{aligned}\mathbb{E}(\mathrm{ADAP}(n,F)) &= \int_0^{\varepsilon_1} \frac{\psi(q_1)}{\alpha_1}\Big[\bar{G}(1-q_1) + \max\{1-q_1, F(v^*)\} \int_{\varepsilon_1}^{\varepsilon_2} \frac{\psi(q_2)}{\alpha_2}\Big[\bar{G}(1-q_2) \\ &\quad + \max\{1-q_2, F(v^*)\} \int_{\varepsilon_2}^{\varepsilon_3} \frac{\psi(q_3)}{\alpha_3}\Big[\bar{G}(1-q_3) + \dots \\ &\quad + \max\{1-q_{n-2}, F(v^*)\} \int_{\varepsilon_{n-2}}^{\varepsilon_{n-1}} \frac{\psi(q_{n-1})}{\alpha_{n-1}}\Big[\bar{G}(1-q_{n-1}) \\ &\quad + \max\{1-q_{n-1}, F(v^*)\} \int_{\varepsilon_{n-1}}^{1} \frac{\psi(q_n)}{\alpha_n}\bar{G}(1-q_n)\,dq_n\Big]\,dq_{n-1}\dots\Big]\,dq_3\Big]\,dq_2\Big]\,dq_1 \\ &\geq \int_0^{\varepsilon_1} \frac{\psi(q_1)}{\alpha_1}\Big[\bar{G}(1-q_1) + (1-q_1) \int_{\varepsilon_1}^{\varepsilon_2} \frac{\psi(q_2)}{\alpha_2}\Big[\bar{G}(1-q_2) + \\ &\quad + (1-q_2) \int_{\varepsilon_2}^{\varepsilon_3} \frac{\psi(q_3)}{\alpha_3}\Big[\bar{G}(1-q_3) + \dots \\ &\quad + (1-q_{n-2}) \int_{\varepsilon_{n-2}}^{\varepsilon_{n-1}} \frac{\psi(q_{n-1})}{\alpha_{n-1}}\Big[\bar{G}(1-q_{n-1}) \\ &\quad + (1-q_{n-1}) \int_{\varepsilon_{n-1}}^{1} \frac{\psi(q_3)}{\alpha_3}\bar{G}(1-q_n)\,dq_n\Big]\,dq_{n-1}\dots\Big]\,dq_3\Big]\,dq_2\Big]\,dq_1\end{aligned}$$

and the latter equals

$$\begin{aligned}&\frac{1}{\alpha_1}\int_0^{\varepsilon_1} \psi(q_1)\bar{G}(1-q_1)\,dq_1 + \frac{1}{\alpha_1}\frac{\int_0^{\varepsilon_1}\psi(q_1)(1-q_1)\,dq_1}{\alpha_2}\int_{\varepsilon_1}^{\varepsilon_2}\psi(q_2)\bar{G}(1-q_2)\,dq_2 + \dots \\ &\quad + \frac{1}{\alpha_1}\frac{\int_0^{\varepsilon_1}\psi(q_1)(1-q_1)\,dq_1}{\alpha_2}\cdot\ldots\cdot\frac{\int_{\varepsilon_{n-2}}^{\varepsilon_{n-1}}\psi(q_{n-1})(1-q_{n-1})\,dq_{n-1}}{\alpha_n}\int_{\varepsilon_{n-1}}^{1}\psi(q_n)\bar{G}(1-q_n)\,dq_n \\ &= \sum_{i=1}^{n}\rho_i\int_{\varepsilon_{i-1}}^{\varepsilon_i}(n-1)(1-q)^{n-2}\bar{G}(1-q)dq\,. \qquad \square\end{aligned}$$

By choosing $\varepsilon_1, \dots, \varepsilon_{n-1}$ appropriately, we can lower bound the expected revenue of the adaptive posted price mechanism against that of Myerson.

Lemma 4.2. *If we choose $\varepsilon_1, \dots, \varepsilon_{n-1}$ such that $\rho_1 = \rho_2 = \ldots = \rho_n$, then*

$$\mathbb{E}(ADAP(n,F)) \geq \frac{1}{n\alpha_1}\mathbb{E}(MY(n,F))\,.$$

Proof. If we choose $\varepsilon_1, \dots, \varepsilon_{n-1}$ such that $\rho_i = \rho_1$ for all i, then by Lemma 4.1 we can bound the expected value of our mechanism by

$$\begin{aligned}\mathbb{E}(\mathrm{ADAP}(n,F)) &\geq \sum_{i=1}^{n}\rho_i\int_{\varepsilon_{i-1}}^{\varepsilon_i}(n-1)(1-q)^{n-2}\bar{G}(1-q)\,dq \\ &= \frac{\rho_1}{n}\sum_{i=1}^{n}\int_{\varepsilon_{i-1}}^{\varepsilon_i} n(n-1)(1-q)^{n-2}\bar{G}(1-q)\,dq \\ &= \frac{1}{n\alpha_1}\int_0^1 n(n-1)(1-q)^{n-2}\bar{G}(1-q)\,dq = \frac{1}{n\alpha_1}\mathbb{E}(\mathrm{MY}(n,F))\,. \qquad \square\end{aligned}$$

Bounding α_1 through a recursion. Since $\rho_{i+1} = \frac{\rho_i}{\alpha_{i+1}} \int_{\varepsilon_{i-1}}^{\varepsilon_i} \psi(q)(1-q)dq$ for all i, choosing $\varepsilon_1, \ldots, \varepsilon_{n-1}$ such that all ρ_i are the same amounts to choosing them such that $\int_{\varepsilon_{i-1}}^{\varepsilon_i} \psi(q)(1-q)dq = \alpha_{i+1}$ for all i. By definition of α_{i+1} and $\psi(q)$, this is equivalent to choosing them such that for all i

$$\int_{\varepsilon_{i-1}}^{\varepsilon_i} \psi(q)(1-q)\, dq = \frac{n-1}{n}\left((1-\varepsilon_{i-1})^n - (1-\varepsilon_i)^n\right)$$

is equal to

$$\int_{\varepsilon_i}^{\varepsilon_{i+1}} \psi(q)\, dq = (1-\varepsilon_i)^{n-1} - (1-\varepsilon_{i+1})^{n-1}\,.$$

Now, substitute $x_i = 1 - \varepsilon_i$. Then, from Lemma 4.2, we obtain the following recursion on x_i:

$$\frac{{x_{i-1}}^n}{n} - \frac{{x_i}^n}{n} = \frac{{x_i}^{n-1}}{n-1} - \frac{{x_{i+1}}^{n-1}}{n-1}\,, \tag{5}$$

where $x_0 = 1$ and $x_n = 0$. Moreover,

$$\alpha_1 = \int_0^{\varepsilon_1} \psi(q)\, dq = 1 - {x_1}^{n-1}\,.$$

Combining this with Lemma 4.2, we see that if $\frac{1}{n(1-{x_1}^{n-1})} \geq \frac{1}{\beta}$, for some $\beta \geq 1$, then the adaptive posted price mechanism has an expected revenue that is at least a $\frac{1}{\beta}$ fraction of the expected revenue of Myerson's optimal auction.

Note that $\frac{1}{n(1-{x_1}^{n-1})} \geq \frac{1}{\beta}$ if and only if $x_1 \geq (1-\frac{\beta}{n})^{1/(n-1)}$. Thus, if we find the minimum value β for which $x_1 < (1-\frac{\beta}{n})^{1/(n-1)} \implies x_n < 0$, we know that $x_1 \geq (1-\frac{\beta}{n})^{1/(n-1)}$ for that value of β. Hence, we show an upper bound on the sequence x_i. For this, we use the following lemma.

Lemma 4.3. *For values $x_0, x_1, \ldots, x_n$ satisfying (5) and $x_0 = 1$ and $x_n = 0$, we have for $i = 1, \ldots, n-1$,*

$$x_{i+1} = \left(\frac{n-1}{n}{x_i}^n + {x_1}^{n-1} - \frac{n-1}{n}\right)^{1/(n-1)}\,.$$

Proof. We prove this lemma by induction. For $i = 1$ equation (5) gives

$$x_2 = \left({x_1}^{n-1} + \frac{n-1}{n}{x_1}^n - \frac{n-1}{n}\right)^{1/(n-1)}\,.$$

Now, suppose the claim is true for $i = 1, \ldots, j$. From (5), we know that

$$\begin{aligned}
{x_{j+1}}^{n-1} &= {x_j}^{n-1} + \frac{n-1}{n}{x_j}^n - \frac{n-1}{n}{x_{j-1}}^n \\
&= \frac{n-1}{n}{x_{j-1}}^n + {x_1}^{n-1} - \frac{n-1}{n} + \frac{n-1}{n}{x_j}^n - \frac{n-1}{n}{x_{j-1}}^n \\
&= \frac{n-1}{n}{x_j}^n + {x_1}^{n-1} - \frac{n-1}{n}\,,
\end{aligned}$$

where the second equality is due to the induction hypothesis. □

Bounding the recursion through a differential equation. In the following, we show that each of the terms x_i in the recursion can be bounded with a function $y(t) : [0,1] \to \mathbb{R}$, defined through the following differential equation. All derivatives of y are with respect to t.

$$\begin{aligned}
y' &= y(\ln(y) - 1) - (\beta - 1)\,, \\
y(0) &= 1\,.
\end{aligned} \tag{ODE}$$

Furthermore, we define $y(1) = \lim_{t\uparrow 1} y(t)$ as the continuous extension of $y(t)$. Later on, we will choose $\beta \approx 1.34$. For this β, we have $y \in [0,1]$, so we restrict our analysis of (ODE) to this interval. We assume $\beta > 1.25$ and $y \in [0,1]$. We validate these assumptions at the end of our analysis.

We now proceed to prove that the solution of (ODE) dominates the terms of the recurrence. In this proof, we make use of the following technical results.

Lemma 4.4. *Differential equation* (ODE) *has a unique solution $y(t)$, which is a decreasing and strictly convex function on the interval $[0,1]$. Furthermore, $y'''(t) > 0$ for $y \in (0,1)$.*

Proposition 4.5. *If $x \in (0,1]$ and $n \geq 2$, then*

$$x + \frac{x(\ln(x) - 1)}{n} + \frac{x(\ln(x) - 1) - (\beta - 1)}{2n^2} \ln(x) \geq \frac{n-1}{n} x^{\frac{n}{n-1}} .$$

Using this inequality, we bound the recurrence by the function $y(t)$ in the following way.

Lemma 4.6. *If $x_1 < (1 - \frac{\beta}{n})^{\frac{1}{n-1}}$, then ${x_i}^{n-1} < y(\frac{i}{n})$ for $i = 1, \ldots, n$, where $y(t)$ is the unique solution of* (ODE).

Proof. First note that $x_0 = y(0) = 1$, by definition. Moreover, a straightforward computation shows that $y'(0) = -\beta$. As $y(t)$ is strictly convex, we know that $y(1/n) > y(0) - \frac{1}{n}\beta > {x_1}^{n-1}$, where the last inequality follows by assumption. Now assume that ${x_i}^{n-1} < y(\frac{i}{n})$, then we prove ${x_{i+1}}^{n-1} < y(\frac{i+1}{n})$. First observe that the Taylor expansion of $y(\frac{i+1}{n})$ around $\frac{i}{n}$ is

$$y(\tfrac{i+1}{n}) = y(\tfrac{i}{n}) + \frac{1}{n} y'(\tfrac{i}{n}) + \frac{1}{2n^2} y''(\tfrac{i}{n}) + \frac{1}{6n^6} y'''(\zeta),$$

with $\zeta \in [\frac{i}{n}, \frac{i+1}{n}]$. As $y''' > 0$, it follows that

$$\begin{aligned} y(\tfrac{i+1}{n}) &> y(\tfrac{i}{n}) + \frac{1}{n} y'(\tfrac{i}{n}) + \frac{1}{2n^2} y''(\tfrac{i}{n}) \\ &= y(\tfrac{i}{n}) + \frac{y(\frac{i}{n})(\ln(y(\frac{i}{n})) - 1) - (\beta - 1)}{n} + \frac{y(\frac{i}{n})(\ln(y(\frac{i}{n}) - 1) - (\beta - 1))}{2n^2} \ln(y(\tfrac{i}{n})) \\ &\geq \frac{n-1}{n} y(\tfrac{i}{n})^{\frac{n}{n-1}} - \frac{\beta - 1}{n} > \frac{n-1}{n} x_i^n - \frac{\beta - 1}{n} > x_{i+1}^{n-1}, \end{aligned}$$

where the second inequality is due to Proposition 4.5 and the last inequality follows from Lemma 4.3 and the assumption that $x_1^{n-1} < 1 - \frac{\beta}{n}$. □

We now finish the proof of Theorem 1.3.

Proof of Theorem 1.3. Choosing $0 = \varepsilon_0 < \varepsilon_1 < \ldots < \varepsilon_{n-1} < \varepsilon_n = 1$ such that for all i $\int_{\varepsilon_{i-1}}^{\varepsilon_i} \psi(q)(1-q)\, dq = \alpha_{i+1}$, we know by Lemma 4.2 that

$$\mathbb{E}(\text{ADAP}(n, F)) \geq \frac{1}{n\alpha_1} \mathbb{E}(\text{MY}(n, F)),$$

where $\alpha_1 = 1 - (1 - \varepsilon_1)^{n-1} = 1 - x_1^{n-1}$. Hence, we want to show $\frac{1}{n(1 - x_1^{n-1})} \geq \frac{1}{\beta}$ for $\beta \approx 1.3415 < \frac{1}{0.745}$.

We prove by contradiction and assume $x_1^{n-1} < 1 - \frac{\beta}{n}$. Then Lemma 4.6 yields $x_n < y(1)$, so we choose β such that $y(1) = 0$ to reach a contradiction with the fact that $x_n = 0$. Note that this indeed implies $y \in [0,1]$ as we assumed. Hereto, note that $y(t)$ is invertible by Lemma 4.4. Hence, we can consider t as a function of y, for which we know $t(1) = 0$, and we want to choose β such that $t(0) = 1$. In particular, we have that

$$t(1) = t(0) + \int_0^1 \frac{dt}{dy} dy = 1 + \int_0^1 \frac{1}{\frac{dy}{dt}} dy = 1 + \int_0^1 \frac{1}{y(\ln(y) - 1) - (\beta - 1)} dy .$$

So β is the value such that the last integral equals -1. This yields $\beta \approx 1.3415 < \frac{1}{0.745}$. □

Extension. As we did in Corollary 2.2 of Section 2, we can extend our result in Theorem 1.3 to an adaptive version of the prophet inequality.

Corollary 4.7. *Given nonnegative i.i.d. random variables, $X_1, \ldots, X_n$, with $X_i \sim F$ for all i, there exist thresholds, $\tau_1, \ldots, \tau_n$, such that for a sequence σ, drawn uniformly at random, the expected value of the first variable that exceeds its threshold according to that sequence, $X_{\sigma(i)} \geq \tau_i$, is at least a $1/\beta$ fraction of the expected value of $\max\{X_1, \ldots, X_n\}$.*

Proof. When F is continuous and strictly increasing, we express the expected value of the maximum in a convenient way:

$$\begin{aligned}\mathbb{E}\left(\max_{i=1,\ldots,n} X_i\right) &= n\int_0^1 tF^{n-1}dF(t) = n\int_0^1 (1-q)^{n-1}F^{-1}(1-q)dq \\ &= n\int_0^1 (n-1)(1-q)^{n-2}\left(\int_0^q F^{-1}(1-\theta)d\theta\right)dq = n\int_0^1 (n-1)(1-q)^{n-2}R(q)qdq ,\end{aligned}$$

where $R(q) = \mathbb{E}(X \mid X > F^{-1}(1-q))$ is the expected value of a random variable given that the probability that that variable attains a larger value is at most q (here, $X \sim F$). As we did in the previous mechanism, we partition $[0,1]$ into n intervals $A_i = [\varepsilon_{i-1}, \varepsilon_i]$, $0 = \varepsilon_0 < \varepsilon_1 < \ldots < \varepsilon_{n-1} < \varepsilon_n = 1$, and we set a threshold $\tau_i = F^{-1}(1-q_i)$ for the random variable arriving at step i, where q_i is drawn from the interval A_i according to the probability density $f_i(q) = \frac{(n-1)(1-q_i)^{n-2}}{\alpha_i}$ with $\alpha_i = \int_{\varepsilon_{i-1}}^{\varepsilon_i} \psi(q)dq$. Since $R(q)$ corresponds to the expected value we get when setting threshold $F^{-1}(1-q)$, one can prove – following the same reasoning as the analogous part in the proof of Theorem 1.3 – that the expected revenue of this strategy is equal to

$$\sum_{i=1}^n \rho_i \int_{\varepsilon_{i-1}}^{\varepsilon_i} (n-1)(1-q)^{n-2}R(q)q\,dq , \tag{6}$$

where $\rho_1 = \frac{1}{\alpha_1}$ and $\rho_{i+1} = \frac{\rho_i}{\alpha_{i+1}} \int_{\varepsilon_{i-1}}^{\varepsilon_i}(n-1)(1-q)^{n-1}dq$ for $i = 1, \ldots, n-1$. Again, if we choose $\varepsilon_1, \ldots, \varepsilon_{n-1}$ such that $\rho_1 = \rho_2 = \ldots = \rho_n$, and solve the recurrence $\{\varepsilon_i\}_{i=1}^{n-1}$ satisfies, then expression (6) equals $\frac{1}{n\alpha_1}\mathbb{E}\left(\max_{i=1,\ldots,n} X_i\right) \geq \frac{1}{\beta}\mathbb{E}\left(\max_{i=1,\ldots,n} X_i\right)$.

If F is not strictly increasing, replacing $F^{-1}(1-q)$ by $\arg\max F^{-1}(1-q)$ maintains the correctness of the proof. In the case that F is not continuous, one must be more careful when expressing the expected value of the maximum. The result still holds provided the thresholds are chosen randomly, after sampling the probability of acceptance q. □

Remark. A routine exercise shows that the sequence a_n defined by Hill and Kertz [13] exactly equals our $n\alpha_1$. Note here that our α_1 does depend on n, though we have omitted this dependency for simplicity of notation. Thus our result implies that $a_n \leq \beta$ and by the work of Kertz [14] we know that this bound is tight.

Acknowledgments

We thank Bobby Kleinberg for pointing out the connection of our Theorem 1.3 and Corollary 4.7 to the work of Hill and Kertz [13].

REFERENCES

[1] M. Abolhassani, S. Ehsani, H. Esfandiari, M.T. Hajiaghayi, R. Kleinberg, and B. Lucier. Beating 1-1/e for Ordered Prophets. In *STOC 2017*.

[2] M. Adamczyk, A. Borodin, D. Ferraioli, B. de Keijzer, and S. Leonardi. Sequential Posted Price Mechanisms with Correlated Valuations. In *WINE 2015*.

[3] Saeed Alaei, Jason Hartline, Rad Niazadeh, Emmanouil Pountourakis, and Yang Yuan. Optimal Auctions vs. Anonymous Pricing. In *FOCS 2015*.

[4] L. Blumrosen and T. Holenstein. Posted Prices vs. Negotiations: An Asymptotic Analysis. In *EC 2008*.

[5] J.R. Bult and T. Wansbeek. Optimal selection for direct mail. *Marketing Science* 14(4):378–394, 1995.

[6] S. Chawla, J.D. Hartline, D.L. Malec, and B. Sivan. Multi-parameter Mechanism Design and Sequential Posted Pricing. In *STOC 2010*.

[7] V. Choudhary, A. Ghose, T. Mukhopadhyay, and U. Rajan. Personalized Pricing and Quality Differentiation. *Management Science* 51(7):1120–1130, 2005.

[8] R. Cominetti, J. Correa, T. Rothvoß, and J. San Martín. Optimal Selection of Customers for a Last-Minute Offer. *Operations Research* 58(4):878–888, 2010.

[9] P. Dütting, F. Fischer, and M. Klimm. Revenue Gaps for Discriminatory and Anonymous Sequential Posted Pricing. arXiv:cs.GT/1607.07105, 2016.

[10] H. Esfandiari, M. Hajiaghayi, V. Liaghat, and M. Monemizadeh. Prophet Secretary. In *ESA 2015*.

[11] J.P. Gilbert and F. Mosteller. Recognizing the Maximum of a Sequence. *J. Amer. Statist. Assoc.* 61 (1966), 35–76.

[12] J. Hartline. Mechanism Design and Approximation, 2016. http://jasonhartline.com/MDnA/

[13] T.P. Hill and R.P. Kertz. 1982. Comparisons of stop rule and supremum expectations of i.i.d. random variables. *The Annals of Probability*10(2):336–345, 1982.

[14] R.P. Kertz. Stop rule and supremum expectations of i.i.d. random variables: A complete comparison by conjugate duality. *Journal of Multivariate Analysis* 19:88–112, 1986.

[15] O. Kharif. 2013. Supermarkets Offer Personalized Pricing. *Bloomberg* (15 Nov. 2013).

[16] R. Kleinberg and S.M. Weinberg. Matroid Prophet Inequalities. In *STOC 2012*.

[17] U. Krengel and L. Sucheston. Semiamarts and finite values. *Bull. Amer. Math. Soc.* 83:745–747, 1977.

[18] D. Mattioli. 2012. On Orbitz, Mac Users Steered to Pricier Hotels. *The Wall Street Journal* (23 Aug. 2012).

[19] R.B. Myerson. Optimal Auction Design. *Mathematics of Operations Research* 6(1):58–73, 1981.

[20] U. Saint-Mont. A simple derivation of a complicated prophet region. *Journal of Multivariate Analysis* 80:67–72, 2002.

[21] E. Samuel-Cahn. Comparisons of threshold stop rule and maximum for independent nonnegative random variables. *The Annals of Probability* 12(4):1213–1216, 1983.

[22] C. Shapiro and H.R. Varian. 1999. *Information Rules: A Strategic Guide to the Network Economy.* Harvard Business School Press, Cambridge, MA.

[23] Q. Yan. Mechanism design via correlation gap. In *SODA 2011*.

Accounting for Strategic Response in an Agent-Based Model of Financial Regulation

FRANK CHENG, University of Michigan
MICHAEL P. WELLMAN, University of Michigan

Due to complex interactions in financial markets, financial regulations can sometimes produce unexpected outcomes, and fail to achieve their macroeconomic goals. We replicate a previous agent-based simulation study which showed that the Basel banking regulations may increase financial instability, counter to their intended purpose. Our replication confirms that this is the case, following the original study's assumption that the financial firms' behaviors are fixed. We then extend the model to account for a possible strategic response, where financial firms adapt to the regulatory regime. Using empirical game-theoretic analysis, we derive equilibria with and without regulation. We find that in the new Basel-regulated equilibria, more funds stay out of default and banks lose less capital. The overall effect of regulation on financial stability becomes benign on most measures when accounting for the strategic adaptation of agents.

Additional Key Words and Phrases: Basel; leverage cycle; game theory; agent-based model; finance; financial regulation; systemic risk

1 INTRODUCTION

The financial crisis in 2008 marked a seismic shift in perceptions of how markets operate. Its reverberations are still being felt now in debt markets around the world [Shaffer, 2016]. The question of how financial crises arise time and again in the midst of sophisticated and logically motivated actors is still incompletely understood. After an initial rush in academic circles to develop new economic models to reflect forensic evidence from the crash and to recommend regulation to prevent future crashes, we have been left with a plethora of different viewpoints.

One approach that has gained influence even in crisis-unrelated research [Healy and Palepu, 2001] focuses on the fact that buyers and sellers do not have the same access to information about assets, especially in the context of debt markets. Based on this asymmetry, Bernanke et al. [1999] showed that periodic, deep financial crashes are endemic due to an overreaction to interest rate changes. The recommendation is clear: force sellers to be more transparent about their wares. Almost everyone agrees that making more information available is a good policy, and regulators commonly work towards this goal.

There are many other convincing perspectives on the crisis. The irrational exuberance [Shiller, 2015] narrative posits a deep behavioral reason for market malfunction. It is also popular to point to systemic factors like lax lending standards and oversight leading to market participants whose priorities move away from the proper valuation of assets [Commission, 2011]. Another body of work points to the seizure of credit markets at the most critical juncture of the crisis for amplifying

Authors' address: Computer Science & Engineering, University of Michigan, Ann Arbor, USA
Email: frcheng@umich.edu, wellman@umich.edu.

EC'17, June 26–30, 2017, Cambridge, Massachusetts, USA. ACM ISBN 978-1-4503-4527-9/17/06...$15.00.

DOI: http://dx.doi.org/10.1145/3033274.3085114

the crisis. This failure has been attributed to either too much refinancing during normal times [Roberts and Sufi, 2009] or a run on liquidity [Ivashina and Scharfstein, 2010] in response to financial panic. Agent-based simulations elaborating on traditional economic models have also been used. Bookstaber et al. [2017] introduce one where agents have fixed fire-sale behavior and the spread of the crisis can subsequently be measured through different pathways.

All of these models can explain some aspects of the financial crisis, and suggest various emphases for macroeconomic policy and regulation. Given the complexity of the financial system, however, it is difficult to draw direct conclusions from underlying causes to ideal policies. An alternative perspective is to start from the policies, and model the situations where they are beneficial or harmful. We take this perspective, focusing on international banking regulations in the ***Basel framework***. Basel's salience follows from its central role in global financial policy, and its force in governing the lending policies of major financial institutions.

Basel regulations consist chiefly of a limit to ***leverage***, or the ratio of gross investment to wealth. By taking on debt, this ratio can become arbitrarily large without regulation. An institution with high leverage cannot pay its obligations if its investments underperform even slightly, so it seems natural that limiting leverage may help control default risk. That leverage levels turned out to predict the financial crisis better than interest rates evidences the centrality of this variable to financial stability.[1] Regulator belief in limiting leverage is so strong that their most prominent operational regulation after the crisis was to simply implement a stricter version of Basel. But as such policies had failed to immunize the financial system, there is some uncertainty about how much the stricter version will help in the future.

The ***leverage cycle*** model of Geanakoplos [2003] describes the ebb and flow of leverage, shedding light on how aggregate leverage may increase to dangerous levels. Importantly, the model *endogenizes* leverage, showing how it evolves through agent decision making. Several key predictions made by this model were borne out by asset behavior during the crisis. First, price fluctuations were disproportionate to fundamental value changes. Second, the failure of a few highly leveraged investors had an outsize impact on prices. Third, the severe tightening of short term credit markets contributed to a deeper crash. All of these predictions were entailed by the model, with leverage choices at Walrasian equilibrium under perfect information.

While the model of Geanakoplos [2003] had the advantage of being fully analytical, it extended only to three periods and thus could not accommodate changing financial regulation over time. In a discrete agent-based extension to the leverage cycle model, Thurner et al. [2012] and Poledna et al. [2014] introduced a Basel-style regulator that imposes a leverage limit on financial firms. As in the latest round of Basel financial regulations, the leverage limit in the model is more stringent in times of high asset price volatility. Using this model, Poledna et al. [2014] argue that Basel regulations could, counter to their purpose, contribute to financial instability. In their model under certain settings, market participants (or ***funds***) defaulted more frequently and produced more volatile asset prices when a Basel-based leverage limit was implemented. Market participants also made less profit. However, funds that defaulted were of a smaller size so that the cost per default decreased. A follow-up study by Aymanns and Farmer [2015] suggests that an inverted Basel regulation would be more effective at preventing financial crises.

Our contribution to this story is to observe that a certain fixed assumption in these models, the ***aggression distribution***, might naturally be considered a strategic choice by agents. We extend the model of Poledna et al. [2014] to a game, where the agents strategically choose their aggression level in response to the regulation regime. We employ simulation-based methods to analyze this

[1] A study by Geanakoplos et al. [2012] established a link between financial crashes and leverage levels that successfully predicted data from 2.2 million American households.

game, identifying aggression distributions that are in approximate Nash equilibrium. Using this approach we reverse in aggregate the finding that Basel causes more defaults. Losses due to default decrease further, and agent profits decrease less. The overall case against Basel is thus weakened by our findings.

In Section 2 we describe the model used by Poledna et al. [2014], and explain the effect of Basel regulations on the leverage cycle in this model. We also describe implementation details and assumptions used in the original work that carry over into our independent implementation. In Section 3 we argue that agent aggression levels in this model should be treated as strategic variables. We propose an approach to analyze the strategic adaptations of agent aggression using Nash equilibrium. Finally, we design an experiment that distinguishes the effect of Basel on the leverage cycle for a fixed set of agents (studied in previous work) from its effect due to strategic adaptations of agents found in equilibrium. We measure the effect of Basel on financial stability by looking at default rate, agent profits, capital losses, and price volatility. The strategic adaptation of agents on its own improved every measure except price volatility, which was unchanged. In aggregate, we find that Basel decreases default rate and capital losses while also decreasing agent profits and increasing price volatility.

2 AN AGENT-BASED MODEL OF THE LEVERAGE CYCLE

Following Poledna et al. [2014], we adopt and extend the basic leverage cycle model of Geanakoplos [2010]. This model has been credited with predicting characteristics of the 2008 financial crisis years in advance. By treating leverage as an endogenous decision, it characterizes equilibrium in financial markets in terms of leverage taken by each agent in addition to the asset price and the interest rate on debt. Since Basel targets leverage as a policy variable, the leverage cycle model seems like a natural candidate for evaluating recent financial regulation.

However, the original leverage cycle model is limited in its ability to express real-world complexity. For example, it cannot be extended for an arbitrary number of periods and short asset positions are not considered. Basel regulation, since it responds to the historical volatility of asset prices, is not easily incorporated. To address such issues, Poledna et al. [2014] develop a discrete agent-based model (ABM). At a high level, this model clears the market in each period for persistent financial agents. Agents carry over their wealth to each new period, where demand undergoes a random shock and new prices are formed. Basel regulation is easily expressed in this new model since a regulator may act in each period with knowledge of historical prices. The flip side is that agents are no longer coming to an intertemporal equilibrium as in the leverage cycle model. But leverage remains an endogenous decision by each market participant.

2.1 Agent-Based Model

Poledna et al. [2014] include four types of agent, who interact in a market for a single risky asset. The asset has a ***fundamental value***, V, and a market ***price*** $p(t)$ at time t, determined by the cumulative demand of all agents. The central actors are informed value investors called ***fund managers***. Fund managers know the fundamental value and adjust their demand for the asset based on a ***mispricing signal*** $m = V - p_t$. The fund managers exhibit heterogeneous demand as a function of m, reflecting their differing levels of ***aggression*** in pursuing investment opportunities. The more aggressive a fund is, the more leverage it will take to pursue a given mispricing signal. Aggression reflects factors such as a fund's confidence that the asset price will return to its fundamental in short order, and its tolerance for risk. A fund manager that buys an asset while it is priced under its fundamental is betting that the price will move back up and make her a profit.

To buy or short-sell assets, fund managers may take loans from the ***bank***, treated as an agent in the ABM of Poledna et al. [2014]. The bank provides credit to funds but requires a set amount of ***collateral*** per unit debt. In effect, this collateral requirement imposes a ***leverage limit***. To see this, consider how a leveraged investor keeps her books. She knows that to borrow a dollar from the bank she must commit some amount of wealth as collateral. Call this collateral requirement X. But she only has so much wealth, W, to commit in total. Thus there is a maximum amount she can borrow, W/X, which is constant given W. The ratio of this maximum amount to her current wealth is $1/X$. If the bank decides to increase X, it effectively decreases the leverage limit. In practice, we refer to the bank setting a leverage limit without relating explicitly to collateral. In general the investor is taking on debt in order to take a larger investment position, which she is free to do until she is over the leverage limit. Then she must wind down her investment position and reduce her debt until she is in compliance with the bank.

Thus, in any given time period, funds are limited in the size of the asset position they can take, either long or short, in response to asset mispricings. Note that the bank may be forced to take losses when fund managers default. These losses are recorded but the bank itself never defaults, as it is assumed that there is an unlimited bailout fund.

Mispricings are made possible by stochastic, weakly mean-reverting asset demand from aptly named ***noise traders***. The noise traders represent a collection of ill-informed investors. Their collective behavior exerts a random shock to total asset demand, which in turn shifts the market-clearing asset price.

The final agent type is the ***fund investor***. The fund investor's role is simply to move capital from fund managers with poor (historical) performance, toward those with good performance.

2.2 The Leverage Cycle and Basel: Intuition

It is easy to see that without any limits on leverage, the price of the asset would always return to its fundamental value, as funds would just increase their position against the direction of the shock until the mispricing disappears. It requires just one fund able to take unlimited size positions on the asset to ensure that there is never any price volatility around V. But with leverage limits, the system exhibits complete leverage cycles over time. The qualitative steps to the cycle are shown in Figure 1.

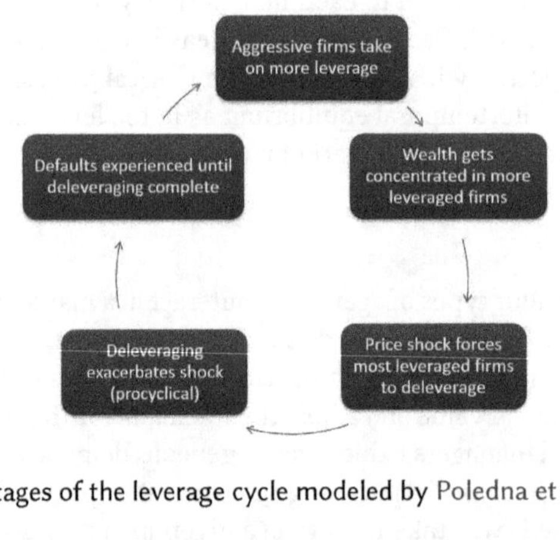

Fig. 1. Stages of the leverage cycle modeled by Poledna et al. [2014].

When shocks are small enough, wealth in the system becomes more and more concentrated in the most aggressive funds as they take more effective leverage in pursuing mispricing opportunities. This gradually increases the sensitivity of total wealth in the system to random price shocks until some investors reach their leverage limit. At that point, a decrease in the asset price would push the leverage ratio over the limit,[2] and so the investor would be forced to sell to get back in compliance when she would actually rather be buying the asset. This action is ***procyclical***, since the act of selling further depresses the price, which can lead to further deleveraging by other funds. It may even induce a mass sell-off (or buy-off for short positions) as other, formerly less leveraged funds struggle to satisfy the leverage limit due to the acceleration of the price movement against their positions. Eventually enough funds have either defaulted or deleveraged that, collectively, they have become insensitive to further price movements, and the cycle begins again. Price volatility, probability of investor default, and losses on defaulted loans are all elevated due to this leverage cycle.

Within this model we can also incorporate Basel-style regulation, which makes leverage limits more stringent during periods of high volatility and less stringent otherwise. Under fixed fund behavior, this increases the probability that investors get into procyclical situations, since the leverage limits themselves will adapt to be procyclical. Intuitively, higher leverage limits in volatile times could allow funds to provide a voice of reason and return the price to the asset's fundamental value. So Basel, by doing the opposite, potentially makes volatility and default more likely. On the other hand, Basel may reduce the losses suffered by the bank on defaulted loans, since the doomed funds were forced to deleverage more quickly before their default.

Our study starts by reimplementing this ABM and replicating the original results. The remainder of this section describes model details; our extension to incorporate strategic response is described in Section 3. To implement the model, we used as references the description of Poledna et al. [2014] together with code provided by these authors in response to our queries. Unless otherwise stated, all of the following modeling decisions and parameters are as implemented in the prior work. We attempt to keep the model as close as possible to prior work in order to isolate the effect that our equilibrium concept has on the evaluation of Basel policies. These assumptions were justified in the original work by drawing parallels with real data on financial crashes.

2.3 Schedule

The state of the market is defined by an equilibrium asset price and the resulting holdings and debt levels of the fund managers. The agent-based simulation iterates between a price formation phase and a wealth update phase. We describe these phases at a high level below to give a sense of the scheduling of tasks.

Price Formation.

(1) Each fund manager has a fixed demand as a function of the mispricing signal and its current wealth. These demand functions depend on the maximum leverage allowed by banks as well as the fund's idiosyncratic aggression parameter.
(2) Noise traders demand the asset according to a stochastic process such that without fund managers the asset price would weakly mean revert around the fundamental value of the asset (an Ornstein-Uhlenbeck process). The noise trader's demand is what makes the mispricing signal nonzero in each period.
(3) The price of the asset is set at a level that clears the market given the collection of demand functions submitted by noise traders and fund managers. This is the Walrasian equilibrium.

Wealth Update of Fund Managers.

[2]For example, consider the investor with \$1 who borrows \$5 to buy assets worth \$6. Her leverage ratio is currently 6. If the asset value decreases to \$5.5, the investor still owes \$5 to the bank, so her wealth is now \$0.5. Her leverage ratio increases to 11, which may be out of compliance with the bank.

(1) The new asset price as determined in the price-formation phase induces revised wealth levels for each of the fund managers based on the market value of their holdings.
(2) The fund investors obtain a new datapoint regarding the profitability of each fund manager by observing the wealth gained or lost in this update. They withdraw or deposit capital into funds accordingly.
(3) Banks enforce leverage limits on funds. Funds that exceed leverage limits are subject to a ***margin call***, requiring they change their position in the asset to comply with the limit. Note that the violation of leverage limits can be triggered by a change in asset price, by the movement of capital by fund investors, or some combination.

2.4 Basic Definitions

We define the key variables describing the state of a fund h at time t.

(1) $D_h(t)$ is the amount of the asset that the fund holds at t. It may be positive, meaning the fund owns a positive amount of the asset, or negative, indicating a short position.
(2) $M_h(t)$ is the cash position of the fund. The cash balance is changed each period based on purchases or sales of the asset. A negative $M_h(t)$ indicates a debt position.
(3) The wealth of a fund is defined by

$$W_h(t) \equiv D_h(t)p(t) + M_h(t).$$

where recall that $p(t)$ is market price of the asset. All nondefaulted funds have $W_h(t) > 0$. This entails in particular that a short asset position is always accompanied by a positive cash position.
(4) The ***leverage*** taken by each firm is defined as

$$\lambda_h(t) \equiv \begin{cases} D_h(t)p(t)/W_h(t) & \text{if } D_h(t) \geq 0 \text{ (long)} \\ M_h(t)/W_h(t) & \text{if } D_h(t) < 0 \text{ (short)} \end{cases}$$

Recalling that $W_h(t)$ within a period is constant and positive, and therefore the numerator is always positive, $\lambda_h(t) \in [0, \infty)$. It can in principle be made arbitrarily large by taking an investment position of sufficient magnitude, although due to leverage restrictions the funds are constrained in the positions they can take. Note that leverage is ill defined for $W_h(t) \leq 0$.

These definitions allow for a fund to have ***short*** and ***long*** positions on an asset. For a given wealth, a fund with a long position has a positive value of asset holdings $D_h(t)p(t)$ with cash $M_h(t)$ unrestricted. A common scenario is negative $M_h(t)$, meaning the fund has taken on debt to finance their long position. This necessarily makes $D_h(t)p(t) > W_h(t)$. Thus any fund indebted to the bank must have $\lambda_h(t) \geq 1$.

On the other hand, a fund with a short position owes future shares to its counterparty ($D_h(t) < 0$) but holds the cash it obtained from the sale of these future shares ($M_h(t) > 0$). If the price of the asset $p(t)$ increases, the wealth of a fund that is long on the asset goes up while the wealth of a fund that is short goes down. The opposite occurs if $p(t)$ decreases.

2.5 Regulatory Environments

In the somewhat misnamed ***unregulated environment***, $\lambda_h(t)$ is constrained to be less than a parameter $\lambda_{\max}$ for all h. The ***Basel environment*** adaptively selects maximum leverage $\lambda_{\max}^{\sigma(t)}$ between periods based on price volatility $\sigma(t)$. $\lambda_{\max}^{\sigma(t)}$ is calculated at the beginning of every timestep

t according to the formula

$$\lambda_{\max}^{\sigma(t)} = \min\{\lambda_{\max}, \max\{1, \frac{\sigma_b}{\sigma(t)}\}\}, \tag{1}$$

where $\sigma_b = 0.0118$ is a set benchmark level of volatility, and $\sigma(t)$ is measured as the average volatility of the log asset price in the previous 10 periods. Before 10 periods are available, all price data is used. Thus, maximum leverage requirements are adjusted downwards in periods of high volatility and are allowed to reach $\lambda_{\max}$ when volatility is low. In the unregulated case, $\lambda_{\max}$ is still a hard limit on leverage but it does not adapt to market conditions.

2.6 Fund Demand

Leverage limits effectively constrain the maximum and minimum demand for each fund manager. Individually, each fund manager h with aggression parameter β_h has a demand $D_h(t)$ of the following form, at time t:

$$D_h(t) \equiv \begin{cases} (1-\lambda_{\max}^{\sigma(t)})W_h(t-1)/p(t) & m(t) \le (1-\lambda_{\max})/\beta_h \\ \lambda_{\max}^{\sigma(t)} W_h(t-1)/p(t) & m(t) > \lambda_{\max}/\beta_h \\ \beta_h m(t) W_h(t-1)/p(t) & \text{otherwise} \end{cases}$$

Here the price $p(t)$ at time t is the free variable and all other quantities are fixed. The fundamental value is set at $V = 1$ and $W_h(t-1)$ denotes the total wealth accumulated by h in the last period. In the original study [Poledna et al., 2014], the aggression parameter β_h is fixed to be $h \times 5$ where $h \in \{1, \ldots, 10\}$ is the index of the fund, of which there are ten in total. In our strategic analysis we allow the funds to choose the β_h's, but for now they are fixed. Notice that in the lower and upper regions of price, demand does not depend on β_h. In particular, demand is fixed in these regions. This comes from the fact that funds have hit their leverage limit and cannot borrow further to pursue investment opportunities. An example of the demand function for two funds with different β_h is shown in Figure 2.

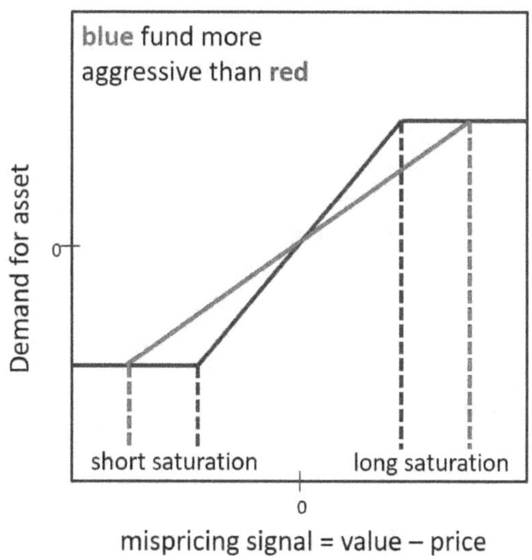

Fig. 2. Demand as a function of mispricing. The mispricing values beyond short saturation and long saturation on either side result in no additional demand for the asset because leverage limits have been reached.

2.7 Market Clearing Price

Every period, prices are used to coordinate asset allocation. Each fund submits their demand function truthfully and an equilibrium is found after the noise traders generate stochastic demand. Each period gets its own independent price. The only thing that transfers information between periods is the wealth that each fund ends up holding.

Given the demand functions of all funds as well as the noise trader demand $C(t)$, prices are formed via the market clearing condition

$$\sum_h D_h(t) = N - C(t), \tag{2}$$

where $C(t)$ is generated by

$$\log C_n(t) = \rho \log C_n(t-1) + \sigma_n \chi(t) + (1-\rho)\log(N).$$

The noise parameter σ_n is set to 0.035 and $\chi(t)$ is an i.i.d. standard Gaussian draw. Parameter ρ is set to 0.99, representing extremely weak mean reversion. This is the Ornstein-Uhlenbeck process, a standard model in finance for asset price dynamics.

We set $N = 10^9$. Equation (2) is a piecewise linear function of $p(t)$ which can be solved using standard methods.

2.8 Wealth Update

Using the $p(t)$ (recall it is embedded in the demand functions $D_h(t)$) obtained as solution to (2), the wealth of each fund $W_h(t)$ can now be updated. Assume for now that $D_h(t-1)$ is positive, that is, fund h takes a long position. There are three possible sources of wealth change in the model: market value of assets, interest payments, and equity flows.

The increase in asset value for each fund is simply $D_h(t-1)[p(t) - p(t-1)]$, and reflects the return on an investment made in the previous period. This is the fund's profit or loss.

In general, funds finance their investment opportunities using debt from the bank. If the amount of cash $M_h(t) = W_h(t) - D_h(t)p(t)$ is negative, then the fund has borrowed from the bank to buy $D_h(t)$ shares of the asset. In this case the fund pays a fixed interest rate $S = 0.015\%$. After paying interest, the fund's total available assets for withdrawal is now

$$M_h^*(t) = D_h(t-1)p(t) + M_h(t-1)(1+S).$$

The other source for changes in wealth is withdrawals or deposits made by fund investors. These make their decisions based on recent performance of each fund. Fund investors examine each fund's rate of return (estimated using an exponential moving average) $r_h(t)$ and withdraw/deposit an amount $F_h(t)$ as follows:

$$F_h(t) = \max\{-1, b(r_h(t) - r_b)\} \max\{0, M_h^*(t)\},$$

where the benchmark return r_b is 0.003 and b, controlling how strongly fund investors react to historical performance, is set at 0.15. The overall motion equation for wealth is then

$$W_h(t) = W_h(t-1) + D_h(t-1)[p(t) - p(t-1)] + F_h(t) + M_h(t-1)(1+S).$$

Analogously, for a short position we have

$$M_h^*(t) = D_h(t-1)p(t) + M_h(t-1) + D_h(t-1)S,$$
$$W_h(t) = W_h(t-1) + D_h(t-1)[p(t) - p(t-1)] + F_h(t) + D_h(t-1)p(t-1)S.$$

Once all fund wealths are updated, the time step is complete and we go back to price formation.

2.9 Default

Each fund starts with $W_0 = 2 \times 10^6$ in wealth. Default occurs when wealth goes below a critical value $W_e = 2 \times 10^5$. In this case, the fund's wealth, demand, and cash positions become zero for 100 timesteps, after which the fund is resuscitated at the same level of aggression β_h and given W_0 to start operations again.

3 SYSTEMIC RISK EVALUATION

The motivation for using this model is to see what effect regulation can have on the leverage cycle, and how this impacts systemic risk. We first develop an approach for evaluating the effect of regulation when fund managers are given the opportunity to adapt strategically according to changing external conditions. Then we define metrics for measuring systemic risk and perform an experiment measuring the effects of the strategic adaptations on systemic risk.

3.1 Strategic Aggression Behavior

Recall from Section 2.6 that each fund is assigned an aggression level. We call these assignments the ***aggression distribution***. Poledna et al. [2014] assume that the aggression distribution is fixed. This assumption is problematic for several reasons, but fundamentally because it limits the responsiveness of fund behavior to environmental conditions, either of the market or the regulatory system.

We focus on this assumption in particular because the entire model appears to be highly sensitive to the aggression distribution. For example, if all funds have low aggression then leverage will almost never be high enough to induce defaults. As circumstantial evidence for this, in all the experiments described in Section 3.4, no fund at an aggression level of 5 ever defaulted. This may be considered an extreme setting, but it is disturbing that one can generate almost any story one wants by manipulating this fixed assumption. It is far better to derive the aggression distribution from something more fundamental, like strategic choice.

Therefore we treat aggression level as an *endogenous* variable, taking account of the dependence of each fund's payoff on the aggression of other players. That is, we cast the entire scenario as a ***game*** played among funds, where aggression distributions are ***strategy profiles*** and aggression levels are ***strategies***. This allows us to search through the space of possible aggression distributions to find a ***Nash equilibrium*** where no fund can make more profit by changing their aggression level. This approach, notably, leaves each fund's aggression level (and thus demand function) in a given period fixed. Within a given time period we still have perfect information and complete markets, so clearing the asset market still produces a Walrasian equilibrium. The only intertemporal choice funds make is aggression level, which is chosen for all periods simultaneously. Thus our strategic analysis is limited to aggression levels, that is, we do not consider other strategic market behavior.[3] This preserves the spirit of the leverage cycle story for a given equilibrium choice of aggression distribution. We see below that the aggregate effect of equilibrating prices in each period and aggression over all periods has a substantial effect on financial stability.

3.2 Experimental Setup

In our approach we evaluate the introduction of Basel into the model on two dimensions. First, given a particular aggression distribution, we measure the effect of regulatory environment on systemic risk measures. This isolates the effect of Basel on the leverage cycle story given fixed aggression levels. Second, given a particular regulatory environment, we look at the effect of

[3]Since funds are not atomic, there could be room for exercising market power. In our setting we view the market as competitive enough at that level to ignore such options.

changing the distribution of fund aggression levels. This isolates the effect of Basel on the strategic choice of aggression levels while leaving its effect on the leverage cycle constant.

Nash Equilibrium. First, some definitions and implementation details. A *pure profile* is an H-dimensional vector β containing a single aggression level, or **strategy**, for each of H funds. For our study we chose a number of funds $H \in \{10, 21\}$ and a set of 7 possible aggression levels/strategies $\Gamma = \{5, 10, 15, 20, 30, 40, 50\}$. Thus a particular fund's **mixed strategy** is a 7-dimensional vector of positive real numbers summing to 1, corresponding to the probabilities that the fund will pick each of the seven strategies for use over the entire simulation. A mixed strategy D induces a probability distribution over pure profiles. Drawing from Γ using the multinomial distribution specified by D assigns a β_h to each of the H funds.

There are many strategy profiles and we cannot evaluate them all. Our focus is on profiles that are strategically stable. A mixed strategy D^* is stable if no fund has an incentive to deviate from drawing its strategy from D^*. In other words, D^* is a ***mixed strategy symmetric Nash equilibrium*** over fund aggression levels. The problem becomes finding D^* in a computationally feasible way, since the number of profiles increases exponentially with the number of players and strategies. To do this, we first need to define how the game is played and how payoffs are generated.

Payoffs and Game Definition. Each run of the model provides a ready made payoff: the fee earned by each fund. To find this fee, we first run the model for $T = 50,000$ periods using $H \in \{10, 21\}$ funds and a given β vector representing the aggression level for each fund. At the end of the simulation, we annualize into 1000 years containing 50 periods each as before. In each year i starting at periods t, we calculate the average size of fund h, $W_h(i) = \sum_t^{t+50} W_h(t)/50$ as well as the profit $\zeta_h(i) = W_h(t + 50) - W_h(t) - \sum_t^{t+50} F_h(t)$, which is simply the change in wealth net of investor withdrawals and deposits over the course of the year. The fee for year i is then defined as $0.2\zeta_h(i) + 0.02W_h(i)$ and the total fees over the entire simulation for fund h are

$$\sum_{i=1}^{1000} 0.2\zeta_h(i) + 0.02W_h(i).$$

This is the specification used by Poledna et al. [2014], based on standard practice in the financial industry. It captures the common 2-and-20 fee structure, which pays hedge funds 2% of assets under management and 20% of value returned to investors annually. This annualization (1000 years that are each 50 periods long) is done according to the original paper [Poledna et al., 2014], where the model was calibrated to real yearly data. Note that the payoff for a given mixed strategy D depends on whether or not Basel is active as well as $\lambda_{\max}$ and is an average over many 50,000-period simulations where pure profiles β are generated from D.

Environmental Settings. In summary, we can view the model input as choice of regulation R, a particular β vector of strategies representing a pure profile, and parameters $\lambda_{\max}$. The model itself can be viewed as a black box function, mapping to the model output which is a vector of rewards, or fees, for each fund. In reality, remember that we are relying on separate Walrasian equilibria in each of the 50,000 periods to set prices.

Finding the Nash equilibrium distribution $D^*(R, \lambda_{\max})$ of such a system requires searching through input β and evaluating fees until an equilibrium is found. We adopt a heuristic approach, inexhaustively exploring a space of strategy profiles and estimating their payoffs through agent-based simulation. This method goes by the name of ***empirical game-theoretic analysis*** [Wellman, 2016], as it applies standard game-theoretic concepts to a game model derived by empirical means. We use a suite of tools developed by Cassell and Wellman [2013] to automate the simulation and data management. We were able to obtain approximate $D^*(R, \lambda_{\max})$ for $R \in \{Basel, Unregulated\}$ and $\lambda_{\max} \in \{8, 20\}$. These levels of $\lambda_{\max}$ were chosen to reflect a wide range of conditions.

Note that we chose to show results for the same set of strategies Γ as that used by Poledna et al. [2014]. This was mainly for comparability, but we did test lower minimum (down to 1), higher maximum (up to 70), and a finer resolution in between for aggression levels. We found that the results were not qualitatively different. For example, a beta of 1 was not adopted in the mixed strategy equilibrium when added to the reported set of strategies. In all tested cases, Basel encouraged less average aggression in equilibrium.

Empirical Game-Theoretic Analysis. Our empirical game approach imposes two major approximations. First, the set of available strategies Γ is restricted to a modest number of enumerated choices. As noted above, we limit attention to $|\Gamma| = 7$ choices of aggression level. Since the number of strategy profiles is exponential in the number of strategies, we have no choice but to impose such a limit. Second, for the $H = 21$ setting we used a technique called ***deviation preserving reduction*** [Wiedenbeck and Wellman, 2012], which employs aggregation to model the 21-player game in terms of a reduced six-player game.

3.3 Systemic Risk Metrics

Our metrics for systemic risk differ from those provided by Poledna et al. [2014] in one key respect. Rather than focusing on the risk of the most aggressive fund manager, we instead evaluate risk aggregated over all fund managers. The aggregate measure reflects a more direct evaluation of the entire economy. Moreover, as we allow distribution of aggression to vary based on endogenous choices, we need a way to evaluate the riskiness across situations with different maximum aggression levels. This difference is only relevant for measuring probability of default and capital losses.[4]

Probability of Default. To calculate probability of default of a single fund for a single run of the model, we record the years during which a default occurred. Then we divide the number of defaults by the number of years during which default was possible, K_h. $K_h \leq 1000$ because defaulted funds go out of operation for 2 years, or 100 time steps, as specified in Section 2.3. Thus, there are entire years during which default is impossible. Note that there are also years during which default is only partially possible as the fund is still in a defaulted state at the beginning of the year. We choose to exclude these years from K_h as well. The overall probability of default is then

$$\sum_h \#defaults_h/(K_h H).$$

Here, recall that H is the total number of funds.

Capital Losses to Banks. Capital losses are the amount of loss banks suffer when a fund manager defaults. It is defined as the wealth $W_h(t)$ of the defaulting fund at default. This is an important metric for systemic risk because these losses are often paid for through bank bailouts, which detract from social welfare.

Capital losses were measured on an annual basis, in the same way as for probability of default. Yearly capital losses are totaled, then averaged across the number of funds and number of years during which default was possible.

[4]We also calculated the original study's metrics and verified that our implementation matched the results reported by Poledna et al. [2014].

Price Volatility. Price volatility is detrimental to the extent it contributes to financial uncertainty. One of the functions of financial markets is efficient price discovery, and one might hope that in a single asset market where some investors have perfect information about the fundamental value of the asset, this function would be performed well. Price volatility is a good proxy for how well price discovery is performed. Indeed, if we allow $\sum_h D_h(t)$ to be large compared to $C(t)$ for all t, we would expect price volatility to be near zero as the effect of the noise traders is minimized. Price volatility is the average of the annual variances of $p(t)$. This metric does not depend on K_h like the other two, since prices can be formed regardless of the default status of any fund.

3.4 Systemic Risk Results

First we note that in every setting we evaluated, the strategy profile that maximized total fees was for every fund to use $\beta_h = 5$. This is the least aggressive strategy available, and is the most limiting in the range of investment choices available to the fund. The only benefit to playing this strategy is that it mitigates the leverage cycle and may prevent crashes from happening. This is circumstantial evidence that defaults are very harmful not only to banks and investors, but also to the funds themselves. It also provides a basis for believing that strategy profiles with low aggression may be better for systemic risk.

Regulation	numFunds	λ_{max}	5	10	15	20	30	40	50	$\beta_{weighted}$
Unregulated	21	20	35%	4%	0%	0%	0%	0%	60%	32.3
Basel	21	20	40%	12%	6%	0%	0%	0%	42%	25.3
Unregulated	21	8	32%	15%	7%	2%	0%	0%	43%	26.3
Basel	21	8	46%	11%	9%	5%	10%	15%	4%	16.7
Unregulated	10	20	46%	5%	0%	0%	0%	0%	49%	27.4
Basel	10	20	51%	14%	8%	0%	0%	0%	26%	18.4
Unregulated	10	8	40%	21%	8%	0%	0%	0%	31%	20.8
Basel	10	8	53%	18%	7%	1%	11%	10%	0%	13.0

Fig. 3. Mixed-strategy symmetric equilibria for different regulatory regimes and leverage restrictions.

Mixed Strategy Nash Equilibria. We found an approximate mixed strategy Nash equilibrium for each of 8 environmental settings, shown in Figure 3. We also report $\beta_{weighted}$, which is the average value of β_h drawn from each distribution over strategies. Notice that decreasing λ_{max} and imposing Basel both decrease the $\beta_{weighted}$ of the Nash equilibrium. When Basel is imposed, it is no longer as lucrative for funds to be aggressive since they will reach their leverage limits immediately. Decreasing λ_{max} has a similar effect. This strategic response has ramifications on our systemic risk measures.

Interestingly, all equilibria are far from the social optimum. This is because it takes coordination to prevent defaults and maximize profits. Unilaterally playing a less aggressive strategy has positive externalities, namely a lower default rate and crash rate for *all* agents, that are not internalized by fund payoffs.

Systemic Risk under Equilibria. When Basel is imposed on a previously unregulated market, two things happen in equilibrium. First, the mechanics of fund behavior change as their leverage limits become more stringent in volatile periods. Second, funds adapt their aggression to fit the regulation, shifting to less aggresive (on average) Nash equilibria over mixed strategies as in Figure 3. To evaluate these two effects on financial stability, we first select an mixed strategy equilibrium. Next, we take 200 draws from the distribution. Each draw is a valid strategy profile. We calculate the metrics from Section 3.3 on each of these 200 strategy profiles both with and without Basel. The averages are presented in Figure 5 and Figure 4.

↑	Volatility	Setting	
Profile	λ_{max} = 20	Basel	Unregulated
	Basel	0.0222	0.0182
	Unregulated	0.0221	0.018

↑	Volatility	Setting	
Profile	λ_{max} = 8	Basel	Unregulated
	Basel	0.0338	0.0205
	Unregulated	0.0341	0.0208

↑	Default Probability	Setting	
Profile	λ_{max} = 20	Basel	Unregulated
	Basel	3.67%	2.99%
	Unregulated	5.02%	3.73%

↓	Default Probability	Setting	
Profile	λ_{max} = 8	Basel	Unregulated
	Basel	1.43%	2.20%
	Unregulated	3.11%	3.55%

↓	Capital Loss	Setting	
Profile	λ_{max} = 20	Basel	Unregulated
	Basel	2.66E+06	3.42E+06
	Unregulated	3.21E+06	3.88E+06

↓	Capital Loss	Setting	
Profile	λ_{max} = 8	Basel	Unregulated
	Basel	5.45E+05	2.13E+06
	Unregulated	9.15E+05	2.76E+06

↓	Fees	Setting	
Profile	λ_{max} = 20	Basel	Unregulated
	Basel	1.80E+05	1.90E+05
	Unregulated	1.78E+05	1.87E+05

↓	Fees	Setting	
Profile	λ_{max} = 8	Basel	Unregulated
	Basel	1.43E+05	2.03E+05
	Unregulated	1.37E+05	1.93E+05

Fig. 4. Three systemic risk metrics evaluated at two levels of $\lambda_{\max}$ for 21 funds. Analagous table for 10 funds in Figure 5. Within a table, each row fixes an equilibrium mixed strategy and applies a different regulatory setting, each column fixes a regulatory setting and switches to a different mixed strategy equilibrium. Down arrows signify that the metric decreased when Basel was applied in the study by Poledna et al. [2014] while up arrows signify that the metric increased. Blue lettering means changing that property results in a metric change that agrees with Poledna et al. [2014] while red means changing that property results in a metric change that goes against their finding. Black means that there was no significant change in the variable. Example: For $\lambda_{\max} = 20$'s default probability table, up arrow means that Poledna et al. [2014] found Basel increased default probability. Fixing profiles and changing settings agrees with this finding, indicating successful replication, while fixing setting and changing profiles goes against this finding.

Each table shows two-dimensional variation across regulatory environments. Along rows, we keep the mixed strategy equilibrium fixed and change the environment. Along columns, we keep the regulatory setting fixed and change the equilibrium. For every metric and setting we tested, shifting between Basel and unregulated environments under a fixed equilibrium resulted in the same effect on the metric as that reported by Poledna et al. [2014]. This should not be surprising since with a fixed aggression distribution, we are essentially repeating their experiment with slightly different aggression settings. This is confirmation that we have done a successful replication.

Something interesting happens when we examine these tables along columns. This is equivalent to fixing the regulatory environment and switching between mixed strategy equilibria. We have already seen that the average β_h for Basel equilibria is substantially lower. It turns out that less aggressive funds increase financial stability by decreasing the probability of default and bank capital losses. For example, at $\lambda_{\max} = 20$, even though Basel makes default more likely for a fixed aggression distribution, the shift towards the Basel equilibrium counteracts and reverses this effect for both $H = 10$ and $H = 21$.

↑	Volatility	Setting	
Profile	$\lambda_{max} = 20$	Basel	Unregulated
	Basel	0.0232	0.0188
	Unregulated	0.0229	0.0188

↑	Volatility	Setting	
Profile	$\lambda_{max} = 8$	Basel	Unregulated
	Basel	0.0317	0.0205
	Unregulated	0.0313	0.0219

↑	Default Probability	Setting	
Profile	$\lambda_{max} = 20$	Basel	Unregulated
	Basel	2.24%	2.11%
	Unregulated	4.17%	3.65%

↓	Default Probability	Setting	
Profile	$\lambda_{max} = 8$	Basel	Unregulated
	Basel	0.52%	1.35%
	Unregulated	1.23%	2.46%

↓	Capital Loss	Setting	
Profile	$\lambda_{max} = 20$	Basel	Unregulated
	Basel	1.43E+06	2.24E+06
	Unregulated	1.91E+06	2.79E+06

↓	Capital Loss	Setting	
Profile	$\lambda_{max} = 8$	Basel	Unregulated
	Basel	3.09E+05	1.41E+06
	Unregulated	3.52E+05	1.56E+06

---	Fees	Setting	
Profile	$\lambda_{max} = 20$	Basel	Unregulated
	Basel	4.25E+05	4.34E+05
	Unregulated	4.28E+05	4.26E+05

↓	Fees	Setting	
Profile	$\lambda_{max} = 8$	Basel	Unregulated
	Basel	3.48E+05	4.63E+05
	Unregulated	3.28E+05	4.34E+05

Fig. 5. 10 funds. See Figure 4 for key.

In aggregate (that is, moving from the Basel/Basel cell to the Unregulated/Unregulated one), the story has changed. Basel decreases probability of default in every measured case. Capital losses, which were already decreasing in the original study, decrease even further. Price volatility still increases with Basel, since the shift in equilibrium did not have an effect. Fees are lower in the Basel setting, but by less than was predicted by Poledna et al. [2014]. Shifting between equilibria increases fees in most cases to cancel out some of the fee loss found in the original study.

3.5 Discussion

So what explains Basel's performance in decreasing systemic risk? We break this question into two parts. First, how does Basel allow less aggressive funds to thrive compared to aggressive ones? And second, why do less aggressive funds allow for better financial stability?

Consider this model with a single fund manager. Suppose she is currently operating in the unregulated environment with $\lambda_{max} = 20$ and she hears that Basel will soon be implemented. This can only lower her leverage limit. We posit that even without any strategic interactions with other funds, she will be inclined to lower her aggression levels. A fund gets more fees by generating higher returns, and higher returns are gotten by taking high leverage when there are large mispricing signals. When leverage limits are high, an aggressive fund will just snap up all the mispriced assets at and profit off of all of them. But when leverage limits become more stringent under Basel, too much aggression will quickly lead to paralysis due to hitting the leverage limit. In contrast, less aggression will preserve some investment capacity for the truly large mispricing signals, generating a better return.

Now consider two funds who each know that Basel is coming. If they both decide to be aggressive, they can mitigate more price movements, reduce price volatility, and operate as if Basel was never implemented. However, if fund A decides to shirk its price enforcing duties by being less aggressive, Basel will restrict maximum leverage since price volatility will rise. This doesn't affect fund A much since it doesn't take much leverage anyway. In fact, in all of our simulations, the funds playing strategy $\beta_h \in \{5, 10\}$ never defaulted a single time. But the leverage limit does affect the more aggressive fund B, and will cause it to default eventually. When this happens, A will have the entire market to itself. When this strategic advantage is coupled with the fact that less aggressive funds stand to make more profit regardless of what other funds do, it is easy to see why Basel induces funds to be less aggressive.

Now why does the shift to a less aggressive set of funds result in better default rates, bank losses, and fees while not having any effect on price volatility? Note that here we are only giving intuition for the effect of the shift in aggression distribution, not the aggregate effect of Basel.

Less aggressive funds simply do not take much leverage before the mispricing signal disappears randomly. Thus, they never get to the point where a price shock can cause them to lose all their wealth. Again we quote the result that not a single low-aggression fund defaulted in our experiments. Thus, default rates decrease when funds are less aggressive.

Funds that are aggressive under equilibrium that end up defaulting also cause less capital loss to banks. Recall the feedback cycle that occurs with Basel. First, aggressive firms accumulate all the wealth in good times since Basel hasn't kicked in yet. Then, a price shock happens that forces the aggressive funds to wind down their positions to comply with collateral requirements. This procyclical unwinding deepens the initial shock, increasing volatility and forcing Basel to make leverage limits more stringent. When there are many less aggressive funds, none of this volatility can be absorbed and the Basel requirements will get extremely stringent. Thus, the funds that end up defaulting will have been trying to reach a lower leverage limit. This reduces their size when they default.

Fees are slightly helped by less aggression for the same reason funds decided to be less aggressive in the first place. And price volatility is definitely hurt in normal times by less aggressive funds, but the decrease in default rate reflects a lower incidence of financial crashes, which helps price volatility. It seems these two effects cancel out.

4 CONCLUSION

When evaluating the effect of financial regulation on markets, we should always be aware that agents in this arena are highly sophisticated and resourceful. It is a good bet that any possible path to profit will eventually be explored. So when economic models make fixed assumptions on behavior, we should always be on guard for the day these assumptions start break down. To become more robust, models can endogenize important behavioral assumptions so that agent response to the environment is as realistic as possible.

We argue for endogenizing the aggression level of funds in an agent based leverage cycle model used to evaluate Basel regulations. We then propose a strategic analysis that endogenizes an important fixed assumption, the aggression distribution. After making appropriate approximations to make finding equilibria feasible, we perform a series of experiments to measure the aggregate effect of Basel on financial stability under our new equilibrium concept. Our findings suggest that the pessimism surrounding Basel's exacerbation of leverage cycles may be overstated. We find that irrecoverable losses on the part of banks and defaulted funds are reduced substantially under Basel. Although fund profits fall, our new equilibrium concept lessens the fall compared to the one without endogenous aggression. Volatility remains a problem, as funds still cannot prevent day to day fluctuations in price effectively.

There is still much work to be done, both in evaluating Basel and in building richer economic models. For the former, the obvious question is how to improve on Basel so that we get its benefits (less aggressive agents on average) without its costs (agents constrained from taking volatility out of prices). There has been some work on this, but not under endogenous aggression levels [Aymanns and Farmer, 2015, Poledna et al., 2015, Poledna and Thurner, 2016]. There are also many other directions where computer science techniques can aid in understanding Basel. For example, using network science and graph theory to model financial networks could help us understand how contagion works and how regulation affects it.

The way we solve for equilibria in agent based models can also be studied further. For example, how close does clearing the market in each period independently come to preserving Pareto efficiency in a multi-period setting? How does imperfect information affect regarding noise traders play into this? In addition, in our analysis we fixed aggression to be constant throughout the entire simulation. This was mainly to not disturb the market clearing process within each time step. But perhaps there is a way to combine the market clearing mechanism and the strategic aggression adjustments so that they interact with each other. This would make for a less interpretable model but may be more realistic for certain markets.

ACKNOWLEDGMENTS

We are grateful to Sebastian Poledna and Stefan Thurner for correspondence that assisted us in replicating their results. Thanks to anonymous reviewers for constructive suggestions about the presentation. This work was supported in part by the National Science Foundation and the Office of Financial Research under NSF grant IIS-1440360.

REFERENCES

Christoph Aymanns and J. Doyne Farmer. 2015. The dynamics of the leverage cycle. *Journal of Economic Dynamics and Control* 50 (2015), 155–179.

Ben S. Bernanke, Mark Gertler, and Simon Gilchrist. 1999. The financial accelerator in a quantitative business cycle framework. In *Handbook of Macroeconomics*, J. B. Taylor and M. Woodford (Eds.). Vol. 1. Elsevier, 1341–1393.

Richard Bookstaber, Mark Paddrik, and Brian Tivnan. 2017. An agent-based model for financial vulnerability. *Journal of Economic Interaction and Coordination* (2017).

Ben-Alexander Cassell and Michael P. Wellman. 2013. EGTAOnline: An experiment manager for simulation-based game studies. In *Multi-Agent Based Simulation XIII*. Lecture Notes in Artificial Intelligence, Vol. 7838. 85–100.

Financial Crisis Inquiry Commission. 2011. *The financial crisis inquiry report: Final report of the national commission on the causes of the financial and economic crisis in the United States.* PublicAffairs.

John Geanakoplos. 2003. Liquidity, default, and crashes: Endogenous contracts in general equilibrium. In *Advances in Economics and Econometrics: Theory and Applications, Eighth World Congress*, Vol. 2. Cambridge University Press, 170–205.

John Geanakoplos. 2010. The leverage cycle. In *NBER Macroeconomics Annual*. Vol. 24. University of Chicago Press, 1–65.

John Geanakoplos, Robert Axtell, J. Doyne Farmer, Peter Howitt, Benjamin Conlee, Jonathan Goldstein, Matthew Hendrey, Nathan M. Palmer, and Chun-Yi Yang. 2012. Getting at systemic risk via an agent-based model of the housing market. *American Economic Review* 102, 3 (2012), 53–58.

Paul M. Healy and Krishna G. Palepu. 2001. Information asymmetry, corporate disclosure, and the capital markets: A review of the empirical disclosure literature. *Journal of Accounting and Economics* 31, 1 (2001), 405–440.

Victoria Ivashina and David Scharfstein. 2010. Bank lending during the financial crisis of 2008. *Journal of Financial Economics* 97, 3 (2010), 319–338.

Sebastian Poledna, José Luis Molina-Borboa, Serafín Martínez-Jaramillo, Marco van der Leij, and Stefan Thurner. 2015. The multi-layer network nature of systemic risk and its implications for the costs of financial crises. *Journal of Financial Stability* 20 (2015), 70–81.

Sebastian Poledna and Stefan Thurner. 2016. Elimination of systemic risk in financial networks by means of a systemic risk transaction tax. *Quantitative Finance* 16, 10 (2016), 1599–1613.

Sebastian Poledna, Stefan Thurner, J. Doyne Farmer, and John Geanakoplos. 2014. Leverage-induced systemic risk under Basle II and other credit risk policies. *Journal of Banking and Finance* 42 (2014), 199–212.

Michael R. Roberts and Amir Sufi. 2009. Renegotiation of financial contracts: Evidence from private credit agreements. *Journal of Financial Economics* 93, 2 (2009), 159–184.

Leslie Shaffer. 2016. Debt is holding back the global economic recovery, say central bankers Dudley, Rajan and Zeti. *CNBC* (Aug. 2016).

Robert J. Shiller. 2015. *Irrational Exuberance.* Princeton University Press.

Stefan Thurner, J. Doyne Farmer, and John Geanakoplos. 2012. Leverage causes fat tails and clustered volatility. *Quantitative Finance* 12, 5 (2012), 695–707.

Michael P. Wellman. 2016. Putting the agent in agent-based modeling. *Autonomous Agents and Multi-Agent Systems* 30 (2016), 1175–1189.

Bryce Wiedenbeck and Michael P. Wellman. 2012. Scaling simulation-based game analysis through deviation-preserving reduction. In *11th International Conference on Autonomous Agents and Multiagent Systems*. 931–938.

Empirical Mechanism Design for Optimizing Clearing Interval in Frequent Call Markets

ERIK BRINKMAN, University of Michigan
MICHAEL P. WELLMAN, University of Michigan

Several recent authors have advocated for financial markets to move from continuous clearing to discrete or batched clearing, as a way to defeat the latency arms race: the never-ending quest for small advantages in time to access markets. How frequently should such a modern batch auction clear? We conduct a systematic simulation-based investigation on the relationship between clearing frequency and metrics of market quality, such as allocative efficiency, comparing the performance of discrete and continuous auction mechanisms under empirical equilibrium behavior of all participating traders. In effect we perform empirical mechanism design on frequent batch auctions. We find that in a wide array of environments, equilibrium efficiency is improved for small positive intervals but falls off dramatically when there are too few opportunities to trade. The result is a large range of batch frequencies that are near optimally efficient; this range is wider in thick markets.

CCS Concepts: • **Theory of computation** → *Algorithmic game theory*;

Additional Key Words and Phrases: call market, computational finance, agent-based simulation

1 INTRODUCTION

The defining feature of a *continuous-time* market mechanism is that orders trade as soon as they match. That is, the moment a buy order arrives that is compatible with an incumbent sell order (or vice versa), the trade executes and the two orders are cleared from the market. If two buyers submit orders compatible with an existing sell order, then whichever arrives to the market first is executed. A consequence of the continuous-time property is that there is no lower bound on the speed differential that could be pivotal in deciding the trade. In consequence, financial markets adopting the standard continuous-time mechanism—termed the *continuous double auction* (CDA)—foster a *latency arms race*, where traders may obtain significant benefit by achieving small access-time advantages over their counterparts.

The apparent first-order cost of the latency arms race has led several to advocate switching from continuous to discrete-time clearing mechanisms [3, 22, 23, 28]. In a discrete-time, or *call market*, orders are accumulated (or *batched*) over specified time intervals, with matches determined only at the end of each interval.

The call market mechanism has been known and in substantial use for a long time; in fact typical financial markets open each day with a call market. What is new is the opportunity to run call markets with short clearing intervals, say on the order of one second. The Chicago Stock

EC'17, June 26–30, 2017, Cambridge, Massachusetts, USA. ACM ISBN 978-1-4503-4527-9/17/06...$15.00.

DOI: http://dx.doi.org/10.1145/3033274.3085153

Exchange recently launched a similar mechanism called a SNAP^{SM} auction,[1] which is roughly a temporary half-second call that occurs in an otherwise standard CDA market. The clearing interval in frequent call markets is intended to be long enough to undermine most of the benefit of tiny speed advantages, yet short enough to avoid imposing serious delays on economic activity. The literature discussing discrete-time markets uses a number of different names, including frequent batch auction [3], periodic auction [19], and frequent call market [28]; we simply refer to them as call markets, with the understanding that the clearing interval will be relatively short.

There are many ways a call market could trigger a clear, such as by volume or time, deterministically or randomly. Random choice of clear time has been proposed as a way to prevent a form of *sniping*, where a fast trader with an edge on information or market access can snipe a stale order. In a call market, this applies only right at the end of the clearing interval, say for a fraction δ of that interval. Randomization prevents such deterministic sniping, but allows the fast trader to snipe with a δ probability of success for the entire time. Thus randomization provides no protection benefit in expectation. It also poses the problem of trusting the mechanism to honestly randomize, which is not easy to audit.

For both of these reasons we focus on deterministic clearing, and the question of how long the interval should be. A specific choice of around one second, which has often been suggested as a reasonable interval, is quite arbitrary. As market designers, we would prefer a principled basis for deciding exactly how much time should elapse between market clears. We investigate this question by examining how the quality of the market—measured as allocative market efficiency—is affected by the clearing interval when traders are strategic and utility maximizing, playing according to an approximate form of Nash equilibrium.

Our model posits finitely many agents trading a single security in a single market, where agents respond to asymmetric private information as they repeatedly enter the market to buy or sell, conditioning on market observations. This model allows us to investigate how the presence of adverse selection, and market parameters that affect it, contribute to the optimal selection of a clearing interval. We do not model agents' response to public information or other important aspects of modern financial markets such as opportunities to invest in better information or faster market access.

We expect the duration of the clearing interval to have certain qualitative effects on a call market. If the clearing interval is sufficiently short, then a frequent call market should behave almost identically to a CDA.[2] Frequent clearing reduces transaction times at the expense of making hasty matching decisions and thereby potentially inefficient trades. If the clearing interval is sufficiently long, then the behavior approaches a *one-shot double auction* [20, 31]. Infrequent clearing produces more efficient trades at the expense of delayed execution. Waiting for the next clear can be costly, for example when other market actions serially depend on the present one. At some point, the efficiency benefit of longer clears will be outweighed by this time cost. The question then becomes, is there some clearing interval where the benefit of more efficient trades outweighs the loss of immediacy, or is the most efficient call market the one that behaves like a CDA?

Our market model is too complex to analyze using traditional means, so we restrict agents to a finite set of strategies, and use simulation in conjunction with game-theoretic analysis [32] to find approximate equilibria in a CDA market and in call markets with a discrete set of clearing intervals. In effect, we perform *empirical mechanism design* [25] with the goal of maximizing allocative

[1] http://www.chx.com/snap/snap-auction-cycle.html

[2] Even at infinite frequency, the behavior is not exactly identical, because the markets price differently. CDAs price at the incumbent order price, whereas call markets price at the midpoint of the clearing range.

efficiency on a much richer model than would be possible to analyze with standard economic analysis.

Our model indicates that frequent batch auctions do not always improve market efficiency, but in markets with low adverse selection, lengthening the clearing interval produces greater efficiency until a point where agent impatience dominates and efficiency falls sharply. We also find that the benefit of switching to a frequent call market is significantly improved in thick markets. These conclusions suggest practical considerations that should be taken when implementing such a mechanism.

2 RELATED WORK

Wah and Wellman [28] and Budish et al. [3] were among the first to propose call markets as a design response to the negative effects of latency arbitrage. Both papers demonstrate that continuous clearing creates arbitrage opportunities that arise at imperceptible frequencies, and that exploiting them reduces market liquidity and efficiency. Budish et al. [3] also roughly calculate what batch interval should be sufficient to prevent the latency arms races for various calibrations of their model. Their results yield a lower bound of one millisecond to one second depending on assumptions about the information arrival process and the magnitude of speed improvement available to high-frequency traders (HFTs). Other studies have also found benefits to frequent call markets. Schnitzlein [21] performed a laboratory experiment comparing a call markets and CDAs and found that the call market was more liquid and better for noise traders, while not harming price efficiency. Baldauf and Mollner [1] compared CDAs, frequent call markets, and delayed CDAs[3] in a model with costly research. Both frequent call markets and delayed CDAs performed at the Pareto frontier of price discovery and spread, but traditional CDAs did not. Madhavan [19] considered a model where risk-averse traders start with some initial endowment of both a risky asset and cash and found that, in equilibrium, call markets offered greater price efficiency than CDAs. Follow-up studies have investigated how frequent call markets could coexist with traditional CDAs [18, 27], have outlined practical considerations necessary to implement a frequent call market compliant with current regulations [2], and present some tangential evidence of a smooth tradeoff between immediacy and batching [29]. All these have relegated the question of optimizing call frequency to future work.

In response, several recent papers have developed stylized analytical models that propose definitions of an optimal clearing interval. Fricke and Gerig [10] studied a financial market model that is very similar to the model used in Garbade and Silber [12]. Like the earlier paper, the authors attempted to determine the optimal clearing frequency based on a version of *liquidity risk*. The authors then calibrated their model with aggregate current market data and estimated that the optimal clearing interval for current S&P 500 securities is somewhere between one and three seconds. Du and Zhu [8] solve for Nash equilibrium in linear strategies of a model with a divisible good and shocks to both common and private information. In this model, faster auctions allow agents to more quickly respond to information, but also cause them to be more aggressive with their demand schedule. A key result is that when information arrives via a Poisson process, then optimal clearing interval can be much longer than the average arrival rate of information, except when there are few traders or a large amount of adverse selection. Their approach is similar to ours, but several aspects of the model, including divisible units, private value shocks, and maintained order books, make it difficult to directly compare results. Haas and Zoican [15] propose a model in which they measure market liquidity as a function of clearing interval in equilibrium. Their market model has two types of participants: HFTs and liquidity agents, where HFTs respond to random information and the liquidity traders are impatient and respond to random private value shocks.

[3] CDAs with delayed submission but immediate cancels.

Their model parallels Budish et al. [3] until the clearing interval gets long enough, at which point traders' impatience gives out and longer clearing intervals cease to improve liquidity. The authors find that liquidity may still be worse in these call markets than in traditional CDAs. Each of these models presents a slightly different view on the role and effect of frequent call markets, which is necessary given the complexity of the modern financial system.

3 MARKET MODEL

Our experiments employ a parameterized financial market model, related to the model in Wah et al. [27]. This model features many of the same qualitative phenomena found in today's financial markets, including adverse selection, multi-unit holdings, and agents with the ability to buy and sell. We model a single security traded in either a CDA or a call market. Agents submit limit orders representing the maximum (minimum) price an agent is willing to buy (sell) a single unit. The market reveals price quotes reflecting the best outstanding orders after the most recent clear; other bids in the market are not visible to agents, and no new information is provided between clears. During a market clear, the mechanism determines the range of prices that would match supply and demand, and executes all compatible trades at a price in this range. If there is an imbalance of supply and demand at the clearing price (due to multiple units with the same price), the ties are broken first by orders that arrived in earlier clears, and then in a random manner. CDAs and call markets differ only in when they clear, and how they set transaction prices. CDAs clear after every market interaction at the price of the incumbent order; call markets clear at discrete intervals at the midpoint of the feasible price range. In this model, prices and times are fine-grained but discrete, and run until a finite horizon T.

3.1 Valuation Model

Each agent has an individual valuation for the security composed of private and common components. The common component is represented as a stochastic *fundamental value*, which determines the common utility of held positions at the end of time. Let f_t denote the fundamental value for the security at time t. The fundamental is generated by a mean-reverting stochastic process:

$$f_t = r\bar{f} + (1-r)f_{t-1} + s_t, \qquad f_0 = \bar{f}, \qquad s_t \sim \mathcal{N}\left(0, \sigma_s^2\right). \tag{1}$$

s_t is a random Gaussian shock at time t. Reversion rate $r \in (0,1)$ specifies the tendency by which the fundamental reverts back to the mean $\bar{f}$; $r = 1$ would correspond to a fundamental process of i.i.d. Gaussian draws around the fundamental mean, while $r = 0$ corresponds to a martingale Gaussian fundamental.

The time-varying fundamental presents agents with an issue of *adverse selection*—trading with agents who have better information—as standing orders reflect outdated information from the time submitted. If the fundamental shifts significantly, subsequently arriving agents are more likely to transact with orders on the side opposite the direction of change. That is, a positive price shock will tend to trigger transactions with stale sell orders, and negative price shocks with stale buys. Strategic agents who leave orders in the order book must shade to account for these events. The degree of adverse selection in our model depends on the fundamental shock variance σ_s^2 and the degree of mean reversion r. With lower mean reversion or higher shock variance the expected shift in the final fundamental estimate after a jump in the fundamental is greater, exposing agents to higher adverse selection.

The private component of an agent's valuation represents its individual motivation for trading this security, for example needs for consumption or investment, and portfolio management. Differences across agents on these motivations are the sole basis for gains in trade, and naturally arise from heterogeneous preferences, time in life cycle, risk attitudes, differences in hedging needs, or other reasons. An agent's private value is represented as a vector $\boldsymbol{\theta}$ containing the agent-specific marginal utility for acquiring one more unit, relative to the fundamental value—similar to the model of Goettler et al. [14]. The vector has length $2q_{\max}$, where $q_{\max} > 0$ is the maximum number of units the agent can be long or short at any time. Element $\theta_q, q \in [-q_{\max}, q_{\max}) \cap \mathbb{Z}$ is the incremental benefit, over the fundamental, to the agent for gaining one unit of the security given current position q, where positive q indicates a long position. We generate an agent's private value vector by sampling $2q_{\max}$ values from $\mathcal{N}\left(0, \sigma_{pv}^2\right)$, sorting the values in descending order, and setting each θ_q respectively. This process ensures agents' valuations exhibit diminishing marginal returns.

At the end of the simulation, an agent's total surplus is the combination of their cash holdings p (from transaction prices), their final position q, and the value of the fundamental at the end of trading f_T.

$$\text{agent surplus} = p + qf_T + \begin{cases} \sum_{i=0}^{q-1} \theta_i & \text{if } q > 0 \\ 0 & \text{if } q = 0 \\ \sum_{i=q}^{-1} -\theta_i & \text{if } q < 0 \end{cases}$$

Since the cash and fundamental terms cancel out in exchange, the total surplus achieved is a result of the differences in transacting agents' private values.

3.2 Trading Strategies

There is an extensive literature on autonomous bidding strategies for CDAs [7, 11, 31]. We consider trading strategies that are variants of the *Zero Intelligence* (ZI) family [13]. The ZI strategy is exceedingly simple, but often employed in agent-based study of financial markets [4, 17], including recent AI studies of market making [5, 30], because they have been found to generate realistic patterns of market behavior [9]. Though ZI agent instances are typically outperformed by more sophisticated alternatives [24, 26], by using game-theoretic selection to set strategy parameters we can produce highly competitive behavior for a given market environment [34]. In rough effect, game-theoretic equilibration serves the parameter-tuning function accomplished through adaptation and evolutionary search in the *ZI Plus* strategies of [6].

In our market model, agents get information about the fundamental according to an independent geometric process with probability λ of observing the fundamental (f_t) at any specific time. Upon observing the fundamental, agents observe the price quote, withdraw any outstanding orders, and have the opportunity to submit new ones. If multiple agents receive information at the same time, they act in a random order. Agents are assigned on each arrival to either buy or sell, with equal probability, and accordingly submit an order to buy or sell a single unit. Agents may trade any number of times, as long as their net positions do not exceed their maximum position ($q_{\max}$) (either long or short).

An agent assesses its expected valuation at the time of market entry t, using an estimate $\hat{f}_t$ of the terminal fundamental f_T. The estimate is based on the current fundamental, f_t, adjusted to account for mean reversion:

$$\hat{f}_t = (1 - \rho)\bar{f} + \rho f_t, \qquad \rho = (1 - r)^{T-t}.$$

The agent then submits a bid *shaded* from this estimate by a random offset—the amount of expected surplus it demands from the trade. The amount of shading is drawn uniformly from the range $[U_{\min}, U_{\max}]$.

The restrictions that agents are assigned to buy or sell randomly, shade in a uniform interval, and shade from the same distribution at every arrival are consistent with the original definition of ZI [13]. Given such limitations, the ZI equilibria cannot be considered true equilibria of the unrestricted game. Nevertheless, evidence for the efficacy of the ZI strategy set, particularly with parameters tuned by equilibration, suggests that it provides a reasonable basis for evaluating market design choices.

We extend the traditional ZI strategy by introducing a threshold parameter $\eta \in [0, 1]$, whereby if the agent could achieve a fraction η of its requested surplus at the current price quote, it would simply take that quote rather than posting a limit order to the book. Setting $\eta = 1$ is equivalent to the strategy without employing the threshold. Thus, an agent's strategic choice is determined by three parameters: U_{min}, U_{max}, and η.

Since the ZI family of trading strategies was conceived for CDA markets, it stands to reason that similarly effective call market strategies would have a different parameterization. To our knowledge, there is no prior literature analyzing strategies for periodic call markets. We propose a simple extension to the ZI class of strategies that allows agents to condition their shading on their location in the clearing interval. Our extension provides the first step in exploring effective call market strategies. An agent that arrives close to a clear has better information about the fundamental than the other agents with orders in the market, and as a result, faces lower adverse-selection. Instead of being parameterized by only U_{min} and U_{max}, this strategy class has four shading parameters $U_{\text{min}\,i}$, $U_{\text{min}\,f}$, $U_{\text{max}\,i}$, and $U_{\text{max}\,f}$, where i and f stand for *initial* and *final* respectively. When an agent arrives, it linearly interpolates its effective U_{min} and U_{max} based on its position in the interval. That is, if an agent arrives α fraction of the way through the interval, then its demanded surplus is drawn uniformly from the range $[(1-\alpha)U_{\text{min}\,i} + \alpha U_{\text{min}\,f}, (1-\alpha)U_{\text{max}\,i} + \alpha U_{\text{max}\,f}]$.

3.3 Environments

Characterizing all possible model parameter settings under all possible agent strategies is infeasible and would be largely uninteresting. Many possible parameter settings are degenerate—they provide no opportunities to trade, or insufficient information to trade safely, or fail to present strategic tradeoffs—for example, as fundamental shock variance diminishes, adverse selection vanishes. We obtain an understanding of how different aspects of a market affect optimal mechanism design by analyzing many discrete parameter settings. We refer to each distinct point in parameter space as an *environment*.

Each environment we study shares a base set of parameter settings. These fixed parameters either have an unimportant effect on the simulation, or can be appropriately scaled by settings of the parameters we do vary. The fundamental mean $\bar{f}$ is 10^9 so that boundary effects at zero never happen in practice. The private value variance σ_{pv}^2 is 5×10^6 and the maximum position q_{max} is 10 so that the importance of public and private value components are loosely balanced. With $q_{\text{max}} = 10$, there is a 0.0002% chance that an agent's optimal position is 10, thus agents rarely reach their maximum position. The arrival rate λ is 5×10^{-3}, which gives agents either 5 or 10 opportunities to trade on average.[4] The remaining parameters are dimensions that we vary in our analysis: the number of agents (market thickness), the simulation length (number of trade opportunities), and the fundamental parameters (mean reversion, shock variance). We explore three different numbers of agents: 25, 58, and 238 respectively referred to as the thin $\downarrow N$, medium $-N$, or thick market $\uparrow N$. We investigate two different simulation lengths: 5000 and 10000 respectively short $\downarrow T$ or long $\uparrow T$. Finally, we consider two different levels of adverse selection: 2×10^{-2} mean reversion with 5×10^6 fundamental shock variance and 2×10^{-4} mean reversion with 5×10^4 fundamental shock variance, respectively $\downarrow A$ or $\uparrow A$. The fundamental parameters were chosen such that the distribution of the

[4]See settings of T in the next paragraph.

final fundamental is roughly equivalent[5] in the long time horizon setting, but the variance of the difference in final fundamental estimates before and after the initial time step—a loose measure of the benefit for obtaining recent information—are markedly different, roughly 0 in $\downarrow A$ but over 900 in $\uparrow A$. An environment is the combination of these three parameter settings, so describe an environment in shorthand as the combination of the associated symbols. For instance, $\uparrow N \downarrow T \downarrow A$ is the environment with 238 agents and time horizon 5000, with a fundamental that has mean reversion of 0.02 and shock variance of 5×10^6.

The ZI strategy space defined in Section 3.2 is continuous, not necessarily compact, and not differentiable with respect to utility. We discretize the strategy space in order to make these games amenable to normal-form analysis. We want a set of discrete strategies such that equilibria in the discrete game have low regret in the continuous game. How to guarantee this property is unknown, but we nevertheless select what we consider a reasonable set of discrete strategies by starting with a set of feasible strategies, and then adding best responses to initial equilibria from a significantly larger set. This technique is similar to that described by Jordan et al. [16]. The strategies we ultimately consider for equilibrium analysis are listed in Table 1.

Table 1. Strategies considered for equilibrium analysis. See Section 3.2 for parameter details. The first strategy is *truth-telling*, and the last strategy is effectively *fill-or-kill* where agents demand between 29 and 30 surplus.

U_{min}	0	0	0	0	0	0	0	0	125	250	500	500	1000	29000
U_{max}	0	125	250	500	1000	1500	2500	2500	1000	500	1000	1000	2000	30000
η	1	1	1	1	1	0.6	0.4	1	0.4	1	0.4	1	0.4	0.001

In order to test the effect of tailoring strategies to the call mechanism, we also found equilibria in environments where agents have access to a select number of call strategies. In the same way we chose a discrete set of standard strategies, we chose this set of call market strategies by looking for best responses from existing equilibria. Table 2 lists the three strategies agents had additional access to when finding equilibria with call strategies. All of these strategies exhibit decreasing levels of shading as the clear approaches, that is, as agents trade in a call market with better information, they shade less.

4 ANALYSIS

In order to understand how clearing interval affects market efficiency, we first demonstrate the effects when agents are non-strategic—specifically, when agents are truth-telling. We measure efficiency by fraction of optimal social welfare: average total trader surplus divided by the expected maximum possible trader surplus for the corresponding environment. This appropriately gives more weight to sampled instances with higher achievable surplus.

When the clearing interval is sufficiently small, we expect efficiency—as well as most other statistics—to be almost identical for call and CDA markets. The market types still will not be identical due to their different pricing schemes, and the discreteness of time. When the clearing interval is sufficiently large, we expect efficiency to degrade, because traders lack sufficient opportunities to trade. In other words, longer clearing intervals increase the friction due to agents' impatience for trading. We also expect that at some point between almost-continuous clearing and a single clear, the efficiency of the call market will exceed CDA efficiency. The optimal clearing interval would ideally balance improvement in matching from aggregation over time, and provision to traders of ample opportunities to trade. In the words of Haas and Zoican [15], when the clearing interval is

[5] $\downarrow A$ has 1.26×10^8 variance versus 1.23×10^8 in $\uparrow A$.

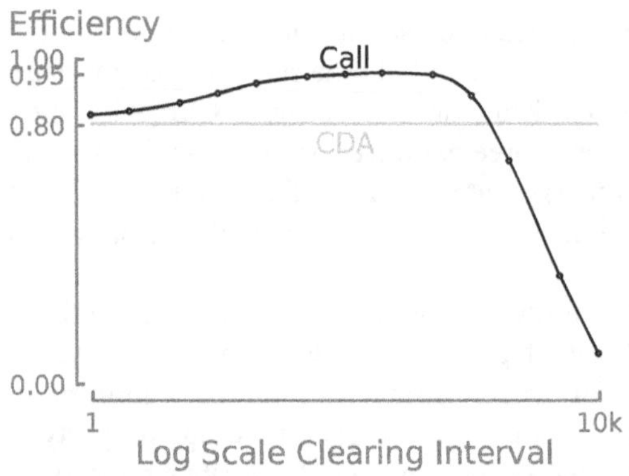

Fig. 1. Call market efficiency in the $-N{\uparrow}T{\downarrow}A$ environment as a function of clearing interval when agents are truthful. In this environment, there is a large region of clearing intervals where call market efficiency is near optimal, and significantly higher than CDA market efficiency. Call market efficiency is slightly higher even when clearing every time step because multiple agents can arrive in a single time step and still benefit from batching.

Table 2. Additional strategies considered for equilibrium analysis with call market strategies. See Section 3.2 for parameter details.

$U_{\min i}$	250	29000	39000
$U_{\max i}$	1250	30000	40000
$U_{\min f}$	0	20000	30000
$U_{\max f}$	1000	21000	31000
η	0.4	0.001	0.001

short, the friction due to trader impatience is minimized, when the clearing interval is long, the friction due to imperfect information is minimized, and ideally at some intermediate interval, the two are balanced.

We simulated environment $-N{\uparrow}T{\downarrow}A$ ten thousand times for each clearing interval when agents submit truthful bids. Figure 1 shows the results of that simulation, which matches our expectations. The call market is generally more efficient than the CDA, as the clearing interval increases, the agents see the allocation benefit of batched clearing, until the point that infrequent trading opportunities dominate the benefit of batching, and there is a sharp decline in efficiency.

Agents are unlikely to behave truthfully in real markets. Evaluating a market effect on all combinations of strategy choices and environments would be infeasible; moreover, the various strategic contexts are not equally relevant. Given the high level of competition between trading firms and the significant financial incentives, we are most interested in effects produced when agents are being *rational*. In other words, we wish to evaluate the impact *in Nash equilibrium*, where the agents are adopting the best strategies, given the setting and other-agent strategy selections.

Since the model we investigate is too complex to support analytical solutions, we compute empirical equilibria using a simulation-based process, known as *empirical game-theoretic analysis* (EGTA) [32]. EGTA employs systematic simulation of strategy profiles to sample from payoff distributions in a specified environment. The simulated payoff data is used to induce a normal-form game model, from which we identify symmetric mixed-strategy equilibria with respect to the strategies in Table 1. A symmetric mixed-strategy equilibrium is an equilibrium where every agent simultaneously and independently chooses a strategy from the same distribution over all possible strategies prior to play. However, direct simulation of all payoff data is prohibitive given that the number of profiles in the largest games we analyze is over 10^{21}. We employ two techniques to reduce the profile space necessary to identify at least one approximate equilibrium. First, we employ an aggregation technique known as *deviation-preserving reduction* [33] to approximate our games with many players as a reduced game with only four players. This reduction heuristic preserves regret of symmetric pure strategies, but only approximates regret of symmetric mixed strategies. The approximation typically works well when the payoff impact of single other agents is small. Second, we use a best-response search to attempt to confirm low-support equilibria, before sampling profiles for large-support equilibria.

Using these techniques we computed approximate empirical equilibria in the environments discussed in Section 3.3. Figure 2 contains plots of clearing interval versus equilibrium efficiency for the six environments with low adverse selection. Since environments may have multiple equilibria, we plot a range of efficiencies for all of the equilibria found at a given clearing interval. In each CDA environment, we found exactly one equilibrium. These methods are not perfect, and occasionally produce *artifacts*—for instance, the dip in Figure 2d—which may be attributable to discretizations imposed in modeling. Despite the few artifacts, the general trends are unmistakable. The trend in efficiency closely matches what was expected and what we see in Figure 1, but to a lesser extent.

The decrease in equilibrium efficiency improvement of call markets relative to truth-telling is likely due in part to the surprising equilibrium efficiency of CDAs [35]. As clearing interval increases, call markets go from being quite similar to CDAs to being significantly more efficient. In most of the environments the optimal call market mechanism reduces inefficiency by half when compared to the CDA. This trend is stronger as the number of agents increases, which we attribute partially to effective batching that does not happen when the markets are thinner. This suggests that frequent call markets would actually benefit thick markets more than thin, matching the result of Du and Zhu [8]. It also suggests that given an ideal market setting, the specific choice of clearing interval is not important to improve efficiency conditioned on it being short enough to not interfere with the patience of investors.

There are other measures of market quality besides allocative efficiency, and the nature of our model allows us to compute arbitrary market statistics in equilibrium. Price discovery is a general measure of how closely the market represents the true price of a security; we calculate it as the *root-mean-square deviation* (RMSD) of the transaction prices relative to the unbiased estimate of the final fundamental at the time of transaction. A market with *worse* price discovery would have a *larger* RMSD. There is a fundamental tension between common and private information aggregation: as the call interval gets longer, orders in the market represent more outdated fundamental information and may be less accurate, but as the call interval gets longer more orders are present in each clear, and so more private information is aggregated in each transaction. Figure 3 presents the median price discovery RMSD for every low adverse-selection environment. CDAs exhibit far better price discovery in every environment except for thick markets, and as for efficiency, when the clearing interval is long, price discovery significantly degrades. The price discovery improvement in thick markets likely arises because batching large numbers of orders helps to reduce the noise caused by private valuations, while still ensuring that orders represent recent information.

A common measure of liquidity is the market *spread*. The spread is the difference between the highest outstanding buy order and the lowest outstanding sell order. The size of the spread roughly corresponds to the transaction cost for impatient traders, as they must meet the quote to trade immediately. Since our model does not contain a dealer or market maker, there are times when spread is not defined, and we therefore report the median spread over all time. Increasing clearing interval should reduce the spread as agents have more protection from mispriced orders, since transactions happen at the midpoint of all orders instead of the incumbent price, and are therefore willing to price closer to their beliefs. This trend is present in Figure 4, where we show the equilibrium median spread for every low adverse-selection environment. The spread decreases

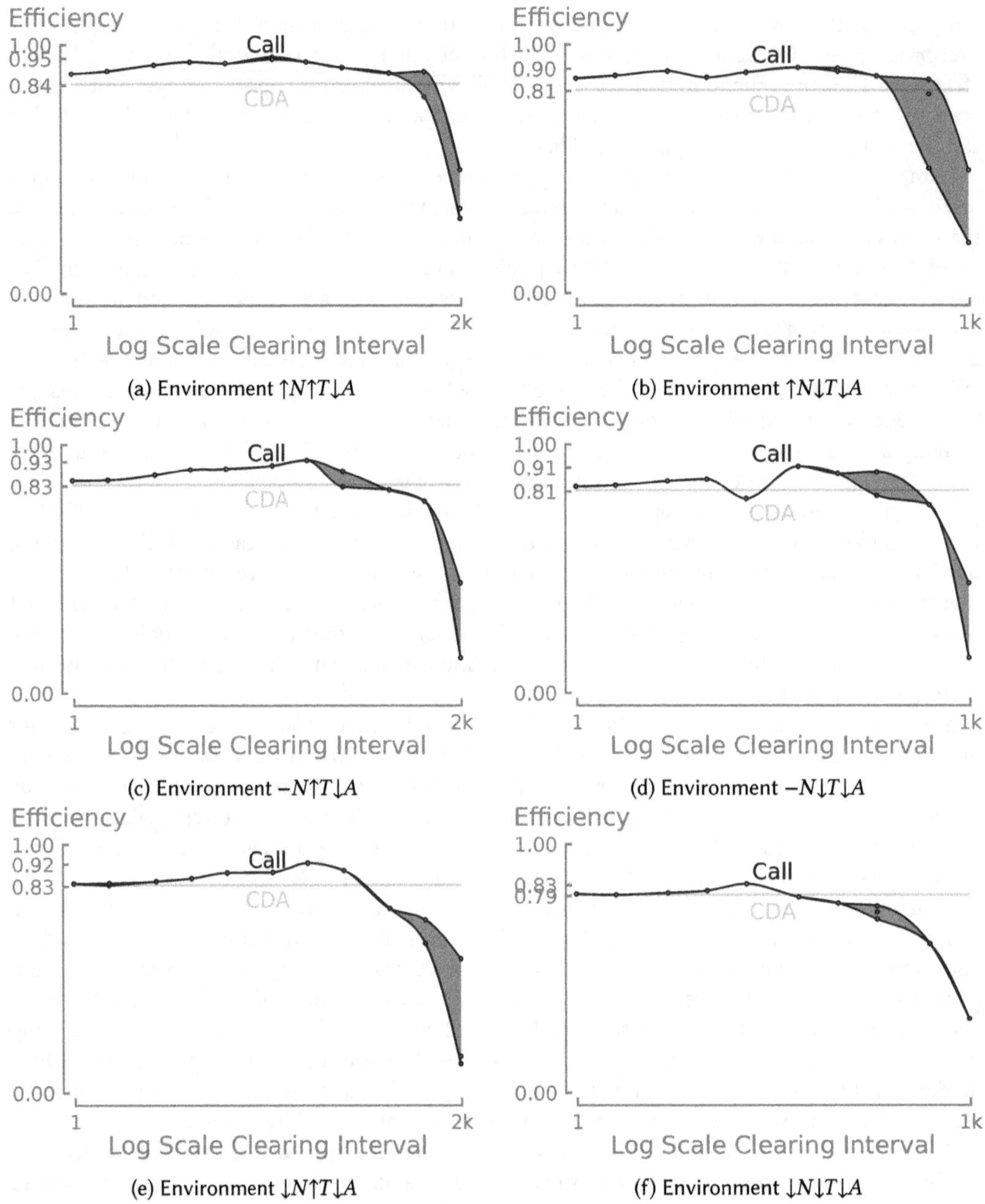

Fig. 2. Equilibrium efficiency as a function of clearing interval in six environments with low adverse selection. Rows from the top represent environments with 238, 58, and 25 agents respectively. The left column has a time horizon of 10000, while the right has a time horizon of 5000. Games where we found multiple equilibria have their efficiency represented as a range. These plots show the expected tradeoff between the benefits of batching and harm of limited execution opportunities. As the markets become thicker, the range of clearing intervals that are near optimal significantly increases.

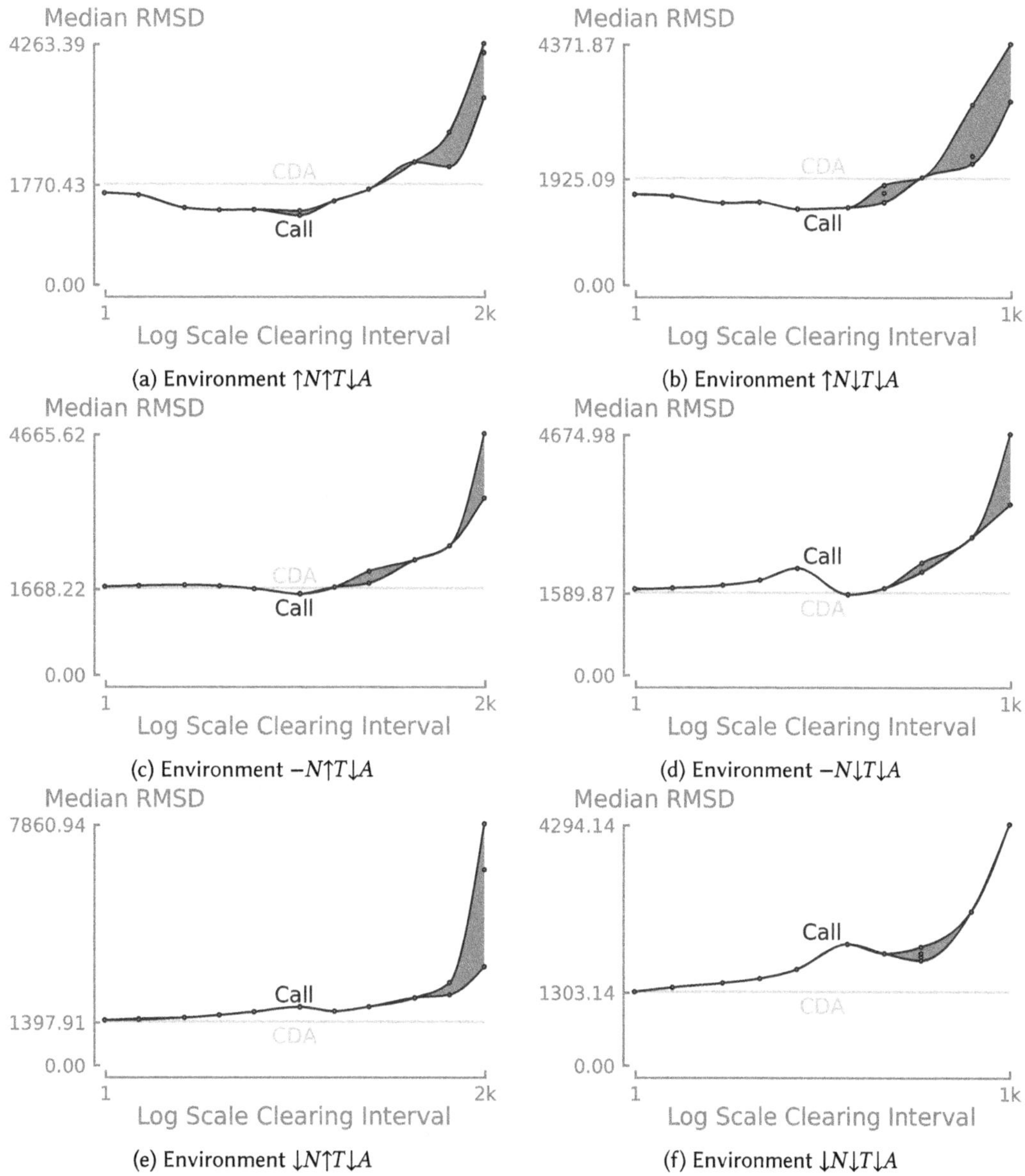

(a) Environment $\uparrow N \uparrow T \downarrow A$

(b) Environment $\uparrow N \downarrow T \downarrow A$

(c) Environment $-N \uparrow T \downarrow A$

(d) Environment $-N \downarrow T \downarrow A$

(e) Environment $\downarrow N \uparrow T \downarrow A$

(f) Environment $\downarrow N \downarrow T \downarrow A$

Fig. 3. Equilibrium price discovery as a function of clearing interval in low adverse-selection environments. Rows from the top represent environments with 238, 58, and 25 agents respectively. The left column has a time horizon of 10000, while the right has a time horizon of 5000. Higher RMSD indicates worse price discovery. Call markets improve price discovery only in thick markets with relatively short clearing intervals.

as the clearing interval increases, but the benefit disappears as the clearing interval becomes prohibitively long.

Our results indicate that long clearing intervals can result in low efficiency, poor price discovery, and large spreads, and the transition to this regime of poor market performance can be very fast.

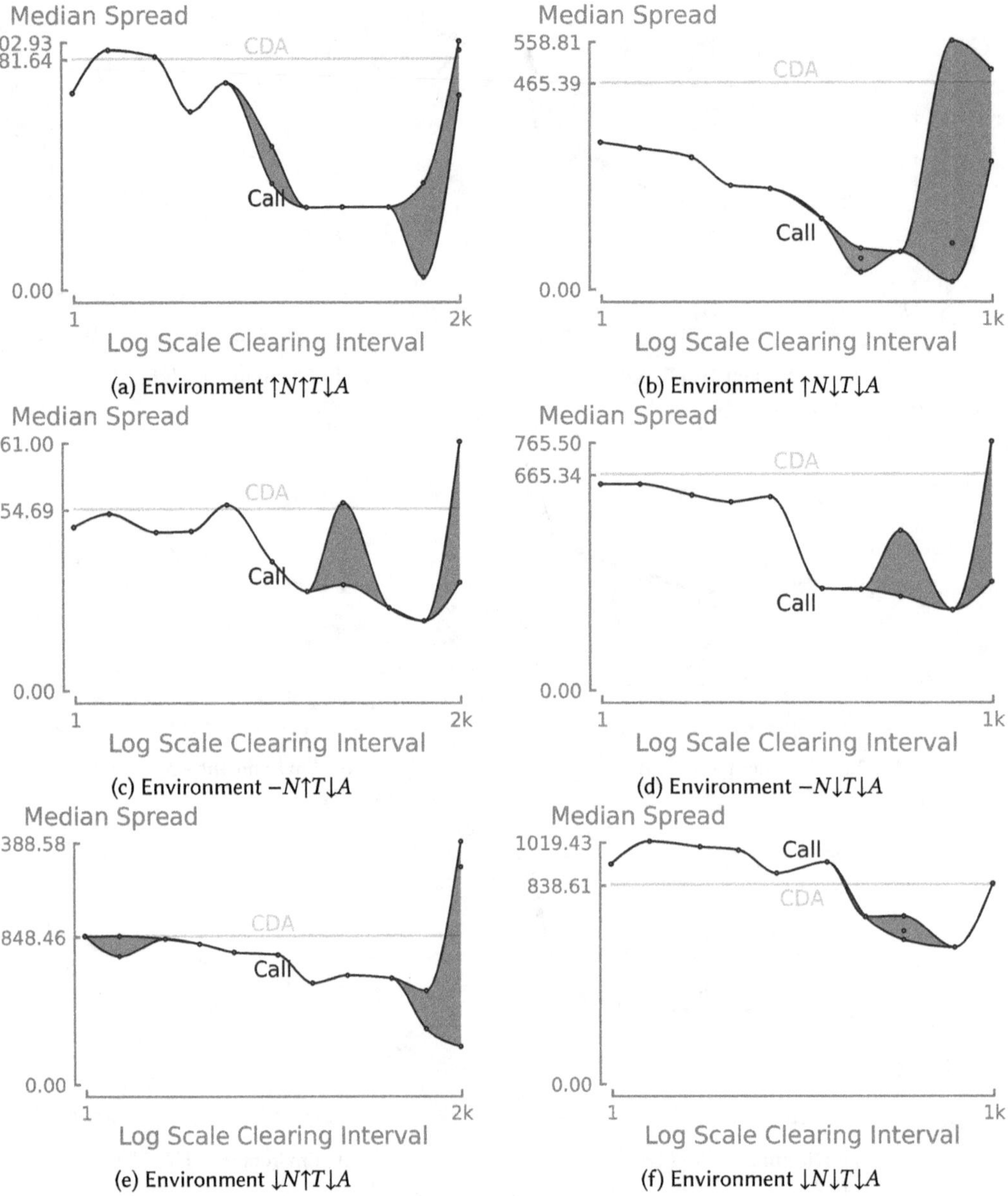

(a) Environment $\uparrow N \uparrow T \downarrow A$

(b) Environment $\uparrow N \downarrow T \downarrow A$

(c) Environment $-N \uparrow T \downarrow A$

(d) Environment $-N \downarrow T \downarrow A$

(e) Environment $\downarrow N \uparrow T \downarrow A$

(f) Environment $\downarrow N \downarrow T \downarrow A$

Fig. 4. Equilibrium median spreads as a function of clearing interval in low adverse-selection environments. Rows from the top are for environments with 238, 58, and 25 agents respectively; columns from the left represent time horizons of 10000 and 5000 respectively. Following intuition, longer clearing intervals decrease the spread; however, excessively long clearing intervals increase the spread.

Our results also indicate that appropriate clearing interval selection in thick markets with low adverse selection can significantly improve performance over CDAs. However, these equilibria contain only strategies intended for use in CDAs. How robust are these results when agents can condition their strategy on their location in the clearing interval? Figure 5 shows the difference

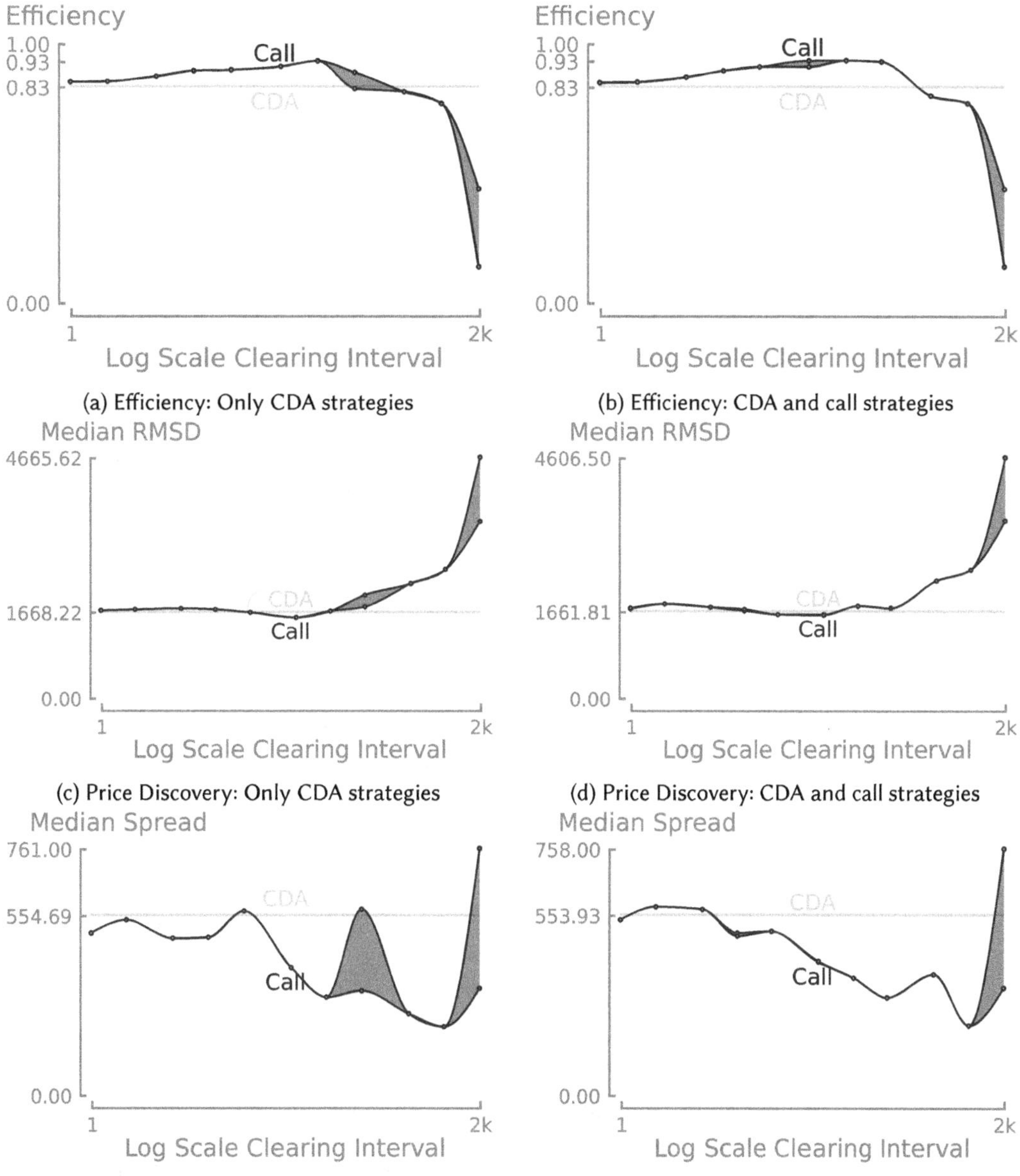

(a) Efficiency: Only CDA strategies

(b) Efficiency: CDA and call strategies

(c) Price Discovery: Only CDA strategies

(d) Price Discovery: CDA and call strategies

(e) Spread: Only CDA strategies

(f) Spread: CDA and call strategies

Fig. 5. How equilibrium statistics change when agents have access to call market specific strategies in environment $-N\uparrow T\downarrow A$. The left column contains equilibria when agents have access only to CDA strategies; the right column contains equilibria when agents additionally have access to call market specific strategies. Call market strategies have negligible effect on the qualitative trends in market quality.

between equilibrium market statistics when call market agents have access to call market strategies. 82% of equilibria and 90% of games had equilibria where at least one call market strategy was in support, which indicates that it can be effective to develop customized strategies for call markets.

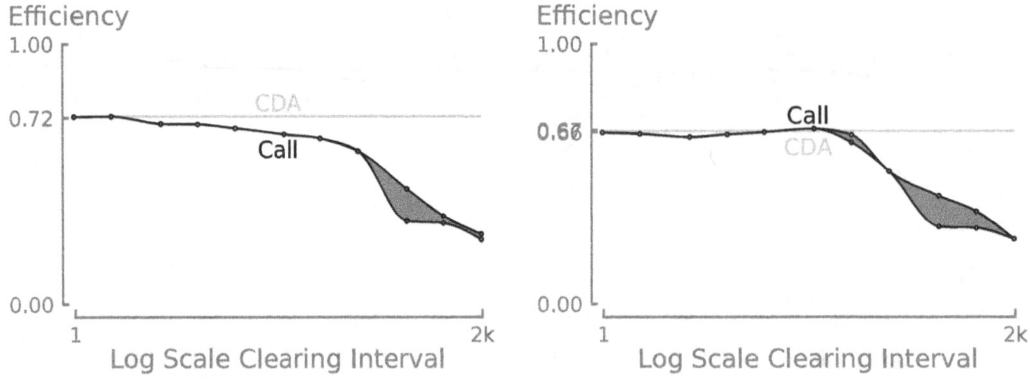

(a) Environment $-N{\uparrow}T{\uparrow}A$ (b) Environment ${\uparrow}N{\uparrow}T{\uparrow}A$

Fig. 6. Equilibrium efficiencies in two environments with high adverse selection. Even in a thick market (Figure b), short clearing intervals are on par with a CDA, but never surpass it.

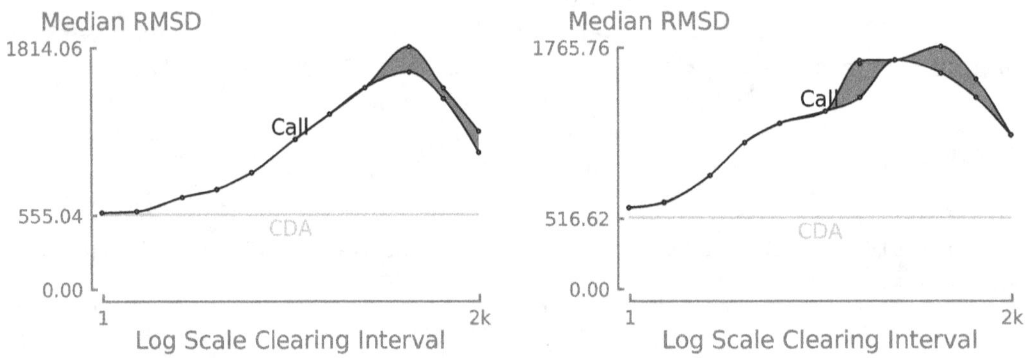

(a) Environment $-N{\uparrow}T{\uparrow}A$ (b) Environment ${\uparrow}N{\uparrow}T{\uparrow}A$

Fig. 7. Equilibrium price discovery with high adverse selection. Unlike with low adverse selection, price discovery in call markets with high adverse selection is consistently worse.

However, despite incorporating some call market strategies, qualitative market performance in equilibrium is essentially the same.

Our analysis to this point has considered only environments with low adverse-selection. Figures 6–8 show the same set of experiments for varying numbers of agents with a long time horizon and large adverse selection. We find that in high adverse-selection environments, the optimally efficient clearing interval approaches a CDA. Even when the number of agents is increased, short clearing intervals match, but do not exceed CDA efficiency. Thick markets do not restore price discovery as they do with low adverse selection, but the spread is generally tighter.

5 CONCLUSION

We employed empirical mechanism design to investigate the effects of clearing interval on market statistics. Given the significant difference between equilibrium trading behavior in a call market and in a CDA, we believe analyses of strategic interaction, like the results presented here, are

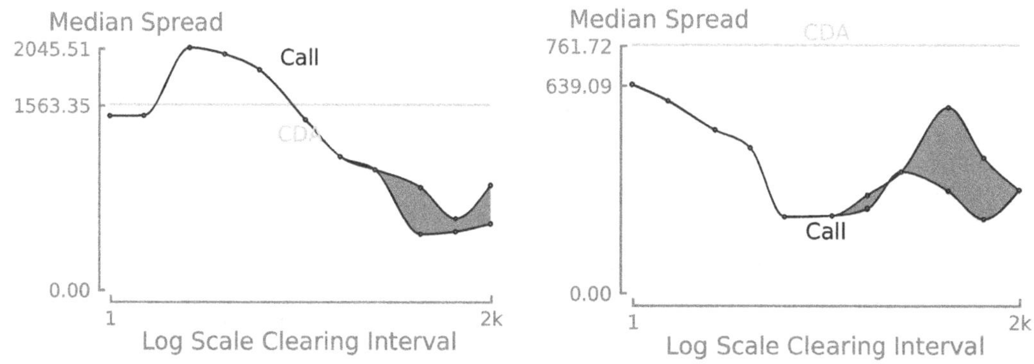

(a) Environment $-N\uparrow T\uparrow A$

(b) Environment $\uparrow N\uparrow T\uparrow A$

Fig. 8. Equilibrium spread with high adverse selection. Spreads are reduced at large clearing intervals, even with high adverse selection.

necessary to characterize expected behavior in call markets where little historic data exists. Our analysis has produced a number of unique insights.

In a first exploration of agent strategies geared toward call markets, we find evidence suggesting that even simple consideration of the call interval can provide gains. However, while these strategies appear in equilibrium, they do not qualitatively change equilibrium market quality in our experiments. Are the lack of qualitative differences due simply to the first-order nature of the call strategies, or does effective call market trading not need a significantly different strategy space? We leave this question for future work.

More to the point, there are a number of practical revelations about frequent call markets that we demonstrate. Environments with high adverse selection may be served more efficiently by CDAs than by frequent call markets. Otherwise, call markets tend to have some clearing interval region where they operate more efficiently, and this region is significantly wider in thick markets. Thick markets also universally saw improved spreads and price discovery than their thinner counterparts. These results roughly parallel those of Du and Zhu [8], who also found long optimal clearing intervals in thick markets with low adverse selection. Our results suggest that contrary to what might seem natural, the markets best suited to frequent call markets are thick with low adverse selection.

More generally, our methodology adapts readily to other metrics of interest, other market designs, and other agent behaviors, and provides a unique perspective on complex problems where models will always be stylized. For example, analyzing the effectiveness of random or volume-based clearing and other market-quality metrics can be easily factored into this model.

ACKNOWLEDGMENTS

Aaron Pollack contributed to the implementation and exploration of call-market strategies. Anonymous referees provided helpful suggestions for improving our exposition. This work was supported in part by grants from the National Science Foundation (IIS-1421391) and Future of Life Institute.

REFERENCES

[1] Markus Baldauf and Joshua Mollner. 2015. *High-Frequency Trade and Market Performance.* Technical Report. University of British Columbia and Northwestern University. Available at SSRN, 2674767.

[2] Eric Budish, Peter Cramton, and John Shim. 2014. Implementation Details for Frequent Batch Auctions: Slowing Down Markets to the Blink of an Eye. *American Economic Review* 104, 5 (2014), 418–424.

[3] Eric Budish, Peter Cramton, and John Shim. 2015. The High-Frequency Trading Arms Race: Frequent Batch Auctions as a Market Design Response. *Quarterly Journal of Economics* 130, 4 (2015), 1547–1621.

[4] Timothy N. Cason and Daniel Friedman. 1996. Price Formation in Double Auction Markets. *Journal of Economic Dynamics and Control* 20, 8 (1996), 1307–1337.

[5] Mithun Chakraborty, Sanmay Das, and Justin Peabody. 2015. Price Evolution in a Continuous Double Auction Prediction Market with a Scoring-Rule Based Market Maker. In *29th AAAI Conference on Artificial Intelligence.* 835–841.

[6] Dave Cliff. 2009. ZIP60: Further explorations in the evolutionary design of trader agents and online auction-market mechanisms. *IEEE Transactions on Evolutionary Computation* 13 (2009), 3–18.

[7] Rajarshi Das, James E. Hanson, Jeffrey O. Kephart, and Gerald Tesauro. 2001. Agent-Human Interactions in the Continuous Double Auction. In *Seventeenth International Joint Conference on Artificial Intelligence.* 1169–1178.

[8] Songzi Du and Haoxiang Zhu. 2017. What is the Optimal Trading Frequency in Financial Markets? *Review of Economic Studies* (2017).

[9] J. Doyne Farmer, Paolo Patelli, and Ilija I. Zovko. 2005. The Predictive Power of Zero Intelligence in Financial Markets. *Proceedings of the US National Academy of Sciences* 102 (2005), 2254–2259.

[10] Daniel Fricke and Austin Gerig. 2016. *Too Fast or Too Slow? Determining the Optimal Speed of Financial Markets.* Technical Report. Available at SSRN, 2363114.

[11] Daniel Friedman and John Rust (Eds.). 1993. *The Double Auction Market: Institutions, Theories, and Evidence.* Addison-Wesley.

[12] Kenneth D. Garbade and William L. Silber. 1979. Structural Organization of Secondary Markets: Clearing Frequency, Dealer Activity and Liquidity Risk. *Journal of Finance* 34, 3 (1979), 577–593.

[13] Dhananjay K. Gode and Shyam Sunder. 1993. Allocative Efficiency of Markets with Zero-intelligence Traders: Market as a Partial Substitute for Individual Rationality. *Journal of Political Economy* (1993), 119–137.

[14] Ronald L. Goettler, Christine A. Parlour, and Uday Rajan. 2009. Informed Traders and Limit Order Markets. *Journal of Financial Economics* 93, 1 (2009), 67–87.

[15] Marlene Haas and Marius A. Zoican. 2016. Beyond the Frequency Wall: Speed and Liquidity on Batch Auction Markets. *Paris Finance Meeting EUROFIDAI* (2016).

[16] Patrick R. Jordan, L. Julian Schvartzman, and Michael P. Wellman. 2010. Strategy Exploration in Empirical Games. In *9th International Conference on Autonomous Agents and Multiagent Systems.* 1131–1138.

[17] Blake LeBaron. 2006. Agent-Based Computational Finance. In *Handbook of Agent-Based Computational Economics,* Leigh Tesfatsion and Kenneth L. Judd (Eds.). Elsevier.

[18] Zhuoshu Li and Sanmay Das. 2016. An Agent-Based Model of Competition between Financial Exchanges: Can Frequent Call Mechanisms Drive Trade Away from CDAs?. In *15th International Conference on Autonomous Agents and Multi-Agent Systems.* 50–58.

[19] Ananth Madhavan. 1992. Trading mechanisms in securities markets. *Journal of Finance* 47, 2 (1992), 607–641.

[20] Mark A. Satterthwaite and Steven R. Williams. 1989. Bilateral Trade with the Sealed Bid k-Double Auction: Existence and Efficiency. *Journal of Economic Theory* 48, 1 (1989), 107–133.

[21] Charles R. Schnitzlein. 1996. Call and Continuous trading Mechanisms under Asymmetric Information: An Experimental Investigation. *Journal of Finance* 51, 2 (1996), 613–636.

[22] Robert A. Schwartz and Liuren Wu. 2013. Equity Trading in the Fast Lane: The Staccato Alternative. *Journal of Portfolio Management* 39 (2013), 3–6. Issue 3.

[23] Chris Sparrow. 2012. The Failure of Continuous Markets. *Journal of Trading* 7, 2 (2012), 44–47.

[24] Gerald Tesauro and Rajarshi Das. 2001. High-Performance Bidding Agents for the Continuous Double Auction. In *Third ACM Conference on Electronic Commerce.* 855–872.

[25] Yevgeniy Vorobeychik, Christopher Kiekintveld, and Michael P. Wellman. 2006. Empirical Mechanism Design: Methods, with Application to a Supply Chain Scenario. In *Seventh ACM Conference on Electronic Commerce.* 306–315.

[26] Perukrishnen Vytelingum, Dave Cliff, and Nicholas R. Jennings. 2008. Strategic Bidding in Continuous Double Auctions. *Artificial Intelligence* 172 (2008), 1700–1729.

[27] Elaine Wah, Dylan R. Hurd, and Michael P. Wellman. 2015. Strategic Market Choice: Frequent call Markets vs. Continuous Double Auctions for Fast and Slow Traders. In *Third EAI Conference on Auctions, Market Mechanisms and Their Applications.*

[28] Elaine Wah and Michael P. Wellman. 2013. Latency Arbitrage, Market Fragmentation, and Dfficiency: A Two-Market Model. In *14th ACM Conference on Electronic Commerce.* 855–872.

[29] Elaine Wah and Michael P. Wellman. 2016. Latency Arbitrage in Fragmented Markets: A Strategic Agent-Based Analysis. *Algorithmic Finance* 5 (2016), 69–93.

[30] Elaine Wah, Mason D. Wright, and Michael P. Wellman. 2017. Welfare Effects of Market Making in Continuous Double Auctions. *Journal of Artificial Intelligence Research* (2017).

[31] Michael P. Wellman. 2011. *Trading Agents.* Morgan & Claypool Publishers.

[32] Michael P. Wellman. 2016. Putting the Agent in Agent-Based Modeling. *Autonomous Agents and Multi-Agent Systems* 30 (2016), 1175–1189.

[33] Bryce Wiedenbeck and Michael P. Wellman. 2012. Scaling simulation-based game analysis through deviation-preserving reduction. In *Eleventh International Conference on Autonomous Agents and Multi-Agent Systems.* 931–938.

[34] Mason Wright. 2016. Using Reinforcement Learning to Validate Empirical Game-Theoretic Analysis: A Continuous Double Auction Study. (2016). arXiv:1604.06710

[35] Wenjie Zhan and Daniel Friedman. 2007. Markups in Double Auction Markets. *Journal of Economic Dynamics and Control* 31, 9 (2007), 2984–3005.

Potential Function Minimizers of Combinatorial Congestion Games: Efficiency and Computation

PIETER KLEER, CWI, Amsterdam, The Netherlands
GUIDO SCHÄFER, CWI and Vrije Universiteit Amsterdam, The Netherlands

We study the inefficiency and computation of pure Nash equilibria in unweighted congestion games, where the strategies of each player i are given implicitly by the binary vectors of a polytope P_i. Given these polytopes, a strategy profile naturally corresponds to an integral vector in the *aggregation polytope* $P_N = \sum_i P_i$. We identify two general properties of the aggregation polytope P_N that are sufficient for our results to go through, namely the *integer decomposition property (IDP)* and the *box-totally dual integrality property (box-TDI)*. Intuitively, the IDP is needed to decompose a load profile in P_N into a respective strategy profile of the players, and box-TDI ensures that the intersection of a polytope with an arbitrary integer box is an integral polytope. Examples of polytopal congestion games which satisfy IDP and box-TDI include common source network congestion games, symmetric totally unimodular congestion games, non-symmetric matroid congestion games and symmetric matroid intersection congestion games (in particular, r-arborescences and strongly base-orderable matroids).

Our main contributions for polytopal congestion games satisfying IDP and box-TDI are as follows:

(1) We derive tight bounds on the price of stability for these games. This extends a result of Fotakis (2010) on the price of stability for symmetric network congestion games to the larger class of polytopal congestion games. Our bounds improve upon the ones for general polynomial congestion games obtained by Christodoulou and Gairing (2016).
(2) We show that pure Nash equilibria can be computed in strongly polynomial time for these games. To this aim, we generalize a recent aggregation/decomposition framework by Del Pia et al. (2017) for symmetric totally unimodular and non-symmetric matroid congestion games, both being a special case of our polytopal congestion games.
(3) Finally, we generalize and extend results on the computation of strong equilibria in bottleneck congestion games studied by Harks, Hoefer, Klimm and Skopalik (2013). In particular, we show that strong equilibria can be computed efficiently for symmetric totally unimodular bottleneck congestion games.

In general, our results reveal that the combination of IDP and box-TDI gives rise to an efficient approach to compute a pure Nash equilibrium whose inefficiency is better than in general congestion games.

1 INTRODUCTION

Background and Motivation. Congestion games constitute an important class of non-cooperative games which have been studied intensively since their introduction by Rosenthal (1973). In a *congestion game*, a (finite) set of players compete over a (finite) set of resources. Each resource is associated with a non-negative and non-decreasing cost (or delay) function which specifies its cost depending on the total number of players using it. Every player chooses a subset of resources from a set of available resource subsets (corresponding to the player's strategies) and experiences a cost equal to the sum of the costs of the chosen resources. The goal of each player is to minimize

EC'17, June 26–30, 2017, Cambridge, Massachusetts, USA. © 2017 ACM ISBN 978-1-4503-4527-9/17/06...$15.00.
DOI: http://dx.doi.org/10.1145/3033274.3085149

her individual cost. Congestion games are both theoretically appealing and practically relevant. For example, they find their applications in network routing, resource allocation and scheduling problems.

In a seminal paper, Rosenthal (1973) establishes the existence of pure Nash equilibria in congestion games. He proves this result through the use of an *exact potential function* which assigns a value to each strategy profile such that the difference in potential value of any two strategy profiles corresponding to a unilateral deviation of a player is equal to the difference in cost experienced by that player. Rosenthal proves that every congestion game admits an exact potential function, also known as *Rosenthal's potential.* As a consequence, every best response sequence must converge to a pure Nash equilibrium because the game is finite. Further, this shows that the set of pure Nash equilibria corresponds to the set of local minima of Rosenthal's potential. Especially this correspondence has helped to shed light on several important aspects of congestion games in recent years.

Rosenthal's Potential: Local vs. Global Minimizers. One of the most predominant aspects that has been studied intensively in recent years is the computational complexity of finding a pure Nash equilibrium. In a seminal paper, Fabrikant, Papadimitriou, and Talwar (2004) show that the problem of finding a pure Nash equilibrium is PLS-complete, both for symmetric congestion games and non-symmetric network congestion games. In particular, this suggests that a polynomial time algorithm for finding a pure Nash equilibrium is unlikely to exist for these games. In their proof they construct instances of non-symmetric network congestion games where any best response sequence has exponential length. Ackermann, Röglin, and Vöcking (2008) strengthen this result by exhibiting instances of symmetric network congestion games for which every best response sequence (from certain initial configurations) has exponential length. On the positive side, they prove that best response dynamics converge in polynomial time for non-symmetric matroid congestion games, where the available resource subsets of the players correspond to bases of a given matroid (see below for formal definitions). The authors also show that basically this is the only class of congestion games for which this property holds true.

Most previous works in this context focus on the analysis of decentralized dynamics to reach a pure Nash equilibrium (see, e.g., Ackermann et al. (2008); Chien and Sinclair (2007); Christodoulou et al. (2012); Even-Dar et al. (2007); Fabrikant et al. (2004); Fotakis (2010); Ieong et al. (2005)); said differently, these works focus on finding a local minimum of Rosenthal's potential. Much less is known about the problem of computing a pure Nash equilibrium that corresponds to a *global* minimum. Fabrikant et al. (2004) use this idea to show that a pure Nash equilibrium can be computed in polynomial time for symmetric network congestion games. The authors observe that in this case a global minimum of Rosenthal's potential can be computed by a reduction to a min-cost flow problem (if all cost functions are non-decreasing). Note that this is in stark contrast with the fact that best response dynamics might need exponential time in this case (Ackermann et al. 2008).

Only very recently, Del Pia, Ferris, and Michini (2017) make further progress along these lines. The authors consider congestion games where the strategy sets of the players are given implicitly by a *polyhedral description* (see also (Chan and Jiang 2016)). More precisely, for each player i the incidence vectors of the strategies are defined as the binary vectors in a polytope $P_i = \{x : A_i x \leq b_i\}$, where A_i is an integral matrix and b_i is an integral vector. They (mostly) focus on the case where the matrix A_i is *totally unimodular* (see below for formal definitions) and thus the describing polytope P_i is integral (i.e., all its extreme points are integral); they term these games *totally unimodular (TU) congestion games.* For symmetric TU congestion games (when all A_i, b_i are identical), they devise an aggregation/decomposition framework that reduces the problem of finding a global minimum of Rosenthal's potential to an integer linear programming problem. Using this framework, they show that pure Nash equilibria can be computed efficiently for symmetric TU congestion games. The authors also show that this problem is PLS-complete for non-symmetric TU congestion games. Further, they show that their framework can be adapted to the case of non-symmetric matroid congestion games.

Another important aspect that has has been the subject of intensive research in recent years is the inefficiency of pure Nash equilibria in congestion games (see, e.g., Aland et al. (2011); Awerbuch et al. (2005); Caragiannis et al. (2006); Christodoulou and Gairing (2016); Christodoulou and Koutsoupias (2005); de Jong et al. (2016); Feldman et al. (2016); Fotakis (2010); Gairing et al. (2008); Koutsoupias and Papadimitriou (1999); Lücking et al. (2008); Roughgarden (2015)). Here the goal is to assess the *social cost* (defined as the sum of the costs of the players) of a pure Nash equilibrium relative to an optimal outcome. Koutsoupias and Papadimitriou (1999) introduced the *price of anarchy* as the ratio between the worst social cost of a Nash equilibrium and the social cost of an optimum. Anshelevich et al. (2004) defined the *price of stability* as the ratio between the best social cost of a Nash equilibrium and the social cost of an optimum.

Fotakis (2010) reveals an intriguing connection between the price of stability of network congestion games and the price of anarchy of their *non-atomic* counterparts. More specifically, he shows that for symmetric network congestion games the ratio between the social cost of a global minimum of Rosenthal's potential and the social cost of a social optimum is at most $\rho(\mathcal{D})$, where $\rho(\mathcal{D})$ is a tight bound on the price of anarchy for *non-atomic* network congestion games with latency functions in class $\mathcal{D}$ introduced by Correa, Schulz, and Stier-Moses (2004). In particular, this implies that the price of stability of symmetric network congestion games with cost functions in $\mathcal{D}$ is at most $\rho(\mathcal{D})$. For example, this parameter equals 4/3 for the class of affine functions and $(27 + 6\sqrt{3})/23 \approx 1.63$ for quadratic functions. These type of bounds fall within Roughgarden's *smoothness framework* (Roughgarden 2015).

Our Contributions. In light of the discussion above a natural question that arises, and which we settle in this paper, is:

> *Which structural properties of the strategy sets of the players are sufficient to*
> *(A) efficiently compute a global minimum of Rosenthal's potential, and*
> *(B) bound the inefficiency of the resulting pure Nash equilibrium?*

In order to tackle this question, we use a polyhedral approach similar to the ones by Chan and Jiang (2016) and Del Pia et al. (2017). But in contrast to these works, we do not restrict our attention to polyhedral descriptions arising from totally unimodular matrices only. Instead, we identify more general polyhedral properties of the describing systems that are sufficient to achieve (A) and (B). Our main contribution in this paper is to unify and extend the results in (Del Pia et al. 2017; Fotakis 2010) to a much larger class of polytopal congestion games.

More specifically, we consider *polytopal congestion games* in which the incidence vectors of the strategies of player i are given by the binary vectors in a polytope $P_i = \{x : Ax \leq b_i\}$, where A is an integral matrix and b_i is an integral vector. Given the polytopes of all players, a strategy profile naturally corresponds to an integral vector in the *aggregation polytope* $P_N = \sum_i P_i$. We identify two general properties of the aggregation polytope P_N which are sufficient for our results to go through, namely the *integer decomposition property (IDP)* and the *box-totally dual integrality property (box-TDI)* (formal definitions are given below). The integer decomposition property is needed to decompose a load profile in P_N to a respective strategy profile of the players. Intuitively, the box-TDI property ensures that the intersection of a polytope with an arbitrary integer box is an integral polytope.

Our main contributions for polytopal congestion games are as follows:

(1) We generalize the upper bound of $\rho(\mathcal{D})$ on the price of stability for symmetric network congestion games by Fotakis (2010) to the much larger class of polytopal congestion games satisfying IDP and box-TDI (Section 4). To this aim, we introduce a novel property, which we term the *symmetric difference decomposition property*, and show that it is satisfied by our polytopal congestion games. By exploiting this property, we can generalize the proof by Fotakis (2010) to these games. We also prove that our bounds are tight for these games.
(2) We provide a framework to derive an efficient algorithm for computing a feasible load profile minimizing Rosenthal's potential for polytopal congestion games satisfying IDP and box-TDI (Section 5). The time complexity of this algorithm is polynomial in the number of players and resources, the largest entry in $\sum_i b_i$ and the complexity of a separation oracle for the aggregation polytope. This generalizes the framework of Del Pia et al. (2017) for symmetric TU congestion games and non-symmetric matroid congestion games, both being special cases of our polytopal congestion games.
(3) We give a series of examples of combinatorial polytopal congestion games satisfying IDP and box-TDI (Section 6). These examples include the symmetric TU congestion games by Del Pia et al. (2017), common source network congestion games, symmetric matroid intersection congestion games (in particular, r-arborescences and strongly base-orderable matroids) and non-symmetric matroid congestion games.
(4) We show that the integer decomposition property and box-total dual integrality can be used to generalize and extend some results on the computation of strong equilibria in bottleneck congestion games studied by Harks, Hoefer, Klimm, and Skopalik (2013) (Section 7). In particular, we obtain the new result that strong equilibria can be computed in strongly polynomial time for symmetric totally unimodular bottleneck congestion games.

Further Implications and Significance. To the best of our knowledge, all previous works addressed either (A) or (B), but not both. Note that the combination of (A) and (B) provides an efficient algorithm for the computation of a pure Nash equilibrium that comes with a provable inefficiency guarantee. Said differently, our contributions (1) and (2) can be seen as an efficient equilibrium selection procedure to find a pure Nash equilibrium whose social cost is at most $\rho(\mathcal{D})$ times the optimal social cost. By exploiting contribution (1), we obtain new bounds on the price of stability which improve upon the ones for general polynomial congestion games: Christodoulou and Gairing (2016) derive tight bounds on the price of stability of congestion games with polynomial cost functions of maximum degree d, which grow like $d + 1$. However, for the class $\mathcal{D}_d$ of polynomial functions of maximum degree d, we have $\rho(\mathcal{D}_d) \approx d/\log(d)$ for large d (see, e.g., (Feldman et al. 2016)), which is a significant improvement over the general case. Also, $\rho(\mathcal{D})$ is well-understood for various classes of delay functions $\mathcal{D}$; for example, a closed form expression is known for $\rho(\mathcal{D}_d)$ (see preliminaries).

Our upper bound of $\rho(\mathcal{D})$ on the price of stability is (asymptotically) tight, even for symmetric singleton congestion games with the class of delay functions $\mathcal{D}$ containing all constant functions and being closed under dilations (see below for formal definitions). Note that singleton congestion games constitute a special case of all polytopal congestion games mentioned in (3). In particular, our results settle the exact price of stability for these applications.

Our results also reveal that the price of stability for matroid congestion games is much more well-behaved than the price of anarchy. de Jong et al. (2016) show that for symmetric k-uniform matroid congestion games with affine cost functions, the price of anarchy lies strictly between 4/3 and $28/13 \approx 2.15$. Obtaining a tight bound for this case seems (highly) non-trivial. In contrast, for the price of stability we provide tight bounds for arbitrary non-symmetric matroid congestion games with arbitrary cost functions.

Our framework in (2) unifies and extends the aggregation/decomposition framework of Del Pia et al. (2017). In particular, the symmetric TU congestion games and non-symmetric matroid congestion games (considered separately in (Del Pia et al. 2017)) fall into our class of polytopal congestion games satisfying IDP and box-TDI. Similarly, all combinatorial TU congestion games (i.e., network, matching, edge cover, vertex cover and stable set congestion games) and their respective extensions to the maximum (or minimum) cardinality versions in (Del Pia et al. 2017) can be handled by our framework.

Contribution (2) can also be regarded as a "black-box" approach for the computation of a pure Nash equilibrium. Given a congestion game that exhibits some combinatorial structure, checking whether our approach applies reduces to the following three tasks: (i) derive a polytopal description P_i for the strategy set of each player i, (ii) verify whether the resulting aggregation polytope P_N satisfies the IDP, (iii) check that the system describing the aggregation polytope P_N is box-TDI. In particular, if the integer decomposition of P_N can be done in polynomial time, then this approach provides an efficient algorithm to compute a pure Nash equilibrium. By exploiting this idea, we derive strongly polynomial time algorithms for the computation of Rosenthal's potential minimum for all applications mentioned in (3).

It is interesting to note that the IDP seems to be the limiting property for our approach to apply. For example, non-symmetric network congestion games can naturally be modeled as polytopal congestion games satisfying box-TDI. But it is easy to see that the IDP does not hold. In fact, it is unlikely that an efficient algorithm to find a pure Nash equilibrium exists because this problem is PLS-complete (Fabrikant et al. 2004).

2 PRELIMINARIES

Congestion Games and Rosenthal's Potential. A congestion game Γ is given by a tuple $(N, E, (\mathcal{S}_i)_{i\in N}, (c_e)_{e\in E})$, where $N = [n]$ is a finite set of players, $E = [m]$ is a finite set of resources (or facilities), $\mathcal{S}_i \subseteq 2^E$ is a set of strategies of player $i \in N$, and $c_e : \mathbb{R}_{\geq 0} \to \mathbb{R}$ is a cost function of resource $e \in E$. Unless stated otherwise, the cost functions are assumed to be non-negative and non-decreasing. For a strategy profile $s = (s_1, \dots, s_n) \in \times_i \mathcal{S}_i$, we define x_e as the number of players using resource e, i.e., $x_e = x_e(s) = |\{i \in N : e \in s_i\}|$. We call x the *load profile* corresponding to strategy profile s. The cost of player $i \in N$ under a strategy profile $s = (s_1, \dots, s_n) \in \times_i \mathcal{S}_i$ is given by $C_i(s) = \sum_{e\in s_i} c_e(x_e)$. If $\mathcal{S}_i = \mathcal{S}_j$ for all $i, j \in N$, the game is called *symmetric.* The *social cost* $C(s)$ of a strategy profile refers to the sum of the players' individual costs, i.e., $C(s) = \sum_i C_i(s)$.

We say that $\Phi : \times_i \mathcal{S}_i \to \mathbb{R}$ is an *exact potential function* for a congestion game Γ if for every strategy profile $s \in \times_i \mathcal{S}_i$, for every player $i \in N$ and every unilateral deviation $s_i' \in \mathcal{S}_i$ of i it holds: $\Phi(s) - \Phi(s_{-i}, s_i') = C_i(s) - C_i(s_{-i}, s_i')$. Rosenthal (1973) shows that $\Phi(s) = \sum_{e\in E} \sum_{k=1}^{x_e} c_e(k)$ is an exact potential. Subsequently, we refer to this potential function simply as *Rosenthal's potential.* Further, a strategy profile minimizing Rosenthal's potential is said to be a *Rosenthal minimizer.*

Inefficiency of equilibria. A strategy profile s is a *Nash equilibrium* if for every player $i \in N$ it holds that $C_i(s) \leq C_i(s_i', s_{-i})$ for all $s_i' \in \mathcal{S}_i$. Further, a strategy profile s is a *strong equilibrium* if for every group of players $I \subseteq N$ and every deviation $s_I' \in \times_{i\in I} \mathcal{S}_i$ of the players in I, it holds that $C_i(s) \leq C_i(s_I', s_{-I})$ for some $i \in I$.

The price of anarchy (POA) and the price of stability (POS) of a game Γ are defined as

$$\mathrm{POA}(\Gamma) = \frac{\max_{s\in \mathrm{NE}} C(s)}{\min_{s^*\in \times_i S_i} C(s^*)} \quad \text{and} \quad \mathrm{POS}(\Gamma) = \frac{\min_{s\in \mathrm{NE}} C(s)}{\min_{s^*\in \times_i S_i} C(s^*)},$$

where NE denotes the set of all Nash equilibria of Γ. For a collection of games $\mathcal{H}$ we define $\mathrm{POA}(\mathcal{H}) = \sup_{\Gamma\in\mathcal{H}} \mathrm{POA}(\Gamma)$ and $\mathrm{POS}(\mathcal{H}) = \sup_{\Gamma\in\mathcal{H}} \mathrm{POS}(\Gamma)$. These notions naturally generalize to the solution concept of strong equilibria.

Smoothness parameter. Correa et al. (2004) show that for *non-atomic* network congestion games with latency functions in class $\mathcal{D}$ the price of anarchy of an instance is at most

$$\rho(\mathcal{D}) := (1-\beta(\mathcal{D}))^{-1}, \quad \text{where} \quad \beta(\mathcal{D}) = \sup_{d\in\mathcal{D}} \sup_{x,y\in\mathbb{R}: x\geq y>0} \frac{y(d(x)-d(y))}{xd(x)}. \tag{1}$$

The value of $\rho(\mathcal{D})$ is well-understood for many important classes of latency functions. For example, let $\mathcal{D}_d = \{g : \mathbb{R}_{\geq 0} \to \mathbb{R}_{\geq 0} : g(\mu x) \geq \mu^d g(x)\ \forall \mu \in [0,1]\}$. In particular, $\mathcal{D}_d$ contains all polynomial latency functions with non-negative coefficients and maximum degree d. We have $\rho(\mathcal{D}_d) = (1 - \frac{d}{(d+1)^{(d+1)/d}})^{-1}$. The parameter $\rho(\mathcal{D})$ plays a crucial role in bounding the price of stability of our congestion games.

Integral polytopes. We review some basic definitions and results from polyhedral combinatorics which are used in this paper. A polytope $P \subseteq \mathbb{R}^m$ is the convex hull of a finite set of vectors in $\mathbb{R}^m$. We say that P is *integral* if all its extreme points are integral vectors. P is said to be *box-integral* if the intersection of P with any integral box, i.e., $P \cap \{x : c \leq x \leq d\}$ for arbitrary integral c and d, yields an integral polytope.

A matrix $A \in \mathbb{Q}^{r\times m}$ is *totally unimodular (TUM)* if the determinant of each square submatrix of A is in $\{0, \pm 1\}$. In particular, each entry of a totally unimodular matrix is in $\{0, \pm 1\}$. If A is totally unimodular and $b \in \mathbb{Z}^m$ is an integer vector, then the polyhedron $P = \{x : Ax \leq b\}$ is integral (Schrijver 1986, Theorem 19.1).

Edmonds and Giles (1977) introduced the powerful notion of total dual integrality. A rational system $Ax \leq b$ with $A \in \mathbb{Q}^{r\times m}$ and $b \in \mathbb{Q}^r$ is *totally dual integral (TDI)* if for every integral $c \in \mathbb{Z}^m$, the dual of minimizing $c^\top x$ over $Ax \leq b$, i.e., $\max\{y^\top b : y \geq 0,\ y^\top A = c^\top\}$, has an integer optimum solution y, if it is finite. If $Ax \leq b$ is a TDI-system and b is integral, then the polyhedron $P = \{x : Ax \leq b\}$ is integral (Schrijver 1986, Corollary 22.1c). Note that TDI is a weaker sufficient condition for the integrality of P than TUM.

The system $Ax \leq b$ is *box-totally dual integral (box-TDI)* if the system $Ax \leq b,\ l \leq x \leq u$ is TDI for all rational vectors l and u. We say that a polytope P is *box-TDI*, if it can be described by a box-TDI system. If P has some box-TDI describing system, then every TDI-system describing P is also box-TDI (Schrijver 1986, Theorem 22.8). We will use the following properties of box-TDI descriptions:

Proposition 2.1. *(Schrijver 1986, Section 22.5) The following statements are equivalent:*

(i) The system $Ax \leq b$, $x \geq 0$ is box-TDI.
(ii) The system $Ax + \mu = b$, $\mu \geq 0$, $x \geq 0$ is box-TDI.
(iii) The system $Ax \leq \alpha b$, $x \geq 0$ is box-TDI for all $\alpha \geq 0$.
(iv) The system $a\zeta_0 + Ax \leq b$ is box-TDI, where a is a column of A and ζ_0 is a new variable.

Moreover, if a polytope P is box-integral, then every edge of P is in the direction of a $\{0, \pm 1\}$-vector.

For our computational results we need the notion of a separation oracle. Let $P \in \mathbb{R}^m$ be a polytope defined by a finite set of rational inequalities. Given a vector $y \in \mathbb{Q}^n$, we assume that there is a *separation oracle* that decides whether $y \in P$ or not, and in the latter case it returns a vector $a \in \mathbb{Q}^n$ such that $a^\mathsf{T} x < a^\mathsf{T} y$ for all $x \in P$. All applications that we consider in this paper are known to have efficient separation oracles. Finally, for a vector $y \in \mathbb{Q}^r$ we define the *size* of y as $\text{size}(y) = \max\{\log(y_i) + 1 : i = 1, \ldots, r\}$.

Matroids. We introduce some general terminology and facts for matroids (an extensive treaty of matroids can be found, e.g., in (Schrijver 2003)). Let E be a finite set of elements and $\mathcal{I} \subseteq 2^E$ be a collection of subsets of E (called *independent sets*). The pair $\mathcal{M} = (E, \mathcal{I})$ is a *matroid* if the following three properties hold: (1) $\emptyset \in \mathcal{I}$, (2) if $A \in \mathcal{I}$ and $B \subseteq A$, then $B \in \mathcal{I}$, (3) if $A, B \in \mathcal{I}$ and $|A| > |B|$, then there exists an $a \in A \setminus B$ such that $B + a \in \mathcal{I}$. An independent set $B \in \mathcal{I}$ of maximum size is called a *basis*. We use $\mathcal{B}$ to denote the set of all bases of $\mathcal{M}$. The matroid $\mathcal{M}$ also has a rank function $r : 2^E \to \{1, \ldots, |E|\}$ which maps every subset $A \subseteq E$ to the cardinality of the largest independent set contained in A.

The *base matroid polytope* is given by

$$P_{\mathcal{M}} = \{x : x(A) \leq r(A)\ \forall A \subset E,\ x(E) = r(E),\ x \geq 0\},$$

where $x(A) = \sum_{a \in A} x_a$ for all $A \subseteq E$. It is the convex hull of the incidence vectors of the bases in $\mathcal{B}$ (Schrijver 2003). If in the description above the equality $x(E) = r(E)$ is replaced by $x(E) \leq r(E)$, we obtain the *independent set polytope* which is the convex hull of the incidence vectors of the independent sets.

We assume that the matroid is given by an *independence oracle* that takes as input a subset $A \subseteq 2^E$ and returns whether or not $A \in \mathcal{I}$. Given an independence oracle, we can determine in time polynomial in $|E|$ and the complexity of the oracle, whether a set is a basis and what the rank of a set is. Further, there exists a separation oracle for $P_{\mathcal{M}}$ that runs in time polynomial in $|E|$ and the complexity of an independence oracle. This follows from the fact that the *most violated inequality problem* can be solved in time polynomial in $|E|$ and the complexity of an independence oracle. The most violated inequality problem takes as input a vector $x \in \mathbb{Q}^m$ and returns whether or not $x \in P$, and if not, it returns a subset A for which $r(A) - x(A)$ is minimized, see, e.g., (Schrijver 2003, Section 40.3).

Given two matroids $\mathcal{M}_1$ and $\mathcal{M}_2$ on a common ground set E, the polytope

$$P_{\mathcal{M}_1, \mathcal{M}_2} = \{x : x(A) \leq r_i(A)\ \forall A \subset E,\ x(E) = r_i(E) \text{ for } i = 1, 2,\ x \geq 0\} \tag{2}$$

is the convex hull of the common bases of matroids $\mathcal{M}_1$ and $\mathcal{M}_2$, see, e.g., (Schrijver 2003, Corollary 41.12d). It follows directly that $P_{\mathcal{M}_1, \mathcal{M}_2}$ also has a separation oracle which runs in time polynomial in $|E|$ and the complexity of the independence oracles for $\mathcal{M}_1$ and $\mathcal{M}_2$.

3 POLYTOPAL CONGESTION GAMES

We consider *polytopal congestion games* $\Gamma = (N, E, (\mathcal{S}_i)_{i \in N}, (c_e)_{e \in E})$ with $N = [n]$ and $E = [m]$, where the set of strategies $\mathcal{S}_i$ of each player $i \in N$ is given implicitly by a polytopal representation. More precisely, let $\mathcal{X}_i$ be the finite set of all incidence vectors of the strategies of player i, i.e., $\mathcal{X}_i = \{\chi_i \in \{0, 1\}^m : \chi_{ie} = 1 \text{ iff } e \in s_i \text{ for } s_i \in \mathcal{S}_i\}$. The polytope P_i representing the strategies of player i is defined as the convex hull of $\mathcal{X}_i$, i.e., $P_i = \text{conv}(\mathcal{X}_i) \subseteq [0, 1]^m$. We assume that P_i is given by $P_i = \{x : Ax \leq b_i\} \subseteq [0, 1]^m$, where $A \in \mathbb{Z}^{r \times m}$ is an integral $r \times m$-matrix and $b_i \in \mathbb{Z}^r$ is an integral vector. Note that $\mathcal{X}_i = P_i \cap \{0, 1\}^m$. For notational convenience, we subsequently use $\mathcal{S}_i$ also to refer to the set of incidence vectors $\mathcal{X}_i$; no confusion shall arise.

We say that $(N, E, (\mathcal{S}_i)_{i \in N})$ is the *polytopal tuple* given by $P_1, \ldots, P_n$, where $\mathcal{S}_i = P_i \cap \{0, 1\}^m$. Moreover, we define $P_N = \{y : Ay \leq \sum_i b_i\} \subseteq \mathbb{R}^m$ to be the *aggregation polytope* of the tuple. If $b_i = b_j = b$ for all $i, j \in N$, the tuple is called *symmetric* and denoted by $(N, E, \mathcal{S})$ where

$\mathcal{S} = P \cap \{0,1\}^m$, with $P = \{x : Ax \le b\}$. If additionally we equip the tuple with cost functions $(c_e)_{e\in E}$, we call $\Gamma = (N, E, (\mathcal{S}_i)_{i\in N}, (c_e)_{e\in E})$ the *polytopal congestion game* given by $P_1, \ldots, P_n$.

3.1 Aggregation Polytope: IDP and box-TDI

We identify two crucial properties that the aggregation polytope P_N has to satisfy for our results to go through:

(1) P_N satisfies the integer decomposition property (IDP).
(2) The system $Ay \le \sum_i b_i$ describing P_N is box-totally dual integral (box-TDI).

The aggregation polytope $P_N = \{y : Ay \le \sum_i b_i\} \subseteq \mathbb{R}^m$ has the *integer decomposition property (IDP)* if every integral $z \in P_N$ can be written as $z = \sum_{i=1}^n z^i$, where $z^i \in P_i \cap \mathbb{Z}^m$ for all $i = 1, \ldots, n$.[1]

We next introduce the notion of a feasible load profile. Given a tuple $(N, E, (\mathcal{S}_i)_{i\in N})$, a load profile $y \in \mathbb{N}^m$ is said to be *feasible* for $(N, E, (\mathcal{S}_i)_{i\in N})$ if there exists a strategy profile $s = (s_1, \ldots, s_n) \in \times_i \mathcal{S}_i$ such that y is the load profile corresponding to s, i.e., $y_e = x_e(s)$ for all $e \in E$. We omit the explicit reference to the tuple if it is clear from the context.

The IDP is crucial to establish a correspondence between feasible load profiles for $(N, E, (\mathcal{S}_i)_{i\in N})$ and the integral vectors in P_N.

Proposition 3.1. *If the aggregation polytope P_N of a polytopal tuple $(N, E, (\mathcal{S}_i)_{i\in N})$ has the IDP, then the feasible load profiles of the tuple correspond precisely to the integral vectors in P_N.*

Proof. Let $s = (s_1, \ldots, s_n) \in \times_i \mathcal{S}_i$ be a strategy profile and let x be the load profile corresponding to s. It follows directly that $x \in P_N$ by definition of P_N. Moreover, any integral vector z in P_N can be decomposed as $z = \sum_{i=1}^n z^i$ where $z^i \in P_i \cap \mathbb{Z}^m$ for all $i = 1, \ldots, n$. This implies that for every i the vector z^i is the incidence vector of some strategy of player i and thus z is a feasible load profile. □

The main reason as to why box-TDI is useful, is that it serves as a sufficient condition to show that the polytope it describes is box-integral.

Proposition 3.2. *If the system $Ax \le b$ describing a polytope P is box-TDI and b is integral, then P is box-integral.*

Proof. By assumption, the describing system $Ax \le b$ of P is box-TDI. Thus the system $Ax \le b$, $l \le y \le u$ is TDI for all rational vectors l and u. In particular, $Ax \le b$, $c \le y \le d$ is TDI for arbitrary integral vectors c and d. Because b, c and d are integral, we can conclude that the polytope $P \cap \{y : c \le y \le d\}$ is integral (see, e.g., (Schrijver 1986, Corollary 22.1c)). □

It seems that most 0/1-polytopes for which the integer decomposition property is known in the literature, also have a box-TDI describing system. We do not know if this is true in general, but it would imply that the box-TDI assumption is redundant in all our statements below.

4 PRICE OF STABILITY

We first introduce the *symmetric difference decomposition property*. This property is crucial to derive the bound on the price of stability.

[1]Note that in the symmetric case ($b_i = b_j$ for all $i, j \in N$) this definition reduces to the integer decomposition property for a polytope $P_N = nP$ as introduced by Baum and Trotter (1978).

4.1 Symmetric Difference Decomposition Property

Definition 4.1 (Symmetric difference decomposition). A tuple $(N, E, (S_i)_{i \in N})$ satisfies the *symmetric difference decomposition property (SDD)* if for all feasible load profiles f and g, there exist vectors $a^1, \ldots, a^q \in \{0, \pm 1\}^m$ such that $g - f = \sum_{k=1}^{q} a^k$, and, for all $k = 1, \ldots, q$, the load profile $f + a^k$ is feasible and a^k satisfies

$$a_e^k = -1 \Rightarrow f_e - g_e > 0 \qquad \text{and} \qquad a_e^k = 1 \Rightarrow f_e - g_e < 0. \tag{3}$$

As an example, let us consider symmetric network congestion games, where the common strategy set of all players is the set of all directed simple s, t-paths in some directed graph $G = (V, A)$ with $s, t \in V$. Here each feasible load profile corresponds to an integral feasible s, t-flows of value $n = |N|$. The symmetric difference of two flows f and g can be written as the sum of unit circuit flows on cycles.[2] The incidence vectors of these unit circuit flows correspond to the vectors a^k in Definition 4.1.

The following theorem establishes the symmetric difference decomposition property.

Theorem 4.2. *Let $(N, E, (S_i)_{i \in N})$ be a polytopal tuple given by $P_1, \ldots, P_n$ and let P_N be the corresponding aggregation polytope. If P_N satisfies the IDP and has a box-TDI description, then the tuple has the symmetric difference decomposition property.*

Proof. We start by adding slack-variables to the system $Ay \leq \sum_{i \in N} b_i$ describing P_N. Note that by Proposition 2.1 (ii) box-TDI is preserved under adding slack variables. As a result, we obtain the polytope

$$Q_N = \{(y, \mu) : Ay + \mu = \textstyle\sum_i b_i,\ \mu \geq 0,\ y \geq 0\}$$

for which its describing system is box-TDI. Also, Q_N is integral.

Let f and g be two feasible load profiles with $f \neq g$. By Proposition 3.1, we have $f, g \in P_N$. Therefore, there are non-negative integral slack vectors τ, σ such that $(f, \tau), (g, \sigma) \in Q_N$. Let $f' = (f, \tau)$ and $g' = (g, \sigma)$. Observe that τ and σ are integral because of the integrality of A, $\sum_i b_i$ and f and g, respectively.

Note that the pairs $f' = (f, \tau)$ and $g' = (g, \sigma)$ are vectors in $\mathbb{Z}^{m+r}$ since A is an $r \times m$-matrix. Let $c, d \in \mathbb{Z}^{m+r}$ be vectors defined by $c_j = \min\{f'_j, g'_j\}$ and $d_j = \max\{f'_j, g'_j\}$ for $j = 1, \ldots, r + m$, and let B be the integral box defined by $B = \{z : c \leq z \leq d\} \subseteq \mathbb{R}^{m+r}$.

Lemma 4.3. *The polytope $Q_N \cap B$ is integral and every edge of $Q_N \cap B$ is in the direction of a $\{0, \pm 1\}$-vector.*

Proof. The integrality follows from box-TDI of the integral system Q_N. For the second part of the claim, we first show that $Q_N \cap B$ is box-integral. Note that Q_N is box-integral by Proposition 3.2. Let $B' = \{x : \gamma \leq x \leq \delta\} \in \mathbb{Z}^{m+r}$ be an arbitrary integral box. Note that $(Q_N \cap B) \cap B' = Q_N \cap (B \cap B')$ and that $B \cap B'$ is again an integral box, since B is integral as well (because f' and g' are integral). It follows that $Q_N \cap (B \cap B')$ is an integral polytope. Thus, $(Q_N \cap B) \cap B'$ is integral which proves that $Q_N \cap B$ is box-integral. The claim now follows from Proposition 2.1. □

Note that $f', g' \in Q_N \cap B$. Further, both f' and g' are extreme points of this polytope because they are extreme points of the box B. We now fix some edge of $Q_N \cap B$ containing f'. Such an edge must exist because $Q_N \cap B$ contains at least two elements (since $f' \neq g'$). Let $(a^1)' = (a^1, \mu^1)$ be the non-zero $\{0, \pm 1\}$-vector describing the direction of the edge.[3] Since $Q_N \cap B$ is an integral polytope we can show that $f' + (a^1)' \in Q_N \cap B$. To see this, let $h(\lambda) = f' + \lambda \cdot (a^1)'$ be a parametrization of

[2] A unit circuit flow is a $\{0, \pm 1\}$-flow that satisfies flow-conservation at every node, including s and t.

[3] Here, μ^1 corresponds to the slack variables, and a^1 to the original variables.

the edge for some range $0 \leq \lambda \leq \lambda^*$, where $h' = h(\lambda^*)$ is the other extreme point of the edge $(a^1)'$. Since f' is integral and $(a^1)'$ a $\{0, \pm 1\}$-vector, it must be that λ^* is a strictly positive integer.

We have shown that $f' + (a^1)' \in Q_N \cap B$. It follows that $A(f + a^1) + (\tau + \mu^1) = \sum_{i \in N} b_i$. Thus, $Aa^1 + \mu^1 = 0$ because $Af + \tau = \sum_{i \in N} b_i$. Moreover, by construction of the box B it follows that

$$(a^1)'_j = -1 \Rightarrow f'_j - g'_j > 0 \qquad \text{and} \qquad (a^1)'_j = 1 \Rightarrow g'_j - f'_j > 0 \tag{4}$$

for $j = 1, \ldots, r + m$. Using the fact that $Aa^1 + \mu_1 = 0$, it now also follows that $g' - (a^1)'_j \in Q_N \cap B$. To see this, note that $A(g - a^1) + (\sigma - \mu^1) = Ag + \sigma - (Aa^1 + \mu^1) = \sum_{i \in N} b_i + 0$. Moreover, we also have $g' - (a^1)' \geq 0$ by construction, since if $(a^1)'_j = 1$ for some j then $g'_j > f'_j \geq 0$, so in particular $g'_j - 1 \geq 0$ (because of the integrality of g'_j).

We can now apply the same argument to the vectors f' and $g' - (a^1)'$ in order to obtain a vector $(a^2)'$ satisfying (4) and for which $f' + (a^2)'$, $g' - (a^1)' - (a^2)' \in Q_N$. Repeating this procedure we find vectors $(a^1)', \ldots, (a^q)'$ satisfying (4), and such that $g' - f' = \sum_{k=1}^{q} (a^k)'$ with $f' + (a^k)' \in Q_N$ for $k = 1, \ldots, q$.[4]

We argue that this process terminates. For the K-th step of this procedure, we have by construction of the $(a^k)'$,

$$T(K) = \left\| \left(g' - \sum_{k=1}^{K} (a^k)' \right) - f' \right\|_1 < \left\| \left(g' - \sum_{k=1}^{K-1} (a^k)' \right) - f' \right\|_1 = T(K-1)$$

where $||\cdot||_1$ is the L_1-norm. Since f', g' and the a^k are all integral this guarantees that the expression $T(K)$ decreases by at least one in every step.

We conclude the proof by showing that f and g can be decomposed according to Definition 4.1. We have $(a^k)' = (a^k, \mu^k)$ as defined before. It then follows that $a^1, \ldots, a^q$ are vectors satisfying (3) such that $g - f = \sum_{k=1}^{q} a^k$ with $f + a^k \in P_N$ for $k = 1, \ldots, q$. Note that a^k might be the zero-vector, if $(a^k)'$ only contained non-zero elements in the part of the vector corresponding to slack variables. These a^k can be left out. It remains to show that $f + a^k$ corresponds to a feasible strategy profile for $k = 1, \ldots, q$. This follows directly from the fact that P_N has the IDP. The decomposition yields the strategies of the players. □

For symmetric polytopal tuples with common polytope P, we have $P_N = nP = \{y : y/n \in P\}$. The latter polytope has a box-TDI description if and only if P has a box-TDI description, which follows from Proposition 2.1 (iii). This yields the following corollary.

Corollary 4.4. *Let $(N, E, \mathcal{S})$ be a symmetric polytopal tuple given by P. If P satisfies the IDP and has a box-TDI description, then the tuple has the symmetric difference decomposition property.*

4.2 Upper bound for price of stability

The following is the main result of this section.

Theorem 4.5 (price of stability). *Let $\Gamma = (N, E, (\mathcal{S}_i)_{i \in N}, (c_e)_{e \in E})$ be a congestion game with cost functions in class $\mathcal{D}$. Suppose that the tuple $(N, E, (\mathcal{S}_i)_{i \in N})$ satisfies the symmetric difference decomposition property. Then POS(Γ) $\leq \rho(\mathcal{D})$. Further, this bound is (asymptotically) tight, even for symmetric singleton congestion games.*

Recall that $\rho(\mathcal{D})$ is defined as in (1) and refers to the price of anarchy of *non-atomic* network congestion games with latency function in class $\mathcal{D}$. We need the following lemma to prove Theorem 4.5. Its proof relies on the symmetric difference decomposition property.

[4]This construction is essentially a *conformal circuit decomposition*, see, e.g., Onn, Rothblum, and Tangir (2005).

Lemma 4.6. *Let $(N, E, (S_i)_{i\in N})$ satisfy the symmetric difference decomposition property and let $(c_e)_{e\in E}$ be arbitrary cost functions. Let f be a feasible load profile that minimizes Rosenthal's potential $\Phi(\cdot)$. Then for every feasible load profile g*

$$\Delta(f,g) := \sum_{e:f_e>g_e} (f_e - g_e)c_e(f_e) - \sum_{e:f_e<g_e} (g_e - f_e)c_e(f_e+1) \le 0.$$

Proof. Let f be a global minimizer of Rosenthal's potential and let g be an arbitrary feasible load profile. Then by the SDD property, there exist vectors $a^1, \dots, a^q$ such that $g - f = \sum_{k=1}^{q} a^k$ for some q. Moreover,

$$\Phi(f) - \Phi(f + a^k) = \sum_{e:\ a_e^k=-1} c_e(f_e) - \sum_{e:\ a_e^k=1} c_e(f_e+1) \le 0$$

for all $k = 1, \dots, q$, where the inequality holds because f minimizes Rosenthal's potential Φ. By adding up these inequalities for all $k = 1, \dots, q$, we obtain that $\Delta(f,g) \le 0$. To see this, note that if $e \in E$ with $f_e > g_e$ then there are precisely $f_e - g_e$ vectors a^k with $a_e^k = -1$; similarly, if $e \in E$ with $g_e > f_e$ then there are precisely $g_e - f_e$ vectors a^k with $a_e^k = 1$. □

Proof of Theorem 4.5. The upper bound proof follows the same line of arguments as in (Fotakis 2010, Lemma 3). We sketch the main ideas here only and refer to (Fotakis 2010) for more details. Let f be a minimizer of Rosenthal's potential and g an arbitrary feasible load profile. Note that f is a pure Nash equilibrium. It can be shown that

$$C(f) \le C(g) + \beta(\mathcal{D})C(f) + \sum_{e:f_e>g_e} (f_e - g_e)c_e(f_e) - \sum_{e:f_e<g_e} (g_e - f_e)c_e(f_e+1).$$

By Lemma 4.6, the sum difference $\Delta(f,g)$ is non-negative. By rearranging terms, we obtain $C(f)/C(g) \le (1 - \beta(\mathcal{D}))^{-1} = \rho(\mathcal{D})$, which establishes the upper bound. The proof that this bound is tight will be given in the full version of the paper. □

5 MINIMIZING ROSENTHAL'S POTENTIAL

Del Pia, Ferris, and Michini (2017) introduce an *aggregation/decomposition method* for computing a global minimum of Rosenthal's potential. It consists of two phases: In the *aggregation phase*, we find a feasible load profile f^* minimizing Rosenthal's potential. In the *decomposition phase*, f^* is then decomposed into a feasible strategy profile. The authors provide an aggregation approach (detailed below) that works for totally unimodular matrices A and one common vector $b = b_i$ for all $i \in N$. Here we extend this result to aggregation polytopes P_N that have a box-TDI description.

Recall from Proposition 3.1 that if the aggregation polytope P_N of a polytopal congestion game has the integer decomposition property, then the feasible load profiles correspond to the integral vectors of P_N. As a result, the problem we need to solve in the aggregation phase is equivalent to

$$(Z) \qquad \min \sum_{e\in E} \sum_{k=1}^{f_e} c_j(k) \quad \text{s.t.} \quad f \in P_N \cap \mathbb{Z}^m$$

Note that this formulation is not a linear program in the variables $(f_e)_{e\in E}$. As in the approach of Del Pia et al. (2017), this problem can be resolved by introducing binary variables $h_j^k \in \{0, 1\}$ for $k = 1, \dots, n$ and $j = 1, \dots, m$. The interpretation is that $h_j^k = 1$ if at least k players are using resource $j \in E$, and $h_j^k = 0$ otherwise. In particular, if the cost functions $(c_e)_{e\in E}$ are non-decreasing, then the aggregation problem (Z) is equivalent to the problem (R) stated below:

$$(R) \qquad \min \sum_{j=1}^{m}\sum_{k=1}^{n} c_j(k)h_j^k$$

$$\text{s.t.} \quad [A, A, \ldots, A](h_1^1, \ldots, h_m^1, h_1^2, \ldots, h_m^2, \ldots, h_1^n, \ldots, h_m^n)^\top \le \textstyle\sum_{i\in N} b_i \qquad (5)$$

$$h_j^k \in \{0,1\} \quad \forall k = 1, \ldots, n,\ j = 1, \ldots, m \qquad (6)$$

The equivalence of (Z) and (R) follows from the following observations: If $f = (f_1, \ldots, f_m) \in P_N \cap Z^m$ is optimal for (Z), we define $h_j^k = 1$ for $k = 1, \ldots, f_j$ and $h_j^k = 0$ for $k = f_j + 1, \ldots, n$. The resulting solution $h = (h_j^k)$ is feasible for (R). Similarly, if $h = (h_j^k)$ is an optimal solution for (R), then the vector f defined by $f_j = \sum_{k=1}^n h_j^k$ is feasible for (Z). Note that here we implicitly exploit that the cost functions are non-decreasing.

We show that the integer program (R) can be solved efficiently for box-TDI aggregation polytopes.

Lemma 5.1. *If P_N has a box-TDI description and A is a $\{0, \pm 1\}$-matrix, then (R) can be solved in time polynomial in n, m,* size$(\sum_i b_i)$ *and the complexity of a separation oracle of P_N.*

Proof. Define $A' = [A, A, \ldots, A] \in \mathbb{Z}^{r\times mn}$ and $h = (h_j^k) \in \mathbb{Q}^{mn}$. The relaxation of the integral system (5) and (6) can then be written as the system $A'h \le \sum_i b_i,\ 0 \le h \le 1$. Let $Q_N = \{h : A'h \le \sum_i b_i,\ 0 \le h \le 1\}$ be the polytope described by this system.

We first show that Q_N is integral. By assumption the description of $P_N = \{f : Af \le \sum_{i\in N} b_i\}$ is box-TDI. In particular, by applying Proposition 2.1(iv) repeatedly, we obtain that the system

$$[A, A, \ldots, A](h_1^1, \ldots, h_m^1, h_1^2, \ldots, h_m^2, \ldots, h_1^n, \ldots, h_m^n)^\top \le \textstyle\sum_{i\in N} b_i$$

is box-TDI as well. In particular, this implies that the system $A'h \le \sum_i b_i,\ 0 \le h \le 1$ is TDI because the intersection of a box-TDI system with an arbitrary box yields a TDI system. Because $\sum_i b_i$ and the restrictions on h are integral vectors, we conclude that Q_N is indeed integral.

We now show how to construct a separation oracle for Q_N from a separation oracle for P_N. For $h = (h_1^1, \ldots, h_m^1, h_1^2, \ldots, h_m^2, \ldots, h_1^n, \ldots, h_m^n) \in \mathbb{Q}^{mn}$, let the aggregated vector $f \in \mathbb{Q}^m$ be defined as $f_j = \sum_{k=1}^n h_j^k$ for $j = 1, \ldots, m$. Then $h \in Q_N$ if and only if $f \in P_N$. We now give a separation oracle for Q_N. Let $y = (y_j^k) \in \mathbb{Q}^{mn}$ be an arbitrary rational vector and let f be defined as above. We use the separation oracle of P_N to check if $f \in P_N$ or not. If $f \in P_N$, then also $h \in Q_N$ and we are done. Otherwise if $f \notin P_N$ the oracle returns a vector $a \in \mathbb{Q}^m$ such that $a^\top x < a^\top f$ for all $x \in P_N$. In particular this means that $(a^\top, a^\top, \ldots, a^\top)z < (a^\top, a^\top, \ldots, a^\top)y$ for all $z = (z_j^k) \in Q_N$. Thus, we obtain a separation oracle for Q_N.

We now conclude the proof with a running-time analysis. From the claims above, it follows that we can efficiently solve (R) with the ellipsoid method. In particular, by (Schrijver 1986, Corollary 14.1a) this can be done in time polynomial in n, m, size$(\sum_i b_i)$, size(c_e) for $e \in E$, and the running time of the separation oracle for P_N. Frank and Tardos (1987) show that for every linear program $\max\{c^\top x : Ax \le b\}$ with a $\{0, \pm 1\}$-matrix A, the objective function c can be replaced by an objective function c', which is polynomially bounded in m, that yields the same set of optimal solutions. The function c' can be computed in strongly polynomial time. This concludes the proof. □

We obtain the following main result from the discussion above.

Theorem 5.2 (Aggregation). *Let $\Gamma = (N, E, (S_i)_{i\in N}, (c_e)_{e\in E})$ be a polytopal congestion game with aggregation polytope P_N that satisfies the IDP and has a box-TDI description. Then a feasible load profile minimizing Rosenthal's potential can be computed in time polynomial in n, m,* size$(\sum_i b_i)$ *and the complexity of a separation oracle of P_N.*

For symmetric polytopal congestion games we obtain the following corollary.

Corollary 5.3. *Let* $\Gamma = (N, E, \mathcal{S}, (c_e)_{e\in E})$ *be a symmetric polytopal congestion game given by* P. *If* P *satisfies the IDP and has a box-TDI description, then a feasible load profile minimizing Rosenthal's potential can be computed in time polynomial in* n, m, $\text{size}(\sum_i b_i)$, *and the complexity of a separation oracle of* P.

To the best of our knowledge, there is no universal algorithm that can perform integer decomposition of an arbitrary polytope satisfying the IDP in time polynomial in n, m, $\text{size}(\sum_i b_i)$ and the complexity of a separation oracle. However, under a slightly stronger integer decomposition property such a decomposition can be done as explained below. Here we focus on symmetric congestion games for clarity; but these arguments can be extended to the non-symmetric case as well (details will be given in the full version of the paper).

We say that a polytope P satisfies the *middle integral decomposition property* (McDiarmid 1983) if for $n \in \mathbb{N}$ and $w \in \mathbb{Z}^m$, the polytope $P \cap (w - (n-1)P)$ is integral. If this property is satisfied, the decomposition algorithm of Baum and Trotter (1978) can then be used to perform the integer decomposition; details are given in the proof of Theorem 5.4.

Theorem 5.4 (Aggregation/Decomposition). *Let* $\Gamma = (N, E, \mathcal{S}, (c_e)_{e\in E})$ *be a symmetric polytopal congestion game given by* P. *If* P *satisfies the middle integral decomposition property and has a box-TDI description, then a feasible strategy profile minimizing Rosenthal's potential can be computed in time polynomial in* n, m, $\text{size}(\sum_i b_i)$ *and the complexity of a separation oracle of* P.

We remark that all results in this section also hold for computing a social optimum of congestion games with *weakly convex* cost functions, since this problem can be reduced to computing a global optimum of Rosenthal's potential (see (Del Pia et al. 2017)).

6 APPLICATIONS

We now give examples of polytopal tuples $(N, E, (\mathcal{S}_i)_{i\in N})$ for which the aggregation polytope has the IDP (or middle integral decomposition property), a box-TDI description and an efficient separation oracle. As a consequence, our results on the price of stability (Theorem 4.5) and the computation of Rosenthal's potential minimizer (Theorem 5.2 and Corollary 5.3) apply.

6.1 Symmetric totally unimodular congestion games

Totally unimodular congestion games (Del Pia et al. 2017) capture a wide range of combinatorial congestion games. Here the common strategy set of the players is described by a polytope $P = \{x : Ax \leq b\}$ with a totally unimodular $r \times m$-matrix A and an integral vector b. In particular, such a system satisfies the IDP and is box-TDI. The integer decomposition property was shown by Baum and Trotter (1978). We argue that the system is box-TDI. The constraint matrix describing the intersection of P with $\{x : c \leq x \leq d\}$ for $c, d \in \mathbb{Q}^m$ is again totally unimodular (Veinott and Dantzig 1968). Any totally unimodular system is TDI (see, e.g., (Schrijver 1986, Section 22.1)), and therefore the system $Ax \leq b, c \leq x \leq d$ is TDI. We conclude that the system $Ax \leq b$ is box-TDI. If, as in (Del Pia et al. 2017), the parameter r is considered as part of the input size as well, then there is a trivial (strongly) polynomial separation oracle that simply checks all inequalities of the system $Ax \leq b$. For all combinatorial applications given in (Del Pia et al. 2017), the parameter r is actually polynomially bounded in n and m, so then this assumption is justified.

6.2 Common source network congestion games

In a *common source network congestion game* we are given a directed graph $G = (V, A)$ and a source $s \in V$. The strategy set of player $i \in N$ is the set of all directed s, t_i-paths for some $t_i \in V$.

Ackermann et al. (2008) already showed that one can compute a global optimum of Rosenthal's potential function for these games. We outline how this case can be cast in our framework. The strategies of player i can be described by a polytope $P_i = \{x : Ax = b_i, 0 \leq x \leq 1\}$, where A is the arc-incidence matrix of the network G, and b is the vector with $(b_i)_s = 1$, $(b_i)_{t_i} = -1$ and zero otherwise.[5] The aggregation polytope is then $P_N = \{y : Ay = \sum_{i \in N} b_i, 0 \leq y \leq n\}$. Any feasible load profile minimizing Rosenthal's potential can be decomposed into a feasible strategy profile, using a similar argument as in (Ackermann et al. 2008). Further, the describing system of P_N is totally unimodular and thus box-TDI.

6.3 Symmetric matroid intersection congestion games

In *symmetric matroid intersection congestion games* the (symmetric) strategy set of all players is given by the common bases of two matroids $\mathcal{M}_1 = (E, \mathcal{I}_1)$ and $\mathcal{M}_2 = (E, \mathcal{I}_2)$ over a common element set E. The polytope P of the players corresponds to the common base polytope $P_{\mathcal{M}_1, \mathcal{M}_2}$ as defined in (2). The describing system of P is box-TDI (see, e.g., (Schrijver 2003, Corollary 41.12e)). Further, as noted in the preliminaries there is a separation oracle for P (and thus P_N) which runs in time polynomial in $|E|$ and the complexity of the independence oracles for $\mathcal{M}_1$ and $\mathcal{M}_2$. However, it is not precisely known for which cases of matroid intersection the integer decomposition property holds.

Example 6.1 (r-Arborescences). Let $D = (V, A)$ be a directed graph. An *r-arboresence* in D is a directed spanning tree rooted in $r \in V$. The set of all r-arboresences can be seen as the set of common bases of two matroids. The first matroid $\mathcal{M}_1$ is the graphic matroid on the undirected graph $D' = (V, A')$, where A' is the set formed by replacing every directed arc in A with its undirected version, i.e., $A' = \{\{u, v\} : (u, v) \in A\}$. The second matroid $\mathcal{M}_2$ is the partition matroid in which independent sets are given by sets of arcs for which there is at most one incoming arc at every node $v \neq r$ (we assume there are no incoming arcs at r). Thus, the common base polytope $P_{\mathcal{M}_1, \mathcal{M}_2}$ describes the arborescences of D and we let $P = P_{\mathcal{M}_1, \mathcal{M}_2}$.

We argue that there is a strongly polynomial time algorithm for computing a minimum of Rosenthal's potential. First note that the describing system of $P_{\mathcal{M}_1, \mathcal{M}_2}$ is box-TDI (see (Schrijver 2003, Corollary 41.12e)). Also, $P_{\mathcal{M}_1, \mathcal{M}_2}$ satisfies the integer decomposition property, which follows from Edmonds' Disjoint Arborescences Theorem (Edmonds 2003). By Corollary 5.3, we can compute a minimum of Rosenthal's potential in time polynomial in n, m, size$(\sum_i b_i)$ and the complexity of a separation oracle for $P_{\mathcal{M}_1, \mathcal{M}_2}$. The elements of the vector b are bounded by $|E|$, by the definition of the rank functions. Moreover, it is not hard to see that there exist independence oracles for both $\mathcal{M}_1$ and $\mathcal{M}_2$ that run in time polynomial in m. These oracles can be used for separation oracles as described in the preliminaries. It is not hard to see that if both base matroid polytopes have a polynomial time separation oracle, then the intersection of these polytopes has one too. This shows that there is an algorithm for computing an optimal feasible load profile in time polynomial in n and m. Integer decomposition can also be done in time polynomial in n and m (see, e.g., (Harks et al. 2013, Theorem 5)).

Example 6.2 (Intersection of strongly base-orderable matroids). A matroid $\mathcal{M} = (E, \mathcal{I})$ is strongly base-orderable if for every pair of bases $B_1, B_2 \in \mathcal{B}$ there exists a bijection $\tau : B_1 \to B_2$ such that for every $X \subseteq B_1$, we have $B_1 - X + \tau(X) \in \mathcal{B}$. As in the previous example, a box-TDI description follows from (Schrijver 2003, Corollary 41.12e). It is also known that the independent set polytope

[5]Technically, this polytope can also contain paths with a finite number of disjoint cycles, but these can always be removed in the end.

of the intersection of strongly base-orderable matroids has the integer decomposition property (McDiarmid 1983, Theorem 5.1).[6]

6.4 Non-symmetric matroid congestion games

In a non-symmetric matroid congestion game $\Gamma = (N, E, (\mathcal{S}_i)_{i\in N}, (c_e)_{e\in E}$, the strategy set of player i is given by the bases $\mathcal{B}_i$ of a matroid $\mathcal{M}_i = (E, \mathcal{I}_i)$ for $i \in N$.[7] The incidence vectors of the bases of $\mathcal{B}_i$ can be described by the base matroid polytope

$$P_i = \{x : x(A) \leq r_i(A), A \subseteq E,\ x(E) = r_i(E),\ x \geq 0\}$$

as introduced in the preliminaries. That is, for every player we have a polytope of the form $P_i = \{x : Ax \leq b_i, x \geq 0\}$ where b_i is the rank function r_i of the matroid $\mathcal{M}_i$. In particular, it follows that the aggregation polytope is given by

$$P_N = \{y : y(A) \leq \textstyle\sum_i r_i(A), A \subseteq E,\ y(E) = \sum_i r_i(E),\ y \geq 0\}.$$

The polytope P_N has a box-TDI description, which follows from (Schrijver 2003, Theorem 46.2).[8] The integer decomposition property is also satisfied (see, e.g., (Schrijver 2003, Corollary 46.2c)). Using similar arguments as for r-arborescences, we can thus derive a strongly polynomial time algorithm to compute a minimum of Rosenthal's potential.

We also derive a result that is of independent interest: We can give a combinatorial approach for computing the symmetric difference decomposition (which is of a specific form) of non-symmetric matroid congestion games. Our analysis also gives rise to a strongly polynomial time local search algorithm that computes a global optimum of Rosenthal's potential function. This local search algorithm can be seen as a natural generalization of best-response dynamics. The details regarding these results will be given in the full version of the paper.

7 BOTTLENECK CONGESTION GAMES.

A *bottleneck congestion game* $\Gamma = (N, E, (\mathcal{S}_i)_{i\in N}, (c_e)_{e\in E})$ is defined similar as a congestion game, with the only difference that the objective of a player is to minimize the *maximum* (rather than the aggregated) congestion over all resources that she occupies. Formally, the cost of player $i \in N$ under strategy profile $s = (s_1, \ldots, s_n)$ is given by $C_i(s) = \max_{e\in s_i} c_e(x_e)$.

Harks, Hoefer, Klimm, and Skopalik (2013) give a *dual greedy algorithm* to compute a strong equilibrium, which uses a *strategy packing oracle* as a subroutine. They give efficient packing oracles for symmetric network congestion games, non-symmetric matroid congestion games, and (a slight generalization of) r-arborescences. In particular, this leads to polynomial time algorithms for computing a strong equilibrium in these cases.

We adapt the algorithm in (Harks et al. 2013) to compute a load profile of a strong equilibrium for bottleneck polytopal congestion games satisfying the IDP and box-TDI property.

THEOREM 7.1 (AGGREGATION). *Let $\Gamma = (N, E, (\mathcal{S}_i)_{i\in N}, (c_e)_{e\in E})$ be a polytopal bottleneck congestion game with aggregation polytope P_N that satisfies the IDP and has a box-TDI description. Then there is an algorithm for computing a load profile of a strong equilibrium in time polynomial in n, m,* size$(\sum_i b_i)$ *and the complexity of a separation oracle of P_N.*

[6]This also implies that the common base polytope has the integer decomposition property, since the integer decomposition property is preserved if we restrict ourselves to a face of a polytope with the integer decomposition property.

[7]Our framework also captures the *independent set congestion games* studied by Del Pia et al. (2017). However, we mainly focus on non-negative cost functions here (because of the inefficiency measures) and then these games are trivial.

[8]To see this, we use the fact that the rank function is submodular and that the sum of submodular functions is again submodular. We can then apply Theorem 46.2 in (Schrijver 2003).

ALGORITHM 1: Load profile-dual greedy algorithm.

```
Input  : Bottleneck congestion game Γ = (N, E, (S_i)_{i∈N}, (c_e)_{e∈E}), load profile oracle 𝔒
Output : Load profile of strong equilibrium of Γ.
set N' = N, u_e = n for all e ∈ E, T = ∅, L = E and a = 𝔒(T ∪ L, (u_e)_{e∈E});
while e ∈ L : u_e > 0 ≠ ∅ do
    choose e' ∈ argmax_{e∈L:u_e>0}{c_e(u_e)}
    u_{e'} := u_{e'} − 1;
    if 𝔒(T ∪ L, (u_e)_{e∈E}) = NO then
        u_{e'} := u_{e'} + 1;
        L = L \ e', T = T ∪ {e'}
    end
    a = 𝔒(T ∪ L, (u_e)_{e∈E})
end
return (u_e)_{e∈E};
```

We adapt the definition of the strategy packing oracle of Harks et al. (2013) to load profiles:

Load profile oracle

Input: finite set of resources $E = T \cup L$ with upper bounds $(u_e)_{e\in E}$ and n collections $\mathcal{S}_1, \dots, \mathcal{S}_n \subseteq 2^E$ (given implicitly by a certain combinatorial property)

Output: yes, if there exists a feasible load profile f such that $f_e = u_e$ for all $e \in T$ and $f_e \leq u_e$ for all $e \in L$; no otherwise.

Our adaptation of the dual greedy algorithm in (Harks et al. 2013) is given in Algorithm 1. Although the ideas are similar to the ones in (Harks et al. 2013), our algorithm only works with load profiles; in particular, we do not have to explicitly compute decompositions of feasible load profiles in intermediate steps of the algorithm (which significantly improves the running time).

Our algorithm works roughly as follows. We start with capacities of n on every resource. In every step we pick a resource $e' \in L$ with maximum cost among all resources that are called *loose*, and check whether there is a feasible load profile if we reduce the capacity on e' by one. If this is not possible, we remove e' from L and add e' to the set T of so-called *tight* resources. Note that after the algorithm has terminated, all resources are in the set T.

Proof of Theorem 7.1. It can be shown that Algorithm 1 computes a load profile of a strong equilibrium (details will be given in the full version of the paper). It is clear that Algorithm 1 can be executed in time polynomial in n, m and the complexity of a load profile oracle. We now give an efficient load profile oracle, based on a separation oracle of P_N. From the fact that P_N has a box-TDI description, it follows that the polytope

$$\{y : Ay \leq \textstyle\sum_{i\in N} b_i\} \cap \{y_e = u_e : e \in T\} \cap \{0 \leq y_e \leq u_e : e \in L\}$$

is integral. We can then use a separation oracle for P_N to find an integral vector in this polytope in time polynomial in n, m, size$(\sum_i b_i)$ and the complexity of the separation oracle. This concludes the proof. □

Once we have obtained the feasible load profile, we can use an integer decomposition algorithm to find the corresponding strategies of the players. If the integer decomposition can be done within the same time bounds as in Theorem 7.1, we obtain a (strongly) polynomial algorithm for computing a strong equilibrium in a polytopal bottleneck congestion game. In particular, this applies to all applications mentioned in Section 6.

For matroid bottleneck congestion games, we can also derive an upper bound on the strong price of stability (SPOS). The proof of the following result essentially relies on the fact that Algorithm 1 actually also calculates a global optimum of Rosenthal's potential in the case of matroid bottleneck congestion games.

Corollary 7.2 (Strong price of stability). *Let $\Gamma = (N, E, (S_i)_{i \in N}, (c_e)_{e \in E})$ be a matroid bottleneck congestion game with cost functions in class $\mathcal{D}$. Then SPOS$(\Gamma) \leq \rho(\mathcal{D})$.*

Acknowledgements. We thank Carla Groenland, Bart de Keijzer and Daniel Dadush for helpful discussions.

REFERENCES

Heiner Ackermann, Heiko Röglin, and Berthold Vöcking. 2008. On the Impact of Combinatorial Structure on Congestion Games. *J. ACM* 55, 6, Article 25 (2008), 22 pages.

Sebastian Aland, Dominic Dumrauf, Martin Gairing, Burkhard Monien, and Florian Schoppmann. 2011. Exact Price of Anarchy for Polynomial Congestion Games. *SIAM J. Comput.* 40, 5 (2011), 1211–1233.

Elliot Anshelevich, Anirban Dasgupta, Jon Kleinberg, Eva Tardos, Tom Wexler, and Tim Roughgarden. 2004. The Price of Stability for Network Design with Fair Cost Allocation. In *Proceedings of the 45th Annual IEEE Symposium on Foundations of Computer Science.* 295–304.

Baruch Awerbuch, Yossi Azar, and Amir Epstein. 2005. The Price of Routing Unsplittable Flow. In *Proceedings of the Thirty-seventh Annual ACM Symposium on Theory of Computing.* 57–66.

Steven P. Baum and Leslie. E. Trotter. 1978. Integer Rounding and Polyhedral Decomposition for Totally Unimodular Systems. In *Optimization and Operations Research: Proceedings of a Workshop Held at the University of Bonn, October 2–8, 1977,* Rudolf Henn, Bernhard Korte, and Werner Oettli (Eds.). 15–23.

Ioannis Caragiannis, Michele Flammini, Christos Kaklamanis, Panagiotis Kanellopoulos, and Luca Moscardelli. 2006. Tight Bounds for Selfish and Greedy Load Balancing. In *Proceedings of the 33rd International Colloquium on Automata, Languages and Programming.* 311–322.

Hau Chan and Albert Xin Jiang. 2016. Congestion Games with Polytopal Strategy Spaces. In *Proceedings of the Twenty-Fifth International Joint Conference on Artificial Intelligence.* 165–171.

Steve Chien and Alistair Sinclair. 2007. Convergence to Approximate Nash Equilibria in Congestion Games. In *Proceedings of the Eighteenth Annual ACM-SIAM Symposium on Discrete Algorithms.* 169–178.

George Christodoulou and Martin Gairing. 2016. Price of Stability in Polynomial Congestion Games. *ACM Transactions on Economics and Computation* 4, 2, Article 10 (2016), 17 pages.

George Christodoulou and Elias Koutsoupias. 2005. The Price of Anarchy of Finite Congestion Games. In *Proceedings of the Thirty-seventh Annual ACM Symposium on Theory of Computing.* 67–73.

George Christodoulou, Vahab S. Mirrokni, and Anastasios Sidiropoulos. 2012. Convergence and approximation in potential games. *Theoretical Computer Science* 438 (2012), 13–27.

José R. Correa, Andreas S. Schulz, and Nicolás E. Stier-Moses. 2004. Selfish Routing in Capacitated Networks. *Mathematics of Operations Research* 29, 4 (2004), 961–976.

Jasper de Jong, Max Klimm, and Marc Uetz. 2016. Efficiency of Equilibria in Uniform Matroid Congestion Games. In *Proceedings of the 9th International Symposium on Algorithmic Game Theory.* 105–116.

Alberto Del Pia, Michael Ferris, and Carla Michini. 2017. Totally Unimodular Congestion Games. In *Proceedings of the Twenty-Eighth Annual ACM-SIAM Symposium on Discrete Algorithms.* 577–588.

Jack Edmonds. 2003. *Combinatorial Optimization — Eureka, You Shrink! Papers Dedicated to Jack Edmonds.* Chapter Submodular Functions, Matroids, and Certain Polyhedra.

Jack Edmonds and Rick Giles. 1977. A Min-Max Relation for Submodular Functions on Graphs. In *Studies in Integer Programming.* Annals of Discrete Mathematics, Vol. 1. Elsevier, 185–204.

Eyal Even-Dar, Alex Kesselman, and Yishay Mansour. 2007. Convergence Time to Nash Equilibrium in Load Balancing. *ACM Transactions on Algorithms* 3, 3 (2007), 1–32.

Alex Fabrikant, Christos Papadimitriou, and Kunal Talwar. 2004. The Complexity of Pure Nash Equilibria. In *Proceedings of the Thirty-sixth Annual ACM Symposium on Theory of Computing.* 604–612.

Michal Feldman, Nicole Immorlica, Brendan Lucier, Tim Roughgarden, and Vasilis Syrgkanis. 2016. The Price of Anarchy in Large Games. In *Proceedings of the Forty-eighth Annual ACM Symposium on Theory of Computing.* 963–976.

Dimitris Fotakis. 2010. Congestion Games with Linearly Independent Paths: Convergence Time and Price of Anarchy. *Theory of Computing Systems* 47, 1 (2010), 113–136.

András Frank and Éva Tardos. 1987. An application of simultaneous diophantine approximation in combinatorial optimization. *Combinatorica* 7, 1 (1987), 49–65.

Martin Gairing, Thomas Lücking, Marios Mavronicolas, Burkhard Monien, and Manuel Rode. 2008. Nash equilibria in discrete routing games with convex latency functions. *J. Comput. System Sci.* 74, 7 (2008), 1199–1225.

Tobias Harks, Martin Hoefer, Max Klimm, and Alexander Skopalik. 2013. Computing pure Nash and strong equilibria in bottleneck congestion games. *Mathematical Programming* 141, 1 (2013), 193–215.

Samuel Ieong, Robert McGrew, Eugene Nudelman, Yoav Shoham, and Qixiang Sun. 2005. Fast and Compact: A Simple Class of Congestion Games. In *Proceedings of the 20th National Conference on Artificial Intelligence.* 489–494.

Elias Koutsoupias and Christos Papadimitriou. 1999. Worst-case Equilibria. In *Proceedings of the 16th Annual Conference on Theoretical Aspects of Computer Science.* 404–413.

Thomas Lücking, Marios Mavronicolas, Burkhard Monien, and Manuel Rode. 2008. A new model for selfish routing. *Theoretical Computer Science* 406, 3 (2008), 187–206.

Colin McDiarmid. 1983. Integral decomposition in polyhedra. *Mathematical Programming* 25, 2 (1983), 183–198.

Shmuel Onn, Uriel G. Rothblum, and Yoav Tangir. 2005. Edge-Directions of Standard Polyhedra with Applications to Network Flows. *Journal of Global Optimization* 33, 1 (2005), 109–122.

Robert W. Rosenthal. 1973. A class of games possessing pure-strategy Nash equilibria. *International Journal of Game Theory* 2 (1973), 65–67.

Tim Roughgarden. 2015. Intrinsic Robustness of the Price of Anarchy. *J. ACM* 62, 5 (2015), 32.

Alexander Schrijver. 1986. *Theory of Linear and Integer Programming.* John Wiley & Sons, Inc., New York, NY, USA.

Alexander Schrijver. 2003. *Combinatorial optimization: polyhedra and efficiency. Vol. B, Matroids, trees, stable sets. Chapters 39–69.* Springer-Verlag.

Arthur F. Veinott and George B. Dantzig. 1968. *Integral Extreme Points.* Defense Technical Information Center.

Surge Pricing Solves the Wild Goose Chase

JUAN CAMILO CASTILLO, Stanford University
DAN KNOEPFLE, Uber Technologies
GLEN WEYL, Microsoft Research and Yale University

ACM Reference format:
Juan Camilo Castillo, Dan Knoepfle, and Glen Weyl. 2017. Surge Pricing Solves the Wild Goose Chase. *ACM Transactions on Economics and Computation* 1, 1, Article 1 (January 2017), 2 pages.
DOI: http://dx.doi.org/10.1145/3033274.3085098

Ride-hailing applications (apps) like Uber and Lyft introduced a matching technology and market design that recent research has found is more efficient than traditional taxi systems [2]. However, unlike traditional street-hailing taxi systems, they are prone to a failure mode first anticipated by [1]. In this paper we model and empirically establish the existence of these dynamics. We then show how surge pricing and, to a lesser extent, other market design interventions can prevent this problem from crippling a ride-hailing market.

An over-burdened dispatch system results in available idle drivers being too thinly spread throughout a city, forcing matches between drivers and passengers that are far away from each other. Cars are thus sent on a *wild goose chase* (WGC) to pick up distant customers, wasting drivers' time and reducing earnings. This effectively removes cars from the road both directly (as the cars are busy making pick-ups) and indirectly (as cars exit in the face of reduced earnings), exacerbating the problem. This harmful feedback cycle results in a dramatic fall in welfare, hurting both drivers and passengers. A ride-hailing market that falls into WGCs frequently might therefore perform worse than traditional street-hailing taxi systems, so it is essential to understand WGCs in order to design markets in a way that avoids WGCs and exploits the potential welfare gains from the new technology.

[1] dismissed WGCs as Pareto-dominated equilibria and thus just a theoretical curiosity. However, we show that when prices are too low relative to demand all equilibria of the market are WGCs when using a first-dispatch protocol, in which an idle driver is immediately dispatched every time a rider requests a trip (as many ride-hailing services have committed to).

This suggests two ways in which pricing can avoid WGCs. First, one might set a single high price all the time, sufficiently high to avoid WGCs even at peak-demand periods. Of course this design has the drawback that prices will

A full version of the paper is available at https://ssrn.com/sol3/abstract=2890666. We appreciate the helpful comments of Susan Athey, Eduardo Azevedo, Timothy Bresnahan, Liran Einav, Matthew Gentzkow, Ramesh Johari, Jonathan Levin, Christopher Snyder, Rory Sutherland, Andy Skrzypacz, and seminar participants at Microsoft Research New York City and Stanford University. Author's addresses: Juan Camilo Castillo, Economics Department, Stanford University, 579 Serra Mall, Stanford, CA, 94305; Dan Knoepfle, Uber Technologies, 1455 Market Street, San Francisco, CA, 94103; Glen Weyl, Microsoft Corporation, One Memorial Drive, Cambridge, MA, 02142.

EC'17, June 26–30, 2017, Cambridge, MA, USA. ACM ISBN 978-1-4503-4527-9/17/06.
 DOI: http://dx.doi.org/10.1145/3033274.3085098

be unnecessarily high, and thus demand inefficiently suppressed, at times of low demand. A more elaborate mechanism is to use dynamic "surge pricing" that responds to market conditions. Such a system was introduced by Uber early in its development. Prices are set high during peak-loads, but can fall when demand is more normal. Thus, against the common perception, surge pricing allows ride-hailing apps to *reduce* prices from the static baseline instead of increasing them.

We build a theoretical model composed of demand, supply and matching in a homogeneous spatial region in order to highlight the phenomenon of WGCs. After calibrating physical features of the transportation process based on Uber data, this theory yields a sharp and simple prediction about conditions causing WGCs. This allows us to empirically investigate the fit of the theory by seeing whether the system does enter a failure mode when these conditions are satisfied. We use data from Uber in Manhattan, and while surge appears sufficiently responsive to avoid WGCs during most of the day, during thin hours and in thin areas, our theoretical conditions for WGCs occur with some regularity. We show that during these periods a variety of negative performance metrics spike: many riders and drivers cancel rides and waiting times jump.

We then use our calibrated model to analyze the welfare effects of surge pricing. The effects of WGCs dominate more traditional price theoretic considerations and imply that welfare and profits fall dramatically as price falls below a certain threshold and only gradually move in price above this point. Thus, the main concern for a ride-hailing platform when deciding how to price is to avoid WGCs and bans on surge pricing would lead to prices that are always close to the surge prices charged at peak times.

Pricing is not the only tool ride-hailing apps can use to avoid WGCs. We discuss two alternative approaches. First, rationing rides when demand is high avoids over-burdening the market and WGCs. However, this makes the service unreliable, eliminating one key advantage of ride-hailing over traditional taxis. Second, setting a small maximum dispatch radius also avoids WGCs, but it creates passenger queues. Passengers then have to wait without being matched to a driver and without knowing how long they will have to wait to be picked up. A maximum dispatch radius is thus in tension with a user interface feature of current ride-hailing apps—that riders know immediately upon request the location and trajectory of a car driving towards them. This feature is considered very appealing to riders and our internal interviews suggest product leaders at Uber would be loath to compromise that element of the rider experience. Hence, although surge pricing is not the only way to avoid WGCs, alternative approaches have drawbacks that limit their appeal to ride-hailing platforms.

In the last few years, ride-hailing apps have promoted the use of pooling services like UberPool and Lyft Line. We find that these services can complicate and exacerbate WGCs.

REFERENCES

[1] Richard Arnott. 1996. Taxi Travel Should Be Subsidized. *Journal of Urban Economics* 40, 3 (1996), 316–333.

[2] Judd Cramer and Alan B. Krueger. 2016. Disruptive Change in the Taxi Business: The Case of Uber. *American Economic Review* 106, 5 (2016), 177–182.

Stable Secretries [Abstract]

YAKOV BABICHENKO, Technion
YUVAL EMEK, Technion
MICHAL FELDMAN, Tel Aviv University
BOAZ PATT-SHAMIR, Tel Aviv University
RON PERETZ, Bar-Ilan University
RANN SMORODINSKY, Technion

We define and study a new variant of the secretary problem. Whereas in the classic setting multiple secretaries compete for a single position, we study the case where the secretaries arrive one at a time and are assigned, in an on-line fashion, to one of *multiple* positions. Secretaries are ranked according to talent, as in the original formulation, and in addition positions are ranked according to attractiveness. To evaluate an online matching mechanism, we use the notion of *blocking pairs* from stable matching theory: our goal is to maximize the number of positions (or secretaries) that do not take part in a blocking pair. This is compared with a *stable matching* in which no blocking pair exists. We consider the case where secretaries arrive randomly, as well as that of an adversarial arrival order, and provide corresponding upper and lower bounds.

CCS Concepts: •**Theory of computation → Online algorithms;** *Algorithmic game theory;* **Algorithmic game theory and mechanism design;**

Additional Key Words and Phrases: Secretary Problem; stable matching; blocking pair

---

A full version of this paper is available at https://arxiv.org/abs/1705.01589.

Author's email addresses: yakovbab@tx.technion.ac.il; yemek@technion.ac.il; mfeldman@tau.ac.il; boaz@tau.ac.il; ron.peretz@biu.ac.il; rann@ie.technion.ac.il.

The work of Y. Babichenko was partially supported by the Israeli Science Foundation, grant number 2021296. The work of M. Feldman was partially supported by the European Research Council under the European Union's Seventh Framework Programme (FP7/2007-2013) / ERC grant agreement number 337122. B. Patt-Shamir was supported in part by the Israel Science Foundation, grant number 1444/14. R. Smorodinsky was supported by Technion VPR grants, the Bernard M. Gordon Center for Systems Engineering at the Technion, and the TASP Center at the Technion.

EC'17, June 26–30, 2017, Cambridge, MA, USA.

ACM ISBN 978-1-4503-4527-9/17/06.
DOI: http://dx.doi.org/10.1145/3033274.3085103

Computing Equilibrium in Matching Markets

SAEED ALAEI, Google Inc.
POOYA JALALY KHALILABADI, Cornell University
ÉVA TARDOS, Cornell University

Market equilibria of matching markets offer an intuitive and fair solution for matching problems without money with agents who have preferences over the items. Such a matching market can be viewed as a variation of Fisher market, albeit with rather peculiar preferences of agents. These preferences can be described by piece-wise linear concave (PLC) functions, which however, are not separable (due to each agent only asking for one item), are not monotone, and do not satisfy the gross substitute property– increase in price of an item can result in increased demand for the item. Devanur and Kannan in FOCS 08 showed that market clearing prices can be found in polynomial time in markets with fixed number of items and general PLC preferences. They also consider Fischer markets with fixed number of agents (instead of fixed number of items), and give a polynomial time algorithm for this case if preferences are separable functions of the items, in addition to being PLC functions.

Our main result is a polynomial time algorithm for finding market clearing prices in matching markets with fixed number of different agent preferences, despite that the utility corresponding to matching markets is not separable. We also give a simpler algorithm for the case of matching markets with fixed number of different items.

CCS Concepts: •**Theory of computation → Exact and approximate computation of equilibria;**

1 INTRODUCTION

We consider the problem of matching without money with n agents who have preferences over m items. This problem models a range of situations from assigning students to schools, applicants to jobs, or people to committees. We call such an assignment problem a matching problem, if all agents are required to get a fixed number of items. An intuitive application is the school choice problem. Students have preferences over schools, and each student needs to get assigned to exactly one school. In this paper we will consider computing the fair randomized solution to this problem proposed by Hylland and Zeckhauser [12] based on market equilibria.

We model the preferences of agents with the value of agent i for being assigned to item j is v_{ij}. Using values allows agents to express the intensity of their preferences. An important property of an allocation is its efficiency. Since agents utilities are meaningless to compare (without money, there is no natural unit to express utility), the best we can hope for is a Pareto-efficient allocation. An allocation is Pareto inefficient if there is an alternate allocation where no agent is worse off, and at least one agent has improved utility. We will consider fractional or randomized allocation. The

EC17, June 26–30, 2017, Cambridge, MA, USA.
ACM ISBN 978-1-4503-4527-9/17/06... $15.00
http://dx.doi.org/10.1145/3033274.3085150

value of an agent i for the fractional allocation x_{ij} is $\sum_j v_{ij} x_{ij}$, if it obeys the matching constraint. This is the agent's expected value, if x_{ij} is the probability of assigning item j to agent i.

Market equilibria offer an intuitive, fair, and Pareto-efficient solution for problems of allocations of resources to agents who have their own (incomparable) preferences over the items in systems with no money. This was proposed by Hylland and Zeckhauser [12] in the context of matching markets, and by Dolev et al. [9] (see also [11] and [13]), in the context of allocation of resources in systems. The idea is to endow each agent with equal resource: a unit of (artificial) money. A set of prices $\mathbf{p}$ for the items is market clearing, if there is a fractional allocation $\mathbf{x}$ of items to agents such that the following conditions hold (i) each item is allocated at most once, (ii) each agents is allocated her favorite set of items subject to the budget constraint[1] that $\sum_j x_{ij} p_j \leq 1$, and (iii) the market clears, meaning that all items not fully allocated have price 0. Hylland and Zeckhauser [12] showed that such market equilibria is guaranteed to exists, see also Appendix C of the full version of our paper Alaei et al. [3]. We view the resulting fractional (or randomized) allocation $\mathbf{x}$ as a fair solution to the allocation problem without money, which is also clearly Pareto-efficient and envy-free (no agent prefers the allocation of another agent).[2] We are concerned with computing this solution efficiently.

Computing Market Equilibria and the Odd Demand Structure of Matching Markets. Market equilibrium problems where demands satisfy the *gross substitute* condition are well understood [7], and can be computed efficiently. The demand structure of our matching problem does not satisfy the gross substitutability condition, which requires that decreasing the price of an item (while keeping all other prices fixed) should never decrease the demand for that item. We show an example in Appendix B of the full version of this paper Alaei et al. [3] that decreased price can cause decreased demand in a matching markets. It is not hard to gain intuition for the phenomena: with the decreased price the agent could get her old allocation, and would have money leftover. In other markets, money can be used to buy additional items. However, in a matching market additional money makes no sense, and instead, the agent may want to exchange his share of a cheaper and less favorable items (possibly the item whose price decreased) for share of a more valuable expensive items.

Devanur and Kannan [8] gave an algorithm to compute market equilibria in markets with a fixed number of items, where agents have piece-wise linear concave (PLC) utility functions, despite the fact that PLC utility functions can give rise to demand not satisfying the gross substitute condition. They also gave a polynomial time algorithm to compute market equilibria in markets with a fixed number of agents, where agents have piece-wise linear concave and *separable* utility functions. They leave as an open problem to give a polynomial time algorithm to compute market equilibria in markets with a fixed number of agents and general PLC utilities that are not separable. We will show in Section 2 that demand structure of the matching market can be modeled by a piece-wise linear concave (PLC) utility function, which however, is neither separable nor monotone. This allows us to use the algorithm of [8] to find a market equilibrium is the number of goods is fixed, but leaves open the question whether market equilibrium can be found in polynomial time if the number of different agents is finite instead.

Our Results. We give a polynomial time exact algorithm for finding market equilibria of matching markets with a fixed number of agents, extending the work of [8] to the case of matching markets with a fixed number of agents, despite the fact that utilities describing matching markets are not separable. Our algorithm in Section 3 is based on the structural Theorem 3.10, and explores a polynomial number of possible player utility values and allocation structures,

[1] Note that agents have no use for the (artificial) money and are simply optimizing their allocated item, subject to their budget.

[2] An alternate way to arrive to the same solution concept is to assign each agent an equal share of each resource, and then look for an equilibrium of the resulting exchange market. To see that this results in an identical outcome, we can think of each agents trade, as a two step-process, where he first sells all his allocated share on the market prices, and then uses the resulting money to buy his optimal allocation.

and finds a market equilibrium in polynomial time when the number of agents is fixed. The algorithm also extend to the case when there are only a finite number of different agent utility types.

In case of large number of items and finite number of agents, when each individual item is insignificant, our allocation can be used for finding an approximately optimal integer solution. We achieve this by showing in Lemma 3.8 that we find an allocation in which the number of items which are shared by the agents is $O(n^2)$, which is constant when the number of agents is constant.

In Appendix A of the full version of this paper Alaei et al. [3], we consider the problem with a fixed number of goods. In this case, the algorithm of [8] can find market equilibria in polynomial time. We give a simpler algorithm which is tailored for matching markets. With m different goods and n agents, our algorithm enumerates a polynomial number of different set of prices and allocation structures for the equilibrium.

Related Work. The problem of fairly allocating items to unit demand agents without money has been studied extensively in both Economics and Computer Science literature. Perhaps the most well known solution to this problem is the *random serial dictatorship (RSD)* [1] — also known as *random priority (RP)* — in which agents are served sequentially according to a random permutation, and each agent in turn receives her most preferred item among the remaining ones. Clearly, serial dictatorship is Pareto efficient, and as a result, RSD is ex post Pareto-efficient, i.e., Pareto-efficient given the order used. However, the expected allocation of RSD may not be Pareto-efficient, i.e., its not interim Pareto-efficient. In Appendix B of the full version of this paper [3], we give an example where the expected allocation of RSD can be Pareto improved just using the order of player preferences, showing that RSD may be Pareto-inefficient even with ordinal preferences.

An alternative solution called probabilistic serial (PS) was proposed by Bogomolnaia and Moulin [6] which is both envy-free and Pareto-efficient with respect to ordinal preferences. The PS mechanism is, however, not Pareto-efficient with cardinal preferences. This is possible, as ordinal preferences are not always sufficient for ranking the randomized (interim) allocations, (i.e., ranking of distributions over outcomes).

The mechanism we study in this paper, based on market equilibrium from equal income, has been proposed in this context by Hylland and Zeckhauser [12], is both envy-free and Pareto-efficient even with respect to cardinal preferences. Note that neither PS nor the market equilibrium mechanism is strategy-proof. However, Zhou [14] shows that for $n \geq 3$ agents there is no mechanism that is strategyproof, Pareto-efficient, and envy-free.

Hylland and Zeckhauser [12] proves that equilibrium is guaranteed to exist (see also Appendix C of the full version of our paper Alaei et al. [3], and propose an exponential time algorithm for finding approximate equilibrium, whereas the current paper proposes an exact algorithm for computing equilibrium which runs in polynomial time when either the number of agents or the number of items is constant. Most of the recent work on the problem of assignment without money has been focused on analyzing the efficiency of RSD and PS mechanism under cardinal and/or ordinal preferences, e.g., Adamczyk et al. [2], Bhalgat et al. [5].

The main techniques used in the current paper are based on the cell decomposition result of Basu et al. [4] which has also been used by Devanur and Kannan [8] to derive a polynomial time algorithm for a related market equilibrium computation problem. We show how to find equilibria of matching problems in polynomial time when the number of agents is fixed. In Appendix A of the full version of this paper [3], we also give an algorithm to find equilibria in matching markets with a fixed number of goods. While the algorithm of [8] can be used for this latter case, our algorithm is simpler: we avoid some complications (for instance their primal dual technique for checking the market clearing conditions), and we use a simpler cell decomposition theorem. The case of fixed number of agents has been studied by [10]. However, they assume that the agents' utility functions are strictly concave and strictly monotone, which does not apply to our problem. They also approximate the Walrasian equilibrium, while our main goal is to find the exact value of equilibrium prices and allocations.

2 PRELIMINARIES

In this section we review the matching problem with additive preferences and the market equilibrium solution we aim to compute. Then we'll discuss our main technical tool, the cell decomposition technique of Basu, Pollack, and Roy [4].

The Matching Problem. The problem is defined by a set of m items, and $C_j \geq 0$ amount available of item j, and a set of n agents. The matching problem requires that we allocate exactly 1 unit of these items to all agents. The amount C_j available of each item j may be very small, so the 1 unit allocated to an agent may need to be combined from small fractions of many different items. An allocation $\{x_{ij}\}$ for all agents i is a feasible solution of the matching problem, if

$$\begin{aligned} \sum_j x_{ij} &= 1 \text{ for all } i \in [n] \\ \sum_i x_{ij} &\leq C_j \text{ for all } j \in [m] \\ x_{ij} &\geq 0 \text{ for all } i \in [n] \text{ and } j \in [m] \end{aligned}$$

We assume agent i has value v_{ij} for a unit of item j. So her value for a set of $\{x_{ij}\}$ amounts of each item j is $\sum_j v_{ij}x_{ij}$, assuming $\sum_j x_{ij} = 1$.

More generally, we can require to allocate different amounts for different agents, and allow the matching constraint to be only an upper bound, that is, allocate at most 1 unit to each agent. For simplicity of presentation, in this paper we will use equal amount required for the agents, and normalize that value to 1. Further, we will assume, also for simplicity of the presentation only, that $\sum_j C_j = n$, so a feasible solution to the matching problem will fully allocate all items.

Fair Allocation: Matching Market. We use the Fisher market proposed by Hylland and Zeckhauser [12] to make the allocation fair. Fisher market is defined by giving each agent a unit of (artificial) money. A market equilibrium is defined by a set of prices $p_j \in \mathbb{R}_{\geq 0}$ for each item j. Given a set of prices, the agent i's optimization problem can be written as follows:

$$\begin{aligned} &\text{maximize} && \sum_j v_{ij}x_{ij} && \\ &\text{subject to} && \sum_j x_{ij} = 1 && \text{(The matching constraint)} \\ & && \sum_j x_{ij}p_j \leq 1 && \text{(The budget constraint)} \\ & && x_{ij} \geq 0 && \forall j \in [m]\,. \end{aligned}$$

A *market equilibrium* for this market is a set of prices $\mathbf{p}$, and a feasible allocation $\mathbf{x}$ such that (i) $\mathbf{x}_i$ is an optimal solution to agent i's optimization problem with respect to prices $\mathbf{p}$ and her budget of 1 unit of money. Note that the requirement of market clearing that all items are allocated, is automatically satisfied due to the matching constraint and our assumption that $\sum_j C_j = n$.

The matching constraint in the agents' preferences creates an odd demand structure. For some prices the agent's optimization problem is not feasible, and even on prices when all agent optimization problems are feasible, the preferences do not satisfy the gross substitute property, i.e increasing price of an item may increase the demand of that item, as explained in the introduction, and an example is shown in Appendix B of the full version of this paper [3].

A natural idea to convert the problem to one with a simpler structure is to allow agents to have free disposal, i.e., if assigned more than 1 unit of item, they value the best unit. Unfortunately, this change in the model significantly changes the structure of the problem, and can result in market equilibria that are simply not feasible for the original problem. Consider the following market with 2 agents and 2 items.

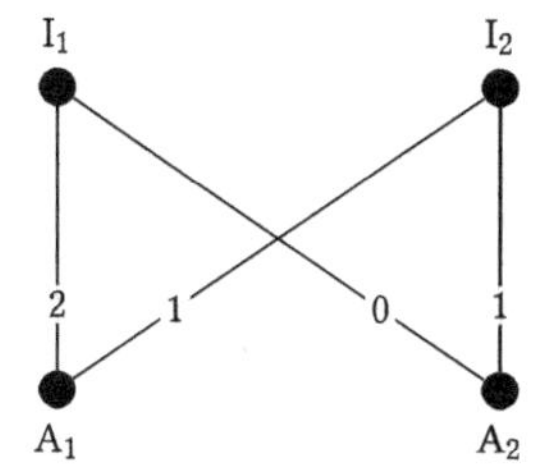

Let $v_1 = (2, 1)$ and $v_2 = (0, 1)$. Assume that the prices are $\mathbf{p} = (0.5, 1.5)$. When agent's have free disposal, these prices are equilibrium, since $\mathbf{x}_1 = (1, \frac{1}{3})$ and $x_2 = (0, \frac{2}{3})$ is optimal for both agents, and also clears the market. However, with matching market preferences these prices are not equilibrium, since A_1 will not get any of I_2 and A_2 cannot afford all of I_2 so the prices are not market clearing.

We note that it is possible to express this matching market problem as a classical Fisher market with agent preferences that are piece-wise linear and concave (general PLC) functions, though non-monotone and non-separable. To do this, we first relax the matching constraint in the agents' optimization problem to requiring only that $\sum_j x_{ij} \leq 1$. We will show that the market clearing condition of a Fisher market requiring that all items are allocated (or have 0 price) will help to enforce that all agents get exactly 1 unit. We can also express the agents' utility as a piece-wise linear and concave function. To do this, let $v_i^* = \max_j v_{ij} + \epsilon$ where $\epsilon > 0$. Let agent i's utility for an allocation $\mathbf{x}_i$

$$\min\Big(\sum_j v_{ij}x_{ij}, \sum_j v_{ij}x_{ij} + v_i^*(1 - \sum_j x_{ij})\Big).$$

When $\sum_j x_{ij} \leq 1$, the first term is smaller, but when $\sum_j x_{ij} \geq 1$ the minimum is taken by the second term, so the total value strictly decreases as the allocated amount exceeds 1. Since the agent's utility decreases with more than one unit allocated, an optimal solution to the agent's optimization problem will allocate at most 1 unit of item to each agent, and hence if the market clears, this is also a solution to the matching market problem.

Devanur and Kannan [8] provides a polynomial time algorithm to find the equilibrium prices and allocation for the case with fixed number of goods. In Appendix A of the full version of this paper [3], we give a simpler exact algorithm for this case, taking advantage of the matching structure. Our main result is to extend this to the case of fixed number of agents, instead of fixed number of items. [8] also offers an algorithm for finding market clearing prices for with fixed number of agents, but only with *separable* PLC utilities, i.e., when the utility of each agent is a separable function of the items allocated to the agents. Note that the utility function of a matching problem is necessarily not separable, as it needs to express the upper bound on the total allocation.

The Cell Decomposition Technique. Our algorithms will search the space of optimal utility values of each agent, and for each possible utility value, will search through the possible structures of allocations. There are only a fixed number of agents, however, the space of possible optimal values is huge. We use a cell decomposition technique to make the search space discrete, facilitated by a characterization of equilibria. The beginning of Section 3 has a more detailed outline.

A main technical tool for our work will be the following theorem concerning the way polynomials divide the space in a d dimensional space. Given a set of polynomials on M variables, the sign of the polynomials define an equivalence between vectors in the M dimensional space $\mathbb{R}^M$, where two vectors y and y' are equivalent if all polynomials have the same sign on y and y'. We call the equivalence sets of this relations the *cells* of the way the polynomials divide up the space. In principle N functions can divide up the space into at many as 3^N cells (as each polynomial can be 0 positive or negative). However, Basu, Pollack, and Roy [4] showed that bounded degree polynomials in small dimensional spaces define much fewer cells.

THEOREM 2.1. *[4] If we have a set of M number of variables, and N number of polynomials whose degree is at most d, then the number of non-empty cells, and the time required to enumerate them is $O(N^{M+1})d^{O(M)}$.*

We will use this decomposition to find the equilibrium for our matching problem. To illustrate the idea, and let $\mathbb{R}^n$ be the space of all possible agent utilities. Roughly speaking the idea is as follows. If we could describe whether a set of utilities $u \in \mathbb{R}^n$ arises from an equilibrium by the signs of a few bounded degree polynomials in these variables, then we could use Theorem 2.1 to enumerate all cells defined by these polynomials, and test which of the cells satisfies the condition required for being an equilibrium. Unfortunately, the equilibrium condition cannot be described this way, so we will need to introduce additional variables (helping us infer the prices and assignment, despite the fact that these are not in fixed dimensional space) to be able to carry out this plan.

3 COMPUTING MARKET EQUILIBRIUM WITH FIXED NUMBER OF AGENTS

In this section, we give an exact algorithm to find an equilibrium in the case where the number of agents n is constant, and the number of different goods is an arbitrary number $m \in \mathbb{N}$, under the mild technical assumption that each agent has a unique most preferred item. More formally, for every agent $i \in [n]$, there is exactly one item j such that $v_{ij} = \max_{k \in [m]}(v_{ik})$. The goal of this section is proving the following theorem.

THEOREM 3.1. *Exact equilibrium (prices and allocations) in a matching market with fixed number of agents, in which agents have additive values one unit of money, and a unique most preferred item, can be found in polynomial time.*

General Outline and Techniques. Our algorithm searches the space of agents' optimal utilities and item prices to find an equilibrium. We divide this space into a polynomial number of cells, where each cell contains utility and price vectors that have the same properties. We use Theorem 2.1 as the basis of the cell decomposition. The space of possible agent utilities is finite dimensional. However, since the number of items is not constant, we cannot use a separate variable for each item price. In section 3.1, we provide a bundling technique and a characterization of the equilibrium structure that allow us to define equilibria using only a finite set of variables.

Cell. Consider the vector of player utilities $\mathbf{u} = \{u_i\}$, a constant dimensional space for fixed number of agents. Now consider the linear functions $u_i - v_{ij}$ for each agent i and item j. A cell of the space of utilities $\mathbf{u}$ defined by these functions is the region of this space in which each of these functions has a fixed sign. Within each region, the items are divided for each agent i into those with value above u_i, same as u_i, and below u_i. This division also has implications on prices: if the utilities are part of an equilibrium, the price p_j of any item j with value $v_{ij} > u_i$ will have to be above 1. We will add further variables and polynomials, until each cell provides enough information for checking all the equilibrium properties.

Layered Cell Decomposition. Next we would like to add the item prices as variables. However, to keep the running time polynomial when using Theorem 2.1, we can only have a constant number of variables, so we cannot afford a variable for each item price. To get around this problem we will try a polynomial number of different structures for the price vector, where for any fixed structure, we can define all item prices via a fixed number of variables. To do this, for each agent we will fix a special item that is at least partially allocated to the agent. Lemma 3.6 will show that given prices for the fixed number of special items, we can infer prices for all items.

Finally, we also need to be able to find the assignment variables. We will show in Lemma 3.8 that each pair of agents only shares a few items (at most 5), and given the set of shared items, as well as the utilities and item prices, the allocation can be fully determined. Our algorithms iterates over all structures of specially assigned items and shared sets of items. For each of these structures, the algorithm iterates over all cells of the cell-decomposition given by agent utilities and prices of special items and the constraint (polynomials) described in the next subsections that ensure that these describe an equilibrium, and finds the ones which correspond to equilibria.[3]

Bundles. Rather than thinking about individual items in isolation, it is useful to think of items in pairs. In equilibria each agent spends exactly one unit of money and gets exactly a total of one unit of items. This means that in equilibrium, if an agent gets some amount an item whose unit price is less than one, she should also get some amount of an item whose unit price is more than one. As suggested by this fact, we pair items of price below and above 1. We define a *bundle* as either a single item of price 1, or fractions of two items of a total of one unit of items, where the total unit price of the bundle is exactly 1. First, we show that in a market equilibrium, the allocations of items to agents, can be rewritten as the allocation of bundles to agents.

LEMMA 3.2. *In an equilibrium pricing* $\mathbf{p}$ *with equilibrium allocation* $\mathbf{x}$*, there exists a bundling* B *of items such that*

a. *Each bundle* b *consists of at most two items. Two items* j *and* k *are in a bundle* $b = (j, k)$ *if and only if* $p_j < 1 < p_k$*. One item* j *forms a bundle* $b = (j)$ *if and only if* $p_j = 1$*.*
b. *Each bundle* $b = (j, k)$*, associated with a unique mix* $0 < \alpha_b < 1$ *such that* $\alpha_b p_j + (1 - \alpha_b)p_k = 1$ *(recall that* $p_j < 1 < p_k$*). For bundles with one item we use* $\alpha_b = 1$*.*
c. *The optimum allocation of items to agent* i *satisfying the matching constraint can be rewritten as allocation of bundles.*

PROOF. Let $\mathbf{p}$ be an equilibrium pricing and $\mathbf{x}$ be an arbitrary allocation associated with $\mathbf{p}$. For each agent i, we know that the total allocation of items to i and the the total cost of i's items is 1 (due to the market clearing condition), i.e.

$$\sum_{j \in [m]} x_{ij} = 1$$

and

$$\sum_{j \in [m]} p_j x_{ij} = 1$$

We start rewriting i's allocation with bundles. Let y_{ib} be the amount of bundle b that i uses in the new allocation (y_{ib} is zero at the beginning). At each step we consider the following cases

(1) For every j that $x_{ij} > 0$, we have $p_j = 1$: in this case all such items should be in a bundle $b = (j)$ ($y_{ib} = x_{ij}$), so our claim is correct.

[3]Recall that by [12] (see also Appendix C of full version of our paper [3]) an equilibrium must exists.

(2) There exists j that $x_{ij} > 0$ and $p_j > 1$: This means that there exists another item j' such that $p_{j'} < 1$ and $x_{ij} > 0$, otherwise if i gets t unit of items, her total cost cannot be t (note that $t = 1$ here). So by the definition, j and j' should be in a bundle $b = (j, j')$.

Let $z = \min(\frac{x_{ij}}{\alpha_b}, \frac{x_{ij'}}{1-\alpha_b})$. In the second case, we increase y_{ib} by z, and reduce x_{ij} by $z\alpha_b$ and $x_{ij'}$ by $z(1 - \alpha_b)$. This means that both the total cost of remaining allocation of **x** and the total remaining items in allocation of **x** decrease by z. Note that by doing this the total allocation of i (counting her allocation in $\mathbf{x}_i$ and y_i) does not change. Furthermore, either x_{ij} or $x_{ij'}$ becomes zero.

If we repeat this process, y_i gives us a way to rewrite the allocation of items to i as an allocation of some bundles (B_i) to i. If we repeat this for all the agents, we get what we want. ∎

For each agent i, the value of a bundle $b = (j, k)$ is $v_{ib} = \alpha_b v_{ij} + (1 - \alpha_b)v_{ik}$, while the value of a single item bundle $b = (j)$ is just the value $v_{ib} = v_{ij}$. Let $B_i \subseteq B$ the set of bundles of maximum value for agent i (called i's optimum bundles).

Corollary 3.3. *The optimum allocation of items to agent i is any allocation of bundles using only bundles in B_i. Furthermore, utility of i in the equilibrium is $u_i = v_{ib}$ for the bundles $b \in B_i$.*

Proof. We prove this by contradiction. Assume that y is the allocation of bundles to agents. Also assume that there exists an agent i and a bundle b for which $y_{ib} > 0$ but there exists another bundle b' such that $v_{ib} < v_{ib'}$. Since the unit price of the bundles is 1, and there is one unit of items in them, i can trade her share of b for the same amount of b' and increase her value. This is a contradiction.

Now since the unit values of bundles that i uses are the same, and i gets exactly one unit of bundles, her utility in equilibrium is equal to the unit value of these bundles. So the second claim is also true. ∎

A key observation for using the bundles to define prices in Lemma 3.6 is the following exchange property of optimal bundles.

Lemma 3.4. *If $b = (j, k)$ and $b' = (j', k')$ are optimum bundles of agent i (are in B_i), such that $p_j, p_{j'} < 1 < p_k, p_{k'}$, then $b'' = (j, k')$ and $b''' = (j', k)$ are also in B_i.*

Proof. We prove this lemma by using contradiction. W.l.o.g assume that $b'' \notin B_i$. If in equilibrium i trade her bundles to get $y_{ib} > 0$ unit of b and $y_{ib'} > 0$ unit of b', then by lemma 3.3, her value will not change. Now, since $x_{ij} > 0$ and $x_{ik'} > 0$, similar to proof of lemma 3.2, we can rewrite her allocation so that it includes some of b'', and similarly rewrite the remaining allocation of i with other bundles. Since the unit value of i for b'' is less than value of i in equilibrium, this is a contradiction with corollary 3.3 and we are done. ∎

3.1 Characterizing the Prices and Optimum Bundles with Polynomials

In this subsection we define a set of variables and polynomials that help us determine agent utilities and prices of all items at equilibrium. We consider assignments in the next subsection.

For each agent i, we define a variable u_i which is i's utility in the equilibrium. By Lemma 3.2, we know that any equilibrium allocates bundles to agents, where each agent only gets one unit of her optimum bundles B_i. Since we did not define variables for the prices yet, we cannot use prices to define bundles, so we start by defining a set of item bundles for each agent just based on the fact from Corollary 3.3 that optimum bundles must give value u_i.

Candidate Bundles. For each agent i, we define a *candidate bundle* to be the items whose value is u_i, or the pair of items j and k such that $v_{ij} < u_i < v_{ik}$, so there exists a unique $0 < \alpha^i_{jk} < 1$ such that $\alpha^i_{jk} v_{ij} + (1 - \alpha^i_{jk}) v_{ik} = u_i$. Note that the optimum bundles of i also satisfy this constraint (by Corollary 3.3). This means that the optimum bundles of an agent is a subset of her candidate bundles. In addition, the price of optimum bundles is exactly 1.

In order to find the set of candidate bundles of agent i, we define a polynomial $v_{ij} - u_i$ for each agent i and item j. This way, each cell tells us for each item j, whether $v_{ij} < u_i$, $v_{ij} = u_i$ or $v_{ij} > u_i$. For any two items $j, k \in [m]$, j and k form a candidate bundle if $v_{ij} < u_i$ and $v_{ik} > u_i$. Similarly if for an item j, if $u_i = v_{ij}$ then j alone forms a candidate bundle. By the information provided by each cell, for each agent $i \in [n]$ and item $j, k \in [m]$ that form a candidate bundle, we define the ratio for the candidate bundle to be $\alpha^i_{jk} = \frac{u_i - u_k}{u_j - u_k}$.

Not all the candidate bundles of agent i are in the set of her optimum bundles, since the price of optimum bundles should be exactly 1. We first observe that the unit price of a candidate bundle cannot be less than 1. This property of candidate bundles is useful in proof of lemma 3.6, allowing us to infer all prices from prices on only a few items.

Lemma 3.5. *In an equilibrium with prices* p, *all candidate bundles have price at least* 1.

Proof. We prove this by contradiction. Assume that there exists an agent i such that the price of one her candidate bundles b is less than one. Assume that i's most preferred item is j. We have the following cases

- $b = (z) \neq (j)$: In this case, since i's most preferred item is unique, there exists an $\epsilon > 0$ such that if i gets $1 - \epsilon$ unit of item z and ϵ unit of item j, her total price is still less than 1, but her utility is more than v_{iz}. This is a contradiction since by the definition of candidate bundles, i's utility in equilibrium cannot be more than v_{iz}.
- $b = (j)$: In this case, we claim that $\mathbf{x}$ does not allocate any item to i other than j. Assume this is not true. If i trades whatever she gets in the equilibrium with j, her price will be less than 1, and since the maximum value for i is unique, her utility will increase. So it should be the case that i does not spend all her money and market will not be cleared. This is a contradiction with the assumption that the prices are market clearing.
- $b = (k, z)$: Since the maximum value item of i is unique, her value b should be less than v_{ij}. Now since the unit price of b is less than one, there exists $\epsilon > 0$ such that $\epsilon p_j + (1 - \epsilon) p_b < 1$. However, if i gets ϵ from item j and $1 - \epsilon$ from bundle b, his utility is more than v_{ib}. This is a contradiction with the definition of candidate bundles.

So all the possible cases reach a contradiction and we are done. ∎

Next we wish to find the prices for all items. We will show that if one knows for each agent her utility, the price of only one item in her optimum bundles, and we use the set of candidate bundles defined above, we can find a the price of all the items which are in one of her optimum bundles.

Lemma 3.6. *Consider an equilibrium where we know for each agent i, the utility u_i of the agent, and the price of a single item j which is in a bundle of B_i with two items. Using these values, and the notion of candidate bundles defined above, we can find the price of all items in polynomial time.*

Proof. The key for finding the prices is the observation that if for a bundle $b = (j, k)$, we have α_b and p_j, then we can find p_k. This fact, combined with lemma 3.4, imply that if for each agent i, we know the price of one item in one of her optimum bundles, then we can find the price of all the items in her optimum bundles. The only problem is that we do not know which one of her candidate bundles is also one of her optimum bundles.

Assume that for each agent i, we know a good $g_i \in [m]$ is in one of her optimum bundles and we have a variable for g_i's price. To find a formula for price of other items with the variables we have defined so far, consider the following game. Assume that i is playing a game, in which she wants to maximize the number of her optimum bundles. She can participate in this game by proposing a price for all the items in her candidate bundles, knowing p_{g_i} and her candidate bundles. W.l.o.g assume that $p_{g_i} < 0$. For each of her candidate bundles $b = (g_i, j)$, i first proposes price $p_j = \frac{1-\alpha_b g_i}{1-\alpha_b}$ for item j, then for each of her candidate bundles $b' = (k, j)$, she proposes price $p_k = \frac{1-(1-\alpha_{b'})p_j}{\alpha_{b'}}$ for item k. Finally she proposes price 1 for all the items which form a bundle alone. By doing this, if any of her proposed prices is chosen, that item will be in her optimum bundles. Now, for each item j, we, the game coordinator, choose the maximum price for j among all the prices which were proposed by the agents for j and set that to be the price of item j.

Note that in equilibrium, we have to choose the maximum proposed price, since if we choose less than that, the agents with higher proposals will have candidate bundles whose price is less than 1, this is a contradiction with lemma 3.5. ■

In order to use the above lemma, we should be able to do two things: (i) For each agent i, select an item j that is in one of i's optimum bundle with two items (if such an item exists), and set its price p_j. (ii) For each item j, find the maximum proposed price among all the proposed prices for that item, with proposed price of 1 of items in single item candidate bundles for any agent (including agents with no special item). We can do the first task by checking all possible assignments of the special items with defining $O(m^n)$ separate equilibrium structures for each possible selection of one special item assigned to each agent, and checking them separately. Since the number of agents is constant, the number of different equilibrium structures is polynomial. For each case, we use $O(n)$ variables, one for agent utility, and one for the price of the proposed special items for agents. To define prices of other items, we use candidate bundles for each agent to define candidate prices, add polynomial comparing the expressions for candidate prices. The actual price of the item is the highest of all prices as shown in the proof of Lemma 3.6, which is now set uniquely in each cell. Note that if an agent i is proposing a price for an item j which is higher than the proposed price of another agent i' and j is the special item of i', then this cell cannot contain equilibria.

Lemma 3.7. *Consider the space of at most $2n$ variables including agents' utilities and price of one item in each agent's optimum bundles. Now we add $O(mn^2)$ polynomials: comparing utilities to item values, and comparing candidate item prices using candidate budges, as defined in Lemma 3.6, the sign of these polynomials gives us a formula for the price of each item as well as the set of optimum bundles of each agent.*

3.2 Characterizing the Equilibria

In this section, we add a set of new variables and polynomials to the set of variables and polynomials defined in Section 3.1, in order to determine whether each cell contains equilibria. The new variables will help us define assignments. We cannot directly define a variable representing the allocation of all goods/bundles to agents, since the number of these is not constant.

The key idea is to show that for every equilibrium pricing, there is a specific allocation of items to agents where the number of items which is being shared between multiple agents is very small, and the allocation has a special structure. This helps us to significantly reduce the number of variables needed to define allocations. Consider two agents $i < j$, and all items of price $p_k < 1$ in sorted by price as shown by Figure 1. We will show that there is an equilibrium allocation with only two of these items shared between i and j, and the structure indicated by the figure, and the analogous structure for items of price $p_k > 1$. If we know the shared items, this structure helps us with finding the owner of the items which only have a single owner in the allocation, hence finding the allocation of each agent using allocation variables only for shared items. Before stating the properties of this allocation in Lemma 3.8, we have to define some notations.

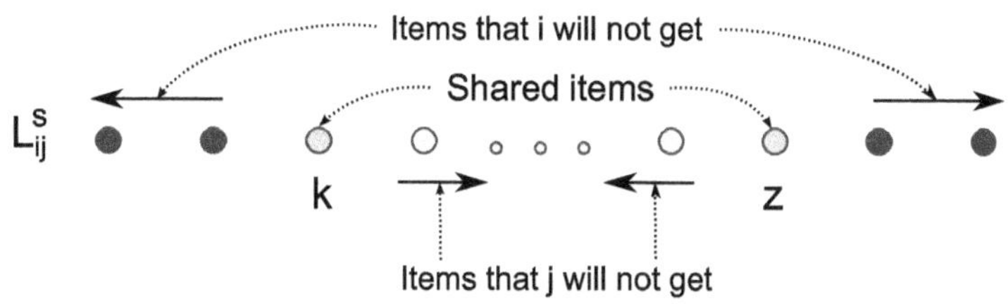

Fig. 1. The nodes are the items in S (one side of G) that are in a optimum bundle of both i and j ($i < j$), which are sorted by their prices. The figure shows the items that i and j share (green nodes), the items that of i or j will not get in the special allocation (blue and yellow nodes).

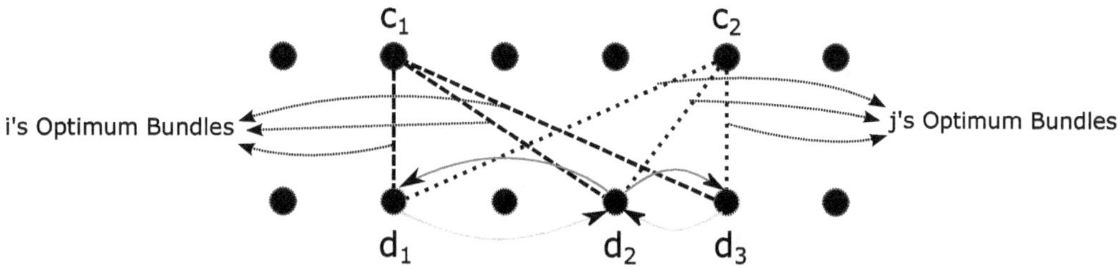

Fig. 2. The arrows show the trades of items between agents i and j in the proof of Lemma 3.8.

Consider a bipartite graph $G = (S, T, E)$ in which vertices in S are the items with price less than 1 and vertices in T are the items with price more than 1. For simplicity, we sort items in each side of G by their price and break ties with items' indexes. Figure 1 is one side of this bipartite graph. For each bundle, we put an edge in the graph which connects the two items in the bundle. For every pair of agents i and j, let $B^S_{ij} = S \cap (V(B_i) \cap V(B_j))$ and $B^T_{ij} = T \cap (V(B_i) \cap V(B_j))$. Furthermore, let H be the set of items whose price is 1 and let B^H_i be the optimum bundles of agent i which has exactly 1 item.

For each pair of agents i and j, let L^S_{ij} and L^T_{ij} be the list of items in B^S_{ij} and B^T_{ij} sorted by their price in increasing order (break ties with index of the items), respectively, the set of items of price above 1 (and below 1) that are part of optimum bundles for both i and j. Figure 2 is showing a part of the above bipartite graph for a pair of agents.

The following Lemma claims that there is an equilibrium allocation of a special structure suggested by Figure 1: on each side of the bipartite graph the agents share at most two items, and the agent with lower index only gets items between the two shared items, while the agent with higher index only gets items outside this interval as shown by Figure 1.

The main idea of the proof is that given any equilibrium allocation, we can make each pair of agents that violate the properties trade their items, as illustrated by the Figure 2. Note that the running time of this trading process is not important, since we only use it to show that for any equilibrium pricing an allocation with the desired structure exists.

Lemma 3.8. *For every equilibrium pricing* $\mathbf{p}$, *there exists an equilibrium allocation* $\mathbf{x}$ *of items to agents such that for every pair of agents* i *and* j ($1 \leq i < j \leq n$)

1. *There are at most 2 items that* X *is allocating to both* i *and* j *on each side of* G. *Furthermore, if* k *and* z *are two items in* S (T) *such that* $p_k \leq p_z$ *and* i *and* j *are sharing* k *and* z, i *only gets items between* k *and* z *in the order sorted by price, while* j *does not get any of the items from* B^S_{ij} (B^T_{ij}) *whose whose position in* L^S_{ij} (L^T_{ij}) *is between* k *and* z *in the order (see Figure 1).*

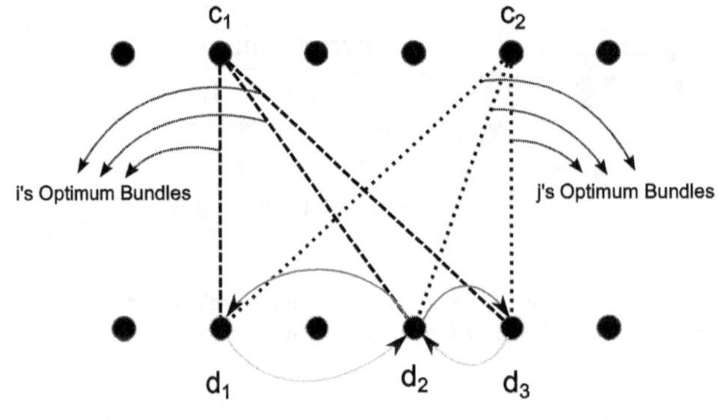

Fig. 3. Red and green arrows shows the trades of items between agent i and j in proof of lemma 3.8.

2. *There is at most one item k in $B_i^H \cap B_j^H$ that is shared by i and j in $\mathbf{x}$, and i only get items from B_i^H whose index is lower than k and j only gets items whose index is higher than k.*

Proof. Suppose that we have an allocation of bundles to agents y in an equilibrium. We want to reallocate these bundles so that it satisfies the conditions of the lemma.

Assume that there exist two agents $1 \le i < j \le n$, such that there are tree bundles $a_1 = (c_1, d_1)$, $a_2 = (c_1, d_2)$ and $a_3 = (c_1, d_3)$ such that $a_1, a_2, a_3 \in B_i$ and three bundles $b_1 = (c_2, d_1)$, $b_2 = (c_2, d_2)$ and $b_3 = (c_2, d_3)$ such that $b_1, b_2, b_3 \in B_j$. Suppose that $p_{d_1} \le p_{d_2} \le p_{d_3}$ and Yy is allocating $y_{id_1}, y_{id_3} > 0$ of a_1 and a_3 to agent i, and $y_{jd_2} > 0$ of d_2 to agent j. Furthermore, assume that $y_{ic_1}, y_{jc_2} > 0$.

Since $p_{d_1} \le p_{d_2} \le p_{d_3}$, there is $0 < \beta < 1$ such that $\beta p_{d_1} + (1-\beta)p_{d_3} = p_{d_2}$. So if we remove βz from y_{id_1} and $(1-\beta)z$ from y_{id_3} and add z to y_{id_2} then the total cost of agent i will be the same. Similarly, if we add βz to y_{jd_1} and $(1-\beta)z$ to y_{jd_3} and remove z from y_{jd_2}, then the total cost of j will not change. Furthermore, it is easy to see that doing this does not affect the matching constraints. Figure 3 demonstrates this procedure.

Now, we have to show that doing this does not change the utility of i and j. From the assumption that Yy is an equilibrium allocation, it follows that by doing this, the utility of i and j cannot increase. Assume that by doing this utility of agent i decreases. We have

$$\begin{aligned} u_i &= \alpha_{a_2} v_{id_2} + (1-\alpha_{a_2}) v_{ic_1} \\ &< \alpha_{a_2}(\beta v_{id_1} + (1-\beta) v_{id_3}) + (1-\alpha_{a_2}) v_{ic_1} \\ &= \beta\alpha_{a_2} v_{id_1} + (1-\beta)\alpha_{a_2} v_{id_3} + (1-\alpha_{a_2}) v_{ic_1} \end{aligned}$$

similarly we have

$$\beta\alpha_{a_2} p_{d_1} + (1-\beta)\alpha_{a_2} p_{d_3} + (1-\alpha_{a_2}) p_{c_1} = 1$$

This means that if agent i only use these three items with these ratios, he gets one unit of item, spends at most 1 unit of money and her utility will be more than u_i. This is a contradiction. The argument for agent j is similar to the argument for agent i.

For each pair of agents $1 \leq i < j \leq n$, we find the cheapest item k and the most expensive item z in S that i owns, if there is an item r in between k and z in the ordered list of items in S that j owns, we switch the allocation we switch the ownership of these items until, one of the following cases happen

- j runs out of item r.
- i runs out of item k.
- i runs out of item z

Let Φ be a potential function which is equal to $|S|$ minus the the position of highest positioned item that i owns in the ordered list, plus the position of the lowest positioned item that i owns in the ordered list, plus the number of items for which j is a shareholder and are between the the two in the ordered list. If we repeat the above procedure, each time this potential function will decrease by 1. Since the potential function is always non-negative, we cannot continue the above procedure forever. This means that at after some iterations, we will reach an equilibrium allocation which satisfies the first condition for this pair of agents.

We repeat this procedure until such pair of agents and set of items with these properties do not exist. We also do the same to the allocation of items on the other side of G (T) to agents. For the items in $B_i^H \cap B_j^H$, one can also transfer items between i and j to satisfy the second condition by finding two items that violate the condition and switch their ownership. The procedure defined for satisfying these conditions are an easier version of the previous procedure. ■

From now on, we focus on finding and characterizing the specific equilibrium allocation which is guaranteed to exist by this lemma. By using Lemma 3.8, for every pair of agents $i, j \in [n]$ we can use 5 item indexes f_{ij}^S, r_{ij}^S, f_{ij}^T, r_{ij}^T, and h_{ij} that tell us which items are shared by agent i and j. We can assume that we know what are these shared items by simply checking all the possible $O(m^{5n^2})$ of these combinations. At the start of the algorithm, we fix the 5 shared items for each pair of agents and an item in optimum bundle of each agent (which we discussed in Section 3.1). We call this set of items associated with each agent and pairs of agents the *structure* of the equilibrium. For each such a structure, we will aim to decide if there is an equilibrium with the given structure.

When considering equilibria of a given structure, we define variables for the allocation of the at most $5n^2$ shared items, but do not define variable for allocations of other items. Next we show that given the allocations of the shared items, we can (i) infer allocations of all other items using the structure of Lemma 3.8, and (ii) can also define polynomials whose sign will tell us if there is an equilibrium with the given structure and allocation of shared items.

Since all the items should be sold in the equilibrium, for each agent i, all the items that are in only in i's optimum bundles, should get allocated to i. Second, we have defined a variable that indicates the share of each agent for the shared items. The only thing left is to consider items that are in the set of the optimum bundles of multiple agents, but are not shared by these agents.

Lemma 3.8 helps us find allocation of this set of items. We start with the agent with the lowest index (agent 1) and one side of G, say S. The items that agent 1 gets, are the ones that satisfy all the constraints given to us by second part of the lemma. In order to check whether for an item j all these constraints hold, for each agent i, we can look at the position of item j in L_{1i}^S. If j's position is between position of f_{1i}^S and r_{1i}^S in the list, for all the choices of $i > 1$, then it satisfies all the constraints. By lemma 3.8, we know this is a necessary and sufficient condition for j to get allocated to agent 1. We do this for S and T separately, and remove the items that get allocated to agent 1. Now, we repeat this procedure for agent 2, but only check the constraints for agents $i > 2$, then remove the items that agent 2 gets. We repeat this for rest of agents based on their indexes. We can do the same procedure for items in H to find which agent is getting what item. Now, we are ready to exactly specify what are the necessary and sufficient conditions for the prices in each cell to be the equilibrium prices. This process is summarized in the following lemma.

LEMMA 3.9. *Consider a structure of special items for agents, and shared items between agents (as defined after Lemma 3.8). Now consider a cell in the space of variables of agent utilities, prices of the special items, and allocation shares of the shared items, defined by the polynomials that help define prices of all items. The prices and allocation of this cell forms an equilibrium, if and only if the allocation defined above satisfies the following constraints*

1. *All the items get fully allocated to agents.*
2. *Each agent gets exactly one unit of items.*
3. *For each agent i, the total cost of buying the items allocated to i is exactly 1.*
4. *For each agent i, each of the items allocated to i is in one of her optimum bundles.*

PROOF. $\Rightarrow$ The first, second and third condition follow from the market clearing conditions. The fourth condition directly follows from part c of lemma 3.2.

$\Leftarrow$ From the first and second condition, we know that the pricing and allocation are market clearing. From the second, third and fourth condition, and the argument in proof of part c of lemma 3.2 we know that the allocation of items to each agent can be rewritten as her optimum bundles to her. So, from the definition of optimum bundles we know that the allocation of items to agents is optimal. Therefore, the prices and allocation are in equilibrium state. ■

The final thing we need to do is to define a set of polynomials for checking the above conditions. The first conditions holds for an item j, if summing up the share of each agent for that item, the sum is equal to C_j. This can be handled by adding one polynomial for each item j.

The second condition holds for an agent i, if when we sum all the items (including the proportion of the shared items) that i gets, this sum is exactly 1. So we can also check this condition by adding a polynomial for each agent. Note that we can do this since we explained how to find out what is the allocation of items to agents for this cell.

The third condition holds by Lemma 3.9 if multiplying the share of each agent for an item by its price and summing over all items, we get 1 for all the agents. We can do this by defining a polynomial for each agent and checking its sign. The fourth condition is guaranteed to hold by definition. The following theorem summarizes how we equilibria are cells of the constraints discussed throughout this section.

THEOREM 3.10. *Consider an equilibrium structure, and the space of the $O(n)$ variables for agents' utilities and price of one special item in each agent's optimum bundle, the $O(n^2)$ variables for allocation of shared items between the agent. Divide this space into cells by the signs of the polynomials defined in the previous section, along with the $O(m^2 + n)$ polynomials defined just above, for checking the existence of the special equilibrium allocation. The sign of these polynomials fully determines either that the vectors in this cell can be extended to form equilibria.*

Using this structure Theorem allows us to prove Theorem 3.1.

Proof of Theorem 3.1. We use theorem 2.1 as the base of our algorithm. We start by fixing the structure of the equilibrium, selecting a single item from the optimum bundles of each agent, and selecting fixing 5 items shared for every pair of agents. We check all the possible combinations, at most $O(m^{n+5n^2})$ options, which is polynomial in m for fixed n.

For a given equilibrium structure, we use the $O(n)$ variables, the agent utilities, and $O(mn)$ polynomials defined in section 3.1 to find a set of candidate bundles for each agent. Then we use an additional $O(n)$ variables, the prices of the special items for each agent, and $O(mn^2)$ polynomials in order to find a formula for the prices and the set of optimum bundles of each agent in each cell. Finally, we use the last set of $O(n^2)$ variables, the assignments of shared items, and $O(m^2 + n)$ additional polynomials, in order to check whether the set of prices in the feasible cell are equilibrium prices with the given structure. The degree of the defined polynomials is polynomial. We check all the non-empty cells of the resulting system, taking time polynomial on m for any fixed n by Theorem 2.1. Since the equilibrium exists, it should be in one of the non-empty cells.

Finally, if the prices of the cell are equilibrium prices, we take any vector from that cell, and extend it to get an equilibrium pricing and allocation. After we have the equilibrium prices $\mathbf{p}$, we can also find each agent's allocation by finding a solution of the following set of inequalities.

$$\sum_{b \in B_i} x_{ib} = 1 \qquad \forall i \in [n]$$

$$\sum_i \Big(\sum_{b:b=(j,k)} \alpha_b x_{ib} + \sum_{b:b=(k,j)} (1-\alpha_b) x_{ib} + \sum_{b:b=(j)} x_{ib} \Big) = C_j \qquad \forall j \in [m]$$

$$x_{ib} \geq 0 \qquad \forall i \in [n], b \in B$$

In which, x_{bi} is the amount of bundle b used by agent i. Note that since we know this bundling is associated with an equilibrium, the feasible region of the above inequalities is not empty. Finally, the allocation of each agent i for item j in this equilibrium is

$$x_{ij} = \sum_{b:b=(j,k)} \alpha_b x_{ib} + \sum_{b:b=(k,j)} (1-\alpha_b) x_{ib} + \sum_{b:b=(j)} x_{ib}$$

3.3 Relaxing Full Budget Spent Assumption of Agents in Equilibria

So far, we have assumed each agent fully spend her budget and introduced an algorithm for finding an equilibrium with this assumption. While equilibria where all agents spend their budget do exists (as shown in Appendix C of the full version of this paper [3]), there may be equilibria where not all agents spend their budgets. In this section, we describe how the same algorithm can be modified to find an equilibrium which does not require this assumption. The following lemma shows that if an agent does not fully spend her budget in an equilibrium, she will get exactly one unit of her most desired item, hence she cannot get any part of the other items. Recall that we assume that for each agent, her most preferred item is unique.

Lemma 3.11. *In an equilibrium, with price vector* $\mathbf{p}$ *and equilibrium allocation* $\mathbf{x}$, *for each agent* i *whose most preferred item is* j, *if* i *does not fully spend her one unit of money then* $x_{ij} = 1$.

Proof. We use contradiction. Assume i is not fully spend her budget in an equilibrium, but there exists an item z such that $x_{iz} > 0$ and z is not her most preferred item. Let b'_i be i's leftover money and j be her most preferred item. If $p_z \geq p_j$ then i can trade her share of item z for the same amount of item j and increase her utility, which contradicts the equilibrium condition. If $p_z < p_j$ then, since i has b'_i unit of extra money, i can afford to trade $\min(\frac{p_j - p_z}{b'_i}, x_{iz}) > 0$ unit of item z with the same amount of item j and increase her utility. This contradicts the fact that in equilibrium, utility of each agent should be optimum and we are done. ∎

Since the number of agents is fixed, we can iterate over all the 2^n settings each of which tells us whether each agent fully spend her budget or not. In each setting, before we start the algorithm, for each agent that does not fully spent her budget, we remove one unit from her most preferred item. From lemma 3.11 we know that if this setting leads to an equilibrium, this will be the only valid allocation of items to these agents. We also remove these agents themselves and continue the algorithm assuming all the remaining agents fully spend their budget as before. If in a setting, enough of the most preferred items of the agents who do not fully spend their budget is not available, then it simply means that the setting cannot lead to an equilibrium, so we ignore the setting and iterate to the next one.

Note that if an agent is not fully spending her budget, from lemma 3.11 we know that the price of her most preferred item should be at most 1. Therefore, in our algorithm after formulating the prices in the algorithm (described in section 3.1), for each item that was partially allocated to the agents who do not fully spent their budget, we add a constraint that its price should be at most 1. Then we continue with the algorithm to find the equilibrium given the initial setting. Because such equilibrium always exists, at least one of the initial settings will lead to finding an equilibrium price vector and allocation.

ACKNOWLEDGMENTS

We want to thank the generous support of NSF via grant CCF-1563714, ONR via grant N00014-08-1-0031, and a Google Research Grant.

REFERENCES

[1] Atila Abdulkadiroglu and Tayfun Sonmez. 1998. Random Serial Dictatorship and the Core from Random Endowments in House Allocation Problems. *Econometrica* 66, 3 (May 1998), 689–702. https://ideas.repec.org/a/ecm/emetrp/v66y1998i3p689-702.html

[2] Marek Adamczyk, Piotr Sankowski, and Qiang Zhang. 2014. Efficiency of Truthful and Symmetric Mechanisms in One-Sided Matching. In *Algorithmic Game Theory - 7th International Symposium, SAGT 2014, Haifa, Israel, September 30 - October 2, 2014. Proceedings.* 13–24.

[3] Saeed Alaei, Pooya Jalaly, and Éva Tardos. 2017. Computing Equilibrium in Matching Markets. *CoRR* abs/1703.10689 (2017). http://arxiv.org/abs/1703.10689

[4] S. Basu, R. Pollack, and M.-F. Roy. 1998. A new algorithm to find a point in every cell defined by a family of polynomials. In *Quantifier Elimination and Cylindrical Algebraic Decomposition (Texts and Mongraphs in Symbolic Computation)*, B. Caviness and J. Johnson (Eds.). Springer-Verlag, 341–350.

[5] Anand Bhalgat, Deeparnab Chakrabarty, and Sanjeev Khanna. 2011. Social Welfare in One-Sided Matching Markets without Money. In *Approximation, Randomization, and Combinatorial Optimization. Algorithms and Techniques - 14th International Workshop, APPROX 2011, and 15th International Workshop, RANDOM 2011, Princeton, NJ, USA, August 17-19, 2011. Proceedings.* 87–98.

[6] Anna Bogomolnaia and Herve Moulin. 2001. A New Solution to the Random Assignment Problem. *Journal of Economic Theory* 100, 2 (2001), 295 – 328. DOI: http://dx.doi.org/10.1006/jeth.2000.2710

[7] Bruno Codenotti and Kasturi Varadarajan. 2007. Computation of market equilibria by convex programming. In *Algorithmic Game Theory*, Noam Nisan, Tim Roughgarden, Eva Tardos, and Vijay V. Vazirani (Eds.). Cambridge University Press, Chapter 6, 135–158.

[8] Nikhil R. Devanur and Ravi Kannan. 2008. Market Equilibria in Polynomial Time for Fixed Number of Goods or Agents. In *Proceedings of the 2008 49th Annual IEEE Symposium on Foundations of Computer Science (FOCS '08)*. IEEE Computer Society, Washington, DC, USA, 45–53. DOI: http://dx.doi.org/10.1109/FOCS.2008.30

[9] Danny Dolev, Dror G. Feitelson, Joseph Y. Halpern, Raz Kupferman, and Nathan Linial. 2012. No Justified Complaints: On Fair Sharing of Multiple Resources. In *Proceedings of the 3rd Innovations in Theoretical Computer Science Conference (ITCS '12)*. ACM, New York, NY, USA, 68–75. DOI: http://dx.doi.org/10.1145/2090236.2090243

[10] Federico Echenique and Adam Wierman. 2012. Finding a walrasian equilibrium is easy for a fixed number of agents.. In *EC*. 495.

[11] Avital Gutman and Noam Nisan. 2012. Fair Allocation Without Trade. In *Proceedings of the 11th International Conference on Autonomous Agents and Multiagent Systems - Volume 2 (AAMAS '12)*. International Foundation for Autonomous Agents and Multiagent Systems, Richland, SC, 719–728. http://dl.acm.org/citation.cfm?id=2343776.2343799

[12] Aanund Hylland and Richard Zeckhauser. 1979. The Efficient Allocation of Individuals to Positions. *Journal of Political Economy* 87, 2 (April 1979), 293–314. https://ideas.repec.org/a/ucp/jpolec/v87y1979i2p293-314.html

[13] Xiaodong Wang and José F. Martínez. 2015. XChange: A market-based approach to scalable dynamic multi-resource allocation in multicore architectures. In *International Symposium on High-Performance Computer Architecture (HPCA)*. Bay Area, CA.

[14] Lin Zhou. 1990. On a conjecture by gale about one-sided matching problems. *Journal of Economic Theory* 52, 1 (1990), 123–135. http://EconPapers.repec.org/RePEc:eee:jetheo:v:52:y:1990:i:1:p:123-135

Communication Requirements and Informative Signaling in Matching Markets

ITAI ASHLAGI, Stanford University
MARK BRAVERMAN, Princeton University
YASH KANORIA, Columbia University
PENG SHI, Microsoft Research

We study how much communication is needed to find a stable matching in a two-sided matching market with private preferences. Segal (2007) and Gonczarowski et al. (2015) showed that in the worst case, any protocol that computes a stable matching requires the communication cost per agent to scale linearly in the total number of agents. In real-world markets with many agents, this communication requirement is implausibly high. This casts doubts on whether stable matching can arise in large markets.

We study markets with realistic structure on the preferences and information of agents, and show that in "typical" markets, a stable matching can be found with much less communication effort. In our model, the preferences of workers are unrestricted, and the preferences of firms follow an additively separable latent utility model. Our efficient communication protocol modifies workers-proposing DA, by having firms signal workers they especially like, while also broadcasting qualification requirements to discourage other workers who have no realistic chances from applying. In the special case of tiered random markets, the protocol can be modified to run in two-rounds and involve only private messages. Our protocols have good incentive properties and give insights on how to mediate large matching markets to reduce congestion.

CCS Concepts: • **Theory of computation → Algorithmic game theory and mechanism design**; *Communication complexity*;

A full version of this paper is available at https://ssrn.com/abstract=2965135.

Authors' email addresses: First: iashlagi@stanford.edu; Second: mbraverm@cs.princeton.edu; Third: kanoria@columbia.edu; Fourth: pengshi46@gmail.com

Ashlagi acknowledges the research support of the National Science Foundation grant (SES-1254768).

EC'17, June 26–30, 2017, Cambridge, Massachusetts, USA. ACM ISBN 978-1-4503-4527-9/17/06.
DOI: http://dx.doi.org/10.1145/3033274.3084093

Complementary Inputs and the Existence of Stable Outcomes in Large Trading Networks

RAVI JAGADEESAN, Harvard University

This paper studies a model of large trading networks with bilateral contracts. Contracts capture exchange, production, and prices, as well as frictions such as complex taxes and the absence of transfers. In our setting, under standard continuity and convexity conditions, a stable outcome exists in any acyclic network, as long as all firms regard sales as substitutes and the market is large. Thus, complementarities between inputs do not preclude the existence of stable outcomes in large markets, unlike in discrete markets. Even when sales are not substitutable, tree stable outcomes exist in our setting.

The model presented in this paper generalizes and unifies versions of general equilibrium models with divisible and indivisible goods, matching models with continuously divisible contracts, models of large (two-sided) matching with complementarities, and club formation models. Additional results provide intuition for the role of uni-directional substitutability conditions and acyclicity in the main existence results, and explain what kinds of equilibria are guaranteed to exist even when these conditions are relaxed. Unlike in two-sided large-market settings, the sufficient conditions described in this paper pin down maximal domains for the existence of equilibria.

CCS Concepts: •**Theory of computation → Market equilibria;** Solution concepts in game theory;

Additional Key Words and Phrases: Economics; Matching with contracts; Large markets; Stability; Substitutability; Trading networks; Complementary inputs

A full version of this paper is available at http://sites.google.com/site/ravijagadeesan/large-networks.pdf.

I would like to thank Sandro Ambuehl, Eduardo Azevedo, Eric Budish, Jeremy Fox, Jerry Green, Ben Golub, John Hatfield, Fuhito Kojima, Ross Rheingans-Yoo, Rachit Singh, Alex Teytelboym, Sahana Vasudevan, seminar audiences at Harvard, and, especially, Scott Kominers for helpful comments. This research was conducted in part while the author was an Economic Design Fellow at the Harvard Center of Mathematical Sciences and Applications.

Author address: R. Jagadeesan, Department of Mathematics, Harvard University, 1 Oxford St, Cambridge, MA 02138. Email address: ravi.jagadeesan@gmail.com.

EC'17, June 26–30, 2017, Cambridge, MA, USA.

 ACM ISBN 978-1-4503-4527-9/17/06
http://dx.doi.org/10.1145/3033274.3085113

Making Right Decisions Based on Wrong Opinions

GERDUS BENADE, ANSON KAHNG, and ARIEL D. PROCACCIA, Carnegie Mellon University

We revisit the classic problem of designing voting rules that aggregate objective opinions, in a setting where voters have noisy estimates of a true ranking of the alternatives. Previous work has replaced structural assumptions on the noise with a worst-case approach that aims to choose an outcome that minimizes the maximum error with respect to any feasible true ranking. This approach underlies algorithms that have recently been deployed on the social choice website RoboVote.org. We take a less conservative viewpoint by minimizing the *average* error with respect to the set of feasible ground truth rankings. We derive (mostly sharp) analytical bounds on the expected error and establish the practical benefits of our approach through experiments.

1 INTRODUCTION

The field of *computational social choice* [4] has been undergoing a transformation, as rigorous approaches to voting and resource allocation, previously thought to be purely theoretical, are being applied to group decision making and social computing in practice [9]. From our biased viewpoint, RoboVote.org, a not-for-profit social choice website launched in November 2016, gives a compelling (and unquestionably recent) example. Its short-term goal is to facilitate effective group decision making by providing free access to optimization-based voting rules. In the long term, one of us has argued [21] that RoboVote and similar applications of computational social choice can change the public's perception of democracy.[1]

RoboVote distinguishes between two types of social choice tasks: aggregation of *subjective preferences*, and aggregation of *objective opinions*. Examples of the former task include a group of friends deciding where to go to dinner or which movie to watch; family members selecting a vacation spot; and faculty members choosing between faculty candidates. In all of these cases, there is no single correct choice — the goal is to choose an outcome that makes the participants as happy as possible overall.

By contrast, the latter task involves situations where some alternatives are objectively better than others, i.e., there is a true *ranking* of the alternatives by quality, but voters can only obtain noisy estimates thereof. The goal is, therefore, to aggregate these noisy opinions, which are themselves rankings of the alternatives, and uncover the true ranking. For example, consider a group of engineers deciding which product prototype to develop based on an objective metric, such as projected market share. Each prototype, if selected for development (and, ultimately, production), would achieve a particular market share, so a true ranking of the alternatives certainly exists. Other examples include a group of investors deciding which company to invest in, based on projected

[1]Of course, many people disagree. We were especially amused by a reader comment on a sensationalist story about RoboVote in the British tabloid Daily Mail: "Bloody robots coming over telling us how to vote! Take our country back!"

EC'17, June 26–30, 2017, Cambridge, Massachusetts, USA.

DOI: http://dx.doi.org/10.1145/3033274.3085108 © 2017 ACM. ISBN 978-1-4503-4527-9/17/06...$15.00.

revenue; and employees of a movie studio selecting a movie script for production, based on projected box office earnings.

In this paper, we focus on the second setting — aggregating objective opinions. This is a problem that boasts centuries of research: it dates back to the work of the Marquis de Condorcet, published in 1785, in which he proposed a random noise model that governs how voters make mistakes when estimating the true ranking. He further suggested — albeit in a way that took 203 years to decipher [30] — that a voting rule should be a *maximum likelihood estimator (MLE)*, that is, it should select an outcome that is most likely to coincide with the true ranking, given the observed votes and the *known* structure of the random noise model. Condorcet's approach is the foundation of a significant body of modern work [1–3, 6, 7, 10, 11, 13, 14, 16, 18, 22, 26–28].

While the MLE approach is conceptually appealing, it is also fragile. Indeed, it advocates rules that are tailor-made for one specific noise model, which is unlikely to accurately represent real-world errors [18]. Recent work [6, 7] circumvents this problem by designing voting rules that are robust to large families of noise models, at the price of theoretical guarantees that only kick in when the number of voters is large — a reasonable assumption in crowdsourcing settings. However, here we are most interested in helping small groups of people make decisions — on RoboVote, typical instances have 4–10 voters — so this approach is a nonstarter.

1.1 The Worst-Case Approach

In recent work, Procaccia et al. [24] have taken another step towards robustness (we will argue shortly that it is perhaps a step too far). Instead of positing a random noise model, they essentially remove all assumptions about the errors made by voters. To be specific, first fix a distance metric d on the space of rankings. For example, the *Kendall tau (KT)* distance between two rankings is the number of pairs of alternatives on which they disagree. We are given a vote profile and an upper bound t on the average distance between the input votes and the true ranking. This induces a set of *feasible* true rankings — those that are within average distance t from the votes. The *worst-case optimal voting rule* returns the ranking that minimizes the maximum distance (according to d) to any feasible true ranking. If this minimax distance is k, then we can guarantee that our output ranking is within distance k from the true ranking. The most pertinent theoretical results of Procaccia et al. are that for any distance metric d, one can always recover a ranking that is at distance at most $2t$ from the true ranking, i.e., $k \leq 2t$; and that for the four most popular distance metrics used in the social choice literature (including the KT distance), there is a tight lower bound of (roughly) $k \geq 2t$.

Arguably the more compelling results of Procaccia et al. [24], though, are empirical. In the case of objective opinions, the measure used to evaluate a voting rule is almost indisputable: the distance (according to the distance metric of interest, say KT) between the output ranking and the *actual* true ranking. And, indeed, according to this measure, the worst-case approach significantly outperforms previous approaches — including those based on random noise models — on real data [18]; we elaborate on this dataset later.

Based on the foregoing empirical results, the algorithms deployed on RoboVote for aggregating objective opinions implement the worst-case approach. Specifically, given an upper bound t on the average KT distance between the input votes and the true ranking,[2] the algorithm computes the set of feasible true rankings (by enumerating the solutions to an integer program), and selects a ranking that minimizes the KT distance to any ranking in that set (by solving another integer program).

[2]This value is set by minimizing the average distance between any input vote and the remaining votes. This choice guarantees a nonempty set of feasible true rankings, and performs extremely well in experiments.

RoboVote also supports two additional output types: single winning alternative, and a subset of alternatives. When the user requests a single alternative as the output, the algorithm computes the set of feasible true rankings as before, and returns the alternative that minimizes the maximum position in any feasible true ranking, that is, the alternative that is guaranteed to be as close to the top as possible. Computing a subset is similar, with the exception that the *loss* of a subset with respect to a specific feasible true ranking is determined based on the *top-ranked* alternative in the subset; the algorithm selects the subset that minimizes the maximum loss over all feasible true rankings. In other words, if this loss is s then any feasible true ranking has an alternative in the subset among its top s alternatives.

1.2 Our Approach and Results

To recap, the worst-case approach to aggregating objective opinions has proven quite successful. Nevertheless, it is very conservative, and it seems likely that better results can be achieved in practice by modifying it. We therefore take a more "optimistic" angle by carefully injecting some randomness into the worst-case approach.

In more detail, we refer to the worst-case approach as "worst case" because the errors made by voters are arbitrary, but there is actually another crucial aspect that makes it conservative: the optimization objective — minimizing the *maximum* distance to any feasible true ranking when the output is a ranking, and minimizing the maximum position or loss in any feasible true ranking when the output is a single alternative or a subset of alternatives, respectively. We propose to modify these objective functions, by replacing (in both cases) the word "maximum" with the word "average". Equivalently, we assume a uniform prior over the set of all rankings, which induces a uniform posterior over the set of feasible true rankings, and replace the word "maximum" with the word "expected".[3] Note that this model is fundamentally different from assuming that the *votes* are random: as we mentioned earlier, it is arguable whether real-world votes can be captured by any particular random noise model, not to mention a uniform distribution.[4] By contrast, we make no structural assumptions about the noise, and, in fact, we do not make any new assumptions about the world; we merely modify the optimization objective with respect to the same set of feasible true rankings.

In Section 3, we study the case where the output is a ranking. We find that for any distance metric, if the average distance between the vote profile and the true ranking is at most t, then we can recover a ranking whose average distance to the set of feasible true rankings is also t. We also establish essentially matching lower bounds for the four distance metrics studied by Procaccia et al. [24]. Note that our relaxed goal allows us to improve their bound from $2t$ to t, which, in our view, is a *qualitative* improvement, as now we can guarantee performance that is at least as good as the average voter. While we would like to outperform the average voter, this is a worst-case (over noisy votes) guarantee, and, as we shall see, in practice we indeed achieve excellent performance.

In Section 4, we explore the case where the output is a subset of alternatives (including the all-important case of a single winning alternative). This problem was not studied by Procaccia et al. [24], in part because their model does not admit nontrivial analytical solutions (as we explain in detail later) — but it is just as important in practice, if not even more so (see Section 1.1). We find significant gaps between the guarantees achievable under different distance metrics. Our main technical result concerns the practically significant KT distance and the closely related *footrule* distance: If the average distance between the vote profile and the true ranking is at most t, we can

[3] Our positive results actually work for any distribution; see Section 6.

[4] That said, some social choice papers do analyze uniformly random vote profiles [20, 25] — a model known as *impartial culture*.

pinpoint a subset of alternatives of size z, whose average loss — that is, the average position of the subset's top-ranked alternative in the set of feasible true rankings (smaller position is closer to the top) — is $O(\sqrt{t/z})$. We also prove a lower bound of $\Omega(\sqrt{t}/z)$, which is tight for a constant subset size z (note that z is now outside of the square root). For the *maximum displacement* distance, we have asymptotically matching upper and lower bounds of $\Theta(t/z)$. Interestingly, for the *Cayley* distance and $z = 1$, we prove a lower bound of $\Omega(\sqrt{m})$, showing that there is no hope of obtaining positive results that depend only on t.

In Section 5, we present empirical results from real data. Our key finding is that our methods are robust to overestimates of the true average level of noise in the vote profile — significantly more so than the methods of Procaccia et al. [24], which are currently deployed on RoboVote. We believe that this conclusion is meaningful for real-world implementation.

2 PRELIMINARIES

Let A be a set of *alternatives* with $|A| = m$. Let $\mathcal{L}(A)$ be the set of possible rankings of A, which we think of as permutations $\sigma : A \to [m]$, where $[m] = \{1, \ldots, m\}$. That is, $\sigma(a)$ gives the position of $a \in A$ in σ, with $\sigma^{-1}(1)$ being the highest-ranked alternative, and $\sigma^{-1}(m)$ being the lowest-ranked alternative. A ranking σ induces a strict total order $\succ_\sigma$, such that $a \succ_\sigma b$ if and only if $\sigma(a) < \sigma(b)$. A *vote profile* $\pi = (\sigma_1, \ldots, \sigma_n) \in \mathcal{L}(A)^n$ consists of n votes, where σ_i is the vote of voter i.

We next introduce notations that will simplify the creation of vote profiles. For a subset of alternatives $A_1 \subseteq A$, let σ^{A_1} be an arbitrary ranking of A_1. For a partition A_1, A_2 of A, $A_1 \succ A_2$ is a *partial order* of A which specifies that every alternative in A_1 is preferred to any alternative in A_2. Similarly, $A_1 \succ \sigma^{A_2}$ is a partial ordering where the alternatives in A_1 are preferred to those in A_2 and the order of the alternatives in A_2 is specified to coincide with σ^{A_2}. An *extension* of a partial order $\mathcal{P}$ is any ranking $\sigma \in \mathcal{L}(A)$ satisfying the partial order. Denote by $\mathcal{F}(\mathcal{P})$ the set of possible extensions of $\mathcal{P}$. For example, $|\mathcal{F}(A_1 \succ A_2)| = |A_1|! \cdot |A_2|!$ and $|\mathcal{F}(A_1 \succ \sigma^{A_2})| = |A_1|!$.

Distance metrics on permutations play an important role in the paper. We pay special attention to the following well-known distance metrics:

- The *Kendall tau (KT)* distance, denoted d_{KT}, measures the number of pairs of alternatives on which the two rankings disagree: $d_{KT}(\sigma, \sigma') \triangleq |\{(a, b) \in A^2 |\ a \succ_\sigma b \text{ and } b \succ_{\sigma'} a\}|$. Equivalently, the KT distance between σ and σ' is the number of swaps between *adjacent* alternatives required to transform one ranking into the other. Some like to think of it as the "bubble sort" distance.
- The *footrule* distance, denoted d_{FR}, measures the total displacement of alternatives between two rankings: $d_{FR}(\sigma, \sigma') \triangleq \sum_{a \in A} |\sigma(a) - \sigma'(a)|$.
- The *maximum displacement* distance, denoted d_{MD}, measures the largest absolute displacement of any alternative between two rankings: $d_{MD}(\sigma, \sigma') \triangleq \max_{a \in A} |\sigma(a) - \sigma'(a)|$.
- The *Cayley* distance, denoted d_{CY}, measures the number of pairwise swaps required to transform one ranking into the other. In contrast to the KT distance, the swapped alternatives need not be adjacent.

We also require the following definitions that apply to any distance metric d. For a ranking $\sigma \in \mathcal{L}(A)$ and a set of rankings $S \subseteq \mathcal{L}(A)$, define the average distance between σ and S in the obvious way,

$$d(\sigma, S) \triangleq \frac{1}{|S|} \sum_{\sigma' \in S} d(\sigma, \sigma').$$

Similarly, define the average distance between two sets of rankings $S, T \subseteq \mathcal{L}(A)$ as

$$d(S,T) \triangleq \frac{1}{|S| \cdot |T|} \sum_{\sigma \in S} \sum_{\sigma' \in T} d(\sigma, \sigma').$$

Finally, let $d^{\downarrow}(k)$ be the largest distance allowed under the distance metric d which is at most k, i.e.,

$$d^{\downarrow}(k) \triangleq \max\{s \leq k : \exists \sigma, \sigma' \in \mathcal{L}(A) \text{ s.t. } d(\sigma, \sigma') = s\}.$$

3 RETURNING THE RIGHT RANKING, IN THEORY

We first tackle the setting where our goal is to return an accurate ranking. We assume that there is an objective ground truth ranking σ^*, and that n voters submit a *vote profile* π of noisy estimates of this true ranking. As in the work of Procaccia et al. [24], an individual vote is allowed to deviate from the ground truth in any way, but we expect that the average error is bounded, that is, the average distance between the vote profile and the ground truth is no more than some parameter t. Formally, for a distance metric d on $\mathcal{L}(A)$, we are guaranteed that

$$d(\pi, \sigma^*) = \frac{1}{n} \sum_{\sigma \in \pi} d(\sigma, \sigma^*) \leq t.$$

There are several approaches for obtaining good estimates for this upper bound t; we return to this point later.

A combinatorial structure that plays a central role in our analysis is the "ball" of feasible ground truth rankings,

$$\mathcal{B}_t(\pi) \triangleq \{\sigma \in \mathcal{L}(A) : d(\pi, \sigma) \leq t\}.$$

If this ball were a singleton (or empty), our task would be easy. But it typically contains multiple feasible ground truths, as the following example shows.

Example 3.1. Suppose that $A = \{a, b, c\}$ and the vote profile consists of 5 votes, $\pi = \{(a \succ b \succ c), (a \succ b \succ c), (b \succ c \succ a), (c \succ a \succ b), (a \succ c \succ b)\}$. For each distance metric, let the bound on average error equal half of the maximum distance allowed by the distance metric; in other words, $t_{KT} = 1.5, t_{FR} = 2, t_{MD} = 1$ and $t_{CY} = 1$. The set of feasible ground truths for the vote profile π under the respective distance metrics may be found in Table 1.

Table 1. The set of feasible ground truths in Example 3.1 for various distance metrics.

d	t	$\mathcal{B}_t(\pi)$
KT	1.5	$\{(a \succ b \succ c), (c \succ a \succ b), (a \succ c \succ b)\}$
FR	2	$\{(a \succ b \succ c), (a \succ c \succ b)\}$
MD	1	
CY	1	

Procaccia et al. [24] advocate a conservative approach — they choose a ranking that minimizes the *maximum* distance to any feasible ground truth. By contrast, we are concerned with the *average* distance to the set of feasible ground truths. In other words, we assume that each of the feasible ground truths is equally likely, and our goal is to find a ranking that has a small expected distance to the set of feasible ground truths $\mathcal{B}_t(\pi)$.

Our first result is that is it always possible to find a ranking $\sigma \in \pi$ that is close to $\mathcal{B}_t(\pi)$.

Theorem 3.2. *Given a profile π of n noisy rankings with average distance at most t from the ground truth according to some distance metric d, there always exists a ranking within average distance t from the set of feasible ground truths $\mathcal{B}_t(\pi)$ according to the same metric.*

Proof. For any $\sigma \in \mathcal{B}_t(\pi)$, $d(\sigma, \pi) \le t$. It follows from the definitions that

$$d(\pi, \mathcal{B}_t(\pi)) = \frac{1}{n \cdot |\mathcal{B}_t(\pi)|} \sum_{\sigma' \in \pi} \sum_{\sigma \in \mathcal{B}_t(\pi)} d(\sigma, \sigma') = \frac{1}{|\mathcal{B}_t(\pi)|} \sum_{\sigma \in \mathcal{B}_t(\pi)} \frac{1}{n} \sum_{\sigma' \in \pi} d(\sigma, \sigma')$$
$$= \frac{1}{|\mathcal{B}_t(\pi)|} \sum_{\sigma \in \mathcal{B}_t(\pi)} d(\sigma, \pi) \le t.$$

To conclude the proof, observe that if the average distance from π to $\mathcal{B}_t(\pi)$ is no more than t, then there certainly exists $\sigma'' \in \pi$ with $d(\sigma'', \mathcal{B}_t(\pi)) \le t$. □

This result holds for any distance metric. Interestingly, it also generalizes to any probability distribution over $\mathcal{B}_t(\pi)$, not just the uniform distribution (see Section 6 for additional discussion of this point).

We next derive essentially matching lower bounds for the four common distance metrics introduced in Section 2.

Theorem 3.3. *For $d \in \{d_{KT}, d_{FR}, d_{MD}, d_{CY}\}$, there exists a profile π of n noisy rankings with average distance at most t from the ground truth, such that for any ranking, its average distance (according to d) from $\mathcal{B}_t(\pi)$ is at least $d^{\downarrow}(2t)/2$.*

The proof of this theorem relies heavily on constructions by Procaccia et al. [24]; it is included in the full version of the paper.[5]

4 RETURNING THE RIGHT ALTERNATIVES, IN THEORY

In the previous section, we derived bounds on the expected distance of the ranking closest to the set of feasible ground truth rankings. In practice, we may not be interested in eliciting a complete ranking of alternatives, but rather in selecting a subset of the alternatives (often a single alternative) on which to focus attention, time, or effort.

In this section, we bound the average position of the *best* alternative in a subset of alternatives, where the average is taken over the set of feasible ground truths as before. This type of utility function, where the utility of a set is defined by its highest utility member, is consistent with quite a few previous papers that deal with selecting subsets of alternatives in different social choice settings [5, 8, 15, 19, 22, 23]. For example, when selecting a menu of movies to show on a three hour flight, the utility of passengers depends on their most preferred alternative. From a technical viewpoint, this choice has the advantage of giving bounds that improve as the subset size increases, which matches our intuition. Of course, in the important special case where the subset is a singleton, all reasonable definitions coincide.

Formally, let $Z \subseteq A$ be a subset of alternatives; the *loss of Z in σ* is $\ell(Z, \sigma) \triangleq \min_{a \in Z} \sigma(a)$, and therefore the *average loss of Z in $\mathcal{B}_t(\pi)$* is

$$\ell(Z, \mathcal{B}_t(\pi)) \triangleq \frac{1}{|\mathcal{B}_t(\pi)|} \sum_{\sigma \in \mathcal{B}_t(\pi)} \ell(Z, \sigma).$$

For given average error t and subset size z, we are interested in bounding

$$\max_{\pi \in \mathcal{L}(A)^n} \min_{Z \subseteq A \text{ s.t. } |Z| = z} \ell(Z, \mathcal{B}_t(\pi)).$$

[5]The full version is accessible from procaccia.info/research.

In words, we wish to bound the the average loss of the best Z (of size z) in $\mathcal{B}_t(\pi)$, in the worst case over vote profiles.

Let us return to Example 3.1. For the footrule, maximum displacement, and Cayley distance metrics, it is clear from Table 1 that selecting $\{a\}$ when $z = 1$ guarantees average loss 1, as $\mathcal{B}_t(\pi)$ only contains rankings that place a first. For the KT distance, the set $\{a\}$ has average loss 4/3, and the set $\{a, c\}$ has average loss 1.

We now turn to the technical results, starting with some lemmas that are independent of specific distance metrics. Throughout this section, we will rely on the following lemma, which is the discrete analogue of selecting a set of z numbers uniformly at random in an interval and studying their order statistics. No doubt someone has proved it in the past, but we include our (cute, if we may say so ourselves) proof, as we will need to reuse specific equations.

Lemma 4.1. *When choosing z elements $Y_1, \ldots, Y_z$ uniformly at random without replacement from the set $[k]$, $\mathbb{E}[\min_{i\in[z]} Y_i] = \frac{k+1}{z+1}$.*

Proof. Let $Y_{min} = \min_{i\in[z]} Y_i$ be the minimum value of the z numbers chosen uniformly at random from $[k]$ without replacement. It holds that

$$\Pr[Y_{min} = y] = \frac{\binom{k-y}{z-1}}{\binom{k}{z}},$$

and therefore

$$\mathbb{E}[Y_{min}] = \sum_{y=1}^{k} y\frac{\binom{k-y}{z-1}}{\binom{k}{z}} = \frac{1}{\binom{k}{z}}\sum_{y=1}^{k} y\binom{k-y}{z-1} = \frac{1}{\binom{k}{z}}\sum_{y=1}^{k-z+1} y\binom{k-y}{z-1}. \tag{1}$$

We claim that

$$\sum_{y=1}^{k-z+1} y\binom{k-y}{z-1} = \binom{k+1}{z+1}. \tag{2}$$

Indeed, the left hand side can be interpreted as follows: for each choice of $y \in [k-z+1]$, elements $\{1, \ldots, y\}$ form a committee of size y. We have y possibilities for choosing the head of the committee. Then we choose $z-1$ clerks among the elements $\{y+1, \ldots, k\}$. We can interpret the right hand side of Equation (2) in the same way. To see how, choose $z+1$ elements from $[k+1]$, and sort them in increasing order to obtain $s_1, \ldots, s_{z+1}$. Now s_1 is the head of the committee, $y = s_2 - 1$ is the number of committee members, and $s_3 - 1, \ldots, s_{z+1} - 1$ are the clerks.

Plugging Equation (2) into Equation (1), we get

$$\mathbb{E}[Y_{min}] = \frac{\binom{k+1}{z+1}}{\binom{k}{z}} = \frac{k+1}{z+1}.$$

□

Our strategy for proving upper bounds also relies on the following lemma, which relates the performance of randomized rules on the worst ranking in $\mathcal{B}_t(\pi)$, to the performance of deterministic rules on average, and is reminiscent of Yao's Minimax Principle [29]. This lemma actually holds for any distribution over ground truth rankings, as we discuss in Section 6.

Lemma 4.2. *Suppose that for a given $\mathcal{B}_t(\pi)$, there exists a distribution D over subsets of A of size z such that*

$$\max_{\sigma\in\mathcal{B}_t(\pi)} \mathbb{E}_{Z\sim D}\left[\ell(Z,\sigma)\right] = k.$$

Then there exists $Z^* \subseteq A$ of size z whose average loss in $\mathcal{B}_t(\pi)$ is at most k.

Proof. Let U be the uniform distribution over rankings in $\mathcal{B}_t(\pi)$. Then clearly

$$\mathbb{E}_{Z\sim D,\sigma\sim U}\left[\ell(Z,\sigma)\right] \le k,$$

as this inequality holds pointwise for all $\sigma \in \mathcal{B}_t(\pi)$. It follows there must exist at least one Z^* such that

$$\ell(Z^*,\mathcal{B}_t(\pi)) = \mathbb{E}_{\sigma\sim U}\left[\ell(Z^*,\sigma)\right] \le k,$$

that is, the average loss of Z^* in $\mathcal{B}_t(\pi)$ is at most k. □

Finally, we require a simple lemma of Procaccia et al. [24].

Lemma 4.3. *Given a profile π of n noisy rankings with average distance at most t from the ground truth according to a distance metric d, there exists $\sigma \in \mathcal{L}(A)$ such that for all $\tau \in \mathcal{B}_t(\pi)$, $d(\sigma,\tau) \le 2t$.*

4.1 The KT and Footrule Distances

We first focus on the KT distance and the footrule distance. The KT distance is by far the most important distance metric over permutations, both in theory, and in practice (see Section 1.1). We study it together with the footrule distance because the two distances are closely related, as the following lemma, due to Diaconis and Graham [12], shows.

Lemma 4.4. *For all $\sigma,\sigma' \in \mathcal{L}(A)$, $d_{KT}(\sigma,\sigma') \le d_{FR}(\sigma,\sigma') \le 2d_{KT}(\sigma,\sigma')$.*

Despite this close connection between the two metrics, it is important to note that it does not allow us to automatically transform a bound on the loss for one into a bound for the other.

The next upper bound is, in our view, our most significant theoretical result. It is formulated for the footrule distance, but, as we show shortly, also holds for the KT distance.

Theorem 4.5. *For $d = d_{FR}$, given a profile π of n noisy rankings with average distance at most t from the ground truth, and a number $z \in [m]$, there always exists a subset of size z whose average loss in the set of feasible ground truths $\mathcal{B}_t(\pi)$ is at most $O(\sqrt{t/z})$.*

At some point in the proof, we will rely on the following (almost trivial) lemma.

Lemma 4.6. *Given two positive sequences of k real numbers, P, and Q, such that P is non-decreasing, Q is strictly decreasing and $\sum_{i=1}^{k} P_i = C$, the sequence P that maximizes $S = \sum_{i=1}^{n} P_i Q_i$ is constant, i.e., $P_i = C/k$ for all $i \in [k]$.*

Proof. Assume for contradiction that P maximizes S and contains consecutive elements such that $P_j < P_{j+1}$. Now moving mass from P_{j+1} and distributing it to all lower positions in the sequence will strictly increase S. Concretely, if $P_{j+1} = P_j + \varepsilon$, we can subtract $j\varepsilon/(j+1)$ from P_{j+1} and add $\varepsilon/(j+1)$ to P_i for all $i \in [j]$. Because Q is strictly decreasing, this increases S by

$$\left(\sum_{i=1}^{j} \frac{Q_i \varepsilon}{j+1}\right) - \frac{Q_{j+1} j\varepsilon}{j+1} > \left(\sum_{i=1}^{j} \frac{Q_j \varepsilon}{j+1}\right) - \frac{Q_{j+1} j\varepsilon}{j+1} = \frac{j\varepsilon}{j+1}(Q_j - Q_{j+1}) > 0,$$

contradicting the assumption that P maximizes S. We may conclude that P is constant. □

Proof of Theorem 4.5. By Lemma 4.2, it is sufficient to construct a randomized rule that has expected loss at most $O(\sqrt{t/z})$ on *any* ranking in $\mathcal{B}_t(\pi)$. To this end, let $\sigma \in \mathcal{L}(A)$ such that $d(\sigma,\tau) \le 2t$ for any $\tau \in \mathcal{B}_t(\pi)$; its existence is guaranteed by Lemma 4.3. Let $k = \sqrt{tz}$, and assume for ease of exposition that k is an integer. For $y = 1,\ldots,k$, let $a_y = \sigma^{-1}(y)$. Our randomized rule simply selects z alternatives uniformly at random from the top k alternatives in σ, that is, from the set $T \triangleq \{a_1,\ldots,a_k\}$. So, fixing some $\tau \in \mathcal{B}_t(\pi)$, we need to show that choosing z elements uniformly at random from the worst-case positions occupied by T in τ has expected minimum position at most $O(\sqrt{t/z})$.

Let Y^{σ}_{min} be the minimum position in σ of a random subset of size z from T. By Lemma 4.1 and Equation (1), we have

$$\mathbb{E}[Y^{\sigma}_{min}] = \sum_{y=1}^{k} y \frac{\binom{k-y}{z-1}}{\binom{k}{z}} = \frac{k+1}{z+1}.$$

However, we are interested in the positions of these elements in $\tau \in \mathcal{B}_t(\pi)$, not σ. Instead of appearing in position y, alternative a_y appears in position $p_y \triangleq \tau(a_y)$. Therefore, the expected minimum position in τ is

$$\mathbb{E}[Y^{\tau}_{min}] = \sum_{y=1}^{k} p_y \frac{\binom{k-y}{z-1}}{\binom{k}{z}}.$$

We wish to upper bound $\mathbb{E}[Y^{\tau}_{min}]$. Equivalently, because $\mathbb{E}[Y^{\sigma}_{min}]$ is fixed and independent of τ, it is sufficient to maximize the expression

$$\begin{aligned}\mathbb{E}[Y^{\tau}_{min}] - \mathbb{E}[Y^{\sigma}_{min}] &= \sum_{y=1}^{k} p_y \frac{\binom{k-y}{z-1}}{\binom{k}{z}} - \sum_{y=1}^{k} y \frac{\binom{k-y}{z-1}}{\binom{k}{z}} \\ &= \sum_{y=1}^{k} (p_y - y) \frac{\binom{k-y}{z-1}}{\binom{k}{z}}.\end{aligned} \tag{3}$$

Let us now assume that $p_y < p_{y+1}$ for all $y \in [k-1]$, that is, τ and σ agree on the order of the alternatives in T; we will remove this assumption later. Since the original positions of the alternatives in T were $\{1, \ldots, k\}$ it follows that $p_y \geq y$ for all $y \in [k]$. Moreover, because

$$\frac{\binom{k-y}{z-1}}{\binom{k}{z}} > \frac{\binom{k-(y+1)}{z-1}}{\binom{k}{z}},$$

the sequence of probabilities

$$Q = \left\{ \frac{\binom{k-y}{z-1}}{\binom{k}{z}} \right\}_{y \in [k]}$$

is strictly decreasing in y. Additionally, the sequence $P = \{p_y - y\}_{y \in [k]}$ is non-decreasing, because $p_{y+1} > p_y$, coupled with the fact that both values are integers, implies that $p_{y+1} \geq p_y + 1$.

In light of these facts, let us return to Equation (3). We wish to maximize

$$\mathbb{E}[Y^{\tau}_{min}] - \mathbb{E}[Y^{\sigma}_{min}] = \sum_{y=1}^{k} (p_y - y) \frac{\binom{k-y}{z-1}}{\binom{k}{z}} = \sum_{y=1}^{k} P_y Q_y.$$

By Lemma 4.6, $p_y - y$ is the same for all $y \in [k]$, that is, all alternatives in T are shifted by the same amount from σ to form τ. Moreover, we have that

$$\sum_{y=1}^{k} (p_y - y) \leq d(\sigma, \tau) \leq 2t.$$

Using $k = |T| = \sqrt{zt}$, we conclude that $p_y - y \leq 2\sqrt{t/z}$ for all $y \in [k]$. Therefore, in the worst $\tau \in \mathcal{B}_t(\pi)$, we have that the alternatives in T occupy positions $2\sqrt{t/z} + 1$ to $2\sqrt{t/z} + \sqrt{tz}$ in τ. By

Lemma 4.1, the expected minimum position of T in τ is

$$2\sqrt{\frac{t}{z}} + \frac{\sqrt{tz}+1}{z+1} = O\left(\sqrt{\frac{t}{z}}\right).$$

To complete the proof, it remains to show that our assumption that $p_y < p_{y+1}$ for all $y \in [k-1]$ is without loss of generality. To see this, note that since we are selecting uniformly at random from T, Y^{τ}_{min} only depends on the positions occupied by T in τ. Moreover, if τ does not preserve the order over T, we can find a ranking τ' that has the following properties:

(1) $d(\sigma, \tau') \leq 2t$.
(2) T occupies the same positions: $\{\tau(a_1), \ldots, \tau(a_k)\} = \{\tau'(a_1), \ldots, \tau'(a_k)\}$.
(3) τ' preserves the order over T: $\tau'(a_y) < \tau'(a_{y+1})$ for all $y \in [k-1]$.

Now all our arguments would apply to τ', and $\mathbb{E}[Y^{\tau}_{min}] = \mathbb{E}[Y^{\tau'}_{min}]$.

In order to construct τ', suppose that $\tau(a_y) > \tau(a_{y+1})$, and consider τ'' that is identical to τ except for swapping a_y and a_{y+1}. Then

$$\begin{aligned} d(\tau'', \sigma) &= d(\tau, \sigma) + \left(|\tau''(a_y) - y| + |\tau''(a_{y+1}) - (y+1)| - |\tau(a_y) - y| - |\tau(a_{y+1} - (y+1)|\right) \\ &\leq d(\tau, \sigma) \leq 2t. \end{aligned}$$

By iteratively swapping alternatives we can easily obtain the desired τ'. □

We next formulate the same result for the KT distance. The proof is very similar, so instead of repeating it, we just give a proof sketch that highlights the differences.

Theorem 4.7. *For $d = d_{KT}$, given a profile π of n noisy rankings with average distance at most t from the ground truth, and a number $z \in [m]$, there always exists a subset of size z whose average loss in the set of feasible ground truths $\mathcal{B}_t(\pi)$ is at most $O(\sqrt{t/z})$.*

Proof sketch. The proof only differs from the proof of Theorem 4.7 in two places.

First, the footrule proof had the inequality

$$\sum_{y=1}^{k}(p_y - y) \leq d_{FR}(\sigma, \tau) \leq 2t.$$

In our case,

$$\sum_{y=1}^{k}(p_y - y) \leq d_{FR}(\sigma, \tau) \leq 2 \cdot d_{KT}(\sigma, \tau) \leq 4t,$$

where the second inequality follows from Lemma 4.4.

Second, if τ does not preserve the order over T, we needed to find a ranking τ' that has the following properties:

(1) $d(\sigma, \tau') \leq 2t$.
(2) T occupies the same positions: $\{\tau(a_1), \ldots, \tau(a_k)\} = \{\tau'(a_1), \ldots, \tau'(a_k)\}$.
(3) τ' preserves the order over T: $\tau'(a_y) < \tau'(a_{y+1})$ for all $y \in [k-1]$.

To construct τ' under $d = d_{KT}$, we use the same strategy as before: Suppose that $\tau(a_y) > \tau(a_{y+1})$, and consider τ'' that is identical to τ except for swapping a_y and a_{y+1}. We claim that $d(\tau', \sigma) \leq d(\tau, \sigma) \leq 2t$. Indeed, notice that all $a \in T$ precede all $b \in A \setminus T$ in σ. Therefore, holding all else equal, switching the relative order of alternatives in T will not change the number of pairwise disagreements on alternatives $b \in T$, $b' \in A \setminus T$, nor will it change the number of pairwise disagreements on alternatives $b, b' \in A \setminus T$. It will only (strictly) decrease the number of disagreements on alternatives in T. □

Our next result is a lower bound of $\Omega(\sqrt{t}/z)$ for both distance metrics. Note that here z is outside the square root, i.e., there is a gap of $\sqrt{z}$ between the upper bounds given in Theorems 4.5 and 4.7, and the lower bound. That said, the lower bound is tight for a constant z, including the important case of $z = 1$.

THEOREM 4.8. *For $d \in \{d_{FR}, d_{KT}\}$, $z \in [m]$, and an even n, there exist $t = O(m^2)$ and a profile π of n noisy rankings with average distance at most t from the ground truth, such that for any subset of size z, its average loss in the set of feasible ground truths $\mathcal{B}_t(\pi)$ is at least $\Omega(\sqrt{t}/z)$.*

PROOF. We first prove the theorem for the KT distance, that is, $d = d_{KT}$. For any $k \geq 1$, let $t = \binom{k}{2}/2$; equivalently, let

$$k = \frac{1 + \sqrt{1 + 16t}}{2} = \Theta\left(\sqrt{t}\right).$$

Let $\sigma = (a_1 \succ \cdots \succ a_m)$, and let $\sigma_{R(k)} = (a_k, a_{k-1}, \ldots, a_1, a_{k+1}, \ldots, a_m)$ be the ranking that reverses the first k alternatives of σ. Consider the vote profile π with $n/2$ copies of each ranking σ and $\sigma_{R(k)}$.

Let $A_k = \{a_1, \ldots, a_k\}$ and denote by σ_{-k} the ranking of $A \setminus A_k$ ordered as in σ. We claim that $\mathcal{B}_t(\pi) = \mathcal{F}(A_k \succ \sigma_{-k})$, i.e., exactly the rankings that have some permutation of A_k in the first k positions, and coincide with σ in all the other positions. Indeed, consider any $\tau \in \mathcal{L}(A)$. This ranking will disagree with exactly one of σ and $\sigma_{R(k)}$ on every pair of alternatives in A_k, so

$$d(\tau, \pi) \geq \frac{\binom{k}{2}}{2} = t.$$

It follows that if $\tau \in \mathcal{B}_t(\pi)$ then τ must agree with σ_{-k} on the remaining alternatives.

Now let Z be a subset of z alternatives. Note that for every $a \in A \setminus A_k$ and $\tau \in \mathcal{B}_t(\pi)$, $\tau(a) > k$, so it is best to choose $Z \subset A_k$. We are interested in the expected loss of Z under the uniform distribution on $\mathcal{B}_t(\pi)$, which amounts to a random permutation of A_k. This is the same as choosing z positions at random from $[k]$. By Lemma 4.1, the expected minimum position of a randomly chosen subset of size z is $\frac{k+1}{z+1}$. Since $k = \frac{1+\sqrt{1+16t}}{2}$, it holds that

$$\mathbb{E}[Y_{min}] = \frac{\frac{1+\sqrt{1+16t}}{2} + 1}{z + 1} = \Omega\left(\frac{\sqrt{t}}{z}\right).$$

For $d = d_{FR}$, the construction is analogous to above, with one minor modification. For any $k \geq 1$, we let $t = \lfloor k^2/2 \rfloor/2$, because the footrule distance between σ and $\sigma_{R(k)}$ is $\lfloor k^2/2 \rfloor$, instead of $\binom{k}{2}$ as in the KT case. Now, the proof proceeds as before. □

An important remark is in order. Suppose that instead of measuring the average loss of the subset Z in $\mathcal{B}_t(\pi)$, we measured the *maximum* loss in any ranking in $\mathcal{B}_t(\pi)$, in the spirit of the model of Procaccia et al. [24]. Then the results would be *qualitatively* different. To see why on an intuitive level, consider the KT distance, and suppose that the vote profile π consists of n copies of the same ranking σ. Then for any $a \in A$, $\mathcal{B}_t(\pi)$ includes a ranking σ' such that $\sigma'(a) \geq t$ (by using our "budget" of t to move a downwards in the ranking). Therefore, for $z = 1$, it is impossible to choose an alternative whose maximum position (i.e., loss) in $\mathcal{B}_t(\pi)$ is smaller than t. In contrast, Theorem 4.5 gives us an upper bound of $O(\sqrt{t})$ in our model.

4.2 The Maximum Displacement Distance

We now turn to the maximum displacement distance. Here the bounds are significantly worse than in the KT and footrule settings. On an intuitive level, the reason is that two rankings that are at maximum displacement distance t from each other can be drastically different, because *every* alternative can move by up to t positions. Therefore, $\mathcal{B}_t(\pi)$ under maximum displacement would typically be larger than under the distance metrics we previously considered. Indeed, this is the case in Example 3.1 if one sets $t_{MD} \geq 1.5$.

THEOREM 4.9. *For $d = d_{MD}$, given a profile π of n noisy rankings with average distance at most t from the ground truth, and a number $z \in [m]$, there always exists a subset of size z whose average loss in the set of feasible ground truths $\mathcal{B}_t(\pi)$ is at most $O(t/z)$.*

PROOF. By Lemma 4.2, it is sufficient to construct a randomized rule that has expected loss at most $O(t/z)$ on *any* ranking in $\mathcal{B}_t(\pi)$. To this end, let $\sigma \in \mathcal{L}(A)$ such that $d(\sigma, \tau) \leq 2t$ for any $\tau \in \mathcal{B}_t(\pi)$; its existence is guaranteed by Lemma 4.3. For $y = 1, \ldots, 3t$, let $a_y = \sigma^{-1}(y)$. Our randomized rule selects z alternatives uniformly at random from the top $3t$ alternatives in σ, that is, from the set $T \triangleq \{a_1, \ldots, a_{3t}\}$.

Let T' be the top t alternatives in a ranking $\tau \in \mathcal{B}_t(\pi)$. Since $d(\sigma, \tau) \leq 2t$, we know that $T' \subset T$. Moreover, for any $a_y \in T$, we have that $p_y \triangleq \tau(a_y) \leq 5t$. Assume without loss of generality that $p_y \leq p_{y+1}$ for all $y \in [3t-1]$; then we have that the vector of positions $(p_1, \ldots, p_{3t})$ is pointwise at least as small as the vector $(1, 2, \ldots, t, 5t, 5t, \ldots, 5t)$. Using Lemma 4.1 and Equation (1), we conclude that the minimum position in τ when selecting z alternatives uniformly at random from T, denoted Y^{τ}_{min}, satisfies

$$\mathbb{E}[Y^{\tau}_{min}] = \sum_{y=1}^{3t} p_y \frac{\binom{3t-y}{z-1}}{\binom{3t}{z}} = \sum_{y=1}^{t-1} p_y \frac{\binom{3t-y}{z-1}}{\binom{3t}{z}} + \sum_{y=t}^{3t} p_y \frac{\binom{3t-y}{z-1}}{\binom{3t}{z}} \leq \sum_{y=1}^{t-1} y \frac{\binom{3t-y}{z-1}}{\binom{3t}{z}} + \sum_{y=t}^{3t} 5t \frac{\binom{3t-y}{z-1}}{\binom{3t}{z}}$$
$$\leq 5 \cdot \sum_{y=1}^{3t} y \frac{\binom{3t-y}{z-1}}{\binom{3t}{z}} = 5 \cdot \frac{3t+1}{z+1} = \Theta\left(\frac{t}{z}\right).$$

□

We next establish a lower bound of $\Omega(t/z)$ on the average loss achievable under the maximum displacement distance. Note that this lower bound matches the upper bound of Theorem 4.9.

THEOREM 4.10. *For $d = d_{MD}$, given $k \in \mathbb{N}$ and $z \in [m]$, there exist $t = \Theta(k)$ and a vote profile π of $k!$ noisy votes at average distance at most t from the ground truth, such that for any subset of size z, its average loss in the set of feasible ground truths $\mathcal{B}_t(\pi)$ is at least $\Omega(t/z)$.*

PROOF. Let $\pi = \mathcal{F}(A_k \succ \sigma^{A \setminus A_k})$, where $|A_k| = k$. For some $\tau \in \pi$, let $t = d(\tau, \pi)$. By symmetry, $\tau' \in \mathcal{B}_t(\pi)$ for all $\tau' \in \pi$.

We first claim that $t = \Omega(k)$. Indeed, t is the average distance between τ and π. Letting U be the uniform distribution over π, we have that $t = \mathbb{E}_{\tau' \sim U}[d(\tau, \tau')]$. Now consider the top-ranked alternative in τ, $a \triangleq \tau^{-1}(1)$. Because U amounts to a random permutation over A_k, it clearly holds that $\mathbb{E}_{\tau' \sim U}[\tau'(a)] = (k+1)/2$, and therefore

$$t = \mathbb{E}_{\tau' \sim U}[d(\tau, \tau')] = \mathbb{E}_{\tau' \sim U}\left[\max_{b \in A} |\tau'(b) - \tau(b)|\right] \geq \mathbb{E}_{\tau' \sim U}[\tau'(a) - \tau(a)] = \frac{k+1}{2} - 1 = \Omega(k).$$

Now, suppose that we have shown that $\mathcal{B}_t(\pi) = \pi$; we argue that the theorem follows. Let $Z \subseteq A$ be a subset of alternatives of size z. We can assume without loss of generality that $Z \subseteq A_k$, as A_k is ranked at the top of every $\tau \in \mathcal{B}_t(\pi)$. But because $\mathcal{B}_t(\pi)$ consists of all permutations of A_k, $\ell(Z, \mathcal{B}_t(\pi))$ is equal to the expected minimum position when z elements are selected uniformly at random from the positions occupied by A_k, namely $[k]$. That is, we have that

$$\ell(Z, \mathcal{B}_t(\pi)) = \frac{k+1}{z+1} = \Omega\left(\frac{t}{z}\right).$$

Therefore, it only remains to show that $\mathcal{B}_t(\pi) = \pi$. Indeed, let $\tau \notin \pi$, then there exists $a \in A_k$ such that $\tau(a) > k$. Without loss of generality assume a is unique and let $\tau(a) = k + 1$. There must then be some $b \in A \setminus A_k$ with $\tau(b) \leq k$. Recall that the alternatives in $A \setminus A_k$ remain in fixed positions in π, and, again without loss of generality, suppose that $\sigma(b) = k + 1$ for all $\sigma \in \pi$. We wish to show that $d(\tau, \pi) > d(\sigma, \pi)$ for all $\sigma \in \pi$.

Let τ' be τ except that a and b are swapped, so $\tau'(a) = \tau(b)$ and $\tau'(b) = \tau(a)$. Observe that $\tau' \in \pi$ since a is unique. By definition, $d(\tau', \pi) = d(\sigma, \pi)$ for all $\sigma \in \pi$. It is therefore sufficient to show that $d(\tau', \pi) < d(\tau, \pi)$.

To this end, we partition the rankings $\sigma \in \pi \setminus \{\tau'\}$ into two sets, analyze them separately, and in both cases show that $d(\tau', \sigma) \leq d(\tau, \sigma)$.

(1) $\sigma(a) \leq \tau'(a)$ (see Figure 1): In this case, we have that $|\sigma(a) - \tau(a)| \geq |\sigma(a) - \tau'(a)|$. Also, because σ and τ' agree on the position of $b \in A \setminus A_k$, $0 = |\sigma(b) - \tau'(b)| \leq |\sigma(b) - \tau(b)|$. We conclude that $d(\tau', \sigma) \leq d(\tau, \sigma)$.

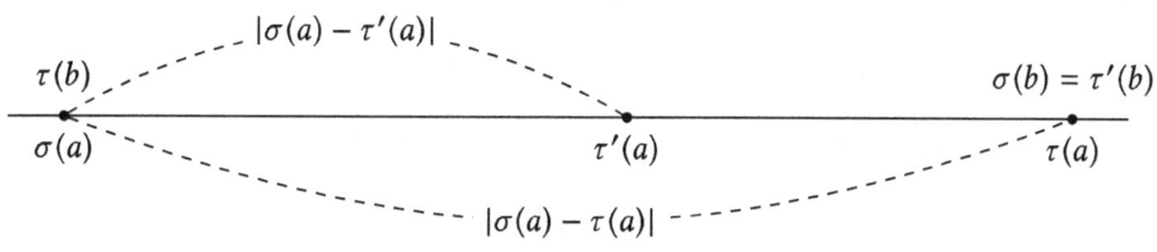

Fig. 1. Illustration of Case 1 of the proof of Theorem 4.10.

(2) $\sigma(a) > \tau'(a)$ (see Figure 2): It again holds that $0 = |\sigma(b) - \tau'(b)| \leq |\sigma(b) - \tau(b)|$, so if $d(\tau', \sigma) > d(\tau, \sigma)$ then $d(\tau', \sigma)$ is determined by a (i.e., a has the maximum displacement). Assume for contradiction that $d(\tau', \sigma) > d(\tau, \sigma)$. Then it holds that

$$d(\tau', \sigma) = |\sigma(a) - \tau'(a)| \leq |\sigma(a) - \tau'(a)| + |\sigma(a) - \tau(a)| = |\sigma(b) - \tau(b)| \leq d(\tau, \sigma),$$

a contradiction. We may conclude that $d(\tau', \sigma) \leq d(\tau, \sigma)$.

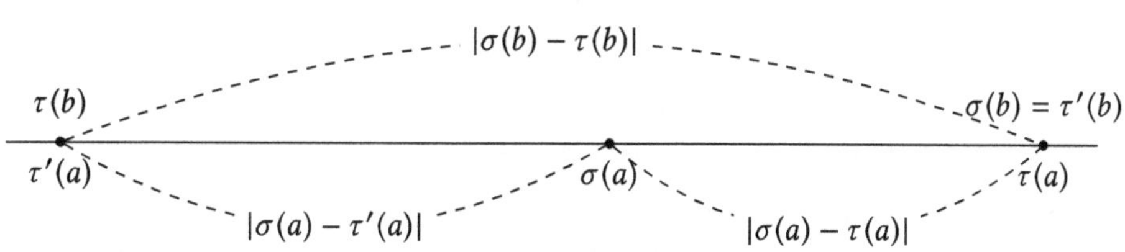

Fig. 2. Illustration of Case 2 of the proof of Theorem 4.10.

Since $d(\tau', \sigma) \leq d(\tau, \sigma)$ for all $\sigma \in \pi \setminus \{\tau'\}$, and $d(\tau', \tau') = 0 < d(\tau, \tau')$ we may conclude that $d(\tau, \pi) > d(\tau', \pi) = t$. It follows that $\mathcal{B}_t(\pi) = \pi$, thereby completing the proof. □

4.3 The Cayley Distance

In the previous sections, we have seen that our bounds are very different for different distance metrics. Still, all those bounds depended on t. By contrast, we establish a lower bound of $\Omega(\sqrt{m})$ on the average loss of any subset with $z = 1$ (i.e., the average position of any alternative) under the

Cayley distance. We view this as a striking negative result: Even if the votes are extremely accurate, i.e., t is very small, the ball $\mathcal{B}_t(\pi)$ could be such that the average position of any alternative is as large as $\Omega(\sqrt{m})$.

Theorem 4.11. *For $d = d_{CY}$ and every $k \in [\sqrt{m}/3]$, there exists $t = \Theta(k)$ and a vote profile π with*

$$n = k!\binom{\sqrt{m}}{k}^2$$

noisy rankings at average distance at most t from the ground truth, such that for any single alternative, its average position in the set of feasible ground truths $\mathcal{B}_t(\pi)$ is at least $\Omega(\sqrt{m})$.

The theorem's proof appears in the full version of the paper. Note that the delicate construction is specific to the case of $z = 1$. It remains open whether the theorem still holds when, say, $z = 2$, and, more generally, how the bound decreases as a function of z.

5 MAKING THE RIGHT DECISIONS, IN PRACTICE

We have two related goals in practice, to recover a ranking that is close to the ground truth, and identify a subset of alternatives with small loss in the ground truth. We compare the optimal rules that minimize the *average* distance or loss on $\mathcal{B}_t(\pi)$, denoted AVG^d, which we developed, to those that minimize the *maximum* distance or loss, denoted MAX^d, which were developed by Procaccia et al. [24]. Importantly, at least for the case where the output is a ranking, Procaccia et al. [24] have compared their methods against a slew of previously studied methods – including MLE rules for famous random noise models like the one due to Mallows [17] – and found theirs to be superior. In addition, their methods are the ones currently used in practice, on RoboVote. Therefore we focus on comparing our methods to theirs.

Datasets. Like Procaccia et al. [24], we make use of two real-world datasets collected by Mao et al. [18]. In both of these datasets – *dots* and *puzzle* – the ground truth rankings are known, and data was collected via Amazon Mechanical Turk. Dataset *dots* was obtained by asking workers to rank four images containing different numbers of dots in increasing order. Dataset *puzzle* was obtained by asking workers to rank four different states of a puzzle according to the minimal number of moves necessary to reach the goal state. Each dataset consists of four different noise levels, corresponding to levels of difficulty, represented using a single noise parameter. In *dots*, higher noise corresponds to smaller differences between the number of dots in the images, whereas in *puzzle*, higher noise entails ranking states that are all a constant number of steps further from the goal state. Overall the two datasets contain thousands of votes – 6367, to be precise.

Experimental design. When recovering complete rankings, the evaluation metric is the distance of the returned ranking to the *actual* (known) ground truth. We reiterate that, although MAX^d is designed to minimize the maximum distance to any feasible ground truth given an input profile π and an estimate of the average noise t, that is, it is designed for the worst case, it is known to work well in practice [24]. Similarly, AVG^d is designed to optimize the average distance to the set of feasible ground truths; our experiments will determine whether this is a useful proxy for minimizing the distance to an unknown ground truth.

When selecting a subset of alternatives, the evaluation metric is the loss of that subset in the *actual* ground truth. As discussed above, the current implementation of RoboVote uses the rule MAX^d that returns the set of alternatives that minimizes the maximum loss in any feasible true ranking. As in the complete ranking setting, the rule AVG^d returns the set of alternatives that minimizes the average loss over the feasible true rankings.

It is important to emphasize that in both these settings, MAX^d and AVG^d optimize an objective over the set of feasible ground truths, but are evaluated on the actual known ground truth. It is therefore impossible to predict in advance which of the methods will perform best.

Our theoretical results assume that an upper bound t on the average error is given to us, and our guarantees depend on this bound. In practice, though, t has to be estimated. For example, the current RoboVote implementation uses $t_{RV} = \min_{\sigma \in \pi} d(\sigma, \pi)/|\pi|$, or the minimum average distance from one ranking in π to all other rankings in π.

In our experiments, we wish to study the impact of the choice of t on the performance of AVG^d and MAX^d. A natural choice is $t^* \triangleq d(\pi, \sigma^*)$, where π is the vote profile and σ^* is the actual ground truth. That is, t^* is the average distance between the vote profile and the actual ground truth. In principle it is an especially good choice because it induces the smallest ball $\mathcal{B}_t(\pi)$ that contains the actual ground truth. However, it is also an impractical choice, because one cannot compute this value without knowing the ground truth. We also consider

$$t_{KEM} \triangleq \min_{\sigma \in \mathcal{L}(A)} d(\sigma, \pi)$$

(named after the *Kemeny* rule) — the minimum possible distance between the vote profile and any ranking.

In order to synchronize results across different profiles, we let $\hat{t}$ be the estimate of t that we feed into the methods, and define

$$r = \frac{\hat{t} - t_{KEM}}{t^* - t_{KEM}}.$$

Note that because t_{KEM} is the minimum value that allows for a nonempty set of feasible ground truths, we know that $t^* - t_{KEM} \geq 0$. For any profile, $r = 0$ implies that $\hat{t} = t_{KEM}$, $r < 1$ implies that $\hat{t} < t^*$, $r = 1$ implies that $\hat{t} = t^*$, and $r > 1$ implies that $\hat{t} > t^*$. In our experiments, as in the work of Procaccia et al. [24], we use $r \in [0, 2]$.

Results and their interpretation. Our results for three output types — ranking, subset with $z = 1$ (single winner), and subset with $z = 2$ — can be found in Figures 3, 4, and 5, respectively. Each has two subfigures, for the KT distance, and the Cayley distance. All Figures show r on the x axis. In Figure 3, the y axis shows the distance between the output ranking and the actual ground truth.

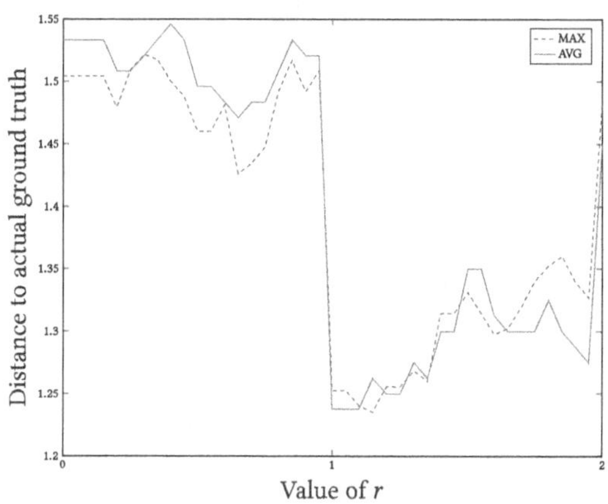

(a) Kendall tau

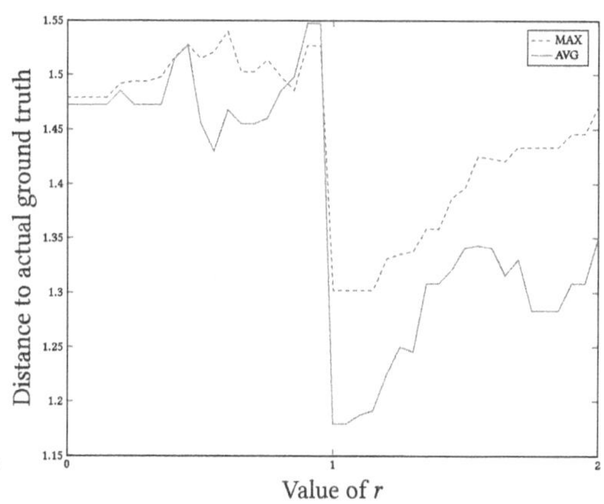

(b) Cayley

Fig. 3. Dots dataset (noise level 4), ranking output.

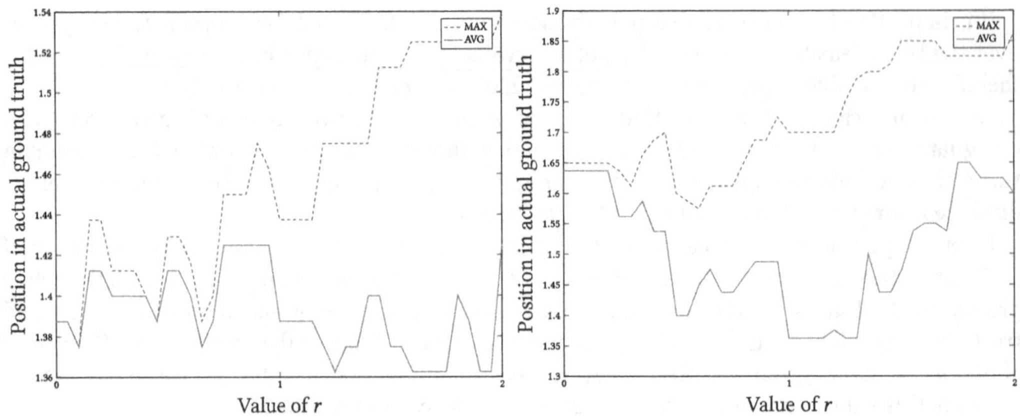

(a) Kendall tau (b) Cayley

Fig. 4. Dots dataset (noise level 4), subset output with $z = 1$.

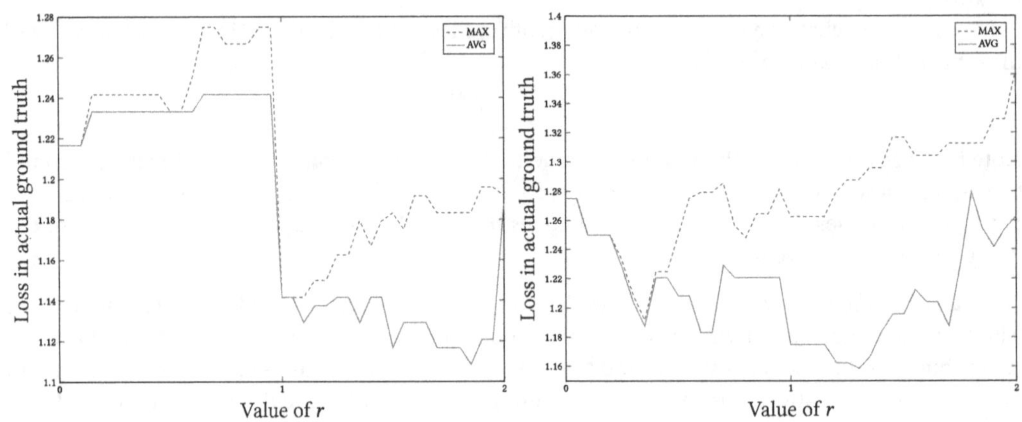

(a) Kendall tau (b) Cayley

Fig. 5. Dots dataset (noise level 4), subset output with $z = 2$.

In Figures 4 and 5, the y axis shows the loss of the selected subset on the actual ground truth. All figures are based on the dots dataset with the highest noise level (4). The results for the puzzle dataset are similar (albeit not as crisp), and the results for different noise levels are quite similar. The results differ across distance functions, but the conclusions below apply to all four, not just the two that are shown here. Additional figures can be found in the full version of the paper.

It is interesting to note that, while in Figure 3 the accuracy of each distance metric is measured using that metric (i.e., KT is measured with KT and Cayley with Cayley), in the other two figures the two distances are measured in the exact same way: based on position or loss in the ground truth. Despite the dismal theoretical results for Cayley (Theorem 4.11), its performance in practice is comparable to KT.

More importantly, we see that although MAX^d and AVG^d perform similarly on low values of r, AVG^d significantly outperforms MAX^d on medium and high values of r, and especially when $r > 1$, that is, $\hat{t} > t^*$. This is true in all cases (including the two distance metrics that are not shown), except for the ranking output type under the KT distance (Figure 3a) and the footrule distance (in the full version of the paper), where the performance of the two methods is almost identical across the board (values of r, datasets, and noise levels).

These results match our intuition. As r increases, so does $\hat{t}$, and the set $\mathcal{B}_{\hat{t}}(\pi)$ grows larger. When this set is large, the conservatism of MAX^d becomes a liability, as it minimizes the maximum distance with respect to rankings that are unlikely to coincide with the actual ground truth. By contrast, AVG^d is more robust: It takes the new rankings into account, but does not allow them to dictate its output.

The practical implication is clear. Because we do not have a way of divining t^*, which is often the most effective choice in practice, we resort to relatively crude estimates, such as the deployed choice of t_{RV} discussed above. Moreover, underestimating t^* is often risky, as the results show, because the ball $\mathcal{B}_{\hat{t}}(\pi)$ does not contain the actual ground truth when $\hat{t} < t^*$. Therefore in practice we try to aim for estimates such that $\hat{t} > t^*$, and robustness to the value of $\hat{t}$ is crucial. In this sense AVG^d is a better choice than MAX^d.

6 DISCUSSION

We wrap up with a brief discussion of several key points.

Non-uniform distributions. All of our upper bound results, namely Theorems 3.2, 4.5, 4.7, and 4.9, apply to any distribution over $\mathcal{B}_t(\pi)$, not just the uniform distribution (when replacing "average" distance/loss with "expected" distance/loss). To see why this is true for the latter three theorems, note that their proofs construct a randomized rule and leverage Lemma 4.2, which easily extends to any distribution. While this is a nice point to make, we do not believe that non-uniform distributions are especially well motivated — where would such a distribution come from? By contrast, the uniform distribution represents an agnostic viewpoint.

Computational complexity. We have not paid much attention to computational complexity. In our experiments there are only four alternatives, so we can easily compute $\mathcal{B}_t(\pi)$ by enumeration. For real-world instances, integer programming is used, as we briefly discussed in Section 1.1. While those implementations are for rules that minimize the *maximum* distance or loss over $\mathcal{B}_t(\pi)$ [24], they can be easily modified to minimize the average distance or loss. Therefore, at least for the purposes of applications like RoboVote, computational complexity is *not* an obstacle.

Real-world implications. As noted in Section 5, our empirical results suggest that minimizing the average distance or loss has a significant advantage in practice over minimizing the maximum distance or loss. We are therefore planning to continue refining our methods, and ultimately deploy them on RoboVote, where they will influence the way thousands of people around the world make group decisions.

ACKNOWLEDGMENTS

Kahng and Procaccia were partially supported by the National Science Foundation under grants IIS-1350598 and CCF-1525932, by the Office of Naval Research, and by a Sloan Research Fellowship.

REFERENCES

[1] H. Azari Soufiani, D. C. Parkes, and L. Xia. 2012. Random Utility Theory for Social Choice. In *Proceedings of the 26th Annual Conference on Neural Information Processing Systems (NIPS)*. 126–134.

[2] H. Azari Soufiani, D. C. Parkes, and L. Xia. 2013. Preference Elicitation For General Random Utility Models. In *Proceedings of the 29th Annual Conference on Uncertainty in Artificial Intelligence (UAI)*. 596–605.

[3] H. Azari Soufiani, D. C. Parkes, and L. Xia. 2014. Computing Parametric Ranking Models via Rank-Breaking. In *Proceedings of the 31st International Conference on Machine Learning (ICML)*. 360–368.

[4] F. Brandt, V. Conitzer, U. Endriss, J. Lang, and A. D. Procaccia (Eds.). 2016. *Handbook of Computational Social Choice.* Cambridge University Press.

[5] I. Caragiannis, S. Nath, A. D. Procaccia, and N. Shah. 2017. Subset Selection Via Implicit Utilitarian Voting. *Journal of Artificial Intelligence Research* 58 (2017), 123–152.

[6] I. Caragiannis, A. D. Procaccia, and N. Shah. 2014. Modal Ranking: A Uniquely Robust Voting Rule. In *Proceedings of the 28th AAAI Conference on Artificial Intelligence (AAAI).* 616–622.

[7] I. Caragiannis, A. D. Procaccia, and N. Shah. 2016. When Do Noisy Votes Reveal the Truth? *ACM Transactions on Economics and Computation* 4, 3 (2016), article 15.

[8] J. R. Chamberlin and P. N. Courant. 1983. Representative Deliberations and Representative Decisions: Proportional Representation and the Borda Rule. *American Political Science Review* 77, 3 (1983), 718–733.

[9] Y. Chen, A. Ghosh, M. Kearns, T. Roughgarden, and J. Wortman Vaughan. 2016. Mathematical Foundations for Social Computing. *Communications of the ACM* 59, 12 (2016), 102–108.

[10] V. Conitzer, M. Rognlie, and L. Xia. 2009. Preference Functions That Score Rankings and Maximum Likelihood Estimation. In *Proceedings of the 21st International Joint Conference on Artificial Intelligence (IJCAI).* 109–115.

[11] V. Conitzer and T. Sandholm. 2005. Common Voting Rules as Maximum Likelihood Estimators. In *Proceedings of the 21st Annual Conference on Uncertainty in Artificial Intelligence (UAI).* 145–152.

[12] P. Diaconis and R. L. Graham. 1977. Spearman's footrule as a measure of disarray. *Journal of the Royal Statistical Society: Series B* 39, 2 (1977), 262–268.

[13] E. Elkind, P. Faliszewski, and A. Slinko. 2010. Good Rationalizations of Voting Rules. In *Proceedings of the 24th AAAI Conference on Artificial Intelligence (AAAI).* 774–779.

[14] E. Elkind and N. Shah. 2014. Electing the Most Probable Without Eliminating the Irrational: Voting Over Intransitive Domains. In *Proceedings of the 30th Annual Conference on Uncertainty in Artificial Intelligence (UAI).* 182–191.

[15] T. Lu and C. Boutilier. 2011. Budgeted Social Choice: From Consensus to Personalized Decision Making. In *Proceedings of the 22nd International Joint Conference on Artificial Intelligence (IJCAI).* 280–286.

[16] T. Lu and C. Boutilier. 2011. Robust Approximation and Incremental Elicitation in Voting Protocols. In *Proceedings of the 22nd International Joint Conference on Artificial Intelligence (IJCAI).* 287–293.

[17] C. L. Mallows. 1957. Non-null ranking models. *Biometrika* 44 (1957), 114–130.

[18] A. Mao, A. D. Procaccia, and Y. Chen. 2013. Better Human Computation Through Principled Voting. In *Proceedings of the 27th AAAI Conference on Artificial Intelligence (AAAI).* 1142–1148.

[19] B. L. Monroe. 1995. Fully Proportional Representation. *American Political Science Review* 89, 4 (1995), 925–940.

[20] G. Pritchard and M. Wilson. 2009. Asymptotics of the minimum manipulating coalition size for positional voting rules under impartial culture behaviour. *Mathematical Social Sciences* 58, 1 (2009), 35–57.

[21] A. D. Procaccia. 2016. Science Can Restore America's Faith in Democracy. (2016). https://www.wired.com/2016/12/science-can-restore-americas-faith-democracy/

[22] A. D. Procaccia, S. J. Reddi, and N. Shah. 2012. A Maximum Likelihood Approach For Selecting Sets of Alternatives. In *Proceedings of the 28th Annual Conference on Uncertainty in Artificial Intelligence (UAI).* 695–704.

[23] A. D. Procaccia, J. S. Rosenschein, and A. Zohar. 2008. On the Complexity of Achieveing Proportional Representation. *Social Choice and Welfare* 30, 3 (2008), 353–362.

[24] A. D. Procaccia, N. Shah, and Y. Zick. 2016. Voting rules as error-correcting codes. *Artificial Intelligence* 231 (2016), 1–16.

[25] I. Tsetlin, M. Regenwetter, and B. Grofman. 2003. The impartial culture maximizes the probability of majority cycles. *Social Choice and Welfare* 21 (2003), 387–398.

[26] L. Xia. 2016. Bayesian Estimators As Voting Rules. In *Proceedings of the 32nd Annual Conference on Uncertainty in Artificial Intelligence (UAI).*

[27] L. Xia and V. Conitzer. 2011. A maximum likelihood approach towards aggregating partial orders. In *Proceedings of the 22nd International Joint Conference on Artificial Intelligence (IJCAI).* 446–451.

[28] L. Xia, V. Conitzer, and J. Lang. 2010. Aggregating preferences in multi-issue domains by using maximum likelihood estimators. In *Proceedings of the 9th International Conference on Autonomous Agents and Multi-Agent Systems (AAMAS).* 399–408.

[29] A. C. Yao. 1977. Probabilistic Computations: Towards a Unified Measure of Complexity. In *Proceedings of the 17th Symposium on Foundations of Computer Science (FOCS).* 222–227.

[30] H. P. Young. 1988. Condorcet's theory of voting. *The American Political Science Review* 82, 4 (1988), 1231–1244.

Voting in the Limelight

RONEN GRADWOHL, Kellogg School of Management, Northwestern University

In many economic and political settings, decisions are made collectively by committees. The committee members who participate in these decision-making processes are partly motivated by the quality of the decisions they reach, but they may additionally be concerned about the ex post consequences of the way their votes are perceived. Moreover, in some of these scenarios the committee members would not like to be seen as voting in *any* particular way, and instead prefer to maintain an ambiguous perception of their vote.

One might conjecture that for committees with such members, it would be desirable to institute voting procedures that hide some or all of the information about how the votes were cast. For instance, anonymous voting, in which only an anonymous tally of the votes is publicized, would be preferable to open voting, in which all individual votes are publicly disclosed. And secret voting, in which nothing beyond the final decision is revealed, would be best. This paper examines the validity of this conjecture by analyzing these three common disclosure rules—open, anonymous, and secret—when voters have a preference for strategic ambiguity. The main result is that the conjecture is false, and that restricting the amount of information disclosed about the votes may actually be harmful.

More specifically, we consider a common-value setting, in which committee members receive signals about the state of the world, and in each state of the world there is a corresponding correct outcome that all members prefer most. The three disclosure rules are compared along two dimensions: the probability that the committee decides on the correct outcome, and the welfare of the committee members. In standard common-value voting models, in which voters do not have preferences over how their votes are perceived by others, the welfare of voters is maximized when the probability of correctness is maximized. In this paper, however, the two dimensions are not perfectly aligned, as welfare is impacted not only by the outcome, but also by the inferences that can be drawn by outsiders about committee members' votes.

We show that the amount of information disclosed may have a non-monotonic effect on both the probability of correctness and on the welfare of the committee members. In particular, the first-best probability of correctness is often attained at the extremes—in open voting, when all information is disclosed, and in secret voting, when no information is disclosed—but is not attained in anonymous voting, when some but not all information is disclosed. Furthermore, the welfare of the committee members, while always minimal in open voting, is sometimes maximal in anonymous rather than secret voting.

To see the intuition for the tradeoffs between open, anonymous, and secret voting, and the non-monotonic effect of information disclosure on correctness and welfare, consider first the case

---

The full version of this paper is available at http://www.kellogg.northwestern.edu/faculty/Gradwohl/htm/papers/voting.pdf.

This work is supported by the National Science Foundation, under grant #1216006. I am grateful to David Austen-Smith, Tim Feddersen, Nicola Persico, and Yuval Salant for helpful conversations about this research. I would also like to thank seminar participants at Hebrew University, Northwestern, Technion, Tel Aviv University, and the Econometric Society Meeting in Minneapolis, MN.

Author's address: MEDS, Kellogg School of Management, Northwestern University, 2211 Campus Drive, Evanston, IL 60208.

EC'17, June 26–30, 2017, Cambridge, MA, USA.

 ACM ISBN 978-1-4503-4527-9/17/06
http://dx.doi.org/10.1145/3033274.3085096

of sincere voting. Under sincere voting, committee members always vote for the outcome that is most likely correct, given their respective signals. In this case, the probability of correctness is always the same, and the welfare of committee members decreases with the amount of information disclosed—it is minimal in open voting and maximal in secret voting.

In order to isolate the effects of the preference for strategic ambiguity, this paper focuses on settings in which there are no other strategic distortions—settings in which, absent concerns for ambiguity, sincere voting is an equilibrium. In these settings, even when committee members have a preference for strategic ambiguity, sincere voting is the unique equilibrium in open voting and often the unique equilibrium in secret voting. However, it is often *not* an equilibrium in anonymous voting. The intuition for this last point is the following: When a committee member obtains a signal, voting sincerely will increase the probability that the more-likely-correct outcome is chosen. However, the probability that one committee member's vote affects the outcome might be small, leading to a possible benefit to voting *non*-sincerely. In particular, if such a deviation does not change the outcome, its effect is to increase the uncertainty about the committee member's vote. However, a deviation will induce some uncertainty, since the identity of the deviator will remain unknown. Such uncertainty is beneficial to the committee member due to her predilection for strategic ambiguity. When the possible benefit from this induced uncertainty outweighs the risk of obtaining the less-likely-correct outcome such deviations are profitable. Thus, in these cases sincere voting is not an equilibrium, and so the probability that the outcome is correct will be less than under the sincere equilibria of open and secret voting.

In fact, the unique equilibrium here under anonymous voting is one in which committee members randomize, sometimes voting for the outcome that is most likely correct given their respective signals, but sometimes voting for a different outcome. By adding noise to the outcome of the decision-making process this randomization increases the ambiguity about committee members' votes, leading to an increase in utility. If in equilibrium the utility gain from increased ambiguity outweighs the loss from a lower probability of correctness, the welfare under anonymous voting will be higher than under secret voting. In that case, the equilibrium in anonymous voting will achieve both lower probability of correctness and higher welfare than the equilibria of open and secret voting.

Determining whether the net gain from randomization is positive or negative *in equilibrium* requires finding the equilibrium. This is a challenging problem in general voting settings, and so we focus on two tractable settings: a setting with only two players and a setting with many players. In the first we compute equilibria, and then show that non-monotonicity in welfare holds when the preference for ambiguity is strong, when signals are accurate, and when utility functions are not too convex. In the second setting we prove asymptotic results, ones that hold when the number of players is large enough. The general intuition driving the results is that as players begin to mix more, the gain from greater ambiguity about votes increases linearly with the amount of mixing. At the same time, the loss due to lower probability of correctness increases at a lower rate: In the asymptotic case, for example, even a fairly large amount of mixing will nonetheless lead to the correct outcome with high probability, and so such mixing will yield a net welfare gain.

Metric Distortion of Social Choice Rules: Lower Bounds and Fairness Properties

ASHISH GOEL, Stanford University
ANILESH K. KRISHNASWAMY, Stanford University
KAMESH MUNAGALA, Duke University

We study social choice rules under the utilitarian distortion framework, with an additional metric assumption on the agents' costs over the alternatives. In this approach, these costs are given by an underlying metric on the set of all agents plus alternatives. Social choice rules have access to only the ordinal preferences of agents but not the latent cardinal costs that induce them. Distortion is then defined as the ratio between the social cost (typically the sum of agent costs) of the alternative chosen by the mechanism at hand, and that of the optimal alternative chosen by an omniscient algorithm. The worst-case distortion of a social choice rule is, therefore, a measure of how close it always gets to the optimal alternative without any knowledge of the underlying costs. Under this model, it has been conjectured that Ranked Pairs, the well-known weighted-tournament rule, achieves a distortion of at most 3 (Anshelevich et al. 2015). We disprove this conjecture by constructing a sequence of instances which shows that the worst-case distortion of Ranked Pairs is at least 5. Our lower bound on the worst-case distortion of Ranked Pairs matches a previously known upper bound for the Copeland rule, proving that in the worst case, the simpler Copeland rule is at least as good as Ranked Pairs. And as long as we are limited to (weighted or unweighted) tournament rules, we demonstrate that randomization cannot help achieve an expected worst-case distortion of less than 3. Using the concept of approximate majorization within the distortion framework, we prove that Copeland and Randomized Dictatorship achieve low constant factor fairness-ratios (5 and 3 respectively), which is a considerable generalization of similar results for the sum of costs and single largest cost objectives. In addition to all of the above, we outline several interesting directions for further research in this space.

CCS Concepts: •**Theory of computation** → *Algorithmic game theory and mechanism design;* Approximation algorithms analysis;

Additional Key Words and Phrases: Social Choice; Metric Distortion; Fairness; Copeland; Ranked Pairs

1 INTRODUCTION

Social choice theory is the science of aggregating the varied preferences of multiple agents into a single collective decision. Ways of doing this aggregation are called social choice rules – functions that map the given preferences of agents, typically in the form of total orderings over a set of alternatives, to a single alternative. The conventional approach to reasoning about the quality of outcomes obtained from these rules has been a normative, axiomatic one. A variety of axiomatic criteria, corresponding to naturally desirable properties, have been proposed, and a great deal of

Anilesh K. Krishnaswamy (anilesh@stanford.edu) and Ashish Goel (ashishg@stanford.edu) were supported by the NSF, under grant CCF-1637418, the ONR, under grant N00014-15-1-2786, and the ARO, under grant W911NF-14-1-0526. Kamesh Munagala (kamesh@cs.duke.edu) was supported by the NSF, under grants CCF-1408784, CCF-1637397, and IIS-1447554.
All details omitted in this paper for want of space are available at https://arxiv.org/abs/1612.02912.

EC'17, June 26–30, 2017, Cambridge, Massachusetts, USA. © 2017 ACM. ISBN 978-1-4503-4527-9/17/06...$15.00.
DOI: http://dx.doi.org/10.1145/3033274.3085138

work has been done to understand which axioms can or cannot be satisfied together, and how the known social choice rules measure up against them. For instance, a few celebrated results (Gibbard 1973; Satterthwaite 1975) rule out the concurrent satisfiability of such basic axioms, and additional spatial assumptions that help sidestep these impossibilities have been identified (Barbera 2001; Moulin 1980).

Another approach, which has received a great deal of attention lately (Boutilier et al. 2015; Caragiannis and Procaccia 2011; Procaccia and Rosenschein 2006), is to assume a ***utilitarian*** view, as is commonplace in economics and algorithmic mechanism design. Every agent has latent cardinal preferences over the alternatives in terms of utility (or cost) and the social utility of an alternative is a function of the agents' utilities. The most commonly used objective is the total sum of agent utilities for an alternative. Social choice rules are then viewed as approximation algorithms which try to choose the best alternative given access only to ordinal preferences. Similar to the competitive ratio of online approximation algorithms, the quantity of interest here is the worst-case value (over all possible underlying utilities) of the *distortion* – the ratio of the social utility of the truly optimal alternative over that of the alternative chosen by the social choice rule at hand (Procaccia and Rosenschein 2006).

Characterizing the worst-case distortion of social choice functions has emerged as the central question within the utilitarian approach to social choice. With no assumptions on the utilities, the distortion of deterministic social choice rules is unbounded (Procaccia and Rosenschein 2006), and that of randomized social choice rules is $\Omega(m)$, where m is the number of alternatives (Boutilier et al. 2015).

Interestingly, some constant factor bounds on the distortion of social choice rules are made possible with an additional *metric* assumption on the cardinal preferences of agents, represented by their costs with respect to alternatives (Anshelevich et al. 2015). These costs are assumed to form an unknown, arbitrary metric space, and distortion is redefined in terms of these costs. In this setting, the best known positive result for deterministic social rules is that the distortion of the Copeland rule, a tournament function, is at most 5 (Anshelevich et al. 2015). It is known that the worst-case distortion of *any* deterministic social choice rule is at least 3, and that Ranked Pairs, a weighted-tournament function, achieves this lower bound given some assumptions on the ordinal preferences of agents. It is also known that the distortion of *any* randomized rule is at least 2, and that of Randomized Dictatorship is at most 3 (Anshelevich and Postl 2016), showing that randomization helps beat the performance of common deterministic rules with respect to worst-case distortion.

An important open question here is whether the worst-case distortion of Ranked Pairs is indeed 3, as has been conjectured (Anshelevich et al. 2015). And given that tournament/weighted-tournament rules provide the best-known bounds in the deterministic case, another interesting question is whether they perform well in the randomized case too, and in particular, better than Randomized Dictatorship. The first half of this paper is devoted to settling these questions, providing answers in the negative for both. The proof for Ranked Pairs is particularly surprising and intricate.

Under the utilitarian metric distortion approach, in addition to reasoning about the total social cost, it is natural to ask how "fair" choosing a particular alternative is in terms of the cost incurred by the agents. For example, let us say there are two agents and two alternatives, and the costs incurred by the agents are x_1, x_2 ($x_1 \neq x_2$) for the first alternative, and $(x_1+x_2)/2$, $(x_1+x_2)/2$ for the second. It seems natural that the second is more "fair" than the first. Various notions of fairness such as lexicographic fairness[1], prefix-based measures, and the more general approximate majorization measure, have been studied in the context of routing, bandwidth allocation and load balancing

[1]This is also called max-min fairness in the resource allocation literature.

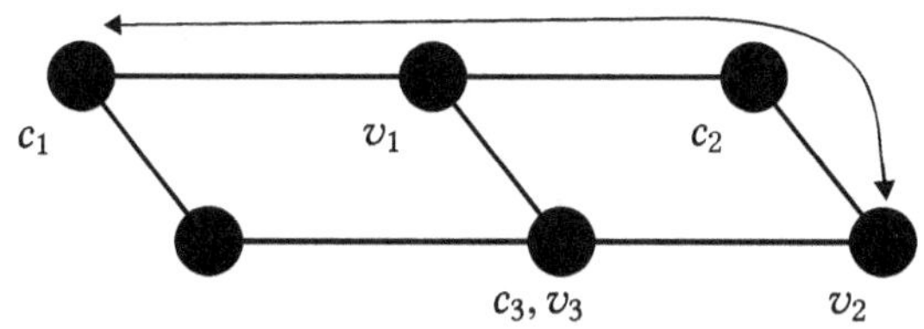

v_2's cost for $c_1 = 3$
= the length of the shortest path.

Fig. 1. Underlying shortest path metric in Example 1 – each edge is of unit weight

problems (Goel et al. 2001; Kleinberg et al. 1999; Kumar and Kleinberg 2000). Other measures of fairness such as envy-freeness (Caragiannis et al. 2009; Chen et al. 2013), maximin-shares (Procaccia and Wang 2014), and leximin (Barbarà and Jackson 1988; Rawls 2009) have also been studied in the context of mechanism design and social choice. We could also look at objectives given by α-percentiles ($\alpha = 0.5$ is the median) for $\alpha \in [0, 1]$. While there are positive results (as achieved by Copeland) for $\alpha \in [0.5, 1)$, it is known that for $\alpha \in [0, 0.5)$, all deterministic social choice rules have unbounded worst-case distortion (Anshelevich et al. 2015).

A question arises as to which one of the above notions of fairness can be adapted to the metric distortion framework, and moreover yields meaningful results. Even if percentiles were the most appropriate, they are too strong for this domain given the lower bounds (Anshelevich et al. 2015) mentioned above; in fact, there are very few resource allocation settings known where simultaneous maximization or approximation of all percentiles is possible. Notions from cake-cutting such as envy-freeness and maximin shares do not apply to social choice settings, since these definitions assume a partition of available goods among agents; in social choice settings, we make a single societal decision rather than partition resources. We will instead look at approximate majorization, which attempts to minimize, simultaneously for all k, the sum of the k-largest costs incurred by agents. This generalizes both lexicographic fairness and total cost minimization, and applies to any setting where agents receive utilities (or costs), regardless of whether the underlying problem is one of cake-cutting, resource allocation, or social choice. Further, an approximate majorization ratio of α guarantees an α-approximation of a large class of fairness measures, including all p-moments of costs for agents, for $p \geq 1$. The second half of this paper states and proves these fairness results. In particular, we show how the simple Copeland rule approximates a broad class of convex cost functions.

Warm-up example of metric costs and distortion. Imagine there are three alternatives c_1, c_2, c_3, and three agents v_1, v_2, v_3 with preferences $c_1 \succ c_2 \succ c_3$, $c_2 \succ c_3 \succ c_1$ and $c_3 \succ c_1 \succ c_2$ respectively. The underlying costs are given by the shortest path metric on the graph in Figure 1. The agent costs are given by $d(.,.)$ as follows:

(i) $d(v_1, c_1) = d(v_1, c_2) = d(v_1, c_3) = 1$;
(ii) $d(v_2, c_2) = d(v_2, c_3) = 1$, $d(v_2, c_1) = 3$;
(iii) $d(v_3, c_3) = 0$, $d(v_3, c_1) = d(v_3, c_2) = 2$.

Let's say that a deterministic rule chooses c_1 as the winner based on the preferences. Then the distortion is given by $\sum_{i=1,2,3} d(v_i, c_1) / \sum_{i=1,2,3} d(v_i, c_3) = 6/2 = 3$. In fact, this metric achieves the worst-case distortion among all possible metrics that agree with the given preferences.

If a randomized rule picks each of the three alternatives with equal probability, the expected distortion will be equal to $(\frac{1}{3}.6 + \frac{1}{3}.4 + \frac{1}{3}.2)/2 = 2$. It can be seen, based on symmetry, that this distribution minimizes the worst-case distortion over all possible metrics that agree with the preferences.

Let us also look at the fairness ratio when we pick c_1 as the winner. The largest cost for c_1 is that of v_2 with $d(v_2, c_1) = 3$. And for the optimal alternative c_3, the largest cost is $d(v_1, c_3) = 1$. The ratio of these values is 3. Similarly if we look at the ratio of the two largest costs, then we have $[d(v_2, c_1) + d(v_3, c_1)]/[d(v_1, c_3) + d(v_2, c_3)] = 5/2$. For the three largest costs, we have a ratio of 3 from above. Therefore, the alternative c_1 achieves a fairness ratio of $\max\{3, 2.5, 3\} = 3$.

1.1 Our contributions

Our first set of results are in the negative: we show that social choice rules of simple forms cannot have worst-case distortion ratios matching the known lower bounds. Our second set of results concern defining fairness in this setting, and upper bounding the fairness ratios of natural social choice rules, in particular the Copeland rule.

Lower Bounds on Distortion. It has been conjectured that the simple Ranked Pairs rule achieves the optimal distortion ratio of 3 (Anshelevich et al. 2015). This conjecture is based on the fact that if the ordinal preferences of agents are restricted to be of a certain form, Ranked Pairs does indeed have a distortion at most 3 (see Theorem 3.1). Our first main result is disproving this conjecture – we show that Ranked Pairs, and the related Schulze rule, have a worst-case distortion ratio at least 5, and in this sense, are no better than the Copeland rule when the preferences are general. We do this by constructing a sequence of instances where the agent preferences are obtained by coupling cyclic permutations of two equally large sets of alternatives in a one to one fashion.

Result 1 (Theorem 3.3). *Ranked Pairs, and the Schulze rule, have a worst-case distortion ratio of at least 5.*

As stated before, a lower bound of 2 is known on the worst-case distortion of any randomized rule (Anshelevich and Postl 2016). We show that this lower bound cannot be achieved by *any* rule that looks at only the pairwise wins/losses among the alternatives, or the margins of these wins/losses (tournament rules and weighted-tournament rules – see Section 2.2 for a definition).

Result 2 (Theorem 3.6). *The worst-case (expected) distortion of any tournament or weighted-tournament rule is at least 3.*

Fairness properties. We introduce a method of quantifying the "fairness" of social choice rules by incorporating the concept of approximate majorization (Goel and Meyerson 2006) within the *metric distortion* framework. For this purpose, we redefine the social cost of any alternative as the sum of its k largest agent costs. How fair a given social choice rule is depends on how well the alternative it chooses performs on this objective compared to every other alternative. To evaluate the fairness of a social choice rule, we then seek to bound the distortion ratio of this objective *simultaneously* over all possible values of k: we call this the *fairness ratio* (we define this measure formally in the next section).

The fairness ratio generalizes both the sum of costs objective (utilitarianism), and maxmin fairness (egalitarianism). Given such a strong definition, it is impossible to achieve a constant fairness ratio in many settings, and surprisingly, for the metric distortion problem we study in this paper, simple social choice rules like Copeland and Randomized Dictatorship achieve small constant fairness ratios that match the best-known distortion bounds for just the sum objective.

Result 3 (Theorem 4.2). *Copeland rule achieves a fairness ratio of at most 5.*

Result 4 (Theorem 4.3). *Randomized Dictatorship achieves a fairness ratio of at most 3.*

Additionally, for deterministic rules, a bound on the fairness ratio translates to an approximation result for a general class of symmetric convex objectives (see Section 2.5). And therefore, the above result leads us to the surprising observation that, assuming metric costs, the simple Copeland rule simultaneously approximates a very broad class of cost functions.

Conjectures and open problems. There are many directions for further research on the metric distortion problem. We mention some of these in context as we go along (Conjectures 3.5, 3.7). More details can be found in the full version of our paper (Goel et al. 2016). For example, for randomized rules, we suggest an interesting variation of the distortion measure, one that is more adversarial than the standard measure.

1.2 Related Literature

Several interesting problems pertaining to the distortion arising from the mapping of cardinal preferences to ordinal information have been studied (Moulin et al. 2016). The worst-case distortion of social choice rules, with unrestricted or normalized utilities, is known to be unbounded (Procaccia and Rosenschein 2006). With randomized mechanisms, it is possible to achieve a distortion of $\Omega(\sqrt{m}\log^* m)$, where m is the number of alternatives (Caragiannis and Procaccia 2011). The standard assumption here is that agents translate cardinal scores into ordinal preferences in the straightforward way – the alternative with the k-th highest utility is placed in the k-th position. If this mapping could be done in any other way, it is possible to construct low distortion embeddings of cardinal preferences into (ordinal) social choice rules like plurality (Caragiannis and Procaccia 2011). Another interesting result here is that is possible to construct a truthful-in-expectation mechanism whose worst-case distortion is $O(m^{3/4})$ (Filos-Ratsikas and Miltersen 2014).

Analysis of cardinal preferences under spatial models of proximity has had a long history in social choice (Enelow and Hinich 1984; Moulin 1980). Such models, especially those with Euclidean spaces, have also been commonly studied in the approximation algorithms literature on facility location problems (Arya et al. 2004; Drezner and Hamacher 1995). In these models, the cost of an agent for an alternative is given by the distance between the two. As mentioned earlier, our work follows the literature on the analysis of distortion of social choice rules under the assumption that agent costs form an unknown metric space (Anshelevich et al. 2015; Anshelevich and Postl 2016). We have already mentioned that several lower and upper bounds for both the sum of costs and percentile objectives are known in this setting. In addition, it is known that a distortion of at most 4 for the median objective can be achieved by a randomized mechanism that chooses from the uncovered set (Anshelevich and Postl 2016). In the deterministic case, an interesting result we must mention is that the distortion of the Single Transferable Vote (STV) is at most $\log(m)$ (Skowron and Elkind 2017).

It is important to note that in the special case of Euclidean metrics, it possible to design low distortion mechanisms, with the additional constraint of their being truthful-in-expectation (Feldman et al. 2016). Additionally, the metric distortion framework has also been used to study other problems such as finding an approximate maximum weight matching with access to only ordinal preferences (Anshelevich and Sekar 2016).

In the distortion framework, both the interpersonal comparison of utilities, and the goal of utility maximization, are implicitly assumed to be valid. While the interpersonal comparison of utilities is more meaningful in some contexts than others (Boutilier et al. 2015), we take it for granted.

While the results on the distortion of the sum of costs (or utilities) objective are extremely interesting, minimization of total cost (or maximization of total utility) is not the only imaginable goal of social choice mechanisms. The first step toward other understanding the distortion of other objectives is apparent in the various results on the distortion of the median cost objective (Anshelevich et al. 2015; Anshelevich and Postl 2016). We take a further step in this direction by drawing on the notions of fairness that have been studied in the context of network problems such as bandwidth allocation and load balancing (Goel et al. 2001; Kleinberg et al. 1999; Kumar and Kleinberg 2000).

2 PRELIMINARIES

2.1 Social Choice Rules

Let $\mathcal{V}$ be the set of agents and C the set of alternatives. We will use N to denote the total number of agents, i.e., $N = |\mathcal{V}|$. Every agent $v \in \mathcal{V}$ has a strict (no ties) preference ordering σ_v on C. For any $c, c' \in C$, we will use $c \succ_v c'$ to denote the fact that agent $v \in \mathcal{V}$ *prefers* c over c' in her ordering σ_v. Let $\mathcal{S}$ be the set of all possible preference orderings on $\mathcal{V}$. We call a profile of preference orderings $\sigma \in \mathcal{S}^N$ as an *instance.*

Based on the preferences of agents, we want to determine a single alternative as the winner, or a distribution over the alternatives and pick a winner according to it. A deterministic social choice rule is a function $f : \mathcal{S}^N \to C$ that maps each instance to an alternative. A randomized social choice rule is a function $g : \mathcal{S}^N \to \Delta(C)$, where $\Delta(C)$ is the space of all probability distributions over the set of alternatives C.

To define the social choice rules that we use in this paper, we need a few additional definitions. An alternative c *pairwise-beats* c' if $|\{v \in \mathcal{V} : c \succ_v c'\}| \geq \frac{N}{2}$, with ties broken arbitrarily. Given an instance σ, a complete weighted digraph $G_t(\sigma)$ with C as the set of nodes, and the weight of any edge $c \to c'$ given by $w(c, c') = |\{v \in \mathcal{V} : c \succ_v c'\}|$, is called the *weighted-tournament* graph induced by σ. An unweighted digraph $G_m(\sigma)$ with C as the set of nodes such that an edge from $c \to c'$ exists iff c pairwise beats c' is called the *tournament* graph induced by σ.

- **Ranked Pairs**: Given an instance σ, sort the edges of the weighted-tournament graph $G_t(\sigma)$ according to the values $w(.,.)$ in some non-decreasing order (breaking ties arbitrarily). Start with a graph $G = (C, \emptyset)$ and iterate over the edges in the order determined above. At each step, add the edge to G if it does not create a cycle, and discard the edge otherwise. The winning alternative is the source node of the resulting directed acyclic graph.
- **Copeland**: Given an instance σ, define a score for each $c \in C$ given by $|\{c' \in C : c \text{ pairwise beats } c'\}|$. The alternative with the highest score (the largest number of pairwise victories) is chosen to be the winner. In other words, the winning alternative is the node in the tournament graph $G_m(\sigma)$ with the maximum out-degree (breaking ties arbitrarily).
- **Randomized Dictatorship**: Choose alternative $c \in C$ with probability $p(c)$ equal to $|V_c|/N$ where $V_c = \{v \in \mathcal{V} : c \succ_v c', \forall c' \neq c\}$.
- **Schulze** (Schulze 2003) In the weighted-tournament graph, a path of strength p from alternative c to alternative c' is a sequence of candidates $c_1, c_2, \ldots, c_n$ with the following properties: (i) $c_1 = c$ and $c_n = c'$, (ii) for all $i = 1, \ldots, (n-1)$, $w(c_i, c_{i+1}) \geq w(c_{i+1}, c_i)$, and (iii) for all $i = 1, \ldots, (n-1)$, $w(c_i, c_{i+1}) \geq p$.

  Let $p(c, c')$ be the strength of the strongest path from c to c'. If there is no path from c to c', then $p(c, c') = 0$.

  Define a relation $\succ^\star$ as follows: $\forall c, c', c \succ^\star c' \iff p(c, c') > p(c', c)$. It can be proven that $\succ^\star$ defines a transitive relation. The alternative (with arbitrary tie-breaking, as there may be many such) $c^\star$, such that $p(c^\star, c) \geq p(c, c^\star)$ for all other alternatives c, is chosen as the winner.

2.2 Tournament and weighted-tournament rules

Any social choice rule that chooses an alternative, or a distribution over the alternatives, based on just the tournament graph is called a tournament rule (Moulin et al. 2016). These are also called C1 functions according to Fishburn's classification (Fishburn 1977). Any rule that is a function of the weighted-tournament graph is a *weighted-tournament* rule, as long as it is not a tournament rule (Moulin et al. 2016). According to Fishburn's classification, these rules are also called C2 functions (Fishburn 1977). Such rules do not need knowledge of all the preferences orderings, just the aggregated information in terms of the tournament/weighted-tournament graph. From the above definitions, we see that Ranked Pairs is a deterministic weighted-tournament rule, and Copeland a tournament rule. Randomized Dictatorship is neither a tournament rule nor a weighted-tournament rule, because it needs to know which alternative is first in each ordering.

2.3 Metric costs

We assume that the agent costs over the alternatives is given by an underlying metric d on $C \cup \mathcal{V}$. $d(v, c)$ is the cost incurred by agent v when alternative c is chosen as the winning alternative.

Definition 2.1. A function $d : C \cup \mathcal{V} \times C \cup \mathcal{V} \rightarrow \mathcal{R}_{\geq 0}$ is a metric iff $\forall x, y, z \in C \cup \mathcal{V}$, we have the following: (1) $d(x, y) \geq 0$, (2) $d(x, x) = 0$, (3) $d(x, y) = d(y, x)$, and (4) $d(x, z) \leq d(x, y) + d(y, z)$.

We can do with a much simpler yet equivalent assumption on the agents' costs (see Lemma 2.3). We need to first define a q-metric ("q" for quadrilateral) by replacing the triangle inequalities by "quadrilateral" inequalities (Condition 2 in the definition below).

Definition 2.2. A function $d : \mathcal{V} \times C \rightarrow \mathcal{R}_{\geq 0}$ is a q-metric iff $\forall v, v' \in \mathcal{V}$, and $\forall c, c' \in C$, we have the following:

(1) $d(v, c) \geq 0$
(2) $d(v, c) \leq d(v, c') + d(v', c') + d(v', c)$

The following equivalence result could be of independent interest in problems involving metrics. We make heavy use of it in later sections to prove our results.

LEMMA 2.3. *If d is a q-metric, then there exists a metric d' such that $d(v, c) = d'(v, c)$ for all $v \in \mathcal{V}$ and $c \in C$.*

PROOF. For all $v, v' \in \mathcal{V}$ and $c, c' \in C$, we define

$$d'(v, c) = d'(c, v) = d(v, c), \quad (1)$$

$$d'(c, c') = \max_{v \in \mathcal{V}} |d(v, c) - d(v, c')|, \quad (2)$$

$$d'(v, v') = \max_{c \in C} |d(v, c) - d(v', c)|. \quad (3)$$

Clearly, by the above definitions, and that of a q-metric, for all $x, y \in C \cup \mathcal{V}$, we have $d(x, y) \geq 0$, $d(x, x) = 0$ and $d(x, y) = d(y, x)$.

Consider $c_1, c_2, c_3 \in C$. Without loss of generality with respect to c_1, c_2, c_3, there exists $u \in \mathcal{V}$ such that

$$\begin{aligned} d'(c_1, c_3) &= d(u, c_1) - d(u, c_3) \\ &= d(u, c_1) - d(u, c_2) + d(u, c_2) - d(u, c_3) \\ &\leq |d(u, c_1) - d(u, c_2)| + |d(u, c_2) - d(u, c_3)| \\ &\leq d'(c_1, c_2) + d'(c_2, c_3). \end{aligned}$$

Consider $v_1, v_2 \in \mathcal{V}$ and $c \in C$. Again without loss of generality with respect to v_1, v_2, there exists $c' \in C$ such that

$$\begin{aligned} d'(v_1, v_2) &= d(v_1, c') - d(v_2, c') \\ &\leq d(v_1, c) + d(v_2, c) \\ &= d'(v_1, c) + d'(v_2, c). \end{aligned}$$

The inequality in the second line of the above follows by Condition 2 in Definition 2.2. Inequalities corresponding to Condition 4 in Definition 2.1 for triangles given by v_1, v_2, v_3 and v, c_1, c_2 for all $v, v_1, v_2, v_3 \in \mathcal{V}$ and $c_1, c_2 \in C$ follow analogously. □

Henceforth, we will deal mainly with *q-metrics* and use the terms *metric* and *q-metric* interchangeably.

2.4 Distortion

We say that a metric d is *consistent* with an instance σ, if whenever any agent v prefers c over c', then the her cost for c must be at most her cost for c', i.e., $c \succ_v c' \implies d(v, c) \leq d(v, c')$. We denote by $\rho(\sigma)$ the set of all metrics d that are consistent with σ.

The social cost of an alternative is taken as the sum of agent costs for it. For any metric d, we define $\phi(c, d) = \sum_{v \in \mathcal{V}} d(v, c)$. For any instance σ, a consistent metric d, and any deterministic social choice rule f, define $\Phi(f(\sigma), d) = \phi(f(\sigma), d)$. If f is a randomized social choice rule, we define $\Phi(f(\sigma), d) = \mathbb{E}[\phi(f(\sigma), d)]$.

As mentioned before, we want to measure how close a social choice rule gets to the optimal alternative in terms of social cost. We view every social choice as trying to approximate the optimal alternative, with knowledge of only the agent preference instance σ, but not the underlying metric cost d that induces σ. To measure this performance, we take the ratio of the social cost of the alternative chosen by the rule for σ, and the optimal alternative according to d. Distortion (Procaccia and Rosenschein 2006) is then defined as the worst-case value of this quantity over all metrics d that are consistent with σ:

$$\text{dist}(f, \sigma) = \sup_{d \in \rho(\sigma)} \frac{\Phi(f(\sigma), d)}{\min_{c \in C} \phi(c, d)}.$$

In other words, the distortion of a rule f on an instance σ is the worst-case ratio of the social cost Φ of $f(\sigma)$, and that of the optimal alternative. By worst-case we mean the largest value of the above over all possible metrics d that could induce σ, since f does not know what the true underlying metric is. In fact, we look to bound the quantity $\text{dist}(f, \sigma)$ over all possible instances, so as to have a measure of performance for the given rule f independent of the what the instance is, i.e., the *worst-case distortion* of f.

2.5 Fairness

Given an underlying metric, based on the alternative chosen, the costs incurred might vary widely among the agents. We want to formally quantify how "fair" choosing a particular alternative is. For this purpose, we look at social cost defined as the sum of k largest agent costs, for all $1 \leq k \leq N$. For any metric d and $c \in C$, we define $\forall 1 \leq k \leq N$,

$$\phi_k(c, d) = \max_{S \subseteq \mathcal{V}: |S| = k} \sum_{v \in \mathcal{V}} d(v, c).$$

For a deterministic social choice rule f, we define $\Phi_k(f(\sigma), d) = \phi_k(f(\sigma), d)$, for all instances σ and consistent metrics d. If f is a randomized social choice rule, we define $\Phi_k(f(\sigma), d) =$

$\mathbb{E}[\phi_k(f(\sigma), d)]^2$, for all instances σ and consistent metrics d. We define the fairness-ratio of f as follows:

$$\text{fairness}(f, \sigma) = \sup_{d \in \rho(\sigma)} \max_{1 \leq k \leq N} \frac{\Phi_k(f(\sigma), d)}{\min_{c \in C} \Phi_k(c, d)}.$$

The fairness ratio of a rule f on an instance σ is a worst-case bound on how well it simultaneously (for all k) approximates the social cost given by Φ_k of $f(\sigma)$, compared to the optimal alternative, over all possible metrics d that could induce σ, without knowing what the true underlying metric is.

Bounds for general convex costs via the fairness ratio. Another reason for studying the fairness ratio is that for deterministic social choice rules, a bound on the fairness-ratio translates to an approximation result with respect to any canonical cost function – a symmetric convex function F of the vector of agent costs such that $F\left(\vec{0}\right) = 0$ and F is non-decreasing in each argument (Goel and Meyerson 2006).

For any $c \in C$, define $\vec{d}(c) = [d(v_1, c), \ldots, d(v_N, c)]$, where $\mathcal{V} = \{v_1, \ldots, v_N\}$.

Theorem 2.4. *For any deterministic social choice rule f, instance σ, consistent metric d, and canonical cost function F, if* fairness$(f, \sigma) \leq \alpha$, *then for any $c \in C$,*

$$F\left(\frac{\vec{d}(f(\sigma))}{\alpha}\right) \leq F\left(\vec{d}(c)\right).$$

Proof. For any vector $\vec{x} \in \mathbb{R}^N$, let $x_{(1)} \geq x_{(2)} \geq \ldots x_{(i)} \geq \ldots x_{(N)}$ denote its components arranged in some non-decreasing order. For any $1 \leq k \leq N$, define $S_k(\vec{x}) = \sum_{i=1}^{k} x_{(i)}$.

A vector $\vec{x}$ is said to be α-submajorized by $\vec{y}$ iff $S_k(\vec{x}) \leq \alpha S_k(\vec{y})$, for all $1 \leq k \leq N$.

If fairness$(f, \sigma) \leq \alpha$, then for any $c \in C$, we have that $\vec{d}(f(\sigma))$ is α-submajorized by $\vec{d}(c)$. This implies that $F\left(\frac{\vec{d}(f(\sigma))}{\alpha}\right) \leq F\left(\vec{d}(c)\right)$ (Theorem 2.3 in (Goel and Meyerson 2006)). □

If a deterministic social choice rule has a fairness ratio of at most α, then for all $p \geq 1$, the l_p norm of the cost vector for the agents under this social choice rule is at most α times the optimum, giving an "all-norms" approximation (Corollary 2.5). As special cases, this gives an α-approximation for many objective functions such as the sum, the maximum, and the ℓ_2 norm of the agentsfi costs for an alternative, using $p = 1, \infty$, and 2 respectively.

Corollary 2.5. *For any deterministic social choice rule f, instance σ, and $p \geq 1$, if* fairness$(f, \sigma) \leq \alpha$, *then for any $c \in C$,*

$$||\vec{d}(f(\sigma))||_p \leq \alpha ||\vec{d}(c)||_p.$$

3 LOWER BOUNDS ON DISTORTION

In this section, we will establish that Ranked Pairs fails to achieve a distortion of at most 3, contrary to what has been conjectured (Anshelevich et al. 2015), thereby falling short of the lower bound on the worst-case distortion of any deterministic rule. We also show a similar result on how tournament/weighted-tournament rules fail to come close to the lower bound of 2 on the worst-case distortion of any randomized rule.

[2]We could define variations of this objective, leading to interesting open questions (Goel et al. 2016).

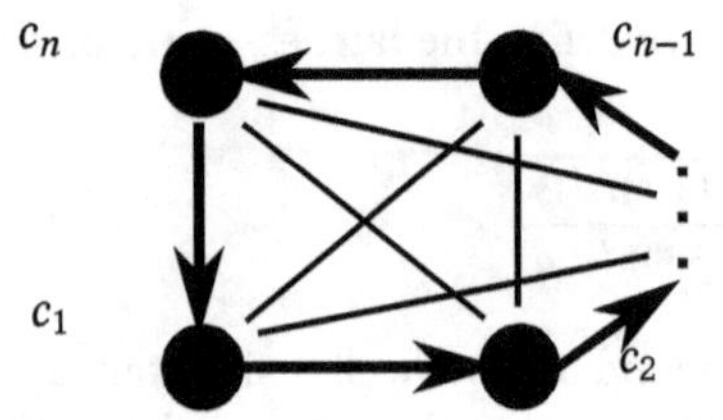

Fig. 2. Weighted-tournament Graph: A cycle of heavy edges making c_1 the Ranked Pairs winner.

3.1 Ranked Pairs

In our first result, we will show that the worst-case distortion of Ranked Pairs is at least 5. (Anshelevich et al. 2015) conjectured that the worst case bound here is 3. This conjecture was based on the result that if the tournament graph does not have cycles of length greater than 4, then the distortion of Ranked Pairs is, in fact, bounded above by 3.

THEOREM 3.1. *(Anshelevich et al. 2015) The distortion of ranked pairs is at most 3, as long as the tournament graph has circumference at most 4.*

Assume for a moment that among the set of alternatives C, c is the Ranked Pairs winner, and c' is the optimal alternative that minimizes the sum of agent costs. To achieve a large distortion, c' must beat c often. And since c is the Ranked Pairs winner, at the step when $c' \to c$ is considered in the Ranked Pairs iteration over edges, a path from c to c' must already be in place.

One way of achieving this structure is to have n agents, each with a preference ordering that is a different *cyclic permutation* of $c_1, c_2, \ldots, c_n$. c_1 is then a Ranked Pairs winner (assuming ties are broken in its favor), and the cycle $c_1 \to c_2, c_2 \to c_3, \ldots, c_{n-1} \to c_n, c_n \to c_1$ has edges of (equal) weight larger than those of edges not on the cycle (Figure 2). The worst-case distortion in this case, however, is only 3.

3.1.1 Coupling of two sets of cyclic permutations. To achieve a larger distortion, we engineer an overall cyclic structure similar to Figure 2 on $2n+1$ alternatives with $n+2$ agents as follows: construct n agents with distinct preference orderings by taking each cyclic permutation of $c_1, \ldots, c_n$ and coupling it with a corresponding permutation of $c_{n+2}, \ldots, c_{2n+1}$, pivoted about c_{n+1}. We add two agents with the preference exactly $c_1, c_2, \ldots, c_{2n+1}$.

To understand this coupling, let us look at a related example when $n = 2$.

Example 3.2. We couple $c_4 \succ c_5$ with $c_2 \succ c_1$, and $c_5 \succ c_4$ with $c_1 \succ c_2$ using c_3 as a pivot to get two agents v_1 and v_2 as in Figure 3. To make c_1 the unique Ranked Pairs winner, we make n copies each of v_1 and v_2, and add $n+1$ copies of a third agent v_0 with preference $c_1 \succ c_2 \succ c_3 \succ c_4 \succ c_5$. We will see in the proof of Theorem 3.3 that the following is a valid metric:

$$\underbrace{c_4 \succ_{v_1} c_5}_{d(v_1,.)=1} \succ_{v_1} \underbrace{c_2 \succ_{v_1} c_3}_{d(v_1,.)=3} \succ_{v_1} \underbrace{c_1}_{d(v_1,.)=5},$$

$$\underbrace{c_5}_{d(v_2,.)=0} \succ_{v_2} \underbrace{c_3 \succ_{v_2} c_4}_{d(v_2,.)=2} \succ_{v_2} \underbrace{c_1 \succ_{v_2} c_2}_{d(v_2,.)=4},$$

$$\underbrace{c_1 \succ_{v_0} c_2 \succ_{v_0} c_3 \succ_{v_0} c_4 \succ_{v_0} c_5}_{d(v_0,.)=2}.$$

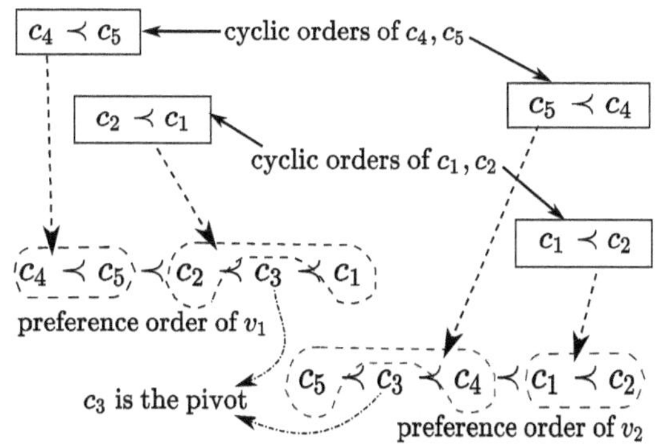

Fig. 3. Coupling example: $n = 2$

The ratio of the total costs of c_1 and c_5 here is $\frac{5(n)+4(n)+2(n+1)}{1(n)+0(n)+2(n+1)} = \frac{11n+2}{3n+2}$, which is more than 3 for $n \geq 3$. This serves as simple counter-example to the conjecture that Ranked Pairs achieves a distortion of 3.

This example can be modified to give a sequence of instances that lead to a distortion of 5 in the limit. In every instance in this sequence, we will see that the Ranked Pairs winner does not depend on how ties are broken.

Theorem 3.3. *There exists a sequence of instances* $\{\sigma^{(n)}\}_{n\geq 2}$ *such that*

$$\lim_{n\to\infty} \text{dist}(\textit{Ranked-Pairs}, \sigma^{(n)}) = 5.$$

Proof. For each $n \geq 2$, construct an instance $\sigma^{(n)}$ and a corresponding metric d as follows: There are $n + 2$ agents given by $\mathcal{V} = \{v_0, v_0', v_1, v_2, \ldots, v_n\}$, and $2n + 1$ alternatives given by $C = \{c_1, c_2, \ldots, c_{2n+1}\}$.

Both v_0 and v_0' have the preference order $c_1 \succ c_2 \succ \ldots \succ c_{2n+1}$, and $d(v_0, c) = d(v_0', c) = 2$ for all $c \in C$.

For $1 \leq i \leq n$, v_i has the preference order

$$\underbrace{c_{n+i+1} \succ \ldots \succ c_{2n+1}}_{d(v_i,.)=1} \succ \underbrace{c_{i+1} \succ \ldots \succ c_{n+i}}_{d(v_i,.)=3} \succ \underbrace{c_1 \succ \ldots \succ c_i}_{d(v_i,.)=5}.$$

Also, define d as follows, for all $c \in C$:

$$d(v_i, c_j) = \begin{cases} 1, & \text{if } n+i+1 \leq j \leq 2n+1, \\ 3, & \text{if } i+1 \leq j \leq n+i, \\ 5, & \text{if } 1 \leq j \leq i. \end{cases}$$

First, we show that d thus constructed is a valid q-metric. For all $(v, c) \in \mathcal{V} \times C$, $d(v, c) \geq 0$ is trivially satisfied. Let $A = \{c_1, c_2, \ldots, c_n\}$ and $B = \{c_{n+1}, \ldots, c_{2n+1}\}$. For all $a, a' \in A$, and $b, b' \in B$, and $v \in \mathcal{V}$,

$$|d(v,a) - d(v,b)| \leq 4,$$
$$|d(v,a) - d(v,a')| \leq 2,$$
$$|d(v,b) - d(v,b')| \leq 2.$$

The first holds with equality when $d(v,a) = 5, d(v,b) = 1$, the second when one of $d(v,a), d(v,a')$ is 5 and the other is 3, and the third when one of $d(v,b), d(v,b')$ is 3 and the other is 1. We also have

$$d(v,a) + d(v,b) \geq 4,$$
$$d(v,a) + d(v,a') \geq 4,$$
$$d(v,b) + d(v,b') \geq 2.$$

The first holds with equality when $d(v,a) = 3, d(v,b) = 1$ or $d(v,a) = d(v,b) = 2$, the second when $d(v,a) = d(v,a') = 2$, and the third when $d(v,b) = d(v,b') = 1$. Putting the above inequalities together, we see that d is a valid q-metric since it satisfies Definition 2.2.

Also from the above, we have $\sum_{v \in \mathcal{V}} d(v, c_1) = 5n + 4$ and $\sum_{v \in \mathcal{V}} d(v, c_{2n+1}) = n + 4$, and so

$$\lim_{n \to \infty} \frac{\sum_{v \in \mathcal{V}} d(v, c_1)}{\sum_{v \in \mathcal{V}} d(v, c_{2n+1})} = 5.$$

We will now show that c_1 is the Ranked Pairs winner, irrespective of how ties are broken, in every $\sigma^{(n)}$.

Recall that $w(i,j) = |\{v \in \mathcal{V} : c_i \succ_v c_j\}|$, the strength of edge $c_i \to c_j$ in the weighted-tournament graph obtained from σ_n. We will first show that for all $1 \leq i \leq 2n$, $w(i, i+1) = n+1$: If $1 \leq i \leq n$, then $w(i, i+1) = n+1$, since $c_i \succ_v c_{i+1}$ for all $v \in \mathcal{V}$ except v_i. If $n+1 \leq i \leq 2n$, then $w(i, i+1) = n+1$, since $c_i \succ_v c_{i+1}$ for all $v \in \mathcal{V}$ except v_{i-n}.

All other edges $i \to j$ fall into the following cases:

- $i < j - 1$: If $j \leq n+1$, then $c_j \succ_{v_k} c_i$ for all $i \leq k \leq j-1$. A similar argument holds when $n+1 \leq i$. If $i \leq n$ and $j \geq n+2$, then $c_j \succ_{v_k} c_i$ at least for $k = i, j-n-1$;
- $i > j$, then $c_j \succ_v c_i$ at least for $v \in \{v_0, v_0'\}$.

In all these cases, $c_j \succ_v c_i$ at least for two agents, and thereby $w(i,j) \leq n$. Therefore, the edges $c_i \to c_{i+1}$ for $1 \leq i \leq 2n$ have the largest weights (with no ties) and consequently c_1 is the Ranked Pairs winner. □

The *Schulze* method (Schulze 2003) also gives priority to edges of larger weight, albeit in a more complicated way. The above result holds for the Schulze rule since it also picks c_1 as the winner in the instances constructed.

Corollary 3.4.

$$\lim_{n \to \infty} \text{dist}(\textit{Schulze}, \sigma^{(n)}) = 5.$$

Proof. The proof follows from the fact that the Schulze rule also chooses c_1 as the winner in every instance in the sequence $\{\sigma^{(n)}\}_{n \geq 2}$, irrespective of how ties are broken. □

Since methods like Ranked Pairs and the Schulze rule (Schulze 2003) fall in the category of weighted-tournament rules (C2 functions), we believe that no weighted-tournament rule can achieve a worst-case distortion of less than 5.

Conjecture 3.5. *Any weighted-tournament rule has a worst-case distortion of at least 5.*

Copeland falls in the category of tournament rules (C1 functions), and we know that Copeland, and other similar rules related to the uncovered set (Moulin 1986), achieve a worst-case distortion of 5 (Anshelevich et al. 2015). In fact, a lower bound of 5 for the worst-case distortion of Copeland is established via an instance where the tournament graph is a 3-node cycle (Anshelevich et al.

2015). It therefore follows that the worst-case distortion of any deterministic tournament rule is at least 5[3] (since such a rule has no way of distinguishing between the 3 nodes).

3.2 Randomized tournament/weighted-tournament rules

We will now turn our attention to randomized social choice rules. The worst-case distortion in this case is at least 2 (Anshelevich and Postl 2016). Continuing our discussion on tournament and weighted-tournament rules, we show that in the worst-case randomized tournament/weighted-tournament rules do not get close to the above lower bound. We will construct a sequence of instances where any randomized tournament or weighted-tournament rule achieves a distortion of 3 in the limit.

THEOREM 3.6. *The worst-case distortion of any randomized tournament/weighted-tournament rule is at least 3.*

PROOF. Construct an instance $\sigma^{(m)}$ and a corresponding metric as follows: There are $m+1$ alternatives given by $C = \{c^*, c_1, c_2, \ldots, c_m\}$. And there are $2m$ agents given by $\mathcal{V}$, and $\mathcal{V}$ is divided into two groups $V = \{v_1, v_2, \ldots, v_m\}$ and $U = \{u_1, \ldots, u_m\}$.

v_1 has the preference order $c^* \succ_{v_1} c_1 \succ_{v_1} \ldots \succ_{v_1} c_m$. For $2 \le i \le m$, agent v_i has the preference order $c^* \succ_{v_i} c_i \succ_{v_i} c_{i+1} \succ_{v_i} \ldots \succ_{v_i} c_m \succ_{v_i} c_1 \succ_{v_i} \ldots c_{i-1}$.

u_1 has the preference order $c_m \succ_{u_1} \ldots \succ_{u_1} c_1 \succ_{u_1} c^*$. For $2 \le i \le m$, agent v_i has the preference order $c_{i-1} \succ_{u_i} \ldots c_1 \succ_{u_i} c_m \succ_{u_i} \ldots \succ_{u_i} c_{i+1} \succ_{u_i} c_i \succ_{u_i} c^*$.

Define a metric d as: $\forall v \in V$, $d(v, c^*) = 0$ and $d(v, c) = 2$, $\forall c \neq c^*$; and $\forall u \in U$, $d(u, c) = 1$, for all $c \in C$. We omit the details, but this is indeed a valid metric (see Figure 4 for a graphical illustration).

For any given distribution $\vec{x}$ over the alternatives C, we must have some alternative a such that $x_a \le \frac{1}{m}$. In this instance, we have $w(a, b) = |\{v \in V \cup U : a \succ_v b\}| = m$ for all $a \neq b \in C$, i.e., $\frac{w(a,b)}{|\mathcal{V}|} = 0.5$. Since the tournament/weighted-tournament graph is completely symmetric (since the edge weight is equal to 0.5 on all directed edges), we can assume without loss of generality that $c^* = a$[4].

The expected cost for c^* is

$$\sum_{v \in V} d(v, c^*) + \sum_{u \in U} d(u, c^*) = m(0) + m(1) = m.$$

The expected cost for the distribution $\vec{x}$ is

$$\sum_{c \in C} x_c \sum_{v \in V} d(v, c) + \sum_{c \in C} x_c \sum_{u \in U} d(u, c) = x_{c^*} \sum_{t \in V \cup U} d(t, c^*) + \sum_{c \neq c^*} x_c \sum_{t \in V \cup U} d(t, c).$$

Since $d(v, c^*) = 0$ for all $v \in V$, and $d(u, c^*) = 1$ for all $u \in U$, we get $\sum_{t \in V \cup U} d(t, c^*) = m$. For any $c \neq c^*$, $t \in V \cup U$, we defined $d(t, c) = 3$, which implies that $\sum_{t \in V \cup U} d(t, c) = 3m$.

Using the above, the expected cost becomes

$$x_{c^*}(m) + \sum_{c \neq c^*} x_c(3m) = x_{c^*}(m) + (1 - x_{c^*})(3m) = 3m - x_{c^*}(2m) \ge 3m - \frac{1}{m}(2m) = 3m - 2.$$

Therefore, the distortion ratio is at least $(3m-2)/m = 3 - 2/m$ which tends to 3 as $m \to \infty$. □

---

[3]We thank Reyna Hulett for pointing this out.

[4]Tournament/weighted-tournament rules are inherently anonymous, but the winner in this case will depend on how ties are broken. We can get around this issue by tailoring the constructed instance appropriately, i.e., swapping the roles of c^* and the chosen winner.

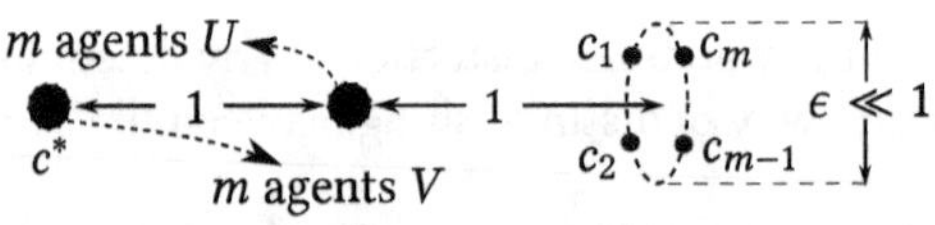

Fig. 4. Underlying metric in proof of Theorem 3.6

Putting Theorems 3.3 and 3.6 together, we see that Copeland does at least as well as Ranked Pairs, and randomized tournament/weighted-tournament rules perform no better than Randomized Dictatorship with respect to the worst-case distortion of the sum of costs objective. In the next section, we will show that the upper bounds on the distortion of the sum of costs, for both Copeland and Randomized Dictatorship, hold much more generally.

3.3 Instance Optimal Distortion

For any given instance, the single alternative that achieves the least worst-case distortion over all consistent metrics can be found in polynomial time (by solving a polynomial number of linear programs). This follows in a straightforward fashion from the fact that the metric inequalities are linear. The same is true also in the randomized case, perhaps not so directly, in that we can find the optimal distribution over alternatives in polynomial time. The technical details of this claim are provided in our full report (Goel et al. 2016). Given the computability of these instance optimal functions, we believe that:

Conjecture 3.7. *There exists a deterministic social choice rule that achieves a worst-case distortion of at most 3, and a randomized rule that achieves a worst-case distortion of at most 2.*

4 FAIRNESS IN DISTORTION

As mentioned before, we introduce a way of quantifying the fairness of social choice rules by using the concept of approximate majorization within the metric distortion framework. One could hope to adapt other notions of fairness like envy-freeness (Lipton et al. 2004) and leximin (Barbarà and Jackson 1988; Rawls 2009) (actually leximax since we are dealing with costs) into the distortion framework. While the standard definition of envy-freeness applies to problems involving the division of goods, and requires no inter-personal comparison of utilities, we could perhaps re-purpose it to our setting by looking at the difference between the largest and smallest costs for any given alternative. This quantity in itself cannot be bounded because it is not scale-invariant – for whenever it is positive, the metric can be scaled to make the envy unbounded. Unfortunately, using this "envy" as the objective in the distortion ratio is also fruitless (see Example 4.1 below).

We know that Copeland achieves a worst-case distortion of 5 for objectives given by α-percentiles for $\alpha \in [0.5, 1)$ (Anshelevich et al. 2015). Here the α-percentile cost with respect to any alternative $c \in C$ corresponds to the smallest value $x \in \{d(v, c) |\ v \in \mathcal{V}\}$ for which $\frac{\#\{v \in \mathcal{V} |\ d(v,c) \leq x\}}{N} > \alpha$. It is easy to see that such an upper bound for all $\alpha \in [0, 1)$ would subsume our results. However, for $\alpha \in [0, 0.5)$, any deterministic rule has unbounded distortion in the worst case. To see this, consider the following example.

Example 4.1. Consider two alternatives c_1, c_2. There are two sets of agents U and V of size $N/2$ each which have preference $c_1 \succ c_2$ and $c_2 \succ c_1$ respectively. Assume without loss of generality that c_1 is picked as the winner by the given social choice rule.

Let $d(v, c_1) = 1 \leq d(v, c_2) = 1$ for all $v \in V$, and $d(u, c_2) = \epsilon < d(u, c_1) = 1$ for all $u \in U$. By invoking Lemma 2.3, we can see that this gives us a consistent metric.

For $\alpha \in [0, 0.5)$, we have that the α-percentile costs for c_1 and c_2 are 1 and ϵ respectively. The distortion ratio is then $\frac{1}{\epsilon}$, which goes to ∞ as $\epsilon \to 0$.

Now assume c_2 is picked as the winner. The maximum envy in this case is $1 - \epsilon$. And in the case of c_1 the maximum envy is 0, leading to an unbounded ratio.

The above example also shows us why a leximax comparison does not work. Ordering the costs for c_1 and c_2 in non-decreasing order, let us compare the costs at the first position at which these orders differ. At the $(N/2+1)$-th position, the cost for c_1 is 1, and that for c_2 is ϵ, leading to an unbounded ratio as $\epsilon \to 0$.

4.1 Bounding the fairness ratio of Copeland rule

In this section, we show that Copeland achieves a fairness ratio of at most 5. Besides Copeland, other weighted-tournament rules such as those selecting winners from the minimal covering set, the bipartisan set, banks set, or any other subset of the uncovered set, also achieve a fairness-ratio of at most 5.

Theorem 4.2. *For any instance σ, if x is the Copeland winner, and z is any other alternative, then*

$$\text{fairness}(Copeland, \sigma) = \sup_{d \in \rho(\sigma)} \max_{1 \le k \le N} \frac{\max_{S \subseteq \mathcal{V}:|S|=k} \sum_{v \in S} d(v,x)}{\max_{S \subseteq \mathcal{V}:|S|=k} \sum_{v \in S} d(v,z)} \le 5.$$

Proof. Fix any $k \in \{1, 2, \ldots, N\}$.
For any $a, b \in C$, denote the set of agents that prefer a over b by $G_{ab} = \{v \in \mathcal{V} : a \succ_v b\}$.
And for any $t \in C$, let

$$S_t \triangleq \arg \max_{S \subseteq \mathcal{V}:|S|=k} \sum_{v \in S} d(v,t).$$

Since x is the Copeland winner, we know, from the connection to the uncovered set (Moulin 1986), that either (A) $|G_{xz}| \ge \frac{N}{2}$, or (B) $\exists y \in C$, such that $|G_{xy}| \ge \frac{N}{2}$ and $|G_{yz}| \ge \frac{N}{2}$. We deal with each case separately.

Case (A): Let $g : \mathcal{V} \to \mathcal{V}$ be any one-one map such that if $v \in S_x \setminus G_{xz}$ then $g(v) \in G_{xz}$. One such map exists because $|S_x \setminus G_{xz}| \le |\mathcal{V} \setminus G_{xz}| \le \frac{N}{2} \le |G_{xz}|$. Let $A = S_x \cap G_{xz}$ and $B = S_x \setminus G_{xz}$.

$$\begin{aligned}
\sum_{v \in S_x} d(v,x) &= \sum_{v \in A} d(v,x) + \sum_{v \in B} d(v,x) \\
&\le \sum_{v \in A} d(v,z) + \sum_{v \in B} d(v,x) \\
&\le \sum_{v \in A} d(v,z) + \sum_{v \in B} (d(g(v),x) + d(g(v),z) + d(v,z)) \\
&= \sum_{v \in S_x} d(v,z) + \sum_{v \in B} (d(g(v),x) + d(g(v),z)) \\
&\le \sum_{v \in S_x} d(v,z) + \sum_{v \in B} 2d(g(v),z) \\
&\le 3 \sum_{v \in S_z} d(v,z).
\end{aligned}$$

In the above sequence, the first inequality follow from the fact that $v \in A \implies v \in G_{xz}$ and for any $v \in G_{xz}$, $d(v,x) \le d(v,z)$ by definition. The second inequality follows after invoking Condition 2 from Definition 2.2. The third inequality is true because $g(v) \in G_{xz}$ by definition, and the fourth because for any $S \subseteq \mathcal{V}$ such that $|S| \le k$, $\sum_{v \in S} d(v,z) \le \sum_{v \in S_z} d(v,z)$ by the definition of S_z.

Case (B): For a complete treatment of this case, we refer the reader to the full version of this paper (Goel et al. 2016). However, a bound of 9 is easy to see from a repeated application of case (A). □

The fact that the inequality in Theorem 4.2 above is tight follows from the known example (Anshelevich et al. 2015) in which Copeland achieves a distortion of 5 with respect to the sum of costs objective.

As mentioned before Copeland also does well with respect to other objectives such as median and α-percentiles for $\alpha \in [0.5, 1)$ (Anshelevich and Postl 2016). These functions are not convex and hence do not fall under the category of functions that can be approximated with the help of the fairness ratio. An interesting question is to characterize the entire class of functions for which Copeland achieves a constant factor bound on the distortion.

4.2 Randomized Dictatorship

For randomized rules, the connection of the fairness-ratio to convex cost functions does not hold in terms of the expectation variants of the quantities involved. However, the fairness ratio in its own right is a generalization of both max-min fairness and total cost minimization, and is hence worth studying in the case of randomized social choice rules.

Our last result is that Randomized Dictatorship, which achieves a worst-case distortion of 3, also achieves a fairness ratio of 3 in expectation.

THEOREM 4.3. *For any instance σ, alternative y, and X chosen according to Randomized Dictatorship*

$$\sup_{d \in \rho(\sigma)} \max_{1 \le k \le N} \frac{\mathbb{E}[\max_{S \subseteq \mathcal{V}:|S|=k} \sum_{v \in S} d(v, X)]}{\max_{S \subseteq \mathcal{V}:|S|=k} \sum_{v \in S} d(v, y)} \le 3.$$

PROOF. Fix any $k \in \{1, 2, \ldots, N\}$, and any alternative $y \in C$.

For all $c \in C$, denote the set of agents with c as their top choice by $V_c = \{v \in \mathcal{V} : c \succ_v c', \ \forall c' \neq c\}$, and the size of this set as $N_c = |V_c|$. Let the total number of agents be given by $N = |\mathcal{V}|$.

For any alternative $c \in C$, denote the set of agents that maximize the sum of k costs for it by $S_c = \arg\max_{S \subseteq \mathcal{V}:|S|=k} \sum_{v \in S} d(v, c)$.

For all $c \in C$, by the triangle inequality we have

$$\begin{aligned} \sum_{v \in S_c} d(v, c) &\le \sum_{v \in S_c} (d(v, y) + d(c, y)) \\ &\le k \cdot d(c, y) + \sum_{v \in S_y} d(v, y), \end{aligned} \tag{4}$$

where the second inequality follows by the definition of S_y.

For any $c \in C$, if $v \in V_c$, we have $d(v, c) \le d(v, y)$ (by the definition of V_c), and $d(v, c) + d(v, y) \ge d(c, y)$ (by the triangle inequality), which together imply $d(v, y) \ge \frac{d(c,y)}{2}$. Therefore,

$$\sum_{v \in \mathcal{V}} d(v, y) = \sum_{c \in C} \sum_{v \in V_c} d(v, y) \ge \sum_{c \in C} N_c \frac{d(c, y)}{2}. \tag{5}$$

Consequently, we get

$$\sum_{v \in S_y} d(v, y) \ge \frac{k}{N} \sum_{v \in \mathcal{V}} d(v, y) \ge \frac{k}{N} \sum_{c \in C} N_c \frac{d(c, y)}{2}, \tag{6}$$

where the first inequality follows by the definition of S_y, and the second from the inequality in 5. We can now bound the expected distortion as follows:

$$\frac{\mathbb{E}[\max_{S\subseteq\mathcal{V}:|S|=k}\sum_{v\in S}d(v,X)]}{\max_{S\subseteq\mathcal{V}:|S|=k}\sum_{v\in S}d(v,y)} = \frac{\sum_{c\in C}\frac{N_c}{N}\sum_{v\in S_c}d(v,c)}{\sum_{v\in S_y}d(v,y)}$$
$$\le \frac{\sum_{c\in C}\frac{N_c}{N}(k\cdot d(c,y)+\sum_{v\in S_y}d(v,y))}{\sum_{v\in S_y}d(v,y)}$$
$$\le 1+\frac{\sum_{c\in C}\frac{N_c}{N}k\cdot d(c,y)}{\sum_{v\in S_y}d(v,y)} \le 1+\frac{\frac{k}{N}\sum_{c\in C}N_c\cdot d(c,y)}{\frac{k}{N}\sum_{c\in C}N_c\frac{d(c,y)}{2}} \le 3.$$

We have made use of 4 and 6 to get the first and third inequalities in the above sequence. □

To make amply clear that the bound on the fairness ratio of randomized does not extend to convex functions, we will now look at an example where the distortion of randomized dictatorship is unbounded when the objective used is the square of the sum of costs.

Example 4.4. Consider two agents $\{c_1, c_2\}$ and $N_1 + N_2$ agents in total divided into two groups V_1 and V_2. Assume all of the above are points in $\mathbb{R}$. $c_1 = 0$ and $c_2 = 1$. Every agent in V_1 is at 0, and every agent in V_2 is at 1. Also assume that $N_1 \ge N_2$.

Let $C(\vec{x}) = (\sum_i x_i)^2$. With C as the cost objective, the optimal alternative is c_1. The social cost of this alternative is equal to N_2^2.

Randomized dictatorship chooses c_1 with probability $\frac{N_1}{N_1+N_2}$ and c_2 with probability $\frac{N_2}{N_1+N_2}$. The expected cost is equal to

$$N_2^2\frac{N_1}{N_1+N_2}+N_1^2\frac{N_2}{N_1+N_2}=N_1N_2.$$

The distortion ratio is $N_1N_2/N_2^2 = N_1/N_2$ which is unbounded in the limit $N_1 \to \infty$ for any fixed N_2.

The fact that the distortion of Randomized Dictatorship with respect to convex cost objectives is unbounded makes the fairness properties of Copeland even more interesting. It seems surprising that a simple rule like Copeland can approximate the optimal alternative over a very general class of cost functions.

5 CONCLUSIONS

In this paper, we further the understanding of the performance of social choice rules under metric preferences with respect to the distortion measure. We provide lower bounds on worst-case distortion for deterministic rules such as Ranked Pairs and Schulze, and randomized tournament/weighted-tournament rules. We introduce a framework to study the fairness properties of social choice rules within the distortion framework, and provide low constant-factor upper bounds on the fairness ratios of some well-known mechanisms like Copeland and Randomized Dictatorship. In particular, what stands out is that Copeland not only achieves the best known upper bound for deterministic rules, but also simultaneously approximates a large class of cost functions. We also point out a few interesting directions for future research.

ACKNOWLEDGMENTS

We would like to thank Brandon Fain for useful discussions.

REFERENCES

Elliot Anshelevich, Onkar Bhardwaj, and John Postl. 2015. Approximating Optimal Social Choice under Metric Preferences. *Association for the Advancement of Artificial Intelligence, 15th Conference of the* (2015).

Elliot Anshelevich and John Postl. 2016. Randomized Social Choice Functions Under Metric Preferences. *25th International Joint Conference on Artificial Intelligence* (2016).

Elliot Anshelevich and Shreyas Sekar. 2016. Blind, Greedy, and Random: Algorithms for Matching and Clustering Using Only Ordinal Information. *Association for the Advancement of Artificial Intelligence, 15th Conference of the* (2016).

Vijay Arya, Naveen Garg, Rohit Khandekar, Adam Meyerson, Kamesh Munagala, and Vinayaka Pandit. 2004. Local search heuristics for k-median and facility location problems. *SIAM Journal on computing* (2004).

Salvador Barberà and Matthew Jackson. 1988. Maximin, leximin, and the protective criterion: characterizations and comparisons. *Journal of Economic Theory* (1988).

Salvador Barbera. 2001. An introduction to strategy-proof social choice functions. *Social Choice and Welfare* (2001).

Craig Boutilier, Ioannis Caragiannis, Simi Haber, Tyler Lu, Ariel D Procaccia, and Or Sheffet. 2015. Optimal social choice functions: A utilitarian view. *Artificial Intelligence* (2015).

Ioannis Caragiannis, Christos Kaklamanis, Panagiotis Kanellopoulos, and Maria Kyropoulou. 2009. On low-envy truthful allocations. *International Conference on Algorithmic Decision Theory* (2009).

Ioannis Caragiannis and Ariel D Procaccia. 2011. Voting almost maximizes social welfare despite limited communication. *Artificial Intelligence* (2011).

Yiling Chen, John K Lai, David C Parkes, and Ariel D Procaccia. 2013. Truth, justice, and cake cutting. *Games and Economic Behavior* (2013).

Zvi Drezner and Horst W Hamacher. 1995. *Facility location.* Springer-Verlag New York, NY.

James M Enelow and Melvin J Hinich. 1984. *The spatial theory of voting: An introduction.* CUP Archive.

Michal Feldman, Amos Fiat, and Iddan Golomb. 2016. On voting and facility location. *Proceedings of the 2016 ACM Conference on Economics and Computation* (2016).

Aris Filos-Ratsikas and Peter Bro Miltersen. 2014. Truthful approximations to range voting. *International Conference on Web and Internet Economics* (2014).

Peter C Fishburn. 1977. Condorcet social choice functions. *SIAM Journal on applied Mathematics* (1977).

Allan Gibbard. 1973. Manipulation of voting schemes: a general result. *Econometrica: journal of the Econometric Society* (1973).

Ashish Goel, Anilesh Kollagunta Krishnaswamy, and Kamesh Munagala. 2016. Metric Distortion of Social Choice Rules: Lower Bounds and Fairness Properties. *arXiv preprint arXiv:1612.02912* (2016).

Ashish Goel and Adam Meyerson. 2006. Simultaneous optimization via approximate majorization for concave profits or convex costs. *Algorithmica* (2006).

Ashish Goel, Adam Meyerson, and Serge Plotkin. 2001. Approximate majorization and fair online load balancing. *Symposium on Discrete Algorithms: Proceedings of the twelfth annual ACM-SIAM symposium on Discrete algorithms* (2001).

Jon Kleinberg, Yuval Rabani, and Éva Tardos. 1999. Fairness in routing and load balancing. *Foundations of Computer Science, 1999. 40th Annual Symposium on* (1999).

Amit Kumar and Jon Kleinberg. 2000. Fairness measures for resource allocation. *Foundations of Computer Science, 41st Annual Symposium on* (2000).

Richard J Lipton, Evangelos Markakis, Elchanan Mossel, and Amin Saberi. 2004. On approximately fair allocations of indivisible goods. *Proceedings of the 5th ACM conference on Electronic commerce* (2004).

Hervé Moulin. 1980. On strategy-proofness and single peakedness. *Public Choice* (1980).

Hervé Moulin. 1986. Choosing from a tournament. *Social Choice and Welfare* (1986).

Hervé Moulin, Felix Brandt, Vincent Conitzer, Ulle Endriss, Ariel D Procaccia, and Jérôme Lang. 2016. *Handbook of Computational Social Choice.* Cambridge University Press.

Ariel D Procaccia and Jeffrey S Rosenschein. 2006. The distortion of cardinal preferences in voting. *International Workshop on Cooperative Information Agents* (2006).

Ariel D Procaccia and Junxing Wang. 2014. Fair enough: Guaranteeing approximate maximin shares. *Proceedings of the fifteenth ACM conference on Economics and computation* (2014).

John Rawls. 2009. *A theory of justice.* Harvard University Press.

Mark Allen Satterthwaite. 1975. Strategy-proofness and Arrow's conditions: Existence and correspondence theorems for voting procedures and social welfare functions. *Journal of economic theory* (1975).

Markus Schulze. 2003. A new monotonic and clone-independent single-winner election method. *Voting matters* (2003).

Piotr Skowron and Edith Elkind. 2017. Social Choice Under Metric Preferences: Scoring Rules and STV. *Association for the Advancement of Artificial Intelligence, 16th Conference of the* (2017).

Of the People: Voting Is More Effective with Representative Candidates

YU CHENG, University of Southern California
SHADDIN DUGHMI, University of Southern California
DAVID KEMPE, University of Southern California

In light of the classic impossibility results of Arrow and Gibbard and Satterthwaite regarding voting with ordinal rules, there has been recent interest in characterizing how well common voting rules approximate the social optimum. In order to quantify the quality of approximation, it is natural to consider the candidates and voters as embedded within a common metric space, and to ask how much further the chosen candidate is from the population as compared to the socially optimal one. We use this metric preference model to explore a fundamental and timely question: does the social welfare of a population improve when candidates are representative of the population? If so, then by how much, and how does the answer depend on the complexity of the metric space?

We restrict attention to the most fundamental and common social choice setting: a population of voters, two candidates, and a majority rule election. When candidates are not representative of the population, it is known that the candidate selected by the majority rule can be thrice as far from the population as the socially optimal one; this holds even when the underlying metric is a line. We examine how this ratio improves when candidates are drawn independently from the population of voters. Our results are two-fold: When the metric is a line, the ratio improves from 3 to $(4-2\sqrt{2}) \approx 1.1716$; this bound is tight. When the metric is arbitrary, we show a lower bound of 1.5 and a constant upper bound strictly better than 2 on the distortion of majority rule.

The aforementioned positive results depend in part on the assumption that the two candidates are independently and identically distributed. However, we show that i.i.d. candidates do not suffice for our upper bounds: if the population of candidates can be different from that of voters, an upper bound of 2 on the distortion is tight for both general metric spaces and the line. Thus, we show a constant gap between representative and non-representative candidates in both cases.

1 INTRODUCTION

> *"[...] and that government of the people, by the people, for the people, shall not perish from the earth."*
>
> — Abraham Lincoln

Abraham Lincoln's Gettysburg Address culminated with the oft-quoted words above. This single sentence gives a remarkably succinct summary of the role of a country's populace in a participatory democracy, identifying three distinct facets: (1) The government should be *of* the people: the members of the government should be drawn from — and by inference representative of — the country's populace. (2) The government should be *by* the people: decisions should be made by the populace. (3) The government should be *for* the people: its objective should be to serve the interests of the populace. In Lincoln's words, the central question we study here is the following:

EC'17, June 26–30, 2017, Cambridge, Massachusetts, USA. © 2017 ACM. ISBN 978-1-4503-4527-9/17/06...$15.00.
DOI: http://dx.doi.org/10.1145/3033274.3085155

> If a government by the people is to be for the people, how important is it that it also be *of* the people?

In quantifying this question, we observe that there is a surprisingly clean mapping of Lincoln's vision onto central concepts of social choice theory:

(1) Who is the government of? Who are the candidates (people or ideas) to be aggregated?
(2) Who is the government by? What are the social choice rules used for aggregation?
(3) Who is the government for? What objective function is to be optimized?

While the exact social choice rules to be used have been a topic of vigorous debate for several centuries [5, 12, 14, 15], the broad class they are drawn from is generally agreed upon: voters provide an ordinal ranking of (a subset of) the candidates, and these rankings are then aggregated to produce either a single winner or a consensus ranking of all (or some) candidates. Social choice is limited by the severe impossibility results of Arrow [5] and Gibbard and Satterthwaite [19, 28], establishing that even very simple combinations of desired axioms are in general unachievable. These impossibility results in turn have resulted in a fruitful line of work exploring restrictions on individuals' preference orders for circumventing the impossibility of social choice.

One of the avenues toward circumventing the impossibility results simultaneously doubles as a framework for addressing the third question: What objective function is to be optimized by the social choice rule? The key modeling assumption is that all candidates (ideas or people) and voters are embedded in a metric space: small distances model high agreement, while large distances correspond to disagreement [6–9, 17, 23, 24, 27]. The metric induces a preference order over candidates for each voter: she simply ranks candidates by distance from herself. When the metric space is specifically the line, we obtain the well-known and much studied special case of single-peaked preferences [8, 24]. Embedding voters and candidates in a metric space has historically served two purposes: (1) Restricting the metric space — for example, by limiting its dimension — defines a restricted class of ordinal preference profiles, and might help circumvent the classic impossibility results of social choice. (2) The distances naturally provide an objective function: the *best* alternative is the one that is closest to the voters on average. Even when the metric space is unrestricted, replacing the hard axioms of social choice theory with this objective function can "circumvent" impossibility results through approximation [25], and permits comparing different social rules by quantifying their worst-case performance.

While distances yield cardinal preferences and a social objective function, it is arguably unrealistic to expect individuals to articulate distances accurately. It is consequently unsurprising that common and well-established voting rules typically restrict voters to providing ordinal information, such as rankings or a single vote. Therefore, we view the metric space as implicit, and a social choice function as optimizing the associated cardinal objective function *using only ordinal information.*

This viewpoint was recently crisply expressed in a sequence of works originating with Anshelevich et al. [1–4, 20]. In particular, Anshelevich et al. [2] examine many of the most widely used election voting rules, guided by the question: "How much worse is the outcome of voting than would be the omniscient choice of the best available candidate?" They showed remarkable separations: while some voting rules guarantee a distortion of no more than a constant factor, others are off by a factor that increases linearly in the number of candidates or — even worse — voters. The simplest, and in some sense canonical, example of such distortion is captured as follows:

Example 1.1. A population consists of voters of whom just below half lean solidly left (at position -1), while just over half are just to the right of center (at position $\epsilon > 0$). The population conducts an election between a solidly left-wing (position -1) and a solidly right-wing (position 1) candidate.

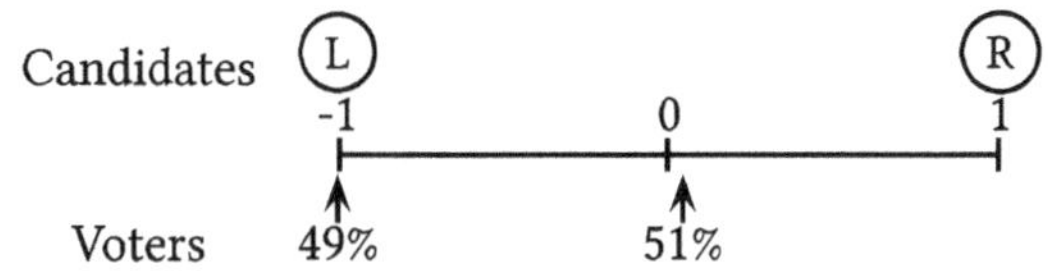

Fig. 1. The winning candidate could have thrice the social cost of the other candidate.

Because the centrist voters express their (slight) preference for the right-wing candidate, he is elected by a small majority. However, the average distance from the population to the right-wing candidate (1.5) is thrice that to the left-wing candidate (0.5), meaning that the majority vote led to a loss of a factor three in the utility.

We follow prior nomenclature [2, 10, 11, 13, 26] and term this utility loss the *distortion*. A closer examination of Example 1.1 suggests a likely culprit for the high distortion: the right-wing candidate was not representative of the population – he was not *of* the people. Had we drawn two candidates from the population, the winner would in fact always be the socially optimal choice in this case. If we wanted to create the possibility of recreating the above example, we would need to move some fraction δ of the population to the right wing. If δ were large, then the election of a right-wing candidate would not be nearly as bad according to the objective function; conversely, if δ were small, then it would be unlikely that a right-wing candidate would run, so most of the time the social choice rule would select an optimal candidate. Thus, intuitively, when candidates are drawn from the population, we would expect the distortion in the social cost to be better than when they are not. The goal of this article is to investigate to what extent this intuition holds.

The Model

Formally, we assume that the candidates and voters are jointly located in a (finite) metric space; the distance between i and j is denoted by $d_{i,j}$. The candidates' locations are given by a probability distribution $\boldsymbol{p}$, while the voters' location distribution is denoted by $\boldsymbol{q}$. In order to isolate the driving question and side-step issues of specific voting rules, we focus on the simplest social choice scenario: two candidates i, i' are drawn i.i.d. from $\boldsymbol{p}$, and a simple majority vote determines the winner between them. Voter j votes for the one of i, i' who is closer[1] to j. The *social cost* of candidate i is $c_i = \sum_j q_j d_{i,j}$. With $w(i, i')$ denoting the winner of the election and $o(i, i')$ the socially optimal candidate, the expected distortion of voting is $\sum_{i,i'} p_i p_{i'} \frac{c_{w(i,i')}}{c_{o(i,i')}}$. Our goal is then to understand how much the distortion decreases when candidates are of the people (when $\boldsymbol{p} = \boldsymbol{q}$).

Our Results

We begin our investigation with arguably the simplest metric space, which nonetheless is frequently used to describe the political spectrum of countries: the line. As we saw in Example 1.1, even for the line, voting between two arbitrary candidates can lead to a distortion of 3. Our first main result (proved in Section 3) is that when two candidates are drawn i.i.d. from $\boldsymbol{p} = \boldsymbol{q}$, the expected distortion is at most $4 - 2\sqrt{2} \approx 1.1716$, and this bound is tight. The lower-bound example is in fact of the type discussed after Example 1.1, obtained by moving a suitable population mass δ from location ϵ to location 1. The more difficult part of the proof is the upper bound, and in particular, the proof that the worst-case distribution of voters/candidates always has support size 3. The proof proceeds by showing that for larger support sizes, there is always a sequence of alterations that gradually shifts the population to fewer locations, without lowering the distortion.

[1] Throughout, we will assume when convenient that the metric and distribution are in general position. Specifically, there are no ties in any voter's preference order, and there are no ties in any election outcome. Ties could in principle be dealt with using suitable tie breaking rules, but the slight gain in generality would not be worth the overhead.

Next, we turn our attention to general metric spaces. For arbitrary metric spaces, the distortion of voting can be larger. In Section 5, we analyze a simple example: just under half the population is located at one point i, while the rest of the population is spread out evenly over $n \gg 1$ locations that are at distances just below 1 from each other and at distance 1 from i. As $n \to \infty$, we show that the expected distortion converges to $\frac{3}{2}$. The upper bound we establish in Section 5 does not match this lower bound: we show that for every metric and every $\boldsymbol{p}$, the expected distortion is at most $2 - \frac{1}{652}$. We conjecture that the bound of $\frac{3}{2}$ is in fact tight — proving or disproving this conjecture is a natural direction for future work, discussed in Section 6.

The significance of our upper bounds on distortion (for the line and for general metric spaces) arises from the contrast to the corresponding bounds when $\boldsymbol{q} \neq \boldsymbol{p}$. In revisiting the improved distortion results we prove, we notice two potential driving factors: (1) The two candidates are independently and identically distributed. (2) The distributions of candidates and voters are the same. One may wonder whether the innocuous-looking assumption of i.i.d. candidates alone could be responsible for the lower distortion, without requiring that candidates be of the people. In Section 4, we rule out this possibility by establishing a (tight) bound of 2 on the distortion of voting when candidates are drawn i.i.d. from $\boldsymbol{p} \neq \boldsymbol{q}$, both in general metrics and on the line. The (small, but constant) gap between the distortions of $2 - \frac{1}{652}$ and 2 in general metric spaces, and the significant gap between the distortions of $4 - 2\sqrt{2} \approx 1.1716$ and 2 on the line, show that government by the people is more efficient when it is also *of the people.* The exact size of the gap between the two distortions in general metric spaces is a natural open question.

Related Work

There has been a lot of interest recently in circumventing the impossibility results of voting and social choice by approximation; see, e.g., [13, 25, 26] and [11] for a recent survey. Of particular interest is the recent direction in which the voters' objective functions are derived from proximity in a metric space [1–4, 18, 20]. One of the important issues is providing incentives for truthful revelation of preferences (e.g., [18]); in this paper, we side-step this issue by considering only elections between two candidates at a time.

Our work is most directly inspired by the recent work of Anshelevich et al. [2, 3], which analyzes the distortion of ordinal voting rules when evaluated for metric preferences. Our work departs from [2, 3] in assuming that the candidates themselves are drawn i.i.d. from underlying distributions, and in analyzing the case when the distributions of candidates and voters are the same.

Anshelevich and Postl [3] consider a condition of instances that also aims to capture that candidates are in some sense "representative" of the voting population. Specifically, they define a notion of *decisiveness* as follows: Let i be a voter, and j_i, j'_i her two closest candidates, with $d_{i,j_i} \leq d_{i,j'_i}$. An instance is α-decisive (for $\alpha \leq 1$) if $d_{i,j_i} \leq \alpha d_{i,j'_i}$ for all i; in other words, when $\alpha \ll 1$, every voter has a strongly preferred candidate. Naturally, the decisiveness condition is applicable only in elections in which the number of candidates is large or the space of voters is highly clustered. In our work, by considering candidates drawn from the voter distribution, we avoid such assumptions.

2 PRELIMINARIES

The candidates and voters are embedded in a finite metric space $\mathcal{D} = (d_{i,j})_{i,j}$ with *points (locations)* $i = 1, \ldots, n$. Depending on the context, we will refer to i as a point, candidate, or voter. The probability for a candidate to be drawn from point i is p_i; we write $\boldsymbol{p} = (p_i)_i$. The fraction of voters at i is q_i, summarized as $\boldsymbol{q} = (q_i)_i$. For a subset of points A, we write $p_A = \sum_{i \in A} p_i$ to denote the total probability mass in A, and similarly for q_A. The *social cost* of a candidate i is his average distance to all voters: $c_i = \sum_j q_j \cdot d_{i,j}$.

When candidates i and i' are competing, each voter j votes for the candidate that is closer[2] to her, i.e., for $\text{argmin}_{i,i'}(d(j,i), d(j,i'))$. The *winner* is the candidate who gets more votes: i wins iff $\sum_{j:d_{i,j} \le d_{i',j}} q_j \ge \frac{1}{2}$. For two candidates i, i', let $w(i,i')$ denote the winner as just described, and let $o(i,i') = \text{argmin}_{j \in \{i,i'\}} c_j$ be the candidate of lower social cost. The *distortion* of an election between two candidates (i,i') is defined as $r_{i,i'} = \frac{c_{w(i,i')}}{c_{o(i,i')}}$.

We are interested in the (expected) *distortion* of the instance $(\mathcal{D}, \boldsymbol{p}, \boldsymbol{q})$, defined as the expected distortion of an election between two candidates drawn i.i.d. from the candidate distribution $\boldsymbol{p}$:

$$C(\mathcal{D}, \boldsymbol{p}, \boldsymbol{q}) = \mathbb{E}_{i,i' \sim \boldsymbol{p}}\left[r_{i,i'}\right] = \mathbb{E}_{i,i' \sim \boldsymbol{p}}\left[\frac{c_{w(i,i')}}{c_{o(i,i')}}\right] = 2\sum_{i<i'} p_i p_{i'} \cdot \frac{c_{w(i,i')}}{c_{o(i,i')}} + \sum_i p_i^2 \cdot 1. \tag{1}$$

In particular, our goal is to analyze the worst-case distortion when the candidates are representative and when they are not, that is, we want to find the gap between

$$\max_{\mathcal{D},\boldsymbol{p},\boldsymbol{q}} C(\mathcal{D}, \boldsymbol{p}, \boldsymbol{q}) \quad \text{and} \quad \max_{\mathcal{D},\boldsymbol{p}} C(\mathcal{D}, \boldsymbol{p}, \boldsymbol{p}).$$

3 IDENTICAL DISTRIBUTIONS ON THE LINE

We begin with the simplest setting: the underlying metric space is the line, and two candidates are drawn independently from the population of voters ($\boldsymbol{p} = \boldsymbol{q}$). We first show a family of examples (a variant of Example 1.1) for which the expected distortion gets arbitrarily close to $4 - 2\sqrt{2} \approx 1.1716$.

Example 3.1. The metric space is the line, denoted by $\mathcal{L}$. There are $p_1 = \frac{1}{2} - \epsilon$ voters at location $x_1 = -1$, $p_2 = 1 - \frac{1}{\sqrt{2}}$ voters at $x_2 = \epsilon$, and $p_3 = \frac{1}{\sqrt{2}} - \frac{1}{2} + \epsilon$ voters at $x_3 = 1$. This example is obtained from Example 1.1 by moving a suitable fraction of voters from location $x_2 = \epsilon$ to $x_3 = 1$, carefully trading off between two factors: (1) decreasing the pairwise distortion between the candidates at -1 and 1, but (2) increasing the chance of a such an election happening.

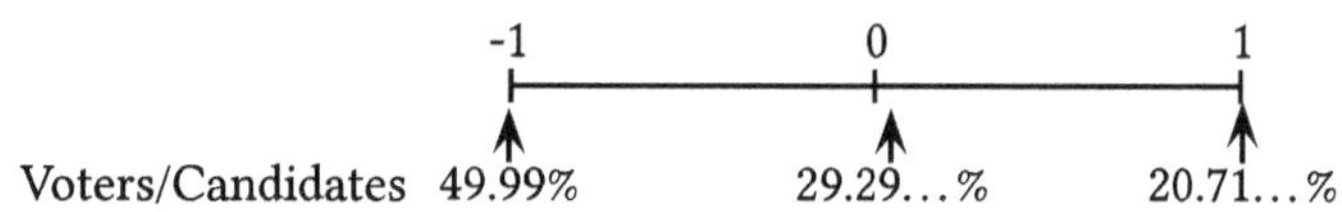

Fig. 2. The worst case instance on the line with $C(\mathcal{L}, \boldsymbol{p}, \boldsymbol{p}) = 4 - 2\sqrt{2}$.

Because the voters at $x_2 = \epsilon$ are slightly closer to 1 than to -1, a candidate drawn from $x_3 = 1$ will win against a candidate drawn from $x_1 = -1$. The costs of the two candidates are

$$c_1 = p_2 d_{1,2} + p_3 d_{1,3} = p_2 + 2p_3 + O(\epsilon) = 1/\sqrt{2} + O(\epsilon),$$
$$c_3 = p_1 d_{1,3} + p_2 d_{2,3} = 2p_1 + p_2 - O(\epsilon) = 2 - 1/\sqrt{2} - O(\epsilon).$$

Because the candidates are drawn independently from $\boldsymbol{p}$, the election between x_1 and x_3 happens with probability $2p_1p_3$. In all other cases (when a candidate from x_2 runs against one from x_1 or x_3, or both candidates are from the same location), the voters elect the socially better candidate. Thus,

$$C(\mathcal{L}, \boldsymbol{p}, \boldsymbol{p}) = (1 - 2p_1p_3) \cdot 1 + (2p_1p_3) \cdot \frac{c_3}{c_1} = 4 - 2\sqrt{2} - O(\epsilon).$$

Our first main result is that Example 3.1 gives the worst distortion on the line.

THEOREM 3.2. *For any distribution $\boldsymbol{p}$, we have $C(\mathcal{L}, \boldsymbol{p}, \boldsymbol{p}) \le 4 - 2\sqrt{2}$.*

We will prove Theorem 3.2 in Section 3.2. In preparation, in Section 3.1, we first provide some structural characterization results about the voting behavior and social cost on the line.

[2]Recall the discussion of tie breaking in Footnote 1.

3.1 Characterizing the Structure of Voting on the Line

Given a distribution on the line with support size n, we label the support points as $1, \ldots, n$ from left to right. Let m be the index of the median[3], and let $L = \{1, \ldots, m-1\}$ and $R = \{m+1, \ldots, n\}$ denote the locations to the left and to the right of the median, respectively. By the definition of the median, $p_L < \frac{1}{2} < p_L + p_m$ and $p_R < \frac{1}{2} < p_m + p_R$.

LEMMA 3.3. *If two candidates (x, y) are drawn, the one closer to m wins the election.*

PROOF. Without loss of generality, we assume that $d_{x,m} < d_{y,m}$ and $x \in L \cup \{m\}$; that is, x lies to the left of the median, or x is the median. There are two cases depending on whether y is also to the left of m.

(1) If $y \in L$, then all voters to the right of the median as well as the median are going to vote for x, so x gets a $p_m + p_R > \frac{1}{2}$ fraction of the votes.
(2) If $y \in R$, then all voters in L as well as m are going to vote for x, so x gets a $p_L + p_m > \frac{1}{2}$ fraction of the votes.

In either case, x gets more than half of the votes and wins the election. □

The next lemma characterizes the social cost ordering on the line.

LEMMA 3.4. *If x, y are on the same side of the median m (including one of them being the median), the one closer to m has smaller social cost.*

PROOF. Without loss of generality, assume that $x \in L \cup \{m\}$, $y \in L$, and $d_{x,m} < d_{y,m}$. Intuitively, x has smaller social cost because more than half of the population need to first get to x before they can get to y. Formally, we have

$$\begin{aligned} c_x = \sum_{i \in L} p_i d_{i,x} + \sum_{i \in \{m\} \cup R} p_i d_{i,x} &= \sum_{i \in L} p_i d_{i,x} + \sum_{i \in \{m\} \cup R} p_i \left(d_{i,y} - d_{x,y}\right) \\ &\overset{p_L \leq p_m + p_R}{\leq} \sum_{i \in L} p_i \left(d_{i,x} - d_{x,y}\right) + \sum_{i \in \{m\} \cup R} p_i d_{i,y} \\ &\overset{\Delta\text{-inequality}}{\leq} \sum_{i \in L} p_i d_{i,y} + \sum_{i \in \{m\} \cup R} p_i d_{i,y} = c_y. \end{aligned}$$

□

As a simple corollary of Lemmas 3.3 and 3.4, notice that if two candidates (x, y) are drawn from the same side of the median (including when one of them is the median), majority voting always elects the socially better candidate. This observation allows us to simplify the expression for $C(\mathcal{D}, \boldsymbol{p}, \boldsymbol{p})$ on the line,

$$C(\mathcal{L}, \boldsymbol{p}, \boldsymbol{p}) = \sum_{i \in [n]} p_i^2 + \sum_{i,j \in [n]} 2 p_i p_j r_{i,j} = 1 + \sum_{i \in L, j \in R} 2 p_i p_j (r_{i,j} - 1).$$

3.2 Proof of the Upper Bound of $4 - 2\sqrt{2}$

In this section, we prove Theorem 3.2, showing that the worst-case distortion on the line is $4 - 2\sqrt{2}$. The high-level idea is that, given any instance $(\mathcal{L}, \boldsymbol{p})$ with support size larger than 3, we can iteratively reduce its support size to 3 using a series of operations (Lemmas 3.5, 3.6 and 3.7), while preserving (or increasing) $C(\mathcal{L}, \boldsymbol{p}, \boldsymbol{p})$. Once the instance has support size 3, we can optimize the locations and probabilities of these 3 points.

[3]Recall that we assume the instance to be in general position, which implies uniqueness of the median.

As before, let m be the index of the median, and let $L = \{1, \ldots, m-1\}$ and $R = \{m+1, \ldots, n\}$ denote the points to the left and to the right of the median, respectively. We can assume that both L and R are non-empty; otherwise, the median is the leftmost or rightmost point, and we always elect the socially better candidate. The proof proceeds by moving probability mass within L or within R to merge points until $|L| = |R| = 1$. None of the operations in this section will change the median m, so the election results are still decided by the candidates' distance to m.

When shifting the probability mass, we will not be able to guarantee that no pairwise election sees a decrease in distortion. Instead, we use a more global argument to show that the operation increases the distortion *on average*. We define r_i to be the expected distortion conditioned on one of the candidates being i, and the other candidate being drawn according to $\boldsymbol{p}$, that is,

$$r_i = \sum_j p_j r_{i,j}.$$

We will show that so long as p_L, p_m, and p_R remain the same, $C(\mathcal{L},\boldsymbol{p},\boldsymbol{p})$ is a linear function of the average distortion on one side of the median. By Lemmas 3.3 and 3.4, the pairwise distortion can be larger than 1 only if two candidates are on different sides of m; therefore,

$$C(\mathcal{L},\boldsymbol{p},\boldsymbol{p}) = 1 + 2 \sum_{i \in L, j \in R} p_i p_j (r_{i,j} - 1) \;=\; 1 + 2 \sum_{i \in L, j \in [n]} p_i p_j (r_{i,j} - 1) \;=\; 1 - 2p_L + 2 \sum_{i \in L} p_i r_i,$$

$$C(\mathcal{L},\boldsymbol{p},\boldsymbol{p}) = 1 - 2p_R + 2 \sum_{i \in R} p_i r_i.$$

The two preceding equations formalize that whenever p_L and p_R stay constant and $\sum_{i \in R} p_i r_i$ (or $\sum_{i \in R} p_i r_i$) does not decrease, $C(\mathcal{L},\boldsymbol{p},\boldsymbol{p})$ also does not decrease. This fact is exploited repeatedly in the proofs of the following lemmas.

Lemma 3.5. *Let $y^* = \operatorname{argmax}_{y \in R} r_y$ be the "worst" candidate in R. Then, moving all probability mass from indices $y > y^*$ to y^* does not decrease $C(\mathcal{L},\boldsymbol{p},\boldsymbol{p})$. (A symmetric claim holds for the worst candidate $x^* = \operatorname{argmax}_{x \in L} r_x$.)*

Proof. Since the operation does not change p_L or p_R, it is sufficient to show that $\sum_{y \in R} p_y r_y$ does not decrease. By Lemma 3.3, all election results between pairs $i, j \le y^*$ are preserved. Let p_i', c_i', and r_i' denote the corresponding values of p_i, c_i and r_i after the operation. Then, for all $1 \le i, j \le y^*$,

$$r'_{i,j} \;=\; \frac{c'_{w(i,j)}}{c'_{o(i,j)}} \;=\; \frac{c_{w(i,j)} - \sum_{y > y^*} p_y d_{y,y^*}}{c_{o(i,j)} - \sum_{y > y^*} p_y d_{y,y^*}} \;\ge\; \frac{c_{w(i,j)}}{c_{o(i,j)}} \;=\; r_{i,j}.$$

After the shift of probability mass, y^* is the largest index. Consider $m < y \le y^*$. Using that elections between two candidates on the same side of the median always result in the socially better candidate winning, we bound

$$r'_y \;=\; \sum_{1 \le i \le y^*} p'_i r'_{i,y} \;=\; \sum_{i \in L} p_i r'_{i,y} + (1 - p_L) \cdot 1 \;\ge\; \sum_{i \in L} p_i r_{i,y} + (1 - p_L) \;=\; r_y.$$

Any candidates that used to be at $y > y^*$ are now at y^*, and y^* used to be the worst candidate in R. Hence, for all of the probability mass from locations $y > y^*$, the expected distortion also weakly increases. Combining these two cases, we get

$$\sum_{m < y \le y^*} p'_y r'_y \;=\; \sum_{m < y < y^*} p_y r'_y + \sum_{y^* \le y \le n} p_y r'_{y^*} \;\ge\; \sum_{m < y \le y^*} p_y r_y + \sum_{y^* \le y \le n} p_y r_{y^*} \;\ge\; \sum_{y \in R} p_y r_y. \quad \square$$

Lemma 3.5 can be applied repeatedly unless the two worst candidates x^* and y^* are the leftmost and rightmost points. We next show that in that case, either all the probability mass of L or all the probability mass of R can be moved to x^* or y^*, respectively.

Lemma 3.6. *Let x^* and y^* be the worst candidates in L and R. Assume w.l.o.g. that $d_{m,x^*} < d_{m,y^*}$. If $x^* = 1$ and $y^* = n$, then moving all probability mass from R to y^* does not decrease $C(\mathcal{L},\mathbf{p},\mathbf{p})$.*

Proof. As for the previous lemma, because we are only shifting probability mass within R, it is sufficient to show that $\sum_{y\in R} p_y r_y$ does not decrease. Because more probability mass moved closer to y^*, we have that $c'_{y^*} \le c_{y^*}$, and because probability mass moved away from L (to the right), we get that $c'_i \ge c_i$ for all $i \in L \cup \{m\}$.

By Lemma 3.3, y^* loses all of his elections both before and after the move. Moreover, by Lemma 3.4, we get $r_{y^*} = (1-p_L) + \sum_{i\in L} p_i r_{i,y^*}$ before the move, and $r'_{y^*} = (1-p'_L) + \sum_{i\in L} p'_i r'_{i,y^*} = (1-p_L) + \sum_{i\in L} p_i r'_{i,y^*}$ after the move. Since $r'_{i,y^*} = \frac{c'_i}{c'_{y^*}} \ge \frac{c_i}{c_{y^*}} = r_{i,y^*}$ for all $i \in L$, we get that $r'_{y^*} \ge r_{y^*}$. Finally, because y^* used to be the worst candidate in R, and after the move of probability mass is the only candidate in R, we bound

$$p'_{y^*} r'_{y^*} = \sum_{y\in R} p_y r'_{y^*} \ge \sum_{y\in R} p_y r_{y^*} \ge \sum_{y\in R} p_y r_y. \qquad \square$$

Once neither Lemma 3.5 nor Lemma 3.6 can be applied, we can apply Lemma 3.7.

Lemma 3.7. *Let $x^* = 1$, $y^* = n$ be the worst candidates in L and R, respectively. If $|R| = 1$ and $d_{m,y^*} > d_{m,x^*}$, then either $C(\mathcal{L},\mathbf{p},\mathbf{p})$ can be strictly increased, or the size of L can be reduced by 1 without decreasing $C(\mathcal{L},\mathbf{p},\mathbf{p})$.*

Proof. Notice that $m = n-1$ and $L = \{1,\ldots,n-2\}$. Recall that the only elections in which the winner could be socially inferior are those involving y^* and a candidate $x \in L$. Because $d_{m,y^*} > d_{m,x^*} \ge d_{m,i}$ for all i, we obtain that y^* loses all elections. We split the proof into two cases.

(1) If there exists an $i \in L$ with $c_i \le c_{y^*}$, then in particular, $c_{n-2} \le c_{y^*}$. Thus, candidate $n-2$ wins all elections against $i \le n-2$ (as he should) and against y^* (as he should), while losing to m (as he should). This implies that $r_{n-2} = 1$.

   Consider the effect of moving all probability mass from $n-2$ to the median $m = n-1$. First, all elections results remain the same. The contribution of the probability mass that used to be at $n-2$ to the distortion does not change. (It was 1 before and is still 1.) Furthermore, c_{y^*} decreases while c_i increases for all $i < n-2$. Because y^* loses all pairwise elections, the overall distortion can only increase.

(2) If $c_i > c_{y^*}$ for all $i \in L$, the expected distortion is exactly

$$C(\mathcal{L},\mathbf{p},\mathbf{p}) = 1 + 2p_{y^*} \sum_{i\in L} p_i \left(\frac{c_i}{c_{y^*}} - 1\right) = 1 + \frac{2p_{y^*}}{c_{y^*}} \cdot \sum_{i\in L} p_i \left(c_i - c_{y^*}\right).$$

   Let x_i denote the position of point i on the line. Writing $Y := \sum_{j>1} p_j |x_n - x_j|$ and $X_i := \sum_{j>1} p_j |x_i - x_j|$, we get that $c_i = X_i + p_1(x_i - x_1)$, and $c_{y^*} = Y + p_1(x_n - x_1)$. Hence, we can rewrite

$$C(\mathcal{L},\mathbf{p},\mathbf{p}) = 1 + \frac{2p_{y^*}}{Y + p_1(x_n - x_1)} \left(\sum_{i\in L, i>1} p_i(X_i - Y - p_1(x_n - x_i)) + p_1\left(\left(\sum_{j>1} p_j(x_j - x_1)\right) - Y - p_1(x_n - x_1)\right)\right).$$

   Treating everything except x_1 as constant, and dividing out constant factors suitably, the relevant part of this expression is of the form $\frac{B+\beta x_1}{A-x_1}$, where A, B, and β are constants independent of x_1. The derivative of this expression with respect to x_1 is $\frac{\beta A+B}{(A-x_1)^2}$; its sign is always the sign of $\beta A + B$. If $\beta A + B \neq 0$, then the expected distortion can be strictly increased by moving x_1 in one direction or the other; otherwise, x_1 can be increased all the way to x_2 without decreasing the expected distortion. □

We are now ready to prove Theorem 3.2.

Proof of Theorem 3.2. By Lemmas 3.5, 3.6 and 3.7, the worst-case instance $(\mathcal{L},\boldsymbol{p},\boldsymbol{p})$ has support size (at most) 3. Let $x_1 \leq x_2 \leq x_3$ be the locations on the line. By rescaling and mirroring, we may assume without loss of generality that $x_1 = 0$, $x_3 = 1$, and $x_2 > \frac{1}{2}$.

If x_2 were not the median of the distribution, then the socially better candidate would always win, giving $C(\mathcal{L},\boldsymbol{p},\boldsymbol{p}) = 1$. So in a worst-case distribution, x_2 must be the median, and the socially worse candidate must win the election between x_1 and x_3. Because $x_2 > \frac{1}{2}$, x_3 is closer to the median, so he wins the election between x_1 and x_3; therefore, x_1 must have lower cost than x_3. The expected distortion is

$$C(\mathcal{L},\boldsymbol{p},\boldsymbol{p}) = (1-2p_1p_3)\cdot 1 + 2p_1p_3\cdot\frac{c_3}{c_1} = (1-2p_1p_3) + 2p_1p_3\cdot\frac{p_1+p_2(1-x_2)}{p_2x_2+p_3}.$$

This expression is monotonically decreasing in x_2 and monotonically increasing in p_1, so it is maximized when we take the limit $x_2 \to \frac{1}{2}$ and $p_1 \to \frac{1}{2}$. In particular,

$$C(\mathcal{L},\boldsymbol{p},\boldsymbol{p}) \leq (1-p_3) + p_3\cdot\frac{1/2+p_2/2}{p_2/2+p_3} = (1-p_3) + p_3\cdot\frac{3-2p_3}{1+2p_3},$$

which is maximized at $p_3 = \frac{\sqrt{2}-1}{2}$ (as in Example 3.1), where it attains a value of $4-2\sqrt{2}$. □

4 DIFFERENT DISTRIBUTIONS

In this section, we prove a tight bound of 2 on the worst-case distortion of voting, when two candidates are drawn i.i.d. from a distribution $\boldsymbol{p}$ which may be different from the voter distribution $\boldsymbol{q}$. This ratio is tight for both general metric spaces and the line, and the lemmas we prove in this section apply to arbitrary metric spaces.

We begin with an example on the line (a variant of Example 1.1) which establishes the lower bound of 2. The candidate distribution $\boldsymbol{p}$ has probability 1/2 at position −1, and the other 1/2 at position 1. The voter distribution $\boldsymbol{q}$ has a $(1/2-\epsilon)$ fraction of the voters at position −1, while the remaining voters are just to the right of center at position $\epsilon > 0$. With probability 1/2, we draw two different candidates, and the distortion is $3 - O(\epsilon)$; otherwise, we draw two candidates from the same location, getting a distortion of 1. Therefore, the expected distortion of the instance is $2 - O(\epsilon) \to 2$ as $\epsilon \to 0$.

The challenge is to establish the matching upper bound. In proving the upper bound, some of the techniques we establish will be useful in Section 5.

Theorem 4.1. *For all instances $(\mathcal{D},\boldsymbol{p},\boldsymbol{q})$, the expected distortion $C(\mathcal{D},\boldsymbol{p},\boldsymbol{q})$ is at most 2.*

The overall proof structure is as follows. First, we show in Lemma 4.2 that if $i = w(i,i')$, then $c_i \leq 3c_{i'}$. That is, while the election winner can be socially worse, he cannot be too much worse.[4] Lemma 4.2 is the only place where we use the metric structure and the voter distribution. Subsequently, we rewrite the social cost function $C(\mathcal{D},\boldsymbol{p},\boldsymbol{q})$ accordingly, and then treat the costs as completely arbitrary numbers.

[4]Lemma 4.2 is a special case of the more general result [2, Theorem 4]; we present a self-contained proof here for completeness.

Second, in Lemma 4.3, we prove that if all pairwise elections have distortion at most $1 \leq \alpha \leq 3$, then $C(\mathcal{D},\boldsymbol{p},\boldsymbol{q}) \leq (1+\alpha)/2$. (While in this section, we will only use the lemma with $\alpha = 3$, the version with general α constitutes a key step in Section 5.)

LEMMA 4.2 ([2]). *Let $i = w(i,i')$. Then, $c_i \leq 3c_{i'}$.*

PROOF. In the following derivation, we will use that:

- Because i beats i', at least half of the voters are at least as close to i as to i'.
- For any voter j who is at least as close to i as to i', the triangle inequality implies that $d_{i',i} \leq d_{i',j} + d_{j,i} \leq 2d_{i',j}$.

Then, we can bound c_i as follows:

$$\begin{aligned} c_i &= \sum_{j:d_{i,j}\leq d_{i',j}} q_j \cdot d_{i,j} + \sum_{j:d_{i,j}>d_{i',j}} q_j \cdot d_{i,j} \\ &\overset{\triangle\text{-inequality}}{\leq} \sum_{j:d_{i,j}\leq d_{i',j}} q_j \cdot d_{i',j} + \sum_{j:d_{i,j}>d_{i',j}} q_j \cdot (d_{i',j} + d_{i,i'}) \\ &\overset{i \text{ beats } i'}{\leq} \sum_{j:d_{i,j}\leq d_{i',j}} q_j \cdot (d_{i',j} + d_{i,i'}) + \sum_{j:d_{i,j}>d_{i',j}} q_j \cdot d_{i',j} \\ &\leq \sum_{j:d_{i,j}\leq d_{i',j}} q_j \cdot (3d_{i',j}) + \sum_{j:d_{i,j}>d_{i',j}} q_j \cdot d_{i',j} \leq 3c_{i'}. \end{aligned}$$

□

LEMMA 4.3. *For any $1 \leq \alpha \leq 3$ and any instance $(\mathcal{D},\boldsymbol{p},\boldsymbol{q})$, if $r_{i,j} = \frac{c_{w(i,j)}}{c_{o(i,j)}} \leq \alpha$ for all (i,j), then $C(\mathcal{D},\boldsymbol{p},\boldsymbol{q}) \leq \frac{1+\alpha}{2}$.*

PROOF. Consider an instance $(\mathcal{D},\boldsymbol{p},\boldsymbol{q})$ and its associated costs $\boldsymbol{c}$. Without loss of generality, assume that $c_1 \leq c_2 \leq \cdots \leq c_n$. For each candidate i, let $\ell_i = \max\{j \mid c_j \leq \alpha c_i\}$. Notice that by the assumption that $r_{i,j} \leq \alpha$ for all i,j, whenever $j > \ell_i$, we have that $w(i,j) = o(i,j)$, resulting in a cost ratio of 1. We can therefore bound the expected distortion (minus 1) as follows:

$$C(\mathcal{D},\boldsymbol{p},\boldsymbol{q}) - 1 \leq 2 \sum_{i<j\leq\ell_i} p_i p_j \cdot \left(\frac{c_j}{c_i} - 1\right) =: \hat{C}(\boldsymbol{p},\boldsymbol{c},\alpha). \tag{2}$$

The upper bound $\hat{C}(\boldsymbol{p},\boldsymbol{c},\alpha)$ assumes that the worse candidate wins whenever the two candidates' social costs are within a factor of α of each other. Note that this upper bound $\hat{C}(\boldsymbol{p},\boldsymbol{c},\alpha)$ makes no more reference to distances or voter distributions. It depends on a distribution over candidates and a cost vector, both of which can be arbitrary, and it assumes that all elections whose candidates' costs are more than a factor α apart choose the socially better candidate, while all other elections choose the socially worse candidate.

We will now argue that $\hat{C}(\boldsymbol{p},\boldsymbol{c},\alpha)$ is at most $\frac{\alpha-1}{2}$. First, we show that the expression is maximized by moving probability mass so that c_i and c_j are at most a factor α apart for every i and j in the support of $\boldsymbol{p}$. Suppose that there exists a pair $i < j$ in the support of $\boldsymbol{p}$ with $j > \ell_i$, i.e., with $c_j > \alpha c_i$. Consider moving ϵ probability mass from p_i to p_j, where a negative value of ϵ moves probability mass from p_j to p_i; call the resulting probability vector $\boldsymbol{p}(\epsilon)$. Because our choice of i and j avoids the bilinear term $p_i p_j$ in (2), $\hat{C}(\boldsymbol{p}(\epsilon),\boldsymbol{c},\alpha)$ is a linear function of ϵ. Therefore, the expression is maximized at an extreme, i.e., by moving all the probability mass from one of i and j to the other.

Once all points in the support of $\boldsymbol{p}$ are at most a factor α apart in social cost, the expression for $\hat{C}(\boldsymbol{p},\boldsymbol{c},\alpha)$ in (2) becomes a sum over all pairs of points. Assume that the support of $\boldsymbol{p}$ has size $n' \geq 3$, and associated costs $c_1 < c_2 < \cdots < c_{n'}$. (The inequalities can be assumed to be strict, because two points i, i' with the same cost can be merged without affecting the value $\hat{C}(\boldsymbol{p}, \boldsymbol{c}, \alpha)$.) Considering all terms except c_2 as constants, $\hat{C}(\boldsymbol{p}, \boldsymbol{c}, \alpha)$ is of the form $\beta_1 + \beta_2 c_2 + \beta_3 / c_2$ (with $\beta_2, \beta_3 \geq 0$), which is convex in c_2. In particular, it attains its maximum at $c_2 = c_1$ or $c_2 = c_3$. In either case, we can merge the probability mass of point 2 with 1 or 3, reducing the support size by 1 without decreasing $\hat{C}(\boldsymbol{p}, \boldsymbol{c}, \alpha)$. By repeating such merges, we eventually arrive at a distribution with support size 2 and $c_2 \leq \alpha c_1$. Finally, we can bound

$$C(\mathcal{D}, \boldsymbol{p}, \boldsymbol{q}) = 1 + \hat{C}(\boldsymbol{p}, \boldsymbol{c}, \alpha) \leq 1 + 2p_1(1 - p_1) \cdot (\alpha - 1) \leq 1 + \frac{1}{2}(\alpha - 1) = \frac{1 + \alpha}{2}. \qquad \square$$

5 IDENTICAL DISTRIBUTIONS IN GENERAL METRIC SPACES

In this section, we examine the setting where the underlying metric space is arbitrary, and the candidates are drawn i.i.d from the population of voters. We establish the following main theorem:

THEOREM 5.1. *The worst-case distortion* $\sup_{(\mathcal{D}, \boldsymbol{p}, \boldsymbol{p})} C(\mathcal{D}, \boldsymbol{p}, \boldsymbol{p})$ *is between* $\frac{3}{2}$ *and* $2 - \frac{1}{652}$.

Key to the upper bound portion of this theorem is the following lemma.

LEMMA 5.2. *Assume that* $\delta \leq \frac{1}{100}$. *Let* $(\mathcal{D}, \boldsymbol{p}, \boldsymbol{p})$ *be an instance with maximum pairwise distortion (exactly)* $3 - \delta$. *Then,* $C(\mathcal{D}, \boldsymbol{p}, \boldsymbol{p}) \leq \frac{3}{2} + 9\sqrt{\delta}$.

We prove Lemma 5.2 in Section 5.2. The proof relies on the following structural characterization: if a pair of candidates has distortion $3 - \delta$ for sufficiently small δ, then the instance must be very structured: nearly half the probability mass must be concentrated very close to the socially optimal candidate, and most of the remaining candidates must be nearly equidistant to the two candidates.

PROOF OF THEOREM 5.1. We begin by proving the lower bound, by constructing a family of instances whose distortion converges to $\frac{3}{2}$. We label the $n + 1$ points $\{0, 1, \ldots, n\}$. We set $p_0 = \frac{1-\epsilon}{2}$, and all other $p_i = \frac{1+\epsilon}{2n}$. The distances[5] are $d_{0,i} = 1$ for all $i > 0$, and $d_{i,j} = 1 - \epsilon$ for all $i, j > 0$. See Figure 3 for an illustration.

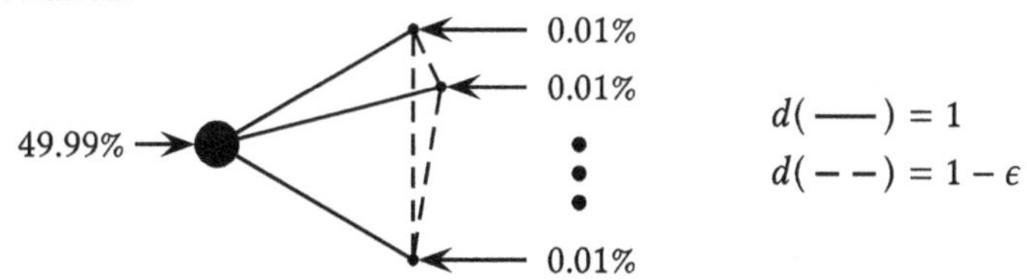

Fig. 3. A class of instances for general metric spaces in which $C(\mathcal{D}, \boldsymbol{p}, \boldsymbol{p})$ approaches $\frac{3}{2}$.

This way, all voters/candidates in the set $\{1, \ldots, n\}$ prefer each other over the voter/candidate 0. Therefore, even though candidate 0 is socially optimal (with a cost $c_0 = \frac{1}{2} + O(\epsilon)$), he loses to any other candidate in the election; the other candidates' costs are $c_i = 1 - O(\frac{1}{n}) - O(\epsilon)$.

With probability $\frac{1}{2} - O(\epsilon)$, an election occurs between candidate 0 and some other candidate $i > 0$, resulting in distortion $2 - O(\epsilon) - O(1/n)$. In the other cases (two candidates from 0, or two candidates $i, j > 0$), the distortion is at least 1. Hence, the overall expected distortion is at least $(\frac{1}{2} - O(\epsilon))(2 - O(\epsilon) - O(1/n)) + \frac{1}{2} = \frac{3}{2} - O(\epsilon) - O(1/n)$, which approaches $\frac{3}{2}$ as $\epsilon \to 0, n \to \infty$.

For the upper bound, let $\delta = \frac{1}{326}$ and consider the following two cases. If all pairwise elections have distortion at most $3 - \delta$, then Lemma 4.3 implies that the overall expected distortion $C(\mathcal{D}, \boldsymbol{p}, \boldsymbol{p})$ is at most $2 - \delta/2 = 2 - \frac{1}{652}$. If some pair of candidates has distortion at least $3 - \delta$, then Lemma 5.2 implies that the overall expected distortion is at most $\frac{3}{2} + 9\sqrt{\delta} \leq 2 - \frac{1}{652}$. Together, these two cases complete the proof of the theorem. $\square$

[5]To avoid tie breaking issues, consider the distances as perturbed by distinct and very small amounts.

As mentioned above, the key insight in the proof of Lemma 5.2 is that when a pair of candidates has $r_{x,y} \geq 3 - \delta$, *nearly* half the probability mass must be concentrated *very close to* the socially optimal candidate, and *most* of the remaining candidates must be *nearly* equidistant to the two candidates. Trading off these four sources of approximation makes the proof of the lemma fairly complex. To illustrate the key ideas more cleanly, we therefore begin by proving the following special case of Lemma 5.2 with $\delta = 0$.

Lemma 5.3. *Let* $(\mathcal{D}, \boldsymbol{p}, \boldsymbol{p})$ *be an instance. If there exists a pair of candidates* x, y *with* $\frac{c_{w(x,y)}}{c_{o(x,y)}} = 3$, *then* $C(\mathcal{D}, \boldsymbol{p}, \boldsymbol{p}) = 1.5$.

As before, we let $p_A = \sum_{i \in A} p_i$ denote the total probability mass in A. Throughout this section, $\boldsymbol{p}_A$ is the conditional candidate/voter distribution given that candidate i is drawn from A; that is, $(\boldsymbol{p}_A)_i = p_i / p_A$. We use $d_{i,A} = \mathbb{E}_{j \sim \boldsymbol{p}_A}\left[d_{i,j}\right]$ to denote the *average* distance from i to the set A.

5.1 Proof of Lemma 5.3

Assume that $y = w(x,y)$ and $x = o(x,y)$. We assume w.l.o.g. that $d_{x,y} = 2$. The fact that $c_y = 3c_x$ implies very stringent conditions on the instance: we begin by showing that half of the probability mass must be at x, x is socially optimal, and all other locations are at distance[6] 1 from x and y.

Let Y be the set of voters preferring y over x, and $X = \overline{Y}$ the set of voters preferring x over y. Then,

$$\begin{aligned} c_y &= p_Y d_{y,Y} + p_X d_{y,X} \\ &\overset{\Delta\text{-inequality}}{\leq} p_Y d_{y,Y} + p_X (d_{y,x} + d_{x,X}) \\ &\overset{y \text{ beats } x}{\leq} p_Y (d_{y,Y} + d_{y,x}) + p_X d_{x,X} \\ &\overset{\Delta\text{-inequality}}{\leq} p_Y (d_{y,Y} + d_{y,Y} + d_{x,Y}) + p_X d_{x,X} \\ &\leq 3(p_Y d_{x,Y} + p_X d_{x,X}) = 3c_x. \end{aligned}$$

Because $c_y = 3c_x$ by assumption, all of the inequalities must be tight, and therefore:

(1) By the second (in)equality, $p_Y = p_X = \frac{1}{2}$.
(2) By the final (in)equality, $d_{x,Y} = d_{y,Y}$, so all points in Y are equidistant from x and y. Furthermore, because $p_X d_{x,X} = 3 p_X d_{x,X}$, we get $d_{x,X} = 0$.
(3) By the first (in)equality, $d_{y,X} = d_{y,x} + d_{x,X} = 2$.
(4) By the third (in)equality, $d_{y,x} = d_{y,Y} + d_{x,Y}$, so $d_{y,i} = d_{x,i} = 1$ for all $i \in Y$.

Because $d_{x,X} = 0$, we can write $p_x = \frac{1}{2}$. We then have that $c_x = \frac{1}{2}$, and $c_y = \frac{3}{2}$. Let A denote the set of all candidates other than x. The expected distortion is then

$$C(\mathcal{D}, \boldsymbol{p}, \boldsymbol{p}) = p_x^2 + 2 p_x p_A \mathbb{E}_{i \sim A}\left[r_{i,x}\right] + p_A^2 \mathbb{E}_{i,j \sim A}\left[r_{i,j}\right] = 1/4 + 1/4 \cdot \mathbb{E}_{i,j \sim A}\left[r_{i,x} + r_{j,x} + r_{i,j}\right].$$

Let $\Delta_{i,j} = r_{i,x} + r_{j,x} + r_{i,j}$. We will show that $\Delta_{i,j} \leq 5$ for all $i, j \in A$, and thus $C(\mathcal{D}, \boldsymbol{p}, \boldsymbol{p}) \leq 1.5$. The three key properties we exploit repeatedly are the following.

(1) x is socially optimal, i.e., $c_i \geq c_x$ for all $i \in A$. This is because $c_x = \frac{1}{2}$, and for each $i \in A$, at least all voters at x are at distance 1.
(2) $c_i \leq 3c_x$ for all $i \in A$. This is because $d_{i,A} \leq d_{i,x} + d_{x,A} = 2$ and $d_{i,x} = 1$, giving a total cost of at most $\frac{3}{2}$.
(3) If some $i \in A$ beats x, then $c_i \leq 2c_x$. This is because everyone in A has to vote for i, implying that $d_{i,A} \leq 1$, giving $c_i \leq 1$.

[6] In a sense, this extreme example *does* rely on tie breaking. Since we are proving an *upper* bound here, this is not a concern.

Now fix some pair $i, j \in A$, and assume without loss of generality that i wins the election over j. For each of the three elections that contribute to $\Delta_{i,j}$ (i vs. x, j vs. x, i vs. j), there is a term which is 1 if the election chooses the socially better candidate (e.g., $w(i,x) = o(i,x)$), and at most 3 otherwise. Thus, if we ever had $\Delta_{i,j} > 5$, at least two of the three elections would have to produce the socially worse candidate as a winner, e.g., $w(i,x) \neq o(i,x)$. We distinguish three possible cases.

(1) If x beats j, then i must beat x and (because we assumed i to beat j) j must have lower cost than i. Because x is socially optimal (in particular having lower social cost than j), using that $c_i \leq 2c_x$, we have that $\Delta_{i,j} = r_{i,x} + r_{j,x} + r_{i,j} = \frac{c_i}{c_x} + 1 + \frac{c_i}{c_j} \leq 1 + \frac{c_i}{c_x} + \frac{c_i}{c_x} \leq 1+2+2 = 5$.

(2) If x beats i, then j must beat x and have lower cost than i. Then we obtain the expression. $\Delta_{i,j} = r_{i,x} + r_{j,x} + r_{i,j} = 1 + \frac{c_j}{c_x} + \frac{c_i}{c_j}$. Treating c_j as a variable t, we have an expression of the form $\frac{t}{c_x} + \frac{c_i}{t}$, which is convex and hence maximized at an extreme point ($t = c_i$ or $t = c_x$), giving an upper bound of $1 + 1 + \frac{c_i}{c_x} \leq 5$.

(3) Finally, we have the case that both i and j beat x (implying that $c_i \leq 2c_x$ and $c_j \leq 2c_x$). If i has lower social cost than j, we can bound $\Delta_{i,j} = r_{i,x} + r_{j,x} + r_{i,j} \leq 2+2+1 = 5$. Otherwise we have $c_x \leq c_j < c_i$, and obtain the expression $\Delta_{i,j} = \frac{c_i}{c_x} + \frac{c_j}{c_x} + \frac{c_i}{c_j}$. Again, the expression $\frac{c_j}{c_x} + \frac{c_i}{c_j}$ is maximized at $c_j = c_x$ or $c_j = c_i$, in both cases giving us a bound of $\frac{c_i}{c_x} + 1 + \frac{c_i}{c_x} \leq 5$. □

5.2 Proof of Lemma 5.2

The proof of Lemma 5.2 follows the same roadmap as the proof of Lemma 5.3, except that we no longer have a point with probability mass 1/2. Instead, close to half of the probability mass will be in a ball B of small radius around x. The three key properties used to bound $\Delta_{i,j}$ will then be replaced with approximate (slightly inferior) versions.

For any pair of candidates i, j, we will be frequently using the following upper bounds on c_i:

$$c_i \leq c_j + d_{i,j}, \tag{3}$$

$$c_i \leq c_j + \frac{d_{i,j}}{2} \quad \text{whenever } i \text{ beats } j. \tag{4}$$

Inequality (3) is simply by the triangle inequality, while Inequality (4) also uses the fact that half of the voters are closer to i, and at most the remaining half can contribute to the cost gap.

Let (x, y) be the election maximizing $r_{x,y}$, having $r_{x,y} = 3-\delta$. Without loss of generality, assume that $y = w(x,y)$ and $d_{x,y} = 2$. Because $c_y = (3-\delta)c_x$ and $c_y \leq c_x + \frac{d_{x,y}}{2} = c_x + 1$, we obtain that $c_x \leq \frac{1}{2-\delta}$.

As before, let X be the set of voters closer to x than to y, and $Y = \overline{X}$ the set closer to y. Then, $p_X \leq \frac{1}{2} \leq p_Y$. Following our intuition from the proof of Lemma 5.3, we partition the points into three disjoint sets A, B and C. Specifically, we will choose (later) a parameter p close to 1/2. As before, the set A captures the points that are "roughly equidistant" between x and y; specifically: $A = \{i \mid d_{i,y} \leq d_{i,x} \leq 1 + \rho_A\} \subseteq Y$, where we will choose ρ_A so that $p_A = p$. The set B captures the points "close to" x: $B = \{i \mid d_{i,x} \leq \rho_B\} \subseteq X$, where we choose ρ_B so that $p_B = p$.[7] The set C consists of the remaining points $C = \overline{A \cup B}$. (C may contain points from both X and Y, and $p_C = 1-2p$.) Observe that the closer p is to 1/2, the larger ρ_A and ρ_B will be, and we will have less

[7] Notice that such ρ_A, ρ_B exist without loss of generality. For if there were a radius ρ such that — say — $B^\circ = \{i \mid d_{i,x} < \rho\}$ had $p_{B^\circ} < p$, while $\overline{B} = \{i \mid d_{i,x} \leq \rho\}$ had $p_{\overline{B}} > p$, we could split a point i on the boundary (that is, i satisfies $d_{i,x} = \rho$) into two points, without affecting any outcomes for the instance.

control over where the points in A and B are located. Contrast this with the proof of Lemma 5.3, where the stringent assumption of $\delta = 0$ allowed us to choose $p = 1/2$ and still get $\rho_A = \rho_B = 0$.

We use the fact that $c_x \approx \frac{1}{2}$ to derive that close to half of the probability mass must be in A, and close to half in B. To lower-bound the probability mass, notice that the cost of x can be lower-bounded term-by-term as follows:

(1) All points in B contribute cost at least 0.
(2) All points in $X \setminus B$ contribute cost at least ρ_B.
(3) All points in A contribute cost at least 1.
(4) All points in $Y \setminus A$ contribute cost at least $1 + \rho_A$.

We can thus lower bound c_x as follows:

$$\frac{1}{2-\delta} \geq c_x \geq (p_X - p_B)\rho_B + p_A \cdot 1 + (p_Y - p_A)(1 + \rho_A) \;=\; p_X\rho_B + p_Y(1+\rho_A) - p_B\rho_B - p_A\rho_A$$
$$\geq \frac{1}{2}\rho_B + \frac{1}{2}(1+\rho_A) - p_B\rho_B - p_A\rho_A \;=\; \frac{1}{2} + (\frac{1}{2} - p)(\rho_A + \rho_B).$$

This implies that $\rho_A + \rho_B \leq \frac{\delta}{(2-\delta)(1-2p)}$. In particular, notice that even while choosing the desired probability p very close to half (e.g., $p = 1/2 - O(\sqrt{\delta})$), the cost bound still guarantees that such a p is achieved with small radii: $\rho_A + \rho_B = O(\sqrt{\delta})$. For notational convenience, we use $\rho = \frac{\delta}{(2-\delta)(1-2p)}$ to denote the upper bound for $\rho_A + \rho_B$, so $\rho_B \leq \rho_A + \rho_B \leq \rho$.

The expected distortion can now be broken into terms based on the three partitions A, B, C.

$$C(\mathcal{D},\mathbf{p},\mathbf{p}) = 2p_C(p_A + p_B)\,\mathbb{E}_{i\sim p_C, j\sim p_{A\cup B}}\left[r_{i,j}\right] + p_C^2 \cdot C(\mathcal{D},\mathbf{p_C},\mathbf{p}) + p_B^2 \cdot C(\mathcal{D},\mathbf{p_B},\mathbf{p})$$
$$+ 2p_Ap_B\mathbb{E}_{i\sim p_A, j\sim p_B}\left[r_{i,j}\right] + p_A^2 \cdot C(\mathcal{D},\mathbf{p_A},\mathbf{p})$$

We bound the terms in the sum separately.

- $\mathbb{E}_{i\sim p_C, j\sim p_{A\cup B}}\left[r_{i,j}\right] \leq 3 - \delta$, simply because we assumed that the worst-case pairwise distortion of any election was $3 - \delta$.
- The same bound of $3 - \delta$ applies to $C(\mathcal{D},\mathbf{p_C},\mathbf{p})$, for the same reason.
- When both candidates i, j are drawn from B, assume that i wins while j has lower social cost. We can use Inequalities (4) (for i and j) and (3) (for j and x, the latter having cost at least $\frac{1}{2}$) to bound $\frac{c_i}{c_j} \leq \frac{c_j + \frac{d_{i,j}}{2}}{c_j} \leq 1 + \frac{\rho_B}{c_j} \leq 1 + \frac{\rho_B}{1/2 - \rho_B} = \frac{1}{1-2\rho_B}$. We apply Lemma 4.3, and obtain that $C(\mathcal{D},\mathbf{p_B},\mathbf{p}) \leq \frac{1}{2}\left(1 + \frac{1}{1-2\rho_B}\right) = \frac{1-\rho_B}{1-2\rho_B} \leq \frac{1-\rho}{1-2\rho}$.
- The most difficult term to bound is
$$2p_Ap_B\mathbb{E}_{i\sim p_A, j\sim p_B}\left[r_{i,j}\right] + p_A^2 \cdot \mathbb{E}_{i,j\sim p_A}\left[r_{i,j}\right] \;=\; p^2 \cdot \mathbb{E}_{i,j\sim p_A, b\sim p_B}\left[r_{i,b} + r_{j,b} + r_{i,j}\right].$$
Similar to the proof of Lemma 5.3, we define $\Delta_{i,j,b} = r_{i,b} + r_{j,b} + r_{i,j}$, and upper-bound $\Delta_{i,j,b}$ for all $i, j \in A$ and $b \in B$ by a quantity which tends to 5 as $p \to 1/2$ and $\rho \to 0$. The proof of the following lemma involves an intricate case analysis, and is relegated to the end of this section.

Lemma 5.4. *$\Delta_{i,j,b} \leq 1 + 2 \cdot \frac{2}{1-\rho} \cdot \frac{1-p+\rho+p\rho}{p(1-\rho)}$ for all $i, j \in A$ and $b \in B$.*

Substituting all the upper bounds into the expected distortion, we obtain that

$$C(\mathcal{D},\mathbf{p},\mathbf{p}) \leq 2p_C \cdot (3-\delta) + p_B^2 \cdot \frac{1-\rho}{1-2\rho} + p^2 \cdot \max_{i,j,b} \Delta_{i,j,b}$$
$$\leq 2(1-2p)\cdot(3-\delta) + p^2 \cdot \frac{1-\rho}{1-2\rho} + p^2\left(1 + 2 \cdot \frac{2}{1-\rho} \cdot \frac{1-p+\rho+p\rho}{p(1-\rho)}\right)$$

Substituting $p = \frac{1-\sqrt{\delta}}{2}$ (which may not be optimal), we get $\rho = \frac{\sqrt{\delta}}{2-\delta}$, and a tedious calculation using the observation that $2 - \sqrt{\delta} - \delta = (1 - \sqrt{\delta})(2 + \sqrt{\delta})$ gives an upper bound of $C(\mathcal{D},\boldsymbol{p},\boldsymbol{p}) \leq \frac{48+196\delta^{0.5}-348\delta-287\delta^{1.5}+275\delta^2+193\delta^{2.5}-39\delta^3-46\delta^{3.5}-8\delta^4}{32(1+\delta^{0.5}/2)^2(1-\delta^{0.5})(1-\delta^{0.5}-\delta/2)}$. Dropping dominated terms (negative in the numerator, positive in the denominator), this expression can be upper-bounded by $C(\mathcal{D},\boldsymbol{p},\boldsymbol{p}) \leq \frac{48+196\sqrt{\delta}}{32(1+\sqrt{\delta}/2)^2(1-2\sqrt{\delta}+\delta/2)}$.

Finally, using the upper bound $\delta \leq \frac{1}{100}$, we obtain that

$$C(\mathcal{D},\boldsymbol{p},\boldsymbol{p}) \leq (\frac{3}{2} + \frac{49}{8}\sqrt{\delta})/(1 - \frac{9}{8}\sqrt{\delta}) \leq (\frac{3}{2} + \frac{49}{8}\sqrt{\delta}) \cdot (1 + \frac{90}{71}\sqrt{\delta}) \leq \frac{3}{2} + 9\sqrt{\delta}.$$

This completes the proof of Lemma 5.2.

Proof of Lemma 5.4. Note that, for all $i \in A$ and $b \in B$, we have

$$1 - \rho_B \leq d_{i,x} - d_{x,b} \leq d_{i,b} \leq d_{i,x} + d_{x,b} \leq 1 + \rho_A + \rho_B.$$

In the proof of Lemma 5.3, the three key properties were that (1) x was socially optimal, (2) any $i \in A$ was at most thrice worse than x, and (3) if $i \in A$ beat x in a pairwise election, then it was at most twice worse than x. The relaxed versions of these key properties are the following:

(1) Every $b \in B$ is close to socially optimal: For all $i \in A$ and $b \in B$,

$$\begin{aligned}\frac{c_b}{c_i} &= \frac{p_A d_{b,A} + p_B d_{b,B} + p_C d_{b,C}}{p_A d_{i,A} + p_B d_{i,B} + p_C d_{i,C}} \leq \frac{(1-p_B) d_{i,b} + p_B d_{b,B}}{p_B d_{i,B}} \\ &\leq \frac{(1-p_B)(1+\rho_A+\rho_B) + p_B 2\rho_B}{p_B(1-\rho_B)} \leq \frac{(1-p)(1+\rho) + 2p\rho}{p(1-\rho)} = \frac{1-p+\rho+p\rho}{p(1-\rho)}.\end{aligned}$$

The first inequality is obtained by bounding $d_{b,A} \leq d_{b,i} + d_{i,A}$ and $d_{b,C} \leq d_{b,i} + d_{i,C}$, then subtracting $d_{i,A}p_A + d_{i,C}p_C$ from both the numerator and denominator. The next step uses that $1 - \rho_B \leq d_{i,b} \leq 1 + \rho_A + \rho_B$. This ratio is at least 1 and approaches 1 as $\rho \to 0$ and $p \to \frac{1}{2}$.

(2) For all $i \in A$ and $b \in B$ (regardless of who wins the pairwise election between them),

$$\frac{c_i}{c_b} \leq \frac{c_b + d_{i,b}}{c_b} \leq 1 + \frac{1+\rho_A+\rho_B}{c_b} \leq 1 + \frac{1+\rho}{\frac{1}{2}(1-\rho)} = \frac{3+\rho}{1-\rho}.$$

This ratio is at least 3 and approaches 3 as $\rho \to 0$.

(3) For any $i \in A$ that wins the pairwise election against $b \in B$,

$$\frac{c_i}{c_b} \leq \frac{c_b + \frac{d_{i,b}}{2}}{c_b} \leq 1 + \frac{\frac{1}{2}(1+\rho_A+\rho_B)}{c_b} \leq 1 + \frac{\frac{1}{2}(1+\rho)}{\frac{1}{2}(1-\rho)} = \frac{2}{1-\rho}.$$

This ratio is at least 2 and approaches 2 as $\rho \to 0$.

We now fix $i,j \in A$ and $b \in B$, and upper-bound $\Delta_{i,j,b}$ through a detailed case analysis based on who wins (and is socially better) in the three elections $(i,j), (i,b), (j,b)$. W.l.o.g., we assume that i wins the election against j. Throughout the analysis, as in the proof of Lemma 5.3, we use repeatedly that $\frac{t}{c_b} + \frac{c_i}{t}$ is a convex function of t, and in particular is maximized at $t = c_i$ or $t = c_b$.

(1) If the socially better candidate wins in at least two of the three elections, then $\Delta_{i,j,b} \leq 1 + 1 + 3 - \delta = 5 - \delta$, because the third election can have distortion at most $3 - \delta$.

(2) If both i and j lose to b, $\Delta_{i,j,b} \leq 2\left(\max_{i \in A, b \in B} \frac{c_b}{c_i}\right) + 3 - \delta \leq 2 \cdot \frac{1-p+\rho+p\rho}{p(1-\rho)} + 3 - \delta$.

(3) If both i and j beat b, then we obtain $\Delta_{i,j,b} = \max\{\frac{c_i}{c_b}, 1\} + \max\{\frac{c_j}{c_b}, 1\} + \max\{\frac{c_i}{c_j}, 1\}$. Because we are not in the first case, at most one of the three maxima can be 1. There are three orderings of the social costs c_b, c_i, c_j which are consistent with these assumptions:

(a) If $c_b \le c_i \le c_j$, then $\Delta_{i,j,b} = \frac{c_i}{c_b} + \frac{c_j}{c_b} + 1 \le 1 + 2 \cdot \frac{2}{1-\rho}$.
(b) If $c_b \le c_j \le c_i$, then $\Delta_{i,j,b} = \frac{c_i}{c_b} + \frac{c_j}{c_b} + \frac{c_i}{c_j} \le \frac{c_i}{c_b} + 1 + \frac{c_i}{c_b} \le 1 + 2 \cdot \frac{2}{1-\rho}$.
(c) If $c_j \le c_b \le c_i$, then

$$\Delta_{i,j,b} = \frac{c_i}{c_b} + 1 + \frac{c_i}{c_j} \le 1 + \left(\max_{i \in A, b \in B, i \text{ beats } b} \frac{c_i}{c_b}\right)\left(1 + \max_{j \in A, b \in B} \frac{c_b}{c_j}\right)$$
$$\le 1 + \frac{2}{1-\rho} \cdot \left(1 + \frac{1-p+\rho+p\rho}{p(1-\rho)}\right).$$

(4) If i beats b and j loses to b, then $\Delta_{i,j,b} = \max\{\frac{c_i}{c_b}, 1\} + \max\{\frac{c_b}{c_j}, 1\} + \max\{\frac{c_i}{c_j}, 1\}$.
Again, because at least two of the three pairwise elections result in the socially worse candidate winning, we have only three cost orderings consistent with the outcome:
(a) If $c_j \le c_i \le c_b$, then $\Delta_{i,j,b} = 1 + \frac{c_b}{c_j} + \frac{c_i}{c_j} \le 1 + \frac{1-p+\rho+p\rho}{p(1-\rho)} + 3 - \delta$.
(b) If $c_b \le c_j \le c_i$, then $\Delta_{i,j,b} = \frac{c_i}{c_b} + 1 + \frac{c_i}{c_j} \le 1 + \frac{2}{1-\rho}\left(1 + \frac{1-p+\rho+p\rho}{p(1-\rho)}\right)$, as in Case 3(c).
(c) If $c_j \le c_b \le c_i$, then

$$\Delta_{i,j,b} = \frac{c_i}{c_b} + \frac{c_b}{c_j} + \frac{c_i}{c_j} \le 1 + 2 \cdot \frac{c_i}{c_j}$$
$$\le 1 + 2\left(\max_{i \in A, b \in B, i \text{ beats } b} \frac{c_i}{c_b} \cdot \max_{j \in A, b \in B} \frac{c_b}{c_j}\right) \le 1 + 2 \cdot \frac{2}{1-\rho} \cdot \frac{1-p+\rho+p\rho}{p(1-\rho)},$$

where the first inequality again used the convexity argument on $\frac{c_i}{c_b} + \frac{c_b}{c_j}$.

(5) In the final case, i loses to b and j beats b, resulting in a cycle in the election results. We now have $\Delta_{i,j,b} = \max\{\frac{c_b}{c_i}, 1\} + \max\{\frac{c_j}{c_b}, 1\} + \max\{\frac{c_i}{c_j}, 1\}$. Again, we have three possible cost orderings consistent with the assumption that at most one of the pairwise elections agrees with the social costs:
(a) If $c_j \le c_i \le c_b$, then $\Delta_{i,j,b} = \frac{c_b}{c_i} + 1 + \frac{c_i}{c_j} \le 1 + \frac{1-p+\rho+p\rho}{p(1-\rho)} + 3 - \delta$.
(b) If $c_i \le c_b \le c_j$, then $\Delta_{i,j,b} = \frac{c_b}{c_i} + \frac{c_j}{c_b} + 1 \le 1 + \frac{1-p+\rho+p\rho}{p(1-\rho)} + \frac{2}{1-\rho}$.
(c) In the final case $c_b \le c_j \le c_i$, we again apply the convexity argument to bound $\Delta_{i,j,b} = 1 + \frac{c_j}{c_b} + \frac{c_i}{c_j} \le 1 + 1 + \frac{c_i}{c_b} \le 2 + \frac{3+\rho}{1-\rho}$.

Collecting all the upper bounds in all cases, we see that they are all equal to (or immediately upper-bounded by) one of the following three terms:

$$\begin{cases} 2 \cdot \frac{1-p+\rho+p\rho}{p(1-\rho)} + 3 - \delta & \text{for cases (1), (2), (4a), (5a)} \\ 1 + 2 \cdot \frac{2}{1-\rho} & \text{for cases (3a), (3b), (5b), (5c)} \\ 1 + 2 \cdot \frac{2}{1-\rho} \cdot \frac{1-p+\rho+p\rho}{p(1-\rho)} & \text{for cases (3c), (4b), (4c)} \end{cases}$$

A tedious calculation shows that because $p \le \frac{1}{2}$, the expressions in the first and second cases are always bounded by the expression in the third case. This completes the proof of Lemma 5.4. □

6 DISCUSSION AND OPEN QUESTIONS

We showed that under the simple model of two i.i.d. candidates and a majority election, government by the people is better for the people if it is also of the people: there is a constant gap between the distortion caused by voting in the case when $\boldsymbol{q} = \boldsymbol{p}$ vs. $\boldsymbol{q} \ne \boldsymbol{p}$. For the case of the line, we pinned down the gap precisely, while for general metric spaces, we proved a small constant gap.

Our results can be construed as providing some mathematical underpinnings for the benefits of *lottocracy*. *Lottocracy* (also called *sortition*) [16, 21, 22] refers to systems of government in which (some) political officials are chosen through lotteries instead of (or in addition to) elections. Two of the arguments put forth in favor of lottocracy are: (1) it is more inclusive [22], in the sense that the office holders will be more representative of the population as a whole and its different subgroups; (2) it leads to more responsive government [21]: because office holders are representative of the population, they will respond more directly to the preferences of the population. The definition of inclusiveness is very closely aligned with our notion of candidates being "of the people;" it is sometimes justified by empirical and simulation studies giving evidence that inclusive groups may be better at problem solving. The notion of responsiveness is similar to our notion of government being "for the people;" in this sense, our results could be – with some latitude – rephrased as stating that inclusiveness may lead to responsiveness.

While most proponents of lottocracy argue in favor of filling offices with randomly selected citizens, our analysis applies to a process wherein voters do have a say, but the slate of candidates is random. Allowing a vote between randomly selected candidates may in fact address one of the main concerns aboud lottocracy, namely, the competency of candidates [21, 22]. It simultaneously addresses a concern about democratic votes: that the slate of candidates could be such that voters make a societally suboptimal choice. While the mathematical model presented here is far too simplistic to provide reliable insights into the merits (or problems) of lottocracy and its variants, it may serve as a point of departure for future more refined models.

In terms of more direct technical questions, the most immediate open question is to obtain the maximum expected distortion in general metric spaces. We conjecture an upper bound of $3/2$. Our conjecture is based on extensive computational experiments, and on several partial results. In particular, we can show that the distortion is upper-bounded by $3/2$ whenever the metric is uniform (i.e., all voters/candidates are equidistant), or when there is a location of the metric space that has half the voters/candidates. Both properties seem to naturally arise in worst-case constructions, although we are unable to prove at this point that they are necessary for worst-case metrics.

Beyond the immediate open question, our work raises a number of other directions for future work. A first natural question is how the distortion depends on the metric space. As we saw, the distortion for the line is $4 - 2\sqrt{2} < \frac{3}{2}$. What is the distortion for d-dimensional Euclidean space? Are there other natural metric spaces that are suitable models of political or similar affiliation, and may be amenable to a detailed analysis?

In this work, in order to isolate the issue of representativeness of candidates, we focused on a majority election between two candidates. When $k > 2$ candidates are running, vote aggregation becomes more complex, and indeed, a large number of different voting rules have been considered throughout history. The work of Anshelevich et al. [2, 3] analyzed the worst-case distortion of some of the most prevalent voting rules. It would be interesting to examine the performance of these voting rules under our model of candidates drawn from the voter population. In particular, would such an analysis reveal a more fine-grained stratification between some of the voting rules that perform equally well (or poorly) under worst-case assumptions?

A further direction is to deviate from the extremes of worst-case candidates or candidates drawn from the voter distribution. How gracefully does the distortion degrade as the voter and candidate distributions become more and more dissimilar? Answering this question first requires a suitable definition of a distance metric between probability distributions. Such a definition will have to be "Earthmover-like," yet also "scale-invariant."

ACKNOWLEDGMENTS

Yu Cheng is supported in part by Shang-Hua Teng's Simons Investigator Award. Shaddin Dughmi is supported by NSF CAREER award CCF-1350900 and NSF Grant CCF-1423618. David Kempe is supported in part by NSF Grant CCF-1423618 and NSF Grant IIS-1619458. The authors would like to thank Elliot Anshelevich and Utkash Dubey for useful conversations, and anonymous reviewers for helpful feedback.

REFERENCES

[1] Elliot Anshelevich. 2016. Ordinal Approximation in Matching and Social Choice. *ACM SIGecom Exchanges* 15, 1 (July 2016), 60–64.

[2] Elliot Anshelevich, Onkar Bhardwaj, and John Postl. 2015. Approximating Optimal Social Choice under Metric Preferences. In *Proc. 30th AAAI Conf. on Artificial Intelligence.* 777–783.

[3] Elliot Anshelevich and John Postl. 2016. Randomized Social Choice Functions Under Metric Preferences. In *Proc. 31st Intl. Joint Conf. on Artificial Intelligence.* 46–59.

[4] Elliot Anshelevich and Shreyas Sekar. 2016. Blind, Greedy, and Random: Algorithms for Matching and Clustering using only Ordinal Information. In *Proc. 31st AAAI Conf. on Artificial Intelligence.* 390–396.

[5] Kenneth Arrow. 1951. *Social Choice and Individual Values.* Wiley.

[6] Salvador Barberà. 2001. An Introduction to Strategy-Proof Social Choice Functions. *Social Choice and Welfare* 18 (2001), 619–653.

[7] Salvador Barberà, Faruk Gul, and Ennio Stacchetti. 1993. Generalized Median Voter Schemes and Committees. *Journal of Economic Theory* 61 (1993), 262–289.

[8] Duncan Black. 1948. On the Rationale of Group Decision Making. *J. Political Economy* 56 (1948), 23–34.

[9] Duncan Black. 1958. *The Theory of Committees and Elections.* Cambridge University Press.

[10] Craig Boutilier, Ioannis Caragiannis, Simi Haber, Tyler Lu, Ariel D. Procaccia, and Or Sheffet. 2015. Optimal social choice functions: A utilitarian view. *Artificial Intelligence* 227 (2015), 190–213.

[11] Craig Boutilier and Jeffrey S. Rosenschein. 2016. Incomplete information and communication in voting. In *Handbook of Computational Social Choice*, Felix Brandt, Vincent Conitzer, Ulle Endriss, Jérôme Lang, and Ariel D. Procaccia (Eds.). Cambridge University Press, Chapter 10, 223–257.

[12] Felix Brandt, Vincent Conitzer, Ulle Endriss, Jérôme Lang, and Ariel D. Procaccia (Eds.). 2016. *Handbook of Computational Social Choice.* Cambridge University Press.

[13] Ioannis Caragiannis and Ariel D. Procaccia. 2011. Voting almost maximizes social welfare despite limited communication. *Artificial Intelligence* 175, 9 (2011), 1655–1671.

[14] Jean-Charles de Borda. 1784. Mémoire sur les élections au Scrutin. *Histoire de l'Académie Royale des Sciences, Paris* (1784), 657–665.

[15] M. J. A. Nicolas de Condorcet. 1785. *Essai sur l'application de l'analyse à la probabilité des décisions rendues à la pluralité des voix.* Imprimerie Royale, Paris.

[16] Oliver Dowlen. 2008. *The political potential of sortition: A study of the random selection of citizens for public office.* Imprint Academic.

[17] Anthony Downs. 1957. An economic theory of political action in a democracy. *The Journal of Political Economy* 65, 2 (1957), 135–150.

[18] Michal Feldman, Amos Fiat, and Iddan Golomb. 2015. On voting and facility location. (2015). arXiv:1512.05868.

[19] Alan F. Gibbard. 1973. Manipulation of voting schemes: a general result. *Econometrica* 41, 4 (1973), 587–601.

[20] Ashish Goel, Anilesh Kollagunta Krishnaswamy, and Kamesh Munagala. 2016. Metric Distortion of Social Choice Rules: Lower Bounds and Fairness Properties. (2016). arXiv:1612.02912.

[21] Alexander A. Guerrero. 2014. Against elections: The lottocratic alternative. *Philosophy & Public Affairs* 42, 2 (2014), 135–178.

[22] Hélène Landemore. 2013. Deliberation, cognitive diversity, and democratic inclusiveness: An epistemic argument for the random selection of representatives. *Synthese* 190, 7 (2013), 1209–1231.

[23] Samuel Merrill and Bernard Grofman. 1999. *A unified theory of voting: Directional and proximity spatial models.* Cambridge University Press.

[24] Hervé Moulin. 1980. On strategy-proofness and single peakedness. *Public Choice* 35 (1980), 437– 455.

[25] Ariel D. Procaccia. 2010. Can approximation circumvent Gibbard-Satterthwaite?. In *Proc. 25th AAAI Conf. on Artificial Intelligence.* 836–841.

[26] Ariel D. Procaccia and Jeffrey S. Rosenschein. 2006. The distortion of cardinal preferences in voting. In *Proc. 10th Int. Workshop Cooperative Inform. Agents X.* 317–331.

[27] Diana Richards, Whitman A. Richards, and Brendan McKay. 1998. Collective Choice and Mutual Knowledge Structures. *Advances in Complex Systems* 1 (1998), 221–236.

[28] Mark A. Satterthwaite. 1975. Strategy-proofness and Arrow's Conditions: Existence and Correspondence Theorems for Voting Procedures and Social Welfare Functions. *Journal of Economic Theory* 10 (1975), 187–217.

A Simple and Approximately Optimal Mechanism for a Buyer with Complements [Abstract]

ALON EDEN, Tel-Aviv University
MICHAL FELDMAN, Tel-Aviv University
OPHIR FRIEDLER, Tel-Aviv University
INBAL TALGAM-COHEN, The Hebrew University of Jerusalem
S. MATTHEW WEINBERG, Princeton University

We consider a revenue-maximizing seller with m heterogeneous items and a single buyer whose valuation v for the items may exhibit both substitutes (i.e., for some S, T, $v(S \cup T) < v(S) + v(T)$) and complements (i.e., for some S, T, $v(S \cup T) > v(S) + v(T)$). We show that the mechanism first proposed by Babaioff et al. [2014] – the better of selling the items separately and bundling them together – guarantees a $\Theta(d)$ fraction of the optimal revenue, where d is a measure on the degree of complementarity. Note that this is the first approximately optimal mechanism for a buyer whose valuation exhibits any kind of complementarity. It extends the work of Rubinstein and Weinberg [2015], which proved that the same simple mechanisms achieve a constant factor approximation when buyer valuations are subadditive, the most general class of complement-free valuations.

Our proof is enabled by the recent duality framework developed in Cai et al. [2016], which we use to obtain a bound on the optimal revenue in this setting. Our main technical contributions are specialized to handle the intricacies of settings with complements, and include an algorithm for partitioning edges in a hypergraph. Even nailing down the right model and notion of "degree of complementarity" to obtain meaningful results is of interest, as the natural extensions of previous definitions provably fail.

CCS Concepts: •**Theory of computation → Algorithmic game theory and mechanism design;**

Additional Key Words and Phrases: Revenue maximization; degree of complementarity; hypergraph representation

A full version of this paper is available at https://arxiv.org/pdf/1612.04746.pdf.

Author's email addresses: alonarden@gmail.com; mfeldmantau@gmail.com; ophirfriedler@gmail.com; inbaltalgam@gmail.com; smweinberg@princeton.edu.

Work done in part while A. Eden and S. M. Weinberg were visiting the Simons Institute for the Theory of Computing. This work was partially supported by the European Research Council under the European Union's Seventh Framework Programme (FP7/2007-2013) / ERC grant agreement number 337122. This work has received funding from the European Union's Horizon 2020 research and innovation programme under the Marie Sklodowska-Curie grant agreement number 708935.

ACM ISBN 978-1-4503-4527-9/17/06. DOI: http://dx.doi.org/10.1145/3033274.3085116

Price Doubling and Item Halving: Robust Revenue Guarantees for Item Pricing

ELLIOT ANSHELEVICH, Rensselaer Polytechnic Institute
SHREYAS SEKAR, Rensselaer Polytechnic Institute

We study approximation algorithms for revenue maximization based on static *item pricing*, where a seller chooses prices for various goods in the market, and then the buyers purchase utility-maximizing bundles at these given prices. We formulate two somewhat general techniques for designing good pricing algorithms for this setting: *Price Doubling* and *Item Halving*. Using these techniques, we unify many of the existing results in the item pricing literature under a common framework, as well as provide several new bicriteria algorithms for approximating both revenue and social welfare simultaneously. More specifically, for a variety of settings with item pricing, we show that it is possible to deterministically obtain a log-approximation for revenue and a constant-approximation for social welfare *simultaneously*: thus one need not sacrifice revenue if the goal is to still have decent welfare guarantees.

The main technical contribution of this paper is a $O((\log m + \log k)^2)$-approximation algorithm for revenue maximization based on the item halving technique, for settings where buyers have XoS valuations, where m is the number of goods and k is the average supply. Surprisingly, ours is the first known item pricing algorithm with polylogarithmic approximation for such general classes of valuations, and partially resolves an important open question from the algorithmic pricing literature about the existence of item pricing algorithms with logarithmic factors for general valuations [4]. We also use the item halving framework to form envy-free item pricing mechanisms for the popular setting of multi-unit markets, providing a log-approximation to revenue in this case.

Additional Key Words and Phrases: Item Pricing; Revenue Maximization; Non-Discriminatory Pricing; Combinatorial Valuations;

1 INTRODUCTION

In this paper, we tackle the following fundamental problem in algorithmic economics:

> Given a market with a set $\mathcal{I}$ of m goods and buyers having complex valuations, compute a set of prices (one per good) that maximize revenue once buyers purchase utility maximizing bundles.

The *item pricing* formulation described above is an abstraction that captures many types of economic interactions between buyers and sellers. Arguably, the appeal of item pricing stems from its simplicity and decentralized nature: the seller posts prices on the goods in advance, and each buyer purchases the most desirable set of available goods at the given prices. Moreover, although

This work was partially supported by NSF awards CNS-1218374 and CCF-1527497.
Author's addresses: E. Anshelevich and S. Sekar, Computer Science Department, Rensselaer Polytechnic Institute, 110, 8th Street, Troy, NY-12180. Email: eanshel@cs.rpi.edu, shreyas.sekar@gmail.com.
The full version of this paper containing proofs of all theorems can be accessed at https://arxiv.org/abs/1611.02442.

EC'17, June 26–30, 2017, Cambridge, Massachusetts, USA. ACM ISBN 978-1-4503-4527-9/17/06...$15.00.

DOI: https://doi.org/10.1145/3033274.3085117

there are exceptions, a seller often cannot choose to charge different prices for different customers, i.e., the item prices are *non-discriminatory.* The lack of price discrimination is the crucial feature that distinguishes our model from the body of work on general posted pricing in mechanism design, where prices are charged per buyer, and not per good as we do in this work. To illustrate the subtleties involved here, for unit-demand [12] and even submodular valuations [9], one can compute per-buyer posted pricing schemes that yield constant factor approximations for revenue, whereas, the item pricing problem that we consider is known to be $O(\log^{1-\epsilon} m)$-hard to approximate for unit-demand valuations [11].

Item pricing (to maximize revenue) occupies a central place in the study of markets (see for example [7, 22]). Despite the substantial body of work in this domain, surprisingly little is known about maximizing revenue for complex buyer valuations such as submodular or XoS; in fact, a long-standing open question [4, 10] is 'whether static item prices can be used to achieve non-trivial revenue guarantees for submodular and more general valuations?'. We attempt to fill this conspicuous void in the literature by presenting *the first item pricing algorithm with a polylogarithmic-approximation for revenue* for such valuations, partially resolving the open question. Previously, logarithmic revenue guarantees using non-discriminative pricing strategies were only known for simpler settings such as markets with unit-demand buyers [22]. In the process, we also develop a general framework for item pricing via black-box reductions that unifies many of the previous revenue-maximization results in the literature and helps us transform pricing mechanisms for revenue maximization into those that yield bicriteria (revenue,welfare) guarantees.

Informal Model. For the majority of this work, we study item pricing mechanisms in which the seller posts a price p_i for each good $i \in \mathcal{I}$, followed by a consumption stage in which buyers arrive in some order and purchase a utility maximizing subset of the available goods at the fixed prices. Each buyer j has a monotone valuation function $v_j : 2^{\mathcal{I}} \to \mathbb{R}^+$ and a utility-maximizing bundle refers to a set $S \subseteq \mathcal{I}$ maximizing $v_j(S) - \sum_{i \in S} p_i$. We refer to this as the *sequential mechanism*: in this model, buyers still see the same prices on items, but once the supply of a good is exhausted, it is no longer available for sale to future buyers. Specifically, we assume that some k_i units of good $i \in \mathcal{I}$ are available to be sold. In Section 4, we also consider the stronger class of *simultaneous mechanisms,* where buyers arrive at the same time and consume utility-maximizing bundles in parallel, with the mechanism ensuring that the supply constraints are not violated. In decentralized markets with limited supply where buyers consume goods in an asynchronous fashion, it is reasonable to assume that the sequential mechanism is a more natural model as compared to the simultaneous one [27]. Finally, we will use the term *item pricing* to encompass all mechanisms that only post a single price per good, including both of the mechanisms mentioned above.

Landscape of Item Pricing Results

To obtain a better understanding of our results, it is important to place them in the context of the larger body of work on item pricing for revenue maximization. The problem of revenue maximization is considered to be well understood for simpler valuations such as *unit-demand* [22] or *single-minded* [14], which admit $O(\log m)$ and $O(\sqrt{m} \log k_{max})$-approximations respectively via simultaneous mechanisms. On other hand, for submodular and XoS valuations, our understanding of this regime is largely incomplete owing to the super-logarithmic gap between the known lower bound of $\Omega(\log m)$ for submodular valuations, and the upper bound of $2^{\tilde{O}(\sqrt{\log m})}$ [4], corresponding to the current best approximation algorithm for revenue maximization with sequential mechanisms[1]. While recent work [18] has yielded sequential item pricing mechanisms with $O(1)$-approximations

[1]The result assumes a unit-supply environment and hence, the bound depends only on the number of goods m

for social welfare, those techniques do not necessarily lead to any direct insights for the revenue problem.

To summarize, for the primary problem studied in this work, i.e., *sequential item pricing for revenue maximization with XoS valuations*: (*i*) the state of the art is a $2^{\tilde{O}(\sqrt{\log m})}$-approximation algorithm, (*ii*) no algorithm can achieve revenue that is within a $\Omega(\log m)$-factor of the optimum welfare for all instances [4], (*iii*) no poly-time algorithm can achieve a $\log^{1-\epsilon} m$-approximation for any $\epsilon > 0$ [11]. Against this backdrop, we present an algorithm whose revenue is within a $O(\log^2 m)$-factor of the optimum welfare for unit-supply settings, significantly narrowing the gap between the upper and lower bounds. Our result generalizes the logarithmic revenue guarantees that were previously obtained only for restricted valuations such as unit-demand functions [22] to the more general XoS class. Prior to this, logarithmic guarantees for XoS valuations were only known for more complex mechanisms involving bundle pricing [20] or price discrimination [10].

Finally, our work is motivated by concerns that are somewhat orthogonal to those prevalent in fields such as mechanism design. Specifically, we are less interested in constructing novel combinatorial auctions for revenue maximization, and more so in gaining a fundamental understanding of how markets with item pricing can operate. Towards this end, as is common in the item pricing literature [14, 20, 22], we eschew concerns such as incentive compatibility, and consider a full information model, where the seller is aware of each buyer's valuation function.

Revenue, Welfare, and Black-box Reductions . A noteworthy aspect of this work is that, as in much of the previous literature, all of our approximation factors are derived by comparing the revenue obtained by our algorithm to the social welfare of the optimum allocation. Measuring revenue in terms of social welfare allows for our results to have some useful implications [2]. For instance, since the optimum welfare is an upper bound on the revenue obtained by any 'individually rational mechanism', our main result implies that no pricing mechanism can improve upon item pricing (specifically, our algorithm's revenue) by a factor larger than $O(\log^2 m)$ for unit-supply settings. This includes, for instance, an algorithm that updates prices dynamically every round or one that charges per-buyer posted prices. Finally, all of the results in this paper are presented in the form of black-box reductions that convert *any given input allocation* to an item pricing solution, whose revenue guarantees depend on the social welfare of the original allocation. Such black-box reductions are highly sought after in the pricing literature since they allow us to apply the extensive techniques developed for the purely algorithmic resource allocation problem to a more game-theoretic pricing problem where the seller can only indirectly control what items are allocated to the buyers.

1.1 Summary of Contributions

In this paper, we consider a typical setting consisting of a set of m goods in limited supply, with k being the supply averaged over all of the goods in the market, and $k_{\max}$ being the maximum supply of any good. There are N buyers in the market having combinatorial valuation functions, and under a given set of prices, each buyer purchases a subset of the available goods that maximizes her quasilinear utility, i.e., value derived minus price paid.

Unifying Charging Framework. At a fundamental level, our main contribution is a simple, but general charging framework that provides a recipe for revenue maximization by *charging* welfare differentials to revenue. In combination with the two complementary algorithmic paradigms of *price doubling* and *item halving*, the framework can be used to derive black-box reductions from 'item pricing' to 'item allocations'. Price doubling, or multiplicative pricing has been previously employed to derive pricing mechanisms with logarithmic guarantees in the literature [22], whereas item halving is a new technique for pricing that we propose in this work. In some senses, item halving can be viewed as a more granular version of the supply-limiting approach in mechanism design [26]: our generalization allows us to apply this technique for general combinatorial valuations. The charging framework serves as a focal point for unifying a number of results in the pricing literature (see Table 1); we add value to these results by transforming them into bicriteria approximation algorithms that simultaneously guarantee good revenue and welfare. Secondly, we leverage our framework to design new approximations for revenue maximization in other settings.

Item Halving + Charging Framework: Sequential Mechanism for XoS Buyers. The main technical contribution of this paper is a new approximation algorithm for revenue maximization based on a novel algorithmic approach that we term item halving. The sequential mechanism that we design achieves the stated revenue guarantee for two models of buyer arrival: (*i*) when the arrival is adversarial within a polynomially bounded set of buyer orders, and (*ii*) when buyers arrive according to an arbitrary probability distribution. For the completely adversarial case, we present a non-polynomial-time algorithm with the same guarantee, that serves as an existence result.

(Centerpiece Result). *For settings where buyers have XoS valuations, we can compute item prices in poly-time such that the sequential mechanism with these prices results in a $O((\log m + \log k)^2)$-approximation to the optimum revenue for random and polynomially adversarial buyer arrival orders.*

Note that XoS valuations are a strict generalization of submodular functions. The above result assumes access to Demand and XoS oracles for accessing buyer valuations (see Section 2). In unit-supply settings ($k = 1$), our approximation guarantee is $O(\log^2 m)$.
Key Features of our Result: The above theorem provides a positive answer to the long standing open question of whether static item pricing could be used to obtain (poly-)logarithmic approximation factors for complex valuations, and in the process, significantly improves upon the previous upper bound of $2^{O(\sqrt{\log(mk)\log\log(mk)})}$ [4]. Prior to this, similar approximation factors were only known for more general pricing schemes such as bundle pricing [20] or discriminatory pricing [10]. In contrast, ours is the first known poly-logarithmic approximation algorithm based on non-discriminatory item pricing. Moreover, we come close to closing the gap between the upper and lower bounds for this setting, the latter being a $\Omega(\log m)$ factor for submodular valuations with unit supply.
Other Implications of our Framework After proving our centerpiece result, we devote the rest of this paper to a more detailed exploration of our charging framework resulting in new item pricing algorithms for other settings. All of the below results are obtained via the simultaneous mechanism, which is stronger than the sequential mechanism (see Section 2). Thereby, we make the case that our charging framework is not specifically tied to any specific mechanism and bears strong implications for future work involving item pricing.

- **Price Doubling and Bicriteria Approximations** By employing the price doubling approach within the confines of our framework, we identify a 'generic algorithm for item pricing' that unifies many of the existing results under a common umbrella. Not only are we able to re-derive guarantees from the item pricing literature, we actually strengthen *all of these results* by transforming them to bicriteria approximation algorithms, whose guarantees are listed in Table 1. Specifically, we present a black-box transformation from revenue maximization to welfare maximization for simultaneous item pricing mechanisms: "*given any α-approximate simultaneous mechanism for welfare maximization, we present a poly-time reduction to compute item prices that ensure a $O(\alpha(\log m + \log k + \log \alpha))$-approximation to the optimal revenue, and simultaneously a 3α-approximation for welfare*". The result holds for arbitrary combinatorial valuations as long as the black-box algorithm satisfies a mild requirement known as 'local welfare maximization' (See Section 4.1).

- **Item Halving for Multi-Unit Valuations** Finally, in Section 4.2 we apply the same item halving machinery developed for XoS valuations to obtain a simultaneous item pricing mechanism with a $O(\log m)$-revenue guarantee for the popular class of *multi-unit valuations,* where a buyer's value depends only on the number of items that she receives. Previously, the best known result for this setting was a $O(\log m + \log N)$-approximation based on sequential mechanisms [4].

Setting	Previous Results (Revenue)	Our Results {Revenue,Welfare}
Unit-Demand	$O(\log m + \log k)$ [22]	$\{O(\log m + \log k), 3\}$
Gross Substitutes	-	$\{O(\log m + \log k), 3\}$
Single-Minded	$O(\sqrt{m} \log k_{max})$ [14]	$\{O(\sqrt{m} \log k_{max}), O(\sqrt{m})\}$
Unlimited Supply	$O(\log m + \log N)$ [4]	$\{O(\log m + \log N), 2\}$
Bundle Pricing	$O(\alpha^* \log N)$ [20]	$\{O(\alpha^* \log N), 6\alpha^*\}$

Table 1. Bicriteria approximation factors obtained for various settings. For a given valuation class, α^* denotes the best known approximation factor for the allocation problem.

Discussion of Bicriteria Results Simultaneous bicriteria (revenue,welfare) approximations have featured previously in single-item auctions [15], and item pricing for special cases of unit-demand and multi-minded buyers [2]. Our result, on the other hand, has a far greater scope since it is not tied to any class of valuation (see Table 1). We also remark that while many revenue maximization algorithms in the literature do lead to implicit bicriteria factors, the bounds obtained for welfare are trivial since any α-approximation for revenue in terms of the optimum social welfare implies an α-approximation for social welfare as well. On the contrary, our framework allows us to derive explicit bicriteria approximations, where both the revenue and social welfare are comparable to their respective optimal lower bounds. For example, while the results of [22] immediately imply a $(O(\log m), O(\log m))$-approximation for (revenue,welfare) for unit-demand buyers, our framework provides an improved $(O(\log m), O(1))$-bicriteria approximation for the unit-supply setting. The main message behind our result is: 'why only maximize revenue when we can get near-optimal welfare at no cost'.

1.2 Related Work

In terms of similarity, the current paper is closest to the extensive body of work on item pricing and more general envy-free schemes [6, 17, 21] for welfare and revenue maximization. Item pricing for maximizing only welfare has traditionally been a sought after area of research as it is equivalent to computing a Walrasian equilibrium minus the market clearing constraints; since our focus is primarily on revenue, we refer the reader to [19, 25] for more recent algorithmic perspectives on the subject. On the other hand, item pricing for revenue maximization has been gaining traction with respect to both sequential and simultaneous mechanisms. A steady stream of research has yielded near-optimal approximation algorithms for a variety of settings including unit demand [7, 13, 22], single minded [3, 14], multi-unit markets [6, 17], and unlimited supply settings [4]. One of the main contributions of this paper is a general framework that captures many of the above results, and provides a recipe for converting them into bicriteria approximations.

Despite the tremendous body of work on revenue maximization, ours is the first known poly-logarithmic approximation algorithm based on static, item pricing for complex valuations such as submodular and XoS functions. Partial exceptions include the $O(\log m)$-approximation for 'simple submodular functions' in [4] and the $O(\log^3 m)$-approximation in [10] for settings consisting of a large number of buyers having the exact same valuation function. Although our central result improves upon the upper bound of $2^{\tilde{O}(\sqrt{\log m})}$ from [4] for XoS functions, it is pertinent to mention that their result holds for a more general information model where the seller is not aware of the buyer valuations. For such a general model, it is reasonable to expect that the only possible strategy would be to price items uniformly (common price), as is done in [4, 10]. The presence of a matching lower bound of $2^{\Omega(\sqrt{\log m})}$ [10] for uniform pricing motivates the need for pricing different goods differently. For such a scheme, we argue that knowledge of buyer valuations is necessary since it allows us to quantify each good's relative value in the market.

As mentioned previously, this work differs considerably from the literature on *sequential posted pricing* in mechanism design (e.g., [5, 8, 12]). With the notable exception of [18], most of the pricing schemes in this area are non-anonymous, i.e., based on offering the same good to different buyers at different prices. On the contrary, our prices are static and do not change across rounds.

2 MODEL AND PRELIMINARIES

We consider a market setting with a set $\mathcal{N}$ of N buyers and set $\mathcal{I}$ of m goods. Each buyer j has a monotone valuation function $v_j : 2^{\mathcal{I}} \rightarrow \mathbb{R}^+$, whereas the seller is bound by a supply constraint on each good, i.e., at most k_i units of good $i \in \mathcal{I}$ are available to be sold. We use $k := \frac{\sum_{i \in \mathcal{I}} k_i}{m}$ to denote the average supply of goods in the market. Given an allocation $\vec{S} = (S_1, S_2, \dots, S_N)$ of goods to the buyers, we will use $SW(\vec{S}) = \sum_{j \in \mathcal{N}} v_j(S_j)$ to represent the social welfare of this allocation. For the same allocation, let $N_i(\vec{S})$ denote the set of buyers who received a copy of good i and $k_i(\vec{S}) = |N_i(\vec{S})|$. An allocation is *feasible* only if it does not violate the supply constraints i.e., for each $i \in \mathcal{I}$, no more k_i buyers receive a copy of this good. Finally, let $\theta(\vec{S}) = \sum_{i \in \mathcal{I}} k_i(\vec{S})$ denote the total number of items allocated to buyers in the given allocation $\vec{S}$.

In this work, we will primarily deal with the XoS class consisting of *fractionally subadditive* valuation functions; this class includes, for example, all submodular functions. A valuation function v is said to belong to this class if there exists a set of additive clauses or functions $(a_1, \dots, a_r)$ such that for any $T \subseteq \mathcal{I}$, $v(T) = \max_{j=1}^{r} a_j(T)$. Each additive function a_j has a single value $a_j(i)$ for each $i \in \mathcal{N}$ so that for a set T of agents, $a_j(T) = \sum_{i \in T} a_j(i)$. We also provide algorithms for the class of *multi-unit valuations*, where a buyer's valuation depends only on the number of items that she receives, i.e., for all $S, T \subseteq \mathcal{I}$ such that $|S| = |T|$, $v(S) = v(T)$. Some of our secondary results are shown for other standard classes of valuations including *unit-demand, gross substitutes, submodular,* and *single-minded* valuations, all of whose definitions can be found in the full version of this work or a standard text such as [24].

Finally, as is common in the literature, we assume that we have black-box access to certain oracles that allow us to query the set functions. Specifically, we consider the following types of oracles with respect to a valuation v: (*i*) *Value Oracle*, that when given a set $S \subseteq \mathcal{I}$ returns the value of $v(S)$, (*ii*) *Demand Oracle* that when queried with a vector of item prices $\vec{p}$ returns a set S that maximizes the quantity $v(S) - \sum_{i \in S} p_i$, and (*iii*) an *XoS oracle* that for an XoS function v and a set $T \subseteq \mathcal{I}$ returns the additive function a_l that maximizes $a_l(T)$. We refer the reader to [16] for a detailed discussion on the power and limitations of different types of oracles.

2.1 Pricing Mechanisms

In the current work, we restrict our attention to two types of mechanisms based on *non-discriminatory item pricing*, where the seller fixes a single price per good in advance, and buyers purchase utility-maximizing bundles at the given prices. The price paid by each buyer equals the sum of item prices of the goods that she receives.

(1) **Simultaneous Mechanism.** In this mechanism, the seller posts a price p_i per good, buyers arrive simultaneously, and purchase a utility-maximizing subset $S_j \subseteq \mathcal{I}$ under the given prices. A pair $(\vec{p}, \vec{S})$ is said to be a *valid outcome* of the simultaneous mechanism if the following constraints are satisfied: (i) for every buyer $j \in \mathcal{N}$, S_j maximizes $v_j(S_j) - \sum_{i \in S_j} p_i$, and (ii) at most k_i buyers are allocated a copy of good i.

(2) **Sequential Mechanism.** The sequential mechanism is very similar to the previous mechanism except that buyers arrive sequentially and once the supply of a good is exhausted, it is no longer available to future buyers. Specifically, this mechanism proceeds as follows:
   (a) Initially, all of the goods are available.
   (b) For each good $i \in \mathcal{I}$, the seller posts a single price p_i and decides on the quantity $0 \leq q_i \leq k_i$ of this good to supply.
   (c) The buyers arrive in some order, and each buyer purchases her utility maximizing bundle from the set of available goods.
   (d) At any stage of the mechanism, if q_i copies of good i are sold (i.e, the good is sold out), then it is marked as unavailable.

   A triple $(\vec{p}, \vec{q}, \vec{S})$ is said to be a valid outcome of the sequential mechanism if by setting the prices p_i and supply constraints q_i, the above mechanism can result in the allocation $\vec{S}$ for some arrival order of the buyers. In fact, we will usually omit $\vec{q}$ from this and simply denote an outcome by $(\vec{p}, \vec{S})$, since if such an outcome is possible, then we can always set $q_i = k_i(\vec{S})$ to obtain the same outcome.

The sequential mechanism is a relaxation of the simultaneous one since any valid outcome of the latter mechanism is also a valid outcome for the sequential mechanism. Moreover, the outcome of the simultaneous mechanism is always *envy-free* as each buyer receives her utility-maximizing bundle and does not envy other buyers, whereas this may not be the case for the sequential mechanism. Finally, we consider three arrival models for buyers in the sequential mechanism: (i) *partially adversarial*, where the buyer arrival order comes from a polynomially bounded set of arrival orders, (ii) *random arrival*, where buyers arrive according to an arbitrary distribution D^{Π} over the arrival orders, and finally (iii) *fully adversarial*, where any of the $N!$ arrival orders are possible. For the objective of revenue maximization, we are able to provide efficient computational mechanisms for the first two arrival models, and a constructive existence result for the fully adversarial case.

Revenue and Surplus Given a valid outcome $(\vec{p}, \vec{S})$ of either item pricing mechanism, we define $Rev(\vec{p}, \vec{S}) := \sum_{i \in \mathcal{I}} p_i k_i(\vec{S}) = \sum_{j \in \mathcal{N}} \sum_{i \in S_j} p_i$ to be the resulting revenue, and $Surp(\vec{p}, \vec{S}) := \sum_{j \in \mathcal{N}} \{v_j(S_j) - \sum_{i \in S_j} p_i\}$ to be the aggregate surplus or buyer utility. It is not hard to see that $SW(\vec{S}) = Rev(\vec{p}, \vec{S}) + Surp(\vec{p}, \vec{S})$.

2.2 Charging Framework and Black-box Reductions

As a first step towards deriving black-box reductions from item pricing (for revenue maximization) to 'item allocations', we present a simple, but general charging framework for identifying pricing solutions with good revenue. The framework is not constructive and merely provides sufficient conditions for revenue approximation. The computationally challenging aspect is to actually design algorithms that compute prices obeying the properties spelled out below, which we do using

Price Doubling and Item Halving. Following a treatment of the charging framework, we briefly introduce the item halving technique that together with the framework yields our central result for fractionally subadditive valuations. In Section 4, we return to a more detailed examination of the charging framework and show how it can be used to unify existing results when applied in conjunction with the price doubling technique.

Revenue-Welfare Charging Property. Our charging framework is composed of Definition 2.1 and Claims 2.2 and 4.1. The driving force behind this framework is the following idea: suppose that we have a sequence of γ benchmark allocations that are provided as input, and we are able to design item pricing mechanisms such that the difference in welfare between successive allocations can be 'charged' to the mechanism's revenue. Then, one of these mechanisms must provide revenue that is comparable to the social welfare of the 'best benchmark allocation'. Finally, we remark that similar techniques based on charging welfare differentials to revenue have been used previously in the literature to compute revenue maximizing item prices for restricted classes of valuations [14, 22]. However, the framework that we present is considerably more general as it is not tied to any specific pricing strategy or class of buyer valuations.

Definition 2.1. Consider a sequence of benchmark allocations $\vec{B}^{(1)}, \vec{B}^{(2)}, \ldots, \vec{B}^{(\gamma)}$, and pricing solutions $(\vec{p}^{(t)}, \vec{S}^{(t)})_{t=1}^{\gamma}$. The sequence of solutions is said to satisfy the *charging* property if $\exists\, \alpha, \beta \geq 1$, such that (*i*) for all $1 \leq t \leq \gamma - 1$, $SW(\vec{B}^{(t)}) - SW(\vec{B}^{(t+1)}) \leq \alpha Rev(\vec{p}^{(t)}, \vec{S}^{(t)}) + \frac{SW(\vec{B}^{(t)})}{\beta}$; (*ii*) $SW(\vec{B}^{(\gamma)}) \leq \alpha Rev(\vec{p}^{(\gamma)}, \vec{S}^{(\gamma)})$.

In most of the applications, γ and α will be $O(\log m)$, and β will be sufficiently large. We now show how to leverage the property to obtain revenue that is within a $O(\gamma\alpha)$-factor of the social welfare of the first benchmark allocation.

Claim 2.2. *Consider a sequence of benchmark allocations $\vec{B}^{(1)}, \ldots, \vec{B}^{(\gamma)}$, and pricing solutions $(\vec{p}^{(t)}, \vec{S}^{(t)})_{t=1}^{\gamma}$ that satisfy the charging property as per Definition 2.1. Then, there exists $1 \leq \ell \leq \gamma$ such that $Rev(\vec{p}^{(\ell)}, \vec{S}^{(\ell)}) \geq \frac{1}{\gamma\alpha} SW(\vec{B}^{(1)}) \left(1 - \frac{\gamma-1}{\beta}\right)$.*

Proof. Suppose that for some $r \geq 1$, $\vec{B}^{(r)}$ represents the allocation with the maximum social welfare among the sequence of benchmark allocations, i.e., $r = \arg\max_{t=1}^{\gamma} SW(\vec{B}^{(t)})$. Define ℓ to be the integer index in the range $[1, \gamma]$ at which the pricing solution obtains the maximum revenue. So, for all $1 \leq t \leq \gamma$, $Rev(\vec{p}^{(\ell)}, \vec{S}^{(\ell)}) \geq Rev(\vec{p}^{(t)}, \vec{S}^{(t)})$. As per Definition 2.1, we know that for any $r \leq t \leq \gamma - 1$, the following property holds: $SW(\vec{B}^{(t)}) - SW(\vec{B}^{(t+1)}) \leq \alpha Rev(\vec{p}^{(t)}, \vec{S}^{(t)}) + \frac{SW(\vec{B}^{(t)})}{\beta}$.

Summing up the above sequence of inequalities from $t = r$ to $t = \gamma - 1$ along with the inequality $SW(\vec{B}^{(\gamma)}) \leq \alpha Rev(\vec{p}^{(\gamma)}, \vec{S}^{(\gamma)})$, we get that

$$\begin{aligned} SW(\vec{B}^{(r)}) &\leq \alpha \sum_{t=1}^{\gamma} Rev(\vec{p}^{(t)}, \vec{S}^{(t)}) + \sum_{t=1}^{\gamma-1} \frac{SW(\vec{B}^{(t)})}{\beta} \\ &\leq \gamma\alpha Rev(\vec{p}^{(\ell)}, \vec{S}^{(\ell)}) + (\gamma - 1)\frac{SW(\vec{B}^{(r)})}{\beta}. \end{aligned}$$

Therefore, we have that $Rev(\vec{p}^{(\ell)}, \vec{S}^{(\ell)}) \geq \frac{1}{\gamma\alpha} SW(\vec{B}^{(r)}) \left(1 - \frac{\gamma-1}{\beta}\right) \geq \frac{1}{\gamma\alpha} SW(\vec{B}^{(1)}) \left(1 - \frac{\gamma-1}{\beta}\right)$. □

Price Doubling, Item Halving, and Revenue Maximization for XoS Buyers

According to our framework, if we are provided with a sequence of benchmark allocations and pricing outcomes that satisfy Definition 2.1, we have essentially solved the revenue maximization problem. In order to obtain a full-fledged black-box reduction from pricing to allocation, we need to generate these solutions using a single input allocation, which we do using the price doubling and item halving approaches. Here, we describe the latter approach in the context of XoS valuations. This provides a natural segue to the central result of this paper: a $O((\log m + \log k)^2)$-revenue approximation for XoS buyers. We defer the treatment of price doubling to Section 4.

Item Halving The main idea behind this technique is that the number of items allocated to buyers in successive allocations decreases by a multiplicative factor of two. Towards this end, each allocation starting with the input allocation $\vec{B}^{(1)}$ is intrinsically tied to a pricing vector so that running either mechanism in conjunction with those prices results in the successive allocation.

Item Halving for XoS Buyers: Challenges and Techniques. Putting aside our framework for the time being, let us consider a fundamental question: how do we price items in unit supply for buyers having complex valuations? Almost *all of the literature has relied on price doubling* to obtain item prices that approximately maximize revenue. Specifically, powerful approximation algorithms have resulted from the simple observation made in [4] that offering a 'single buyer' a random price (on all goods) from the set $\{2^t \frac{H}{m^2}\}_{t=1}^{1+\log^2 m}$, for a suitable choice of H, is sufficient to ensure good revenue in expectation. Unfortunately, it is known [10] that static pricing based on this technique could be rather sub-optimal ($2^{\Omega(\sqrt{\log m})}$) even for two buyers, since the earlier buyer could have large valuations for low revenue goods intended for the later buyer. The natural next step is to then consider pricing items differently based on the value they generate for buyers in some allocation, for e.g., as in [18]. However, this need not result in good revenue either for similar reasons. Therefore, we infer that current pricing techniques including price doubling are ineffectual in a static setting since they do not take into account the dependencies introduced by limited supply.

The crucial observation that enables our centerpiece result is inspired by Definition 2.1. Suppose that we compute prices for each good based on the average value that it generates for buyers in some benchmark allocation multiplied by a conservative scaling parameter, and that the sequential mechanism based on these prices results in poor revenue. If the prices truly reflect each item's value and the scaling parameter is judiciously chosen so that the items do not get sold out too early, then we can infer that every utility-maximizing buyer would purchase a high-value bundle with only a few items. More specifically, our result is powered by the following *dichotomous black-box reduction*: given a benchmark allocation, either the mechanism with the above prices results in good revenue, or we can identify a dense sub-allocation that only uses half the number of items as the original benchmark allocation, but whose social welfare is close to the benchmark. Recursively applying this reduction, we either obtain a pricing strategy with good revenue or we simply end up with one good, for which revenue maximization is trivial. We refer to this technique as item halving as each successive application of our black-box mechanism decreases the number of allocated items by a multiplicative factor of two.

3 ITEM PRICING FOR REVENUE MAXIMIZATION WITH XOS BUYERS

In this section, we present the central result of this paper: a computationally efficient, sequential posted pricing mechanism that achieves a $O((\log m + \log k)^2)$-approximation to the optimum revenue. In fact, as discussed previously, our approximation factor is obtained with respect to the social welfare maximizing allocation. Depending on the arrival order, our $O((\log m + \log k)^2)$ sequential mechanism comes in two flavors: the partially adversarial model, where the arrival order is adversarial within a bounded set of arrival orders, and the random model, where the buyers arrive according to an arbitrary distribution D^{Π}.

Notation We will implicitly assume that we are dealing with XoS valuations for the rest of the section. Given an allocation $\vec{S} = (S_1, S_2, \ldots, S_N)$, we use $x_j^{S_j}$ to denote the XoS clause that maximizes buyer j's valuation for the set S_j of goods, i.e., $x_j^{S_j}(S_j) = v_j(S_j)$. Then, we can define the total value derived by buyers from any given good $i \in \mathcal{I}$ with respect to an allocation $\vec{S}$ as $U_i(\vec{S}) = \sum_{j \in N_i(\vec{S})} x_j^{S_j}(i)$. Additionally, for any integer $1 \leq r \leq k_i(\vec{S})$, we define $Top_i(r, \vec{S}) \subseteq N_i(\vec{S})$ to be the (r) buyers in $N_i(\vec{S})$ with the r highest values of $x_j^{S_j}(i)$.

Now, we are ready to define our first black-box algorithm that takes as input an allocation $\vec{A}$ and a parameter $\gamma \geq 1$, and computes a series of benchmark allocations $(\vec{B}^{(1)}, \ldots, \vec{B}^{(\gamma)})$ as well as pricing solutions $((\vec{p}^{(1)}, \vec{S}^{(1)}) \ldots, (\vec{p}^{(\gamma)}, \vec{S}^{(\gamma)}))$ that are in accordance with Definition 2.1. We present our black-box reduction (the core algorithm) in two parts, where the first part handles the main reduction and the computation of successive benchmark allocations, and the second part handles the boundary or tail condition, where a buyer has a large valuation for a single item. Note that the purpose of our core algorithm is to simply compute prices (and supply limits) for our eventual poly-logarithmic sequential mechanism.

Algorithm 1: Core Algorithm

input : Allocation $\vec{A}$, parameter $\gamma \geq 1$.

Define $\vec{B}^{(1)} = \vec{A}$;
for $t \leftarrow 1$ **to** $\gamma - 1$ **do**
  Set $\vec{p}^{(t)} = Prices(\vec{B}^{(t)}, \gamma)$ [See Figure 1];
  Let π be an arrival order chosen by an arbitrary function $\Gamma(\vec{p}^{(t)}, \vec{B}^{(t)})$ *(to be fixed later)*;
  Let $\vec{S}^{(t)}$ be an allocation obtained upon running the sequential mechanism with prices $\vec{p}^{(t)}$, supply $\vec{k}(\vec{B}^{(t)})$, and buyer arrival order π;
  `/* Case I: less than half the goods from` $\vec{B}^{(t)}$ `are sold in` $\vec{S}^{(t)}$ `*/`
  if $2\theta(\vec{S}^{(t)}) \leq \theta(\vec{B}^{(t)})$ **then**
    Set $\vec{B}^{(t+1)} = \vec{S}^{(t)}$;
  end
  `/* Case II: more than half the goods from` $\vec{B}^{(t)}$ `are sold in` $\vec{S}^{(t)}$ `*/`
  else Set $\vec{B}^{(t+1)} =$ Alloc-Unsold$(\vec{B}^{(t)}, \vec{S}^{(t)})$ [See Figure 2];
end

`/* Tail Conditions */`
Define j^*, i^* to be a buyer, good pair that maximizes $v_j(\{i\})$;
Set $\vec{p}_{i^*}^{(\gamma)} = v_{j^*}(\{i^*\}) - \epsilon$, for some sufficiently small $\epsilon > 0$, and $\vec{p}_i^{(\gamma)} = \infty$, for $i \neq i^*$;
Let $\vec{S}^{(\gamma)}$ be the allocation in which j^* receives the item i^*, and no one else receives anything;

Informal Description of Core Algorithm. The core algorithm presented here (Algorithm 1) is the main workhorse behind all of our results. The purpose of this algorithm is to take an arbitrary allocation $\vec{A}$ as input along with an arrival order determining function Γ and return a sequence of benchmark allocations and pricing solutions that satisfy the charging property. By varying the formulation of the function Γ, we can use the same core procedure to derive revenue maximization algorithms for all three arrival orders discussed previously (see Section 3.1). Beginning with the input allocation $\vec{A}$, in each iteration, we use the function $Prices(\vec{S}, \gamma)$ from Figure 1 to compute a price for each good that depends on the average value it generates in allocation $\vec{S} = \vec{B}^{(t)}$ scaled down by a factor of 2γ. Following this, we run the sequential mechanism with the computed prices for the arrival order π determined by Γ and obtain the pricing solution $(\vec{p}^{(t)}, \vec{S}^{(t)})$. Now, if the number of items allocated in $\vec{S}^{(t)}$ is at most half the number allocated in $\vec{B}^{(t)}$, then we set the benchmark allocation for the next iteration $\vec{B}^{(t+1)}$ to be $\vec{S}^{(t)}$. If the condition does not hold, then we invoke the function *Alloc-Unsold* and set $\vec{B}^{(t+1)}$ to be the allocation comprising of all the items which were allocated in $\vec{B}^{(t)}$ but *unsold* in $\vec{S}^{(t)}$. Thus, at each iteration the number of items allocated in the benchmark solution reduces by at least a factor of two. Finally, the *tail conditions* provide a means for revenue maximization when the benchmark allocation consists of a single good.

Return $\vec{p}$ such that:

$$p_i = \frac{U_i(\vec{S})}{2\gamma k_i(\vec{S})} \qquad \text{if } k_i(\vec{S}) \neq 0$$

$$p_i = \infty \qquad \text{otherwise.}$$

Fig. 1. Function $Prices(\vec{S}, \gamma)$

Construct an allocation $\vec{C}$ as follows:

(1) For each good $i \in \mathcal{I}$:
(2) Define $q_i := k_i(\vec{B}) - k_i(\vec{S})$.
(3) if $q_i > 0$:
(4) Allocate item i to each of the buyers in $Top_i(q_i, \vec{B})$.

Return the allocation $\vec{C}$.

Fig. 2. Function Alloc-Unsold$(\vec{B}, \vec{S})$

We now prove the main theorem of this section, which allows us to use the charging property for the allocations generated by the above algorithm. In Section 3.1, we show how to apply this algorithm and the charging property to actually produce mechanisms with high revenue. The modular nature of Algorithm 1 allows us to use the same core algorithm to obtain revenue maximizing prices for all three arrival orders: partially adversarial, random arrival, and fully adversarial (existence result) by simply varying the formulation of the function Γ .

THEOREM 3.1. *For $\gamma = \log m + \log k$, the benchmark allocations $\{\vec{B}^{(t)}\}_{t=1}^{t=\gamma}$ and pricing solutions $\{(\vec{p}^{(t)}, \vec{S}^{(t)})\}_{t=1}^{t=\gamma}$ generated by the above algorithm for any input allocation $\vec{A}$ satisfy the charging property (Definition 2.1) with $\alpha = \beta = 2\gamma$, and thus for some ℓ we have that*

$$SW(\vec{A}) \leq 4(\log m + \log k)^2 Rev(\vec{p}^{(\ell)}, \vec{S}^{(\ell)}).$$

Note that although this theorem immediately implies that at least one solution $(\vec{p}^{(\ell)}, \vec{S}^{(\ell)})$ has high revenue compared to the welfare of the starting allocation $\vec{A}$, this does not yet give us the result we need since the allocation $\vec{S}^{(\ell)}$ is specific to one particular arrival order of buyers, whereas the actual arrival order is either random or adversarial.

Proof of Theorem 3.1. By Claim 2.2, it suffices if we show that for every $1 \leq t \leq \gamma - 1$: (*i*) $SW(\vec{B}^{(t)}) - SW(\vec{B}^{(t+1)}) \leq 2\gamma Rev(\vec{p}^{(t)}, \vec{S}^{(t)}) + \frac{SW(\vec{B}^{(t)})}{2\gamma}$ and (*ii*) $SW(\vec{B}^{(\gamma)}) \leq 2\gamma Rev(\vec{p}^{(\gamma)}, \vec{S}^{(\gamma)})$. We assume without loss of generality that the number of items allocated in $\vec{B}^{(t+1)}$ is exactly half the number of copies allocated in the previous benchmark allocation $\vec{B}^{(t)}$ for all $1 \leq t \leq \gamma - 1$. We begin with an outline of the proof.

(1) Consider some iteration t of our core algorithm where the benchmark solution is $\vec{B}^{(t)}$. As mentioned in the algorithm, let $\vec{S}^{(t)}$ denote the allocation obtained upon running the sequential posted pricing mechanism with prices that are a scaled down version of each good's average value in $\vec{B}^{(t)}$, (as in $Prices(\vec{B}^{(t)}, \gamma)$). Then, we claim and prove that $SW(\vec{B}^{(t)}) - SW(\vec{S}^{(t)})$ can be bounded in terms of the mechanism's revenue and the welfare of $\vec{B}^{(t)}$, analogous to Definition 2.1. This has obvious implications in showing that our solutions satisfy Definition 2.1 for a given value of t as long as the core algorithm chooses $\vec{B}^{(t+1)}$ to be the output of the sequential mechanism.
(2) Given a benchmark allocation vector $\vec{B}^{(t)}$, once again consider running the sequential mechanism with scaled down prices, and let $\vec{T}$ denote a sub-allocation of $\vec{B}^{(t)}$ obtained by allocating the 'unsold' items back to the original buyers (as in Alloc-Unsold($\vec{B}^{(t)}, \vec{S}^{(t)}$)). Then, $SW(\vec{B}^{(t)}) - SW(\vec{T})$ can be bounded purely in terms of the revenue of the above sequential mechanism. Therefore, our solutions satisfy Definition 2.1 in the second case where $\vec{B}^{(t+1)}$ is defined to be the output of Alloc-Unsold.
(3) In the final act, we prove that for each t, $\vec{B}^{(t+1)}$ allocates at most half the total number of items as $\vec{B}^{(t)}$, and so at most two items are allocated in $\vec{B}^{(\gamma)}$. In this case, the tail part of our core algorithm, where exactly one good is sold, results in a revenue that is only a constant factor away from the social welfare of $\vec{B}^{(\gamma)}$.

General Claims. We now show two general claims that can be used to bound the difference in welfare of any two consecutive benchmark solutions in our core algorithm.

Claim 3.2. *Given any allocation $\vec{B}$ and some parameter $\alpha \geq 1$, consider the sequential posted pricing mechanism with arbitrary buyer arrival order for supply constraint $q_i = k_i(\vec{B})$, and price $p_i = \frac{U_i(\vec{B})}{\alpha q_i}$ for all $i \in \mathcal{I}$. Suppose that $\vec{S}$ denotes the output allocation of this mechanism. Then, $SW(\vec{B}) - SW(\vec{S}) \leq \alpha Rev(\vec{p}, \vec{S}) + \frac{SW(\vec{B})}{\alpha}$.*

The next claim is useful in showing that Definition 2.1 holds in the (second) case when our core algorithm uses the function Alloc-Unsold($\vec{B}^{(t)}, \vec{S}^{(t)}$) to select the next benchmark allocation.

Claim 3.3. *Given any allocation $\vec{B}$ and some parameter $\alpha \geq 1$, consider the sequential posted pricing mechanism with arbitrary buyer arrival order for supply constraint $q_i = k_i(\vec{B})$, and price $p_i = \frac{U_i(\vec{B})}{\alpha q_i}$ for all $i \in \mathcal{I}$. Suppose that $\vec{S}^M$ denotes the output allocation of this mechanism, and $\vec{S}$ is the allocation returned by Alloc-Unsold($\vec{B}, \vec{S}^M$). Then, $SW(\vec{B}) - SW(\vec{S}) \leq \alpha Rev(\vec{p}, \vec{S}^M)$.*

Tail Conditions. Applying Claims 3.2 and 3.3 in the context of our core algorithm, we can prove that the first half of the charging property is obeyed by our solutions. It only remains for us to show that $SW(\vec{B}^{(\gamma)}) \leq \alpha Rev(\vec{p}^{(\gamma)}, \vec{S}^{(\gamma)})$. We begin by highlighting the 'item halving' nature of our algorithm. Note that in the initial allocation to our core algorithm $\vec{A}$ (and hence $\vec{B}^{(1)}$), at most mk copies of goods are allocated since k denotes the average supply. In every successive round, the number of items in the (next) benchmark solution is at least halved. Therefore, after $\log(mk) - 1$ rounds, i.e., in $\vec{B}^{(\gamma)}$, at most 2 items are allocated to the buyers. The next lemma follows from this reasoning.

Lemma 3.4. *Define* $(i^*, j^*) := \arg\max_{i \in I, j \in N} v_j(i)$. *The social welfare of the allocation* $\vec{B}^{(\gamma)}$ *is at most* $2v_{j^*}(i^*)$.

Thus, since the revenue obtained by $(\vec{p}^{(\gamma)}, \vec{S}^{(\gamma)})$ is $v_{j^*}(i^*) - \epsilon$, we know that for a small enough epsilon it must be that $SW(\vec{B}^{(\gamma)}) \leq 2\gamma Rev(\vec{p}^{(\gamma)}, \vec{S}^{(\gamma)})$, as desired.

Wrapping up the Proof. Equipped with the various pieces, we can now complete the proof of our black-box reduction by showing that our solutions obey the conditions outlined in Definition 2.1. Fix the inputs to the core algorithm, i.e., allocation $\vec{A}$, and γ as defined previously. Consider any iteration $t \leq \gamma - 1$ of our algorithm. Let us proceed in two cases depending on the algorithm's choice of $\vec{B}^{(t+1)}$. In the first case, suppose that our algorithm identifies $\theta(\vec{B}^{(t)}) \geq 2\theta(\vec{S}^{(t)})$ and defines $\vec{B}^{(t+1)} = \vec{S}^{(t)}$. Then, we apply Claim 3.2 with $\vec{B} = \vec{B}^{(t)}$, $\vec{S} = \vec{S}^{(t)} = \vec{B}^{(t+1)}$, and $\alpha = 2\gamma$ and get that: $SW(\vec{B}^{(t)}) - SW(\vec{B}^{(t+1)}) \leq 2\gamma Rev(\vec{p}^{(t)}, \vec{S}^{(t)}) + \frac{SW(\vec{B}^{(t)})}{2\gamma}$.

In the second case, we have that $\theta(\vec{B}^{(t)}) < 2\theta(\vec{S}^{(t)})$ and so, we set $\vec{B}^{(t+1)} = \text{Alloc-Unsold}(\vec{B}^{(t)}, \vec{S}^{(t)})$. For this case, we refer to Claim 3.3 with $\vec{B} = \vec{B}^{(t)}$, $\vec{S}^M = \vec{S}^{(t)}$, and $\alpha = 2\gamma$ to obtain the same result as above. Finally, the last condition that $SW(\vec{B}^{(\gamma)}) \leq 2Rev(\vec{p}^{(\gamma)}, \vec{S}^{(\gamma)})$ comes from Lemma 3.4. Therefore, our solutions satisfy Definition 2.1 and as a consequence, we can apply Claim 2.2 with $\alpha = \beta = 2\gamma$ to complete the proof. □

3.1 Applying the Item Halving Framework to Form Pricing with High Revenue

We are now in a position to leverage Theorem 3.1 as a black-box mechanism to obtain computationally efficient posted price mechanisms with good revenue guarantees for different arrival orders. Specifically, for instances having XoS valuations, we can use the $\frac{e}{e-1}$-approximation algorithm for the allocation problem [16] to form an initial allocation $\vec{A}$ with high welfare. The item-halving algorithm gives us a pricing and allocation $(\vec{p}, \vec{S})$ whose revenue is a $O((\log m + \log k)^2)$-approximation to the optimum social welfare. However, $\vec{S}$ is a specific allocation and only arises for some buyer arrival order. By choosing the function Γ appropriately, we can make sure that the revenue resulting from all other arrival orders is no worse than that of $\vec{S}$.

3.1.1 *Adversarial Buyer Arrival.*

Theorem 3.5. ***(Computational Result)*** *Given a set of arrival orders* Π, *we can compute in time polynomial in* N, m, *and* $|\Pi|$, *prices* $\vec{p}$ *and supply constraints* $\vec{q}$ *such that the revenue guaranteed by the sequential posted pricing mechanism with these parameters for all* $\pi \in \Pi$ *is a* $\frac{4e}{e-1}(\log m + \log k)^2$-*approximation to the optimum welfare, and thus to the optimum revenue as well.*

For the case where the buyer arrival order is adversarial with $|\Pi|$ being of polynomial size, Theorem 3.5 immediately gives us an efficient algorithm for forming a sequential pricing mechanism which achieves a $O((\log m + \log k)^2)$ approximation for maximum revenue. For the case where Π consists of all possible arrival orders (truly adversarial), this still gives us an interesting existence result: for every instance, there exist *fixed* prices and supply constraints such that, no matter what order the buyers arrive, the revenue of the outcome is a $O((\log m + \log k)^2)$ approximation to the maximum possible welfare.

(Description of Mechanism for Partially Adversarial Case) Set $\vec{A}$ to be the allocation which yields an $\frac{e}{e-1}$-approximation to maximum social welfare; this can be obtained from [16]. Set $\Gamma(\vec{p}, \vec{B})$ to be as follows. For each $\pi \in \Pi$, run the sequential posted price mechanism with prices $\vec{p}$ and supply constraints $\vec{q} = k(\vec{B})$, and choose π to be the arrival order that results in the smallest revenue. Set $\Gamma(\vec{p}, \vec{B})$ to be this arrival order π. We can now run the core algorithm with $\vec{A}$, Γ as defined previously and $\gamma = \log m + \log k$. □

3.1.2 *Random Arrival Orders.*

We now consider a more realistic model [23] of buyer arrival that is determined by an arbitrary distribution D^{Π} over the set of arrival orders. We make the standard assumption that we have access to an oracle from which we can draw samples corresponding to the distribution D^{Π}. Building on our machinery from the previous sections, we design a mechanism that with high probability achieves a $O((\log m + \log k)^2)$-approximation for revenue, which is the same asymptotic factor that was obtained for the partially adversarial model.

THEOREM 3.6. *Given oracle access to a distribution D^{Π} over the buyer arrival orders, we can design in poly-time a sequential posted pricing mechanism $\mathcal{M}$ such that with high probability,*

$$SW(OPT) \leq \frac{8e}{e-1}(\log m + \log k)^2 E_{\pi \sim D^{\Pi}}[Rev(\mathcal{M}, \pi)],$$

where $Rev(\mathcal{M}, \pi)$ is the revenue achieved by the mechanism $\mathcal{M}$ when the buyer arrival order is given by π.

We remark here that while the revenue achieved by our mechanism is in expectation over the arrival orders, the 'high probability' refers to the randomization of the algorithm itself. The core algorithm that achieves the desired approximation guarantee is the same as before; the only difference is in the function Γ, which is shown in Figure 3.

Set $T = \log((\log m + \log k)Nm)$

(1) For $r = 1$ to T
(2) Draw a sample π_r independently from D^{Π}
(3) Suppose that $\vec{S}(\pi_r)$ is the allocation obtained by the sequential posted price mechanism with prices $\vec{p}$ and supply constraints $k(\vec{B})$ when the buyer arrival order is π_r.
(4) Let $Rev(\pi_r)$ be the revenue of the same mechanism.

Return the arrival order π_r with the smallest revenue $Rev(\pi_r)$.

Fig. 3. Function $\Gamma(\vec{p}, \vec{B})$ specifically for random arrival orders

Instead of iterating over a finite set of arrival orders Π as we did previously, the new sequential mechanism function draws a logarithmic (in N, m) number of arrival orders according to the input distribution, and for each of these orders simulates the sequential posted pricing mechanism with the same set of prices and supply constraints. Finally, the function returns the outcome of the posted pricing mechanism (corresponding to some arrival order), which has the worst revenue.

(Description of Mechanism for Random Arrival Case) Run the core algorithm with $\vec{A}$ being the allocation obtained via the algorithm in [16], $\Gamma(\vec{p}, \vec{B})$ as defined in Figure 3 and $\gamma = \log m + \log k$.

4 IMPLICATIONS OF THE CHARGING FRAMEWORK

In this section, we return to the charging framework that we defined in Section 2. Previously, we only defined the parts of the framework that were necessary to prove our $O((\log m + \log k)^2)$-revenue result for XoS valuations. Here, we will show some additional properties associated with this framework and show how it can be leveraged to unify many of the results in the item pricing literature and generate new results for other classes of valuations.

In contrast to the previous section, all of the results from this section are obtained using the simultaneous mechanism, in which all buyers purchase bundles in parallel. Recall that simultaneous mechanisms are harder to design owing to the fact that the prices need to be chosen in a manner that ensures that every buyer receives a utility-maximizing bundle without violating the supply constraints. We reiterate that for any given instance, a valid solution $(\vec{p}, \vec{S})$ of the simultaneous mechanism is also a valid solution for the sequential mechanism.

4.1 Price Doubling and Bicriteria Approximations via Simultaneous Mechanisms

The field of item pricing has been witness to a rich algorithmic literature with near-optimal guarantees for revenue. A few of the notable contributions in this landscape include the logarithmic approximations to revenue for unit-demand [22] and unlimited-supply markets [4], and a $O(\sqrt{m}\log k_{max})$-approximation for single-minded valuations [14]. Somewhat surprisingly, we observe that our charging framework is found lurking beneath the hood of all of the above results. Applying the price doubling technique along with our framework, we present a single black-box revenue maximization theorem for a general class of market: *all of the results* mentioned above are obtained as corollaries. Further, we strengthen these results by also extracting welfare guarantees without any loss in the asymptotic factors for revenue. We begin by informally describing the price doubling technique and then show how the charging framework can be leveraged to obtain multi-objective guarantees.

Price Doubling Also known as multiplicative pricing, this technique is based on generating pricing solutions by running the mechanism on a sequence of pricing vectors such that the prices across successive solutions differ by a multiplicative factor (usually two). Following this, we charge the difference in social welfare between the allocations (obtained via the mechanism) to the mechanism's revenue so that we can apply the charging property.

Claim 4.1. *Consider a sequence of benchmark allocations $\vec{B}^{(1)}, \vec{B}^{(2)}, \ldots, \vec{B}^{(\gamma)}$, and pricing solutions $(\vec{p}^{(t)}, \vec{S}^{(t)})_{t=1}^{\gamma}$ that satisfy the charging property. Further, suppose that for all $1 \le t \le \gamma$, $\vec{B}^{(t)} = \vec{S}^{(t)}$. Then, for any target welfare parameter $c \in [1, \gamma\alpha]$, there exists an $1 \le \ell \le \gamma$ such that*

$$SW(\vec{S}^{(\ell)}) \geq \frac{SW(\vec{B}^{(1)})}{c}(1 - \frac{\gamma-1}{\beta}) \text{ and } Rev(\vec{p}^{(\ell)}, \vec{S}^{(\ell)}) \geq (1 - \frac{1}{c})\frac{SW(\vec{B}^{(1)})}{\gamma\alpha}(1 - \frac{\gamma-1}{\beta}).$$

Essentially, the claim states that as long as the benchmark solution coincides with the allocation obtained via the pricing mechanism, one can obtain excellent bicriteria (revenue,welfare) guarantees.

Black-Box Reduction for Item Pricing. Our main result in this section involves a reduction from revenue to welfare maximization via a simultaneous mechanism. Informally, the result indicates that in order to design item pricing mechanisms with good revenue, it is sufficient to design item pricing mechanisms that approximate welfare; this is true even for arbitrary combinatorial valuations. We now define some pertinent concepts. We say that a buyer has a (monotone) *single-item valuation* if and only if $v(\{i\}) > 0$ for at most one good $i \in \mathcal{I}$. Secondly, an allocation, and by extension an algorithm, is said to be *locally welfare maximizing* if for any buyer j who is not allocated any good, and any set of goods T that are not *sold out*, $v(T) = 0$. For instance, observe that any mechanism that outputs a socially optimal solution trivially satisfies this property. The following theorem takes as input a black-box algorithm for a simultaneous item pricing mechanism whose social welfare is an α-approximation to $SW(OPT)$ and creates an item pricing algorithm for revenue with a log factor increase in the approximation factor and a small loss in welfare.

THEOREM 4.2. *Let $\mathcal{V}$ be a class of buyer valuations that includes all single-item valuations. Suppose that we are given black-box access to a locally welfare maximizing algorithm Alg, that provides an α-approximate pricing solution for the problem of designing a simultaneous mechanism for welfare maximization for instances where buyer valuations belong to $\mathcal{V}$. Then, we can efficiently compute prices such that the simultaneous mechanism with these prices provides a $O(\alpha(\log(\alpha) + \log(m) + \log(k)))$-approximation to revenue and a (3α)-approximation to social welfare.*

We remark that the logarithmic gap between welfare and revenue is tight even when all buyers have single item valuations [18]. Further, even though the above result applies to XoS valuations, it does not replace Theorem 3.5 since simultaneous mechanisms cannot achieve good approximations to welfare for this class [19]. Hence, we need sequential mechanisms and the item halving technique to obtain good revenue for XoS buyers.

Black-box Reduction: For a fixed instance G and 'reserve price' $r \geq 0$, suppose that $(\vec{p}(r), \vec{S}(r))$ denotes the outcome of the item pricing mechanism *Alg* for this instance augmented by a set of $m(k+1)$ dummy buyers. Specifically for each good $i \in \mathcal{I}$, there are $k_i + 1$ dummy buyers all of whom have single item valuations with $v(\{i\}) = r$. Let $Rev'(\vec{p}^{(r)}, \vec{S}^{(r)})$ be the revenue obtained by the mechanism only from the original set of buyers. Now, we define our black-box reduction for $\gamma = 1 + \log(\alpha mk)$, and $SW^0 = SW(Alg(G))$, which is the social welfare of the allocation returned by *Alg* for the original instance G.

(1) For $t = 1$ to $t = \gamma$
(2) Set reserve price $r_t = 2^{t-1}\frac{SW^0}{2mk}$.
(3) Return the smallest index $1 \leq \ell \leq \gamma$ at which $Rev'(\vec{p}^{(\ell)}, \vec{S}^{(\ell)}) \geq \frac{SW(\vec{S}^{(1)})}{6\gamma}$.

It suffices to show that the sequence of solutions $(\vec{p}^{(t)}, \vec{S}^{(t)})_{t=1}^{\gamma}$ satisfy Claim 4.1.

Unifying Previous Results in Item Pricing. The next theorem of this paper is a collection of bicriteria approximation algorithms that use simultaneous item pricing mechanisms based on Theorem 4.2 to maximize both revenue and welfare for a number of settings. In the full version, we show how the theorem can be applied to derive bicriteria bounds even for pricing mechanisms that do not fall under the purview of item pricing, for e.g., bundle pricing [20].

THEOREM 4.3. *We can compute the following {revenue, welfare}-approximations in poly-time*

(1) *A $\{O(\log m + \log k), 3\}$-approximation when buyers have gross substitutes valuation.*
(2) *A $\{O(\sqrt{m}\log(k_{max})), O(\sqrt{m})\}$-approximation for single-minded valuations.*
(3) *A $\{O(\log(N) + \log m), 3\}$-approximation for arbitrary combinatorial valuations (that includes single-item valuations) and unlimited supply.*

Here k_{max} refers to the maximum available supply of any good.

Recall that any c-approximation algorithm for revenue obtained in terms of the optimum social welfare is trivially a (c, c)-bicriteria approximation. What makes Theorem 4.3 appealing is that the bound for welfare is much better than c, i.e., there is no asymptotic loss in the approximation factors for both revenue and welfare from the state of the art.

4.2 Simultaneous Mechanism: Item Halving applied to Multi-unit Markets

Previously, we used the item halving technique to derive a sequential mechanism with poly-logarithmic revenue guarantees for fractionally subadditive buyers. We now highlight the versatility of this technique by showing that it leads to good approximations even when buyer valuations may not belong to the XoS class. Specifically, we consider the popular multi-unit market setting [17] where buyers only care about the number of items they receive, and show that a small variant of our previously developed algorithm yields a $O(\log m)$-approximation for revenue. Previously [4] provided a sequential mechanism with a $O(\log m + \log(N))$ guarantee for revenue; not only do we remove the dependence on N, but we provide a stronger (simultaneous) mechanism with the given approximation factor.

A multi-unit market consists of a single good and each buyer's valuation depends only on the number of copies of this good that she receives. For the purpose of notational consistency, we assume that the market consists of a set $\mathcal{I}$ of m goods with one copy each and every buyer's valuation depends only on the cardinality of the set of goods, i.e., for any $j \in \mathcal{N}$, and any $S, T \subseteq \mathcal{I}$, $v_j(T) = v_j(S)$ if $|S| = |T|$; thus we will sometimes overload notation and refer to $v_j(S)$ for $|S| = q$ as $v_j(q)$. Note that such valuations can exhibit complementarities, and therefore do not fall under the XoS class. Additionally, we make the fairly standard assumption (e.g., see [4]) that no single buyer wishes to buy out more than half of the entire supply of goods in the market.

Definition 4.4. We say that an instance with multi-unit valuations satisfies the *no overwhelming buyer assumption* if for every buyer j, $v_j(\frac{m}{2} + q) = v_j(\frac{m}{2})$ for any non-negative integer q.

THEOREM 4.5. *Given any instance of a multi-unit market that satisfies the no overwhelming buyer assumption and an input allocation $\vec{A}$, we can compute in poly-time a single price $\tilde{p}$ such that the simultaneous mechanism with price $\tilde{p}$ on all copies of the good achieves a $O(\log m)$-revenue approximation to the optimum social welfare (and hence, optimum revenue) as long as $m \geq 2$.*

5 CONCLUSION AND OPEN QUESTIONS

The contributions made by this work can be evaluated at two levels. The fundamental contribution is a general framework for revenue maximization that captures the essence of a number of revenue maximization algorithms, previously developed in an ad-hoc fashion for specific settings and transforms all of these results into bicriteria approximation algorithms with only a constant factor loss in revenue. Our second contribution is more technical: we present the first known algorithm with a log-squared approximation factor for revenue with XoS buyers. In doing so, we partially resolve a decade long open question [4, 10] about the existence of polylogarithmic approximations for revenue maximization based on static item pricing. Our result is surprisingly powerful: it implies that even for quite general combinatorial valuations, we can use arguably the simplest pricing scheme known to us (one number per good) and approximate an all-encompassing benchmark, that is the optimum welfare.

An immediate open question is whether our central result for XoS buyers can be generalized to obtain a bicriteria bound. We make some progress towards answering this question in the full version. A more fundamental question is whether our results extend to a Bayesian information setting, where the seller is only aware of the distribution from which buyers' valuations are drawn. Unfortunately, it is known that no posted price obtains a reasonable revenue in comparison to the optimum welfare [1] in Bayesian environments even for unit-demand. One way to circumvent this would be to develop better benchmarks as in [8]; alternatively, we could assume some natural properties on the distributions such as monotone hazard rate.

REFERENCES

[1] Saeed Alaei, Jason D. Hartline, Rad Niazadeh, Emmanouil Pountourakis, and Yang Yuan. 2015. Optimal Auctions vs. Anonymous Pricing. In *Proceedings of FOCS 2015.*

[2] Elliot Anshelevich, Koushik Kar, and Shreyas Sekar. 2016. Pricing to Maximize Revenue and Welfare Simultaneously in Large Markets. In *Proceedings of WINE 2016.*

[3] Maria-Florina Balcan and Avrim Blum. 2007. Approximation Algorithms and Online Mechanisms for Item Pricing. *Theory of Computing* 3, 1 (2007), 179–195. https://doi.org/10.4086/toc.2007.v003a009

[4] Maria-Florina Balcan, Avrim Blum, and Yishay Mansour. 2008. Item pricing for revenue maximization. In *Proceedings of ACM EC 2008.*

[5] Avrim Blum, Anupam Gupta, Yishay Mansour, and Ankit Sharma. 2011. Welfare and Profit Maximization with Production Costs. In *Proceedings of FOCS 2011.* 77–86.

[6] Simina Brânzei, Aris Filos-Ratsikas, Peter Bro Miltersen, and Yulong Zeng. 2016. Envy-Free Pricing in Multi-unit Markets. *CoRR* abs/1602.08719 (2016). http://arxiv.org/abs/1602.08719

[7] Patrick Briest and Piotr Krysta. 2011. Buying Cheap Is Expensive: Approximability of Combinatorial Pricing Problems. *SIAM J. Comput.* 40, 6 (2011), 1554–1586.

[8] Yang Cai, Nikhil R. Devanur, and S. Matthew Weinberg. 2016. A duality based unified approach to Bayesian mechanism design. In *Proceedings of the ACM STOC 2016.*

[9] Yang Cai and Mingfei Zhao. 2017. Simple Mechanisms for Subadditive Buyers via Duality. In *Proceedings of STOC 2017.*

[10] Tanmoy Chakraborty, Zhiyi Huang, and Sanjeev Khanna. 2013. Dynamic and Nonuniform Pricing Strategies for Revenue Maximization. *SIAM J. Comput.* 42, 6 (2013), 2424–2451.

[11] Parinya Chalermsook, Julia Chuzhoy, Sampath Kannan, and Sanjeev Khanna. 2012. Improved Hardness Results for Profit Maximization Pricing Problems with Unlimited Supply. In *Proceedings of APPROX-RANDOM 2012.*

[12] Shuchi Chawla, Jason D. Hartline, David L. Malec, and Balasubramanian Sivan. 2010. Multi-parameter mechanism design and sequential posted pricing. In *Proceedings of STOC 2010.* 311–320.

[13] Ning Chen and Xiaotie Deng. 2014. Envy-free pricing in multi-item markets. *ACM Trans. Algorithms* 10, 2 (2014), 7.

[14] Maurice Cheung and Chaitanya Swamy. 2008. Approximation Algorithms for Single-minded Envy-free Profit-maximization Problems with Limited Supply. In *Proceedings of FOCS 2008.* 35–44.

[15] Ilias Diakonikolas, Christos H. Papadimitriou, George Pierrakos, and Yaron Singer. 2012. Efficiency-Revenue Trade-Offs in Auctions. In *Proceedings of ICALP 2012.* 488–499.

[16] Shahar Dobzinski, Noam Nisan, and Michael Schapira. 2010. Approximation Algorithms for Combinatorial Auctions with Complement-Free Bidders. *Math. Oper. Res.* 35, 1 (2010), 1–13. https://doi.org/10.1287/moor.1090.0436

[17] Michal Feldman, Amos Fiat, Stefano Leonardi, and Piotr Sankowski. 2012. Revenue maximizing envy-free multi-unit auctions with budgets. In *Proceedings of ACM EC 2012.*

[18] Michal Feldman, Nick Gravin, and Brendan Lucier. 2015. Combinatorial Auctions via Posted Prices. In *Proceedings of SODA 2015.* 123–135.

[19] Michal Feldman, Nick Gravin, and Brendan Lucier. 2015. On Welfare Approximation and Stable Pricing. *arXiv* abs/1511.02399 (2015). http://arxiv.org/abs/1511.02399

[20] Michal Feldman, Nick Gravin, and Brendan Lucier. 2016. Combinatorial Walrasian Equilibrium. *SIAM J. Comput.* 45, 1 (2016), 29–48. https://doi.org/10.1137/13094339X

[21] Amos Fiat and Amiram Wingarten. 2009. Envy, Multi Envy, and Revenue Maximization. In *Internet and Network Economics, 5th International Workshop, WINE 2009, Rome, Italy, December 14-18, 2009. Proceedings.* 498–504.

[22] Venkatesan Guruswami, Jason D. Hartline, Anna R. Karlin, David Kempe, Claire Kenyon, and Frank McSherry. 2005. On profit-maximizing envy-free pricing. In *Proceedings of SODA 2005.*

[23] Thomas Kesselheim, Robert D. Kleinberg, and Rad Niazadeh. 2015. Secretary Problems with Non-Uniform Arrival Order. In *Proceedings of STOC 2015.* 879–888. https://doi.org/10.1145/2746539.2746602

[24] Noam Nisan, Tim Roughgarden, Eva Tardos, and Vijay V Vazirani. 2007. *Algorithmic game theory.* Vol. 1. Cambridge University Press Cambridge.

[25] Tim Roughgarden and Inbal Talgam-Cohen. 2015. Why Prices Need Algorithms. In *Proceedings of the Sixteenth ACM Conference on Economics and Computation, EC '15, Portland, OR, USA, June 15-19, 2015.* 19–36.

[26] Tim Roughgarden, Inbal Talgam-Cohen, and Qiqi Yan. 2012. Supply-limiting mechanisms. In *ACM Conference on Electronic Commerce, EC '12, Valencia, Spain, June 4-8, 2012.* 844–861.

[27] Asher Wolinsky. 1988. Dynamic markets with competitive bidding. *The Review of Economic Studies* 55, 1 (1988), 71–84.

The Competition Complexity of Auctions: A Bulow-Klemperer Result for Multi-Dimensional Bidders [Abstract]

ALON EDEN, Tel-Aviv University
MICHAL FELDMAN, Tel-Aviv University
OPHIR FRIEDLER, Tel-Aviv University
INBAL TALGAM-COHEN, The Hebrew University of Jerusalem
S. MATTHEW WEINBERG, Princeton University

A seminal result of Bulow and Klemperer [1989] demonstrates the power of competition for extracting revenue: when selling a single item to n bidders whose values are drawn i.i.d. from a regular distribution, the simple welfare-maximizing VCG mechanism (in this case, a second price-auction) with one additional bidder extracts at least as much revenue in expectation as the optimal mechanism. The beauty of this theorem stems from the fact that VCG is a *prior-independent* mechanism, where the seller possesses no information about the distribution, and yet, by recruiting one additional bidder it performs better than any prior-dependent mechanism tailored exactly to the distribution at hand (without the additional bidder).

In this work, we establish the first *full Bulow-Klemperer* results in *multi-dimensional* environments, proving that by recruiting additional bidders, the revenue of the VCG mechanism surpasses that of the optimal (possibly randomized, Bayesian incentive compatible) mechanism. For a given environment with i.i.d. bidders, we term the number of additional bidders needed to achieve this guarantee the environment's *competition complexity*.

Using the recent duality-based framework of Cai et al. [2016] for reasoning about optimal revenue, we show that the competition complexity of n bidders with additive valuations over m independent, regular items is at most $n + 2m - 2$ and at least $\log(m)$. We extend our results to bidders with additive valuations subject to downward-closed constraints, showing that these significantly more general valuations increase the competition complexity by at most an additive $m - 1$ factor. We further improve this bound for the special case of matroid constraints, and provide additional extensions as well.

CCS Concepts: •**Theory of computation → Algorithmic game theory and mechanism design;**

Additional Key Words and Phrases: Revenue maximization; prior-independence; simple auctions

A full version of this paper is available at https://arxiv.org/pdf/1612.08821.pdf.

Author's email addresses: alonarden@gmail.com; mfeldmantau@gmail.com; ophirfriedler@gmail.com; inbaltalgam@gmail.com; smweinberg@princeton.edu.

Work done in part while A. Eden and S. M. Weinberg were visiting the Simons Institute for the Theory of Computing. This work was partially supported by the European Research Council under the European Union's Seventh Framework Programme (FP7/2007-2013) / ERC grant agreement number 337122. This work has received funding from the European Union's Horizon 2020 research and innovation programme under the Marie Sklodowska-Curie grant agreement number 708935.

ACM ISBN 978-1-4503-4527-9/17/06. DOI: http://dx.doi.org/ 10.1145/3033274.3085115

Assortment Optimisation under a General Discrete Choice Model: A Tight Analysis of Revenue-Ordered Assortments

GERARDO BERBEGLIA, Melbourne Business School, University of Melbourne
GWENAËL JORET, Computer Science Department, Université Libre de Bruxelles

The assortment problem in revenue management is the problem of deciding which subset of products to offer to consumers in order to maximise revenue. A simple and natural strategy is to select the best assortment out of all those that are constructed by fixing a threshold revenue π and then choosing all products with revenue at least π. This is known as the *revenue-ordered assortments* strategy. Our first contribution is an analysis of the performance of the revenue-ordered assortments strategy making only minimal assumptions about the underlying discrete choice model: We assume that consumers behave rationally, in the sense that the probability of choosing a specific product $x \in S$ when given a choice set S cannot increase if S is enlarged. This rationality assumption, known as *regularity*, is satisfied by almost all models studied in the revenue management and choice theory literature. This includes in particular all random utility models, as well as other models introduced recently such as the additive perturbed utility model, the hitting fuzzy attention model, and models obtained using a non-additive random utility function. We provide three types of revenue guarantees for revenue-ordered assortments: If there are k distinct revenues $r_1, r_2, \ldots, r_k$ associated with the products (listed in increasing order), then revenue-ordered assortments approximate the optimum revenue to within a factor of

(A) $1/k$;
(B) $1/(1 + \ln(r_k/r_1))$, and
(C) $1/(1 + \ln v)$,

where v is defined with respect to an optimal assortment S^* as the ratio between the probability of just buying a product and that of buying a product with highest revenue in S^*. These three guarantees are in general incomparable, that is, (A), (B), or (C) can be the largest depending on the instance. We also show that the three bounds (A), (B), and (C) are exactly tight, in the sense that none of the bounds remains true if multiplied by a factor $(1 + \epsilon)$ for any $\epsilon > 0$.

When applied to the special case of Mixed MNL models, bound (B) improves the recent analysis of revenue-ordered assortments by Rusmevichientong et al. [1], who showed a bound of $1/(e(1 + \ln(r_k/r_1)))$.

Our second contribution is to draw a connection between assortment optimisation and some pricing problems studied in the theoretical computer science literature by showing that these pricing problems can be restated as an assortment problem under a discrete choice model satisfying the above-mentioned rationality assumption. This includes unit demand envy-free pricing problems and the Stackelberg minimum spanning tree problem. Building on that connection, we then observe that a well-studied heuristic in that area called *uniform pricing* corresponds in fact to the revenue-ordered assortment strategy for the specifically constructed discrete choice models. As a consequence, our revenue guarantees for revenue-ordered assortments apply. Interestingly, the resulting bounds match and unify known results on uniform pricing that were proved separately in the literature for the envy-free pricing problems and the Stackelberg minimum spanning tree problem.

This paper is available at https://arxiv.org/abs/1606.01371

ACM ISBN 978-1-4503-4527-9/17/06. DOI: http://dx.doi.org/10.1145/3033274.3084084

REFERENCES

[1] Paat Rusmevichientong, David Shmoys, Chaoxu Tong, and Huseyin Topaloglu. 2014. Assortment optimization under the multinomial logit model with random choice parameters. *Production and Operations Management* 23, 11 (2014), 2023–2039.

Optimal Signaling Mechanisms in Unobservable Queues with Strategic Customers

DAVID LINGENBRINK, Cornell University
KRISHNAMURTHY IYER, Cornell University

We study the problem of optimal information sharing in the context of a service system. In particular, we consider an unobservable single server queue offering a service at a fixed price to a Poisson arrival of delay-sensitive customers. The service provider can observe the queue, and may share information about the state of the queue with each arriving customer. The customers are Bayesian and strategic, and incorporate any information provided by the service provider into their prior beliefs about the queue length before making the decision whether to join the queue or leave without obtaining service. We pose the following question: which signaling mechanism and what price should the service provider select to maximize her revenue?

We formulate this problem as an instance of Bayesian persuasion in dynamic settings. The underlying dynamics make the problem more difficult because, in contrast to static settings, the signaling mechanism adopted by the service provider affects the customers' prior beliefs about the queue (given by the steady state distribution of the queue length in equilibrium). The core contribution of this work is in characterizing the structure of the optimal signaling mechanism. We summarize our main results as follows.

(1) Structural characterization: Using a revelation-principle style argument, we find that it suffices to consider signaling mechanisms where the service provider sends a binary signal of "join" or "leave", and under which the equilibrium strategy of a customer is to follow the service provider's recommended action.

(2) Optimality of threshold policies: For a given fixed price for service, we use the structural characterization to show that the optimal signaling mechanism can be obtained as a solution to a linear program with a countable number of variables and constraints. Under some mild technical conditions on the waiting costs, we establish that there exists an optimal signaling mechanism with a threshold structure, where service provider sends the "join" signal if the queue length is below a threshold, and "leave" otherwise. (In addition, at the threshold, the service provider randomizes.) For the special case of linear waiting costs, we derive an analytical expression for the optimal threshold in terms of the two branches of the Lambert-W function.

(3) Revenue comparison: Finally, we show that with the optimal choice of the fixed price and using the corresponding optimal signaling mechanism, the service provider can achieve the same revenue as with the optimal state-dependent pricing mechanism in a fully-observable queue. This implies that in settings where state-dependent pricing is not feasible, the service provider can effectively use optimal signaling (with the optimal fixed price) to achieve the same revenue.

CCS Concepts: •**Mathematics of computing → Queueing theory; Markov processes;** *Linear programming;* •**Theory of computation → Algorithmic mechanism design;**

Additional Key Words and Phrases: Bayesian persuasion; optimal pricing in queues; throughput optimization; threshold strategies

The second author gratefully acknowledges support from the NSF under grants CMMI-1462592 and CMMI-1633920. The full version of this paper is available at https://ssrn.com/abstract=2964093.

Contact author's address: dal299@cornell.edu.

DOI: http://dx.doi.org/10.1145/3033274.3085135

EC'17, June 26–30, 2017, Cambridge, MA, USA.
ACM ISBN 978-1-4503-4527-9/17/06.

Information Sharing and Privacy in Networks

RONEN GRADWOHL, Kellogg School of Management, Northwestern University

Users of social, economic, or medical networks share personal information in exchange for tangible benefits, but may be harmed by leakage and misuse of the shared information. This paper analyzes the effects of privacy enhancements on the tradeoffs faced by such privacy-concerned individuals. The main insights are that different privacy enhancements may have opposite effects on the volume of information sharing, and that although they always seem beneficial to non-strategic users, privacy enhancements may backfire when users are strategic.

The observation that privacy regulation may be harmful is not new, and the burgeoning empirical and experimental literature on the topic has shown that the effects of regulation may be positive or negative, depending on the context [1]. The theoretical literature on privacy has its roots in the work of [3] and [4], who derive a similar conclusion in a signaling context: under stronger privacy regimes individuals can more readily hide negative traits, which may be harmful to other market participants and to social welfare.

This paper's goal is to identify properties of interactions that determine the effects of various privacy regulations. The point of departure is the observation that the conception of privacy commonly studied in the theory literature—namely, as a technology for altering the signaling capabilities of individuals—misses a key dimension of privacy harm: a concern not about third parties' inferences about individuals' types, but rather about misuse of the information itself. identity theft, spam, harassment, stalking, re-identification, online tracking, excessive profiling, and targeted advertising care less about whether the information leaked about them is positive or negative, and more about the fact that information has been leaked and misused in the first place.

We frame the paper within the context of online social networks, but describe its applicability in other contexts as well. In the model, agents are not concerned about what the leaked information signals about their type, but rather about the quantity of personal information leaked. As a preliminary formalization, consider a user of a social network who wishes to share some information. The user derives a benefit from sharing information on the platform, a benefit captured by an increasing function of the amount of information shared. However, there is some chance λ of information leakage and misuse, in which case the user incurs a cost, captured by another increasing function of the amount of information shared. The user thus faces a tradeoff between benefit and cost. Is a privacy enhancement, in the form of lowering λ, beneficial to the user? The answer is easily seen to be positive.

Of course, this simple example ignores the collective nature of social networks. More realistically, suppose there are many users of the network, each deciding on the amount of information to share. The interaction between users is captured by two opposing forces: First, users enjoy network effects from participation in the platform: the more information others share, the more benefit an individual user derives from his own participation. Second, a key feature of personal information on social networks is its interdependent nature: Individuals hold information not only about themselves, but

The full version of this paper is available at https://ssrn.com/abstract=2910655.

This work is supported by the National Science Foundation, under grant #1216006.

Author's address: MEDS, Kellogg School of Management, Northwestern University, 2211 Campus Drive, Evanston, IL 60208.

EC'17, June 26–30, 2017, Cambridge, MA, USA.
DOI: http://dx.doi.org/10.1145/3033274.3085095
ACM ISBN 978-1-4503-4527-9/17/06.

also about others [2]. If others share information about a particular user, that user may suffer from the leakage of information that he did not himself share.

Given these forces shaping interaction, we study two distinct privacy enhancements for online social networks: lowering the probability λ of leakage and misuse of information, and reducing the level of interdependence in users' information. The main results are that although both enhancements have a positive direct effect on user welfare, they have opposite effects on the volume of information sharing. The impact on the volume of sharing drives an indirect effect on user welfare, and its direction depends on the tradeoff between network effects and interdependencies. If the indirect effect is positive—when the privacy enhancement increases sharing and network effects dominate interdependencies, or when the enhancement decreases sharing and interdependencies dominate network effects—then the net effect of the privacy enhancement on user welfare is positive. However, if the indirect effect is negative, then the net effect depends on the structure and intensity of the interdependencies.

To further the analysis in the latter case we examine two extreme forms of interdependencies: overlapping information and additive information. Under overlapping information, the information shared by one user about another overlaps what the other shares about himself, and so contributes additional information only if he shares more of it. For example, on Facebook, profile information shared about others with third-party apps is overlapping information. Under additive information, in contrast, the information shared by one user about another is distinct from what the other has shared about himself. For example, original photos shared by two users of a social network are distinct, and so the facial-feature information they contain about a third user is additive. We show that enhancing privacy by lowering the leakage probability is beneficial when information is overlapping, but not necessarily when it is additive. In contrast, enhancing privacy by decreasing the level of interdependence is harmful when information is overlapping, but beneficial when it is additive.

The general intuition underlying these results is that under overlapping information, the interaction between users is locally similar to an interaction with no informational interdependencies. Hence, the response to small changes in λ is driven by its direct effects. Furthermore, small changes to the interdependencies have no direct effect, and so the response to those is driven by its indirect effects. Under additive information, in contrast, the indirect effect of varying the level of interdependencies is neutralized, and so only the direct effect influences utility.

Finally, we show that user-optional privacy enhancements lead to privacy "paradoxes", in which an enhancement is welfare-improving but each user optimally refrains from implementing it.

REFERENCES

[1] Alessandro Acquisti, Curtis R Taylor, and Liad Wagman. 2016. The economics of privacy. *Journal of Economic Literature* 54, 2 (2016), 442–492.

[2] danah boyd. 2012. Networked privacy. *Surveillance & Society* 10, 3/4 (2012), 348.

[3] Richard A. Posner. 1981. The economics of privacy. *The American Economic Review* (1981), 405–409.

[4] George J Stigler. 1980. An introduction to privacy in economics and politics. *The Journal of Legal Studies* (1980), 623–644.

Algorithmic Persuasion with No Externalities

SHADDIN DUGHMI, University of Southern California
HAIFENG XU, University of Southern California

We study the algorithmics of information structure design — a.k.a. persuasion or signaling — in a fundamental special case introduced by Arieli and Babichenko: multiple agents, binary actions, and no inter-agent externalities. Unlike prior work on this model, we allow many states of nature. We assume that the principal's objective is a monotone set function, and study the problem both in the public signal and private signal models, drawing a sharp contrast between the two in terms of both efficacy and computational complexity.

When private signals are allowed, our results are largely positive and quite general. First, we use linear programming duality and the equivalence of separation and optimization to show polynomial-time equivalence between (exactly) optimal signaling and the problem of maximizing the objective function plus an additive function. This yields an efficient implementation of the optimal scheme when the objective is supermodular or anonymous. Second, we exhibit a $(1-1/e)$-approximation of the optimal private signaling scheme, modulo an additive loss of ϵ, when the objective function is submodular. These two results simplify, unify, and generalize results of [3, 4], extending them from a binary state of nature to many states (modulo the additive loss in the latter result). Third, we consider the binary-state case with a submodular objective, and simplify and slightly strengthen the result of [4] to obtain a $(1-1/e)$-approximation via a scheme which (i) signals independently to each receiver and (ii) is "oblivious" in that it does *not* depend on the objective function so long as it is monotone submodular.

When only a public signal is allowed, our results are negative. First, we show that it is NP-hard to approximate the optimal public scheme, within any constant factor, even when the objective is additive. Second, we show that the optimal private scheme can outperform the optimal public scheme, in terms of maximizing the sender's objective, by a polynomial factor.

Additional Key Words and Phrases: Bayesian Persuasion; Signaling; Information Structure.

1 INTRODUCTION

Information structure design studies how beliefs influence behavior, both of individuals and of groups, and how to shape those beliefs in order to achieve desired outcomes. The key object of study here is the *information structure*, which describes "who knows what" about the parameters governing the payoff function of a game of incomplete information. These parameters, collectively termed the *state of nature*, encode uncertainty in the environment, and their prior distribution together with the information structure determine agents' equilibrium behavior.

When studied descriptively, information structures lend structural insight into the space of potential equilibria of a game of incomplete information (termed Bayes correlated equilibria in [6]), and can provide answers to comparative statics questions regarding the provision or withholding

This work is supported by NSF grant CCF-1350900.
Contact information: {shaddin, haifengx}@usc.edu .

EC'17, June 26–30, 2017, Cambridge, Massachusetts, USA. © 2017 ACM ISBN 978-1-4503-4527-9/17/06...$15.00.
DOI: http://dx.doi.org/10.1145/3033274.3085152

of information. The associated prescriptive questions are fundamentally algorithmic, and are often termed *persuasion* or *signaling*. Persuasion is the task faced by a principal — call her the *sender* — who has privileged access to the state of nature, and can selectively provide information to the agent(s) in the game — call him/them the *receiver(s)* — in order to further her own objectives. Such a sender effectively *designs* the information structure, and faces the algorithmic problem of selecting which of her information to reveal, to whom, and whether and how to add noise to this information. As in much of the prior work in this area, when we think of the information structure as an algorithm implemented by the sender, we call it a *signaling scheme*.

Both descriptive and prescriptive questions in this space have enjoyed an explosion of research interest of late, in particular at the intersection of economics and computer science. Our discussion can not do justice to the large literature in this area, including the wealth of work on related models. We therefore refer the curious reader to the recent survey by [16] and the references therein. The model we focus on in this paper, and for which we provide a thorough exploration through the algorithmic lens, is the fundamental special case of the multi-agent persuasion problem when restricted to binary actions and no externalities.

Our Model and its Significance

Our technical and conceptual starting point, and arguably the most influential model in this area, is the *Bayesian persuasion* model of [22]. Here the sender faces a single receiver, and her task is to persuade the receiver to take an action which is more favored by the sender. As in persuasion more generally, the sender's "leverage" is her informational advantage — namely, access to the realization of the state of nature, which determines the payoffs of the actions to both the receiver and the sender. The receiver, in contrast, a-priori knows nothing about the state of nature besides its prior distribution (the common prior). Kamenica and Gentzkow [22] assume that the sender can *commit* to her policy for revealing the information prior to realization of the state of nature, and study how and when this signaling scheme can increase the sender's utility.

The model we use is one recently proposed by Arieli and Babichenko [3], both generalizing and restricting aspects of the model of [22]. Here the sender interacts with multiple receivers, each of whom is restricted to a binary choice of actions. Without loss, we denote these actions by 1 and 0. As mentioned in [3, 4], settings like this arise when a manager seeks to persuade investors to invest in a project, or when a principal persuades opinion leaders in a social network with the goal of maximizing social influence. Each receiver's utility depends only on his own action and the state of nature, but crucially not on the actions of other receivers — the *no externality* assumption. The sender's utility, on the other hand, depends on the state of nature as well as the *profile* of receiver actions — since actions are binary, the sender's utility can be viewed as a *set function* on receivers. As in [22], the state of nature is drawn from a common prior, and the sender can commit to a policy of revealing information regarding the realization of the state of nature. Since there are multiple receivers, this policy — the information structure — is more intricate, since it can reveal different, and correlated, information to different receivers. As made clear in [3], such flexibility is crucial to the sender unless receivers are homogeneous and the sender's utility function highly structured (for example, additively separable across receivers). In particular, if restricted to a *public communication channel*, the sender is limited in her ability to discriminate between receivers and correlate their actions, whereas a *private communication channel* provides more flexibility.

Our results, and the models of Kamenica and Gentzkow [22] and Arieli and Babichenko [3], are crucially underlied by the assumption that the sender has the power of commitment to a signaling scheme. The commitment assumption is not as unrealistic as it might first sound, and a number of arguments to that effect are provided in [16, 22, 24]. We mention one of those arguments here:

commitment arises organically at equilibrium if the sender and receiver(s) interact repeatedly over a long horizon, in which case commitment can be thought of as a proxy for "establishing credibility."

If one permits commitment by the sender, restricts attention to a common prior distribution, and postulates that receiver(s) are not privately informed through channels not controlled by the sender, then the model of [22] is *the* special case of persuasion for a single receiver, and the model of [3] is *the* special case of persuasion for multiple receivers with binary actions and no externalities. Viewed this way, both are fundamental special cases of the general information structure design problem, meaningfully restricted. It is thus only fitting that they be thoroughly explored via an algorithmic lens, en-route to a more general understanding of the algorithmics of information in multi-agent settings. A computational study of the single-receiver Bayesian persuasion model of [22] was undertaken by Dughmi and Xu [18]. As for multi-agent persuasion with binary actions and no externalities, a partial algorithmic understanding is provided by [3, 4] in the special case of a binary state of nature, and this paper picks up there.

Context: Private and Public Persuasion

At their most general, signaling schemes can reveal different information to different receivers, through *private* communication channels. Such schemes play a dual role: they *inform* receivers, possibly asymmetrically, and they *coordinate* their behavior by correlating the information provided. In some settings, however, such private communication channels are unrealistic, and the sender is constrained to a *public* communication channel. Work on both descriptive and prescriptive questions regarding information structure design in multi-agent settings can be classified along these lines, and the extent to which a public communication channel limits the sender's powers of persuasion is a fundamental question which has not been thoroughly explored.

Much of the earlier work on information structure design, in particular its computational aspects, focused on public signaling models. This includes work on signaling in auctions [8, 17, 19, 21], voting [2], routing [7], and abstract game models [7, 14, 15, 25]. The work of [14] is relevant to this paper, in that they identify conditions under which public persuasion problems are tractable to approximate, and prove impossibility results in some cases where those conditions are violated. Our hardness proof in Section 6 is in part based on some of their ideas.

Private persuasion has been less thoroughly explored, particularly through the computational lens. The space of (private channel) information structures is studied by Bergemann and Morris [6], who observe that these information structures and their associated equilibria form a generalization of correlated equilibria, and term the generalization the *Bayes Correlated Equilibrium (BCE)*. The space of BCEs is characterized in two-agent two-action games by [26]. Moreover, recent work explores private persuasion in the context of voting [5, 13, 27].

Arieli and Babichenko [3] pose the model we consider in this paper, with the goal of studying private persuasion. We believe that their model wisely simplifies the general multi-agent persuasion problem by removing the most thorny aspect limiting progress in the study of private schemes: externalities. Specifically, by assuming that receivers only influence each others' payoffs through the choices of the sender, they sidestep the equilibrium selection and computation concerns which would arise in more general settings. Assuming a binary state of nature, Arieli and Babichenko [3] provide explicit characterizations of the optimal private signaling scheme for three of the most natural classes of sender objective functions: viewing the sender's objective as a set function on receivers, those are supermodular, anonymous monotone submodular, and supermajority functions. In all three cases, their characterization can be easily converted to an efficient algorithm. Moreover Arieli and Babichenko [3] provide necessary and sufficient conditions under which public signaling schemes match the performance of private signaling schemes. In follow-up work, Babichenko and

Barman [4] also consider the binary state setting, and reduce the private persuasion problem to the problem of computing the concave closure of the sender's utility function. This connection yields a $(1 - \frac{1}{e} - \epsilon)$-approximate private signaling scheme for monotone submodular utility functions, and an optimal private scheme for anonymous utility functions. Moreover, they show that the former approximation result is almost tight, assuming $P \neq NP$.

Our Results and Techniques

In Section 3, we examine private signaling in our model in the presence of many states of nature. When the sender's set-function objective is monotone non-decreasing, and the prior distribution is given as input, we show the polynomial-time equivalence of optimal (private) persuasion and the algorithmic problem of maximizing the sender's objective function plus an additive function (subject to no constraints).[1] The proof relies on a linear programming formulation of private persuasion, LP duality, and the equivalence of separation and optimization. This leads to polynomial-time persuasion algorithms when the sender's objective is anonymous or supermodular. Our results here are similar to the line of research on optimal mechanism design [9–11], in that both relate economic design problems with Bayesian incentive constraints to purely algorithmic problems. However, our techniques are different from those in [9–11].

Next, we consider a sender with a monotone submodular objective, and efficiently compute a private signaling scheme which is $(1 - \frac{1}{e})$-approximately optimal for the sender, modulo an arbitrarily small additive ϵ. This generalizes the result of [4] from two states of nature to many states, modulo the additive loss. The techniques used in [4] do not appear to help in the presence of many states of nature, since they are tied to several structural properties which only hold in the case of a binary state. Therefore, our algorithm uses a different approach, and crucially relies on a new structural property of (approximately) optimal private signaling schemes. Specifically, we prove that there always exists an ϵ-optimal "simple" private signaling scheme which is a uniform mixture of polynomially many deterministic schemes, i.e., a scheme that deterministically sends a signal to each receiver upon receiving a state of nature. Notably, this property only depends on the monotonicity of the sender's utility function, and does not rely on submodularity. Using this property, we then use ideas from the literature on submodular function optimization to compute a $(1 - \frac{1}{e})$-approximation to the best "simple" scheme.

We note that our algorithmic results from Sections 3 and 4 can be approximately extended to the sample oracle model, in which our algorithm is only given sample access to the prior distribution, using ideas from [18]. The resulting schemes suffer an arbitrarily small additive loss in the sender's objective and in persuasiveness of their recommendations, and this loss is unavoidable for information theoretic reasons.

In Section 5, we examine private signaling in the special case with two states of nature and a monotone submodular objective. We give a simple and explicit construction of a polynomial-time private signaling scheme that serves as a $(1 - \frac{1}{e})$-approximation to the optimal scheme, which is the best possible assuming $P \neq NP$ as shown by [4]. This result simplifies, and slightly strengthens, a result of [4]. Moreover, the constructed private scheme has the following distinctive properties: (i) it is *independent* in that it signals independently to each receiver in each of the two states of nature; (ii) it is *oblivious* in the sense that it does not depend on the sender's utility function, and the approximation ratio is guaranteed so long as the function is monotone submodular. To obtain this result, we first use the idea of the *correlation gap* [1] to argue that there always exists an independent signaling scheme which is a $(1 - \frac{1}{e})$ approximation to the optimal private scheme. We

[1] We mention that the reduction from our persuasion problem to the set function maximization problem does not require monotonicity, but the opposite reduction does.

then exploit the fact that there are two states of nature to argue that our scheme is the optimal independent scheme, simultaneously for all monotone objectives. We then show two respects in which this result cannot generalize to many states of nature. First, we show that it is NP-hard to obtain a $(1-\frac{1}{e})$-approximation to the best independent signaling scheme in multi-state settings. Second, we show that oblivious schemes cannot guarantee more than a $\frac{1}{\sqrt{m-1}}$ fraction of the optimal sender utility where $m > 1$ is the number of states of nature.

Finally, in Section 6, we consider public signaling in our model, and present two negative results. First, we show via a simple example that the optimal private scheme can outperform the optimal public scheme, in terms of maximizing the sender's objective, by a polynomial factor. Second, we employ a reduction from an NP-hard graph coloring promise problem to rule out an algorithm for approximating the optimal public scheme to within any constant factor, and also to rule out an additive PTAS for the problem.

2 PRELIMINARIES

2.1 Basic Setup

As in [3], we consider the special case of multi-agent persuasion with binary actions, no inter-agent externalities, and a monotone objective function. Here, we adopt the perspective of *sender* facing n *receivers*. Each receiver has two actions, which we denote by 0 and 1. The receiver's payoff depends only on his own action and a random *state of nature* θ supported on Θ. In particular, we use $u_i(\theta, 1)$ and $u_i(\theta, 0)$ to denote receiver i's utility for action 1 and action 0, respectively, at the state of nature θ; as shorthand, we use $u_i(\theta) = u_i(\theta, 1) - u_i(\theta, 0)$ to denote how much receiver i prefers action 1 over action 0 given state of nature θ. Note that $u_i(\theta)$ may be negative. The sender's utility (our objective) is a function of all the receivers' actions and the state of nature θ. We use $f_\theta(S)$ to denote the sender's utility when the state of nature is θ and S is the set of receivers who choose action 1. We assume throughout the paper that f_θ is a monotone non-decreasing set function for every θ. For convenience in stating our approximation guarantees, we assume without loss of generality that f_θ is normalized so that $f_\theta(\emptyset) = 0$ and $f_\theta(S) \in [0, 1]$ for all $\theta \in \Theta$ and $S \subseteq [n]$.

As is typical in information structure design, we assume that θ is drawn from a common prior distribution λ, that the sender has access to the realized state of nature, and that the sender can publicly *commit* to a policy— termed a *signaling scheme* — for mapping the realized state of nature to a *signal* for each receiver. The signaling scheme may be randomized, and hence reveals noisy partial information regarding the state of nature. The order of events is as follows: (1) The sender commits to a signaling scheme φ; (2) Nature draws $\theta \sim \lambda$; (3) Signals $(\sigma_1, \dots, \sigma_n) \sim \varphi(\theta)$ are drawn, and each receiver i receives the signal σ_i; (4) Receivers select their actions.

A general signaling scheme permits sending different signals to different receivers through a private communication channel — we term these *private signaling schemes* to emphasize this generality. We also study the special case of *public signaling schemes* — these are restricted to a public communication channel, and hence send the same signal to all receivers. We discuss these two signaling models in Sections 2.2 and 2.3, including the equilibrium concept and the induced sender optimization problem for each. In both cases, we are primarily interested in the optimization problem faced by the sender in step (1), the goal of which is to maximize the sender's expected utility. When φ yields expected sender utility within an additive [multiplicative] ϵ of the best possible, we say it is ϵ*-optimal* [ϵ-approximate] in the additive [multiplicative] sense.

2.2 Private Signaling Schemes

A *private signaling scheme* φ is a randomized map from the set of states of nature Θ to a set of *signal profiles* $\Sigma = \Sigma_1 \times \Sigma_2 \ldots \times \Sigma_n$, where Σ_i is the *signal set* of receiver i. We use $\varphi(\theta, \sigma)$ to denote the probability of selecting the signal profile $\sigma = (\sigma_1, \ldots, \sigma_n) \in \Sigma$ given a state of nature θ. Therefore, $\sum_{\sigma \in \Sigma} \varphi(\theta, \sigma) = 1$ for every θ. With some abuse of notation, we use $\varphi(\theta)$ to denote the random signal profile selected by the scheme φ given the state θ. Moreover, for each $\theta \in \Theta$, $i \in [n]$, and $\sigma_i \in \Sigma_i$, we use $\varphi_i(\theta, \sigma_i) = \mathbf{Pr}[\varphi_i(\theta) = \sigma_i]$ to denote the marginal probability that receiver i receives signal σ_i in state θ. An algorithm *implements* a signaling scheme φ if it takes as input a state of nature θ, and samples the random variable $\varphi(\theta)$.

Given a signaling scheme φ, each signal $\sigma_i \in \Sigma_i$ for receiver i is realized with probability $\mathbf{Pr}(\sigma_i) = \sum_{\theta \in \Theta} \lambda(\theta)\varphi_i(\theta, \sigma_i)$. Upon receiving σ_i, receiver i performs a Bayesian update and infers a posterior belief over the state of nature, as follows: the realized state is θ with posterior probability $\lambda(\theta)\varphi_i(\theta, \sigma_i)/\mathbf{Pr}(\sigma_i)$. Receiver i then takes the action maximizing his posterior expected utility. In case of indifference, we assume ties are broken in favor of the sender (i.e., in favor of action 1). Therefore, receiver i chooses action 1 if

$$\frac{1}{\mathbf{Pr}(\sigma_i)} \sum_{\theta \in \Theta} \lambda(\theta)\varphi_i(\theta, \sigma_i)u_i(\theta, 1) \geq \frac{1}{\mathbf{Pr}(\sigma_i)} \sum_{\theta \in \Theta} \lambda(\theta)\varphi_i(\theta, \sigma_i)u_i(\theta, 0),$$

or equivalently

$$\sum_{\theta \in \Theta} \lambda(\theta)\varphi_i(\theta, \sigma_i)u_i(\theta) \geq 0,$$

where $u_i(\theta) = u_i(\theta, 1) - u_i(\theta, 0)$.

A simple revelation-principle style argument [3, 22] shows that there exist an optimal private signaling scheme which is *direct* and *persuasive*. By *direct* we mean that signals correspond to actions — in our setting $\Sigma_i = \{0, 1\}$ for each receiver i — and can be interpreted as action recommendations. A direct scheme is *persuasive* if the strategy profile where all receivers follow their recommendations forms an equilibrium of the resulting Bayesian game.[2] Due to the absence of inter-receiver externalities in our setting, such an equilibrium would necessarily also satisfy the stronger property of being a dominant-strategy equilibrium — i.e., each receiver i maximizes his posterior expected utility by following the recommendation, regardless of whether other receivers follow their recommendations.

When designing private signaling schemes, we restrict attention (without loss) to direct and persuasive schemes. Here, a signal profile can be equivalently viewed as a set $S \subseteq [n]$ of receivers — namely, the set of receivers who are recommended action 1. Using this alternative representation, a scheme can be specified by variables $\varphi(\theta, S)$ for all $\theta \in \Theta, S \subseteq [n]$. We can now encode the sender's optimization problem of computing the optimal scheme using the following exponentially-large linear program; note the use of auxiliary variables $x_{\theta,i}$ to denote the marginal probability of recommending action 1 to receiver i in state θ.

$$\begin{array}{lll} \text{maximize} & \sum_{\theta \in \Theta} \lambda(\theta) \sum_{S \subseteq [n]} \varphi(\theta, S) f_\theta(S) & \\ \text{subject to} & \sum_{S: i \in S} \varphi(\theta, S) = x_{\theta,i}, & \text{for } i \in [n], \theta \in \Theta. \\ & \sum_{\theta \in \Theta} \lambda(\theta) x_{\theta,i} u_i(\theta) \geq 0, & \text{for } i = 1, \ldots, n. \\ & \sum_{S \subseteq [n]} \varphi(\theta, S) = 1, & \text{for } \theta \in \Theta. \\ & \varphi(\theta, S) \geq 0, & \text{for } \theta \in \Theta; S \subseteq [n]. \end{array} \tag{1}$$

The second set of constraints in LP (1) are *persuasiveness constraints*, and state that each receiver i should maximize his utility by taking action 1 whenever that action 1 is recommended. Note that the persuasiveness constraints for action 0, which can be written as $\sum_{\theta \in \Theta} \lambda(\theta)(1 - x_{\theta,i})u_i(\theta) \leq 0$ for each $i \in [n]$, are intentionally omitted from this LP. This omission is without loss when f_θ is a

[2]Persuasiveness has also been called *incentive compatibility* or *obedience* in prior work.

non-decreasing set function for each θ: any solution to the LP in which a receiver prefers action 1 when recommended action 0 can be improved by always recommending action 1 to that receiver.

2.3 Public Signaling Schemes

A public signaling scheme π can be viewed as a special type of private signaling schemes in which each receiver must receive the same signal, i.e., only a public signal is sent. Overloading the notation of Section 2.2, we use Σ to denote the set of public signals and $\sigma \in \Sigma$ to denote a public signal. A public signaling scheme π is fully specified by $\{\pi(\theta, \sigma)\}_{\theta,\sigma}$, where $\pi(\theta, \sigma)$ denotes the probability of sending signal σ at state θ. Upon receiving a signal σ, each receiver performs the same Bayesian update and infers a posterior belief over the state of nature, as follows: the realized state is θ with probability $\lambda(\theta)\pi(\theta, \sigma)/\mathbf{Pr}(\sigma)$, where $\mathbf{Pr}(\sigma) = \sum_{\theta\in\Theta} \pi(\theta, \sigma)$. This induces a subgame for each signal σ, one in which all receivers share the same belief regarding the state of nature.

Whereas in more general settings than ours receivers may play a mixed Nash equilibrium in each subgame, our restriction to a setting with no externalities removes this complication. Given a posterior distribution on states of nature (say, one induced by a signal σ), our receivers face disjoint single-agent decision problems, each of which admits an optimal pure strategy. We assume that receivers break ties in favor of the sender (specifically, in favor of action 1), which distinguishes a unique pure response for each receiver. Therefore, our solution concept here distinguishes a unique action profile for each posterior distribution, and hence for each signal. A simple revelation-principle style argument then allows us to conclude that there is an optimal public signaling schemes which is *direct*, meaning that the public signals are action profiles, and *persuasive*, meaning that in the subgame induced by signal $\sigma = (\sigma_1, \ldots, \sigma_n)$ each receiver i's optimal decision problem (which breaks ties in favor of action 1) solves to action σ_i.

Restricting attention to direct and persuasive public signaling schemes, each signal can also be viewed as a subset $S \subseteq [n]$ of receivers taking action 1. The sender's optimization problem can then be written as the following exponentially-large linear program.

$$\begin{array}{lll} \text{maximize} & \sum_{\theta\in\Theta} \lambda(\theta) \sum_{S\subseteq[n]} \pi(\theta, S) f_\theta(S) & \\ \text{subject to} & \sum_{\theta\in\Theta} \lambda(\theta)\pi(\theta, S) \cdot u_i(\theta) \geq 0, & \text{for } S \subseteq [n] \text{ with } i \in S. \\ & \sum_{S\subseteq[n]} \pi(\theta, S) = 1, & \text{for } \theta \in \Theta. \\ & \pi(\theta, S) \geq 0, & \text{for } \theta \in \Theta; S \subseteq [n]. \end{array} \tag{2}$$

The first set of constraints are persuasiveness constraints corresponding to action 1. Note that the persuasiveness constraints for action 0, which can be written as $\sum_{\theta\in\Theta} \lambda(\theta)\pi(\theta, S) \cdot u_i(\theta) \leq 0$ for each $S \subseteq [n]$ and $i \notin S$, are intentionally omitted from this LP. This omission is without loss when f_θ is non-decreasing for each state θ: if signal S with $i \notin S$ is such that receiver i prefers action 1 in the resulting subgame, then we can replace it with the signal $S \cup i$ without degrading the sender's utility. We remark that LP (2) and LP (1) only differ in their persuasiveness constraints.

2.4 Input Models

We distinguish two input models for describing persuasion instances in this paper. The first is the *explicit* model, in which the prior distribution λ is given explicitly as a probability vector. The second is the *sample oracle* model, where Θ and λ are provided implicitly through sample access to λ. In both models, we assume that given a state of nature θ, we can efficiently evaluate $u_i(\theta)$ for each $i \in [n]$ and $f_\theta(S)$ for each $S \subseteq [n]$. In the explicit input model, by *computing* a signaling scheme φ (whether private or public) we mean that we explicitly list the non-zero variables $\varphi(\theta, S)$ on which the scheme is supported. In the implicit model, computing a signaling scheme φ (whether private or public) amounts to providing an algorithm which takes as input a state of nature θ, and samples the random variable $\varphi(\theta)$.

2.5 Set Functions and Submodularity

Given a finite ground set X, a *set function* is a map $f : 2^X \to \mathbb{R}$. Such a function is *nonnegative* if $f(S) \geq 0$ for all $S \subseteq X$, *monotone non-decreasing* (or *monotone* for short) if $f(S) \leq f(T)$ for all $S \subseteq T$. Most importantly, f is *submodular* if for any $S, T \subseteq X$, we have $f(S \cup T) + f(S \cap T) \leq f(S) + f(T)$.

We also consider continuous functions G from the solid hypercube $[0, 1]^X$ to the real numbers. Such a function is *nonnegative* if $G(x) \geq 0$ for all x, *monotone non-decreasing* (or *monotone* for short) if $G(x) \leq G(y)$ whenever $x \preceq y$ (coordinate wise), and *smooth submodular* (in the sense of [12]) if its second partial derivatives exist and are non-positive everywhere.

The Multilinear Extension of a Set Function. Given any set function $f : 2^X \to \mathbb{R}$, the *multilinear extension* of f is the continuous function $F : [0, 1]^X \to \mathbb{R}$ defined as follows:

$$F(x) = \sum_{S \subseteq X} f(S) \prod_{i \in S} x_i \prod_{i \notin S} (1 - x_i), \tag{3}$$

Notice that, $F(x)$ can be viewed as the expectation of $f(S)$ when the random set S independently includes each element i with probability x_i. In particular, let p^I_x denote the *independent distribution* with marginals x, defined by $p^I_x(S) = \prod_{i \in S} x_i \prod_{i \notin S}(1 - x_i)$, then $F(x) = \mathbf{E}_{S \sim p^I_x} f(S)$. If f is nonnegative/monotone then so is F. Moreover, if f is submodular then F is smooth submodular. For our results, we will need to maximize $F(x)$ subject to a set of linear constraints on x. This problem is NP-hard in general, yet can be approximated by the *continuous greedy process* of Calinescu et al. [12] for fairly general families of constraints. Note that though we cannot exactly evaluate $F(x)$ in polynomial time, it is sufficient to approximate $F(x)$ within a good precision in order to apply the continuous greedy process. By an additive FPTAS evaluation oracle for F, we mean an algorithm that evaluates $F(x)$ within additive error ϵ in poly$(n, \frac{1}{\epsilon})$ time.

Theorem 2.1 (Adapted form [12]). *Let $F : [0, 1]^n \to [0, 1]$ be a non-negative, monotone, smooth submodular function. Let $\mathcal{P} \subseteq [0, 1]^n$ be a down-monotone polytope*[3]*, specified explicitly by its linear constraints. Given an additive FPTAS evaluation oracle for F, there is a* poly$(n, \frac{1}{\epsilon})$ *time algorithm that outputs $\overline{x} \in \mathcal{P}$ such that $F(\overline{x}) \geq (1 - \frac{1}{e})OPT - \epsilon$, where $OPT = \max_{x \in \mathcal{P}} F(x)$.*

Correlation Gap. A general definition of the correlation gap can be found in [1]. For our results, the following simple definition will suffice. Specifically, for any $x \in [0, 1]^X$, let $D(x)$ be the set of all distributions p over 2^X with fixed marginal probability $\mathbf{Pr}_{S \sim p}(i \in S) = x_i$ for all i. Let p^I_x, as defined above, be the independent distribution with marginal probabilities x. Note that $p^I_x \in D(x)$. For any set function $f(S)$, the correlation gap κ is defined as follows:

$$\kappa = \max_{x \in [0,1]^X} \max_{p \in D(x)} \frac{\mathbf{E}_{S \sim p} f(S)}{\mathbf{E}_{S \sim p^I_x} f(S)}. \tag{4}$$

Loosely speaking, the correlation gap upper bounds the "loss" of the expected function value over a random set by ignoring the correlation in the randomness.

Theorem 2.2 ([1]). *The correlation gap κ is upper bounded by $\frac{e}{e-1}$ for any non-negative monotone non-decreasing submodular function.*

[3] A polytope $\mathcal{P} \subseteq \mathbb{R}^n_+$ is called *down-monotone* if for all $x, y \in \mathbb{R}^n_+$, if $y \in P$ and $x \preceq y$ (coordinate-wise) then $x \in P$.

3 EQUIVALENCE BETWEEN PRIVATE SIGNALING AND OBJECTIVE MAXIMIZATION

In this section, we relate the computational complexity of private persuasion to the complexity of maximizing the sender's objective function, and show that the optimal private signaling scheme can be computed efficiently for a broad class of sender objectives. Let $\mathcal{F}$ denote any collection of monotone set functions. We use $\mathcal{I}(\mathcal{F})$ to denote the class of all persuasion instances in our model in which the sender utility function f_θ is in $\mathcal{F}$ for all states of nature θ. We restrict attention to the explicit input model for most of this discussion, though discuss how to extend our results to the sample oracle model, modulo an arbitrarily small additive loss in both the sender's objective and the persuasiveness constraints, at the end of this section.

The following theorem establishes the polynomial-time equivalence between computing the optimal private signaling scheme and the problem of maximizing the objective function plus an additive function. Note that although the number of variables in LP (1) is exponential in the number of receivers, a vertex optimal solution of this LP is supported on $O(n|\Theta|)$ variables.

Theorem 3.1. *Let $\mathcal{F}$ be any collection of monotone set functions. There is a polynomial-time algorithm which computes the optimal private signaling scheme given any instance in $\mathcal{I}(\mathcal{F})$ if and only if there is a polynomial time algorithm for maximizing $f(S) + \sum_{i \in S} w_i$ given any $f \in \mathcal{F}$ and any set of weights $w_i \in \mathbb{R}$.*

Proof. We first reduce optimal private signaling to maximizing the objective function plus an additive function, via linear programming duality. In particular, consider the following dual program of LP (1) with variables $w_{\theta,i}, \alpha_i, y_\theta$.

$$\begin{array}{lll} \text{minimize} & \sum_{\theta \in \Theta} y_\theta & \\ \text{subject to} & \sum_{i \in S} w_{\theta,i} + y_\theta \geq \lambda(\theta) f_\theta(S), & \text{for } S \subseteq [n], \theta \in \Theta. \\ & w_{\theta,i} + \alpha_i \lambda(\theta) u_i(\theta) = 0, & \text{for } i = 1, \ldots, n. \\ & \alpha_i \geq 0, & \text{for } i \in [n]. \end{array} \tag{5}$$

We can obtain a separation oracle for LP (5) given an algorithm for maximizing $f_\theta(S)$ plus an additive function. Given any variables $w_{\theta,i}, \alpha_i, y_\theta$, separation over the first set of constraints reduces to maximizing the set function $g_\theta(S) = f_\theta(S) - \frac{1}{\lambda(\theta)} \sum_{i \in S} w_{\theta,i}$ for each $\theta \in \Theta$. The other constraints can be checked directly in linear time. Given the resulting separation oracle, we can use the Ellipsoid method to obtain a vertex optimal solution to both LP (5) and its dual LP (1) in polynomial time [20].

We now prove the converse. Namely, we construct a polynomial-time Turing reduction from the problem of maximizing f plus an additive function to a private signaling problem in $\mathcal{I}(\mathcal{F})$. At a high level, we first reduce the set function maximization problem to a certain linear program, and then prove that solving the dual of the linear program reduces to optimal private signaling for a set of particularly constructed instances in $\mathcal{I}(\mathcal{F})$.

Given $f \in F$ and weights w, our reduction concerns the following linear program, parameterized by $\mathbf{a} = (a_1, \ldots, a_n)$ and b, with variables $\mathbf{z} = (z_1, \ldots, z_n)$ and v.

$$\begin{array}{lll} \text{minimize} & \sum_{i \in [n]} a_i z_i + bv & \\ \text{subject to} & \sum_{i \in S} z_i + v \geq f(S), & \text{for } S \subseteq [n]. \end{array} \tag{6}$$

Let $\mathcal{P}$ denote the feasible region of LP (6). As the first step of our reduction, we reduce maximizing the set function $g_w(S) = f(S) + \sum_{i \in S} w_i$ to the separation problem for $\mathcal{P}$. Let $z_i = -w_i$ for each i. Notice that $(\mathbf{z}, v)$ is feasible (i.e., in $\mathcal{P}$) if and only if $v \geq \max_{S \subseteq [n]} f(S) - \sum_{i \in S} z_i$. Therefore, we can binary search for a value $\widetilde{v}$ such that $(\mathbf{z}, \widetilde{v})$ is almost feasible, but not quite. More precisely, let B denote the bit complexity of the $f(S)$'s and the w_i's, then binary search returns the exact optimal value of the set function maximization problem after $O(B)$ steps. We then set $\widetilde{v}$ to equal that value minus 2^{-B}. Feeding $(\mathbf{z}, \widetilde{v})$ to the separation oracle, we obtain a violated constraint which must correspond to the maximizer of $f(S) + \sum_{i \in S} w_i$.

As the second step of our reduction, we reduce the separation problem for $\mathcal{P}$ to solving LP (6) for every choice of objective coefficients a and b. This polynomial-time Turing reduction follows from the equivalence of separation and optimization [20].

Third, we reduce solving LP (6) for arbitrary a and b to the special case where $\mathbf{a} \in [0,1]^n$ and $b = 1$. The reduction involves a case analysis. (a) If any of the objective coefficients are negative, then the fact that $\mathcal{P}$ is upwards closed implies that LP (6) is unbounded. (b) If $b = 0$ and $a_i > 0$ for some i, then the LP is unbounded since we can make v arbitrarily small and z_i arbitrarily large. Normalizing by dividing by b, we have reduced the problem to the case when $b = 1$ and $a \geq 0$ (coordinate-wise). (c) Now suppose that $a_i > 1 = b$ for some i; the LP is unbounded by making z_i arbitrarily small and v arbitrarily large. This analysis leaves the case of $b = 1$ and $\mathbf{a} \in [0,1]^n$.

Fourth, we reduce LP (6) with parameters $\mathbf{a} \in [0,1]^n$ and $b = 1$ to its dual shown below, with variables p_S for $S \subseteq [n]$.

$$\begin{array}{lll} \text{maximize} & \sum_{S \subseteq [n]} p_S f(S) & \\ \text{subject to} & \sum_{S: i \in S} p_S \leq a_i, & \text{for } i \in [n]. \\ & \sum_{S \subseteq [n]} p_S = 1 & \\ & p_S \geq 0, & \text{for } S \subseteq [n]. \end{array} \tag{7}$$

We note that LP (7) is not the standard dual of LP (6); in particular the first set of constraints are inequality rather than equality constraints. It is easy to see that LP (7) is equivalent to the standard dual when f is monotone non-decreasing, and that an optimal solution to one of the two duals can be easily converted to an optimal solution of the other.

The fifth and final step of our reduction will reduce LP (7) to a private signaling problem in $\mathcal{I}(\mathcal{F})$. There are n receivers and two states of nature θ_0, θ_1 with $\lambda(\theta_0) = \lambda(\theta_1) = 1/2$. Define $u_i(\theta_1) = 1$ and $u_i(\theta_0) = -\frac{1}{a_i}$ $(-\infty$ if $a_i = 0)$ for all i. The sender's utility function satisfies $f_{\theta_1} = f_{\theta_0} = f$. Let φ^* be an optimal signaling scheme, in particular an optimal solution to the instantiation of LP (1) for our instance. Note that all receivers prefer action 1 in state θ_1; therefore, it is easy to see that φ^* can be weakly improved, without violating the persuasiveness constraints, by modifying it to always recommend action 1 to all receivers when in state θ_1. After this modification, φ^* is an optimal solution to the following LP, which optimizes over all signaling schemes satisfying $\varphi(\theta_1, [n]) = 1$.

$$\begin{array}{lll} \text{maximize} & \frac{1}{2} f([n]) + \frac{1}{2} \sum_{S \subseteq [n]} \varphi(\theta_0, S) f(S) & \\ \text{subject to} & \sum_{S: i \in S} \varphi(\theta_0, S) = x_{\theta_0, i}, & \text{for } i \in [n]. \\ & x_{\theta_0, i} \leq a_i, & \text{for } i = 1, \ldots, n. \\ & \sum_{S \subseteq [n]} \varphi(\theta_0, S) = 1 & \\ & \varphi(\theta_0, S) \geq 0, & \text{for } \theta \in \Theta; S \subseteq [n]. \end{array} \tag{8}$$

It is now easy to see that setting $p_S = \varphi^*(\theta_0, S)$ yields an optimal solution to LP (7) □

As an immediate corollary of Theorem 3.1, the optimal private signaling scheme can be computed efficiently when the sender's objective function is supermodular or anonymous. Recall that a set function $f : 2^{[n]} \to \mathbb{R}$ is anonymous if there exists a function $g : \mathbb{Z} \to \mathbb{R}$ such that $f(S) = g(|S|)$.

Corollary 3.2. *There is a polynomial time algorithm for computing the optimal private signaling scheme when the sender objective functions are either supermodular or anonymous.*

Proof. Since a supermodular function plus an additive function is still supermodular, and the problem of unconstrained supermodular maximization can be solved in polynomial time, Theorem 3.1 implies that the optimal private signaling scheme can also be computed in polynomial time. As for anonymous objectives, there is a simple algorithm for maximizing an anonymous set function plus an additive function. In particular, consider the problem of maximizing $f(S) + \sum_{i \in S} w_i$ where $f(S) = g(|S|)$. Observe that fixing $|S| = k$, the optimal set S_k corresponds to the k highest-weight elements in w. Enumerating all k and choosing the best S_k yields the optimal set. □

Finally, we make two remarks on Theorem 3.1, particularly on the reduction from optimal private signaling to set function maximization. First, we note that the assumption of monotonicity is not necessary to the reduction from signaling to optimization. In other words, even without the monotonicity assumption for the sender's objective function, one can still efficiently compute the optimal private signaling scheme for instances in $\mathcal{I}(\mathcal{F})$ given access to an oracle for maximizing $f(S) + \sum_{i \in S} w_i$ for any $f \in \mathcal{F}$ and weight vector w. This can be verified by adding back the persuasiveness constraints for action 0 to LP (1) and examining the corresponding dual, which has similar structure to LP (5). We omit the trivial details here. Consequently, Corollary 3.2 applies to non-monotone supermodular or anonymous functions as well.

Second, our reduction assumes that the prior distribution λ over the state of nature is explicitly given. This can be generalized to the sample oracle model. In particular, when our only access to λ is through random sampling, we can implement an ϵ-optimal and ϵ-persuasive[4] private signaling scheme in $poly(n, \frac{1}{\epsilon})$ time using an idea from [18] (assuming $u_i(\theta) \in [-1, 1]$). The algorithm is as follows: given any input state θ, we first take $poly(n, \frac{1}{\epsilon})$ samples from λ, and then solve LP (1) on the empirical distribution of the samples plus θ, with relaxed (by ϵ) persuasiveness constraints. Finally, we signal for θ as the solution to the LP suggests. The analysis of this algorithm is very similar to that in [18], thus is omitted here. Moreover, the bi-criteria loss is inevitable in this oracle model due to information theoretic reasons [18].

4 PRIVATE SIGNALING WITH SUBMODULAR OBJECTIVES

In this section we consider optimal private signaling for submodular sender objectives, and show that there is a polynomial time $(1 - \frac{1}{e})$-approximation scheme, modulo an additive loss of ϵ. This is almost the best possible: Babichenko and Barman [4] show that even in the special case of two states of nature, it is NP-hard to approximate the optimal private signaling scheme within a factor better than $(1 - \frac{1}{e})$ for monotone submodular sender objectives.

Theorem 4.1. *Consider private signaling with monotone submodular sender objectives. Let OPT denote the optimal sender utility. For any $\epsilon > 0$, a private signaling scheme achieving expected sender utility at least $(1 - \frac{1}{e})OPT - \epsilon$ can be implemented in* $\text{poly}(n, |\Theta|, \frac{1}{\epsilon})$ *time.*

The main technical challenge in proving Theorem 4.1 is that a private signaling scheme may have exponentially large support, as apparent from linear program (1). To overcome this difficulty, we prove a structural characterization of (approximately) optimal persuasive private schemes, i.e., solutions to LP (1). Roughly speaking, we show that LP (1) always has an approximately optimal solution with polynomial-sized support and nicely structured distributions. This greatly narrows down the solution space we need to search over. Recall that for any θ, $\varphi(\theta)$ is a random variable supported on $2^{[n]}$. We say $\varphi(\theta)$ is *K-uniform* if it follows a uniform distribution on a multiset of size K. The following lemma exhibits a structural property regarding (approximately) optimal solutions to LP (1). Notably, this property only depends on monotonicity of the sender's objective functions and does not depend on submodularity. Its proof is postponed to the end of this section.

[4] This is the natural relaxation of persuasiveness. In our setting, a receiver approximately maximizes his posterior expected payoff, to within an additive ϵ, by following the scheme's recommendation. This is regardless of the actions of other receivers.

Lemma 4.2. *Let f_θ be monotone for each θ. For any $\epsilon > 0$, there exists an ϵ-optimal persuasive private signaling scheme $\overline{\varphi}$ such that $\overline{\varphi}(\theta)$ is K-uniform for every θ, where $K = \frac{108n\log(2n|\Theta|)}{\epsilon^3}$.*

By Lemma 4.2, we can, without much loss, restrict our design of $\varphi(\theta)$ to the special class of K-uniform distributions. Note that a K-uniform distribution $\varphi(\theta)$ can be described by variables $x^j_{\theta,i} \in \{0,1\}$ for $i \in [n], j \in [K]$, where $x^j_{\theta,i}$ denotes the recommended action to receiver i in the j'th profile in the support of $\varphi(\theta)$. Relaxing our variables to lie in $[0,1]$, this leads to optimization problem (9), where $F_\theta(x) = \sum_{S\subseteq[n]} f_\theta(S)\prod_{i\in S} x_i \prod_{i\notin S}(1-x_i)$ is the multi-linear extension of f_θ.

$$\begin{array}{lll} \text{maximize} & \sum_{\theta\in\Theta}\frac{\lambda(\theta)}{K}\sum_{j=1}^{K}F_\theta(x^j_\theta) & \\ \text{subject to} & \sum_{\theta\in\Theta}\frac{\lambda(\theta)}{K}\sum_{j=1}^{K}x^j_{\theta,i}u_i(\theta)\geq 0, & \text{for } i=1,\dots,n. \\ & 0\leq x^j_{\theta,i}\leq 1, & \text{for } i=1,\dots,n;\theta\in\Theta. \end{array} \tag{9}$$

As a high level, our algorithm first approximately solves Program (9) and then signals according to its solution. Details are in Algorithm 1, which we instantiate with $\epsilon > 0$ and $K = \frac{108n\log(2n|\Theta|)}{\epsilon^3}$. Since $F_\theta(x) = \mathbf{E}_{S\sim p^I_x} f(S)$ where p^I_x is the independent distribution over $2^{[n]}$ with marginal probability x, the expected sender utility induced by the signaling scheme in Algorithm 1 is precisely the objective value of Program (9) at the obtained solution. Theorem 4.1 then follows from two claims: 1. The optimal objective value of Program (9) is ϵ-close to the optimal sender utility (Claim 4.3); 2. The continuous greedy process [12] can be applied to Program (9) to efficiently compute a $(1-1/e)$-approximate solution, modulo a small additive loss (Claim 4.4). We remark that Theorem 4.1 can be generalized to the sample oracle model, but with an additional ϵ-loss in persuasiveness constraints (assuming $u_i(\theta) \in [-1,1]$), using the idea from [18].

Algorithm 1 Private Signaling Scheme for Submodular Sender Objectives

---

Parameter: $\epsilon > 0$
Input: Prior distribution λ supported on Θ
Input: $u_i(\theta)$'s and value oracle access to the sender utility $f_\theta(S)$
Input: State of nature θ
Output: A set $S \subseteq [n]$ indicating the set of receivers who will be recommended action 1.
Approximately solve Program (9). Let $\{\overline{x}^j_{\theta,i}\}_{\theta\in\Theta, i\in[n], j\in[K]}$ be the returned solution.
Choose j from $[K]$ uniformly at random; For each receiver i, add i to S independently with probability $\overline{x}^j_{\theta,i}$.
Return S.

Claim 4.3. *When $K = \frac{108n\log(2n|\Theta|)}{\epsilon^3}$, the optimal objective value of Program (9) is at least $OPT - \epsilon$, where OPT is the optimal sender utility in private signaling.*

Proof. By Lemma 4.2, there exists a private signaling scheme $\overline{\varphi}$ such that: (i) $\overline{\varphi}$ achieves sender utility at least $OPT - \epsilon$; (ii) for each θ, there exists K sets $S^1_\theta, \dots, S^K_\theta \subseteq [n]$ such that $\overline{\varphi}_\theta$ is a uniform distribution over $\{S^1_\theta, \dots, S^K_\theta\}$. Utilizing $\overline{\varphi}$, we can construct a feasible solution $\overline{x}$ to Program (9) with objective value at least $OPT - \epsilon$. In particular, let $\overline{x}^j_\theta \in \{0,1\}^n$ be the indicator vector of the set S^j_θ, formally defined as follows: $\overline{x}^j_{\theta,i} = 1$ if and only if $i \in S^j_\theta$. By referring to the feasibility of $\overline{\varphi}$ to LP (1), it is easy to check that $\overline{x}^j_{\theta,i}$'s are feasible to Program (9). Moreover, since $F_\theta(\overline{x}^j_\theta) = f_\theta(S^j_\theta)$, the objective value of Program (9) at the solution $\overline{x}$ equals the objective value of Program (1) at the solution $\overline{\varphi}$, which is at least $OPT - \epsilon$. Therefore, the optimal objective value of Program (9) is at least $OPT - \epsilon$, as desired. □

Claim 4.4. *There is an algorithm that runs in* $\text{poly}(n, |\Theta|, K, \frac{1}{\epsilon})$ *time and computes a* $(1 - 1/e)$*-approximate solution, modulo an additive loss of* ϵ/e*, to Program* (9).

Proof. The objective function of Program (9) is a linear combination, with non-negative coefficients, of multilinear extensions of monotone submodular functions, thus is smooth, monotone and submodular. Moreover, the function value can be evaluated within error ϵ by $\text{poly}(n, \frac{1}{\epsilon})$ random samples, thus in $\text{poly}(n, \frac{1}{\epsilon})$ time. To apply Theorem 2.1, we only need to prove that the feasible region is a down-monotone polytope. Observe that there always exists an optimal solution to Program (9) such that $x_{\theta,i} = 1$ for any θ, i such that $u_i(\theta) \geq 0$. Therefore, w.l.o.g., we can pre-set these variables to be 1 and view the program as an optimization problem over $x_{\theta,i}$'s for all θ, i such that $u_i(\theta) < 0$. It is easy to check that these $x_{\theta,i}$'s form a down-monotone polytope determined by polynomially many constraints, as desired. □

Proof of Lemma 4.2

Our proof is based on the probabilistic method. Recall that the optimal private signaling scheme can be computed by solving the exponentially-large LP (1). Roughly speaking, given any optimal private scheme φ^*, we will take polynomially many samples from $\varphi^*(\theta)$ for each θ, and prove that with strictly positive probability the corresponding empirical distributions form a solution to LP (1) that is close to optimality. However, the sampling approach usually suffers from ϵ-loss in both the objective and persuasiveness constraints. It turns out that the ϵ-loss to persuasiveness constraints can be avoided in our setting with carefully designed pre-processing steps.

At a high level, to get rid of the ϵ-loss in persuasiveness constraints, there are two main technical barriers. The first is to handle the estimation error in the receiver's utilities, which is inevitable due to sampling. We address this by adjusting the φ^* to strengthen the persuasiveness constraints so that a small estimation error would still preserve the original persuasiveness constraints. The second barrier arises when some $x^*_{\theta,i}$'s are smaller than inverse polynomial of the precision ϵ, then $poly(\frac{1}{\epsilon})$ samples cannot guarantee a good multiplicative estimate of $x^*_{\theta,i}$. We deal with this issue by making "honest" recommendation, i.e., action 0, at these cases, and show that such modification will not cause much loss to our objective.

We first introduce some convenient notations. For any receiver i, let set $\Theta_i^+ = \{\theta : u_i(\theta) \geq 0\}$ be the set of states at which receiver i (weakly) prefers action 1; Similarly, $\Theta_i^- = \{\theta : u_i(\theta) < 0\}$ be the set of states at which receiver i prefers action 0. Moreover, for any state of nature θ, let $I_\theta^+ = \{i : u_i(\theta) \geq 0\}$ be the set of receivers who (weakly) prefer action 1 at state θ. It would be convenient to think of $\{\Theta_i^+\}_{i\in[n]}$ and $\{I_\theta^+\}_{\theta\in\Theta}$ as two different partitions of the set $\{(\theta, i) : u_i(\theta) \geq 0\}$.

Observe that by monotonicity there always exists an optimal signaling scheme φ^* such that $x^*_{\theta,i} = 1$ for every $\theta \in \Theta_i^+$. Let φ^* be such an optimal signaling scheme and OPT denote the optimal sender utility. We now adjust the scheme φ^* such that they do not degrade the objective value by much but is more suitable for applying concentration bounds for our probabilistic argument.

Adjustment 1: Always Recommend Action 0 When $x^*_{\theta,i} < \frac{\epsilon}{3n}$

Note that $x^*_{\theta,i} < \frac{\epsilon}{3n}$ only when $\theta \in \Theta_i^-$, i.e., action 0 is the best action for receiver i conditioned on θ. We first adjust φ^* to obtain a new scheme $\widetilde{\varphi}$, as follows: $\widetilde{\varphi}$ is the same as φ^* except that for every θ, i such that $x^*_{\theta,i} < \frac{\epsilon}{3n}$, $\widetilde{\varphi}$ always recommends action 0 to receiver i given the state of nature θ. As a result, $\widetilde{x}_{\theta,i}$ equals $x^*_{\theta,i}$ whenever $x^*_{\theta,i} \geq \frac{\epsilon}{3n}$ and equals 0 otherwise. Note that the signaling scheme still satisfies the persuasiveness constraints.

Naturally, each adjustment above, corresponding to θ, i satisfying $x^*_{\theta,i} < \frac{\epsilon}{3n}$, could decrease the objective value since the marginal probability of recommending action 1 decreases. Nevertheless, this loss, denoted as $L(\theta, i)$, can be properly bounded as follows:

$$\begin{aligned} L(\theta,i) &= \lambda(\theta)\cdot\left[\sum_{S:i\in S}\varphi^*(\theta,S)f_\theta(S) - \sum_{S:i\in S}\varphi^*(\theta,S)f_\theta(S\setminus\{i\})\right] \\ &\le \lambda(\theta)\cdot\left[\sum_{S:i\in S}\varphi^*(\theta,S)\right] \\ &= \lambda(\theta)x^*_{\theta,i} \le \frac{\lambda(\theta)\epsilon}{3n}. \end{aligned}$$

As a result, the aggregated loss of all the adjustments made in this step can be upper bounded by $\sum_{\theta\in\Theta}\sum_{i=1}^n \frac{\lambda(\theta)\epsilon}{3n} = \frac{\epsilon}{3}$. That is, the objective value of $\widetilde{\varphi}$ is at least $OPT - \frac{\epsilon}{3}$.

Adjustment 2: Strengthen the Persuasive Constraints by Scaling Down $x_{\theta,i}$'s

We now strengthen the persuasiveness constraints by further adjusting the $\widetilde{\varphi}$ obtained from above so that a small estimation error due to sampling will still maintain the original persuasiveness constraints. For any θ, we define $\varphi'(\theta,S) = \frac{3}{3+\epsilon}\widetilde{\varphi}(\theta,S)$ for all $S \neq I^+_\theta$, and define $\varphi'(\theta, I^+_\theta) = 1 - \sum_{S\neq I^+_\theta}\varphi'(\theta,S)$. Obviously, φ'_θ is still a distribution over $2^{[n]}$. Moreover, we claim that $x'_{\theta,i} = \mathbb{E}_{S\sim\varphi'_\theta}\mathbb{I}(i\in S) = 1$ whenever $\widetilde{x}_{\theta,i} = 1$, i.e., $\theta\in\Theta^+_i$. That is, given state θ, any receiver $i \in I^+_\theta$ will still aways be recommended action 1. This is because, to construct φ'_θ, we moved some probability mass from all other sets S to the set I^+_θ, therefore the marginal probability of recommending action 1 to any receiver $i\in I^+_\theta$ will not decrease. However, this marginal probability is originally 1 in the solution of $\widetilde{\varphi}$. Therefore, $x'_{\theta,i}$ still equals 1 for any $i\in I^+_\theta$, or equivalently, for any $\theta\in\Theta^+_i$. Similarly, we also have $x'_{\theta,i} = 0$ whenever $\widetilde{x}_{\theta,i} = 0$.

Let $Val(\varphi)$ denote the objective value of a scheme φ. We claim that $Val(\varphi') \ge OPT - \frac{2\epsilon}{3}$ and φ' satisfies $x'_{\theta,i} = \frac{3}{3+\epsilon}\widetilde{x}_{\theta,i}$ for every $\theta\in\Theta^-_i$. For any $i\in[n], \theta\in\Theta^-_i$ (which means $i\notin I^+_\theta$), we have

$$x'_{\theta,i} = \sum_{S:i\in S}\varphi'(\theta,S) = \frac{3}{3+\epsilon}\sum_{S:i\in S}\widetilde{\varphi}(\theta,S) = \frac{3}{3+\epsilon}\widetilde{x}_{\theta,i},$$

since the summation excludes the term $\varphi'(\theta, I^+_\theta)$. We now prove the guarantee of the objective value. Observe that $\varphi'(\theta, I^+_\theta) \ge \frac{3}{3+\epsilon}\widetilde{\varphi}(\theta, I^+_\theta)$ also holds in our construction. Therefore, we have

$$\begin{aligned} Val(\varphi') &= \sum_{\theta\in\Theta}\lambda(\theta)\sum_{S\subseteq[n]}\varphi'(\theta,S)f_\theta(S) \\ &\ge \frac{3}{3+\epsilon}\sum_{\theta\in\Theta}\lambda(\theta)\sum_{S\subseteq[n]}\widetilde{\varphi}(\theta,S)f_\theta(S) \\ &= \frac{3}{3+\epsilon}\cdot Val(\widetilde{\varphi}) \\ &\ge OPT - \frac{2\epsilon}{3}, \end{aligned}$$

where we used the upper bound $Val(\widetilde{\varphi}) \le 1$.

Existence of An ϵ-Optimal Solution of Small Support.

The above two steps of adjustment result in a feasible $\frac{2\epsilon}{3}$-optimal solution φ' to LP (1) that satisfies the following properties: (i) $x'_{\theta,i} = x^*_{\theta,i} = 1$ whenever $u_i(\theta) \geq 0$; (ii) $x'_{\theta,i} = \frac{3}{3+\epsilon}\widetilde{x}_{\theta,i} = \frac{3}{3+\epsilon}x^*_{\theta,i} \geq \frac{\epsilon}{4n}$ when $x^*_{\theta,i} \geq \frac{\epsilon}{3n}$ and $\theta \in \Theta_i^-$; (iii) $x'_{\theta,i} = 0$ when $x^*_{\theta,i} < \frac{\epsilon}{3n}$ and $\theta \in \Theta_i^-$. Utilizing such a φ' we show that there exists an ϵ-optimal solution $\overline{\varphi}$ to LP (1) such that the distribution $\overline{\varphi}_\theta$ is a K-uniform distribution for every θ, where $K = \frac{108n\log(2n|\Theta|)}{\epsilon^3}$.

Our proof is based on the probabilistic method. For each θ, independently take $K = \frac{108n\log(2n|\Theta|)}{\epsilon^3}$ samples from random variable $\varphi'(\theta)$, and let $\overline{\varphi}_\theta$ denote the corresponding empirical distribution. Obviously, $\overline{\varphi}_\theta$ is a K-uniform distribution. We claim that with strictly positive probability over the randomness of the samples, $\overline{\varphi}$ is feasible to LP (1) and achieves utility at least $Val(\varphi') - \frac{\epsilon}{3} \geq OPT - \epsilon$.

We first examine the objective value. Observe that the objective value $Val(\varphi')$ can be viewed as the expectation of the random variable $\sum_{\theta\in\Theta}\lambda(\theta)f_\theta(S_\theta) \in [0,1]$, where S_θ follows the distribution of $\varphi'(\theta)$. Our sampling procedure generates K samples for the random variable $\{S_\theta\}_{\theta\in\Theta}$, therefore by the Hoeffding bound, with probability at least $1 - \exp(-2K\epsilon^2/9) > 1 - 1/(2n|\Theta|)$, the empirical mean is at least $Val(\varphi') - \epsilon/3$.

Now we only need to show that all the persuasiveness constraints are preserved with high probability. First, observe that if $x'_{\theta,i} = 0$, then $\overline{x}_{\theta,i}$ induced by $\overline{\varphi}$ also equals 0. This is because $x'_{\theta,i} = \mathbf{E}_{S\sim\varphi'(\theta)}\mathbb{I}(i \in S) = 0$ implies that i is not contained in any S from the support of $\varphi'(\theta)$, therefore, also not contained in any sample. Similarly, $x'_{\theta,i} = 1$ implies $\overline{x}_{\theta,i} = 1$. To show that all the persuasiveness constraints hold, we only need to argue that $\overline{x}_{\theta,i} \leq x^*_{\theta,i}$ for every $\theta \in \Theta_i^-$ satisfying $x^*_{\theta,i} \geq \frac{\epsilon}{3n}$. This holds with high probability by tail bounds. In particular, $x'_{\theta,i} = \mathbf{E}_{S\sim\varphi'(\theta)}\mathbb{I}(i \in S)$ and we take K samples from $\varphi'(\theta)$. By the Chernoff bound, with probability at least

$$1 - \exp(-\frac{K\epsilon^2 x'_{\theta,i}}{27}) \geq 1 - \exp(-\frac{K\epsilon^3}{108n}) > 1 - \frac{1}{2n|\Theta|},$$

the empirical mean $\overline{x}_{\theta,i}$ is at most $(1+\epsilon/3)x'_{\theta,i} = x^*_{\theta,i}$.

Note that there are at most $n|\Theta|$ choices of such θ, i. By union bound, with probability at least $1 - (n|\Theta|+1)/(2n|\Theta|) > 0$, $\overline{\varphi}$ satisfies all the persuasiveness constraints thus is feasible to LP (1), and achieves objective value at least $Val(\varphi') - \frac{\epsilon}{3} \geq OPT - \epsilon$. So there must exist a feasible ϵ-optimal solution $\overline{\varphi}$ to LP (1) such that $\overline{\varphi}_\theta$ is K-uniform for every θ. This concludes our proof of Lemma 4.2.

5 AN OBLIVIOUS PRIVATE SCHEME FOR BINARY-STATE SETTINGS

In this section, we consider the special case with two states of nature, denoted by θ_0 and θ_1, and submodular sender utility functions. We show that a $(1-\frac{1}{e})$-approximate private signaling scheme can be *explicitly* constructed. The approximation ratio is tight by [4]. Moreover, the constructed signaling scheme has the following distinctive properties: (i) it signals independently to each receiver, which we term an *independent signaling scheme*; (ii) it is *oblivious* in the sense that it does not depend on the sender's utility function so long as it is monotone submodular. All proofs in this section are omitted due to space constraints, and can be found in the full version on arXiv.

In particular, we consider the independent signaling scheme φ_I that simply maximizes the probability of recommending action 1 to each receiver i independently. Such a scheme can be easily constructed by alway recommending action 1 to receiver i whenever $u_i(\theta) \geq 0$, and recommend action 1 with probability as high as possible subject to the persuasiveness constraints. We refer the reader to the Appendix for an explicit construction. Notice that φ_I is determined by the receiver's payoffs, and does *not* depend on the sender's payoff function $f_\theta(S)$. Nevertheless, the following theorem shows that φ_I is approximately optimal.

Theorem 5.1. *In the binary-state setting with monotone submodular sender objectives, the scheme φ_I is a $(1 - \frac{1}{e})$-approximate private signaling scheme.*

Theorem 5.1 follows from the following two lemmas. The proof of Lemma 5.2 employs the idea of the correlation gap from the robust stochastic optimization literature [1].

Lemma 5.2. *In the multiple-state setting with monotone submodular sender objectives, the optimal independent signaling scheme is a $(1 - \frac{1}{e})$-approximation to the optimal private signaling scheme.*

Lemma 5.3. *In the binary-state setting with monotone sender objectives, the φ_I defined above is the optimal independent signaling scheme.*

We conclude this section with two negative results regarding generalizing Theorem 5.1 to many states of natures. We first show that it is NP-hard to approximate the optimal independent signaling scheme within a factor better than $(1 - \frac{1}{e})$ when there are multiple states of nature (Proposition 5.4). We then prove that the best oblivious scheme can perform poorly in terms of the sender utility when there are multiple states (Proposition 5.5).

Proposition 5.4. *In the multiple-state setting with monotone submodular sender objectives, it is NP-hard to compute an independent signaling scheme that $(1 - 1/e)$-approximates the optimal independent scheme.*

Proposition 5.5. *For any integer $m > 1$, there exists an instance with m states of nature such that any oblivious private scheme can achieve at most $\frac{1}{\lfloor\sqrt{m-1}\rfloor}$ fraction of the optimal sender utility.*

6 INEFFICACY AND HARDNESS OF PUBLIC PERSUASION

In this section, we turn our attention to the design of optimal public signaling schemes, and show a stark contrast with private signaling, both in terms of their efficacy at optimizing the sender's utility, and in terms of their computational complexity.

We start with an example illustrating how the restriction to public signaling can drastically reduce the sender's expected utility. The example is notably simple: two states of nature, and a binary sender utility function which is independent of the state of nature. We show a multiplicative gap of $\Omega(n)$, and an additive gap of $1 - \frac{1}{\Omega(n)}$, between the expected sender utility from the optimal private and public signaling schemes, where n is the number of receivers.

Example 6.1 (Inefficacy of Public Signaling Schemes). Consider an instance with n identical receivers and two states of nature $\Theta = \{\mathrm{H}, \mathrm{L}\}$. Each receiver has the same utility function, defined as follows: $u_i(\mathrm{H}) = 1$ and $u_i(\mathrm{L}) = -1$, for all i. The state of nature H occurs with probability $\frac{1}{n+1}$, and L occurs with probability $\frac{n}{n+1}$. The sender's utility function is $f_\theta(S) = f(S) = \min(|S|, 1)$. In other words, the sender gets utility 1 precisely when at least one receiver takes action 1.

The persuasiveness constraints imply that each receiver can take action 1 with probability no more than $\frac{2}{n+1}$. This is achievable by always recommending action 1 to the receiver in state H, and recommending action 0 with probability $\frac{1}{n}$ in state L. The sender's expected utility depends on how these recommendations are correlated.

The optimal private scheme anti-correlates the receivers' recommendations in order to guarantee that at least one receiver takes action 1 always, which achieves an expected sender utility of 1, the maximum possible. Specifically, in state H the scheme always recommends action 1 to every receiver, and in state L the scheme chooses one receiver uniformly at random and recommends action 1 to that receiver, and action 0 to the other receivers.

We argue that no public scheme can achieve sender utility more than $\frac{2}{n+1}$. Indeed, since receivers are identical, our solution concept implies that they choose the same action for every realization of a public signal. Therefore, the best that a public scheme can do is to recommend action 1 to all receivers simultaneously with probability $\frac{2}{n+1}$ in aggregate, and recommend action 0 with the remaining probability, yielding an expected sender utility of $\frac{2}{n+1}$. This is achievable: in state **H** the scheme always recommends action 1 to every receiver, and in state **L** the scheme recommends action 1 to all receivers with probability $\frac{1}{n}$, and action 0 to all receivers with probability $1 - \frac{1}{n}$.

Our next result illustrates the computational barrier to obtaining the optimal public signaling scheme, even for additive sender utility functions. Our proof is inspired by a reduction in [14] for proving the hardness of computing the best posterior distribution over Θ, a problem termed *mixture selection* in [14], in a voting setting. That reduction is from the maximum independent set problem. Since a public signaling scheme is a combination of posterior distributions, one for each signal, we require a more involved reduction from a graph-coloring problem to prove our result.

THEOREM 6.2. *Consider public signaling in our model, with sender utility function $f_\theta(S) = f(S) = \frac{|S|}{n}$. It is NP-hard to approximate the optimal sender utility to within any constant multiplicative factor. Moreover, there is no additive PTAS for evaluating the optimal sender utility, unless P = NP.*

PROOF. We prove by reducing from the following NP-hard problem. In particular, [23] prove that for any positive integer k, any integer q such that $q \geq 2^k + 1$, and an arbitrarily small constant $\epsilon > 0$, given an undirected graph G, it is NP-hard to distinguish between the following two cases:

- **Case 1**: There is a q-colorable induced subgraph of G containing a $(1-\epsilon)$ fraction of all vertices, where each color class contains a $\frac{1-\epsilon}{q}$ fraction of all vertices.
- **Case 2**: Every independent set in G contains less than a $\frac{1}{q^{k+1}}$ fraction of all vertices.

Given graph G with vertices $[n] = \{1, \dots, n\}$ and edges E, we will construct a public persuasion instance so that the desired algorithm for approximating the optimal sender utility can be used to distinguish these two cases. Our construction is similar to that in [14]. We let there be n receivers, and let $\Theta = [n]$. In other words, both receivers and states of nature correspond to vertices of the graph. We fix the uniform prior distribution over states of nature — i.e., the realized state of nature is a uniformly-drawn vertex in the graph. We define the receiver utilities as follows: $u_i(\theta) = \frac{1}{2}$ if $i = \theta$; $u_i(\theta) = -1$ if $(i, \theta) \in E$; and $u_i(\theta) = -\frac{1}{4n}$ otherwise. We define the sender's utility function, with range $[0, 1]$, to be $f_\theta(S) = f(S) = \frac{|S|}{n}$. The following claim is proven in [14].

CLAIM 6.3 ([14]). *For any distribution $x \in \Delta_\Theta$, the set $S = \{i \in [n] : \sum_{\theta \in \Theta} x_\theta u_i(\theta) \geq 0\}$ is an independent set of G.*

Claim 6.3 implies that upon receiving any public signal with any posterior distribution x over Θ, the players who take action 1 always form an independent set of G. Therefore, if the graph G is from **Case 2**, the sender's expected utility in any public signaling scheme is at most $\frac{1}{q^{k+1}}$.

Now supposing that G is from **Case 1**, we fix the corresponding coloring of $(1-\epsilon)n$ vertices with colors $k = 1, \dots, q$, and we use this coloring to construct a public scheme achieving expected sender utility at least $\frac{(1-\epsilon)^2}{q}$. The scheme uses $q + 1$ signals, and is as follows: if θ has color k then deterministically send the signal k, and if θ is uncolored then deterministically send the signal 0. Given signal $k > 0$, the posterior distribution on states of nature is the uniform distribution over the vertices with color k — an independent set S_k of size $\frac{1-\epsilon}{q} n$. It is easy to verify that receivers $i \in S_k$ prefer action 1 to action 0, since $\sum_{\theta \in S_k} \frac{1}{|S_k|} u_i(\theta) = \frac{1}{|S_k|}(\frac{1}{2} - \frac{|S_k|-1}{4n}) > \frac{1}{4|S_k|} \geq 0$. Therefore, the sender's utility is $f(S_k) = \frac{|S_k|}{n} = \frac{1-\epsilon}{q}$ whenever $k > 0$. Since signal 0 has probability ϵ, we conclude that the sender's expected utility is at least $\frac{(1-\epsilon)^2}{q}$, as needed.

Since distinguishing **Case 1** and **Case 2** is NP-hard for arbitrarily large constants k and q, we conclude that it is NP-hard to approximate the optimal sender utility to within any constant factor. Moreover, by setting $k = 1, q = 3$, we conclude that the sender's utility cannot be approximated additively to within $(1 - \epsilon)^2/3 - 1/3^2 > 1/9$, and thus there is no additive PTAS, unless P=NP. □

REFERENCES

[1] Shipra Agrawal, Yichuan Ding, Amin Saberi, and Yinyu Ye. 2010. Correlation Robust Stochastic Optimization. In *Proceedings of the Twenty-first Annual ACM-SIAM Symposium on Discrete Algorithms (SODA '10)*. Society for Industrial and Applied Mathematics, Philadelphia, PA, USA, 1087–1096.

[2] Ricardo Alonso and Odilon Câmara. 2016. Persuading voters. *The American Economic Review* 106, 11 (2016), 3590–3605.

[3] Itai Arieli and Yakov Babichenko. 2016. Private Bayesian persuasion. *Available at SSRN 2721307* (2016).

[4] Yakov Babichenko and Siddharth Barman. 2017. Algorithmic Aspects of Private Bayesian Persuasion. In *Proceedings of the 2017 ACM Conference on Innovations in Theoretical Computer Science (ITCS)*.

[5] Arjada Bardhi and Yingni Guo. 2016. Modes of Persuasion Toward Unanimous Consent. *Working paper* (2016).

[6] Dirk Bergemann and Stephen Morris. 2016. Bayes correlated equilibrium and the comparison of information structures in games. *Theoretical Economics* 11, 2 (2016), 487–522.

[7] U. Bhaskar, Y. Cheng, Y. Kun Ko, and C. Swamy. 2016. Hardness Results for Signaling in Bayesian Zero-Sum and Network Routing Games. In *Proceedings of the 2016 ACM Conference on Economics and Computation (EC)*. ACM, 18.

[8] Peter Bro Miltersen and Or Sheffet. 2012. Send Mixed Signals: Earn More, Work Less. In *Proceedings of the 13th ACM Conference on Electronic Commerce (EC '12)*. ACM, New York, NY, USA, 234–247.

[9] Y. Cai, C. Daskalakis, and S M. Weinberg. 2012. An algorithmic characterization of multi-dimensional mechanisms. In *Proceedings of the forty-fourth annual ACM symposium on Theory of computing*. ACM, 459–478.

[10] Y. Cai, C. Daskalakis, and S M. Weinberg. 2012. Optimal multi-dimensional mechanism design: Reducing revenue to welfare maximization. In *2012 IEEE 53rd Annual Symposium on Foundations of Computer Science (FOCS)*. 130–139.

[11] Yang Cai, Constantinos Daskalakis, and S Matthew Weinberg. 2013. Understanding incentives: Mechanism design becomes algorithm design. In *Foundations of Computer Science (FOCS), 2013 IEEE 54th Annual Symposium on*. 618–627.

[12] Gruia Calinescu, Chandra Chekuri, Martin Pál, and Jan Vondrák. 2011. Maximizing a monotone submodular function subject to a matroid constraint. *SIAM J. Comput.* 40, 6 (2011), 1740–1766.

[13] Jimmy Chan, Seher Gupta, Fei Li, and Yun Wang. 2016. Pivotal Persuasion. *Available at SSRN* (2016).

[14] Yu Cheng, Ho Yee Cheung, Shaddin Dughmi, Ehsan Emamjomeh-Zadeh, Li Han, and Shang-Hua Teng. 2015. Mixture selection, mechanism design, and signaling. In *IEEE 56th Annual Symposium on Foundations of Computer Science (FOCS)*. IEEE, 1426–1445.

[15] Shaddin Dughmi. 2014. On the Hardness of Signaling. In *Proceedings of the 55th Symposium on Foundations of Computer Science (FOCS '14)*. IEEE Computer Society.

[16] S. Dughmi. 2017. Algorithmic Information Structure Design: A Survey. *ACM SIGecom Exchanges* 15 (2017), 2–24.

[17] S. Dughmi, N. Immorlica, and A. Roth. 2014. Constrained Signaling in Auction Design. In *Proceedings of the Twenty-five Annual ACM-SIAM Symposium on Discrete Algorithms (SODA)*. Society for Industrial and Applied Mathematics.

[18] Shaddin Dughmi and Haifeng Xu. 2016. Algorithmic Bayesian Persuasion. In *Proceedings of the Forty-eighth Annual ACM Symposium on Theory of Computing (STOC '16)*. ACM, 412–425.

[19] Yuval Emek, Michal Feldman, Iftah Gamzu, Renato Paes Leme, and Moshe Tennenholtz. 2012. Signaling Schemes for Revenue Maximization. In *Proceedings of the 13th ACM Conference on Electronic Commerce (EC '12)*. ACM, 514–531.

[20] Martin Grötschel, László Lovász, and Alexander Schrijver. 2012. *Geometric algorithms and combinatorial optimization*. Vol. 2. Springer Science & Business Media.

[21] Mingyu Guo and Argyrios Deligkas. 2013. Revenue Maximization via Hiding Item Attributes. In *Proceedings of the Twenty-Third International Joint Conference on Artificial Intelligence (IJCAI '13)*. AAAI Press, 157–163.

[22] Emir Kamenica and Matthew Gentzkow. 2011. Bayesian persuasion. *The American Economic Review* 101, 6 (2011), 2590–2615.

[23] Subhash Khot and Rishi Saket. 2012. Hardness of finding independent sets in almost q-colorable graphs. In *IEEE 53rd Annual Symposium on Foundations of Computer Science (FOCS)*. IEEE, 380–389.

[24] Luis Rayo and Ilya Segal. 2010. Optimal Information Disclosure. *Journal of Political Economy* 118, 5 (2010), pp. 949–987.

[25] Aviad Rubinstein. 2017. Honest signaling in zero-sum games is hard...and lying is even harder!. In *Proceedings of the 44th international colloquium conference on Automata, Languages, and Programming*. Springer-Verlag.

[26] Ina A Taneva. 2015. Information design. (2015).

[27] Yun Wang. 2015. Bayesian persuasion with multiple receivers. *Available at SSRN 2625399* (2015).

Fairness Incentives for Myopic Agents

SAMPATH KANNAN, University of Pennsylvania
MICHAEL KEARNS, University of Pennsylvania
JAMIE MORGENSTERN, University of Pennsylvania
MALLESH PAI, Rice University
AARON ROTH, University of Pennsylvania
RAKESH VOHRA, University of Pennsylvania
ZHIWEI STEVEN WU, University of Pennsylvania

We consider settings in which we wish to incentivize myopic agents (such as Airbnb landlords, who may emphasize short-term profits and property safety) to treat arriving clients *fairly*, in order to prevent overall discrimination against individuals or groups. We model such settings in both classical and contextual bandit models in which the myopic agents maximize rewards according to current empirical averages, but are also amenable to exogenous *payments* that may cause them to alter their choices. Our notion of fairness asks that more qualified individuals are never (probabilistically) preferred over less qualified ones [8].

We investigate whether it is possible to design inexpensive subsidy or payment schemes for a principal to motivate myopic agents to play fairly in all or almost all rounds. When the principal has full information about the state of the myopic agents, we show it is possible to induce fair play on every round with a subsidy scheme of total cost $o(T)$ (for the classic setting with k arms, $\tilde{O}(\sqrt{k^3T})$, and for the d-dimensional linear contextual setting $\tilde{O}(d\sqrt{k^3T})$). If the principal has much more limited information (as might often be the case for an external regulator or watchdog), and only observes the number of rounds in which members from each of the k groups were selected, but not the empirical estimates maintained by the myopic agent, the design of such a scheme becomes more complex. We show both positive and negative results in the classic and linear bandit settings by upper and lower bounding the cost of fair subsidy schemes.

1 INTRODUCTION

Recent uses of machine learning to make decisions of consequence for individual citizens (such as credit, employment and criminal sentencing) have led to concerns about the potential for these techniques to be discriminatory or unfair ([1], [4], [2]). Existing research has emphasized discriminatory outcomes originating from biases encoded into the data sets on which algorithms are trained.[1] In this paper, we consider a different source of unfairness in a stochastic bandit setting. The key friction we examine is when a forward-looking principal concerned with fairness (such as a regulator or technology platform) is not the one directly making the choices. Instead, a sequence of myopic agents are making the choices. To prevent unfair choices by these agents, the principal

[1] For example, Boston's Street Bump program, which uses smartphones to determine where road repairs are needed, results in certain areas being underserved because of the sparsity of smartphones traversing them ([12]).

This work is supported by the National Science Foundation, under grant CNS-0435060, grant CCR-0325197 and grant EN-CS-0329609. A full version of the paper can be found on the arXiv preprint site.

EC'17, June 26–30, 2017, Cambridge, Massachusetts, USA. ACM ISBN 978-1-4503-4527-9/17/06...$15.00.

DOI: http://dx.doi.org/10.1145/3033274.3085154

may offer targeted monetary rewards to agents to incentivize them to make different choices than they would have in the absence of such payments. Our concern in this paper is how much the principal needs to be prepared to pay in order to incentivize fair decisions by myopic agents.

To help fix ideas and motivate our problem, consider a challenge faced by peer-to-peer (P2P) platforms such as Prosper (P2P lending) or Airbnb (P2P short-stay housing). The platform cannot dictate to their users who to extend loans or rent to. Nevertheless, it may wish to ensure the choices its users make are fair, either to avoid criticism,[2] or to comply with existing regulations. P2P lending, for example, is subject to the Equal Credit Opportunity Act (ECOA). One provision of the Act is a requirement that lenders furnish reasons for adverse lending decisions. This obligation falls on the shoulders of the platform, and is challenging to discharge because the platform aggregates the decisions of many different lenders.[3]

In our model, an agent arrives at each period and must choose amongst a set of available alternatives. (For instance, the agent might be a lender on Prosper choosing to whom they will grant a loan, or an Airbnb host choosing which guest to accept.) We model this as a choice of which arm to pull in a stochastic bandit setting. We consider both the classic and contextual bandit cases. In the classic setting, each arm represents an individual, who will over time repeatedly be considered for service. In the contextual setting, each arm represents a group, and individual members of that group are represented by contexts (i.e. sets of individual features) which change at each round. A stochastic reward from the pull of an arm models the uncertain payoff associated with serving an individual (i.e. extending a loan, or having the individual rent). Each agent is myopic in the sense that they are occasional users of this platform, and thus care only about their current expected payoff. Because of myopia, the agent chooses the arm with the highest empirical mean in the classical case, and the context with the highest predicted reward according to a fixed one-shot learning procedure known to the principal (e.g. ordinary least squares regression, or ridge regression). Each agent is limited to pulling a single arm to model their limited resources (e.g., they may only have the funds to grant one loan, or host one guest on any particular night), and of course this simplifies our analysis.

The platform, motivated by a need for "accountability," would like to be fair. Our formal definition of fairness (Joseph et al. [8]) may be found in Section 2, and can be informally described as follows: Suppose an auditor knew the expected reward of each arm (or more generally, in the contextual case, of each context), and looked back at the platform's decisions. Fairness requires that a worse individual was never favored over a better individual. More precisely, if a platform is fair, then on any day t, the probability p_x that the agent pulls arm x is such that if the expected reward of x is at least that of x', then $p_x \geq p_{x'}$. Fairness as defined in this paper does not address inequities "outside the model." For example, if one group has lower expected payoff for every context than another, perhaps due to historical inequities, and there are no additional features available to the learning algorithm, our notion of fairness permits the agent to favor the higher expected group. In this sense our fairness notion is aligned with (apparent) meritocracy.

Intuitively, there are two impediments to fairness in this model. First, neither the platform nor the agents know the distribution of rewards of each arm. If these were known, the problem would be trivial: it would be both fair and agent-optimal to always pull the arm with highest expected reward. Second, the agents are myopic – they have no incentive to directly invest in fairness or learning.

We examine whether it is possible for the platform, hereafter called the *principal*, to incentivize the agents to make fair choices by offering the agent payments for selecting particular arms. These

[2] Airbnb has very recently received scrutiny over both anecdotal reports and systematic studies of racist behavior by landlords on their platform ([5]). This study also suggests that myopia may play a role in discrimination, in the sense that landlords with no prior exposure to minority renters were more likely to discriminate.

[3] Lenders on Prosper must agree to comply with the relevant provisions of the ECOA, but there is still evidence of discrimination; see [14].

	Full Information	Partial Information
Classical	$\tilde{O}(\sqrt{k^3T})$ cost	$O(\sqrt{T})$ cost for $k = 2$ $\Omega(T)$ cost for $k \geq 3$ $\tilde{O}(\sqrt{k^3T})$ cost allowing $\tilde{O}(k^2)$ unfair rounds
Linear Contextual	$\tilde{O}(d\sqrt{k^3T})$ cost	$o(T)$ unfair rounds $\to \Omega(T)$ cost $o(T)$ cost $\to \Omega(T)$ unfair rounds

Table 1. Summary of cost to incentivize perfect fairness and fairness in all but a limited number of rounds.

payments can be randomized. Because the agents behave identically in our model (they are all myopic), we treat them as if they are a single myopic entity, whom we term the *agent.* We investigate how much information a principal needs to incentivize fair behavior. Characterizing the information requirements is important, since sometimes the principal may be an external regulator or other entity tasked with oversight without the full information available to the platform. At one extreme, called partial information, we suppose the principal observes only which decisions were made by the agent in each of the previous rounds but not the rewards. In the P2P context, rewards might be unobservable because the reward an agent experiences is a function of both observed characteristics of the borrower or renter and a private type of the agent. At the other extreme of full information, the principal has the same information as the agent.

We ask each of these questions in both the classic and linear contextual bandits settings. In the classic case, individual i is better than individual j if the mean of distribution i is higher than that of distribution j. In the contextual case, individual i on day t is represented by a set of features, or a context x_i^t, and that individual's expected reward is defined as $f_i(x_i^t)$ for some $f_i \in C$.

1.1 Our Results

Table 1 summarizes our results for characterizing the cost of incentivizing fair play in myopic agents. Informally, we show a stark separation: in the partial information model, any fair payment scheme must cost $\Omega(T)$; while in the full information model there are payment schemes which cost $\tilde{O}(d\sqrt{k^3T})$. In both the classic and contextual settings, the full information upper bounds effectively incentivize the agent to play known fair algorithms. The lower bounds for the partial information model look somewhat different. For the classic setting, our lower bound simply shows that the first round at which the principal doesn't offer a payment of 1 will be unfair with constant probability; for the contextual setting, *every* round must either be unfair or offer $\Omega(1)$ payment.

We additionally show that in partial information model, the classic problem is somewhat easier in two cases. When there are only 2 arms, we give a simple payment scheme that only incurs a cost of $O(\sqrt{T})$ and guarantees with high probability that the agent is fair at every round. Even when $k \geq 3$, a principal who is allowed $\tilde{O}(k^2)$ unfair rounds can design a payment scheme which costs only $\tilde{O}(\sqrt{k^3T})$.[4] In the full information model, we exhibit a payment scheme for the principal which, with high probability, is fair in *every* round, and has cost $\tilde{O}(\sqrt{k^3T})$.

It is interesting to observe that all our payment schemes that guarantee fairness (either in each period, or except at a constant number of periods) and achieve sublinear costs also induce the agent to play so as to experience sublinear regret. If we think of sub-linear regret as a proxy for efficiency, our full information results say we can achieve *both* efficiency and fairness with subsides that grow

[4]In other words, we show that by allowing a constant number of unfair rounds, independent of T, one can achieve sublinear costs.

slowly over time. Under certain conditions, this is also possible in the partial information setting, which does not require the principal to "open the books" of the agent.

1.2 Related Work

Our work is closely related to the literature on incentivizing experimentation in bandit settings. In these papers, a sequence of agents arrives one at a time and each is allowed to select an arm to pull. Each agent "lives" for one period and therefore pulls the arm that has the highest current estimated payoff given the history. The agents' myopia means that they do not explore sufficiently and the patient principal must encourage it.

In this context, Frazier et al. [6] explore the achievable set between the monetary rewards the principal must pay to incentivize exploration and the time discounted expected reward to the principal. In this paper the history of actions and outcomes is observed by the principal and there is, therefore, no examination of what happens with limited information. More importantly, there is no consideration of fairness, which is our primary interest.

A different string of papers does not explicitly allow for monetary payments, but instead the principal discloses information about past agents' realized rewards to the future agents, see e.g. Kremer et al. [9], a more general exploration in Mansour et al. [10, 11], or an analytical solution in a continous time Poisson bandit setting by Che and Horner [3] and the same in a discrete time setting in Papanastasiou et al. [13]. The key point of departure for our work is that for us, the principal is not explicitly interested in the long term reward of the agent, but is instead interested in promoting "fairness" (although this will incidentally have the property of increasing long-term reward of the agent by encouraging experimentation).

Joseph et al. [8] originally proposed our definition of contextual fairness. They consider the tradeoffs between requiring this form of fairness and achieving no-regret in both classic and contextual bandit settings. This notion was also employed in Joseph et al. [7], when specialized to the linear contextual bandits case.

2 PRELIMINARIES

A principal faces a sequence of homogeneous myopic agents, each operating in a *contextual bandit* setting. For simplicity, we view the agents as a single agent repeatedly making myopic choices.

2.1 Contextual Bandits

Let $\{k\}$ refer to a set of arms. In each round $t \in [T]$, an adversary reveals to the agent a *context* $x_j^t \in \mathcal{X}$, where $\mathcal{X}$ is the common domain of contexts, for each arm $j \in [k]$.

Fix some class C of functions of the form $f : \mathcal{X} \to [0,1]$. Associated with each arm j is a function $f_j \in C$, unknown to both the agent and the principal.[5]. An agent who chooses an arm j in period t with context is x_j^t receives a stochastic reward $r_j^t \sim \mathcal{F}_j^{x_j^t}$, where $\mathbb{E}[r_j^t] = f_j(x_j^t)$, for some distribution $\mathcal{F}_j^{x_j^t}$ over $[0,1]$.

Remark 1 (Linear Contextual Bandits). The results in this paper which involve contexts are for the case where the set of contexts $\mathcal{X} = \{x \in [0,1]^d : ||x|| \leq 1\}$ for some number $d > 0$, and

$$C = \left\{ f_j : \text{ there exists some } \theta_j \in [0,1]^d, ||\theta_j|| \leq 1, \text{ s.t. } f_j(x_j) = \langle \theta_j, x_j \rangle, \ \forall x_j \in \mathcal{X} \right\}.$$

Remark 2 (Classic Bandits). The *classic* bandits problem is a special case of the contextual bandits problem where the set of possible contexts is a singleton. Then $\mathcal{F}_j^{\cdot} = \mathcal{F}_j$ and $r_j^t \sim \mathcal{F}_j$.

[5]Often, the contextual bandit problem is defined so that there is a single function f associated with all of the arms. Our model is only more general.

In the running example of P2P lending, $\mathcal{X}$ represents possible profiles of attributes that a lender can observe about a potential borrower. The exact relationship between a profile of attributes at time t, denoted x_j^t, and the expected reward earned from extending a loan to a borrower with this profile is $f_j(x_j^t)$; this functional form is unknown to the lender, the platform, and the agent.

2.2 The Myopic Agent and the Principal

In each period t, the principal can offer a vector of payments $p^t \in \mathfrak{R}_+^k$ to the agent. Here p_i^t is to be interpreted as the monetary incentive the agent receives from the principal if they selects arm i on top of any reward that would accrue from the arm itself.

We assume the agent makes *myopic* choices facing empirical estimates of the reward from each arm (we describe how these empirical estimates are constructed momentarily). We use $\hat{\mu}_i^t$ to denote the empirical estimated reward for selecting arm i in round t. When the agent receives a proposed subsidy vector $p^t \sim \gamma^t(\cdot)$, they choose the arm which maximizes the sum of empirical expected reward and payment, i.e. chooses $i^t \in \arg\max_i(\hat{\mu}_i^t + p_i^t)$. This is the sense in which the agent is myopic—they maximize (their estimate of) today's net reward plus payment, with no concern for the future. Note that we assume that rewards are expressed in monetary terms, i.e. that they are directly comparable to offered payments.

For concreteness and without loss of generality, we fix a tie-breaking rule—if $M = \arg\max_i(\hat{\mu}_i^t + p_i^t)$ contains multiple elements, the agent chooses uniformly at random amongst the members of M that also maximize payment, i.e. from the set $\arg\max_{i \in M} p_i^t$.[6] The principal experiences cost $p_{i^t}^t$ at round t, and total cost $\sum_{t=1}^T p_{i^t}^t$ over the course of T rounds. The payments offered by the principal, and the empirical estimates of the agent, depend on what they know about past choices and outcomes. We define these next.

2.3 Information and Histories

The agent will, in any period t, recall history $h^t \in \left(\mathcal{X}^k \times \mathfrak{R}_+^k \times [k] \times [0,1]\right)^{t-1} = \mathcal{H}^t$. This is a record of the previous $t-1$ rounds experienced by the agent: $t-1$ 4-tuples encoding the realization of the contexts for each arm in a given period, the payments the principal offered, the arm chosen, and the realized reward observed.

In the linear contextual case, let $\hat{\theta}_i^t$ represent an estimate of the linear model θ_i based on the history h^t (this could, for example, be the ordinary least-squares or regularized ridge regression estimator — the important thing is that whichever method is used is known to the principal). The myopic decision maker, at day t, when facing contexts $x_1^t, \ldots, x_k^t$ will have empirical estimated reward $\hat{\mu}_i^t = \langle \hat{\theta}_i^t, x_i^t \rangle$. In the classic setting,

$$\hat{\mu}_i^t = \frac{\sum_{t'<t} r_i^{t'}}{|\{t' < t : i \text{ played in round } t'\}|}$$

that is, it represents the empirical average for the set of previous rewards observed from arm i in previous rounds.

Note that during the first several rounds, the myopic reward estimates $\hat{\mu}_i^t$ are not necessarily defined, e.g. if in the classic setting, the agent has not yet observed any rewards from arm i, or if in the linear contextual case, the agent has not observed sufficiently many reward/context pairs to uniquely define the OLS estimator. To get around this issue, we assume that the agent has previously observed sufficiently many observations from each arm to make these estimates well

[6]Our results do not depend in any important way on the particulars of the tie-breaking rule—we chose this one to simplify parts of the lower bound proof.

defined — i.e. at least one observation per arm in the classic case, and observations corresponding to contexts that combined form a full rank matrix in the linear case.

We consider two information models for the principal. In the *full information* model, the principal observes everything the agent observes, i.e. there is no information asymmetry between the two. In the *partial information* model, the principal observes neither the contexts faced by the agents, nor the realized reward of the arm the agent pulled. We will denote this by $\underline{h}^t \in \left(\mathfrak{R}_+^k \times [k]\right)^{t-1} = \underline{\mathcal{H}}^t$. The principal's information scheme is a function of the information they have.

In what follows, we define various notions of performance of algorithm. This is without loss: the payments that the principal offers, and the resulting choices made by the agents choices, taken together, can be thought of as an algorithm making choices in a stochastic bandit setting.

2.4 Fairness and Regret

A standard method for measuring the performance of a bandit algorithm is to measure its *regret*. If one knew $\{f_j\}_{j\in[k]}$, selecting the arm with highest expected reward in each period would be optimal. Fix an algorithm $\mathcal{A}$ and let π^t be the distribution over arms at round t of the algorithm: the **regret** of $\mathcal{A}$ is the difference between the reward of the optimal policy, and the reward of the agent:

$$\text{Regret}(x^1, \ldots, x^T) = \sum_t \max_j \left(f_j(x_j^t)\right) - \mathbb{E}_{i^t \sim \pi^t}[\sum_t f_{i^t}(x_{i^t}^t)].$$

We say that $\mathcal{A}$ satisfies regret bound $R(T)$, if $\max_{x^1,\ldots,x^T} \text{Regret}(x^1, \ldots, x^T) \leq R(T)$.

We denote by $\pi_{j|h^t}^t$ the probability that $\mathcal{A}$ chooses arm j after observing contexts x^t in period t, given h^t. For economy, we will often drop the superscript t on the history when referring to the distribution over arms: $\pi_{j|h}^t := \pi_{j|h^t}^t$.

We now define what it means for an algorithm $\mathcal{A}$ to be fair in a particular round t. Informally, this will mean that $\mathcal{A}$ will play arm i with higher probability than arm j in round t only if i has higher *true* expected reward than j in round t.

Definition 2.1 (Round Fairness). Fix some history h^t. Recall $\pi_{j|h^t}^t$ is the probability that $\mathcal{A}$ plays arm j in round t given the history h^t. We will say $\mathcal{A}$ is fair in round t if, for any context x^t, for all pairs of arms $j, j' \in [k]$,

$$\pi_{j|h}^t > \pi_{j'|h}^t \text{ only if } f_j(x_j^t) > f_{j'}(x_{j'}^t).$$

Similarly, a payment scheme is fair in round t if the selection by the myopic agent under the payment distribution is fair.

Remark 3. When this definition is specialized to the classic (noncontextual) case, the reward distributions do not vary with time, i.e. $\mathcal{F}_j^t = \mathcal{F}_j$ for all t. Thus, "noncontextual" fairness reduces to guaranteeing that if arm i is played with higher probability than arm j, it must be that the average reward drawn from distribution $\mathcal{F}_i$ is higher than the average reward drawn from distribution $\mathcal{F}_j$.

Remark 4. To be clear about this definition in the partial information model, and what we mean by probabilities: note that the "algorithm" has access to h^t at the beginning of time t. By this we mean that, the principal has access to $\underline{h}^t$. The principal then offers payments to the agent, possibly randomizing. The agent sees the full history h^t, and the realized payments drawn from a distribution, and makes a choice. The principal's randomization, and then, if there are ties, the agent's randomization in period t, can be amalgamated into a net probability of each arm being selected in period t after history h^t. These are the π's that the definition refers to.

We now introduce a notion of fairness which holds at every round with high probability over the history of observed rewards.

Definition 2.2 (Contextual Fairness). $\mathcal{A}(\cdot)$ is **fair** if, for any input $\delta \in (0,1)$, for all sequences of contexts, $x^1, \ldots, x^t$ and all reward distributions $\mathcal{F}_1^t, \ldots, \mathcal{F}_k^t$, with probability at least $1-\delta$ over the realization of the history h, for all rounds $t \in [T]$, $\mathcal{A}(\delta)$ is fair in round t.

Contextual fairness, introduced in Joseph et al. [8], formalizes the idea that highly qualified individuals should be treated at least as well as less qualified individuals. Here, an individual's qualification is measured in terms of their expected reward for $\mathcal{A}$. If two individuals have different profiles (or contexts) but generate the same expected reward to the learner, this definition enforces that both be played with *equal* probability every round. We also introduce a relaxation of contextual fairness, which allows for an algorithm to have some number of unfair rounds.

Definition 2.3 (g-Contextual Fairness). $\mathcal{A}(\delta)$ is g-**fair** if, for any input $\delta \in (0,1)$, for all sequences of contexts, and all reward distributions, with probability at least $1-\delta$ over the realization of the history h, for all but g rounds $t \in [T]$, $\mathcal{A}(\delta)$ is fair in round t.

Our principal is willing to incentivize the agent's behavior to ensure contextual fairness (and, incidentally, low regret). We investigate what subsidy schemes incentivize fair choices by a myopic agent, and the cumulative cost of such subsidies. We show this answer depends upon the kind of information the principal has access to: incentivizing fair play with partial information is in general very expensive, while incentivizing fair play under full information need not be so.

3 A PRINCIPAL WITH PARTIAL INFORMATION CANNOT ENSURE T FAIR ROUNDS

In this section, we give a lower bound on the total payments needed in the partial information setting to ensure contextual fairness in every round. In fact, we don't even need to move to the contextual case: this section focuses on the classic bandit setting (where the context x_j^t is invariant with respect to t for each arm j). We show that in the partial information setting, any principal who incentivizes a myopic agent to satisfy contextual fairness in each round must incentivize uniformly random play in each of the T rounds, which has cumulative cost $\Omega(T)$.

Theorem 3.1. *Suppose $k \geq 3$. There is an instance such that any fair payment scheme in the partial information model must, with probability $1-\delta$, (where δ is the fairness parameter passed to the principal) spend $\Omega(T)$ in payments over T rounds and incur regret $\Omega(T)$.*

The lower bound proceeds from the following idea: at the first round, the principal has no information about what the instance is. Hence, in order to guarantee fairness against all instances, they must proceed cautiously and use a payment scheme that is able to induce uniformly random play (the only distribution that is fair for all instances) for every possible realization of empirical means. Because empirical means can range between 0 and 1, this will cost 1. However, because this payment distribution (by design) induces identical behavior on every possible instance, it does not allow the principal to learn anything about the instance. Thus, in every round before which fair play has been guaranteed, the principal has the same informational disadvantage. By induction, therefore, they must induce uniformly random play at every round, at a cost of 1 per round.

We show that fairness at every round, against all instances is equivalent to the payment scheme in each round being what we term *peaked.* A peaked payment rule is one that can always incentivize the play of some arm regardless of the empirical means the myopic agent currently has. This is equivalent to saying that there is some arm $i \in [k]$ for which $p_i \geq p_{i'} + 1$ for all $i' \neq i$. This will imply the payment scheme must spend $\Omega(1)$ in each round to incentivize fair play, or $\Omega(T)$ in total.

Definition 3.2 (Peaked). Let $p \in \mathbb{R}^k$. If for some $i \in [k]$, $p_i \geq \max_{i' \neq i} p_{i'} + 1$, we say p is *peaked.* If

$$\mathbb{P}_{p \sim \mathcal{D}}[p \text{ is peaked}] = 1$$

then we call distribution $\mathcal{D}$ peaked.

Observation 1. If a principal uses a peaked distribution $\mathcal{D}$ in a round, they learn nothing about the instance the agent faces from the agent's play in that round.

Proof. By Definition 3.2, every payment scheme drawn from $\mathcal{D}$ is peaked. In other words, for every $p_\ell \sim \mathcal{D}$: there is some i_ℓ such that $p_{i_\ell} \geq \max_{i' \neq i_\ell} p_{i'} + 1$. Thus, the myopic agent will choose i_ℓ when presented with p_ℓ regardless of the instance the agent faces. □

The main idea behind Theorem 3.1 is in proving that any fair payment scheme must be peaked in every round. Technically, we use the fact that the principal learns nothing about the instance from a peaked distribution to allow us freedom to design a lower bound instance as a function of the first distribution $\mathcal{D}^t$ deployed by the principal that is not peaked. Because this distribution, by virtue of being the first non-peaked distribution, cannot be a function of the underlying instance, we are unconstrained in our ability to tailor the instance as a function of $\mathcal{D}^t$. We then show this instance forces an unfair round for $\mathcal{D}^t$; we can conclude that with probability $1-\delta$, the principal must *never* deploy any distribution over payments that is not peaked.

Lemma 3.3. *For any fairness parameter δ, a fair payment scheme must with probability $1-\delta$ generate a sequence of payment distributions $\mathcal{D}^1, \ldots, \mathcal{D}^T$ such that each D^t is peaked.*

We now conclude the proof of Theorem 3.1 before presenting the proof of Lemma 3.3.

Proof. Lemma 3.3 implies that a fair payment scheme must with probability $1-\delta$ generate T peaked payment distributions. Since $\max_i p_i \geq \max_{j \neq i} p_j + 1$, and $\hat{\mu}_i^t \in [0, 1]$ for all i, the payment scheme's largest payment is always at least 1, and is always accepted. Thus, the myopic agent will receive a payment of at least 1 in every round, for a total cost of $\Omega(T)$.

To prove the regret of this payment scheme may be $\Omega(T)$ on some instances, consider each of the k instances in which one arm has mean 1 and the remaining $k-1$ arms have mean 0. By Observation 1, the principal has no information about which of these instances is realized. Therefore to be to be fair with respect to all of these instances, each arm must be assigned the largest payment with equal probability, which induces uniformly random play amongst all k arms, $\Omega(1)$ regret per round, and cumulative regret $\Omega(T)$. □

We now present the proof of the main lemma for this section: that in order for a payment distribution to be fair, it must be peaked. Informally, we first show that any fair payment distribution must be "invariant under permutation": any coordinate i should have have an equal probability of having the largest payment, and have an equal probability of j being the second-largest payment with margin c, for each value of j and c. We then show in the first round t at which the payment distribution is unpeaked, $\mathcal{D}^t$ is unfair for some instance I constructed as a function of $\mathcal{D}^t$.

Proof of Lemma 3.3. We consider some round t. Suppose that for every round $t' < t$, the payment distribution $\mathcal{D}^{t'}$ was peaked. If the payment distribution $\mathcal{D}^t = \mathcal{D}$ at round t is fair, we show that it too must be peaked. Observe that by Observation 1, $\mathcal{D}$ must be defined independently of the underlying instance I, and because fairness is defined in the worst case over instances, we continue to have complete freedom in choosing I.

We first claim that in round t, if $\mathcal{D}$ is fair, for any two distinct $i, i', \in [k]$ and any $c \in [0, 1]$, that

$$\mathbb{P}_{p \sim \mathcal{D}}[p_i \geq \max_{\ell \in [k], \ell \neq i} p_\ell + c] = \mathbb{P}_{p \sim \mathcal{D}}[p_i' \geq \max_{\ell \in [k], \ell \neq i'} p_\ell + c]. \tag{1}$$

Suppose Equation 1 does not hold. We construct an instance for which $\mathcal{D}$ will not be fair, a contradiction. Suppose the left-hand side is larger than the right-hand side. Consider an instance where $\mu_i = \mu_{i'} = 1 - c$, and all other arms (of which there is at least 1) have means $\mu_j = 1$. Suppose further that the distribution over i's reward is deterministic point mass at $1 - c$, whereas i''s reward distribution yields reward $1 - c + \epsilon$ with probability $\frac{1}{2}$ and $1 - c - \epsilon$ with probability $\frac{1}{2}$. Then, with probability at least $\frac{1}{4}$, $\hat{\mu}_{i'} < \hat{\mu}_i$.[7] Thus, with probability $\frac{1}{4}$ over the history of rewards observed, i wins with higher probability than i', since i wins whenever i's payment is the largest by c, and i' can only win when i''s payment is the largest by at least c for any history for which $\hat{\mu}_{i'} < \mu_{i'}$. This is a violation to fairness for $\delta < \frac{1}{4}$.

Notice that Equation 1 implies that each arm receives the highest payment with probability $\frac{1}{k}$, and that this also holds conditioning on any gap c between highest and second-highest payments.

Now, since $\mathcal{D}$ is not peaked,

$$\mathbb{P}_{p \sim \mathcal{D}}[\exists i : p_i \geq \max_{i' \neq i} p_{i'} + 1] < 1.$$

Define c as follows:

$$c = \sup_{y \geq 0} \text{ s.t. } \mathbb{P}_{p \sim \mathcal{D}}[\exists i : p_i \geq \max_{i' \neq i} p_{i'} + y] = 1.$$

Notice, this implies that:

$$\forall \epsilon > 0, \exists \eta > 0 \text{ s.t. } \mathbb{P}_{p \sim \mathcal{D}}[\exists i : p_i \geq \max_{i' \neq i} p_{i'} + c + \epsilon] \leq 1 - \eta. \tag{2}$$

We now construct an instance as a function of c. There are two cases – either $c > 0$ or $c = 0$.

Case 1: $c > 0$. Consider the following instance, defined in terms of c and a constant $0 < \epsilon < c$: arm 1 has mean $1 - c$ with deterministic rewards, arm 2 has mean $1 - c$ with reward $1 - c - \epsilon$ with probability $\frac{1}{2}$ and reward $1 - c + \epsilon$ with probability $\frac{1}{2}$, and arms $3, \ldots, k$ have a deterministic reward of 1. Note that by definition of c, and the deterministic nature of arm 1's distribution, we have that for every history h, $\pi^t_{1|h} \geq 1/k$. By the fairness constraint, we must therefore also have that for every other arm $i > 1$, $\pi^t_{i|h} \geq 1/k$, since no other arm has lower mean. This implies that for every arm i, it must be that $\pi^t_{i|h} = 1/k$.

Note, as we argued in footnote 7, that with probability at least $\frac{1}{4}$, for any t, $\hat{\mu}_2 < \hat{\mu}_1 = 1-c$, by construction. In this case, there is some $\epsilon' > 0$ such that arm 2 is not played unless $p_2 > \max_{i \neq 2} p_i + c + \epsilon'$. However, by definition of c, this occurs with probability strictly less than $1/k$, contradicting the assertion that $\mathcal{D}$ is a fair distribution.

Case 2: $c = 0$. Consider the instance in which arms $1, \ldots, k-1$ have mean $\frac{1}{2}$ and deterministic reward distributions, while arm k has mean $1/2$, and stochastic rewards that are $\frac{1}{2} - \epsilon$ with probability $\frac{1}{2}$ and $\frac{1}{2} + \epsilon$ with probability $\frac{1}{2}$. Note that in this case, fairness requires that all arms be played with identical probabilities. With probability at least $\frac{1}{4}$, arm k has empirical mean lower than its true mean. Condition on $\hat{\mu}_k < \mu_k$. In this case, since $c = 0$, with arm k must be selected with probability less than $\frac{1}{k}$ since the payment to arm k will be strictly less than $\mu_k - \hat{\mu}_k$ with strictly positive probability (2), and therefore unfair. □

3.1 A Fair Payment Scheme for Two Arms

We now show that having at least three arms is necessary for our lower bound result. Indeed, in the classic stochastic partial information setting with two arms there exists a simple payment scheme that can ensure fairness in every round while achieving sublinear regret and payment.

The key idea in this payment scheme is to maintain confidence intervals around empirical reward means for the two arms. The following lemma tells us how to construct confidence intervals.

[7] For t odd it is $\frac{1}{2}$, for even t it is $\frac{1}{2}\left(1 - \cdot\binom{t}{t/2}\right) \cdot \frac{1}{2^t} \geq \frac{1}{4}$, achieved at $t = 2$ and increasing in t.

Lemma 3.4 (Lemma 1, [8]). *Suppose arm i has been pulled n_i^t times before round t. Let $\ell_i^t = \hat{\mu}_i^t - \sqrt{\frac{\ln\frac{(\pi(t+1))^2}{3\delta}}{2n_i^t}}$, and $u_i^t = \hat{\mu}_i^t + \sqrt{\frac{\ln\frac{(\pi(t+1))^2}{3\delta}}{2n_i^t}}$. Then, with probability at least $1-\delta$, for every $i \in [k], t \in [T]$, $\ell_i^t \le \mu_i \le u_i^t$.*

In the light of this result, we will define the function ConfidenceWidth as follows, which will also be useful for describing our payment scheme in the following section.

$$\textsc{ConfidenceWidth}(\delta, t, n) = 2\sqrt{\frac{\ln\left(\frac{(\pi\cdot(t+1))^2}{3\delta}\right)}{n}} \tag{3}$$

Given this confidence width function, our payment scheme is the following: in each round t, choose an arm a^t uniformly at random, and offer payment $p(\delta, t, n_1^t, n_2^t)$ for playing arm a^t and offer 0 for playing the other arm, where

$$p(\delta, t, n_1^t, n_2^t) = \textsc{ConfidenceWidth}(\delta, t, n_1^t) + \textsc{ConfidenceWidth}(\delta, t, n_2^t)$$

and n_1^t, n_2^t denote the number of times that the two arms are played before round t. Whenever the agent selects the arm associated with zero payment, the principal will then offer zero payment for both arms in all future rounds.

Theorem 3.5. *Consider the classic case with $k = 2$ arms in the partial information setting. Then the payment scheme above instantiated with parameter δ is fair in every round with probability at least $1-\delta$. Moreover, the incurred total cost and expected regret are at most $\tilde{O}(\sqrt{T})$.*

4 CLASSIC SETTING: SUBLINEAR PAYMENTS WITH ONLY $\tilde{O}(K^2)$ UNFAIR ROUNDS

The necessity of linear growth in subsidies (Theorem 3.1) was driven by the requirement that the agent satisfy contextual fairness in each period. It is natural to ask what would happen if one relaxed this requirement. In this section, we describe how to design a payment scheme which will satisfy contextual fairness in all but $\tilde{O}(k^2)$ rounds. We show that it is possible to achieve payments and regret which grow sub-linearly with T.

The rough idea behind this upper bound is inspired by Joseph et al. [8] who show that fairness can be achieved by maintaining confidence intervals around empirical arm means, and enforcing the constraint that any pair of arms with overlapping confidence intervals are played with equal probability: in particular, a fair no-regret algorithm can play uniformly at random amongst the set of arms "chained" to the arm with highest upper confidence bound by the confidence intervals, called the *chained set X*.

Denote the confidence interval associated with arm i at round t by $[\ell_i^t, u_i^t]$. Fix a set of confidence intervals at round t, $[\ell_1^t, u_1^t], \dots, [\ell_k^t, u_k^t]$. We say i is *linked* to j if $[\ell_i^t, u_i^t] \cap [\ell_j^t, u_j^t] \ne \emptyset$, and i is *chained* to j if i and j are in the same component of the transitive closure of the linked relation. We refer to the set of arms chained to the arm with highest upper confidence bound as the *chained set X*. We say the sequence of confidence intervals are *valid* if, with probability $1-\delta$, they contain the true and empirical averages of every arm in every round.

In the absence of explicit knowledge of the sample means, the principal does not have sufficient information to incentivize uniformly random play amongst exactly the set of arms chained to the arm with highest upper confidence bound X[8]. The principal does not know the empirical means of the arms, and therefore cannot compute the arms contained in X directly.

The principal can, however, incentivize the myopic agent to play an arm j with a payment vector p^t such that $p_j^t \ge \max_i p_i^t + |\max_i \hat{\mu}_i^t - \hat{\mu}_j^t|$. Unfortunately, the principal neither knows *which* arms

[8]Indeed, the ability to do so would contradict Theorem 3.1 by acheiving sublinear regret with zero unfair rounds.

belong to X, nor how many arms are in X, nor how far apart the empirical means are in X. Instead, the principal can maintain upper bounds on all of these quantities. Namely, the principal tracks a superset of the chained set X, called the *active set* $\hat{X}$. $|\hat{X}|$ will then act as an upper bound on the size of the chained set, and $|\hat{X}| \cdot x_{\hat{X}}$ will upper bound the difference between the highest arm mean and the lowest chained arm's means, where $x_{\hat{X}}$ is the width of the largest confidence interval of any arm in $\hat{X}$. By offering a payment of $|\hat{X}| \cdot x_{\hat{X}}$ to an arm selected uniformly from $\hat{X}$ (and zero for all other arms), the principal will cause uniformly random play amongst $\hat{X}$ if all arms in $\hat{X}$ have empirical means within $|\hat{X}| \cdot x_{\hat{X}}$ of the best empirical mean.

This is fair if in every round $\hat{X} = X$: all means will then be within $|\hat{X}| \cdot x_{\hat{X}}$ by the definition of chaining and $x_{\hat{X}}$, and so this will induce uniformly random play amongst the chained set, exactly the behavior shown to be fair in Joseph et al. [8]. On the other hand, if $\hat{X} \setminus X \neq \emptyset$, this behavior could be unfair, either because not all arms within $\hat{X}$ have empirical means within $|\hat{X}| \cdot x_{\hat{X}}$ of one another (i.e., not all arms in the set are chained together), or because some arms in $\hat{X}$ chain to other arms outside of $\hat{X}$, or because some arms in $\hat{X}$ are "below" arms outside of $\hat{X}$. We will guarantee the latter issues do not occur, by always ensuring $\hat{X}$ contains any arms "above" or chained to any arm in $\hat{X}$. The former issue (that some arms in $\hat{X}$ may not be chained to others in $\hat{X}$, and their empirical means may then not be close enough for the payment to change the myopic agent's behavior in all cases) cannot be entirely avoided. However, we can quickly discover if any arm in $\hat{X}$ has empirical mean less than $|\hat{X}| \cdot x_{\hat{X}}$ below the best empirical mean: in $O(\hat{X}) = \tilde{O}(k)$ rounds, that arm will be offered the subsidy and it won't change the agent's decision. Those $\tilde{O}(k)$ rounds will be unfair, as are several rounds which follow this discovery and update the set $\hat{X}$.

The following lemma, a generalization of the analysis of Joseph et al. [8], can be interpreted to mean the following. Fix a definiton of confidence intervals which are all valid over all rounds for all arms with probability $1 - \delta$. Consider any set of arms S which (a) contains the "upper chain" (all arms chained to the arm with highest upper confidence bound), (b) contains any arms "above" the confidence intervals of any arm in the set, and (c) is closed under chaining. Then, playing uniformly at random amongst S will satisfy contextual fairness.

Lemma 4.1. *Suppose, with probability $1 - \delta$, at every round t and for every arm i, $\mu_i^t \in [\ell_i^t, u_i^t]$. Consider a set S of arms with the k' highest upper confidence bounds for some $k' < k$. Then, it is fair to play uniformly at random over $S \cup \{i$ chained to an arm in $S\}$.*

The pseudo-code in Figure 1 describes the payment scheme, which we analyze thereafter. The performance of this payment scheme is summarized in the following theorem.

Theorem 4.2. *For any δ, PlayAll is $O(k^2 \ln(k/\delta))$-fair, and has expected cost and regret*

$$O\left(k \cdot \sum_t \text{ConfidenceWidth}(\delta, t, \frac{t}{k})\right) = O\left(\sqrt{k^3 T \ln \frac{T}{\delta}}\right).$$

We present the proof to this theorem after stating several lemmas describing the behavior of PlayAll. Observation 2 states that using x as a confidence interval width for all arms in $\hat{X}$ yields valid confidence intervals. Hereafter, we use $[\ell_i^t, u_i^t] = [\hat{\mu}_i^t - x, \hat{\mu}_i^t + x]$ as valid confidence intervals for all $i \in \hat{X}$, $t \in [T]$. Lemma 4.3 shows that FindChained outputs a set which contains the upper confidence chain in its output round. Lemma 4.4 states that FindChained's output is closed under chaining (e.g., that every arm in its output is only chained to arms also belonging to the output set) and contains all arms "above" any arms in its output. Lemma 4.5 argues that the empirical means of every arm in the set output by FindChained are within 4 confidence interval widths of some other arm in the set. Lemma 4.6 shows that when this is the case (that the empirical means

ALGORITHM 1: $O(k^2 \ln \frac{k}{\delta})$-fair Payment Scheme

```
Function PlayAll (δ, T)
    x ← 1;
    X̂ ← {1, ..., k};
    while t ≤ T do
        (x, X̂) ← ChainedFair(δ, x, X̂);
    end
Function ChainedFair (δ, x, X̂)
    Choose j^t ∈_UAR X̂ ;  // Pick arm to incentivize
    x ← min(x, ConfidenceWidth(δ, t, min_{j∈X̂} n_j^t));
    Offer p^t : p^t_{j^t} = 4x · |X|, p^t_{i'≠j^t} = 0;
    i^t ← the myopic player's choice;
    if i^t ≠ j^t then
        X̂ ← FindChained(x, X̂, t);
    end
    return (x, X̂)

Function FindChained (x, X̂, t)
    Offer p^t = 0⃗;
    i^t ← the myopic player's choice;
    R ← {i^t};
    Offer p^t = p^{t-1} + 2 · x · Σ_{i∈X̂\R} e_i;
    while i^t ← the myopic player's choice
    and i^t ∉ R do
        R = R ∪ {i^t};
        t ← t + 1;
        Offer p^t = p^{t-1} + 2 · x · Σ_{i∈X̂\R} e_i
        ;  // add 2 · x to payments
        of arms in X̂ not yet chosen
    end
    return R
```

are within $4x$ of each other, as is the case right after a call to FindChained), that ChainedFair induces uniformly random play amongst $\hat{X}$. Lemma 4.7 upper-bounds the number of rounds before which ChainedFair will discover when it is inducing unfair play. All proofs of these lemmas can be found in the full version of this paper.

Observation 2. With probability $1 - \delta$, for all $t \in [T]$, $i \in \hat{X}^t$, $\mu_i \in [\hat{\mu}_i^t - x, \hat{\mu}_i^t + x]$.

Lemma 4.3. *FindChained$(x, \hat{X}, t)$ contains all arms chained to the arm with highest upper confidence bound in its output round t'.*

Lemma 4.4. *Any arm chained to the set R = FindChained$(x, \hat{X}, t)$ belongs to R. Moreover, any arm $i \notin R$ must have $u_i^t < \min_{i' \in R} \ell_{i'}^t$.*

Lemma 4.5. *Let t' be the round in which R = FindChained$(x, \hat{X}, t')$ outputs R. Then, for any $j \in R$ = FindChained$(x, \hat{X}, t')$,*

$$\hat{\mu}_j^{t'} \geq \min_{j' \in R \setminus \{j\}} \hat{\mu}_{j'}^{t'} - 4 \cdot x.$$

Moreover, $\max_{j \in R} \hat{\mu}_j^{t'} - \min_{j \in R} \hat{\mu}_j^{\prime t} \leq (2|R| + 2) \cdot x$.

Lemma 4.6. *Suppose $\max_{i,j \in \hat{X}} |\hat{\mu}_i^t - \hat{\mu}_j^t| \leq 4|\hat{X}| \cdot x$. Then ChainedFair$(\delta, \hat{X})$ induces uniformly random play amongst $\hat{X}$.*

Lemma 4.7. *Whenever there is an arm i such that $\max_{j \in \hat{X}} |\hat{\mu}_j^t - \hat{\mu}_i^t| > 4|\hat{X}| \cdot x$, with probability $1 - \delta$, FindChained will be called within $O(k \cdot \ln(1/\delta))$ many rounds.*

Proof of Theorem 4.2. We first upper-bound the number of rounds in which PlayAll might violate the fairness condition.

We argue iteratively about the set $\hat{X}$: that (a) all arms chained to the top arm belong to $\hat{X}$, and (b) all arms chained to any arm in $\hat{X}$ belong to $\hat{X}$. This is trivially true initially as $\hat{X} = \{1, \ldots, k\}$. $\hat{X}$ is only updated as the result of a call to FindChained. By Lemma 4.3, any arm chained to the top arm will remain in $\hat{X}$. Furthermore, by Lemma 4.4, any arm chained to an arm in its output also belongs to its output. Thus, (a) and (b) hold for $\hat{X}$ for all rounds.

So, in rounds in which ChainedFair induces uniformly random play from $\hat{X}$, (a) and (b) imply ChainedFair satisfies the fairness condition. For any round in which $\max_{i,j\in\hat{X}} |\hat{\mu}_i^t - \hat{\mu}_j^t| \leq 2|\hat{X}| \cdot x$, Lemma 4.6 implies ChainedFair induces uniformly random play from $\hat{X}$. By Lemma 4.4, $\hat{X}$ contains any arms either above or chained to arms in $\hat{X}$. Thus, Lemma 4.1 applies and these rounds are fair.

We now upper-bound the number of rounds for which ChainedFair does not induce uniformly random play amongst $\hat{X}$. For any particular i and round t such that $\max_{j\in\hat{X}} |\hat{\mu}_j^t - \hat{\mu}_i^t| > 4|\hat{X}| \cdot x$, Lemma 4.7 implies that this will be found in $O(k\ln(1/\delta))$ rounds, and FindChained will be called. In any future round $t' \geq t$, since the confidence intervals are valid, we know that $\max_{j\in\hat{X}} |\hat{\mu}_j^{t'} - \hat{\mu}_i^{t'}| > 4(|\hat{X}| - 2) \cdot x$, since either of the two means can change but by at most x each. Lemma 4.5 will return $\hat{X}$ such that $\max_{i,j\in\hat{X}} |\hat{\mu}_i^t - \hat{\mu}_j^t| \leq (2|\hat{X}| + 2) \cdot x$. Thus, as $|\hat{X}| \geq 2$, then arm i will be removed at the first round in which it was the impetus for FindChained to be called as $\max_{i,j\in\hat{X}} |\hat{\mu}_j^{t'} - \hat{\mu}_i^{t'}| \leq 2(|\hat{X}| + 2) \cdot x \leq 4(|\hat{X}| - 2) \cdot x < \max_{j\in\hat{X}} |\hat{\mu}_j^t - \hat{\mu}_i^t|$, a contradiction if $i \in \hat{X}$.

Since x is non-increasing, so is $\hat{X}$: thus, at most k calls to FindChained are made. Thus, the total number of unfair rounds is equal to the number of rounds in which $\max_{i,j\in\hat{X}} |\hat{\mu}_i^t - \hat{\mu}_j^t| > 4|\hat{X}| \cdot x$ plus the number of rounds in FindChained. The former is bounded by $O(k^2 \ln(k/\delta))$ (With probability $1 - \delta/k$ it will take at most $O(k\ln(k/\delta))$ rounds of unfair play before FindChained is called when this is the case, and each call will reduce the size of $\hat{X}$ so it can be called at most k times. In total, this bound holds for all k rounds with probability $1 - \delta$.); the latter by $O(k^2)$ (each call of FindChained uses $O(k)$ rounds, and there are at most $O(k)$ calls to FindChained).

We now upper-bound the cost of this payment scheme and the regret of the agent. In the $O(k^2 \ln(k/\delta))$ unfair rounds, the payments might be $\Omega(1)$; similarly, the regret of the algorithm in those rounds might be $\Omega(1)$. In all other rounds, the myopic agent is playing uniformly at random amongst a set of arms whose true means are within $2k \cdot x$ of the best true mean, so $2k \cdot x$ in each fair round is an upper-bound on per-round regret. The maximum payment offered in any round is $4k \cdot x$ as well, so that also upper bounds the cost. The overall upper bound follows from some basic algebra and the fact that each arm in $\hat{X}$ will have been played $\tilde{\Omega}\left(\frac{t}{k}\right)$ times in round t. □

5 CONTEXTUAL SETTING WITH PARTIAL INFORMATION: LINEAR PAYMENTS OR UNFAIR ROUNDS

In this section, we argue that the partial information model is much harder in the linear contextual case — in *every* round that the principal does not pay $\Omega(1)$, an adversary can force the myopic agent to behave unfairly. This implies that on an adversarially chosen instance, every round is either unfair or has constant cost: thus, either the sum of the payments must be $\Omega(T)$, or the number of unfair rounds must be $\Omega(T)$, or both. This rules out positive results in the partial information model of the sort we were able to obtain in the classic bandits setting. In the following, we assume that the myopic agent is using an ordinary least squares estimator, for simplicity. Identical results can also be proven for other natural estimators, like ridge regression estimators.

Theorem 5.1. *Suppose $k \geq 3$. Consider any payment scheme in the partial information model in the linear contextual bandit setting. For any $\eta \in (0, 1)$, there is an instance for which with probability $1 - \delta$, in every round, either the round is unfair, or the expected cost for the principal is $\frac{k-1}{k} \cdot (1 - \eta)$.*

The proof of the theorem relies on the fact that the principal cannot observe the adversarially chosen contexts; the expected rewards in any round then can be (almost) arbitrary. In the classic case, it was only in the first unpeaked round that we had the freedom to design our lower bound instance arbitrarily – after that, the principal would have learned some information about the instance, and hence the payment distribution could be a function of the instance. In the linear contextual case, we have sufficient freedom to design a lower bound instance at -every- round. Although the principal may have learned a great deal about the underlying linear functions, she by definition has no information about the realized contexts at the current round, which we use to our advantage. As in the classic setting, in any round where the payment scheme is not peaked, the largest payment is strictly less than 1 larger than the other payments with probability more than zero. We will use this to construct an instance over which there is constant probability (over the history) that the myopic agent chooses an unfair distribution over arms. Additional complications arise from the fact that the principal learns about the instance from the set of previous unfair rounds (which, in the classic case, we did not have, since we only argued there had to be a single unfair round if the payment scheme was not peaked). We circumvent this problem by arguing that the principal must deploy a peaked distribution to be fair, even if the principal knows everything about the instance I and even if the principal knows the empirical estimates $\hat{\theta}_i^t$ for all $t \in [T], i \in [k]$.

Proof. Consider the one-dimensional case, where $\theta_i \in \mathbb{R}_{\geq 0}$. We construct an instance I such that even for a principal who has full information about I, and $\hat{\theta}_i^t$ for all $t' \leq t, i$, in order to guarantee that the payment distribution in round t is fair for any set of arriving contexts x^t, the largest payment must be at least $1-\eta$ with probability $\frac{k-1}{k}$. This clearly holds for any round in which a peaked payment distribution is used, and so for the remainder, we assume that the distribution in round t is not peaked.

Let $\theta_i = 1-\eta \in (0,1)$ for all i, and let arm 1 have deterministic rewards equal to their mean, so that $\theta_1 x_1^t = x_1^t$ for all t. As the rewards are deterministic and the agent is using an ordinary least squares estimator, the myopic agent's prediction $\hat{\theta}_1^t = \theta_1^t$ as well for all t. For all $i \neq 1$, let $\mathcal{D}_{i,x_i^t}^t = U[\theta_i x_i^t - \epsilon, \theta_i x_i^t + \epsilon]$ for some very small ϵ. $\mathbb{P}_{r_i^t \sim \mathcal{D}_{i,x_i^t}^t}[r_i^t > \theta_i x_i^t] = \frac{1}{2} = \mathbb{P}_{r_i^t \sim \mathcal{D}_{i,x_i^t}^t}[r_i^t < \theta_i x_i^t]$: the rewards drawn from these distributions have the right expectation but are always larger or smaller than their expectation, and each with equal probability. Then, again by properties of the ordinary least squares estimator, this will imply that with probability $\frac{1}{2}$ over observations, in any round t and for any $i \in [k] \setminus \{1\}$, $\hat{\theta}_i^t > \theta_i^t$, and with probability $\frac{1}{2}$, $\hat{\theta}_i^t < \theta_i^t$, for any round t. Furthermore, with probability 1, in every round t, every empirical estimate of the coefficients is distinct: $\hat{\theta}_i^t \neq \hat{\theta}_j^t$ for all $i \neq j \in [k]$.

We begin by arguing that every coordinate i must have equal probability of receiving the largest payment in any round t if the round is to be fair (with probability $1-\delta$ over the history). Precisely, fix some history h^t, and let

$$d_i = \mathbb{P}_{p \sim \gamma^t(h^t)}[i \text{ wins with payment vector } p, x_i^t = \vec{0}, \forall i | h^t].$$

Since for all $i \in [k]$ and any h^t, $\theta_i \cdot x_i^t = 0$, it must be that $d_i = \frac{1}{k}$ for all i if round t is fair for this h^t.

We have assumed the payment scheme is not peaked in round t, conditioned on h^t. Thus,

$$\mathbb{P}_{p \sim \gamma^t(h^t)}[\max_i p_i - \max_{j \neq i} p_j \geq 1] < 1.$$

We argue round t must be unfair conditioned on h^t, or with probability $\frac{k-1}{k}$, $\max_i p_i \geq 1-\eta$. Let

$$c = \sup_c : \mathbb{P}_{p \sim \gamma^t(h^t)}[\max_i p_i - \max_{j \neq i} p_j \geq c] = 1;$$

we again know that some such $c \geq 0$ must exist, and that $c < 1$ because the payment scheme is unpeaked. Let arm $\bar{i}$ have the largest empirical coefficient: $\hat{\theta}_{\bar{i}}^t > \max_{i' \neq \bar{i}} \hat{\theta}_{i'}^t$ in round t and arm $\underline{i}$ have the smallest empirical coefficient, $\hat{\theta}_{\underline{i}}^t < \min_{i' \neq \underline{i}} \hat{\theta}_{i'}^t$. Further define

$$c_{i'} = \sup_c : \mathbb{P}_{p \sim \gamma^t(\cdot)}[p_{i'} - p_{\bar{i}} \geq c | p_{i'} \geq \max_{i'' \neq i'} p_{i''}] = 1,$$

e.g. that $c_{i'}$ is the margin by which i' has payment larger than arm $\bar{i}$ when i' has largest payment. Note $c_{i'} \in [0,1]$ for all i'. Let $i_{\max} \in \arg\max_{i'} c_{i'}$ be an arm with largest payment margin over $\bar{i}$ and $i_{\min} = \text{argmin}_{i'} c_{i'}$ be the arm with the smallest payment margin over i. We consider three cases: when $c_{i_{\max}} > 1-\eta$, when $1-\eta \geq c_{i_{\max}} > c_{i_{\min}}$, and when $1-\eta \geq c_{i_{\max}} = c_{i_{\min}}$. In each case, we show that either the largest payment is at least $1-\eta$ with probability at least $\frac{k-1}{k}$, or the round is unfair.

Case 1: $c_{i_{\max}} > 1-\eta$. We claim here that either $c_{i_{\min}} > 1-\eta$ or the round is unfair: this will imply that with probability $\frac{k-1}{k}$, $\max_i p_i \geq 1-\eta$. Suppose the round is fair. Consider the context $x^t_{\bar{i}} = \frac{1-\eta}{\hat{\theta}^t_{\bar{i}}}$ and $x^t_{i'} = 0$ for all $i' \neq \bar{i}$. Then, $\hat{\theta}^t_{\bar{i}} x^t_{\bar{i}} = 1-\eta$, and $\hat{\theta}^t_i x^t_i = 0 = \theta_i x^t_i$ for all other i. Fairness will imply that all $i \neq 1$ should be played with equal probability. Notice that $i_{\max}$ is played with probability $\frac{1}{k}$: precisely when $i_{\max}$ has the largest payment (which must be largest by $c_{i_{\max}} > 1-\eta$). $i_{\min}$ wins only when her payment is largest (which happens with probability $\frac{1}{k}$) and larger than $\bar{i}$'s by at least $1-\eta$. So, if $\pi^t_{i_{\min}|h^t} = \pi^t_{i_{\max}|h^t} = \frac{1}{k}$, it must be that $c_{i_{\min}} \geq 1-\eta$.

Case 2: $1-\eta \geq c_{i_{\max}} > c_{i_{\min}}$. We argue that the round must be unfair if $c_{i_{\max}} > c_{i_{\min}}$.

Choose contexts x^t_i such that $\hat{\theta}^t_{\bar{i}} x^t_{\bar{i}} = c_{i_{\max}} \leq 1-\eta$ and $x^t_{i'} = 0$ for all other i'. Then, since $\theta_i x^t_i = 0$ for all $i \neq \bar{i}$, if this round is to be fair, all arms $i \neq \bar{i}$ must be played with equal probability. Arm $i_{\max}$ wins whenever it has the largest payment, since $p_{i_{\max}} \geq p_{\bar{i}} + c_{i_{\max}}$ whenever $i_{\max}$ has the largest payment. Therefore $i_{\max}$ wins with probability $\frac{1}{k}$.

$i_{\min}$, on the other hand, wins only when they have the largest payment and beat i's payment by $c_{i_{\max}} > c_{i_{\min}}$, which happens with strictly less probability than $i_{\min}$ having largest payment (probability $\frac{1}{k}$) by the definition of $c_{i_{\min}}$. So, $i_{\min}$ wins with probability strictly less than that of $i_{\max}$; this round must be unfair.

Case 3: $1-\eta \geq c_{i_{\max}} = c_{i_{\min}}$. In this case, $c_a = c_b = \beta$ for all $a, b \in [k] \setminus \{\bar{i}\}$. If $\beta \geq 1-\eta$, the claim holds (the largest payment is at least $1-\eta$ with probability at least $\frac{k-1}{k}$, so assume $\beta < 1-\eta$.

Suppose $\beta > 0$. We exhibit a set of contexts for which this payment scheme combined with the agent is unfair. Fix some $D \in (\beta, 1-\eta)$; define the contexts

- $x^t_{\bar{i}} : \hat{\theta}^t_{\bar{i}} x^t_{\bar{i}} = D > \beta$
- $x^t_j : \hat{\theta}^t_j x^t_j = D - \beta > 0$ for j the arm with second-largest empirical coefficient,
- $x^t_{i'} = x^t_j$ for all $i' \notin \{\bar{i}, j\}$.

Then, $\hat{\theta}^t_{i'} x^t_{i'} < \hat{\theta}^t_j x^t_j$, and so arm j is played whenever j has the largest payment, since j (and all other arms) has margin over $\bar{i}$ of at least β when they have the largest payment; thus j is played with probability $\frac{1}{k}$. Since $\theta_j x^t_j = \theta_{i'} x^t_{i'}$ for all $i' \neq \bar{i}$, if this round is fair, each i' must also be played with probability $\frac{1}{k}$, in particular for i' with smallest $\hat{\theta}^t_{i'}$. However, $\hat{\theta}^t_{i'} x^t_{i'} < D - \beta$; i' can only win if her payment is the largest and it beats the payment of i by strictly more than β, which happens with probability strictly less than $\frac{1}{k}$ by definition of β. Thus i' cannot win with probability as large as j and so round t is unfair if $c_a = c_b = \beta > 0$ for all $a, b \neq i$.

Finally, we consider the case where $\beta = 0$ and separately argue that this round cannot be fair. The contexts $x^t_{i'} = 1$ for all i' should prove this: arm $\bar{i}$ will be played with probability $\frac{1}{k}$ (precisely the probability that $\bar{i}$ gets the weakly largest payment), but arms with smaller empirical means will need to have the largest payment by some margin, which happens with strictly less probability than them having the largest payment by the definition of β, so they win with probability less than $\frac{1}{k}$, meaning fairness is violated in this round, since $\theta_{\bar{i}} x^t_{\bar{i}} = 1-\eta = \theta_{i'} x^t_{i'}$. □

6 FULL INFORMATION: PERFECT FAIRNESS WITH SUBLINEAR PAYMENTS

In this section, we show that a principal with full information about the state of a myopic agent can design a payment scheme which is fair in every round and has sublinear cost for both the classic and linear contextual bandits problems. This contrasts with the partial information model, where for $k \geq 3$ arms, in both the classic and linear contextual settings, in which there must be unfair rounds for any payment scheme with total cost $o(T)$.

Roughly, the fair payment scheme operates as follows. In each round, the scheme knows the empirical estimates of rewards used by the myopic agent. Moreover, the scheme can compute confidence intervals around these estimates (the scheme knows how many times each arm was pulled, and, in a contextual setting, the contexts for each previous choice). In such a round, the payment scheme then will choose an arm i uniformly at random from the set of arms chained to the arm with highest upper confidence bound, and offer a payment for choosing i equal to the difference between the empirical estimate of i's reward and the empirical estimate of the highest reward in that round. This induces uniformly random play amongst the top set of arms, and by Lemma 4.1, this will be a fair distribution.

We now present the pseudocode in Figure 2 a parametrized family of payment schemes described informally above. A payment scheme in this family is instantiated by giving a method of constructing valid confidence intervals around myopic predictions.

ALGORITHM 2: A Fair Full Information Payment Scheme

Function *Fair-Payments*(δ, T)
  $\hat{X} \leftarrow \{1, \ldots, k\}$;
  while $t \leq T$ **do**
    $i^t = \arg\max_i \hat{\mu}^t_{i^t}$;
    Let $\hat{X}^t = \{i$ chained to i^t by δ-valid confidence intervals from round $t\}$;
    Choose $j^t \in_{\text{UAR}} \hat{X}$;   `// Pick an arm in the upper chain to incentivize`
    Offer $p^t : p^t_{j^t} = \hat{\mu}^t_{i^t} - \hat{\mu}^t_{j^t}, p^t_{i' \neq j^t} = 0$;
  end

Theorem 6.1. *Consider an instance of Fair-Payments(δ, T) instantiated with confidence intervals $[\ell^t_i, u^t_i]$ such that $\hat{\mu}^t_i = \frac{u^t_i - \ell^t_i}{2}$, and with probability $1-\delta$, for all $i \in [k], t \in [T]$, $\mu^t_i \in [\ell^t_i, u^t_i]$. Then, Fair-Payments($\delta, T$) is fair at every round, and has cost and regret $O(k \sum_t w(t) + \delta T)$, where $w(t)$ is the maximum width of any confidence interval in the top chained set.*

Before proving Theorem 6.1, we mention that this theorem, when combined with standard methods of constructing confidence intervals, implies the existence of fair payment schemes with sublinear cost and regret, both in the classic and linear contextual settings.

Corollary 6.2. *Consider the classic bandits problem. Then, Fair-Payments(δ, T) using the confidence interval for arm i introduced by* ConfidenceWidth*(δ, T, n^t_i) is fair and has cost and regret $O(\sqrt{k^3 T \ln \frac{kT}{\delta}})$.*

Proof. By Lemma 3.4, with probability $1-\delta$, these confidence intervals are all valid for all $t \in [T], i \in [k]$. So, Theorem 6.1 applies, and states that this payment scheme is fair, and has regret $O(k \cdot \sum_t w(t))$, where $w(t)$ is the maximum width of any arm in the active set at round t. Since the chained set is monotone, at round t every arm in the chained set has been chained for t rounds. Therefore, in expectation each arm in the chain has been pulled $\frac{t}{k}$ times. An additive Chernoff bound implies that any particular arm has, with probability at least $1 - \frac{\delta}{2kt^2}$, been pulled in round t at least $\frac{t}{k} - \sqrt{\frac{t\ln\left(\frac{2t^2k}{\delta}\right)}{2}}$ times, and so this bound holds for all rounds and all arms with probability at lest $1 - \frac{\delta}{2}$ summing up over all k arms and all t. Then, by Lemma 3 in Joseph et al. [8], we know that $w(t) \leq 2\sqrt{\frac{\ln((\pi t)^2/3\delta)}{2\frac{t}{k} - \sqrt{\frac{t\ln\left(\frac{2kt^2}{\delta}\right)}{2}}}}$. Summing over all t we have the desired result. □

Corollary 6.3. *Consider the linear contextual bandits problem. Suppose the myopic agent uses a ridge regression estimator:* $\hat{\theta}_i^t = \left(X_i^T X_i + \lambda I\right)^{-1} X_i^T Y_i$*, where* X_i, Y_i *are the design matrices and observations before round* t*. Then, define*

$$w_i^t = ||x_i^t||_{(X_i^T X_i + \lambda I)^{-1}}(m\sqrt{d \ln \frac{1 + t/\lambda}{\delta}} + \sqrt{\lambda},$$

and

$$\ell_i^t = \langle \hat{\theta}_i^t, x_i^t \rangle - w_i^t, \qquad u_i^t = \langle \hat{\theta}_i^t, x_i^t \rangle + w_i^t.$$

Then, Fair-Payments(δ, T) *is fair and has cost and regret* $O\left(md\sqrt{k^3 T}\ln^2 \frac{T^2 k}{d\lambda\delta}\right)$.

Proof. The analysis in the proof of Theorem 2 of Joseph et al. [7] shows that these confidence intervals are valid with probability $1 - \delta$. Their analysis upper-bounds $k\sum_t w(t)$ where $w(t)$ is the largest width of any confidence interval in the chained set in round t, by

$$O\left(md\sqrt{k^3 T}\ln^2 \frac{T^2 k}{d\lambda\delta}\right).$$

Thus, the resulting algorithm is fair, and the bounds on cost and regret follow from Theorem 6.1. □

We now proceed with the proof of Theorem 6.1.

Proof. We begin by proving that Fair-Payments(δ, T) is fair in every round. By assumption, with probability $1 - \delta$, for all $i \in [k], t \in [T]$, $\mu_i^t \in [\ell_i^t, u_i^t]$. Thus it follows from Lemma 4.1 that it suffices to show that these payments suffice to induce uniformly random play amongst the set of arms chained to the arm with upper confidence bound. By definition, the top chain in round t is exactly $\hat{X}^t$. The distribution over payments in round t chooses each $j^t \in \hat{X}^t$ with probability $\frac{1}{|\hat{X}^t|}$ and accordingly a p^t such that $p_{j^t}^t = \hat{\mu}_{i^t}^t - \hat{\mu}_{j^t}^t$ and $p_{i'}^t = 0$. This induces the myopic agent to choose j^t in all such cases. Thus, each $j^t \in \hat{X}^t$ is chosen by the myopic agent with probability $\frac{1}{|\hat{X}^t|}$. So, Fair-Payments(δ, T) is fair.

Condition on all confidence intervals being valid. The myopic agent under this payment scheme chooses uniformly at random from the top chain, which has regret in round t bounded by $\sum_{i \in \hat{X}^t} u_i^t - \ell_i^t \leq kw(t)$, where $w(t) = \max_{i \in \hat{X}^t} u_i^t - \ell_i^t$. Thus, in total, the regret is upper bounded by $k\sum_t w(t)$. Moreover, the payment in round t is $\hat{\mu}_{i^t}^t - \hat{\mu}_{j^t}^t \leq u_{i^t}^t - \ell_{j^t}^t \leq \sum_{i \in \hat{X}^t} u_i^t - \ell_i^t \leq kw(t)$, and so the same bound holds for the cost of the payment scheme. With probability δ, the widths of the confidence intervals could be arbitrary, as could the inaccuracy of the sampled means. An additive δT bounds the additional expected regret. □

REFERENCES

[1] Solon Barocas and Andrew D Selbst. 2016. Big Data's Disparate Impact. *CALIFORNIA LAW REVIEW* 104 (2016), 671.

[2] FTC Commisioner Brill. 2015. Navigating the "Trackless Ocean": Fairness in Big Data Research and Decision Making. Keynote Address at the Columbia University Data Science Institute. (April 2015).

[3] Yeon-Koo Che and Johannes Horner. 2015. *Optimal Design for Social Learning.* Technical Report. Cowles Foundation for Research in Economics, Yale University.

[4] Cary Coglianese and David Lehr. 2016. Regulating by Robot: Administrative Decision-Making in the Machine-Learning Era. *Georgetown Law Journal* Forthcoming (2016), Forthcoming.

[5] Benjamin Edelman, Michael Luca, and Dan Svirsky. 2017. Racial discrimination in the sharing economy: Evidence from a field experiment. *American Economic Journal: Applied Economics* 9, 2 (2017), 1–22.

[6] Peter Frazier, David Kempe, Jon Kleinberg, and Robert Kleinberg. 2014. Incentivizing exploration. In *Proceedings of the fifteenth ACM conference on Economics and computation.* ACM, ACM, New York, NY, 5–22.

[7] Matthew Joseph, Michael Kearns, Jamie Morgenstern, Seth Neel, and Aaron Roth. 2016. *Rawlsian fairness for machine learning.* Technical Report. University of Pennsylvania.

[8] Matthew Joseph, Michael Kearns, Jamie H Morgenstern, and Aaron Roth. 2016. Fairness in Learning: Classic and Contextual Bandits. In *Advances in Neural Information Processing Systems 29*, D. D. Lee, M. Sugiyama, U. V. Luxburg, I. Guyon, and R. Garnett (Eds.). Curran Associates, Inc., Red Hook, NY, 325–333.

[9] Ilan Kremer, Yishay Mansour, and Motty Perry. 2014. Implementing the "Wisdom of the Crowd". *Journal of Political Economy* 122, 5 (2014), 988–1012.

[10] Yishay Mansour, Aleksandrs Slivkins, and Vasilis Syrgkanis. 2015. Bayesian incentive-compatible bandit exploration. In *Proceedings of the Sixteenth ACM Conference on Economics and Computation.* ACM, ACM, New York, NY, 565–582.

[11] Yishay Mansour, Aleksandrs Slivkins, Vasilis Syrgkanis, and Zhiwei Steven Wu. 2016. Bayesian Exploration: Incentivizing Exploration in Bayesian Games. In *Proceedings of the 2016 ACM Conference on Economics and Computation, EC '16, Maastricht, The Netherlands, July 24-28, 2016.* 661. DOI: http://dx.doi.org/10.1145/2940716.2940755

[12] Daniel O'Leary. 2013. Exploiting Big Data from Mobile Device Sensor-Based Apps: Challenges and Benefits. *MIS Quarterly Executive* 12, 4 (December 2013), 179–187.

[13] Yiangos Papanastasiou, Kostas Bimpikis, and Nicos Sava. 2017. Crowdsourcing Exploration. *Management Science* (2017). Forthcoming.

[14] Devin Pope and Justin Snyder. 2011. What's in a Picture? Evidence of Discrimination from Prosper.com. *Journal of Human Resources* 101, 1 (2011), 53–92.

Combinatorial Cost Sharing

SHAHAR DOBZINSKI, Weizmann Institute of Science
SHAHAR OVADIA, Weizmann Institute of Science

We introduce a combinatorial variant of the cost sharing problem: several services can be provided to each player and each player values every combination of services differently. A publicly known cost function specifies the cost of providing every possible combination of services. A combinatorial cost sharing mechanism is a protocol that decides which services each player gets and at what price. We look for dominant strategy mechanisms that are (economically) efficient and cover the cost, ideally without overcharging (i.e., budget balanced). Note that unlike the standard cost sharing setting, combinatorial cost sharing is a multi-parameter domain. This makes designing dominant strategy mechanisms with good guarantees a challenging task.

We present the Potential Mechanism – a combination of the VCG mechanism and a well-known tool from the theory of cooperative games: Hart and Mas-Colell's potential function. The potential mechanism is a dominant strategy mechanism that always covers the incurred cost. When the cost function is subadditive the same mechanism is also approximately efficient. Our main technical contribution shows that when the cost function is submodular the potential mechanism is approximately budget balanced in three settings: supermodular valuations, symmetric cost function and general symmetric valuations, and two players with general valuations.

1 INTRODUCTION

In the cost sharing problem the cost of a public good (e.g., a bridge, a park, or a networking infrastructure) has to be partitioned among the players. The challenge is to decide whether to provision the public good, and if so, which players will receive usage permissions and for what prices, all while making sure that the payments cover the cost.

The problem was extensively studied in both economics and algorithmic game theory and many variants were suggested and analyzed (e.g., [2, 3, 8, 16–19, 21, 23]). However, in almost all variants only a single good is considered.

In this paper we attempt to fill this lacuna and introduce *combinatorial cost sharing*, where multiple goods can be provisioned and both costs and preferences depend on the selected combination of goods. While combinatorial cost sharing is a natural generalization of the basic cost sharing scenario, from a technical perspective it is radically different as we leave the relatively safe single parameter world and cross the bridge to the realm of multi parameter mechanism design. Nevertheless, we will see that good mechanisms for combinatorial cost sharing do exist.

The first author is the incumbent of the Lilian and George Lyttle Career Development Chair. Work supported in part by the I-CORE program of the planning and budgeting committee and the Israel Science Foundation 4/11 and by EU CIG grant 618128. Emails: shahar.dobzinski@weizmann.ac.il, shaharov59@gmail.com.

EC'17, June 26–30, 2017, Cambridge, Massachusetts, USA. © 2017 ACM. ISBN 978-1-4503-4527-9/17/06...$15.00.
DOI: http://dx.doi.org/10.1145/3033274.3085141

Simple Cost Sharing

The standard cost sharing setting (from now on, "simple cost sharing") involves a set N of players ($|N| = n$), where the value of player i is v_i if player i receives a usage permission and 0 otherwise. A known cost function $C : 2^N \to \mathbb{R}^+$ specifies the cost of serving each subset of the players. A (direct) mechanism for this problem receives as input the valuations of the players and outputs the set of served players and the payment p_i of every player i. It is standard to assume that the mechanism is individually rational (for every i, $p_i \leq v_i$), that $p_i \geq 0$ (no positive transfers) and moreover $p_i = 0$ if player i is not served.

Work on cost sharing in the AGT community mostly focuses on incentive compatible mechanisms, either dominant strategy or groupstrategyproof, that at the very least always cover the cost. That is, in an instance where the mechanism serves the set ALG of players, $C(ALG) \leq \Sigma_i p_i$. Ideally, we will also not overcharge the players, at least not by much: a mechanism is β-budget balanced if in every instance $C(ALG) \leq \Sigma_i p_i \leq \beta \cdot C(ALG)$.

We look for mechanisms that are economically efficient. Economic efficiency can be interpreted in several ways, with the *social welfare* being the standard definition: $SW(S) = \Sigma_{i \in S} v_i - C(S)$. Unfortunately, Feigenbaum et al. [10] show that no dominant strategy and budget balanced mechanism provides a finite approximation to the social welfare, and this result holds even if we only require the mechanism to cover the cost[1].

To overcome this, Roughgarden and Sundararajan [23] suggest an alternative quantification of efficiency. First, one can use additive approximations, i.e., if OPT is the allocation that maximizes the welfare, then in every instance $SW(OPT) - SW(ALG) \leq \alpha \cdot C(OPT)$, for some reasonable $\alpha > 0$. This benchmark allows the designer to shift the focus from instances with "low" welfare – which are the raison d'etre of the impossibilities – to instances in which using a cost sharing mechanism should yield a noticeable improvement in the efficiency.

A related notion discussed in [23] is minimizing the *social cost*, $\pi(S) = C(S) + \Sigma_{i \notin S} v_i$, which is the construction cost plus the "lost value" from not serving some of the players. Interestingly, the social cost and the social welfare induce the same order on the allocations (i.e., if $SW(S) \geq SW(T)$ then $\pi(S) \leq \pi(T)$). Moreover, additive approximations to the social welfare imply multiplicative guarantees on the social cost: $SW(OPT) - SW(ALG) \leq \alpha \cdot C(OPT)$ implies $\pi(ALG) \leq (\alpha+1) \cdot \pi(OPT)$. Following [23], many papers study social cost minimization in various settings (e.g., [2, 3, 5, 7, 14, 18]. For the sake of compatibility with the literature, we state our results in terms of approximation to the social cost, but in fact we prove essentially the same guarantees with respect to the stronger notion of additive approximation.

The cost sharing literature is rich in beautiful results, but the jewel in the crown is probably the Shapley value mechanism [21], which is a groupstrategyproof mechanism that exactly shares the cost whenever C is a submodular function [21]. Roughgarden and Sundararajan [23] show that it gives an approximation ratio of $\mathcal{H}_n = \Sigma_{i=1}^{n} \frac{1}{n}$ to the social cost. It is known that the approximation ratio of any mechanism that always covers the cost is $\Omega(\log n)$ and that this is true even if we relax the incentive compatibility requirement to strategyproofness [9][2].

[1]This impossibility is typical for mixed sign objectives, like the social welfare. The simple proof is instructive: consider two players, each with $v_i = 1$. The cost of serving any non-empty set is 1. The social welfare of the optimal allocation (which is to serve both players) is 1, whereas the social welfare of any other allocation is 0. Therefore, in any mechanism that provides a finite approximation to the welfare both players are served. To cover the cost, one of the players, without loss of generality player 1, must pay $p > 0$. Consider now an instance with $v_1 = \frac{p}{2} > 0$ and $v_2 = 1$. The mechanism is incentive compatible so player 1 is not served. Hence, no matter whether the mechanism serves player 2 or none of the players, the social welfare is 0. However, the optimal social welfare is $v_1 > 0$.

[2]This impossibility of [9] is stated for budget balanced mechanisms, but the proof applies even to cost recovering mechanisms.

The Model

The main purpose of this paper is to go beyond the single good setting. Toward this end, we introduce *combinatorial cost sharing*. We present two formulations of combinatorial cost sharing. The first is a more direct formulation which might help the reader to digest the setting more easily. The second formulation – which is the one that is studied throughout the paper – is equivalent in power but is notationally more involved. We use it since it makes the technical proofs more readable.

A First Attempt. As in simple cost sharing, there is a set N which consists of n players, but now there is a set M of public goods (for example, a pool, a gym, etc.). The mechanism has to decide which goods to construct and if a good is constructed, which subset of the players will be allowed to use it. Players might have complicated preferences over the goods in M (e.g., a combined membership for the pool and the gym might be more valuable than the sum of the values of each membership alone), thus the private valuation of player i is $v_i : 2^M \to \mathbb{R}$. Note that this assumes that there are no externalities in the sense that value of each player is determined only by the goods he is served (in particular, the value does not depend on the other players who use these services).

Let $C' : (2^N)^m \to \mathbb{R}$ be a known function that specifies the cost of every possible combination of services. For example, $C(S_1, \ldots, S_n)$ is the cost of serving the first good in M to the players in S_1 while serving the second good in M to the players in S_2, and so on. We stress that we do not make any assumptions on $S_1, \ldots, S_n$ and in particular these sets are typically not disjoint.

The Main Formulation. The issue with the first formulation is that we often would like to assume that the cost function belongs to some standard class, e.g., C' is submodular or subadditive. However, as defined C' is not even a set function (its domain is $(2^N)^m$). We thus use a different formulation that is equivalent in power. Define – for notational convenience – for each player i a set M_i with $M_i \cap M_{i'} = \emptyset$ for $i \neq i'$, where each $j \in M_i$ represents a permission to consume a different good. For example, if M is the set of public goods that can be constructed, we define for each player i a set M_i, $|M_i| = |M|$, and think about the j'th item in M_i as permission *for player* i to use the j'th public good in M. In particular player i is never interested in items from $M_{i'}$, for $i \neq i'$. The private valuation of player i is $v_i : 2^{M_i} \to \mathbb{R}$. The cost function $C : 2^{M_1} \times \cdots \times 2^{M_n} \to \mathbb{R}$ specifies the cost of every possible combination of services. Note that it is straightforward to express every cost function in the first formulation as a cost function in the main formulation. In particular, C is now a set function (the set of items is $M_1 \cup \cdots \cup M_n$ – recall that $M_i \cap M_j$ for $i \neq j$), so standard notions such as subadditivity and submodularity are defined in the usual sense.

Other Requirements. Due to the combinatorial richness of our domain, we are not able to develop good *group*strategyproof mechanisms. Instead, we focus on dominant strategy ones. Following the literature, we focus on mechanisms that satisfy individual rationality, no positive transfers and always cover the cost or maybe are even β-budget balanced, for some reasonable β. We naturally extend the social cost definition of [23] to multiple goods: $\pi(\vec{S}) = C(\vec{S}) + \sum_{i \in N} [v_i(M_i) - v_i(S_i)]$. I.e., we still want to minimize the construction cost plus the lost value. We note that the extended definition preserves the properties discussed above, e.g., additive approximations to the welfare lead to multiplicative approximations to the social cost. We refer the reader to the preliminaries section for exact definitions.

Cost Recovering Mechanisms and the Potential Mechanism

The simple cost sharing domain is a single parameter one, where the private information of every player consists of one number. Thus, to design a dominant strategy mechanism one can focus on the quite powerful family of monotone algorithms. In fact, the literature contains powerful techniques for designing groupstrategyproof mechanisms, for various notions of groupstrategyproofness (e.g., the Moulin family of mechanisms [19] and acyclic mechanisms [18]).

In contrast, the combinatorial cost sharing domain is a multi-parameter one. The difficulty of designing useful mechanisms for multi-parameter domains is well known. The root of evil is the lack of general design techniques except the VCG family. For example, if the domain is unrestricted, then the only possible dominant strategy mechanisms are affine maximizers [22], a slight variation of VCG mechanisms. In general, more restricted domains as ours do exhibit non VCG mechanisms, but the VCG family remains the main tool at our disposal.

However, while VCG is effective for welfare maximization, in cost sharing settings we also need to cover the construction cost. Unfortunately, conventional wisdom has it that the revenue of the VCG mechanism is uncontrollable and tends to be low[3] [1]. The main technical contribution of this paper challenges this – we do manage to "tame" the VCG beast and obtain VCG based mechanisms that are approximately budget balanced.

For simplicity, we start our journey by constructing VCG based mechanisms that always cover the cost for simple cost sharing, so the valuation of each player i can be described by a single number: v_i if served and 0 otherwise. In general, affine maximizers can have both (multiplicative) player weights and (additive) allocations weights. The former does not seem to be very useful, so we focus on affine maximizers of the form:

$$\arg\max_{S \subseteq N} \sum_{i \in S} v_i - H(S) \tag{1}$$

where $H : 2^N \to \mathbb{R}$ is a function that does not depend on the v_i's. If S is the allocation that maximizes (1) for the valuation profile v, then the payment of player i is:

$$p_i = \sum_{j \in S_{-i}} v_j - H(S_{-i}) - \left[\sum_{j \in S - \{i\}} v_j - H(S) \right] \tag{2}$$

where S_{-i} is the allocation that maximizes (1) when the valuation of player i is identically 0.

When H is the cost function C, we get a welfare maximizing mechanism. However, it is common for this mechanism to run a deficit, e.g., in the special case of excludable public good ($C(S) = 1$ for every $S \neq \emptyset$), if $v_i > 1$ for every player i, the revenue is 0.

Thus, to cover the incurred cost we need some other function $H \neq C$. Notice that from the definition of S_{-i} that $\sum_{j \in S_{-i}} v_j - H(S_{-i}) \geq \sum_{j \in S - \{i\}} v_j - H(S - \{i\})$. Hence, the payment of the i'th player p_i is at least $H(S) - H(S - \{i\})$. A function H with the property that for every set $S \subseteq N$ it holds that $\sum_{i \in S} H(S) - H(S - \{i\}) \geq C(S)$ will lead to a dominant-strategy mechanism for simple cost sharing that always collects payments that cover the incurred cost. For example, in the special case of excludable public good, we can choose $H(S) = \mathcal{H}_{|S|}$, so if a set S is selected the marginal cost to H of each player $i \in S$ is at least $H(S) - H(S - \{i\}) = \frac{1}{|S|}$ and the total payment is at least 1 (this special case was analyzed by Blumrosen and Dobzinski [4]).

Interestingly, for *every* cost function C the *potential function* of Hart and Mas-Colell [15] satisfies these properties. Given a cooperative game with a set N of players and a cost function C, the potential function is the unique function for which the sum of marginal contributions of every coalition equals its cost, i.e., for every $S \subseteq N$, $\sum_{i \in S} P_C(S) - P_C(S - \{i\}) = C(S)$.

[3] Some papers attempt to control the revenue of VCG in simpler auction settings by rebating the players, e.g., [6, 13, 20]. Also relevant is the work of Blumrosen and Dobzinski [4] which is the closest in spirit to ours (and in fact is the inspiration to our work). One of their results essentially provide a cost-recovering VCG based mechanism for the excludable public good problem. Their mechanism can be derived as a special case of our constructions.

The potential function has several interesting properties, e.g., the marginal contribution $P_C(i|S)$ coincides with the Shapley value of player i in the coalition $S \cup \{i\}$. In addition, it is also known that the worst-case welfare loss of the Shapley mechanism for simple cost sharing is given by $P_C(OPT)$ [21].

We generalize and adapt the potential function to our needs: the potential function as defined in [15] considers cooperative games, i.e., the cost function defined on subsets of N. Our generalization considers allocations. Specifically, we define the marginal contribution of player i to the allocation $(S_1, ..., S_n)$ by $P_C(S_1, ..., S_{i-1}, S_i, S_{i+1}, ..., S_n) - P_C(S_1, ..., S_{i-1}, \emptyset, S_{i+1}, ..., S_n)$.

We set the function H as in (1) to be our generalization of the potential function, and name the new mechanism, a VCG mechanism using the potential function, the *Potential Mechanism.* Notice that this gives a dominant strategy cost-recovering mechanism for *every* cost function C. We are also able to prove efficiency guarantees if the cost function C is subadditive. Combined together, we get the following general result:

Theorem: Let C be a subadditive cost function. Then, the Potential mechanism always recovers the cost and provides an approximation ratio of $2\mathcal{H}_n$ to the social cost. If C is submodular (or even XOS) the approximation ratio improves to $\mathcal{H}_n$.

Again, the approximation ratio is essentially tight due to the impossibility of [9]. For simple cost sharing, there is a dominant-strategy cost recovering mechanism that provides an approximation ratio of $\mathcal{H}_n$ for any cost function, by running the Shapley value mechanism "on top" of the VCG mechanism [25]. Other works that focus on cost recovering mechanisms are [11, 12]. In particular, [12] handles some multi-parameter domains. However, their results are obtained via a reduction to the single parameter setting, e.g., by assuming additive valuations or considering "all or nothing" solutions. This approach leads to poor approximation ratios – linear in the number of goods.

The Main Result

The main technical effort of this work is in identifying three settings in which the potential mechanism is not only efficient and cost recovering, but also budget balanced.

Theorem: Let C be a submodular cost function. The Potential Mechanism is $\mathcal{H}_n$-budget-balanced and provides an approximation ratio of $\mathcal{H}_n$ to the social cost in each of the following settings:

- Supermodular valuations.
- General symmetric valuations and player-wise symmetric cost function[4].
- Two players ($n = 2$) with general valuations.

Some results were already known for some special cases of the symmetric setting, but even then submodular valuations are required: Mehta et al. [18] consider *non-metric fault-tolerant uncapacitated facility location.* Bleischwitz and Schoppmann [3] study *metric fault tolerant uncapacitated facility location.* The mechanisms of Mehta et al. and of Bleischwitz and Schoppmann are actually generalizations of Moulin mechanisms [19, 21] and rely in their core on pushing single parameter cost sharing techniques to their limit. In contrast, in the symmetric setting our mechanism does not make any assumption on the valuations, except monotonicity.

[4]A valuation is symmetric if $v_i(S) = v_i(T)$ whenever $|S| = |T|$. A cost function is player-symmetric if $C(\vec{S}) = C(\vec{T})$ whenever $|S_i| = |T_i|$ for all i.

Limitations and Impossibilities

Our results are tight in several aspects. First, even for excludable public good there is an instance in which the approximation ratio of the potential mechanism is $\Theta(\log n)$ and the mechanism is $\Theta(\log n)$ budget balanced. Actually, this is true for every VCG-based mechanism that uses a symmetric function[5] (i.e., for $\vec{S}, \vec{T}$ with $|\vec{S}| = |\vec{T}|$, $H(\vec{S}) = H(\vec{T})$):

Theorem: Let A be a symmetric VCG-based mechanism for the excludable public good problem (i.e., a mechanism that maximizes $\sum_i v_i(S_i) - H(\vec{S})$ for some symmetric H) which always covers the incurred cost. Suppose that A provides an approximation ratio of $n^{1-\epsilon}$ to the social cost, for some $\epsilon > 0$. Then, there is an instance in which both the approximation ratio is $\Omega(\log n)$ and the sum of payments collected by the mechanism is $\Omega(\log n)$ times the incurred cost.

Next we show that one cannot forgo the assumption of a restricted cost function since there is a (non-subadditive) cost function for which the approximation ratio of the potential mechanism is $\Omega(n)$. Moreover, the potential mechanism is $\Omega(n)$-budget-balanced for a submodular cost function and unit demand valuations (a simple case of submodular valuations). A full mapping of the families for which the potential mechanism provides good approximation ratios is an open problem.

We also show that while one have many possible choices for the function H in (1), the choice to use the potential function is not arbitrary: consider a cost-recovering VCG based mechanism $\sum_i v_i(S_i) - H(\vec{S})$ where H is normalized. Then, $H(\vec{S}) \geq P_C(\vec{S})$ for every $\vec{S}$.

Open Questions

Our work leaves many exciting questions open. We discuss some of them now.

Computational Issues. In this work we focused on proving the existence of mechanisms with good guarantees. An interesting question is to understand whether there are mechanisms with good guarantees that are computationally efficient. We do not know the answer in general, but we do note that in the case of supermodular valuations and a submodular cost function the potential mechanism is computationally efficient whenever the value of the potential function is easy to compute. To see this, we point out that one of our results states that the potential function of a submodular cost function is submodular as well. Therefore, maximizing $\sum_i v_i(S_i) - P_C(\vec{S})$ reduces to the problem of maximizing a supermodular function, which is equivalent to minimizing submodular function. Minimizing a submodular function can be done in polynomial time [24] assuming oracle access to the potential function.

Now observe that the potential function is easy to evaluate given the Shapley values (since the marginals of the potential function correspond to Shapley values). We conclude that in this case the potential mechanism is easy to compute whenever computing Shapley values is easy.

The Performance of the Potential Mechanism. We identified three settings in which the potential mechanism is $\mathcal{H}_n$-budget-balanced and provides an approximation ratio of $\mathcal{H}_n$ to the social cost. When the cost function is subadditive, the social cost approximation is $2\mathcal{H}_n$, but it is not clear whether we get budget balance for some interesting classes of valuations. A first step in this direction will be to determine the overcharging of the potential mechanism for simple cost sharing when the cost function is subadditive.

---

[5] Note that the potential mechanism is symmetric when C is symmetric, and in particular is symmetric for excludable public good.

Other Mechanisms for Combinatorial Cost Sharing. The potential mechanism is a VCG-based mechanism. Are there non VCG-based mechanisms with good guarantees, especially for settings in which the potential mechanism fails to deliver, e.g., submodular cost and valuation functions?

The Power of GSP vs. Strategyproof Mechanisms. We know very little about groupstrategyproof mechanisms for combinatorial cost sharing. In the full version we provide a mechanism that guarantees a poor approximation ratio of $\Omega(n)$. Are there better groupstrategyproof mechanisms?

Impossibilities for Combinatorial Cost Sharing. The potential mechanism provides an approximation ratio of $\mathcal{H}_n$ to the social cost and is $\mathcal{H}_n$-budget-balanced for supermodular valuations and submodular cost functions. Is there a strategyproof combinatorial cost-sharing mechanism for submodular cost function and supermodular valuation functions which is β-budget-balanced and provides approximation ratio of ρ to the social cost, where $\beta, \rho < \mathcal{H}_n$?

In particular, the only unrestricted impossibility result that applies to combinatorial cost sharing is the $\Omega(\log n)$ bound to the social cost of [9] which is proved for the restricted case of excludable public good. It seems that completely new ideas are needed to prove the optimality of the potential mechanism in richer combinatorial settings.

2 PRELIMINARIES

In combinatorial cost sharing we have a set N of n players and $M = \bigcup_{i=1}^{n} M_i$ a set of services, where for every $i \neq j$: $M_i \cap M_j = \emptyset$. Every player $i \in N$ has a valuation function $v_i : 2^{M_i} \to \mathbb{R}^+$. There is a cost function $C : 2^{M_1} \times \ldots \times 2^{M_n} \to \mathbb{R}^+$ that specifies the cost of every possible allocation of services. The output is $(\vec{S}, \vec{p})$ where $S_i \subseteq M_i$ is the allocation of services to player i, and $p_i \geq 0$ is player i's payment.

We assume that the cost function and the valuations are *monotone* (i.e., $S \subseteq T$ implies $C(S) \leq C(T)$ and $v_i(S) \leq v_i(T)$) and *normalized* (i.e., $C(\emptyset) = 0$ and $v_i(\emptyset) = 0$).

We note that since the M_i's are disjoint then $2^M = 2^{M_1} \times \ldots \times 2^{M_n}$. Thus, we sometimes refer to functions from $2^{M_1} \times \ldots \times 2^{M_n}$ as functions from 2^M, e.g., $C(S_1, \ldots, S_n)$ will be denoted $C\left(\bigcup_{i=1}^{n} S_i\right)$, where $S_i \subseteq M_i$ for each $1 \leq i \leq n$. In addition, For a vector of pairwise disjoint sets $\vec{S} = (S_1, \ldots, S_n)$ and a set $T \subseteq M_i$ we let $\vec{S} - T$ be the vector $(S_1, ..., S_{i-1}, S_i - T, S_{i+1}, ..., S_n)$. We similarly define the usual set operations (e.g., union) between two vectors of disjoint sets $\vec{S}, \vec{T}$ as applying this operation on all pairs of the form (S_i, T_i).

Note that simple cost sharing is a special case of combinatorial cost sharing: set $|M_i| = 1$ for every player i. In this case $|M| = |N|$ and we may think of $S \subseteq N$ as a set of served players: $i \in S$ if $S_i \neq \emptyset$. An important special case of simple cost sharing is *excludable public good*: $C(\vec{S}) = 1$ for every $\vec{S} \neq (\emptyset, ..., \emptyset)$ and $C(\emptyset) = 0$.

A (direct) combinatorial cost sharing mechanism takes the valuations of the players and outputs an allocation of services and prices. In this paper we consider only mechanisms that satisfy *individual rationality* (IR), if the mechanism charges player i an amount p_i, then $p_i \leq v_i(S_i)$. A second requirement is *no positive transfers* (NPT), meaning that $p_i \geq 0$. We now discuss other desired properties of mechanisms.

Incentive Compatibility. The focus of most this paper is in dominant-strategy mechanisms: a combinatorial cost-sharing mechanism is *strategyproof* or *truthful* (in dominant strategies), if for every player i with valuation function v_i and for every other valuation function v_i' it holds that $v_i(S_i) - p_i \geq v_i(S_i') - p_i'$ where $(\vec{S}, \vec{p})$ and $(\vec{S}', \vec{p}')$ are the outputs of the mechanism for $\vec{v}$ and $(v_i', \vec{v}_{-i})$, respectively. Groupstrategyproofness will be defined when needed, in the full version.

Budget Balance. A cost-sharing mechanism is *budget-balanced* if the payments charged from the players cover exactly the incurred cost, i.e. if the mechanism's output is $(\vec{S}, \vec{p})$ then $\sum_{i \in N} p_i = C(\vec{S})$. This notion can be relaxed: a cost-sharing mechanism is *β-budget-balanced* (for $\beta \geq 1$) if for every valuation profile and every cost function the mechanism outputs a services allocation $\vec{S}$ and payments vector $\vec{p}$ such that $C(\vec{S}) \leq \sum_{i \in N} p_i \leq \beta \cdot C(\vec{S})$.

Economic Efficiency. Roughgarden and Sundararajan [23] suggested to quantify the inefficiency of cost-sharing mechanisms by the notion of *social cost*, denoted $\pi(S)$, which is the incurred cost of the mechanism plus the excluded values. We extend the definition of the social cost to the combinatorial setting:

$$\pi(\vec{S}) = C(\vec{S}) + \sum_{i \in N} [v_i(M_i) - v_i(S_i)]$$

A cost sharing mechanism is a ρ-approximation to the social cost if for every valuation profile the social cost of its outcome $\vec{S}$ is at most $\rho \geq 1$ times that of the allocation $\overrightarrow{OPT}$ that minimizes the social cost: $\pi(\vec{S}) \leq \rho \cdot \pi(\overrightarrow{OPT})$.

Cost and Valuation Functions. A function $C : 2^M \to \mathbb{R}^+$ is submodular if for every two sets $S, T \subseteq M$, $C(S) + C(T) \geq C(S \cup T) + C(S \cap T)$. Equivalently, a function C is submodular if for every two sets $T \subseteq S \subseteq M$ and an element $x \in M - S$ it holds that $C(T \cup \{x\}) - C(T) \geq C(S \cup \{x\}) - C(S)$. A cost function C is *subadditive* if for every $S, T \subseteq M$, $C(S) + C(T) \geq C(S \cup T)$. A cost function C is *player-wise symmetric* if for every two allocations $\vec{S}, \vec{T} \in 2^{M_1} \times \cdots \times 2^{M_n}$ with $|S_i| = |T_i|$ for every $i \in N$ in holds that $C(\vec{T}) = C(\vec{S})$.

v is *supermodular* if for every two sets $S, T \subseteq M_i$, it holds that $v(S) + v(T) \leq v(S \cup T) + v(S \cap T)$. Equivalently, for every two sets $T \subseteq S$ and an element $x \in M - S$ it holds that $v(T \cup \{x\}) - v(T) \leq v(S \cup \{x\}) - v(S)$. A function $v : 2^M \to \mathbb{R}$ is *symmetric* if for every two sets $S, T \subseteq M_i$ with $|S| = |T|$ it holds that $v(S) = v(T)$. v is *additive* if for every S it holds that $v(S) = \sum_{j \in S} v(\{j\})$. v is XOS if there exists additive valuations $a_1, \ldots, a_t$ such that for every S, $v(S) = \max_r a_r(S)$. The class of submodular valuations is contained in the class of XOS valuations which is contained in the class of subadditive valuations, and these containments are strict.

3 THE POTENTIAL FUNCTION AND ITS PROPERTIES

The potential mechanism is an affine maximizer whose output allocation is defined by:

$$\arg \max_{\vec{S}=(S_1,\ldots,S_n)} \sum_i v_i(S_i) - H(\vec{S})$$

where $H : 2^{M_1} \times \cdots \times 2^{M_n} \to \mathbb{R}$ is a publicly known function. In this section we describe the function H we use and its properties.

The function H we use is an adaptation of the *Potential Function* of Hart and Mas-Colell [15]. Given a cooperative game with N players and cost function C, Hart and Mas-Colell define a potential function to be a normalized function in which the sum of discrete gradients of any set of players N' equals the cost $C(N')$. We naturally extend this definition:

Definition 3.1 (potential function for combinatorial cost sharing). Given a normalized cost function $C : 2^{M_1} \times \cdots \times 2^{M_n} \to \mathbb{R}^+$ we define a potential function $P_C : 2^{M_1} \times \cdots \times 2^{M_n} \to \mathbb{R}^+$ to be any normalized function with the following property:

- For every allocation $\vec{S} = (S_1, ..., S_n)$ such that $S_i \subseteq M_i$, the sum of discrete gradients of the function is exactly the cost: $\sum_{i \in N} \left[P_C\left(\vec{S}\right) - P_C\left(\vec{S} - S_i\right)\right] = C\left(\vec{S}\right)$.

Notice that for simple cost sharing the definitions of [15] and ours coincide. The proof of the next proposition essentially follows from [15]. We bring it in the full version for completeness.

Proposition 3.2. *For every normalized cost function C there is a unique potential function P_C. Moreover, it holds that $P_C(\vec{S}) = \Sigma_{I \subseteq N} \frac{C(\cup_{i \in I} S_i)}{|I| \cdot \binom{n}{|I|}}$.*

Following [15], there are a couple of useful observations related to the potential function. First, by rearranging:

$$P_C(\vec{S}) = \sum_{I \subseteq N} \frac{C(\cup_{i \in I} S_i)}{|I| \cdot \binom{n}{|I|}} = \sum_{l=1}^{n} \sum_{I \subseteq N, |I|=l} \frac{C(\cup_{i \in I} S_i)}{|I| \cdot \binom{n}{|I|}}$$

Let $D(\vec{S}, l) = \Sigma_{I \subseteq N, |I|=l} \frac{C(\cup_{i \in I} S_i)}{|I| \cdot \binom{n}{|I|}}$. Notice the $D(\vec{S}, l)$ is the expected density (cost divided by the number of players) of a set I of players that is chosen uniformly at random among all sets of size l, when each player $i \in I$ is served S_i and player $i \notin I$ is not served at all. Thus, $P_C(\vec{S})$ equals the sum of expected densities of sets of size $1, \ldots, n$.

A second observation (again, following [15]) is that the marginal utility $P_C(\vec{S}) - P_C(\vec{S} - S_i)$ equals the Shapley value of player i in the cooperative game with N players and cost function C', where the cost of serving a set T is $C'(T) = C(\cup_{i \in T} S_i)$.

We now use these observations to prove several useful properties of our potential function.

Claim 3.3. *Let C be a monotone cost function. The potential function P_C is monotone as well. Furthermore, if C is submodular then P_C is submodular as well.*

Proof. Observe that $P_C(\cdot)$ is a sum of functions $C(\cup_{i \in I} S_i)$, each multiplied by a constant $\frac{1}{|I| \cdot \binom{n}{|I|}}$. Each of these functions is monotone because C is monotone. Since a sum of monotone functions is monotone as well, we conclude that P_C is monotone.

The second part of the claim is almost identical, by replacing "monotone" with "submodular" in the previous paragraph. □

Next we prove that for every submodular cost function C and $\vec{S}$, $\mathcal{H}_n \cdot C(\vec{S}) \geq P_C(\vec{S}) \geq C(\vec{S})$. We also prove a similar bound for subadditive cost functions.

Proposition 3.4. *Let C be an XOS (in particular, submodular) cost function. Then, for every $\vec{S}$, $P_C(\vec{S}) \geq C(\vec{S})$. If C is subadditive then for every $\vec{S}$, $P_C(\vec{S}) \geq \frac{C(\vec{S})}{2}$.*

Proof. We will need the following folklore claim:

Claim 3.5. *Let $C' : 2^N \to \mathbb{R}$ be a monotone function. Choose a set T of size l uniformly at random among all such sets. Then:*

(1) If C' is XOS then $\frac{n}{l} \cdot E[C'(T)] \geq C'(N)$.
(2) If C' is subadditive then $\lceil \frac{n}{l} \rceil \cdot E[C'(T)] \geq C'(N)$.

Proof. (of Claim 3.5)

(1) By the definition of an XOS valuation, there is some additive valuation a such that $a(N) = C'(N)$. Moreover, for every S, $C'(S) \geq a(S)$. Consider choosing at random a set T of size l. Each element j is selected with probability $\frac{l}{N}$. Let A_j be the random variable that gets the value $a(\{j\})$ if j is selected and 0 otherwise. Observe that:

$$E[C'(T)] \geq E[a(T)] = \Sigma_{j \in N} A_j = \Sigma_{j \in N} \frac{l}{n} \cdot a(\{j\}) = \frac{l}{n} \cdot C'(N)$$

(2) Let $t = \lfloor \frac{n}{l} \rfloor$. Choose t disjoint sets $T_1, \ldots, T_t$ each of size l, uniformly at random. If n does not divide l, construct an additional set T_{t+1} from taking $N - \cup_j T_j$ in addition to $l - |N - \cup_j T_j|$ items that are chosen uniformly at random. Now choose a set R by choosing one of the sets $T_1, \ldots, T_{\lceil \frac{n}{l} \rceil}$ uniformly at random. Notice that by subadditivity $\Sigma_{i=1}^{\lceil \frac{n}{l} \rceil} C'(T_i) \geq C'(N)$. Thus, $E[R] \geq \frac{1}{\lceil \frac{n}{l} \rceil} \cdot C'(N)$. The proposition follows since R is a set of size l which is chosen uniformly at random.

□

We can now prove Proposition 3.4. Fix $\vec{S} = (S_1, \ldots, S_n)$. Obtain a function $C' : 2^N \to \mathbb{R}$ by $C'(I) = C(\cup_{i \in I} S_i)$. Observe that if C is subadditive (XOS) then C' is subadditive (XOS). For every l, let $D'(l) = D(\vec{S}, l)$ denote the expected density of a set of size l in C'. Notice that by Claim 3.5 for XOS functions we have that $D'(l) \geq \frac{l}{n} \cdot C'(N)$. Now, if C' is XOS, then:

$$P_C(\vec{S}) = \Sigma_{l=1}^{n} D'(l) \geq \Sigma_{l=1}^{n} \frac{\frac{l}{n} \cdot C'(N)}{l} = \Sigma_{l=1}^{n} \frac{C'(N)}{n} = C'(N)$$

The proof is similar if C' is subadditive:

$$P_C(\vec{S}) = \Sigma_{l=1}^{n} D'(l) \geq \Sigma_{l=1}^{n} \frac{C'(N)}{\lceil \frac{n}{l} \rceil \cdot l} \geq \frac{C'(N)}{2}$$

□

Claim 3.6. *Let C be a monotone cost function. Then, for every $\vec{S}$, $P_C(\vec{S}) \leq \mathcal{H}_n \cdot C(\vec{S})$.*

Proof. C is monotone, so for every $\vec{S}$ and l we have the following bound on the average density of a random set of size l: $D(\vec{S}, l) \leq \frac{C(\vec{S})}{l}$. Thus, $P_C(\vec{S}) = \Sigma_{l=1}^{n} D(\vec{S}, l) \leq \Sigma_{l=1}^{n} C(\vec{S}) \cdot \frac{1}{l} = C(\vec{S}) \cdot \mathcal{H}_n$. □

4 THE MAIN RESULT: THE POTENTIAL MECHANISM

In this section we present our main result, the Potential Mechanism. Specifically, given a cost function $C : 2^{M_1} \times \ldots \times 2^{M_n} \to \mathbb{R}^+$ and its potential function P_C, define the *Potential Mechanism* be the following affine maximizer:

$$\overrightarrow{ALG} = \arg \max_{\vec{S}=(S_1,\ldots,S_n)} \sum_{i \in N} v_i(S_i) - P_C(\vec{S}) \tag{3}$$

We charge player i his VCG payment which is given by the formula:

$$p_i = \left[\sum_{j \in N} v_j(ALG_j^{-i}) - P_C(\overrightarrow{ALG^{-i}}) \right] - \left[\sum_{j \in N \setminus \{i\}} v_j(ALG_j) - P_C(\overrightarrow{ALG}) \right]$$

where $\overrightarrow{ALG^{-i}} = (ALG_1^{-i}, \ldots, ALG_{i-1}^{-i}, \emptyset, ALG_{i+1}^{-i}, \ldots, ALG_n^{-i})$ is the allocation that maximizes (3) with the additional constraint $ALG_i^{-i} = \emptyset$. Note that there might be several allocations that maximize (3), hence the mechanism is defined up to the implementation of a tie breaking rule.

Theorem 4.1. *For every valuation profile and cost function C the Potential Mechanism is strategyproof, individually rational, always covers the incurred cost and satisfies no positive transfers. Moreover:*

1. *When C is subadditive the mechanism provides an approximation ratio of $2\mathcal{H}_n$ to the social cost. When C is XOS (in particular, submodular) the mechanism provides an approximation ratio of $\mathcal{H}_n$ to the social cost.*
2. *When C is submodular the mechanism is $\mathcal{H}_n$-budget-balanced in each of the following settings:*

(a) *The valuation functions are supermodular.*
(b) *The valuation functions are symmetric and the cost function C is player-wise symmetric.*
(c) *There are two players.*

Notice that the potential mechanism exhibits a "one size fits all" property: the performance guarantees improve as the more restricted the functions are although the mechanism is defined identically for all cost and valuation functions.

We note that strategyproofness, individual rationality, and no positive transfers of the potential mechanism follow directly from the properties of the VCG mechanism. The rest of the section is devoted to proving that the mechanism always recovers the cost and is approximately efficient and budget balanced in certain settings and in Section 6 we discuss some of the limitations of the potential mechanism.

The Potential Mechanism: Cost Recovering and Efficiency

Lemma 4.2. *The potential mechanism always covers the incurred cost, i.e. for every outcome* $\left(\overrightarrow{ALG}, \vec{p}\right)$, *it holds that* $\sum p_i \geq C(\overrightarrow{ALG})$.

Proof. The payment of player i is given by:

$$p_i = \left[\sum_{j \in N} v_j(ALG_j^{-i}) - P_C\left(\overrightarrow{ALG^{-i}}\right)\right] - \left[\sum_{j \in N \setminus \{i\}} v_j(ALG_j) - P_C(\overrightarrow{ALG})\right]$$

Notice that $\sum_{j \in N} v_j(ALG_j^{-i}) - P_C\left(\overrightarrow{ALG^{-i}}\right) \geq \sum_{j \in N \setminus \{i\}} v_j(ALG_j) - P_C(\overrightarrow{ALG} - ALG_i)$ since $\overrightarrow{ALG} - ALG_i$ is one of the alternatives that are considered for ALG^{-i}, therefore

$$\begin{aligned} p_i &\geq \left[\sum_{j \in N \setminus \{i\}} v_j(ALG_j) - P_C(\overrightarrow{ALG} - ALG_i)\right] - \left[\sum_{j \in N \setminus \{i\}} v_j(ALG_j) - P_C(\overrightarrow{ALG})\right] \\ &= P_C(\overrightarrow{ALG}) - P_C(\overrightarrow{ALG} - ALG_i) \end{aligned}$$

summing over all players, we get

$$\sum_{i \in N} p_i \geq \sum_{i \in N} P_C(\overrightarrow{ALG}) - P_C(\overrightarrow{ALG} - ALG_i) = C(\overrightarrow{ALG})$$

where the last equality is by the definition of the potential function. □

Next we analyze the efficiency guarantees of the mechanism. For completeness in the full version we prove guarantees for both the social cost and additive approximations, although the latter implies the former [23].

Lemma 4.3. *Let C be a subadditive cost function. Then the approximation ratio of the Potential Mechanism to the social cost is* $2\mathcal{H}_n$. *If C is XOS then the approximation ratio improves to* $\mathcal{H}_n$. *Similarly,* $SW(\overrightarrow{OPT}) - SW(\overrightarrow{ALG}) \leq (\mathcal{H}_n - 1) \cdot C(\overrightarrow{OPT})$ *if C is XOS and* $SW(\overrightarrow{OPT}) - SW(\overrightarrow{ALG}) \leq (2\mathcal{H}_n - 1) \cdot C(\overrightarrow{OPT})$ *if C is subadditive.*

Interestingly, up until now we have not used the property that the M_i's are disjoint. That is, consider the usual setting of a combinatorial auction with n players and a set of M items. Let C be a function that specifies the cost of every allocation. The same proofs imply that the potential mechanism always recovers the cost in this general setting. Furthermore, if C is subadditive then the output is approximately efficient.

The Potential Mechanism: Budget Balance

Most of the technical difficulty in the proof of Theorem 4.1 is showing that the mechanism is $\mathcal{H}_n$-budget-balanced. We have already shown that the potential mechanism always cover the cost (Lemma 4.2). We remain with showing that the sum of payments of the mechanism is bounded from above by $\mathcal{H}_n$ times the incurred cost.

Lemma 4.4. *In each one of the settings (2a), (2b) and (2c) of theorem 4.1 the following holds: for every outcome of the mechanism $(\overrightarrow{ALG}, \vec{p})$ we have that $\sum_{i \in N} p_i \leq \mathcal{H}_k \cdot C(\overrightarrow{ALG})$.*

Recall that the potential mechanism is defined up to a tie-breaking rule. For supermodular valuations and $n = 2$ the proofs below work directly for any tie breaking rule. For the symmetric setting, we start with an arbitrary tie-breaking rule and modify it. We prove budget balance for the modified tie-breaking rule and see that this implies budget balance for the original tie breaking rule. The modified rule is defined as follows: for every player i define an arbitrary order on M_i and denote its elements as $M_i = \left\{1^i, \ldots, |M_i|^i\right\}$. If player i gets s items in the original rule then allocate player i items $\{1^i, \ldots, s^i\}$. Notice that due to symmetry all costs and values remain the same, so this new allocation still maximizes the affine maximizer. Finally, observe that since that player i is always indifferent between the bundles he receives in the original and modified rules, we may assume that the price of these bundles is identical as well, so his payment remains the same. Hence, budget balance for the modified rule implies budget balance for the original rule as well.

In order to prove lemma 4.4 we use the following claim:

Claim 4.5. *In each one of settings (2a), (2b) and (2c) of theorem 4.1:*

$$\sum_{i=1}^{n} \left[\sum_{j \in N} v_j(ALG_j^{-i}) - P_C(\overrightarrow{ALG^{-i}}) \right] \leq (n-1) \cdot \left[\sum_{j=1}^{n} v_j(ALG_j) - P_C(\overrightarrow{ALG}) \right] \tag{4}$$

Before providing the proof of claim 4.5 in subsection 4.1, we show how it implies lemma 4.4.

Proof. (of lemma 4.4) Consider the sum of the payments:

$$\sum_{i=1}^{n} p_i = \sum_{i=1}^{n} \left[\left[\sum_{j \in N} v_j(ALG_j^{-i}) - P_C(\overrightarrow{ALG^{-i}}) \right] - \left[\sum_{j \in N \setminus \{i\}} v_j(ALG_j) - P_C(\overrightarrow{ALG}) \right] \right]$$

by claim 4.5 the RHS is bounded from above by:

$$(n-1) \cdot \left[\sum_{j=1}^{n} v_j(ALG_j) - P_C(\overrightarrow{ALG}) \right] - \sum_{i=1}^{n} \left[\sum_{j \in N \setminus \{i\}} v_j(ALG_j) - P_C(\overrightarrow{ALG}) \right]$$

re-arranging, we observe that $\sum_{i=1}^{n} \sum_{j \in N \setminus \{i\}} v_j(ALG_j) = (n-1) \cdot \sum_{j=1}^{n} v_j(ALG_j)$. Therefore the above equals to:

$$(n-1) \cdot \left[\sum_{j=1}^{n} v_j(ALG_j) - P_C(\overrightarrow{ALG}) \right] - (n-1) \cdot \left[\sum_{j=1}^{n} v_j(ALG_j) \right] + n \cdot P_C(\overrightarrow{ALG}) = P_C(\overrightarrow{ALG})$$

By proposition 3.6 we get that $P_C(\overrightarrow{ALG}) \leq \mathcal{H}_n \cdot C(\overrightarrow{ALG})$. Hence, $\sum_{i=1}^{n} p_i \leq \mathcal{H}_n \cdot C(\overrightarrow{ALG})$. □

4.1 Proof of Claim 4.5

The proof consists of several steps: Claim 4.7 shows a lower bound on $\sum_{i=1}^{n} P_C(\overrightarrow{ALG^{-i}})$, Claim 4.8 gives an upper bound on $\sum_{i=1}^{n}\sum_{j\in N} v_j(ALG_j^{-i})$ for supermodular valuations and $n = 2$, and claim 4.9 gives a similar bound for the symmetric setting. The following technical claim will be used:

Claim 4.6. *Let $H : 2^M \to \mathbb{R}$ be a normalized function, and consider $\left\{T^i\right\}_{i=1}^{n}$ such that for every i, $T^i \in 2^M$ and $\bigcap_{i=1}^{n} T^i = \emptyset$. Suppose that either (1) H is supermodular or (2) for every $1 \leq i, j \leq n$, $T^i \cup T^j \in \left\{T^i, T^j\right\}$. Then it holds that $\sum_{i=1}^{n} H(T^i) \leq \sum_{i=1}^{n-1} H\left(T^{i+1} \cup \left(\cap_{\ell=1}^{i} T^\ell\right)\right)$.*

Proof. If H is supermodular, then beginning with the first two summands of the LHS of the claim, by supermodularity of H:

$$H(T^1) + H(T^2) \leq H(T^1 \cup T^2) + H(T^1 \cap T^2)$$

shifting our focus to $H(T^1 \cap T^2)$ and the third summand $H(T^3)$ yields

$$H(T^1 \cap T^2) + H(T^3) \leq H\left(\left(T^1 \cap T^2\right) \cup T^3\right) + H\left(T^1 \cap T^2 \cap T^3\right)$$

iterating the above for n times shows

$$H\left(T^1 \cap \ldots \cap T^{n-1}\right) + H(T^n) \leq H\left(\left(\bigcap_{i=1}^{n-1} T^i\right) \cup T^n\right) + H\left(\bigcap_{i=1}^{n} T^i\right)$$

by combining everything we get

$$\sum_{i=1}^{n} H(T^i) \leq \sum_{i=1}^{n-1} H\left(T^{i+1} \cup \left(\bigcap_{\ell=1}^{i} T^\ell\right)\right) + H\left(\bigcap_{i=1}^{n} T^i\right)$$

since $\bigcap_{i=1}^{n} T^i = \emptyset$ and $H(\emptyset) = 0$, the claim follows.

If $T^i \cup T^j \in \{T^i, T^j\}$ for every $1 \leq i, j \leq n$, then without loss of generality when $T^i \cup T^j = T^j$ we have that $T^i \cap T^j = T^i$. Thus, a similar proof can be applied on $\left\{T^i\right\}_{i\in N}$ with strict equality. □

The next claim bounds the sum of the P_C's as they appear in Claim 4.5.

Claim 4.7. *Suppose that the cost function C is submodular and normalized, then*

$$-\sum_{i=1}^{n} P_C(\overrightarrow{ALG^{-i}}) \leq -\sum_{i=1}^{n-1} P_C\left(\overrightarrow{ALG^{-[i+1]}} \bigcup \left(\cap_{\ell=1}^{i} \overrightarrow{ALG^{-\ell}}\right)\right)$$

Proof. Since C is submodular, by Proposition 3.3 it holds that P_C is submodular as well. Hence, $-P_C$ is supermodular and we can apply Claim 4.6 with $-P_C$ and $\left\{\overrightarrow{ALG^{-i}}\right\}_{i=1}^{n}$ (observe that for every i, $ALG_i^{-i} = \emptyset$ hence $\bigcap_{i=1}^{n} \overrightarrow{ALG^{-i}} = \emptyset$). □

The next two claims bound the sum of valuations $\sum_{i=1}^{n}\sum_{j=1}^{n} v_j(ALG_j^{-i})$. Each of the claims refers to different settings of Theorem 4.1.

Claim 4.8. *Suppose that each v_i is supermodular or that $n = 2$. Then*

$$\sum_{i=1}^{n}\sum_{j=1}^{n} v_j(ALG_j^{-i}) \leq \sum_{i=1}^{n-1}\sum_{j=1}^{n} v_j\left(ALG_j^{-[i+1]} \bigcup \left(\cap_{\ell=1}^{i} ALG_j^{-\ell}\right)\right)$$

Proof. Define $V : 2^{M_1} \times \cdots \times 2^{M_n} \to \mathbb{R}$ by $V(\vec{T}) = \sum_{j=1}^{n} v_j(T_j)$. It is easy to see that V is normalized. Also, since $ALG_i^{-i} = \emptyset$, it holds that $\bigcap_{i=1}^{n} \overrightarrow{ALG^{-i}} = \emptyset$. Observe that if the v_i's are supermodular then V is supermodular as well. Applying claim 4.6 with V and $\left\{\overrightarrow{ALG^{-i}}\right\}_{i=1}^{n}$:

$$\sum_{i=1}^{n} V(\overrightarrow{ALG^{-i}}) \leq \sum_{i=1}^{n-1} V\left(\overrightarrow{ALG^{-[i+1]}} \bigcup \left(\cap_{\ell=1}^{i} \overrightarrow{ALG^{-\ell}}\right)\right) = \sum_{i=1}^{n-1}\sum_{j=1}^{n} v_j\left(ALG_j^{-[i+1]} \bigcup \left(\cap_{\ell=1}^{i} ALG_j^{-\ell}\right)\right)$$

For $n = 2$ we have that:

$$\sum_{i=1}^{2} V(\overrightarrow{ALG^{-i}}) = v_1(ALG_1^{-2}) + v_2(ALG_2^{-1}) = \sum_{j=1}^{2} v_j\left(ALG_j^{-2} \bigcup ALG_j^{-1}\right)$$

□

Claim 4.9. *Suppose that each v_i is symmetric and C is a player-wise symmetric cost function. Then:*

$$\sum_{i=1}^{n}\sum_{j=1}^{n} v_j(ALG_j^{-i}) \leq \sum_{i=1}^{n-1}\sum_{j=1}^{n} v_j\left(ALG_j^{-[i+1]} \bigcup \left(\cap_{\ell=1}^{i} ALG_j^{-\ell}\right)\right)$$

Proof. We prove the claim assuming the tie breaking rule described earlier. Consider the LHS of the claim and change the order of summation:

$$\sum_{i=1}^{n}\sum_{j=1}^{n} v_j(ALG_j^{-i}) = \sum_{j=1}^{n}\sum_{i=1}^{n} v_j(ALG_j^{-i})$$

Fix player j and consider $\sum_{i=1}^{n} v_j(ALG_j^{-i})$. By the implementation, for every $1 \leq i \leq n$, $ALG_j^{-i} = \{1^j, \ldots, |ALG_j^{-i}|^j\}$. Therefore, for every $1 \leq i, k \leq n$ it holds that $ALG_j^{-i} \cup ALG_j^{-k} \in \left\{ALG_j^{-i}, ALG_j^{-k}\right\}$. Moreover, since $ALG_j^{-j} = \emptyset$, $\bigcap_{i=1}^{n} ALG_j^{-i} = \emptyset$. Applying claim 4.6 on v_j and $\left\{ALG_j^{-i}\right\}_{i=1}^{n}$:

$$\sum_{i=1}^{n} v_j(ALG_j^{-i}) \leq \sum_{i=1}^{n-1} v_j\left(ALG_j^{-[i+1]} \bigcup \left(\cap_{\ell=1}^{i} ALG_j^{-\ell}\right)\right)$$

Summing over all players, we get

$$\sum_{j=1}^{n}\sum_{i=1}^{n} v_j(ALG_j^{-i}) \leq \sum_{j=1}^{n}\sum_{i=1}^{n-1} v_j\left(ALG_j^{-[i+1]} \bigcup \left(\cap_{\ell=1}^{i} ALG_j^{-\ell}\right)\right)$$

Changing the order of summation, the RHS equals to

$$\sum_{i=1}^{n-1}\sum_{j=1}^{n} v_j\left(ALG_j^{-[i+1]} \bigcup \left(\cap_{\ell=1}^{i} ALG_j^{-\ell}\right)\right)$$

□

We can now finish the proof of claim 4.5.

Proof. (of claim 4.5) By combining claims 4.7, 4.8 and 4.9:

$$\sum_{i=1}^{n}\left[\sum_{j=1}^{n} v_j(ALG_j^{-i}) - P_C(\overrightarrow{ALG^{-i}})\right]$$

$$\leq \sum_{i=1}^{n-1}\left[\sum_{j=1}^{n} v_j\left(ALG_j^{-[i+1]} \cup \left(\cap_{\ell=1}^{i} ALG_j^{-\ell}\right)\right) - P_C\left(\overrightarrow{ALG^{-[i+1]}} \cup \left(\cap_{\ell=1}^{i} \overrightarrow{ALG^{-\ell}}\right)\right)\right]$$

We define $n-1$ allocations: for every $1 \le i \le n-1$ we let $\overrightarrow{S^i} = \overrightarrow{ALG^{-[i+1]}} \cup \left(\bigcap_{\ell=1}^{i} \overrightarrow{ALG^{-\ell}}\right)$. $\overrightarrow{ALG}$ maximizes (3) so $\sum_{j=1}^{n} v_j(S_j^i) - P_C(\overrightarrow{S^i}) \le \sum_{j=1}^{n} v_j(ALG_j) - P_C(\overrightarrow{ALG})$ for every $\overrightarrow{S^i}$. Hence:

$$\sum_{i=1}^{n}\left[\sum_{j\neq i} v_j(ALG_j^{-i}) - P_C(\overrightarrow{ALG^{-i}})\right] \le (n-1)\cdot\left(\sum_{j=1}^{n} v_j(ALG_j) - P_C(\overrightarrow{ALG})\right)$$

□

5 LIMITATIONS OF VCG-BASED MECHANISMS

In this section we discuss some limitations of VCG-based mechanisms. We first ask whether our analysis of the potential mechanism is tight and prove that this is indeed the case. Our result is in fact more general: no symmetric VCG-based mechanism can do much better. We then show that the potential function is the "minimal" choice for $H(\cdot)$ in the affine maximizer in a concrete technical sense.

A word is in place regarding the definition of an affine maximizer. In general an affine maximizer does not have to maximize over all allocations. This can be implemented by setting $H(\vec{S}) = \infty$ for an allocation $\vec{S}$ that is never selected by the affine maximizer. However, it is more convenient to work with a function H that is monotone. This can be assumed without loss of generality: suppose that there is $\vec{S}, j \in M$ such that $H(\vec{S}) > H(\vec{S} + \{j\})$. Note that by the monotonicity of the valuations this implies that the affine maximizer never outputs $\vec{S}$. To make H monotone, we can set $H(\vec{S}) = H(\vec{S} + \{j\})$ – we still have that the affine maximizer always gives higher value to $\vec{S} + \{j\}$ and in case of equality we can assume that $\vec{S}$ is not selected by defining an appropriate tie breaking rule.

A Lower Bound for Symmetric VCG-Based Mechanisms. We show that every VCG-based mechanism that always covers the cost and uses a symmetric function does not provide better guarantees than the potential mechanism for the excludable public good problem. Note that the potential mechanism is symmetric in this setting since the potential function is symmetric if C is symmetric.

THEOREM 5.1. *Let $\mathcal{A}$ be a VCG-based mechanism for the excludable public good problem. I.e. $\mathcal{A}$ is a mechanism that outputs*

$$ALG = \arg\max_{S\subseteq N} \sum_{i\in S} v_i - H(S) \tag{5}$$

where $H : 2^N \to \mathbb{R}^+ \cup \{\infty\}$ is normalized, monotone and symmetric function (i.e. for every two allocations $S, T \subseteq N$ with $|S| = |T|$ it holds that $H(S) = H(T)$). Suppose that $\mathcal{A}$ always covers the cost and provides an approximation ratio of $\rho < \frac{n^{(1-\delta)/2}}{4}$ to the social cost, for some constant $0 < \delta < 1$. Then, there is an instance in which the good is constructed at cost 1, the sum of payments is at least $\left(\frac{1-\delta}{2}\cdot \log n - 1\right)$ and the approximation ratio to the social cost is no better than $(\delta \cdot \log n - 1)$.

In order to prove the theorem, we need the following claim. Proof is in the full version.

CLAIM 5.2. *Let $\mathcal{A}$ be a VCG-based mechanism for the excludable public good problem where $H : 2^N \to \mathbb{R}^+$ is normalized, monotone and symmetric. Suppose that $\mathcal{A}$ always covers the cost and provides a finite approximation ratio ρ to the social cost. Then, for every $S \subseteq N$ and $i \in S$ it holds that $H(S) - H(S - \{i\}) \ge \frac{1}{|S|}$.*

We now turn to proving Theorem 5.1.

PROOF. (of theorem 5.1) Note that since the mechanism provides a ρ approximation, $H(N) < \infty$. Otherwise, for every i, set $v_i = 2\rho$. The optimal social cost is 1, serve all players, but at least one player is excluded so $\pi(\overrightarrow{ALG}) \geq 2\rho$, a contradiction. Fix a set $S \subseteq N$ of size $n^{1-\delta}$. We now divide the analysis, depending on whether there is some set T, with $|T| < n^{(1-\delta)/2}$ such that $\frac{H(T)}{|T|} \leq \frac{H(S)}{|S|}$.

Assume that there is a set T with $|T| < n^{(1-\delta)/2}$ such that $\frac{H(T)}{|T|} \leq \frac{H(S)}{|S|}$. In this case we get that $H(S) \geq n^{(1-\delta)/2} \cdot H(T)$. By the monotonicity of H and claim 5.2 it holds that $H(T) \geq H(\{1\}) \geq 1$, therefore $H(S) \geq n^{(1-\delta)/2}$.

Choose an arbitrary set $S' \subseteq N$ with $S' = 2 \cdot n^{1-\delta} < n$. Consider the following valuation profile: set $v_i = \frac{1}{4 \cdot n^{(1-\delta)/2}}$ if $i \in S'$, and $v_i = 0$ otherwise. Observe that in this profile the mechanism does not output a set of size more than $n^{1-\delta}$: consider some set $S'' \subseteq S'$ with $|S''| \geq n^{1-\delta}$. By monotonicity of H it holds that $H(S'') \geq H(S) \geq n^{(1-\delta)/2}$. Moreover it holds that $\sum_{i \in S''} v_i \leq 2 \cdot n^{1-\delta} \cdot \frac{1}{4 \cdot n^{(1-\delta)/2}} \leq \frac{n^{(1-\delta)/2}}{2}$, hence $\sum_{i \in S''} v_i - H(S'') < 0$.

Therefore, the mechanism outputs a set of size at most $n^{1-\delta}$, meaning that at least $n^{1-\delta}$ players among S' with value $\frac{1}{4 \cdot n^{(1-\delta)/2}}$ are not served. We get that the optimal optimal allocation is $\pi(OPT) = \pi(N) = 1$, but the social cost of the output of the mechanism is at least $\frac{n^{(1-\delta)/2}}{4}$. Hence the approximation ratio of the mechanism is no better than $\frac{n^{(1-\delta)/2}}{4}$.

Therefore, from now on assume that for every T with $|T| < n^{(1-\delta)/2}$ it holds that $\frac{H(T)}{|T|} > \frac{H(S)}{|S|}$. We construct a valuation profile in which the mechanism does not serve players whose sum of values is at least $\delta \cdot \log n - 1$, hence the approximation ratio of the social cost is no better than $\delta \cdot \log n - 1$. In addition, in the same profile the total sum of payments that the mechanism collects is at least $\frac{1-\delta}{2} \cdot \log n - 1$.

Let W be the minimal set that minimizes the density $\frac{H(W)}{|W|}$ among all sets of size at most $n^{1-\delta}$, i.e., for every $W' \subset W$ it holds that $\frac{H(W)}{|W|} < \frac{H(W')}{|W'|}$. Notice that $|W| \geq n^{(1-\delta)/2}$, since the density of S, which is of size $|S| = n^{1-\delta}$, is smaller than the density of any set of size at most $n^{(1-\delta)/2}$.

Consider the following instance: for every $i \in W$ set $v_i = \frac{H(W)}{|W|} + \varepsilon$ where $\varepsilon > 0$ is such that $\varepsilon < \min\left\{\frac{1}{n^3}, \min_{W' \subset W}\left\{\frac{H(W')}{|W'|} - \frac{H(W)}{|W|}\right\}\right\}$. We get that $\sum_{i \in W} v_i > H(W)$, but for every $W' \subset W$, it holds that $\sum_{i \in W'} v_i = |W'| \cdot \left[\frac{H(W)}{|W|} + \varepsilon\right] < |W'| \cdot \frac{H(W)}{|W|} + H(W') - |W'| \cdot \frac{H(W)}{|W|} = H(W')$. In addition, consider a set $L \subseteq N \backslash W$, with $n - n^{1-\delta}$ players. Without loss of generality, $L = \left\{n^{1-\delta} + 1, n^{1-\delta} + 2, ..., n\right\}$. For every $i \in L$ set $v_i = \frac{1}{i} - \varepsilon$.

We observe that the mechanism outputs $ALG = W$ and that for every $i \in W$, $ALG^{-i} = \emptyset$: by claim 5.2, for any two disjoint sets $W', L' \subseteq N$, $H(W' \cup L') - H(W') \geq \sum_{i=|W'|+1}^{|W'|+|L'|} \frac{1}{i}$, therefore for every subset $L' \subseteq L$ and for every subset $W' \subseteq W$ (which is of size at most $n^{1-\delta}$) the mechanism prefers the allocation W' over $W' \cup L'$:

$$\begin{aligned}
\sum_{i \in W' \cup L'} v_i - H(W' \cup L') &\leq \sum_{i \in W'} v_i + \sum_{i \in L'} v_i - \sum_{i=|W'|+1}^{|W'|+|L'|} \frac{1}{i} - H(W') \\
&< \sum_{i \in W'} v_i + \sum_{i=|W'|+1}^{|W'|+|L'|} \frac{1}{i} - \sum_{i=|W'|+1}^{|W'|+|L'|} \frac{1}{i} - H(W') \\
&= \sum_{i \in W'} v_i - H(W')
\end{aligned}$$

where the second inequality holds since $\sum_{i \in L'} v_i < \frac{1}{n^{1-\delta}+1} + \cdots + \frac{1}{n^{1-\delta}+|L'|} < \sum_{i=n^{1-\delta}+1}^{n^{1-\delta}+|L'|} \frac{1}{i} \leq \sum_{i=|W'|+1}^{|W'|+|L'|} \frac{1}{i}$. Hence no player from L is in ALG nor in ALG^{-i}. Recall that we have already observed that for any $W' \subset W$, the mechanism prefers the empty set over W' since $\sum_{i \in W'} v_i < H(W')$.

We get that the mechanism outputs W, the only allocation that provides a non-negative value. Similarly, for every $i \in W$ it holds that $ALG^{-i} = \emptyset$. Therefore, the payment of every player $i \in W$ is:

$$\begin{aligned} p_i &= \left[\sum_{j \in ALG^{-i}} v_j - H(ALG^{-i}) \right] - \left[\sum_{j \in W - \{i\}} v_j - H(W) \right] \\ &= H(W) - \frac{|W|-1}{|W|} \cdot H(W) - \frac{|W|-1}{|W|} \cdot \varepsilon > \frac{H(W)}{|W|} - \frac{1}{n^3} \end{aligned}$$

Summing over all $i \in W$ we get that the sum of the payments is at least $H(W) - \frac{1}{n^2}$. By claim 5.2, $H(W) \geq \mathcal{H}_{|W|}$. Recall that $|W| \geq n^{(1-\delta)/2}$, therefore $H(W) \geq \mathcal{H}_{n^{(1-\delta)/2}} \approx \frac{1-\delta}{2} \cdot \log n$. Hence, the sum of payments that the mechanism collects is at least $\frac{1-\delta}{2} \cdot \log n - 1$.

We now analyze the social cost in this instance. Note that $\sum_{i \in L} v_i > \sum_{i=n^{1-\delta}+1}^{n} \frac{1}{i} - |L| \cdot \frac{1}{n^3} > \mathcal{H}_n - \mathcal{H}_{n^{1-\delta}} - 1 \approx \log n - \log n^{1-\delta} - 1 = \delta \cdot \log n - 1$ whereas the optimal allocation is N, with social cost 1. The approximation ratio to the social cost is therefore no better than $\delta \cdot \log n - 1$. □

Minimality of the Potential Function. The potential mechanism is an affine maximizer that uses the potential function as the function H in the affine maximizer. Other choices for H also guarantee that the mechanism will always cover the cost. However, we show that our choice of the potential function is not arbitrary in the sense that the potential function is the minimal function that always covers the cost. Proof is in the full version.

THEOREM 5.3. *Let $\mathcal{A}$ be a VCG-based combinatorial cost-sharing mechanism for a domain that contains additive valuations and always covers the cost. I.e., $\mathcal{A}$ is a mechanism that outputs*

$$\overrightarrow{ALG} = \arg \max_{\vec{S} \in 2^{M_1} \times \cdots \times 2^{M_n}} \sum_i v_i(S_i) - H(\vec{S}) \tag{6}$$

where $H : 2^{M_1} \times \cdots \times 2^{M_n} \to \mathbb{R} \cup \{\infty\}$ is normalized and monotone. Then, for every $\vec{S} \in 2^{M_1} \times \cdots \times 2^{M_n}$ it holds that $H(\vec{S}) \geq P_C(\vec{S})$.

6 LIMITATIONS OF THE POTENTIAL MECHANISM

In this section we revisit the potential mechanism and consider relaxing some of our assumptions on the valuations and on the cost function. We first show that the potential mechanism provides a bad approximation ratio to the social cost for some non-subadditive functions. We then show that the potential mechanism is not budget balanced with a submodular cost function and simple submodular valuations such as unit demand. Both proofs appear in the full version.

PROPOSITION 6.1. *In the simple cost sharing setting, there is a non-subadditive cost function such that the Potential Mechanism provides an approximation ratio of $\Omega(n)$ to the social cost.*

PROPOSITION 6.2. *The Potential Mechanism is $\Omega(n)$-*budget-balanced *for submodular cost function and unit demand valuations.*

REFERENCES

[1] Lawrence M. Ausubel and Paul Milgrom. 2006. The Lovely but Lonely Vickrey Auction. In *Combinatorial Auctions, chapter 1.* MIT Press.

[2] Yvonne Bleischwitz, Burkhard Monien, and Florian Schoppmann. 2007. To be or not to be (served). In *International Workshop on Web and Internet Economics*. Springer, 515–528.

[3] Yvonne Bleischwitz and Florian Schoppmann. 2008. Group-strategyproof cost sharing for metric fault tolerant facility location. In *International Symposium on Algorithmic Game Theory*. Springer, 350–361.

[4] Liad Blumrosen and Shahar Dobzinski. 2014. Reallocation mechanisms. *EC* (2014).

[5] Janina Brenner and Guido Schäfer. 2007. Cost sharing methods for makespan and completion time scheduling. In *Annual Symposium on Theoretical Aspects of Computer Science*. Springer, 670–681.

[6] Ruggiero Cavallo. 2006. Optimal decision-making with minimal waste: Strategyproof redistribution of VCG payments. In *Proceedings of the fifth international joint conference on Autonomous agents and multiagent systems*. ACM, 882–889.

[7] Shuchi Chawla, Tim Roughgarden, and Mukund Sundararajan. 2006. Optimal cost-sharing mechanisms for steiner forest problems. In *International Workshop on Internet and Network Economics*. Springer, 112–123.

[8] Rajat Deb and Laura Razzolini. 1999. Voluntary cost sharing for an excludable public project. *Mathematical Social Sciences* 37, 2 (1999), 123–138.

[9] Shahar Dobzinski, Aranyak Mehta, Tim Roughgarden, and Mukund Sundararajan. 2008. Is Shapley cost sharing optimal?. In *International Symposium on Algorithmic Game Theory*. Springer, 327–336.

[10] Joan Feigenbaum, Arvind Krishnamurthy, Rahul Sami, and Scott Shenker. 2002. Hardness results for multicast cost sharing. In *International Conference on Foundations of Software Technology and Theoretical Computer Science*. Springer, 133–144.

[11] Hu Fu, Brendan Lucier, Balasubramanian Sivan, and Vasilis Syrgkanis. 2013. Cost-recovering Bayesian algorithmic mechanism design. In *Proceedings of the fourteenth ACM conference on Electronic commerce*. ACM, 453–470.

[12] Konstantinos Georgiou and Chaitanya Swamy. 2013. Black-box reductions for cost-sharing mechanism design. *Games and Economic Behavior* (2013).

[13] Mingyu Guo and Vincent Conitzer. 2009. Worst-case optimal redistribution of VCG payments in multi-unit auctions. *Games and Economic Behavior* 67, 1 (2009), 69–98.

[14] Anupam Gupta, Jochen Könemann, Stefano Leonardi, R Ravi, and Guido Schäfer. 2015. Efficient cost-sharing mechanisms for prize-collecting problems. *Mathematical Programming* 152, 1-2 (2015), 147–188.

[15] Sergiu Hart and Andreu Mas-Colell. 1989. Potential, value, and consistency. *Econometrica: Journal of the Econometric Society* (1989), 589–614.

[16] Kazuhiko Hashimoto and Hiroki Saitoh. 2015. Strategy-proof cost sharing under increasing returns: Improvement of the supremal welfare loss. *Games and Economic Behavior* 89 (2015), 101–121.

[17] Stephen C Littlechild and Guillermo Owen. 1973. A simple expression for the Shapley value in a special case. *Management Science* 20, 3 (1973), 370–372.

[18] Aranyak Mehta, Tim Roughgarden, and Mukund Sundararajan. 2007. Beyond moulin mechanisms. In *Proceedings of the 8th ACM Conference on Electronic Commerce*. ACM, 1–10.

[19] Hervé Moulin. 1999. Incremental cost sharing: Characterization by coalition strategy-proofness. *Social Choice and Welfare* 16, 2 (1999), 279–320.

[20] Hervé Moulin. 2009. Almost budget-balanced VCG mechanisms to assign multiple objects. *Journal of Economic Theory* 144, 1 (2009), 96 – 119. DOI:http://dx.doi.org/10.1016/j.jet.2008.03.003

[21] Hervé Moulin and Scott Shenker. 2001. Strategyproof sharing of submodular costs: budget balance versus efficiency. *Economic Theory* 18, 3 (2001), 511–533.

[22] Kevin Roberts. 1979. Aggregation and revelation of preferences. *The Characterization of Implementable Choice Rules* (1979), 321–348.

[23] Tim Roughgarden and Mukund Sundararajan. 2009. Quantifying inefficiency in cost-sharing mechanisms. *Journal of the ACM (JACM)* 56, 4 (2009), 23.

[24] Alexander Schrijver. 2000. A combinatorial algorithm minimizing submodular functions in strongly polynomial time. *Journal of Combinatorial Theory, Series B* 80, 2 (2000), 346–355.

[25] Mukund Sundararajan. 2009. *Trade-offs in cost sharing*. Ph.D. Dissertation. Stanford University.

Makespan Minimization via Posted Prices

MICHAL FELDMAN*, Tel Aviv University
AMOS FIAT†, Tel Aviv University
ALAN ROYTMAN‡, University of Copenhagen

We consider job scheduling settings, with multiple machines, where jobs arrive online and choose a machine selfishly so as to minimize their cost. Our objective is the classic makespan minimization objective, which corresponds to the completion time of the last job to complete. The incentives of the selfish jobs may lead to poor performance. To reconcile the differing objectives, we introduce posted machine prices. The selfish job seeks to minimize the sum of its completion time on the machine and the posted price for the machine. Prices may be static (i.e., set once and for all before any arrival) or dynamic (i.e., change over time), but they are determined only by the past, assuming nothing about upcoming events. Obviously, such schemes are inherently truthful.

We consider the competitive ratio: the ratio between the makespan achievable by the pricing scheme and that of the optimal algorithm. We give tight bounds on the competitive ratio for both dynamic and static pricing schemes for identical, restricted, related, and unrelated machine settings. Our main result is a dynamic pricing scheme for related machines that gives a constant competitive ratio, essentially matching the competitive ratio of online algorithms for this setting. In contrast, dynamic pricing gives poor performance for unrelated machines. This lower bound also exhibits a gap between what can be achieved by pricing versus what can be achieved by online algorithms.

CCS Concepts: • **Theory of computation → Online algorithms**; **Algorithmic game theory and mechanism design**;

Additional Key Words and Phrases: Pricing Schemes, Load Balancing, Job Scheduling, Makespan

1 INTRODUCTION

Online algorithms can be viewed as follows: events arrive over time, and upon the arrival of an event, the algorithm makes a decision, based only on the prior and current event, without knowing future events. There is a function that maps outcomes to costs or benefits, where the goal of such an algorithm is either to minimize costs or to maximize benefits. The competitive ratio of an online algorithm seeks to compare the outcome of the online algorithm with the optimal outcome. The

*Blavatnik School of Computer Science, Tel Aviv University, email: mfeldman@tau.ac.il.
†Blavatnik School of Computer Science, Tel Aviv University, email: fiat@tau.ac.il.
‡Department of Computer Science, University of Copenhagen, email: alanr@di.ku.dk.

The work of M. Feldman and A. Roytman was partially supported by the European Research Council under the European Union's Seventh Framework Programme (FP7/2007-2013) / ERC grant agreement number 337122. The work of A. Roytman was also partially supported by Thorup's Advanced Grant DFF-0602-02499B from the Danish Council for Independent Research. The work of A. Fiat and A. Roytman was also supported in part by grant number 822/10 from the Israel Science Foundation, and by the Israeli Centers for Research Excellence (ICORE) program.

EC'17, June 26–30, 2017, Cambridge, Massachusetts, USA. © 2017 ACM ISBN 978-1-4503-4527-9/17/06...$15.00.
http://dx.doi.org/10.1145/3033274.3085129

term competitive analysis was coined in [28] and gives the ratio between the outcome (cost or benefit) achieved by an online algorithm and the outcome of an offline optimal solution. Herein we only deal with cost problems so this ratio is ≥ 1.

We consider a setting where every online event is associated with a selfish agent. The agents have some associated true type that describes the nature of the event. Agents have some utility (or disutility) associated with the outcome. For many online algorithms, the decisions made by the algorithm might not be in the best interest of the agent. This may result in the agent misrepresenting her type so as to achieve a better outcome for herself.

The design of *mechanisms* mitigates the problem of strategic behavior described above. In a mechanism, agents report their type, and the mechanism decides upon an outcome and upon payments, where payments are used to align the incentives of the agents with that of the mechanism. A mechanism is truthful if it is always in the best interest of any agent to report her type truthfully. In online settings, agents arrive sequentially, and the mechanism decides upon an outcome and payment for each arriving agent as they arrive[1].

With few notable exceptions (e.g., [33]), problems studied in mechanism design (both online and offline settings) involve *maximizing* social welfare or revenue. Although optimal solutions to maximization/minimization objectives can be cast as the other, the competitive ratio is quite different in the two settings. Online algorithms have been devised with both maximization and minimization objectives. The technique of "classify and randomly select" [6] often gives simple randomized algorithms for maximization objectives which also naturally translate into truthful mechanisms. In contrast, minimization objectives (e.g., k-server and makespan) require entirely different techniques. Converting online algorithms into mechanisms without performance degradation opens up an entire new class of problems for which incentive compatible mechanism design is applicable.

Dynamic posted prices. We consider truthful online mechanisms that take the form of *dynamic posted prices.* Dynamic pricing schemes are truthful online mechanisms that post prices for every possible outcome, before the next agent arrives. Then, the agent chooses the preferred outcome — minimizing the cost for the outcome plus the price tag associated with the outcome.

Such a mechanism is inherently truthful, since prices are determined irrespective of the type of the next agent. Posted price mechanisms have many additional advantages over arbitrary truthful online mechanisms. In particular such mechanisms are simple [24]: agents need not trust nor understand the logic underlying the truthful mechanism, agents are not required to reveal their type, and there is no need to verify that the agents indeed follow the decision made by the truthful online mechanism. A discussion comparing online truthful mechanisms to dynamic pricing schemes can be found in Appendix A.

A posted price mechanism is a truthful online algorithm, and as such, can perform no better than the best online algorithm. Our main goal in this paper is to study the performance of dynamic posted price mechanisms (quantified by the competitive ratio measure) and compare them with the performance of the best online algorithm. One may think of this problem as analogous to one of the central questions in algorithmic mechanism design in offline settings: compare the performance of the best truthful mechanism (quantified by the approximation ratio measure) with the performance of the best non-truthful algorithm.

Makespan minimization in job scheduling. In this paper we study the design of online mechanisms for makespan minimization in job scheduling. Events represent jobs, the job type contains the job's processing times on various machines. Agents seek to complete their job as soon

[1]Such online mechanisms are called *prompt* in that outcomes and payments are determined immediately, non-prompt online mechanisms have also been studied where, for example, the payment is only determined later.

as possible, and therefore prefer to be assigned to a machine whose load (including the new job) is minimized[2]. For simplicity of exposition, we assume that all jobs arrive (sequentially) at time zero. However, our positive results hold even if jobs arrive at arbitrary times. Clearly, adding options (arbitrary arrival times) does not invalidate impossibility results. Existing online algorithms for the problem (e.g., [3]) are not truthful; in that a job may misrepresent its size so as to get a preferential assignment to a machine.

An online truthful mechanism for this setting determines an allocation and payment for each arriving agent upon arrival. That is, upon the arrival of a job, based on the job's processing times, the mechanism assigns the job to some machine and determines the payment the agent should make. The cost of an agent is the sum of the machine's load (including her own processing time) and the payment. Each agent seeks to minimize her cost.

A dynamic posted price mechanism for this setting sets prices on each machine, *before* the next agent arrives (prices may change over time). The next agent to arrive seeks to minimize her cost, i.e., the load on the chosen machine (including her own load) plus the posted price on the machine. The agent breaks ties arbitrarily.

We consider this question for the goal of makespan minimization in job scheduling, where the dynamic pricing scheme seeks to minimize the makespan, whereas selfish jobs seek to minimize their own completion time. We assume FIFO processing within a machine, so the completion time of a job is the sum of the current load (prior to the arrival of the job) plus the job's own processing time on the machine. This problem has many applications, including managing queues at banks, cloud computing settings where customers submit jobs and can lie about their processing times, and crowdsourcing settings where taskmasters wish to hire workers to complete tasks while lying about how long their task takes to complete. In all such applications, we are interested in balancing loads appropriately. To this end, we consider online makespan minimization for identical, restricted, related, and unrelated machine models.

Examples. To clarify the issue of selfish jobs, consider the following small toy problem: the setting is that of machines with speeds, machine #1 has speed 1, machine #2 has speed $1/2$. There are also two jobs, job a is of size $1/2$ and job b is of size 1. Clearly, the minimal makespan is achieved by assigning job a to machine #2 and job b to machine #1. This gives a makespan of one. Assume that the order of arrival is a, b. Job a will prefer machine #1 (completion time $1/2$) to machine #2 (completion time 1). Job b will also prefer machine #1 (completion time 1.5) to machine #2 (completion time 2).

In this specific case a static pricing of $1/2 + \epsilon$ for machine #1 and a price of zero for machine #2 will result in the optimal makespan irrespective of the order of arrival of the jobs. If the order is a, b then job a prefers machine #2 (completion time $1 +$ price $0 = 1$) over machine #1 (completion time $1/2 +$ price $1/2 + \epsilon = 1 + \epsilon$). The second job to arrive, job b, prefers machine #1 (completion time $1 +$ price $1/2 + \epsilon = 1.5 + \epsilon$) over machine #2 (completion time $3 +$ price $0 = 3$). One can verify that the order b, a will also achieve the same minimal makespan result.

The above example is somewhat misleading as we do not want to derive prices for a specific set of arriving jobs but for any arbitrary set and arbitrary order. In fact, we show that, in general, static prices are no better than a complete lack of prices (see Section 4), and only dynamic prices can guarantee a constant competitive ratio. A more detailed example that also illustrates the use of our dynamic pricing scheme for related machines (see Section 2) appears in the full version of the paper [19].

[2]In this interpretation "load" is the time required by the server to deal with all current jobs in the server queue, and jobs are processed in a first-in first-out manner, i.e., jobs enter a server queue. In some papers "load" is used in the context of round-robin processing.

1.1 Our Model

We have m machines and n jobs which arrive in an online manner. Unrelated, related, restricted, and identical machine models are defined as follows:

(1) For unrelated machines, the processing time of job j on machine i is given by p_{ij}.
(2) In the related machines model, each machine i has some speed s_i and each job j has some associated size p_j. The processing time of job j on machine i is given by $p_{ij} = \frac{p_j}{s_i}$.
(3) In the restricted machines model, each job j has some associated size p_j. The processing time of job j on machine i is either p_j or ∞.
(4) In the identical machines model, each job j has some associated size p_j, which is job j's processing time on all machines.

In the online setting, neither processing times, p_{ij}, nor size, p_j, are known until job j arrives. Machine speeds s_i are known in advance. While jobs do arrive in adversarial order, by renaming we can assume that job j is the jth job to arrive.

We denote by σ an input sequence consisting of jobs 1 through n. For a machine i, we let $M_i(j)$ denote the set of jobs that have been assigned to machine i after jobs 1 through j have arrived. We denote the load on machine i after jobs 1 through j have arrived by $\ell_i(j) = \sum_{b \in M_i(j)} p_{ib}$. For the makespan objective, the goal is to minimize $\max_i \ell_i(n)$. Given an input sequence σ, we denote by $L^*(\sigma)$ an optimal solution that is omniscient and knows the entire input sequence σ in advance (i.e., an optimal solution that knows all jobs' processing times). When clear from the context, we omit the parameter σ and simply write L^*.

A *dynamic pricing scheme* D, given an input sequence σ, outputs a sequence of n vectors $\pi_1, \ldots, \pi_n \in \mathbb{R}^m$, where each $\pi_j = (\pi_{1j}, \ldots, \pi_{mj})$ represents a vector of prices for each of the m machines. Each vector π_j is determined before the jth job arrives. We view jobs as rational selfish agents who must choose the machine to which they wish to be assigned. In particular, we model each arriving agent j's cost on machine i as $c_{ij} = \ell_i(j-1) + p_{ij} + \pi_{ij}$, where $\ell_i(j-1)$ is the load on machine i before j arrives, p_{ij} is the processing time of job j on machine i, and π_{ij} is the price on machine i (determined before j arrives). Hence, agent j's cost on machine i represents how long agent j must wait in order to be processed by machine i, given the load of the machine upon j's arrival, plus some price amount determined by the dynamic pricing scheme. We assume that agents are rational and wish to minimize their cost. That is, agent j chooses a machine that attains the minimum value $\min_i c_{ij}$.

Note that, in our model, each player is a job, not a machine. Hence, a job (i.e., player) may potentially misreport its processing times to the scheme in order to lower its incurred cost. However, dynamic pricing schemes are inherently truthful (since the prices are set independently of reported processing times), and hence jobs never benefit from lying regarding their processing times on machines. We denote by $D(\sigma)$ the makespan of the schedule produced by the dynamic pricing scheme D given input σ, $D(\sigma) = \max_i \ell_i(n)$ — the maximum load of any machine.

We can similarly define a *static pricing scheme*, which simply sets one m-dimensional vector of prices π (i.e., a single value for each machine) before any agents arrive. We do not permit static pricing schemes to change prices over time (so that $\pi_{i1} = \pi_{ij}$ for all i and $j \geq 1$). For this reason, when referring to static pricing schemes, we simply use one subscript instead of two. In particular, we write π_{i*} to denote the price on machine i (at all times), so that $\pi = (\pi_{1*}, \ldots, \pi_{m*})$.

We say that a dynamic pricing scheme is c-competitive if, given any input sequence σ, the scheme always produces a schedule with a makespan satisfying $D(\sigma) \leq c \cdot L^*(\sigma) + a$ (assuming that agents behave selfishly), where we allow some additive constant a.

Table 1. Competitive ratio comparison of the greedy algorithm, the best online algorithm, static pricing schemes, and dynamic pricing schemes. Here, the greedy algorithm denotes the algorithm that assigns each job to the machine that minimizes the current load plus processing time of the job on the machine. Results in the Static Pricing and Dynamic Pricing columns are from this paper.

Machine Model	Greedy	Best Online	Static Pricing	Dynamic Pricing
Identical	$O(1)$ [23]	$O(1)$ [23]	$O(1)$	$O(1)$
Related	$\Theta(\log m)$ [3]	$O(1)$ [3]	$\Theta(\log m)$	$O(1)$
Restricted	$\Theta(\log m)$ [9]	$\Theta(\log m)$ [9]	$\Theta(\log m)$	$\Theta(\log m)$
Unrelated	$\Theta(m)$ [3]	$\Theta(\log m)$ [3, 9]	$\Theta(m)$	$\Theta(m)$

1.2 Our Contributions

We give tight results for the competitive ratios that can be achieved via dynamic and static pricing schemes for the problem of minimizing makespan. We study identical, related, restricted, and unrelated machine models. Our results, in comparison with previous work, are summarized in Table 1. Our main results are as follows (m denotes the number of machines).

(1) A dynamic pricing scheme that achieves an $O(1)$ competitive ratio for the related machines model. This matches the $O(1)$-competitive result (of a non-truthful online algorithm) given in [3].
(2) A lower bound on the competitive ratio of any dynamic pricing scheme of $\Omega(m)$ for unrelated machines. Our lower bound holds for any randomized dynamic pricing scheme, even assuming an oblivious adversary.

To the best of our knowledge, the lower bound for unrelated machines exhibits the first gap between what can be achieved by dynamic pricing schemes versus what can be achieved by online algorithms. That is, a gap of $\Omega(m)$ (for randomized dynamic pricing) versus $O(\log m)$ (achieved via deterministic online algorithms [3]).

Our $O(1)$-competitive dynamic pricing scheme for related machines also holds in a more general model where jobs arrive in real time (as opposed to arriving in sequence). Jobs arrive over time and are processed sequentially in a first-in first-out manner. The objective is to minimize the completion time of the last job to complete. For simplicity of presentation, we give the proof when jobs arrive in sequence. We describe the changes that need to be made to carry out the argument in the more general setting of arbitrary arrival times in the full version of the paper [19].

In addition, we show that static pricing schemes and the online greedy algorithm[3] achieve the same performance up to a constant factor. Clearly, the static pricing scheme that sets all prices to zero mimics the greedy algorithm. Furthermore, we show that any lower bound on the competitive ratio of the greedy algorithm translates to the same lower bound on any static pricing scheme[4] (up to constant factors), for all machine models considered in this paper. We note that such a greedy algorithm is $O(1)$-competitive for identical machines [23], $\Theta(\log m)$-competitive for related machines [3], $\Theta(\log m)$-competitive for the restricted assignment model [9], and $\Theta(m)$-competitive for unrelated machines [3]. These results appear in the columns labeled Greedy and Static Pricing in Table 1.

[3]We refer to the online greedy algorithm as the greedy algorithm that assigns each job to a machine that minimizes the current load plus processing time of the job on the machine.
[4]This result holds for any deterministic pricing scheme. For randomized schemes, it holds as long as the lower bound for the greedy algorithm does not depend on the tie-breaking rule.

1.3 Techniques

Positive results for related machines. Our $O(1)$-competitive dynamic pricing scheme for the related machines model is inspired by the corresponding related machines algorithm given in [3], referred to as Slow-Fit in [8].

We now describe the main ideas behind our main result by discussing Slow-Fit. We assume that machines are sorted in increasing order of their speed, so that $s_1 \leq \cdots \leq s_m$. In particular, Slow-Fit operates in phases, where each phase maintains a lower bound Λ on the current optimal solution. The estimate Λ doubles from phase to phase. A job j is said to be feasible on machine i if $\ell_i(j-1) + \frac{p_j}{s_i} \leq 2\Lambda$. Slow-Fit assigns the job to the lowest index (slowest) machine on which it is feasible. If no machine is feasible, Slow-Fit doubles Λ. This doubling process repeats until Λ exceeds the value of the optimal solution (i.e., Λ becomes an upper bound), after which, for any incoming job, some machine is feasible (and hence such jobs can be assigned). Clearly, Slow-Fit depends on the incoming job's size. The challenge in emulating Slow-Fit via a dynamic pricing scheme is that prices must be set before the size of the next job is revealed.

To show the underlying ideas, we now make several assumptions for which we show how to set prices for two machines that perfectly emulate Slow-Fit. The assumptions are (a) Both machines have different speeds, (b) Selfish jobs break ties in favor of machine 1, and (c) Λ is a known upper bound on the optimal solution.

Without loss of generality the price on machine 1 is zero. Slow-Fit assigns job j to machine 1 if and only if job j is feasible on machine 1, hence, we would like to set a price on machine 2, π_{2j}, so that

$$\ell_1(j-1) + \frac{p_j}{s_1} \leq \ell_2(j-1) + \frac{p_j}{s_2} + \pi_{2j} \iff \ell_1(j-1) + \frac{p_j}{s_1} \leq 2\Lambda.$$

This is achieved by setting

$$\pi_{2j} = \ell_1(j-1) - \ell_2(j-1) + s_1\left(\frac{1}{s_1} - \frac{1}{s_2}\right)(2\Lambda - \ell_1(j-1)).$$

As the price π_{2j} is independent of p_j this gives a valid dynamic pricing scheme. Substitution and rearrangement show that a job is assigned to machine 1 if and only if it is feasible on machine 1, as required. Note that this does not hold for equal speed machines, and if tie-breaking is not in favor of machine 1.

It follows from the simple example above, that the following issues must be considered so as to construct a dynamic pricing scheme that attempts to emulate Slow-Fit, these are:

- *Equal Speed Machines*: Imagine that machines i and $i+1$ have the same speed, and job j is feasible on both, then job j should be scheduled on machine i. However, it may be that a larger job j is infeasible on i but still feasible on $i+1$, in this case it should be assigned to $i+1$. However, if the machines have the same speed, then irrespective of any prices and job size, the same machine will always be chosen (as the difference in costs between machines i and $i+1$ is constant).
- *New Phase Recognition*: A new phase starts when the job has no feasible machine. However, the pricing scheme cannot tell that a new phase is about to begin because it does not know the size of the next job to arrive.
- *Machine Tie-Breaking*: Beyond the issue of feasibility (which is also a problem, see above), as the job size increases, different machines (of different speeds) will attain the minimal cost, irrespective of the prices and the current loads. Ergo, a job cannot be assumed to choose the lowest index machine.

If none of these issues were to arise, then it would be possible to come up with a dynamic pricing scheme that would precisely mimic the decisions made by Slow-Fit (as in the two machine example above). To deal with these issues, we design a new online algorithm, Flex-Fit, a variant of Slow-Fit (see Algorithm 1). Flex-Fit allows more flexibility in assigning jobs to multiple machines, and in deciding when to start a new phase. This new algorithm does lend itself to dynamic pricing schemes with the same competitive ratio, up to a constant factor.

The dynamic pricing scheme that emulates Flex-Fit is described in Algorithm 3. We carefully choose a subset of machines that have strictly increasing speeds on which to place finite prices. Other machines get a price of infinity. The prices are set such that the job prefers lower indexed machines to higher indexed machines if and only if the job is feasible on the lower indexed machine.

Impossibility results for unrelated machines. We next describe techniques used in our $\Omega(m)$ lower bound on the competitive ratio of dynamic pricing for unrelated machines. As a warm up, we give a deterministic lower bound. The lower bound job sequence consists of two types of jobs, depending on two cases regarding the behavior of the deterministic dynamic pricing scheme. In case 1, we introduce a type 1 job that results in an increase in the sum of machines' loads, for the dynamic pricing scheme. In contrast, any type 1 job is assigned in an optimal solution without an increase in any machine load. In case 2, we introduce a type 2 job, which always chooses machine 1 (under the dynamic pricing scheme). On the other hand, an optimal solution can always spread out any sequence of m type 2 jobs. This input sequence shows a gap of $\Omega(m)$ for the competitive ratio of deterministic dynamic pricing schemes.

Our randomized lower bound holds against oblivious adversaries (i.e., adversaries that must construct the entire input sequence in advance, before seeing any coin flips of the algorithm). To achieve our randomized lower bound, we use the same two types of jobs as in the deterministic case. We show how to construct such a sequence obliviously, depending on the relative probability of being in case 1 or in case 2.

Static pricing ≡ Greedy. The non trivial direction is to show that every static pricing scheme can be as bad as the greedy algorithm. To do so, we observe that static pricing schemes can be viewed as starting the online process with some initial (arbitrary) imbalance in the loads. For deterministic static pricing schemes we show how to flatten out the effective loads (= load + price) so that they are all equal. Once this is done, we can then apply the greedy lower bound sequence, obtaining a similar lower bound result for any static pricing scheme.

For randomized schemes, we give a different construction, that holds as long as the lower bound for the greedy algorithm does not depend on the tie-breaking rule. The idea is to blow up the job sizes in the greedy lower bound sequence so that the initial imbalance in the effective load becomes negligible.

1.4 Related Work

Online Algorithms. Introduced in the context of self-adjusting search trees [35], paging, list update [34], and snoopy caching [27], there soon arose a vast host of online problems for which competitive analysis was applied. These include problems such as metrical task systems [11], the k-server problem [30, 31], scheduling problems, routing problems, and many more. One particular class of problems that has been widely studied is that of online makespan minimization [3, 7, 9, 32].

Online Makespan Minimization. The literature on online makespan minimization is vast, we only discuss the most relevant works. Online load balancing results for a variety of machine models appear in [3]. An $O(\log m)$-competitive algorithm for unrelated machines and an 8-competitive algorithm for related machines were given (i.e., the Slow-Fit algorithm). It was also shown that greedy is $\Theta(m)$-competitive for unrelated machines and $\Theta(\log m)$-competitive for related machines. The greedy algorithm was shown to be $\Theta(\log m)$-competitive for the restricted assignment model (moreover, no online algorithm can do better) [9]. Results for the identical machines model appear in [10] and [2], where a $(2-\epsilon)$-competitive online algorithm for a small fixed $\epsilon > 0$ and a 1.923-competitive algorithm were given, respectively.

Many other makespan minimization problems have been studied in the online setting, including different objectives such as minimizing the L_p norm for $p \geq 1$ [4] (the classic makespan minimization problem corresponds to minimizing the L_∞ norm), settings where machines have activation costs [7, 32], and load balancing in the multidimensional setting [25, 32].

Static and Dynamic Pricing Schemes for Online Settings. Dynamic pricing schemes for a variety of problems appear in [16]. In particular, [16] gave an $O(k)$-competitive algorithm for the k-server problem on a line, an $O(m)$-competitive algorithm for metrical task systems (where m denotes the number of states), and a competitive ratio that is logarithmic in the ratio of the maximum to minimum distances between points for metrical matching on a line. Additional static and dynamic pricing schemes appear in [22], where queue management problems were studied, and constant competitive ratios were obtained for social welfare. Dynamic pricing schemes were also considered in [29], in which the revenue maximization problem where a seller has an unlimited supply of identical goods was studied. A dynamic pricing scheme for routing small jobs (relative to the edge capacities) through a network was considered in [5].

Posted Prices for Social Welfare and Revenue. Posted pricing schemes [12, 13, 21] need not be online, may use non-anonymous pricing, and often assume something is known about the future (e.g., public valuations, Bayesian settings, etc.). There is a large body of works on posted price mechanisms for social welfare and revenue maximization. In the full information setting (only the order of arrival is unknown), a static posted pricing scheme was given that obtains the optimal welfare for unit-demand buyers, and at least half of the optimal welfare for any valuation function [17]. This uses ideas from [20]. The Bayesian setting was considered in [21], where agents' valuations are drawn from a product distribution over XOS valuations. A static posted pricing scheme was given that achieves at least half the optimal welfare (in expectation). A general framework for the design of posted price mechanisms for welfare maximization in Bayesian settings was devised in [18]. Pricing schemes for revenue maximization in Bayesian settings were considered in [12–14]. In these settings agents arrive sequentially and are offered (non-anonymous) prices. It was shown that the optimal revenue can be approximated to within a constant factor in various single-parameter and multi-parameter settings.

Coordination Mechanisms for Job Scheduling. There is also a research agenda within the price of anarchy literature that studies the notion of coordination mechanisms. This body of work focuses on non-truthful mechanisms in the offline setting, where jobs are selfish agents (note that jobs are also selfish agents in our work). Here, performance is measured in terms of the price of anarchy. A coordination mechanism for identical machines appears in [15], where it was shown that the price of anarchy is $\frac{4}{3} - \frac{1}{3m}$. Various local policies for a variety of machine models appear in [26]. It was shown that any deterministic coordination mechanism has a price of anarchy of $O(\log m)$ for the related and restricted models, and an $\Omega(\log m)$ lower bound was given for the price of anarchy for the restricted model. For unrelated machines, a $\Theta(m)$ bound was given for a simple randomized policy. The weighted sum of completion times objective has also been studied [1].

2 PRICING RELATED MACHINES

We begin by giving an online algorithm for the load balancing problem on related machines with a constant competitive ratio. Our online algorithm is inspired by the Slow-Fit algorithm [3]. We do this to aid us in designing a dynamic pricing scheme that can mimic the behavior of the online algorithm. This ensures that our dynamic pricing scheme will have the same competitive ratio as the online algorithm.

We first assume that machines are sorted in increasing order of speed, so that $s_1 \leq s_2 \leq \cdots \leq s_m$ (i.e., the first machine is the slowest machine, and the mth machine is the fastest machine). Our algorithm and dynamic pricing scheme proceed in phases, where each phase depends on our current estimate Λ of the optimal makespan L^*. A new phase begins upon realizing that the current estimate is too small, at which point we update the estimate accordingly. We use the notion of virtual loads in our algorithms, which we denote by $\hat{\ell}_i(j)$. Virtual loads capture the real load within a particular phase, and are reset to zero once a new phase begins. The real load on a machine is essentially given by the sum of virtual loads over all phases. All loads and virtual loads begin at zero.

Our algorithms use the notion of representative machines, which are determined by the current virtual loads $\hat{\ell}_i(j)$.

Definition 2.1 (Representative). Fix any machine i and job j. Let $R = \{k : s_k = s_i\}$ be the set of machines with the same speed as i. We say the representative of machine i when job j arrives is an arbitrary machine $k \in R$ that minimizes $\hat{\ell}_k(j-1)$. We denote the representative of machine i when j arrives by $r_i(j)$.

Note that, for any machine i, if i is the only machine with a speed of s_i, then we have $r_i(j) = i$ (for all j). Hence, the notion of a representative is mainly useful when there are multiple machines with the same speed. In particular, the notion of representatives enables us to choose one machine out of many that have the same speed (note that representatives may change over time as jobs arrive). Moreover, we always have the property that $s_{r_i(j)} = s_i$.

2.1 Flex-Fit: A Variant of Slow-Fit

ALGORITHM 1: Flex-Fit: A Variant of Slow-Fit

```
Assign job 1 to machine r_m(j)
Λ ← p_1 / s_m
ℓ̂_i(1) ← 0 for all i
while job j arrives do
    T ← {i : ℓ̂_i(j − 1) + p_j/s_i ≤ (2 + ε)Λ}
    if T ≠ ∅ then
        S ← {i : ℓ̂_i(j − 1) + p_j/s_i ≤ 2 · Λ}
        if S = ∅ then
            | Optionally call New-Phase(j) and continue with the next job
        end
        k ← minimum machine index in S (set k ← m if S = ∅)
        Assign j to an arbitrary machine r* ∈ {r_i(j) : s_i ≤ s_k and i ∈ T}
        ℓ̂_{r*}(j) ← ℓ̂_{r*}(j − 1) + p_j/s_{r*}
        ℓ̂_{i'}(j) ← ℓ̂_{i'}(j − 1) for all i' ≠ r*
    end
    else
        | New-Phase(j)
    end
end
```

ALGORITHM 2: New-Phase

input: Job j

Assign j to any machine with a speed of s_m

$\Lambda \leftarrow \max\{2, 2^{\left\lceil \log_2 \frac{p_j}{s_m \Lambda} \right\rceil}\} \cdot \Lambda$

$\hat{\ell}_i(j) \leftarrow 0$ for all i

For any fixed $\epsilon > 0$, we give Algorithm Flex-Fit (which is inspired by the Slow-Fit algorithm in [3]). The main theorem we show in this section is that Flex-Fit is $O(1)$-competitive for the makespan minimization problem on related machines.

We give some intuition for the algorithm. Initially, we assign the first job to some fastest machine and obtain a lower bound estimate of L^*, the optimal makespan. The algorithm considers two sets: $T = \{i : \hat{\ell}_i(j-1) + \frac{p_j}{s_i} \leq (2+\epsilon)\Lambda\}$ and $S = \{i : \hat{\ell}_i(j-1) + \frac{p_j}{s_i} \leq 2 \cdot \Lambda\}$ (note that $S \subseteq T$). In particular, a job is feasible on machine i if and only if $i \in S$. The set T consists of machines that are slightly infeasible for job j.

If $T = \emptyset$, then the algorithm simply begins a new phase. Starting a new phase corresponds to assigning the job j to any machine of speed s_m, along with updating Λ appropriately and resetting virtual loads. If $S \neq \emptyset$, then the algorithm finds the lowest indexed machine in S, namely machine k. In this case, it is free to assign j to the representative $r_i(j)$ of any machine i such that $s_i \leq s_k$ and $i \in T$. If $S = \emptyset$, then Flex-Fit is allowed to take one of two options: begin a new phase and then wait to process the next job, or assign j to the representative $r_i(j)$ of any machine i such that $i \in T$. We need this flexibility in order to mimic the online algorithm via a dynamic pricing scheme. In particular, tie-breaking issues in our dynamic pricing scheme may arise, where a job can be indifferent between choosing a machine of speed strictly less than s_m (in which case a new phase does not begin), or a machine of speed s_m (in which case a new phase may possibly begin). Since we do not have control over which machine agents choose, our online algorithm must be sufficiently flexible and allow either of the two options to be taken.

Note that we assume job 1 has $p_1 > 0$ (otherwise our initial estimate $\Lambda = 0$). If this is not the case, we simply wait until such a job j arrives, and reindex jobs so that $j = 1$.

To show the theorem, we first prove two lemmata, Lemma 2.2 and Lemma 2.3.

Lemma 2.2 says that, as long as $S \neq \emptyset$ when a particular job j arrives, the load on the machine to which j is assigned is within a constant of our estimate Λ. We defer the proof of Lemma 2.2 to the full version of the paper [19].

Lemma 2.2. *For any job $j > 1$, if $S \neq \emptyset$, Flex-Fit always assigns job j to a machine i such that $\hat{\ell}_i(j-1) + \frac{p_j}{s_i} \leq (2+\epsilon)\Lambda$.*

Lemma 2.3 says that once our estimate Λ is at least the optimal makespan, then no more new phases are initiated (the proof is similar to the proof that Slow-Fit is competitive [3], although it must be adapted appropriately).

Lemma 2.3. *If $\Lambda \geq L^*$, then $S \neq \emptyset$ for all jobs $j > 1$.*

Proof. Suppose $\Lambda \geq L^*$, and let $j > 1$ be any arriving job after our estimate Λ exceeds L^*. Note that, once $\Lambda \geq L^*$, virtual loads are reset to zero, and hence we only consider jobs that have arrived since then. Assume towards a contradiction that $S = \emptyset$. Let f be the fastest machine satisfying $\hat{\ell}_f(j-1) \leq L^*$, namely $f = \max\{i : \hat{\ell}_i(j-1) \leq L^*\}$. If such a machine does not exist, we set $f = 0$ (in fact, we will show that such a machine must exist). For any machine i such that $s_i = s_m$, we must have $\hat{\ell}_i(j-1) > L^*$, since otherwise we would have a contradiction to the fact that $S = \emptyset$:

$\hat{\ell}_i(j-1) + \frac{p_j}{s_i} = \hat{\ell}_i(j-1) + \frac{p_j}{s_m} \leq L^* + L^* \leq 2 \cdot \Lambda$ (note that $\frac{p_j}{s_m} \leq L^*$). In particular, we have $s_f < s_m$ (assuming $f \geq 1$).

Now, let $\Gamma = \{i : s_i > s_f\}$, and note that each machine in Γ has load strictly more than L^* (if $f = 0$, we let Γ be the set of all machines). By the fact that $s_f < s_m$, we know that $\Gamma \neq \emptyset$ (if $f = 0$, this is also the case). Let J_i be the set of jobs assigned to machine i after the estimate $\Lambda \geq L^*$, and define J_i^* to be the set of jobs that the optimal solution assigns to i after $\Lambda \geq L^*$. Then we have:

$$\sum_{i \in \Gamma} \sum_{j \in J_i} \frac{p_j}{s_m} = \frac{1}{s_m} \sum_{i \in \Gamma} s_i \sum_{j \in J_i} \frac{p_j}{s_i} > \frac{1}{s_m} \sum_{i \in \Gamma} s_i \cdot L^* \geq \frac{1}{s_m} \sum_{i \in \Gamma} s_i \sum_{j \in J_i^*} \frac{p_j}{s_i} = \sum_{i \in \Gamma} \sum_{j \in J_i^*} \frac{p_j}{s_m}.$$

This implies that there must exist at least one job $b \leq j-1$ such that the online algorithm assigns b to a machine $i' \in \Gamma$ while the optimal solution assigns b to a machine $i^* \notin \Gamma$. Hence, the set Γ is neither empty nor the entire set of machines (note this shows that $f \geq 1$, and hence there always exists a machine i satisfying $\hat{\ell}_i(j-1) \leq L^*$).

Since b was assigned by the optimal solution to a machine $i^* \notin \Gamma$, we have the property that $\frac{p_b}{s_{i^*}} \leq L^*$. Moreover, since $i^* \notin \Gamma$, we know that $s_{i^*} \leq s_f$. Hence, we have $\frac{p_b}{s_f} \leq \frac{p_b}{s_{i^*}} \leq L^*$. In addition, since $\hat{\ell}_f(j-1) \leq L^*$, we have $\hat{\ell}_f(b-1) + \frac{p_b}{s_f} \leq \hat{\ell}_f(j-1) + \frac{p_b}{s_f} \leq 2 \cdot L^* \leq 2 \cdot \Lambda$ (since $b \leq j-1$ and virtual loads can only grow within a phase). Thus, when job b arrived, the set S was nonempty (and hence, T was also nonempty). This implies that the online algorithm assigned job b to the representative $i' = r_i(b)$ of some machine $i \in T$ where $s_i \leq s_k$ (recall that k is the minimum machine index in S). In particular, machine $f \in S \subseteq T$, and hence $s_i \leq s_k \leq s_f$. Since $r_i(b) \in \Gamma$, we have $s_i \leq s_f < s_{r_i(b)} = s_i$, which yields a contradiction and gives the lemma. □

We now conclude the proof of the main theorem in this section.

Theorem 2.4. *Flex-Fit is $O(1)$-competitive for the makespan minimization problem on related machines.*

Proof. Observe that the final makespan of the online algorithm is at most (a) the sum of the maximal loads over all phases, plus (b) any additional processing times incurred due to explicitly assigning jobs to some fastest machine. That is, (b) refers to the very first job, along with all jobs that cause a phase to end.

We let $\Lambda_1 = \frac{p_1}{s_m}$ (i.e., the online algorithm's first estimate once job 1 arrives), and in general define Λ_h to be the value of Λ during phase $h \geq 1$. Observe that the estimate Λ_h is always of the form $2^{a_h} \cdot \Lambda_1$ for some integer $a_h \in \{0, 1, 2, \ldots\}$ (i.e., $\frac{\Lambda_h}{\Lambda_1}$ is always a power of 2 for every phase h). Moreover, we have $\Lambda_{h+1} \geq 2 \cdot \Lambda_h$ (since its new value is always its old value, multiplied by $\max\{2, 2^{\lceil \log_2 \frac{p_j}{s_m \Lambda_h} \rceil}\}$, where j is the current job that caused a new phase to begin). Hence, $a_h < a_{h+1}$.

Let k be the number of phases, where $k \geq 1$. We first show that $\Lambda_k \leq 2 \cdot L^*$, where Λ_k denotes the value of Λ during the final phase. If there is only one phase, we are done since the final estimate is $\Lambda_k = \Lambda_1 = \frac{p_1}{s_m} \leq L^* \leq 2 \cdot L^*$. Now, suppose there are $k \geq 2$ phases. Consider the $(k-1)^{st}$ phase (i.e., the phase just before the last phase). The reason why the algorithm ended phase $k-1$ and started phase k is because the set S was empty when some job arrived. By Lemma 2.3, it must have been the case that the estimate Λ_{k-1} was strictly less than L^*. There are two cases: $\Lambda_k = 2 \cdot \Lambda_{k-1}$ or $\Lambda_k = 2^{\lceil \log_2 \frac{p_j}{s_m \Lambda_{k-1}} \rceil} \cdot \Lambda_{k-1}$ (where j is the job that caused phase k to begin). In the first case, we have $\Lambda_k = 2 \cdot \Lambda_{k-1} < 2 \cdot L^*$. In the second case, we also have $\Lambda_k = 2^{\lceil \log_2 \frac{p_j}{s_m \Lambda_{k-1}} \rceil} \cdot \Lambda_{k-1} \leq 2 \cdot \frac{p_j}{s_m \Lambda_{k-1}} \cdot \Lambda_{k-1} \leq 2 \cdot L^*$ (since $\frac{p_j}{s_m} \leq L^*$).

By Lemma 2.2, the total load that accumulates during a phase h (i.e., while $T \neq \emptyset$, or possibly until $S = \emptyset$) is at most $(2 + \epsilon)\Lambda_h$. In addition, the algorithm also assigns jobs to a machine with the fastest speed (e.g., job 1, and all jobs that cause a new phase to begin). Such jobs j add at most $\frac{p_j}{s_m}$ to the makespan. Note that the job j which causes some phase h to begin satisfies $\frac{p_j}{s_m} \leq 2^{\lceil \log_2 \frac{p_j}{s_m \Lambda_{h-1}} \rceil} \cdot \Lambda_{h-1} \leq \Lambda_h$ (recall that $\frac{p_1}{s_m} = \Lambda_1$ by definition). Hence, each phase h incurs a makespan of at most $\Lambda_h + (2+\epsilon)\Lambda_h$. Let $a_h \in \{0, 1, 2, \ldots\}$ be the integer such that $\Lambda_h = 2^{a_h} \cdot \Lambda_1$. In all, the final makespan is at most:

$$\sum_{h=1}^{k}(3+\epsilon)\Lambda_h = (3+\epsilon)\Lambda_1 \sum_{h=1}^{k} 2^{a_h} \leq (3+\epsilon)\Lambda_1 \cdot 2^{a_k+1} = 2 \cdot (3+\epsilon) \cdot 2^{a_k}\Lambda_1 \leq 4 \cdot (3+\epsilon) \cdot L^*.$$

This concludes the proof of the theorem. □

2.2 Dynamic Pricing Scheme

We now give our dynamic pricing scheme, Dynamic-Related, which mimics the behavior of Flex-Fit. That is, the dynamic prices set by Dynamic-Related (prior to the arrival of each job) have the following property. Any incoming rational job j will choose some machine k such that Flex-Fit is free to assign job j to machine k.

As before, assume that machines are sorted such that $s_1 \leq s_2 \leq \cdots \leq s_m$. We now give some intuition behind the dynamic pricing algorithm and discuss some of its properties. Initially, the algorithm sets prices so that the first job is incentivized to choose machine m (i.e., a machine with the fastest speed), and then obtains an initial estimate Λ (in a manner similar to Flex-Fit). The algorithm then enters an outer while loop which is responsible for setting prices before each next job j arrives. It begins by sorting the values $\mu_i(j) = s_i(2 \cdot \Lambda - \hat{\ell}_i(j-1))$ so that $\mu_{i_1}(j) \leq \cdots \leq \mu_{i_m}(j)$. This is useful since a job is feasible on machine $i \Leftrightarrow \hat{\ell}_i(j-1) + \frac{p_j}{s_i} \leq 2 \cdot \Lambda \Leftrightarrow p_j \leq \mu_i(j)$.

The inner while loop in Dynamic-Related is responsible for obtaining a carefully selected subsequence of machines with strictly increasing speeds. In particular, the inner while loop constructs a set B with the property that for all $1 \leq b \leq |B|$, we have $s_{t_1} < s_{t_2} < \cdots < s_{t_{|B|}}$ (after renaming the machine indices in B by $t_1 < t_2 < \cdots < t_{|B|}$). This property holds due to the process by which the set B is created. Note that machine t_1 has the same speed as the slowest machine (i.e., $s_1 = s_{t_1}$), since the first machine added to set B is the machine in the rightmost position in the sorted ordering $\mu_{i_1}(j) \leq \cdots \leq \mu_{i_m}(j)$ satisfying the property that it has the same speed as the slowest machine (i.e., machine 1's speed). The inner while loop then removes all machines that appear earlier in the sorted ordering than machine t_1 from set A (including machine t_1 itself). This implies that all machines of speed s_{t_1} (i.e., the slowest machine speed) are removed from A, and hence the slowest machine remaining in set A must have strictly larger speed. Therefore, when adding the second machine to set B, namely machine t_2, we get that the speed of t_2 satisfies $s_{t_2} > s_{t_1}$. Repeating this process, we get that $s_{t_1} < s_{t_2} < \cdots < s_{t_{|B|}}$. In addition, we have the property that $\mu_{t_1}(j) \leq \cdots \leq \mu_{t_{|B|}}(j)$, since each time we add a machine to set B that appears later in the sorted order $\mu_{i_1}(j) \leq \mu_{i_2}(j) \leq \cdots \leq \mu_{i_m}(j)$.

The for loop is essentially responsible for determining which machines are given finite prices (in addition to computing the actual prices). Note that the algorithm only sets finite prices on representatives of machines, namely the representatives of machines $t_1, \ldots, t_{|B|}$ (possibly in addition to the representative of machine m). Hence, jobs can only be assigned to the representatives of machines $t_1, \ldots, t_{|B|}$, and possibly the representative of machine m. Dynamic-Related then updates Λ as necessary (in a manner similar to Flex-Fit).

Our goal now is to prove that the prices determined by Dynamic-Related are such that for any sequence of rational selfish jobs, the jobs will choose machines that are consistent with the choices available to Flex-Fit. This is the same as saying that the competitive ratio of the Dynamic-Related

ALGORITHM 3: Dynamic-Related: A Dynamic Pricing Scheme for Related Machines

$\pi_{m1} \leftarrow 0$, $\pi_{i1} \leftarrow \infty$ for all $i < m$
After agent 1 chooses a machine q:
  $\Lambda \leftarrow \frac{p_1}{s_q}$
  $\hat{\ell}_i(1) \leftarrow 0$ for all i
while *job j arrives* **do**
  $\mu_i(j) \leftarrow s_i(2 \cdot \Lambda - \hat{\ell}_i(j-1))$
  Sort the values $\mu_i(j)$ in ascending order so that $\mu_{i_1}(j) \le \mu_{i_2}(j) \le \cdots \le \mu_{i_m}(j)$ (breaking ties arbitrarily)
  $A \leftarrow [m]$, $B = \emptyset$
  while $A \neq \emptyset$ **do**
    $s \leftarrow \min\{s_i : i \in A\}$
    $w \leftarrow \max\{a : s_{i_a} = s\}$
    $B \leftarrow B \cup \{i_w\}$
    $A \leftarrow A \setminus \{i_a : a \le w\}$
  end
  Index the elements in B such that $t_1 < t_2 < \cdots < t_{|B|}$, where t_1 is the smallest element, t_2 is the second smallest, etc.
  $\pi_{r_{t_1}(j)j} = 0$
  for $b = 2$ *to* $|B|$ **do**
    $\pi_{r_{t_b}(j)j} = \ell_{r_{t_{b-1}}(j)}(j-1) - \ell_{r_{t_b}(j)}(j-1) + \left(1 - \frac{s_{t_{b-1}}}{s_{t_b}}\right)((2+\epsilon)\Lambda - \hat{\ell}_{t_{b-1}}(j-1)) + \pi_{r_{t_{b-1}}(j)j}$
  end
  if $s_m \neq s_{t_{|B|}}$ **then**
    $\pi_{r_m(j)j} = \ell_{r_{t_{|B|}}(j)}(j-1) - \ell_{r_m(j)}(j-1) + \left(1 - \frac{s_{t_{|B|}}}{s_m}\right)((2+\epsilon)\Lambda - \hat{\ell}_{t_{|B|}(j)}(j-1)) + \pi_{r_{t_{|B|}}(j)j}$
  end
  Set all other prices to ∞
  After agent j chooses a machine q:
    if $s_q = s_m$ and $S = \{i : \hat{\ell}_i(j-1) + \frac{p_j}{s_i} \le 2 \cdot \Lambda\} = \emptyset$ **then**
      $\Lambda \leftarrow \max\{2, 2^{\left\lceil \log_2 \frac{p_j}{s_m \Lambda} \right\rceil}\} \cdot \Lambda$
      $\hat{\ell}_i(j) \leftarrow 0$ for all i
    end
    else
      $\hat{\ell}_q(j) \leftarrow \hat{\ell}_q(j-1) + \frac{p_j}{s_q}$
      $\hat{\ell}_i(j) \leftarrow \hat{\ell}_i(j-1)$ for all $i \neq q$
    end
end

dynamic pricing scheme is the same as the competitive ratio of the Flex-Fit algorithm, which we know is $O(1)$ by Theorem 2.4. To summarize, we now seek to prove the following theorem:

THEOREM 2.5. *Dynamic-Related is an $O(1)$-competitive dynamic pricing scheme for the makespan minimization problem on related machines.*

We use *FF* and *DR* as shorthand when referring to Flex-Fit and Dynamic-Related, respectively. The plan for the proof is to argue that the behavior of *DR* is consistent with the behavior of *FF*. Note that, at certain points, *FF* is free to assign a job to one of multiple machines. Additionally, *FF* may be free to start a new phase (or not). Hence, by the phrase "*DR behaves consistently with FF*," we mean that *DR* sets prices so that any rational job to arrive will choose one of the permissible actions that *FF* is free to take.

Throughout the proof, we make use of notation present in both algorithms. In addition, when referring to the representative of a machine i when job j arrives, we write r_i instead of $r_i(j)$ and μ_i instead of $\mu_i(j)$ for ease of notation (we always refer to the current job j). Recall that $T = \{i : \hat{\ell}_i(j-1) + \frac{p_j}{s_i} \le (2+\epsilon)\Lambda\}$, $S = \{i : \hat{\ell}_i(j-1) + \frac{p_j}{s_i} \le 2 \cdot \Lambda\}$, and k is the minimum machine index in S ($k = m$ if $S = \emptyset$).

Theorem 2.5 follows from the following four lemmas, the first of which explores some properties of the prices *DR* assigns, while the remaining three argue that *DR* behaves consistently with *FF* in three disjoint, exhaustive cases. The proofs of the following lemmas are deferred to the full version of the paper [19].

Lemma 2.6. *If $|B| \ge 2$, then for all $1 \le b \le |B|-1$, we have $c_{r_{t_b}(j)j} \le c_{r_{t_{b+1}}(j)j}$ if and only if $t_b \in T$. Similarly, if $s_{t_{|B|}} \ne s_m$, then $c_{r_{t_{|B|}}(j)j} \le c_{r_m(j)j}$ if and only if $t_{|B|} \in T$.*

We now argue that *DR* behaves consistently with *FF* for every fixed job j. Clearly, for $j = 1$, both *FF* and *DR* behave in the same manner (including updating Λ). Now, consider any job $j > 1$. We split the proof up into three disjoint and exhaustive cases, classified as follows: set T is empty (Lemma 2.7), set T is nonempty but set S is empty (Lemma 2.8), and finally set S is nonempty (Lemma 2.9). Note that we always have $S \subseteq T$, so it is not possible for T to be empty while S is nonempty.

Lemma 2.7. *If $T = \emptyset$, then DR assigns prices so that a rational job j chooses a machine of speed s_m. DR also updates Λ, and resets virtual loads to zero (precisely in the same manner as FF).*

Lemma 2.8. *If $T \ne \emptyset$ and $S = \emptyset$, then DR processes job j in one of two ways. DR either (a) Sets prices so that a rational job j chooses a machine of speed s_m, updates Λ, and resets virtual loads to zero, or (b) DR sets prices so that a rational job j chooses some representative r_i where $i \in T$. Both options (a) and (b) are consistent with FF.*

Lemma 2.9. *If $S \ne \emptyset$, then DR sets prices so that j chooses some representative r_i where $s_i \le s_k$ and $i \in T$ (which is consistent with FF).*

This concludes the proof of Theorem 2.5.

3 LOWER BOUNDS FOR UNRELATED MACHINES

In this section, we first give a lower bound which shows that no deterministic dynamic pricing scheme can achieve a competitive ratio better than $\Omega(m)$ for the unrelated machine setting. Note that this competitive ratio can be achieved by the online greedy algorithm that assigns each job j to a machine that minimizes $\ell_i(j-1) + p_{ij}$. Moreover, this behavior can be mimicked by a dynamic pricing scheme, simply by setting all prices $\pi_{ij} = 0$.

Theorem 3.1. *No deterministic dynamic pricing scheme can achieve a competitive ratio better than $\Omega(m)$ for the unrelated machine setting.*

Proof. Let D denote the dynamic pricing scheme, and let *OPT* denote an optimal solution (i.e., a solution that minimizes the makespan). Our lower bound consists of some number of phases k, where k can be arbitrarily large. At the end of all k phases, we argue that the makespan of the dynamic pricing scheme is at least $k \cdot m$, while *OPT* only has a makespan of at most $(1 + 2\epsilon) \cdot k$ for an arbitrarily small $\epsilon > 0$. If we can maintain this property, this would imply a lower bound of $\Omega(m)$ on the competitive ratio.

The input consists of the following sequence of jobs. Suppose the adversary has already introduced $j-1$ jobs, and the dynamic pricing scheme D has processed these jobs. Hence, the dynamic pricing scheme must now set prices π_{ij} on each machine i (before job j arrives). Then, we introduce job j according to the following two cases (depending on how the dynamic pricing scheme D behaves):

(1) If there exist two distinct machines i, i' such that $\ell_i(j-1) + \pi_{ij} + \epsilon < \ell_{i'}(j-1) + \pi_{i'j}$, introduce the job j with $p_{ij} = \epsilon$, $p_{i'j} = 0$, and $p_{bj} = \infty$ for all $b \neq i, i'$.
(2) Otherwise, introduce the job j with $p_{1j} = 1$ and $p_{ij} = 1 + 2\epsilon$ for all $i > 1$.

Note that, if in the second case all prices are ∞, then we assume job j (i.e., agent j) breaks ties by preferring machine 1. Each phase consists of m occurrences of the second case.

The first claim we argue is that there exists an assignment of jobs to machines such that the load on each machine grows by at most $1 + 2\epsilon$ at the end of each phase. This implies that, after k phases have concluded, there is an optimal solution with a makespan of at most $(1 + 2\epsilon) \cdot k$. We construct such an assignment as follows. Observe that each time D assigns prices to machines such that we fall into the first case, we simply assign the constructed job j to machine i' (i.e., the machine satisfying $p_{i'j} = 0$). Hence, each time case 1 occurs, the load of each machine remains the same. On the other hand, consider the jobs introduced due to the second case during a phase, of which there are m. We simply assign these m jobs to m distinct machines. Each such job causes the load on the machine to which it is assigned to increase by at most $1 + 2\epsilon$. Hence, there is an assignment of jobs to machines that causes the load on every machine to increase by at most $1 + 2\epsilon$ after each phase completes.

We now argue that, after each phase completes, the dynamic pricing scheme D sets prices such that jobs choose machines in a way that the load on the first machine increases by m. This implies that, after k phases, the load on the first machine (according to the assignment given by D) is at least $k \cdot m$, and hence the makespan must be at least $k \cdot m$. We first consider the case where D sets prices such that we fall into case 1, and argue that the load for some machine increases by ϵ. In this case, there exist two machines i and i' such that $\ell_i(j-1) + \pi_{ij} + \epsilon < \ell_{i'}(j-1) + \pi_{i'j}$. We argue that machine i attains the minimum cost c_{ij} for job j. This holds since $c_{ij} = \ell_i(j-1) + p_{ij} + \pi_{ij} = \ell_i(j-1) + \epsilon + \pi_{ij} < \ell_{i'}(j-1) + \pi_{i'j} = \ell_{i'}(j-1) + p_{i'j} + \pi_{i'j}$ (recall that $p_{ij} = \epsilon$ while $p_{i'j} = 0$). Moreover, $c_{bj} = \infty$ for all $b \neq i, i'$, since $p_{bj} = \infty$. Hence, the dynamic pricing scheme D causes job j to be assigned to machine i, which increases the load on machine i by ϵ.

We now consider the case where D sets prices such that we fall into case 2, and argue that each such job always chooses machine 1 (causing the load on machine 1 to increase by 1, since $p_{1j} = 1$ for each such job j). Since m such jobs are introduced during each phase, this would show that the load on machine 1 increases by m after each phase completes. In the second case, if $\pi_{1j} = \infty$, then all prices must be ∞ (since there does not exist another machine i satisfying $\ell_i(j-1)+\pi_{ij}+\epsilon < \ell_1(j-1)+\pi_{1j} = \infty$). Hence, since we assumed that such a job j breaks ties in favor of machine 1, the job j prefers machine 1 over all other machines (which increases the load on machine 1 by 1). On the other hand, if π_{1j} is finite, we argue that job j is also assigned to machine 1. Observe that in the second case, for any two machines i and i', we have $\ell_i(j-1)+\pi_{ij}+\epsilon \geq \ell_{i'}(j-1)+\pi_{i'j}$. Hence, for any machine $i > 1$, we have $c_{1j} = \ell_1(j-1)+p_{1j}+\pi_{1j} = \ell_1(j-1)+1+\pi_{1j} \leq \ell_i(j-1)+1+\epsilon+\pi_{ij} < \ell_i(j-1)+1+2\epsilon+\pi_{ij} = c_{ij}$. This implies that machine 1 minimizes job j's cost, which in turn implies that the load on machine 1 increases by 1.

Finally, observe that we can always eventually force the dynamic pricing scheme D to produce prices such that we fall into case 2. This holds since, each time we fall into case 1, there is an optimal solution which satisfies the property that the load on every machine does not change. On the other hand, D causes such jobs j to be assigned to some machine for which the processing time is ϵ. This implies that the assignment determined by D causes the load on some machine to increase by ϵ, while in an optimal solution the load on every machine remains the same. This process cannot go on forever, since the makespan of the schedule produced by D can be made arbitrarily bad while the makespan of an optimal solution does not change (which would result in an arbitrarily bad competitive ratio). □

We now give a lower bound of $\Omega(m)$ on the expected competitive ratio for any randomized dynamic pricing scheme, which even holds against an oblivious adversary.

THEOREM 3.2. *No randomized dynamic pricing scheme can achieve an expected competitive ratio better than $\Omega(m)$ for the unrelated machine setting.*

PROOF. Let D denote the randomized dynamic pricing scheme, and let OPT denote an optimal solution (i.e., a solution that minimizes the makespan). Our lower bound draws on ideas from the proof of our deterministic lower bound (i.e., the proof of Theorem 3.1). Let $\epsilon > 0$ be arbitrarily small. The input sequence will consist of some number of jobs n, where we make n arbitrarily large.

In particular, the input sequence is iteratively constructed by the adversary in a deterministic manner. After the first $j-1$ jobs have been determined (independent of the randomness of the algorithm), the adversary constructs job j according to the following two cases, one of which must happen with probability at least $\frac{1}{2}$ (depending on the code of the dynamic pricing scheme D, but independent of any random coin flips). Here, the probability is taken over the coin flips of the algorithm, and the probability is computed as if the first $j-1$ jobs constructed so far are given as input to D (note that the jobs are only imagined to be given as input):

(1) There exist two distinct machines i, i' such that $\ell_i(j-1) + \pi_{ij} + \epsilon < \ell_{i'}(j-1) + \pi_{i'j}$ with probability at least $\frac{1}{2}$. Note that, conditioned on this event occurring, there must exist a fixed pair of machines (i, i') (obtained deterministically) such that the event $\ell_i(j-1) + \pi_{ij} + \epsilon < \ell_{i'}(j-1) + \pi_{i'j}$ occurs with probability at least $\frac{1}{m^2}$, since there are at most m^2 such pairs. For this fixed pair (i, i'), the adversary constructs the job j with $p_{ij} = \epsilon$, $p_{i'j} = 0$, and $p_{bj} = \infty$ for all $b \neq i, i'$.

(2) Otherwise, introduce the job j with $p_{1j} = 1$ and $p_{ij} = 1 + 2\epsilon$ for all $i > 1$.

Observe that one of these two cases must happen with probability at least $\frac{1}{2}$. Hence, the adversary constructs job j depending on which such case occurs with higher probability. Note that, if in the second case all prices are ∞, then we assume job j (i.e., agent j) breaks ties by preferring machine 1.

Let n_1 be the number of jobs constructed due to case 1, and n_2 be the number of jobs constructed due to case 2. Note that n_1 and n_2 are fixed (i.e., they are not random variables), and moreover we have $n_1 + n_2 = n$. Using similar reasoning as in the proof of Theorem 3.1, $OPT \leq (1 + 2\epsilon) \cdot \lceil \frac{n_2}{m} \rceil$, since we can always assign case 1 jobs to the machine on which a load of 0 is incurred. Moreover, for every m jobs constructed due to case 2, we can always put the m jobs on m distinct machines, increasing the makespan by at most $(1 + 2\epsilon)$.

On the other hand, we argue that the expected makespan of the dynamic pricing scheme D must be large. Observe that for each job j constructed due to case 1, the dynamic pricing scheme's expected sum of loads increases as follows: $\mathbb{E}[\sum_i \ell_i(j) - \ell_i(j-1)] \geq \epsilon \cdot \frac{1}{2m^2}$. This holds since, for each such job j, if the event $\ell_k(j-1) + \pi_{kj} + \epsilon < \ell_{k'}(j-1) + \pi_{k'j}$ occurs for the fixed pair of machines (k, k'), which happens with probability at least $\frac{1}{2m^2}$, then job j induces a load of ϵ on machine k. Hence, we have $\mathbb{E}[\sum_i \ell_i(n)] \geq n_1 \cdot \epsilon \cdot \frac{1}{2m^2}$. Moreover, for each job j constructed due to case 2, the load on machine 1 increases by 1 with probability at least $\frac{1}{2}$ (since if the event corresponding to case 2 occurs, which happens with probability at least $\frac{1}{2}$, job j is assigned to machine 1). Hence, we have $\mathbb{E}[\ell_1(n)] \geq n_2 \cdot \frac{1}{2}$. Putting it all together, we get $\mathbb{E}[\max_i \ell_i(n)] \geq \mathbb{E}\left[\max\left\{\frac{1}{m}\sum_i \ell_i(n), \ell_1(n)\right\}\right] \geq \max\left\{\frac{\epsilon \cdot n_1}{2m^3}, \frac{n_2}{2}\right\}$.

We consider the following two cases. In the first case, we have $n_2 \le t \cdot m$ for some large integer t, and in the other case we have $n_2 > t \cdot m$. Note that we assume $n_2 > 0$, as otherwise $OPT = 0$ and the competitive ratio is arbitrarily bad. In the first case, the expected competitive ratio is at least $\frac{\epsilon \cdot (n-n_2)}{2m^3 \cdot (1+2\epsilon) \cdot \lceil \frac{n_2}{m} \rceil} \ge \frac{\epsilon \cdot (n-t \cdot m)}{2m^3 \cdot (1+2\epsilon) \cdot (t+1)} = \Omega(\sqrt{n})$, which can be made arbitrarily bad (note that we choose n sufficiently large so that $\sqrt{n} \gg t \cdot m^3$). In the second case, the expected competitive ratio is at least $\frac{n_2}{2(1+2\epsilon) \cdot \lceil \frac{n_2}{m} \rceil} = \Omega(m)$. Note that, in the second case, OPT is large and hence our lower bound rules out additive constants in the competitive ratio of the dynamic pricing scheme.

□

4 GREEDY AND STATIC PRICING ARE EQUIVALENT

In this section, we relate the greedy algorithm and static pricing schemes. Our main theorem, Theorem 4.1, is given below. The proof of Theorem 4.1 appears in the full version of the paper [19].

THEOREM 4.1. *If the greedy algorithm that assigns each job j to a machine i that minimizes $\ell_i(j-1)+p_{ij}$ is c-competitive in some machine model (either identical, related, restricted, or unrelated), then the static pricing scheme that sets all prices to zero is also c-competitive. Moreover, a lower bound of c on the (expected) competitive ratio of the greedy algorithm implies a lower bound of $\Omega(c)$ for any deterministic or randomized static pricing scheme (for all machine models). The randomized lower bound holds as long as the greedy lower bound does not specify how ties are broken.*

REFERENCES

[1] Fidaa Abed, José R. Correa, and Chien-Chung Huang. 2014. Optimal coordination mechanisms for multi-job scheduling games. In *Proceedings of the 22nd annual European Symposium on Algorithms.*

[2] Susanne Albers. 1997. Better bounds for online scheduling. In *Proceedings of the 29th annual ACM Symposium on Theory of Computing.*

[3] James Aspnes, Yossi Azar, Amos Fiat, Serge Plotkin, and Orli Waarts. 1993. On-line load balancing with applications to machine scheduling and virtual circuit routing. In *Proceedings of the 25th annual ACM Symposium on Theory of Computing.*

[4] Baruch Awerbuch, Yossi Azar, Edward Grove, Ming-Yang Kao, P. Krishnan, and Jeffrey Vitter. 1995. Load balancing in the L_p norm. In *Proceedings of the 36th annual IEEE Symposium on Foundations of Computer Science.*

[5] Baruch Awerbuch, Yossi Azar, and Adam Meyerson. 2003. Reducing truth-telling online mechanisms to online optimization. In *Proceedings of the 35th annual ACM Symposium on Theory of Computing.*

[6] Baruch Awerbuch, Yair Bartal, Amos Fiat, and Adi Rosén. 1994. Competitive non-preemptive call control. In *Proceedings of the 5th annual ACM-SIAM Symposium on Discrete Algorithms.*

[7] Yossi Azar, Umang Bhaskar, Lisa Fleischer, and Debmalya Panigrahi. 2013. Online mixed packing and covering. In *Proceedings of the 24th annual ACM-SIAM Symposium on Discrete Algorithms.*

[8] Yossi Azar, Bala Kalyanasundaram, Serge Plotkin, Kirk Pruhs, and Orli Waarts. 1997. On-line load balancing of temporary tasks. *Journal of Algorithms* 22, 1 (1997), 93–110.

[9] Yossi Azar, Joseph (Seffi) Naor, and Raphael Rom. 1992. The competitiveness of on-line assignments. In *Proceedings of the 3rd annual ACM-SIAM Symposium on Discrete Algorithms.*

[10] Yair Bartal, Amos Fiat, Howard Karloff, and Rakesh Vohra. 1992. New algorithms for an ancient scheduling problem. In *Proceedings of the 24th annual ACM Symposium on Theory of Computing.*

[11] Allan Borodin, Nathan Linial, and Michael E. Saks. 1992. An optimal on-line algorithm for metrical task system. *J. ACM* 39, 4 (1992), 745–763.

[12] Shuchi Chawla, Jason D. Hartline, and Robert Kleinberg. 2007. Algorithmic pricing via virtual valuations. In *Proceedings of the 8th ACM Conference on Electronic Commerce.*

[13] Shuchi Chawla, Jason D. Hartline, David L. Malec, and Balasubramanian Sivan. 2010. Multi-parameter mechanism design and sequential posted pricing. In *Proceedings of the 42nd annual ACM Symposium on Theory of Computing.*

[14] Shuchi Chawla, David L. Malec, and Balasubramanian Sivan. 2010. The power of randomness in bayesian optimal mechanism design. In *Proceedings of the 11th ACM Conference on Electronic Commerce.*

[15] George Christodoulou, Elias Koutsoupias, and Akash Nanavati. 2004. Coordination mechanisms. In *Proceedings of the 31st International Colloquium on Automata, Languages, and Programming.*

[16] Ilan Reuven Cohen, Alon Eden, Amos Fiat, and Łukasz Jeż. 2015. Pricing online decisions: beyond auctions. In *Proceedings of the 26th annual ACM-SIAM Symposium on Discrete Algorithms.*
[17] Vincent Cohen-Addad, Alon Eden, Michal Feldman, and Amos Fiat. 2016. The invisible hand of dynamic market pricing. In *Proceedings of the 17th ACM Conference on Economics and Computation.*
[18] Paul Dütting, Michal Feldman, Thomas Kesselheim, and Brendan Lucier. 2016. Posted prices, smoothness, and combinatorial prophet inequalities. *CoRR* abs/1612.03161 (2016).
[19] Michal Feldman, Amos Fiat, and Alan Roytman. 2017. Makespan minimization via posted prices. *CoRR* abs/1705.01965 (2017).
[20] Michal Feldman, Nick Gravin, and Brendan Lucier. 2013. Combinatorial walrasian equilibrium. In *Proceedings of the 45th annual ACM Symposium on Theory of Computing.*
[21] Michal Feldman, Nick Gravin, and Brendan Lucier. 2015. Combinatorial auctions via posted prices. In *Proceedings of the 26th annual ACM-SIAM Symposium on Discrete Algorithms.*
[22] Amos Fiat, Yishay Mansour, and Uri Nadav. 2008. Competitive queue management for latency sensitive packets. In *Proceedings of the 19th annual ACM-SIAM Symposium on Discrete Algorithms.*
[23] Ronald L. Graham. 1966. Bounds for certain multiprocessing anomalies. *Bell System Technical Journal* 45, 9 (1966), 1563–1581.
[24] Jason D. Hartline and Tim Roughgarden. 2009. Simple versus optimal mechanisms. In *Proceedings of the 10th ACM Conference on Electronic Commerce.*
[25] Sungjin Im, Nathaniel Kell, Janardhan Kulkarni, and Debmalya Panigrahi. 2015. Tight bounds for online vector scheduling. In *Proceedings of the 56th annual IEEE Symposium on Foundations of Computer Science.*
[26] Nicole Immorlica, Li Li, Vahab S. Mirrokni, and Andreas Schulz. 2005. Coordination mechanisms for selfish scheduling. In *Proceedings of the 1st International Workshop on Internet and Network Economics.*
[27] Anna R. Karlin, Mark S. Manasse, Larry Rudolph, and Daniel D. Sleator. 1986. Competitive snoopy caching. In *Proceedings of the 27th annual Symposium on Foundations of Computer Science.*
[28] Anna R. Karlin, Mark S. Manasse, Larry Rudolph, and Daniel D. Sleator. 1988. Competitive snoopy caching. *Algorithmica* 3, 1 (1988), 79–119.
[29] Robert Kleinberg and Tom Leighton. 2003. The value of knowing a demand curve: bounds on regret for online posted-price auctions. In *Proceedings of the 44th annual IEEE Symposium on Foundations of Computer Science.*
[30] Elias Koutsoupias and Christos H. Papadimitriou. 1995. On the k-server conjecture. *J. ACM* 42, 5 (1995), 971–983.
[31] Mark S. Manasse, Lyle A. McGeoch, and Daniel D. Sleator. 1990. Competitive algorithms for server problems. *Journal of Algorithms* 11, 2 (1990), 208–230.
[32] Adam Meyerson, Alan Roytman, and Brian Tagiku. 2013. Online multidimensional load balancing. In *Proceedings of the 16th International Workshop on Approximation Algorithms for Combinatorial Optimization Problems.*
[33] Noam Nisan and Amir Ronen. 1999. Algorithmic mechanism design (extended abstract). In *Proceedings of the 31st annual ACM Symposium on Theory of Computing.*
[34] Daniel D. Sleator and Robert E. Tarjan. 1985. Amortized efficiency of list update and paging rules. *Commun. ACM* 28, 2 (1985), 202–208.
[35] Daniel Dominic Sleator and Robert Endre Tarjan. 1985. Self-adjusting binary search trees. *J. ACM* 32, 3 (1985), 652–686.

A COMPARISON OF ONLINE TRUTHFUL MECHANISMS TO DYNAMIC PRICING

The connection between online mechanisms and dynamic pricing schemes is not entirely trivial[5]. Dynamic pricing schemes are obviously truthful mechanisms, but converting an arbitrary online mechanism into a dynamic pricing scheme may not be possible. Online mechanisms with certain performance guarantees that also have properties (a) – (c) below can be converted into dynamic pricing schemes with the same guarantee. (a) The online mechanism must be prompt (where the payments are determined immediately), (b) Ties in agent utilities do not arise, or can be resolved arbitrarily without harming performance guarantees — this is not an issue in the mechanism design setting because the mechanism may decide how to break ties, but it is an issue with pricing schemes, and (c) The mechanism does not require "voluntary revelation" of agent types, in pricing schemes the only information available to the dynamic pricing scheme is what the previous agents actually choose, pricing schemes are *not* direct revelation schemes.

[5]Many thanks to Moshe Babaioff, Liad Blumrosen, Yannai A. Gonczarowski, and Noam Nisan for discussions helpful in clarifying this point.

Truth and Regret in Online Scheduling

SHUCHI CHAWLA, University of Wisconsin-Madison
NIKHIL DEVANUR, Microsoft Research
JANARDHAN KULKARNI, Microsoft Research
RAD NIAZADEH, Cornell University

We consider a scheduling problem where a cloud service provider has multiple units of a resource available over time. Selfish clients submit jobs, each with an arrival time, deadline, length, and value. The service provider's goal is to implement a truthful online mechanism for scheduling jobs so as to maximize the social welfare of the schedule. Recent work shows that under a stochastic assumption on job arrivals, there is a single-parameter family of mechanisms that achieves near-optimal social welfare. We show that given any such family of near-optimal online mechanisms, there exists an online mechanism that in the worst case performs nearly as well as the best of the given mechanisms. Our mechanism is truthful whenever the mechanisms in the given family are truthful and prompt, and achieves optimal (within constant factors) regret.

We model the problem of competing against a family of online scheduling mechanisms as one of learning from expert advice. A primary challenge is that any scheduling decisions we make affect not only the payoff at the current step, but also the resource availability and payoffs in future steps. Furthermore, switching from one algorithm (a.k.a. expert) to another in an online fashion is challenging both because it requires synchronization with the state of the latter algorithm as well as because it affects the incentive structure of the algorithms.

We further show how to adapt our algorithm to a non-clairvoyant setting where job lengths are unknown until jobs are run to completion. Once again, in this setting, we obtain truthfulness along with asymptotically optimal regret (within polylogarithmic factors).

Additional Key Words and Phrases: Cloud Computing; Online Learning; Pricing

1 INTRODUCTION

We consider an online mechanism design problem inspired by the allocation and scheduling of cloud services. A scheduler allocates scarce resources to jobs arriving over time with the goal of maximizing economic efficiency or social welfare. The jobs are submitted by selfish users who can lie about the job's value, length, arrival, or deadline, so as to obtain a better allocation or pay a cheaper price. Our goal is to design an online mechanism that is truthful and obtains good welfare guarantees in the worst case.

The primary motivation for our work comes from resource allocation in the context of cloud computing. The scheduling model we study is motivated by spot markets for virtual machines in "the cloud", such as the one run by Amazon. A similar model, called the economic resource

A full version of this paper is available at https://arxiv.org/abs/1703.00484.

Authors' email addresses: shuchi@cs.wisc.edu; nikdev@microsoft.com; jakul@microsoft.com; rad@cs.cornell.edu.

Shuchi Chawla was supported in part by NSF grants CCF-1320854 and CCF-1617505. Rad Niazadeh was supported by NSF grant CCF-1512964 and by a Google Ph.D. Fellowship. Portions of this work were completed while the first author was a visitor and the fourth author an intern at Microsoft Research Redmond.

ACM ISBN 978-1-4503-4527-9/17/06...$15.00. DOI: http://dx.doi.org/10.1145/3033274.3085119

allocation or ERA model, has been proposed in the context of Microsoft's Azure as described by Babaioff et al. [2017].

There is a vast and rich literature on online mechanism design in settings where selfish agents participate in the mechanism over time. What makes the scheduling problem described above interesting is that even ignoring the users' incentive constraints, there are strong lower bounds in the worst case for the purely algorithmic problem of scheduling jobs with deadlines to maximize welfare. Canetti and Irani [1998] showed, in particular, that no online algorithm can achieve a less than polylogarithmic competitive ratio for this problem in comparison to the hindsight optimal schedule. On the other hand, Lavi and Nisan [2015] showed that no deterministic mechanism that is truthful with respect to all of the parameters can approximate social welfare better than a factor T in the worst case, where T is the time horizon, even for unit length jobs on a single machine. In the face of these strong negative results, a number of works have considered weakening various aspects of the model in order to obtain positive results, such as requiring a slackness condition on the jobs' deadlines [Azar et al., 2015], allowing the algorithm to make tardy decisions [Hajiaghayi et al., 2005], satisfying incentive compatibility with respect to only a few of the jobs' parameters [Azar and Khaitsin, 2011, Cole et al., 2008], etc.

A Bayesian benchmark. In this paper we follow an alternate approach of competing against a benchmark inspired by a stochastic model for job arrivals. For many online problems, the hindsight optimum is too pessimistic and strong a benchmark to compete against. A classic example from algorithmic mechanism design is the digital goods auction for which no mechanism can compete against the hindsight optimum that obtains the entire social welfare. But picking the right benchmark to compete against, namely the optimal posted price, has led to the design of many beautiful mechanisms with robust and strong revenue guarantees. Hartline and Roughgarden [2008] advocate a general framework for generating an appropriate benchmark for such online problems—determine the class of all mechanisms that are optimal for the problem in an appropriate stochastic setting; compete against the best of these Bayesian optimal mechanisms for a worst case instance.

In this paper we apply the Hartline and Roughgarden approach to online scheduling.[1] *We show that for any given finite class of truthful scheduling mechanisms, we can design an online mechanism that is competitive against the best of the given mechanisms. Our mechanism is truthful with respect to all of the parameters of the jobs' types, is computationally efficient, and requires no assumptions on the input instance. We achieve asymptotically optimal regret guarantees with respect to all of the involved problem parameters.*

While the Hartline and Roughgarden agenda has been successfully applied in mechanism design settings, it has not yet seen much use in algorithmic settings where the worst case optimization problem is hard but positive results are known under stochastic assumptions.[2] Our hope is that this work will spur future work in this direction.

Our work is inspired by the recent work of Chawla et al. [2017] that shows that when jobs are drawn from an i.i.d. distribution in every time period, a family of simple mechanisms achieves near-optimal social welfare. Chawla et al.'s mechanism is a simple greedy best-effort mechanism based on posted prices. The mechanism announces a price per-unit of resource for each time period into the future. When a job arrives it gets scheduled in a best-effort FIFO manner in the cheapest slots that satisfy its requirements. Chawla et al. show that if the number of resources per time

[1]Note, however, that while Hartline and Roughgarden advocate competing against the Bayesian optimal mechanism, we compete against a suite of mechanisms that contain an approximately optimal one in any Bayesian setting.

[2]The idea of combining several online algorithms into one that is nearly as good as the best of them has been explored previously, but in the limited context of metrical task systems and adaptive data structures. See, e.g., Blum and Burch [2000], Blum et al. [2002].

period is large enough, then for any underlying distribution over job types, there exists a set of prices such that this posted-pricing-FIFO mechanism achieves a $1 - \epsilon$ approximation to expected social welfare. Unfortunately, finding the best price to offer requires knowing the fine details of the distribution over job types and solving a large linear program.

Chawla et al.'s mechanisms are parameterized by a single price. Machine learning techniques have been succesfully used to tune parameters of heuristics for a wide variety of problems [Hutter et al., 2009, Xu et al., 2008]. This is typically done in a batch setting, where past data is used to find a good setting of parameters for the heuristic. For an inherently online problem such as scheduling, we seek to do the parameter tuning itself in an online manner. Can we search for the right parameters as we are running the heuristic?

We model the online mechanism design problem as a sort of "learning from expert advice" problem where the experts are algorithms in the set of all Bayesian optimal algorithms. We present a general black-box reduction from the online scheduling problem to online learning algorithms for the experts setting. Previous work along these lines has looked at online settings where the mechanism gets a new instance of the problem in every time step, and the learning algorithm can adapt the parameters of the mechanism as more and more instances are seen. In the scheduling setting the algorithms run on a single instance of the problem, and we want to achieve low regret over all Bayesian optimal mechanisms for this specific instance.

Challenges. There are several novel challenges that the scheduling context imposes. First, in our setting, jobs can grab resources for multiple consecutive units of time. So the decision of scheduling a job in the current time step can affect the availability of resources in many future steps. Furthermore it is unclear at what time an algorithm should receive credit for scheduling a job – when the job starts, or when it ends, or throughout its execution? What if the algorithm uses preemption?

Second, while an online algorithm for the experts problem can cleanly switch from one expert to another during execution, in the scheduling setting switching can be tricky. On the one hand, we cannot abandon jobs that have already been started but not finished by the previous algorithm. On the other hand, we must try to match the state of the new algorithm that we are following, so as to obtain the same reward. Most importantly, switching impacts the *incentive properties* of the underlying mechanisms. Indeed there are several ways in which jobs may lie to affect their outcomes in the combined mechanism, even if they cannot in the underlying algorithms. For example, jobs may be able to influence the time at which a switch happens, or the next algorithm that is selected. Moreover, a job may be able to benefit indirectly by influencing the schedule of the algorithm that is used just prior to the algorithm that determines the job's allocation.

Our techniques. We design a switching procedure that overcomes all of these challenges. Each switch takes a few time steps to finish previously scheduled jobs, synchronize with the state of the new mechanism, as well as handle the scheduling of intermediate jobs in a manner so as to preserve their incentive structure. As a consequence of this "switching delay" our algorithm incurs a bounded cost for every switch. Using this switching procedure in tandem with a reduction to experts with switching costs allow us to obtain a sublinear regret guarantee in addition to truthfulness.

Our truthful switching technique is oblivious to the details of the underlying truthful mechanisms and works as long as the underlying mechanisms are prompt, that is, they announce the allocation and payment of a job right at the time of the job's arrival. To our knowledge this is the first result that combines truthful mechanisms online into an overall truthful mechanism.

Non-clairvoyance. Finally, one challenge faced by schedulers in a real-world setting is that jobs may not know how long they would take to run. Fortunately, the benchmark suggested by Chawla et al. [2017], namely the optimal posted-pricing-FIFO mechanism, continues to obtain near-optimal welfare—the mechanism does not need to know jobs' lengths in order to make scheduling decisions, although the existence of a good posted price assumes that lengths along with other job parameters are drawn from some i.i.d. distribution.

Non-clairvoyance poses extra challenges in the online scheduling setting. We can no longer keep track of different algorithms' rewards or their states at the time of a switch. Synchronization with an algorithm's state at the time of a switch is crucial because for some algorithms, such as posted-price-FIFO in particular, out of sync execution can cost almost the entire social welfare of the algorithm. (See, e.g., Example 4.1.)[3] We therefore consider a slightly modified benchmark where the performance of an algorithm is measured according to the welfare it accumulates if it is periodically (randomly) restarted with an empty state. These random restarts do not significantly affect the performance of algorithms such as posted-price-FIFO in the stochastic setting.

We give a reduction from the non-clairvoyant setting to a multi-armed bandit (MAB) problem. The main challenge in this reduction is to couple the random restarts of the expert algorithms with the times at which the MAB algorithm decides to switch experts, in a manner that ensures that the restarts are independent of the internal coin flips of the MAB algorithm. To do so, we partition the scheduling process into mini-batches synchronized with random restarts, and run the MAB algorithm over this batched instance. Because switching between algorithms happens exactly at the time of a random restart, it becomes possible for us to sync with the states of the expert algorithms.

Random restarts can once again break the incentive properties of the overall mechanism. We need to take care to ensure that jobs that are caught in the middle of a restart cannot benefit by misreporting their arrival or deadline. This necessitates a careful redesign of the switching protocol for non-clairvoyant settings. As in the clairvoyant setting, we obtain the optimal dependence within polylogarithmic factors of the regret on the time horizon.

Outline. In Section 3 we present a truthful online algorithm for the clairvoyant setting along with an upper bound on its regret. We extend both the truthfulness and regret guarantees to the non-clairvoyant setting in Section 4. Section 5 presents matching lower bounds on regret.

2 MODEL AND DEFINITIONS

2.1 The online job scheduling problem

An instance of the online job scheduling problem consists of a finite set of jobs $\mathcal{J}$, a time horizon T, and the number m of resources (machines) available per unit of time. Each job $j \in \mathcal{J}$ arrives at time $a_j \in [T]$, has a deadline $d_j \in [a_j, a_j + d_{\max}]$ and a processing length $l_j \in [0, \ell_{\max}]$. Assume all the deadlines are in the time horizon $[T]$. Completing each time unit of job $j \in \mathcal{J}$ generates a value-per-length $v_j \in [0, v_{\max}]$.

Online scheduling algorithms. An online scheduler is an algorithm that determines which jobs to schedule and when, and how much to charge each scheduled job. Each job j, at the time of its arrival, reports its arrival time, deadline, length, and value; this four-tuple is called the job's type. The scheduling algorithm determines whether or not to schedule the job (*admission control step*) and, if the job is scheduled, maps it to a set τ_j of time units (*scheduling step*) and charges it a payment p_j. If $|\tau_j \cap [a_j, d_j]| \geq l_j$, that is, the job is allocated at least l_j time units before its deadline, then the job obtains a utility of $(v_j - p_j) \cdot l_j$. The schedule produced by the algorithm is feasible if no more than m jobs are assigned to each time unit.

We now discuss various features of online scheduling algorithms:

[3] In the full version of the paper we also show that in a continuous time setting no algorithm can get a sub-linear regret.

Preemption: We say that the algorithm is *non-preemptive* if the set τ_j consists of contiguous time units for every job j. In other words, when a job is started, the algorithm processes it without pausing until it is finished.

Truthfulness: A scheduling algorithm is *truthful* if for every job j, fixing the reported types of jobs in $\mathcal{J}_{-j}$, job j's utility is maximized by reporting its true type. Jobs can misreport any of the four components of their type, however, following convention we assume that jobs cannot report an earlier arrival time.

Promptness: A scheduling algorithm is *prompt* if for every job j, the job's allocation and payment, (τ_j, p_j), are determined at the time of the job's arrival. At times we will refer to a weaker property: an algorithm is *order respecting* if for every job j, the job's allocation and payment, (τ_j, p_j), are functions of jobs in $\mathcal{J}$ that arrive prior to j and not of those jobs that arrive after j.

Clairvoyance: The *clairvoyant scheduling* problem is the setting where every job j reports its length l_j to the scheduling mechanism, together with other parts of its type, upon its arrival, whereas in the *non-clairvoyant scheduling problem* jobs do not report their lengths upon arrival. In fact, the scheduling mechanism observes the length of a job only after it completes the job. Since the length of job j is unknown prior to its completion in the non-clairvoyant scheduling, we have to slightly modify other aspects of the setting:

- we change the definition of deadline d_j to denote the latest time that j can be started.[4]
- We do not allow preemption in the non-clairvoyant setting.

With these two modifications, it is indeed guaranteed that if a job j is allocated at a time no later than its deadline, then it will be scheduled properly, i.e. it will be given enough time to be completed.

Let ONL denote an online scheduling algorithm, and let $J(\mathsf{ONL}) = \mathcal{J} \cap \{j : |\tau_j \cap [a_j, d_j]| \geq l_j\}$ denote the set of jobs that receive service in ONL. We use $W_t(\mathsf{ONL}, \mathcal{J})$ to denote the value generated by the algorithm at time unit t:

$$W_t(\mathsf{ONL}, \mathcal{J}) = \sum_{j \in J(\mathsf{ONL}):\, t \in \tau_j} v_j$$

The total value generated by the algorithm, a.k.a. its *social welfare*, is given by:

$$W(\mathsf{ONL}, \mathcal{J}) = \sum_{t=1}^{T} W_t(\mathsf{ONL}, \mathcal{J}) = \sum_{j \in J(\mathsf{ONL})} v_j l_j$$

We drop the argument $\mathcal{J}$ when it is clear from the context.

Regret minimization in online scheduling. We consider an online learning problem, where we are given a finite set of scheduling algorithms and our goal is to compete with the best one in hindsight with respect to the social welfare objective. Let $\{\mathsf{ALG}_1, \ldots, \mathsf{ALG}_n\}$ be the set of n online schedulers. Given an instance $\mathcal{J}$, let $\mathsf{OPT}(\mathcal{J}) = \max_{i \in [n]} W(\mathsf{ALG}_i, \mathcal{J})$ denote the social welfare obtained by the hindsight optimal algorithm on this instance. Let ONL denote our online scheduling algorithm. The regret of ONL is defined as:

$$\textsc{Reg}(\mathsf{ONL}) \triangleq \max_{\mathcal{J}} \left(\mathsf{OPT}(\mathcal{J}) - W(\mathsf{ONL}, \mathcal{J})\right)$$

[4]Note the difference with deadlines in the clairvoyant setting, where d_j was defined to be the latest time that j could be completed.

2.2 Learning from expert advice

We will reduce the regret minimization problem for online scheduling to the problem of learning from expert advice. In the latter, we are given n experts indexed by i. In each time step $t \in [T]$, the online algorithm must choose a (potentially random) expert, $i_t \in [n]$, to follow. An adversary then reveals a reward vector $\{r_t^{(i)}\}$. We assume that the adversary is oblivious, that is, it cannot observe the internal coin flips of the algorithm. The total payoff of expert i is given by $\sum_{t\in[T]} r_t^{(i)}$. The payoff of the algorithm is given by $\mathbf{E}\left[\sum_{t\in[T]} r_t^{(i_t)}\right]$, where the expectation is taken over the algorithm's internal coin flips. The regret of the algorithm is:

$$\left(\max_{i\in[n]} \sum_{t\in[T]} r_t^{(i)}\right) - \mathbf{E}\left[\sum_{t\in[T]} r_t^{(i_t)}\right]$$

Let R denote an upper bound on $r_t^{(i)}$ for any $i \in [n]$ and $t \in [T]$. Then, several different online algorithms are known to achieve a regret of $O(R\sqrt{T \log n})$, and this bound is tight [Cesa-Bianchi and Lugosi, 2006, Freund and Schapire, 1995, Kalai and Vempala, 2005].

Experts with switching costs. This is a variant of the problem of learning from expert advice in which the algorithm faces a *switching cost* of C units every time it switches from one expert to another in consecutive time steps. In particular, the payoff of the algorithm is given by $\mathbf{E}\left[\sum_{t\in[T]} r_t^{(i_t)}\right] - C\,|\{t \in [T] : i_t \neq i_{t-1}\}|$. The first term corresponds to the rewards and the second corresponds to the switching cost. Accordingly, the regret of the algorithm is:

$$\left(\max_{i\in[n]} \sum_{t\in[T]} r_t^{(i)}\right) - \mathbf{E}\left[\sum_{t\in[T]} r_t^{(i_t)}\right] + C\,\mathbf{E}[|\{t \in [T] : i_t \neq i_{t-1}\}|]$$

THEOREM 2.1 (KALAI AND VEMPALA [2005]). *There is an algorithm* Expert-ALG(C) *for the experts problem with a switching cost of C such that*

$$\textit{Reg}(\texttt{Expert-ALG}(C)) \leq O\left(\sqrt{R(R+C)T\log n}\right).$$

Multi-armed bandit setting. In the multi-armed bandit (MAB) setting, the online algorithm may only observe the reward $r_t^{(i_t)}$ of the expert that it selects at time t, and cannot observe the remaining rewards. Algorithms for MAB typically mix some exploration alongside following the recommendation of an online learning algorithm for the full-information setting.

THEOREM 2.2 (AUER ET AL. [1995]). *There is an algorithm* Bandit-ALG *for the MAB problem with*

$$\textit{Reg}(\texttt{Bandit-ALG}) \leq O\left(R\sqrt{Tn\log n}\right).$$

We can further consider an extension of the MAB setting to the setting with a switching cost. For this problem, we mainly use that there is no algorithm with a regret of $o(T^{2/3})$ [Dekel et al., 2014], to get a similar lower bound for our problem. The precise statement of their result is in Section 5.

3 THE CLAIRVOYANT SETTING

In this section we consider the online scheduling problem in the clairvoyant setting, namely where every job reports its length (in addition to the rest of its type) at the time of its arrival. We are given n online scheduling algorithms, $\texttt{ALG}_1, \ldots, \texttt{ALG}_n$, and our goal is to design an online algorithm that minimizes regret relative to the best of the n algorithms in hindsight. We begin by showing how to switch between algorithms in a way that preserves truthfulness in Section 3.1. In Section 3.2 we present a reduction from this problem to the problem of learning from expert advice with switching costs. In Section 5 we prove that the regret guarantee we obtain from the reduction is optimal.

3.1 Truthful switching

In this section, we show how to switch between truthful mechanisms while preserving truthfulness and making sure the loss in welfare is bounded. We consider the following setting. Let A and B be two order respecting truthful scheduling mechanisms. Our goal is to switch from mechanism A to mechanism B at time 0. (This is just a normalization of the time index for ease of notation.) We consider show how to perform this switch in the clairvoyant setting, and extend our algorithm to the non-clairvoyant setting in Section 4.2. The loss in welfare from our switching algorithm is captured in the following lemma.

Lemma 3.1. *Given order respecting truthful mechanisms A and B, there exists an order respecting truthful mechanism C that obtains welfare at least*

$$\sum_{t\leq 0} W_t(A) + \sum_{t\geq 1} W_t(B) - 2v_{\max}d_{\max}m.$$

In particular, all jobs that arrive by time 0 and are completed by mechanism A are also completed by C. We can compose any number of "switching" steps, losing an additive $2v_{\max}d_{\max}m$ amount in welfare each time.

Theorem 3.2. *Suppose we wish to switch among many order respecting truthful mechanisms as follows: start with A_0 at time 1, switch to A_1 at time t_1, then to A_2 at time t_2 and so on till you switch to A_L at time t_L for some $L \in \mathbb{Z}_+$. Let $t_0 = 0$ and $t_{L+1} = T$ for notational convenience. Then there is an order respecting truthful mechanism whose welfare is at least*

$$\sum_{i=0}^{L} \sum_{t\in(t_i,t_{i+1}]} W_t(A_i) - 2Lv_{\max}md_{\max}.$$

Proof. Let B_1 be the mechanism obtained by applying Lemma 3.1 to switch from A_0 to A_1 at time t_1. Apply the lemma again to switch from B_1 to A_2 at time t_2; let the resulting mechanism be B_2. Continuing this way, we apply the lemma to switch from B_i to A_{i+1} at time t_{i+1}, to get mechanism B_{i+1}, for all i up to $L-1$. The resulting mechanism at the end, B_L, is the one we want. □

In the rest of this section we prove Lemma 3.1.

3.1.1 *The online switching algorithm.*

Definition 3.3. The mechanism C (Lemma 3.1) is as follows.

1. For jobs that arrive by time 0, mimic mechanism A and return the same allocation, schedule and prices. Observe that jobs that are scheduled in this step are terminated by time $d_{\max}$.
2. Mark the remaining time slots in $[1, d_{\max}]$ as *unavailable*. This means that for all jobs j that were not considered in the previous step (because $a_j > 0$) and have deadline $d_j \leq d_{\max}$, we decline service and charge a price of 0.
3. For all remaining jobs, i.e., jobs j with $a_j > 0$ and $d_j > d_{\max}$, consider the jobs in the order of arrival, and do the following:
   (a) If B rejects j, then reject j.
   (b) If there are not enough slots available to cover j's length prior to its deadline, reject j.
   (c) Otherwise, accept and schedule j in a "best effort" manner. Specifically, assign to the job all of the slots that it gets in B and that are still available in C's schedule. If any of these

slots is unavailable, replace it with the earliest available slot in C's schedule. We call these newly assigned slots the "replacement" slots for job j. Charge j the same payment as in mechanism B.

Design choices. We explain the design choices made in the above mechanism. In step (1) we continue to process jobs that arrive by time 0 according to mechanim A. If we abruptly stop mechanism A, then there may be an incentive for some jobs to lie so that they get scheduled by time 0. In step (2) we make the remaining slots unavailable. Why not directly go to step (3) and schedule jobs that B has accepted in a best effort manner? One of the properties we need for truthfulness to hold is that jobs that arrive after time 0 finish at a time in mechanism C that is no earlier than their finish time in mechanism B. Otherwise there may be an incentive for a job to lie so that it gets accepted in B but is scheduled to finish after its true deadline, whereas mechanism C ends up scheduling it within its true deadline. Lemma 3.4 below shows that the algorithm C satisfies this property. Another option is to simply reject all jobs that arrive during the time interval $[1, d_{\max}]$. This would not be truthful since it incentivizes a job that arrives in this interval to report a later arrival time. In step (3) (a) if we start considering jobs that B rejected because we have some more available slots than B, we might break the truthfulness of B. Finally, in step (3) (c) we first assign the same slots to the job as in B in order to ensure the no early completion property. Assigning the remaining available slots in the chronological order is crucial for the welfare analysis.

3.1.2 *Truthfulness.* We begin by proving the no early completion property.

Lemma 3.4. *Any replacement slot assigned in step (3) (c) is always later in time relative to the unavailable slot it replaces.*

Proof. Suppose one of the slots assigned to a job j in mechanism B, say at time t, is unavailable in mechanism C. If $t \leq d_{\max}$ then by construction the replacement slot is later. Otherwise, t itself is a replacement slot for some other job j'. The arrival time of j', $a_{j'}$ is no larger than a_j because jobs are processed in FIFO order. Since replacement slots are assigned in chronological order, all slots in $[a_{j'}, t-1]$ must have been unavailable when t was assigned to j'. Now all slots in $[a_j, t]$ are unavailable when we consider job j, so its replacement for slot t can only be later. □

Lemma 3.5. *Mechanism C is truthful.*

Proof. We consider three cases depending on which step of the mechanism handles the job. Recall that we assume that jobs cannot report an earlier arrival time.

(1) Suppose that $a_j \leq 0$, which means that the job gets processed in step (1) and gets an allocation and payment as per mechansim A. If the job reports an arrival time > 0, then it is not processed in step (1) and gets none of the slots in $[a_j, d_j]$, because $d_j \leq d_{\max}$, and all those slots are marked unavailable at the beginning of step (2). Any other misreport means that the job still gets processed in step (1). Now we can appeal to the fact that algorithm A is truthful to assert that the job does not benefit from misreporting its type.

(2) Suppose that $a_j > 0$ and $d_j \leq d_{\max}$, which means it is processed in step (2). In this case, regardless of its actual report the job gets no slots in its time window.

(3) Suppose that $a_j > 0$ and $d_j > d_{\max}$, which means it is processed in step (3). Since the job cannot report an earlier arrival time, it cannot be processed in step (1), and reporting a deadline $\leq d_{\max}$ means it gets no slots. Hence the only misreports we need to consider are such that the job is still processed in step (3).

The truthfulness of B should now imply that no misreport can be beneficial in C as well. This is almost true since, for instance, the price paid is the same in both (on acceptance). However, there is a possibility that misreporting a later deadline in B (possibly combined with a misreport of other parameters) results in a lower price, but that in B's schedule the job finishes after its true deadline d_j. This would be a non-beneficial misreport in B but could be beneficial in C if it actually finishes earlier than d_j in C, while enjoying the lower price. Lemma 3.4 ensures this does not happen.

□

3.1.3 Welfare. Define a time slot $t > d_{\max}$ to be "free" if mechanism C schedules fewer jobs in time t than mechanism B. The *number* of free slots at time t is the difference, given that it is non-negative, and zero otherwise. We first argue that there are few free slots in C's schedule.

Lemma 3.6. *All replacement slots occur before the first free slot.*

Proof. Let t be the first free slot. Consider a job that arrives before t. This job is not assigned any replacement slots after t since t is free and hence available, and replacement slots are assigned in chronological order. We will argue that jobs arriving after t have no replacement slots, i.e., they get the same slots as in B. This is by induction on the arrival order of these jobs. Consider the very first such job. All earlier jobs arrive before t by definition, and have no replacement slots after t as already argued, therefore all of the slots assigned to this job in B's schedule are available. This is the base case. The argument for the inductive case is almost exactly the same. □

Lemma 3.7. *The total number of free slots is at most md_{max}. In particular, if t is the earliest time of a free slot, then all the free slots are in the interval $[t, t + d_{max}]$. In other words, mechanisms B and C get synchronized after time $t + d_{max}$.*

Proof. From Lemma 3.6, there are no replacement slots after t. Any job that arrives at t or later and is scheduled in B gets the same slots in C as in B, and hence there are no free slots corresponding to such a job. All the free slots must correspond to jobs that arrive before t, and are therefore in the interval $[t, t + d_{\max}]$. □

We are now ready to prove the main lemma of this section.

Proof of Lemma 3.1. It is easy to see that mechanism C is also order respecting. Since we already showed that the mechanism is truthful in Lemma 3.5, we only need to argue about the welfare.

Any job that arrives before time 0 and is accepted by A is also accepted by C and completed, therefore it gets the same welfare as A upto time 0. Now we argue about the total loss in welfare during the time $t \geq 1$. Let $\ell_B(t)$ (resp. $\ell_C(t)$) be the number of jobs scehduled at time $t \geq 1$ by mechanism B (resp. mechanism C), and let $\ell_F(t)$ be the number of free slots at time t. By the definition of a free slot, we have that

$$\sum_{t\geq 1} \ell_B(t) \leq \sum_{t \geq d_{\max}+1} (\ell_C(t) + \ell_F(t)) + md_{\max}.$$

The set of jobs accepted by C is a subset of the set of jobs accepted by B, due to steps (2) and (3a). The total length of all jobs that are accepted by B but not by C is equal to $\sum_{t\geq 1} (\ell_B(T) - \ell_C(t)) \leq \sum_{t\geq d_{\max}+1} \ell_F(t) + md_{\max} \leq 2md_{\max}$, where the last inequality is from Lemma 3.7. Thus the total loss is at most $2mv_{\max}d_{\max}$. □

3.2 Reduction to experts with switching costs

Let `Expert-ALG`(C) denote an online algorithm for the problem of learning from expert advice with switching cost C that achieves the regret guarantee of Theorem 2.1. `Expert-ALG` is given an instance with n experts, indexed by $i \in [n]$. It specifies for every time step $t \in [T]$ a random expert i_t, and then receives a reward vector $\{r_t^{(i)}\}$. Our online scheduling algorithm, that we call *Follow-The-Switcher* or FTS, simulates Expert-ALG in a black-box fashion and follows its advice on which expert, a.k.a. algorithm, to run at every time step.

Definition 3.8. Given the n online scheduling algorithms, $\mathsf{ALG}_1, \ldots, \mathsf{ALG}_n$, the Follow-The-Switcher, a.k.a. FTS, algorithm simulates the online algorithm Expert-ALG(C) with C set to $2v_{\max}d_{\max}m$. It then proceeds as follows.

At each time $t \in [T]$:

(1) Simulate algorithms $\mathsf{ALG}_1, \ldots, \mathsf{ALG}_n$ on the freshly arrived set of jobs.

(2) Query Expert-ALG to obtain the index $i_t \in [n]$.

(3) If $i_t \neq i_{t-1}$, then switch from $\mathsf{ALG}_{i_{t-1}}$ to ALG_{i_t} as described in Section 3.1. Otherwise continue running the same algorithm $\mathsf{ALG}_{i_{t-1}} = \mathsf{ALG}_{i_t}$.

(4) Set $r_t^{(i)} \leftarrow W_t(\mathsf{ALG}_{i_t})$ for all $i \in [n]$. Send the reward vector $\{r_t^{(i)}\}$ to Expert-ALG.

The following theorem now immediately follows from Theorem 3.2.

Theorem 3.9. *Let $C = 2v_{max}d_{max}m$. Then the Follow-The-Switcher (FTS) algorithm, described in Definition 3.8, admits the following regret-bound:*

$$\textsc{Reg}(\mathsf{FTS}) \leq \textsc{Reg}(\mathsf{Expert\text{-}ALG}(C)) \leq O\left(mv_{max}\sqrt{Td_{max}\log n}\right) .$$

4 NON-CLAIRVOYANT SETTING

In this section, we look at regret minimization in the non-clairvoyant setting; we recall the main differences here. Every job reports all parts of its type except its length, and the algorithm only observes the length of a job when (and if) it is completed. Hence a non-clairvoyant algorithm cannot plan for a complete schedule ahead of time. The algorithm maintains a queue of unfinished jobs and at every time t decides which job to schedule from this queue at that time. The deadline for a job is now the number of time slots that the job is willing to wait out. If a job passes its deadline, which means that the number of time slots that a job j waits since its arrival exceeds a threshold d_j, then the job is deleted from the queue. Due to this reason, the notion of promptness is not quite applicable to the non-clairvoyant setting. In its place, we use the order respecting property, which states that only jobs arriving earlier can influence the allocation and payments for a given job. We assume that there is a total order on the arrival time of the jobs, by breaking ties arbitrarily in case multiple jobs arrive at the same time.

Similar to the clairvoyant setting, we have a set of n online scheduling algorithms, $\mathsf{ALG}_1, \ldots, \mathsf{ALG}_n$, and we aim to design an online algorithm that minimizes the regret relative to the best of these algorithms in hindsight. We begin our discussion in Section 4.1, where we show that this benchmark by itself is impossible to compete with, which motivates a reasonable modification. In Section 4.2 we show how to switch between two mechanisms truthfully. Finally in Section 4.3, we show how to use multi-armed bandit algorithms to get tight regret bounds.

4.1 Scheduling algorithms with random restarts

Robustness of the benchmark. In the non-clairvoyant setting, it is easy to come up with examples showing that the welfare obtained by an online scheduling mechanism is very sensitive to *timing* in the adversarial model of jobs, i.e., by slightly changing the starting time of the mechanism the obtained welfare can be drastically different. This has been demonstrated in Example 4.1.

Example 4.1. Consider running FIFO scheduling with pricing admission control at $p = 1$. Suppose we have two sets of jobs J_1 and J_2, with $v_j = 1$ for all the jobs. Suppose $(a_j, l_j) = (4i + 1, 4)$ for all $j \in J_1$ and $(a_{j'}, l_{j'}) = (4i + 4, 2)$ for all $j' \in J_2$, where $i = 0, 1, \ldots (\frac{T}{4} - 1)$. All of them have immediate deadlines, which means they need to be scheduled when they arrive. If we schedule jobs in J_1, we generate a welfare equal to T. Now consider starting at a time t which does not corresponds to the arrival times of jobs in J_1. Then we only end up scheduling jobs in J_2 (and in the non-clairvoyant setting we will not even notice how valuable jobs in J_1 were!) and get only welfare equal to $T/2$.

The example is robust to variations such as picking a random job when you start (by having many identical copies of jobs in J_2), or picking a random starting time.

As it is clear from this example, the welfare obtained form such a mechanism cannot be a reasonable benchmark for our regret minimization, as one has to think very carefully about when to start running such a mechanism to calculate the benchmark. Otherwise, the benchmark mechanism could easily get tricked into a false start. In other words, we need to define the benchmark in a way that is *robust* to this sort of timing issues, independent of the choice of scheduling mechanism defining the benchmark.

Syncing issues. In the non-clairvoyant setting, our scheduling mechanism is not able to *simulate* an arbitrary candidate scheduling mechanism ALG_i starting from an arbitrary time, since there is no way of knowing its state. Accordingly, following the decisions of a bandit algorithm, similar to what we did in Section 3.2, is generally not possible in the non-clairvoyant setting.

However, if both our mechanism and the new switched scheduling mechanism restart from a fresh state at exactly the same time after switching (e.g. slightly after the switching time when our mechanism is done with its current jobs) then our mechanism can sync with the new scheduling mechanism.

To address above concerns and to be able to design a truthful online scheduling mechanism that achieves a meaningful regret bound, we introduce a couple of new ingredients in our model and redefine our benchmark. We start by defining the notion of a *random restart* formally as following. An important property of the way we restart is that it preserves truthfulness: a mechanism that was truthful to begin with is still truthful with a restart. We use ideas from the clairvoyant truthful switching: think of the restart as a switch from A to A.

Definition 4.2. Given an online scheduling mechanism A, we define the *restart* at time t as follows.

- During $[t : t + (\ell_{\max} + d_{\max})]$, mechanism $\mathcal{M}$ continues working on the jobs that have arrived before t.
- If a job j arrives during $[t : t + (\ell_{\max} + d_{\max})]$, modify it as follows.
  - Shift its arrival time to the end of this interval, i.e. $a_j \leftarrow t + (\ell_{\max} + d_{\max}) + 1$.
  - Adjust the deadline of the job so that it reflects the time lost during the interval $[t, t + d_{\max} + \ell_{\max}]$. This might mean some jobs are past their deadline. These jobs are rejected.
  - Preserve the arrival order. Use the tie breaking rule to make sure the arrival order of jobs whose starting time was set to $t + d_{\max} + \ell_{\max}$ is the same as in the original instance.

Having the formal definition of a restart, we ask the following question: how can one define a robust benchmark in the non-clairvoyant scheduling problem, given a set of candidate scheduling mechanisms? Here is an adaptation of our previous benchmark, i.e. welfare of the best-in-hindsight scheduling mechanism, for the non-clairvoyant setting.

Definition 4.3. Given candidate scheduling mechanisms $\mathsf{ALG}_1, \ldots, \mathsf{ALG}_n$, and a parameter $\gamma \in [0, 1]$, the *random-restarting* mechanisms $\overline{\mathsf{ALG}}_1, \ldots, \overline{\mathsf{ALG}}_n$ are defined to be the original candidate mechanisms accompanied by independent random restarts of probability γ at every time $t \in [T]$. We define the *random-restarting benchmark* for an instance $\mathcal{J}$ to be $\overline{\mathsf{OPT}}(\mathcal{J}) = \max_{i\in[n]} \mathbf{E}\left[W(\overline{\mathsf{ALG}}_i, \mathcal{J})\right]$.

The benefits of using benchmark $\overline{\mathsf{OPT}}(\mathcal{J})$ are twofold. First, this benchmark is robust to timing issues, because the scheduling mechanism generating the benchmark restarts independently at random at every time t with probability γ. Therefore, the benchmark loses no more than the generated welfare between two consecutive random-restarts due to timing issues. Second, while this property does not hold in general, for a large family of scheduling mechanisms (such as posted-pricing-FIFO) and under the *stochastic model* of jobs (e.g. see [Chawla et al., 2017]), the welfare loss due to independent (but infrequent) random restarts will easily be bounded. This property of the pair (stochastic model, online scheduling mechanisms), which we call *robustness-to-welfare-loss*, is formalized as following.

Definition 4.4. Given a distribution over jobs $\mathcal{D}$, the random-restarting benchmark $\overline{\mathsf{OPT}}(\mathcal{J})$ with parameter γ is robust-to-welfare-loss in expectation over stochastic jobs $\mathcal{D}$ if

$$\mathbf{E}_{\mathcal{J}\sim\mathcal{D}}\left[\overline{\mathsf{OPT}}(\mathcal{J})\right] \geq \mathbf{E}_{\mathcal{J}\sim\mathcal{D}}[\mathsf{OPT}(\mathcal{J})] - \gamma \cdot T \cdot v_{\max}(\ell_{\max} + d_{\max})$$

Moreover, a random-restarting online scheduling mechanism $\overline{\mathsf{ALG}}_i$ with parameter γ is robust-to-welfare-loss in expectation under stochastic jobs $\mathcal{D}$ if

$$\mathbf{E}_{\mathcal{J}\sim\mathcal{D}}\left[\sum_{t\in[T]} W_t(\overline{\mathsf{ALG}}_i, \mathcal{J})\right] \geq \mathbf{E}_{\mathcal{J}\sim\mathcal{D}}\left[\sum_{t\in[T]} W_t(\mathsf{ALG}_i, \mathcal{J})\right] - \gamma \cdot T \cdot v_{\max}(\ell_{\max} + d_{\max})$$

Clearly, if all of the random-restarting mechanisms $\mathsf{ALG}_1, \ldots, \mathsf{ALG}_n$ are robust-to-welfare-loss under stochastic job model $\mathcal{D}$, then $\overline{\mathsf{OPT}}(\mathcal{J})$ will also be robust-to-welfare-loss under $\mathcal{D}$.

4.2 Truthful switching in the non-clairvoyant setting

We now show how to switch between truthful non-clairvoyant mechanisms. We reiterate a subtle aspect of truthfulness in the non-clairvoyant setting: a job that tries to influence the mechanism by switching its position in the arrival order can be treated the same way as a job reporting a later arrival time: it cannot be beneficial to do this given that the mechanism is truthful. Posted-pricing-FIFO is an example of a mechanism that is both truthful and order respecting: all jobs whose values are less than a threshold price are rejected, and the rest of the jobs are scheduled in arrival order.

We claim that the random restart algorithm of Definition 4.2 preserves the truthfulness of the underlying scheduling mechanism. The following lemma is proved in the full version of the paper.

Lemma 4.5. *If A is an order respecting truthful mechanism, then A with (arbitrary) restarts is also order respecting and truthful.*

Combining ideas from the truthful switching algorithm in the clairvoyant setting and the truthful random restart algorithm, we develop a truthful switching algorithm for non-clairvoyant settings that switches from a mechanism A to a mechanism B at time 0.

Definition 4.6. The mechanism C is as follows.

(1) For jobs that arrive by time 0, mimic mechanism A and return the same allocation, schedule and prices as A. All these jobs are completed by time $d_{\max} + \ell_{\max}$.
(2) For all remaining jobs, i.e., jobs j with $a_j \geq 1$ run mechanism B on these with the following modifications.
    (a) If the arrival time of a job is $< d_{\max} + \ell_{\max}$, set its arrival time to $d_{\max} + \ell_{\max} + 1$.

(b) Adjust the deadline of the job so that it reflects the time lost during the interval $[1, d_{\max} + \ell_{\max}]$. This might mean some jobs are past their deadline. These jobs are rejected.
(c) Preserve the arrival order. Use the tie breaking rule to make sure the arrival order of jobs whose starting time was set to $d_{\max} + \ell_{\max}$ is the same as in the original instance.

Lemma 4.7. *The state of the algorithm C at time $d_{max} + \ell_{max}$ is the same as the state of the algorithm B at time $d_{max} + \ell_{max}$, given that B is restarted during the interval $[1, d_{max} + \ell_{max}]$.*

Proof. This follows by observing that Step (2) of mechanism C is identical to the modifications made during a restart. Any job that arrives by time 0 does not influence the state of mechanism B at time $d_{\max} + \ell_{\max}$ in either case. □

We obtain the following theorem (see the full version for a proof).

Theorem 4.8. *Given order respecting truthful mechanisms A and B in the non-clairvoyant setting, switching mechanism C in Definition 4.6 is order respecting, truthful, and obtains welfare at least*

$$\textstyle\sum_{t \leq d_{max}+\ell_{max}} W_t(A) + \sum_{t \geq 1+d_{max}+\ell_{max}} W_t(B),$$

given that A and B are restarted at time 1.

4.3 Reduction to multi-armed bandits

In this section, we show how to design a truthful online learning algorithm that minimizes the regret relative to the random-restarting benchmark, i.e. best-in-hindsight of random-restarting truthful mechanisms $\overline{\mathsf{ALG}}_1, \ldots, \overline{\mathsf{ALG}}_n$. Similar to Section 3.2, we consider a relevant adversarial Multi-Armed Bandits problem or MAB, where we have an arm for each of the n online scheduling mechanisms and we have bandit feedback, meaning that any algorithm only observes the reward of the arm it plays and not the other arms.

In such a setting, we assume having query access to a MAB algorithm `Bandit-ALG` that admits the optimal regret bound $O(R\sqrt{Tn\log n})$ in Theorem 2.2, where n is the number of arms, T is the time horizon and R is an upper-bound on the reward of an arm. Moreover, for the sake of simplicity, we assume `Bandit-ALG` does not need to know the time horizon T or rewards range R in advance, and it only needs to know these quantities are bounded. This assumption can be removed by using a *doubling trick*: given black-box access to a bandit algorithm $\mathsf{Bandit\text{-}ALG}_1(R, T)$ that requires knowing R and T, one can come up with another black-box algorithm $\mathsf{Bandit\text{-}ALG}_2$ with the same asymptotic regret bound that does not need this information. This reduction is explained in the full version of the paper.

Our proposed algorithm, which we call *Follow-The-Bandit-Switcher* or *FTBS*, uses `Bandit-ALG` in a black-box fashion when looped in with the right rewards. It then follows `Bandit-ALG`'s advice by truthful switching between arms, as suggested by Theorem 4.8. This helps the FTBS to aggregate truth and welfare guarantees of mechanisms $\overline{\mathsf{ALG}}_1, \ldots, \overline{\mathsf{ALG}}_n$ even in the non-clairvoyant setting. We formally define the FTBS as following.

Definition 4.9. Given the n online scheduling mechanisms, $\mathsf{ALG}_1, \ldots, \mathsf{ALG}_n$, query access to online bandit algorithm `Bandit-ALG`, and parameter $\gamma \in [0, 1]$, the Follow-The-Bandit-Switcher mechanism proceeds as follows.

Initialize $\hat{t} = 1$. `(This index is counter for number of Heads)`
Query `Bandit-ALG` for the initial arm i_1, and run algorithm ALG_{i_1}.
At each time $t \in [T]$:

(1) Flip an independent coin $\kappa(t)$ with $\Pr(\kappa(t) = \mathsf{Heads}) = \gamma$.

(2) If coin $\kappa(t)$ shows a Heads,
   (a) Let $t' = \max\{t'' < t : \kappa(t'') = \text{Heads}\}$. If no such an integer exists, let $t' = 1$.
   (b) Update the sequence of bandit rewards between two consecutive Heads:

$$r_x^{(i_{\hat{t}})} = \begin{cases} 0, & \text{if } x \in [t', \min(t' + \ell_{\max} + d_{\max}, t-1)] \\ W_x(\mathsf{FTBS}), & \text{if } x \in [\min(t' + \ell_{\max} + d_{\max}, t-1) + 1, t-1] \end{cases}$$

   (c) Set $R_{\hat{t}}^{(i_{t'})} \leftarrow \sum_{x \in [t', t-1]} r_x^{(i_{t'})}$ and send this bandit feedback to Bandit-ALG.
   (d) Set $\hat{t} \leftarrow \hat{t} + 1$.
   (e) Let the new arm chosen by Bandit-ALG be $i_{\hat{t}} \in [n]$.
   (f) If $i_{\hat{t}} \neq i_{\hat{t}-1}$, switch from $\mathsf{ALG}_{i_{\hat{t}-1}}$ to $\mathsf{ALG}_{i_{\hat{t}}}$ using the mechanism in Section 4.2.
   (g) Otherwise, restart ALG_{i_t} at time t.

(3) If coin $\kappa(t)$ shows a Tails, continue running $\mathsf{ALG}_{i_{\hat{t}}}$.

We now state and prove a tight regret bound (up to logarithmic factor) for FTBS.

Theorem 4.10. *The Follow-The-Bandit-Switcher (FTBS) scheduling mechanism, described in Definition 4.9, admits the following regret-bound if $\gamma = (\ell_{max} + d_{max})^{-2/3} T^{-1/3} (n \log(n))^{1/3}$:*

$$\textsc{Reg}(\mathsf{FTBS}) \leq O(m \cdot v_{max} (\ell_{max} + d_{max})^{1/3} (n \log(n))^{1/3} T^{2/3} \log T) = \tilde{O}(T^{2/3})$$

where $\textsc{Reg}(\mathsf{FTBS})$ is the regret relative to $\overline{\mathsf{OPT}}$, i.e. the random-restarting benchmark as in Definition 4.3.

We finally consider stochastic jobs, and we focus on benchmarks that are robust-to-welfare-loss in expectation under this stochastic model, as described in Definition 4.4. The following corollary is immediate.

Corollary 4.11. *Given a distribution $\mathcal{D}$ over jobs and a robust-to-welfare-loss benchmark $\mathsf{OPT}(\mathcal{J})$ as in Definition 4.4, there exists a scheduling mechanism whose expected regret relative to $\mathbf{E}_{\mathcal{J} \sim \mathcal{D}}[\mathsf{OPT}(\mathcal{J})]$ is bounded by $\tilde{O}(T^{2/3})$.*

Proof of Theorem 4.10. Let $C_1 \triangleq v_{\max}(\ell_{\max} + d_{\max})m$ and $C_2 \triangleq v_{\max} m$ be constants. Fix a sequence of coins $\mathbf{K}[T] \triangleq [\kappa(1), \ldots, \kappa(T)]$ and let $t_1, t_2, \ldots, t_{\hat{T}}$ be the times $t \in [T]$ that coin $\kappa(t)$ shows a Heads. As a convention, let $t_0 \triangleq 1$ and $t_{\hat{T}+1} \triangleq \tilde{T} \geq T$ be the next time that coin $\kappa(t)$ flips a Heads if we continue flipping after T. By abuse of notation, we will use $\overline{\mathsf{ALG}_i}$ to denote mechanism ALG_i restarted at exactly these times. For each $i \in [n]$ and $x \in [1, \hat{T}]$, let $R_x^{(i)}$ be:

$$R_x^{(i)} \triangleq \sum_{t=\min(t_{x-1}+\ell_{\max}+d_{\max}, t_x-1)+1}^{t_x-1} W_t(\overline{\mathsf{ALG}_i}) \geq \sum_{t=t_{x-1}}^{t_x-1} W_t(\overline{\mathsf{ALG}_i}) - C_1$$

Also, for the last interval $[t_{\hat{T}}, T]$ and for each $i \in [n]$, let $R_{\hat{T}+1}^{(i)}$ be

$$R_{\hat{T}+1}^{(i)} \triangleq \sum_{t=\min(t_{\hat{T}}+\ell_{\max}+d_{\max}, t_x-1)+1}^{T} W_t(\overline{\mathsf{ALG}_i}) \geq \sum_{t=t_{\hat{T}}}^{T} W_t(\overline{\mathsf{ALG}_i}) - C_1$$

Therefore, by summing over all intervals $\{[t_{x-1}, t_x]\}_{x \in [\hat{T}]} \cup [t_{\hat{T}}, T]$, we have:

$$\forall i \in [n] : \sum_{x \in [\hat{T}+1]} R_x^{(i)} \geq W(\overline{\mathsf{ALG}_i}) - C_1(\hat{T} + 1) \tag{1}$$

Note that after the coin shows a Heads at time t_x, our mechanism either stays with the same algorithm and does a restart or the truthful switching from $\mathsf{ALG}_{i_{x-1}}$ to ALG_{i_x} as in Section 4.2. Also, Theorem 4.8 and the definition of truthful restart in Definition 4.2 guarantee that our scheduling mechanism will be synced with the restarting algorithms $\overline{\text{ALG}_{i_x}}$ after $\ell_{\max} + d_{\max}$ units of time, and therefore the mechanism generates a welfare that is at least the welfare generated by the new arm in the interval $[\min(t_{x-1} + \ell_{\max} + d_{\max}, t_x - 1) + 1, t_x - 1]$. Formally speaking,

$$\forall x \in [\hat{T}] : \sum_{t=t_{x-1}}^{t_x} W_t(\text{FTBS}) \geq R_x^{(i_x)}, \qquad \sum_{t=t_{\hat{T}}}^{T} W_t(\text{FTBS}) \geq R_{\hat{T}}^{(i_{\hat{T}})}$$

and therefore, by summing over all intervals $\{[t_{x-1}, t_x]\}_{x\in[\hat{T}]} \cup [t_{\hat{T}}, T]$, we have:

$$W(\text{FTBS}) \geq \sum_{x\in[\hat{T}+1]} R_x^{(i_x)} \tag{2}$$

Conditioned on the sequence of coin flips $\mathbf{K}[T]$ (and therefore times $t_1, t_2, \ldots, t_{\hat{T}}$), the rewards $\{R_x^{(i)}\}_{x\in[\hat{T}+1], i\in[n]}$ define an (oblivious) adversarial instance of a MAB problem. For this adversarial instance, time horizon is indeed the random variable $(\hat{T} + 1)$, i.e. number of Heads in the sequence $\mathbf{K}[T]$ plus one. Moreover, if we let $\hat{U} = \max_{j\in[\hat{T}+1]} U_j$ where

$$j \in [1, \hat{T} + 1] : U_j \triangleq t_j - t_{j-1}$$

then the rewards of this instance would also be upper-bounded by the random variable $C_2\hat{U}$. Then, due to the optimal regret bound of Bandit-ALG (Theorem 2.2), we have:

$$\forall i \in [n] : \mathbf{E}\left[\sum_{x\in[\hat{T}+1]} R_x^{(i)} | \, \mathbf{K}[T]\right] - \mathbf{E}\left[\sum_{x\in[\hat{T}+1]} R_x^{(i_x)} | \, \mathbf{K}[T]\right] \leq O(\hat{U}\hat{T}^{1/2} C_2 (n \log n)^{1/2}) \tag{3}$$

Combining Inequalities (1), (2) and (3) and taking expectations:

$$\textsc{Reg}(\text{FTBS}) \leq O(\mathbf{E}\left[\hat{U}\hat{T}^{1/2} C_2 (n \log n)^{1/2}\right]) + \mathbf{E}\left[C_1(\hat{T} + 1)\right] \tag{4}$$

Now, $\mathbf{E}\left[C_1(\hat{T} + 1)\right] = O(\gamma \cdot C_1 T)$. To bound the other term, we use the following fact, proved in [Eisenberg, 2008], about independent and identically distributed geometric random variables.

Lemma 4.12 ([Eisenberg, 2008]). *If $g_1, \ldots, g_k$ are i.i.d. and $g_i \sim$ Geometric(γ), then*

$$\mathbf{E}\left[\max_{j\in[k]} g_j\right] \leq H_k \cdot \gamma^{-1} = O(\gamma^{-1} \log k)$$

.

Note that conditioned on $\hat{T}$, random variables $\{U_j\}_{j\in\hat{T}+1}$ are $(\hat{T} + 1)$ i.i.d. Geometric(γ) random variables. Using Lemma 4.12 we have:

$$\mathbf{E}\left[\hat{U}\hat{T}^{1/2} | \hat{T}\right] = \hat{T}^{1/2}\mathbf{E}\left[\max_{j\in[\hat{T}]} U_j | \hat{T}\right] \leq \hat{T}^{1/2} \cdot H_{\hat{T}} \cdot \gamma^{-1} = \gamma^{-1} \cdot O(\hat{T}^{1/2} \log(\hat{T}))$$

Now, function $f(x) = x^{1/2} \log(x)$ is concave. By taking expectation and using Jensen's inequality, we further upper-bound this term. Hence:

$$\mathbf{E}\left[\hat{U}\hat{T}^{1/2}\right] \leq \gamma^{-1}.O(f(\mathbf{E}\left[\hat{T}\right])) = \gamma^{-1/2} \cdot T^{1/2} \log(\gamma T)$$

So, we can upper-bound the RHS of (4) by

$$O(\gamma^{-1/2} T^{1/2} \log(\gamma T) C_2 (n \log n)^{1/2}) + O(\gamma.C_1 T)$$

By setting $\gamma = (\frac{C_2}{C_1})^{2/3} T^{-1/3} (n \log n)^{1/3}$, we get the desired regret bound. □

5 LOWER BOUNDS

We first state a lower bound of $\Omega(\sqrt{T})$ on the regret for the clairvoyant scheduling problem. The proof of this theorem can be found in the full version of the paper. We note that this lower bound can be extended to $\Omega(m\sqrt{T})$ when there are m machines by simply having m copies of the same set of jobs every time. Similarly the lower bound can be made to scale linearly with $v_{\max}$ and $\sqrt{d_{\max}}$, matching the upper bound we give in Theorem 3.9.

Theorem 5.1. *There exists an instance of the clairvoyant scheduling problem where the regret of any online algorithm relative to the hindsight optimal posted-pricing-FIFO algorithm is $\Omega(\sqrt{T})$.*

Next we show a lower bound of $\tilde{\Omega}(T^{2/3})$ on the regret for the non-clairvoyant setting that matches our upper bound within polylogarithmic factors. Our lower bound follows by a reduction from the lower bound given in [Dekel et al., 2014] for the multi-armed bandit problem with switching costs.

For the bandit problem with switching costs with n actions, [Dekel et al., 2014] show that there exists a sequence of loss functions $\ell_1, \ell_2, \dots \ell_T$, where $\ell_i : [n] \to [0,1]$, such that any online algorithm incurs a regret of at least $\tilde{\Omega}(n^{1/3}T^{2/3})$. We use this loss sequence to define an instance of the non-clairvoyant scheduling problem as follows. First we give a reduction to regret against the welfare benchmark without random restarts. Later we show how to extend the lower bound to apply against the random restart benchmark. In our lower bound instance, we fix $n = 2$, and

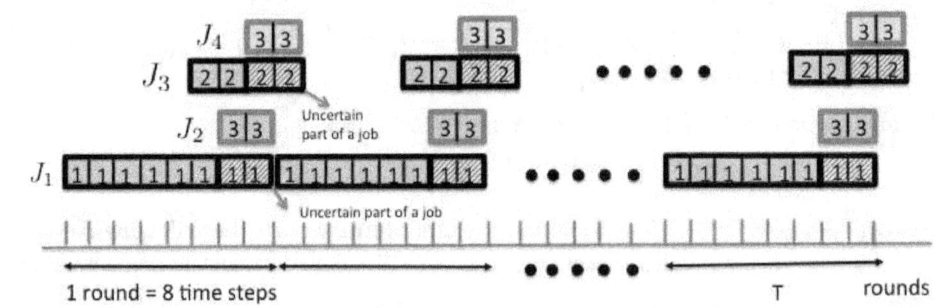

let $\ell_i(1)$ and $\ell_i(2)$ denote the losses of actions 1 and 2 in round i as defined in [Dekel et al., 2014]. We map each round of the game to 8 time steps; that is, round i corresponds to the time interval $[8i, 8(i+1)-1]$. Our instance has 4 sets of jobs J_1, J_2, J_3, and J_4, as shown in the above figure. In each round, one job from each set arrives. Jobs in the set J_1 arrive at the beginning of each round; that is, at time steps $8i$ for $i = 0, 1, 2, \dots .. T$. The processing length of a job $j \in J_1$ that arrives in the round i is 6 with probability $p_i(1)$ and 8 with probability $(1 - p_t(1))$, where $p_i(1) = 1/2 + \ell_i(1)/2$. Observe that processing lengths of the jobs in J_1 depend on losses defined by [Dekel et al., 2014]. Further, the jobs in J_1 have a value of 1 per unit length. In round i, a job from J_2 arrives at time $8(i+1) - 2$ for $i = 0, 1, 2, 3, \dots .. T$, and has a processing length of 2. The value per unit length of jobs in J_2 is 3.

The set J_3 consists of jobs that arrive at time instants $8i - 3$ for $i = 1, 2, \dots T$, and have value per unit length of 2. The processing length of job $j \in J_3$ released in the round i is 4 with probability $p_i(2)$ and 2 with probability $1 - p_i(2)$, where $p_i(2) = \ell_i(2)$. Similar to the jobs in J_1, the processing lengths of jobs in J_3 depend on the losses defined by the result of [Dekel et al., 2014]. Finally, the jobs in set J_4 are released at time steps $8i - 1$ for $i = 1, 2, \dots T$, and have a processing length of 2 and value per unit length of 3.

The deadlines of all jobs are equal to their arrival times. (This condition is not necessary but simplifies the construction.) Hence, if a job is not scheduled upon its arrival, the algorithm loses the job.

Let ALG_1 and ALG_2 denote the two posted price scheduling mechanisms with prices 1 and 2 and FIFO scheduling policy. (Note that other posted price mechanisms, for example one that posts a price of 3, lose a constant factor in each round, hence we do not consider them.) The algorithms ALG_1 and ALG_2 correspond to the action set in the bandit problem with switching costs. The following two lemmas follow from the construction of lower bound instance. See the full version of the paper for a proof.

Lemma 5.2. *For all rounds $i = 0, 1, \dots T$, the expected value of ALG_1 in round i is $10 - 2\ell_i(1)$ and expected value of ALG_2 in round i is $10 - 2\ell_i(2)$.*

Lemma 5.3. *If an online algorithm switches from ALG_2 to ALG_1 in any round i, it incurs a loss of at least 6.*

From Lemmas 5.2 and 5.3, we get the following theorem.

Theorem 5.4. *Minimax regret of non-clairvoyant scheduling problem is at least $\tilde{\Omega}(T^{2/3})$.*

Proof. Consider an online scheduling algorithm for the non-clairvoyant scheduling problem. At the beginning of each round i, it can either follow ALG_1 and obtain a value of $10 - 2\ell_i(1)$ or follow ALG_2 and get a value $10 - 2\ell_i(2)$. Furthermore, since we are in the non-clairvoyant setting, the online algorithm won't know the value it can obtain from the algorithm it is not following. Since, the value obtained by ALG_1 and ALG_2 are exactly the same in each round except for the terms $-\ell_i(1)$ and $-\ell_i(2)$, the regret of the non-clairvoyant scheduling algorithm is equal to the regret it suffers on the losses at each round i. Moreover, switching from ALG_2 to ALG_1 in any round incurs a cost of 6. Hence, our scheduling instance corresponds to bandit with switching cost problem, where switching from action 2 to action 1 incurs a cost. The result of [Dekel et al., 2014] shows that the problem has a minimax regret of least $\tilde{\Omega}(T^{2/3})$, when there is a switching cost between any pair of actions. However, it is easy to modify the proof in [Dekel et al., 2014], where there is a switching cost only between action 2 to action 1, losing a factor of 2 in the regret bound [Dekel et al., 2014]. This completes our reduction. □

Now we argue that Theorem (5.4) can be extended to random restarting benchmarks. Before that we make the following simple observation regarding the lower bound instance in Theorem (5.4). Consider the posted price mechanisms ALG_1 and ALG_2 as defined in the proof of Theorem (5.4). $\overline{\mathsf{ALG}_1}(\gamma), \overline{\mathsf{ALG}_2}(\gamma)$ denote the random restarting versions of them with restart parameter γ.

Lemma 5.5. *For some constant $c \geq 11$, we have:*

$$j \in \{1,2\} : \mathbf{E}[W(\overline{\mathsf{ALG}_j}(\gamma), J)] \geq W(\mathsf{ALG}_j, J) - c \cdot \gamma \cdot T$$

Proof. Proof of the lemma follows immediately from the observation that if ALG_j for $j = 1, 2$ restarts at time t, and t is in round i, then it loses values of jobs in that round. The expected number of restarts by the algorithms is at most $\gamma \cdot T$. As the total value of jobs in each round is at most 11, the statement of the lemma holds for $c \geq 11$. □

To extend the lower bound to random restarting benchmarks, we need the following theorem from [Dekel et al., 2014] for the bandit with switching costs problem.

Theorem 5.6 ([Dekel et al., 2014]). *Let $\mathcal{A}$ be a multi-armed bandit algorithm that guarantees an expected regret (without switching costs) of $O(T^{\alpha})$ then there exists a sequence of loss functions that forces $\mathcal{A}$ to make $\tilde{\Omega}(T^{2(1-\alpha)})$ switches.*

Combining Lemma 5.5 and above theorem, we prove the following theorem.

Theorem 5.7. *No online algorithm can achieve a regret $O(T^{2/3-\epsilon})$ for any $\epsilon > 0$ against a random restarting benchmark with restart parameter $\gamma \in (T^{-1}, T^{-1/3}]$.*

Proof. Proof is by contradiction. Suppose there is an online non-clairvoyant algorithm $\mathcal{A}$ that achieves a regret of $O(T^{2/3-\epsilon})$ for some $\epsilon > 0$. From Lemma 5.5, this implies that it achieves a regret of at most $O(T^{2/3-\epsilon})$ against the non-restarting benchmark of Theorem 5.4. Our proof of Theorem 5.4 gives a reduction from the bandit with switching cost problem to the non-clairvoyant scheduling problem. Therefore, we can invoke Theorem 5.6, which implies that $\mathcal{A}$ does at least $\tilde{\Omega}(T^{2(1-(2/3-\epsilon))})$ switches. Since there are only two actions in our lower bound instance, $\mathcal{A}$ still pays a switching cost of at least $\tilde{\Omega}(T^{2(1-(2/3-\epsilon))}) = \tilde{\Omega}(T^{2/3+2\epsilon})$ in switching from ALG_2 to ALG_1. This is gives a contradiction to the regret of $\mathcal{A}$ being $O(T^{2/3-\epsilon})$ against the non-restarting benchmark, and completes the proof. □

REFERENCES

Peter Auer, Nicolo Cesa-Bianchi, Yoav Freund, and Robert E Schapire. 1995. Gambling in a rigged casino: The adversarial multi-armed bandit problem. In *Foundations of Computer Science, 1995. Proceedings., 36th Annual Symposium on*. IEEE, 322–331.

Yossi Azar, Inna Kalp-Shaltiel, Brendan Lucier, Ishai Menache, Joseph Seffi Naor, and Jonathan Yaniv. 2015. Truthful Online Scheduling with Commitments. In *Proceedings of the Sixteenth ACM Conference on Economics and Computation*. ACM, 715–732.

Yossi Azar and Ety Khaitsin. 2011. Prompt mechanism for ad placement over time. In *International Symposium on Algorithmic Game Theory*. Springer, 19–30.

Moshe Babaioff, Yishay Mansour, Noam Nisan, Gali Noti, Carlo Curino, Nar Ganapathy, Ishai Menache, Omer Reingold, Moshe Tennenholtz, and Erez Timnat. 2017. ERA: A Framework for Economic Resource Allocation for the Cloud. In *Proceedings of the 26th International Conference on World Wide Web Companion*. 635–642.

Avrim Blum and Carl Burch. 2000. On-line Learning and the Metrical Task System Problem. *Machine Learning* 39, 1 (2000), 35–58. DOI: http://dx.doi.org/10.1023/A:1007621832648

Avrim Blum, Shuchi Chawla, and Adam Kalai. 2002. Static Optimality and Dynamic Search-optimality in Lists and Trees. In *Proceedings of the Thirteenth Annual ACM-SIAM Symposium on Discrete Algorithms (SODA '02)*. Society for Industrial and Applied Mathematics, Philadelphia, PA, USA, 1–8. http://dl.acm.org/citation.cfm?id=545381.545382

Ran Canetti and Sandy Irani. 1998. Bounding the power of preemption in randomized scheduling. *SIAM J. Comput.* 27, 4 (1998), 993–1015.

Nicolo Cesa-Bianchi and Gábor Lugosi. 2006. *Prediction, learning, and games*. Cambridge university press.

Shuchi Chawla, Nikhil Devanur, Alexander Holroyd, Anna Karlin, James Martin, and Balasubramanian Sivan. 2017. Stability of service under time-of-use pricing. In *STOC*. To appear.

Richard Cole, Shahar Dobzinski, and Lisa Fleischer. 2008. Prompt mechanisms for online auctions. In *International Symposium on Algorithmic Game Theory*. Springer, 170–181.

Ofer Dekel, Jian Ding, Tomer Koren, and Yuval Peres. 2014. Bandits with Switching Costs: T2/3 Regret. In *Proceedings of the Forty-sixth Annual ACM Symposium on Theory of Computing (STOC '14)*. ACM, New York, NY, USA, 459–467. DOI: http://dx.doi.org/10.1145/2591796.2591868

Bennett Eisenberg. 2008. On the expectation of the maximum of IID geometric random variables. *Statistics & Probability Letters* 78, 2 (2008), 135–143.

Yoav Freund and Robert E Schapire. 1995. A desicion-theoretic generalization of on-line learning and an application to boosting. In *European conference on computational learning theory*. Springer, 23–37.

Mohammad T. Hajiaghayi, Robert D. Kleinberg, Mohammad Mahdian, and David C. Parkes. 2005. Online auctions with re-usable goods. In *Proceedings of the 6th ACM conference on Electronic commerce*. ACM, 165–174.

J. Hartline and T. Roughgarden. 2008. Optimal Mechanism Design and Money Burning. In *Proc. 39th ACM Symp. on Theory of Computing*.

Frank Hutter, Holger H Hoos, Kevin Leyton-Brown, and Thomas Stützle. 2009. ParamILS: an automatic algorithm configuration framework. *Journal of Artificial Intelligence Research* 36, 1 (2009), 267–306.

Adam Kalai and Santosh Vempala. 2005. Efficient algorithms for online decision problems. *J. Comput. System Sci.* 71, 3 (2005), 291–307.

Ron Lavi and Noam Nisan. 2015. Online ascending auctions for gradually expiring items. *Journal of Economic Theory* 156 (2015), 45–76.

Lin Xu, Frank Hutter, Holger H Hoos, and Kevin Leyton-Brown. 2008. SATzilla: portfolio-based algorithm selection for SAT. *Journal of artificial intelligence research* 32 (2008), 565–606.

Cost-Sharing Methods for Scheduling Games under Uncertainty

GIORGOS CHRISTODOULOU, University of Liverpool
VASILIS GKATZELIS, Drexel University
ALKMINI SGOURITSA, University of Liverpool

We study the performance of cost-sharing protocols in a selfish scheduling setting with load-dependent cost functions. Previous work on selfish scheduling protocols has focused on two extreme models: omnipotent protocols that are aware of every machine and every job that is active at any given time, and oblivious protocols that are aware of nothing beyond the machine they control. The main focus of this paper is on a well-motivated middle-ground model of *resource-aware* protocols, which are aware of the set of machines that the system comprises, but unaware of what jobs are active at any given time. Apart from considering budget-balanced protocols, to which previous work was restricted, we augment the design space by also studying the extent to which *overcharging* can lead to improved performance.

We first show that, in the omnipotent model, overcharging enables us to enforce the optimal outcome as the unique equilibrium, which largely improves over the $\Theta(\log n)$-approximation of social welfare that can be obtained by budget-balanced protocols, even in their best equilibrium [32]. We then transition to the resource-aware model and provide price of anarchy (PoA) upper and lower bounds for different classes of cost functions. For concave cost functions, we provide a protocol with PoA of $1 + \epsilon$ for arbitrarily small $\epsilon > 0$. When the cost functions can be both convex and concave we construct an overcharging protocol that yields PoA≤ 2; a spectacular improvement over the bounds obtained for budget-balanced protocols, even in the omnipotent model. We complement our positive results with impossibility results for general increasing cost functions. We show that any resource-aware budget-balanced cost-sharing protocol has PoA of $\Theta(n)$ in this setting and, even if we use overcharging, no resource-aware protocol can achieve a PoA of $o(\sqrt{n})$.

CCS Concepts: • **Theory of computation → Quality of equilibria**;

Additional Key Words and Phrases: cost-sharing; price of anarchy; resource-aware protocols

1 INTRODUCTION

We consider a very basic resource allocation setting from a game theoretic point of view. There is a collection of m available machines and a set of n users, each of which needs access to one of the machines in order to process some task. For each user i there is a weight w_i associated with his task, that may represent its duration or its complexity; the higher the weight of a task, the higher the cost incurred by the machine that processes it. More precisely, each machine j is described by a cost function c_j that is weakly increasing in the total weight of the jobs assigned to it, and each machine's users need to cover the processing costs of their jobs.

The first author was supported by EPSRC EP/M008118/1 and Royal Society LT140046. The second author was supported by the National Science Foundation, under grants CCF-1216073, CCF-1161813, CCF-1408635. Part of this work took place while the authors were visiting the Simons Institute for the Theory of Computing.

EC'17, June 26–30, 2017, Cambridge, Massachusetts, USA. © 2017 ACM ISBN 978-1-4503-4527-9/17/06...$15.00.
DOI: http://dx.doi.org/10.1145/3033274.3085151

From the perspective of a user in this setting, the goal is to minimize the cost that he needs to cover (be it monetary payment, delay, or some other type of inconvenience) for processing his job. Therefore, the decision of each user regarding which machine to utilize depends directly on how the induced cost of each machine is shared among its users, and different approaches regarding how the cost is to be shared may lead to vastly different outcomes. A *cost-sharing protocol* in this setting provides the rules regarding how the cost of each machine is to be shared among its users. Given such a protocol, the users strategically select which machine to use, taking both the protocol and the anticipated congestion into consideration. This forms a non-cooperative game whose equilibria can be quite inefficient, even for very natural cost-sharing protocols and extremely simple instances [2]. The focus of this paper is on the design of cost-sharing methods aiming to maximize the efficiency of the equilibria.

Motivated by the observation that such protocols can have a significant impact on the quality of the outcome, Chen et al. [8] were the first to address cost-sharing design questions. They focused on network cost-sharing, i.e., the case when the players can choose multiple machines but the cost functions are all constant. They gave a characterization of protocols that satisfy some natural axioms and they thoroughly studied their worst-case performance. Building on top of this work, von Falkenhausen and Harks [32] focused on the case where each player needs to choose a single machine or a matroid of machines, but allowed general cost functions as we also do in this work.

One essential way in which our work deviates from this previous work has to do with the informational constraints applied to the cost-sharing protocol. The information that the protocol is assumed to have access to plays a very important role in the extent to which efficient outcomes can be achieved. For instance, can the decisions of the protocol regarding how to distribute the cost of a machine depend on which other machines exist in the system? Can it depend on the set of users that are populating the system at each time? The more information the protocol possesses, the higher its power to reach high quality outcomes. Previous work focused on the following two informational assumptions.

- **Omnipotent protocols**[1]. The protocol of each machine has *full knowledge* of the instance. The cost-sharing decisions on that machine can depend arbitrarily on the state of the system: on the set of available machines and their cost functions, as well as on the set of active users and their weights.
- **Oblivious protocols**[2]. The protocol of each machine has *no knowledge* of the instance, except the set of users who chose to utilize that particular machine.

These assumptions lie at two extremes of the information spectrum. The former applies to a very static, or centralized, system where each machine always has access to up-to-date information regarding the users and the machines. The latter, on the other hand, is very pessimistic, assuming that the cost-sharing decisions of each machine need to be oblivious to the state of the system. Aiming for a middle-ground, we study a compromise between these extremes which is much more reasonable for many settings. Following the "adversarial" model of [12], we maintain the assumption that the cost-sharing protocol of a machine is aware of the other machines that are available in the system, but we restrict it to depend only on the particular machine's users.

- **Resource-aware protocols**. The protocol of each machine knows the set of available machines and their cost functions, but is aware only of the set of users who chose to utilize that particular machine.

[1]Previous work has also referred to these protocols as "non-uniform" protocols.

[2]Previous work has also referred to these protocols as "uniform" protocols.

This model is more realistic than the oblivious one when the machines of the system do not change often, which is the case in many scenarios. In that case, this information can be taken into consideration when designing or updating the cost-sharing protocol. For instance, if the machines correspond to computers in a static network, the designer could take the structure of the network into consideration when selecting which protocol to use. On the other hand, the set of active users in a system may change more often, as users arrive and depart. In fact, even if the machines had access to up-to-date information on the whole set of active users, protocols that depend on such dynamic information would complicate the user's decision, and could thus be less stable.

Hence, knowing the set of machines and their cost functions, the designer wishes to design a protocol that defines how the cost of each machine is to be shared among the users that utilize it, depending only on this particular set of users. In designing such protocols, the goal is to ensure that the worst-case equilibria of the induced game approximate the optimal social welfare within some small factor. We measure the performance of these protocols using the worst-case price of anarchy (PoA) measure, i.e., the ratio of the social welfare in the worst equilibrium over that in the optimal solution. Essentially, once the designer selects the protocol on each machine, then an adversary chooses the requested subset of players so that the PoA of the induced game is maximized.

Overcharging. A second important way in which our work deviates from previous work is the fact that we do consider protocols that use overcharging. Specifically, Chen et al. [8] and von Falkenhausen and Harks [32] restricted themselves to *budget-balanced* protocols, i.e., protocols such that the costs of the users using some machine add up to *exactly* the cost of the machine. Similarly to the framework of "coordination mechanisms" [9], we relax this assumption and seek to optimize the welfare via overcharging: although we maintain the restriction that the users need to pay at least as much as the cost that they create, in total, our protocols can also choose to charge the users additional costs in order to better align their incentives. It is important to note that, once we introduce increased costs in our protocols, we compare the performance of the equilibria in the induced game with the *increased* costs to the original optimal solution with the *initial* cost functions. Therefore, using this technique requires a careful trade-off between the benefit of improved incentives and the drawback of penalties suffered.

1.1 Our Results

We begin with a simple observation that demonstrates the power of overcharging for omnipotent protocols (Sec. 3). We show that, using overcharging, the designer can achieve the optimal outcome. In fact, no user actually suffers these extra charges in equilibrium, so this approach yields a PoA of 1 for arbitrary cost functions. This is in contrast to the $\Omega(\log n)$ bound obtained by budget-balanced omnipotent protocols, even for the best possible equilibria (price of stability) in [32].

We then move on to study resource-aware protocols, where our main results are the following.

- (Sec. 4) We provide a budget-balanced resource-aware cost-sharing protocol that achieves the optimal outcome, i.e., a PoA of 1, for functions with decreasing marginals (strictly concave functions). In contrast, we show that the PoA for oblivious protocols is lower bounded by $\Omega(n)$ for the same class of functions.
- (Sec. 5) We construct an overcharging resource-aware protocol that yields a PoA of at most 2 for the much more challenging case when both convex and concave cost functions appear in the system. This result holds only for unweighted players. For this class of functions, budget-balanced protocols, even omnipotent ones, are known to yield an $\Omega(\log n)$ approximation in their best equilibrium.
- (Sec. 6) We complement our positive results by proving lower bounds for resource-aware protocols. We show that, no policy can achieve a $o(\sqrt{n})$ PoA, even by the use of overcharging.

In the case of budget-balanced protocols we show that the respective bound is $\Theta(n)$. We stress that showing lower bounds for resource-aware mechanisms that allow overcharging is much more involved than the corresponding proofs for budget-balanced mechanisms, since the design space is considerably larger.

All our lower bounds hold for the unweighted case, so they immediately carry over to the weighted case. We should also point out that the lower bounds for resource-aware protocols hold also for oblivious protocols (but not vice versa). Finally, in Sec. 7 we provide results for the special case of two machines with general cost functions and unweighted players. We propose a protocol which does not fall into the class of the generalized weighted Shapley mechanisms [17], but still always possesses pure Nash equilibria. This protocol achieves a PoA of 2. We also show a PoA lower bound of 1.36 for all resource-aware protocols (with overcharging). Note that this lower bound applies also to the case of both convex and concave functions of Sec. 5, for which we achieved a PoA of 2.

1.2 Related Work

Cost-sharing protocols for resource selection games have been the focus of a lot of recent work [16, 17, 20, 24]. Harks and Miller [20] study the performance of several cost-sharing methods in a slightly modified setting, where each player declares a different demand for each resource. Marden and Wierman [24] studied various cost-sharing methods in a utility maximization model for the players, while Gopalakrishnan et al. [17] characterized the space of admissible cost-sharing methods as the set of generalized weighted Shapley values. Gkatzelis et al. [16] explored the space of cost-sharing methods and identified the Shapley value as the optimal one with respect to the price of anarchy for a class of general resource selection games.

Christodoulou et al. [10] studied network design games with constant cost functions under the Bayesian setting, where the position of the players' sources on the graph is drawn from a distribution over all vertices. They considered overcharging, where they could use any non-budget-balanced policy under the restriction of preserving budget-balance in all equilibria. In contrast to the scheduling games we study here, where the costs are functions of the machines' loads, in [10] the costs are functions of the set of players using a resource. Therefore, it turns out that their overcharging scheme is equivalent to the one that defines new cost (set) functions and then uses a budget-balanced protocol, similarly to our scheme.

An interesting family of resource selection games is the class of weighted congestion games. There has been a long line of work on these games focusing on the proportional sharing method, according to which the players share their joint cost in proportion to the size of their demands, [3, 6, 15, 18, 19, 25, 26, 31]. Proportional sharing does not always guarantee the existence of a pure Nash equilibrium, except for special cases, such as when the costs are quadratic or exponential functions of the load [14, 18]. Kollias and Roughgarden [23] were the first to propose the use of Shapley value based methods in congestion games in order to restore stability.

The impact of cost-sharing methods on the quality of equilibria has also been studied in other models: Moulin and Shenker [30] focused on participation games, while Moulin [29] and Mosk-Aoyama and Roughgarden [27] studied queueing games. Also, very closely related in spirit is previous work on coordination mechanisms, beginning with Christodoulou et al. [9] and subsequently in [1, 4, 5, 7, 11, 13, 21, 22]. Most work on coordination mechanisms concerns scheduling games and how the price of anarchy varies with the choice of local machine policies (i.e., the order in which to process jobs assigned to the same machine).

2 PRELIMINARIES

The games that we study comprise a set $N = \{1, \ldots, n\}$ of players, and a set $M = \{1, \ldots, m\}$ of available machines. Each player i needs to schedule a job to one of the machines and he can choose which machine to schedule it on; hence, the set of strategies corresponds to the set M. We consider "weighted" instances, where each agent may have a different weight $w_i \geq 1$, as well as "unweighted" instances, where $w_i = 1$ for every i. We denote the total weight of the players in the game by $W = \sum_{i \in N} w_i$. Each machine j is characterized by a cost function $c_j(\cdot)$ which is increasing in the total load on the machine and satisfies $c_j(0) = 0$.

Given a strategy profile (or schedule) $\mathbf{s} = (s_1, s_2, ..., s_n)$, let $S_j(\mathbf{s}) = \{i \in N : s_i = j\}$ be the set of players scheduling their jobs on machine j, and let $\ell_j(\mathbf{s}) = \sum_{i \in S_j(\mathbf{s})} w_i$ be the load on machine j. The cost of j in this schedule is $c_j(\ell_j(\mathbf{s}))$, and this cost needs to be covered by the set of players using this machine, $S_j(\mathbf{s})$. In this paper we design *cost-sharing methods*, i.e., protocols that decide how the cost of each machine will be distributed among its users. A cost-sharing protocol Ξ defines, at each schedule $\mathbf{s}$, a cost share $\xi_{ij}(\mathbf{s})$ for each $i \in N$ and $j \in M$. Since the machine that i uses, i.e., s_i, is implicitly part of $\mathbf{s}$, we may also denote this cost share as $\xi_i(\mathbf{s})$.

Our goal is to design policies that yield efficient outcomes in all games within a broader class. Formally, a class of scheduling games $\mathcal{G} = (\mathcal{N}, \mathcal{M}, C, \Xi)$ comprises a universe of players $\mathcal{N}$, a universe of machines $\mathcal{M}$, whose cost functions are chosen from the set C, and a cost sharing protocol Ξ. A game $G \in \mathcal{G}$ then consists of a set $M \subseteq \mathcal{M}$ of machines with cost functions from C, a set of agents $N \subseteq \mathcal{N}$, and the cost sharing protocol Ξ.

Based on the information that the cost sharing protocol can depend on, previous work has focused on two extreme protocol design domains. On one extreme is the class of *oblivious protocols*, in which the cost shares $\xi_{ij}(\mathbf{s})$ for a machine j can depend only on the cost function $c_j(\cdot)$ of that machine and on the set $S_j(\mathbf{s})$ of players using j in $\mathbf{s}$. In other words, two machines with the same cost function are identical in terms of the way they share the cost, and their cost sharing is independent of what other machines or players are participating in the game at hand. On the other extreme, in an *omnipotent protocol* the cost shares $\xi_{ij}(\mathbf{s})$ for machine j can depend on *any* information regarding the game at hand. That is, apart from the set $S_j(\mathbf{s})$, the protocol is also aware of the set of participating players, N, the set of machines, M, and the cost functions of all these machines. In this paper we propose the class of *resource-aware protocols* that strike a balance between these two extremes. In particular, apart from the set of jobs $S_j(\mathbf{s})$, these protocols allow $\xi_{ij}(\mathbf{s})$ to depend on the set of machines M and their cost functions. They cannot, however, depend on the set of other jobs, $N \setminus S_j(\mathbf{s})$, that participate in the specific game.

A change of the cost-sharing protocol leads to a different class of games and, hence, to possibly very different outcomes. As a result, the efficiency of a game crucially depends on the choice of the protocol. In evaluating the performance of a cost-sharing protocol, we measure the quality of the pure Nash equilibria that arise in the games that it induces. A strategy vector $\mathbf{s}$ is a *pure Nash equilibrium* (PNE) of a game G if for every player $i \in S_j(\mathbf{s})$, and every other strategy $s'_i \in M$

$$\xi_i(\mathbf{s}) = \xi_i(s_i, \mathbf{s}_{-i}) \leq \xi_i(s'_i, \mathbf{s}_{-i}).$$

As a measure of efficiency of a schedule $\mathbf{s}$, we use the total cost $C(\mathbf{s}) = \sum_{j \in M} c_j(\ell_j(\mathbf{s}))$, and we quantify the performance of the cost-sharing protocol using the price of anarchy metric. Given a cost sharing protocol Ξ, the *price of anarchy* (PoA) of the induced class of games $\mathcal{G} = (\mathcal{N}, \mathcal{M}, C, \Xi)$ is the worst-case ratio of equilibrium cost to optimal cost over all games in $\mathcal{G}$. That is, if $E(G)$ is the set of pure Nash equilibria of the game G, and $F(G)$ the set of schedules of G, then

$$\mathrm{PoA}(\mathcal{G}) = \sup_{G \in \mathcal{G}} \frac{\max_{\mathbf{s} \in E(G)} C(\mathbf{s})}{\min_{\mathbf{s}^* \in F(G)} C(\mathbf{s}^*)}.$$

We say that a cost sharing protocol is *budget-balanced* if the cost that it distributes to the users of each machine adds up to exactly the cost of the machine, i.e., $\forall j \in M$, $c_j(\ell_j(\mathbf{s})) = \sum_{i \in S_j(\mathbf{s})} \xi_{ij}(\mathbf{s})$. A protocol is *stable* within a class of games $\mathcal{G}$ that it induces, if every $G \in \mathcal{G}$ always possesses at least one PNE. In this paper, we restrict our attention to protocols that are stable.

If the mechanism is not budget-balanced, it may define cost functions such that $\hat{c}_j(\ell) > c_j(\ell)$ for some loads ℓ. As a result, the social cost of a given schedule $\mathbf{s}$ may be increased from $C(\mathbf{s})$ to $\hat{C}(\mathbf{s})$. In these mechanisms, we measure the quality of the equilibria using the new costs, but we compare their performance to the optimal solutions based on the original cost functions. If $\hat{G}$ is the game induced by the new cost functions $\hat{c}_j(\ell)$, and $E(\hat{G})$ is the set of pure Nash equilibria of $\hat{G}$,

$$\mathrm{PoA}(\mathcal{G}) = \sup_{G \in \mathcal{G}} \frac{\max_{\mathbf{s} \in E(\hat{G})} \hat{C}(\mathbf{s})}{\min_{\mathbf{s}^* \in F(G)} C(\mathbf{s}^*)}.$$

Some of our results focus on the games induced by specific classes of functions C. In particular, a large part of this paper focuses on convex functions (exhibiting non-decreasing marginal costs), concave cost functions (exhibiting non-increasing marginal costs), or combinations of the two. Apart from these functions, a class of functions that plays an important role is that of *capacitated constant* cost functions. That is, functions such that $c(\ell) = c_1$ when $\ell \leq c_2$ and $c(\ell) = \infty$ when $\ell > c_2$, for positive constants c_1 and c_2. These functions correspond to a machine whose cost is constant as long as the load does not exceed its capacity. It is important to point out that these functions are not concave, since our cost functions satisfy $c_j(0) = 0$. In fact, as we show, this class of functions poses significant obstacles to cost-sharing protocols.

2.1 Related Results for Machines with Convex Functions

We now briefly consider the class of games where all the cost functions are convex, and we present a simple oblivious protocol proposed by Moulin [28]. In Section 5 we use this protocol as a component of our own protocol for the larger class of instances that include both convex and concave functions. Moulin's *incremental cost-sharing protocol*, like many of the known cost-sharing protocols in the related work, uses a global ordering over the universe of players in deciding how to distribute the cost. Some of our mechanisms use this ordering as well, so we provide a definition below.

Definition 2.1. For a class of games $\mathcal{G} = (\mathcal{N}, \mathcal{M}, C, \Xi)$, the *global ordering* π is an ordering of all the players in $\mathcal{N}$ in a non-increasing order with respect to their weight.

Definition 2.2. Given a schedule $\mathbf{s}$ and a machine j, the *prior load*, $\ell_j^{<i}(\mathbf{s})$, for a player $i \in S_j(\mathbf{s})$ is the load on j in $\mathbf{s}$ due to jobs that precede i in π, i.e.,

$$\ell_j^{<i}(\mathbf{s}) = \sum_{k \in S_j(\mathbf{s}): \pi(k) < \pi(i)} w_k.$$

In games with convex cost functions and unweighted jobs the optimal assignment can be computed via a greedy algorithm that assigns each job to the machine where it causes the smallest marginal contribution to the cost function. The incremental cost-sharing protocol charges each user its marginal contribution with respect to the prior load.

Definition 2.3. The *incremental cost-sharing protocol* defines the cost-share of each $i \in S_j(\mathbf{s})$ to be its marginal contribution if only players preceding it in π were using machine j.

$$\xi_{ij}(\mathbf{s}) = c_j(\ell_j^{<i}(\mathbf{s}) + w_i) - c_j(\ell_j^{<i}(\mathbf{s}))$$

The incremental cost-sharing protocol is oblivious, budget-balanced, and stable [28]. Furthermore, when the players are unweighted, it achieves a PoA of 1.

Theorem 2.4. *[28] For convex cost functions and unweighted jobs, the incremental cost-sharing protocol induces games with PoA = 1.*

Although the equilibria of this protocol are optimal when the players are unweighted, for weighted jobs, the incremental cost-sharing protocol induces games with unbounded PoA [32].

3 OMNIPOTENT PROTOCOLS

In this section, we demonstrate the power of overcharging for omnipotent protocols. We show that overcharging can dramatically decrease the PoA of the game. In particular, even for unweighted instances, no budget-balanced omnipotent mechanism can achieve a PoA better than the harmonic number $\mathcal{H}_n = \Omega(\log n)$. In fact, this bound applies even to the best equilibria of the induced games (the price of stability). However, a simple overcharging scheme enables us to reach a PoA of 1 for weighted instances.

Given any problem instance, using an optimal schedule $\mathbf{s}^*$, following the approach of [32], we define the set of "foreign" players of machine j in an outcome $\mathbf{s}$ as the subset of players using j in $\mathbf{s}$ but not in $\mathbf{s}^*$. We then define an efficient omnipotent protocol that overcharges foreign players.

Definition 3.1. The set of *foreign players* of j in $\mathbf{s}$ is $F_j(\mathbf{s}) := \{i \in S_j(\mathbf{s}) \setminus S_j(\mathbf{s}^*)\}$.

Definition 3.2. Given some large constant $D > \sum_{j \in M} c_j(W)$ and the players' ordering π, the *omnipotent overcharging protocol* defines the *modified* costs $\hat{c}_j(\cdot)$ of the machines and the cost shares $\xi_{ij}(\cdot)$ as follows:

$$\hat{c}_j(\ell) = \begin{cases} c_j(\ell), & \text{if } \ell \leq \sum_{i \in S_j(\mathbf{s}^*)} w_i; \\ D, & \text{otherwise,} \end{cases}$$

and

$$\xi_{ij}(\mathbf{s}) = \begin{cases} \frac{w_i}{\sum_{k \in S_j(\mathbf{s})} w_k} \hat{c}_j(\ell_j(\mathbf{s})), & \text{if } F_j(\mathbf{s}) = \emptyset; \\ \hat{c}_j(\ell_j(\mathbf{s})), & \text{if } F_j(\mathbf{s}) \neq \emptyset \text{ and } i = \arg\min_k \{\pi(k) | k \in F_j(\mathbf{s})\}; \\ 0, & \text{otherwise.} \end{cases}$$

This protocol keeps the costs of each machine unaffected, unless the total load on this machine exceeds its total load in $\mathbf{s}^*$, in which case the cost jumps up to some large constant D. If there are no foreign players on a machine j, its cost is divided among its users in a proportional manner. Otherwise, all of its cost, which need not be D, is charged to a single foreign player (the one that appears earliest in π) and every other user suffers no cost.

The next lemma shows that this protocol is stable and that every equilibrium corresponds to an optimal schedule. Furthermore, we show that, despite the extra charges this protocol introduces, no charges are used in any equilibrium, leading to a PoA of 1.

Lemma 3.3. *The omnipotent overcharging protocol is stable and it has PoA 1.*

Proof. We first show that (i) $\mathbf{s}^*$ is a Nash equilibrium of the game induced by the omnipotent overcharging protocol, and (ii) for any other Nash Equilibrium $\tilde{\mathbf{s}}$, it is $\hat{C}(\tilde{\mathbf{s}}) \leq C(\mathbf{s}^*)$.

To show (i) note that, since there are no foreign players on any machine j at $\mathbf{s}^*$, then $\hat{c}_j(\ell_j(\mathbf{s}^*)) = c_j(\ell_j(\mathbf{s}^*))$. Hence, in $\mathbf{s}^*$, the cost of every player is $\xi_i(\mathbf{s}^*) \leq c_j(\ell_j(\mathbf{s}^*)) \leq D$. If some player i can improve his cost by unilaterally deviating from s_i^* to some other machine j, his new cost should be less than D. But, this deviation makes i the *only foreign player* on that machine, since every other player i' is still using $s_{i'}^*$. The cost for this machine after this deviation is $\hat{c}_j(\ell_j(\mathbf{s}^*) + w_i) = D$, and all of this cost is charged to i, i.e., $\xi_i(j, \mathbf{s}_{-i}^*) = D$, proving that $\mathbf{s}^*$ is a Nash equilibrium.

To see (ii), let $\tilde{\mathbf{s}}$ be a Nash equilibrium of the induced game. If there is a machine with $\ell_j(\tilde{\mathbf{s}}) > \ell_j(\mathbf{s}^*)$, then clearly there is a "foreign" player i using this machine that pays a cost of D. But, if i were to deviate to machine $j' = s_i^*$, his cost would be less than D, contradicting that $\tilde{s}$ is an equilibrium. To verify this fact note that if $F_{j'}(\tilde{s}) \neq \emptyset$, then i would suffer a cost of 0 and if $F_{j'}(\tilde{s}) = \emptyset$, then i would suffer a cost of $\xi_i(j', \tilde{s}_{-i}) \leq c_{j'}(s^*) < D$. Therefore, for any equilibrium $\tilde{s}$ and every machine j, the loads are $\ell_j(\tilde{s}) \leq \ell_j(s^*)$, which implies $\hat{C}(\tilde{s}) \leq \hat{C}(s^*) = C(s^*)$. □

4 MACHINES WITH CONCAVE COST FUNCTIONS

In Section 2 we showed that, for the class of convex cost functions, there exists a simple oblivious, stable, and budget-balanced mechanism with PoA of 1. We begin this section by showing that this is far from true when it comes to concave functions. In particular, Theorem 4.1 shows that the PoA of any oblivious, stable, and budget-balanced mechanism grows linearly with n, even for strictly concave functions. We then complement this result with a resource-aware, stable, and budget-balanced mechanism that achieves a PoA of 1 for strictly concave cost functions. We conclude this section by showing how we can apply a negligible amount of overcharging in order to extend our positive result to general (non-strictly) concave cost functions. In particular, we use overcharging to transform the function into a strictly concave one and then apply our resource-aware protocol over the new cost functions, leading to a PoA of $1 + \varepsilon$ for an arbitrarily small constant $\varepsilon > 0$.

4.1 Oblivious Budget-Balanced Protocols

Theorem 4.1. *Any oblivious, stable, and budget-balanced cost-sharing policy has PoA of at least n, even for the class of strictly concave cost functions and in the unweighted setting.*

Proof. Aiming for a contradiction, assume that there exists some oblivious, stable, and budget-balanced policy with PoA of at most $n - \delta$ for some constant $\delta > 0$. Consider the outcomes of this policy for an instance comprising n unweighted agents and n machines with cost functions $c_j(\ell) = \ell + \varepsilon - \varepsilon/\ell$, for some arbitrarily small constant $\varepsilon > 0$.

Since this policy is stable, it is guaranteed to possess an equilibrium for this instance. We show that in any such equilibrium s, every player needs to pay a cost of at most 1. If, in s, each agent is matched to a different machine, this is obvious, since the policy is budget-balanced, and $c_j(1) = 1$. Also, if more than one agent use some machine j in s, the cost share of each one of these agents should be at most 1, otherwise, any agent with a cost share greater than 1 would benefit from a unilateral deviation to one of the "empty" machines (there is always one, since the number of machines and agents is the same).

Now, consider the outcomes of this same policy in an instance where, apart from the same set of jobs and same set of machines, we introduce an extra machine $n + 1$ with cost $c_{n+1}(\ell) = 1 + \varepsilon - \varepsilon/\ell$. Since the protocol is oblivious, the cost functions of the old machines are not affected by the existence of this new machine, and any equilibrium s of the previous instance, remains an equilibrium in the new instance. To verify this fact, note that the cost of the new machine is at least 1 and, as we showed above, the cost of every player in s is at most 1. But, any such equilibrium has social cost at least $n - \varepsilon$, when the optimal solution would be for all agents to use the last machine with social cost of at most $1 + \varepsilon$. Hence, for small enough values of ε, this protocol's PoA is greater than $n - \delta$, leading to a contradiction. □

4.2 Resource-Aware Budget-Balanced Protocol

We now present the main result of this section, which is an efficient resource-aware protocol that is both stable and budget-balanced. We begin by assuming that the cost functions are *strictly* concave and then also address the general concave functions case.

The result of Theorem 4.1 implies that, in order to achieve a good PoA, a resource-aware protocol would need to take advantage of the additional information that it has access to, compared to an oblivious protocol. In particular, this protocol will need to use the information regarding the available machines and their cost functions in such a way that the agents are incentivized to avoid inefficient outcomes. But, what information regarding the machines of the system should such a protocol use, and how can we describe such a protocol that works for *all* possible instances, in a concise way? Also, note that the protocol is not going to be aware of what subset of agents is active, so it needs to work for *any* such subset. Before presenting our protocol, we begin with a few definitions and observations.

Definition 4.2. Given a schedule, s, and a global ordering of the players, π, the *highest priority player* of some non-empty machine j in s, denoted by $h_j(\mathbf{s})$, or simply h_j, is the player $i \in S_j(\mathbf{s})$ with the highest priority in π, i.e.,

$$h_j(\mathbf{s}) = \arg \min_{i' \in S_j(\mathbf{s})} \{\pi(i')\}.$$

The following definition provides the information regarding the set of machines in the system that our resource-aware protocol uses in order to outperform any oblivious protocol.

Definition 4.3. Given a set of machines and some load ℓ, let $\phi(\ell) = \min_{j \in M} c_j(\ell)$ be the smallest cost over all the machines for serving this load, and note that this function $\phi : \mathbb{R}_+ \to \mathbb{R}_+$ is concave as minimum of concave functions. Also, let $X_{\min}(\ell)$ be the set of machines with the smallest cost when their load is ℓ, i.e., $X_{\min}(\ell) = \arg\min_{j \in M}\{c_j(\ell)\}$.

Remark 4.4. *If the total load in the game is W, then an optimal allocation assigns all the load to a machine $j^* \in X_{\min}(W)$. To verify this fact note that, due to the concavity of $\phi(\cdot)$, for any profile* s,

$$\sum_{j \in M} c_j(\ell_j(\mathbf{s})) \geq \sum_{j \in M} \phi(\ell_j(\mathbf{s})) \geq \phi\left(\sum_{j \in M} \ell_j(\mathbf{s})\right) = \phi(W) = c_{j^*}(W).$$

We now define the concave cost-sharing protocol. In its description, for notational simplicity we have dropped the dependence of $h_j(\mathbf{s})$ on s, thus replacing it with h_j.

Definition 4.5. According to the *concave cost-sharing protocol*, given a machine j and a schedule s, the cost share of player $i \in S_j(\mathbf{s})$ is

$$\xi_{ij}(\mathbf{s}) = \begin{cases} c_j(\ell_j(\mathbf{s})) & \text{if } j \notin X_{\min}(\ell_j(\mathbf{s})) \text{ and } i = h_j \\ 0 & \text{if } j \notin X_{\min}(\ell_j(\mathbf{s})) \text{ and } i \neq h_j \\ \phi(w_i) & \text{if } j \in X_{\min}(\ell_j(\mathbf{s})) \text{ and } i = h_j \\ w_i \frac{c_j(\ell_j(\mathbf{s})) - \phi(w_{h_j})}{\ell_j(\mathbf{s}) - w_{h_j}} & \text{if } j \in X_{\min}(\ell_j(\mathbf{s})) \text{ and } i \neq h_j \end{cases}$$

Note that, according to Remark 4.4, the optimal solution can change radically, depending on the set of jobs that are active in the system. Being unaware of which jobs are active, a resource-aware cost-sharing mechanism is therefore unable to guess which machine it should be incentivizing the players to use. In the absence of this information, our cost-sharing policy essentially treats the players that use a machine j as if they are the only active ones in the system. Hence, if the load of this machine is $\ell_j(\mathbf{s})$, but $j \notin X_{\min}(\ell_j(\mathbf{s}))$, then s should not be permitted as an equilibrium, and the protocol incentivizes the $h_j(\mathbf{s})$ to leave the machine by charging the whole cost to him.

Of course, this high level intuition does not go far enough in explaining why the protocol actually works. For instance, one could come up with schedules s such that two (or more) different machines $j1$ and $j2$ have positive loads that satisfy $j1 \in X_{\min}(\ell_{j1}(\mathbf{s}))$ and $j2 \in X_{\min}(\ell_{j2}(\mathbf{s}))$. In such schedules, the myopic view of the protocol for each one of these machines is that s may as well be optimal. Therefore, the most interesting part of this protocol is the way in which it distributes the costs in these circumstances, using the $\phi(w_i)$ function, which ensures that such "locally optimal" but globally inefficient schedules will not be equilibrium outcomes.

Since the protocol depends only on the cost functions of the machines, but not on the total number of agents and their weights, it is a valid resource-aware protocol. As we show below, it is also budget-balanced, stable, and its PoA is 1.

Lemma 4.6. *The concave cost-sharing protocol is budget-balanced.*

Proof. Given some problem instance, we show that for any schedule s and any machine j, the sum of the cost shares of the players in $S_j(\mathbf{s})$ adds up to exactly $c_j(\ell_j(\mathbf{s}))$. If $j \notin X_{\min}(\ell_j(\mathbf{s}))$, then every player $i \neq h_j(\mathbf{s})$ has a cost of 0, and player $h_j(\mathbf{s})$ suffers the whole cost $c_j(\ell_j(\mathbf{s}))$. On the other hand, if $j \in X_{\min}(\ell_j(\mathbf{s}))$, the cost of $h_j(\mathbf{s})$ is $\phi(w_{h_j})$, while the total cost of all the other players is

$$\sum_{i \in S_j(\mathbf{s}) \setminus \{h_j\}} w_i \frac{c_j(\ell_j(\mathbf{s})) - \phi(w_{h_j})}{\ell_j(\mathbf{s}) - w_{h_j}} = (\ell_j(\mathbf{s}) - w_{h_j}) \frac{c_j(\ell_j(\mathbf{s})) - \phi(w_{h_j})}{\ell_j(\mathbf{s}) - w_{h_j}} = c_j(\ell_j(\mathbf{s})) - \phi(w_{h_j}).$$

□

Lemma 4.7. *The concave cost-sharing protocol is stable.*

Proof. To prove the stability of this protocol, we show that for any problem instance, the schedule s in which every player uses the same machine $j \in X_{\min}(W)$ is a Nash equilibrium.

In this schedule, the cost share of the highest priority player $i = h_j(\mathbf{s})$ is $\phi(w_i)$. Also, by Lemma 4.8, the cost share of every other player i is strictly less than $\phi(w_i)$. Therefore, every player i's cost in s is at most $\phi(w_i)$. But, if some player i were to deviate to another machine j', his new cost would be $c_{j'}(w_i) \geq \phi(w_i)$, so nobody has an incentive to deviate. □

The following lemma will help to prove the PoA bound of Theorem 4.9. It argues that for any machine j with load ℓ and $j \in X_{\min}(\ell)$, the cost-share of any agent $i \neq h_j(\mathbf{s})$ using j is strictly less than $\phi(w_i)$.

Lemma 4.8. *At any profile* s *and every machine $j \in X_{\min}(\ell_j(\mathbf{s}))$, the concave cost-sharing protocol assigns to every $i \in S_j(\mathbf{s}) \setminus \{h_j(\mathbf{s})\}$ a cost share $\xi_{ij}(\mathbf{s}) < \phi(w_i)$.*

Proof. Since $j \in X_{\min}(\ell_j(\mathbf{s}))$, the cost on j satisfies $c_j(\ell_j(\mathbf{s})) = \phi(\ell_j(\mathbf{s}))$. Therefore, for every player i who is not highest priority on j, i.e., $i \neq h_j$,

$$\xi_{ij}(\mathbf{s}) = w_i \frac{c_j(\ell_j(\mathbf{s})) - \phi(w_{h_j})}{\ell_j(\mathbf{s}) - w_{h_j}} = w_i \frac{\phi(\ell_j(\mathbf{s})) - \phi(w_{h_j})}{\ell_j(\mathbf{s}) - w_{h_j}} \leq w_i \frac{\phi(\ell_j(\mathbf{s}) - w_{h_j})}{\ell_j(\mathbf{s}) - w_{h_j}}.$$

Note that the denominator $\ell_j(\mathbf{s}) - w_{h_j}$ is always positive, since there is at least one more job $i \neq h_j$ using machine j in s. In fact, $\ell_j(\mathbf{s}) - w_{h_j} \geq w_i$ so, using the fact that the cost functions are strictly concave, the previous inequality implies

$$\xi_{ij}(\mathbf{s}) \leq w_i \frac{\phi(\ell_j(\mathbf{s}) - w_{h_j})}{\ell_j(\mathbf{s}) - w_{h_j}} < \phi(w_i).$$

□

Theorem 4.9. *The concave cost-sharing protocol has PoA = 1.*

Proof. According to Remark 4.4, the schedule s in which all the players use a machine $j \in X_{\min}(W)$ is optimal. We now show that the social cost of any Nash equilibrium also equals $c_j(W)$. Aiming for a contradiction, assume that there exists some Nash equilibrium $\mathbf{s}'$ with cost greater than $c_j(W)$.

If, in $\mathbf{s}'$, every player uses the same machine $j' \notin X_{\min}(W)$, then the total cost is $c_{j'}(W) > c_j(W)$. If i is the highest priority player among them, then he pays a share equal to $c_{j'}(W)$. But, if this player deviated to machine j, his cost would become $c_j(w_i) \leq c_j(W) < c_{j'}(W)$, so this cannot be an equilibrium.

If, on the other hand, two or more machines are being used in $\mathbf{s}'$, let a and b be two of these machines, and let α and β be the corresponding highest priority players in $\mathbf{s}'$. Without loss of generality, assume that α has higher global priority than β, i.e., $\pi(\alpha) < \pi(\beta)$. According to the definition of the protocol, if $b \in X_{\min}(\ell_b(\mathbf{s}'))$, the cost share of β in $\mathbf{s}'$ is $\xi_\beta(\mathbf{s}') = \phi(w_\beta)$ and, if $b \notin X_{\min}(\ell_b(\mathbf{s}'))$ it is

$$\xi_\beta(\mathbf{s}') = c_b(\ell_b(\mathbf{s}')) \geq c_b(w_\beta) \geq \phi(w_\beta).$$

Therefore, in both cases, $\xi_\beta(\mathbf{s}') \geq \phi(w_\beta)$. But, if player β deviates to machine a, he is not the highest priority player on that machine (player α is), so his cost is less than $\phi(w_\beta)$. To verify this fact, we consider two different scenarios depending on whether, after this deviation, $a \in X_{\min}(\ell_a(\mathbf{s}')+w_\beta)$ or $a \notin X_{\min}(\ell_a(\mathbf{s}')+w_\beta)$. In the former case, Lemma 4.8 implies that the cost of β after the deviation is less than $\phi(w_\beta)$. In the latter, according to the definition of the protocol, the cost of β is 0. Therefore this cannot be an equilibrium either, which conclude the proof. □

4.3 General Concave Cost Functions

Since the positive result of the previous section focused on strictly concave functions, we now show how we can leverage overcharging in order to transform any weakly concave cost function into a strictly concave one. This way, we reduce this problem to the one we solved above and, as we show, the loss in PoA can be arbitrarily small. In particular, by overcharging, we define a cost-sharing protocol with PoA = $1 + \varepsilon$, where $\varepsilon > 0$ is an arbitrarily small constant.

The main observation is that we can implement this transformation by updating each $c_j(\ell)$ to $\hat{c}_j(\ell) = c_j(\ell) + \varepsilon/\ell$. Once we have done this, the $\hat{c}_j(\ell)$ is strictly concave, and the cost difference between $\hat{c}_j(\ell)$ and $c_j(\ell)$ is no more than ε. Although this overcharging may affect the set of equilibrium outcomes, the social cost of the optimal schedule will not be affected by more than some insignificant constant. Therefore, the PoA of this game will be arbitrarily close to 1, as ϵ goes to zero.

5 MACHINES WITH A MIX OF CONCAVE AND CONVEX COST FUNCTIONS

Unlike the previous two sections, the rest of the paper focuses exclusively on instances with unweighted jobs. We now consider the case where the cost function of each machine is either a concave or a convex function. If we focus on budget-balanced cost-sharing policies, the price of stability is known to be $\Omega(\log n)$ *even for omnipotent protocols* [32]. In stark contrast to this fact, we propose a non-budget-balanced resource-aware policy whose PoA is at most 2. Once again, this demonstrates the power of overcharging. In Section 7.2 we complement this positive result by proving that no resource-aware protocol can achieve a PoA better than 1.36 even for instances with just two machines with convex and concave cost functions, and even if overcharging is used.

5.1 Budget-Balanced Cost-Sharing

As shown in [32], even in the omnipotent case, where the designer has full knowledge of the instance, and even the *best* Nash equilibrium can be a $\Omega(\log n)$ factor away of the optimal cost. We describe here the lower bound for completeness.

Lower bound for budget balanced protocols. Consider the load balancing game of $m+1$ machines, such that each machine j of the first m has a cost function $c_j(\ell)$ with $c_j(1) = 1/j$ and $c_j(\ell) = \infty$ for $\ell > 1$. The last machine has a cost of $c_{m+1}(\ell) = 1 + \varepsilon$ for all ℓ. Let m be the number of agents that require to be served (we can even assume that this is known to the designer). Suppose now that $m' \geq 1$ of agents are served by the last machine. By budget-balance, there is at least one with share more that $1/m'$, whereas from the first m machines there should be at least one empty with cost at most $1/m'$ (there are $m - m' + 1$ machines with cost at most $1/m'$). So, such an outcome cannot be stable. Therefore, the only outcome that may be stable with bounded cost is for every agent to use a distinct machine from the m first. This results to a PoA and PoS of $\Omega(\log m)$.

5.2 Cost-Sharing with Overcharging

Let M_v, M_c be the subset of machines with convex and concave cost functions, respectively. Also, let ξ^{v} denote the incremental cost-sharing protocol defined in Sec. 2.1 for convex functions and ξ^{c} denote the protocol of Sec. 4 for concave functions. We now define a protocol that combines them.

Definition 5.1 (Convex-Concave (VC) cost-sharing protocol). Using the global order π of the players, we define the Ξ^{vc} as follows:

$$\xi^{\mathrm{vc}}_{ij}(\mathbf{s}) = \begin{cases} \xi^{\mathrm{v}}_{ij}(\mathbf{s}) & \text{if } j \in M_v \\ \xi^{\mathrm{c}}_{ij}(\mathbf{s}) & \text{if } j \in M_c \end{cases}$$

where for ϕ and $X_{\min}$ (used to define ξ^{c}) are defined only over the set of concave functions.

Lemma 5.2. *The Convex-Concave cost-sharing protocol is stable.*

Proof. Let $\phi(\ell) = \min_{j \in M_c} c_j(\ell)$ be the minimum cost incurred by load ℓ, over all concave machines. Without loss of generality we assume that the identity of each player matches her position according to π, i.e. $\pi(i) = i$.

We define a profile $\mathbf{s}$ which is a pure Nash equilibrium. The first k (possibly zero) players with respect to the global ordering π, use only convex functions from M_v. The condition that needs to be satisfied is that k is the maximum integer such that $\xi^{v}_{k}(\mathbf{s}) \leq \phi(1)$. The rest of the players use the concave machine with the minimum cost for $n - k$ load, i.e. machine $X_{\min}(n - k)$.

If $k = 0$ (all players use concave machines), then as shown in Section 4, each player pays a share of at most $\phi(1)$, while for any $j \in M_v$ $c_j(1) > \phi(1)$. If $k = n$, (all players use convex machines), $\mathbf{s}$ is an equilibrium by the analysis of Section 2.1. Notice that each player pays share of at most $\phi(1)$ (by definition of k), so no player will deviate to a concave machine.

It is clear why a player will not switch from a convex to a convex and from a concave to a concave machine, by analysis similar to Sections 2.1 and 4. Now, observe that a player that uses a convex machine precedes, according to π, any player using a concave machine. Therefore, if she switches to any concave machine, she will pay at least $\phi(1)$. Moreover, recall that each player that uses the concave machine $X_{\min}(n - k)$, pays a share of at most $\phi(1)$, while if she deviates to a convex machine, she will be the last according to π, and will pay the next marginal cost, which exceeds $\phi(1)$, by definition of k. □

The following Lemma reveals a useful structural property of optimal schedules when the cost functions are either convex or concave. Due to space constraints, the proof of this Lemma is deferred to the full version of the paper.

Lemma 5.3. *If for n players some optimal schedule assigns $n_c > 0$ agents to concave machines and n_v agents to convex machines, then for $n' > n$ players there is an optimal schedule such that the number of players assigned to convex machines is at most n_v.*

Using the VC cost-sharing protocol, which is budget-balanced, we now define the VC-Overcharing protocol, which combines the VC protocol with appropriate overcharging to circumvent the limitations of budget-balanced protocols shown above. Given a set of machines, let $n^{\max}$ be the maximum number of players such that, when $n \leq n^{\max}$, there is no optimal schedule $OPT(n)$ of n unweighted jobs to these machines that uses a concave machine. Also, let $n_j^{\max}$ be the number of players assigned to machine $j \in M_v$ in the $OPT(n^{\max})$ allocation.

Definition 5.4 (VC-Overcharging cost-sharing protocol). Apply the VC cost-sharing protocol to cost functions $\hat{c}_j(\ell)$ such that $\hat{c}_j(\ell) = c_j(\ell)$, unless $j \in M_v$ and $\ell \geq n_j^{max}$, in which case

$$\hat{c}_j(\ell) = \max\left\{\max_{j' \in M_c} c_{j'}(1)\ ,\ c_j(\ell)\right\}.$$

Remark 5.5. *The minimum number of players for which at least one concave machine is used by the optimum allocation is $n^{max} + 1$. Moreover, by Lemma 5.3 for any $n > n^{max}$ there is an optimal schedule that assigns at most n^{max} players in total to convex machines. Therefore the optimal cost is not affected by the overcharging of the VC-Overcharging protocol. Furthermore, the arguments of Lemma 5.2 can be applied to show that the VC-Overcharging protocol is stable as well.*

Theorem 5.6. *For instances with concave and convex cost functions the VC-Overcharging protocol yields PoA at most 2.*

Proof. Recall that M_c, M_v are the sets of concave and convex machines respectively. Further, let $\phi_c(\ell)$ and $\phi_v(\ell)$ be the cost of optimally assigning ℓ players to only concave or only convex machines, respectively. Observe that ϕ_c, and ϕ_v are concave and convex respectively.

Let s be any Nash equilibrium, and s* be the optimal allocation with at most n^{max} players in convex machines; the existence of such an optimal allocation is guaranteed by Remark 5.5. Let $n_c = \sum_{j \in M_c} \ell_j(\mathbf{s})$, and $n_v = \sum_{j \in M_v} \ell_j(\mathbf{s})$ be the total number of players using concave and convex machines, respectively, in the Nash equilibrium, and n_c^*, n_v^* the same numbers w.r.t $\mathbf{s}^*$.

Claim 5.7. *The total number of players using concave machines in $\mathbf{s}^*$ is at least as high as in $\mathbf{s}$, i.e., $n_c^* \geq n_c$, and hence $n_v^* \leq n_v$.*

Proof. Aiming for a contradiction, assume that $n_c^* < n_c$ and $n_v^* > n_v$. By optimality of n_c^*, n_v^*,

$$\phi_v(n_v^*) - \phi_v(n_v) < \phi_c(n_c) - \phi_c(n_c^*). \tag{1}$$

Let i^* be the smallest player w.r.t π that uses a concave machine in s, and let j^* be the index of that machine (recall that all players that use concave machines, are assigned to j^*). Notice that there is such a player since by assumption $n_c > n_c^*$.

The share of i^* is $\xi_{i^*}(\mathbf{s}) = \xi_{i^*j^*}(\mathbf{s}) = \phi_c(1)$. Using Inequality (1), the fact that $n_v < n_v^*$, as well as convexity and concavity of ϕ_v and ϕ_c, respectively, we get

$$\phi_v(n_v + 1) - \phi_v(n_v) \leq \frac{\phi_v(n_v^*) - \phi_v(n_v)}{n_v^* - n_v} < \frac{\phi_c(n_c) - \phi_c(n_c^*)}{n_c - n_c^*} \leq \phi_c(1) = \xi_{i^*}(\mathbf{s}).$$

So, player i^* has a reason to deviate to a convex machine, which contradicts the assumption that s is a Nash equilibrium. □

If $n \leq n^{max}$, then the the optimal cost is $\phi_v(n)$, i.e. $n_v^* = n$, based on the definition of n^{max}. By Claim 5.7 it is $n = n_v^* \leq n_v$, so trivially, $n = n_v$, and the PoA is 1.

Otherwise, based on the definition of n^{max} and on the VC-Overcharging cost-sharing protocol, both the optimal allocation and the Nash equilibrium assign at most n^{max} players to the convex machines. Therefore,

$$\begin{aligned} C(\mathbf{s}) &= \phi_c(n_c) + \phi_v(n_v) \leq \phi_c(n_c) + \phi_v(n_v^*) + \phi_c(n_v - n_v^*) \\ &= \phi_c(n_c) + \phi_v(n_v^*) + \phi_c(n_c^* - n_c) \leq \phi_c(n_c^*) + \phi_v(n_v^*) + \phi_c(n_c^*) \leq 2C(\mathbf{s}^*), \end{aligned}$$

	$c_1(\ell)\dots c_m(\ell)$	$c_{m+1}(\ell)$
$\ell = 0$	0	0
$\ell = 1$	1	1
$2 \leq \ell \leq m$	∞	1
$\ell \geq m+1$	∞	∞

Table 1. The lower bound construction for budget-balanced resource-aware cost-sharing protocols

where for the first inequality, observe that if there were only n_v players, the optimal cost would be $\phi_v(n_v)$, since $n_v \leq n^{max}$. This means that, since by Claim 5.7 $n_v \geq n_v^*$, it holds that $\phi_v(n_v) \leq \phi_v(n_v^*) + \phi_c(n_v - n_v^*)$. □

6 MACHINES WITH GENERAL COST FUNCTIONS

In this section we show that the positive results of the previous sections do not carry over to general increasing cost functions. Remarkably, the instances that we construct in our PoA lower bounds use just capacitated constant cost functions, a seemingly mild extension beyond convex and concave functions.

We first focus on budget-balanced protocols and show that the PoA of any budget-balanced resource-aware cost-sharing protocol is $\Omega(n)$, even for unweighted players. It is not hard to check that the PoA is guaranteed to be $O(n)$ for any budget-balanced resource-aware cost-sharing protocol, with unweighted players,[3] so this bound is tight.

Theorem 6.1. *Every stable budget-balanced resource-aware cost-sharing mechanism has a PoA of $\Omega(n)$ for the class of capacitated constant cost functions.*

Proof. Consider a class of games comprising a set of $m+1$ machines with costs as in Table 1. A resource-aware cost-sharing protocol for each one of these machines can depend arbitrarily on all this information, so even the first m machines can have a different protocol, although they have the same cost function. However, the cost-sharing cannot depend on the number, n, of jobs that are participating in the game.

First, assume that the number of jobs in the game is $n = 2m$. In this case, an optimal schedule assigns exactly one player to each of the first m machines and the remaining m players are assigned to the last machine. This allocation results in a total cost of $m+1$, and any other allocation would lead to an infinite total cost. Since the cost-sharing protocol is stable, this game has at least one Nash equilibrium and, if any sub-optimal schedule is an equilibrium, then the PoA is unbounded. Otherwise, if an optimal schedule is an equilibrium, let S be the set of m players using the first m machines in this equilibrium. Then, none of them can decrease their cost by deviating to any other one of the first m machines.

Now, consider the different game from the same class where only the set S of players participate, i.e., $n = m$. Then, assigning them to the same machines that they were assigned to in the equilibrium of the previous game, would have to be an equilibrium for the new game: they do not want to deviate to each other's machines, and they also do not want to deviate to the unused machine since

[3] If the allocation in the pure Nash equilibrium is different from the optimal allocation, there should exist a machine j with n_j and n_j^* players in the equilibrium and in the optimal allocation, respectively, such that $n_j < n_j^*$. The cost of any player in machine j is upper bounded by $c_j(n_j) \leq c_j(n_j^*)$ and the cost of any other player is upper bounded by $c_j(n_j+1) \leq c_j(n_j^*)$, because she has no benefit to deviate to j. $c_j(n_j^*)$ is trivially upper bounded by the cost of the optimal allocation and by summing up over all players the $O(n)$ bound follows.

their cost would remain the same, due to budget-balance. However, the optimal schedule in the new game would assign them all to the last machine, achieving a social cost of 1 instead of n. □

We now prove that the PoA of any resource-aware, not necessarily budget-balanced, cost-sharing protocol is $\Omega(\sqrt{n})$ even for unweighted players. We should emphasize that showing lower bounds for resource-aware mechanisms that allow overcharging is much more involved than the corresponding proofs for budget-balanced mechanisms, since the design space is considerably larger. In particular, we would like to direct the reader's attention to the second half of the following proof, which provides some intuition regarding the difficulty involved.

Theorem 6.2. *Every stable resource-aware cost-sharing mechanism has a PoA of $\Omega(\sqrt{n})$ for the class of capacitated constant cost functions.*

Proof. In the instances that we consider, $n = \Theta(m)$, so we just prove the bound as a function of m, and the same bound as a function of n is implied.

Consider the following family of problem instances involving $m + 1$ machines. The first group contains m machines that have a cost function $c_j(\ell)$, such that $c_j(1) = 1$ and $c_j(\ell) = \infty$ for $\ell > 1$. The second group contains a single machine with a cost of $c_{m+1}(\ell) = \sqrt{m}$ for $\ell \le m$ and $c_{m+1}(\ell) = \infty$ for $\ell > m$. The resource-aware protocol can change the cost functions by increasing the induced costs that need to be shared among the agents, but the following case analysis shows that, no matter how the designer changes the shared costs, the price of anarchy of the induced game is $\Omega(\sqrt{m})$.

Let m' be the number of machines from the first group whose, possibly overcharged, cost functions are $\hat{c}_i(1) < \sqrt{m}$ and therefore, there exist $m + 1 - m'$ machines with cost at least $\sqrt{m}$. If $m' < m/2$, consider the instance in which the number of agents that are active is $n = 2m$. In this case, the only equilibrium is the one in which m players are matched to the first m machines, and the remaining m players are assigned to the last machine, leading to a social cost of at least $m' + (m + 1 - m')\sqrt{m} \in \Omega(m\sqrt{m})$. The same assignment prior to the overcharging costs though would yield a cost of $m + \sqrt{m}$, which implies that the price of anarchy would be $\Omega(\sqrt{m})$.

If, on the other hand $m' \ge m/2$, then consider the instance in which the number of agents that arrive at the system is $n = m'$. If all these agents were matched, in equilibrium, to one of the m' machines whose cost is less than $\sqrt{m}$, then this would also lead to a PoA of $\Omega(\sqrt{m})$. To verify this fact, note that the total cost of this assignment would be at least m', while the social optimum cost would be $\sqrt{m}$, if all of them chose the last machine. Therefore the price of anarchy for any such setting would be at least $m'/\sqrt{m} \in \Omega(\sqrt{m})$.

However, why this assignment of the m' agents to the m' machines of the first group would be an equilibrium is unclear. It is true that the cost of each player in this assignment would be at most $\sqrt{m}$, i.e., less than any other machine that is not occupied by another player. But, we cannot exclude the possibility of at least one of these players has an incentive to deviate to one of the other $m' - 1$ occupied machines. Such a deviation would lead to a cost of infinity on that machine, but the protocol could just charge all of this cost to the existing occupant, thus charging the new occupant 0! Such a cost-sharing protocol would then incentivize this player to deviate, in turn forcing the previous occupant to move to another machine. In fact, each machine could have a different ordering over which players to give higher priority to aiming to prevent any such equilibrium from arising.

So, how can we prove that for any stable resource-aware protocol there exists a set of m' players such that the assignment described above is an equilibrium? We consider what would happen if $n = 2m$ agents arrived instead. The crucial observation is that, since the protocol is stable, it *must* possess an equilibrium in this instance as well. The only equilibrium that may exist is the one in which m players are matched to the first m machines, and the remaining m players are assigned to the last machine. Since this assignment is an equilibrium, the agents occupying the m' "cheaper" machines of the first group have no incentive to deviate to another one of these m' machines. Hence, if we remove everyone else, except these m' players, the remaining assignment needs to be an equilibrium. In particular, it needs to be an equilibrium because the protocol is resource-aware, so its cost sharing cannot depend on whether the other $2m - m'$ players exist or not. □

7 COST-SHARING FOR TWO MACHINES

We finally focus on the special case of instances comprising two machines and unweighted jobs. We show that for general cost-functions, there is a budget-balanced cost-sharing protocol with PoA = 2. Notably, this mechanism does not belong to the class of generalized weighted Shapley mechanisms [8], yet we show that it always induces Nash equilibria. Then we show a lower bound of 1.36 for resource-aware protocols with overcharging.

7.1 Budget-Balanced Cost-Sharing

Let $\alpha(\mathbf{s}) = \arg\min_i\{\pi(i)|i \in S_1(\mathbf{s})\}$ and $\beta(\mathbf{s}) = \arg\max_i\{\pi(i)|i \in S_2(\mathbf{s})\}$ be the first player of the first machine and the last player of the second machine in $\mathbf{s}$, with respect to the global ordering π.

Definition 7.1 (Increasing-Decreasing protocol). For any profile $\mathbf{s}$, player $\alpha(\mathbf{s})$ is charged the whole cost of the first machine and player $\beta(\mathbf{s})$ is charged the whole cost of the second. The rest of the players are charged 0:

$$\xi_{ij}(\mathbf{s}) = \begin{cases} c_j(\ell_j(\mathbf{s})), & \text{if } j = 1 \text{ and } i = \alpha(\mathbf{s}) \\ c_j(\ell_j(\mathbf{s})), & \text{if } j = 2 \text{ and } i = \beta(\mathbf{s}) \\ 0, & \text{otherwise.} \end{cases}$$

THEOREM 7.2. *For instances with two machines, unweighted jobs, and general cost functions, the Increasing-Decreasing protocol is stable and it yields a PoA of 2.*

PROOF. We verify that this protocol is stable by constructing a pure Nash equilibrium. Starting from a schedule where all the jobs are assigned to the first machine, while the first player (w.r.t. π) using machine 1 prefers to deviate to machine 2 we let him do so, until this is not the case. It is easy to verify that this schedule $\mathbf{s}$ is an equilibrium with n_1 jobs on the first machine and n_2 on the second, such that $c_1(n_1) \le c_2(n_2 + 1)$ and $c_2(n_2) \le c_1(n_1 + 1)$. The only two players suffering a cost are the last player to deviate (and he preferred to do so) and the first player who did not want to deviate (who also preferred not to). The only alternative choice of these two players is to deviate and suffer the full cost of the other machine.

Now, assume that the optimal allocation assigns n_1^* and n_2^* players to machines 1 and 2, respectively. The case of $n_1^* = n_1$ and $n_2^* = n_2$, trivially results in a PoS of 1. Without loss of generality, let $n_1^* > n_1$ and $n_2^* < n_2$. Then PoA ≤ 2 since,

$$c_1(n_1) + c_2(n_2) \;\le\; c_1(n_1^*) + c_1(n_1 + 1) \;\le\; 2c_1(n_1^*) \;\le\; 2(c_1(n_1^*) + c_2(n_2^*)).$$

The example of Figure 1, with two players and two machines, shows that this bound is tight. Assume that $\pi(1) = 1$ and $\pi(2) = 2$. Then, the allocation where player 1 uses machine 2 and player 2 uses machine 1 is a Nash equilibrium. Indeed, if player 1 deviates to machine 1, he should pay 1, whereas he currently pays $1 - \varepsilon$. If player 2 deviates to machine 2, he should pay 2, whereas he currently pays 1. The optimal schedule would assign both players to machine 1, with a total cost 1. Hence, the PoA is at least $2 - \varepsilon$. For an arbitrarily small $\varepsilon > 0$. □

	$c_1(\ell)$	$c_2(\ell)$
$\ell = 0$	0	0
$\ell = 1$	1	$1 - \varepsilon$
$\ell = 2$	1	2

Fig. 1. Tight lower bound on the PoA of the Increasing-Decreasing protocol.

7.2 Cost-Sharing with Overcharging

We conclude by demonstrating that we cannot avoid losing a constant factor in games with just two machines, even if we used overcharging.

THEOREM 7.3. *There is no stable overcharging resource-aware cost-sharing protocol that achieves PoA* $\leq (1+\sqrt{3})/2 \approx 1.36$, *even for instances with two machines with concave and convex cost functions.*

PROOF. Consider two machines with the cost functions as shown in the Figure 2, where $c \in (0, 1/2)$ is some constant to be defined later.

	$c_1(\ell)$	$c_2(\ell)$
$\ell = 0$	0	0
$\ell > 0$	1	$2(\ell - 1) + c$

Fig. 2. Lower bound on the PoA of any resource-aware protocol, after overcharging. $0 < c < 1/2$.

Assume that two players appear and consider any budget-balanced protocol. Observe that the profile where both players choose the second machine is not a Nash equilibrium, since the cost would be more than 2 and, hence, at least one of the players would be paying more than 1. The profile where both players choose the first machine is not a Nash equilibrium either, since at least one of the players would be paying at least $\frac{1}{2}$, giving him reason to deviate to the second machine. Therefore, the only Nash equilibrium is the schedule where one player chooses the first machine and the other one chooses the second machine. The PoA then is $1 + c$.

The only way to achieve a better PoA for this case is to force the player that chooses the second machine to move to the first machine. In order to achieve this, the cost of the second machine for $\ell = 1$ should be raised at least to the value of $\frac{1}{2}$. But then, for instances where only one player appears the PoA becomes $\frac{1/2}{c}$. Choosing the value of c that satisfies the equality $1 + c = \frac{1}{2c}$, the PoA cannot be better than $1 + c = \frac{1+\sqrt{3}}{2}$ even with overcharging. □

REFERENCES

[1] Fidaa Abed and Chien-Chung Huang. 2012. Preemptive coordination mechanisms for unrelated machines. In *European Symposium on Algorithms*. Springer, 12–23.

[2] Elliot Anshelevich, Anirban Dasgupta, Jon Kleinberg, Eva Tardos, Tom Wexler, and Tim Roughgarden. 2008. The price of stability for network design with fair cost allocation. *SIAM J. Comput.* 38, 4 (2008), 1602–1623.

[3] Baruch Awerbuch, Yossi Azar, and Amir Epstein. 2005. The price of routing unsplittable flow. In *ACM Symposium on Theory of Computing*. ACM, 57–66.

[4] Yossi Azar, Lisa Fleischer, Kamal Jain, Vahab S. Mirrokni, and Zoya Svitkina. 2015. Optimal Coordination Mechanisms for Unrelated Machine Scheduling. *Operations Research* 63, 3 (2015), 489–500.

[5] Sayan Bhattacharya, Sungjin Im, Janardhan Kulkarni, and Kamesh Munagala. 2014. Coordination mechanisms from (almost) all scheduling policies. In *5th conference on Innovations in theoretical computer science*. ACM, 121–134.

[6] Kshipra Bhawalkar, Martin Gairing, and Tim Roughgarden. 2014. Weighted congestion games: Price of anarchy, universal worst-case examples, and tightness. *ACM Transactions on Economics and Computation* 2, 4 (2014), 14.
[7] Ioannis Caragiannis. 2013. Efficient coordination mechanisms for unrelated machine scheduling. *Algorithmica* 66, 3 (2013), 512–540.
[8] Ho-Lin Chen, Tim Roughgarden, and Gregory Valiant. 2010. Designing network protocols for good equilibria. *SIAM J. Comput.* 39, 5 (2010), 1799–1832.
[9] George Christodoulou, Elias Koutsoupias, and Akash Nanavati. 2009. Coordination mechanisms. *Theor. Comput. Sci.* 410, 36 (2009), 3327–3336.
[10] George Christodoulou, Stefano Leonardi, and Alkmini Sgouritsa. 2016. Designing Cost-Sharing Methods for Bayesian Games. In *Algorithmic Game Theory - 9th International Symposium, SAGT 2016.* 327–339.
[11] Giorgos Christodoulou, Kurt Mehlhorn, and Evangelia Pyrga. 2014. Improving the price of anarchy for selfish routing via coordination mechanisms. *Algorithmica* 69, 3 (2014), 619–640.
[12] George Christodoulou and Alkmini Sgouritsa. 2016. Designing Networks with Good Equilibria under Uncertainty. In *Proceedings of the Twenty-Seventh Annual ACM-SIAM Symposium on Discrete Algorithms, SODA 2016.* 72–89.
[13] Richard Cole, José R. Correa, Vasilis Gkatzelis, Vahab S. Mirrokni, and Neil Olver. 2015. Decentralized utilitarian mechanisms for scheduling games. *Games and Economic Behavior* 92 (2015), 306–326.
[14] Dimitris Fotakis and Paul G. Spirakis. 2008. Cost-balancing tolls for atomic network congestion games. *Internet Mathematics* 5, 4 (2008), 343–363.
[15] Martin Gairing and Florian Schoppmann. 2007. Total latency in singleton congestion games. In *Internet and Network Economics.* Springer, 381–387.
[16] Vasilis Gkatzelis, Konstantinos Kollias, and Tim Roughgarden. 2016. Optimal Cost-Sharing in General Resource Selection Games. *Operations Research* 64, 6 (2016), 1230–1238.
[17] Ragavendran Gopalakrishnan, Jason R. Marden, and Adam Wierman. 2014. Potential games are necessary to ensure pure Nash equilibria in cost sharing games. *Mathematics of Operations Research* (2014).
[18] Tobias Harks and Max Klimm. 2012. On the existence of pure Nash equilibria in weighted congestion games. *Mathematics of Operations Research* 37, 3 (2012), 419–436.
[19] Tobias Harks, Max Klimm, and Rolf H. Möhring. 2011. Characterizing the existence of potential functions in weighted congestion games. *Theory of Computing Systems* 49, 1 (2011), 46–70.
[20] Tobias Harks and Konstantin Miller. 2011. The worst-case efficiency of cost sharing methods in resource allocation games. *Operations Research* 59, 6 (2011), 1491–1503.
[21] Nicole Immorlica, Li Erran Li, Vahab S. Mirrokni, and Andreas S. Schulz. 2009. Coordination mechanisms for selfish scheduling. *Theoretical Computer Science* 410, 17 (2009), 1589–1598.
[22] Konstantinos Kollias. 2013. Nonpreemptive coordination mechanisms for identical machines. *Theory of Computing Systems* 53, 3 (2013), 424–440.
[23] Konstantinos Kollias and Tim Roughgarden. 2015. Restoring pure equilibria to weighted congestion games. *ACM Transactions on Economics and Computation* 3, 4 (2015), 13–46.
[24] Jason R. Marden and Adam Wierman. 2013. Distributed welfare games. *Operations Research* 61, 1 (2013), 155–168.
[25] Igal Milchtaich. 1996. Congestion games with player-specific payoff functions. *Games and Economic Behavior* 13, 1 (1996), 111–124.
[26] Dov Monderer and Lloyd S. Shapley. 1996. Potential games. *Games and Economic Behavior* 14, 1 (1996), 124–143.
[27] Damon Mosk-Aoyama and Tim Roughgarden. 2009. Worst-case efficiency analysis of queueing disciplines. In *International Colloquium on Automata, Languages and Programming.* Springer, 546–557.
[28] Hervé Moulin. 1999. Incremental cost sharing: Characterization by coalition strategy-proofness. *Social Choice and Welfare* 16, 2 (1999), 279–320.
[29] Hervé Moulin. 2008. The price of anarchy of serial, average and incremental cost sharing. *Economic Theory* 36, 3 (2008), 379–405.
[30] Hervé Moulin and Scott J. Shenker. 2001. Strategyproof sharing of submodular costs: budget balance versus efficiency. *Economic Theory* 18, 3 (2001), 511–533.
[31] Robert W. Rosenthal. 1973. The network equilibrium problem in integers. *Networks* 3, 1 (1973), 53–59.
[32] Philipp von Falkenhausen and Tobias Harks. 2013. Optimal cost sharing protocols for scheduling games. *Mathematics of Operations Research* 38, 1 (2013), 184–208.

Convex Program Duality, Fisher Markets, and Nash Social Welfare

RICHARD COLE, New York University
NIKHIL R. DEVANUR, Microsoft Research
VASILIS GKATZELIS, Drexel University
KAMAL JAIN, Faira
TUNG MAI, VIJAY V. VAZIRANI, and SADRA YAZDANBOD, Georgia Institute of Technology

CCS Concepts: • **Theory of computation → Approximation algorithms analysis; Market equilibria;**

Additional Key Words and Phrases: Nash social welfare; Fisher market; convex program duality

The main focus of this paper is on the problem of maximizing the Nash social welfare (NSW). In particular, given a collection of indivisible goods that needs to be allocated to a set of agents, our goal is to compute an allocation that maximizes the geometric mean of the agents' utilities. This objective has been studied since the fifties, and is known to provide a natural balance between fairness and efficiency. For additive agent utilities, Cole and Gkatzelis [1] gave the first constant factor approximation algorithm. The natural integer program for maximizing the NSW in this setting is closely related to the Fisher market model: if we relax the integrality constraint of the allocation, i.e., assume that the the goods are divisible, this program reduces to the Eisenberg-Gale (EG) convex program, whose solutions correspond to market equilibria for the linear Fisher market. Therefore, a canonical approach for designing a NSW approximation algorithm would be to compute a fractional allocation via the EG program, and then "round" it to get an integral one. However, Cole and Gkatzelis observed that this program's integrality gap is unbounded, and they were forced to follow an unconventional approach in designing and analyzing their algorithm. This algorithm used an alternative fractional allocation, the *spending-restricted* (SR) equilibrium, and they had to come up with an independent upper bound of the optimal NSW in order to prove that the approximation factor is at most $2e^{1/e} \approx 2.89$.

The absence of a conventional analysis for this problem could be, in part, to blame for the lack of progress on important follow-up problems. For instance, the SR equilibrium introduces constraints that are incompatible with the EG program so, instead of a convex program, Cole and Gkatzelis had to use a complicated algorithm for computing this allocation. Generalizing such an algorithm and proving new upper bounds for the optimal NSW may be non-trivial. In this paper we remove this obstacle by uncovering the underlying structure of the NSW problem and shedding new light on the results of Cole and Gkatzelis. Specifically, we propose a new integer program which, as we show, computes the optimal NSW allocation. More importantly, we prove that the relaxation of

This work was supported by National Science Foundation, under grants CCF-1216019, CCF-1216073, CCF-1161813, CCF-1408635, and CCF-1527568. A full version of this paper is available at https://arxiv.org/abs/1609.06654.
 EC'17, June 26–30, 2017, Cambridge, MA, USA. ACM ISBN 978-1-4503-4527-9/17/06.
 DOI: http://dx.doi.org/10.1145/3033274.3085109

this program computes the SR equilibrium, and, quite surprisingly, we also show that the objective of this program happens to be precisely the upper bound that was used by Cole and Gkatzelis. As a result, this new integer program yields a convex program for computing the SR equilibrium and, unlike the standard program, it has an integrality gap that is bounded by 2.89. In addition to this, we provide a tight analysis of the algorithm of Cole and Gkatzelis to show that its approximation factor is 2, which also puts an upper bound of 2 on the integrality gap of the new program. Further, we prove a lower bound of $e^{1/e} \approx 1.44$ on the integrality gap.

Apart from the results regarding the NSW problem, we also reveal interesting connections between seemingly disparate results, and we provide convex programs for computing market equilibria in generalizations of Fisher's market model. For instance, besides the EG program, there is another very different convex program for the linear Fisher market, due to Shmyrev [2]; however, there were no known connections between these two programs. Using our convex program duality techniques (see below), we show that one can define a dual program for each of them, and the two duals are the same, up to a change of variables. Furthermore, by adding suitable constraints to Shmyrev's program, we obtain the convex program that captures the SR equilibria used by the NSW algorithm.

The spending-restricted market model generalizes Fisher's market model and has potential use beyond its NSW application. Under this model, sellers can declare an upper bound on the money they wish to earn in the market (and take back their unsold good). Therefore, the total amount of money that the buyers can spend on this seller's good is bounded. Another generalization of the linear Fisher model that we study is the *utility restricted* (UR) model. In this model, buyers can declare an upper bound on the amount of utility they wish to derive (and take back the unused part of their money). Thus, in the SR model, the supply of a good is a function of the prices and, in the UR model, the amount of money a buyer spends in the market is a function of the prices. In the presence of these additional constraints, we give a convex program for the second model as well, this time by generalizing the EG program. Existence of equilibria for both models follows from these convex programs. We further show that both models admit rational equilibria, i.e., prices and allocations are rational numbers if all parameters specified in the instance are rational. As a result, the ellipsoid algorithm will find a solution to the convex programs in polynomial time.

For some of the aforementioned results, we use convex program duality. For convex programs with convex objective functions and *linear* constraints, we show that the duals can be constructed using a set of rules almost as simple as those for linear programs. Convex programming duality is usually stated in its most general form, with convex objective functions and convex constraints, and the process of constructing their dual is quite tedious. Following an earlier version of this paper[1], these rules have found several applications in deriving convex programs such as for Fisher markets with spending constraint utilities, transaction costs, and reserve prices, or Arrow-Debreu market with linear utilities. They have also been used in the design of algorithms, such as simplex-like algorithms for spending constraint utilities and perfect price discrimination markets, online algorithms for scheduling and welfare maximization with production costs, as well as for bounding the price of anarchy of certain games and analyzing the convergence of the tatonnement process.

REFERENCES

[1] Richard Cole and Vasilis Gkatzelis. Approximating the Nash social welfare with indivisible items. In *Proceedings of the Forty-Seventh Annual ACM on Symposium on Theory of Computing*, pages 371–380, 2015.

[2] VI Shmyrev. An algorithm for finding equilibrium in the linear exchange model with fixed budgets. *Journal of Applied and Industrial Mathematics*, 3(4):505–518, 2009.

[1]The part of the current paper about convex programming duality had been available online since 2010 as an unpublished manuscript: N. R. Devanur, Fisher Markets and Convex Programs. The manuscript is now incorporated into this paper.

Controlled Dynamic Fair Division

ERIC J. FRIEDMAN, ICSI and UC Berkeley
CHRISTOS-ALEXANDROS PSOMAS, UC Berkeley
SHAI VARDI, California Institute of Technology

In the single-resource dynamic fair division framework there is a homogeneous resource that is shared between agents dynamically arriving and departing over time. When n agents are present, there is only one truly "fair" allocation: each agent receives $1/n$ of the resource. Implementing this static solution in the dynamic world is notoriously impractical; there are too many disruptions to existing allocations: for a new agent to get her fair share, all other agents must give up a small piece.

A natural remedy is simply to restrict the number of allowed disruptions when a new agent arrives. [16] considered this setting, and introduced a natural benchmark - the *fairness ratio* - the ratio of the minimal share to the ideal share ($1/k$ when there are k agents in the system). They described an algorithm that obtains the optimal fairness ratio when $d \geq 1$ disruptions are allowed per arriving agent. However, in systems with high arrival rates even one disruption per arrival can be too costly. We consider the scenario when fewer than one disruption per arrival is allowed. We show that we can maintain high levels of fairness even with significantly fewer than one disruption per arrival. In particular, we present an instance-optimal algorithm (the input to the algorithm is a vector of allowed disruptions) and show that the fairness ratio of this algorithm decays logarithmically with c, where c is the longest number of consecutive time steps in which we are not allowed any disruptions.

We then consider dynamic fair division with multiple, heterogeneous resources. In this model, agents demand the resources in fixed proportions, known in economics as Leontief preferences. We show that the general problem is NP-hard, even if the resource demands are binary and known in advance. We study the case where the fairness criterion is *Dominant Resource Fairness* (DRF), and the demand vectors are binary. We design a generic algorithm for this setting using a reduction to the single-resource case. To prove an impossibility result, we take an integer program for the problem and analyze an algorithm for constructing dual solutions to a "residual" linear program; this approach may be of independent interest.

Additional Key Words and Phrases: Fair Division; Resource Allocation; Dynamic Fair Division

1 INTRODUCTION

Fair division has been a central topic in economics and mathematics (e.g., [2–4, 6, 13, 35, 42, 43]). More recently, it has received more attention in computer science due to its applications to resource sharing in data centers and the cloud (e.g., [5, 12, 18, 37, 46]). Traditionally, research on fair division has focused on static allocations; contemporary resource allocation protocols, however, need to be dynamic in nature. This has led to more research on fairness in the dynamic setting (e.g., [1, 16, 29, 45]): There is some finite amount of resource(s), agents arrive and depart, and the goal is to constantly maintain allocations that are "fair". There are several accepted notions of fairness in the literature, for example, *envy-freeness* (no agent would like to exchange shares with

This work is supported by the National Science Foundation, under grants NSF-1216073, NSF-1161813, CCF1408635, CCF0964033, Templeton Foundation grant 3966, the Leventis Foundation and by the I-CORE in Algorithms Postdoctoral Fellowship.

EC'17, June 26–30, 2017, Cambridge, Massachusetts, USA. © 2017 ACM. ISBN 978-1-4503-4527-9/17/06...$15.00.
DOI: http://dx.doi.org/10.1145/3033274.3085123

any other agent) and *equitability* (every agent has the same utility). Arguably the most widely accepted notion is *proportionality*: if there are n agents in the system, each agent is allocated at least a $1/n$ fraction of what she would receive if she were allocated all of the resource. If there are multiple resources and agents have heterogeneous demands, the notions of fairness become more complex; two of the most common notions in this setting are *Competitive Equilibrium from Equal Incomes* (CEEI) and *Dominant Resource Fairness* (DRF). We elaborate more on these later on.

A major difficulty in maintaining fairness in dynamic settings comes from the price of reallocating resources. Even if there exist good solutions for k agents and for $k+1$ agents, these solutions do not typically include instructions for transitioning from one solution to the other without reclaiming and reallocating all the resources. As an example, consider the case of a single homogeneous resource. If reallocating resources is cheap and efficient, it is trivial to satisfy any and all of the above fairness notions in the dynamic setting: when there are k agents, allocate each one $1/k$ of the resource. When a new agent arrives, reallocate the resource evenly once more; note that this necessitates reducing the allocation of *all* agents, whenever a new agent arrives. If there are many successive arrivals, much of the time could be spent on reallocation, instead of resource consumption. This is an important issue in practice (e.g., [26, 31, 44]).

> "The offline scheduler is not applicable . . . because, if we simply called it each time a resource freed up, we might have to reallocate a large number of machines to obtain the configuration it returns. " [19].

Motivated by these issues, we study dynamic fair division problems where the amount of disruption is a hard constraint.

1.1 The Dynamic Fair Division Model

We first consider the case of a single homogeneous resource.

Dynamic fair division of a single resource. One unit of a homogeneous resource is shared among agents that arrive and depart over time. An allocation for t agents is denoted by a vector $X^t \in [0,1]^t$. The utility of agent j at step t is proportional to $X^t(j)$. An allocation is *feasible* if $S^t = \sum_{j=1}^{t} X^t(j) \le 1$. X and S are usually defined with respect to a resource allocation algorithm; this is omitted from the notation when the algorithm is obvious from context. An allocation algorithm is feasible if it always outputs a feasible allocation. An allocation is *Pareto optimal* if $S^t = 1$. An allocation algorithm is Pareto optimal if it always outputs Pareto optimal allocations. An allocation for t agents is σ_t-*fair* if $\min_{j=1,\dots,t} \{X^t(j)\} \ge \frac{\sigma}{t}$. An allocation algorithm A is σ-fair if it outputs a σ_t-*fair* allocation in the presence of t agents, and $\sigma \le \min_t\{\sigma_t\}$. σ_t is called A's *fairness ratio*.

We restrict our algorithms to disrupt a small number of agents when a new agent arrives: An allocation algorithm is d-disruptive if it is allowed to decrease the allocation of at most d agents at every arrival. Upon departure, the algorithm is not allowed to reduce the allocation of any agent except the departing agent (this is known as *population monotonicity*). Augmenting the resource of any agent is always allowed (for both arrivals and departures).

Example 1.1. Assume we would like to design a Pareto optimal 1-disruptive algorithm for a system with a capacity for 3 agents. The naïve algorithm divides the largest available share equally at each arrival: When the first agent arrives, she is allocated the entire resource; $\sigma_1 = 1$. When the second agent arrives, she is given half of the resource, and the first agent's resource is halved: $\sigma_2 = \frac{\min_i\{X^2(i)\}}{1/2} = 1$. When the third agent arrives, one agent is allocated half of the resource and the two other agents are allocated one quarter of the resource each: $\sigma_3 = \frac{1/4}{1/3} = \frac{3}{4}$. The fairness ratio of this algorithm is $\sigma = \min_i\{\sigma_i\} = \frac{3}{4}$. It is easy to verify that there is no algorithm that guarantees perfect fairness ($\sigma = 1$), even in this simple scenario.

The optimal algorithm is the following [16]: when the second agent arrives, she is given 3/7 of the resource; $\sigma_2 = \frac{3/7}{1/2} = \frac{6}{7}$. When the third agent arrives, the first agent's share is split evenly between the first and third agents, giving the allocation $(2/7, 3/7, 2/7)$; $\sigma_3 = \frac{2/7}{1/3} = \frac{6}{7}$. This fairness ratio of this algorithm is $\frac{6}{7}$.

Define $\sigma^*(d)$ to be the optimal fairness ratio of any d-disruptive mechanism (with an unbounded number of agents). [16] show that $\sigma^*(d) = \left((d+1)\ln\left(\frac{d+1}{d}\right)\right)^{-1}$, for all (integer) $d \geq 1$, and describe an algorithm that achieves this fairness ratio. They also give a $\frac{3(d+1)^2}{2d^2}$ bound on the *envy ratio* of this algorithm, the ratio of the maximum and minimum allocations. In addition, the algorithm accommodates arbitrary arrivals and departures of agents, and it satisfies population monotonicity as well as Pareto optimality. Their analysis relies on a characterization of the optimal allocation as an LP, reducing its feasible region to a certain class of allocations, and then bounding the fairness ratio for this class.

At first glance, one might think that a single disruption per arrival is the best we can hope for; this is true if, for example, we require Pareto optimality (Lemma 1.2). However, if n agents arrive, this still mandates n disruptions overall! We consider what can be done with even fewer disruptions. In particular, we study the problem of maximizing the fairness ratio, when fewer than one disruption is allowed per arrival.

Fewer than one disruption per arrival. Consider the following scenario: an algorithm designer is given a list of constraints: one constraint per arrival, denoting the number of disruptions allowed. The algorithm designer's goal is to design an algorithm that maximizes the fairness ratio subject to these constraints. For now, assume that there are only arrivals - agents arrive and stay in the system indefinitely; we will remove this restriction later on. Ideally, the algorithm designer should design an *instance-optimal* algorithm: one that takes the list of constraints as an input and outputs a set of allocations that maximizes the fairness ratio for that list. We consider the case that fewer than one disruption is allowed per arrival, and model it as follows: the algorithm takes as input a vector ψ (which we call a *control vector*), and is allowed to use d_i donors when the ith agent arrives if $\psi[i] = d_i$. We call this problem *Controlled Dynamic Fair Division (CDFD)*. For simplicity, we only consider *binary* control vectors (i.e., at each time step, the algorithm is either not allowed to use a donor or allowed to use exactly one); it is straightforward to extend the results to non-binary vectors. If ψ has at most c consecutive zeros, we call it a c-control vector. To align with the notation of [16], we say that a c-control vector implies a $\frac{1}{c+1}$-disruptive algorithm. Notice that the setting of [16] is a special case; for d donors per arrival, ψ has "d" at every coordinate.

Let $\sigma^*(\psi)$ be the optimal fairness ratio for a given control vector ψ. We overload the notation and define $\sigma^*\left((c+1)^{-1}\right)$ to be the optimal fairness ratio for all c-control vectors ψ, i.e., $\sigma^*\left((c+1)^{-1}\right) = min_\psi\{\sigma^*(\psi)\}$. Note that, with fewer than one disruption per arrival, Pareto optimality is impossible.

Lemma 1.2. *For any $c > 0$, there is no Pareto optimal algorithm for CDFD that guarantees a fairness ratio of $\sigma((c+1)^{-1}) > 0$.*

Proof. Assume that such an algorithm exists. Let i be the first coordinate for which $\psi[i] = 0$. As the algorithm is Pareto optimal, there is no available resource, and agent i receives nothing. □

One can also consider a more adversarial online setting, in which the control vector is revealed online. If there are no restrictions on the adversary, it is easy to see that no algorithm can guarantee a good fairness ratio: the adversary can simply give the algorithm an arbitrarily long all-zero control vector. We therefore restrict our attention to adversaries limited to control vectors that have bounded length and/or at most c consecutive zeros, for some constant c.

Multi-resource fairness. Consider the case of multiple heterogeneous resources. Let r be the number of resources in the system and, without loss of generality, assume there is one unit of each resource available. As in the single resource case, define $X^t(j)$ to be the allocation of the j-th agent at step t. Notice that the allocation of agent j this time is a vector, not a number.

Every agent i has a demand vector $\mathcal{D}_j \in [0, 1]^r$ over the resources. Let $\mathcal{D}^t$ (or simply $\mathcal{D}$) be the t by r matrix of demands for t agents. For example, if 3 agents with demands $\mathcal{D}_1 = [1, 1/2]$, $\mathcal{D}_2 = [0, 1]$, and $\mathcal{D}_3 = [1, 1]$ are present $\mathcal{D} = \begin{bmatrix} 1 & 1/2 \\ 0 & 1 \\ 1 & 1 \end{bmatrix}$.

Assume that the agents demand the resources in fixed proportions, known in economics as Leontief preferences, and have binary demand vectors. Let $u_j(X^t(j))$ be the utility of agent j for an allocation $X^t(j)$. It is convenient to think of $\mathcal{D}_{j,l}$ as the amount of resource l agent j needs to execute a task. For example, if $r = 3$, agent j with demand vector $\mathcal{D}_j = [1, 0, 1]$, needs one unit of resource 1 and one unit of resource 3 to execute a task. In this example, Leontief preferences imply that given the resource vector $X^t(j) = (\frac{1}{2}, 0, \frac{1}{2})$, the agent would have utility $u_j(X^t(j)) = \frac{1}{2}$. The agent would have the same utility for resource vector $(1, 0, \frac{1}{2})$.

In the case of multiple resources, the definition of fairness is not as straightforward. One could define fairness in a very general way: at every step t the minimum utility of an agent should be $L(t)$, for some non increasing function $L(t)$, and the maximum utility should be $U(t)$. $L(t)$ dictates the lower bound on the satisfaction of each agent, maintaining fairness in terms of proportionality. $U(t)$ maintains fairness in the sense of envy-freeness: $\min_t \left\{\frac{U(t)}{L(t)}\right\}$ is an upper bound on the envy of such an allocation. (Intuitively, an allocation of $\left(\frac{1}{3}, \frac{1}{4}, \frac{1}{4}\right)$ is more fair than an allocation of $\left(\frac{1}{2}, \frac{1}{4}, \frac{1}{4}\right)$.) Define *General Dynamic Fair Division* (*GDFD*) to be this problem; the inputs are agents' demands $\mathcal{D}$, the number of resources r, and vectors L and U, and the algorithm is asked to decide whether there exist feasible allocations (i.e., ones that satisfy all the constraints).

Dominant Resource Fairness. In the full version of this paper we show that *GDFD* is computationally intractable (assuming P ≠ NP), even in simple settings and clairvoyant allocation algorithms (ones that know in advance the number of agents that will arrive and their demands). We focus on a less general, well-studied notion of fairness: *Dominant Resource Fairness* (DRF), introduced by [18].

The *dominant resource* of an agent is the resource for which the agent's task requires the largest fraction of total availability. The *dominant share* of an agent is the fraction of her dominant resource that she receives. The DRF algorithm seeks to maximize the minimum dominant share. DRF can also be interpreted as the leximin mechanism, i.e., it maximizes the minimum utility, and subject to that, maximizes the second minimum utility, and so on, when applied to Leontief utilities [30]. DRF has multiple advantages: it is Pareto optimal, strategy-proof, envy-free, and proportional: it guarantees to each agent a utility of

$$DRF_{\mathcal{D}^t} = \left(\max_{l=1,\ldots,r} \sum_{j=1}^{t} \mathcal{D}_{j,l}^t\right)^{-1}.$$

The notion of DRF is naturally extendable to the dynamic case:

Dynamic fairness for multiple resources. An allocation is σ_t-*DRF* fair at step t, if

$$\min_{j=1,\ldots,t} \{u_j(X^t(j))\} \geq \sigma_t DRF_{\mathcal{D}^t}.$$

An allocation algorithm is σ-*DRF* fair if outputs a σ_t-*DRF* fair allocation when t agents are present, and $\sigma \geq \min_t\{\sigma_t\}$. Let $\sigma^*(d,r)$ be the optimal fairness ratio in the case of $r > 1$ resources, when d donors are allowed at every arrival, over all possible agent demands $\mathcal{D}$. We allow d to be less than 1; we discuss this in more detail later on. Define *Dynamic Dominant Resource Fairness* (DDRF) to be the problem of maximizing $\sigma^*(d,r)$.

1.2 Main Results and Techniques

Controlled dynamic fair division. Given a binary control vector ψ as an input, the goal is to output a set of allocations that gives the best possible fairness ratio. We describe an instance-optimal algorithm for this case, which we call Skip. Skip has two stages; in the first (which we sometimes refer to as the *preprocessing* stage), it computes the optimal fairness ratio $\sigma^*(\psi)$; in the second, it allocates the resource frugally, giving each agent the least amount of resource possible in order to maintain $\sigma^*(\psi)$.

Theorem 1.3. *Skip is an instance-optimal algorithm for controlled dynamic fair division.*

To prove Theorem 1.3, we show that for any allocation algorithm $\mathcal{A}$ and any control vector ψ, if the allocations produced by $\mathcal{A}$ for ψ give a fairness ratio of σ, then the allocations produced by Skip do too. Although, by Lemma 1.2, Skip cannot be Pareto optimal, it can accommodate departures, and is population-monotone - it does not disrupt any agent when there is a departure (except the departing agent); it is only allowed to re-allocate the departing agent's share.

We would like to provide a lower bound[1] σ on the fairness ratio of Skip. This is particularly important for unbounded systems; while Skip is optimal for any finite control vector ψ,[2] it is not defined on infinite vectors, which are necessary for systems that can accommodate an arbitrary number of agents. In such a case, we skip the preprocessing stage of Skip, and simply give Skip σ as an auxiliary input. As long as σ is upper bounded by the worst fairness ratio possible for any number of agents, the allocations produced by Skip will be feasible. We bound $\sigma^*\left((c+1)^{-1}\right)$, the optimal fairness ratio possible for all control vectors ψ with at most c consecutive zeros (in particular, including infinite vectors such as $(1,0,0,0,1,0,0,0,\ldots)$). This also gives us a bound on the performance of Skip in the adversarial online setting, when the adversary is limited to selecting vectors with at most c consecutive zeros. (In the adversarial online an adversary chooses the control vector and it is revealed online - when the ith agent arrives, the ith coordinate of the control vector is revealed.)

Showing bounds for $\sigma^*\left((c+1)^{-1}\right)$ is much more complicated than for $\sigma^*(d)$, $d \geq 1$: there are infinitely many possible control vectors (as opposed to exactly one for constant $d \geq 1$), and the allocations Skip produced for each of these are different; furthermore, they are not as "well behaved" as the allocations for $d \geq 1$. Compare Figures 1 and 2.[3]. Figure 1 shows the allocations created by the optimal algorithm when 1 donor is allowed at every step (for an unbounded number of agents, truncated at 100). Figure 2 shows the allocations created for 4 different infinite control vectors (truncated at 30 agents). The difficulty in the second setting comes from several facts: the allocations are not monotone, they are not pointwise comparable, and they are not simple transformations one of the other. Furthermore, the allocations do not necessarily take their maxima at the limit. Still, in both cases, the total allocation converges to a limit as the number of agents grows (in the

[1]Note that upper bounds on the fairness ratio are negative results, while lower bounds are positive results.

[2]We do not explicitly compute the running times of the algorithms in this paper, but all are easily implemented in time linear in the size of the input.

[3]The graphs are normalized by artificially setting $\sigma = 1$, and then running the respective optimal algorithms without any constraints on the amount of available resource. While this obviously leads to the total allocation being greater than 1, it is still instructive, as the optimal fairness ratio of these algorithms can be easily be deduced from these plots - it is simply the inverse of the maximal total allocation created

second case, *all* infinite allocations that obey certain natural requirements converge to the *same* limit (Theorem 1.6)). The horizontal line in both figures denotes this limit. It is easy to see (this is formally proved for the two cases in [16] and Section 2 respectively), that the first set of allocations takes its maximum at the limit, while the second case does not.[4]

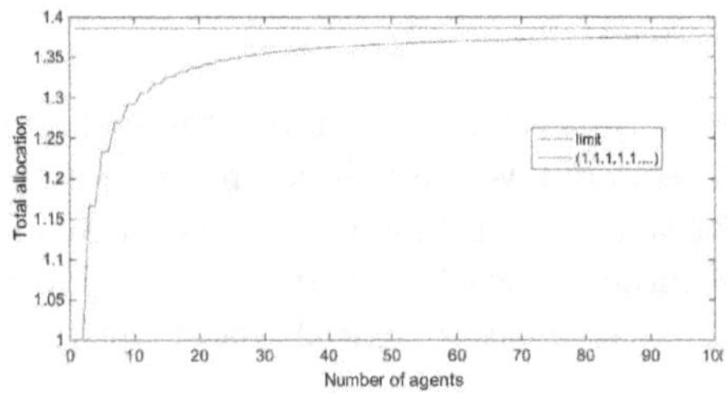

Fig. 1. Optimal values of S for $d = 1$.

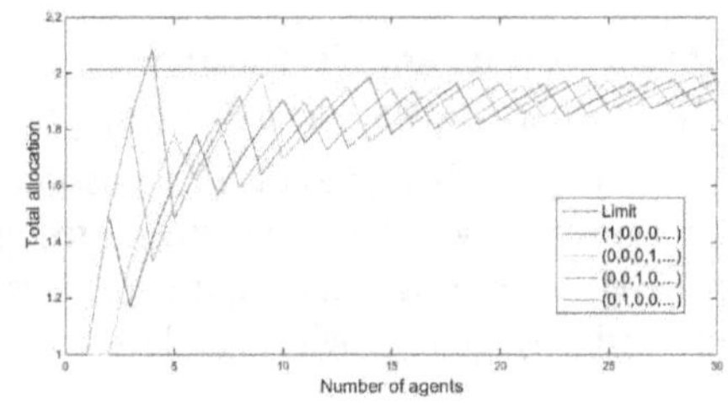

Fig. 2. Optimal values of S for some 2-control vectors.

We show almost matching upper and lower bounds for the optimal fairness ratio attainable for any (possibly infinite) c-control vector. Let $H_n = \sum_{i=1}^{n} \frac{1}{i}$ be the n-th harmonic number.

Theorem 1.4. *The optimal fairness ratio of CDFD for any c-control vector is bounded by*

$$(H_{c+1})^{-1} \geq \sigma^* \left((c+1)^{-1}\right) \geq \left(H_{2c+3} - \tfrac{1}{2}\right)^{-1}.$$

In order to prove Theorem 1.4, we need to be able to argue about allocations of optimal algorithms for *any* ψ. For this, we define *basic* control vectors - vectors that always have exactly 1 donor every $c+1$ agents, and show that for any c-control vector, there exists some basic c-control vector whose allocations are pointwise greater. For any c, there are exactly $c+1$ basic control vectors, therefore it remains to reason about them. For the cases $c = 1$ and $c = 2$, it turns out that the worst allocations are always at the limit. In order to show this, we consider allocations (of the basic control vectors) that are a certain distance apart (specifically $(c+1)(c+2)$), and show that these special allocations are monotone increasing, and each is greater than the $(c+1)(c+2)$ allocations that came before it. This gives exact bounds:

Theorem 1.5. *The optimal fairness ratio of CDFD for any c control vector for $c = 1$ and $c = 2$ are*

$$\sigma^* \left((2)^{-1}\right) = 2(3\ln 3)^{-1} \quad \textit{and} \quad \sigma^* \left((3)^{-1}\right) = 3(4\ln 4)^{-1}.$$

For details on the proof we refer the reader to the full version of this paper. For $c > 2$, we consider a set of allocations that are pointwise greater than the allocations for all basic vectors simultaneously, and bound them, to obtain Theorem 1.4. In addition, we show that as the number of agents grows, the optimal allocations for all basic c-control vectors converge to the same value:

Theorem 1.6. *There exists a number n_0 such that, for all $c > 2$, all c-control vectors, and present agents $t > n_0$, the allocation of* Skip *is σ_t-fair, where $\sigma_t = (c+1)\left((c+2)\ln(c+2)\right)^{-1}$.*

[4]It might be tempting to think that, as in Figure 2, there always exists *some* basic c-control vector (see Section 2 for a definition of basic c-control vectors) that takes its maximum at the limit, and this is indeed the case for $c < 8$ (we do not prove this, but it is easy to verify). However, for $c \geq 8$, *every* basic c-control vector has its maximum at a finite number of agents. For more details we refer the reader to the full version of this paper.

We show that SKIP can accommodate departures, and therefore all the bounds on $\sigma^*\left((c+1)^{-1}\right)$ hold even when we allow agents to depart. We omit the proof due to lack of space. For more details we refer the reader to the full version of this paper. We summarize our main results for $\sigma^*\left((c+1)^{-1}\right)$ in Table 1.

Disruptions	**Bound on the fairness ratio**
$d \geq 1$	$\left((d+1)\ln\left(\frac{d+1}{d}\right)\right)^{-1}$ (tight) [16]
2^{-1}	$2\,(3\ln 3)^{-1}$ (tight)
3^{-1}	$3\,(4\ln 4)^{-1}$ (tight)
$(c+1)^{-1}, c > 2$	$(H_{c+1})^{-1} \geq \sigma^*\left((c+1)^{-1}\right) \geq \left(H_{2c+3} - \frac{1}{2}\right)^{-1}$
	$(c+1)\,((c+2)\ln(c+2))^{-1}$ (asymptotic bound, tight)

Table 1. Results for a single resource

The adversarial online case. In the adversarial online case, if there are no restrictions on the adversary, there is no lower bound on the fairness ratio, as the adversary can give an infinite vector of zeros. If, however, there is an a-priori upper bound n on the number of agents that can arrive (with no restriction on the number of consecutive zeros), SKIP obtains a fairness ratio of $\sigma = \frac{1}{H_n}$.

Multiple resource dynamic fair division. In the multiple resource case, we consider the *uncontrolled* setting. The input to the algorithm is a demand matrix $\mathcal{D}$ and the number of disruptions allowed per arrival, d. We consider two scenarios: in the first, the *clairvoyant* setting, $\mathcal{D}$ is known in advance. In the *non-clairvoyant* (or online) setting, row i of $\mathcal{D}$ is revealed upon arrival of agent i. We focus on two notions of fairness, *GDFD* and *DDRF*.

Our first result is that *GDFD* is NP-hard:

THEOREM 1.7. *GDFD is* NP*-hard, even for* 2 *resources,* 1 *donor, binary demand vectors, and clairvoyant algorithms.*

Due to lack space we omit the proof; for more details we refer the reader to the full version of this paper. We do not know if the same is true for less general notions of fairness.

OPEN PROBLEM 1. *Is there a polynomial time algorithm for computing $\sigma^*(d,r)$ for DDRF?*

OPEN PROBLEM 2. *Is there a polynomial time algorithm for computing $\sigma^*(d,r)$ when the notion of fairness is CEEI?*

In Section 3 we consider *DDRF*, for binary demand vectors. To see why the techniques of the single resource case do not extend to the multi-resource case, consider the following simple example for $d = 1$: Three agents arrive; the first has a demand vector $[1,0]$, the second $[0,1]$, and the third $[1,1]$. The following algorithm gives the optimal allocation of $2/3$ (see Section 4 for the upper bound): the first two agents receive $2/3$ of their respective resource (we do not use a donor at the second arrival), and at the third arrival, one of the two agents has her allocation reduced by half, and the arriving agent is given $1/3$ of that resource. $1/3$ of the other resource is taken from the "bank" - the resource that was left unallocated. It is easy to see that a non-clairvoyant algorithm can never do as well as a clairvoyant one (in contrast to the single resource case): in the non-clairvoyant case, if an agent with demand $[0,1]$ arrives, how much do we allocate her? Even if we know three agents will arrive in total, and the second one has demand $[1, 0]$, if the third agent has demand vector $[1, 0]$, we "should have" given the first agent all of the first resource, to get a fairness ratio of 1, but we have to allow for the possibility of the third agent's demand being $[1, 1]$. To complicate matters further, it is possible to find examples where solutions that seem intuitively correct are wrong; consider the following set of demands:

$$[0, 1], [1, 0], [0, 1], [1, 0], \mathbf{[1, 0]}, [1, 1], [1, 1].$$

Surprisingly, the only optimal algorithm uses an agent with demand $[0, 1]$ as a donor when the fifth agent (who has demand $[1, 0]$) arrives![5]

We prove upper and lower bounds on $\sigma^*(d, r)$ for *DDRF* for the non-clairvoyant setting for three cases: (1) $d = kr$ for integer k, (2) $d = 1$ and (3) $d = (c + 1)^{-1}$ for $c > 0$. For the lower bounds (positive results), we use the single resource algorithms as subroutines. The challenge is choosing which donor to use when only one donor is allowed. Our negative results use reductions to single resource upper bounds.

Theorem 1.8. *The optimal fairness ratio of DDRF for $d = k \cdot r$ donors and r resources is bounded by*

$$\left((kr + 1)\ln\left(\frac{kr + 1}{kr}\right)\right)^{-1} \geq \sigma^*(kr, r) \geq \left((k + 1)\ln\left(\frac{k + 1}{k}\right)\right)^{-1}.$$

Theorem 1.9. *The optimal fairness ratio of DDRF for $d = 1$ donors and $r \geq 2$ resources is bounded by*

- $\sigma^*(1, 2) \geq 2(3\ln 3)^{-1} \approx 0.6068$
- $\sigma^*(1, 3) \geq 3(4\ln 4)^{-1}$
- $\sigma^*(1, r) \geq \left(H_{2r+1} - \frac{1}{2}\right)^{-1}, r > 3.$

Theorem 1.10. *The optimal fairness ratio of DDRF for r resources and $(c + 1)^{-1}$ donors (1 donor allowed per $c + 1$ arrivals) is bounded by*

$$(H_{c+1})^{-1} \geq \sigma^*\left((c + 1)^{-1}, r\right) \geq \left(H_{2r(c+1)+1} - \frac{1}{2}\right)^{-1}.$$

The gap between the upper and lower bounds for *DDRF* is far from tight. Even for $d = 1$, $r = 2$, a seemingly simple case, the best lower bound we can show is is $2(3\ln 3)^{-1} \approx 0.6068$, by using the single resource algorithm with 1-control vectors ($c = 1$). An immediate upper bound is $(\ln 4)^{-1} \approx 0.7213$: the fairness ratio $\sigma^*(d, r)$ is non-increasing in the number of resources r, and we have tight bounds for $\sigma^*(d, 1)$ from [16] (a subtle but necessary condition for this argument to go through is that *DRF* reduces to proportionality when there is only one resource). In Section 4 we improve this upper bound to the following.

Theorem 1.11. *The optimal fairness ratio of DDRF for $d = 1$ and $r \geq 2$ resources is bounded by*

$$\sigma^*(1, r) \leq 0.6318\ldots$$

Our proof technique for Theorem 1.11 may be of independent interest. We first identify a set of bad inputs (demand matrices $\mathcal{D}$): n $[0, 1]$'s followed by n $[1, 0]$'s, followed by a series of $2n$ $[1, 1]$'s. We describe the optimal mixed integer program for maximizing the fairness ratio. Let Z be the set of all integer variables. Given an algorithm for *DDRF* we can simulate its execution on the bad input and fix these integer variables. Fixing Z allows us to use LP duality! We take the dual with respect to the remaining (non-integer) variables, and give a procedure for constructing feasible dual solutions, for any choice of Z, and therefore any algorithm for *DDRF*.

[5] This can be verified by optimizing the fairness for each choice of donors - when the donors are fixed, finding the optimal fairness can be easily computed by a linear program, as we show in Section 4.

Notice that the bound is independent of r. For $r > 2$, the same technique does not seem to provide better results, at least not for choices of $\mathcal{D}$ that are the most natural; for example, for $r = 3$, one would expect that the worst inputs are n $[0, 0, 1]$'s, followed by n $[0, 1, 0]$'s, followed by n $[1, 0, 0]$'s, followed by a series of $3n$ $[1, 1, 1]$'s. Surprisingly, the fairness ratio for these inputs is an increasing function of n, at least for n small enough for us to verify computationally.

An interesting open problem is finding tight bounds for $\sigma^*(d, r)$. Our algorithms so far rely on a reduction to *CDFD*. We conjecture that this is not necessary. Constructing algorithms that accommodate departures is also an intriguing open direction.

Open Problem 3. *Compute the exact value of $\sigma^*(d, r)$ for DDRF, for all $d > 0, r > 1$.*

Open Problem 4. *Compute the exact value of $\sigma^*(d, r)$ for DDRF, for all $d > 0$, $r > 1$, when allowing departures.*

Note that our results for multiple resources only apply to binary demand vectors.

Open Problem 5. *Compute the value of $\sigma^*(d, r)$ for DDRF, for all $d > 0$, $r > 1$ for arbitrary demand vectors.*

Our main results for the optimal fairness ratio of *DDRF* are summarized in the following table.

Resources	**Disruptions**	**Bound on the fairness ratio**
2	1	$0.6318\ldots \geq \sigma^*(1,2) \geq 2\,(3\ln 3)^{-1} \approx 0.6068$
3	1	$0.6318\ldots \geq \sigma^*(1,3) \geq 3\,(4\ln 4)^{-1}$
$r > 3$	1	$0.6318\ldots \geq \sigma^*(1,r) \geq \left(H_{2r+1} - \frac{1}{2}\right)^{-1}$
r	kr	$\left((kr+1)\ln\left(\frac{kr+1}{kr}\right)\right)^{-1} \geq \sigma^*(kr,r) \geq \left((k+1)\ln\left(\frac{k+1}{k}\right)\right)^{-1}$
r	$(c+1)^{-1}$	$(H_{c+1})^{-1} \geq \sigma^*\left((c+1)^{-1}, r\right) \geq \left(H_{2r(c+1)+1} - \frac{1}{2}\right)^{-1}$

Table 2. Results for many resources and DRF

1.3 Related Work

Competitive Equilibrium from Equal Incomes (CEEI) was introduced by [32] and has been studied extensively in the economics and theoretical computer science literature (for some recent results see [11], [7], [33], [10], [8]). Dominant Resource Fairness was proposed by [18]. DRF attracted significant attention from the computer systems community [17, 25, 27, 41], as well as the theoretical computer science community [15, 24, 29, 34]. It is interesting to note that DRF can also be interpreted as the Kalai-Smorodinsky bargaining solution [28].

[45] was the first to study the problem of online fair cake cutting when agents arrive, receive a piece and depart. He showed how several well-known fair division solutions (cut-and-choose, Dubins-Spanier, etc) can be adapted to satisfy desirable properties in an online setting with a single (heterogeneous) divisible cake. More recently, and closer to our problem, [29] introduced a model of dynamic allocations. However, their model only considers arrivals and their main algorithm reserves resources for future arrivals; it does not allow the reallocation of resources, or agents to depart. This leads to allocations that satisfy neither fairness nor Pareto efficiency, as resources are left idle.

[21] study the problem of repeatedly allocating a single item between competing agents, and give allocation algorithms that don't allow monetary transfers with good competitive ratios with

respect to optimal allocation algorithms with payments. [39] studied the problem of re-dividing a two-dimensional resource, subject to fairness and "geometric" constraints on the allocations.

The idea of making a small number of alterations to maintain a good solution in online settings had been studied for other problems. In online scheduling, one of the earliest works is by [36], who show that linear preemption in the number of tasks yields a competitive ratio of $O(\log n)$ on makespan, where n is the number of tasks. Preemption in their context means reassigning jobs to a different machine. [38] study online scheduling when the migration is bounded by a constant, and [14] who study a similar problem with bounded migrations, where the capacity of change is based on the size of the new input. [23] consider online matching, online flow and online scheduling, and the number of changes they allow is an amortized constant per step. For scheduling they show a $O(\log\log(nm))$ approximation to the makespan, where n is the number of tasks and m is the number of machines. Other examples include [20] and [22] who show how to maintain an online Steiner tree, vertices arriving online, where the algorithm can change an edge at every arrival; [9] and [40] who consider reoptimization with costs.

2 SINGLE RESOURCE

In this section we study CDFD. The algorithm is given as input a binary c-control vector ψ (Definition 2.1). A solution consists of a fairness ratio σ and a set of allocations $A_1, \ldots, A_{|\psi|}$, one for each number of agents present t, such that: (1) for every $1 \le t \le |\psi|$, the fairness ratio σ_t is at least σ, and (2) some agent's resource is reduced from step t to step $t+1$ if and only if $\psi[t+1] = 1$. Note that (as we only consider binary vectors) only one agent can have their resource reduced at any time. In some cases (for example, when the control vectors are unbounded), we allow the algorithm to receive σ as an auxiliary input, in which case a possible output is "infeasible", if no such set of allocations exists. For now, we assume that agents only arrive, and do not depart; we can use t both for the time and the number of agents present. We show how to augment Skip to accommodate departures in the full version of this paper.

Definition 2.1. [Control vector] Let ψ^N be a binary vector of length N. $\psi^N[i] = 1$ means that we use a donor when agent i arrives, and a $\psi^N[i] = 0$ means we do not. If the maximal number of consecutive 0s is c, we call this a *c-control vector.*

We define a *basic c-control vector* to be one in which there is exactly one donor every $c+1$ arrivals; otherwise the control vector is non-basic. There are $c+1$ possible basic control vectors.

Example 2.2. For $c = 2$, the three possible basic control vectors are:

(1) (0,1,0,0,1,0,0,1,0,...), denoted $(0,1,0)^\infty$,
(2) (0,0,1,0,0,1,0,0,1,...), denoted $(0,0,1)^\infty$, or $(0^2,1)^\infty$.
(3) (1,0,0,1,0,0,1,0,0,...), denoted $(1,0,0)^\infty$, or $(1,0^2)^\infty$.

We also use the following definition.

Definition 2.3. Let $A = (a_1, \ldots, a_t)$ and be $B = (b_1, \ldots, b_t)$ be two sorted vectors. We say that *A dominates B*, denoted $A \succeq B$, if $\forall i \in [1,t]$, $a_i \ge b_i$.

2.1 Skip - an Instance-Optimal Algorithm

Definition 2.4 (Algorithm Skip). Algorithm Skip receives as an input a control vector ψ. Set $n = |\psi|$. Skip has a preprocessing stage (which we describe after the main algorithm description), in which it computes the optimal σ. When agent $1 \le i \le n$ arrives, allocate her $\frac{\sigma}{i}$ of the resource. If $\psi[i] = 1$, take the agent with the most resource to be the donor, and reduce her allocation to $\frac{\sigma}{i}$ as well.

The preprocessing stage is the following: simulate the arrivals of the agents $1, \ldots, n$, with $\sigma = 1$, and compute the sum of allocations at each step, S_i. Set the optimal fairness ratio to be $\sigma = (\max_{1 \le i \le n}\{S_i\})^{-1}$.

First, note that the allocations created by Skip are always feasible, by the choice of σ. We prove Skip is optimal among all feasible allocation algorithms, for any control vector.

Theorem 1.3. *Skip is an instance-optimal algorithm for controlled dynamic fair division.*

Proof. Let ψ be an input for any allocation algorithm $\mathcal{A}$ and Skip. Let σ be the maximum fairness ratio achievable by $\mathcal{A}$ and σ' the maximum fairness ratio achievable by Skip. We consider Skip when σ' is replaced by σ during its execution. We show that Skip is feasible in this case, therefore $\sigma' \ge \sigma$. We assume w.l.o.g. that $\mathcal{A}$ never increases the allocation of any agent (except the arriving agents).

Let $\mathcal{A}^t$ and Skip^t be the sorted allocations of $\mathcal{A}$ and Skip, respectively, for t agents in the system. It suffices to show that $A^t \succeq \text{Skip}^t$ for all $t \le |\psi|$. The proof is by induction on the number of agents in the system, t.

The base case: By the definition of Skip, $\text{Skip}^1(1) = \sigma$. Because $\mathcal{A}$'s fairness ratio is σ, it must hold that $\mathcal{A}^1(1) \ge \sigma$.

The inductive step: Assume the statement holds for $t-1$ agents. We show it holds for t. There are two cases: $\psi[t] = 0$ and $\psi[t] = 1$.

Case $\psi[t] = 0$ **:** Let the allocation of Skip at time $t-1$ be $(\text{Skip}_1^{t-1}, \ldots, \text{Skip}_{t-1}^{t-1})$. Then, at time t we have $\text{Skip}^t = (\text{Skip}_1^{t-1}, \ldots, \text{Skip}_{t-1}^{t-1}, \frac{\sigma}{t})$. Algorithm $\mathcal{A}$ will allocate an amount of resource $x \ge \frac{\sigma}{t}$ to the incoming agent. Let the allocation of $\mathcal{A}$ at time $t-1$ be $(\mathcal{A}_1^{t-1}, \mathcal{A}_2^{t-1}, \ldots, \mathcal{A}_{t-1}^{t-1})$. Then

$$\mathcal{A}^t = (\mathcal{A}_1^{t-1}, \mathcal{A}_2^{t-1}, \ldots, \mathcal{A}_j^{t-1}, x, \mathcal{A}_{j+1}^{t-1}, \ldots, \mathcal{A}_{t-1}^{t-1}),$$

for some $0 \le j \le t-1$. It is easy to see that $\mathcal{A}^t \succeq \left(A_1^{t-1}, A_2^{t-1}, \ldots, A_{t-1}^{t-1}, \frac{\sigma}{t}\right)$ for any such value of j. Furthermore, by the induction hypothesis,

$$\left(\mathcal{A}_1^{t-1}, \mathcal{A}_2^{t-1}, \ldots, \mathcal{A}_{t-1}^{t-1}, \frac{\sigma}{t}\right) \succeq (\text{Skip}_1^{t-1}, \ldots, \text{Skip}_{t-1}^{t-1}, \frac{\sigma}{t}) = \text{Skip}^t.$$

This concludes the proof for $\psi[t] = 0$.

Case $\psi[t] = 1$ **:** Starting with the allocation vector at time $t-1$, $\mathcal{A}^{t-1}$, we break the allocation changes at time t into two steps:

(1) Reduce the share of the donor, to get $\hat{\mathcal{A}}^{t-1}$.
(2) Allocate x to the incoming agent, to obtain $\mathcal{A}^t$.

Denote $\mathcal{A}^{\min} = (\mathcal{A}_2^{t-1}, \ldots \mathcal{A}_{t-1}^{t-1}, \frac{\sigma}{t})$. We show that at the end of the first step, $\hat{\mathcal{A}}^{t-1} \succeq \mathcal{A}^{\min}$. The second step is identical to the $\psi[t] = 0$ case, hence we can combine the two results to conclude that $A^t \succeq \text{Skip}^t$. Assume algorithm $\mathcal{A}$ reduced the allocation of an agent from $\mathcal{A}_j^{t-1}$ to y, where $1 \le j \le t-1$ (possibly $\mathcal{A}_j^{t-1} = y$). There is some $k, j \le k \le t-1$ such that $\mathcal{A}_k^{t-1} \ge y \ge \mathcal{A}_{k+1}^{t-1}$. Then,

$$\hat{\mathcal{A}}^{t-1} = (\mathcal{A}_1^{t-1}, \mathcal{A}_2^{t-1}, \ldots, \mathcal{A}_{j-1}^{t-1}, \mathcal{A}_{j+1}^{t-1}, \mathcal{A}_{j+2}^{t-1}, \ldots, \mathcal{A}_k^{t-1}, y, \mathcal{A}_{k+1}^{t-1}, \ldots \mathcal{A}_{t-1}^{t-1}).$$

For $i \in [1, j-1]$, $\hat{\mathcal{A}}_i^{t-1} \ge \mathcal{A}_i^{\min}$. For $i \in [j, k]$, $\hat{\mathcal{A}}_i^{t-1} = \mathcal{A}_i^{\min}$. Then, by definition of y, $\hat{\mathcal{A}}_{k+1}^{t-1} = y \ge \mathcal{A}_{k+1}^{t-1} = A_{k+1}^{\min}$. Similarly, $\hat{A}_i^{t-1} \ge \mathcal{A}_i^{\min}$, for all $i \in [k+1, t-2]$. For the last term, we note that since $\mathcal{A}$ is σ-fair, $\mathcal{A}_{t-1}^{t-1} \ge \frac{\sigma}{t-1} \ge \frac{\sigma}{t}$ (possibly y is the last share, but then $y \ge \frac{\sigma}{t}$ as $\mathcal{A}$ is σ-fair). □

2.2 Reduction to Basic Control Vectors

We wish to compute a lower bound (positive result) on the fairness ratio of Skip for *all* control vectors, but the optimal fairness ratio for any control vector depends on the vector itself. We show that basic control vectors have the worst fairness ratio; hence in order to provide a lower bound on the fairness ratio, it suffices to analyze basic control vectors. We allow Skip to receive a fairness ratio, σ as an auxiliary input. Denote the (possibly infinite) set of allocations of Skip when ψ^N is the control vector and σ is the fairness ratio by $\text{Skip}(\psi^N, \sigma)$. It will be useful to think of the unallocated resource as a "bank": Let $\text{bank}(\psi^N, t) = 1 - S(\psi^N, t)$.

We want to show that for any legal c-control vector ψ^N and real number σ, it holds that if $\text{Skip}(\hat{\psi}^N, \sigma)$ is feasible, then $\text{Skip}(\psi^N, \sigma)$ is feasible, where $\hat{\psi}^N$ is a basic c-control vector. To this end, we define a series of control vectors $\hat{\psi}^N = \psi_1^N, \psi_2^N, \ldots, \psi_k^N = \psi^N$ such that if $\text{Skip}(\psi_i^N, \sigma)$ is feasible, then $\text{Skip}(\psi_{i+1}^N, \sigma)$ is feasible, for all $1 \le i < k$. We define these vectors inductively: Let t_i^* be the leftmost coordinate on which ψ_i^N and ψ^N differ. The first $t_i^* - 1$ entries of ψ_{i+1}^N are the same as ψ_i^N, the t_i^*-th entry becomes the same as $\psi^N[t_i^*]$, and the remainder continues as $(0^c1)^\infty$.

Example 2.5. Let $\psi^7 = (0, 1, 1, 1, 0, 1, 0, 0, 1)$. We derive the ψ_i^7s.

$$\begin{aligned}\hat{\psi}^N = \psi_1^7 &= (0, 1), (0, 0, 1)^\infty,\\ \psi_2^7 &= (0, 1, 1), (0, 0, 1)^\infty,\\ \psi_3^7 &= (0, 1, 1, 1), (0, 0, 1)^\infty\\ \psi_4^7 &= (0, 1, 1, 1, 0, 1), (0, 0, 1)^\infty = \psi^7(0, 0, 1)^\infty\end{aligned}$$

Lemma 2.6. *For every c-control vector ψ, there exists some basic c-control vector ψ' such that $\sigma^*(\psi) \ge \sigma^*(\psi')$.*

Proof. We prove that, if $\text{Skip}(\psi_i^N, \sigma)$ is feasible, then $\text{Skip}(\psi_{i+1}^N, \sigma)$ is feasible, for all steps t such that $t = t_i^* \pmod{c+1}$ in Lemma 2.7. We then show the same holds for steps $t \ne t_i^* \pmod{c+1}$ in Lemma 2.8. □

Notice that $X(\psi_i^N)$ and $X(\psi_{i+1}^N)$ are identical up to step $t_i^* - 1$. Then, on step t_i^*, necessarily $\psi_i^N[t_i^*] = 0$, $\psi_{i+1}^N[t_i^*] = 1$.

Lemma 2.7. *$X(\psi_i^N, t) \ge X(\psi_{i+1}^N, t)$ for all $t = t_i^* \pmod{c+1}$.*

The proof of Lemma 2.7 is by simple induction and is deferred to the full version of this paper. Showing that if $\text{Skip}(\psi_i^N, \sigma)$ is feasible, then $\text{Skip}(\psi_{i+1}^N, \sigma)$ is feasible, for steps $t \ne t_i^* \pmod{c+1}$ is more involved. First observe that there exists some t_{max} such that, for all steps $t > t_{max}$, $X(\psi_{i+1}^N, t)$ is identical to the allocation of some basic control vector at step t (as the allocations produced by Skip are memoryless). Hence, it suffices to show the result for all $t \le t_{max}$. The value of t_{max} is computed as follows: Let p be number of 0s between t_i^* and the previous 1, and $p' = c + 1 - p$. In Example 2.5, for ψ_4^7, $p = 1$, $p' = 2$. Set $k = t_i^* - (c + 2) + p'$. Once the largest share is $\frac{\sigma}{k}$ (and the second largest is strictly smaller), the allocation is the same as it would have been at time k for some basic control vector (in Example 2.5, this allocation is $\left(\frac{1}{4}, \frac{1}{5}, \frac{1}{6}, \frac{1}{6}, \ldots\right)$). A straightforward calculation gives $t_{max} = t_i^* + (c + 1)(k - 1) = (c + 2)t_i^* + (c + 1)(p' - c - 3)$. Note that this is *exactly* the time at which the allocations converge.

Lemma 2.8. *For all $t \ne t_i^* \pmod{c+1}$, $t \in [t_i^*, t_{max}]$, $\text{bank}(\psi_{i+1}^N, t) \ge \sum_{j=1}^{c} \frac{\sigma}{t+j}$.*

The proof for this Lemma is quite technical; as it mostly involves applications of known techniques, it is deferred to the full version of this paper.

2.3 Bounding the Fairness Ratio of Skip

The allocations created by Skip have a particular structure: they resemble a segment of the harmonic series, with some doubled entries (see Example 2.9). Even though we showed that in order to bound the fairness ratio, it is enough to consider only basic control vectors, each basic control vector has a different fairness ratio. Nevertheless, we would like to provide some upper bound on the fairness ratio of Skip, for each c. We give two types of bounds: an upper bound that applies to all control vectors for any number of agents, and an asymptotic bound. The asymptotic bound is particularly useful for systems that wish to be able to accommodate an unbounded number of agents, and in which the amount of time the system will have fewer than n_0 agents (for some constant n_0) is vanishingly small. In this case, one can set the fairness ratio to be the asymptotic fairness ratio, with an arbitrary "quick fix" heuristic for when there are fewer than n_0 agents in the system (for example, allowing slightly more disruptions to guarantee the asymptotic fairness ratio).

To better characterize these allocations, we need some notation. Elements of an allocation (an element is a real number[6]) that appear once are called *singletons*, and those that appear twice *doubles*. We use the following to make our notation more compact.

$\bowtie_c$ represents a double followed by c singletons, followed by a double, and so on, ending in c singletons. Let the share before $\bowtie_c$ be $\frac{\sigma}{i}$; the first double of $\bowtie_c$ is $\frac{\sigma}{i+1}, \frac{\sigma}{i+1}$. Let the share after $\bowtie_c$ be $\frac{\sigma}{j}$; the last singleton of $\bowtie_c$ is $\frac{\sigma}{j-1}$.

$\rightharpoonup_k$ represents $k-1$ more singletons continuing the series, $k \geq 1$. We use $k = 0$ is used to denote no singletons, not even the one before $\rightharpoonup_k$. (This may seem strange at first, but will greatly simplify the notation.)

Example 2.9. The following are possible allocations, written in full and abbreviated.

(1) $\left(\frac{\sigma}{3}, \frac{\sigma}{4}, \frac{\sigma}{5}, \frac{\sigma}{5}, \frac{\sigma}{6}, \frac{\sigma}{7}, \frac{\sigma}{8}, \frac{\sigma}{8}, \frac{\sigma}{9}, \frac{\sigma}{10}\right)$ or $\left(\frac{\sigma}{3} \rightharpoonup_2, \bowtie_2, \frac{\sigma}{8}, \frac{\sigma}{8}, \frac{\sigma}{9} \rightharpoonup_2\right)$.

(2) $\left(\frac{\sigma}{2}, \frac{\sigma}{3}, \frac{\sigma}{4}, \frac{\sigma}{5}, \frac{\sigma}{5}, \frac{\sigma}{6}, \frac{\sigma}{7}, \frac{\sigma}{8}\right)$, or $\left(\frac{\sigma}{2} \rightharpoonup_3, \frac{\sigma}{5}, \frac{\sigma}{5}, \frac{\sigma}{6} \rightharpoonup_3\right)$.

(3) $\left(\frac{\sigma}{4}, \frac{\sigma}{4}, \frac{\sigma}{5}, \frac{\sigma}{6}, \frac{\sigma}{7}, \frac{\sigma}{8}, \frac{\sigma}{8}, \frac{\sigma}{9}, \frac{\sigma}{10}, \frac{\sigma}{11}, \frac{\sigma}{12}, \frac{\sigma}{12}, \frac{\sigma}{13}, \frac{\sigma}{14}, \frac{\sigma}{15}\right)$ or $\left(\frac{\sigma}{3} \rightharpoonup_0, \bowtie_3, \frac{\sigma}{12}, \frac{\sigma}{12}, \frac{\sigma}{13} \rightharpoonup_3\right)$.

Instead of individually analyzing each basic control vector, for any $c > 0$, we define a set of allocations:

$$S^c = S^c_{1,1}, \dots S^c_{1,c+1}, S^c_{2,0}, S^c_{2,1} \dots, S^c_{2,c+1}, S_{3,0}, S^c_{3,1} \dots, S^c_{3,c+1}, \dots$$

that simultaneously upper bounds all allocations created by all basic control vectors, for a fixed c. (This series is not a series of valid allocations; it is only used for the analysis.) At a high level, $S_{t,i}$ is the allocation created by some basic control vector ψ, such that the largest share is $\frac{1}{t}$ (all of the allocations in Example 2.9 are such allocations; they correspond to $S^2_{3,2}, S^3_{2,3}$ and $S^3_{3,0}$ respectively). For ψ, the allocation at this time is necessarily greater than the previous c allocations (as there was no donor for c rounds). The following observation is a characterization of the allocations just before the round when a donor is used. Note that the control vector is characterized by the variable k, which does not appear in the expression; we only claim that for every k and every round t that is just before the donor, there is some i for which the expression holds.

Definition 2.10. For $t = 1$ and $j \in \{1, \dots, c+1\}$,

$$S^c_{t,j} = \sigma \rightharpoonup_{(j)} .$$

For $t > 1$ and $j \in \{0, 1, \dots, c+1\}$, $t'_{t,j} = (t-1)(c+2) + j - c$,

$$S^c_{t,j} = \frac{\sigma}{t} \rightharpoonup_{(j)}, \bowtie_c, \frac{\sigma}{t'}, \frac{\sigma}{t'}, \frac{\sigma}{t'+1} \rightharpoonup_{(c)} .$$

[6]In all of the algorithms that we describe, shares are rational numbers.

It is easy to verify that these are exact descriptions of all possible allocations of Skip in the round before a donor is used; we invite the reader to consult Example 2.9 in which the allocations correspond to $S^2_{3,2}$, $S^3_{2,3}$ and $S^3_{4,0}$ respectively.

Lemma 2.11. *The fairness ratio of Skip for any $t > 1, j$ is at most*

$$\left(\arg\max_{t\in\mathbb{N}^+, j\in\{0,\ldots,c+1\}} \sum_{i=t}^{(t-1)(c+2)+j} \frac{1}{i} + \sum_{i=0}^{t-2} \frac{1}{t+i(c+1)+j}\right)^{-1}.$$

Proof. The maximal allocation of S^c is an upper bound on the maximal allocation of Skip, with a basic c-control vector. The allocation of $S_{t,j}$ is

$$\sum_{i=t}^{(t-1)(c+2)+j} \frac{1}{i} + \sum_{i=0}^{t-2} \frac{1}{t+i(c+1)+j},$$

by straightforward summation over the allocation vector of Definition 2.10, where the first is a sum of all the values appearing in the allocation vector and the second part is a sum of the duplicates. □

The following is our bound for basic control vectors, for $c > 3$. For the cases of $c = 1$ and $c = 2$, we get a stronger bounds. We note that this discrepancy between $c = 1, 2$ and $c = 3$ is unavoidable, as the asymptotic bound holds for all time periods for $c = 1, 2$, but not for $c = 3$. The plot for $c = 3$ is slightly misleading, in that it appears that for some control vectors, the asymptotic bound holds. While this is true for all $c < 8$, it ceases to be true thereafter. I can be shown that no control vector has fairness ratio at most the asymptotic bound (see the full version of this paper for more details). The missing proofs and the analysis for $c = 1$ and $c = 2$ are omitted due to lack of space.

Theorem 2.12. *For all $c > 2$, the fairness ratio, $\sigma^*\left((c+1)^{-1}\right)$ for all c-control vectors and all steps t satisfies:*

$$\frac{1}{H_{c+1}} \geq \sigma^*\left((c+1)^{-1}\right) \geq \frac{1}{H_{2c+3} - \frac{1}{2}}.$$

Proof. We consider two cases: $t = 1$ and $t > 1$. For the former, the allocation simply is $1 + \frac{1}{2} + \cdots + \frac{1}{j}$. For control vector $(10^c)^\infty$ this is the first $c+1$ elements of the harmonic progression. For $t > 1$, the total resource allocated is:

$$\sum_{i=t}^{(t-1)(c+2)+j} \frac{1}{i} + \sum_{i=0}^{t-2} \frac{1}{t+i(c+1)+j} \leq \sum_{i=t}^{(t-1)(c+2)+c+1} \frac{1}{i} + \sum_{i=0}^{t-2} \frac{1}{t+i(c+1)}.$$

We bound each term separately. For the term on the left, one can show that the expression is decreasing in t, and therefore is upper bounded by $\sum_{i=2}^{2c+3} \frac{1}{i} = H_{2c+3} - 1$. The term on the right is upper bounded by $\frac{1}{2}$. Combined, we get that the total resource allocated is at most $H_{2c+3} - \frac{1}{2}$. $H_{2c+3} - \frac{1}{2} > H_{c+1}$, for all $c \geq 2$. Furthermore, the bound of the total resource for $t = 1$, is tight. See the full version of this paper for the missing proofs. □

We show a tight asymptotic bound on the fairness ratio of Skip as the number of agents tends to infinity.

Theorem 1.6. *There exists a number n_0 such that, for all $c > 2$, all c-control vectors, and present agents $t > n_0$, the allocation of Skip is σ_t-fair, where $\sigma_t = (c+1)\left((c+2)\ln(c+2)\right)^{-1}$.*

Proof. We use the following fact about harmonic sums: $\sum_{x=a}^{b} \frac{1}{x} \leq \ln\left(\frac{b}{a-1}\right)$.

We bound the total allocation at step t, as it appears in Lemma 2.11. For the first term:

$$\sum_{i=t}^{(t-1)(c+2)+j} \frac{1}{i} \leq \ln\left(\frac{(t-1)(c+2)+j}{t-1}\right) = \ln\left(c+2+\frac{j}{t-1}\right),$$

which approaches $\ln(c+2)$ as $t \to \infty$. For the second term:

$$\sum_{i=0}^{t-2} \frac{1}{t+i(c+1)+j} \leq \sum_{i=0}^{t-2} \frac{1}{t+i(c+1)} = \frac{1}{c+1} \sum_{i=0}^{t-2} \frac{1}{\frac{t}{c+1}+i} = \frac{1}{c+1} \sum_{i=\frac{t}{c+1}}^{\frac{t}{c+1}+t-2} \frac{1}{i}$$

$$\leq \frac{1}{c+1} \ln\left(\frac{\frac{t}{c+1}+t-2}{\frac{t}{c+1}-1}\right) = \frac{1}{c+1} \ln\left(\frac{t+(t-2)(c+1)}{t-c-1}\right),$$

which approaches $\frac{1}{c+1}\ln(c+2)$ as $t \to \infty$. Combining gives a bound of $(c+1)^{-1}\left((c+2)\ln(c+2)\right)$ on S^t as t goes to infinity; the theorem follows. □

3 MULTIPLE RESOURCES

We show lower and upper bounds for the optimal fairness ratio of *DDRF*. In Section 4 we show a tighter upper bound for the case $d = 1$ and r resources. We describe algorithms for the following cases:

(1) the number of donors allowed is a multiple of the number of resources ($d = kr$), for some integer $k \geq 1$ (we omit the proof due to lack of space),
(2) $d = 1$, (r is any integer),
(3) one disruption is allowed for per $c+1$ arrivals, for $c \geq 1$.

Our algorithms use solutions to the single resource algorithms as subroutines: For each resource ℓ, we run a copy of a single resource algorithm. Let $\mathcal{SR}$ be an algorithm for the single resource case (we expand shortly about the exact nature of $\mathcal{SR}$). When the t-th agent arrives with demand $\mathcal{D}_t = (\mathcal{D}_{t,1}, \mathcal{D}_{t,2}, \ldots, \mathcal{D}_{t,r})$, the ℓ-th copy of $\mathcal{SR}$ is given as an input the number $D_{t,\ell} \in \{0,1\}$. If $D_{t,\ell} = 1$, $\mathcal{SR}$ behaves as if an agent arrived. If the number is $D_{t,\ell} = 0$, $\mathcal{SR}$ "ignores" it. The total amount of resource ℓ allocated to agent i is dictated by the ℓ-th copy. The following Lemma, whose proof is deferred to the full version of this paper, allows us to combine the single resource algorithms:

Lemma 3.1. *Let $\mathcal{MR}$ be a multiple resource algorithm that executes a single resource algorithm $\mathcal{SR}$ with fairness ratio σ^* for each resource. Then, $\mathcal{MR}$ is σ^*-DRF fair.*

Theorem 1.9. *The optimal fairness ratio of DDRF for $d = 1$ donors and $r \geq 2$ resources is bounded by*

- $\sigma^*(1,2) \geq 2(3\ln 3)^{-1} \approx 0.6068$
- $\sigma^*(1,3) \geq 3(4\ln 4)^{-1}$
- $\sigma^*(1,r) \geq \left(H_{2r+1} - \frac{1}{2}\right)^{-1}, r > 3.$

Proof. Our algorithm for $d = 1$ will run r copies of the Skip algorithm, one for each resource, where every copy can use a at least one donor for every r arrivals.

The algorithm maintains a priority list O_t over the copies of Skip. Let $O_1 = (1, 2, \ldots, r)$: at step $t = 1$, the first copy has the highest priority, the second copy has the second highest, and so on. At the arrival of the t-th agent with demand $D_t = (D_{t,1}, D_{t,2}, \ldots, D_{t,r})$, the ℓ-th copy of the single resource algorithm will be given as an input the number $D_{t,\ell}$ if that number is non-zero (otherwise it receives no input). All copies that received a non-zero input request a donor. Copies with no input stay idle. If there are conflicts, (two or more copies request *different* donors), then the copy with the highest priority in O_t, among those that requested a donor, is the only one allowed to use a donor, and is moved to have the lowest priority in O_{t+1}. The total amount of resource ℓ allocated to agent i is dictated by the ℓ-th copy of Skip.

Clearly, only one donor is used per step. Therefore we only need to show that the algorithm guarantees a $\sigma^*\left(r^{-1}\right)$ fraction of the *DRF* utility for each agent (recall that here $\sigma^*\left(r^{-1}\right)$ is the fairness ratio of Skip when one donor every r arrivals is allowed). Notice that for each step that a copy requests a donor but is not allowed to use one, it moves up one spot in the priority list. A copy cannot be denied a donor more than $r-1$ times consecutively. This implies that the ℓ-th copy, if seen independently, behaves identically to Skip, and therefore, by Lemma 3.1 the algorithm is $\sigma^*\left(r^{-1}\right)$-*DRF* fair. □

Using a similar approach we can show positive results for $d=(c+1)^{-1}$. The main observation here is that each single resource subroutine cannot be denied a donor for more than $r(c+1)-1$ steps. The upper bound on the fairness ratio is implied by the upper bound on the single resource case.

Theorem 1.10. *The optimal fairness ratio of DDRF for r resources and* $(c+1)^{-1}$ *donors (1 donor per* $c+1$ *arrivals) is bounded by* $(H_{c+1})^{-1} \geq \sigma^*\left((c+1)^{-1}, r\right) \geq \left(H_{2r(c+1)+1} - \frac{1}{2}\right)^{-1}$.

4 IMPOSSIBILITY RESULT FOR $\sigma^*(1, R)$

We prove the following theorem. The complete proof is deferred to the full version of this paper:

Theorem 1.11. *The optimal fairness ratio of DDRF for* $d=1$ *and* $r \geq 2$ *resources is bounded by* $\sigma^*(1, r) \leq 0.6318\ldots$

The high level of our approach to the proof of Theorem 1.11 is the following.

1. Write the optimal mixed integer program for a general number of donors d and fix an input $\mathcal{D}$ (to be described later).
2. Notice that the only integer variables are variables $Z_{t,i} \in \{0,1\}$, encoding whether the i-th agent is a donor at step t. If we fix these variables, the remaining program is an LP. Treat these variables as constants Z and consider the dual of this LP.
3. Show an algorithm that, given Z, outputs a feasible solution for the dual with a value of at most $\sigma^* \approx 0.6318$.

The main difficulty is showing that no matter what the adversary picks Z to be, a feasible dual solution can always be constructed, such that we get the desired bound. The optimal integer program for general d is:

$$\begin{aligned}
&\max \sigma \\
&\text{subject to: } \forall i \leq t, t \in [N]: \quad u_i^t \geq \frac{\sigma}{DRF_t} \\
&\forall r \in [R], t \in [N]: \quad \sum_{i=1}^{t} u_{ir}^t D_{i,r} \leq 1, \qquad \forall t \in [N]: \quad \sum_{i=1}^{t} Z_{t,i} \leq d \\
&\forall i, t \in [N]: \quad u_i^t - u_i^{t-1} \leq 1 - Z_{t,i}, \qquad u_i^t - u_i^{t-1} \geq -z_i^t \\
&Z_{t,i} \in \{0,1\}
\end{aligned}$$

Fixing our integer variables $Z_{t,i}$ and taking the dual for the resulting linear program gives:

$$
\begin{aligned}
\min \quad & \sum_{t,r} f(t,r) + \sum_{t,i} x(t,i)\,(1 - Z_{t,i}) + \sum_{t,i} y(t,i) Z_{t,i} \\
\text{subject to} \quad & \sum_{t,i} l(t,i) \geq 1 \\
\forall t \in [N-1], i \in [t]: \quad & \sum_{r} D_{i,r} f(t,r) + x(t,i) - x(t+1,i) + y(t+1,i) - y(t,i) \geq \frac{1}{DRF_t} l(t,i) \\
\forall i \in [N]: \quad & \sum_{r} D_{i,r} f(N,r) + x(N,i) - y(N,i) \geq \frac{1}{DRF_N} l(N,i)
\end{aligned}
$$

Acknowledgements

We thank Ophir Friedler for helpful discussions and the anonymous referees for their useful comments.

REFERENCES

[1] Martin Aleksandrov, Haris Aziz, Serge Gaspers, and Toby Walsh. 2015. Online fair division: analysing a food bank problem. In *Proceedings of the 24th International Conference on Artificial Intelligence.* AAAI Press, 2540–2546.

[2] Noga Alon. 1987. Splitting necklaces. *Advances in Mathematics* 63, 3 (1987), 247–253.

[3] Haris Aziz and Simon Mackenzie. 2016. A Discrete and Bounded Envy-Free Cake Cutting Protocol for Any Number of Agents. *arXiv preprint arXiv:1604.03655* (2016).

[4] Haris Aziz and Simon Mackenzie. 2016. A discrete and bounded envy-free cake cutting protocol for four agents. In *Proceedings of the 48th Annual ACM SIGACT Symposium on Theory of Computing.* ACM, 454–464.

[5] Arka A. Bhattacharya, David Culler, Eric Friedman, Ali Ghodsi, Scott Shenker, and Ion Stoica. 2013. Hierarchical Scheduling for Diverse Datacenter Workloads. In *Proceedings of the 4th Annual Symposium on Cloud Computing (SOCC '13).* 4:1–4:15.

[6] Steven J Brams and Alan D Taylor. 1995. An envy-free cake division protocol. *Amer. Math. Monthly* (1995), 9–18.

[7] Eric Budish. 2011. The combinatorial assignment problem: Approximate competitive equilibrium from equal incomes. *Journal of Political Economy* 119, 6 (2011), 1061–1103.

[8] Ioannis Caragiannis, David Kurokawa, Hervé Moulin, Ariel D Procaccia, Nisarg Shah, Junxing Wang, et al. 2016. *The Unreasonable Fairness of Maximum Nash Welfare.* Technical Report.

[9] Edith Cohen, Graham Cormode, Nick G. Duffield, and Carsten Lund. 2016. On the Tradeoff between Stability and Fit. *ACM Trans. Algorithms* 13, 1 (2016), 7:1–7:24.

[10] Richard Cole and Vasilis Gkatzelis. 2015. Approximating the Nash social welfare with indivisible items. In *Proceedings of the Forty-Seventh Annual ACM on Symposium on Theory of Computing.* ACM, 371–380.

[11] Nikhil R Devanur, Christos H Papadimitriou, Amin Saberi, and Vijay V Vazirani. 2008. Market equilibrium via a primal–dual algorithm for a convex program. *Journal of the ACM (JACM)* 55, 5 (2008), 22.

[12] Danny Dolev, Dror G. Feitelson, Joseph Y. Halpern, Raz Kupferman, and Nathan Linial. 2012. No Justified Complaints: On Fair Sharing of Multiple Resources. In *Proceedings of the 3rd Innovations in Theoretical Computer Science Conference (ITCS '12).* ACM, New York, NY, USA, 68–75. https://doi.org/10.1145/2090236.2090243

[13] Lester E Dubins and Edwin H Spanier. 1961. How to cut a cake fairly. *American mathematical monthly* (1961), 1–17.

[14] Leah Epstein and Asaf Levin. 2011. Robust algorithms for preemptive scheduling. In *European Symposium on Algorithms.* Springer, 567–578.

[15] Eric Friedman, Ali Ghodsi, and Christos-Alexandros Psomas. 2014. Strategyproof allocation of discrete jobs on multiple machines. In *Proceedings of the fifteenth ACM conference on Economics and computation.* ACM, 529–546.

[16] Eric J. Friedman, Christos-Alexandros Psomas, and Shai Vardi. 2015. Dynamic Fair Division with Minimal Disruptions. In *Proceedings of the Sixteenth ACM Conference on Economics and Computation, EC '15, Portland, OR, USA, June 15-19, 2015.* 697–713. https://doi.org/10.1145/2764468.2764495

[17] Ali Ghodsi, Vyas Sekar, Matei Zaharia, and Ion Stoica. 2012. Multi-resource fair queueing for packet processing. *ACM SIGCOMM Computer Communication Review* 42, 4 (2012), 1–12.

[18] Ali Ghodsi, Matei Zaharia, Benjamin Hindman, Andy Konwinski, Scott Shenker, and Ion Stoica. 2011. Dominant Resource Fairness: Fair Allocation of Multiple Resource Types. In *Proceedings of the 8th USENIX Conference on Networked Systems Design and Implementation (NSDI'11).* 24–24.

[19] Ali Ghodsi, Matei Zaharia, Scott Shenker, and Ion Stoica. 2013. Choosy: Max-min Fair Sharing for Datacenter Jobs with Constraints. In *Proceedings of the 8th ACM European Conference on Computer Systems (EuroSys '13).* 365–378.

[20] Albert Gu, Anupam Gupta, and Amit Kumar. 2016. The power of deferral: maintaining a constant-competitive steiner tree online. *SIAM J. Comput.* 45, 1 (2016), 1–28.

[21] Mingyu Guo, Vincent Conitzer, and Daniel M Reeves. 2009. Competitive repeated allocation without payments. In *International Workshop on Internet and Network Economics.* Springer, 244–255.

[22] Anupam Gupta and Amit Kumar. 2014. Online steiner tree with deletions. In *Proceedings of the Twenty-Fifth Annual ACM-SIAM Symposium on Discrete Algorithms.* Society for Industrial and Applied Mathematics, 455–467.

[23] Anupam Gupta, Amit Kumar, and Cliff Stein. 2014. Maintaining assignments online: Matching, scheduling, and flows. In *Proceedings of the Twenty-Fifth Annual ACM-SIAM Symposium on Discrete Algorithms.* Society for Industrial and Applied Mathematics, 468–479.

[24] Avital Gutman and Noam Nisan. 2012. Fair allocation without trade. In *Proceedings of the 11th International Conference on Autonomous Agents and Multiagent Systems-Volume 2.* International Foundation for Autonomous Agents and Multiagent Systems, 719–728.

[25] Benjamin Hindman, Andy Konwinski, Matei Zaharia, Ali Ghodsi, Anthony D Joseph, Randy H Katz, Scott Shenker, and Ion Stoica. 2011. Mesos: A Platform for Fine-Grained Resource Sharing in the Data Center.. In *NSDI,* Vol. 11. 22–22.

[26] Michael Isard, Vijayan Prabhakaran, Jon Currey, Udi Wieder, Kunal Talwar, and Andrew Goldberg. 2009. Quincy: fair scheduling for distributed computing clusters. In *Proceedings of the ACM SIGOPS 22nd symposium on Operating systems principles.* ACM, 261–276.

[27] Carlee Joe-Wong, Soumya Sen, Tian Lan, and Mung Chiang. 2013. Multiresource allocation: Fairness-efficiency tradeoffs in a unifying framework. *IEEE/ACM Transactions on Networking (TON)* 21, 6 (2013), 1785–1798.

[28] Ehud Kalai and Meir Smorodinsky. 1975. Other solutions to Nash's bargaining problem. *Econometrica: Journal of the Econometric Society* (1975), 513–518.

[29] Ian Kash, Ariel D Procaccia, and Nisarg Shah. 2013. No agent left behind: Dynamic fair division of multiple resources. In *Proceedings of the 2013 international conference on Autonomous agents and multi-agent systems.* 351–358.

[30] David Kurokawa, Ariel D Procaccia, and Nisarg Shah. 2015. Leximin allocations in the real world. In *Proceedings of the Sixteenth ACM Conference on Economics and Computation.* ACM, 345–362.

[31] Dejan S Milojičić, Fred Douglis, Yves Paindaveine, Richard Wheeler, and Songnian Zhou. 2000. Process migration. *ACM Computing Surveys (CSUR)* 32, 3 (2000), 241–299.

[32] John F Nash Jr. 1950. The bargaining problem. *Econometrica: Journal of the Econometric Society* (1950), 155–162.

[33] Abraham Othman, Christos Papadimitriou, and Aviad Rubinstein. 2014. The complexity of fairness through equilibrium. In *Proceedings of the fifteenth ACM conference on Economics and computation.* ACM, 209–226.

[34] David C. Parkes, Ariel D. Procaccia, and Nisarg Shah. 2012. Beyond Dominant Resource Fairness: Extensions, Limitations, and Indivisibilities. In *Proceedings of the 13th ACM Conference on Electronic Commerce (EC '12).* 808–825.

[35] Elisha A Pazner and David Schmeidler. 1978. Egalitarian equivalent allocations: A new concept of economic equity. *The Quarterly Journal of Economics* (1978), 671–687.

[36] Steven Phillips and Jeffery Westbrook. 1993. Online load balancing and network flow. In *Proceedings of the twenty-fifth annual ACM symposium on Theory of computing.* ACM, 402–411.

[37] Lucian Popa, Gautam Kumar, Mosharaf Chowdhury, Arvind Krishnamurthy, Sylvia Ratnasamy, and Ion Stoica. 2012. FairCloud: sharing the network in cloud computing. In *Proceedings of the ACM SIGCOMM 2012 conference on Applications, technologies, architectures, and protocols for computer communication.* ACM, 187–198.

[38] Peter Sanders, Naveen Sivadasan, and Martin Skutella. 2009. Online scheduling with bounded migration. *Mathematics of Operations Research* 34, 2 (2009), 481–498.

[39] Erel Segal-Halevi. 2016. How to Re-Divide a Cake Fairly. *arXiv preprint arXiv:1603.00286* (2016).

[40] Hadas Shachnai, Gal Tamir, and Tami Tamir. 2012. A Theory and Algorithms for Combinatorial Reoptimization. In *LATIN 2012: Theoretical Informatics - 10th Latin American Symposium, Proceedings.* 618–630.

[41] David Shue, Michael J Freedman, and Anees Shaikh. 2012. Performance isolation and fairness for multi-tenant cloud storage. In *Presented as part of the 10th USENIX Symposium on Operating Systems Design and Implementation (OSDI 12).* 349–362.

[42] Hugo Steinhaus. 1948. The problem of fair division. *Econometrica* 16, 1 (1948).

[43] Walter Stromquist. 1980. How to cut a cake fairly. *Amer. Math. Monthly* (1980), 640–644.

[44] Abhishek Verma, Luis Pedrosa, Madhukar Korupolu, David Oppenheimer, Eric Tune, and John Wilkes. 2015. Large-scale cluster management at Google with Borg. In *Proceedings of the Tenth European Conference on Computer Systems.* ACM, 18.

[45] Toby Walsh. 2011. Online cake cutting. In *Algorithmic Decision Theory.* Springer, 292–305.

[46] Wei Wang, Baochun Li, and Ben Liang. 2014. Dominant resource fairness in cloud computing systems with heterogeneous servers. In *INFOCOM, 2014 Proceedings IEEE.* IEEE, 583–591.

A Lower Bound for Equitable Cake Cutting

ARIEL D. PROCACCIA and JUNXING WANG, Carnegie Mellon University

We are interested in the problem of dividing a cake — a heterogeneous divisible good — among n players, in a way that is *ε-equitable*: every pair of players must have the same value for their own allocated pieces, up to a difference of at most ε. It is known that such allocations can be computed using $O(n \ln(1/\varepsilon))$ operations in the standard *Robertson-Webb Model*. We establish a lower bound of $\Omega(\ln(1/\varepsilon)/\ln\ln(1/\varepsilon))$ on the complexity of this problem, which is almost tight for a constant number of players. Importantly, our result implies that allocations that are exactly equitable cannot be computed.

1 INTRODUCTION

While in hiding during World War II, the Polish mathematician Hugo Steinhaus initiated the study of fair division. His model [27] involves a single, infinitely divisible, heterogeneous good — the *cake*, represented by the interval $[0, 1]$ — and a set of players $1, \ldots, n$ with possibly different valuation functions $v_1, \ldots, v_n$ over the cake. Although mathematical models for everyday fair division problems like splitting rent or allocating indivisible goods have proven more directly practical [11, 18], *cake cutting* is still considered to be the paradigmatic model of fair division, and gives rise to some of the most fundamental problems in the field.

From the computational viewpoint, the key challenges have to do with the complexity of computing allocations of the cake that satisfy certain fairness properties. For example, we say that an allocation $A_1, \ldots, A_n$ of the cake, where A_i is the piece of cake given to player i, is *proportional* if each player receives a piece of cake that he values at least at $1/n$ of his value for the entire cake. It has long been known that a proportional allocation can be computed using $O(n \ln n)$ operations [17]. (Allowable operations are specified by the standard *Robertson-Webb* model [25], which we discuss in Section 2.) A decade ago, Edmonds and Pruhs [16] proved that this bound is tight: Any algorithm that computes a proportional allocation requires $\Omega(n \ln n)$ operations in the worst case.

While the complexity of proportional cake cutting is well understood, other fairness properties are more enigmatic. *Envy-freeness*, in particular, has attracted much attention over the years; it requires that for every two players i, j, $v_i(A_i) \geq v_i(A_j)$, that is, each player must (weakly) prefer his own piece to the piece allocated to any other player. In a breakthrough result, Brams and Taylor [8] designed a discrete envy-free cake cutting algorithm. But it is *unbounded*, in the sense that the number of operations cannot be bounded as a function of the number of players — for any $k \in \mathbb{N}$, one can set the valuation functions so that the algorithm would require at least k operations. For two decades, the existence of *bounded* envy-free cake cutting algorithms had arguably been one of the most important open questions in theoretical computer science, until it was answered last year in the positive by Aziz and Mackenzie [3].[1]

[1]However, their algorithm's running time is astronomical even for small n, and the only unconditional lower bound currently known is $\Omega(n^2)$ [22].

EC'17, June 26–30, 2017, Cambridge, Massachusetts, USA.
DOI: http://dx.doi.org/10.1145/3033274.3085107
© 2017 ACM. ISBN 978-1-4503-4527-9/17/06...$15.00.

The third major fairness property studied in the cake cutting literature is *equitability* [6, 7]. It requires that for every two players i, j, $v_i(A_i) = v_j(A_j)$, that is, every two players must have the same value for their pieces (compare with envy-freeness, which requires that the value of player i for his piece be at least as high as *his own value* for the piece of j). Herreiner and Puppe [20] demonstrate empirically that equitability, or the lack thereof, has a major impact on whether people perceive allocations as fair; this conclusion is supported by the recent work of Gal et al. [18]. Equitability also plays a key role in the study of fair divorce settlements (where spite can lead to acrimony); it underlies the design of the *Adjusted Winner* algorithm of Brams and Taylor [9] for dividing homogeneous divisible goods, which can be viewed as a special case of cake cutting with so-called *piecewise constant* [14] valuations, between two players. This algorithm was deployed on the fair division website *Spliddit*[2] [19] between November 2014 and May 2016.

To develop some intuition about the computational aspects of equitable cake cutting, it is instructive to understand why an equitable allocation even *exists*. Consider the case of two players, and assume for convenience that both players have value 1 for the entire cake $[0, 1]$. Let $f(x) = v_1([0, x]) - v_2([x, 1])$, and note that f is continuous (this follows from standard assumptions listed in Section 2), $f(0) = -1$, and $f(1) = 1$. By the intermediate value theorem, there is x^* such that $f(x^*) = 0$, that is, the allocation $A_1 = [0, x^*], A_2 = [x^*, 1]$ is equitable. As observed by Cechlárová and Pillárová [12], this argument can be used to compute an *ε-equitable* allocation — which guarantees that for all i, j, $|v_i(A_i) - v_j(A_j)| \leq \varepsilon$ — using $O(\ln(1/\varepsilon))$ operations, via binary search for x^*. This approach extends to the case of n players [13], leading to an upper bound of $O(n \ln(1/\varepsilon))$ on the complexity of ε-equitable cake cutting.

By contrast, very little is known about *lower bounds* on the complexity of this problem. Cechlárová and Pillárová [13] show that there is no algorithm that computes (exactly) equitable allocations, but under two restrictive assumptions: the allocated pieces must be connected,[3] and the allocation must satisfy an additional property called Pareto efficiency, which greatly reduces the space of equitable allocations [6].

In this paper, we establish a lower bound of $\Omega(\ln(1/\varepsilon)/\ln\ln(1/\varepsilon))$ on the complexity of ε-equitable cake cutting (in the Robertson-Webb model), for any number of players. Note that this bound is almost tight — up to a $\ln\ln(1/\varepsilon)$ factor — for a constant number of players. More importantly, it directly implies the nonexistence of cake cutting algorithms — even unbounded ones — that are exactly equitable (see Section 5 for additional discussion of this point).

It is natural to ask whether the lower bound can be improved in a way that grows with n. We answer this question in the negative by establishing a new *upper* bound of $O((1/\varepsilon)\ln(1/\varepsilon))$, which implies that the complexity of ε-equitable cake cutting need not depend on n at all. Nevertheless, for $n \geq 1/\varepsilon$, we leave open a significant gap between the upper bound of $O((1/\varepsilon)\ln(1/\varepsilon))$, and the lower bound of $\Omega(\ln(1/\varepsilon)/\ln\ln(1/\varepsilon))$.

2 PRELIMINARIES

Let $N = \{1, \dots, n\}$ be the set of *players*. The *cake* is represented as the interval $[0, 1]$; a *piece of cake* is a finite union of disjoint intervals. Each player $i \in N$ is associated with a *valuation function* v_i which assigns a non-negative value to any given piece of cake. Like almost all of the cake cutting literature [24], we assume that the valuation functions satisfy the following standard properties for all $i \in N$:

[2] `http://www.spliddit.org`

[3] One way to see that this assumption is indeed very restrictive is that envy-free allocations with connected pieces cannot be computed even for three players [28], whereas the classic Selfridge-Conway algorithm easily computes envy-free allocations for three players, which may consist of disconnected pieces.

- *Additivity:* For two disjoint pieces of cake X and Y, $v_i(X \cup Y) = v_i(X) + v_i(Y)$.
- *Divisibility:* For any interval $[x, z] \subseteq [0, 1]$ and $\lambda \in [0, 1]$ there exists a point $y \in [x, z]$ such that $v_i([x, y]) = \lambda \cdot v_i([x, z])$.
- *Normalization:* $v_i([0, 1]) = 1$.

The normalization assumption is without loss of generality for the purposes of this paper. Also note that divisibility implies that the valuation functions are *non-atomic*, in the sense that $v_i([x, x]) = 0$ for any $x \in [0, 1]$. We can therefore consider two intervals that overlap only at the boundary as disjoint.

A cake cutting algorithm outputs an allocation $A = (A_1, \ldots, A_n)$, where A_i is the piece of cake allocated to $i \in N$, and the pieces form a partition of the cake (they are disjoint and their union is the entire cake).

2.1 Fairness Properties

In Section 1 we discussed three fairness properties; here we define them formally. We say that an allocation $A_1, \ldots, A_n$ is

- *proportional* if for all $i \in N$, $v_i(A_i) \geq 1/n$,
- *ε-envy free* if for all $i, j \in N$, $v_i(A_i) \geq v_i(A_j) - \varepsilon$, and simply *envy free* if it is 0-envy free,
- *ε-equitable* if for all $i, j \in N$, $|v_i(A_i) - v_j(A_j)| \leq \varepsilon$, and simply *equitable* if it is 0-equitable.

2.2 The Robertson-Webb Model

Over the years, the Robertson-Webb (RW) model [25] has emerged as the standard model in which the complexity of cake cutting algorithms is analyzed [3–5, 10, 15, 16, 21–24, 29]. In this model, a cake cutting algorithm is allowed to interact with the players via two types of queries:

- *Evaluation:* An $\texttt{eval}_i(x, y)$ query returns $v_i([x, y])$.
- *Cut:* A $\texttt{cut}_i(x, \beta)$ query returns a point y such that $v_i([x, y]) = \beta$.

Consider, for example, the classic *Cut and Choose* algorithm for two players, where player 1 cuts the cake into two pieces that he values equally, and player 2 chooses the piece that he prefers. This algorithm is envy free and proportional, but, for obvious reasons (if one already believes our lower bound), it is not equitable. Cut and Choose can be simulated using two queries in the RW model: $y = \texttt{cut}_1(0, 1/2)$, and then $\texttt{eval}_2(0, y)$. More generally, all classic discrete cake cutting algorithms can be simulated in this model.

The goal of an algorithm in the RW model is to gather enough information about the valuation functions of the players to *guarantee* a certain property — ε-equitability in our case. Formally, we say that an algorithm in the RW model is ε-equitable if, when it terminates, there *exists* an allocation A such that *for any* valuation functions $v_1, \ldots, v_n$ that are *consistent with the answers to the algorithm's queries*, it holds for all $i, j \in N$ that $|v_i(A_i) - v_j(A_j)| \leq \varepsilon$. Note that the actual *computation* of the allocation A is "free".

As usual, the complexity of an algorithm is its worst-case running time, and the complexity of a problem is the complexity of the best algorithm that solves the problem. We are interested in the complexity of the ε-equitable cake cutting problem.

3 MAIN RESULT

As the reader is surely aware by now, our main result is the following theorem.

THEOREM 3.1. *For any number of players $n \geq 2$, the complexity of ε-equitable cake cutting in the RW model is*

$$\Omega\left(\frac{\ln(1/\varepsilon)}{\ln\ln(1/\varepsilon)}\right).$$

The rest of this section is devoted to the theorem's proof, divided into three parts: defining a variant of the RW model that simplifies the exposition (and proving that a lower bound in the adjusted model implies a lower bound in the standard model); proving the theorem for the case of two players; and extending the proof to the general case.

Before jumping into the details of the proof, we give an overview of the main ideas. The adjusted RW model allows us to view the cake cutting process as a process of splitting *indivisible goods* (i.e., any allocation must give each of these goods to a single player) into smaller indivisible goods (Lemma 3.2). For the case of two players, we design an adversary that answers the algorithm's queries in a way that whenever a good is split into two goods, the ratio of the two player's values for each of the new goods is close to the ratio of these values for the old good (Lemma 3.5). But we do create some discrepancy in the values, and the degree of discrepancy is carefully chosen so that we can upper-bound the number of non-zero digits *in the base 3 representation* of $\bar{v}(a)$, where a belongs to a certain subset of the goods, and $\bar{v}(a) = v_1(a) + v_2(a)$ is the *total value* of a (Lemma 3.6). We show that this implies an upper bound on the number of ones *in the base 3 representation* of $\bar{v}(A_1)$ (Lemmas 3.7 and 3.8). But it is easy to see that, when players' values for the entire cake are normalized to $1/2$ (which they are throughout the proof), ε-equitability is equivalent to the condition $|\bar{v}(A_1) - 1/2| \leq \varepsilon$ (Lemma 3.3), and $1/2$ is $0.111\cdots$ in base 3. We can therefore find a sufficiently significant digit in which $\bar{v}(A_1)$ disagrees with $1/2$, and the 2-player case of the theorem (stated as Lemma 3.9) follows. Finally, we prove the theorem by (essentially) reducing the 2-player case to the n-player case (using Lemma 3.10).

3.1 The Adjusted Robertson-Webb Model

Instead of directly analyzing algorithms that operate in the RW model, we define a related model, and show that a lower bound in the alternative model holds, up to a constant factor, in the standard model.

In the *adjusted RW* model, we keep track of a partition of the cake into disjoint intervals. We think of these intervals as *indivisible* goods, which are denoted by small letters such as a and b. An allocation A may only allocate these indivisible goods. Initially there is only one good — the entire cake $[0, 1]$. The algorithm may create new goods using a single type of query:

- $\texttt{split}_i(a, \beta)$: Replace good a with two goods a' and a'' such that $v_i(a') = \beta \leq v_i(a)$, and return the value $v_j(a')$ for each other player $j \in N \setminus \{i\}$.

Note that in the adjusted RW model, the algorithm always knows the value of each good to each player. Indeed, if $v_i(a)$ and $v_i(a')$ are both known, then $v_i(a'') = v_i(a) - v_i(a')$ is also known.

LEMMA 3.2. *Suppose there is an algorithm that finds an ε-equitable allocation using at most $f(n, \varepsilon)$ queries in the RW model. Then there is an algorithm that finds an ε-equitable allocation using at most $2 \cdot f(n, \varepsilon)$ queries in the adjusted RW model.*

Equivalently, the lemma says that a lower bound of $2 \cdot f(n, \varepsilon)$ in the adjusted RW model implies a lower bound of $f(n, \varepsilon)$ in the RW model. In other words, any asymptotic lower bound established in the adjusted model also holds in the standard model.

PROOF OF LEMMA 3.2. Consider algorithm $\mathcal{B}$ that finds an ε-equitable allocation using $f(n, \varepsilon)$ queries in the RW model. Imagine that each query makes two marks in the cake. An $\texttt{eval}_i(x, y)$

query makes marks at x and y, whereas a $\texttt{cut}_i(x, \beta)$ query makes marks at x and at the point y such that $v_i([x, y]) = \beta$. Initially there are two marks at 0 and 1.

We first claim that for any allocation A that is guaranteed to be ε-equitable when algorithm $\mathcal{B}$ terminates, there is an allocation A'' that is guaranteed to be ε-equitable and never splits any interval between adjacent marks in the cake, i.e., each such interval is entirely allocated to a single player.

Indeed, let I be an interval between adjacent marks that is split by A between several players, including player i^*; let $J \subsetneq I$ be the subinterval allocated to i^*. Define an allocation A' that is identical to A, except that $I \subseteq A'_{i^*}$, i.e., the entire interval I is allocated to player i^*.

Now, let $v_1, \ldots, v_n$ be valuations consistent with the answers to the queries of algorithm $\mathcal{B}$; we know that A is ε-equitable according to $v_1, \ldots, v_n$ (as the allocation is guaranteed to have this property). Create $v'_1, \ldots, v'_n$ by modifying each v_i so that $v'_i(J) = v_i(I)$ for all $i \in N$, i.e., each player thinks the value of I is concentrated entirely in J. Note that

$$\forall i \in N,\ v'_i(A_i) = v'_i(A'_i). \tag{1}$$

Indeed, for all $i \in N$ it holds that $v'_i(I \setminus J) = 0$, player i^* gets J either way, and the two allocations A_i and A'_i are identical except on I. Furthermore,

$$\forall i \in N,\ v_i(A'_i) = v'_i(A'_i). \tag{2}$$

This equality holds because i^* receives the entire interval I either way, so it does not matter how the valuations of the players are distributed on I (which is the only difference between the two sets of valuations).

Crucially, $v'_1, \ldots, v'_n$ are also consistent with the answers to the queries, as $\mathcal{B}$ has no information about how value is distributed between adjacent marks. Therefore, A must be ε-equitable according to $v'_1, \ldots, v'_n$. It follows from Equation (1) that A' is ε-equitable according to $v'_1, \ldots, v'_n$. We conclude using Equation (2) that A' is ε-equitable according to $v_1, \ldots, v_n$. We have constructed an allocation A' that does not split one of the intervals split by A, and is ε-equitable for any valuation functions that are consistent with the queries of $\mathcal{B}$. Finally, we can repeat this argument for any interval between adjacent marks that is split, ultimately obtaining the desired allocation A''.

So far we have shown that we can assume that the ε-equitable algorithm $\mathcal{B}$ does not split intervals between adjacent marks, i.e., we can treat these intervals as indivisible goods. In the remainder of the proof we construct an Algorithm C in the adjusted RW model, which simulates Algorithm $\mathcal{B}$. At each step Algorithm C receives the next (cut or evaluation) query of Algorithm $\mathcal{B}$, and then issues at most two split queries that provide enough information to answer the original query. An invariant that is maintained throughout the execution of Algorithm C is that each interval between adjacent marks $[z, z']$ is associated with an indivisible good (and vice versa), and $v_j([z, z'])$ is known to the algorithm for all $j \in N$.

Let us now turn to the details of the simulation. First, suppose the next query of Algorithm $\mathcal{B}$ is a $\texttt{cut}_i(x, \beta)$ query. If x is an existing mark, let z and z' be the adjacent marks such that $v_i([x, z]) < \beta$ and $v_i([x, z']) \geq \beta$; note that these values are known by the invariant mentioned above. If $v_i([x, z']) = \beta$, Algorithm C returns the point z' as the answer to the cut query issued by Algorithm $\mathcal{B}$. Otherwise (a strict inequality holds), let $y = (z + z')/2$. Algorithm C issues a $\texttt{split}_i([z, z'], \beta - v_i([x, z]))$ query, which splits the good $[z, z']$ into two goods $[z, y]$ and $[y, z']$, such that $v_i([z, y]) = \beta - v_i([x, z])$. Note that the query reveals the values of the new goods for all players, hence the invariant is maintained (this is also true for the other cases discussed below, although we do not mention it explicitly). Finally, Algorithm C returns the point y as the answer to the cut query issued by Algorithm $\mathcal{B}$.

If x is not an existing mark, let z and z' be the adjacent marks such that $x \in (z, z')$. Algorithm C starts by issuing a $\texttt{split}_i([z, z'], 0)$ query that splits $[z, z']$ into two goods $[z, x]$ and $[x, z']$, such that $v_i([z, x]) = 0$. Now x coincides with one of the existing marks (equivalently, with the boundary of one of the existing goods), and algorithm C requires only one additional split query, as described above.

Second, suppose the next query of Algorithm $\mathcal{B}$ is an $\texttt{eval}_i(x, y)$ query. Using the procedure just described, we can assume that x is an existing mark. If y is an existing mark, Algorithm C returns $v_i([x, y])$ as the answer to the evaluation query issued by Algorithm $\mathcal{B}$. Otherwise, let z and z' be the adjacent marks such that $y \in (z, z')$. Algorithm C issues a $\texttt{split}_i([z, z'], 0)$ query, which splits the good $[z, z']$ into two goods $[z, y]$ and $[y, z']$, such that $v_i([z, y]) = 0$. Finally, Algorithm C returns the value $v_i([x, y]) = v_i([x, z])$ as the answer to the cut query issued by Algorithm $\mathcal{B}$.

By assumption, Algorithm $\mathcal{B}$ terminates after $f(n, \varepsilon)$ queries (hence Algorithm C issues at most $2 \cdot f(n, \varepsilon)$ queries). At that point, there exists an allocation A that is ε-equitable with respect to all valuation functions $v_1, \ldots, v_n$ that are consistent with the answers to the queries of Algorithm $\mathcal{B}$. By the first part of this proof, we can assume that A does not split intervals between adjacent marks.

To complete the proof, we claim that the same allocation A — which can be seen as an allocation of the indivisible goods created by Algorithm C — is ε-equitable with respect to all valuation functions $v_1, \ldots, v_n$ that are consistent with the answers to the queries of Algorithm C. The reason is simple: At each step the answer to the query of Algorithm $\mathcal{B}$ is deduced from the answers to the queries of Algorithm C, which means that any valuation functions that are consistent with the answers to the queries issued by the latter algorithm are also consistent with respect to those issues by the former. □

3.2 The Case of Two Players

In this subsection we assume that there are exactly two players, i.e., $n = 2$. We will show how to relax this assumption in Section 3.3.

It will be somewhat easier to consider an equivalent formulation of ε-equitability. Let $\bar{v}(a)$ be the *total value* of good a. For our current case of $n = 2$, it is $\bar{v}(a) = v_1(a) + v_2(a)$. For a set of goods (piece of cake) X, let $\bar{v}(X) = \sum_{a \in X} \bar{v}(X)$ be the total value of X. We also deviate a bit from the standard cake cutting formulation (Section 2) by normalizing the value of the whole cake to $1/2$ for both players, i.e., $v_1([0, 1]) = v_2([0, 1]) = 1/2$. This is purely for ease of exposition — it allows us to work with numbers in base 3 and cleanly achieve the desired result.

LEMMA 3.3. *The allocation $A = (A_1, A_2)$ is ε-equitable if and only if*

$$|\bar{v}(A_1) - 1/2| \leq \varepsilon.$$

PROOF. It holds that

$$\begin{aligned} |\bar{v}(A_1) - 1/2| &= |v_1(A_1) + v_2(A_1) - 1/2| \\ &= |v_1(A_1) - (1/2 - v_2(A_1))| \\ &= |v_1(A_1) - v_2(A_2)|. \end{aligned}$$

□

Next, we introduce an adversary *framework*. (Recall that we aim to design an adversary to frustrate an algorithm trying to achieve ε-equitability.) For a good a and $i \in \{1, 2\}$, let

$$\rho_i(a) = \frac{v_i(a)}{v_{3-i}(a)},$$

and

$$\tilde{\rho}(a) = \min\{\rho_1(a), \rho_2(a)\}.$$

The framework can now be described as in Algorithm 1.

Algorithm 1 Adversary framework with parameters $\vec{\gamma} = (\gamma_1, \ldots, \gamma_K) \in [0,1]^K$.

For $k = 1, 2, \cdots, K$ (the number of rounds):

(1) Receive the query $\texttt{split}_i(a, \beta)$, where $i \in \{1, 2\}$. It splits a into a' and a'' such that $v_i(a') = \beta$. Assume without loss of generality that $0 < \beta \le v_i(a)/2$, otherwise we can reverse the roles of a' and a''.

(2) Choose a value for the other player, $v_{3-i}(a')$, so that

$$v_i(a') \cdot \rho_{3-i}(a) \cdot (1 - \gamma_k) \le v_{3-i}(a') \le v_i(a') \cdot \rho_{3-i}(a). \tag{3}$$

Lemma 3.4. *Suppose that queries are answered in a way that is consistent with Algorithm 1. Then for each good a generated in the first k rounds, it holds that*

$$\tilde{\rho}(a) \ge \prod_{i=1}^{k}(1 - \gamma_i).$$

Proof. We prove the lemma by induction on the number of rounds. The lemma is clearly true at round 0, because $\tilde{\rho}([0,1]) = 1$, and the empty product equals 1 by convention.

Suppose that the lemma holds after $k-1$ rounds, and in round k we get a $\texttt{split}_i(a, \beta)$ query that splits a into a' and a''. By the induction assumption, it is sufficient to show that $\tilde{\rho}(a')$ and $\tilde{\rho}(a'')$ satisfy the desired inequality. By Equation (3), we have that

$$\begin{aligned}
\rho_{3-i}(a') &= \frac{v_{3-i}(a')}{v_i(a')} \\
&\ge \frac{v_i(a') \cdot \rho_{3-i}(a) \cdot (1 - \gamma_k)}{v_i(a')} \\
&\ge \tilde{\rho}(a) \cdot (1 - \gamma_k) \\
&\ge \left(\prod_{i=1}^{k-1}(1 - \gamma_i)\right) \cdot (1 - \gamma_k) \\
&= \prod_{i=1}^{k}(1 - \gamma_i),
\end{aligned} \tag{4}$$

where the fourth transition follows from the induction assumption. In addition,

$$\rho_i(a') = \frac{v_i(a')}{v_{3-i}(a')} \ge \frac{v_i(a')}{v_i(a') \cdot \rho_{3-i}(a)} = \frac{1}{\rho_{3-i}(a)} = \rho_i(a) \ge \tilde{\rho}(a) \ge \prod_{i=1}^{k-1}(1 - \gamma_i). \tag{5}$$

Using Equations (4) and (5),

$$\tilde{\rho}(a') = \min\{\rho_{3-i}(a'), \rho_i(a')\} \ge \prod_{i=1}^{k}(1 - \gamma_i).$$

For the other newly generated good a'', we have that

$$\rho_i(a'') = \frac{v_i(a'')}{v_{3-i}(a'')} = \frac{v_i(a'')}{v_{3-i}(a) - v_{3-i}(a')}$$

$$\begin{aligned}
&\geq \frac{v_i(a'')}{v_i(a) \cdot \rho_{3-i}(a) - v_i(a') \cdot \rho_{3-i}(a) \cdot (1-\gamma_k)} \\
&= \frac{v_i(a'')}{v_i(a'') \cdot \rho_{3-i}(a) + v_i(a') \cdot \rho_{3-i}(a) \cdot \gamma_k} \\
&\geq \frac{v_i(a'')}{v_i(a'') \cdot \rho_{3-i}(a) + v_i(a'') \cdot \rho_{3-i}(a) \cdot \gamma_k} \\
&= \frac{1}{\rho_{3-i}(a) \cdot (1+\gamma_k)} \\
&\geq \tilde{\rho}(a) \cdot (1-\gamma_k) \\
&\geq \prod_{i=1}^{k} (1-\gamma_i),
\end{aligned}$$

where the third transition follows from the definition of ρ and Equation (3), and the fifth holds due to the assumption that $0 < v_i(a') \leq v_i(a)/2$, which implies that $v_i(a') \leq v_i(a'')$. Furthermore,

$$\begin{aligned}
\rho_{3-i}(a'') &= \frac{v_{3-i}(a'')}{v_i(a'')} \\
&= \frac{v_{3-i}(a) - v_{3-i}(a')}{v_i(a'')} \\
&= \frac{v_i(a) \cdot \rho_{3-i}(a) - v_i(a') \cdot \rho_{3-i}(a)}{v_i(a'')} \\
&= \rho_{3-i}(a) \\
&\geq \tilde{\rho}(a) \geq \prod_{i=1}^{k-1} (1-\gamma_i).
\end{aligned}$$

As before, it follows that $\tilde{\rho}(a'') = \min\{\rho_i(a''), \rho_{3-i}(a'')\} \geq \prod_{i=1}^{k}(1-\gamma_i)$. □

Our next step is to instantiate the adversary framework of Algorithm 1 as Algorithm 2. We show that the algorithm is indeed consistent with the abstract framework.

Lemma 3.5. *Algorithm 2 with parameters $\vec{\gamma}$ is consistent with the framework of Algorithm 1 with parameters $\vec{\gamma}$, i.e., it satisfies Equation (3) for all k.*

Proof. First, let us prove the correctness of the left inequality of (3), that is,

$$v_i(a') \cdot \rho_{3-i}(a) \cdot (1-\gamma_k) \leq v_{3-i}(a'). \tag{6}$$

Denote $\psi = v_i(a') + v_i(a') \cdot \rho_{3-i}(a)$. We have that

$$\psi - \bar{v}(a') = v_i(a') + v_i(a') \cdot \rho_{3-i}(a) - (v_i(a') + v_{3-i}(a')) = v_i(a') \cdot \rho_{3-i}(a) - v_{3-i}(a'). \tag{7}$$

We also know that

$$\psi - \bar{v}(a') = \left(0.00 \cdots 0 d_{t+\ell_k} d_{t+\ell_k+1} \cdots\right)_3. \tag{8}$$

Algorithm 2 Adversary protocol with parameters $\vec{\gamma} = (\gamma_1, \ldots, \gamma_K) \in [0,1]^K$.

For $k = 1, 2, \cdots, K$ (the number of rounds):

(1) Receive the query $\texttt{split}_i(a, \beta)$, where $i \in \{1, 2\}$. It splits a into a' and a'' such that $v_i(a') = \beta$. Assume without loss of generality that $0 < \beta \le v_i(a)/2$, otherwise we can reverse the roles of a' and a''.

(2) Let
$$\delta_k = \frac{\rho_{3-i}(a) \cdot \gamma_k}{1 + \rho_{3-i}(a)}$$
and
$$\ell_k = \left\lceil \log_3 \delta_k^{-1} \right\rceil + 1.$$

(3) Compute the base-3 representation of the expression $v_i(a') + v_i(a') \cdot \rho_{3-i}(a)$. (Intuition: This expression is the total value of a' that would guarantee that $\tilde{\rho}(a') = \tilde{\rho}(a)$.) Denote this representation by $(0.d_1 d_2 d_3 \cdots)_3$ where $d_i \in \{0, 1, 2\}$ for all i.

(4) Let $\bar{v}(a') = \left(0.00 \cdots 0 d_t d_{t+1} \cdots d_{t+\ell_k - 1}\right)_3$, where d_t is the first non-zero digit among $d_1, d_2, \ldots$

(5) Determine the valuation of player $3-i$ via $v_{3-i}(a') = \bar{v}(a') - v_i(a')$.

Since $\psi = (0.d_1 d_2 d_3 \cdots)_3$, we can deduce that

$$\begin{aligned}
\left(0.00 \cdots 0 d_{t+\ell_k} d_{t+\ell_k+1} \cdots\right)_3 &\le \frac{\psi}{3^{\ell_k - 1}} \\
&= \frac{\psi}{3^{\lceil \log_3 \delta_k^{-1} \rceil}} \\
&\le \psi \cdot \delta_k \\
&= \psi \cdot \frac{\rho_{3-i}(a) \cdot \gamma_k}{1 + \rho_{3-i}(a)} \\
&= (v_i(a') + v_i(a') \cdot \rho_{3-i}(a)) \cdot \frac{\rho_{3-i}(a) \cdot \gamma_k}{1 + \rho_{3-i}(a)} \\
&= v_i(a') \cdot \rho_{3-i}(a) \cdot \gamma_k.
\end{aligned} \tag{9}$$

Combining Equations (7), (8), and (9), we conclude that
$$v_i(a') \cdot \rho_{3-i}(a) - v_{3-i}(a') \le v_i(a') \cdot \rho_{3-i}(a) \cdot \gamma_k.$$
By rearranging, we immediately obtain Equation (6).

We now turn to the right inequality of Equation (3),
$$v_{3-i}(a') \le v_i(a') \cdot \rho_{3-i}(a). \tag{10}$$
Clearly $\bar{v}(a') \le \psi$, because (according to Algorithm 2) the positive digits of $\bar{v}(a')$ in base 3 representation are a subset of those of ψ. Using the definitions, we can rewrite this inequality as $v_i(a') + v_{3-i}(a') \le v_i(a') + v_i(a') \cdot \rho_{3-i}(a)$, which is equivalent to Equation (10). □

Suppose that in round k we split good a into a' and a'', as in Algorithms 1 and 2. Let us denote the good a' by $a^{(k)}$, and the good a (the one that will be split in this round) by $b^{(k)}$. In particular, $a^{(0)}$ is the entire cake.

Lemma 3.6. *Let*
$$\gamma_k^* = \frac{1}{K - k + 1}$$

for $k = 1, \ldots, K$. Then under Algorithm 2 with parameters $\vec{\gamma^*}$, the total number of non-zero digits in the base-3 representations of $\bar{v}(a^{(0)}), \bar{v}(a^{(1)}), \cdots, \bar{v}(a^{(K)})$ is $O(K \ln K)$.

Proof. It is clearly sufficient to show that

$$\sum_{k=1}^{K} \ell_k = O(K \ln K),$$

because for all $k = 1, \ldots, K$, $\bar{v}(a^{(k)})$ has at most ℓ_k non-zero digits (by Algorithm 2).

By Lemma 3.4, we have that

$$\tilde{\rho}\left(b^{(k)}\right) \geq \prod_{i=1}^{k-1} (1 - \gamma_i^*).$$

It follows that

$$\delta_k = \frac{\rho_{3-i}\left(b^{(k)}\right) \cdot \gamma_k^*}{1 + \rho_{3-i}\left(b^{(k)}\right)} \geq \frac{\tilde{\rho}\left(b^{(k)}\right) \cdot \gamma_k^*}{1 + \tilde{\rho}\left(b^{(k)}\right)} \geq \frac{\gamma_k^* \cdot \prod_{i=1}^{k-1}(1 - \gamma_i^*)}{2}, \tag{11}$$

where the first inequality holds because $h(x) = \gamma_k^* \cdot x/(1 + x)$ is monotone non-decreasing, as $h'(x) = \gamma_k^*/(1 + x)^2 \geq 0$, and the second holds because $\tilde{\rho}(a) \leq 1$ for any a.

Next, let us bound the expression we are interested in.

$$\begin{aligned}
\sum_{k=1}^{K} \ell_k &= \sum_{k=1}^{K} \left(\left\lceil \log_3 \delta_k^{-1} \right\rceil + 1\right) \\
&\leq 2K + \sum_{k=1}^{K} \log_3 \delta_k^{-1} \\
&\leq 2K + \sum_{k=1}^{K} \log_3 \left(\frac{2}{\gamma_k^* \cdot \prod_{i-1}^{k-1} (1 - \gamma_i^*)}\right) \\
&\leq 3K - \sum_{k=1}^{K} \log_3 \left(\gamma_k^* \prod_{i=1}^{k-1} (1 - \gamma_i^*)\right) \\
&= 3K - \sum_{k=1}^{K} \left(\log_3 \gamma_k^* + \sum_{i=1}^{k-1} \log_3 (1 - \gamma_i^*)\right) \\
&= 3K - \sum_{k=1}^{K} \log_3 \gamma_k^* - \sum_{k=1}^{K} \sum_{i=1}^{k-1} \log_3 (1 - \gamma_i^*) \\
&= 3K - \sum_{k=1}^{K} \log_3 \gamma_k^* - \sum_{k=1}^{K} (K - k) \cdot \log_3 (1 - \gamma_k^*) \\
&= 3K - \sum_{k=1}^{K} \left(\log_3 \gamma_k^* + (K - k) \cdot \log_3 (1 - \gamma_k^*)\right) \\
&= 3K - \sum_{k=1}^{K} f_{K-k}(\gamma_k^*),
\end{aligned}$$

where the third transition follows from Equation (11), and $f_t(x) = \log_3 x + t \cdot \log_3 (1 - x)$ in the last line.

Let us consider the function f_t. On the domain $x \in (0, 1)$, it is maximized when

$$\frac{df_t(x)}{dx} = \frac{1}{\ln 3} \cdot \left(\frac{1}{x} - \frac{t}{1-x}\right) = 0,$$

or, equivalently, $1 - x - tx = 0$. Hence, the function value is maximized at $1/(t+1)$ — which explains our choice of y_k^*. We have that

$$\begin{aligned} f_t\left(\frac{1}{t+1}\right) &= \log_3\left(\frac{1}{t+1}\right) + \log_3\left(1 - \frac{1}{t+1}\right)^t \\ &\geq \log_3\left(\frac{1}{t+1}\right) + \log_3(1/e) \\ &= -\log_3(t+1) - \frac{1}{\ln 3}. \end{aligned} \tag{12}$$

Plugging (12) into our upper bound on $\sum_{k=1}^{K} \ell_k$, we get

$$\begin{aligned} \sum_{k=1}^{K} \ell_k &\leq 3K - \sum_{k=1}^{K} f_{K-k}\left(\frac{1}{K-k+1}\right) \\ &\leq 3K - \sum_{k=1}^{K}\left(-\log_3(K-k+1) - \frac{1}{\ln 3}\right) \\ &\leq 4K + \sum_{k=1}^{K} \log_3(K-k+1) \\ &\leq 4K + K \cdot \log_3(K+1) \\ &= O(K \ln K). \end{aligned}$$

□

The next lemma formalizes a simple fact about numbers represented in base 3. It is useful because Lemma 3.6 already gives us a bound on the number of non-zero digits in the total values of the goods we are interested in.

Lemma 3.7. *For any t real numbers $x_1, x_2, \cdots, x_t \in \mathbb{R}$, if they have m non-zero digits in total in their base-3 representation, then their sum $\sum_{i=1}^{t} x_i$ has at most $2m$ ones in its base-3 representation.*

Proof. We assume without loss of generality that the numbers are integers (otherwise we can multiply them by a sufficiently large power of 3). Our strategy is to sum up the integers one non-zero digit at a time, and check that the number of ones in the sum increases by at most two in each step.

Suppose that at some point in this process we have a positive partial sum, and we add to it a single positive digit, i.e., a number of the form $(10 \cdots 0)_3$ or $(20 \cdots 0)_3$ in base 3. This possibly results in a sequence of addition operations, as each one can create a carry to the next digit. Crucially, we get a new digit that is 1 only from $1 + 0$ or from $2 + 2$. Now, since the carry is at most 1, $2 + 2$ can only happen in the initial addition. Any additional ones will be created in a $1 + 0$ operation, but this operation has no carry, hence the process ends. Overall this process creates at most two ones.

Next, suppose we have a positive partial sum, and we add to it a single *negative* digit. Again, this may lead to a sequence of subtraction operations with a borrow. In this case, a 1 is generated only from $0 - 2$ and $2 - 1$. As before, $0 - 2$ can only happen once, as the borrow is at most 1. Moreover, the process ends after a $2 - 1$ operation, which has no borrow. Overall, at most two ones are generated.

The remaining two cases (negative partial sum and positive digit, negative partial sum and negative digit) are analogous to the two cases analyzed above. □

The next lemma may seem unrelated at first glance, but its application will become clear momentarily.

LEMMA 3.8. *Consider a binary tree where each node is colored either red or blue, each internal node has one red child and one blue child, and the root is red. Furthermore, each leaf i is labeled with a number x_i, and the label of each internal node is the sum of the labels of its two children. Then for any subset of leaves S, the sum $\sum_{i \in S} x_i$ can be represented as a weighted sum of the labels of red nodes, where the weights are in $\{-1, 0, 1\}$.*

PROOF. Given the subset of leaves S, we can compute the weight vector $\vec{w}$ via Algorithm 3.

Algorithm 3 Computing weights given a subset S of leaves

```
w⃗ ← 0⃗
while there are at least two nodes in the tree do
    j, k ← two sibling leaves (j is red)
    i ← parent of j and k
    if j, k ∈ S then
        S ← S ∪ {i}
    end if
    if j ∈ S and k ∉ S then
        w_j ← 1
    end if
    if j ∉ S and k ∈ S then
        w_j ← −1
        S ← S ∪ {i}
    end if
    S ← S \ {j, k}
    remove nodes j and k from the tree
end while
if S = {i} then                                    ▷ S contains only the root
    w_i ← 1
    S ← ∅
end if
```

Denoting the set of red nodes by R, it holds throughout the execution of the algorithm that the sum $\sum_{i \in S} x_i + \sum_{i \in R} w_i x_i$ remains constant (here we are assigning weight 0 unless the algorithm explicitly assigns a weight of 1 or −1). Moreover, initially this sum is equal to $\sum_{i \in S} x_i$ for the given S, and when the algorithm terminates it is equal to $\sum_{i \in R} w_i x_i$, as at that point $S = \emptyset$. □

Finally, we have all the machinery in place to prove Theorem 3.1 for the case of two players.

LEMMA 3.9. *For two players, the complexity of ε-equitable cake cutting in the RW model is*

$$\Omega\left(\frac{\ln(1/\varepsilon)}{\ln\ln(1/\varepsilon)}\right).$$

Proof. After K rounds of the adversary protocol given by Algorithm 2, the cake is partitioned into $K+1$ goods, as in each round the number of goods increases by one (one good is split into two). By Lemmas 3.2 and Lemma 3.3, it is sufficient to guarantee that no subset of these $K+1$ goods provides total value within ε of $1/2$.

In order to show this, we think of the execution of Algorithm 2 as building a binary tree. Indeed, initially there is a red root associated with the entire cake, and its label is the total value $1/2+1/2=1$. Each query splits the good a into a' and a'', and splits its total value $\bar{v}(a)$ into $\bar{v}(a')$ and $\bar{v}(a'')$; note that $\bar{v}(a)=\bar{v}(a')+\bar{v}(a'')$. We associate a red child with a' and label it with $\bar{v}(a')$, and label another blue child with $\bar{v}(a'')$. Now, Lemma 3.8 implies that there is a subset of goods (where the total value of each good is the label of the corresponding leaf) whose total value is within ε of $1/2$ if and only if there are $w_0,\ldots,w_k\in\{-1,0,1\}$ such that

$$\left|\sum_{k=0}^{K} w_i\cdot\bar{v}(a^{(k)})-\frac{1}{2}\right|\leq\varepsilon.$$

By Lemma 3.6, we know that if the adversary follows Algorithm 2 with parameters $\vec{\gamma}^*$, the total number of non-zero digits in the base-3 representation of $\bar{v}(a^{(0)}),\ldots,\bar{v}(a^{(K)})$ can be upper-bounded by $O(K\ln K)$. Therefore, Lemma 3.7 implies that the base-3 representation of $\sum_{k=0}^{K} w_i\cdot\bar{v}(a^{(k)})$ has at most $O(K\ln K)$ ones.

Note that $1/2=(0.111\cdots)_3$. By contrast, a number with no more than m ones in its base-3 representation must have a zero in the first $m+1$ positions. Taking $m=O(K\ln K)$, it follows that

$$\left|\sum_{k=0}^{K} w_i\cdot\bar{v}(a^{(k)})-\frac{1}{2}\right|\geq 3^{-O(K\ln K)}.$$

Consequently, a necessary condition to guarantee ε-equitability is

$$3^{-O(K\ln K)}\leq\varepsilon.$$

The lemma directly follows by solving for K. □

3.3 Extension to Any Number of Players

At this point, it only remains to extend the lower bound for two players to a lower bound for n players, i.e., to show that ε-equitable cake cutting for n players is at least as hard as for two players. This is not as trivial as it sounds. Indeed, one's first thought might be that it is possible to just focus on players 1 and 2; if the n-player allocation is ε-equitable, then, in particular, $|v_1(A_1)-v_2(A_2)|\leq\varepsilon$. However, the allocation to players 1 and 2 is only a *partial* allocation, i.e., the union of A_1 and A_2 may not be the entire cake.

A slightly more sophisticated approach reduces the 2-player case to the n-player case by creating copies of the two players. This approach only takes us halfway: We obtain an initial lower bound that *decreases* as n increases.

Lemma 3.10. *For any number of players $n\geq 2$, the complexity of ε-equitable cake cutting in the RW model is*

$$\Omega\left(\frac{\ln(1/(n\varepsilon))}{\ln\ln(1/(n\varepsilon))}\right).$$

Proof. Assume for ease of exposition that the number of players n is even (the proof for odd n is very similar, but a bit more cumbersome notation-wise). Our goal is to use an algorithm for ε-equitable cake cutting in the n-player case to compute an ε'-equitable allocation in the 2-player case for $\varepsilon' = n\varepsilon/2$. This means that the former problem is at least as hard as the latter, and using Lemma 3.9 with ε', we get the stated bound.

Turning to the reduction, we start from a 2-player instance, consisting of two players $\{1, 2\}$ with valuation functions v_1 and v_2. Now create an n-player instance with a set N_1 of $n/2$ players with valuation function v_1, and a set N_2 of $n/2$ players with valuation function v_2. Suppose we have an ε-equitable allocation A for the latter instance, then for all $i \in N_1$ and $j \in N_2$, $|v_1(A_i) - v_2(A_j)| \le \varepsilon$. Now let $A'_1 = \bigcup_{i\in N_1} A_i$, and $A'_2 = \bigcup_{i\in N_2} A_i$. Let $\sigma : N_1 \hookrightarrow\!\!\!\!\rightarrow N_2$ be a bijection (meaning we simply pair up players from N_1 and N_2); then

$$|v_1(A'_1) - v_2(A'_2)| \le \sum_{i\in N_1} |v_1(A_i) - v_2(A_{\sigma(i)})| \le \frac{n}{2} \cdot \varepsilon.$$

□

Even though Lemma 3.10 does not quite give us Theorem 3.1, we only need one additional idea to complete the theorem's proof.

Proof of Theorem 3.1. Our strategy is to prove an additional (trivial) lower bound on the complexity of ε-equitable cake cutting, by focusing on the case where all players have the same valuation function. We will combine it with the lower bound of Lemma 3.10 to obtain the theorem.

Consider first the case where $n < 1/\varepsilon$. Because we have assumed that $v_i = v_j$ for all $i, j \in N$, and using the additivity of the valuation functions, for any allocation A there must exist a player i such that $v_i(A_i) \ge 1/n > \varepsilon$. Therefore, in order for A to be ε-equitable, each player must receive a piece with positive value. It follows that ε-equitability requires at least $n - 1$ split queries in the adjusted RW model, as we must generate at least n goods. Combining this lower bound with the bound of Lemma 3.10, we get a lower bound of

$$\max\left\{\Omega\left(\frac{\ln(1/(n\varepsilon))}{\ln\ln(1/(n\varepsilon))}\right), n-1\right\} \ge \max\left\{\Omega\left(\frac{\ln(1/\varepsilon)}{\ln\ln(1/\varepsilon)}\right) - O\left(\ln(n)\right), n-1\right\}. \tag{13}$$

The right hand side of Equation (13) is minimized when $n = n^*$, where

$$\Omega\left(\frac{\ln(1/\varepsilon)}{\ln\ln(1/\varepsilon)}\right) - O\left(\ln(n^*)\right) = n^* - 1.$$

Clearly it holds that

$$n^* = \Omega\left(\frac{\ln(1/\varepsilon)}{\ln\ln(1/\varepsilon)}\right),$$

and it follows that the lower bound of Equation (13) is $\Omega(\ln(1/\varepsilon)/\ln\ln(1/\varepsilon))$, as desired.

Next consider the other case, where $n \ge 1/\varepsilon$. Similarly to the previous case, the number of players receiving pieces with nonzero value must be at least $1/\varepsilon$ — otherwise one of those players would have value greater than ε (recall that the players are identical), and some others would have value 0. It follows that at least $1/\varepsilon - 1$ split queries are required. Of course,

$$\frac{1}{\varepsilon} - 1 = \Omega\left(\frac{\ln(1/\varepsilon)}{\ln\ln(1/\varepsilon)}\right).$$

□

4 AN UPPER BOUND THAT IS INDEPENDENT OF THE NUMBER OF PLAYERS

As discussed in Section 1, Cechlárová and Pillárová [13] establish an upper bound of $O(n \ln(1/\varepsilon))$ on the complexity of ε-equitable cake cutting. By contrast, the lower bound of Theorem 3.1 is independent of n. While it is almost tight for a small number of players, it is natural to ask whether it is possible to prove a lower bound that grows larger with the number of players. In this section we answer this question in the negative. Specifically, we prove the following theorem.

THEOREM 4.1. *For any number of players n, the complexity of ε-equitable cake cutting in the RW model is*

$$O\left(\min\left\{n, \frac{1}{\varepsilon}\right\} \ln\left(\frac{1}{\varepsilon}\right)\right).$$

The proof is quite simple and we opt for an informal exposition. Our goal is to give an algorithm that finds an ε-equitable allocation using $O((1/\varepsilon)\ln(1/\varepsilon))$ queries; together with the upper bound of Cechlárová and Pillárová [13], this implies the theorem.

The intuition behind our algorithm comes from the elegant Even-Paz algorithm [17] that finds a proportional allocation using $O(n \ln n)$ queries. We will describe the algorithm recursively, and assume for ease of exposition that n is a power of 2. The input to the algorithm is a subset of players $1, \ldots, m$ (itself a power of 2) and a piece of cake $[x, z]$; initially these are N and $[0, 1]$. If the given set of players is a singleton, give $[x, z]$ to that player. Otherwise, the algorithm asks each player i an $\texttt{eval}_i(x, z)$ query that returns $v_i([x, z])$; and then a $\texttt{cut}_i(x, v_i([x, z]/2))$ query, which returns a point y_i that partitions the interval $[x, z]$ into two subintervals that i values equally. These marks are sorted so that $y_{i_1} \leq y_{i_2} \leq \cdots \leq y_{i_m}$, and the algorithm is called recursively with the subset of players $\{i_1, \ldots, i_{m/2}\}$ and the piece of cake $[x, y_{i_{m/2}}]$, and the subset of players $\{i_{m/2+1}, \ldots, i_m\}$ and the piece of cake $[y_{i_{m/2}}, z]$. The crux of the proportionality argument is that in each recursive call exactly half of the players that participated in the previous call share a piece of cake that they value at least at half their value for the previous piece. The height of the recursion tree is exactly $\log_2 n$, so the value of each player for his piece of cake is at least $1/2^{\log_2 n} = 1/n$.

Now, suppose that $n \geq 1/\varepsilon$, and assume for ease of exposition that $1/\varepsilon$ is a power of 2. Choose a subset of players N' of size $1/\varepsilon$. The idea is to find an *anti-proportional* allocation that gives each player in N' a piece that he values *at most* at $1/|N'| = \varepsilon$. Since players in $N \setminus N'$ receive empty pieces that they value at 0, this is an ε-equitable allocation.

In order to find an anti-proportional allocation for N', we run a variant of the Even-Paz algorithm. The only difference is that we swap the pieces in the recursive calls, that is, we call the algorithm with the subset of players $\{i_1, \ldots, i_{m/2}\}$ and the piece of cake $[y_{i_{m/2}}, z]$, and the subset of players $\{i_{m/2+1}, \ldots, i_m\}$ and the piece of cake $[x, y_{i_{m/2}}]$. Now in each recursive call exactly half of the players that participated in the previous call share a piece of cake that they value *at most* at half their value for the previous piece, which implies that each player in N' receives a piece worth *at most* $1/2^{\lg(1/\varepsilon)} = \varepsilon$.

5 DISCUSSION

The algorithm just presented (in Section 4) is clearly a very bad method for cutting a cake, even though it achieves ε-equitability.[4] We mainly included it to make a technical point about the (lack of) dependence of the problem on the number of players. But it also illustrates that equitability, in and of itself, is not a sufficiently strong property to guarantee good outcomes — it should be sought

[4]It is worth noting that there is a trivial, even worse method of achieving equitability: giving each player an empty piece (or, equivalently, throwing away the entire cake). Being able to throw away cake is known to provide significant advantages for some cake cutting problems [2, 26]. However, we work in the standard cake cutting model, where the foregoing "algorithm" is not valid, as the allocation A must form a partition of the cake.

together with other desirable properties, as it has in the past [7, 9]. Of course, our main result is a lower bound, so it holds for any combination of properties that includes ε-equitability. For example, it implies that an allocation that is both proportional and equitable cannot be computed, even though one always exists [1].

A somewhat subtle point has to do with the implications of Theorem 3.1 for exact equitability, which are stronger than they may seem at first glance. Its statement directly implies that there is no *bounded* algorithm for equitable cake cutting. Indeed, for any $K \in \mathbb{N}$ we can take ε to be small enough so that our lower bound is at least K. This approach does not rule out the existence of an *unbounded* equitable algorithm, which always terminates with an equitable allocation, but has running time that cannot be bounded as a function of the number of players. To see why such algorithms do not exist, note that instead of choosing γ_k^* that depends on the number of rounds K (as we did in Lemma 3.6), we can choose, e.g., $\gamma_k^* = 1/2$. Then Lemma 3.6 would still give an upper bound (albeit not as small as before) on the number of non-zero digits in the base-3 representation of $\bar{v}(a^{(0)}), \bar{v}(a^{(1)}), \cdots, \bar{v}(a^{(K)})$ for any K, which implies (by the rest of the proof of Lemma 3.9) that $|\bar{v}(A_1) - 1/2|$ must be strictly positive after any number of rounds. In other words, Algorithm 2 maintains a gap between the values of any allocation and the values needed for equitability, which grows smaller as the number of rounds grows larger, but always remains strictly positive. Therefore, the adversary can keep fooling an equitable algorithm forever.

Finally, it is interesting to to note that achieving ε-envy freeness requires $O(n^2/\varepsilon)$ queries in the RW model [24],[5] but *bounded* envy-free algorithms exist [3]. By contrast, ε-equitable cake cutting requires only $O(n \ln(1/\varepsilon))$ queries, yet equitable algorithms do not exist. This conceptual discrepancy highlights the richness of the cake cutting model, and of the space of problems it gives rise to.

ACKNOWLEDGMENTS

This work was partially supported by the National Science Foundation under grants IIS-1350598 and CCF-1525932, by the Office of Naval Research, and by a Sloan Research Fellowship.

REFERENCES

[1] N. Alon. 1987. Splitting necklaces. *Advances in Mathematics* 63 (1987), 241–253.

[2] O. Arzi, Y. Aumann, and Y. Dombb. 2011. Throw One's Cake — and Eat It Too. In *Proceedings of the 4th International Symposium on Algorithmic Game Theory (SAGT)*. 69–80.

[3] H. Aziz and S. Mackenzie. 2016. A Discrete and Bounded Envy-Free Cake Cutting Protocol for Any Number of Agents. In *Proceedings of the 57th Symposium on Foundations of Computer Science (FOCS)*. 416–427.

[4] H. Aziz and S. Mackenzie. 2016. A Discrete and Bounded Envy-Free Cake Cutting Protocol for Four Agents. In *Proceedings of the 48th Annual ACM Symposium on Theory of Computing (STOC)*. 454–464.

[5] E. Balkanski, S. Brânzei, D. Kurokawa, and A. D. Procaccia. 2014. Simultaneous Cake Cutting. In *Proceedings of the 28th AAAI Conference on Artificial Intelligence (AAAI)*. 566–572.

[6] S. J. Brams, M. Feldman, J. Morgenstern, J. K. Lai, and A. D. Procaccia. 2012. On Maxsum Fair Cake Divisions. In *Proceedings of the 26th AAAI Conference on Artificial Intelligence (AAAI)*. 1285–1291.

[7] S. J. Brams, M. A. Jones, and C. Klamler. 2006. Better Ways to Cut a Cake. *Notices of the AMS* 53, 11 (2006), 1314–1321.

[8] S. J. Brams and A. D. Taylor. 1995. An Envy-Free Cake Division Protocol. *The American Mathematical Monthly* 102, 1 (1995), 9–18.

[9] S. J. Brams and A. D. Taylor. 1996. *Fair Division: From Cake-Cutting to Dispute Resolution*. Cambridge University Press.

[10] S. Brânzei and P. B. Miltersen. 2015. A Dictatorship Theorem for Cake Cutting. In *Proceedings of the 24th International Joint Conference on Artificial Intelligence (IJCAI)*. 482–488.

[11] I. Caragiannis, D. Kurokawa, H. Moulin, A. D. Procaccia, N. Shah, and J. Wang. 2016. The Unreasonable Fairness of Maximum Nash Product. In *Proceedings of the 17th ACM Conference on Economics and Computation (EC)*. 305–322.

[5] This is the best known upper bound, but there is no matching lower bound.

[12] K. Cechlárová and E. Pillárová. 2012. A Near Equitable 2-Person Cake Cutting Algorithm. *Optimization* 61, 11 (2012), 1321–1330.

[13] K. Cechlárová and E. Pillárová. 2012. On the Computability of Equitable Divisions. *Discrete Optimization* 9, 4 (2012), 249–257.

[14] Y. Chen, J. K. Lai, D. C. Parkes, and A. D. Procaccia. 2013. Truth, Justice, and Cake Cutting. *Games and Economic Behavior* 77 (2013), 284–297.

[15] J. Edmonds and K. Pruhs. 2006. Balanced Allocations of Cake. In *Proceedings of the 47th Symposium on Foundations of Computer Science (FOCS)*. 623–634.

[16] J. Edmonds and K. Pruhs. 2006. Cake Cutting Really Is Not a Piece of Cake. In *Proceedings of the 17th Annual ACM-SIAM Symposium on Discrete Algorithms (SODA)*. 271–278.

[17] S. Even and A. Paz. 1984. A Note on Cake-Cutting. *Discrete Applied Mathematics* 7 (1984), 285–296.

[18] Y. Gal, M. Mash, A. D. Procaccia, and Y. Zick. 2016. Which Is the Fairest (Rent Division) of Them All?. In *Proceedings of the 17th ACM Conference on Economics and Computation (EC)*. 67–84.

[19] J. Goldman and A. D. Procaccia. 2014. Spliddit: Unleashing Fair Division Algorithms. *SIGecom Exchanges* 13, 2 (2014), 41–46.

[20] D. K. Herreiner and C. D. Puppe. 2009. Envy freeness in experimental fair division problems. *Theory and decision* 67, 1 (2009), 65–100.

[21] D. Kurokawa, J. K. Lai, and A. D. Procaccia. 2013. How to Cut a Cake Before the Party Ends. In *Proceedings of the 27th AAAI Conference on Artificial Intelligence (AAAI)*. 555–561.

[22] A. D. Procaccia. 2009. Thou Shalt Covet Thy Neighbor's Cake. In *Proceedings of the 21st International Joint Conference on Artificial Intelligence (IJCAI)*. 239–244.

[23] A. D. Procaccia. 2013. Cake Cutting: Not Just Child's Play. *Communications of the ACM* 56, 7 (2013), 78–87.

[24] A. D. Procaccia. 2016. Cake Cutting Algorithms. In *Handbook of Computational Social Choice*, F. Brandt, V. Conitzer, U. Endress, J. Lang, and A. D. Procaccia (Eds.). Cambridge University Press, Chapter 13.

[25] J. M. Robertson and W. A. Webb. 1998. *Cake Cutting Algorithms: Be Fair If You Can*. A. K. Peters.

[26] E. Segal-Halevi, A. Hassidim, and Y. Aumann. 2016. Waste Makes Haste: Bounded Time Algorithms for Envy-Free Cake Cutting with Free Disposal. *ACM Transactions on Economics and Computation* 13, 1 (2016), article 15.

[27] H. Steinhaus. 1948. The Problem of Fair Division. *Econometrica* 16 (1948), 101–104.

[28] W. Stromquist. 2008. Envy-Free Cake Divisions Cannot Be Found by Finite Protocols. *The Electronic Journal of Combinatorics* 15 (2008), #R11.

[29] G. J. Woeginger and J. Sgall. 2007. On the Complexity of Cake Cutting. *Discrete Optimization* 4 (2007), 213–220.

Online Auctions and Multi-scale Online Learning

SÉBASTIEN BUBECK, Microsoft Research
NIKHIL R. DEVANUR, Microsoft Research
ZHIYI HUANG, The University of Hong Kong
RAD NIAZADEH, Cornell University

We consider revenue maximization in online auctions and pricing. A seller sells an identical item in each period to a new buyer, or a new set of buyers. For the online posted pricing problem, we show regret bounds that scale with the *best fixed price*, rather than the range of the values. We also show regret bounds that are *almost scale free*, and match the offline sample complexity, when comparing to a benchmark that requires a *lower bound on the market share*. These results are obtained by generalizing the classical learning from experts and multi-armed bandit problems to their *multi-scale* versions. In this version, the reward of each action is in a *different range*, and the regret w.r.t. a given action scales with its *own range*, rather than the maximum range.

1 INTRODUCTION

Consider the following revenue maximization problem in a repeated setting, called the *online posted pricing* problem. In each period, the seller has a single item to sell, and a new prospective buyer. The seller offers to sell the item to the buyer at a given price; the buyer buys the item if and only if the price is below his private valuation for the item. The private valuation of the buyer itself is never revealed to the seller. How should a monopolistic seller iteratively set the prices if he wishes to maximize his revenue? What if he also cares about market share?

Estimating price sensitivities and demand models in order to optimize revenue and market share is the bedrock of econometrics. The emergence of online marketplaces has enabled sellers to costlessly change prices, as well as collect huge amounts of data. This has renewed the interest in understanding best practices for data driven pricing. The extreme case of this when the price is updated for each buyer is the online pricing problem described above; one can always use this for less frequent price updates. Moreover this problem is intimately related to classical experimentation and estimation procedures.

This problem has been studied from an *online learning* perspective, as a variant of the *multi-armed bandit* problem. The revenue of a pricing algorithm is compared to the revenue of the best fixed posted price, in hindsight, and the difference between the two, called the *regret*, is analyzed. No assumption is made on the distribution of values; the regret bounds are required to hold for the *worst case* sequence of values. Blum et al. [10] assume that the buyer valuations are in $[1, h]$, and show the following multiplicative + additive bound on the regret: for any $\epsilon \in (0, 1)$, the regret is at most ϵ times the revenue of the optimal price, + $O(\epsilon^{-2} h \log h \log\log h)$. Blum and Hartline [9] show that the additive factor can be made to be $O(\epsilon^{-3} h \log\log h)$, trading off a $\log h$ factor for an extra ϵ^{-1} factor.

An undesirable aspect of these bounds is that they scale *linearly with* h; this is particularly problematic when h is an estimate and we might set it to be a generous upper bound on the range

Zhiyi Huang is supported by a RGC grant HKU17202115E. Rad Niazadeh is supported by a NSF grant CCF-1512964 and by a Google Ph.D. Fellowship. Part of this work were completed while Zhiyi and Rad were visiting Microsoft Research Redmond.

EC'17, June 26–30, 2017, Cambridge, MA, USA. © 2017 Association for Computing Machinery.
ACM ISBN 978-1-4503-4527-9/17/06...$15.00. DOI: http://dx.doi.org/10.1145/3033274.3085145

of prices we wish to consider. A typical use case is when the same algorithm is used for many different products, with widely varying price ranges. We may not be able to manually tune the range for each product separately.

This dependency on h seems unavoidable, as is reflected by the lower bounds for the problem. (Lower bounds are discussed later in the introduction.) Yet, somewhat surprisingly, **our first contribution in this paper is to show that we can replace h by the best fixed price** [1] (that is used in the definition of the benchmark). In particular, we show that the additive bound can be made to be $O(\epsilon^{-2}p^* \log h)$, where p^* is the best fixed price in hindsight. This allows us to use a very generous estimate for h; we only lose a $\log h$ factor. The algorithm balances exploration probabilities of different prices carefully and automatically zooms in on the relevant price range. This does not violate known lower bounds, since in those instances p^* is close to h.

Bar-Yossef et al. [7], Blum et al. [10], and Blum and Hartline [9] also consider the "full information" version of the problem, or what we call the *online auction* problem, where the valuations of the buyers are revealed to the algorithm after the buyer has made a decision. Such information may be available in a context where the buyers have to bid for the items, and are awarded the item if their bid is above a hidden price. In this case, the additive term can be improved to $O(\epsilon^{-1}h \log(\epsilon^{-1}))$, which is tight. Once again, *we show that h can be replaced with p^**; in particular, we show that the additive term can be made to be $O(\epsilon^{-1}p^* \log(h\epsilon^{-1}))$.

1.1 Purely multiplicative bounds and sample complexity

The regret bounds mentioned above can be turned into a purely multiplicative factor in the following way: for any $\epsilon > 0$, the algorithm is guaranteed to get a $1 - O(\epsilon)$ fraction of the best fixed price revenue, provided the number of periods $T \geq E/\epsilon$, where E is the additive term in the regret bounds above. This follows from the observation that a revenue of T is a lower bound on the best fixed price revenue. Call the number of periods required to get a $1 - \epsilon$ multiplicative approximation (as a function of ϵ) as the *convergence rate* of the algorithm.

A $1 - \epsilon$ multiplicative factor is also the target in the recent line of work on the *sample complexity* of auctions started by Cole and Roughgarden [12], Dhangwatnotai et al. [16]. (We give a more comprehensive discussion of this line of work in Section 1.3.) Here, *i.i.d.* samples of the valuations are given from a *fixed but unknown distribution*, and the goal is to find a price such that its revenue w.r.t. the hidden distribution is a $1 - \epsilon$ fraction of the optimum revenue for this distribution. The sample complexity is the minimum number of samples needed to guarantee this (as a function of ϵ).

The sample complexity and the convergence rate (for the full information setting) are closely related to each other. The sample complexity is always smaller than the convergence rate: the problem is easier because of the following.

(1) The valuations are i.i.d. in case of sample complexity whereas they can be arbitrary (worst case) in case of convergence rate.
(2) Sample complexity corresponds to an offline problem: you get all the samples at once. Convergence rate corresponds to an online problem: you need to decide what to do on a given valuation without knowing what valuations arrive in the future.

This is formalized in terms of an *online to offline reduction* [folklore] which shows that a convergence rate upper bound can be automatically translated to a sample complexity upper bound. This lets us convert sample complexity lower bounds into lower bounds on the convergence rate, and in turn into lower bounds on the additive error E in an additive + multiplicative regret bound. E.g.,

[1] Standard bounds allow regret to depend on the loss of the best action instead of the worst case loss. However, even such bounds still depend linearly on the range of the losses, and thus they would not allow to replace h by the best fixed price.

the additive error for the online auction problem (and hence also for the posted pricing problem[2]) cannot be $o(h\epsilon^{-1})$ [19]. Moreover, it is insightful to compare convergence rates we show with *the best known sample complexity upper bound; proving better convergence rates would mean improving these bounds as well.*

A natural target convergence rate for a problem is therefore the corresponding sample complexity, but achieving this is not always trivial. An interesting version of the sample complexity bound for auctions did not have an analogous convergence rate bound. This version takes into account *both revenue and market share*, and surprisingly, gets sample complexity bounds that are *scale free*; there is no dependence on h, which means it works for unbounded valuations! For any $\delta \in (0, 1)$, the best fixed price benchmark is relaxed to ignore those prices whose market share (or equivalently probability of sale) is below a δ fraction; as δ increases the benchmark is lower. This is a meaningful benchmark since in many cases revenue is not the only goal, even if you are a monopolist. A more reasonable goal is to maximize revenue subject to the constraint that the market share is above a certain threshold. What more, this gives a sample complexity of $O(\epsilon^{-2}\delta^{-1}\log(\delta^{-1}\epsilon^{-1}))$ [19]. In fact δ can be set to h^{-1} without loss of generality, when the values are in $[1, h]$,[3] and the above bound then matches the sample complexity w.r.t. the best fixed price revenue. In addition, this bound gives a precise interpolation: as the target market share δ increase, the number of samples needed decreases almost linearly.

The second contribution of this paper is to show a convergence rate that almost matches the above sample complexity, for the full information setting. We have a mild dependence on h; the rate is proportional to $\log\log h$. Further, we also show a near optimal convergence rate for the posted pricing problem.[4]

Multiple buyers: All of our results in the full information (online auction) setting extend to the multiple buyer model. In this model, in each time period, a new set of n buyers compete for a single item. The seller runs a truthful auction that determines the winning buyer and his payment. The benchmark here is the set of all "Myerson-type" mechanisms. These are mechanisms that are optimal when each period has n buyers of potentially different types, and the value of each buyer is drawn independently from a type dependent distribution. In fact, our convergence rates also imply new sample complexity bounds for these problems (except that they are not computationally efficient).

The various bounds and comparison to previous work are summarized in Tables 1 and 2.

1.2 Multi-scale online learning

The main technical ingredients in our results are variants of the classical problems of learning from expert advice and multi-armed bandit. We introduce the multi-scale versions of these problems, where each action has its reward bounded in a different range. **Our third contribution is to give an algorithm for this problem whose regret w.r.t. a certain action scales with the range of rewards for that particular action.** To contrast, the regret bounds in the standard versions scale with the maximum range. We expect such bounds to be of independent interest.

The multi-scale versions of these problems exhibit subtle variations that don't appear in the standard versions. First of all, our applications to auctions and pricing has non-negative rewards, and this actually makes a difference. For both the expert and the bandit versions, the minimax regret bounds for non-negative rewards are *provably better* than those when rewards could be negative. Further, for the bandit version, we can prove a better bound if we only require the bound

---

[2] We conjecture that the lower bound for the posted pricing problem should be worse by a factor of ϵ^{-1}, since one needs to explore about ϵ^{-1} differnet prices.

[3] When the values are in $[1, h]$, we can guarantee a revenue of T by posting a price of 1, and to beat this, any other price (and in particular a price of h) would have to sell at least T/h times.

[4] Unfortunately, we cannot yet guarantee that our online algorithm itself gets a market share of δ, although we strongly believe that it does. Showing such bounds on the market share of the algorithm is an important avenue for future research.

	Lower bound	Upper bound		
		Best known (Sample complexity)	Best known (Convergence rate)	This paper (Thm. 2.5)
Online single buyer auction	$\Omega\left(\frac{h}{\epsilon^2}\right)$ *	$\tilde{O}\left(\frac{h}{\epsilon^2}\right)$ †	$\tilde{O}\left(\frac{h}{\epsilon^2}\right)$ †	$\tilde{O}\left(\frac{p^*}{\epsilon^2}\right)$
Online posted pricing	$\Omega\left(\max\{\frac{h}{\epsilon^2}, \frac{1}{\epsilon^3}\}\right)$ *§	-	$\tilde{O}\left(\frac{h}{\epsilon^3}\right)$ †	$\tilde{O}\left(\frac{p^*}{\epsilon^3}\right)$
Online multi buyer auction	$\Omega\left(\frac{h}{\epsilon^2}\right)$ *	$O\left(\frac{nh}{\epsilon^3}\right)$ ‡	-	$\tilde{O}\left(\frac{nh}{\epsilon^3}\right)$

* Huang et al. [19]; † Blum et al. [10]; ‡ Devanur et al. [14], Gonczarowski and Nisan [18]; § Kleinberg and Leighton [20].

Table 1. Number of rounds/samples needed to get a $1 - \epsilon$ approximation to the best offline price/mechanism. Sample complexity is for the offline case with i.i.d. samples from an unknown distribution. Convergence rate is for the online case with a worst case sequence. Sample complexity is always no larger than the convergence rate. Lower bounds hold for sample complexity too, except for the online posted pricing problem for which there is no sample complexity version. The additive + multiplicative regret bounds are converted to convergence rates by dividing the additive error by ϵ. In the last row, n is the number of buyers. In the last column, p^* denotes the optimal price.

	Lower bound (Sample Complexity)	Upper bound	
		Best known (Sample complexity)	This paper (Thm. 2.6)
Online single buyer auction	$\Omega\left(\frac{1}{\epsilon^2\delta}\right)$ *	$\tilde{O}\left(\frac{1}{\epsilon^2\delta}\right)$ *	$\tilde{O}\left(\frac{1}{\epsilon^2\delta}\right)$
Online posted pricing	$\Omega\left(\max\{\frac{1}{\epsilon^2\delta}, \frac{1}{\epsilon^3}\}\right)$ *†	-	$\tilde{O}\left(\frac{1}{\epsilon^4\delta}\right)$
Online multi buyer auction	$\Omega\left(\frac{1}{\epsilon^2\delta}\right)$ *	-	$\tilde{O}\left(\frac{n}{\epsilon^3\delta}\right)$

* Huang et al. [19]; † Kleinberg and Leighton [20].

Table 2. Sample complexity & convergence rate w.r.t. the opt mechanism/price with market share $\geq \delta$.

to hold w.r.t. the *best* action, rather than *all* actions (for non-negative rewards). The various regret bounds and comparison to standard bounds are summarized in Tables 3.

	Standard regret bound $O(\cdot)$	Multi-scale bound (this paper)	
		Upper bound $O(\cdot)$	Lower bound $\Omega(\cdot)$
Experts/non-negative	$c_{\max}\sqrt{T\log(k)}$ *	$c_i\sqrt{T\log(kT)}$	$c_i\sqrt{T\log(k)}$
Bandits/non-negative	$c_{\max}\sqrt{Tk\log(k)}$ †	$c_iT^{\frac{2}{3}}(k\log(kT))^{\frac{1}{3}}$	$c_i\sqrt{TK}$
		$c_{i^*}\sqrt{Tk\log(k)}$, i^* is the best action	-
Experts/symmetric	$c_{\max}\sqrt{T\log(k)}$ *	$c_i\sqrt{T\log(k\cdot\frac{c_{\max}}{c_{\min}})}$	$c_i\sqrt{T\log(k)}$
Bandits/symmetric	$c_{\max}\sqrt{Tk\log(k)}$ †	$c_i\sqrt{Tk\cdot\frac{c_{\max}}{c_{\min}}\log(kT\cdot\frac{c_{\max}}{c_{\min}})}$	$c_i\sqrt{Tk\cdot\frac{c_{\max}}{c_{\min}}}$

* Freund and Schapire [17]; † Auer et al. [4].

Table 3. Pure-additive regret bounds for non-negative rewards, i.e. when reward of any action i at any time is in $[0, c_i]$, and symmetric range rewards, i.e. when reward of any action i at any time is in $[-c_i, c_i]$ (suppose T is the time horizon, A is the actions set, and k is the number of actions).

We use algorithms based on online (stochastic) mirror descent (OSMD) [11], with a weighted negative entropy as the Legendre function. This framework gives regret bounds in terms of a "local norm" as well as an "initial divergence", which we then bound differently for each version of the problem. In the technical sections we highlight how the subtle variations arise as a result of different techniques used to bound these two terms.

1.3 Other related work

The online pricing problem, also called *dynamic pricing*, is a much studied topic, across disciplines such as operations research and management science [26], economics [24], marketing, and of course computer science. The multi-armed bandit approach to pricing is particularly popular. See den Boer [13] for a recent survey on various approaches to the problem.

Kleinberg and Leighton [20] consider the online pricing problem, under the assumption that the values are in $[0, 1]$, and considered purely additive factors. They showed that the minimax additive regret is $\tilde{\Theta}(T^{2/3})$, where T is the number of periods. This is similar in spirit to regret bounds that scale with h, since one has to normalize the values so that they are in $[0, 1]$. The finer distinction about the magnitude of the best fixed price is absent in this work. Recently, Syrgkanis [25] also consider the online auction problem, with an emphasis on a notion of "oracle based" computational efficiency. They assume the values are all in $[0, 1]$ and don't consider the scaling issue that we do; this makes their contribution orthogonal to ours.

Starting with Dhangwatnotai et al. [16], there has been a spate of recent results analyzing the sample complexity of pricing and auction problems. Cole and Roughgarden [12] and Devanur et al. [14] consider multiple buyer auctions with regular distributions (with unbounded valuations) and give sample complexity bounds that are polynomial in n and ϵ^{-1}, where n is the number of buyers. Morgenstern and Roughgarden [21] consider arbitrary distributions with values bounded by h, and gave bounds that are polynomial in n, h, and ϵ^{-1}. Huang et al. [19], Roughgarden and Schrijvers [23] give further improvements on the single- and multi-buyer versions respectively; tables 1 and 2 give a comparison of these results with our bounds, for the problems we consider. The dynamic pricing problem has also been studied when there are a given number of copies of the item to sell (limited supply) [1, 5, 6, 8]. There are also variants where the seller interacts with the same buyer repeatedly, and the buyer can strategize to influence his utility in the future periods [2, 15].

2 MODEL AND MAIN RESULTS

We consider a variety of online algorithmic problems that are all parts of the *multiscale online learning* framework. We start by defining this framework and expressing our results in terms of *action-specific* regret bounds for this general problem. Next, we investigate different auction design problems that are covered by this framework, and show how to get multiplicative cum additive approximations for these problems by the help of the multi-scale learning framework. We then consider competing with *δ-guarded benchmarks* and show how our algorithms get pure multiplicative approximations with respect to these benchmarks. We can then translate the convergence rate of our online algorithms to sample complexity of auctions to 1) generalize many sample complexity upper-bounds to the online adversarial auction settings, 2) compare our bounds with the known sample complexity lower-bounds, and 3) design new algorithms achieving near-optimal sample complexity bounds for the offline Bayesian auction problem.

2.1 Multi-scale online learning framework

Our multi-scale online learning framework is basically the classical learning from expert advice problem (under full-information) or multi-armed bandit problem (under partial-information). The main difference is that the *range* of different experts/arms could be different. Suppose there is a set of actions A. The problem proceeds in T rounds, and in each round $t \in [T]$:[5]

- The algorithm picks an action $i_t \in A$
- The adversary picks a reward function $\mathbf{g}(t)$ simultaneously, where action i has reward $g_i(t)$.
- The algorithm gets the reward $g_{i_t}(t)$.
- In the *full information* setting, the algorithm sees the entire reward function $\mathbf{g}(t)$. In the *bandit* setting, the algorithm sees only its own reward, $g_{i_t}(t)$.

The total reward of the algorithm is denoted by

$$G_{\text{ALG}} := \textstyle\sum_{t=1}^{T} g_{i_t}(t).$$

The standard "best fixed action" benchmark is

$$G_{\text{MAX}} := \max_{i\in A} \textstyle\sum_{t=1}^{T} g_i(t).$$

We consider both full-information and the bandit setting:

- **Multi-scale experts:** The action set is countable. If the action set is finite of size k, we identify $A = [k]$. The reward $\mathbf{g}(t)$ is such that for all $i \in A$, $g_i(t) \in [0, c_i]$. The entire reward function $\mathbf{g}(t)$ is revealed to the algorithm after round t.
- **Multi-scale bandit learning:** The same as before, in the bandit setting.

We prove *action-specific regret* bounds, which we call also *multi-scale regret guarantees.* Towards this end, we define the following quantities.

$$G_i := \textstyle\sum_{t\in[T]} g_i(t)\,, \tag{1}$$

$$\text{REGRET}_i := G_i - G_{\text{ALG}}\,. \tag{2}$$

The regret bound w.r.t. action i, i.e., an upper bound on $\mathbf{E}[\text{REGRET}_i]$, depends on the range c_i, as well as any *prior* distribution $\boldsymbol{\pi}$ over the action set A; this way, we can handle countably many actions. Let $c_{\min} = \inf_{i\in A} c_i$ and $c_{\max} = \sup_{i\in A} c_i$ (if applicable) be the minimum and the maximum range. We first state a version of the regret bound which is parameterized by $\epsilon > 0$; such bounds are stronger than $\sqrt{T}$ type bounds which are more standard.

Theorem 2.1. *There exists an algorithm for the multi-scale experts problem that takes as input any distribution $\boldsymbol{\pi}$ over A, the ranges c_i, $\forall\, i \in A$, and a parameter $0 < \epsilon \leq 1$, and satisfies:*

$$\forall i \in A:\ \mathbf{E}[\mathit{REGRET}_i] \leq \epsilon \cdot G_i + O\left(\frac{1}{\epsilon}\log\left(\frac{1}{\epsilon\pi_i}\right)\cdot c_i\right) \tag{3}$$

Compare this to what you get by using the standard analysis for the experts problem [3], where the second term in the regret bound is $O\big(\frac{1}{\epsilon}\log(k)\cdot c_{\max}\big)$. Choosing $\boldsymbol{\pi}$ to be the uniform distribution in the above theorem gives $O\big(\frac{1}{\epsilon}\log\left(\frac{k}{\epsilon}\right)\cdot c_i\big)$. Also, one can compare the pure-additive version of this bound with the classic pure-additive regret bound $O\big(c_{\max}\cdot\sqrt{T\log(k)}\big)$ for the experts problem by setting $\epsilon = \sqrt{\frac{\log(kT)}{T}}$ (Corollary 2.2).

Corollary 2.2. *There exists an algorithm for the multi-scale experts problem that takes as input the ranges c_i, $\forall\, i \in A$, and satisfies:*

$$\forall i \in A:\ \mathbf{E}[\mathit{REGRET}_i] \leq O\left(c_i\cdot\sqrt{T\log(kT)}\right) \tag{4}$$

[5] We use the notation $[n] := \{1, 2, \ldots, n\}$, for any $n \in \mathbb{N}$.

For the bandit version, we can get a similar regret guarantee, but only for the *best* action. If we require the regret bound to hold for all actions, then we can only get a weaker bound, where the second term has ϵ^{-2} instead of ϵ^{-1}. The difference between the bounds for the bandit and the full information setting is essentially a factor of k, which is unavoidable.

Theorem 2.3. *There exists an algorithm for the online multi-scale bandits problem that takes as input the ranges c_i, $\forall\, i \in A$, and a parameter $0 < \epsilon \leq 1$, and satisfies,*

- *for $i^* = \arg\max_{i \in A} G_i$,*

$$\mathrm{E}\left[\textit{REGRET}_{i^*}\right] \leq \epsilon \cdot G_{i^*} + O\left(\tfrac{1}{\epsilon} k \log\left(\tfrac{k}{\epsilon}\right) \cdot c_{i^*}\right). \tag{5}$$

- *for all $i \in A$,*

$$\mathrm{E}\left[\textit{REGRET}_{i}\right] \leq \epsilon \cdot G_{i} + O\left(\tfrac{1}{\epsilon^2} k \log\left(\tfrac{k}{\epsilon}\right) \cdot c_{i}\right). \tag{6}$$

Also, one can compute the pure-additive versions of the bounds in Theorems ?? by setting $\epsilon = \sqrt{\frac{k\log(kT)}{T}}$ and $\epsilon = (\frac{k\log(kT)}{T})^{\frac{1}{3}}$ resepctively (Corollary 2.4), and compare with the pure-additive regret bound $O\left(c_{\max} \cdot \sqrt{Tk\log k}\right)$ for the adversarial multi-armed bandit problem [4].

Corollary 2.4. *There exist algorithms for the online multi-scale bandits problem that satisfies,*

- *For $i^* = \arg\max_{i \in A} G_i$,*

$$\mathrm{E}\left[\textit{REGRET}_{i^*}\right] \leq O\left(c_{i^*} \cdot \sqrt{Tk\log(kT)}\right) \tag{7}$$

- *For all $i \in A$,*

$$\mathrm{E}\left[\textit{REGRET}_{i}\right] \leq O\left(c_{i} \cdot T^{\frac{2}{3}} (k\log(kT))^{\frac{1}{3}}\right) \tag{8}$$

2.2 Online auction design

The auction design problems that we consider are as follows.

- **Online single buyer auction:** The action set $A = [1, h]$. The reward function is such that the adversary picks a *value* $v(t) \in [1, h]$ and for any *price* $i \in A$, the reward $g_i(t) := p \cdot \mathbf{1}(v(t) \geq i)$. This is the full information setting, where the value $v(t)$ is revealed to the algorithm after round t.
- **Online posted pricing:** The same as above, in the bandit setting. The algorithm only learns the indicator function $\mathbf{1}(v(t) \geq i_t)$ where i_t is the price it picks in round t.
- **Online multi buyer auction:** The action set is the set of all "Myerson-type" mechanisms for n buyers, for some $n \in \mathbb{N}$. (See Definition 5.1.) The adversary picks a valuation vector $\mathbf{v}(t) \in [1, h]^n$ and the reward of a mechanism M is its revenue when the valuation of the buyers is given by $\mathbf{v}(t)$; this is denoted by $\text{REV}_M(\mathbf{v}(t))$. The algorithm sees the full vector of valuations $\mathbf{v}(t)$.

We show how to get a multiplicative cum additive approximations for these problems with G_{MAX} as the benchmark, à la Blum and Hartline [9], Blum et al. [10]. The main improvement over these results is that the additive term scales with the best price rather than h. Let p^* be the best fixed price on hindsight, which is the price that achieves G_{MAX}.

Theorem 2.5. *There are algorithms for the online single buyer auction, online posted price auction, and the online multi buyer auction problems that take as input a parameter $\epsilon > 0$, and satsify $G_{ALG} \geq (1-\epsilon)G_{MAX} - O(E)$, where respectively (for the three problems mentioned above)*

$$E = \frac{p^* \log(\log h/\epsilon)}{\epsilon}, \ \frac{p^* \log h \log(\log h/\epsilon)}{\epsilon^2}, \ \textit{and}\ \frac{hn\log h \log(n\log h/\epsilon)}{\epsilon^2}.$$

Even if h is not known upfront, we can still get the similar approximation guarantee for online single buyer auction and online multi buyer auction with:

$$E = \frac{p^* \log(p^*/\epsilon)}{\epsilon}, \textit{ and } \frac{hn \log h \log(n \log h/\epsilon)}{\epsilon^2}.$$

Bounds on the *sample complexity* of auctions imply that the first bound in this theorem is tight up to log factors: the lower bound is $h\epsilon^{-1}$ in an instance where $p^* = h$, and the best upper bound known is $h\epsilon^{-1}\log(1/\epsilon)$. We conjecture that our bound for the online posted pricing problem is tight up to log factors, and leave resolving this as an open problem. The third bound is not comparable to the best sample complexity for the multi buyer auction problem by Roughgarden and Schrijvers [23]; it is better than theirs for large ϵ (when $1/\epsilon \le o(nh)$), and is worse for smaller ϵ (when $1/\epsilon \ge \omega(nh)$). Also, compare these to the corresponding upper bounds for the first two problems by Blum and Hartline [9], Blum et al. [10], which are respectively

$$\frac{h\log(1/\epsilon)}{\epsilon}, \text{ and } \min\left\{\frac{h \log h \log\log h}{\epsilon^2}, \frac{h \log\log h}{\epsilon^3}\right\}.$$

2.3 Competing with δ-guarded benchmarks

For the single buyer auction/pricing problem, we define a δ-guarded benchmark, for any $\delta \in [0, 1]$. This benchmark is restricted to only those prices that sell the item in at least a δ fraction of the rounds.

$$G_{\text{MAX}}(\delta) := \max\left\{\textstyle\sum_{t=1}^{T} g_p(t) : p \in A, \sum_{t=1}^{T} \mathbf{1}(v_t \ge p) \ge \delta T\right\}.$$

As observed in Footnote 3, one can replace δ with $1/h$ and get the corresponding guarantees for G_{MAX} rather than $G_{\text{MAX}}(\delta)$. However, the main point of these results is to show a graceful improvement of the bounds as δ is chosen to be larger.

Multiple buyers: For the multi buyer auction problem, we define the δ-guarded benchmark as follows. For any sequence of value vectors $\mathbf{v}(1), \mathbf{v}(2), \dots, \mathbf{v}(T)$, let $\bar{V}$ denote the largest value such that there are at least δT distinct $\mathbf{v}(t)$'s with $\max_{i\in[n]} v_i(t) \ge \bar{V}$. Define the δ-guarded benchmark to be

$$G_{\text{MAX}}(\delta) = \max_M \textstyle\sum_{t=1}^{T} Rev_M\left(\min(\bar{V}\vec{1}, \mathbf{v}(t)))\right),$$

where the min is to be understood to be applied co-ordinate wise, and the max is over all Myerson-type mechanisms.

We focus on purely multiplicative approximation factors when competing with $G_{\text{MAX}}(\delta)$. In particular, for any given $\epsilon > 0$, we are interested in a $1-\epsilon$ approximation. We state our results in terms of the *convergence rate.* We say that $T(\epsilon, \delta)$ is the convergence rate of an algorithm if for all time horizon $T \ge T(\epsilon, \delta)$, we are guaranteed that $G_{\text{ALG}} \ge (1-\epsilon)G_{\text{MAX}}(\delta)$. Our main results are as follows.

Theorem 2.6. *There are algorithms for the online single buyer auction, online posted pricing, and the online multi buyer auction problems with convergence rates respectively of*

$$O\left(\frac{\log(\log h/\epsilon)}{\epsilon^2\delta}\right), O\left(\frac{\log h}{\epsilon^4\delta}\right), \textit{ and } O\left(\frac{n\log(1/\epsilon\delta)\log(n\log(1/\epsilon\delta)/\epsilon)}{\epsilon^3\delta} + \frac{\log(\log h/\epsilon)}{\epsilon^2\delta}\right).$$

Even if h is not known upfront, we can still get the following similar convergence rates for online single buyer auction and online multi buyer auction respectively:

$$O\left(\frac{\log(p^*/\epsilon)}{\epsilon^2\delta}\right), \textit{ and } O\left(\frac{n\log(1/\epsilon\delta)\log(n\log(1/\epsilon\delta)/\epsilon)}{\epsilon^3\delta} + \frac{\log(h/\epsilon)}{\epsilon^2\delta}\right).$$

Once again, we compare to the sample compexity bounds: our first is within a $\log\log h$ factor of the best sample complexity upper bound in Huang et al. [19]. The lower bound for the online single buyer auction is $\Omega(\delta^{-1}\epsilon^{-2})$, which is also the best lower bound known for the pricing and the multi-buyer problem.[6] For the online posted pricing problem, we conjecture that the right dependence on ϵ should be ϵ^{-3}. No sample complexity bounds for the multi-buyer problem were known before; in fact we introduce the definition of a δ-guarded benchmark for this problem.

2.4 Multi-scale online learning with symmetric range

The standard analysis for the experts and the bandit problems holds even if the range of $g_i(t)$ is $[-c_i, c_i]$, rather than $[0, c_i]$ as we have assumed. In contrast, there are subtle differences on the best acheivable multi-scale regret bounds between the non-negative and the symmetric range. We first show the following upper bound for the full information setting when the range is symmetric. This bounds follows the same style of action-specific regret bounds as in Theorem 2.1. More detailed discussion on how the choice of initial distribution $\boldsymbol{\pi}$ affects the bound is deferred to the full version due to space constraint.

Theorem 2.7. *There exists an algorithm for the multi-scale experts problem with symmetric range that takes as input any distribution $\boldsymbol{\pi}$ over A, the ranges c_i, $\forall\, i \in A$, and a parameter $0 < \epsilon \leq 1$, and satisfies:*

$$\forall i \in A: \ \mathbf{E}\left[\textit{REGRET}_i\right] \leq \epsilon \cdot \mathbf{E}\left[\textstyle\sum_{t\in[T]} \left|g_t(i)\right|\right] + O\left(\frac{1}{\epsilon}\log\left(\frac{1}{\pi_i}\cdot\frac{c_i}{c_{\min}}\right)\cdot c_i\right). \tag{9}$$

Similar to Section 2.1, we can compute the pure-additive version of the bound in Theorem 2.7 by setting $\epsilon = \sqrt{\frac{\log(k\cdot\frac{c_{\max}}{c_{\min}})}{T}}$, as in Corollary 2.2.

Corollary 2.8. *There exists an algorithm for the online multi-scale experts problem with symmetric range that takes as input the ranges c_i, $\forall\, i \in A$, and satisfies:*

$$\forall i \in A: \ \mathbf{E}\left[\textit{REGRET}_i\right] \leq O\left(c_i \cdot \sqrt{T\log(k\cdot\tfrac{c_{\max}}{c_{\min}})}\right) \tag{10}$$

If we compare the above regret bound with the standard $O(c_{\max}\sqrt{T\log k})$ regret bound for the experts problem, we see that we replace the dependency on $c_{\max}$ in the standard bound with $c_i\sqrt{\log(\frac{c_{\max}}{c_{\min}})}$. It is natural to ask whether we could get rid of the dependence on $\log(c_i/c_{\min})$ and show regret bound of $O(c_i\sqrt{T\log k})$, like we did for non-negative rewards. However, the next theorem shows that this dependence on $\log(c_i/c_{\min})$ in the above bound is necessary, in a weak sense: where the constant in the $O(\cdot)$ is universal and does not depend on the ranges c_i. This is because the lower bound only holds for "small" values of the horizon T, which nonetheless grows with the c_is.[7]

Theorem 2.9. *There exists an action set of size k, and ranges $c_i, \forall i \in [k]$, and time horizon T, such that for all algorithms for the online multi-scale experts problem with symmetric range, there is a sequence of T gain vectors such that*

$$\exists i \in A: \ \mathbf{E}\left[\textit{REGRET}_i\right] > \frac{c_i}{4}\cdot\sqrt{T\log(k\cdot\tfrac{c_{\max}}{c_{\min}})}$$

We then show the following upper bound for the bandit setting when the range is symmetric. This bound also follows the same style of action-specific regret bounds as in Theorem 2.3.

[6] Cole and Roughgarden [12] show that at least a linear dependence on n is necessary when the values are drawn from a regular distribution, but as is, their lower bound needs unbounded valuations. The lower bound probably holds for "large enough h" but it is not clear if it holds for all h.

[7] For this reason we chose not to include this bound in Table 3.

THEOREM 2.10. *There exists an algorithm for the multi-scale bandits problem with symmetric range that takes as input the ranges c_i, $\forall\, i \in A$, and a parameter $0 < \epsilon \leq 1/2$, and satisfies:*

$$\forall i \in A: \ \mathrm{E}\left[\textit{REGRET}_i\right] \leq O\Big(\epsilon T + \tfrac{k}{\epsilon}\tfrac{c_{\max}}{c_{\min}} \log\left(\tfrac{k}{\epsilon}\tfrac{c_{\max}}{c_{\min}}\right)\Big) \cdot c_i. \tag{11}$$

Also, similar to Section 2.1, we can compute the pure-additive version of the bound in Theorem 2.10 by setting $\epsilon = \sqrt{\frac{k \frac{c_{\max}}{c_{\min}} \log(kT \cdot \frac{c_{\max}}{c_{\min}})}{T}}$, as in Corollary 2.2. This bound is comparable to the standard regret bound of $O(c_{\max}\sqrt{kT \log k})$ [4] for the adversarial multi-armed bandits problem.

COROLLARY 2.11. *There exists an algorithm for the online multi-scale bandits problem with symmetric range that satisfies:*

$$\forall i \in A: \ \mathrm{E}\left[\textit{REGRET}_i\right] \leq O\left(c_i \cdot \sqrt{Tk \cdot \tfrac{c_{\max}}{c_{\min}} \log(kT \cdot \tfrac{c_{\max}}{c_{\min}})}\right). \tag{12}$$

Once again, for the bandit problem, the following theorem shows that this bound cannot be improved beyond log factors (to get a guarantee like that of Theorem 2.3, for instance).

THEOREM 2.12. *There exists an action set of size k, and ranges $c_i, \forall i \in [k]$, such that for all algorithms for the online multi-scale bandit problem with symmetric range, for all sufficiently large time horizon T, there is a sequence of T gain vectors such that*

$$\exists i \in A: \ \mathrm{E}\left[\textit{REGRET}_i\right] > \frac{c_i}{8\sqrt{2}} \cdot \sqrt{Tk \cdot \frac{c_{\max}}{c_{\min}}}.$$

Organization. We start in Section 3 by showing regret upper bounds for the multi-scale experts problem with non-negative rewards (Theorem 2.1). The corresponding upper bounds for the bandit version are in section 4 (Theorem 2.3). In Section 5 we show how the multi-scale regret bounds (Theorems 2.1 and 2.3) imply the corresponding bounds for the auction/pricing problems (Theorems 2.5 and 2.6). Finally, the regret (upper and lower) bounds for the symmetric range are deferred to the full version due to space constraints (Theorems 2.7, 2.9, 2.10, and 2.12).

3 MULTI-SCALE ONLINE LEARNING WITH FULL INFORMATION

In this section, we look at the full information multi-scale learning problem, in which different experts have different ranges. We exploit this structure to achieve expert-specific regret bounds.

Here is a map of this section. In Section 3.1 we propose an algorithm that exploits the aforementioned structure, and later in Section 3.2 we show how this algorithm is an online mirror descent with weighted negative entropy as the Legendre function. For reward-only instances, we prove the regret bound *without* dependency on $\log(c_i/c_{\max})$ in Section 3.3.

3.1 Multi-Scale Multiplicative-Weight (MSMW) algorithm

We propose the "*Multi-Scale Multiplicative-Weight*" (MSMW) algorithm as a multiplicative-weight update style learning for our problem. The algorithm is presented in Algorithm 1. The main idea behind this algorithm is taking into account different ranges for different experts, and therefore

(1) Normalizing reward of each expert accordingly, i.e. dividing the reward of expert i by c_i.
(2) Projecting the updated weights accordingly, by performing a *smooth multi-scale projection* into the simplex that will be described later.

3.2 Equivalence to Online Mirror Descent (OMD) with weighted negative entropy

While it is possible to analyze the regret of MSMW algorithm (Algorithm 1) by using first principles (Look at the proof of Lemma 3.7 in the appendix, Section ??), we take a different approach . We

Algorithm 1 MSMW

input initial distribution μ over A, learning rate $0 < \eta \leq 1$.
initialize $\mathbf{p}(1)$ such that $p_i(1) = \mu_i$ for all $i \in A$.
for $t = 1, \ldots, T$ **do**
  Randomly pick an action drawn from $\mathbf{p}(t)$, and observe $\mathbf{g}(t)$.
  $\forall i \in A: \ w_i(t+1) \leftarrow p_i(t) \cdot \exp(\eta \cdot \frac{g_i(t)}{c_i})$.
  Find λ^* (e.g., binary search) s.t. $\sum_{i \in A} w_i(t+1) \cdot \exp(-\frac{\lambda^*}{c_i}) = 1$.
  $\forall i \in A: \ p_i(t+1) \leftarrow w_i(t+1) \cdot \exp(-\frac{\lambda^*}{c_i})$.
end for

show how this algorithm is indeed an instance of Online Mirror Descent (OMD) algorithm for a particular choice of *Legendre function.*

3.2.1 Preliminaries on online mirror descent. Fix an open convex set $\mathcal{D}$ and its closure $\bar{\mathcal{D}}$, which in our case are $\mathbb{R}^A_{>0}$ and $\mathbb{R}^A_+$ respectively, and a closed-convex action set $\mathcal{A} \subset \bar{\mathcal{D}}$, which in our case is Δ_A, i.e. the set of all probability distributions over experts in A. At the heart of an OMD algorithm there is a *Legendre* function $F : \bar{\mathcal{D}} \to \mathbb{R}$, i.e. a strictly convex function that admits continuous first order partial derivatives on $\mathcal{D}$ and $\lim_{x \to \bar{\mathcal{D}} \backslash \mathcal{D}} ||\nabla F(x)|| = +\infty$, where $\nabla F(.)$ denotes the gradient map of F. One can think of OMD as a member of *projected gradient descent* algorithms, where the *gradient update* happens in the *dual space* $\nabla F(\mathcal{D})$ rather than in primal $\mathcal{D}$, and the *projection* is defined by using the *Bregman divergence* associated with F rather than ℓ_2-distance.

Definition 3.1 (Bregman Divergence [11]). Given a Legendre function F over Δ_A, the Bregman divergence associated with F, denoted as $D_F : \Delta_A \times \Delta_A \to \mathbb{R}$, is defined by

$$D_F(x, y) = F(x) - F(y) - (x - y)^T \nabla F(y)$$

Definition 3.2 (Online Mirror Descent [11]). Suppose F is a Legendre function. At every time $t \in [T]$, the online mirror descent algorithm with Legendre function F selects an expert drawn from distribution $\mathbf{p}(t)$, and then updates $\mathbf{w}(t)$ and $\mathbf{p}(t)$ given rewards $\mathbf{g}(t)$ by:

Gradient update:

$$\nabla F(\mathbf{w}(t+1)) = \nabla F(\mathbf{p}(t)) + \eta \cdot \mathbf{g}(t) \Rightarrow \mathbf{w}(t+1) = (\nabla F)^{-1} (\nabla F(\mathbf{p}(t)) + \eta \cdot \mathbf{g}(t)) \tag{13}$$

Bregman projection:

$$\mathbf{p}(t+1) = \operatorname*{argmin}_{\mathbf{p} \in \Delta_A} (D_F(\mathbf{p}, \mathbf{w}(t+1))) \tag{14}$$

where $\eta > 0$ is called the learning rate of OMD.

We use the following standard regret bound of OMD (Refer to [11] for a thorough discussion on OMD. For completeness, a proof is also provided in the appendix, Section ??).

Lemma 3.3. *For any learning rate parameter* $0 < \eta \leq 1$ *and any benchmark distribution* $\mathbf{q}$ *over* A, *the OMD algorithm with Legendre function* $F(.)$ *admits the following:*

$$\textstyle\sum_{t \in [T]} \mathbf{g}(t) \cdot \left(\mathbf{q} - \mathbf{p}(t)\right) \leq \frac{1}{\eta} \sum_{t \in [T]} D_F(\mathbf{p}(t), \mathbf{w}(t+1)) + \frac{1}{\eta} D_F(\mathbf{q}, \mathbf{p}(1)) \tag{15}$$

3.2.2 MSMW algorithm as an OMD. For our application, we focus on a particular choice of Legendre function that captures different learning rates proportional to c_i^{-1} for different experts, as we saw earlier in Algorithm 1. We start by defining the *weighted negative entropy* function.

Definition 3.4. Given expert-ranges $\{c_i\}_{i\in A}$, the *weighted negative entropy* is defined by

$$F(x) = \textstyle\sum_{i\in A} c_i \cdot x_i \ln(x_i) \tag{16}$$

Corollary 3.5. *It is straightforward to see $F(x) = \sum_{i\in A} c_i \cdot x_i \ln(x_i)$ is a non-negative Legendre function over $\mathbb{R}_+^A$. Moreover, $\nabla F(x)_i = c_i(1 + \ln(x_i))$ and $D_F(x, y) = \sum_{i\in A} c_i \cdot (x_i \ln(\frac{x_i}{y_i}) - x_i + y_i)$.*

We now have the following lemma that shows Algorithm 1 is indeed an OMD algorithm.

Lemma 3.6. *The MSMW algorithm, i.e. Algorithm 1, is equivalent to an OMD algorithm associated with the weighted negative entropy $F(x) = \sum_{i\in A} c_i \cdot x_i \ln(x_i)$ as its Legendre function.*

Proof. Look at the gradient update step of OMD, as in Equation (13), with Legendre transform $F(x) = \sum_{i\in A} c_i \cdot x_i \ln(x_i)$. By using Corollary 3.5 we have

$$\nabla F(\mathbf{w}(t+1)) = \nabla F(\mathbf{p}(t)) + \eta \cdot \mathbf{g}(t) \Rightarrow c_i(1 + ln(w_i(t+1))) = c_i(1 + ln(p_i(t))) + \eta \cdot g_i(t)\,,$$

and therefore, $w_i(t+1) = p_i(t) \cdot \exp(\eta \cdot \frac{g_i(t)}{c_i})$. Moreover, for Bregman projection step we have

$$\mathbf{p}(t+1) = \operatorname*{argmin}_{\mathbf{p}\in\Delta_A} (D_F(\mathbf{p}, \mathbf{w}(t+1))) = \operatorname*{argmin}_{\mathbf{p}\in\Delta_A} \left(\sum_{i\in A} c_i \cdot (p_i \ln(\frac{p_i}{w_i(t+1)}) - p_i + w_i(t+1)) \right) \tag{17}$$

This is a convex-minimization over a convex set. To find a closed form solution, we look at the Lagrangian dual function $\mathcal{L}(\mathbf{p}, \lambda) \triangleq \sum_{i\in A} c_i \cdot (p_i \ln(\frac{p_i}{w_i(t+1)}) - p_i + w_i(t+1)) + \lambda(\sum_{i\in A} p_i - 1)$ and the Karush-Kuhn-Tucker (KKT) conditions $\nabla\mathcal{L}(\mathbf{p}^*, \lambda^*) = 0$. We have

$$c_i \cdot \ln(\frac{p_i^*}{w_i(t+1)}) + \lambda^* = 0 \Rightarrow p_i^* = w_i(t+1) \cdot \exp(-\frac{\lambda^*}{c_i}) \tag{18}$$

As $\sum_{i\in A} p_i^* = 1$, λ^* should be unique number s.t. $\sum_{i\in A} w_i(t+1) \cdot \exp(-\frac{\lambda^*}{c_i}) = 1$, and then $p_i(t+1) = w_i(t+1) \cdot \exp(-\frac{\lambda^*}{c_i})$. So, Algorithm 1 is equivalent to OMD with weighted negative entropy as its Legendre transform. □

Lemma 3.7. *For any initial distribution $\boldsymbol{\mu}$ over A, and any learning rate parameter $0 < \eta \le 1$, and any benchmark distribution $\mathbf{q}$ over A, the MSMW algorithm satisfies that:*

$$\sum_{i\in A} q_i \cdot G_i - \mathbf{E}[G_{\text{ALG}}] \le \eta \sum_{t\in[T]} \sum_{i\in A} p_i(t) \frac{(g_i(t))^2}{c_i} + \frac{1}{\eta} \cdot \sum_{i\in A} c_i \left(q_i \ln\left(\frac{q_i}{\mu_i}\right) - q_i + \mu_i \right).$$

3.3 Regret bound for non-negative rewards - proof of Theorem 2.1

Proof of Theorem 2.1. Suppose $i_{\min}$ is an action with the minimum c_i. Let $\boldsymbol{\mu} = (1-\eta)\cdot\mathbf{1}_{i_{\min}} + \eta\cdot\boldsymbol{\pi}$, and let $\mathbf{q} = (1-\eta)\cdot\mathbf{1}_i + \eta\cdot\boldsymbol{\pi}$ in Lemma 3.7. If $i \ne i_{\min}$, we get that (note that $\mu_j = q_j$ for any $j \ne i, i_{\min}$):

$$\begin{aligned}(1-\eta)\cdot G_i + \eta \cdot \sum_{j\in A} \pi_j \cdot G_j - \mathbf{E}[G_{\text{ALG}}] &\le \eta \cdot \mathbf{E}[G_{\text{ALG}}] + \frac{1}{\eta} \cdot c_i \cdot \left(q_i \ln\left(\frac{q_i}{\mu_i}\right) - q_i + \mu_i \right) \\ &\quad + \frac{1}{\eta} \cdot c_{i_{\min}} \cdot \left(q_{i_{\min}} \ln\left(\frac{q_{i_{\min}}}{\mu_{i_{\min}}}\right) - q_{i_{\min}} + \mu_{i_{\min}} \right)\end{aligned}$$

By $1 \ge q_i > \mu_i \ge \eta\pi_i$, the 2nd term on the RHS is upper bounded as:

$$\frac{1}{\eta} \cdot c_i \cdot \left(q_i \ln\left(\frac{q_i}{\mu_i}\right) - q_i + \mu_i \right) \le \frac{1}{\eta} \cdot c_i \cdot \ln\left(\frac{1}{\eta\pi_i}\right)$$

Similarly, by $1 \geq \mu_{i_{\min}} > q_{i_{\min}} \geq 0$, the 3rd term on the RHS is upper bounded as

$$\frac{1}{\eta} \cdot c_{i_{\min}} \cdot \left(q_{i_{\min}} \ln\left(\frac{q_{i_{\min}}}{\mu_{i_{\min}}}\right) - q_{i_{\min}} + \mu_{i_{\min}} \right) \leq \frac{1}{\eta} \cdot c_{i_{\min}} \leq \frac{1}{\eta} \cdot c_i$$

Finally, note that $G_j \geq 0$ for all $j \in A$ in reward-only instances. So the LHS is lower bounded by

$$(1-\eta) \cdot G_i - \mathbf{E}[G_{\text{ALG}}] = (1-\eta) \cdot \text{REGRET}_i - \eta \cdot \mathbf{E}[G_{\text{ALG}}].$$

Putting together we get that

$$\mathbf{E}[\text{REGRET}_i] \leq \frac{2\eta}{1-\eta} \cdot \mathbf{E}[G_{\text{ALG}}] + O\left(\frac{1}{\eta} \ln\left(\frac{1}{\eta\pi_i}\right) \cdot c_i\right) \leq 3\eta \cdot \mathbf{E}[G_{\text{ALG}}] + O\left(\frac{1}{\eta} \ln\left(\frac{1}{\eta\pi_i}\right) \cdot c_i\right).$$

The theorem then follows by choosing $\eta = \frac{\epsilon}{3}$ and rearranging terms. □

4 MULTI SCALE ONLINE LEARNING WITH BANDIT FEEDBACK

In this section, we look at the bandit feedback version of multi scale online learning. Inspired by online stochastic mirror descent algorithm, we introduce *Bandit-MSMW* algorithm. Our algorithm follows the standard bandit route of using unbiased estimators for the rewards in a full information strategy (in this case MSMW). We also mix the MSMW distribution with an extra uniform exploration, and use a tailored initial distribution for our multi-scale learning setting.

Here is a map of this section. In Section 4.1 we propose our bandit algorithm and prove its general regret guarantee for non-negative rewards. Then in Section 4.2 we show how to get a multi-scale style regret guarantee for the best arm c_{i^*}, and a weaker guarantee for all arms $\{c_i\}_{iA}$.

4.1 Bandit Multi-Scale Multiplicative Weight (Bandit-MSMW) algorithm

We present our Bandit algorithm (Algorithm 2) when the set of actions A is finite (with $|A| = k$). Let η be the learning rate and γ be the exploration probability. We show the following regret bound.

Algorithm 2 Bandit-MSMW

input exploration parameter $\gamma > 0$, learning rate $\eta > 0$.
initialize $\mathbf{p}(1) = (1-\gamma)\mathbf{1}_{i_{\min}} + \frac{\gamma}{k}\mathbf{1}$, where $i_{\min}$ is the arm with minimum range $c_{i_{\min}}$.
for $t = 1, \ldots, T$ **do**
  Let $\tilde{\mathbf{p}}(t) = (1-\gamma)\mathbf{p}(t) + \frac{\gamma}{k}\mathbf{1}$.
  Randomly pick an expert i_t drawn from $\tilde{\mathbf{p}}(t)$, and observe $g_{i_t}(t)$.
  Let $\tilde{\mathbf{g}}(t)$ be such that

$$\tilde{g}_i(t) = \begin{cases} \frac{g_i(t)}{\tilde{p}_i(t)} & \text{if } i = i_t; \\ 0 & \text{otherwise.} \end{cases}$$

  $\forall i \in A: \; w_i(t+1) \leftarrow p_i(t) \cdot \exp(\frac{\eta}{c_i} \cdot \tilde{g}_i(t))$.
  Find λ^* (e.g., binary search) s.t. $\sum_{i \in A} w_i(t+1) \cdot \exp(-\frac{\lambda^*}{c_i}) = 1$.
  $\forall i \in A: \; p_i(t+1) \leftarrow w_i(t+1) \cdot \exp(-\frac{\lambda^*}{c_i})$.
end for

Lemma 4.1. *For any exploration probability $0 < \gamma \leq \frac{1}{2}$ and any learning rate parameter $0 < \eta \leq \frac{\gamma}{k}$, the Bandit-MSMW algorithm achieves the following regret bound when the gains are non-negative :*

$$\forall i \in A: \mathbf{E}[\textit{REGRET}_i] \leq O\left(\frac{1}{\eta}\log\left(\frac{k}{\gamma}\right) \cdot c_i + \eta \sum_{j \in A} G_j + \gamma \cdot G_i\right)$$

Proof. We further define:

$$\widetilde{G}_{\text{ALG}} \triangleq \textstyle\sum_{t\in[T]} g_{i_t}(t) = \sum_{t\in[T]} \tilde{\mathbf{p}}(t)\cdot\tilde{\mathbf{g}}(t)\ ,$$
$$\widetilde{G}_j \triangleq \textstyle\sum_{t\in[T]} \tilde{g}_j(t)\ .$$

In expectation over the randomness of the algorithm, we have:

(1) $\mathbf{E}\left[G_{\text{ALG}}\right] = \mathbf{E}\left[\widetilde{G}_{\text{ALG}}\right]$; and
(2) $G_j = \mathbf{E}\left[\widetilde{G}_j\right]$ for any $j \in A$.

Hence, to upper bound $\mathbf{E}\left[\text{REGRET}_i\right] = G_i - \mathbf{E}\left[G_{\text{ALG}}\right]$, it suffices to upper bound $\mathbf{E}\left[\widetilde{G}_i - \widetilde{G}_{\text{ALG}}\right]$. By the definition of the probability that the algorithm picks each arm, i.e., $\tilde{\mathbf{p}}(t)$, we have:

$$\mathbf{E}\left[\widetilde{G}_{\text{ALG}}\right] \ge (1-\gamma)\textstyle\sum_{t\in[T]} \mathbf{p}(t)\cdot\tilde{\mathbf{g}}(t)\ .$$

Hence, we have that for any initial distribution $\mathbf{q}$ over A:

$$\sum_{j\in A} q_j\cdot\mathbf{E}\left[\widetilde{G}_j\right] - \mathbf{E}\left[\widetilde{G}_{\text{ALG}}\right] \le \mathbf{E}\left[\textstyle\sum_{j\in A} q_j\cdot\widetilde{G}_j - \sum_{t\in[T]}\mathbf{p}(t)\cdot\tilde{\mathbf{g}}(t)\right] + \tfrac{\gamma}{1-\gamma}\mathbf{E}\left[\widetilde{G}_{\text{ALG}}\right]$$
$$\le \mathbf{E}\left[\textstyle\sum_{j\in A} q_j\cdot\widetilde{G}_j - \sum_{t\in[T]}\mathbf{p}(t)\cdot\tilde{\mathbf{g}}(t)\right] + 2\gamma\mathbf{E}\left[\widetilde{G}_{\text{ALG}}\right]\ . \tag{19}$$

Next, we upper bound the 1st term on the RHS. Note that $\mathbf{p}(t)$'s are the probability of choosing experts by MSMW when the experts have rewards $\tilde{\mathbf{g}}(t)$'s. By Lemma 3.7, we have that for any benchmark distribution $\mathbf{q}$ over S, the Bandit-MSMW algorithm satisfies that:

$$\sum_{j\in A} q_j\cdot\widetilde{G}_j - \sum_{t\in[T]}\mathbf{p}(t)\cdot\tilde{\mathbf{g}}(t) \le \eta\sum_{t\in[T]}\sum_{j\in A}\frac{p_j(t)}{c_j}\cdot\left(\tilde{g}_j(t)\right)^2 + \frac{1}{\eta}\sum_{j\in A} c_j\left(q_j\ln\left(\frac{q_j}{p_j(1)}\right) - q_j + p_j(1)\right)\ . \tag{20}$$

For any $t\in[T]$ and any $j\in A$, by the definition of $\tilde{g}_j(t)$, it equals $\frac{g_j(t)}{\tilde{p}_j(t)}$ with probability $\tilde{p}_j(t)$, and equals 0 otherwise. Thus, if we fix the random coin flips in the first $t-1$ rounds and, thus, fix $\tilde{\mathbf{p}}(t)$, and take expectation over the randomness in round t, we have that:

$$\mathbf{E}\left[\frac{p_j(t)}{c_j}\cdot\left(\tilde{g}_j(t)\right)^2\right] = \frac{p_j(t)}{c_j}\cdot\tilde{p}_j(t)\cdot\left(\frac{g_j(t)}{\tilde{p}_j(t)}\right)^2 = \frac{p_j(t)}{\tilde{p}_j(t)}\frac{(g_j(t))^2}{c_j}\ .$$

Further note that $\tilde{p}_j(t) \ge (1-\gamma)p_j(t)$, and $g_j(t)\le c_j$, the above is upper bounded by $\frac{1}{1-\gamma}g_j(t) \le 2g_j(t)$. Putting together with (20), we have that for any $0<\eta\le\frac{\gamma}{n}$:

$$\mathbf{E}\left[\sum_{j\in A} q_j\cdot\widetilde{G}_j - \sum_{t\in[T]}\mathbf{p}(t)\cdot\tilde{\mathbf{g}}(t)\right] \le \eta\sum_{t\in[T]}\sum_{j\in A}2g_j(t) + \frac{1}{\eta}\sum_{j\in A}c_j\left(q_j\ln\left(\frac{q_j}{p_j(1)}\right) - q_j + p_j(1)\right)$$
$$= 2\eta\sum_{j\in A}G_j + \frac{1}{\eta}\sum_{j\in A}c_j\left(q_j\ln\left(\frac{q_j}{p_j(1)}\right) - q_j + p_j(1)\right)$$

Combining with (19), we have:

$$\sum_{j\in A} q_j\cdot\mathbf{E}\left[\widetilde{G}_j\right] - \mathbf{E}\left[\widetilde{G}_{\text{ALG}}\right] \le 2\eta\sum_{j\in A}G_j + \frac{1}{\eta}\sum_{j\in A}c_j\left(q_j\ln\left(\frac{q_j}{p_j(1)}\right) - q_j + p_j(1)\right) + 2\gamma\mathbf{E}\left[\widetilde{G}_{\text{ALG}}\right]$$

Let $\mathbf{q} = (1-\gamma)\mathbf{1}_i + \frac{\gamma}{k}\mathbf{1}$. Recall that $\mathbf{p}(1) = (1-\gamma)\mathbf{1}_{i_{\min}} + \frac{\gamma}{k}\mathbf{1}$ (recall $i_{\min}$ is the arm with minimum range $c_{i_{\min}}$). Similar to the discussion for the expert problem in Section 3.3, the 2nd term on the

RHS is upper bounded by $O\left(\frac{1}{\eta}\log\left(\frac{k}{\gamma}\right)\cdot c_i\right)$. Hence, we have:

$$\sum_{j\in A} q_j \cdot \mathbf{E}\left[\widetilde{G}_j\right] - \mathbf{E}\left[\widetilde{G}_{\text{ALG}}\right] \le 2\eta \sum_{j\in A} G_j + O\left(\frac{1}{\eta}\log\left(\frac{k}{\gamma}\right)\cdot c_i\right) + 2\gamma \mathbf{E}\left[\widetilde{G}_{\text{ALG}}\right] . \tag{21}$$

Further, the LHS is lower bounded as:

$$(1-\gamma)\mathbf{E}\left[\widetilde{G}_i\right] + \frac{\gamma}{k}\sum_{j\in A}\mathbf{E}\left[\widetilde{G}_j\right] - \mathbf{E}\left[\widetilde{G}_{\text{ALG}}\right] \ge (1-\gamma)\mathbf{E}\left[\widetilde{G}_i\right] - \mathbf{E}\left[\widetilde{G}_{\text{ALG}}\right] .$$

The lemma then follows by putting it back to (21) and rearranging terms. □

4.2 Regret bounds for non-negative rewards - proof of Theorem 2.3

Proof of Theorem 2.3. Let $\gamma = \epsilon$ and $\eta = \frac{\gamma}{k} = \frac{\epsilon}{k}$ in Lemma 4.1, we get that the expected regret w.r.t. an action $i \in A$ is bounded by:

$$O\left(\epsilon \cdot G_i + \tfrac{\epsilon}{k}\textstyle\sum_{j\in A} G_j + c_i \cdot \tfrac{k}{\epsilon}\ln\left(\tfrac{k}{\epsilon}\right)\right) .$$

When $i = i^*$ (best arm), regret is bounded by $O\left(\epsilon \cdot G_{i^*} + c_i^* \cdot \frac{k}{\epsilon}\ln\left(\frac{k}{\epsilon}\right)\right)$, as desired.

For the regret w.r.t. an arbitrary action, note that $\mathbf{E}\left[G_{\text{ALG}}\right] \ge \frac{\gamma}{k}\sum_{j\in A} G_j$. Thus, the regret bound w.r.t. an action $i \in A$ in Lemma 4.1 is further upper bounded by:

$$O\left(\tfrac{1}{\eta}\log\left(\tfrac{k}{\gamma}\right)\cdot c_i + \left(\tfrac{\eta k}{\gamma} + \gamma\right)\cdot \mathbf{E}\left[\widetilde{G}_{\text{ALG}}\right]\right)$$

The theorem then follows by letting $\gamma = \epsilon$ and $\eta = \frac{\gamma}{k} = \frac{\epsilon^2}{k}$. □

5 AUCTIONS AND PRICING

5.1 Auctions and pricing as multi-scale online learning problems

Online single buyer auction and posted pricing. Recall that in each round, the algorithm chooses an action, i.e., a price, $p_t \in [1, h]$; the adversary picks a value $v(t) \in [1, h]$; and the algorithm collects reward $g_{p_t}(t) = p_t \cdot \mathbf{1}(v(t) \ge p_t)$. In order to obtain a $1-\epsilon$ approximation of the optimal revenue, it suffices to consider prices of the form $(1+\epsilon)^j$ for $0 \le j \le \lfloor \log_{1+\epsilon} h \rfloor = O(\frac{\log h}{\epsilon})$. As a result, we reduce the online single buyer auction problem and the online posted pricing problem to a multi-sclae online learning problem with full information and bandit feedback respectively with $k = O(\frac{\log h}{\epsilon})$ actions whose ranges form a geometric sequence $(1+\epsilon)^j$, $0 \le j < k$.

Online multi buyer auction. In multi buyer auctions, we consider the set of all discretized Myerson-type auctions as the action space. We start by defining Myerson-type auctions:

Definition 5.1 (Myerson-type auctions). A *Myerson-type auction* is defined by n non-decreasing virtual value mappings $\phi_1, \ldots, \phi_n : [1, h] \mapsto [-\infty, h]$. Given a value profile $v_1, \ldots, v_n$, the item is given to the bidder j with the largest virtual value $\phi_j(v_j)$. Then, bidder j pays the minimum value that would keep him as the the winner.

Myerson [22] shows that when the bidders' values are drawn from independent (but not necessarily identical) distributions, the revenue-optimal auction is a Myerson-type auction. Devanur et al. [14, Lemma 5] observe that to obtain a $1-\epsilon$ approximation, it suffices to consider the set of discretized Myerson-type auctions that treat each bidder's value as if it is equal to the closest power of $1+\epsilon$ from below. As a result, it suffices to consider the set of discretized Myerson-type auctions, each of which is defined by the virtual values of $(1+\epsilon)^j$'s, i.e., by $O(n \log h/\epsilon)$ real numbers $\phi_\ell((1+\epsilon)^j)$, for $\ell \in [n]$, and $0 \le j \le \lfloor \log_{1+\epsilon} h \rfloor$. Devanur et al. [14], Gonczarowski and Nisan [18] further note that a discretized Myerson-type auction is in fact completely characterized by the total ordering of $\phi_\ell((1+\epsilon)^j)$'s; their actual values do not matter. Indeed, both the allocation rule and the payment rule are determined by the ordering of virtual values. As a result, our action space is a finite set with at most $O((n \log h/\epsilon)!)$ actions. The range of an action, i.e., a discretized Myerson-type auction, is the largest price ever charged by the auction, i.e., the largest value v of the form $(1+\epsilon)^j$ such that there exists $\ell \in [n]$, $\phi_\ell(v) > \phi_\ell((1+\epsilon)^{-1}v)$.

5.2 Proof of Theorem 2.5

Proof. *Online single buyer auction.* Recall the above formulation of the problem as an online learning problem with full information. The case when h is known then follows by Theorem 2.1, letting π be the uniform distribution over the $k = O(\log h/\epsilon)$ actions, i.e., discretized prices.

When h is not known upfront, we consider a countably infinite action space comprised of all prices of the form $(1+\epsilon)^j$, for $j \geq 0$. Then, let the prior distribution π be such that for any price $p = (1+\epsilon)^j$, $\pi_p = \epsilon(1+\epsilon)^{-j-1} = \frac{\epsilon}{1+\epsilon} \cdot \frac{1}{p}$. The approximation guarantee then follows by Theorem 2.1.

Online posted pricing. Recall the above formulation of the problem as an online learning problem with bandit feedback. This part then follows by Theorem 2.3 with $k = O(\log h/\epsilon)$ actions.

Online multi buyer auction. Recall the above formulation of the problem as an online learning problem with full information. The case when h is known then follows by Theorem 2.1, where we let π be the uniform distribution over the $k = O((n \log h/\epsilon)!)$ actions, i.e., Myerson-type auctions.

When h is not known upfront, we consider a countably infinite action space A as follows. For any $p = (1+\epsilon)^j$, $j \geq 0$, let the $k_p = O((n \log p/\epsilon)!)$ Myerson-type auctions for values in $[1, p]$ be in A; we assume these auctions treat any values greater than p as if they were p. Further, we choose the prior distribution π such that the probability mass of each auction for range $[1, p]$ is equal to $\frac{\epsilon}{1+\epsilon} \cdot \frac{1}{p} \cdot \frac{1}{k_p}$. The approximation guarantee then follows by Theorem 2.1. □

5.3 Proof of Theorem 2.6

Proof. *Online single buyer auction.* When h is known, by Theorem 2.1, letting π be the uniform distribution over the $k = O(\log h/\epsilon)$ actions, i.e., discretized prices, we have that for any price p (recall that $c_p = p$):

$$G_{\text{ALG}} \geq (1-\epsilon) \cdot G_p - O\left(\frac{\log(\log h/\epsilon)}{\epsilon} \cdot p\right) .$$

For the δ-guarded optimal price p^* (i.e., subject to selling in at least δT rounds), we have $G_{p^*} \geq \delta T \cdot p^*$. Therefore, when $T \geq O\left(\log(\log h/\epsilon)/\epsilon^2\delta\right)$, the additive term of the above approximation guarantee is at most $\epsilon \cdot G_{p^*}$. So the theorem holds.

The treatment for the case when h is not known upfront is essentially the same as in Theorem 2.5. We consider a countably infinite action space comprised of all prices of the form $(1+\epsilon)^j$, for $j \geq 0$. Then, let the prior distribution π be such that for any price $p = (1+\epsilon)^j$, $\pi_p = \epsilon(1+\epsilon)^{-j-1} = \frac{\epsilon}{1+\epsilon} \cdot \frac{1}{p}$.

Online posted pricing. Recall the above formulation of the problem as an online learning problem with bandit feedback. By Theorem 2.3 with $k = O(\log h/\epsilon)$ actions, we have that for any price p:

$$G_{\text{ALG}} \geq (1-\epsilon) \cdot G_p - O\left(\frac{\log h \log(\log h/\epsilon)}{\epsilon^3} \cdot p\right) .$$

Again, for the δ-guarded optimal price p^* (i.e., subject to selling in at least δT rounds), we have $G_{p^*} \geq \delta T \cdot p^*$. Therefore, when $T \geq O\left(\log h \log\left(\log h/\epsilon\right)/\epsilon^4\delta\right)$, the additive term of the above approximation guarantee is at most $\epsilon \cdot G_{p^*}$. So the theorem holds.

Online multi buyer auction. Suppose i^* is the δ-guarded best Myerson-type auction. Recall that $\bar{V}$ is the largest value such that there are at least δT distinct $v(t)$'s with $\max_{\ell \in [n]} v_\ell(t) \geq \bar{V}$. So we may assume without loss of generality that i^* does not distinguish values greater than $\bar{V}$. Hence:

$$c_{i^*} \leq \bar{V} . \tag{22}$$

Further, note that running a 2nd-price auction with anonymous reserve $\bar{V}$ is a Myerson-type auction (e.g., mapping values less than $\bar{V}$ to virtual value $-\infty$ and values greater than or equal to $\bar{V}$ to virtual value $\bar{V}$), and it gets revenue at least $\delta T \cdot \bar{V}$. So we have that:

$$G_{p^*} \geq \delta T \cdot \bar{V} . \tag{23}$$

Finally, the above implies that to obtain a $1-\epsilon$ approximation, it suffices to consider prices that are at least $\epsilon\delta\bar{V}$. Hence, it suffices to consider Myerson-type auctions that, for a given $\bar{V}$, do not distinguish among values greater than $\bar{V}$, and do not distinguish among values smaller than $\epsilon\delta\bar{V}$. There are $O(\log h/\epsilon)$ different values of $\bar{V}$. Further, given $\bar{V}$, there are only $O(\log(1/\epsilon\delta)/\epsilon)$ distinct values to be considered and, thus, there are at most $O((n\log(1/\epsilon\delta)/\epsilon)!)$ distinct Myerson-type auctions of this kind. Hence, the total number of distinct Myerson-type actions that we need to consider is at most:

$$k = O\left(\frac{\log h}{\epsilon} \cdot \left(\frac{n\log(1/\epsilon\delta)}{\epsilon}\right)!\right) .$$

When h is known, letting π be the uniform distribution over the k actions in Theorem 2.1, we have that (recall Eqn. (22)):

$$G_{\text{ALG}} \geq (1-\epsilon) \cdot G_{i^*} - O\left(\frac{n\log(1/\epsilon\delta)\log(n\log(1/\epsilon\delta)/\epsilon)}{\epsilon^2} + \frac{\log(\log h/\epsilon)}{\epsilon}\right) \cdot \bar{V} .$$

When $T \geq O\left(\frac{n\log(1/\epsilon\delta)\log(n\log(1/\epsilon\delta)/\epsilon)}{\epsilon^3\delta} + \frac{\log(\log h/\epsilon)}{\epsilon^2\delta}\right)$, the additive term of the above approximation guarantee is at most $\epsilon \cdot G_{i^*}$ due to Eqn. (23). So the theorem holds.

Again, the treatment for the case when h is not known upfront is similar to that in Theorem 2.5. When h is not known upfront, we consider a countably infinite action space A as follows. For any $\bar{V} = (1+\epsilon)^j$, $j \geq 0$, let the $k' = O((n\log(1/\epsilon\delta)/\epsilon)!)$ Myerson-type auctions that do not distinguish among values greater than $\bar{V}$, and do not distinguish among values smaller than $\epsilon\delta\bar{V}$ be in A. Further, we choose the prior distribution π such that the probability mass of each Myerson-type auction for a given $\bar{V}$ is equal to $\frac{\epsilon}{1+\epsilon} \cdot \frac{1}{\bar{V}} \cdot \frac{1}{k'}$. The approximation guarantee then follows by Theorem 2.1 and essentially the same argument as the known h case. □

Remark. Devanur et al. [14] show that when the values are drawn from independent regular distributions, the ϵ-guarded optimal is a $1-\epsilon$ approximation of the unguarded optimal. So our convergence rate for the online multi buyer auction problem in Theorem 2.1 implies a $\tilde{O}(n\epsilon^{-4})$ sample complexity modulo a mild $\log\log h$ dependency on the range, almost matching the best known sample complexity upper bound for regular distributions.

REFERENCES

[1] Shipra Agrawal and Nikhil R Devanur. 2014. Bandits with concave rewards and convex knapsacks. In *Proceedings of the fifteenth ACM conference on Economics and computation.* ACM, 989–1006.

[2] Kareem Amin, Afshin Rostamizadeh, and Umar Syed. 2013. Learning prices for repeated auctions with strategic buyers. In *Advances in Neural Information Processing Systems.* 1169–1177.

[3] Sanjeev Arora, Elad Hazan, and Satyen Kale. 2012. The Multiplicative Weights Update Method: a Meta-Algorithm and Applications. *Theory of Computing* 8, 1 (2012), 121–164.

[4] Peter Auer, Nicolo Cesa-Bianchi, Yoav Freund, and Robert E Schapire. 1995. Gambling in a rigged casino: The adversarial multi-armed bandit problem. In *Foundations of Computer Science, 1995. Proceedings., 36th Annual Symposium on.* IEEE, 322–331.

[5] Moshe Babaioff, Shaddin Dughmi, Robert Kleinberg, and Aleksandrs Slivkins. 2015. Dynamic pricing with limited supply. *ACM Transactions on Economics and Computation* 3, 1 (2015), 4.

[6] Ashwinkumar Badanidiyuru, Robert Kleinberg, and Aleksandrs Slivkins. 2013. Bandits with knapsacks. In *Foundations of Computer Science (FOCS), 2013 IEEE 54th Annual Symposium on.* IEEE, 207–216.

[7] Ziv Bar-Yossef, Kirsten Hildrum, and Felix Wu. 2002. Incentive-compatible online auctions for digital goods. In *Proceedings of the thirteenth annual ACM-SIAM symposium on Discrete algorithms.* Society for Industrial and Applied Mathematics, 964–970.

[8] Omar Besbes and Assaf Zeevi. 2009. Dynamic pricing without knowing the demand function: Risk bounds and near-optimal algorithms. *Operations Research* 57, 6 (2009), 1407–1420.

[9] Avrim Blum and Jason D Hartline. 2005. Near-optimal online auctions. In *Proceedings of the sixteenth annual ACM-SIAM symposium on Discrete algorithms.* Society for Industrial and Applied Mathematics, 1156–1163.

[10] Avrim Blum, Vijay Kumar, Atri Rudra, and Felix Wu. 2004. Online learning in online auctions. *Theoretical Computer Science* 324, 2-3 (2004), 137–146.

[11] Sébastien Bubeck. 2011. Introduction to online optimization. *Lecture Notes* (2011), 1–86.

[12] Richard Cole and Tim Roughgarden. 2014. The sample complexity of revenue maximization. In *Symposium on Theory of Computing, STOC 2014, New York, NY, USA, May 31 - June 03, 2014.* 243–252. DOI: http://dx.doi.org/10.1145/2591796.2591867

[13] Arnoud V den Boer. 2015. Dynamic pricing and learning: historical origins, current research, and new directions. *Surveys in operations research and management science* 20, 1 (2015), 1–18.

[14] Nikhil R Devanur, Zhiyi Huang, and Christos-Alexandros Psomas. 2016. The sample complexity of auctions with side information. In *Proceedings of the 48th Annual ACM SIGACT Symposium on Theory of Computing.* ACM, 426–439.

[15] Nikhil R Devanur, Yuval Peres, and Balasubramanian Sivan. 2014. Perfect bayesian equilibria in repeated sales. In *Proceedings of the Twenty-Sixth Annual ACM-SIAM Symposium on Discrete Algorithms.* SIAM, 983–1002.

[16] Peerapong Dhangwatnotai, Tim Roughgarden, and Qiqi Yan. 2014. Revenue maximization with a single sample. *Games and Economic Behavior* (2014).

[17] Yoav Freund and Robert E Schapire. 1995. A desicion-theoretic generalization of on-line learning and an application to boosting. In *European conference on computational learning theory.* Springer, 23–37.

[18] Yannai A Gonczarowski and Noam Nisan. 2017. Efficient Empirical Revenue Maximization in Single-Parameter Auction Environments. In *Proceedings of the ACM STOC.*

[19] Zhiyi Huang, Yishay Mansour, and Tim Roughgarden. 2015. Making the most of your samples. In *Proceedings of the Sixteenth ACM Conference on Economics and Computation.* ACM, 45–60.

[20] Robert Kleinberg and Tom Leighton. 2003. The value of knowing a demand curve: Bounds on regret for online posted-price auctions. In *Foundations of Computer Science, 2003. Proceedings. 44th Annual IEEE Symposium on.* IEEE, 594–605.

[21] Jamie H Morgenstern and Tim Roughgarden. 2015. On the pseudo-dimension of nearly optimal auctions. In *Advances in Neural Information Processing Systems.* 136–144.

[22] Roger B. Myerson. 1981. Optimal Auction Design. *Mathematics of Operations Research* 6, 1 (1981), 58–73.

[23] Tim Roughgarden and Okke Schrijvers. 2016. Ironing in the dark. In *Proceedings of the 2016 ACM Conference on Economics and Computation.* ACM, 1–18.

[24] Ilya Segal. 2003. Optimal pricing mechanisms with unknown demand. *The American economic review* 93, 3 (2003), 509–529.

[25] Vasilis Syrgkanis. 2017. A Sample Complexity Measure with Applications to Learning Optimal Auctions. *arXiv preprint arXiv:1704.02598* (2017).

[26] Kalyan T Talluri and Garrett J Van Ryzin. 2006. *The theory and practice of revenue management.* Vol. 68. Springer Science & Business Media.

Joint Pricing and Inventory Management with Strategic Customers

YIWEI CHEN, Singapore University of Technology and Design
CONG SHI, University of Michigan

We consider a joint pricing and inventory management problem wherein a seller sells a single product over an infinite horizon via dynamically determining anonymous posted prices and inventory replenishment quantities. Customers arrive over time with a deterministic arrival rate but heterogeneous product valuations. A customer's arrival time and product valuation are his private information. Customers are forward-looking, who can strategize their times of purchases. Customer unsatisfied demand is backlogged. A customer incurs disutility from delaying making the purchasing decision and incurring product delivery delay. The seller incurs fixed ordering cost and inventory holding cost. The seller seeks a joint pricing and inventory policy that maximizes her long-run average profit. We show that the optimal policy is cyclic, i.e., the seller repeats the pricing and ordering decisions over cycles of the same length. Under the optimal policy, strategic customer equilibrium behaviors are proven to be myopic. The seller's optimal long-run average profit in the presence of strategic customers is the same as her optimal profit in an auxiliary classical backlogging model wherein customers are myopic that they make their purchasing decisions immediately upon their arrivals. We adopt a mechanism design approach to prove the optimality of our proposed policy in the presence of strategic customers.

CCS Concepts: • **Theory of computation → Dynamic programming**; **Algorithmic mechanism design**; **Computational pricing and auctions**;

Additional Key Words and Phrases: Mechanism design; joint pricing and inventory control; strategic customers; cyclic policy

---

A full version of this paper is available at https://papers.ssrn.com/sol3/papers.cfm?abstract_id=2770242.

Authors' email addresses: First: yiwei_chen@sutd.edu.sg; Second: shicong@umich.edu.

This collaboration is supported by the ARCHES Award for Research Cooperation and High Excellence in Science.

EC'17, June 26–30, 2017, Cambridge, Massachusetts, USA.

ACM ISBN 978-1-4503-4527-9/17/06.

DOI: http://dx.doi.org/10.1145/3033274.3084086

Pricing and Optimization in Shared Vehicle Systems: An Approximation Framework

SIDDHARTHA BANERJEE, Cornell University
DANIEL FREUND, Cornell University
THODORIS LYKOURIS, Cornell University

Optimizing shared vehicle systems (bike-sharing/car-sharing/ride-sharing) is more challenging compared to traditional resource allocation settings due to the presence of *complex network externalities*. In particular, changes in the demand/supply at any location (via dynamic pricing, rebalancing of empty vehicles, etc.) affect future supply throughout the system within short timescales. Such externalities are well captured by steady-state Markovian models, which are therefore widely used to analyze and design shared vehicle systems. However, using such models to design pricing/control policies is computationally difficult since the resulting optimization problems are high-dimensional and non-convex.

To this end, we develop a general approximation framework for designing pricing policies in shared vehicle systems, based on a novel convex relaxation which we term *elevated flow relaxation*. Our approach provides the first efficient algorithms with *rigorous approximation guarantees* for a wide range of objective functions (throughput, revenue, welfare). For any shared vehicle system with n stations and m vehicles, our framework provides a pricing policy with an approximation ratio of $1 + (n - 1)/m$. This guarantee is particularly meaningful when m/n, the average number of vehicles per station is large, as is often the case in practice.

Further, the simplicity of our approach allows us to extend it to more complex settings. Apart from pricing, shared vehicle systems enable other control levers for modulating demand and supply, e.g. rebalancing empty vehicles, redirecting riders to nearby vehicles, etc. Our approach yields efficient algorithms with the same approximation guarantees for all these problems, and in the process, obtains as special cases several existing heuristics and asymptotic guarantees. We also extend our approach to obtain bi-criterion guarantees in multi-objective settings; we illustrate this with the example of Ramsey pricing.

From a technical perspective, our work develops a new approach for obtaining control policies with approximation guarantees in steady-state Markovian models. Our approach can be distilled into the following three-step program: (i) construct an upper bound via a relaxation to the original problem that encodes essential conservation laws of the system, (ii) identify a family of control policies inducing known steady-state distributions that achieve the value of the relaxed solution in an appropriate scaling limit (in our case, *state-independent* policies in the limit $m \to \infty$), and (iii) characterize the performance loss between the finite system (i.e. fixed m) and the scaling limit. This technique may be of independent interest for other settings.

Additional Key Words and Phrases: Queueing systems; Revenue management; Sharing Economy

---

A draft of our full paper is available at https://arxiv.org/abs/1608.06819.

The email addresses of the authors are: sbanerjee@cornell.edu (S. Banerjee), df365@cornell.edu (D. Freund), and teddlyk@cs.cornell.edu (T. Lykouris).

This work has been supported by the NSF under grants CCF-1526067, CMMI-1537394, CCF-1522054, and CCF-1563714, the ARL under grant W911NF-17-1-0094, the ONR under grant N00014-08-1-0031, and a Google faculty research award.

The authors thank Anton Braverman, David Shmoys, Éva Tardos, and Jim Dai for fruitful conversations.

ACM ISBN 978-1-4503-4527-9/17/06. DOI: http://dx.doi.org/10.1145/3033274.3085099

Multidimensional Dynamic Pricing for Welfare Maximization

AARON ROTH, University of Pennsylvania
ALEKSANDRS SLIVKINS, Microsoft Research
JONATHAN ULLMAN, Northeastern University
ZHIWEI STEVEN WU, University of Pennsylvania

We study the problem of a seller dynamically pricing d distinct types of indivisible goods, when faced with the online arrival of unit-demand buyers drawn independently from an unknown distribution. The goods are not in limited supply, but can only be produced at a limited rate and are costly to produce. The seller observes only the bundle of goods purchased at each day, but nothing else about the buyer's valuation function. Our main result is a dynamic pricing algorithm for optimizing welfare (including the seller's cost of production) that runs in time and a number of rounds that are polynomial in d and the approximation parameter. We are able to do this despite the fact that (i) the price-response function is not continuous, and even its fractional relaxation is a non-concave function of the prices, and (ii) the welfare is not observable to the seller.

We derive this result as an application of a general technique for optimizing welfare over *divisible* goods, which is of independent interest. When buyers have strongly concave, Hölder continuous valuation functions over d divisible goods, we give a general polynomial time dynamic pricing technique. We are able to apply this technique to the setting of unit demand buyers despite the fact that in that setting the goods are not divisible, and the natural fractional relaxation of a unit demand valuation is not strongly concave. In order to apply our general technique, we introduce a novel price randomization procedure which has the effect of implicitly inducing buyers to "regularize" their valuations with a strongly concave function. Finally, we also extend our results to a limited-supply setting in which the number of copies of each good cannot be replenished.

Additional Key Words and Phrases: Dynamic Pricing, Welfare Maximization, Learning, Revealed Preferences

1 INTRODUCTION

Consider the problem of an online retailer who sells a large variety of goods. The seller can in principle produce or procure more copies of each good as needed, but only at a limited rate, and at some per-unit production /procurement cost that varies by good. In each round, the seller can dynamically set the price for each type of good. Each buyer has an unknown valuation function defined (in general) over bundles of goods, and quasi-linear utility for money. Each buyer chooses which item to buy to optimize his utility function given the prices. The seller observes the purchased bundle—i.e. the *revealed preferences of the buyer*—but not the buyer's valuation of the purchased bundle (or of any other bundle). The buyer's valuation function is drawn independently from a fixed but *unknown* distribution, called the *buyer distribution.* The seller's objective is to optimize social welfare: the expected buyer valuation of the purchased good minus its production cost.

This work was partially supported by NSF grant CNS-1253345, a Sloan Foundation Fellowship, and a DARPA grant. A full version of the paper can be found on arXiv: https://arxiv.org/abs/1607.05397.

EC'17, June 26–30, 2017, Cambridge, Massachusetts, USA. ACM ISBN 978-1-4503-4527-9/17/06...$15.00.

DOI: http://dx.doi.org/10.1145/3033274.3085106

Social welfare, like profit, is a natural objective for the seller: in particular, sellers attempting to grow their market (rather than exploit an existing monopoly position) might prefer to optimize social welfare rather than profit in the short term.

A tempting first attempt at solving this problem would be to simply set the price for each good to be equal to its cost of production, which would indeed maximize social welfare if there were no other constraints on the bundles of items purchased by buyers. However, this solution is unsatisfactory when additional supply can only be generated at a bounded rate, because the cost of production bears no relationship to the buyers' values for a good. Because of this, setting prices equal to costs can result, for example, in every buyer demanding the largest possible quantity of the same good, which the seller may not be able to accommodate. In a more realistic setting, there will be constraints on the rate of production and resupply for each good. Hence, we study the welfare maximization problem in which we impose the additional constraint that the *expected bundle* purchased (in expectation over the draw of the buyer) lies in a bounded set. Because constraints of this sort bind *across* buyers, setting prices equal to costs fails, and the problem requires a nontrivial solution.

Since the buyer distribution is unknown, the seller cannot directly compute the prices that optimize social welfare. Instead, she faces a learning problem: she can try different prices over time and observe the responses from random buyers drawn from the distribution, and try to learn the optimal price vector. More formally, the goal is to use a small number of rounds to learn a price vector that nearly optimizes expected social welfare. We want the algorithm's guarantees hold in the worst case over the choice of distributions over buyer valuation functions.

Essentially, we are studying a welfare-optimization version of the well-known *dynamic pricing* problem, also known as *learn-and-earn*, with $d > 1$ goods for sale. (Prior work on dynamic pricing focused on profit maximization.) At a very high level, the main challenge presented is to learn the price response function—i.e. the function mapping prices to expected bundles purchased—and then optimize it with respect to welfare. Moreover, this is a high dimensional function (for large d), and so one must overcome the curse of dimensionality. Prior work on non-Bayesian dynamic pricing (e.g., [4, 10, 11, 14, 19, 26, 33]) dealt with this challenge by making strong assumptions on the price response function itself. Typical assumptions include Lipschitzness [10, 11, 33] (which allows for discretization in low-dimensional problems), and particularly for high dimensional problems, linearity [19, 26] or concavity [4, 10, 33].[1] However, assumptions of this sort are not well supported by a micro-economic foundation. In fact, natural assumptions on the buyer valuations do not necessarily result in price-response function with these properties.

In this paper, we pursue a different approach which stands on stronger microeconomic foundations: we make assumptions on the form of the valuation functions directly (and no assumptions on the distribution over valuation functions), and show that we can work with the price response function that results. This is the case *despite* the fact that our problem is high dimensional, and the price response function that results from our assumptions is not concave. We also face an additional challenge: unlike profit, welfare is not observable, and we can observe the purchased bundle but not the buyer's valuation for that bundle. Nevertheless, we design algorithms that find a near-optimal price vector with respect to welfare, in a number of rounds that is polynomial in d and the accuracy parameter. (Whereas, for example, a naive solution based on discretization and Lipschitzness of the price-response function requires a number of rounds that is exponential in d.) Our results also extend to the limited-supply setting.

[1] Prior work that does *not* make assumptions on the shape of valuations or demand curves is either restricted to selling a single good ($d = 1$) [4, 27], or suffers from the curse of dimensionality *and* comes with performance guarantees relative to the discretized prices rather than all prices [5].

1.1 Our Contributions

Our main result solves the problem in the setting of *indivisible goods* when buyers are unit-demand or, alternatively, when the seller only allows each customer to buy a single item. Surprisingly, no other assumptions are needed! Further, we give a general result for the setting of *divisible goods* under certain assumptions on the valuation functions. In fact, we show how this general result can be leveraged to yield the result for unit demands.

Both settings work as follows. There are d goods. In each round, prices are set and one buyer arrives and purchases her most preferred bundle from the set of feasible bundles. The seller incurs production/procurement costs for each sale, which are linear in the sold bundle.

We give a computationally efficient and round efficient algorithm for finding a nearly welfare-maximizing price vector subject to a constraint on the expected consumption. Let $\mathsf{SW}(p)$ be the expected social welfare that results from setting prices p. The seller would like to set prices to ensure that the expected per-round purchase of each good j, denoted $x_j(p)$, is bounded above by some supply s_j. This models a realistic scenario in which the seller's inventory can be replenished, but only at a limited rate. For example, perhaps at most one truckload of goods can be stocked per day. Approximating a restocking period constraint with a constraint on the expected per-customer purchase is reasonable if the restocking period corresponds to a large number of rounds, because then the realized consumption over these rounds concentrates around is expectation. In the following, we will write $x(p) = (x_1(p), \dots, x_d(p))$ to denote the bundle *induced* by prices p.

Divisible goods. Departing from previous work, instead of making assumptions about the functional form of the price-response function, which depends on the buyers' valuations in aggregate, we make assumptions on the individual buyers' valuations themselves. Specifically, we assume the buyers' valuations are strongly concave and Hölder continuous. (These assumptions are satisfied by a large class of well-studied valuation, including *CES* and *Cobb-Douglas* as shown in [29]). The sold bundles are constrained to lie in the bounded set $\mathcal{F} \subset \mathbb{R}^d_+$ (e.g. $\mathcal{F} = [0, 1]^d$ means at most one unit of each good can be purchased).

Theorem 1.1 (Divisible Goods). *Assume divisible goods, and buyers with strongly concave and and Hölder-continuous valuations. There is an algorithm that takes as input parameters $d, \alpha, \delta > 0$ and a supply vector $s \in \mathbb{R}^d_{>0}$, such that with probability at least $1 - \delta$, the algorithm outputs a price vector $p \in \mathbb{R}^d_+$ such that*

$$x(p) \leq s \quad \text{and} \quad \mathsf{SW}(p) \geq \max_{p \in \mathbb{R}^d_+ \colon x(p) \leq s} \mathsf{SW}(p) - \alpha. \tag{1}$$

The number of rounds and the total computation time are polynomial in d, $\frac{1}{\alpha}$ and $\log \frac{1}{\delta}$.

Unit-demand buyers and indivisible goods. We use our result for divisible goods to give a polynomial time dynamic pricing algorithm for welfare maximization in the *indivisible goods* setting when buyers have unit demand valuations. Here we consider *distributions* $\mathcal{D}$ over price vectors $p \in \mathbb{R}^d_+$, rather than fixed price vectors p. To extend our notation, let $x(\mathcal{D}) = \mathbb{E}_{p \sim \mathcal{D}}[x(p)]$ and $\mathsf{SW}(\mathcal{D}) = \mathbb{E}_{p \sim \mathcal{D}}[\mathsf{SW}(p)]$. We prove:

Theorem 1.2 (Indivisible Goods). *Assume indivisible goods, and buyers with unit-demand valuations. There is an algorithm that takes as input parameters $d, \alpha, \delta > 0$ and a supply vector $s \in \mathbb{R}^d_+$, such that with probability at least $1 - \delta$ the algorithm outputs a distribution $\mathcal{D}$ over price vectors $p \in \mathbb{R}^d_+$ such that*

$$x(\mathcal{D}) \leq s \quad \text{and} \quad \mathsf{SW}(\mathcal{D}) \geq \max_{\text{distributions } \mathcal{D}' \colon x(\mathcal{D}') \leq s} \mathsf{SW}(\mathcal{D}') - \alpha. \tag{2}$$

The number of rounds and the total computation time are polynomial in d, $\frac{1}{\alpha}$ and $\log\frac{1}{\delta}$.

In the generality that we state our theorem, using a *distribution* over prices rather than a fixed price vector is unavoidable. The reason has to do with how the buyers break ties when they are indifferent between goods. As shown in [25], without further genericity assumptions, it can be that *no* fixed pricing can induce optimal (or even feasible) allocations if buyers use uncoordinated tie breaking rules. Instead, tie-breaking needs to be *coordinated* amongst the buyers: the tie-breaking rule needs to be different for different buyers, and essentially needs to be specified by the mechanism. The randomness in our pricing scheme serves as a coordination mechanism amongst buyers (since each buyer faces a different realization of prices).

Remark. In both settings, we prove more general theorems in which we express our results in terms of a stronger benchmark–the welfare of the optimal lottery over allocations, without restriction to those that can be induced by posted pricing.[2]

The above theorems can be reformulated in terms of cumulative regret for a given time horizon T. Then the execution of the algorithm in the respective theorem corresponds to an *exploration phase* of bounded length. The price vector p computed by the algorithm is used in an *exploitation phase* consisting of all subsequent rounds. Theorem 1.1 guarantees that OWEL completes in $\text{poly}(d, \log\frac{1}{\delta}) \cdot \alpha^{-m}$ rounds, for some constant m. Expected regret relative to the best fixed price vector can be upper-bounded by 1 for every round of exploration, and $\alpha+\delta$ per round of exploitation. Optimizing the choice of α and δ, we obtain regret $\text{poly}(d, \log T) \cdot T^{m/(m+1)}$. Theorem 1.2 implies a similar corollary for the unit-demands setting.

Extension to limited supply. We extend our results to a limited-supply setting. In our model, there is a fixed horizon of T rounds and the seller has a non-replenishable supply of Ts_j units of each good j. T and $s \in [0,1]^d$ are known in advance. Each day, the seller will set prices and a random buyer will purchase their preferred bundle until either the time horizon or the sellers' supply is exhausted, whichever comes first.

For a pricing policy π, we use $\mathsf{SW}_{\mathsf{tot}}(\pi)$ to denote its expected total welfare.[3] A "fixed-vector" pricing policy uses the same price vector p in all rounds. Likewise, "fixed-distribution" pricing policy always draws the price vector independently from the same fixed distribution $\mathcal{D}$. The expected total welfare of these policies is denoted, resp., $\mathsf{SW}_{\mathsf{tot}}(p)$ and $\mathsf{SW}_{\mathsf{tot}}(\mathcal{D})$.

In the setting of divisible goods, we simply use the algorithm from Theorem 1.1 with the same constraint vector s. The price vector p computed by this algorithm achieves high expected total welfare for a given problem instance: we prove that it is nearly optimal compared to the best fixed-vector pricing policy. Further, it is nearly optimal compared to *any* pricing policy.

Likewise, in the setting of unit demands, we use the algorithm from Theorem 1.2 with the same constraint vector s. The distribution $\mathcal{D}$ computed by this algorithm is nearly optimal compared to the best fixed-distribution pricing policy with $x(\mathcal{D}) \leq s$.

THEOREM 1.3. *Consider dynamic pricing with limited supply. Fix constraint vector $s \in \mathbb{R}_+^d$ and time horizon $T > 32\log(T)/s^*$, where $s^* = \min_j s_j$.*

[2] A posted price vector (resp., distribution over them) computed by an algorithm can only hope to compete with the best posted price vector (resp., distribution). Thus, the mathematical statement behind (ii) is that the posted price benchmarks used in the theorems are in fact equivalent to the stronger benchmark.

[3] Considering expected welfare per round is not enough, as one pricing policy may halt sooner than another.

(a) *Consider the setting of divisible goods. When the algorithm from Theorem 1.1 is given as input d, s, α, δ, with probability $1 - \delta$ it outputs a price vector $p \in \mathbb{R}_+^d$ such that*

$$\mathsf{SW}_{\mathsf{tot}}(p) \geq \sup_{\text{pricing policies } \pi} \mathsf{SW}_{\mathsf{tot}}(\pi) - \alpha T - O\left(\sqrt{T \log(T)/s^*}\right).$$

(b) *Assume indivisible goods and unit demands. When the algorithm from Theorem 1.2 is given as input d, s, α, δ, with probability $1 - \delta$ it outputs distribution $\mathcal{D}$ over price vectors such that*

$$\mathsf{SW}_{\mathsf{tot}}(\mathcal{D}) \geq \sup_{\text{distributions } \mathcal{D}' \text{ with } x(\mathcal{D}') \leq s} \mathsf{SW}_{\mathsf{tot}}(\mathcal{D}') - \alpha T - O\left(\sqrt{T \log(T)/s^*}\right).$$

The number of rounds and the total computation time are polynomial in d, $\frac{1}{\alpha}$ and $\log \frac{1}{\delta}$.

1.2 Our Techniques

Our general results for divisible goods build on a crucial structural property: even though the expected welfare of the induced bundle $x(p)$ is not concave in the price vector p, it becomes concave if we treat the bundle itself as the decision variable. We illustrate this via a simple 1-dimensional example, adapted from [29]:

Example 1.4. There is a single good ($d = 1$), and a single buyer with valuation $v(x) = \sqrt{x}$. he seller's cost function is $c(x) = x$. If price p is posted, the buyer's utility for x units is $\sqrt{x} - p \cdot x$, so she would purchase $x^*(p) = \frac{1}{4p^2}$ units of the good. Consequently, the welfare is

$$\mathsf{SW}(p) = v(x^*(p)) - c(x^*(p)) = \frac{1}{2p} - \frac{1}{4p^2}.$$

Note that welfare is not a concave function of the price. However, if we write the welfare as a function of $x = x^*(p)$, the purchased amount of good, this function is concave:

$$\mathsf{SW}(x) = v(x) - c(x) = \sqrt{x} - x.$$

Thus, we would like to optimize expected welfare as a function of the induced bundle. However, we only control prices and not induced bundles. To address this, our algorithm has two "layers," where the outer layer optimizes over induced bundles, and the inner layer finds a price vector which approximately induces a given bundle. Another challenge is that welfare is not observed, since we do not observe buyer valuations. Instead, we find a way to approximate the *subgradients* of welfare, and use noise-tolerant subgradient descent to optimize over the bundles.

We build on and extend the result of [29] for the special case of a single buyer and unlimited supply (which focuses on profit rather than welfare). The main distinction is single buyer vs. distributions over buyers; in other words, [29] assume that for a given price vector the outcome is deterministic, whereas in our paper it is drawn from a fixed but unknown distribution over the possible outcomes.

The "inner layer" of our algorithm extends the algorithm in [29] from a single buyer to distributions over buyers. This extension presents several technical challenges, and answers one of their main open questions. In particular, we analyze a generalization of the convex programming technique used in [29] to accommodate a distribution over (arbitrarily many) buyers. We cannot use the "outer layer" from [29] because it requires direct observations of the objective function to feed into a procedure for zeroth-order optimization, and our seller cannot directly observe the buyers' welfare (unlike profit, which is observable). Instead, we develop a new technique to obtain the subgradient for the welfare function so as to enable first-order optimization. Also, we remove a major assumption of homogenous buyer valuations.

As stated, our general result does not apply to unit demand buyers over indivisible goods. In order to cast this problem as a divisible goods problem, we view buyers as having *linear* valuations over divisible goods, optimizing over the set of bundles that have at most unit ℓ_1 norm. The bundle that maximizes a linear function is always at a vertex of the feasible region, and hence is integral. That is, it is the bundle purchased by a unit-demand buyer in the indivisible goods setting. However, there is a substantial difficulty: our general technique relies on buyer valuation functions being *strongly* concave, a condition not satisfied by linear functions. A standard way to obtain strong convexity in the convex optimization literature is to add a strongly convex *regularizer* to the objective function. However, we do not get to modify the buyer's objective function in this way. Instead, we perturb the price vectors proposed by our general dynamic pricing algorithm with Gumbel noise. Doing so has the property that the expected bundle purchased by each buyer (where expectation is taken over the price perturbation) is the bundle that maximizes the buyer's linear valuation function, plus an entropy regularization term [34]. Thus, in expectation over our perturbations, we can view buyers as optimizing valuation functions which are strongly concave over the ℓ_1 norm—even though for every fixed perturbation, buyers are maximizing some linear function and thus buy a unit bundle of indivisible goods. By perturbing the price vectors used over the run of our algorithm for divisible goods, therefore, we can optimize welfare over these "regularized" buyers. By reducing the noise rate (and hence the implicit regularization parameter), we approach the optimal welfare of the actual, unit-demand buyers.

The extension to limited supply (Theorem 1.3(a)) relies on a structural result about *bandits with knapsacks* [5], a general framework of which dynamic pricing with limited supply is a special case. We use a non-standard "embedding" of dynamic pricing into this framework, and a concentration inequality for total welfare that requires a somewhat delicate proof.

1.3 Related Work

Our setting is related to several lines of work. First, dynamic pricing, a.k.a. *learn-and-earn*, focuses on a seller with a large inventory of each good, facing a stream of buyers with unknown valuations. This is a large line of work, mainly in operations research – see [13] for a review. Most related are non-Bayesian approaches. As mentioned above, the main distinction is that we make assumptions on the buyer valuations rather than on the price response function. Also, the learn-and-earn literature does not consider welfare-optimization, to the best of our knowledge.

Second, our problem can be viewed as an instance of the *multi-armed bandits* problem [16, 23], a well-studied abstract framework in which an algorithm repeatedly chooses actions (e.g., price vectors) and receives rewards (e.g., revenue from a sale). The main issue is the tension between acquisition and usage of information, a.k.a. the *exploration-exploitation tradeoff.* Bandit algorithms are directly applicable to dynamic pricing either via discretization [4, 5, 27] or via assumptions on expected revenue.[4] The main distinction is (again) that solutions to bandit problems tend to make assumptions directly on the rewards, in part because they do not model the finer structure behind the rewards (such as valuation functions).

Third, there are several papers on welfare-optimizing posted pricing in combinatorial auctions [6, 12, 18, 21]. These papers tackle more difficult scenarios with non-divisible goods and non-IID valuations, and accordingly obtain weaker, multiplicative guarantees. Also, the pricing is either static [6, 21] (not changing over time), or changing over time but not adapting to the observed purchases [12, 18]. This research is mainly motivated by connections to mechanism design for combinatorial auctions.

Fourth, there is a large literature on *revealed preferences*, starting from Samuelson [31], see [28, 30, 32] for background. Most work in economics has focused on the construction of utility functions that explain or *rationalize* a given sequence of price/bundle observations, e.g. [1]. A

[4] E.g., if expected revenue is concave in prices, one can apply bandit algorithms for concave rewards [2, 17, 22, 24].

recent literature studies the problem of predicting purchase decisions given past observations at different price points [8, 9, 35]. More related to our paper is Amin et al. [3] who study the problem of iteratively setting prices to maximize the profit obtained from a single budgeted buyer (who repeatedly makes purchase decisions) with a linear utility function. The most related paper in this line is [29], as discussed in the previous subsection. Ours is the first paper in this line of work able to handle indivisible goods. A related, but distinct literature focuses on *learning valuation functions* from example evaluations of those functions [7], rather than from example *maximizations* of those functions (as in the revealed preference literature).

1.4 Map of the Paper

Section 3 contains the our general result for divisible goods (a generalization of Theorem 1.1). Our application to unit demand valuations over indivisible goods, and the perturbation techniques that go into deriving this result are presented in Section 4. The limited supply setting and some technical details are deferred to the full version.

2 MODEL AND PRELIMINARIES

There is a *seller* selling d different types of goods to a sequence of *buyers* arriving one after another in rounds. Each buyer's valuation v is drawn independently from an unknown distribution ψ over a finite class $\mathcal{V}$ of valuation functions over the goods, where $|\mathcal{V}| = n$.[5] [6] Both ψ and $\mathcal{V}$ are unknown to the seller. Throughout, we will use i to index the buyer's types in $\mathcal{V}$, and write v_i for the valuation function for a buyer of type i, and $\psi(v_i)$ for the probability mass on buyers of type i.

At each round t, the seller posts a price vector $p = p^t \in \mathbb{R}^d_+$, and the t-th buyer with valuation $v \sim \psi$ makes a purchase to maximize his utility under these prices. In particular, we consider two different settings: one with divisible goods and the other with indivisible goods.

Divisible goods. Each valuation $v\colon \mathbb{R}^d_+ \to \mathbb{R}_+$ is a function from (fractional) bundles of goods to values. Under prices p, the buyer with valuation v will purchase the utility-maximizing bundle

$$x^*_v(p) \equiv \operatorname*{argmax}_{x\in\mathcal{F}}[v(x) - \langle x,p\rangle]$$

where $\mathcal{F} \subset \mathbb{R}^d_+$ denotes the set of feasible bundles available for purchase.

Indivisible goods. We consider unit-demand buyers, who will either purchase exactly 1 unit of some good or nothing. Each buyer's valuation is defined by a value vector $v \in \mathbb{R}^d_{>0}$ such that v_j denotes her value for 1 unit of the j-th good. At round t, a buyer with valuation v purchases

$$x^*_v(p) \equiv \operatorname*{argmax}_{j\in[d]\cup\{\perp\}} \left[v_j - p_j\right].$$

where $\perp$ denotes the choice of buying nothing (we define $v_\perp = p_\perp = 0$), and we allow arbitrary tie-breaking rules.

The seller has a *(known) cost vector* $c \in \mathbb{R}^d_+$ such that the cost of producing a unit of good j is c_j. The seller wishes to set prices so as to optimize the expected *social welfare* — the expected valuation of the buyer's purchased bundle or item minus its production cost. In particular, if the seller posts a price vector p over the goods, the expected social welfare is

$$\mathsf{SW}(p) = \mathop{\mathbb{E}}_{v\sim\psi}\left[v(x^*_v(p)) - c(x^*_v(p))\right]. \tag{3}$$

[5]We take $\mathcal{V}$ to be finite only for convenience. Our results do not depend on $n = |\mathcal{V}|$, so it can be arbitrarily large.
[6]Throughout, $\mathbb{R}_+ = \{x \in \mathbb{R} \mid x \geq 0\}$ and $\mathbb{R}_{>0} = \{x \in \mathbb{R} \mid x > 0\}$ denote non-negative reals and positive reals, resp.

where we write $c(x^*_v(p))$ to denote the production cost for the purchase $x^*_v(p)$. For any distribution $\mathcal{D}$ over prices, the expected welfare is defined as $\mathsf{SW}(\mathcal{D}) = \mathbb{E}_{p\sim\mathcal{D}}[\mathsf{SW}(p)]$.

Computational model. We will think of the algorithm as having access to a *revealed preference* oracle $\mathsf{ReP}(\psi)$: given any input price vector $p \in \mathbb{R}^d_+$, it will draw a random valuation v from ψ, and return the purchase decision $x^*_v(p)$. Our goal is to design computationally efficient algorithms to compute optimal prices using only polynomially many queries to ReP. Notably, the expected or realized social welfare is not observable to the algorithm, since it cannot observe $v(x^*_v(p))$.

2.1 Noisy Subgradient Descent

A key ingredient in our algorithms is the ability to minimize a convex function (or maximize a concave function), given access only to noisy sub-gradients of the function. We accomplish this using the gradient descent algorithm. Below we recap some necessary background.

Let $C \subseteq \mathbb{R}^d$ be a compact and convex set of diameter at most D (w.r.t. ℓ_2 norm). A *subgradient* of a function $f : C \to R$ at point $x \in C$ is any vector $g \in C$ that satisfies the inequality $f(y) \geq f(x) + \langle g, y - x\rangle$ for any point $y \in C$. The set of all subgradients at x is denoted $\partial f(x)$. If f is differentiable, the only subgradient g is the gradient $\nabla f(x)$.

The basic subgradient descent method is an iterative algorithm that starts at some point $x_1 \in C$ and iterates the following equations

$$y_{t+1} = x_t - \eta\, g_t, \qquad \text{and} \qquad x_{t+1} = \Pi_C(y_{t+1})$$

where η is the learning rate and $g_t \in \partial f(x_t)$ is a subgradient of the function f at point x_t, and $\Pi_C(x) = \operatorname{argmin}_{y\in C} \|x - y\|$ denote the projection operator onto C.

Now, we will assume that g_t and/or x_t are subject to noise. We will use two variants of the algorithm, which operate under two different models of noise. In the first model, the algorithm only has access to *unbiased estimates* of the subgradient.

Theorem 2.1 ([36]). *Suppose that f is convex, and for some constant D,G, the estimates of the subgradients satisfy $\mathbb{E}[g_t] \in \partial f(x_t)$ and $\|g_t\| \leq G$ for all steps t, and the diameter of the set satisfies $\|C\| \leq D$. Then if we run the subgradient descent method with step size $\eta = D/(G\sqrt{T})$, then for any T and any initial point $x_1 \in C$, the point $z = \frac{1}{T}\sum_{t=1}^T x_t$ satisfies*

$$\mathbb{E}[f(z)] \leq \min_{x\in C} f(x) + 2DG/\sqrt{T}.$$

In the second model, the algorithm has access to the noiseless subgradients, but the points x^t are adversarially perturbed after the projection.

Theorem 2.2. *Suppose that f is convex, fix constants $D, E,$ and G. Suppose that the gradient descent algorithm performs the following update in each iteration*

$$y_{t+1} = x_t - \eta\, g_t \qquad \textit{and} \qquad x_{t+1} = \Pi_C(y_{t+1}) + \xi_t$$

such that $g_t \in \partial f(x_t)$ and $\xi_t \in \mathbb{R}^d$ is a noise vector. Suppose that $\|g_t\| \leq G$ and $\|\xi_t\| \leq E$, $x_t \in C$ for all steps t, and the diameter of the set satisfies $\|C\| \leq D$. Then if we run the subgradient descent method with step size $\eta = D/(G\sqrt{T})$, for any T and any initial point $x_1 \in C$, the point $z = \frac{1}{T}\sum_{t=1}^T x_t$ satisfies

$$f(z) \leq \min_{x\in C} f(x) + DG/\sqrt{T} + GE\sqrt{T}.$$

The proof is similar to the standard analysis of gradient descent (e.g., see Theorem 3.1 in [15]). For the sake of completeness, we provide a self-contained proof of this result in the full version.

3 A GENERAL ALGORITHM IN THE DIVISIBLE GOODS SETTING

This section is dedicated to the divisible good setting: we give a computationally efficient algorithm for finding a price vector that approximately optimizes social welfare subject to the constraint that the expected per-round demand of each good j is no more than s_j. Specifically, let $x^*_\psi(p)$ denote the expected bundle purchased by a random buyer under the prices p (or the *induced bundle* by p), that is

$$x^*_\psi(p) = \mathop{\mathbb{E}}_{v\sim\psi}\left[x^*_v(p)\right].$$

Given access to the revealed preference oracle RePr, the algorithm finds an approximately optimal price vector p using polynomially queries to RePr and guarantees that $x^*_\psi(p) \leq s$. Our algorithm consists of two layers, and we present it in three main steps.

(1) First, we analyze a pertinent convex program and derive several structural results. In particular, we show that the expected social welfare can be expressed as a concave function of the induced bundle.
(2) Next, we present the inner layer of the algorithm: given any target bundle $\hat{x}$, we can iteratively find price vectors p^t such that the induced bundle $x^*_\psi(p^t)$ converges to $\hat{x}$ over time.
(3) Finally, we show how to derive subgradients of the expected social welfare function from information available. The outer layer of the algorithm will then use (noisy) subgradient descent to optimize the welfare function over the bundle space.

We make the following assumptions on the feasible set $\mathcal{F}$ and each valuation function $v \in \mathcal{V}$.

Assumption 3.1 (Feasible set). *For the set $\mathcal{F} \subset \mathbb{R}^d_+$ of feasible bundles, a canonical example is $\mathcal{F} = [0,1]^d$: each buyer can simultaneously buy up to one unit of each good. More generally, we assume that $\mathcal{F}$ is convex, closed, has a non-empty interior.*[7]

Assumption 3.2 (Valuations). *Each valuation function v in $\mathcal{V}$ satisfies:*

(1) *v is monotonically increasing in each coordinate. (This can be relaxed to Assumption 3.4.)*
(2) *v is (λ,β)-Hölder continuous with respect to the ℓ_1 norm over $\mathcal{F}$, for some $\lambda \geq 1$ and some absolute constant $\beta \in (0,1]$. Namely: $|v(x) - v(x')| \leq \lambda \cdot \|x - x'\|_1^\beta$ for all $x, x' \in \mathcal{F}$.*
(3) *v is σ-strongly concave over $\mathcal{F}$ — for all $x, x' \in \mathcal{F}$, $v(x') \leq v(x) + \langle\nabla v(x), x' - x\rangle - (\sigma/2) \cdot \|x - x'\|_2^2$.*

These assumptions on the valuations are satisfied by a large class of well-studied valuation functions, including *Constant Elasticity of Substitution (CES)* and *Cobb-Douglas* (See [29] for a proof). We crucially rely on a use property of strongly concave functions: any point in the domain that is close to the minimum in objective value is also close to the minimum in Euclidean distance.

3.1 A Stochastic Convex Program

Let us say that a bundle $\hat{x} \in \mathbb{R}^d_+$ is *inducible* if there exists a price vector $p \in \mathbb{R}^d_+$ such that $x^*_\psi(p) = \hat{x}$. Note that each inducible bundle $\hat{x}$ is a convex combination of n bundles (purchased by all the buyers) in $\mathcal{F}$, so it must lie in the set $\mathcal{F}$.

A centerpiece in our analysis is the following welfare maximization convex program that characterizes the relation between the posted prices and inducible bundles.

[7] For a set $C \subset \mathbb{R}^d$ and a norm $\|\cdot\|$, we write $\|C\| = \sup_{x\in C}\|x\|$. When the norm is unspecified, it is assumed to be ℓ_2.

Definition 3.3. For any bundle $\hat{x} \in \mathcal{F}$, let convex program $\mathsf{SCP}(\hat{x})$ be the following

$$\max_{x \in \mathcal{F}^n} \quad \sum_{v_i \in \mathcal{V}} \psi(v_i)\, v_i(x_i) \tag{4}$$

$$\text{such that} \quad \sum_{v_i \in \mathcal{V}} \psi(v_i)\, x_{ij} \le \hat{x}_j \quad \text{for every } j \in [d] \tag{5}$$

$$x_i \in \mathcal{F} \quad \text{for every } v_i \in \mathcal{V} \tag{6}$$

Let $\mathsf{VAL}(\hat{x})$ be the optimal value of the convex program $\mathsf{SCP}(\hat{x})$. We also say that $\mathsf{SCP}(\hat{x})$ is *supply-saturating* if its optimal solution $x^\bullet$ saturates all of the supply constraints defined by eq. (5), that is $\sum_i \psi(v_i)\, x^\bullet_{ij} = \hat{x}_j$ for all j.

To interpret the above as a stochastic welfare maximization program, consider a market in which there are d types of goods and each good j has supply $\hat{x}_j$. For each valuation function $v_i \in \mathcal{V}$, we introduce a buyer i with this valuation, who shows up to the market with probability $\psi(v_i)$. We use a vector $x_i = (x_{i1}, \ldots, x_{id}) \in \mathcal{F}$ to represent the bundle of goods allocated to a buyer i if he shows up. Then the program is precisely computing an allocation over all buyers to maximize the expected welfare subject to the constraint that the expected demand is no more than the supply given by $\hat{x}$.[8]

Assumption 3.4 (Relaxing monotonicity in valuations). *In fact, the assumption that each valuation in the class $\mathcal{V}$ is increasing can be relaxed. Our algorithm works as long as the class $\mathcal{V}$ and the feasible set $\mathcal{F}$ guarantees that $\mathsf{SCP}(\hat{x})$ is supply-saturating for any $\hat{x} \in \mathcal{F}$. For the sake of generality, our analysis will rely on the supply saturation condition instead of the monotonicity of the valuations. This will be useful for applying the algorithm to the indivisible goods setting.*

If the valuations in the class $\mathcal{V}$ are increasing functions, the optimal solution of $\mathsf{SCP}(\hat{x})$ will saturate all of the supply constraints in eq. (5).

Claim 3.5. *Suppose that each valuation $v \in \mathcal{V}$ is monotonically increasing in each coordinate. Then for any $\hat{x} \in \mathcal{F}$, the convex program $\mathsf{SCP}(\hat{x})$ is supply-saturating.*

For each of the supply constraints in eq. (5), we can introduce a dual (price) variable p_j and write down the following *partial Lagrangian*

$$\mathcal{L}_{\hat{x}}(x,p) = \sum_{v_i \in \mathcal{V}} \psi(v_i)\, v_i(x_i) - \sum_{j=1}^{d} p_j \left(\sum_{v_i \in \mathcal{V}} \psi(v_i)\, x_{ij} - \hat{x}_j \right) \tag{7}$$

We can also consider the *Lagrange dual function* of the convex program $g_{\hat{x}} : \mathbb{R}^d \to \mathbb{R}$:

$$g_{\hat{x}}(p) = \max_{x \in \mathcal{F}^n} \mathcal{L}_{\hat{x}}(x,p). \tag{8}$$

We will mostly focus on the case where $\hat{x} \in \left(\mathcal{F} \cap \mathbb{R}^d_{>0}\right)$, which we can show is a sufficient condition for inducibility.[9]

Lemma 3.6. *Let $\hat{x} \in \left(\mathcal{F} \cap \mathbb{R}^d_{>0}\right)$ be a bundle, then $\hat{x}$ is inducible.*

[8] Similar construction of such stochastic convex programs also appeared in [20].

[9] The restriction that the bundle be positive in each coordinate is necessary — a bundle with zero in some coordinate may not be inducible. Consider the same simple setting in Theorem 1.4 where $d = 1$ and there is a single buyer with valuation $v(x) = \sqrt{x}$. Because the marginal valuation at 0 is infinity, there is no bounded price to induce the buyer to purchase 0 units of the good.

Proof. Consider the convex program $\mathsf{SCP}(\hat{x})$. Since the convex program satisfies the *Slater's condition*, strong duality gives

$$\max_{x\in\mathcal{F}^n}\min_{p\in\mathbb{R}^d_+}\mathcal{L}_{\hat{x}}(x,p) = \min_{p\in\mathbb{R}^d_+}\max_{x\in\mathcal{F}^n}\mathcal{L}_{\hat{x}}(x,p) = \mathsf{VAL}(\hat{x})$$

Furthermore, since $\mathsf{SCP}(\hat{x})$ is supply-saturating, the optimal solution satisfies $\mathbb{E}_{v_i\sim\psi}\left[x_i^\bullet\right] = \hat{x}$. Let $p^\bullet$ be the optimal dual solution. It follows that

$$x^\bullet = \operatorname*{argmax}_{x\in\mathcal{F}^n}\mathcal{L}(x,p^\bullet) = \operatorname*{argmax}_{x\in\mathcal{F}^n}\sum_i \psi(v_i)\,v_i(x_i) - \sum_{j=1}^d p_j^\bullet\left(\sum_{v_i\in\mathcal{V}}\psi(v_i)\,x_{ij} - \hat{x}_j\right)$$

$$= \operatorname*{argmax}_{x\in\mathcal{F}^n}\sum_i \psi(v_i)\left(v_i(x_i) - \langle p_j^\bullet, x_i\rangle + \langle p^\bullet,\hat{x}\rangle\right)$$

Note that the expression inside the argmax is linearly separable across i. Therefore,

$$x_i^\bullet = \operatorname*{argmax}_{x_i\in\mathcal{F}}\left[v_i(x_i) - \langle p^\bullet, x_i\rangle + \langle p^\bullet,\hat{x}\rangle\right] = \operatorname*{argmax}_{x_i\in\mathcal{F}}\left[v_i(x_i) - \langle p^\bullet, x_i\rangle\right] \tag{9}$$

It follows that $x_i^\bullet = x^*_{v_i}(p^\bullet)$ for each i, and hence the price vector $p^\bullet$ induces the bundle $\hat{x}$. □

Next, we show that the prices that induce the bundle $\hat{x}$ are an optimal solution of the Lagrangian dual, and the bundles purchased by each buyer in response to these prices form the unique primal optimal solution.

Lemma 3.7. *Let $\hat{x} \in \left(\mathcal{F}\cap\mathbb{R}^d_{>0}\right)$ be a bundle, and let $\hat{p}\in\mathbb{R}^d_+$ be a price vector such that $x^*_\psi(\hat{p}) = \hat{x}$. Then*

- *the price vector $\hat{p}$ is an optimal dual solution for $\mathsf{SCP}(\hat{x})$, and*
- *the vector $x^\bullet \in \mathcal{F}^n$ such that $x_i^\bullet = x^*_{v_i}(\hat{p})$ for each i is the unique optimal primal solution.*

A very nice consequence of Lemma 3.7 is that whenever the induced bundle $\hat{x}$ is fixed, the realized bundles purchased by buyers of each type are also fixed. This allows us to express the expected social welfare as a function only of the induced bundle. In particular, the expected valuation for inducing $\hat{x}$ in expectation is exactly $\mathsf{VAL}(\hat{x})$. This suggests a different way to express the welfare: as a function of the induced bundle (as opposed to a function of the price vector defined in eq. (3)). For each $\hat{x}\in\mathcal{F}$, we can define

$$\mathsf{SW}(\hat{x}) = \mathsf{VAL}(\hat{x}) - \langle c,\hat{x}\rangle. \tag{10}$$

We can show that the expected social welfare for inducing $\hat{x}$ in expectation is exactly $\mathsf{SW}(\hat{x})$. More importantly, by rewriting the welfare as a function of the bundle, we obtain a *concave* objective function. This is crucial for us to obtain an efficient algorithm later.

Lemma 3.8. *The expected social welfare function $\mathsf{SW}\colon \mathcal{F}\to\mathbb{R}$ as defined in eq. (10) is concave.*

With all of structural results above, we are ready to give our two-layered algorithm for finding the welfare-maximizing prices.

3.2 Inner Layer: Converting Target Bundles to Prices

Even though we can express the expected welfare as a concave function of the induced bundle, we still cannot directly optimize the function because the seller only controls the prices of the goods instead of the expected induced bundle itself. To optimize over the bundle space, we give an algorithm that finds a price vector that approximately induces any target expected bundle $\hat{x}$. Specifically, suppose that the seller has some target bundle $\hat{x}$ in mind, we can learn a price vector $\hat{p}$ such that the expected induced bundle is close to the target bundle: $\left\|\hat{x} - x^*_\psi(\hat{p})\right\| \le \varepsilon$.

In Lemma 3.7, we show that the prices that exactly induce the target bundle $\hat{x}$ are the optimal dual solution for the convex program $\mathsf{SCP}(\hat{x})$, which is the price vector p that minimizes the Lagrangian dual function $g_{\hat{x}}$. We will show that if we can find an approximate minimizer for $g_{\hat{x}}$, we can then approximately induce the target expected bundle $\hat{x}$. In particular, we will apply the noisy gradient descent method (Theorem 2.1) to minimize the function $g_{\hat{x}}$, and for the sake of convergence of the algorithm, we will restrict the search space for the price vector to be

$$\mathcal{P}(\varepsilon) = \left\{ p \in \mathbb{R}^d_+ \mid \|p\|_2 \leq \sqrt{d}\lambda^{(1/\beta)} \left(\frac{4d}{\varepsilon^2 \sigma} \right)^{(1-\beta)/\beta} \right\} \tag{11}$$

where ε is the target accuracy parameter. First, we will show that the minimax value of the Lagrangian remains close to $\mathsf{VAL}(\hat{x})$ even when we restrict the dual variables/prices to be in $\mathcal{P}(\varepsilon)$.

Lemma 3.9. *Let $\hat{x} \in \left(\mathcal{F} \cap \mathbb{R}^d_{>0}\right)$. There exists a value* R-OPT *such that*

$$\max_{x \in \mathcal{F}^n} \min_{p \in \mathcal{P}(\varepsilon)} \mathcal{L}_{\hat{x}}(x,p) = \min_{p \in \mathcal{P}(\varepsilon)} \max_{x \in \mathcal{F}^n} \mathcal{L}_{\hat{x}}(x,p) = \text{R-OPT}$$

Moreover, $\mathsf{VAL}(\hat{x}) \leq \text{R-OPT} \leq \mathsf{VAL}(\hat{x}) + \frac{\varepsilon^2 \sigma}{4}$.

The next result translates the approximation error in minimizing the function $g_{\hat{x}}$ to the error in inducing the target bundle $\hat{x}$ by making use of the strong concavity of the valuations in $\mathcal{V}$.

Lemma 3.10. *Let $\hat{x} \in \left(\mathcal{F} \cap \mathbb{R}^d_{>0}\right)$ and p' be a price vector in $\mathcal{P}(\varepsilon)$ such that $g_{\hat{x}}(p') \leq \min_{p \in \mathcal{P}(\varepsilon)} g_{\hat{x}}(p) + \alpha$ for some $\alpha > 0$. Let $x' = x^*_\psi(p')$ be the expected bundle induced by prices p'. Then $\|x' - \hat{x}\|_2 \leq 2\sqrt{\alpha/\sigma}$.*

Therefore, in order to (approximately) induce a target bundle in expectation, we just need to compute an (approximate) minimizer for the Lagrangian dual function $g_{\hat{x}}$. We first show that we can compute an unbiased estimate of the gradient of $g_{\hat{x}}$ by using the observed bundle purchased by a random buyer.

Lemma 3.11. *Let $p \in \mathbb{R}^d_+$ be any price vector, and $x^*_v(p)$ be bundle purchased by a buyer with valuation function v under prices p. Then*

$$\mathop{\mathbb{E}}_{v \sim \psi} \left[\hat{x} - x^*_v(p)\right] = \hat{x} - x^*_\psi(p) = \nabla g_{\hat{x}}(p).$$

The result of Theorem 3.11 shows that we can obtain unbiased estimates of the gradients of the function $g_{\hat{x}}$ at different prices, as long as we can obtain unbiased estimates for the expected demand $x^*_\psi(p)$. In the next section, we will give another technique to obtain unbiased estimates for the gradients. Given access to unbiased estimate of the gradients of $g_{\hat{x}}$, we can rely on the noisy subgradient descent method (and its guarantee in Theorem 2.1) to minimize the function $g_{\hat{x}}$. Note that the algorithm will only find a point that approximately minimizes the function in expectation, but we can get an approximate minimizer with high probability using a standard amplification technique — running the subgradient descent method for logarithmically many times, so that one of the output price vectors is guaranteed to be accurate with high probability. More formally:

Lemma 3.12. *Let $\hat{x} \in \left(\mathcal{F} \cap \mathbb{R}^d_{>0}\right)$ be any target bundle. There exists an algorithm that given any target accuracy ε and confidence parameter δ as input, outputs a list P of $\log(1/\delta)$ price vectors such that with probability at least $1-\delta$, there exists a price vector $\hat{p} \in P$ that satisfies $\left\|x^*_\psi(\hat{p}) - \hat{x}\right\| \leq \varepsilon$. Furthermore, the running time, the length of the list and the number of queries to* ReP *is bounded by* $\mathrm{poly}(d, 1/\varepsilon, \log(1/\delta))$.

Lastly, we have one remaining technical problem to solve: given a set of price vectors P in which at least one price vector can approximately induce the target expected bundle $\hat{x}$, we need to identify one such price vector. To accomplish this, we will simply post each price vector $p \in P$ repeatedly, to obtain polynomially many observations from the buyers and compute the empirical average bundles over these polynomially many rounds. We select the price vector whose empirical average purchased bundle is closest to the target bundle $\hat{x}$. Putting all the pieces together, we obtain our full algorithm BunToPrice (formal description in the full version).

Theorem 3.13. *Let $\hat{x} \in \left(\mathcal{F} \cap \mathbb{R}^d_{>0}\right)$ be any target bundle. For any target accuracy parameter ε and confidence parameter δ, the instantiation* BunToPrice$(\hat{x}, \varepsilon, \delta)$ *outputs a price vector $\hat{p}$ that with probability at least $1 - \delta$ satisfies $\|\hat{x} - x^*_{\psi}(\hat{p})\| \leq \varepsilon$. Furthermore, the number of queries to* ReP *is bounded by* $\mathrm{poly}(d, 1/\varepsilon, \log(1/\delta))$.

3.3 Outer Layer: Welfare Maximization

Finally, we combine the subroutine BunToPrice with subgradient descent to find the welfare maximizing prices. At a high level, we will use subgradient descent to optimize the function SW over the bundle space, and along the way use the algorithm BunToPrice to obtain prices which induce each target bundle that arises along subgradient descent's optimization path. To ensure that the per-round expected demand for each good j is bounded by some supply s_j, the algorithm will optimize over bundles in the set $S = \{x \in \mathcal{F} \mid x_j \leq s_j \text{ for each } j \in [d]\}$.

There are several technical challenges remaining. First, in order to optimize the concave function SW using subgradient descent, we need to compute a subgradient for each bundle the subgradient descent method chooses at intermediate steps. The following result establishes a very nice property that the price vector that induces each target bundle $\hat{x}$ gives us a simple way to compute a subgradient in $\partial \mathsf{SW}(\hat{x})$. In particular, this means we can obtain a subgradient of the function SW using our subroutine BunToPrice.

Lemma 3.14. *Let $\hat{x} \in \left(\mathbb{R}^d_{>0} \cap \mathcal{F}\right)$, and $\hat{p}$ be the price vector that induces $\hat{x}$. Then $(\hat{p} - c) \in \partial \mathsf{SW}(\hat{x})$.*

Second, at each iteration t, subgradient descent may require a subgradient at some bundle x^t, but because of the error in BunToPrice, we only find prices to *approximately* induce the target bundle. To overcome this issue, we will rely on the analysis of subgradient descent under *adversarial noise* (given in Theorem 2.2).

Lastly, instead of optimizing over the entire set S, we will optimize over a slightly smaller set

$$S_\xi = \{x \in \mathcal{F} \mid \xi \leq x_j \leq s_j - \xi\}.$$

This allows us to settle two issues: (1) we can guarantee that all of the induced bundles lie in the set S despite the error of BunToPrice and (2) each bundle in S_ξ is guaranteed to be inducible since it is strictly positive in every coordinate (as required by Theorem 3.13).

Lemma 3.15. *For any $\xi \in (0, 1)$, $\max_{x \in S} \mathsf{SW}(x) - \max_{x' \in S_\xi} \mathsf{SW}(x') \leq \lambda (d\xi)^\beta + \sqrt{d}\xi \|c\|$.*

Putting all the pieces together, we obtain our main algorithm OWel (full description presented in the full version). To establish the welfare guarantee of $\hat{\mathcal{D}}$, we will compare to an even stronger benchmark—the welfare of the optimal lottery over allocations. In particular, given any constraint vector $s \in \mathbb{R}^{d+1}_+$, a feasible lottery over allocations is a randomized mapping $\pi \colon [n] \to \mathcal{F}$ that assigns each buyer to a randomized bundle such that $\mathbb{E}_{v_i \sim \psi}[\pi(i)] \leq s$. Let $\mathrm{OPT}^{\mathrm{lot}}$ be the optimal social welfare achieved by a lottery over allocations. The following is the formal guarantee of OWel (corresponding to Theorem 1.1).

Theorem 3.16. *For any accuracy parameter $\alpha > 0$, confidence parameter $\delta > 0$, and subset $S = \{x \in \mathcal{F} \mid x_j \leq s_j$ for each $j \in [d]\}$ given by a supply vector s. Given query access to* ReP*, the instantiation* OWel(α,δ,s) *outputs a price vector p' that with probability at least $1-\delta$ satisfies $x^*_\psi(p') \leq s$ and*

$$\mathsf{SW}(p') \geq \mathrm{OPT}^{\mathrm{lot}} - \alpha.$$

Furthermore, both the run-time of the algorithm and the number of queries to ReP *is bounded by* $\mathrm{poly}(d, 1/\alpha, 1/\sigma, 1/\lambda, \log(1/\delta))$.

Remark. The only part of the algorithm that interacts with the oracle ReP (or the buyers) is BunToPrice of the inner layer. Since the BunToPrice only requires a bounded and unbiased estimate of $x^*_\psi(p)$ for each price vector p it queries, we can replace ReP by any procedure that can compute such unbiased estimate. This is crucial for solving the unit-demand problem.

4 UNIT-DEMAND BUYERS WITH INDIVISIBLE GOODS

We now switch to the setting of indivisible goods and unit-demand buyers. Our goal is to develop a computationally and query efficient algorithm to find an approximately optimal *distribution* over prices subject to the constraint that the per-round expected demand of each good j is bounded by s_j. In particular, we will use the algorithm OWel in Section 3 as a main tool for our solution. Throughout, we impose the following mild boundedness assumption on the values.

Assumption on valuations. There exists a constant upper bound V_{max} such that for any buyer $i \in [n]$ and item $j \in [d]$, $0 < v_{ij} \leq V_{\mathsf{max}}$.

Overview: relax and regularize. A natural starting point for solving our problem with OWel is to consider the *linear relaxation* of unit demand valuations: that is we can view the buyers as having linear valuation functions over divisible goods, and optimizing over a feasible set of bundles that is the non-negative orthant of the ℓ_1 ball. This relaxation maintains the property that buyers buy integral quantities of each good. However, this approach runs into a substantial difficulty, because linear valuation functions are not *strongly* concave, and strong concavity was an important ingredient in our analysis of OWel. Instead, we will imagine that we have access to a regularized version of the linear relaxation of our original problem: that is, we imagine that each buyer has a regularized valuation function of the form $\langle v, x\rangle + \eta H(x)$, where H is the entropy function (of course, in reality, we cannot modify the valuations of the buyers). We show that we can solve the (imagined) regularized version of the problem, and also that we can induce buyers to behave (in expectation) as if their valuation functions were regularized by appropriately perturbing the price vectors we present to them. Our solution then consists of the following three steps:

(1) We show that the algorithm OWel can compute an approximately optimal price vector for the regularized version of problem, as long as the algorithm has access to an unbiased estimate of the expected demand of a random regularized buyer.
(2) Next, we show that we can obtain such unbiased estimates given access to the revealed preference oracle ReP(ψ) in the original un-regularized instance. The key ingredient is a novel price perturbation technique.
(3) Finally, we show how to construct an approximately optimal price distribution based on the price vector output by OWel.

To facilitate the discussion, we will introduce a dummy good (indexed as $(d+1)$) to represent the buyer's option of buying nothing. The seller's price and each buyer's value for this item is always 0, and the per-round demand upper bound is simply $s_{d+1} = 1$. Moreover, we will write Δ_{d+1} to denote the set of all probability distributions over the $(d+1)$ items (or simply the simplex over the items). For any $x \in \Delta_{d+1}$, the entropy of x is defined as $H(x) = \sum_{j \in [d+1]} x_j \log \frac{1}{x_j}$. The function H is strongly concave with respect to the ℓ_1 norm over the simplex.

4.1 Solving the regularized problem

Given a probability distribution ψ over value vectors and a parameter η, we imagine a corresponding η-regularized problem with a distribution $\tilde{\psi}$ over valuation functions: for each valuation vector v_i in the support of ψ, create a regularized valuation function $\tilde{v}_i \colon \Delta_{d+1} \to \mathbb{R}_{>0}$ with the same probability mass $\tilde{\psi}_{v_i} = \psi_{v_i}$ such that $\tilde{v}_i(x) = \langle v_i, x \rangle + \eta H(x)$.

The regularized problem is an instance of the divisible good setting, with feasible set $\mathcal{F} = \Delta_{d+1}$. Suppose that we have access to an unbiased estimate for $x^*_{\tilde{\psi}}(p)$ for any price vector p: then we can apply OWEL from Section 3 to compute approximately optimal prices. There is a small obstacle in the analysis—the regularized valuations defined above are not monotonically increasing in each coordinate (because of the entropy term). However, recall that we were able to substitute monotonicity for Assumption 3.4— that the convex program $\mathsf{SCP}(\hat{x})$ is supply-saturating for each $\hat{x}$ in our feasible region $\mathcal{F} = \Delta_{d+1}$. This is indeed satisfied in our setting:

Lemma 4.1. *Let $\mathcal{F} = \Delta_{d+1}$ and $\tilde{\psi}$ be a distribution over the regularized valuation functions of the form $[\langle v, x \rangle + \eta H(x)]$. Then the convex program $\mathsf{SCP}(\hat{x})$ defined as*

$$\max_{x \in \Delta^n_{d+1}} \sum_{v_i \in \mathcal{V}} \tilde{\psi}(v_i) \; [\langle v_i, x_i \rangle + \eta H(x_i)] \qquad \text{such that} \quad \sum_{v_i \in \mathcal{V}} \tilde{\psi}(v_i) \, x_{ij} \le \hat{x}_j \quad \text{for every } j \in [d+1]$$

is supply-saturating for any $\hat{x} \in \Delta_{d+1}$.

Proof. Let $x^\bullet$ be an optimal solution to $\mathsf{SCP}(\hat{x})$. The convex combination $\mathbb{E}_{\tilde{\psi}}\left[x^\bullet_i\right] \in \Delta_{d+1}$, so we must have $\sum_{j \in [d+1]} \mathbb{E}_{\tilde{\psi}}\left[x^\bullet_{ij}\right] = 1$. Note that $\hat{x}$ also lies in Δ_{d+1} (these are the only inducible average bundles for unit demand buyers), so $\sum_{j \in [d+1]} \hat{x}_j = 1$. It follows that all of the constraints $\mathbb{E}_{\tilde{\psi}}\left[x^\bullet_{ij}\right] \le \hat{x}_j$ are saturated. □

Moreover, the feasible set Δ_{d+1} is convex, closed, has a non-empty interior, and each of the regularized valuations is η-strongly concave with respect to the ℓ_2 norm,[10] and $((\sqrt{d+1} + V_{\mathsf{max}}, 1/2)$-Hölder continuous (see the full versionfor a proof). Thus we satisfy all conditions needed to apply OWEL, so long as we have access to unbiased estimates of $x^*_{\tilde{\psi}}(p)$ for any price vector $p \in \mathbb{R}^{d+1}_+$.

4.2 From price perturbation to value regularization

Solving the regularized problem using OWEL requires an unbiased estimate for $x_{\tilde{\psi}}(p)$ for any price vector p that the algorithm queries, but in our problem instance the valuations are actually drawn from ψ (without the entropy term). To obtain such an estimate, we give a price perturbation technique that allows us to simulate the response for the regularized buyers: given any price vector p, we will perturb each coordinate to obtain a noisy price vector p', with the effect that the random item purchased by the unit-demand buyer in expectation over the perturbation equals the bundle purchased by her regularized counterpart.[11]

[10] This follows from the fact that the ℓ_1 norm of any vector is bigger than its ℓ_2 norm.

[11] The technique of simulating regularization through perturbation was also used to establish the equivalence between "Follow the Regularized Leader" and "Follow the Perturbed Leader" [34]. In our setting, it is important that we can obtain this effect by perturbing the price vector, rather than the valuation vector, because we do not have control over buyer valuations.

Lemma 4.2 ([34]). *Fix any $\eta > 0$ and any vector $u \in \mathbb{R}^{d+1}_{>0}$. For each $j \in [d+1]$, let G_j be a random number drawn independently and uniformly at random from $[0,1]$, then*

$$x^* = \operatorname*{argmax}_{x \in \Delta_{d+1}}[\langle u, x\rangle + \eta H(x)] = \mathbb{E}\left[\operatorname*{argmax}_{x \in \Delta_{d+1}}\left[\langle u, x\rangle + \eta \sum_{j\in[d+1]} x_j \ln\left(\ln(1/G_j)\right)\right]\right].$$

The random variable $\ln\ln(G_j)$ is distributed according to the *Gumbel* distribution. One immediate technical issue we have is that the Gumbel distribution is unbounded, so the perturbed prices might be negative. We also need to guarantee that the price on the dummy good $\perp$ is 0. To overcome this issue, we will translate the perturbed price vector p into a non-negative price vector p' with the following procedure: set $p'_{d+1} = 0$ and $p'_j = (p_j - p_{d+1}) - \min\{0, \min_{j'\in[d]}(p_{j'} - p_{d+1})\}$. We will refer to this procedure as Convert, and show that the choice made by any unit-demand buyer remains the same under the new price vector p'.

Lemma 4.3. *Let $p \in \mathbb{R}^{d+1}$ any real-valued vector and let $p' = \texttt{Convert}(p)$. Then for any vector $v \in \mathbb{R}^{d+1}_{>0}$ such that $v_{d+1} = 0$,*

$$\operatorname*{argmax}_{j\in[d+1]}[v_j - p_j] = \operatorname*{argmax}_{j\in[d+1]}[v_j - p'_j]$$

Furthermore, $p'_j \geq 0$ for all $j \in [d]$.

Combining the Gumbel noise addition and the procedure Convert, we can now obtain unbiased estimates for $x^*_{\tilde{\psi}}(p)$ using feedback from $\mathsf{ReP}(\psi)$, the revealed preference oracle for the original problem instance. More formally, for any fixed price vector p, consider the following distribution $\mathcal{D}(p)$ of random prices:

(1) For each $j \in [d+1]$, let G_j be a random number drawn independently and uniformly at random from $[0,1]$, and let $\tilde{p}_j = p_j + \ln\ln(G_j)$ for each $j \in [d+1]$.
(2) Output $p' = \texttt{Convert}(\tilde{p})$.

Given this subroutine for generating random prices, we have a procedure Sim (presented in Algorithm 1) for obtaining an unbiased estimate of $x^*_{\tilde{\psi}}(p)$ for any price vector p. We will establish the correctness of Sim in Theorem 4.4.

Algorithm 1 Simulate the response of a regularized buyer Sim(p, η)

Input: A price vector p and regularization parameter η
Let p' a price vector drawn from $\mathcal{D}(p)$
Query the oracle $\mathsf{ReP}(\psi)$ with p' (i.e. post p' to a random consumer) and obtain feedback x'
Output: x' as an unbiased estimate for $x^*_{\tilde{\psi}}(p)$

Lemma 4.4. *Fix any price vector $p \in \mathbb{R}^{d+1}_+$, parameter $\eta > 0$, and any distribution ψ over value vectors in $\mathbb{R}^{d+1}_{>0}$. Let x' be the estimate output by Sim(p, η), then $\mathbb{E}_{\psi,\text{Sim}}[x'] = x^*_{\tilde{v}}(p)$.*

Using the subroutine Sim to obtain unbiased estimate of $x^*_{\tilde{\psi}}(p)$ for different price vectors p, we can now instantiate OWel to solve the η-regularized problem.

4.3 Wrap-up: An approximately optimal distribution over prices

Let $\hat{p}$ be the price vector output by OWEL when solving the η-regularized problem, and consider the distribution over prices $\hat{\mathcal{D}} = \mathcal{D}(\hat{p})$. Similar to the divisible goods setting, we will again compare to the optimal lottery over allocations. In particular, the optimal lottery is given by

$$\max_{x \in \Delta^n_{d+1}} \sum_{i \in [n]} \psi(v_i)[\langle v_i - c, x_i \rangle] \qquad \text{such that} \qquad \sum_{i \in [n]} \psi(v_i) x_{ij} \le s_j \quad \text{for each } j \in [d+1]$$

Let $x^\star$ and $\mathrm{OPT}^{\mathrm{lot}}$ be the optimal solution and value for the program defined above. Since any distribution of prices is just inducing a lottery over allocations, we know that

$$\max_{\mathcal{D} \text{ s.t. } x^*_\psi(\mathcal{D}) \le s} \mathsf{SW}(\mathcal{D}) \le \mathrm{OPT}^{\mathrm{lot}}$$

where we write $x^*_\psi(\mathcal{D}) = \mathbb{E}_{p \sim \mathcal{D}, v \sim \psi}[x^*_v(p)]$ to denote expected demand over the goods.

The following lemma bounds the sub-optimality of $\hat{\mathcal{D}}$ compared to $\mathrm{OPT}^{\mathrm{lot}}$ in terms of the regularization parameter η and accuracy guarantee of the price vector $\hat{p}$.

LEMMA 4.5. *Fix any regularization parameter η. Suppose that $\hat{p}$ is an ε-approximately optimal price vector for the η-regularized problem. Then the distribution of prices $\hat{\mathcal{D}} = \mathcal{D}(\hat{p})$ satisfies*

$$\mathsf{SW}(\hat{\mathcal{D}}) \ge \mathrm{OPT}^{\mathrm{lot}} - \varepsilon - \eta \log(d+1).$$

Therefore, to achieve a target accuracy of α, it suffices to instantiate OWEL with accuracy parameter $\varepsilon = \alpha/2$ to solve the η-regularized problem with $\eta = \alpha/(2\log(d+1))$. Putting all the pieces together, we have our algorithm OWEL-UD (formally presented in the version) that achieves the following main result, which recovers Theorem 1.2.

THEOREM 4.6. *For any accuracy parameter $\alpha > 0$, confidence parameter $\delta > 0$, and subset $S = \{x \in \mathcal{F} \mid x_j \le s_j \text{ for each } j \in [d]\}$ given by a supply vector s. Given query access to* ReP*, the instantiation* OWEL-UD(α, δ, s) *outputs a distribution $\hat{\mathcal{D}}$ over prices such that with probability at least $1 - \delta$ satisfies $x^*_\psi(\hat{\mathcal{D}}) \le s$ and*

$$\mathsf{SW}(\hat{\mathcal{D}}) \ge \mathrm{OPT}^{\mathrm{lot}} - \alpha.$$

Furthermore, both the run-time of the algorithm and the number of queries to ReP *is bounded by* $\mathrm{poly}(d, 1/\alpha, V_{\mathsf{max}}, \log(1/\delta))$.

REFERENCES

[1] Sydney Afriat. 1967. The Construction of Utility Functions from Expenditure Data. *International Economic Review* 8, 1 (1967), 67–77.

[2] Alekh Agarwal, Dean P. Foster, Daniel J. Hsu, Sham M. Kakade, and Alexander Rakhlin. 2013. Stochastic Convex Optimization with Bandit Feedback. *SIAM Journal on Optimization* 23, 1 (2013), 213–240.

[3] Kareem Amin, Rachel Cummings, Lili Dworkin, Michael Kearns, and Aaron Roth. 2015. Online Learning and Profit Maximization from Revealed Preferences. In *Twenty-Ninth AAAI Conference on Artificial Intelligence (AAAI-15).*

[4] Moshe Babaioff, Shaddin Dughmi, Robert D. Kleinberg, and Aleksandrs Slivkins. 2015. Dynamic Pricing with Limited Supply. *ACM Trans. on Economics and Computation* 3, 1 (2015), 4. Special issue for *13th ACM EC*, 2012.

[5] Ashwinkumar Badanidiyuru, Robert Kleinberg, and Aleksandrs Slivkins. 2013. Bandits with Knapsacks. In *54th IEEE Symp. on Foundations of Computer Science (FOCS).*

[6] Maria-Florina Balcan, Avrim Blum, and Yishay Mansour. 2008. Item pricing for revenue maximization. In *9th ACM Conf. on Electronic Commerce (EC).* 50–59.

[7] Maria-Florina Balcan, Florin Constantin, Satoru Iwata, and Lei Wang. 2012. Learning Valuation Functions.. In *23rd.*

[8] Maria-Florina Balcan, Amit Daniely, Ruta Mehta, Ruth Urner, and Vijay V Vazirani. 2014. Learning Economic Parameters from Revealed Preferences. In *Web and Internet Economics.* Springer. 338–353.

[9] Eyal Beigman and Rakesh Vohra. 2006. Learning from revealed preference. In *Proceedings of the 7th ACM Conference on Electronic Commerce*. ACM, 36–42.

[10] Omar Besbes and Assaf Zeevi. 2009. Dynamic Pricing Without Knowing the Demand Function: Risk Bounds and Near-Optimal Algorithms. *Operations Research* 57 (2009), 1407–1420. Issue 6.

[11] Omar Besbes and Assaf J. Zeevi. 2012. Blind Network Revenue Management. *Operations Research* 60, 6 (2012), 1537–1550.

[12] Avrim Blum, Anupam Gupta, Yishay Mansour, and Ankit Sharma. 2011. Welfare and Profit Maximization with Production Costs. In *52nd IEEE Symp. on Foundations of Computer Science (FOCS)*. 77–86.

[13] Arnoud V. Den Boer. 2015. Dynamic pricing and learning: Historical origins, current research, and new directions. *Surveys in Operations Research and Management Science* 20, 1 (June 2015).

[14] Josef Broder and Paat Rusmevichientong. 2012. Dynamic Pricing Under a General Parametric Choice Model. *Operations Research* 60, 4 (2012), 965–980.

[15] Sébastien Bubeck. 2015. Convex Optimization: Algorithms and Complexity. *Foundations and Trends in Machine Learning* 8, 3-4 (2015), 231–357.

[16] Sébastien Bubeck and Nicolo Cesa-Bianchi. 2012. Regret Analysis of Stochastic and Nonstochastic Multi-armed Bandit Problems. *Foundations and Trends in Machine Learning* 5, 1 (2012).

[17] Sébastien Bubeck, Ofer Dekel, Tomer Koren, and Yuval Peres. 2015. Bandit Convex Optimization: \(\sqrt{T}\) Regret in One Dimension. In *28th Conf. on Learning Theory (COLT)*. 266–278.

[18] Tanmoy Chakraborty, Zhiyi Huang, and Sanjeev Khanna. 2013. Dynamic and Nonuniform Pricing Strategies for Revenue Maximization. *SIAM J. on Computing (SICOMP)* 42, 6 (2013), 2424–2451. Preliminary version in *IEEE FOCS 2009*.

[19] Arnoud V. den Boer and Bert Zwart. 2014. Simultaneously Learning and Optimizing Using Controlled Variance Pricing. *Management Science* 60, 3 (2014), 770–783.

[20] Nikhil R. Devanur, Balasubramanian Sivan, and Yossi Azar. 2012. Asymptotically optimal algorithm for stochastic adwords. In *ACM Conference on Electronic Commerce, EC '12, Valencia, Spain, June 4-8, 2012*. 388–404.

[21] Michal Feldman, Nick Gravin, and Brendan Lucier. 2015. Combinatorial Auctions via Posted Prices. In *26th ACM-SIAM Symp. on Discrete Algorithms (SODA)*. 123–135.

[22] Abraham Flaxman, Adam Kalai, and H. Brendan McMahan. 2005. Online Convex Optimization in the Bandit Setting: Gradient Descent without a Gradient. In *16th ACM-SIAM Symp. on Discrete Algorithms (SODA)*. 385–394.

[23] J. C. Gittins. 1989. *Multi-Armed Bandit Allocation Indices*. John Wiley & Sons.

[24] Elad Hazan and Kfir Y. Levy. 2014. Bandit Convex Optimization: Towards Tight Bounds. In *27th Advances in Neural Information Processing Systems (NIPS)*. 784–792.

[25] Justin Hsu, Jamie Morgenstern, Ryan Rogers, Aaron Roth, and Rakesh Vohra. 2016. Do prices coordinate markets?. In *Proceedings of the 48th Annual ACM SIGACT Symposium on Theory of Computing*. ACM, 440–453.

[26] N. Bora Keskin and Assaf J. Zeevi. 2014. Dynamic Pricing with an Unknown Demand Model: Asymptotically Optimal Semi-Myopic Policies. *Operations Research* 62, 5 (2014), 1142–1167.

[27] Robert Kleinberg and Tom Leighton. 2003. The Value of Knowing a Demand Curve: Bounds on Regret for Online Posted-Price Auctions.. In *44th IEEE Symp. on Foundations of Computer Science (FOCS)*. 594–605.

[28] Andreu Mas-Colell, Michael D. Whinston, and Jerry R. Green. 1995. *Microeconomic Theory*. Oxford University Press.

[29] Aaron Roth, Jonathan Ullman, and Zhiwei Steven Wu. 2016. Watch and learn: optimizing from revealed preferences feedback. In *Proc. of the 48th Annual ACM SIGACT Symp. on Theory of Computing, STOC 2016*.

[30] Ariel Rubinstein. 2012. *Lecture notes in microeconomic theory: the economic agent*. Princeton University Press.

[31] Paul A. Samuelson. 1938. A Note on the Pure Theory of Consumers' Behavior. *Economica* 5, 17 (1938), 61–71.

[32] Hal R. Varian. 2006. Revealed preference. In *Samuelsonian economics and the twenty-first century*, Michael Szenberg, Lall Ramrattan, and Aron A. Gottesman (Eds.). Oxford University Press, 99–115.

[33] Zizhuo Wang, Shiming Deng, and Yinyu Ye. 2014. Close the Gaps: A Learning-While-Doing Algorithm for Single-Product Revenue Management Problems. *Operations Research* 62, 2 (2014), 318–331.

[34] Manfred Warmuth. 2009. A perturbation that makes "Follow the leader" equivalent to "Randomized weighted majority". (2009).

[35] Morteza Zadimoghaddam and Aaron Roth. 2012. Efficiently Learning from Revealed Preference. In *Internet and Network Economics - 8th International Workshop, WINE 2012 (Lecture Notes in Computer Science)*, Vol. 7695. Springer, 114–127.

[36] Martin Zinkevich. 2003. Online Convex Programming and Generalized Infinitesimal Gradient Ascent. In *Machine Learning, Proceedings of the Twentieth International Conference (ICML 2003), August 21-24, 2003, Washington, DC, USA*. 928–936.

The Tragedy of your Upstairs Neighbors: Is the Negative Externality of Airbnb Internalized?

APOSTOLOS FILIPPAS, New York University
JOHN JOSEPH HORTON, New York University

A criticism of home-sharing platforms such as Airbnb, HomeAway, VRBO, and CouchSurfing is that their business model has hosts (those renting out properties) impose costs on their neighbors, particularly when long-term tenants are in close proximity. If hosts bring in loud or disreputable guests but, critically, still collect payment, then the platform would seem to help create a classic case of un-internalized externalities that existing illegal hotel laws are intended to prevent: the host gets the money and her neighbors get the noise.

Motivated by the public policy question raised by home-sharing, we develop a model of the market for both home-sharing and long-term rentals, and examine the outcomes under different policy regimes. We examine the regimes where hosting decision rights are allocated to (1) individual tenants, (2) building owners, (3) cities, or (4) a national or supra-national regulatory body that acts as a utilitarian social planner. For each of the four policy regimes, we derive the market equilibrium of the short-term rental market, and characterize the surplus of tenants (both hosting and non-hosting), building owners, and guests.

In our model, tenants consider only their financial pay-off from hosting: they host if the income they receive from home-sharing guests exceeds their individual hosting cost and are allowed to host. The income obtainable from home-share hosting is endogenous in the model, in that it depends on how many other tenants choose to host. Critically, would-be hosts do not consider the cost that their guests might impose on their fellow tenants.

Our analysis shows that when individual tenants decide, there is too much hosting in equilibrium, in that the costs created by the marginal host exceed the benefits. Consequently, the equilibrium following the introduction of home-sharing might offer less surplus than an equilibrium before the introduction. Setting aside for a moment the case where building owners decide, we find that when the city sets the quantity, there is too little hosting. Essentially, the city behaves as a monopolist, reducing supply to raise prices, thereby transferring surplus from guests to hosts. In practice, if cities are "already" picking the profit-maximizing quantity through their regulation and taxation of the hotel industry, the city might find it optimal to ban home-sharing altogether, as the increase in supply is unwanted.

The efficient quantity of hosting is obtained when the decision is left to building owners. This occurs despite the fact that owners only consider rents from long-term tenants in their building. The reason is that rents in a competitive long-term rental market must be the same regardless of the home-sharing policy of the respective building. Rents are equal because the building policy imposes no direct cost on the building owner; if a premium could be charged for one policy or the other, profit-maximizing building owners would choose whatever policy offered the premium. With long-term rental rates equalized, the marginal long-term tenant—the one who is indifferent between buildings that allow home-share hosting and those that do not—has a private benefit of hosting that is equal to the full costs of living in such a building. The full cost includes not only the tenants' private cost of hosting, but also the costs imposed from home-sharing hosts in the same building. The indifference of the marginal tenant combined with the indifference of all building

A full version of this paper is available at http://dx.doi.org/10.2139/ssrn.2443343.

Authors' email addresses: Filippas: apostolosfilippas@gmail.com; Horton: john.joseph.horton@gmail.com.

EC'17, June 26–30, 2017, Cambridge, MA, USA. © 2017 Copyright is held by the owner/author(s).
ACM ISBN 978-1-4503-4527-9/17/06. DOI: http://dx.doi.org/10.1145/3033274.3085097

owners are the drivers of the efficiency result. Note that in this analysis, we do not have to explicitly model the surplus of the guests, as the marginal guest at the market-clearing short-term rental rate is the same as the private benefit to the host.

Our model suggests that allowing individual building owners discretion in setting home-sharing policies is likely to be socially efficient. The social welfare obtained in the case where individual owners set building-wide policies coincides with that obtained in a market regulated by a social planner. The reason is that in a competitive long-term rental market terms are equalized between different types of buildings, and the marginal host's individual benefit does not exceed the full cost of her living in such a building. The two alternatives we examined—allocating decision rights to the individual tenant or to the city—are likely to lead to too much, and too little hosting, respectively.

Additional Key Words and Phrases: Online platforms, negative externalities, public policy

Interacting User Generated Content Technologies: How Q&As Affect Ratings & Reviews

SHRABASTEE BANERJEE, Questrom School of Business, Boston University
CHRYSANTHOS DELLAROCAS, Questrom School of Business, Boston University
GEORGIOS ZERVAS, Questrom School of Business, Boston University

In this paper, we study the question and answer (Q&A) feature of electronic commerce platforms, an increasingly common form of user-generated content (UGC) that allows consumers to publicly ask product-specific questions and receive responses, either from the platform or from other customers. Using data from a major online retailer, we show that Q&As complement reviews and ratings: unlike reviews, Q&As primarily happen pre-purchase, focus on clarification of product attributes (rather than discussion of quality), and convey fit-specific information in a sentiment-free way. Our main hypothesis is that Q&As mitigate product fit uncertainty, leading to better matches between products and consumers, and therefore improved product ratings. We show that when low-rated products start receiving Q&As, their subsequent ratings improve by approximately 0.5 stars. We further show that the extent of the rating increase due to Q&As is moderated by the degree of ex-ante fit uncertainty. Overall, our findings suggest that, by resolving product fit uncertainty in an e-commerce setting, the addition of Q&As can be a viable way for retailers to improve ratings and sales of low-rated products, particularly those products that have incurred low ratings due to customer-product fit mismatch[1].

[1]Full paper link: http://sites.google.com/view/shrabastee/working-papers

EC'17, June 26–30, 2017, Cambridge, MA, USA.
 ACM ISBN 978-1-4503-4527-9/17/06
http://dx.doi.org/10.1145/3033274.3084087

Learning in the Repeated Secretary Problem

DANIEL G. GOLDSTEIN, Microsoft Research
R. PRESTON MCAFEE, Microsoft Corporation
SIDDHARTH SURI, Microsoft Research
JAMES R. WRIGHT, Microsoft Research

In the classical secretary problem, one attempts to find the maximum of an unknown and unlearnable distribution through sequential search. In many real-world searches, however, distributions are not entirely unknown and can be learned through experience. To investigate learning in such a repeated secretary problem we conduct a large-scale behavioral experiment in which people search repeatedly from fixed distributions. In contrast to prior investigations that find no evidence for learning in the classical scenario, in the repeated setting we observe substantial learning resulting in near-optimal stopping behavior. We conduct a Bayesian comparison of multiple behavioral models which shows that participants' behavior is best described by a class of threshold-based models that contains the theoretically optimal strategy. In fact, fitting such a threshold-based model to data reveals players' estimated thresholds to be surprisingly close to the optimal thresholds after only a small number of games.

For the full version of this paper see: http://www.dangoldstein.com/papers/Goldstein_McAfee_Suri_Wright_Learning_Repeated_Secretary.pdf.

 EC'17, June 26–30, 2017, Cambridge, MA, USA. ACM ISBN 978-1-4503-4527-9/17/06.

DOI: http://dx.doi.org/10.1145/3033274.3085112

Diffusion in Networks and the Unexpected Virtue of Burstiness

MOHAMMAD AKBARPOUR, Stanford University
MATTHEW JACKSON, Stanford University

Whether an idea, information, disease, or innovation diffuses throughout a society depends not only on the structure of the network of interactions, but also on the timing of those interactions. Recent studies have shown that diffusion can fail on a network in which people are only active in "bursts", active for a while and then silent for a while, but diffusion could succeed on the same network if people were active in a more random Poisson manner. Those studies generally consider models in which nodes are active according to the same random timing process and then ask which timing is optimal. In reality, people differ widely in their activity patterns – some are bursty and others are not. We model diffusion on networks in which agents differ in their activity patterns. We show that bursty behavior does not always hurt the diffusion, and in fact having some (but not all) of the population be bursty significantly helps diffusion. We prove that maximizing diffusion requires heterogeneous activity patterns across agents, and the overall maximizing pattern of agents' activity times does not involve any Poisson behavior.

Additional Key Words and Phrases: Diffusion, Social Networks, Dynamic Networks, Heterogeneous Agents.

Financial support from the NSF under grant SES-1155302 and from grant FA9550-12-1-0411 from the AFOSR and DARPA, and ARO MURI award No. W911NF-12-1-0509. We thank Shayan Oveis Gharan for helpful conversations and Songyuan Ding for coding some of the simulations reported here.

EC'17, June 26–30, 2017, Cambridge, Massachusetts, USA. ACM ISBN 978-1-4503-4527-9/17/06.
DOI: http://dx.doi.org/10.1145/3033274.3085105

Truthful Allocation Mechanisms Without Payments: Characterization and Implications on Fairness

GEORGIOS AMANATIDIS, Athens University of Economics and Business
GEORGIOS BIRMPAS, Athens University of Economics and Business
GEORGE CHRISTODOULOU, University of Liverpool
EVANGELOS MARKAKIS, Athens University of Economics and Business

We study the mechanism design problem of allocating a set of indivisible items without monetary transfers. Despite the vast literature on this very standard model, it still remains unclear how do truthful mechanisms look like. We focus on the case of two players with additive valuation functions and our purpose is twofold. First, our main result provides a complete characterization of truthful mechanisms that allocate all the items to the players. Our characterization reveals an interesting structure underlying all truthful mechanisms, showing that they can be decomposed into two components: a *selection part* where players pick their best subset among prespecified choices determined by the mechanism, and an *exchange part* where players are offered the chance to exchange certain subsets if it is favorable to do so. In the remaining paper, we apply our main result and derive several consequences on the design of mechanisms with fairness guarantees. We consider various notions of fairness, (indicatively, maximin share guarantees and envy-freeness up to one item) and provide tight bounds for their approximability. Our work settles some of the open problems in this agenda, and we conclude by discussing possible extensions to more players.

CCS Concepts: •**Theory of computation → Algorithmic mechanism design; Algorithmic game theory;**

Additional Key Words and Phrases: mechanism design without money; fair division; maximin share fairness; envy-freeness up to one item

1 INTRODUCTION

We study a very elementary and fundamental model for allocating indivisible goods from a mechanism design viewpoint. Namely, we consider a set of indivisible items that need to be allocated to a set of players. An outcome of the problem is an allocation of all the items to the players, i.e., a partition into bundles, and each player evaluates an allocation by his own additive valuation function. Our primary motivation originates from the fair division literature, where such models have been considered extensively. However, the same setting also appears in several domains, including job scheduling, load balancing and many other resource allocation problems.

The focus of our work is on understanding the interplay between truthfulness and fairness in this setting. Hence, we want to identify the effects on fairness guarantees, imposed by eliminating any incentives for the players to misreport their valuation functions. This type of questions has been posed already in previous works and for various notions of fairness, such as envy-freeness, or for the concept of maximin shares [see, among others, 1, 9, 22]. However, the results so far have been rather scarce in the sense that a) in most cases, they concern impossibility results which

EC'17, June 26–30, 2017, Cambridge, Massachusetts, USA. © 2017 ACM. ISBN 978-1-4503-4527-9/17/06...$15.00.
DOI: http://dx.doi.org/10.1145/3033274.3085147

are far from being tight and b) the proof techniques are based on constructing specific families of instances that do not enhance our understanding on the structure of truthful mechanisms, with the exception of Caragiannis et al. [9] which, however, is only for two players and two items.

In order to comprehend the trade-offs that are inherent between incentives and fairness, we first take a step back and focus solely on truthfulness itself. As is quite common in fair division models, we will not allow any monetary transfers, so that a mechanism simply outputs an allocation of the items. Hence, the question we want to begin with is: *what is the structure of truthful allocation mechanisms?*

There has been already a significant volume of works on characterizing truthful allocation mechanisms for indivisible items, yet there are some important differences from our approach. First, a typical line of work studies this question under the additional assumption of Pareto efficiency or related notions [15, 21, 26]. The characterization results that have been obtained show that the combination of truthfulness together with Pareto efficiency tends to make the class of available deterministic mechanisms very poor; only some types of dictatorship survive when imposing both criteria. Second, in some cases the analysis is carried out without any restrictions on the class of valuation functions, which again often results in a very limited class of mechanisms [see, e.g., 27]. When moving to a specific class, such as the class of additive functions which is usualy assumed in fair division, it is conceivable that we can have a much richer class of truthful mechanisms. The results above indicate that the known characterizations of truthful mechanisms are also dependent on further assumptions, which may be well justified in various scenarios, but they are not aligned with the goal of fair division.

1.1 Contribution

Our main result is a characterization of deterministic truthful mechanisms that allocate all the items to two players with additive valuations. In doing so, we identify some important allocation properties that every truthful mechanism should satisfy. One such crucial property is the notion of *controlling* items (Definition 3.10); we say that a player controls an item, whenever it is possible to report values that will guarantee him this item, regardless of the other player's valuation function. We show that truthfulness implies that every item is controlled by some player. Exploiting this property further, greatly helps us in understanding how a mechanism operates. Consequently, our analysis and the characterization we eventually obtain reveals an interesting structure underlying all truthful mechanisms; they can all be essentially decomposed into two components: (i) a *selection part* where players pick their best subset among prespecified choices determined by the mechanism, and (ii) an *exchange part* where players are offered the chance to exchange certain subsets if it is favorable to do so. Hence, we call them *picking-exchange mechanisms.*

Next, we apply our main result and derive several consequences on the design of mechanisms with (approximate) fairness guarantees. We consider various notions of fairness in Section 4, starting our discussion with the more standard ones such as proportionality and envy-freeness, and explaining why such concepts cannot be attained—even approximately—by truthful mechanisms. We then focus on more recently studied relaxations of either envy-freeness or proportionality where positive algorithmic results have been obtained (e.g., finding allocations that are envy-free up to one item, or achieve approximate maximin share guarantees). For these notions, we provide tight bounds on the approximation guarantees of truthful mechanisms, settling some of the open problems in this area [1, 9]. Interestingly, our results also reveal that the best truthful approximation algorithms for fair division are achieved by *ordinal* mechanisms, i.e., mechanisms that exploit only the relative ranking of the items and not the cardinal information of the valuation functions.

The heart of our approach for obtaining lower bounds on the approximability of fairness criteria, is a necessary condition for fairness in view of our notion of control, which we call *no control of pairs*. It states that no player should control more than one item. We show how this condition summarizes minimum requirements for various fairness concepts previously studied in the literature. Although this condition does not offer an alternative fairness criterion, it is a useful tool for showing lower bounds.

Finally, in Section 5 we provide a general class of truthful mechanisms for the case of multiple players. This class generalizes picking-exchange mechanisms in a non-trivial way. As indicated by our mechanisms, there is a much richer structure in the case of multiple players. In particular, the notion of control does not convey enough information anymore. Instead, there seem to exist several different levels of control.

1.2 Related Work

The only work we are aware of, in which a full characterization is given for truthful mechanisms with indivisible items, additive valuations, and no further assumptions is by Caragiannis et al. [9]. However, this is only a characterization for two players and two items. Apart from characterizations, there have been several works that try to quantify the effects of truthfulness on several concepts of fairness. For the performance of truthful mechanisms with respect to envy-freeness, see Caragiannis et al. [9] and Lipton et al. [22], whereas for max-min fairness see Bezakova and Dani [4]. Coming to more recent results and along the same spirit, Amanatidis et al. [1] and Markakis and Psomas [23] study the notion of maximin share allocations, and a related notion of worst-case guarantees respectively. They obtain separation results, showing that the approximation factors achievable by truthful mechanisms are strictly worse than the known algorithmic (nontruthful) results. Obtaining a better understanding for the structure of truthful mechanisms and how they affect fairness has been an open problem underlying all the above works. For a better and more complete elaboration on fairness and the numerous fairness concepts that have been suggested, we refer the reader to the books [7, 25, 32] and the recent surveys [5, 30].

There has been a long series of works on characterizing mechanisms with indivisible items beyond the context of fair divison. Many works characterize the allocation mechanisms that arise when we combine truthfulness with Pareto efficiency [see, e.g., 15, 21, 26]. Typically, such mechanisms tend to be dictatorial, and it is also well known that economic efficiency is mostly incompatible with fairness [see, e.g., 5]. Another assumption that has been used is nonbossiness, which means that one cannot change the outcome without affecting his own bundle. For instance, Svensson [34] assumes nonbossiness in a setting where each player is interested in acquiring only one item. For general valuations, this also leads to dictatorial algorithms [27]. In most of these works ties are ignored by considering strict preference orders over all subsets of the items, while in some cases it is also allowed for the mechanism not to allocate all the items.

There have also been relevant works for the setting of divisible goods [see, among others, 10, 13]. We note that for additive valuation functions, a mechanism for divisible items can be interpreted as a randomized mechanism for indivisible items. This connection is already discussed and explored in Aziz et al. [3], Guo and Conitzer [19]. In our work, we do not study randomized mechanisms, however it is an interesting question to have characterization results for such settings as well. Along this direction, see Mennle and Seuken [24] where a relaxed notion of truthfulness is studied.

Related to our work is also the literature on exchange markets. These are models where players are equipped with an initial endowment, e.g., a house or a set of items. For the case where players can have multiple indivisible items as their initial endowment, see Pápai [28, 29]. Exchange markets provide an example where the existing characterizations go well beyond dictatorships and are closely related to the exchange component of our mechanisms.

Finally, for settings with payments, the work of Dobzinski and Sundararajan [14], and independently of Christodoulou et al. [11], provided a characterization of truthful mechanisms with two players and additive valuations when all items are allocated. However, their characterization does not apply to our setting because they make an additional assumption, namely *decisiveness*. It roughly requires that each player should be able to receive any possible bundle of items, by making an appropriate bid. Their motivation is the characterization of truthful mechanisms with bounded makespan (maximum finishing time) for the scheduling problem, and in their case decisiveness is necessary in order to achieve bounded guarantees. In our case, our motivation is fairness, and decisiveness is a very strong assumption which has the opposite effects of what we need; e.g., assigning the full-bundle to a player is unacceptable in terms of fairness. Finally, Christodoulou and Kovács [12] give a global characterization of envy-free and truthful mechanisms for settings with payments, when there are multiple players but only two items.

2 PRELIMINARIES AND NOTATION

With the exception of Section 5, we consider a setting with two players and a set of m indivisible items, $M = \{1, \ldots, m\} = [m]$, to be allocated to the players. We assume that each player i has an additive valuation function v_i over the items, so that for every $S \subseteq M$, $v_i(S) = \sum_{j \in S} v_i(\{j\})$. For $j \in M$, we write v_{ij} instead of $v_i(\{j\})$.

We say that $(S_1, S_2, \ldots, S_k)$ is a *partition* of a set S, if $\bigcup_{i \in [k]} S_i = S$, and $S_i \cap S_j = \emptyset$ for any $i, j \in [k]$ with $i \neq j$. Note that we do not require that $S_i \neq \emptyset$ for all $i \in [n]$. An allocation of M to the players is a partition in the form $S = (S_1, S_2)$. By $\mathcal{M}$ we denote the set of all allocations of M.

The set $\mathcal{V}_m$ of all possible profiles is $\mathbb{R}_+^m \times \mathbb{R}_+^m$, i.e., we assume that $v_{ij} > 0$ for every $i \in \{1, 2\}$ and $j \in M$. For some statements we need the assumption that the players' valuation functions are such that no two sets have the same value. So, let $\mathcal{V}_m^{\neq}$ denote the set of such profiles, i.e.,

$$\mathcal{V}_m^{\neq} = \left\{ (v_1, v_2) \in \mathcal{V}_m \;\middle|\; \forall S, T \subseteq [m] \text{ with } S \neq T, \text{ and } \forall i \in \{1, 2\}, \sum_{j \in S} v_{ij} \neq \sum_{j \in T} v_{ij} \right\}.$$

A *deterministic allocation mechanism with no monetary transfers*, or simply a *mechanism*, for allocating all the items in $M = [m]$, is a mapping $\mathcal{X}$ from $\mathcal{V}_m$ to $\mathcal{M}$. That is, for any profile $\mathbf{v}$, the outcome of the mechanism is $\mathcal{X}(\mathbf{v}) = (X_1(\mathbf{v}), X_2(\mathbf{v})) \in \mathcal{M}$, and $X_i(\mathbf{v})$ denotes the set of items player i receives.

A mechanism $\mathcal{X}$ is *truthful* if for any instance $\mathbf{v} = (v_1, v_2)$, any player $i \in \{1, 2\}$, and any v_i':

$$v_i(X_i(\mathbf{v})) \geq v_i(X_i(v_i', v_{-i})).$$

Since we will repeatedly argue about intersections of $X_i(\mathbf{v})$ with various subsets of M, we use $X_i^S(\mathbf{v})$ as a shortcut for $X_i(\mathbf{v}) \cap S$, where $S \subseteq M$.

2.1 Fairness concepts[1]

Several notions have emerged throughout the years as to what can be considered a fair allocation. We define below the concepts that we will examine in Section 4. Although all concepts can be clearly defined for any number of players, we provide the definitions for two players, since this is the focus of the paper.

We start with two of the most dominant solution concepts in fair division, namely proportionality and envy-freeness.

[1] The material of this subsection is needed in the sequel only within Section 4.

Definition 2.1. An allocation $S = (S_1, S_2)$ is

(1) *proportional*, if $v_i(S_i) \geq \frac{1}{2}v_i(M)$, for $i \in \{1, 2\}$.
(2) *envy-free*, if $v_1(S_1) \geq v_1(S_2)$, and $v_2(S_2) \geq v_2(S_1)$.

Proportionality was considered in the very first work on fair division by Steinhaus [33]. Envy-freeness was suggested later by Gamow and Stern [17], and with a more formal argumentation by Foley [16] and Varian [35].

Envy-freeness is a stricter notion than proportionality, but even for the latter existence cannot be guaranteed under indivisible goods. One can also consider approximation versions of these problems as follows: Given an instance I, let $E(I)$ be the minimum possible envy that can be achieved at I, among all possible allocations. We say that a mechanism achieves a ρ-approximation, if for every instance I, it produces an allocation where the envy between any pair of players is at most $\rho E(I)$. Similarly for proportionality, suppose that an instance I admits an allocation where every player receives a value of at least $\frac{c(I)}{2}v_i(M)$ for some $c(I) \leq 1$. Then a ρ-approximation would mean that each player is guaranteed a bundle with value at least $\frac{\rho c(I)}{2}v_i(M)$.

Apart from the approximation versions, the fact that we cannot always have proportional or envy-free allocations gives rise to relaxations of these definitions, with the hope of obtaining more positive results. We describe below three such relaxations, all of which admit either exact or constant-factor approximation algorithms (not necessarily truthful) in polynomial time.

The first such relaxation is the concept of envy-freeness up to one item, where each person may envy another player by an amount which does not exceed the value of a single item in the other player's bundle. Formally:

Definition 2.2. An allocation $S = (S_1, S_2)$ is *envy-free up to one item*, if there exists an item $a_1 \in S_1$, and an item $a_2 \in S_2$, such that $v_i(S_i) \geq v_i(S_j \setminus \{a_j\})$, for $i, j \in \{1, 2\}$.

It is quite easy to achieve envy-freeness up to one item, e.g., a round-robin algorithm that alternates between the players and gives them in each step their best remaining item suffices. Other algorithms are also known to satisfy this criterion [see 22].

A more interesting relaxation from an algorithmic point of view, comes from the notion of maximin share guarantees, recently proposed by Budish [8]. For two players, the maximin share of a player i is the value that he could achieve by being the cutter in a discretized form of the cut and choose protocol. This is a guarantee for player i, if he would partition the items into two bundles so as to maximize the value of the least valued bundle. We define below the approximate version of this notion.

Definition 2.3. Given a set of items $[m]$, the *maximin share* of a player $i \in \{1, 2\}$, is

$$\mu_i = \max_{S \in \mathcal{M}} \min\{v_i(S_1), v_i(S_2)\} .$$

For $\rho \leq 1$, an allocation $S = (S_1, S_2)$ is called a ρ-approximate maximin share allocation if $v_i(S_i) \geq \rho \cdot \mu_i$, for $i \in \{1, 2\}$.

For two players maximin share allocations always exist and even though they are NP-hard to compute, we have a PTAS by reducing this to standard job scheduling problems. Hence each player can receive a value of at least $(1 - \epsilon)\mu_i$. For a higher number of players, constant factor approximation algorithms also exist [see 2, 31].

Finally, a related approach was undertaken by Hill [20]. This work examined what is the worst case guarantee that a player can have as a function of the total number of players and the maximum value of an item across all players. For two players, the following function was identified precisely as the guarantee that can be given to each player. Note that the total value of the items is normalized to 1 in this case.

Definition 2.4. Let $V_2 : [0,1] \longrightarrow [0,1/2]$ be the unique nonincreasing function satisfying $V_2(\alpha) = 1/2$ for $\alpha = 0$, whereas for $\alpha > 0$:

$$V_2(\alpha) = \begin{cases} 1 - k\alpha & \text{if } \alpha \in I(2,k) \\ 1 - \frac{(k+1)}{2(k+1)-1} & \text{if } \alpha \in NI(2,k) \end{cases}$$

where for any integer $k \geq 1$, $I(2,k) = \left[\frac{k+1}{k(2(k+1)-1)}, \frac{1}{2k-1}\right]$ and $NI(2,k) = \left(\frac{1}{2(k+1)-1}, \frac{k+1}{k(2(k+1)-1)}\right)$.

Markakis and Psomas [23] proved that for two players, there always exists an allocation such that each player i receives at least $V_2(\alpha_i)$, where $\alpha_i = \max_{j \in [m]} v_{ij}$. The approximation version of this notion would be to construct allocations where each player receives a value of at least $\rho V_2(\alpha_i)$. Recently, a stricter variant of this guarantee has been provided by Gourvès et al. [18] (also see Remark 4.9).

3 CHARACTERIZATION OF TRUTHFUL MECHANISMS

We present our main characterization result in this section. We start in subsection 3.1 with the main definitions and illustrating examples, and then we state our result in subsection 3.2 along with a road map of the proof. To avoid repetition, when referring to a truthful mechanism $\mathcal{X}$, we mean a truthful mechanism for allocating all the items in M to two players with additive valuation functions.

3.1 A Non-Dictatorial Class of Mechanisms

The main result of this section is that every truthful mechanism is a picking-exchange mechanism (Theorem 3.9). Before we make a precise statement, we formally define the types of mechanisms involved and provide illustrating examples.

Picking Mechanisms. We start with a family of mechanisms where players make a selection out of choices that the mechanism offers to them. Given a subset S of items, we define a *set of offers* $\mathcal{O}$ on S, as a nonempty collection of proper subsets of S that exactly covers S (i.e., $\bigcup_{T \in \mathcal{O}} T = S$), and in which there is no common element that appears in all subsets (i.e., $\bigcap_{T \in \mathcal{O}} T = \emptyset$).

Definition 3.1. A mechanism $\mathcal{X}$ is a *picking mechanism*[2] if there exists a partition (N_1, N_2) of M, and sets of offers $\mathcal{O}_1$ and $\mathcal{O}_2$ on N_1 and N_2 respectively, such that for every profile v,

$$X_i(\mathrm{v}) \cap N_i \in \arg\max_{S \in \mathcal{O}_i} v_i(S).$$

Technical nuances aside, such a mechanism can be implemented by first letting player 1 choose his best offer from $\mathcal{O}_1$ and giving what remains from N_1 to player 2. Then it lets player 2 choose his best offer from $\mathcal{O}_2$ and gives what remains from N_2 to player 1. The following example illustrates a picking mechanism.

Example 3.2. Consider the following mechanism $\mathcal{X}$ on a set $M = \{1, \ldots 6\}$, which first partitions M into $N_1 = \{1,2,3,4\}$, $N_2 = \{5,6\}$ and then constructs the offer sets $\mathcal{O}_1 = \{\{1,2\},\{2,3\},\{4\}\}$, $\mathcal{O}_2 = \{\{5\},\{6\}\}$. On input v, $\mathcal{X}$ first gives to player 1 his best set—with respect to v_1—among $\{1,2\}$, $\{2,3\}$ and $\{4\}$, and then gives what remains from N_1 to player 2. Next, $\mathcal{X}$ gives to player 2 his best set—according to v_2—among $\{5\}$ and $\{6\}$, and then gives what remains from N_2 to player 1. $\mathcal{X}$ resolves ties lexicographically, e.g., in case of a tie, $\{1,2\}$ is preferred to $\{4\}$.

[2] Picking mechanisms are a generalization of *truthful* picking sequences for two players [see 6].

It is not hard to see that $\mathcal{X}$ is truthful. For the following input v, the circles denote the allocation.

$$v = \begin{pmatrix} 3 & \textcircled{5} & \textcircled{5} & 10 & 4 & \textcircled{2} \\ \textcircled{2} & 3 & 6 & \textcircled{1} & \textcircled{5} & 3 \end{pmatrix}.$$

Exchange Mechanisms. We now move to a quite different class of mechanisms. Let X, Y be two disjoint subsets of M. We call the ordered pair (X, Y) an exchange deal. Moreover, we say that an exchange deal (X, Y) is *favorable with respect to* $\mathbf{v}$ if $v_1(Y) > v_1(X)$ and $v_2(Y) < v_2(X)$, while it is *unfavorable with respect to* $\mathbf{v}$ if $v_1(Y) < v_1(X)$ or $v_2(Y) > v_2(X)$. Let S and T be two disjoint subsets of items and let $S_1, S_2, \ldots, S_k$ and $T_1, \ldots, T_k$ be two collections of nonempty and pairwise disjoint subsets of S and T respectively. We say then that the set of exchange deals $D = \{(S_1, T_1), (S_2, T_2), \ldots, (S_k, T_k)\}$ on (S, T) is *valid.*

Definition 3.3. A mechanism $\mathcal{X}$ is an *exchange mechanism*[3] if there exists a partition (E_1, E_2) of M, and a valid set of exchange deals $D = \{(S_1, T_1), \ldots, (S_k, T_k)\}$ on (E_1, E_2), such that for every profile $\mathbf{v}$, there exists a set of indices $I = I(\mathbf{v}) \subseteq [k]$ for which

$$X_1(\mathbf{v}) = \left(E_1 \setminus \bigcup_{i \in I} S_i\right) \cup \bigcup_{i \in I} T_i, \quad X_2(\mathbf{v}) = M \setminus X_1 .$$

Moreover, I contains the indices of every favorable exchange deal with respect to $\mathbf{v}$, but no indices of unfavorable exchange deals.

On a high level, an exchange mechanism initially partitions the items into endowments for the players, and then examines a list of possible exchange deals. Every exchange that improves both players is performed, while every exchange that reduces the value of even one player is avoided. The mechanism may also perform other exchanges where one player is indifferent and the other player can be either indifferent or improved. Whether such exchange deals are materialized or not is up to the tie-breaking rule employed by the mechanism. The following example illustrates an exchange mechanism.

Example 3.4. Let $M = \{1, \ldots 5\}$, and consider the following mechanism $\mathcal{Y}$, with $E_1 = \{1, 2, 3\}$, $E_2 = \{4, 5\}$, and a valid set of exchange deals $D = \{(\{2, 3\}, \{4\})\}$ on (E_1, E_2): One can think of such a mechanism as if $\mathcal{Y}$ initially reserves the set E_1 for player 1 and the set E_2 for player 2. Then it examines whether exchanging $\{2, 3\}$ with $\{4\}$ strictly improves both players, and performs the exchange only if the answer is yes. Mechanism $\mathcal{Y}$ is an example of an *exchange mechanism* with only one possible *exchange deal.* Again, one can see that no player has an incentive to lie.

For the following input v, the circles denote the allocation produced.

$$v = \begin{pmatrix} \textcircled{6} & 2 & 3 & \textcircled{7} & 1 \\ 1 & \textcircled{6} & \textcircled{1} & 4 & \textcircled{7} \end{pmatrix}.$$

Picking-Exchange Mechanisms. Finally, we define the class of picking-exchange mechanisms which is a generalization of both picking and exchange mechanisms.

Definition 3.5. A mechanism $\mathcal{X}$ is a *picking-exchange mechanism* if there exists a partition (N_1, N_2, E_1, E_2) of M, sets of offers $\mathcal{O}_1$ and $\mathcal{O}_2$ on N_1 and N_2 respectively, and a valid set of exchange deals $D = \{(S_1, T_1), \ldots, (S_k, T_k)\}$ on (E_1, E_2), such that for every profile $\mathbf{v}$, $X_i(\mathbf{v}) \cap N_i \in \arg\max_{S \in \mathcal{O}_i} v_i(S)$ and $X_1(\mathbf{v}) \cap (E_1 \cup E_2) = (E_1 \setminus \bigcup_{i \in I} S_i) \cup \bigcup_{i \in I} T_i$, where $I = I(\mathbf{v}) \subseteq [k]$ contains the indices of all favorable exchange deals, but no indices of unfavorable exchange deals.

[3]If we think about E_1, E_2 as fixed a priori, then exchange mechanisms are a generalization of fixed deal exchange rules in general exchange markets for two players [see 29].

It is helpful to think that a picking-exchange mechanism runs independently a picking mechanism on $N_1 \cup N_2$ and an exchange mechanism on $E_1 \cup E_2$, like in Example 3.6. Although this is true under the assumption that the players' valuation functions are such that no two sets have the same value, it is not true for general additive valuations. The reason is that the tie-breaking for choosing the offers from O_1 and O_2 may not be independent from the decision of whether to perform each exchange that is neither favorable nor unfavorable.

The following example illustrates a picking exchange mechanism.

Example 3.6. Let $M = \{1, \ldots, 11\}$, and consider the mechanism $\mathcal{Z}$ that partitions M into $N_1 = \{1, 2, 3, 4\}, N_2 = \{5, 6\}, E_1 = \{7, 8, 9\}$ and $E_2 = \{10, 11\}$, and is the combination of $\mathcal{X}$ and $\mathcal{Y}$ from the previous two examples: On input v, $\mathcal{Z}$ runs $\mathcal{X}$ on $N_1 \cup N_2$ and $\mathcal{Y}$ on $E_1 \cup E_2$. It outputs the union of the outputs of $\mathcal{X}$ and $\mathcal{Y}$.

For the following input v, the circles denote the final allocation.

$$v = \begin{pmatrix} 3 & \textcircled{5} & \textcircled{5} & 10 & 4 & \textcircled{2} & \textcircled{6} & 2 & 3 & \textcircled{7} & 1 \\ \textcircled{2} & 3 & 6 & \textcircled{1} & \textcircled{5} & 3 & 1 & \textcircled{6} & \textcircled{1} & 4 & \textcircled{7} \end{pmatrix}.$$

3.2 Truthfulness and Picking-Exchange Mechanisms

Essentially, we show that a mechanism is truthful if and only if it is a picking-exchange mechanism. We begin with the easier part of our characterization, namely that under the assumption that each valuation function induces a strict preference relation over all possible subsets, every picking-exchange mechanism is truthful. Recall that the set of such profiles is denoted by $\mathcal{V}_m^{\neq}$.

Theorem 3.7. *When restricted to $\mathcal{V}_m^{\neq}$, every picking-exchange mechanism $\mathcal{X}$ for allocating m items is truthful.*

Remark 3.8. For simplicity, Theorem 3.7 is stated for a subclass of additive valuation functions. However, it holds for general additive valuations as long as the mechanism uses a sensible tie-breaking rule (e.g., label-based or welfare-based).[4]

We are now ready to state the main result of this work.

Theorem 3.9. *Every truthful mechanism $\mathcal{X}$ can be implemented as a picking-exchange mechanism.*

The rest of this subsection is a road map to the proof of Theorem 3.9. The proof is long and technical, so for the sake of presentation, it is broken down to several lemmata. In order to illustrate the high-level ideas, the proofs of those lemmata are deferred to the full version of the paper.

For the rest of this subsection we assume a truthful mechanism $\mathcal{X}$ for allocating all the items in $M = [m]$ to two players with additive valuation functions. Every statement is going to be with respect to this $\mathcal{X}$.

3.2.1 *The Crucial Notion of Control.*

We begin by introducing the notions of *strong desire* and of *control*, which are of key importance for our characterization. We say that player i *strongly desires* a set S if each item in S has more value for him than all the items of $M \setminus S$ combined, i.e., if for every $x \in S$ we have $v_{ix} > \sum_{y \in M \setminus S} v_{iy}$.

Definition 3.10. We say that player i *controls* a set S with respect to $\mathcal{X}$, if every time he strongly desires S he gets it whole, i.e., for every $\mathrm{v} = (v_1, v_2)$ in which player i strongly desires S, then we have that $S \subseteq \mathcal{X}_i(\mathrm{v})$.

[4]Describing all such tie-breaking rules seems to be an interesting, nontrivial question for future work, but not our main focus here. It is not hard to see, though, that there exist tie-breaking rules that make a picking-exchange mechanism nontruthful, e.g., break ties on offers of player 1 so that the value that player 2 gets from N_1 is minimized.

Clearly, given $\mathcal{X}$, any set S can be controlled by at most one player.

The following is a key lemma for understanding how truthful mechanisms operate. The lemma together with Corollary 3.12 below show that every item is controlled by some player under any truthful mechanism.

Lemma 3.11 (Control Lemma). *Let $S \subseteq M$. If there exists a profile $\mathbf{v} = (v_1, v_2)$ such that both players strongly desire S, and $S \subseteq X_i(\mathbf{v})$ for some $i \in \{1, 2\}$, then player i controls every $T \subseteq S$ with respect to $\mathcal{X}$.*

Proof. Let $\mathbf{v} = (v_1, v_2)$ be a profile such that both players strongly desire S and $S \subseteq X_1(\mathbf{v})$ (the case where $S \subseteq X_2(\mathbf{v})$ is symmetric). We first prove the statement for $T = S$. Let $\mathbf{v}' = (v_1', v_2')$ be any profile in which player 1 strongly desires S, i.e., $v_{1x}' > \sum_{y \in M \setminus S} v_{1y}', \forall x \in S$. Initially, consider the intermediate profile $\mathbf{v}^* = (v_1, v_2')$. If $S \cap X_2(\mathbf{v}^*) \neq \emptyset$ then player 2 would deviate from profile $\mathbf{v}$ to $\mathbf{v}^*$ in order to strictly improve his total utility. So by truthfulness we derive that $S \subseteq X_1(\mathbf{v}^*)$. Similarly, in the profile $\mathbf{v}'$, if $S \cap X_2(\mathbf{v}') \neq \emptyset$ then player 1 would deviate from $\mathbf{v}'$ to $\mathbf{v}^*$ in order to strictly improve. Thus by truthfulness we have $S \subseteq X_1(\mathbf{v}')$. We conclude that player 1 controls S.

Now, suppose that $\mathbf{v}'' = (v_1'', v_2'')$ is any profile in which player 1 strongly desires $T \subsetneq S$. If $T \nsubseteq X_1(\mathbf{v}'')$ then player 1 could strictly improve his utility by playing v_1' from before (i.e., he declares that he strongly desires S) and getting $S \supsetneq T$. Thus, by truthfulness, $T \subseteq X_1(\mathbf{v}'')$, and we conclude that player 1 controls T. □

Notice here that the existence of sets that are controlled by some player is always guaranteed. Specifically, each singleton $\{x\}$ is always controlled (only) by one of the players. Indeed, when both players strongly desire $\{x\}$, it is always the case that $\{x\} \subseteq X_i(\mathbf{v})$ for some $i \in \{1, 2\}$. This is summarized in the following corollary.

Corollary 3.12. *Let $\mathcal{X}$ be a truthful mechanism for allocating the items in M to two players with additive valuations. For every $x \in M$ there exists $i \in \{1, 2\}$ such that only player i controls $\{x\}$ with respect to $\mathcal{X}$.*

Aside from its use in the current proof, the corollary has implications on fairness, that will be explored in Section 4.

3.2.2 Identifying the Components of a Mechanism. Our goal now is to determine the "exchange component" and the "picking component" of mechanism $\mathcal{X}$. Every picking-exchange mechanism is completely determined by the seven sets N_1, N_2, O_1, O_2, E_1, E_2, and D mentioned in Definition 3.5 (plus a deterministic tie-breaking rule). Below we try to identify these sets. Later we show that the mechanism's behavior is identical to that of a picking-exchange mechanism defined by them.

To proceed, we will need to consider the collection of all maximal sets controlled by each player. For $i \in \{1, 2\}$, let

$$\mathcal{A}_i = \{S \subseteq M \mid \text{player } i \text{ controls } S \text{ and for any } T \supsetneq S, i \text{ does not control } T\}.$$

Clearly, every set controlled by player i is a subset of an element of $\mathcal{A}_i$. According to Lemma 3.11, if we consider the set $C_i = \bigcup_{S \in \mathcal{A}_i} S$, i.e., the union of all the sets in $\mathcal{A}_i$, this is exactly the set of items that are controlled—as singletons—by player i.

Corollary 3.13. *The sets C_1 and C_2 define a partition of M.*

Using the $\mathcal{A}_i$s and the C_is, we define the sets of interest that determine the mechanism. We begin with $E_i = \bigcap_{S \in \mathcal{A}_i} S$ for $i \in \{1, 2\}$. As we are going to see eventually in Lemma 3.21, the "exchange component" of $\mathcal{X}$ is observed on $E_1 \cup E_2$.

Defining the corresponding valid set of exchange deals D is trickier, and we need some terminology. Recall that $X_i^S(\mathbf{v}) = X_i(\mathbf{v}) \cap S$. For $S \subseteq E_1$ and $T \subseteq E_2$, we say that (S,T) is a *feasible exchange*, if there exists a profile $\mathbf{v}$, such that $X_1^{E_1 \cup E_2}(\mathbf{v}) = (E_1 \setminus S) \cup T$. In such a case, each of S and T is called *exchangeable.* An exchangeable set S is called *minimally exchangeable* if any $S' \subsetneq S$ is not exchangeable. Finally, a feasible exchange (S,T) is a *minimal feasible exchange,* if at least one of S and T is minimally exchangeable. Now let

$$D = \{(S,T) \mid (S,T) \text{ is a minimal feasible exchange with respect to } \mathcal{X}\}.$$

Of course, at this point it is not clear whether D is well defined as a valid set of exchange deals, and this is probably the most challenging part of the characterization.

Next, we define $N_i = C_i \setminus E_i$ and $O_i = \{S \setminus E_i \mid S \in \mathcal{A}_i\}$ for $i \in \{1,2\}$. As shown in Lemmata 3.14 and 3.15, we identify the "picking component" of $\mathcal{X}$ on $N_1 \cup N_2$, and O_i will correspond to the set of offers.

Note that by Corollary 3.13 and the above definitions, (N_1, N_2, E_1, E_2) is a partition of M. The intuition behind breaking C_i into N_i and E_i is that player i has different levels of control on those two sets. The fact that E_i is contained in every maximal set controlled by player i will turn out to mean that $\mathcal{X}$ gives the ownership of E_i to player i. On the other hand, the control of player i on N_i is much more restricted as shown below.

3.2.3 Cracking the Picking Component. The first step is to show that the O_is defined above, greatly restrict the possible allocations of the items of $N_1 \cup N_2$. In particular, whatever player i receives from N_i must be contained in some set of O_i.

Lemma 3.14. *For every profile* $\mathbf{v}$ *and every* $i \in \{1,2\}$, *there exists* $S \in O_i$ *such that* $X_i^{N_i}(\mathbf{v}) \subseteq S$.

The idea behind the proof of Lemma 3.14 is that by receiving some $X_i^{N_i}(\mathbf{v})$ not contained in any set of O_i, player i is able to extend his control to subsets not contained in C_i, thus leading to contradiction. The proof, as many of the proofs of the remaining lemmata, includes the careful construction of a series of profiles, where in each step one has to argue about how the allocation does or does not change.

Given the restriction implied by Lemma 3.14, next we can prove that the subset of N_i that player i receives must be the best possible from his perspective, hence the mechanism behaves as a picking mechanism on each N_i. Intuitively, suppose that player 1 receives a subset S of N_1 which is not an element of O_1. By Lemma 3.14, S is contained in an element S' of O_1. Since player 1 controls S', this means that he gave up part of his control to gain something that he was not supposed to. Actually, it can be shown that it is the case where player 2 also gave part of his control (either on N_2 or E_2). This mutual transfer of control, combined with truthfulness, eventually leads to profiles where some of the items must be given to both players at the same time, hence a contradiction.

Lemma 3.15. *For every profile* $\mathbf{v}$ *and every* $i \in \{1,2\}$ *we have* $X_i^{N_i}(\mathbf{v}) \in \arg\max_{S \in O_i} v_i(S)$.

Now we know that $\mathcal{X}$ behaves as the "right" picking-exchange mechanism on $N_1 \cup N_2$. For most of the rest of the proof we would like to somehow ignore this part of $\mathcal{X}$ and focus on $E_1 \cup E_2$.

3.2.4 Separating the Two Components. As mentioned right after Definition 3.5, there is some kind of independence between the two components of a picking-exchange mechanism, at least when restricted on $\mathcal{V}_m^{\neq}$. This independence should be present in $\mathcal{X}$ as well; in fact we are going to exploit it to get rid of $N_1 \cup N_2$ until the last part of the proof.

Lemma 3.16. *Let* $\mathbf{v} = (v_1, v_2), \mathbf{v}' = (v_1', v_2') \in \mathcal{V}_m^{\neq}$ *such that* $v_{ij} = v_{ij}'$ *for all* $i \in \{1,2\}$ *and* $j \in E_1 \cup E_2$. *Then* $X_1^{E_1 \cup E_2}(\mathbf{v}) = X_1^{E_1 \cup E_2}(\mathbf{v}')$.

The lemma states that assuming strict preferences over all subsets, the allocation of $E_1 \cup E_2$ does not depend on the values of either player for the items in $N_1 \cup N_2$. What allows this separation is the complete lack of ties in the restricted profile space.

Without loss of generality we may assume that $E_1 \cup E_2 = [\ell]$. We can define a mechanism $\mathcal{X}_E$ for allocating the items of $[\ell]$ to two players with valuation profiles in $\mathcal{V}_\ell^{\neq}$ as

$$\mathcal{X}_E(\mathbf{v}) = (X_1^{E_1 \cup E_2}(\mathbf{v}'), X_2^{E_1 \cup E_2}(\mathbf{v}')), \text{ for every } \mathbf{v} \in \mathcal{V}_\ell^{\neq},$$

where $\mathbf{v}'$ is any profile in $\mathcal{V}_m^{\neq}$ with $v_{ij} = v'_{ij}$ for all $i \in \{1, 2\}$ and $j \in [\ell]$. This new mechanism is just the projection of $\mathcal{X}$ on $E_1 \cup E_2$ restricted on a domain where it is well-defined. The truthfulness of $\mathcal{X}_E$ on $\mathcal{V}_\ell^{\neq}$ follows directly from the truthfulness of $\mathcal{X}$ on $\mathcal{V}_m^{\neq}$. Moreover, it is easy to see that player i controls E_i with respect to $\mathcal{X}_E$, for $i \in \{1, 2\}$.

The plan is to study $\mathcal{X}_E$ instead of $\mathcal{X}$, show that $\mathcal{X}_E$ is an exchange mechanism, and finally sew the two parts of $\mathcal{X}$ back together and show that everything works properly for any profile in $\mathcal{V}_m$. One issue here is that maybe the set of feasible exchanges with respect to $\mathcal{X}_E$ is greatly reduced, in comparison to the set of feasible exchanges with respect to $\mathcal{X}$, because of the restriction on the domain. In such a case, it will not be possible to argue about exchanges in D that are not feasible anymore. It turns out that this is not the case; the set of possible allocations (of $E_1 \cup E_2$) is the same, whether we consider profiles in $\mathcal{V}_m$ or in $\mathcal{V}_m^{\neq}$.

Lemma 3.17. *For every profile* $\mathbf{v} \in \mathcal{V}_m$ *there exists a profile* $\mathbf{v}' \in \mathcal{V}_m^{\neq}$ *such that* $\mathcal{X}(\mathbf{v}) = \mathcal{X}(\mathbf{v}')$.

In particular, the set of feasible exchanges on $E_1 \cup E_2$ is exactly the same for $\mathcal{X}$ and $\mathcal{X}_E$, and thus we will utilize the following set of exchanges.

$$D = \{(S, T) \mid (S, T) \text{ is a minimal feasible exchange with respect to } \mathcal{X}_E\}.$$

3.2.5 Cracking the Exchange Component. In the attempt to show that $\mathcal{X}_E$ is an exchange mechanism, the first step is to show that D is indeed a valid set of exchange deals.

Lemma 3.18. *D is a valid set of exchange deals on* (E_1, E_2).

The above lemma involves three main steps. First we show that each minimally exchangeable set is involved in exactly one exchange deal. Then, we guarantee that minimally exchangeable sets can be exchanged only with minimally exchangeable sets, and finally, we show that minimally exchangeable sets are always disjoint. There is a common underlying idea in the proofs of these steps: whenever there exist two feasible exchanges that overlap in any way, we can construct a profile where both of them are favorable but the two players disagree on which of them is best. On a high level, each player can "block" his least favorable of the conflicting exchanges, and this leads to violation of truthfulness.

Lemma 3.18 implies that every exchangeable set $S \subseteq E_1$ can be decomposed as $S = W \cup \bigcup_{i \in I} S_i$, where $W = S \setminus \bigcup_{i \in I} S_i$ does not contain any minimally exchangeable sets. Ideally, we would like two things. First, the set W in the above decomposition to always be empty, i.e., every exchangeable set should be a union of minimally exchangeable sets. Second, we want every union of minimally exchangeable subsets of E_1 to be exchangeable only with the corresponding union of minimally exchangeable subsets of E_2, and vice versa. It takes several lemmas and a rather involved induction to prove those. A key ingredient of the inductive step is a carefully constructed argument about the value that each player must gain from any exchange.

Lemma 3.19. *For every exchangeable set* $S \subseteq E_1$, *there exists some* $I \subseteq [k]$ *such that* $S = \bigcup_{i \in I} S_i$. *Moreover,* S *is exchangeable with* $T = \bigcup_{i \in I} T_i$ *and only with* T.

Finally, we have all the ingredients to fully describe $\mathcal{X}_E$ as an exchange mechanism on $E_1 \cup E_2$ and set of exchange deals D.

Lemma 3.20. *Given any profile $\mathbf{v} \in \mathcal{V}_\ell^{\neq}$, each exchange in D is performed if and only if it is favorable, i.e., $X_1^{E_1 \cup E_2}(\mathbf{v}) = (E_1 \setminus \bigcup_{i \in I} S_i) \cup \bigcup_{i \in I} T_i$, where $I \subseteq [k]$ contains exactly the indices of all favorable exchange deals in D.*

3.2.6 Putting the Mechanism Back Together. As a result of Lemma 3.20 (combined, of course, with Lemmata 3.15 and 3.16), the characterization is complete for truthful mechanisms defined on $\mathcal{V}_m^{\neq}$. For general additive valuation functions, however, we need a little more work. This is to counterbalance the fact that in the presence of ties the allocations of $N_1 \cup N_2$ and $E_1 \cup E_2$ may not be independent.

By Lemmata 3.17 and 3.19, we know that for any $\mathbf{v} \in \mathcal{V}_m$, $X_1^{E_1 \cup E_2}(\mathbf{v})$ is the result of some exchanges of D taking place. There are two things that can go wrong: $\mathcal{X}$ performs an unfavorable exchange, or it does not perform a favorable one. In either of these cases it is possible to construct some profile in $\mathcal{V}_m^{\neq}$ that leads to contradiction. Hence we have the following lemma.

Lemma 3.21. *Given any profile $\mathbf{v} \in \mathcal{V}_m$, $X_1^{E_1 \cup E_2}(\mathbf{v}) = (E_1 \setminus \bigcup_{i \in I} S_i) \cup \bigcup_{i \in I} T_i$, where $I \subseteq [k]$ contains the indices of all favorable exchange deals in D, but no indices of unfavorable exchange deals.*

Clearly, Lemma 3.21, together with Lemma 3.15 concludes the proof of Theorem 3.9.

3.3 Immediate Implications of Theorem 3.9

As mentioned in Section 1.2, there are several works characterizing truthful mechanisms in combination with other notions, such as Pareto efficiency, nonbossiness, and neutrality (these results are usually for unrestricted, not necessarily additive valuations). Pareto efficiency means that there is no other allocation where one player strictly improves and none of the others are worse-off. Nonbossiness means that a player cannot affect the outcome of the mechanism without changing his own bundle of items. Finally, neutrality refers to a mechanism being consistent with a permutation on the items, i.e., permuting the items results in the corresponding permuted allocation.

Although such notions are not our main focus, the purpose of this short discussion is twofold. On one hand, we illustrate how our characterization immediately implies a characterization for mechanisms that satisfy these extra properties under additive valuations, and on the other hand we see how these properties are either incompatible with fairness or irrelevant in our context.

To begin with, nonbossiness comes for free in our case, since we have two players and all the items must be allocated. Neutrality and Pareto efficiency, however, greatly reduce the space of available mechanisms. Note that it makes more sense to study neutral mechanisms when the valuation functions induce a strict preference order over all sets of items.

Corollary 3.22. *Every neutral, truthful mechanism $\mathcal{X}$ on $\mathcal{V}_m^{\neq}$ can be implemented as a picking-exchange mechanism, such that*

(1) *there exists $i \in \{1, 2\}$ such that $E_i = [m]$*, or
(2) *there exists $i \in \{1, 2\}$ such that $N_i = [m]$ and $O_i = \{S \subseteq [m] \mid |S| = \kappa\}$ for some $\kappa < m$.*

Corollary 3.23. *Every Pareto efficient, truthful mechanism $\mathcal{X}$ can be implemented as a picking-exchange mechanism, such that*

(1) *there exists $i \in \{1, 2\}$ such that $E_i = [m]$*, or
(2) *there exists $j \in [m]$ such that $E_{i_1} = \{j\}$, $E_{i_2} = [m] \setminus \{j\}$, where $\{i_1, i_2\} = \{1, 2\}$, and $D = \{(E_1, E_2)\}$*, or
(3) *there exists $i \in \{1, 2\}$ such that $N_i = [m]$ and $O_i = \{S \subseteq N_i \mid |S| = m - 1\}$.*

It is somewhat surprising that the resulting mechanisms are a strict superset of dictatorships, even when we impose both properties together. Pareto efficiency, however, allows only mechanisms that are rather close to being dictatorial, and thus cannot guarantee fairness of any type. On the other hand, most of the mechanisms defined and studied in Section 4 are neutral, yet neutrality is not implied by the fairness concepts we consider, nor the other way around.

4 A NECESSARY FAIRNESS CONDITION AND ITS IMPLICATIONS

In this section, we explore some implications of Theorem 3.9 on fairness properties, i.e., on the design of mechanisms where on top of truthfulness, we would like to achieve fairness guarantees.

In Section 4.1 we show that the Control Lemma implies that truthfulness prevents any bounded approximation for envy-freeness and proportionality. Then, we move on describing a necessary fairness condition, in terms of our notion of "control", that summarizes a common feature of several relaxations of fairness and provide a restricted version of our characterization that follows this fairness condition. This will allow us, in Section 4.2, to examine what this new class of mechanisms can achieve in each of these fairness concepts.

4.1 Implications of the Control Lemma.

4.1.1 Control of singletons. The basic restriction that truthfulness imposes to every mechanism (leading to poor results for some fairness concepts) comes from Corollary 3.12, an immediate corollary of the Control Lemma, stating that every single item is controlled by some player.

We begin by studing how the above corollary affects two of the most researched notions in the fair division literature, namely *proportionality* and *envy-freeness.* It is well known that even without the requirement for truthfulness, it is impossible to achieve any of these two objectives, simply because in the presence of indivisible goods, envy-free or proportional allocations may not exist. [5]

This leads to the definition of approximation versions of these two concepts for settings with indivisible goods. For example, one could try to construct algorithms such that for every instance, an approximation to the minimum possible envy admitted by the instance is guaranteed. Similarly, approximate proportionality can be considered, i.e., find allocations that achieve an approximation to the best possible value that an instance can guarantee to all agents. See also the discussion in Section 2 on defining the approximation versions of these problems. Note that if time complexity is not an issue, we can always identify the allocation with the best possible envy or with the best possible proportionality, achievable by a given instance.

We are now ready to state our first application, showing that truthfulness prohibits us from having any approximation to the minimum envy or to proportionality. This greatly improves the conclusions of Lipton et al. [22] and Caragiannis et al. [9] that truthful mechanisms cannot attain the optimal minimum envy allocation.

Application 4.1. *For any truthful mechanism that allocates all the items to two players with additive valuations, the approximation achieved for either proportionality or the minimum envy is arbitrarily bad (i.e., not lower bounded by any positive function of m).*

Proof. Consider a setting with m items, and a truthful mechanism $\mathcal{X}$. Suppose now that item 1 is controlled by player 1 with respect to $\mathcal{X}$. This means that in the profile $\mathrm{v} = ([m\ 1\ 1\ \dots\ 1], [m^d\ 1\ 1\ \dots\ 1])$ player 1 must obtain item 1, and player 2 ends up with a negligible fraction of his total value for large enough d. The optimal solution would be to assign the first item to the

[5] Consider, for instance, a profile where both players desire only the first item and have a negligible value for the other items. Then one of the players will necessarily remain unsatisfied and receive a value close to zero, no matter what the allocation is.

second player and the last m items to the first player, which provides an envy-free and proportional allocation. We conclude that the approximation guarantee that can be obtained by a truthful mechanism is arbitrarily high. □

So far, the conclusion is that even approximate proportionality or envy-freeness are quite stringent and incompatible with truthfulness because of the Control Lemma. The next step would be to relax these notions. There have been already a few approaches on relaxing proportionality and envy-freeness under indivisible goods, leading to solutions such as the maximin share fairness, envy-freeness up to one item [8], as well as the type of worst-case guarantees proposed by Hill [20] (recall Definitions 2.2, 2.3 and 2.4 in Section 2). The fact that a truthful mechanism $\mathcal{X}$ yields control of singletons does not seem to have such detrimental effects on these notions. However, if even a single pair of items is controlled by a player, the same situation arises.

4.1.2 Control of pairs. We propose the following *necessary* (but not sufficient) condition that captures a common aspect of all these relaxations of fairness. This allows us to treat all the above concepts of fairness in a unified way.

Definition 4.2. We say that a mechanism $\mathcal{X}$ *yields control of pairs* if there exists $i \in \{1, 2\}$ and $S \subseteq [m]$ with $|S| = 2$, such that player i controls S with respect to $\mathcal{X}$.

The following lemma states that in order to obtain impossibility results for the above concepts, it is enough to focus on mechanisms with control of pairs.

Lemma 4.3. *In order to achieve (either exactly or within a bounded approximation) the above mentioned relaxed fairness criteria, a truthful mechanism that allocates all the items to two players with additive valuations cannot yield control of pairs.*

So now we are ready to move to a complete characterization of truthful mechanisms that do not yield control of pairs. Of course such mechanisms are picking-exchange mechanisms, but our fairness condition allows only singleton offers, and the exchange part is completely degenerate.

Definition 4.4. A mechanism $\mathcal{X}$ for allocating all the items in $[m]$ to two players is a *singleton picking-exchange mechanism* if it is a picking-exchange mechanism where for each $i \in \{1, 2\}$ at most one of N_i and E_i is nonempty, $|E_i| \le 1$, and

$$O_i = \begin{cases} \{\{x\} \mid x \in N_i\} & \text{when } N_i \neq \emptyset \\ \{\emptyset\} & \text{otherwise} \end{cases}$$

i.e., the sets of offers contain all possible singletons.

Hence, typically, in a singleton picking-exchange mechanism player i receives from $N_i \cup E_i$ only his best item. Moreover, for $m \ge 3$, no exchanges are allowed.[6]

Lemma 4.5. *Every truthful mechanism for allocating all the items to two players with additive valuation functions that does not yield control of pairs can be implemented as a singleton picking-exchange mechanism.*

It is interesting to note that, in contrast to Application 4.1, proving Lemma 4.5 without Theorem 3.9 is not straightforward. In fact, it requires a partial characterization which (on a high level) is similar to characterizing the picking component of general mechanisms.

[6]The only exceptions—and the only such mechanisms where both E_1 and E_2 are nonempty—are two mechanisms for the degenerate case of $m = 2$, e.g., $N_1 = N_2 = \emptyset$, $O_1 = O_2 = \{\emptyset\}$, $E_1 = \{a\}$, $E_2 = \{b\}$ and $D = \{(\{a\}, \{b\})\}$, where $\{a, b\} = \{1, 2\}$.

4.2 Applications to Relaxed Notions of Fairness

It is now possible to apply Lemma 4.5 on each fairness notion separately, and characterize every truthful mechanism that achieves each criterion.

Envy-freeness up to one item. We start with a relaxation of envy-freeness. Below we provide a complete description of the mechanisms that satisfy this criterion.

APPLICATION 4.6. *For $m \leq 3$, every singleton picking-exchange mechanism achieves envy-freeness up to one item. For $m = 4$ every singleton picking-exchange mechanism with $|N_1| = |N_2| = 2$ achieves envy-freeness up to one item. Finally, for $m \geq 5$ there is no truthful mechanism that allocates all the items to two players and achieves envy-freeness up to one item.*

Maximin share fairness and related notions. For maximin share allocations a truthful mechanism was suggested by Amanatidis et al. [1] for any number of items and any number of players. For two players, their mechanism is the singleton picking-exchange mechanism with $N_1 = [m]$ and produces an allocation that guarantees to each player a $\frac{1}{\lfloor m/2 \rfloor}$-approximation of his maximin share. It was left as an open problem whether a better truthful approximation exists. Here we show that this approximation is tight; in fact, almost any other singleton picking-exchange mechanism performs strictly worse. Note that the best previously known lower bound for two players was $1/2$.

APPLICATION 4.7. *For any m there exists a singleton picking-exchange mechanism that guarantees to player i a $\lfloor \max\{2, m\}/2 \rfloor^{-1}$-approximation of $\boldsymbol{\mu}_i$, for $i \in \{1, 2\}$. There is no truthful mechanism that allocates all the items to two players and achieves a better guarantee with respect to maximin share fairness.*

Regarding now allocations that guarantee an approximation of the function $V_2(\alpha_i)$ defined by Hill [20] (recall the definition in Section 2), the singleton picking-exchange mechanism with $N_1 = [m]$ was also suggested by Markakis and Psomas [23] as a $\frac{1}{\lfloor m/2 \rfloor}$-approximation of $V_2(\alpha_i)$.[7] This comes as no surprise, since there exists a strong connection between maximin shares and the function V_n, especially for two players. This is illustrated in the following corollary, where both the positive and the negative results coincide with the ones for the maximin share fairness.

APPLICATION 4.8. *For any m there exists a singleton picking-exchange mechanism that guarantees to player i a $\lfloor \max\{2, m\}/2 \rfloor^{-1}$-approximation of $V_2(\alpha_i)$, for $i \in \{1, 2\}$, where $\alpha_i = \max_{j \in [m]} v_{ij}$. There is no truthful mechanism that allocates all the items to two players and achieves a better guarantee with respect to the $V_2(\alpha_i)$s.*

Again, the best previously known lower bound for two players was constant, namely $2/3$ due to Markakis and Psomas [23]. In Applications 4.7 and 4.8, it is stated that there exists a $\frac{1}{\lfloor m/2 \rfloor}$-approximate singleton picking-exchange mechanism. It is interesting that *any* singleton picking-exchange mechanism does not perform much worse. Following the corresponding proofs, we have that even the worst singleton picking-exchange mechanism achieves a $\frac{1}{m-1}$-approximation in each case.

Remark 4.9. Gourvès et al. [18] introduced a variant of V_n, called W_n, and showed that there always exists an allocation such that each player i receives $W_n(\alpha_i) \geq V_n(\alpha_i)$ (where the inequality is often strict). Since the definition of W_n is rather involved even for $n = 2$, we defer a formal discussion about it to the full version of the paper. However, it is not hard to show that for every valuation function v_i we have $V_2(\alpha_i) \leq W_2(\alpha_i) \leq \boldsymbol{\mu}_i$ and thus the analog of Application 4.8 holds.

[7] The approximation factor in [23] is expressed in terms of $V_2(1/m)$, but it simplifies to $\lfloor m/2 \rfloor^{-1}$.

Remark 4.10. Amanatidis et al. [1] made the following interesting observation: every single known truthful mechanism achieving a bounded approximation of maximin share fairness is *ordinal*, in the sense that it only needs a ranking of the items for each player rather than his whole valuation function. Finding truthful mechanisms that explicitly take into account the players' valuation functions in order to achieve better guarantees was posed as a major open problem. Note that, weird tie-breaking aside, all singleton picking-exchange mechanisms are ordinal! Therefore, from the mechanism designer's perspective, it is impossible to exploit the extra cardinal information given as input and at the same time maintain truthfulness and some nontrivial fairness guarantee.

5 TRUTHFUL MECHANISMS FOR MANY PLAYERS

We introduce a family of non-dictatorial, truthful mechanisms for any number of players. Our mechanisms are defined recursively; in analogy to serial dictatorships, the choices of a player define the sub-mechanism used to allocate the items to the remaining players. Here, however, this serial behavior is observed "in parallel" in several sets of a partition of M.

A *generalized deal* between k players is a collection of (up to $k(k-1)$) exchange deals between pairs of players. A set D of generalized deals is called *valid* if all the sets involved in all these exchange deals are nonempty and pairwise disjoint. Given a profile $\mathbf{v} = (v_1, v_2, \ldots, v_n)$ we say that a generalized deal is *favorable* if it strictly improves all the players involved, while it is *unfavorable* if there exists a player involved whose utility strictly decreases.

Definition 5.1. A mechanism $\mathcal{X}$ for allocating all the items in $[m]$ to n players is called a *serial picking-exchange mechanism* if

(1) when $n = 1$, $\mathcal{X}$ always allocates the whole $[m]$ to player 1.
(2) when $n \geq 2$, there exist a partition $(N_1, \ldots, N_n, E_1, \ldots, E_n)$ of $[m]$, sets of offers O_i on N_i for $i \in [n]$, a valid set D of generalized deals, and a mapping f from subsets of M to serial picking-exchange mechanisms for $n-1$ players, such that for every profile $\mathbf{v} = (v_1, \ldots, v_n)$ we have for all $i \in [n]$:
   - $X_i^{N_i}(\mathbf{v}) \in \arg\max_{S \in O_i} v_i(S)$,
   - $X_i^E(\mathbf{v})$, where $E = \bigcup_{j \in [n]} E_j$, is the result of starting with E_i and performing some of the deals in D, including all the favorable deals but no unfavorable ones,
   - the items of $N_i \setminus X_i^{N_i}(\mathbf{v})$ are allocated to players in $[n] \setminus \{i\}$ using the serial picking-exchange mechanism $f\big(N_i \setminus X_i^{N_i}(\mathbf{v})\big)$.

Clearly, serial picking-exchange mechanisms are a generalization of picking-exchange mechanisms studied in Section 3. The following example illustrates how such a mechanism looks like for three players.

Example 5.2. Suppose that we have three players with additive valuations. For simplicity, assume that each player's valuation induces a strict preference over all possible subsets of items. Let $M = [100]$ be the set of items, and consider the following relevant ingredients of our mechanism:

- $N_1 = \{1, 2, \ldots, 20\}$, $O_1 = \{\{1, 2, 3\}, N_1 \setminus \{1\}\}$
- $N_2 = \{21, 22, \ldots, 50\}$, $O_2 = \{S \subseteq N_2 \mid |S| = 6\}$
- $N_3 = \{51, 52, \ldots, 70\}$, $O_3 = \{\{51, \ldots, 60\}, \{61, \ldots, 70\}\}$
- $E_1 = \{71, \ldots, 80\}$, $E_2 = \{81, \ldots, 90\}$, $E_3 = \{91, \ldots, 100\}$
- $D = \big\{\big[(\{75, 79\}, \{83\})^{1,3}\big], \big[(\{71\}, \{88\})^{1,2}, (\{72, 80\}, \{95\})^{1,3}, (\{85\}, \{99, 100\})^{2,3}\big]\big\}$
- f is a mapping from subsets of M to picking-exchange mechanisms (for 2 players)

The above sets are the analog of the corresponding sets of a picking-exchange mechanism. The deals, however, are a bit more complex. E.g., by $\left[(\{71\},\{88\})^{1,2},(\{72,80\},\{95\})^{1,3},(\{85\},\{99,100\})^{2,3}\right]$ we denote the deal in which:

- player 1 gives item 71 to player 2 and items 72, 80 to player 3
- player 2 gives item 88 to player 1 and item 85 to player 3
- player 3 gives item 95 to player 1 and items 99, 100 to player 2

The mapping f suggests which truthful mechanism should be used every time there are items left to be allocated to only two players.

We are ready to describe our mechanism $\mathcal{X}$:

(1) The mechanism gives endowments E_1, E_2, E_3 to the three players and then performs each exchange deal that strictly improves all the players involved.
(2) Then, for each $i \in \{1, 2, 3\}$, the mechanism gives to player i his best set in O_i, say S_i.
(3) Finally, for each $i \in \{1, 2, 3\}$, $\mathcal{X}$ uses mechanism $f(N_i \setminus S_i)$ to allocate the items of $N_i \setminus S_i$ to players in $\{1, 2, 3\} \setminus i$.

Like picking-exchange mechanisms, serial picking-exchange mechanisms are truthful, given an appropriate tie-breaking rule (e.g., a label-based tie-breaking rule). To bypass a general discussion about tie-breaking, however, we may assume that each player's valuation induces a strict preference over all subsets of M. We denote by $\mathcal{V}^{\neq}_{n,m}$ the set of profiles that only include such valuation functions. Following almost the same proof, however, we have that for general additive valuations every serial picking-exchange mechanism is truthful when using label-based tie-breaking.

THEOREM 5.3. *When restricted to $\mathcal{V}^{\neq}_{n,m}$, every serial picking-exchange mechanism $\mathcal{X}$ for allocating m items to n players is truthful.*

6 DISCUSSION

We obtained a nontrivial characterization for truthful mechanisms, that has immediate implications on fairness. A natural question to ask is whether our characterization can be extended for more than two players. Characterizing the truthful mechanisms without money for any number of additive players is, undoubtedly, a fundamental open problem. However, as indicated by Definition 5.1, there seems to be a much richer structure when one attempts to describe such mechanisms, even though serial picking-exchange mechanisms are only a subset of nonbossy truthful mechanisms. In particular, the notion of control that was crucial for identifying the structure of truthful mechanisms for two players does not convey enough information anymore. Instead, there seem to exist several different levels of control, and understanding this structure still remains a very interesting and intriguing question.

ACKNOWLEDGMENTS

This work has been partly supported by the COST Action IC1205 on Computational Social Choice, and by an internal grant of the Athens University of Economics and Business. George Christodoulou was supported by EPSRC EP/M008118/1 and Royal Society LT140046. We also wish to acknowledge the Simons institute for hosting the program on Economics and Computation, as some ideas and preliminary discussions began there.

REFERENCES

[1] G. Amanatidis, G. Birmpas, and E. Markakis. 2016. On Truthful Mechanisms for Maximin Share Allocations. In *Proceedings of the Twenty-Fifth International Joint Conference on Artificial Intelligence, IJCAI 2016*. 31–37.

[2] G. Amanatidis, E. Markakis, A. Nikzad, and A. Saberi. 2015. Approximation Algorithms for Computing Maximin Share Allocations. In *Automata, Languages, and Programming, ICALP 2015, Proceedings, Part I*. 39–51.

[3] H. Aziz, A. Filos-Ratsikas, J. Chen, S. Mackenzie, and N. Mattei. 2016. Egalitarianism of Random Assignment Mechanisms: (Extended Abstract). In *International Conference on Autonomous Agents & Multiagent Systems, AAMAS 2016*. 1267–1268.

[4] I. Bezakova and V. Dani. 2005. Allocating Indivisible Goods. *ACM SIGecom Exchanges* 5 (2005), 11–18.

[5] S. Bouveret, Y. Chevaleyre, and N. Maudet. 2016. Fair Allocation of Indivisible Goods. In *Handbook of Computational Social Choice*, F. Brandt, V. Conitzer, U. Endriss, J. Lang, and A.D. Procaccia (Eds.). Cambridge University Press, Chapter 12.

[6] S. Bouveret and J. Lang. 2014. Manipulating picking sequences. In *ECAI 2014 - 21st European Conference on Artificial Intelligence*. 141–146.

[7] S. J. Brams and A. D. Taylor. 1996. *Fair Division: from Cake Cutting to Dispute Resolution*. Cambridge University press.

[8] E. Budish. 2011. The Combinatorial Assignment Problem: Approximate Competitive Equilibrium from Equal Incomes. *Journal of Political Economy* 119, 6 (2011), 1061–1103.

[9] I. Caragiannis, C. Kaklamanis, P. Kanellopoulos, and M. Kyropoulou. 2009. On Low-Envy Truthful Allocations. In *First International Conference on Algorithmic Decision Theory, ADT 2009*. 111–119.

[10] Y. Chen, J. Lai, D. Parkes, and A. Procaccia. 2013. Truth, Justice, and Cake Cutting. *Games and Economic Behavior* 77, 284–297.

[11] G. Christodoulou, E. Koutsoupias, and A. Vidali. 2008. A characterization of 2-Player Mechanisms for Scheduling. In *Algorithms - ESA, 16th Annual European Symposium*. 297–307.

[12] G. Christodoulou and A. Kovács. 2011. A Global Characterization of Envy-Free Truthful Scheduling of Two Tasks. In *Internet and Network Economics - 7th International Workshop, WINE 2011, Proceedings*. 84–96.

[13] R. Cole, V. Gkatzelis, and G. Goel. 2013. Mechanism design for fair division: allocating divisible items without payments. In *ACM Conference on Electronic Commerce, EC '13*. ACM, 251–268.

[14] S. Dobzinski and M. Sundararajan. 2008. On Characterizations of Truthful Mechanisms for Combinatorial Auctions and Scheduling. In *ACM Conference on Electronic Commerce (EC '08)*.

[15] L. Ehlers and B. Klaus. 2003. Coalitional strategy-proof and resource-monotonic solutions for multiple assignment problems. *Social Choice and Welfare* 21, 2 (2003), 265–280.

[16] D. Foley. 1967. Resource Allocation and the Public Sector. *Yale Economics Essays* 7 (1967), 45–98.

[17] G. Gamow and M. Stern. 1958. *Puzzle-Math*. Viking press.

[18] L. Gourvès, J. Monnot, and L. Tlilane. 2015. Worst case compromises in matroids with applications to the allocation of indivisible goods. *Theoretical Computer Science* 589 (2015), 121–140.

[19] M. Guo and V. Conitzer. 2010. Strategy-proof allocation of multiple items between two agents without payments or priors. In *9th International Conference on Autonomous Agents & Multiagent Systems AAMAS 2010*. 881–888.

[20] T. Hill. 1987. Partitioning general probability measures. *The Annals of Probability* 15, 2 (1987), 804–813.

[21] B. Klaus and E. Miyagawa. 2002. Strategy-proofness, Solidarity and Consistency for Multiple Assignment Problems. *International Journal of Game Theory* 30, 3 (2002), 421–435.

[22] R. J. Lipton, E. Markakis, E. Mossel, and A. Saberi. 2004. On approximately fair allocations of indivisible goods. In *ACM Conference on Electronic Commerce (EC)*. 125–131.

[23] E. Markakis and C.-A. Psomas. 2011. On Worst-Case Allocations in the Presence of Indivisible Goods. In *7th Workshop on Internet and Network Economics (WINE 2011)*. 278–289.

[24] T. Mennle and S. Seuken. 2014. An axiomatic approach to characterizing and relaxing strategyproofness of one-sided matching mechanisms. In *ACM Conference on Economics and Computation, EC '14*. 37–38.

[25] H. Moulin. 2003. *Fair division and collective welfare*. MIT Press.

[26] S. Pápai. 2000. Strategyproof Multiple Assignment Using Quotas. *Review of Economic Design* 5, 1 (2000), 91–105.

[27] S. Pápai. 2001. Strategyproof and Nonbossy Multiple Assignments. *Journal of Public Economic Theory* 3, 3 (2001), 257–271.

[28] S. Pápai. 2003. Strategyproof exchange of indivisible goods. *Journal of Mathematical Economics* 39, 8 (2003), 931–959.

[29] S. Pápai. 2007. Exchange in a General Market with Indivisible Goods. *Journal of Economic Theory* 132 (2007), 208–235.

[30] A. D. Procaccia. 2016. Cake Cutting Algorithms. In *Handbook of Computational Social Choice*, F. Brandt, V. Conitzer, U. Endriss, J. Lang, and A.D. Procaccia (Eds.). Cambridge University Press, Chapter 13.

[31] A. D. Procaccia and J. Wang. 2014. Fair enough: guaranteeing approximate maximin shares. In *ACM Conference on Economics and Computation, EC '14*. 675–692.

[32] J. M. Robertson and W. A. Webb. 1998. *Cake Cutting Algorithms: be fair if you can*. AK Peters.

[33] H. Steinhaus. 1948. The Problem of Fair Division. *Econometrica* 16 (1948), 101–104.

[34] L. Svensson. 1999. Strategy-proof Allocation of Indivisible Goods. *Social Choice and Welfare* 16 (1999), 557–567.

[35] H. Varian. 1974. Equity, Envy and Efficiency. *Journal of Economic Theory* 9 (1974), 63–91.

From Monetary to Non-Monetary Mechanism Design via Artificial Currencies

ARTUR GOROKH, Cornell University
SIDDHARTHA BANERJEE, Cornell University
KRISHNAMURTHY IYER, Cornell University

Non-monetary mechanisms for repeated resource allocation are gaining widespread use in many real-world settings. Our aim in this work is to study the allocative efficiency and incentive properties of simple repeated mechanisms based on artificial currencies. Within this framework, we make three main contributions:

- We provide a general black-box technique to convert any static monetary mechanism M to a dynamic mechanism M^* with artificial currency, that simultaneously guarantees *vanishing loss in efficiency*, and *vanishing gains from non-truthful bidding* over time.
- On a computational front, we show how such a mechanism can be implemented using only sample-access to the agents' type distributions, and requires roughly twice the amount of computation as needed to run the monetary mechanism alone.
- For settings with two agents, we show that a particular artificial currency mechanism also results in a *vanishing price of anarchy*. Moreover, we show how to leverage this result to demonstrate the existence of a Bayesian incentive-compatible mechanism with vanishing efficiency loss in this setting.

We informally describe our main result below: Consider a repeated allocation setting with n agents over T periods, where, in each period t, an agent s has a type $\theta_s^t \in \Theta_s$, drawn independently from a distribution F_s. Agents declare their types to a central mechanism, which then chooses an allocation X_t from a set of feasible allocations $\mathcal{X}$. We assume that for a single instance of this allocation problem we are given access to a BIC direct-revelation mechanism M that uses non-negative payments; moreover, we assume that for every agent s there exists a report θ_s that guarantees zero payment.

Given access to T samples $\theta_s^t \in \Theta_s$ for each agent s, we compute c_s^T, the sample average payment of agent s in M under truthful reporting, and allocate each agent s with a budget $B_s = (1+\delta)Tc_s$ of *artificial credits*. We then run M in each period using these credits instead of money. If an agent s runs out of credits, we replace their reports from then on with randomly generated types. Let $u_s(A_s; M)$ be the expected utility of agent s when playing some dynamic strategy A_s under truthful play of other agents. Our main result is as follows:

Theorem. *Let $\lambda > 1$, then for the black-box reduction M^* with $\delta = \Theta(\sqrt{\lambda \log T/T})$, we have*

(1) Truthful reporting Tr *is an $\alpha = O(\lambda/logT)$-equilibrium under M^*, i.e., for any agent s, assuming all other agents play truthfully, we have: $u_s(\mathrm{Tr}; M^*)/T \geq \sup_{A_s} (u_s(A_s; M^*)/T) - \alpha$.*

(2) M achieves the maximum welfare up to an additive loss $\beta = o(T^{-\lambda})$ per period under truthful reporting, as compared to monetary mechanism M: $W(M^*)/T \geq W(M)/T - \beta$.

CCS Concepts: •**Theory of computation → Algorithmic game theory and mechanism design;** •**Applied computing** → *Electronic commerce; Economics;*

Additional Key Words and Phrases: Mechanisms without money; Artificial currencies; Dynamic mechanisms

---

A draft of our full paper is available at https://papers.ssrn.com/abstract_id=2964082.
We gratefully acknowledge support from the NSF (under grants CMMI-1633920 and CMMI-1462592), and the ARL (under grant W911NF-17-1-0094).

EC'17, June 26–30, 2017, Cambridge, Massachusetts, USA.

ACM ISBN 978-1-4503-4527-9/17/06.
DOI: http://dx.doi.org/10.1145/3033274.3085140

Gibbard-Satterthwaite Success Stories and Obvious Strategyproofness

SOPHIE BADE, Royal Holloway, University of London and
Max Planck Institute for Research on Collective Goods, Bonn
YANNAI A. GONCZAROWSKI, The Hebrew University of Jerusalem and Microsoft Research

The Gibbard-Satterthwaite Impossibility Theorem [Gibbard, 1973, Satterthwaite, 1975] holds that dictatorship is the only Pareto optimal and strategyproof social choice function on the full domain of preferences. Much of the work in mechanism design aims at getting around this impossibility theorem. Three grand success stories stand out. On the domains of single-peaked preferences, of object assignment, and of quasilinear preferences, there are appealing Pareto optimal and strategyproof social choice functions. We investigate whether these success stories are robust to strengthening strategyproofness to obvious strategyproofness, a stronger incentive property that was recently introduced by Li [2015] and has since garnered considerable attention.

For single-peaked preferences, we characterize the class of OSP-implementable and unanimous social choice functions as *dictatorships with safeguards against extremism* — mechanisms (which turn out to also be Pareto optimal) in which the dictator can choose the outcome, but other agents may prevent the dictator from choosing an outcome that is too extreme. Median voting is consequently not OSP-implementable. Moreover, even when there are only two possible outcomes, majority voting is not OSP-implementable, and unanimity is the only OSP-implementable supermajority rule. For object assignment, we characterize the class of OSP-implementable and Pareto optimal matching rules as *sequential barter with lurkers* — a significant generalization over bossy variants of bipolar serially dictatorial rules. While Li [2015] shows that second-price auctions are OSP-implementable when only one good is sold, we show that this positive result does not extend to the case of multiple goods. Even when all agents' preferences over goods are quasilinear and additive, no welfare-maximizing auction where losers pay nothing is OSP-implementable when more than one good is sold. Our analysis makes use of a gradual revelation principle, an analog of the (direct) revelation principle for OSP mechanisms that we present and prove, and believe to be of independent interest.

An integrated examination, of all of these negative and positive results, on the one hand reveals that the various mechanics that come into play within obviously strategyproof mechanisms are considerably richer and more diverse than previously demonstrated and can give rise to rather exotic and quite intricate mechanisms in some domains, however on the other hand suggests that the boundaries of obvious strategyproofness are significantly less far-reaching than one may hope in other domains. We thus observe that in a natural sense, obvious strategyproofness is neither "too strong" nor "too weak" a definition for capturing "strategyproofness that is easy to see," but in fact while it performs as intuitively expected on some domains, it "overshoots" on some other domains, and "undershoots" on yet other domains.

Additional Key Words and Phrases: Pareto efficient; house matching; house allocation; object allocation

A full version of this paper is available at https://arxiv.org/abs/1610.04873.

Authors' email addresses: Bade: sophie.bade@rhul.ac.uk; Gonczarowski: yannai@gonch.name.

This collaboration is supported by the ARCHES Award for Research Cooperation and High Excellence in Science. Yannai Gonczarowski is supported by the Adams Fellowship Program of the Israel Academy of Sciences and Humanities; his work is supported by ISF grants 230/10 and 1435/14 administered by the Israeli Academy of Sciences, and by Israel-USA Bi-national Science Foundation (BSF) grant 2014389.

EC'17, June 26–30, 2017, Cambridge, MA, USA.

 ACM ISBN 978-1-4503-4527-9/17/06
http://dx.doi.org/10.1145/3033274.3085104

Planning with Multiple Biases

JON KLEINBERG, Cornell University
SIGAL OREN, Ben-Gurion University of the Negev
MANISH RAGHAVAN, Cornell University

Recent work has considered theoretical models for the behavior of agents with specific behavioral biases: rather than making decisions that optimize a given payoff function, the agent behaves inefficiently because its decisions suffer from an underlying bias. These approaches have generally considered an agent who experiences a single behavioral bias, studying the effect of this bias on the outcome.

In general, however, decision-making can and will be affected by multiple biases operating at the same time. How do multiple biases interact to produce the overall outcome? Here we consider decisions in the presence of a pair of biases exhibiting an intuitively natural interaction: present bias – the tendency to value costs incurred in the present too highly – and sunk-cost bias – the tendency to incorporate costs experienced in the past into one's plans for the future.

We propose a theoretical model for planning with this pair of biases, and we show how certain natural behavioral phenomena can arise in our model only when agents exhibit both biases. As part of our model we differentiate between agents that are aware of their biases (sophisticated) and agents that are unaware of them (naive). Interestingly, we show that the interaction between the two biases is quite complex: in some cases, they mitigate each other's effects while in other cases they might amplify each other. We obtain a number of further results as well, including the fact that the planning problem in our model for an agent experiencing and aware of both biases is computationally hard in general, though tractable under more relaxed assumptions.

1 INTRODUCTION

A rich genre of work at the interface of economics and psychology has studied the ways in which behavioral and cognitive biases can lead people to make consistently sub-optimal decisions [3, 7, 11, 23]. Research in this area has provided a useful organization of these types of biases, including broad categories such as treating losses and gains asymmetrically [12], treating the present inconsistently relative to the future [9], and systematically mis-estimating probabilities [17, 24]. Drawing on these results, a recent line of research has developed theoretical models of planning by biased agents, seeking to bound the gap between the quality of the plans produced by these biased agents and the quality of optimal plans [2, 10, 13, 14, 20].

These analyses have generally considered a single bias at a time, which serves as a way to decompose a complex pattern of behavior into a set of conceptually distinct parts. But it is natural to ask what phenomena might emerge if we were to build models of multiple biases acting at once. Would they reinforce each other, or partially "cancel each other out," or would it be situationally dependent?

A full version is available from https://arxiv.org. Supported in part by a Simons Investigator Award, an ARO MURI grant, a Google Research Grant, and a Facebook Faculty Research Grant.

EC'17, June 26–30, 2017, Cambridge, Massachusetts, USA. © 2017 ACM. ISBN 978-1-4503-4527-9/17/06...$15.00.
DOI: http://dx.doi.org/10.1145/3033274.3085156

In this paper we investigate the prospect of analyzing multiple biases simultaneously, using a theoretical model as our underlying approach. We focus on two well-studied behavioral biases that fit naturally together: *present bias* — the tendency to value costs and benefits incurred in the present too highly relative to future costs and benefits [1, 16, 19] — and *sunk-cost bias* — the tendency to incorporate costs incurred in the past into one's plans for the future, even when these past costs are no longer relevant to optimal planning [4, 21, 22]. Sunk cost bias is a fundamental bias in planning, studied in various disciplines under different names. For example, it appears in the organizational behavior literature as "Escalation of Commitment" [18], and it is known as the "Concorde Fallacy" [6, 25] in behavioral ecology, named after the famous supersonic airplane whose development was continued long after it was clear that it had no economic justification.

Present Bias and Sunk-Cost Bias. Present bias and sunk-cost bias on their own are qualitatively quite different, though each operates on perceptions of costs and benefits over time, and each is easily recognizable at an intuitive level. A canonical example of present bias (familiar from many people's experience) is the scenario in which an individual buys a membership to a gym, but then actually goes to the gym very few times [8]. Viewed at the moment when the gym membership was purchased, the long-range health benefits of regular exercise seemed to outweigh the cost in effort required to go to the gym regularly; but when the time comes to actually go to the gym, the cost of the effort seems larger than it did previously, even relative to the other costs and benefits under consideration. This leads to sub-optimal decision-making: either it would have been preferable to buy the membership and then regularly go to the gym, or to not buy the membership, but it can't be optimal to buy a membership and then not use it.

A canonical example of sunk-cost bias (also familiar from everyday experience) lies in the contrast between the following two scenarios [21, 22]:

(i) You have bought an expensive and non-refundable ticket to a concert or sporting event that you are very interested in attending, but on the day of the event, a major snowstorm makes travel dangerous. Should you go to it anyway?

(ii) You were given a free ticket to a concert or sporting event that you are very interested in attending, but on the day of the event, a major snowstorm makes travel dangerous. Should you go to it anyway?

In examples of these and similar situations, many people view the two scenarios differently — they would risk the dangerous travel conditions in scenario (i) so as not to "throw away the cost of the ticket," while they'd conclude in scenario (ii) that it's not worth the risk just to make it to the free event. Yet if we think of the two scenarios strictly as an optimization of costs and benefits, they are effectively equivalent: since the cost of the ticket is unrecoverable in scenario (i), in both cases the question is whether the enjoyment of attending the event (given that you are already in possession of the ticket) outweighs the costs associated with traveling under risky conditions. The fact that the two scenarios feel different at an intuitive level suggests some of the deep ways in which people take into account *sunk costs* — costs incurred in the past that can no longer be recovered — and use these sunk costs in their decision-making even when they are formally irrelevant to the optimization aspects of the planning problem ahead.

Interactions of Present Bias and Sunk-Cost Bias. Although present bias and sunk-cost bias involve different types of reasoning, they both connect costs and benefits incurred at different stages of a planning problem to decisions about future behavior. As such, one could ask about the behavior of an agent in such a planning problem if they were experiencing both biases. Do we learn something new by considering the two biases together?

We argue here that modeling the interaction of present bias and sunk-cost bias in planning leads to an interesting and natural set of phenomena that don't arise when we model either of the two biases individually. To get some intuition for what we learn by combining them, let's first return to a synthesis of the two scenarios discussed above. In particular, consider the reasoning (again familiar from everyday life) of a person who decides they're going to buy a gym membership so that when the time comes to go to the gym, their desire not to waste the money spent on the membership will help motivate them to go regularly. Although the sentiment is expressed in a pithy format, it is intrinsically based on an interaction among multiple ingredients: first, the person suffers from present bias, which will make it harder to attend the gym when the time comes; second, they exhibit sunk cost bias so once they buy a gym membership they will be more inclined to visit the gym to avoid wasting the money they already spent; and third, they are *sophisticated* in that they realize they will experience these biases in the future, so they plan to use their sunk-cost bias associated with prepaying the gym membership as a commitment device to overcome their present bias when it arises.

1.1 Planning with Multiple Biases: A Basic Model

We now describe a simple theoretical model in which we can express this type of planning, and discuss the basic framework for reasoning within the model. The model has the following components, building on a graph-theoretic formalism from our prior work on present bias [13, 14]. First, the planning problem is represented by a directed graph G with non-negative costs on its edges. An agent starts at a node s in G with the goal of reaching a node t in G. There is a reward R at the node t. The agent's payoff if it reaches t is equal to the reward R minus the sum of the costs on all the edges it traverses. In case the agent traverses some of the edges but doesn't reach t its negative payoff is simply the total cost of all edges traversed. (The agent achieves a payoff of 0 if it never starts traversing the graph.)

Figure 1 shows a small instance of this type of planning problem. The optimal plan would be to traverse the upper path through v, achieving a payoff of $R - 1 - 12 = 6$. Note that if we set the reward R to be 10 instead of 19, then the optimal plan would be not to start, thus achieving a payoff of 0.

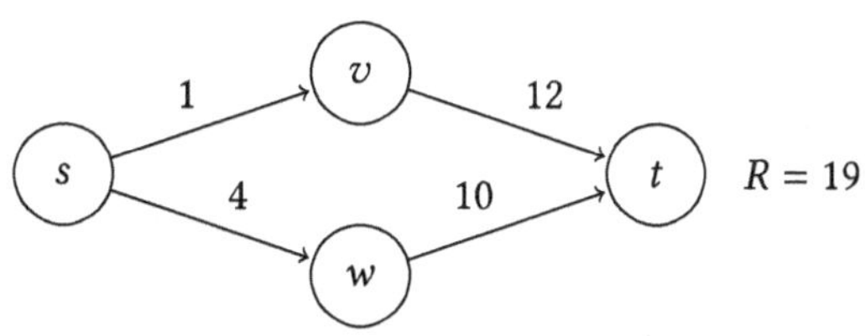

Fig. 1. An instance of the planning problem.

(b, λ)-agents. Now, let's consider how to model the behavior of biased agents on such a graph G. Biased agents can deviate from optimal behavior in two ways: first in how they misperceive the costs of paths in G (and hence how they misperceive payoffs), and second in their potential misunderstanding of how they will behave in the future. We describe these two components in turn, and then illustrate them by showing how biased agents behave in the example of Figure 1.

Our agents will exhibit both present bias and sunk-cost bias in general, and we specify them using parameters $b \geq 1$ and $\lambda \geq 0$.

- The quantity b is a present-bias parameter: when the agent is at a node u and considering the prospect of traversing a path P beginning with the edge (u, v), it *perceives* the cost of the u-v edge as being scaled up by a multiplicative factor of b. It adds this scaled-up cost to the actual costs of the remaining edges on P, resulting in a total *perceived cost* for P. This reflects the overweighting of costs incurred in the present — in this case, the next edge to be traversed — that is associated with agents exhibiting this bias [15].[1] Thus, for example, an agent with present-bias parameter b located at s in Figure 1 would perceive the cost of the upper path as $b + 12$ and the lower path as $4b + 10$.

- The quantity λ is a sunk-cost parameter: if the agent decides to *abandon* the traversal — stopping at its current node u and thus incurring no future cost or reward — it exhibits a mental cost equal to λ times the total cost it has incurred thus far.

  This reflects the agent's aversion to giving up when it already has incurred sunk cost in the traversal thus far; incurring this as a final cost is motivated by constructions in the literature on *mental accounting* [21, 22] and *realization utility* [5].

We will refer to a biased agent with parameters b and λ as a (b, λ)-*agent*. Note that an agent who experiences neither present bias nor sunk-cost bias has $b = 1$ and $\lambda = 0$, and hence is a $(1, 0)$-agent.

Future Selves, Naivete, and Sophistication. So far we have described the way a biased agent perceives costs; now we need to describe the process by which it forms a plan on the graph G. Since our focus is on agents who may have different preferences in the future than they do in the present, we adopt a style of exposition used in behavioral economics and consider agents who reason about what their "future selves" will do. This style of description is useful in our gym membership scenarios, for example, where the person buying the gym membership would like his or her "future self" to go to the gym regularly, but is worried that this future self will not feel like going when the time comes to actually do it.

This is also a useful formulation for our graph-theoretic model, because biased agents may differ in how they believe their future selves are going to behave. Suppose a (b, λ)-agent is currently located at a node u, and is considering whether to traverse an edge (u, v). It imagines that when it reaches the node v, it will hand off control of future planning to its "node-v self." Now, how does the agent believe its node-v self will reason about the remainder of the planning problem? An agent who is *naive* about its biases believes that its node-v self will plan optimally starting from node v, whereas an agent who is *sophisticated* about its biases believes that its node-v self will continue to behave like a (b, λ)-agent. Since in our model, an agent's parameters remain constant for the duration of the planning problem, a sophisticated agent is correct in its belief about its node-v self, while a naive agent is incorrect in its belief. Importantly, both types of agents care about the costs incurred by their future selves as well as their own costs; they just scale up the cost of the immediate next edge by a factor of b when they determine the total cost of a path, reflecting the fact that they value costs to themselves a factor of b higher than they value costs to their future selves.

There is extensive empirical evidence that people can behave more like naive agents or more like sophisticated agents in different scenarios — sometimes we make a plan believing that we'll be fully motivated to follow through on it when the time comes, and sometimes we factor into our planning the belief that we might not be inclined to take the necessary step in the future [9].

There are thus multiple types of agents, and as we will see next, they exhibit a range of intuitively natural behaviors that reflect how their biases — and their awareness of these biases — interact. In keeping with the fact that there are two kinds of biases under consideration, we will refer to the two types of agents discussed above as *doubly naive* and *doubly sophisticated*, indicating that such

[1] The model proposed by Laibson [15] also include an exponential decay on costs and rewards incurred in the future, where for a decay parameter δ, quantities experienced τ steps in the future are reduced by a factor of δ^τ. In this paper we consider the case of $\delta = 1$, where there is no decay into the future, so as to focus our attention on the present-bias parameter b.

agents are either naive about both biases or sophisticated about both biases. Later we will consider the natural question of agents who are naive about one bias and sophisticated about the other.

1.2 Two Examples

With the core definitions established, it is very useful to consider the behavior of these agents in some basic examples, for two reasons. First, given the subtle distinctions among different agent types, it is useful to see these distinctions through simple illustrations; and second, these examples help establish that the behaviors we are modeling are all intuitively quite natural.

Health Club Memberships. We'll start with the behavior of these agents on the instance in Figure 1. To begin with, we note that the planning problem described by the graph in Figure 1 has a direct interpretation in terms of decisions about gym membership, as follows.

> A local health club offers a range of classes, and you're interested in taking its yoga class. The effort required to take the yoga class is 10, and the long-term reward from having taken it is 19. To take the yoga class you need to get a membership at the health club, and there are two options for memberships. With a *basic membership*, you pay 1 up front, and pay 2 for each class at the time you attend it. With a *deluxe membership*, you pay 4 up front, but then all classes are free. You know that you only want to take the yoga class, not any of the other classes (since none of the other classes at the health club appeal to you). What should you do?

It is easy to check that the graph in Figure 1 encodes this story, with node v corresponding to the state in which you've purchased a basic membership (but haven't yet taken the class), node w corresponding to the state in which you've purchased a deluxe membership (but haven't yet taken the class), and node t corresponding to the state in which you've completed the yoga class (and so can now achieve the reward of 19). An optimal agent would buy the basic membership (using the path through v), since there's no reason to pay 4 for a deluxe membership when just the yoga class can be taken for a cost of $1 + 12 = 13$.

Now, what would doubly naive or a doubly sophisticated agent do in this situation? For concreteness, let's use $b = 2$ and $\lambda = 1/2$ as the parameters for our example. In particular, this means that both types of biased agents — doubly naive and doubly sophisticated — will perceive the cost on the first edge out of s as being multiplied by a factor of 2; they differ in how they reason about the remainder of the planning problem. As part of this reasoning, it is important to distinguish between an agent's *perceived payoff* at a given point in the traversal, and the actual payoff it incurs, which is determined entirely by the true costs and rewards on the graph, rather by the agent's biases.

- A doubly naive agent would perceive the path through v as costing $2 \cdot 1 + 12 = 14$ and the path through w as costing $2 \cdot 4 + 10 = 18$. It also believes that it will behave optimally starting from whichever node it visits next. It thus traverses the edge from s to v. Once it is at v, however, it now evaluates the cost of the v-t edge as $2 \cdot 12 = 24$, which means that paying this cost to get the reward of 19 leads to a perceived payoff of -5. On the other hand, abandoning the path incurs a sunk cost penalty of $1 \cdot \lambda = 1/2$; since this perceived payoff of $-1/2$ is preferable to the perceived payoff of -5 from continuing, the agent abandons the path at v. In summary: the doubly naive agent buys the basic membership, but when the time comes to take the yoga class, it lets the membership go to waste.
- A doubly sophisticated agent first reasons about how it would expect to behave starting from node v and from node w. From node v, with a sunk cost of 1, it would behave the way the doubly naive agent actually behaved when it reached v — comparing a perceived

payoff of -5 from continuing with a perceived payoff of $-1/2$ from abandoning — and so it would abandon the path if it were at node v. From node w, with a sunk cost of 4, it would get a perceived payoff of $19 - 2 \cdot 10 = -1$ from continuing to t, and a perceived payoff of $-4\lambda = -2$ (from the sunk-cost penalty of 2) if it were to abandon the path at w. Thus, from w it would continue to t. Finally, back at s, the agent reasons that the path through w to t has perceived cost $2 \cdot 4 + 10 = 18$ and hence a perceived payoff of $19 - 18 = 1$ to its present self, since it knows it will continue from w. Thus it chooses to go to w. The informal summary is that the doubly sophisticated agent buys the deluxe membership, since it knows the fear of wasting the price of the deluxe membership (as manifested through its sunk-cost bias) will motivate it to take the yoga class, leading to a positive payoff.

The upshot is that the optimal agent, the doubly naive agent, and the doubly sophisticated agent all pursue different plans: the optimal agent makes effective use of the basic membership; the doubly naive agent foolishly buys the basic membership and then doesn't actually take the yoga class; and the doubly sophisticated agent buys the deluxe membership as a commitment device to follow through on the yoga class.

It is also instructive to compare these outcomes to the plans pursued by naive and sophisticated present-biased agents — that is, $(b, 0)$-agents who experience only present bias without sunk-cost bias. A naive present-biased agent will follow the same plan as the doubly naive agent above. But a sophisticated present-biased agent will follow a plan distinct from all the ones we've seen so far: it will correctly recognize that it wouldn't continue from either node v or node w, and consequently it wouldn't start out from s. In other words, a sophisticated present-biased agent wouldn't buy either type of membership in the health club, because it realizes that it won't take the yoga class when the time comes.

Completing Assignments in a Class. We briefly consider a second example where the contrasts between the agents turn out differently — a version of an example from [13] involving assigned work in a class, adapted to the types of agents we are considering here.

Suppose you're taking a 4-week class, and you must complete three short projects by the end of the class. In each week you can choose to do 0, 1, or 2 of the projects; doing 0 projects in a given week costs 0, doing 1 project costs 4, and doing 2 projects costs 10. If you complete all three projects by the end of the 4 weeks, then you pass the class, which comes with a reward of $R = 17.5$. The graph G associated with this planning problem is shown in Figure 2: the node v_{ij} corresponds to the state in which you're i weeks into the class and you've completed j projects so far.

An optimal agent would choose to do one project in each of 3 separate weeks, for any 3 out of the 4 weeks, incurring a total cost of 12 and hence a payoff of $17.5 - 12 = 5.5$. Let's consider the behavior of biased agents with $b = 2$ and $\lambda = 3/4$; we only sketch the reasoning for this example.

- A doubly naive agent will do one project in week 2, planning to do one more project in each of weeks 3 and 4. In week 3, it chooses to defer both projects to week 4 (since $2 \cdot 4 + 4 > 10$). In week 4, it would incur a perceived payoff (due to sunk cost) of $-4\lambda = -3$ from abandoning, and a perceived payoff of $17.5 - 2 \cdot 10 = -2.5$ from continuing, so it will do both projects and finish the class.
- A doubly sophisticated agent correctly anticipates that it will do two projects in week 4, for a cost of 10. Thus, when the time comes to do the first project, its perceived cost will be $2 \cdot 4 + 10 = 18 > 17.5$, and since it has no sunk cost at this point, it will choose to abandon the path. Given this, a doubly sophisticated will choose not to start out from s, thus deciding not to take the class. (Essentially, the doubly sophisticated agent says,

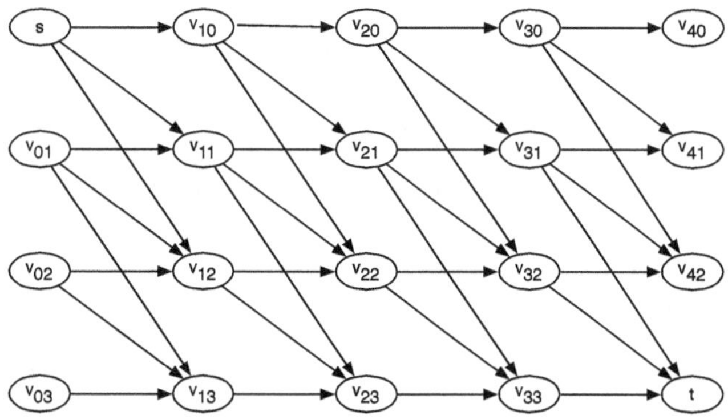

Fig. 2. A biased agent must choose a path from s to t.

correctly, "I know that once I put some work into the class, I'm going to end up pushing the rest of the work to the very end and overdo things in week 4.")

- A naive agent with only present bias – i.e. a naive $(2, 0)$-agent – will, like the doubly naive agent, get to week 4 needing to do two projects. At that point, since it has no sunk cost bias, abandoning the path has a payoff of 0, while continuing has a perceived payoff of $17.5 - 2 \cdot 10 = -2.5$. Thus it will abandon the path (dropping the class) in week 4.
- A sophisticated agent with only present bias – i.e. a sophisticated $(2, 0)$-agent – actually behaves optimally. It correctly anticipates that if it reaches week 4 with two projects left to do, it will abandon the path (since it has no sunk-cost bias), and so it does one project in each of weeks 2, 3, and 4.

It's interesting that in contrast to the case of health club memberships, where the doubly sophisticated agent reached the goal and the sophisticated present-biased agent didn't, here the roles are reversed; the contrast is that this second example is one in which (i) the doubly sophisticated agent realizes that its present bias combined with its sunk-cost bias will lead it down a path where it pays too high a price; and (ii) there's an alternate path that the sophisticated present-biased agent can take.

One conclusion from all these examples is that relatively small graphs can encode scenarios that would otherwise be quite complicated to reason about; and the interplay between present bias and sunk-cost bias in these examples is producing intuitively natural behaviors that inherently require both biases.

1.3 Mixed Forms of Sophistication

Since we are considering two biases at once, we should also consider the possibility that an agent might be naive about one of its two biases and sophisticated about the other. Thus, a (b, λ)-agent at a node u, considering the traversal of edge (u, v), would be naive about its sunk-cost bias but sophisticated about its present bias if it believed that its node-v self will behave like a $(b, 0)$-agent who is sophisticated about its present bias. Alternately, it would be naive about its present bias but sophisticated about its sunk-cost bias if it believed that its node-v self will behave like a $(1, \lambda)$-agent who is sophisticated about its sunk-cost bias.

It is not hard to show that in our model this latter type of agent, who is naive about present bias and sophisticated about sunk-cost bias, is indistinguishable in its behavior from an agent who is naive about both biases.[2] Thus, we will focus on agents that are sophisticated about their present bias and naive about their sunk-cost bias. We refer to such agents as *singly sophisticated* agents.

It is interesting to consider how a singly sophisticated agent behaves in the examples from Figure 1 and 2. In the health club example of Figure 1, the singly sophisticated agent doesn't appreciate that sunk-cost bias will play a role in its reasoning at nodes v and w, and so at node s it reasons like a sophisticated $(b, 0)$-agent and decides not to start out from s. In the class-projects example of Figure 2, the singly sophisticated agent again starts out reasoning like a sophisticated $(b, 0)$-agent and plans to do one project in each of weeks 2, 3, and 4. Once it does the first project in week 2, however, it now has acquired some sunk cost, and so it changes its plan to do both of the remaining projects in week 4. Thanks to the sunk-cost bias it goes ahead and does this, since the perceived payoff of $17.5 - 2 \cdot 10$ from finishing in week 4 is preferable to the perceived payoff of $-4\lambda = -3$ from abandoning in week 4. This second example shows that despite the agent's sophistication about its present bias, its naivete about its sunk-cost bias means that it can still sometimes be time-inconsistent in its behavior, changing plans in the middle of its traversal of the graph G.

Perceived Rewards. We now describe an equivalent way of representing the payoff to an agent with sunk-cost bias. Thus far, if a (b, λ)-agent stops without reaching t, it incurs a negative payoff equal to λ multiplied by the total cost of edges it has traversed. In deciding whether to continue, it compares this negative payoff from stopping to the perceived payof from continuing to t (equal to the reward R minus the perceived cost of upcoming edges). An equivalent way to express this comparison is to add λ times the cost incurred so far to the reward, creating a new (larger) *perceived reward.* The agent continues if and only if this perceived reward is at least as large as the perceived cost of the upcoming edges it plans to traverse. In this way, there is no explicit sunk-cost penalty from stopping; rather, the sunk-cost bias is reflected in the growing reward that the agent perceives, incorporating λ times the cost experienced so far. We will use this equivalent formulation in the remainder of the paper.

1.4 Overview of Results

In the remainder of the paper, we provide a set of performance guarantees and algorithmic results for the types of biased agents defined in this section. We give a brief summary of some of the main results here.

We first consider doubly sophisticated agents, and in particular the planning problem for such agents. Algorithmically, such agents face a non-trivial planning task, since in choosing a next step, they must consider what their future selves will do not just from every node, but for every possible value of the sunk cost they might experience from that node. We give an algorithm for solving the planning problem for doubly sophisticated agents that runs in time polynomial in the number of nodes n and the total sum C of edge costs in the graph. This is a *pseudo-polynomial* algorithm in that its running time depends on the actual magnitudes of the costs in the instance, and it is natural to ask whether there might be some better algorithm that avoids this form of dependence on the costs. We show, however, that this dependence is necessary (assuming $P \neq NP$), by proving that the planning for a doubly sophisticated agent is NP-hard when the edge costs are presented in binary notation (and hence the input has size polynomial in n and $\log C$).

In a positive direction, we are able to show that doubly sophisticated agents always achieve reasonably good payoffs. In particular, we find that if C_o denotes the cost incurred by an optimal

[2]To see why this is the case, first observe that an agent who has no present bias (i.e. $b = 1$) will behave the same in our graph traversal problem regardless of whether or not it has sunk-cost bias, and whether or not it is aware of it. Since an agent who is naive about present bias plans paths on the assumption that it will have $b = 1$ in the future, the plan it makes from any node is indistinguishable from the plan of an agent who is naive about both biases.

agent that reaches t in a given instance, then the payoff of a doubly sophisticated agent is smaller than the payoff of an optimal agent by an additive amount of at most $(b-1)C_o$. As one direct consequence of this fact, a doubly sophisticated agent will reach the target node t in any instance for which the reward R is at least bC_o. We show similar additive gaps between the payoff of a doubly sophisticated agent and the payoff of a sophisticated present-biased agent (with no sunk-cost bias, and hence parameters $(b, 0)$); there are instances in which either can achieve a better payoff than the other, but the gap between them always remains bounded by $(b-1)C_o$.

For doubly naive agents, we show that their sunk-cost bias can push them to incur costs that are much higher than the available reward R. In particular, they can incur a cost that is exponential in the size of the graph. We find upper and lower bounds on the worst-case cost, with exponential bases that are close to one another between the two bounds.

Using a more complex construction, we can show that exponentially bad bounds apply to the singly sophisticated agent as well. Despite its sophistication about its present bias, it is possible for a singly sophisticated agent to incur exponentially large cost before abandoning the traversal without reaching t. We complement this with a nearly matching upper bound, which also shows that the cost incurred by a singly sophisticated agent is only exponential in the number of "switches" — nodes at which the agent changes its plan.

2 DOUBLY SOPHISTICATED AGENTS

In this section we consider doubly sophisticated agents. Recall that these are agents that are sophisticated about both their present bias and sunk cost bias. A doubly sophisticated agent accurately predicts the decisions that its future selves will make, meaning that the agent will follow the path it plans to take. In particular, this means that the agent won't begin traversing the graph unless it is sure that it will reach the target.

Path-planning for an agent that is sophisticated but has no sunk cost bias is straightforward - at a node v, the agent's action is purely a function of its decisions at later nodes in the topological ordering, so its decisions can be recursively computed. With sunk cost bias, however, this is no longer the case. An agent's decision depends not only on its future decisions but also on its past decisions and particularly on the cost it has incurred reaching v. Thus, to plan its path it needs to know its future behavior for all possible values of the cost incurred. In the next section we will see that when the number of possible values of the cost incurred at every node is small the agent can efficiently recursively compute the path it will take and discuss the special case in which the cost on the edges have integer values.

2.1 Integer Doubly-Sophisticated Path Computation

As we will later see the general path computation problem for a doubly sophisticated agent is NP-hard. Let k be an upper bound on the number of possible different values of the costs for reaching a node. In the full version we present a recursive algorithm for path computation that runs in time polynomial in k and n. Here we present an iterative dynamic program algorithm for the case that the edges have integers costs. For this case we take k to be the sum of all edge costs and exhibit a pseudo polynomial algorithm. Such an algorithm is both easier to follow and illustrates well the way that a doubly sophisticated agent reasons about the behavior of its future selves to plan its path.

Proposition 2.1. *The integer doubly sophisticated path computation problem can be solved in time polynomial in n and C, where n is the number of vertices in G and C is the sum of the costs of the edges.*

Proof. **Algorithm** 1 solves the integer doubly-sophisticated path computation problem in time polynomial in n and C. The algorithm relies on the observation that path that the agent will choose from some node u only depends on the total cost of the path it took to get to u and not on the explicit path. Since the costs on the edges are integers, we can compute for each node u and for each possible cost of the path reaching u what the cost of going from u to t is. This can be done in reverse topological order – at node u with some sunk cost i, if we know what the agent will do at every subsequent node v with sunk cost $i + c(u, v)$, we can determine the agent's behavior at u.

In the algorithm we define two arrays – *choices* and *costs* – that hold the choice and cost of the path that the agent would take if it reached a vertex u with a sunk cost of i. We begin filling in these arrays in reverse topological order, since at t, there is no decision to be made, and the cost of the remaining path is 0. If the agent reaches some vertex u having incurred a cost of i along the way, then its choice of where to go next is uniquely determined by the successor vertices it can go to. Since we do the computation in reverse topological order, we know that for any successor v', the *choices* and *costs* values have already been computed. Therefore, the agent can simulate what would happen along each potential path simply by looking up the *costs* value of reaching v' with an incurred cost of $i + c(u, v')$. Out of all potential successors v', the agent chooses the v that minimizes its perceived cost, where perceived cost is given by $b \cdot c(u, v') + costs[v][i + c(u, v)]$. If this perceived cost is larger than the perceived reward, which is given by R plus λ times the cost incurred so far, then the agent would abandon upon reaching u after an incurred cost of i. Otherwise, it would proceed to v, and the total cost of the path it would take from u to v would be $c(u, v) + costs[v]$. In either case, the algorithm correctly computes the action of the agent.

At the start of the traversal, the agent is at s with an incoming cost of 0. Therefore, we can look up $choices[s][0]$ to see where the agent would go next, and so on until we find the path that the agent would take to t, updating the incurred cost so far as we go. □

2.2 The Gap Between a Doubly Sophisticated Agent and an Optimal Agent

As the payoff of a doubly sophisticated agent is always non-negative, the only instances that can admit a positive gap are ones in which the optimal agent reaches the target. Let $C_o(u)$ be the cost of the optimal agent for reaching the target from u, which means that $C_o(s) = C_o$. We show that there can be an additive gap of at most $(b - 1)C_o$ between the payoffs of an optimal agent and a doubly sophisticated agent. We note that the source of the gap could be either because the doubly sophisticated agent did not traverse the graph or because both agents traversed the graph but the cost of the doubly sophisticated agent was higher.

Instead of proving the gap directly we show that a similar claim holds in a more general setting. An agent currently at v that exhibits sunk cost bias perceives a different reward based on the path it took to v. In particular if the agent took a path P to get to v then its perceived reward at v is $R + \lambda \cdot c(P)$, where $c(P)$ is the total cost of the path P. To generalize this, we define a reward schedule H as a mapping from paths beginning at s to rewards. When computing a path for a graph G with reward schedule H, an agent makes its calculations as if after following a path, the reward it will get when it reaches t is given by the reward schedule.

PROPOSITION 2.2. *Given a graph G and a path-dependent reward schedule H, if the perceived reward according to H at each vertex v on the optimal path from s to t is at least $b \cdot C_o(v)$, then a present-bias sophisticated agent will traverse the graph and incur a cost of at most $b \cdot C_o(s)$.*

PROOF. Let P be the optimal path from s to t. We will prove by induction that from each vertex v along P, there exists a path of cost at most $b \cdot C_o(v)$ from v to t that the agent would be willing to take for the reward schedule H, regardless of the path taken to get to v. Let $C_H(v)$ denote the cost for a sophisticated present-biased agent to reach t from v given the schedule H.

Base case: At t, the claim is trivially true.

Algorithm 1 IntegerDoublySophisticated(G, R, b, λ)

```
n ← |V|
C ← sum of the edge costs
choices ← array[n][C] initialized to null
costs ← array[n][C] initialized to 0
for u ∈ V\{t} in reverse topological order do
    for i ← 0 ... C do
        v ← argmin_{v'∈N(u)} b · c(u, v') + costs[v'][i + c(u, v')]
        perceived ← b · c(u, v) + costs[v][i + c(u, v)]
        if perceived > R + λ · i then
            choices[u][i] ← null
            costs[u][i] ← ∞
        else
            choices[u][i] ← v
            costs[u][i] ← c(u, v) + costs[v][i + c(u, v)]
if choices[s][0] == null then
    return no path
path ← []
cost ← 0
u ← s
while u ≠ t do
    Append u to path
    v ← choices[u][cost]
    cost ← cost + c(u, v)
    u ← v
Append t to path
```

Inductive hypothesis: $C_H(v) \leq b \cdot C_o(v)$, and v is never abandoned under H.

Inductive step: Consider some vertex u on P and assume that the inductive hypothesis holds for all the vertices after u on P. Let v be the next vertex after u on P. By assumption, the perceived reward at u is some $R_u \geq b \cdot C_o(u)$. We know by induction that if the agent reaches v, the rest of the path will cost $C_H(v) \leq b \cdot C_o(v)$. Therefore, the perceived cost of going from u to v and then from v to t is

$$b \cdot c(u, v) + C_H(v) \leq b \cdot c(u, v) + b \cdot C_o(v) = b \cdot C_o(u) \leq R_u$$

Thus, the agent would be willing to take this path, so u could never be abandoned. Furthermore, this implies that the agent will take some path (either the one discussed above or a different one) that its perceived cost is at most $b \cdot C_o(u)$. As the total cost is always smaller than the perceived cost this implies that the total cost of the path that the agent will take is at most $b \cdot C_o(u)$ as required. □

We can now use Proposition 2.2 to bound the gap between an optimal agent and a doubly sophisticated agent.

Proposition 2.3. *Consider a task graph G with a reward R on the target. The payoff of an optimal agent can be higher than the payoff of a (b, λ)-doubly sophisticated agent by an additive amount of at most $(b - 1)C_o$.*

Proof. First, observe that if $R \leq b \cdot C_o$ then the payoff of the optimal agent is at most $(b-1) \cdot C_o$ and the proposition holds. Next, recall that the reward schedule that is used to describe the behavior of a doubly sophisticated agent is monotonically increasing: the perceived reward at any vertex v along a path P is $R + \lambda \cdot C_P(v)$, where $C_P(v)$ is the cost for reaching v on the path P. This means that if $R \geq b \cdot C_o$ we can apply Proposition 2.2 and get that the doubly sophisticated agent will reach the target and pay a cost of at most $b \cdot C_o$. Hence, in this case as well, the difference in the payoffs of the optimal agent and doubly sophisticated agents is at most $b \cdot C_o - C_o = (b-1)C_o$. □

Lastly the fact that the agent is always willing to traverse the graph for a reward of $R = b \cdot C_o$ leads us to the following corollary:

Corollary 2.4. *The minimum reward R for which a (b, λ)−doubly sophisticated agent would be willing to traverse a graph G is at most $b \cdot C_o$.*

In the full version, we present results for similar comparisons between doubly sophisticated and sophisticated present-biased agents.

2.3 Doubly-Sophisticated Path Computation is NP-Hard

We will show that the problem of determining whether there exists a path that a doubly sophisticated agent will traverse is NP-hard. Formally, we show

Theorem 2.5. *This problem is NP-hard: Given a graph G, a reward R, present bias b, and sunk cost bias λ, determine whether there exists a path that a doubly sophisticated agent can take from s to t.*

We show that for any parameter $1/2 \leq \lambda < 1$ there exists $b > 0$ such that this problem is NP-hard by using a reduction from the Subset Sum problem. Recall that in the Subset Sum problem we ask, given a set S of integers $x_1, \ldots, x_n$ and a target T, is there some subset of S that adds up to T. Given an instance of the subset sum problem, we construct a graph G as follows: The vertices are $s, v_1, \ldots, v_{n+1}, w_1, \ldots, w_n, t$. There is an edge of cost 0 from s to v_1 and an edge of cost T from v_{n+1} to t. For each i between 1 and n, there is an edge of cost 0 from v_i to w_i and an edge of cost 0 from w_i to v_{i+1}. Finally from each v_i to v_{i+1}, there is a sequence of vertices and edges such that the path from v_i to v_{i+1} has total cost x_i. The first two edges on each sequence have cost $\frac{1}{2b}$, and each subsequent edge has twice the cost of the previous edge. This sequence ends when the total cost of the sequence is exactly x_i (meaning that the last edge has at most twice the cost of the second-to-last edge, and the sum of the costs of the edges is x_i). For example, if $x_i = 4$, then the sequence of edges will be $\frac{1}{5}, \frac{1}{5}, \frac{2}{5}, \frac{4}{5}, \frac{8}{5}, \frac{4}{5}$. The agent's present bias for $\lambda > 0$ is $b = 2 + \lambda$ and the reward is $R = (b - \lambda)T + \lambda - \varepsilon = 2T + \lambda - \varepsilon$. A sketch of the reduction can be found in Figure 3

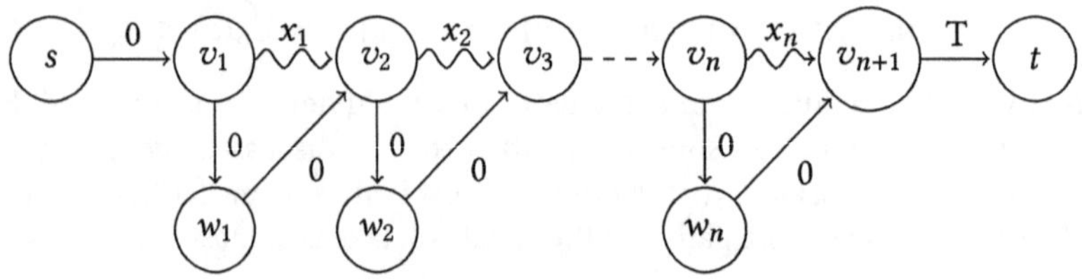

Fig. 3. A sketch of the graph G created by the reduction

It is not hard to show that for each x_i the number of edges we create in G is linear in $\log x_i$, [3] thus, the size of G is polynomial in the size of the input. In the next two claims we prove that the

[3]The formal proof can be found in the full version

subset sum instance has a solution $\Longleftrightarrow$ there is some path in G that the doubly sophisticated agent will traverse for the given reward.

Claim 1. The subset sum instance has a solution $\Longrightarrow$ there is some path in G that the doubly sophisticated agent will traverse for the given reward.

Proof. Let $I \subseteq \{1, \ldots, n\}$ be the solution to the subset sum instance, i.e. $\sum_{i \in I} x_i = T$. If there are multiple solutions, then let I be the one which has the largest minimum index (with ties broken by the second-smallest index, and so on). Then, consider a path through G such that for $i \in I$, the agent takes the sequence of edges from v_i to v_{i+1} for a cost of x_i, and for $j \notin I$, the agent takes the edges (v_i, w_i) and (w_i, v_{i+1}). Then, when the agent gets to v_{n+1}, it will have incurred a total cost of T, so when it takes the last edge from v_{n+1} to t, the final incurred cost will be $2T$. We will show that if the agent follows this path, at every vertex that the agent passes through, the perceived cost will always be smaller than R, meaning this is a valid path. Finally, we will show that the agent cannot take any other path.

Call the path described above P. We proceed by induction, proving the claim that if the agent reaches v_i along P, then the agent will reach t along P.

Base case: $i = n + 1$. If the agent reaches v_{n+1} along P, it will have incurred a total cost of T. The only outgoing edge from v_{n+1} goes to t for a cost of T, so the perceived cost of taking that edge is $b \cdot T$ which is smaller than the perceived reward of $(b - \lambda)T + \lambda - \varepsilon + \lambda T = b \cdot T + \lambda - \varepsilon$. Thus, if the agent reaches v_{n+1} along P, it will reach t along P.

Inductive hypothesis: If the agent reaches v_i along P, it will continue along P to t without abandoning.

Inductive step: Assume that the agent reaches v_{i-1} along P. Then, in order to prove the claim, we must show that it proceeds from v_{i-1} to v_i along P, at which point we can use induction to prove that from v_i, it continues to t along P. Since the agent has reached v_{i-1} along P, we know that at this point, it has incurred a cost of $K_{i-1} = \sum_{j \in I, j < i-1} x_j$. We consider two cases:

Case 1: $i - 1 \in I$. In this case, we must show that the agent takes the sequence of edges from v_{i-1} to v_i. Assume towards contradiction that the agent takes the $v_{i-1} \to w_{i-1} \to v_i$ path instead. In order for w_{i-1} not to be abandoned for this incoming cost, there must be some path that reaches t from w_{i-1} with a sunk cost of K_{i-1} without abandoning. In order for the agent to take the edge from v_{n+1} to t, the total cost of the path from s to v_{n+1} should be at least T. Thus, any valid path from w_{i-1} to v_{n+1} must have a total cost of at least $T - K_{i-1}$. However, if this path does have a total cost of exactly $T - K_{i-1}$, then following it would yield a valid solution to the subset sum instance. Moreover, this solution I' would have a larger minimum index than our original solution I, as $x_{i-1} \in I$ and $x_{i-1} \notin I'$, and for all $j < i - 1$, either j is in both I and I' or it is in neither. Thus, by contradiction, the path from w_{i-1} to v_{n+1} must have a total cost strictly greater than $T - K_{i-1}$. As all edge costs are integers this implies that the path should have a cost of at least $T - K_{i-1} + 1$. As a result the perceived cost of completing this path by going from v_{n+1} to t would is at least $2T - K_{i-1} + 1$. On the other hand the perceived cost of going from v_{i-1} to v_i is

$$b \cdot \frac{1}{2b} + 2T - K_{i-1} - \frac{1}{2b} < \frac{1}{2} + 2T - K_{i-1} < 2T - K_{i-1} + 1$$

This is because by induction, if the agent begins on the path from v_{i-1} to v_i, it will follow P from v_i to t, meaning the total remaining cost is $2T - K_{i-1} - 1/(2b)$. Furthermore, the agent will not abandon at v_{i-1}, as the perceived cost is less than the reward for $\lambda > 1/2$ and $\varepsilon \leq \frac{1}{2b}$: $b \cdot \frac{1}{2b} + 2T - K_{i-1} - \frac{1}{2b} < \frac{1}{2} + 2T - \frac{1}{2b} < 2T + \lambda - \varepsilon$.

For any vertex between v_i and v_{i+1} along the sequence of edges, we must show that the perceived cost is no more than the perceived reward. Let y be the cost of the edge leading out of some intermediate vertex along this sequence. Since the cost of each edge increases by a factor of two, the incurred cost so far along the sequence of edges is also y. This also means that after following this edge of cost y, the remaining cost is at most $2T - 2y$ (because the agent has already incurred a cost of at least y, and the next edge also has a cost of y). Thus, the perceived cost is no more than $by + (2T - 2y) = \lambda y + 2T$ while the perceived reward is at least $R + \lambda y = 2T + \lambda - \varepsilon + \lambda y$ meaning that the agent does not abandon.

Case 2: $i - 1 \notin I$. As before, we know that any path from v_{i-1} to t must have a total cost of at least $2T - K_{i-1}$. The perceived cost of going to w_{i-1} is $2T - K_{i-1}$. The perceived cost of beginning the sequence of edges from v_{i-1} to v_i is at least $b \cdot \frac{1}{2b} + 2T - (K_{i-1} + \frac{1}{2b}) = (b-1)\frac{1}{2b} + 2T - K_{i-1}$ (assuming $x_{i-1} \geq 1$). Therefore, the perceived cost of following P is smaller than the perceived cost of following the sequence of edges from v_{i-1} to v_i, so the agent chooses to go to w_{i-1}. Furthermore, the agent will not abandon at either v_{i-1} or w_{i-1} because at both vertices, the perceived cost is $2T - K_{i-1} < R$.

Since the claim holds in both cases, the induction holds. Thus, if the agent follows P to v_1, it must continue to follow P until it reaches t without abandoning. However, the only way to reach v_1 from s is along P. Thus, all that remains to be shown is that the agent will not abandon at s. However, this must be the case, as the total cost of the path is $2T$ and the (s, v_1) edge has cost 0, so the perceived cost at s is $2T < R$. □

Claim 2. The subset sum instance has a solution $\Longleftarrow$ there is some path in G that the doubly sophisticated agent will traverse for the given reward.

Proof. Let P be the path that the agent traverses. Since P must pass through v_{n+1}, let K_{n+1} be the sunk cost when the agent reaches v_{n+1}. The total cost of the path is $K_{n+1} + T$, so the perceived cost for the agent at s is $K_{n+1} + T$. In order for the agent to be willing to begin along P, the perceived cost must be no more than the reward, so $K_{n+1} + T \leq 2T + \lambda - \epsilon$. Because K_{n+1} must be an integer this implies that $K_{n+1} \leq T$. When the agent reaches v_{n+1}, in order for it to be willing to take the (v_{n+1}, t) edge the perceived cost at that point must also be no more than the reward, so

$$b \cdot T \leq 2T + \lambda - \epsilon + \lambda K_{n+1}$$

By plugging in $b = 2 + \lambda$ and rearranging we get that $T - 1 + \epsilon/\lambda \leq K_{n+1}$ and because K_{n+1} must be an integer we conclude that $T \leq K_{n+1}$. Since we have both $K_{n+1} \leq T$ and $K_{n+1} \geq T$, $K_{n+1} = T$. Then, we can construct a solution to the subset sum instance by letting $I = \{i \mid P \text{ does not include } w_i\}$. $\sum_{i \in I} x_i = K_{n+1} = T$ because $i \in I$ iff P follows the sequence of edges of total cost x_i from v_i to v_{i+1}, and all other edges in P have cost 0. Thus, I is a solution to the subset sum instance. □

3 DOUBLY NAIVE AGENTS

Consider an agent which has both present bias and sunk cost bias, and is naive about both. We know that a naive present-biased agent might abandon partway through a task. This is still the case for a doubly-naive agent, but in contrast to a naive present-biased agent (whose cost is bounded by R), because the perceived reward keeps increasing the doubly-naive agent can actually incur an arbitrary amount of cost along the way. We first provide a bound on the cost a doubly naive agent incurs and then show this upper bound is almost tight. Note that since the payoff of an optimal agent is at most R the claim also establishes an asymptotic exponential additive gap between the payoff of a doubly naive agent and an optimal agent.

Claim 3. A (b, λ)-doubly naive agent with $b > 1$ and $\lambda > 0$ traversing any graph G on n nodes incurs a cost of at most $O\left(R\left(1 + \frac{\lambda}{b}\right)^n\right)$.

Proof. Consider the path that the doubly naive agent takes through G. Let R_i denote the perceived reward when the agent is at node i and let z_i denote the cost of the edge that the agent takes leaving i. In order for the agent to continue at node i, it must be the case that the perceived cost is no more than R_i, so $bz_i \leq R_i$. Since $R_{i+1} = R_i + \lambda z_i$, it must be that $R_{i+1} \leq R_i(1 + \lambda/b)$. Thus, if R_n is the perceived reward when the agent has reached the target, $R_n \leq R_0(1 + \lambda/b)^n$ where $R_0 = R$. Since $R_n - R_0 = \lambda \sum_{i=1}^{n} z_n$, we have $\sum_{i=1}^{n} z_n \leq R((1 + \lambda/b)^n - 1)/\lambda = O(R(1 + \lambda/b)^n)$. □

Next, we show that the above bound is nearly tight.

Claim 4. There exists a fan type graph on n nodes (Figure 4) in which a doubly naive agent with $b > 1$ and $\lambda > 0$ traversing G incurs cost $\Theta\left(R\left(\frac{b(b+\lambda)}{b^2+\lambda}\right)^n\right)$.

Proof. The full proof can be found in the full version. Consider the instance in Figure 4 with the following definitions:

$$x_i = y_0 \frac{b(b-1)}{b^2+\lambda}\left(\frac{b(b+\lambda)}{b^2+\lambda}\right)^{i-1}; \qquad y_i = y_0\left(\frac{b(b+\lambda)}{b^2+\lambda}\right)^{i}; \qquad R = by_0$$

Note that the costs are increasing exponentially with base $b(b+\lambda)/(b^2+\lambda)$. Because the perceived reward is increasing as the agent traverses the graph, it will be willing to continue along the outer edge of the fan, incurring total cost exponential in the size of the graph. □

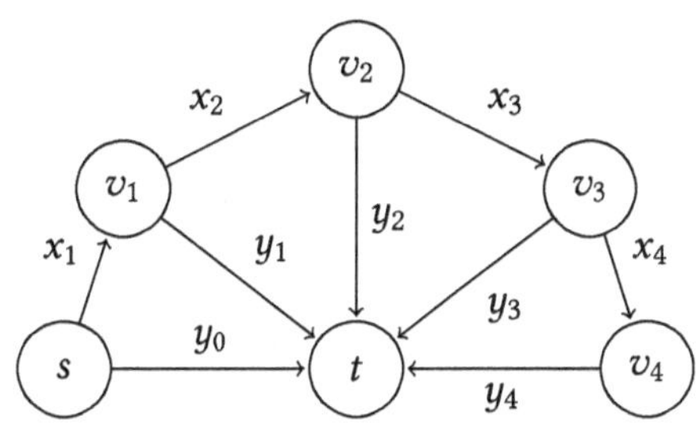

Fig. 4. Graph for which doubly naive agent incurs exponential cost

It is not always the case that a doubly naive agent does worse than a naive present-biased agent. As we will see next, sometimes sunk cost bias may actually help the agent reach the goal and achieve a positive payoff. In the full version, we bound the possible gain due to sunk cost bias and prove the following claim:

Claim 5. The payoff of a doubly naive agent can be greater by $R(1 - \frac{1}{b}))$ than the payoff of a naive present-biased agent. The bound is tight.

4 SINGLY SOPHISTICATED AGENTS

A singly sophisticated agent is an agent who is sophisticated about its present bias but is naive about its sunk cost bias. In contrast to sophisticated present-biased agents, singly sophisticated agents can't plan their whole path ahead of time, as their beliefs about the reward are time-inconsistent. Such an agent, for example, can abandon a task, as demonstrated in Figure 5. In this example a singly sophisticated agent standing at s will plan to follow the path $s \to u \to v \to t$ as it believes that since the reward is only 11, its future self at v will go straight to t instead of taking the $v \to w \to t$ path. However, because of sunk cost bias, once it reaches u its perceived reward is

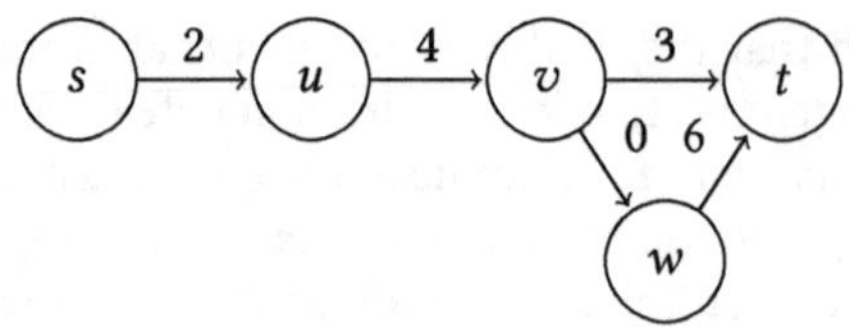

Fig. 5. For $b = 2$ and $R = 11$, a singly sophisticated agent with $\lambda = 1/2$ would abandon.

increased to 12. As a result, it now believes that its future self at v will take the path $v \to w \to t$. When standing at u, the perceived cost of this path is $13 > 12$, and hence the agent abandons.

Next, we bound the loss of a singly sophisticated agent in comparison to an optimal agent. We will later show that this bound is close to tight by putting together many instances similar to the one in Figure 5 to amplify the sunk cost of a singly sophisticated agent.

Claim 6. The additive gap between the payoffs of an optimal agent and a singly sophisticated agent is at most $\frac{(1+\lambda)^k-1}{\lambda}R + R$.

Proof. Recall that a singly sophisticated agent can plan to take one path and then change its plan. Denote the nodes in which the agent decides to change the path it takes by $v_1, \ldots, v_k$ and let $s = v_0$. Denote the cost accumulated between v_{i-1} and v_i by c_{i-1}. Note that between every two adjacent change points v_{i-1} and v_i the agent behaves the same as a present-biased sophisticated agent with no sunk cost bias, and hence its cost is less than the perceived reward at node v_i, which we denote by R_i. Thus we have that $c_i \leq R_i$ and $R_i = R_{i-1} + \lambda c_{i-1}$. Putting this together we get that $R_i \leq (1+\lambda)R_{i-1}$ which implies that $R_i \leq (1+\lambda)^i \cdot R$. Hence,

$$\sum_{j=1}^{k} c_j \leq \sum_{j=1}^{k} (1+\lambda)^{j-1} \cdot R = \frac{(1+\lambda)^k - 1}{\lambda} \cdot R$$

This concludes the claim as the payoff of an optimal agent is at most R. □

In the next claim we show that this gap is essentially tight:

Claim 7. The additive gap between a singly sophisticated agent with $b > 2$ and $\lambda > 0$ and an optimal agent can be as high as $\frac{(1+\alpha\cdot\lambda)^n-1}{\lambda}R + R(1-\alpha-\frac{1}{b})$ where $\alpha = \min\{\frac{1}{2b\lambda}, \frac{b-1}{b^2+2\lambda}\}$.

Proof. Consider the instance in Figure 6. For simplicity, we define the different costs as a function of the perceived rewards, where as before R_i is the perceived reward at node v_i:

$$x_i = \alpha \cdot R_{i-1}; \qquad z_i = \frac{R_{i-1}}{b^2} + \varepsilon; \qquad y_i = \frac{R_i}{b} - \frac{R_{i-1}}{b^2}; \qquad R_0 = R$$

In the full version we show that a singly sophisticated agent will take the path $v_1 \to v_2 \to \ldots \to v_n$ and then abandon at v_n. In particular at every node v_{i-1} (for this purpose $s = v_0$) the agent plans to follow the path $v_{i-1} \to v_i \to u_i \to t_i \to t$. Once it reaches v_i since the perceived reward has increased, the path $v_i \to u_i \to t_i \to t$ is no longer an option and the only path it can take to get to t_i is $v_i \to u_i \to w_i \to t_i \to t$. As the latter path has a perceived cost greater than the perceived reward, the agent plans to follow the path $v_i \to v_{i+1} \to u_{i+1} \to t_{i+1} \to t$ instead.

To compute the total cost the agent incurred, recall that $R_i = R_{i-1} + \lambda\alpha R_{i-1}$ this implies that $(1+\alpha\lambda)^i \cdot R$. Note that

$$\sum_{i=1}^{n} x_i = \frac{R_n - R}{\lambda} = \frac{(1+\alpha\lambda)^n - 1}{\lambda} \cdot R$$

Lastly, observe that an optimal agent will take the path $s \to v_1 \to u_1 \to t_1 \to t$ for a payoff of $R(1 - \alpha - \frac{1}{b})$. □

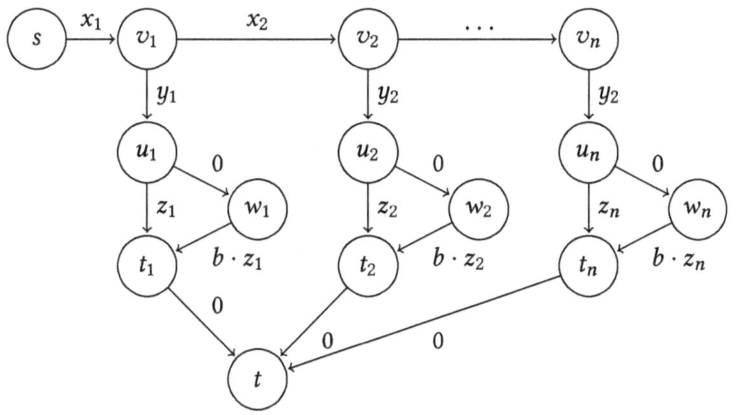

Fig. 6. A graph in which a singly sophisticated agent incurs an exponential cost

To understand the role naivety regarding sunk cost plays in agents that are sophisticated about their present bias we now compare between the payoff of singly sophisticated agents and doubly sophisticated agents. By Proposition 2.3 we have that the payoff of a doubly sophisticated agent is at most an additive amount of $(b - 1)C_o$ from the payoff of an optimal agent. Hence by Claim 6 we have that a singly sophisticated can do worse than a doubly sophisticated agent by an exponential additive factor. However, in some cases being naive about its sunk cost can actually help the agent avoid taking a more costly path or reach the target. As the payoff of a doubly sophisticated agent is at most an additive factor of $(b - 1)C_o$ of from the payoff of an optimal agent, even in cases in which a singly sophisticated agent surpasses a doubly sophisticated one, the payoff of the singly sophisticated agent is greater by at most $(b - 1)C_o$. In the full version we provide an example demonstrating this is tight. This proves the following claim:

Claim 8. The payoff of a singly sophisticated agent can be better than the payoff of a doubly sophisticated agent by an additive amount of $(b - 1)C_o$.

5 CONCLUSION

We have studied the interaction between two behavioral biases that both play an important role in planning contexts: present bias and sunk-cost bias. We find that in conjunction, they give rise to natural behavioral phenomena that cannot be seen with either in isolation. Through these biases, we also gain new insights about subtleties in the behavior of naive and sophisticated agents. We show that sophistication about these two biases makes path-planning computationally hard, though we are still able to provide performance bounds for agents with different forms of sophistication.

This work leads to several open questions. While we showed that path-planning for doubly sophisticated agents is NP-hard, we do not know whether or not the problem is in NP. Moreover, in the case where the reward R exceeds b times the optimal cost — which implies that a feasible path for the doubly sophisticated agent is guaranteed to exist — is it possible to find such a path efficiently? We also showed that there exist instances in which singly sophisticated agents incur exponentially large cost; is there a structural characterization (e.g. a graph minor result) for the graphs on which singly sophisticated agents incur exponential cost, in the style of [13]? More broadly, the rich interplay between these two biases demonstrates how considering multiple behavioral biases together can yield a wider set of natural phenomena. With this in mind, we believe there are many further opportunities to enhance theoretical models of behavior through the analysis of agents with multiple biases.

REFERENCES

[1] George A. Akerlof. 1991. Procrastination and Obedience. *American Economic Review: Papers and Proceedings* 81, 2 (May 1991), 1–19.

[2] Susanne Albers and Dennis Kraft. 2016. Motivating Time-Inconsistent Agents: A Computational Approach. In *Web and Internet Economics - 12th International Conference, WINE 2016, Montreal, Canada, December 11-14, 2016, Proceedings.* 309–323. DOI: http://dx.doi.org/10.1007/978-3-662-54110-4_22

[3] Dan Ariely. 2008. *Predictably irrational.* HarperCollins New York.

[4] Hal R Arkes and Catherine Blumer. 1985. The psychology of sunk cost. *Organizational behavior and human decision processes* 35, 1 (1985), 124–140.

[5] Nicholas Barberis and Wei Xiong. 2012. Realization Utility. *Journal of Financial Economics* 104 (2012), 251–271.

[6] Richard Dawkins. 1976. The selfish gene. *Oxford university Press* 1 (1976), 976.

[7] Stefano DellaVigna. 2009. Psychology and Economics: Evidence from the Field. *Journal of Economic Literature* 47, 2 (2009), 315–372.

[8] Stefano DellaVigna and Ulrike Malmendier. 2006. Paying not to go to the gym. *The American Economic Review* (2006), 694–719.

[9] Shane Frederick, George Loewenstein, and Ted O'Donoghue. 2002. Time Discounting and Time Preference. *Journal of Economic Literature* 40, 2 (June 2002), 351–401.

[10] Nick Gravin, Nicole Immorlica, Brendan Lucier, and Emmanouil Pountourakis. 2016. Procrastination with Variable Present Bias. In *Proceedings of the 2016 ACM Conference on Economics and Computation, EC '16, Maastricht, The Netherlands, July 24-28, 2016.* 361. DOI: http://dx.doi.org/10.1145/2940716.2940774

[11] Daniel Kahneman. 2013. *Thinking Fast and Slow.* Farrar, Straus and Giroux.

[12] Daniel Kahneman and Amos Tversky. 1979. Prospect Theory: An Analysis of Decision Under Risk. *Econometrica* 47, 2 (1979), 263–292.

[13] Jon M. Kleinberg and Sigal Oren. 2014. Time-inconsistent planning: a computational problem in behavioral economics. In *ACM Conference on Economics and Computation, EC '14, Stanford , CA, USA, June 8-12, 2014.* 547–564. DOI: http://dx.doi.org/10.1145/2600057.2602890

[14] Jon M. Kleinberg, Sigal Oren, and Manish Raghavan. 2016. Planning Problems for Sophisticated Agents with Present Bias. In *Proceedings of the 2016 ACM Conference on Economics and Computation, EC '16, Maastricht, The Netherlands, July 24-28, 2016.* 343–360. DOI: http://dx.doi.org/10.1145/2940716.2940764

[15] David Laibson. 1997. Golden eggs and hyperbolic discounting. *Quarterly Journal of Economics* 112, 2 (1997), 443–478.

[16] R. A. Pollak. 1968. Consistent Planning. *Review of Economic Studies* 35, 2 (1968).

[17] Matthew Rabin. 2002. Inference by Believers in the Law of Small Numbers. *Quarterly Journal of Economics* 117, 3 (2002), 775–816.

[18] Barry M Staw. 1976. Knee-deep in the big muddy: A study of escalating commitment to a chosen course of action. *Organizational behavior and human performance* 16, 1 (1976), 27–44.

[19] R. H. Strotz. 1955. Myopia and inconsistency in dynamic utility maximization. *Review of Economic Studies* 23, 3 (1955), 165–180.

[20] Pingzhong Tang, Yifeng Teng, Zihe Wang, Shenke Xiao, and Yichong Xu. 2017. Computational Issues in Time-Inconsistent Planning. In *AAAI Conference on Artificial Intelligence.*

[21] Richard H. Thaler. 1980. Toward a Positive Theory of Consumer Choice. *Journal of Economic Behavior and Organization* 1 (1980), 39–60.

[22] Richard H. Thaler. 1999. Mental Accounting Matters. *Journal of Behavioral Decision Making* 12 (1999), 183–206.

[23] Richard H Thaler. 2015. *Misbehaving: The making of behavioral economics.* WW Norton & Company.

[24] Amos Tversky and Daniel Kahneman. 1971. The Belief in the Law of Small Numbers. *Psychological Bulletin* 2 (1971), 105–110.

[25] Patrick J Weatherhead. 1979. Do savannah sparrows commit the Concorde fallacy? *Behavioral Ecology and Sociobiology* 5, 4 (1979), 373–381.

Multidimensional Binary Search for Contextual Decision-Making

ILAN LOBEL, NYU Stern
RENATO PAES LEME, Google Research
ADRIAN VLADU, MIT Math

We consider a multidimensional search problem that is motivated by questions in contextual decision-making, such as dynamic pricing and personalized medicine. Nature selects a state from a d-dimensional unit ball and then generates a sequence of d-dimensional directions. We are given access to the directions, but not access to the state. After receiving a direction, we have to guess the value of the dot product between the state and the direction. Our goal is to minimize the number of times when our guess is more than ϵ away from the true answer. We construct a polynomial time algorithm that we call Projected Volume achieving regret $O(d \log(d/\epsilon))$, which is optimal up to a $\log d$ factor. The algorithm combines a volume cutting strategy with a new geometric technique that we call cylindrification.

Additional Key Words and Phrases: Online Learning; Online Pricing; Contextual Learning

A full version of this paper is available at https://arxiv.org/abs/1611.00829.

Adrian Vladu was partially supported by NSF grants CCF-1111109 and CCF-1553428.

EC'17, June 26–30, 2017, Cambridge, MA, USA.

 ACM ISBN 978-1-4503-4527-9/17/06
http://dx.doi.org/10.1145/3033274.3085100

Bifurcation Mechanism Design – From Optimal Flat Taxes to Improved Cancer Treatments

GER YANG, University of Texas at Austin
GEORGIOS PILIOURAS, Singapore University of Technology and Design
DAVID BASANTA, H. Lee Moffitt Cancer Center and Research Institute

Small changes to the parameters of a system can lead to abrupt qualitative changes of its behavior, a phenomenon known as bifurcation. Such instabilities are typically considered problematic, however, we show that their power can be leveraged to design novel types of mechanisms. *Hysteresis mechanisms* use transient changes of system parameters to induce a permanent improvement to its performance via optimal equilibrium selection. *Optimal control mechanisms* induce convergence to states whose performance is better than even the best equilibrium. We apply these mechanisms in two different settings that illustrate the versatility of bifurcation mechanism design. In the first one we explore how introducing flat taxation can improve social welfare, despite decreasing agent "rationality", by destabilizing inefficient equilibria. From there we move on to consider a well known game of tumor metabolism and use our approach to derive novel cancer treatment strategies.

CCS Concepts: • **Theory of computation → Quality of equilibria; Convergence and learning in games**;

Additional Key Words and Phrases: preference and decision theory; price of anarchy; bifurcation; quantal response equilibrium; game theory; taxation

Link to the full version: https://arxiv.org/abs/1704.08754
Georgios Piliouras would like to acknowledge SUTD grant SRG ESD 2015 097 and MOE AcRF Tier 2 Grant 2016-T2-1-170. Part of the work was completed while Ger Yang and Georgios Piliouras were visiting scientists at the Simons Institute for the Theory of Computing.
Author's addresses: Ger Yang, Department of Electrical and Computer Engineering, University of Texas at Austin, email: geryang@utexas.edu; Georgios Piliouras, Engineering Systems and Design (ESD), Singapore University of Technology and Design, email: georgios.piliouras@gmail.com; David Basanta, Integrated Mathematical Oncology, H. Lee Moffitt Cancer Center and Research Institute, email: david.Basanta@moffitt.org .

EC'17, June 26–30, 2017, Cambridge, MA, USA. ACM ISBN 978-1-4503-4527-9/17/06.
https://doi.org/http://dx.doi.org/10.1145/3033274.3085144

Approximating Gains from Trade in Two-sided Markets via Simple Mechanisms

JOHANNES BRUSTLE, McGill University
YANG CAI, McGill University
FA WU, McGill University and Zhejiang University
MINGFEI ZHAO, McGill University

We design simple mechanisms to approximate the Gains from Trade (GFT) in two-sided markets with multiple unit-supply sellers and multiple unit-demand buyers. A classical impossibility result by Myerson and Satterthwaite [2] showed that even with only one seller and one buyer, no Bayesian Incentive Compatible (BIC), Individually Rational (IR), and Budget-Balanced (BB) mechanism can achieve full GFT (trade whenever buyer's value is higher than the seller's cost). The same paper also proposed the "second-best" mechanism that maximizes the GFT subject to BIC, IR, and BB constraints, which is unfortunately rather complex for even the single-seller single-buyer case. Our mechanism is simple, BIC, IR, and BB and achieves 1/2 of the optimal GFT among all BIC, IR, and BB mechanisms. The result holds for arbitrary distributions of the buyers' and sellers' values and can accommodate any downward-closed feasibility constraints over the allocations. The analysis of our mechanism is facilitated by extending the Cai-Weinberg-Devanur duality framework [1] to two-sided markets.

CCS Concepts: •**Theory of computation → Algorithmic game theory and mechanism design; Algorithmic mechanism design;**

Additional Key Words and Phrases: Bilateral Trading; Double Auction; Two-sided Market; Simple Mechanism; Gains from Trade; Duality

We study the problem of maximizing the Gains from Trade (GFT) in two-sided markets. Unlike one-sided markets, such as auctions, the items are owned by a group of selfish agents known as sellers who form one side of the market, and the other side of the market – the buyers wish to purchase the items from the sellers. Sellers and buyers both have values for the items. Both sides are assumed to act strategically to maximize their utilities. Usually, the two-sided market is studied in the Bayesian model, where we assume that both the buyers' and sellers' values are drawn from some known distributions. The goal is to design a mechanism to facilitate trade between the two groups and optimize the expected GFT, which is the difference between the social welfare achieved by the mechanism and the sum of the sellers' values.

The simplest two-sided market is usually referred to as the bilateral trading, in which there is a single seller who owns an item and a single buyer who wants to purchase the item. Both the buyer and the seller have quasi-linear utility functions, and the buyer's value for the item b and the seller's value s are drawn independently from two known distributions D^B and D^S.

A full version of this paper is available at http://cs.mcgill.ca/~cai/ec17.pdf.

Authors' email addresses: Johannes Brustle: johannes.brustle@mail.mcgill.ca; Yang Cai: cai@cs.mcgill.ca; Fa Wu: wufa85@zju.edu.cn; Mingfei Zhao: mingfei.zhao@mail.mcgill.ca.

EC'17, June 26–30, 2017, Cambridge, MA, USA.

ACM ISBN 978-1-4503-4527-9/17/06
http://dx.doi.org/10.1145/3033274.3085148

A classical impossibility result [2] states that even in bilateral trading there is no Bayesian Incentive Compatible (BIC), Individual Rational (IR), and Budget Balance (BB) (if the mechanism does not gain or lose any money from the market) mechanism that achieves full GFT. They also provided a mechanism that maximizes the GFT among all BIC, IR, and BB mechanisms. However, such a "second-best" mechanism has extremely complex allocation and price rules determined by solving a system of differential equations that depend on the buyer's and seller's distributions. It is difficult to imagine how to implement it in practice.

Our Results and Contributions: In this paper, we provide simple mechanisms to approximate the optimal GFT obtainable by any BIC, IR, and BB mechanisms. Prior work has either focused on approximating a different objective – the social welfare or has made assumptions on the value distributions of the agents. Here we list the three major contributions of our paper.

(1) We provide a simple BIC, IR, and BB mechanism that achieves at least 1/2 of the optimal GFT in bilateral trading for *arbitrary seller and buyer value distributions.*

(2) We extend the 2-approximation to the *double auction* setting with *arbitrary downward-closed feasibility constraints* and *arbitrary value distributions for the sellers and buyers.*

(3) We demonstrate the applicability of the Cai-Devanur-Weinberg duality framework for two-sided markets. Although our results only concern single-dimensional settings, our duality based upper bound applies to multi-dimensional settings as well.

In particular, for the bilateral trading setting, we consider the following two simple BIC, IR, BB mechanisms and show that the better of the two achieves 1/2 of the optimal GFT.

Seller-Offering Mechanism(SOM): The seller offers a price for the item to the buyer. The buyer receives the item if she pays the offered price to the seller. Otherwise, the seller keeps the item and no payment is transferred. The seller chooses the price that maximizes her expected utility depending on her true value s and the distribution of the buyer's value D^B.

Buyer-Offering Mechanism(BOM): The buyer offers a price for the item to the seller. If the seller accepts the offered price, the buyer receives the item and pays the seller the offered price. Otherwise, the seller keeps the item and no payment is transferred. The buyer chooses the price that maximizes her expected utility depending on her true value b and the distribution of the seller's value D^S.

Our result can be generalized to a broader setting known as the *double auction*, in which there is a single type of item on the market. Each buyer wants a single copy of the item and each seller owns a single copy of it. Assume buyers' and sellers' values are all drawn independently from possibly different distributions. Moreover, we allow any downward-closed feasibility constraint on which buyer-seller pairs can trade. We show that for any double auction with arbitrary downward-closed feasibility constraint, the better of two simple BIC, IR, BB mechanisms, which are natural generalizations of SOM and BOM, achieves 1/2 of the optimal GFT.

Our Techniques: Our result is facilitated by applying the Cai-Devanur-Weinberg duality framework to two-sided markets. We first characterize the set of dual variables that has finite dual objective values as flows. By choosing a specific set of dual variables, we derive an upper bound for the optimal GFT achievable by any BIC, IR, and BB mechanism. Interestingly, the upper bound has a natural format and suggests the allocation rule of our simple mechanisms.

REFERENCES

[1] Yang Cai, Nikhil R. Devanur, and S. Matthew Weinberg. 2016. A Duality Based Unified Approach to Bayesian Mechanism Design. In *the 48th Annual ACM Symposium on Theory of Computing (STOC).*

[2] Roger B Myerson and Mark A Satterthwaite. 1983. Efficient mechanisms for bilateral trading. *Journal of economic theory* 29, 2 (1983), 265–281.

Approximately Efficient Two-Sided Combinatorial Auctions

RICCARDO COLINI-BALDESCHI, Dipartimento di Economia e Finanza, LUISS
PAUL W. GOLDBERG, University of Oxford
BART DE KEIJZER, Centrum Wiskunde & Informatica (CWI)
STEFANO LEONARDI, Sapienza, University of Rome
TIM ROUGHGARDEN, Stanford University
STEFANO TURCHETTA, KPMG Italy and University of Oxford

We develop and extend a line of recent work on the design of mechanisms for two-sided markets. The markets we consider consist of buyers and sellers of a number of items, and the aim of a mechanism is to improve the social welfare by arranging purchases and sales of the items. A mechanism is given prior distributions on the agents' valuations of the items, but not the actual valuations; thus the aim is to maximise the expected social welfare over these distributions. As in previous work, we are interested in the worst-case ratio between the social welfare achieved by a truthful mechanism, and the best social welfare possible.

Our main result is an incentive compatible and budget balanced constant-factor approximation mechanism in a setting where buyers have XOS valuations and sellers' valuations are additive. This is the first such approximation mechanism for a two-sided market setting where the agents have combinatorial valuation functions. To achieve this result, we introduce a more general kind of demand query that seems to be needed in this situation. In the simpler case that sellers have unit supply (each having just one item to sell), we give a new mechanism whose welfare guarantee improves on a recent one in the literature. We also introduce a more demanding version of the *strong budget balance* (SBB) criterion, aimed at ruling out certain "unnatural" transactions satisfied by SBB. We show that the stronger version is satisfied by our mechanisms.

Additional Key Words and Phrases: Auctions; mechanism design; market intermediation; two-sided markets; pricing; approximation algorithms

1 INTRODUCTION

One-sided markets have been studied in economics for several decades and more recently in computer science. Mechanism design in one-sided markets aims to find an efficient (high-welfare) allocation of a set of items to a set of agents, while ensuring that truthfully reporting the input data is the best strategy for the agents. The cornerstone method in mechanism design is the Vickrey-Clarke-Groves (VCG) mechanism [4, 13, 23] that optimises the social welfare while providing the right incentives for truth-telling: VCG mechanisms are *dominant strategy incentive compatible (DSIC)*, and in many mechanism design settings VCG is also *individually rational (IR)*. The IR requirement demands that participating in the mechanism is not harmful to any agent. The DSIC requrement demands that truthfully reporting one's preferences to the mechanism is a dominant strategy for each agent, independently of what the other agents report.

Recently, increased attention has turned to the problems that arise in two-sided markets, in which the set of agents is partitioned into *buyers* and *sellers*. In contrast with the one-sided setting (where one could say that the mechanism itself initially holds the items), in the two-sided setting the items

EC17, June 26–30, 2017, Cambridge, MA, USA. Copyright 2017 ACM ISBN 978-1-4503-4527-9/17/06...$15.00
DOI: http://dx.doi.org/10.1145/3033274.3085128

are initially held by the sellers, who have valuations over the items they hold, and who are assumed to act rationally and strategically. The mechanism's task is now to decide which buyers and sellers should trade, and at which prices. The growing interest in two-sided markets can be attributed to various important applications. Relevant examples are selling display-ads on ad exchange platforms, the US FCC spectrum license reallocation, and stock exchanges. Two-sided markets are usually studied in a Bayesian setting: there is public knowledge of probability distributions, one for each buyer and one for each seller, from which the valuations of the buyers and sellers are drawn.

In two-sided markets, a further important requirement is *strong budget balance (SBB)*, which states that monetary transfers happen only among the agents in the market, i.e., the buyers and sellers are allowed to trade without leaving to the mechanism any share of the payments, and without the mechanism adding money to the market. A weaker version of SBB often considered in the literature is *weak budget balance (WBB)*, which only requires the mechanism not to inject money into the market. However, it is known from the work of Myerson and Satterthwaite [17] that it is generally impossible for an IR, BIC, and WBB mechanism to maximise social welfare in such a market, even in the *bilateral trade* setting, i.e., when there is just one seller and one buyer.[1]

The practical contexts noted above need the application of two-sided market mechanisms that can work in a *combinatorial* setting, i.e., where there are multiple distinct items in the market and agents having possibly complex valuations over the subsets of items that they may receive. However, we are not aware of any such mechanism that approximates the social welfare while meeting the IR, DSIC and SBB requirements. The purpose of this paper is to provide mechanisms that satisfy these requirements and achieve an $O(1)$-approximation to the social welfare for a broad class of agents' valuation functions. We do, in fact, design mechanisms that work under the assumption of the valuations being *fractionally subadditive (XOS)*, a generalisation of submodular functions that are contained in the class of subadditive functions.

Our results extend and improve on previous work which targeted an important special case of a two-sided market: each seller holds a single item, items are identical, and each agent is only interested in holding a single item. In this setting, the valuations of the agents are thus given by a single number, representing the agent's utility for holding an item. A mechanism for this setting is known in the literature as a *double auction*. The goal of several works on double auctions [15, 20, 21] has been that of trading off the achievable social welfare with the strength of the incentive compatibility and budget balance constraints. In our present work, we investigate this question for the much more general class of combinatorial two-sided markets.

1.1 The Model

As stated above, the set of agents is partitioned into a set of *sellers*, each of which is initially endowed with a set of heterogeneous items, and a set of *buyers*, having no items initially. Buyers have money that can be used to pay for items. Every agent has its own, private valuation function, which maps subsets of the items to numbers, and agents are assumed to optimise their (quasi-linear) utility, which is given by the valuation of the set of items that the mechanism allocates to an agent, minus the payment that the mechanism collects from the agent. A seller will typically receive money (instead of pay money), which we treat as a negative payment.

For each agent we are given a (publicly known) probability distribution over a set of valuation functions, from which we assume her valuation function is drawn. The mechanism and the other

[1]The VCG mechanism can also be applied to two-sided markets; however, in this setting, VCG is either not IR or it does not satisfy WBB.

agents have no knowledge of the actual valuation function of the i-th agent, but only of her probability distribution. The general aim of the mechanism is to reallocate the items so as to maximise the expected social welfare (the sum of the agents' valuations of the resulting allocation).

Let OPT be the expected social welfare of an optimal allocation of the items. Note that this is a well-defined quantity, even though computing an optimal allocation may be computationally hard, and even though there might not exist an appropriate mechanism (satisfying IR, SBB, and DSIC), that is guaranteed to always output an optimal allocation.

We are interested in mechanisms that satisfy IR, SBB, and DSIC (or failing that, the weaker notion of *Bayesian incentive compatibility (BIC)*), and that reallocate the items in such a way that the expected social welfare is within some constant fraction of OPT, where expectation is taken over the given probability distributions of the agents' valuations, and over the randomness of the allocation that the mechanism outputs. In contrast with one-sided combinatorial auction design (where the main challenge is polynomial-time implementability), for the two-sided case our primary goal is to design (and thus show the existence of) IR, SBB, and DSIC/BIC mechanisms that $O(1)$-approximate OPT. Such mechanisms circumvent the aformentioned impossibility result of Myerson and Satterthwaite [17] by weakening the requirement of optimal social welfare to that of *approximately* optimal social welfare (while nonetheless strengthening the WBB contraint into SBB).

1.2 Our Results and their Significance

The present paper starts off by showing that there is a straightforward technical trick that one may apply to turn any WBB mechanism into an SBB one, with a small loss in the approximation factor. Technically, one could e.g. apply it to the WBB mechanism of Blumrosen and Dobzinski [1] for combinatorial exchange markets; however, the trick is unsatisfactory in practice as it essentially consists of giving the leftover money to a random agent. This demonstrates a weakness in the current definition of SBB, which motivates the introduction of a strengthened version, that we call *direct-trade strong budget balance (DSBB)*.

Our goal is the design of individually rational, incentive compatible, and direct-trade strongly budget balanced mechanisms for combinatorial two-sided markets, that achieve a constant approximation to the optimal social welfare. We present two mechanisms adhering to these constraints for general families of combinatorial two-sided markets, as summarized in the table below.

Mechanism	Buyers' valuations	Sellers' valuations	Approximation ratio	IR	IC	BB
$\mathbb{M}_{\text{1-supply}}$	XOS	unit-supply	6	ex-post IR	DSIC	DSBB
$\mathbb{M}_{\text{add}}$	XOS	additive	6	interim IR	BIC	DSBB
$\mathbb{M}_{\text{add}}$	additive	additive	6	ex-post IR	DSIC	DSBB

Table 1. Summary of our results.

Our $\mathbb{M}_{\text{1-supply}}$ mechanism handles the setting where all sellers have a single item for sale, and buyers have *fractionally subadditive* (XOS) valuation functions over the set of items in the market. Our $\mathbb{M}_{\text{add}}$ mechanism can handle the more general case where sellers have multiple items for sale and have additive valuation functions over the items they possess, though $\mathbb{M}_{\text{add}}$ satisfies weaker IC and IR notions than $\mathbb{M}_{\text{1-supply}}$. More precisely, $\mathbb{M}_{\text{add}}$ is DSIC and IR on the sellers' side and BIC and interim-IR on the buyers' side. However, for the special case where buyers have additive valuation functions, $\mathbb{M}_{add}$ does satisfy the stronger IC and IR notions for both buyers and sellers. In all three cases, DSBB is satisfied (a strengthened variant of SBB), and our mechanisms achieve an $O(1)$-approximation to the optimal social welfare.

To our knowledge, these are the first mechanisms for combinatorial two-sided markets that simultaneously are IC, (D)SBB, IR, and approximate the optimal social welfare to within a constant factor. Notice that with non-unit-supply sellers, a constant approximation was not previously known even in the context of WBB or standard SBB.[2] Furthermore, we note that our mechanisms not only work for a more general setting than that of [5], but also improve the approximation ratio for double auctions from 16 to 6.

In the case of $\mathbb{M}_{add}$, buyers are required to answer a generalised type of demand query, in which the mechanism gives prices for the items, and asks a buyer which bundle she would like *if, for each item in that bundle, she were to receive it with probability* $1/2$. Our usage of these queries could be criticised for imposing an excessive cognitive burden on the agents. Although we are not concerned here with that issue (we model agents as computationally unbounded as well as rational), our apparent need for such queries highlights the general question of how agents' computational limitations affect what outcomes can be achieved.[3]

1.3 Overview of the Techniques

The main challenge in two-sided market design is to find prices that stimulate truthful behavior and are suitable for both buyers and sellers, which have contrasting interests. In fact, even in the simplest imaginable setting – the bilateral trade – it is impossible to design a socially efficient mechanism satisfying IR, BIC and WBB [17].

A first feature all our mechanisms share to guarantee DSBB is being a generalised version of two-sided *sequential posted price mechanisms (SPMs)* [5] for double auctions to combinatorial two-sided markets. These mechanisms assign fixed, pre-computed prices to each item so that these prices are the only ones for which the items can be traded. This yields a sequence of bilateral trades in which the amount paid by the buyer equals the amount received by the seller.

While one-sided SPMs provide IR and IC for free, two-sided SPMs require additional conditions to be met. In combinatorial two-sided markets, if prices are fixed for every single item, it cannot be guaranteed that a bundle of items chosen by a buyer will surely be allocated to her, in case at that point the corresponding seller has not been queried yet about her willingness to sell the item. Symmetrically, when a seller would communicate to an SPM mechanism which bundle of items she is willing to sell given the proposed item prices, then the mechanism cannot guarantee to the seller that this bundle will surely be traded in case it has not yet queried the buyers which item sets they demand. The situation is further complicated by the fact that there may exist strong interdependencies among items within an agent's valuation function, which implies that the choice of bundle that a buyer requests (or that a seller makes available) depends strongly on the set of items that the sellers are prepared to sell (or that the buyers request). Therefore, a mechanism designer needs to be careful in proposing prices that are suitable for both sides of the market, and needs to be particularly careful in selecting the side of the market to process first. The choice that the mechanism made here can depend crucially on the types of valuation functions of the agents. Indeed, one main difference between our two mechanisms is the order in which we process each side of the market. Anyway all the mechanisms proposed in this paper are oblivious to the order in which sellers and buyers are presented.

[2]The mechanism proposed in [1] achieves a constant approximation to the optimal social welfare if the size of the initial endowment of each agent is bounded by a constant; otherwise the approximation factor is of logarithmic order.

[3]This question also applies to standard demand queries [10], which may be computationally hard to answer or may involve a high communication complexity, depending on the computational model used and on the way in which the valuation functions are represented.

To additionally achieve a mechanism that results in a high social welfare, we exclude some items from trade and introduce randomness into the mechanism. The main idea is to suppose that all the items are available to the set of buyers as in a one-sided auction, and to compute the *expected marginal contribution of an item to the social welfare* [11] under this assumption. Then, the mechanism compares this contribution to the seller's value for the item: if the seller's value is much higher, then we exclude the item from trade and leave it with the seller. Thus, the mechanism only trades items that are of relatively high expected value to the buyers' side of the market.

To estimate the expected marginal contribution of an item to the social welfare, $\mathbb{M}_{\text{1-supply}}$ and $\mathbb{M}_{\text{add}}$ make use of an algorithm $\mathbb{A}$ that, given a buyers' valuation profile and a set of items, allocates the items to the buyers, without considering the sellers and their valuations. If one is not interested in achieving a low runtime, one can take $\mathbb{A}$ to be an exact algorithm that outputs an optimal allocation. Alternatively, by using a technique of Feldman et al. [11], one may take for $\mathbb{A}$ a polynomial time approximation algorithm and combine this with sampling a sufficiently number of valuation profiles from the distribution, in order to estimate the expected marginal contribution of an item to the social welfare accurately in polynomial time. This yields polynomial-time implementable approximation mechanisms. In particular, in case $\mathbb{A}$ is a polynomial time α-approximation algorithm, it will run within time $POLY(1/\epsilon, n, m)$, and approximate the optimal social welfare within an $O(\alpha)$ multiplicative factor and an ϵ additive term, where ϵ is a parameter that results from the sampling procedure. This technique is described in further detail in [11] and works for distributions with bounded support.

Randomness is added to make sure every seller independently sells her bundle of items with a fixed probability of 1/2; which is used to bound the social welfare loss on both sides of the market by no more than a constant factor.

1.4 Related Work

Due to the impossibility result of Myerson and Satterthwaite [17], no two-sided mechanism can simultaneously achieve optimal social welfare and satisfy the BIC, IR, WBB constraints, even in the simple bilateral trade setting. Follow-up work thus had to focus on designing mechanisms that trade off among these properties.

The following papers of the Economics literature studied the convergence rate to the optimal social welfare as a function of the number of agents when all sellers' and buyers' valuations are independently respectively drawn from identical regular distributions, while satisfying IR and WBB. Gresik and Satterthwaite [12] showed that duplicating the number of agents by τ results in a market where the optimal IR, IC, WBB mechanism's expected social welfare approximation factor approaches 1 at a rate of $O(\log \tau/\tau^2)$. Rustichini et al. [18] and Satterthwaite and Williams [21] investigated a family of non-IC double auctions, and study the inefficiency and the extent to which agents misreport their valuations in these double auctions. We remark that these results only hold for unit-demand buyers and unit-supply sellers, identical valuation distributions, and the hidden constants in these asymptotic results depend on the specific valuation distributions. In contrast, our interest is in finding *universal* constant approximation guarantees for combinatorial settings and not necessarily identical distributions.

In McAfee [15], an IC, WBB, IR double auction is proposed that extracts at least a $(1 - 1/\ell)$ fraction of the maximum social welfare, where ℓ is the number of traders in the optimal solution.

Optimal revenue-maximising Bayesian auctions were characterized in Myerson [16], which provides an elegant tool applicable to single-parameter, one-sided auctions. Various subsequent articles dealt with extending these results. Related to our work is the work of Deng et al. [6], which studied maximising the auctioneer's revenue in Bayesian double auctions. The same objective was studied by Deshmukh et al. [7] yet in the *prior-free* model. In [22], mechanisms for some special cases of two-sided markets are presented that work by a combination of random sampling and random serial dictatorship. The mechanism is IR, SBB and DSIC and its *gain from trade* approaches the optimum when the market is sufficiently large. Mechanisms that are IC, IR, and SBB have been given for bilateral trade in [1]. In addition to this, the authors proposed a WBB mechanism for a general class of combinatorial exchange markets. We will use this result to construct our initial mechanism.

Sequential posted price mechanisms (SPMs) in one-sided markets have been introduced by Sandholm and Gilpin [19] and have gained attention due to their simplicity, robustness to collusion, and their easy implementability in practical applications. One of the first theoretical results concerning SPMs is an asymptotic comparison among three different types of single-parameter mechanisms [2]. They were later studied by Chawla et al. [3] for the objective of revenue maximisation. Additionally, Kleinberg and Weinberg [14] and Dütting and Kleinberg [8] strengthen these results further. Very relevant to our work is the paper of Feldman et al. [11], showing that sequential posted price mechanisms can approximate social welfare up to a constant factor of 1/2 for XOS valuation functions if the published price for an item is equal to the expected additive contribution of the item to the social welfare.

A line of recent work addressed the problem of approximating social welfare in double auctions and related problems under the WBB requirement. Dütting et al. [9] indeed proposed a greedy strategy that combines the one-sided VCG mechanism, independently applied to buyers and to sellers with the trade-reduction mechanism of McAfee [15]. They obtain IR, DSIC, WBB mechanisms with a good approximation of the social welfare, for knapsack, matching and matroid allocation constraints. More recently, Colini-Baldeschi et al. [5] presented the first double auction that satisfies IR, DSIC, and SBB, and approximates the optimal (expected) social welfare up to a constant factor. These results hold for any number of buyers and sellers with arbitrary, independent distributions on valuations. The mechanisms are also extended to the setting where there is an additional matroid constraint on the set of buyers who can purchase an item.

2 PRELIMINARIES

As a general convention, we use boldface notation for vectors and use $[a]$ to denote the set $\{1, \ldots, a\}$. We will use $\mathbb{I}(X)$ to denote the indicator function that maps to 1 if and only if event/fact X holds.

2.1 Markets

A *two-sided market* comprises a set of two distinct types of agents: the *sellers*, who initially hold items for sale, and the *buyers*, who are interested in buying the sellers' items. All agents possess a monotone and normalized valuation function, mapping subsets of items to $\mathbb{R}_{\geq 0}$.[4] Formally, we represent a two-sided market as a tuple $(n, m, k, \boldsymbol{I}, \boldsymbol{G}, \boldsymbol{F})$, where $[n]$ denotes the set of buyers, $[m]$ denotes the set of sellers, $[k]$ denotes the set of all items for sale, $\boldsymbol{I} := (I_1, \ldots, I_m)$ is a vector of (mutually disjoint) sets of items called the *initial endowment*, where I_j is the set of items that is initially held by seller $j \in [m]$. It holds that $\bigcup_{j=1}^{m} I_j = [k]$. Vectors $\boldsymbol{G} = (G_1, \ldots, G_n)$ and $\boldsymbol{F} = (F_1, \ldots, F_m)$ are vectors of probability distributions, from which the buyers' and sellers' valuation functions are assumed to be drawn: The valuation function of buyer $i \in [n]$ is drawn from distribution G_i, and similarly the valuation function of seller $j \in [m]$ is drawn from distribution F_j.

A *(combinatorial) exchange market* is a more general version of the above defined two-sided market where an agent can act as both a buyer and a seller. Thus, everyone may initially own items

[4]By a *monotone* valuation function v we mean that $v(S) \geq v(T)$ for all sets of items $T \subseteq S$. That is, getting more items cannot decrease an agent's overall valuation. By *normalized* we mean that $v(\emptyset) = 0$.

and may both sell and buy items. As a result, in this setting, we override the notation and simply use n to denote the total number of agents. Formally, an exchange market is thus a tuple $(n, k, \boldsymbol{I}, \boldsymbol{F})$.

In two-sided markets, sellers are assumed to only value items in their initial bundle and are therefore not interested in buying from other sellers, i.e., $\forall j \in [m]$ and $\forall S \subseteq [k]$, $w_j(S) = w_j(S \cap I_j)$. Conversely, in exchange markets, no such restriction on the valuation functions exists.

Throughout the paper, we reserve the usage of the letter i to denote a single buyer, the letter j to denote a single seller, and the letter ℓ to denote a single item. Moreover, we use v_i to denote buyer i's valuation function and w_j to denote seller j's valuation function.

2.2 Mechanism Design Goals

The following discussion is specific to two-sided markets (the main focus of this paper), but these concepts can be extended straightforwardly to combinatorial exchange markets. Given a two-sided market, our aim is to redistribute the items among the agents so as to maximise the *social welfare* (the sum of the agents' valuations). An *allocation* for a two-sided market $(n, m, k, \boldsymbol{I}, \boldsymbol{G}, \boldsymbol{F})$ is a pair of vectors $(\boldsymbol{X}, \boldsymbol{Y}) = ((X_1, \ldots, X_n), (Y_1, \ldots, Y_m))$ such that the union of $X_1, \ldots, X_n, Y_1, \ldots, Y_m$ is $[k]$, and $X_1, \ldots, X_n, Y_1, \ldots, Y_m$ are mutually disjoint. When discussing a given two-sided market, we will denote by $\mathcal{A}$ the set of all allocations for that market.

Redistribution of the items is done by running a *mechanism* $\mathbb{M}$. A mechanism interacts with and receives input from the agents, and outputs an *outcome*, consisting of an allocation $(\boldsymbol{X}, \boldsymbol{Y})$ and a payment vector $(\boldsymbol{\rho}^B, \boldsymbol{\rho}^S) \in \mathbb{R}^n \times \mathbb{R}^m$, where $\boldsymbol{\rho}^B$ refers to the buyers' vector of payments and $\boldsymbol{\rho}^S$ to the sellers' one. An outcome is therefore a tuple $(\boldsymbol{X}, \boldsymbol{Y}, \boldsymbol{\rho}^B, \boldsymbol{\rho}^S)$. Note that when an agent is charged a negative payment, this should be interpreted as an agent receiving money. The payment of a seller is usually negative in a reasonable two-sided market mechanism, and this is also the case for the mechanisms proposed in the present paper.

Agents are assumed to maximise their *utility*, which is defined as the valuation for the bundle of items that they possess with respect to the allocation vector, minus the payment charged by the mechanism. In particular, the utility $u_i^B(v_i, (\boldsymbol{X}, \boldsymbol{Y}, \boldsymbol{\rho}^B, \boldsymbol{\rho}^S))$ of a buyer $i \in [n]$ with valuation function v_i is $v_i(X_i) - \rho_i^B$, whereas for a seller $j \in [m]$ with valuation function w_j it is $u_j^S(w_j, (\boldsymbol{X}, \boldsymbol{Y}, \boldsymbol{\rho}^B, \boldsymbol{\rho}^S)) = w_j(Y_j) - \rho_j^S$.[5]

Furthermore, agents are assumed to be fully rational, so that they will strategically interact with the mechanism to achieve their goal of maximising utility. Our goal is to design a mechanism such that there is a dominant strategy or Bayes-Nash equilibrium for the agents under which the mechanism returns an allocation with a high social welfare. For an allocation $(\boldsymbol{X}, \boldsymbol{Y})$, the social welfare $\mathrm{SW}(\boldsymbol{X}, \boldsymbol{Y})$ is defined as

$$\mathrm{SW}(\boldsymbol{X}, \boldsymbol{Y}) = \sum_{i \in [n]} v_i(X_i) + \sum_{j \in [m]} w_j(Y_j).$$

We now describe three main economic properties our mechanisms must satisfy. For each of these constraints we first introduce the strictest version and then a more relaxed one. We aim to satisfy the strictest versions, whenever possible.

- **Incentive compatibility (IC)**[6]

[5]Note that Y_j represents the bundle of items that remains in the seller's possession after execution of the mechanism.

[6]Technically, as can be inferred, the DSIC properties are reserved for *direct revelation mechansims*, i.e., where the buyer solely interacts with the mechanism reporting her valuation function. It is well-known that mechanisms admitting a dominant strategy can be transformed into DSIC direct revelation mechanisms, and those with a Bayes-Nash equilibrium can be transformed into BIC direct revelation mechanisms. This way, the DSIC and BIC definitions naturally extend to non-direct revelation mechanisms.

  - *Dominant strategy incentive compatibility (DSIC):* It is a dominant strategy for every agent to report her true valuation sincerely. I.e., for every agent i and for every vector of valuations of all other players, it is impossible for agent i to increase her expected utility by misreporting her valuation.
  - *Bayesian incentive compatibility (BIC):* It is a Bayes-Nash equilibrium (BNE) for the agents to truthfully report their valuations to the mechanism. I.e., each agent i maximizes her expected utility by truthfully reporting her valuation if all other players also truthfully report their valuations.
- **Individual rationality (IR)**
  - *Ex-post individual rationality (ex-post IR):* It is not harmful for any agent to participate in the mechanism, i.e., there is guaranteed to be a strategy for an agent that yields the agent a utility that is not less than her initial utility. (The initial utility of a seller with bundle I_j is $w_j(I_j)$, and the initial utility of a buyer is $v_i(\emptyset) = 0$.)
  - *Interim individual rationality (interim IR):* There is a strategy for each agent that yields her an *expected* utility that is not less than her initial utility (where expectation is over the random outcome of the mechanism, resulting from internal randomness of the mechanism and randomized strategies adopted by the agents).
- **Budget balance (BB)**
  - *Strong Budget Balance (SBB):* The sum of all agents' payments output by the mechanism *is equal to* zero. Conceptually, this means that no money ends up at an external party, and no external party needs to subsidise the mechanism.
  - *Weak Budget Balance (WBB):* The sum of all payments is *at least* zero. In two sided-markets, this generally means that the buyers' payments are at least as large as the payments received by the sellers. No external party needs to subsidise the mechanism.

For valuation profiles $(\boldsymbol{v}, \boldsymbol{w})$, $\mathsf{OPT}(\boldsymbol{v}, \boldsymbol{w}) := \max\{\mathsf{SW}(X, Y) : (X, Y) \in \mathcal{A}\}$ denotes the *optimal social welfare.* The *expected optimal social welfare* is the value $\mathsf{OPT} = \mathbb{E}_{\boldsymbol{v},\boldsymbol{w}}[\mathsf{OPT}(\boldsymbol{v}, \boldsymbol{w})]$. We say that a mechanism $\mathbb{M}$ *α-approximates the optimal social welfare* for some $\alpha > 1$ if and only if $\mathsf{OPT} \leq \alpha\mathbb{E}_{\boldsymbol{v},\boldsymbol{w}}[\mathsf{SW}(\mathbb{M}(\boldsymbol{v}, \boldsymbol{w}))]$. Our goal is to find mechanisms that α-approximate the optimal social welfare for a low α, are DSIC (or BIC), SBB, and ex-post IR (or interim IR).

2.3 Valuation Functions

We will consider probability distributions over the following classes of valuation functions. Let $v : 2^{[k]} \to \mathbb{R}_{\geq 0}$ be a valuation function. Then,

- v is *additive* if and only if there exist numbers $\alpha_1, \ldots \alpha_k \in \mathbb{R}_{\geq 0}$ such that $v(S) = \sum_{j \in S} \alpha_j$ for all $S \subseteq [k]$.
- v is *fractionally subadditive (or XOS)* if and only if there exists a collection of additive functions $a_1, \ldots, a_d$ such that for every bundle $S \subseteq [k]$ it holds that $v(S) = \max_{i \in [d]} a_i(S)$.
- v is *subadditive* if and only if for for all $S, T \subseteq [k]$ it holds that $v(S \cup T) \leq v(S) + v(T)$.

It is easy to see that every additive function is a XOS function. Further, it is well-known that the class of submodular functions are contained in the class of XOS functions, and XOS functions are contained in the class of the subadditive functions.

3 AN INITIAL MECHANISM AND DIRECT TRADE STRONG BUDGET BALANCE

Blumrosen and Dobzinski [1] present a mechanism for exchange markets with subadditive valuation functions. They prove the following for this mechanism, which we name $\mathbb{M}_{\text{bd}}$.

Theorem 3.1 (Blumrosen and Dobzinski [1]). *Mechanism $\mathbb{M}_{\text{bd}}$ is a DSIC, WBB, ex-post IR randomized direct revelation mechanism that $4H(s)$-approximates the optimal social welfare for combinatorial exchange markets $(n,k,\boldsymbol{I},\boldsymbol{F})$ with subadditive valuation functions, where $s = \min\{n, |I_i| : i \in [n]\}$ is the minimum of the number of agents and the number of items in an agent's initial endowment, and $H(\cdot)$ denotes the harmonic numbers.*

In particular, this mechanism gives us a constant approximation factor if the number of starting items of the agents is bounded by a constant.

Now consider a mechanism $\mathbb{M}_{\text{sbb}}$ that selects an agent $i \in [n]$ uniformly at random, runs $\mathbb{M}_{\text{bd}}$ on the remaining agents, and allocates the surplus money of $\mathbb{M}_{\text{bd}}$ to agent i. We are then able to prove the following.

Theorem 3.2. *Mechanism $\mathbb{M}_{\text{sbb}}$ is DSIC, ex-post IR, SBB, and achieves an $8nH(s)/(n-1)$-approximation to the optimal social welfare for exchange markets with subadditive valuations and at least 3 agents.*[7]

Because of space constraints, the proof of this theorem and of various other results in the remainder of this paper, has been omitted. This yields an ex-post IR, SBB, DSIC mechanism that $O(1)$-approximates the social welfare if the number of items initially posessed by an agent is bounded by a constant. The principle that we used to construct Mechanism $\mathbb{M}_{\text{sbb}}$ can more generally be used to turn any WBB mechanism into an SBB one, while preserving the DSIC and ex-post IR properties. It also reveals a problematic aspect of the notion of SBB: it allows for agents to receive money, while they are not involved in any trade. This motivates a strengthened notion of strong budget balance, which we call *direct trade strong budget balance.*

Definition 3.3. A mechanism for an exchange market satisfies *direct trade strong budget balance (DSBB)* if and only if the outcome it generates can be achieved by a set of bilateral trades, where each trade consists of a reallocation of an item from an agent i to an agent j, and a monetary transfer from agent j to agent i. Moreover, each item may only be traded once.

DSBB strengthens the traditional SBB notion and seems to be a reasonable requirement in most two sided markets and exchange markets settings. Note that the way in which we strengthen SBB is rather mild: DSBB still allows an arbitrarily large amount of money to be transfered from one agent to another as long as at least one item is exchanged in the opposite direction. DSBB does not even require such a bilateral exchange to be profitable for both parties, but does nonetheless seem to rule out the rather unsatisfactory type construction such as the one used in $\mathbb{M}_{\text{sbb}}$.

It can be seen that Mechanism $\mathbb{M}_{\text{sbb}}$ does not satisfy DSBB. In the remainder of the paper we will proceed to design mechanisms for two-sided markets that do satisfy DSBB.[8] Moreover, two of our results provide an $O(1)$-approximation even in settings where $\mathbb{M}_{\text{sbb}}$ would only provide an approximation factor of logarithmic order.

4 A MECHANISM FOR UNIT-SUPPLY SELLERS AND XOS BUYERS

In this section we present a DSIC, ex-post IR, and DSBB mechanism for two-sided markets, when sellers initially possess a single item and buyers have XOS valuation functions. This mechanism achieves a constant approximation to the optimal social welfare. In this setting, we use $[k]$ to denote both the set of items and the set of sellers, where item j is owned by seller j (so $I_j = \{j\}$ for all $j \in [k]$). For each seller $j \in [k]$, we then treat F_j as a distribution over $\mathbb{R}_{\geq 0}$ instead of a distribution over functions.

We assume throughout this section that $(n,k,k,\boldsymbol{I},\boldsymbol{G},\boldsymbol{F})$ is a given two-sided market, on which we run the mechanism to be defined. For an allocation $(\boldsymbol{X},\boldsymbol{Y}) \in \mathcal{A}$, we shall use the notation

[7]For two agents, it is straightforward to come up with alternative mechanisms that have the desired properties.

[8]We note that the double auctions given in [5] also satisfy the DSBB property.

$\mathsf{SW}^B, \mathsf{SW}^S$ to respectively denote the buyers' and the sellers' contribution to the social welfare, i.e.,

$$\begin{aligned} \mathsf{SW}^B(\boldsymbol{X},\boldsymbol{Y}) &:= \sum_{i=1}^{n} v_i(X_i), \\ \mathsf{SW}^S(\boldsymbol{X},\boldsymbol{Y}) &:= \sum_{i=1}^{k} w_j(Y_j) = \sum_{j=1}^{k} w_j \mathbb{I}[j \in Y_j]. \end{aligned} \tag{1}$$

Our mechanism requires fixing a price for every item in the market. For a bundle of available items Λ and an item price vector $\boldsymbol{p} = (p_1, \ldots, p_k) \in \mathbb{R}^k_{\geq 0}$, we define the *demand correspondence* of buyer $i \in [n]$ with valuation function v_i as

$$\mathcal{D}(v_i, \boldsymbol{p}, \Lambda) := \left\{ S \subseteq \Lambda : v_i(S) - \sum_{j \in S} p_j \geq v_i(T) - \sum_{j \in T} p_j \text{ for all } T \subseteq \Lambda \right\},$$

i.e., $\mathcal{D}(v_i, \boldsymbol{p}, \Lambda)$ is the set of bundles of items in Λ that maximise i's utility under the given item prices.

For a buyer i with valuation function v_i, we define the *additive representative function* for bundle $T \subseteq [k]$ as any additive function $a(v_i, T, \cdot) : 2^{[k]} \to \mathbb{R}_{\geq 0}$ such that $v_i(T) = a(v_i, T, T)$, and $v_i(S) \geq a(v_i, T, S)$ for all $S \subseteq [k]$. The additive representative function of a bundle is guaranteed to exist for each buyer i and for each valuation function in the support of G_i, by the definition of XOS functions.

4.1 Mechanism

Let $\mathbb{A}$ be an algorithm that, given a buyers' valuation profile $\boldsymbol{v}$ and a set of items $[k]$, allocates the items to the buyers, without considering the sellers and their valuations. $\mathbb{A}$ can either be an exact algorithm that outputs an optimal allocation of $[k]$ to the buyers (if one is not interested in the runtime) or an approximately optimal one (in the case that one insists on polynomial-time implementability). Our mechanism uses $\mathbb{A}$ as a black-box for the computation of item prices.

Let $\boldsymbol{X}^{\text{all}}(\boldsymbol{v}) = (X_1^{\text{all}}(\boldsymbol{v}), \ldots, X_n^{\text{all}}(\boldsymbol{v}))$ (where the superscript "all" stands for "allocation") be the output allocation of $\mathbb{A}(\boldsymbol{v})$. Let $\mathsf{SW}(\boldsymbol{X}^{\text{all}}(\boldsymbol{v}))$ be the total social welfare of the allocation $\boldsymbol{X}^{\text{all}}(\boldsymbol{v})$.

We define for each item $j \in [k]$ its *contribution* $\mathit{SW}_j^B(\boldsymbol{v})$ *to the social welfare* $\mathit{SW}(\boldsymbol{X}^{\text{all}}(\boldsymbol{v}))$ as follows: if there exists a buyer i that receives item j in allocation $X_i^{\text{all}}(\boldsymbol{v})$, then $\mathsf{SW}_j^B(\boldsymbol{v}) = a(v_i, X_i^{\text{all}}(\boldsymbol{v}), \{j\})$. Otherwise, if j is not allocated to any buyer in $X_i^{\text{all}}(\boldsymbol{v})$, then $\mathsf{SW}_j^B(\boldsymbol{v}) = 0$.

This notion allows us to make a distinction between *high welfare items* and *low welfare items*. An item $j \in [k]$ is said to have *high welfare with respect to* $\mathit{SW}(X_i^{\text{all}}(\boldsymbol{v}))$ if and only if $\mathbb{E}_{\boldsymbol{v}}[\mathsf{SW}_j^B(\boldsymbol{v})] \geq 4\mathbb{E}[w_j]$, i.e., the expected social welfare contribution of j if we would allocate j according to $\boldsymbol{X}^{\text{all}}(\boldsymbol{v})$ is at least four times as high as the social welfare that results from leaving item j with its seller.

Formally, let H be the set of high welfare items, i.e., $H := \{\ell \in [k] : \mathbb{E}[\mathsf{SW}_\ell^B(\boldsymbol{v})] \geq 4\mathbb{E}[w_j]\}$, and let L be the set of low welfare items, i.e. $L := [k] \setminus H$. For each high welfare item $j \in H$, the mechanism makes use of the following associated *item price* p_j:

$$p_j := \frac{1}{2}\mathbb{E}_{\boldsymbol{v}}[\mathsf{SW}_j^B(\boldsymbol{v})].$$

Observe that $p_j \geq 2\mathbb{E}[w_j]$ for all $j \in H$, by our definition of high welfare items.

The reason why H is chosen in such a way is twofold: first, the items in L if kept by their sellers provide a welfare loss of at most a constant factor; second, every item in H is guaranteed to be sold (if sold) at a high price, to make sure that the buyer receiving the item has a high valuation for it.

Our (randomized) mechanism does the following. First, it considers the sellers with an item in H (in any order) and asks each of them whether they would sell their item for a price of p_j. As mentioned above, by definition of the prices, every seller $j \in H$ accepts the price with probability at least $1/2$, by Markov's inequality (recall that $p_j \geq 2\mathbb{E}[w_j]$ for all $j \in H$).

To make sure that this probability is exactly $1/2$, the seller j is only given the opportunity to sell her item at the price p_j with probability q_j such that (in expectation) the offer is accepted with probability exactly $1/2$. Formally this means that the mechanism makes an offer to the seller j with probability

$$q_j := \frac{1}{2F_j(p_j)}, \text{ where } F_j(p_j) = \Pr[w_j \leq p_j].$$

An item in H is considered to be "in the market" if the corresponding seller accepts the mechanism's offer. After the mechanism has made the offers to the sellers of H, it knows which items are in the market and then asks each buyer (sequentially, in any order) for her favorite bundle of items among those items that are still in the market. If an item j gets requested by a buyer, then j is transferred from its corresponding seller j, and the buyer pays p_j to seller j. Item j is then removed from the set of items in the market, and the mechanism proceeds to the next buyer.

We call the mechanism sketched above $\mathbb{M}_{\text{1-supply}}$, which we now present more precisely:

(1) Let $H := \{j \in [k] : \mathbb{E}_{\boldsymbol{v}}[\mathrm{SW}_j^B(\boldsymbol{v})] \geq 4\mathbb{E}[w_j]\}$.
(2) For all $j \in H$, set $p_j := \frac{1}{2}\mathbb{E}_{\boldsymbol{v}}[\mathrm{SW}_j^B(\boldsymbol{v})]$.
(3) Let $\Lambda_1 := \emptyset, X_i := \emptyset$ for all $i \in [n]$ and $Y_j := \{j\}$ for all $j \in [k]$.
(4) For all $j \in H$:
   (a) Set $q_j := 1/(2\Pr[w_j \leq p_j])$.
   (b) With probability q_j, offer payment p_j in exchange for her item.
   (c) If j accepts the offer, set $\Lambda_1 := \Lambda_1 \cup \{j\}$.
(5) For all $i \in [n]$:
   (a) Buyer i chooses a bundle $B_i \in \mathcal{D}(v_i, \boldsymbol{p}, \Lambda_i)$ that maximises her utility.
   (b) Allocate the accepted items to buyer i, i.e., $X_i := B_i$ and $Y_j := \emptyset$ for all $j \in B_i$.
   (c) Remove the selected items from the available items, i.e., $\Lambda_{i+1} := \Lambda_i \setminus B_i$.
(6) Return the outcome consisting of allocation $(\boldsymbol{X} = (X_1, \ldots, X_n), \boldsymbol{Y} = (Y_1, \ldots, Y_k))$ and payments $\boldsymbol{\rho} = (\boldsymbol{\rho}^B, \boldsymbol{\rho}^S)$, where $\rho_i^B = \sum_{j \in X_i} p_j$ for $i \in [n]$ and $\rho_j^S = -p_j \mathbb{I}[Y_j = \emptyset]$ for $j \in [k]$.

Note that Algorithm $\mathbb{A}$ is only used in the first steps of mechanism $\mathbb{M}_{\text{1-supply}}$, where $\mathbb{E}_{\boldsymbol{v}}[\mathrm{SW}_j^B(\boldsymbol{v})]$ is computed. Let α be the factor by which $\mathbb{A}$ is guaranteed to approximate the social welfare of the buyers.

4.2 Results

Now, we are ready to present the main result of this section:

THEOREM 4.1. $\mathbb{M}_{\text{1-supply}}$ *is ex-post IR, DSIC, DSBB, and* $(2 + 4\alpha)$*-approximates the optimal social welfare.*

In particular, taking for $\mathbb{A}$ an optimal algorithm (i.e., $\alpha = 1$), we obtain that there exists a mechanism that is ex-post IR, DSIC, DSBB, and 6-approximates the optimal social welfare. As mentioned in Section 1.3, one may alternatively take for $\mathbb{A}$ a polynomial time α-approximation algorithm and use the technique of [11], to obtain a mechanism with runtime $POLY(1/\epsilon, n, m)$ that approximates the optimal social welfare within a $2 + 4\alpha$ multiplicative factor and an ϵ additive term.

We split the proof of Theorem 4.1 into two lemmas that separately bound the sellers' and the buyers' relative contributions to the social welfare. We use the notation OPT as defined in Section 2, and we use ALG to denote the expected social welfare of the mechanism, i.e., $\mathbb{E}_{\boldsymbol{v},\boldsymbol{w}}[\mathrm{SW}(\mathbb{M}_{\text{1-supply}}(\boldsymbol{v}, \boldsymbol{w}))]$. Moreover, the superscripts S, B respectively denote the sellers' and buyers' contributions to the social welfare, e.g., $\mathrm{OPT} = \mathrm{OPT}^S + \mathrm{OPT}^B$ and $\mathrm{ALG} = \mathrm{ALG}^S + \mathrm{ALG}^B$, consistent with the notation of (1).

The following lemma is a simple consequence of the fact that $\mathbb{M}_{\text{1-supply}}$ lets every seller in H accept an offer with probability exactly $1/2$.

Lemma 4.2. *If every seller $j \in H$ puts her item into the market with probability exactly $1/2$, then*

$$2\text{ALG}^S \geq \sum_{j=1}^{k} \mathbb{E}[w_j] \geq \text{OPT}^S.$$

Proof. The second inequality is trivial, so we focus on the first inequality. First, observe that

$$\Pr[w_j > p_j] \leq \Pr[w_j > 2\mathbb{E}[w_j]] < \frac{1}{2},$$

where the first inequality holds because $j \in L$, and the second inequality follows by Markov's inequality. Thus, with probability at least $1/2$ a seller j is happy to sell her item at price p_j. But every seller receives an offer from the mechanism with probability $q_j := 1/(2\Pr[w_j \leq p_j])$, so every seller in H accepts to trade with probability exactly $1/2$. This implies that every seller $j \in H$ contributes in expectation at least $\mathbb{E}[w_j]/2$ to the social welfare. Moreover, every seller in L never trades, so that such a seller contributes her full expected valuation to the expected social welfare. □

Next, we provide a more difficult bound that relates ALG^B and ALG^S to OPT^B.

Lemma 4.3. *The buyers' contributions to the optimal social welfare is bounded by*

$$4\alpha\text{ALG}^B + 4\alpha\text{ALG}^S \geq \text{OPT}^B.$$

Intuitively, Lemma 4.3 uses two main ingredients:

- the partition of the items between high-welfare (H) items and low-welfare items (L), and
- the definition of $\text{SW}_j^B(\boldsymbol{v})$ w.r.t. a one-sided (approximation) algorithm $\mathbb{A}$.

The latter tells us that the sum of the expected contributions of all the items, i.e. $\sum_{j=1}^{k} \mathbb{E}[\text{SW}_\ell^B(\boldsymbol{v})]$, is an upper-bound on OPT^B/α. From the former we know that:

- the sellers do not trade items in L, and this is enough to ensure that their contribution to the expected social welfare is greater than a constant fraction of the expected contribution of the items in L, i.e. $\text{ALG}^S > \frac{1}{4}\sum_{j \in L} \mathbb{E}[\text{SW}_j^B(\boldsymbol{v})]$. Moreover,
- the only items that the agents can trade are those that have a high welfare w.r.t. $\text{SW}(X_i^{\text{all}}(\boldsymbol{v}))$. From that we can infer that the contribution of the buyers to the expected social welfare is greater than a constant fraction of the expected contribution of the items in H, i.e. $\text{ALG}^B > \frac{1}{4}\sum_{j \in H} \mathbb{E}[\text{SW}_j^B(\boldsymbol{v})]$.

By combining these bounds, the claim of Lemma 4.3 follows. Theorem 4.1 is then obtained straightforwardly from Lemma 4.2 and Lemma 4.3.

Proof of Theorem 4.1. The bound on the approximation ratio follows from the sum of the inequalities of Lemma 4.2 and Lemma 4.3. Moreover, it is a dominant strategy for a seller to accept if and only if the payment offered to her exceeds her valuation, and it is a dominant strategy for a buyer to choose a utility-maximising bundle for the items and item prices offered to her. Thus, when viewed as a direct revelation mechanism, $\mathbb{M}_{\text{1-supply}}$ is DSIC. It is clear that participating in the mechanism can never lead to a decrease in utility for both buyers and sellers, and therefore the mechanism is also ex-post IR. Lastly, it is straightforward to see that the mechanism is DSBB, as the definition of $\mathbb{M}_{\text{1-supply}}$ which we gave in terms of sequential posted pricing naturally yields us the required set of bilateral trades. □

5 A MECHANISM FOR ADDITIVE SELLERS AND XOS BUYERS

We now consider the setting in which sellers may own multiple distinct items and have an additive valuation function over them. We design a DSBB mechanism that is DSIC and ex-post IR on the sellers' side, and BIC and interim IR on the buyers' side. At the end of the section we show that, in the case that both buyers and sellers have additive valuation functions, the mechanism we present is DSIC and ex-post IR on both sides of the market.

We assume throughout this section that $(n, m, k, \boldsymbol{I}, \boldsymbol{G}, \boldsymbol{F})$ is a given two-sided market with XOS buyers and additive sellers, on which we run the mechanism to be defined. Like in the previous section, the buyers are still assumed to have XOS valuation functions over the items. Since now the number of items and sellers is different in general, we use m to denote the number of sellers and k for the number of items. The valuation w_j of a seller j is now an additive function. We reuse the following notation from Section 4: the allocation $(X_1^{\text{all}}(\boldsymbol{v}), \dots, X_n^{\text{all}}(\boldsymbol{v}))$ returned by an allocation algorithm $\mathbb{A}$ on input $\boldsymbol{v}$ returns an allocation of $[k]$ to $[n]$. We let $\alpha \geq 1$ again denote the approximation factor by which $\mathbb{A}$ approximates the social welfare. For XOS valuation v_i and bundle $T \subseteq [k]$ we use $a(v_i, T, \cdot)$ to denote the additive representative function of v_i for T. Also we use the buyers' social welfare contribution $\text{SW}_\ell^B(\boldsymbol{v})$ for item $\ell \in [k]$ and buyers' valuation profile $\boldsymbol{v}$, as defined in Section 4.

Furthermore, we define the *sellers' social welfare contribution* $\text{SW}_\ell^S(\boldsymbol{w})$ for item $\ell \in I_j$ and sellers' valuation profile $\boldsymbol{w}$ as $\text{SW}_\ell^S(\boldsymbol{w}) := w_j(\{\ell\})$. Due to the fact that for $j \in [m]$, w_j is an additive function, there is no need for defining the notion of an additive representative function for a seller.

5.1 Mechanism

We aim to design a BIC, interim IR, and DSBB mechanism that approximates the optimal social welfare within a constant. We propose the following mechanism, which we refer to as $\mathbb{M}_{\text{add}}$. We let $H_j := \{\ell \in I_j : \mathbb{E}[\text{SW}_\ell^B(\boldsymbol{v})] \geq 4\mathbb{E}[\text{SW}_\ell^S(\boldsymbol{w})]\}$ and $L_j := I_j \setminus H_j$ for all $j \in [m]$, and we let $H := \bigcup_{j=1}^m H_j$ and $L := [k] \setminus H$ denote the sets of high-welfare items and low-welfare items, respectively. Our mechanism will only allow trading items in H. We define for $\ell \in H$ the item price

$$p_\ell := \frac{1}{2}\mathbb{E}[\text{SW}_\ell^B(\boldsymbol{v})],$$

similar to what we did for $\mathbb{M}_{\text{1-supply}}$.

An essential difference between $\mathbb{M}_{\text{add}}$ and $\mathbb{M}_{\text{1-supply}}$ is that the order in which buyers and sellers are processed is reversed. Mechanism $\mathbb{M}_{\text{add}}$ roughly works as follows. It first asks every buyer which set of items it would like to receive from those items in H that have not been requested yet. Then $\mathbb{M}_{\text{add}}$ offers every seller $j \in [m]$ a payment in exchange for the subset of all items in I_j that have been requested. This offer is made with probability q_j, chosen in such a way that the requested items of seller j are transferred to the buyers with probability $1/2$. The items of the sellers accepting the offer are transferred to the buyers for the corresponding item prices. Buyers act strategically, and will request a bundle of items that maximises their expected utility, knowing that the item sets requested from each seller will be assigned to them with probability $1/2$.[9] In our mechanism, the sellers will each have a dominant strategy, while the buyers' aformentioned behaviour relies on the sellers playing their dominant strategies. This reliance results in a BIC (rather than a DSIC) mechanism. Below we describe the mechanism in more detail and we subsequently provide an example of the mechanism's execution on a simple instance.

[9]Buyers may need to make complex calculations in order to establish which bundle maximises her expected utility.

(1) For $\ell \in [k]$, compute $\mathbb{E}[\mathrm{SW}_\ell^B(\boldsymbol{v})]$ and $\mathbb{E}[\mathrm{SW}_\ell^S(\boldsymbol{w})]$.
(2) For all $j \in [m]$, compute H_j.
(3) Compute H and L.
(4) Let $\Lambda_1 := H, X_i := \emptyset$ for all $i \in [n]$, and $Y_j := I_j$ for all $j \in [m]$.
(5) For each buyer $i \in [n]$:
 (a) Ask buyer i to select an expected-utility maximising bundle $B_i \subseteq \Lambda_i$ given the prices $\{p_\ell : \ell \in \Lambda_i\}$ from the set of available items Λ_i (where the expectation is taken w.r.t. the randomness of the valuations and the mechanism).
 (b) Update the set of available items $\Lambda_{i+1} := \Lambda_i \setminus B_i$.
(6) Let $B := \bigcup_{i=1}^n B_i$ be the set of all items demanded by the buyers.
(7) For each seller $j \in [m]$:
 (a) Let $S_j := B \cap H_j$ be the set of items owned by seller j that are demanded.
 (b) Let $p(S_j) := \sum_{\ell \in S_j} p_\ell$ and let $q_j = 1/(2\Pr[w_j(S_j) \le p(S_j)])$.
 (c) With probability q_j, offer payment $p(S_j)$ in exchange for the bundle S_j. Otherwise, skip this seller.
 (d) If the seller accepts the offer, allocate each items in S_j to the buyer that requested it (i.e., remove S_j from Y_j and add $S_j \cap B_i$ to X_i for all $i \in [n]$)
(8) Return the outcome consisting of allocation $(\boldsymbol{X} = (X_1, \ldots, X_n), Y = (Y_1, \ldots, Y_k))$ and payments $\rho = (\rho^B, \rho^S)$, where $\rho_i^B = \sum_{\ell \in X_i} p_\ell$ for $i \in [n]$ and $\rho_j^S = \sum_{\ell \in I_j \setminus Y_j} -p_\ell$ for $j \in [m]$.

Notice the mechanism $\mathbb{M}_{\text{add}}$ runs in polynomial time, but it makes use of a variant of a standard demand query in which the mechanism gives prices for the items, and asks a buyer which bundle she would like *if, for each item in that bundle, she were to receive it with probability* 1/2. This places a heavier computational and cognitive burden on the agent than with standard demand queries. We will not address in the present paper the complexity aspects of the buyer's task to answer such queries, though we believe that it is an interesting open question to investigate.

The following example illustrates some important aspects of $\mathbb{M}_{\text{add}}$, and the strategies of the buyers under a BNE.

Example 5.1. There is one buyer and two unit-supply sellers. Each seller has one item. The buyer has two XOS valuation functions v_1 and v_2, each chosen with probability 1/2. Valuation v_1 is composed of 3 additive functions a_1, a_2, and a_3, i.e., $v_1(S) = \max\{a_1(S), a_2(S), a_3(S)\}$. Valuation v_2 consists of a single additive function a_4. Each seller j has a valuation function $w_j = 0$. Recall that a function a is additive if there exists $\alpha_1, \ldots, \alpha_k$ such that $a(S) = \sum_{j \in S} \alpha_j$ for all $S \subseteq [k]$. The functions a_1 to a_4 are described in the table below by listing the values α_1 and α_2.

Function	item 1 (α_1)	item 2 (α_2)
a_1	0	2
a_2	8	0
a_3	7	2
a_4	1	6

Let us compute the prices offered by the mechanism $\mathbb{M}_{\text{add}}$ when $\mathbb{A}$ is an optimal algorithm. Thus, we need to compute the expected contribution to the optimal social welfare of every item. First, notice that the optimum allocates the items 1 and 2 to the buyer when her valuation is v_1. In this case the contribution to the optimal social welfare of item 1 is 7, and the contribution of item 2 is 2. Similarly, if the buyer has valuation v_2, the optimum still allocates items 1 and 2 to her, but in this case the contribution to the optimal social welfare of item 1 is 1, and the contribution of item 2 is 6. Thus, the expected contribution of every item to the optimal social welfare is 4, i.e.,

$\mathbb{E}[\mathrm{SW}_j^B(\boldsymbol{v})] = 4$ for all $j = 1, 2$. Since the price p_j of each item is defined to be half of the expected contribution to the optimal social welfare, $p_j = 2$ for all the items.

When the mechanism asks a buyer to select a bundle that maximizes her expected utility, the buyer has to answer by taking into account the fact that each item in her requested bundle will be allocated with probability 1/2. First, consider the case when the buyer has valuation v_1. In this case the expected utility for the different bundles are:

$$u(\{1\}) = \frac{1}{2} \cdot (8-2) + \frac{1}{2} \cdot 0 = 3,$$
$$u(\{2\}) = \frac{1}{2} \cdot (2-2) + \frac{1}{2} \cdot 0 = 0,$$
$$u(\{1,2\}) = \frac{1}{4} \cdot (8-2) + \frac{1}{4} \cdot (2-2) + \frac{1}{4} \cdot (9-4) + \frac{1}{4} \cdot 0 = \frac{11}{4}.$$

The utility-maximising bundle that will be requested by the buyer in case of v_1 is $\{1\}$, in which case the mechanism will let the buyer pay Seller 1 a price of 2 in exchange for the item. Instead, if the valuation of the buyer is v_2, then the requested bundle will be $\{1, 2\}$, in which case the mechanism will let the buyer pay both sellers a price of 2 in exchange for their items.

5.2 Results

Our main result for $\mathbb{M}_{\text{add}}$ is the following theorem.

THEOREM 5.2. *The mechanism $\mathbb{M}_{\text{add}}$ is interim IR, BIC, DSBB, and $(2+4\alpha)$-approximates the optimal social welfare.*

By taking for $\mathbb{A}$ an optimal algorithm (i.e., $\alpha = 1$), we obtain a mechanism that is ex-post IR, DSIC, SBB, and 6-approximates the optimal social welfare. Again, we split the proof of this theorem 5.2 into two lemmas that separately bound the sellers' and the buyers' relative contributions to the social welfare. Like the previous section, we use the notation OPT as defined in Section 2, and we use ALG to denote the expected social welfare of the mechanism. Moreover, we use again the superscripts B and S to refer to the buyers' and sellers' expected contribution to the social welfare of a given allocation, as we did in Section 4.

Let us first discuss how we bound the sellers' expected contribution to the optimal allocation.

LEMMA 5.3.

$$2\mathrm{ALG}^S \geq \mathrm{OPT}^S.$$

PROOF. The only items that our mechanisms potentially reallocates are the ones belonging to H. Every item in L stays with its seller. For the items in H, the mechanism ensures every seller sells her demanded bundle with probability exactly 1/2, so for each seller it holds that she retains her full initial endowment with probability at least 1/2, which implies the claim. □

Similarly, we want to provide an upper bound on the buyers' expected contribution to the optimal allocation. To do that we need two auxiliary propositions.

The first proposition exploits the partition of the items among high-welfare items and low-welfare items. Since the low-welfare items are not traded, the sum of the expected contribution of the buyers on the high-welfare items and the expected contribution of the sellers on the low-welfare items gives us an upper bound on the buyers' expected contribution in the allocation computed by $\mathbb{A}$.

PROPOSITION 5.4.

$$\sum_{\ell \in H} \mathbb{E}_{\boldsymbol{v}}[SW_\ell^B(\boldsymbol{v})] + 4 \sum_{\ell \in L} \mathbb{E}_{\boldsymbol{w}}[SW_\ell^S(\boldsymbol{w})] > \sum_{i=1}^{n} \mathbb{E}_{\boldsymbol{v}}[v_i(X_i^{\text{all}}(\boldsymbol{v}))].$$

Proof. Let $a(v_i, X_i^{\text{all}}(\boldsymbol{v}), \cdot)$ be the representative additive function of v_i for the bundle $X_i^{\text{all}}(\boldsymbol{v})$. Then,

$$\begin{aligned}
\sum_{i=1}^{n} \mathbb{E}[v_i(X_i^{\text{all}}(\boldsymbol{v}))] &= \sum_{i=1}^{n} \mathbb{E}\left[\sum_{\ell \in X_i^{\text{all}}(\boldsymbol{v})} a(v_i, X_i^{\text{all}}(\boldsymbol{v}), \{\ell\})\right] \\
&= \sum_{i=1}^{n}\sum_{\ell=1}^{k} \mathbb{E}[a(v_i, X_i^{\text{all}}(\boldsymbol{v}), \{\ell\})\mathbb{I}[\ell \in X_i^{\text{all}}(\boldsymbol{v})]] \\
&= \sum_{\ell=1}^{k} \mathbb{E}[\text{SW}_\ell^B(\boldsymbol{v})] \\
&= \sum_{\ell \in H} \mathbb{E}[\text{SW}_\ell^B(\boldsymbol{v})] + \sum_{\ell \in L} \mathbb{E}[\text{SW}_\ell^B(\boldsymbol{v})] \\
&< \sum_{\ell \in H} \mathbb{E}[\text{SW}_\ell^B(\boldsymbol{v})] + 4\sum_{\ell \in L} \mathbb{E}[\text{SW}_\ell^S(\boldsymbol{w})].
\end{aligned}$$

The last inequality follows because by definition of L,

$$4\sum_{\ell \in L} \mathbb{E}[\text{SW}_\ell^S(\boldsymbol{w})] > \sum_{\ell \in L} \mathbb{E}[\text{SW}_\ell^B(\boldsymbol{v})].$$

□

Now, since buyers can obtain only high-welfare items, their contribution to the expected social welfare of $\mathbb{M}_{\text{add}}$ is greater than a constant fraction of the expected contribution of the high-welfare items to the allocation computed by $\mathbb{A}$.

Proposition 5.5.

$$\text{ALG}^B \geq \frac{1}{4}\sum_{\ell \in H} \mathbb{E}_{\boldsymbol{v}}[SW_\ell^B(\boldsymbol{v})].$$

Thus, using Proposition 5.4 and Proposition 5.5 we can prove that the sum of the buyers' expected contribution and the sellers' expected contribution of $\mathbb{M}_{\text{add}}$ provides a constant approximation to the buyers' expected contribution in the optimal allocation.

Lemma 5.6.

$$4\alpha\text{ALG}^B + 4\alpha\text{ALG}^S > \text{OPT}^B.$$

Proof. By Proposition 5.5, $4\text{ALG}^B \geq \sum_{\ell \in H} \mathbb{E}_{\boldsymbol{v}}[\text{SW}_\ell^B(\boldsymbol{v})]$. Moreover, our mechanism leaves every item $\ell \in L$ with its seller, and so $\text{ALG}^S \geq \sum_{\ell \in L} \mathbb{E}_{\boldsymbol{w}}[\text{SW}_\ell^S(\boldsymbol{w})]$. Therefore,

$$4\text{ALG}^B + 4\text{ALG}^S \geq \sum_{\ell \in H} \mathbb{E}_{\boldsymbol{v}}[\text{SW}_\ell^B(\boldsymbol{v})] + 4\sum_{\ell \in L} \mathbb{E}_{\boldsymbol{w}}[\text{SW}_\ell^S(\boldsymbol{w})] > \sum_{i=1}^{n} \mathbb{E}_{\boldsymbol{v}}[v_i(X_i^{\text{all}}(\boldsymbol{v}))] \geq \frac{1}{\alpha}\text{OPT}^B.$$

The second inequality holds by Proposition 5.4, and the last inequality follows because we defined α to be the approximation factor of algorithm $\mathbb{A}$, which is the algorithm that we assumed to generate allocation $X^{\text{all}}(\boldsymbol{v})$. □

Finally, we are ready to prove the main theorem of this section.

Proof of Theorem 5.2. On the sellers' side, the mechanism is ex-post IR and DSIC: the sellers solely have to decide between accepting or rejecting a single offer to receive a proposed payment in exchange for a bundle of items, and it is clearly a dominant strategy to accept if and only if such an exchange leads to an improvement in the seller's utility. Every buyer chooses a bundle that maximises her expected utility, and this choice depends solely on the choice of strategies of the sellers. Therefore, the mechanism has a BNE in which the sellers play a dominant strategy, and the mechanism is thus ex-interim IR and BIC. The fact that the mechanism is DSBB follows from its definition, which makes clear that payments are defined by the appropriate sequence of trades and payments from buyers to sellers. The approximation guarantee follows by the sum of the inequalities of the above Lemmas 5.3 and 5.6. □

It is important to notice that the mechanism $\mathbb{M}_{\text{add}}$ turns into a DSIC and ex-post IR mechanism if the buyers have additive valuations instead of XOS valuations.

Corollary 5.7. *For the special case that for all $i \in [n]$, distribution G_i is over additive valuation functions, $\mathbb{M}_{\text{add}}$ is ex-post IR, DSIC, DSBB and $(2 + 4\alpha)$-approximates the optimal social welfare.*

Proof. If a buyer $i \in [n]$ has an additive valuation function, it is a dominant strategy to request the items in $\Lambda_i(\boldsymbol{v}_{<i}))$ for which it holds that $v_i(\{\ell\}) > p_\ell$. This follows from the simple fact that by additivity, the utility that a buyer has for any bundle of items S can be written as $\sum_{\ell \in S} v_i(\{\ell\}) - p_\ell$. Thus, for every item $\ell \in [k]$ that a buyer requests (recall that this item is then allocated to her for price p_ℓ with probability 1/2), a term of $(1/2)(v_i(\{\ell\}) - p_\ell)$ gets added to her expected utility. So including ℓ in her requested bundle is profitable if and only if $v_i(\{\ell\}) - p_\ell \geq 0$. Using the same argument, the ex-post IR property is also satisfied by following this strategy. □

6 DISCUSSION

An open problem is to extend or refine our mechanisms so that they satisfy the DSIC and ex-post IR properties for the case of XOS buyers and additive sellers. The first naive approach for doing so might be trying to consider every additive seller as a set of distinct unit-supply sellers and then run $\mathbb{M}_{\text{1-supply}}$. However, this is not guaranteed to work due to the fact that an additive valuation function may have intrinsic interdependencies among the items (e.g. if there are duplicates among the items) and so the independence of these distinct unit-supply sellers is not guaranteed. Something we might additionally consider to do is to ask every seller for her favorite bundle to place in the market, yet this may cause a seller to regret having chosen that particular bundle after seeing the realizations of the buyers' valuations. On the other hand, it also seems highly challenging to establish any sort of impossibility result for any reasonably defined class of posted price mechanisms for two-sided markets.

Another natural direction is to extend the above mechanism to the setting in which both buyers and sellers possess an XOS valuation function over bundles of items. A first challenge consists in finding a suitable definition of the sellers' social welfare contribution of an item using the corresponding representative additive function.

ACKNOWLEDGMENTS

The authors thank anonymous referees for their helpful comments. Tim Roughgarden is supported by the NSF Grant CCF-1524062. Stefano Leonardi is partly supported by the Google Focused Award on "Algorithms for Large-scale Data Analysis". Part of this work was done while Stefano Leonardi and Tim Roughgarden were visiting the Economics and Computation semester at the Simons Institute for the Theory of Computing.

REFERENCES

[1] Liad Blumrosen and Shahar Dobzinski. 2014. Reallocation mechanisms. In *Proceedings of the 15th ACM Conference on Economics and Computation (EC)*. ACM, 617–617.

[2] Liad Blumrosen and Thomas Holenstein. 2008. Posted Prices vs. Negotiations: an Asymptotic Analysis. In *Proceedings of the 9th ACM conference on Electronic Commerce (EC)*. ACM, 49–49.

[3] Shuchi Chawla, Jason D. Hartline, David L. Malec, and Balasubramanian Sivan. 2010. Multi-parameter mechanism design and sequential posted pricing. In *Proceedings of the 42nd ACM Symposium on Theory of Computing (STOC)*. ACM, 311–320.

[4] Edward H. Clarke. 1971. Multipart Pricing of Public Goods. *Public Choice* 11, 1 (1971), 17–33.

[5] Riccardo Colini-Baldeschi, Bart De Keijzer, Stefano Leonardi, and Stefano Turchetta. 2016. Approximately Efficient Double Auctions with Strong Budget Balance. In *Proceedings of the 27th Annual ACM-SIAM Symposium on Discrete Algorithms (SODA '16)*. ACM-SIAM, 1424–1443.

[6] Xiaotie Deng, Paul W. Goldberg, Bo Tang, and Jinshan Zhang. 2014. Revenue Maximization in a Bayesian Double Auction Market. *Theoretical Computer Science* 539, 1 (2014), 1–12.

[7] Kaustubh Deshmukh, Andrew V. Goldberg, Jason D. Hartline, and Anna R. Karlin. 2002. Truthful and Competitive Double Auctions. In *Proceedings of the 10th Annual European Symposium on Algorithms (ESA)*. Springer, 361–373.

[8] Paul Dütting and Robert Kleinberg. 2015. Polymatroid Prophet Inequalities. In *Proceedings of the 23rd Annual European Symposium on Algorithms (ESA)*. 437–449.

[9] Paul Dütting, Inbal Talgam-Cohen, and Tim Roughgarden. 2014. Modularity and Greed in Double Auctions. In *Proceedings of the 15th ACM Conference on Economics and Computation (EC)*. ACM, 241–258.

[10] Uriel Feige and Shlomo Joseph. 2014. Demand Queries with Preprocessing. In *Proceedings of the 41st Int'l Colloquium on Automata, Languages, and Programming (ICALP)*. Springer LNCS 8572, 477–488.

[11] Michal Feldman, Nick Gravin, and Brendan Lucier. 2015. Combinatorial Auctions via Posted Prices. In *Proceedings of the 26th Annual ACM-SIAM Symposium on Discrete Algorithms (SODA)*. ACM-SIAM, 123–135.

[12] Thomas A. Gresik and Mark A. Satterthwaite. 1989. The Rate at Which a Simple Market Converges to Efficiency as the Number of Traders Increases: An Asymptotic Result for Optimal Trading Mechanisms. *Journal of Economic Theory* 48, 1 (1989), 304–332.

[13] Theodore Groves. 1973. Incentives in Teams. *Econometrica* 41, 4 (1973), 617–631.

[14] Robert Kleinberg and Seth M. Weinberg. 2012. Matroid Prophet Inequalities. In *Proceedings of the 44th Annual ACM Symposium on Theory of Computing (STOC)*. ACM, 123–136.

[15] R. Preston McAfee. 1992. A Dominant Strategy Double Auction. *Journal of Economic Theory* 56, 2 (1992), 434–450.

[16] Roger B. Myerson. 1981. Optimal Auction Design. *Mathematics of Operations Research* 6, 1 (1981), 58–73.

[17] Roger B. Myerson and Mark A. Satterthwaite. 1983. Efficient Mechanisms for Bilateral Trading. *Journal of Economic Theory* 29 (1983), 265–281.

[18] Aldo Rustichini, Mark A. Satterthwaite, and Steven R. Williams. 1994. Convergence to Efficiency in a Simple Market with Incomplete Information. *Econometrica* 62, 5 (1994), 1041–1063.

[19] Tuomas Sandholm and Andrew Gilpin. 2004. *Sequences of Take-It-or-Leave-It Offers: Near-Optimal Auctions Without Full Valuation Revelation.* Springer, 73–91.

[20] Mark A. Satterthwaite and Steven R. Williams. 1989. The Rate of Convergence to Efficiency in the Buyer's Bid Double Auction as the Market Becomes Large. *The Review of Economic Studies* 56, 4 (1989), 477–498.

[21] Mark A. Satterthwaite and Steven R. Williams. 2002. The Optimality of a Simple Market Mechanism. *Econometrica* 70, 5 (2002), 1841–1863.

[22] Erel Segal-Halevi, Avinatan Hassidim, and Yonatan Aumann. 2016. A Random-Sampling Double-Auction Mechanism. *CoRR* abs/1604.06210 (2016).

[23] William Vickrey. 1961. Counterspeculation, Auctions, and Competitive Sealed Tenders. *The Journal of Finance* 16, 1 (1961), 8–37.

Learning in Repeated Auctions with Budgets: Regret Minimization and Equilibrium [Abstract]

SANTIAGO R. BALSEIRO, Duke University
YONATAN GUR, Stanford University

In online advertising markets, advertisers often purchase ad placements through bidding in repeated auctions based on realized viewer information. We study how budget-constrained advertisers may bid in the presence of competition, when there is uncertainty about future bidding opportunities as well as competitors' heterogenous preferences and budgets. We formulate this problem as a sequential game of incomplete information, where bidders know neither their own valuation distribution, nor the budgets and valuation distributions of their competitors. We introduce a family of dynamic bidding strategies we refer to as *adaptive pacing* strategies, in which advertisers adjust their bids *throughout* the campaign according to the sample path of observed expenditures. We analyze the performance of this class of strategies under different assumptions on competitors' behavior. Under arbitrary competitors' bids, we establish through matching lower and upper bounds the asymptotic optimality of this class of strategies as the number of auctions grows large. When adopted by all the bidders, the dynamics converge to a tractable and meaningful steady state. Moreover, we show that these strategies constitute an approximate Nash equilibrium in dynamic strategies: The benefit of unilaterally deviating to other strategies, including ones with access to complete information, becomes negligible as the number of auctions and competitors grows large. This establishes a connection between regret minimization and market stability, by which advertisers can essentially follow equilibrium bidding strategies that also ensure the best performance that can be guaranteed off-equilibrium.

Additional Key Words and Phrases: sequential auctions; online advertising; online learning; stochastic optimization; stochastic approximation; incomplete information; regret analysis; dynamic games.

A full version of this paper is available at https://ssrn.com/abstract=2921446.

Authors' email addresses: First: srb43@duke.edu; Second: ygur@stanford.edu.

DOI: http://dx.doi.org/10.1145/3033274.3084088
EC'17, June 26–30, 2017, Cambridge, MA, USA.
ACM ISBN 978-1-4503-4527-9/17/06.

Nash Social Welfare Approximation for Strategic Agents

SIMINA BRÂNZEI, Hebrew University of Jerusalem
VASILIS GKATZELIS, Drexel University
RUTA MEHTA, University of Illinois at Urbana-Champaign

The fair division of resources among strategic agents is an important age-old problem that has led to a rich body of literature. At the center of this literature lies the question of whether there exist mechanisms that can implement fair outcomes, despite the agents' strategic behavior. A fundamental objective function used for measuring the fairness of an allocation is the geometric mean of the agents' values, known as the *Nash social welfare* (NSW). This objective function is maximized by widely known solution concepts such as Nash bargaining and the competitive equilibrium with equal incomes.

In this work we focus on the question of (approximately) implementing this objective. The starting point of our analysis is the Fisher market, a fundamental model of an economy, whose benchmark is precisely the (weighted) Nash social welfare. We begin by studying two extreme classes of valuations functions, namely perfect substitutes and perfect complements, and find that for perfect substitutes, the Fisher market mechanism yields a constant approximation: at most 2 and at least $e^{\frac{1}{e}}$ (≈ 1.44). However, for perfect complements, the Fisher market mechanism does not work well, its bound degrading linearly with the number of players.

Strikingly, the Trading Post mechanism—an indirect market mechanism also known as the Shapley-Shubik game—has significantly better performance than the Fisher market on its own benchmark. Not only does Trading Post achieve an approximation of 2 for perfect substitutes, but this bound holds for any concave utilities, and it becomes essentially optimal for perfect complements, where it reaches $(1 + \epsilon)$ for any $\epsilon > 0$. Moreover, we show that all the Nash equilibria of the Trading Post mechanism are pure (hence the approximation factors extend to all Nash equilibria), and satisfy an important notion of individual fairness known as proportionality.

CCS Concepts: • **Theory of computation → Quality of equilibria; Market equilibria;**

Additional Key Words and Phrases: Nash social welfare; Fisher market; Trading post

1 INTRODUCTION

The question of allocating resources among multiple participants in a way that is fair is as old as human society itself [52], with some of the earliest recorded instances dating back to more than 2500 years ago[1]. The mathematical study of fair division began with the work of Steinhaus during the second world war, which led to an extensive and growing body of work on fair division

[1]See, e.g., Hesiod's Theogony, where a protocol known as *Cut and Choose* is mentioned.

Simina was supported by ISF grant 1435/14 administered by the Israeli Academy of Sciences and Israel-USA Bi-national Science Foundation (BSF) grant 2014389, and the I-CORE Program of the Planning and Budgeting Committee and The Israel Science Foundation. This project has received funding from the European Research Council (ERC) under the European Union's Horizon 2020 research and innovation programme (grant agreement No 740282). Vasilis was supported by NSF grants CCF-1408635, CCF-1216073, and CCF-1161813. This work was done in part while the authors were research fellows at the Simons Institute for the Theory of Computing.

EC'17, June 26–30, 2017, Cambridge, Massachusetts, USA. © 2017 ACM. ISBN 978-1-4503-4527-9/17/06...$15.00.
DOI: http://dx.doi.org/10.1145/3033274.3085143

protocols within economics and political science, e.g., [6, 9, 52, 61, 65]. Recent years have seen an increased amount of work on fair division coming from computer science (see, e.g., [10, Part II]), partly motivated by problems related to allocating computational resources—such as CPU, memory, and bandwidth—among the users of a computing system. This work has focused on settings with both divisible goods (e.g., [11, 14, 20, 24, 57, 59]) and indivisible ones (e.g., [4, 16, 23, 60]).

One of the basic questions underlying the fair division problem is that of *defining fairness* to begin with, and a large body of work in economics, particularly social choice theory, is concerned with this very question, with numerous solution concepts proposed in response. Our fairness concept of choice herein is the *Nash social welfare* (NSW), which dates back to the fifties [45, 54] and has been proposed by Nash as a solution for bargaining problems, using an axiomatic approach. This objective aims to choose an outcome $\mathbf{x}$ maximizing the geometric mean of the utilities $(u_i(\mathbf{x}))$ of the n participating agents and, like other standard welfare objectives, it is captured by a family of functions known as generalized (power) means:

$$M_p(\mathbf{x}) = \left(\frac{1}{n}\sum_i [u_i(\mathbf{x})]^p\right)^{1/p}.$$

In particular, the NSW corresponds to $M_0(\mathbf{x})$, the limit of $M_p(\mathbf{x})$ as p goes to zero, i.e., $(\Pi_i u_i(\mathbf{x}))^{\frac{1}{n}}$.

While an extended treatment of the NSW can be found, for example, in [52], we highlight a fundamental property of the NSW objective, namely that it achieves *a natural compromise between individual fairness and efficiency.* Two other well-studied functions captured by $M_p(\mathbf{x})$ are the (*i*) *egalitarian* (max-min) objective attained as $p \to -\infty$, and (*ii*) *utilitarian* (average) objective attained at $p = 1$, which correspond to extreme fairness and extreme efficiency, respectively. However, the former may cause vast inefficiencies, while the latter can completely neglect how unhappy some agents might be. The NSW objective lies between these two extremes and strikes a natural balance between them, since maximizing the geometric mean leads to more balanced valuations, but without neglecting efficiency.

The highly desired fairness and efficiency trade-off that the NSW objective provides can be verified via its close connection with market equilibrium outcomes in the *Fisher market* model—one of the fundamental resource allocation models in mathematical economics. This model was developed by Fisher [8] and studied in an extensive body of literature [17, 21, 28, 32, 33, 36–38, 44, 56]. The basic setting involves a seller who brings multiple divisible goods to the market and a set of buyers equipped with monetary endowments (budgets). The goal of the seller is to extract as much money as possible from the buyers, by charging money for the goods (through prices), while each buyer aims to acquire the best possible bundle of goods at the given prices. A *market equilibrium* is an outcome where supply meets demand, and has been shown to exist for very general models of an economy. When the buyers have the same budgets, this outcome is known as a *competitive equilibrium from equal incomes* (CEEI) [64]. For a broad family of valuations, including the ones considered in this paper, the market equilibrium allocation is known to maximize the NSW objective when the budgets are equal. In other words, the seller's goal can be achieved by computing the allocation of the goods that maximizes the NSW which, in turn, implies the desired price for each good.

A fundamental problem in implementing the Nash social welfare objective is informational: the seller needs to know the valuations of the participants. When these valuations are private information of the buyers, a natural candidate is the mechanism induced by the Fisher market, known as the *Fisher market mechanism*: ask the buyers to report their valuations, and then compute the NSW maximizing allocation based on the reports. Unfortunately, it is well known that buyers can feign different interests and eventually get better allocations [1, 5, 12, 18, 19]. This strategic behavior can result in the mechanism computing market equilibria with respect to preferences having little to do with reality, leading to unfair allocations. In this work we address the following basic question:

> *How well does the Fisher market mechanism optimize its own objective—the Nash social welfare—when the participants are strategic? Are there better mechanisms?*

This question falls under the general umbrella of implementation theory [27], and particularly, of implementing markets [7, 31, 41, 53, 58]. In this literature, the goal is to identify mechanisms (game forms) for which the set of Nash equilibria coincides with the set of market equilibrium allocations for every possible state of the world [27]. In general this can be achieved only in the limit, as the number of players goes to infinity and every player is infinitesimal compared to the entire economy [30].

In this work we show that even for small markets there exist classic mechanisms achieving outcomes that closely approximate the optimal NSW on every instance while simultaneously guaranteeing individual fairness. We measure the quality of a mechanism using the *Price of Anarchy* (PoA) [55], defined as the ratio between the optimal NSW and the NSW of the worst Nash equilibrium outcome obtained by the mechanism.

1.1 Our Results

We study the question of approximately implementing the NSW objective starting with two extensively studied classes of valuations, namely linear (or additive) and Leontief [21, 36, 55], two extremes, and generalize many of our results to arbitrary concave valuations. Recall that additive valuations capture goods that are *perfect substitutes*, i.e., that can replace each other in consumption, such as Pepsi and Coca-Cola. Leontief valuations capture *perfect complements*, i.e., goods that have no value without each other, such as left and right shoes.

In addition to the aggregate measure of wealth captured through the Nash welfare, we will analyze mechanisms that guarantee *proportionality*, one of the fundamental fairness notions in fair division. Proportionality requires that every agent i gets at least a fraction $B_i/\mathcal{B}$ of its utility for everything, where B_i is its budget and $\mathcal{B}$ the sum of all budgets.

Our first set of results concerns the Fisher market mechanism, which collects the bidders valuations in the form of bids and then computes the market equilibrium based on those bids:

Theorem (informal) *Any Nash equilibrium of the Fisher market mechanism approximate the NSW objective within a factor of 2 for linear valuations. For Leontief valuations, the approximation degrades linearly with the number of players. Every Nash equilibrium of the mechanism is proportional for all concave utilities.*

These bounds reveal significant differences between the quality of the Nash equilibria of the Fisher market mechanism for complements and substitutes.

Much more strikingly, we find that a classic mechanism known as *Trading Post*, originally introduced by Shapley and Shubik [1977] and studied in a long line of work in different scenarios [30, 43, 46, 49], offers very strong guarantees. At a high level, rather than collecting the players' preferences and computing the market equilibrium, the Trading Post mechanism gives each participant direct control over how to spend its budget. Once the agents choose how to distribute their budget over the available goods, they receive a fraction from each good that is proportional to the amount they spent on it. Our results for the Trading Post mechanism are:

Theorem (informal) *Any Nash equilibrium of the Trading Post mechanism approximates the NSW objective within a factor of 2 for all concave valuations. For Leontief valuations, the Trading Post mechanism achieves in the equilibrium an approximation of $1 + \epsilon$ for every $\epsilon > 0$. Moreover, all the Nash equilibria of Trading Post are pure and proportional for all concave utilities, while their existence is guaranteed for all CES utilities.*

In other words, not only does the Trading Post mechanism achieve the same approximation as the Fisher market mechanism for additive valuations, but the bound holds for all concave valuations, and is arbitrarily close to the optimum for Leontief valuations! We view this as an important result that testifies to the usefulness and robustness of the Trading Post mechanism. A good Nash welfare approximation implies the geometric mean of values is high, and so utility is well distributed across the participants. Trading Post also ensures proportionality in any equilibrium outcome, thus the mechanism guarantees a surprising combination of both individual and aggregate fairness for very general utilities.

An interpretation of the Leontief result is that the Trading Post mechanism limits the extent to which an agent can affect the outcome, thus also limiting the extent to which things can go awry. Specifically, when an agent deviates in the Trading Post mechanism, this deviation has no effect on the way that the other agents are spending their money. On the other hand, an agent's deviation in the Fisher market mechanism can lead to a market equilibrium where the other agents' spending and allocation has changed significantly. In addition to this, in the Fisher market mechanism an agent can affect the price of an item even if the agent does not end up spending on that item in the final outcome. This is in contrast to the Trading Post mechanism where an agent can affect only the prices of the items that this agent is spending on, so the agents are forced to "put their money where their mouth is".

Finally, we prove that the set of mixed Nash equilibria of the Trading Post mechanism coincides with the set of pure Nash equilibria even with concave valuations, which extends our approximation bounds for this mechanism to mixed PoA. Moreover, both mechanisms achieve a classic notion of individual fairness in the equilibrium, namely proportionality. All of the above results work for the weighted version of the Nash social welfare, where agent i has a w_i fraction of the total budget, and the NSW objective becomes $\Pi_i [u_i(\mathbf{x})]^{w_i}$. In the process of obtaining a near optimal bound for Leontief in the Trading Post mechanism, we show that ϵ-approximate market equilibria for Leontief utilities approximate its Nash social welfare by a factor of $\frac{1}{(1+\epsilon)}$. We believe that this as well as the technique that we developed to show the bounds of 2 may be of independent interest.

1.2 Related Work

The paper most closely related to our work is that of [24] which proposes *truthful* mechanisms for approximately maximizing the Nash social welfare objective. One of the truthful mechanisms that they propose, the Partial Allocation mechanism, guarantees a 2.718 approximation of the optimal NSW for both linear and Leontief valuations. In fact, the Partial Allocation mechanism guarantees that *every agent* receives a 2.718 approximation of the value that it would receive in the market equilibrium. But, in order to ensure truthfulness, this mechanism is forced to keep some of the goods unallocated, which makes it inapplicable for many real world settings. Complementing this mechanism, our work analyzes simple and well-studied mechanisms that allocate everything.

Most of the literature on fair division starting from the 1940's deals with the cake-cutting problem, which models the allocation of a divisible heterogeneous resource such as land, time, and mineral deposits, among agents with different preferences [6, 9, 52, 61, 65]. Some recent work has studied the agents' incentives in cake cutting. In particular, [20] study truthful cake-cutting with agents having piecewise uniform valuations and provide a polynomial-time mechanism that is truthful, proportional, and envy-free, while [51] shows that for general valuations there exists a protocol that is truthful in expectation, envy-free, and proportional for any number of players. The work of [48] shows that truthfulness comes at a significant cost in terms of efficiency for direct revelation mechanisms, while [14] show that the only strategyproof mechanisms in the standard query model for cake cutting are dictatorships (even for two players; a similar impossiblity holds for $n > 2$). The standard cake cutting model assumes additive valuations, and so it does not capture resources with Leontief valuations, which we also analyze in this paper.

The resource allocation literature has seen a resurgence of work studying fair and efficient allocation for Leontief valuations [29, 40, 42, 57]. These valuations exhibit perfect complements and they are considered to be natural valuation abstractions for computing settings where jobs need resources in fixed ratios. [40] defined the notion of Dominant Resource Fairness (DRF), which is a generalization of the egalitarian social welfare to multiple types of resources. This solution has the advantage that it can be implemented truthfully for this specific class of valuations. [57] assessed DRF in terms of the resulting efficiency, showing that it performs poorly. [29] proposed an alternate fairness criterion called Bottleneck Based Fairness, which [42] subsequently showed is satisfied by the proportionally fair allocation. [42] also posed the study of incentives related to this latter notion as an interesting open problem. It is worth noting that [40] acknowledge that the CEEI, i.e., the NSW maximizing allocation would actually be the preferred fair division mechanism in their setting, and that the main drawback of this solution is the fact that it cannot be implemented truthfully. Our results show that the Trading Post mechanism can, in fact, approximate the CEEI outcome arbitrarily well, thus shedding new light on this setting.

The Trading Post mechanism, also known as the Shapley-Shubik game [62], has been studied in an extensive body of literature over the years, sometimes under very different names, such as Chinese auction [47], proportional sharing mechanism [35], and the Tullock contest in rent seeking [34, 50, 63], the latter being a variant of the game with a different success probability for items that nobody bid on. Trading Post can also be interpreted as a congestion game (see, e.g., [39]), or an all-pay auction when the budgets are intrinsically valuable to the players.

The fact that, facing the Fisher mechanism, the agents may gain by bidding strategically is well known. [1] studied the agents' incentives and proved existence and structural properties of Nash equilibria for this mechanism. Extending this work, [18, 19] proved bounds on the extent to which an agent can gain by misreporting for various classes of valuation functions, including additive and Leontief. Finally, [12] showed bounds for the price of anarchy of this mechanism with respect to the social welfare objective, and [26] studied large markets under mild randomness and showed that this price of anarchy converges to one.

Finally, recent work on the NSW has revealed additional appealing properties of this objective. For indivisible items the NSW can be approximated in polynomial time [2, 3, 22, 23] and its optimal allocation is approximately envy-free [15]. On the other hand, for divisible items, it can be used as an intermediate step toward approximating the normalized social welfare objective [25].

2 PRELIMINARIES

Let $N = \{1, \ldots, n\}$ be a set of players (agents) and $M = \{1, \ldots, m\}$ a set of divisible goods. Player i's utility for a bundle of goods is represented by a non-decreasing non-negative concave valuation function $u_i : [0,1]^m \to \mathbb{R}_+$. An allocation $\mathbf{x}$ is a partition of the goods to the players such that $x_{i,j}$ represents the amount of good j received by player i. Our goal will be to allocate all the resources fully; it is without loss of generality to assume that a single unit of each good is available, thus the set of feasible allocations is $\mathcal{F} = \left\{\mathbf{x} \mid x_{i,j} \geq 0 \text{ and } \sum_{i=1}^{n} x_{i,j} = 1\right\}$.

Our measure for assessing the quality of an allocation is its Nash social welfare. At a given allocation $\mathbf{x}$ it is defined as follows

$$\text{NSW}(\mathbf{x}) = \left(\prod_{i=1}^{n} u_i(\mathbf{x}_i)\right)^{\frac{1}{n}}.$$

In order to also capture situations where the agents may have different importance or priority, such as clout in bargaining scenarios, we also consider the weighted version of the Nash social welfare objective. Note this is the objective maximized by the Fisher market equilibrium solution when the buyers have different budgets. We slightly abuse notation and refer to the weighted objective as the Nash social welfare (NSW) as well. If $B_i \geq 1$ is the budget of agent i and $\mathcal{B} = \sum_{i=1}^{n} B_i$ is the total budget, the induced market equilibrium in Fisher's model maximizes the objective:

$$\text{NSW}(\mathbf{x}) = \left(\prod_{i=1}^{n} u_i(\mathbf{x}_i)^{B_i}\right)^{\frac{1}{\mathcal{B}}}.$$

Note that we get back the original definition when all players have the same budget. We would like to find mechanisms that maximize the NSW objective in the presence of strategic agents whose goal is to maximize their own utility.

We measure the quality of the mechanisms using the *price of anarchy* [55] with respect to the NSW objective. Given a problem instance $\mathcal{I}$ and some mechanism $\mathcal{M}$ that yields a set of pure Nash equilibria E, the price of anarchy (PoA) of $\mathcal{M}$ for $\mathcal{I}$ is the maximum ratio between the optimal NSW—obtained at some allocation $\mathbf{x}^*$—and the NSW at an allocation $\mathbf{x} \in E$: $\text{PoA}(\mathcal{M}, I) = \max_{\mathbf{x} \in E} \left\{\frac{\text{NSW}(\mathbf{x}^*)}{\text{NSW}(\mathbf{x})}\right\}$. The price of anarchy of $\mathcal{M}$ is the maximum of this value over all possible instances: $\max_{\mathcal{I}}\{\text{PoA}(\mathcal{M}, \mathcal{I})\}$.

Valuation Functions. We start with two very common and extensively studied valuation functions that lie at the two extremes of a spectrum: *perfect substitutes* and *perfect complements*. For both, let $\boldsymbol{v}_i = (v_{i,1}, \dots, v_{i,m}) \in \mathbb{R}_+^m$ be a vector of valuations for agent i, where $v_{i,j}$ captures the liking of agent i for good j.

Perfect substitutes, defined mathematically through *linear (additive) valuations*, represent goods that can replace each other in consumption, such as Pepsi and Coca-Cola. In the additive model, the utility of a player i for bundle $\mathbf{x}_i$ is $u_i(\mathbf{x}_i) = \sum_{j=1}^{m} v_{i,j} \cdot x_{i,j}$.

Perfect complements, represented by *Leontief utilities*, capture scenarios where one good may have no value without the other, such as a left and a right shoe, or the CPU time and computer memory required for the completion of a computing task. In the Leontief model, the utility of a player i for a bundle $\mathbf{x}_i$ is $u_i(\mathbf{x}_i) = \min_{j=1}^{m} \{x_{i,j}/v_{i,j}\}$; that is, player i desires the items in the ratio $v_{i,1} : v_{i,2} : \dots : v_{i,m}$. Coefficients can be rescaled freely in the Leontief model, so w.l.o.g. $v_{i,j} \geq 1$.

Finally, perfect substitutes and complements are extreme points of a much more general class of valuations known as CES (constant elasticity of substitution), mathematically defined as

$$u_i(\mathbf{x}_i) = \Big(\sum_{j=1}^{m} v_{ij} \cdot x_{ij}^{\rho}\Big)^{\frac{1}{\rho}}$$

where ρ parameterizes the family, and $-\infty < \rho \leq 1,\ \rho \neq 0$. The Leontief and additive utilities are obtained when ρ approaches $-\infty$ and equals 1, respectively.

3 THE FISHER MARKET MECHANISM

In the Fisher market model, given prices $\boldsymbol{p} = (p_1, \dots, p_m)$, each buyer i demands a bundle $\boldsymbol{x}_i$ that maximizes her utility subject to her budget constraints; we call this an optimal bundle of buyer i at prices $\boldsymbol{p}$. Prices $\boldsymbol{p}$ induce a market equilibrium if buyers get their optimal bundle and market clears. Formally, prices $\boldsymbol{p}$ and allocation $\boldsymbol{x}$ constitute a market equilibrium if

(1) Optimal bundle: $\forall i \in N$ and $\forall \boldsymbol{y} : \boldsymbol{y} \cdot \boldsymbol{p} \leq B_i,\ u_i(\mathbf{x}_i) \geq u_i(\boldsymbol{y})$
(2) Market clearing: Each good is fully sold or has price zero, i.e., $\forall j \in M,\ \sum_{j=1}^{m} x_{i,j} \leq 1$, and equality holds if $p_j > 0$. Each buyer exhausts all its budget, i.e., $\forall i \in N,\ \sum_{j=1}^{m} x_{i,j} p_j = B_i$.

For linear and Leontief valuations, the market equilibria can be computed using the Eisenberg-Gale (EG) convex program formulations that follow.

$$\begin{array}{llcll} & \textbf{Linear} & & & \textbf{Leontief} \\ \max & \sum_{i=1}^{n} B_i \cdot \log u_i & & \max & \sum_{i=1}^{n} B_i \cdot \log u_i \\ \text{s.t.} & u_i = \sum_{j=1}^{m} v_{i,j} x_{i,j}, \forall i \in N & & \text{s.t.} & u_i \leq \frac{x_{i,j}}{v_{i,j}},\ \forall i \in N, j \in M \\ & \sum_{i=1}^{n} x_{i,j} \leq 1,\ \ \forall j \in M & & & \sum_{i=1}^{n} x_{i,j} \leq 1,\ \ \forall j \in M \\ & x_{i,j} \geq 0,\ \ \forall i \in N, j \in M & & & x_{i,j} \geq 0,\ \ \forall i \in N, j \in M \end{array} \qquad (1)$$

Let p_j be the dual variable of the second inequality (for good j) in both cases, which corresponds to price of good j. Since due to strong duality Karush-Kuhn-Tucker (KKT) conditions capture solutions of the formulations, we get the following characterization for market equilibria.

For linear valuations, an outcome $(\boldsymbol{x}, \boldsymbol{p})$ is a market equilibrium if and only if,

Lin$_1$ $\forall i \in N$ and $\forall j \in M$, $x_{i,j} > 0 \Rightarrow \frac{v_{i,j}}{p_j} = \max_{k \in M} \frac{v_{i,k}}{p_k}$.
Lin$_2$ $\forall i \in N$, $\sum_{j \in M} x_{i,j} p_j = B_i$. $\forall j \in M$, either $\sum_{i \in N} x_{i,j} = 1$ or $p_j = 0$.

For Leontief valuations, an outcome $(\boldsymbol{x}, \boldsymbol{p})$ is a market equilibrium if and only if.

Leo$_1$ $\forall i \in N$ and $\forall j \in M$, $v_{i,j} > 0 \Rightarrow u_i = \frac{x_{i,j}}{v_{i,j}} = \frac{B_i}{\sum_{j \in M} v_{i,j} p_j}$. Note that $\sum_{j \in M} v_{i,j} p_j$ is the amount buyer i has to spend to get unit utility.
Leo$_2$ $\forall i \in N$, $\sum_{j \in M} x_{i,j} p_j = B_i$. $\forall j \in M$, either $\sum_{i \in N} x_{i,j} = 1$ or $p_j = 0$.

The Fisher market mechanism asks that the agents report their valuations and then it computes the market equilibrium allocation with respect to the reported valuations using the EG formulations.

Definition 3.1 (Fisher Market Mechanism). The *Fisher Market Mechanism* is such that:

- The strategy space of each agent i consists of all possible valuations the agent may pose: $S_i = \{\mathbf{s}_i \mid \mathbf{s}_i \in \mathbb{R}^m_{\geq 0}\}$. We refer to an agent's strategy as a *report.*
- Given a strategy profile $\mathbf{s} = (\mathbf{s}_i)_{i=1}^n$, the outcome of the game is a market equilibrium of the Fisher market given by $\langle B_i, \mathbf{s}_i \rangle$, after removing the items j for which $\sum_{i \in N} s_i(j) = 0$. If there exists a market equilibrium $\mathcal{E}$ preferred by all the agents (with respect to their true valuations), then $\mathcal{E}$ is the outcome of the game on $\langle B_i, \mathbf{s}_i \rangle$. Otherwise, the outcome is any fixed market equilibrium.

It is well known that the buyers have incentives to hide their true valuations in a Fisher market mechanism. We illustrate this phenomenon through an example.

Example 3.2. Consider a Fisher market with players $N = \{1, 2\}$, items $M = \{1, 2\}$, additive valuations $v_{1,1} = 1$, $v_{1,2} = 0$, $v_{2,1} = v_{2,2} = 0.5$, and budgets equal to 1. If the players are truthful, the market equilibrium allocation is $\mathbf{x}_1 = (1, 0)$, $\mathbf{x}_2 = (0, 1)$. However, if player 2 pretended that its value for item 2 is a very small $v'_{2,2} = \epsilon > 0$, then player 2 would not only get item 2, but also a fraction of item 1.

In the rest of this section we study the performance of the Fisher mechanism when the goods are substitutes and complements, respectively.

3.1 Fisher Market: Perfect Substitutes

In this section we study efficiency loss in the Fisher market due to strategic agents with additive valuations. We note that pure Nash equilibria in the induced game are known to always exist due to [1].[2] Our first main result states that the Fisher market approximates the Nash Social Welfare within a small constant factor, even when the players are strategic.

THEOREM 3.3. *The Fisher Market Mechanism with linear valuations has price of anarchy at most 2.*

We first prove a useful lemma, which bounds the change in prices due to a unilateral deviation in the Fisher market with additive valuations.

LEMMA 3.4. *Let* $\mathbf{p}$ *be the prices in a Fisher market equilibrium. Suppose that buyer* i *unilaterally changes its reported values to* $\mathbf{v}_i'$*, leading to new market equilibrium prices* $\mathbf{p}'$*. Then,*

$$\sum_{j:\, p_j' > p_j} p_j' \;\le\; B_i + \sum_{j:\, p_j' > p_j} p_j.$$

PROOF. Let M^+, M^-, and $M^=$ be the sets of goods whose prices have strictly increased, strictly decreased, and remained unchanged, respectively, when transitioning from $\mathbf{p}$ to $\mathbf{p}'$. If some player $k \neq i$ is buying any fraction of a good from M^- or $M^=$ at $\mathbf{p}'$, then the player cannot be buying anything from M^+ at $\mathbf{p}'$. To verify this fact, assume that player k was spending on some item $\alpha \in M^- \cup M^=$ at prices $\mathbf{p}$ and is now spending on some item $\beta \in M^+$ at prices $\mathbf{p}'$. Since both these allocations are market equilibria, $\mathbf{Lin}_1$ implies that $\frac{v_{k,\alpha}}{p_\alpha} \ge \frac{v_{k,\beta}}{p_\beta}$ at prices $\mathbf{p}$ and $\frac{v_{k,\alpha}}{p_\alpha'} \le \frac{v_{k,\beta}}{p_\beta'}$ at prices $\mathbf{p}'$. Since $p_\alpha' \le p_\alpha$ and $p_\beta' > p_\beta$, this leads to the contradiction that $v_{k,\alpha} > v_{k,\alpha}$.

Thus, any player, other than i, who is buying goods from M^+ at prices $\mathbf{p}'$ had to be spending all its budget on these items at prices $\mathbf{p}$. This implies that the only reason why the sum of the prices of the goods in M^+ could increase is because player i is contributing more money on these items. Since the budget of i is B_i, the total increase in these prices is at most B_i. This concludes the proof. □

In addition to this, we will be using a folklore weighted arithmetic and geometric mean inequality stated in the following lemma.

LEMMA 3.5. *For any nonnegative numbers* $\rho_1, \rho_2, \dots, \rho_n$ *and* $w_1, w_2, \dots, w_n$ *with* $W = \sum_{i=1}^n w_i$*, we have* $\left(\prod_{i=1}^n \rho_i^{w_i}\right)^{1/W} \le \frac{\sum_{i=1}^n \rho_i w_i}{W}$.

We can now prove the main theorem.

PROOF. (of Theorem 3.3) Given a problem instance with additive valuations, let $\mathbf{x}^*$ be the allocation that maximizes the Nash social welfare—i.e., the market equilibrium allocation with respect to the true valuations—and $\tilde{\mathbf{x}}$ and $\tilde{\mathbf{p}}$ the allocation and prices respectively obtained under some Nash equilibrium of the market, where the players report fake valuations $\tilde{\mathbf{v}}$. Additionally, for each player i, let $\mathbf{x}^i$ be the allocation that would arise if every player $k \neq i$ reported $\tilde{\mathbf{v}}_k$ while i reported its true value v_{ij} for every item j with $x_{ij}^* > 0$, and zero elsewhere.

Since $\tilde{\mathbf{v}}$ is an equilibrium, this unilateral deviation of i cannot increase its utility:

$$u_i(\tilde{\mathbf{x}}_i) \;\ge\; u_i(\mathbf{x}_i^i) \;=\; \sum_{j=1}^m x_{ij}^i v_{ij}. \tag{2}$$

[2]The existence is shown under a *conflict-free* tie breaking rule, which tries to allocate best bundle to as many agents as possible when there is a choice.

Since $\mathbf{x}^i$ is a market equilibrium with respect to the reported values, according to the KKT condition (**Lin**$_1$), $x^i_{ij} > 0$ implies $v_{ij}/p^i_j \geq v_{ik}/p^i_k$ for any other item k, where p^i_j is the price of item j in $\mathbf{x}^i$. Also, the KKT condition (**Lin**$_2$) imply that $\sum_j x^i_{ij}p^i_j = B_i$ for every bidder i. Therefore, $\mathbf{x}^i_i$ provides i at least as much value as any other bundle that i can afford facing prices p^i, i.e., any bundle that costs at most B_i. In particular, consider the allocation $\mathbf{x}'$ such that

$$x'_{ij} = \frac{B_i x^*_{ij}}{\sum_{k=1}^m x^*_{ik}p^i_k}.$$

For this allocation we have:

$$\sum_{j=1}^m x'_{ij}p^i_j = \sum_{j=1}^m \left(\frac{B_i x^*_{ij}}{\sum_{k=1}^m x^*_{ik}p^i_k}\right) \cdot p^i_j = \frac{B_i \sum_{j=1}^m x^*_{ij}p^i_j}{\sum_{k=1}^m x^*_{ik}p^i_k} = B_i.$$

Therefore, player i can afford this bundle of items using the budget B_i, which implies that $\mathbf{x}^i_i$ provides i at least as much value, i.e.,

$$u_i(\mathbf{x}^i_i) \geq u_i(\mathbf{x}'_i) = \sum_{j=1}^m v_{i,j}x'_{i,j} = \frac{B_i u_i(\mathbf{x}^*_i)}{\sum_{j=1}^m x^*_{i,j}p^i_j}.$$

Let ρ_i denote the ratio $\frac{u_i(\mathbf{x}^*)}{u_i(\tilde{\mathbf{x}}_i)}$. Using the Nash equilibrium inequality (2), we get:

$$u_i(\tilde{\mathbf{x}}_i) \geq \frac{B_i u_i(\mathbf{x}^*_i)}{\sum_{j=1}^m x^*_{i,j}p^i_j} \Rightarrow \frac{u_i(\mathbf{x}^*)}{u_i(\tilde{\mathbf{x}}_i)} \leq \frac{\sum_{j=1}^m x^*_{i,j}p^i_j}{B_i} \Rightarrow \rho_i B_i \leq \sum_{j=1}^m x^*_{i,j}p^i_j.$$

Using Lemma 3.4, we get:

$$\rho_i B_i \leq \sum_{j=1}^m x^*_{i,j}p^i_j \leq \sum_{j:\, p^i_j \leq \tilde{p}_j} x^*_{i,j}\tilde{p}_j + \sum_{j:\, p^i_j > \tilde{p}_j} x^*_{i,j}p^i_j \leq B_i + \sum_{j=1}^m x^*_{i,j}\tilde{p}_j,$$

and summing over all players:

$$\sum_{i=1}^n \rho_i B_i \leq \sum_{i=1}^n \left(B_i + \sum_{j=1}^m x^*_{i,j}\tilde{p}_j\right) \leq 2\mathcal{B}. \tag{3}$$

Substituting B_i for w_i in Lemma 3.5 and using Inequality (3) yields:

$$\left(\prod_{i=1}^n \rho_i^{B_i}\right)^{1/\mathcal{B}} \leq \frac{\sum_{i=1}^n \rho_i B_i}{\mathcal{B}} \leq 2.$$

□

Next we show a lower bound for the price of anarchy of the Fisher mechanism. We construct a collection of problem instances whose PoA goes to $e^{1/e}$ as number of players grows.

Theorem 3.6. *The Fisher Market mechanism with additive valuations has a price of anarchy no better than* $e^{1/e} \approx 1.445$.

Given some value of n, we construct a market with $n+2$ agents and $n+1$ goods. Fix an integer $k \leq n$; we will set its value later. Each player $i \leq k$ likes only good i, *i.e.*, $v_{i,i} = 1$ and all other $v_{i,j} = 0$. On the other hand, every agent $i \in [k+1, n]$, apart from having $v_{i,i} = 1$, also has some small, but positive, value $v_{i,j} = \epsilon$ for all items $j \leq k$. The rest of that agent's $v_{i,j}$ values are zero. Agent $n+1$ has a small but positive value ϵ' for goods $j \in [k+1, n]$ and value 2 for good $n+1$. Finally, agent $n+2$ values only good $n+1$ at value 2. Here $\epsilon << \epsilon'$, and we will set their values later. In the allocation where every agent $i \in [1, n]$ gets all of good i, while agents $n+1$ and $n+2$ share good $n+1$ equally, the NSW is equal to 1. Next, we construct a Nash equilibrium strategy profile $\mathbf{s}$ of the above market where the NSW approaches $(1/e)^{1/e}$ as $n \to \infty$.

We define a strategy profile $\mathbf{s}$ where the first k agents and the last agent, i.e., agent $n+2$, bid truthfully, while every bidder $i \in [k+1, n]$ misreports in a way such that it ends up spending some small amount $\delta = 2\epsilon'$ on item i and the rest of its budget, namely $(1-\delta)$, is equally divided on items in $[1, k]$. We later set a value for δ such that agent $n+1$ would want to buy only good $n+1$.

We now show that the above profile is a Nash equilibrium for carefully chosen values of ϵ, and ϵ'. Note that, since bidders $i \in [1, k]$ and bidder $n+2$ bids truthfully and values just one item, each one of these bidders will spend all of its budget on the corresponding items, no matter what the remaining bidders report. Therefore, the price of items $j \in [1, k]$ and item $n+1$ will be exactly 1 if we exclude the spending of bidders $i \in [k+1, n+1]$, no matter what these bidders report. Also, if the price of items $j \in [k+1, n]$ is equal to δ in profile $\mathbf{s}$, then this price will not drop below δ, irrespective of what bidder $n+1$ reports. In the next two lemmas, we show that a deviation from $\mathbf{s}$ does not help the bidders, even when the prices are held constant for the goods where an agent starts spending more money.

Lemma 3.7. *If $\delta = 2\epsilon'$ then, even if the prices of goods $j \in [k+1, n]$ are fixed at δ, the $(n+1)^{th}$ bidder has no incentive to spend money on any good other than good $n+1$.*

Proof. If agent $n+1$ spends all of its budget on item $n+1$, then its price becomes 2 and the agent receives half of that item, i.e., a utility of 1. On the other hand, if the agent spends at total of $\gamma > 0$ on goods $j \in [k+1, n]$ then, even if the price of these items remains δ, her utility would be $\epsilon' \frac{\gamma}{\delta} + 2\frac{1-\gamma}{2-\gamma}$. For this to be strictly greater than 1 we have to have $\delta < 2\epsilon' - \gamma\epsilon'$, which contradicts our assumption that $\delta = 2\epsilon'$. □

Furthermore, using a similar analysis as that of Lemma 3.7, it follows that if agent $i \in [k+1, n]$ deviates in a way that decreases its spending on good i to $2\epsilon' - \tau$ for $\tau > 0$, then the Fisher market mechanism outcome will have the $(n+1)^{th}$ agent spending at least $\frac{\tau}{1+\epsilon'}$ on that item. Thus, such a deviation would cause agent i to lose its monopoly on good i. Next, we show that this is not advantageous for agent i if we set $\epsilon = \frac{1}{n^4}$ and $\epsilon' = \frac{1}{n}$, which implies $\delta = \frac{2}{n}$.

Lemma 3.8. *For any $\tau \geq 0$, if agent i is spending $\delta - \tau$ on good i and agent $(n+1)$ is spending $\frac{\tau}{1+\epsilon'}$, when others are bidding according to $\mathbf{s}$, then agent i's utility is maximized at $\tau = 0$.*

Proof. Note that at $\tau = 0$, agent $i \in [k+1, n]$ is spending $\delta = 2\epsilon'$ on good i and, according to Lemma 3.7, agent $n+1$ would not be interested in spending on good i. Thus, agent i is buying good i exclusively and spends $\frac{1-\delta}{k}$ on each of the first k goods. Thus the price each one of the first k goods is $1 + (n-k)\frac{1-\delta}{k}$. Agent i's utility at this allocation is

$$1 + \frac{\frac{1-\delta}{k}}{1 + (n-k)\frac{1-\delta}{k}} k\epsilon = 1 + \frac{(1-\delta)k\epsilon}{k + (n-k)(1-\delta)}$$

As mentioned above, if agent i reduces spending on good i by τ, then the $(n+1)^{th}$ agent will end up spending at least $\frac{\tau}{1+\epsilon'}$ on this item. This may lead to increased prices for the first k goods, but we show that this deviation would not benefit i even if these prices remained the same. The utility of agent i after such a deviation would be

$$\frac{\delta - \tau}{\delta - \tau + \frac{\tau}{1+\epsilon'}} + \frac{(1-\delta+\tau)k\epsilon}{k + (n-k)(1-\delta)}$$

The latter utility is greater than the former only when

$$\frac{\tau k\epsilon}{k+(n-k)(1-\delta)} > \frac{\frac{\tau}{1+\epsilon'}}{\delta-\tau+\frac{\tau}{1+\epsilon'}} \Rightarrow \epsilon > \frac{k+(n-k)(1-\delta)}{k(\delta+\delta\epsilon'-\tau\epsilon')} > 1,$$

which contradicts the fact that $\epsilon = \frac{1}{n^4}$. □

Lemmas 3.7 and 3.8 imply that s is a Nash equilibrium. The price of the first k goods at this Nash equilibrium is $1 + \frac{(n-k)(1-\delta)}{k} = \frac{k+(n-k)(1-\delta)}{k}$. Thus, the utility of buyer $i \in [1, k]$, who spends all of its \$1 on good i, is $u_i = \frac{k}{k+(n-k)(1-\delta)}$. On the other hand, the utility of buyer $i \in [k+1, n]$, who gets all of good i and some of the first k goods, is $u_i = 1 + \frac{(1-\delta)k\epsilon}{k+(n-k)(1-\delta)}$. Agents $(n+1)$ and $(n+2)$ get half of good $n+1$ and thereby get utility of 1 each. Since $\epsilon = \frac{1}{n^4}$ and $\epsilon' = \frac{1}{n}$, then $\forall i \in [1, k]$, $\lim_{n\to\infty} u_i = \frac{k}{n}$ and $\forall i \in [k+1, n]$ $\lim_{n\to\infty} u_i = 1$. Thus, NSW at this bid profile as $n \to \infty$ is $(\frac{k}{n})^{\frac{k}{n}}$, and thereby PoA is at least $(\frac{n}{k})^{k/n}$. Letting $k = \frac{n}{e}$, this becomes $e^{1/e}$, which concludes the proof of Theorem 3.6.

3.2 Fisher Market: Perfect Complements

On the other hand, the Fisher market with perfect complements has a price of anarchy that grows linearly with the number of players.

Theorem 3.9. *The Fisher Market Mechanism with Leontief valuations has a price of anarchy of n, the number of players, and the bound is tight.*

Remark. We observe that PoA of Fisher Market Mechanism degrades continuously within CES as we move from additive to Leontief. For the complements range, *i.e.*, $\rho < 0$, the example achieving n lower bound for Leontief can be modified to show that as ρ decreases the PoA increases. The modification is in the Nash equilibrium profile, where agent i reports $v_{i,i} = 1 + \epsilon$ instead of 1 for an appropriately chosen $\epsilon \geq 0$ depending on ρ and number of players n.

4 THE TRADING POST MECHANISM

The important difference between the Trading Post mechanism and the Fisher Market mechanism is the strategy space of the agents. More precisely, unlike the Fisher market mechanism, where the agents' are asked to report their valuations, the Trading Post mechanism instead asks the agents to directly choose how to distribute their budgets. Once the agents have chosen how much of their budget to spend on each of the goods, the total spending on each good j is treated as its price, and each agent i is allocated a fraction of good j proportional to the amount that i is spending on j. Therefore, the strategy set of each player i is $\mathcal{S}_i = \left\{\mathbf{b}_i \in [0, B_i]^m \mid \sum_{j=1}^m b_{i,j} = B_i\right\}$.

Given a bid profile $\mathbf{b} = (\mathbf{b}_1, \ldots, \mathbf{b}_n)$, the induced allocation is:

$$x_{i,j} = \begin{cases} \frac{b_{i,j}}{\sum_{k=1}^n b_{k,j}} & \text{if } b_{i,j} > 0 \\ 0 & \text{otherwise} \end{cases}$$

In this section we analyze Trading Post for additive and Leontief valuations, extending a number of results to CES and arbitrary concave functions under a mild technical condition known as *perfect competition*, which states that for each good j, there exist at least two buyers that demand strictly positive amount of j when the good is priced at zero. For additive and Leontief valuations, the condition is equivalent to $v_{i,j} > 0, v_{k,j} > 0$, for some $i, k \in N$, $i \neq k$. If this were not satisfied, we could either discard the good or give it away for free.

Our main results in this section are that the *pure* Nash equilibria of Trading Post approximate the NSW objective within a factor of 2 for linear valuations, and within a factor of $1 + \epsilon$ for every $\epsilon > 0$ for Leontief valuations. In fact we extend the approximation factor of 2 to CES and more generally to concave utilities. Moreover, in all of these cases, all the Nash equilibria of the game are pure and their existence is guaranteed for CES utilities.

4.1 Trading Post: Perfect Substitutes

The existence of pure Nash equilibria in the Trading Post mechanism for additive valuations was established by Feldman, Lai, and Zhang [35] under perfect competition. Without competition, even very simple games may not have pure Nash equilibria. To see this, consider for instance a game with two players, two items, and additive valuations $v_{1,1} = 1$, $v_{1,2} = 0$, $v_{2,1} = v_{2,2} = 0.5$. Through a case analysis it can be seen that both players will compete for item 1, while player 2 is the only one that wants item 2, reason for which this player will successively reduce its bid for 2 to get a higher fraction from item 1. However, in the limit of its bid for the second item going to zero, player 2 loses the item.

Our first result shows that Trading Post matches the Fisher market for additive valuations.

Theorem 4.1. *The Trading Post Mechanism with linear valuations has price of anarchy at most 2.*

Proof. Given a problem instance with linear valuations, let $\mathbf{x}^*$ be the allocation that maximizes the NSW and p^* be the corresponding market equilibrium prices. Also, let $\tilde{\mathbf{x}}$ be the allocation in a Nash equilibrium where each player i bids $\tilde{\boldsymbol{b}}_i$ and the price of each item j is $\tilde{p}_j = \sum_i \tilde{b}_{i,j}$.

For some player i, let $\mathbf{x}'$ be the allocation that arises if every player $k \neq i$ bids $\tilde{\boldsymbol{b}}_k$ while agent i unilaterally deviates to $b'_{i,j}$ for each item j. In this deviation, player i first withdraws all of its money, leaving the price of item j to be $p'_j = \tilde{p}_j - \tilde{b}_{i,j}$, and then it redistributes it by spending $b'_{i,j}$ on each item j. The perfect competition condition ensures that, once player i withdraws its money, the prices remain positive ($p'_j > 0,\ \forall j$), as at least two agents are interested in each good. Let the new bid $b'_{i,j}$ be such that for some $\beta_i > 0$ and every item j:

$$\frac{b'_{i,j}}{p'_j + b'_{i,j}} = \frac{x^*_{i,j}}{\beta_i}. \tag{4}$$

Bid $\mathbf{b}'_i$ is implied by the solution of the following program.

$$\text{min: } \beta_i \quad \text{s.t.: } \frac{1}{\beta_i} = \frac{b'_{i,j}}{x^*_{i,j}(p'_j + b'_{i,j})} \quad \text{and} \quad b'_{i,j} \geq 0 \quad \forall j \in M; \qquad \sum_{j \in M} b'_{i,j} \leq B_i$$

Setting $\boldsymbol{b}'_{i,j} = 0$ and $\beta_i = \infty$ gives a feasible point in the above program, and therefore it has a minimum. The allocation induced by this unilateral deviation of i is $x'_{i,j} = \frac{b'_{i,j}}{p'_j + b'_{i,j}} = \frac{x^*_{i,j}}{\beta_i}$. Therefore, the utility of player i after this deviation is $u_i(\mathbf{x}^*)/\beta_i$. But the outcome $\tilde{\mathbf{x}}$ is a Nash equilibrium, so this deviation cannot yield a higher utility for i, which implies that $u_i(\tilde{\mathbf{x}}) \geq u_i(\mathbf{x}^*)/\beta_i$. By definition of b', we get $\sum_j b'_{i,j} = \sum_j x'_{i,j}(p'_j + b'_{i,j}) = B_i$; all the money is spent at optimum β_i. Therefore, replacing for $x'_{i,j} = x^*_{i,j}/\beta_i$, we get

$$B_i \beta_i = \sum_{j=1}^{m} x^*_{i,j}(p'_j + b'_{i,j}) \tag{5}$$

Since $0 \leq x^*_{i,j} \leq 1$ and $p'_j \leq \tilde{p}_j$ for each item j, for agent i we have,

$$\sum_{j=1}^{m} x^*_{i,j}(p'_j + b'_{i,j}) \leq \sum_{j=1}^{m} x^*_{i,j} b'_{i,j} + \sum_{j=1}^{m} x^*_{i,j} \tilde{p}_j \leq B_i + \sum_{j=1}^{m} x^*_{i,j} \tilde{p}_j. \tag{6}$$

Using Inequalities (5) and (6), and summing over all players gives

$$\sum_{i=1}^{n} B_i \frac{u_i(\mathbf{x}_i^*)}{u_i(\tilde{\mathbf{x}}_i)} \le \sum_{i=1}^{n} B_i \beta_i \le \sum_{i=1}^{n} \left(B_i + \sum_{j=1}^{m} x_{i,j}^* \tilde{p}_j \right) \le 2\mathcal{B}. \tag{7}$$

Using the inequality of weighted arithmetic and geometric means provided by Lemma 3.5 on β_i's of (7), we conclude that $\prod_{i=1}^{n} \left(\frac{u_i(\mathbf{x}_i^*)}{u_i(\tilde{\mathbf{x}}_i)} \right)^{B_i/\mathcal{B}} = \prod_{i=1}^{n} (\beta_i)^{B_i/\mathcal{B}} \le 2.$ □

The next theorem complements the upper bound on the price of anarchy with a lower bound of approximately 1.445.

Theorem 4.2. *The Trading Post mechanism has a price of anarchy no better than* $e^{1/e} \approx 1.445$.

Proof. In order to prove this theorem we can use the same family of problem instances used in the proof of Theorem 3.6. In fact, verifying that the market equilibrium outcome induced by the strategy profile $\boldsymbol{s}$ in that construction is a Nash equilibrium for the Trading Post mechanism as well is much more straightforward since an agent's deviation may affect only the way that particular agent ends up spending its budget. □

The upper and lower bounds of Trading Post with additive valuations given by Theorems 4.1 and 4.2 are same as that of Fisher market mechanism. However, next we show this symmetry breaks as soon as we move away from additive valuations, and Trading Post fares significantly better.

4.2 Trading Post: Perfect Complements

We first characterize the precise conditions under which the Trading Post mechanism has exact pure Nash equilibria for Leontief utilities; the missing proofs of this section may be found in the full version [13].

Theorem 4.3. *The Trading Post mechanism with Leontief utilities has pure Nash equilibria if and only if the corresponding market equilibrium prices are all strictly positive. When this happens, the Nash equilibrium utilities in Trading Post are unique and the price of anarchy is* 1.

This theorem shows a correspondence between the pure Nash equilibria of Trading Post and the corresponding market equilibria with respect to the agents' (true) valuations. We observe however that existence of pure Nash equilibria in Trading Post is not guaranteed for Leontief utilities.

Example 4.4. Consider a game with two players and two items, where player 1 has values $v_{1,1} = v_{1,2} = 0.5$ and player 2 has $v_{2,1} = 0.9$, $v_{2,2} = 0.1$. Assume there is a pure Nash equilibrium profile $\mathbf{b}$. Since both players require a non-zero amount from every item for their utility to be positive, we have that $b_{i,j} > 0$ for all $i, j \in \{1, 2\}$. Denote $b_1 = b_{1,1}$ and $b_2 = b_{2,1}$; then $b_{1,2} = 1 - b_1$ and $b_{2,1} = 1 - b_2$. Note that each player must receive the two items in the same ratio relative to its valuation; that is:

$$u_i(\mathbf{b}) = \left(\frac{b_i}{b_1 + b_2} \right) \frac{1}{v_{i,1}} = \left(\frac{1 - b_i}{b_1 + b_2} \right) \frac{1}{v_{i,2}} \tag{8}$$

Otherwise, if the two ratios were not equal, then a player could transfer weight among the items to improve the smaller fraction. Then the requirement in 8 are equivalent to the following equations:

$$\left(\frac{b_1}{b_1 + b_2} \right) \frac{1}{0.5} = \left(\frac{1 - b_1}{b_1 + b_2} \right) \frac{1}{0.5} \iff b_1 = b_2 \tag{9}$$

and

$$\left(\frac{b_2}{b_1 + b_2} \right) \frac{1}{0.9} = \left(\frac{1 - b_2}{b_1 + b_2} \right) \frac{1}{0.1} \iff 8b_2^2 + 8b_1 b_2 = 9b_1 + 7b_2 \tag{10}$$

Combining equations 9 and 10, we get that $b_1 = 1$ and $b_2 = 1$, which contradicts the requirement that $b_1, b_2 \in (0, 1)$. Thus the equilibrium profile $\mathbf{b}$ cannot exist.

The issue illustrated by this example is that the Trading Post cannot implement market outcomes when there exist items priced at zero in the corresponding market equilibrium. This motivates us to introduce an entrance fee in the Trading Post mechanism, denoted by a parameter $\Delta > 0$, which is the minimum amount that an agent needs to spend on an item in order to receive any of it. We denote the corresponding mechanism by $\mathcal{TP}(\Delta)$. The value of Δ can be arbitrarily small, so its impact on the outcome of the game is insignificant.

Formally, given a bid profile $\mathbf{b} = (\mathbf{b}_1, \ldots, \mathbf{b}_n)$, let $\overline{\mathbf{b}} = (\overline{\mathbf{b}}_1, \ldots, \overline{\mathbf{b}}_n)$ be the "effective" bid profile which, for every $i \in N$ and $j \in M$, satisfies $\overline{b}_{i,j} = b_{i,j}$ if $b_{i,j} \geq \Delta$, and $\overline{b}_{i,j} = 0$ otherwise. Then, the bid profile $\mathbf{b}$ yields the allocation:

$$x_{i,j} = \frac{\overline{b}_{i,j}}{\sum_{k=1}^{n} \overline{b}_{k,j}} \quad \text{if } \overline{b}_{i,j} > 0, \quad \text{and} \quad x_{i,j} = 0 \text{ otherwise}$$

Clearly, in any Nash equilibrium, we have that for every player i and item j we have that $b_{i,j} \geq \Delta$ or $b_{i,j} = 0$ (the latter identity holds for those goods j that are outside of player i's demand).

The main result of this section is that, for every $\epsilon \in (0, 1/m)$, the Trading Post mechanism with $\Delta \leq \epsilon/m^2$ has a price of anarchy of at most $1 + \epsilon$. We first show that Trading Post has a pure Nash equilibrium for Leontief utilities for every strictly positive entrance fee. The proof uses an application of Glicksberg's theorem for continuous games.

THEOREM 4.5. *The parameterized Trading Post mechanism $\mathcal{TP}(\Delta)$ is guaranteed to have a pure Nash equilibrium for every $\Delta > 0$.*

We start by defining a notion of approximate market equilibrium that will be useful

Definition 4.6 (ϵ-market equilibrium). Given a problem instance and some $\epsilon > 0$, an outcome $(\mathbf{p}, \mathbf{x})$ is an ϵ-market equilibrium if and only if: (*i*) All the goods with a positive price are completely sold. (*ii*) All the buyers exhaust their budget. (*iii*) Each buyer gets an ϵ-optimal bundle at prices $\mathbf{p}$; that is, for every bundle $\mathbf{y} \in [0, 1]^m$ that i could afford at these prices ($\mathbf{p} \cdot \mathbf{y} \leq B_i$), we have $u_i(\mathbf{y}) \leq u_i(\mathbf{x}_i)(1 + \epsilon)$.

The following theorem states that for every small enough $\epsilon > 0$, all the PNE of the Trading Post game with a small enough entrance fee correspond to ϵ-market equilibrium outcomes.

THEOREM 4.7. *Let $\epsilon > 0$. Then for every $0 < \Delta < \min\left\{\frac{\epsilon}{m^2}, \frac{1}{m}\right\}$, every pure Nash equilibrium of the mechanism $\mathcal{TP}(\Delta)$ with Leontief valuations corresponds to an ϵ-market equilibrium.*

PROOF. Let $\tilde{\boldsymbol{b}}$ be a pure Nash equilibrium of $\mathcal{TP}(\Delta)$ and $\mathbf{x}$ the induced allocation. For each player i, let $D_i = \{j \in M \mid v_{i,j} > 0\}$ be the set of items that i requires, and let $m_i = |D_i|$. We also override notation and refer to $u_i(\mathbf{b})$ as the utility of player i when the strategy profiles are $\mathbf{b}$.

First note that $\tilde{b}_{i,j} > 0$ for each player i and item $j \in D_i$. If this were not the case, then player i would get zero utility at strategy profile $\tilde{\boldsymbol{b}}$; this is worse than playing the uniform strategy $\mathbf{z}_i = (B_i/m, \ldots, B_i/m)$, which guarantees i a positive value regardless of the strategies of the other players $\tilde{\boldsymbol{b}}_{-i}$, namely:

$$u_i(\mathbf{z}_i, \tilde{\boldsymbol{b}}_{-i}) = \min_{j \in D_i} \left\{ \frac{z_{i,j}}{z_{i,j} + \sum_{k \neq i} \tilde{b}_{k,j}} \cdot \frac{1}{v_{i,j}} \right\} \geq \min_{j \in D_i} \left\{ \frac{B_i/m}{B_i/m + \sum_{k \neq i} B_k} \cdot \frac{1}{v_{i,j}} \right\} > 0$$

For each player i and item $j \in D_i$, denote the fraction of utility that i derives from j by:

$$\phi_{i,j} = \frac{\tilde{b}_{i,j}}{\sum_{k=1}^{n} \tilde{b}_{k,j}} \cdot \frac{1}{v_{i,j}}.$$

Then $u_i(\tilde{\boldsymbol{b}}) = \min_{j \in D_i} \phi_{i,j}$. Sort the items in D_i increasingly by their contribution to i's utility: $\phi_{i,i_1} \leq \phi_{i,i_2} \leq \ldots \leq \phi_{i,i_{m_i}}$; it follows that $u_i(\tilde{\boldsymbol{b}}) = \phi_{i,i_1}$. Let $S_i = \{j \in D_i \mid \phi_{i,j} = \phi_{i,i_1}\}$ be the items received in the smallest fraction (equal to i's utility). If $S_i = M$, then the analysis is similar to the exact equilibrium case, where the prices are strictly positive. The difficult case is when $S_i \neq M$. Then player i is getting a higher than necessary fraction from some resource $j \in M \setminus S_i$. Thus i would improve by shifting some of the mass from item j to the items in S. Since $\tilde{\boldsymbol{b}}$ is an equilibrium, no such deviation is possible. Then it must be the case that $\tilde{b}_{i,j} = \Delta$ for all $j \in D_i \setminus S_i$.

Now interpret the bids and allocation as a market equilibrium with Leontief utilities $\mathbf{v}$ and budgets B_i, by setting the prices to $\mathbf{p} = (p_1, \ldots, p_m)$, where $p_j = \sum_{i=1}^{n} \tilde{b}_{i,j}$ for all $j \in M$, and the allocation to $\mathbf{x}$, the same as the one induced by the bids $\tilde{\boldsymbol{b}}$ in the trading post game. We argue that $(\mathbf{p}, \mathbf{x})$ is an ϵ-market equilibrium. Clearly at the outcome $(\mathbf{p}, \mathbf{x})$ all the goods are sold and each buyer exhausts their budget. Moreover observe that all the prices are strictly positive. We must additionally show that each player gets an ϵ-optimal bundle at $(\mathbf{p}, \mathbf{x})$.

Fix an arbitrary buyer i. Let $\mathbf{y}_i$ be an optimal bundle for i given prices p, and let $q_{i,j}$ be the amount of money spent by i to purchase $y_{i,j}$ units of good j at these prices. An upper bound on the optimal value $u_i(\mathbf{y}_i)$ is attained when buyer i shifts *all* the money spent on purchasing items outside S_i to purchase instead higher fractions from the items in S_i. Since the strategy profile $\mathbf{b}$ is an exact equilibrium in the game $\mathcal{TP}(\Delta)$, the amount of money spent by player i on items outside S_i is at most $(m-1)\Delta$; thus i spends at most $B_i - (m-1)\Delta$ on the remaining items in S_i.

By an averaging argument, there exists a good $j \in S_i$ on which i spends the greatest amount of its money, i.e. $\tilde{b}_{i,j} \geq \frac{B_i - (m-1)\Delta}{|S_i|}$. This will be the item for which the gain brought by the deviation in spending is modest. Formally, the maximum fraction of utility that i can get from item j—without decreasing the ratios at which the other items in S_i are received—is:

$$\begin{aligned} \phi'_{i,j} &= \frac{q_{i,j}}{p_j \cdot v_{i,j}} \leq \frac{\tilde{b}_{i,j} + (m-1)\Delta}{\left(\sum_{k=1}^{n} \tilde{b}_{k,j}\right) \cdot v_{i,j}} = \phi_{i,j} + \frac{(m-1)\Delta}{\left(\sum_{k=1}^{n} \tilde{b}_{k,j}\right) \cdot v_{i,j}} \\ &\leq \phi_{i,j} + \frac{\tilde{b}_{i,j} \cdot \epsilon}{\left(\sum_{k=1}^{n} \tilde{b}_{k,j}\right) \cdot v_{i,j}} = \phi_{i,j} \cdot (1+\epsilon) = u_i(\mathbf{x}_i)(1+\epsilon) \end{aligned}$$

where in the inequalities we additionally used that $\Delta < \epsilon^2/m$, $B_i \geq 1\ \forall i \in N$, and $S_i \leq m-1$. The identities hold since item j is in the tight set S_i. Then $u_i(\mathbf{y}_i) \leq \phi'_{i,j} \leq u_i(\mathbf{x}_i)(1+\epsilon)$. Thus each player gets an ϵ-optimal bundle, and so $(\mathbf{p}, \mathbf{x})$ is an ϵ-market equilibrium. □

The following theorem, which we believe is of independent interest, states that in Fisher markets with Leontief utilities, approximate market equilibria are close to exact equilibria in terms of their Nash Social Welfare.

Theorem 4.8. *The Nash social welfare at an ϵ-market equilibrium for Leontief utilities is at least a $\frac{1}{(1+\epsilon)}$ factor of the optimal Nash social welfare.*

Finally, we can state the main result of this section.

THEOREM 4.9. *For every $\epsilon > 0$, the Trading Post game $\mathcal{TP}(\Delta)$ with entrance fee $0 < \Delta < \min\left\{\frac{\epsilon^2}{m}, \frac{1}{m}\right\}$ has a price of anarchy of $1 + \epsilon$, even for arbitrary budgets.*

PROOF. By Theorem 4.7, every PNE of $\mathcal{TP}(\Delta)$ corresponds to an ϵ-market equilibrium. By Theorem 4.8, every ϵ-market equilibrium attains at least a fraction $\frac{1}{1+\epsilon}$ of the optimal Nash social welfare. Thus, the price of anarchy of $\mathcal{TP}(\Delta)$ is $1 + \epsilon$, which completes the proof. □

4.3 Trading Post: Beyond Perfect Substitutes and Complements

In general market equilibrium theory the valuations of the agents are considered to be arbitrary concave, non-decreasing and non-negative functions. Next we extend the upper bound of 2 achieved by Trading Post to this most general setting. The missing proofs are in the full version [13].

THEOREM 4.10. *The Trading Post game with concave valuations has price of anarchy at most 2.*

Moreover, the existence of pure Nash equilibria holds for all CES utilities.

THEOREM 4.11. *The Trading Post game with no minimum bid has exact pure Nash equilibria for all CES utilities with perfect competition and $\rho \in (-\infty, 1]$.*

4.4 Trading Post: Beyond Pure Nash Equilibria

A natural remaining question is whether there exist mixed Nash equilibria with bad Nash social welfare. In the case of Trading Post mechanism we rule out this case by showing that all its Nash equilibria are pure, be it for linear, Leontief, or concave valuations. Details of this result may be found in the full version [13], where we show the following theorem.

THEOREM 4.12. *For markets with linear utilities, every Nash equilibrium of the corresponding Trading Post game is pure. Further, the result extends to concave valuations if a mild condition of* enough competition *is satisfied . For markets with Leontief utilities, every Nash equilibrium of the corresponding Δ Trading Post game $TP(\Delta)$, for $\Delta > 0$, is pure.*

Given such an efficiency achieved by Trading Post mechanism one may wonder if these mechanisms in-fact have unique equilibrium. We rule this out through constructions for additive and Leontief valuations, given in the full version [13].

5 FAIRNESS GUARANTEES

Finally, for concave utilities all the Nash equilibria of the two mechanisms satisfy an important notion of individual fairness: proportionality. That is, each player i achieves a fraction of at least $B_i/\mathcal{B}$ of its maximum utility in any PNE. For equal budgets, the guarantee is $1/n$.

THEOREM 5.1. *Every Nash equilibrium of the Fisher market mechanism with concave utilities, and of the Trading Post mechanism with concave and strictly increasing utilities is proportional. Moreover, for every $0 < \Delta < 1/m$, every Nash equilibrium of the parameterized Trading Post game $TP(\Delta)$ with concave and strictly increasing utilities is approximately proportional, guaranteeing at least $\frac{B_i}{\mathcal{B}}(1 - \rho_i)$ of the optimum for each player i, where $\rho_i = \frac{\Delta\cdot(m-1)}{B_i}$, B_i is the player's budget, $\mathcal{B}$ the sum of budgets, and m the number of items.*

6 DISCUSSION

Our results show great differences between the Fisher market mechanism and Trading Post, with Trading Post simultaneously achieving a Nash social welfare within a factor of two of the optimum and fairness (in the form of proportionality) for all concave utilities. Existence of pure Nash equilibria in Trading Post is guaranteed for all CES utilities.

Our most unexpected and important contribution is for Leontief utilities, where Trading Post approximates the NSW arbitrarily close, while still guaranteeing fair outcomes to each individual. This result may have implications beyond theory, since Leontief utilities have played a starring role in the emerging literature on allocating computer resources. One of the most influential papers in this literature [40] suggested that the NSW maximizing outcome would be the ideal solution, its only drawback being the fact that it cannot be reached in the presence of strategic participants.

An interesting open question is that of achieving good approximations of the NSW objective using truthful, but non-wasteful, mechanisms.

REFERENCES

[1] B. Adsul, Ch. Sobhan Babu, J. Garg, R. Mehta, and M. Sohoni. 2010. Nash equilibria in Fisher market. In *SAGT*. 30–41.

[2] N. Anari, T. Mai, S. Oveis Gharan, and V. V. Vazirani. 2016. Nash Social Welfare for Indivisible Items under Separable, Piecewise-Linear Concave Utilities. *ArXiv e-prints* (Dec. 2016). arXiv:cs.GT/1612.05191

[3] N. Anari, S. Oveis-Gharan, A. Saberi, and M. Singh. 2017. Nash social welfare, matrix permanent, and stable polynomials. In *ITCS*.

[4] H. Aziz and S. Mackenzie. 2016. A Discrete and Bounded Envy-free Cake Cutting Protocol for Four Agents. In *STOC*.

[5] M. Babaioff, B. Lucier, N. Nisan, and R. Paes Leme. 2014. On the Efficiency of the Walrasian Mechanism. In *EC*. 783–800.

[6] J.B. Barbanel. 2004. *The Geometry of Efficient Fair Division*. Cambridge Univ. Press.

[7] C. Bevia, L. Corchón, and S. Wilkie. 2003. Implementation of the Walrasian correspondence by market games. *Review of Economic Design* 7 (2003), 429–442.

[8] W. C. Brainard and H. E. Scarf. 2000. How to compute equilibrium prices in 1891. *Cowles Foundation Discussion Paper* 1270 (2000).

[9] S. Brams and A. Taylor. 1996. *Fair Division: from cake cutting to dispute resolution*. Cambridge University Press, Cambridge.

[10] F. Brandt, V. Conitzer, U. Endriss, J. Lang, and A. D. Procaccia. 2016. *Handbook of Computational Social Choice*. Cambridge University Press.

[11] S. Brânzei, I. Caragiannis, D. Kurokawa, and A.D. Procaccia. 2016. An Algorithmic Framework for Strategic Fair Division. In *AAAI*.

[12] S. Brânzei, Y. Chen, X. Deng, A. Filos-Ratsikas, S. Frederiksen, and J. Zhang. 2014. The Fisher Market Game: Equilibrium and Welfare. In *AAAI*. 587–593.

[13] S. Branzei, V. Gkatzelis, and R. Mehta. 2017. Nash Social Welfare Approximation for Strategic Agents. (2017). arxiv/abs/1607.01569.

[14] S. Brânzei and P. B. Miltersen. 2015. A Dictatorship Theorem for Cake Cutting. In *IJCAI*. 482–488.

[15] I. Caragiannis, D. Kurokawa, H. C. Moulin, A. D. Procaccia, N. Shah, and J. Wang. 2016. The Unreasonable Fairness of Maximum Nash Welfare. In *EC*. 305–322.

[16] D. Chakrabarty, J. Chuzhoy, and S. Khanna. 2009. On Allocating Goods to Maximize Fairness. In *FOCS*. 107–116.

[17] N. Chen, Xiatie Deng, Xiaoming Sun, and Andrew Yao. 2004. Fisher Equilibrium Price with a class of Concave Utility Functions. In *ESA*. 169–179.

[18] N. Chen, X. Deng, H. Zhang, and J. Zhang. 2012. Incentive Ratios of Fisher Markets. In *ICALP*.

[19] N. Chen, X. Deng, and J. Zhang. 2011. How Profitable Are Strategic Behaviors in a Market?. In *ESA*.

[20] Y. Chen, J.K. Lai, D.C. Parkes, and A.D. Procaccia. 2013. Truth, justice, and cake cutting. *Games and Economic Behavior* 77, 1 (2013), 284–297.

[21] B. Codenotti and K. Vardarajan. 2004. Equlbrium for Markets with with Leontief Utilities. In *ICALP*.

[22] R. Cole, N.R. Devanur, V. Gkatzelis, K. Jain, T. Mai, V.V. Vazirani, and S. Yazdanbod. 2017. Convex Program Duality, Fisher Markets, and Nash Social Welfare. In *EC*.

[23] R. Cole and V. Gkatzelis. 2015. Approximating the Nash Social Welfare with Indivisible Items. In *STOC*. 371–380.

[24] R. Cole, V. Gkatzelis, and G. Goel. 2013. Mechanism design for fair division: allocating divisible items without payments. In *EC*. 251–268.

[25] R. Cole, V. Gkatzelis, and G. Goel. 2013. Positive results for mechanism design without money. In *AAMAS*. 1165–1166.

[26] R. Cole and Y. Tao. 2016. Large Market Games with Near Optimal Efficiency. In *Proceedings of the 2016 ACM Conference on Economics and Computation, EC 2016,*. 791–808.

[27] P. Dasgupta, P. Hammond, and E. Maskin. 1979. The implementation of social choice rules: Some general results on incentive compatibility. *The Review of Economic Studies* 46, 2 (1979), 185–216.

[28] N. Devanur, C.H. Papadimitriou, A. Saberi, and V. V. Vazirani. 2008. Market equilibrium via a primal-dual algorithm for a convex program. *JACM* 55, 5 (2008).

[29] D. Dolev, D.G. Feitelson, J.Y. Halpern, R. Kupferman, and N. Linial. 2012. No justified complaints: on fair sharing of multiple resources. In *ITCS*. 68–75.

[30] P. Dubey and J. Geanakoplos. 2003. From Nash to Walras via Shapley-Shubik. *Journal of Mathematical Economics* 39, 5 (2003), 391–400.

[31] P. Dubey and M. Shubik. 1978. The noncooperative equilibria of a closed trading economy with market supply and bidding strategies. *JET* 17 (1978), 1–20.

[32] B.C. Eaves. 1976. A finite algorithm for the linear exchange model. *J. Math. Econ.* 3 (1976), 197–203.

[33] E. Eisenberg and D. Gale. 1959. Consensus of subjective probabilities: the Pari-Mutuel method. *The Annals of Mathematical Statistics* 30 (1959), 165–168.

[34] H. Fang. 2002. Lottery versus all-pay auction models of lobbying. *Public Choice* 112, 3-4 (2002), 351–71.

[35] M. Feldman, K. Lai, and L. Zhang. 2009. The Proportional-Share Allocation Market for Computational Resources. *ITPDS* 20, 8 (2009).

[36] D. Gale. 1960. *Theory of Linear Economic Models.* McGraw Hill, N.Y.

[37] D. Gale. 1976. The Linear exchange Model. *J. Math. Econ.* 3 (1976), 205–209.

[38] R. Garg, S. Kapoor, and V. V. Vazirani. 2004. An Auction-Based Market Equilbrium Algorithm for the Separable Gross Substitutibility Case. In *APPROX.*

[39] C. Georgiou, T. Pavlides, and A. Philippou. 2006. Network uncertainty in selfish routing. In *International Parallel and Distributed Processing Symposium.*

[40] A. Ghodsi, M. Zaharia, B. Hindman, A. Konwinski, S. Shenker, and I. Stoica. 2011. Dominant resource fairness: fair allocation of multiple resource types. In *NSDI.*

[41] G. Giraud. 2003. Strategic market games: an introduction. *Journal of Mathematical Economics* 39 (2003), 355–375.

[42] A. Gutman and N. Nisan. 2012. Fair allocation without trade. In *AAMAS*. 719–728.

[43] M. O. Jackson and J. Peck. 1999. Asymmetric information in a competitive market game: Reexamining the implications of rational expectations. *Econ. Theory* 13 (1999), 603–628.

[44] K. Jain, V. V. Vazirani, and Y. Ye. 2005. Market Equilibrium for Homothetic, Quasi-Concave Utilities and Economies of Scale in Production. In *SODA.*

[45] M. Kaneko and K. Nakamura. 1979. The Nash Social Welfare Function. *Econometrica* 47, 2 (1979), 423–435.

[46] C. G. Korpeoglu and S. E. Spear. 2015. The Market Game with Production: Coordination Equilibrium and Price Stickiness. (2015). CMU, Tepper School of Business.

[47] A. Matros. 2007. Chinese auctions. (2007). Mimeo, University of Pittsburgh.

[48] A. Maya and N. Nisan. 2012. Incentive Compatible Two Player Cake Cutting. In *WINE.*

[49] J.-F. Mertens and S. Sorin (eds). 2013. *Game-theoretic methods in general equilibrium analysis.* Springer Science & Business Media.

[50] B. Moldovanu and A. Sela. 2001. The optimal allocation of prizes in contests. *AER* 91, 3 (2001), 542–558.

[51] E. Mossel and O. Tamuz. 2010. Truthful Fair Division. In *SAGT.* 288–299.

[52] H. Moulin. 2003. *Fair Division and Collective Welfare.* The MIT Press.

[53] S. Nakamura. 1990. A feasible Nash implementation of Walrasian equilibria in the two-agent economy. *Economics Letters* 34, 1 (1990), 5–9.

[54] J. Nash. 1950. The Bargaining Problem. *Econometrica* 18, 2 (April 1950), 155–162.

[55] N. Nisan, T. Roughgarden, E. Tardos, and V. Vazirani. 2007. *Algorithmic Game Theory.* Cambridge University Press.

[56] J. B. Orlin. 2010. Improved algorithms for computing Fisher's market clearing prices. In *STOC.* 291–300.

[57] D.C. Parkes, A.D. Procaccia, and N. Shah. 2012. Beyond dominant resource fairness: extensions, limitations, and indivisibilities. In *EC.* 808–825.

[58] A. Postlewaite and D. Schmeidler. 1986. Implementation in Differential Information Economies. *JET* 39 (1986), 14–33.

[59] A.D. Procaccia. 2013. Cake Cutting: Not Just Child's Play. *Commun. ACM* 56, 7 (2013), 78–87.

[60] A.D. Procaccia and Junxing Wang. 2014. Fair enough: guaranteeing approximate maximin shares. In *EC.* 675–692.

[61] J.M. Robertson and W.A. Webb. 1998. *Cake-cutting algorithms - be fair if you can.* A K Peters. I–X, 1–181 pages.

[62] L. Shapley and M. Shubik. 1977. Trade using one commodity as a means of payment. *Journal of Political Economy* 85(5) (1977), 937–968.

[63] G. Tullock. 1980. Efficient rent-seeking. In *Toward a theory of the rent-seeking society,* G. Tullock J.M. Buchanan, R.D. Tollison (Ed.). Texas A. & M, University Press.

[64] H.R. Varian. 1974. Equity, envy, and efficiency. *Journal of Economic Theory* 9, 1 (1974), 63–91.

[65] H.P. Young. 1995. *Equity.* Princeton University Press.

Fair Public Decision Making

VINCENT CONITZER, Duke University
RUPERT FREEMAN, Duke University
NISARG SHAH, Harvard University

We generalize the classic problem of fairly allocating indivisible goods to the problem of *fair public decision making*, in which a decision must be made on several social issues simultaneously, and, unlike the classic setting, a decision can provide positive utility to multiple players. We extend the popular fairness notion of proportionality (which is not guaranteeable) to our more general setting, and introduce three novel relaxations – *proportionality up to one issue, round robin share, and pessimistic proportional share* – that are also interesting in the classic goods allocation setting. We show that the Maximum Nash Welfare solution, which is known to satisfy appealing fairness properties in the classic setting, satisfies or approximates all three relaxations in our framework. We also provide polynomial time algorithms and hardness results for finding allocations satisfying these axioms, with or without insisting on Pareto optimality.

1 INTRODUCTION

The literature on mathematically rigorous fair division dates back to the work of Steinhaus [33]. In the field's long history, most work focuses on the fair division of *private goods*, in which a set of m items must be divided among a set of n players. Agents express their preferences by specifying their value for each good, and our goal is to find a division of the goods that is fair to all players.

One particularly appealing notion of fairness is *envy-freeness* [18], which says that no player should want to switch her set of items with that of another player. This is a natural and strong notion of fairness that has long been the subject of fair division research [8, 9, 13, 21, 22, 32, 34]. It actually implies many other fairness notions such as *proportionality* [33] – each player should get at least a $1/n$ fraction of her value for the entire set of goods – and *envy-freeness up to one good (EF1)* [26] – no player should envy another player after removing at most one good from the latter player's bundle. Unfortunately, envy-freeness cannot always be guaranteed, and therefore its relaxations have been focused on [11, 14, 26, 30].

Division of private goods, however, is not the only application in which we may desire a fair outcome. Often, we may need to make decisions where every alternative gives positive utility to many players, rather than to just one player as in the case of private goods. For instance, consider a couple, Alice and Bob, deciding where to go to dinner. Alice likes Italian food the most, but does not like Indian, whereas Bob prefers Indian food but does not like Italian. When there is only a single decision to make, we are simply in a classic bargaining game where players must attempt to arrive at a mutually agreeable solution. Nash [28] proposed maximizing the product of players' utilities (the *Nash welfare*) as an elegant solution that uniquely satisfies several appealing properties. But no matter how we arrive at a decision – and there is a myriad of work in computational social

EC'17, June 26–30, 2017, Cambridge, Massachusetts, USA. ACM ISBN 978-1-4503-4527-9/17/06...$15.00.

DOI: http://dx.doi.org/10.1145/3033274.3085125

choice [10] discussing how exactly we should do so – some tradeoff must necessarily be made, and we may not be able to make everyone happy.

However, if we have several public decisions to make, maybe we can reach a compromise by making sure that all players are happy with at least some of the decisions. For example, if Alice and Bob are to follow their dinner with a movie, then maybe Bob will be willing to eat Italian food for dinner if he gets to pick his favorite movie, and maybe Alice will agree to this compromise.

Note that this setting generalizes the classic private goods setting, because in this special case we can view each public decision as the allocation of a single good. While envy is a compelling notion in the private goods setting, it makes less sense for public decisions. In our example, irrespective of where Alice and Bob go for dinner, because they are eating the same food, it is not clear what it would mean for Alice to envy Bob. If she could somehow trade places with Bob, she would still be sitting at the other end of the dinner table, eating the same food, and not be any better off. Thankfully, proportionality still has a sensible interpretation: Each player should get at least a $1/n$ fraction of the utility she would get if her most desired alternative was chosen for each decision. Unfortunately, as with envy-freeness, proportionality cannot always be guaranteed. Therefore in this work we consider relaxations of proportionality in order to arrive at fairness notions that can be guaranteed.

1.1 Our Results

Formally, a public decision making problem consists of m issues, where each issue has several associated alternatives. Each of n players has a utility for each alternative of each issue. Making a decision on an issue amounts to choosing one of the alternatives associated with the issue, and choosing an overall outcome requires making a decision on each issue simultaneously. The utility to a player for an outcome is the sum of her utilities for the alternatives chosen for different issues. This is a very simple setting, but one in which the problem of fairness is already non-trivial.

We propose relaxations of proportionality in two directions. The first, *proportionality up to one issue (Prop1)*, is similar in spirit to EF1, stating that a player should be able to get her proportional share if she gets to change the outcome of a single issue in her favor. The second direction is based on the guarantees provided by the round robin mechanism. This mechanism first orders the set of players, and then repeatedly goes through the ordering, allowing each player to make her favorite decision on any single issue, until decisions are made on all the issues. Our first relaxation in this direction, the *round robin share (RRS)*, guarantees each player the utility that she would have received under the round robin mechanism if she were the last player in the ordering. Note that the round robin mechanism lets each player make decisions on roughly the same number of issues. A further relaxation in this direction, the *pessimistic proportional share (PPS)*, guarantees each player the utility that she would get if her favorite alternatives were chosen for (approximately) a $1/n$ fraction of the issues, where these issues are chosen adversarially.

We examine the possibility and computational complexity of satisfying combinations of these fairness desiderata. We first observe that the round robin mechanism satisfies both Prop1 and RRS (and thus PPS). However, it fails to satisfy even the most basic efficiency property, Pareto optimality (PO), which requires that no other outcome should be able to make a player strictly better off without making at least one player strictly worse off.

When insisting on Pareto optimality, we observe that the leximin mechanism — informally, it chooses the outcome that maximizes the minimum utility to any player — satisfies RRS (therefore PPS) and PO via a simple argument. However, this argument does not extend to establishing Prop1, although we show that RRS implies a $1/2$ approximation to Prop1. To that end, we prove that the maximum Nash welfare (MNW) solution — informally, it chooses the outcome that maximizes

	PO	PPS	RRS	Prop1
MNW, Private goods	✓	✓ (Theorem 3.10)	$\frac{1}{2}$ (Theorem 3.10)	✓ (Theorem 3.4)
MNW, Public decisions	✓ (Theorem 3.4)	$\frac{1}{n}$ (Theorem 3.8)	$\frac{1}{n}$ (Theorem 3.8)	✓ (Theorem 3.4)
Leximin Mechanism	✓	✓ (Theorem 3.2)	✓ (Theorem 3.2)	$\frac{1}{2}$ (Theorem 3.2)
Round Robin Method	×	✓ (Theorem 3.1)	✓ (Theorem 3.1)	✓ (Theorem 3.1)

Table 1. Axioms satisfied or approximated by the mechanisms we consider. The MNW solution is split into private goods and general decisions because we obtain significantly stronger results for private goods. Results for the leximin mechanism and the round robin method apply equally to private goods and public decisions. The approximation results are lower bounds; we omit the upper bounds from the table for simplicity.

the *product* of utilities to players — that is known for its many desirable fairness properties in dividing private goods [14] satisfies Prop1 and PO in our public decision making framework, and simultaneously provides a $1/n$ approximation to both RRS and PPS. We also show that this approximation is tight up to a factor of $O(\log n)$. For division of private goods, these approximations improve significantly: the MNW solution completely satisfies PPS, and provides an $n/(2n-1) > 1/2$ approximation (but not better than $2/3$ approximation in the worst case) to RRS. Table 1 provides a summary of these results.

However, both the MNW outcome and the leximin outcome are $\mathcal{NP}$-hard to compute. It is therefore natural to consider whether our fairness properties can be achieved in conjunction with PO in polynomial time. For public decision making, the answer turns out to be negative for PPS and RRS, assuming $\mathcal{P} \neq \mathcal{NP}$. For division of private goods, however, we show that there exists a polynomial time algorithm that satisfies PPS and PO.

1.2 Related Work

Two classic fair division mechanisms — the leximin mechanism and the maximum Nash welfare (MNW) solution — play an important role in this paper. Both mechanisms have been extensively studied in the literature on private goods division. In particular, Kurokawa et al. [23] (Section 3.2) show that the leximin mechanism satisfies envy-freeness, proportionality, Pareto optimality, and a strong game-theoretic notion called group strategyproofness, which prevents even groups of players from manipulating the outcome to their benefit by misrepresenting their preferences, in a broad fair division domain with private goods and a specific form of non-additive utilities. On the other hand, the MNW solution has been well studied in the realm of additive utilities [14, 31]. For divisible goods, the MNW solution coincides with another well-known solution concept called *competitive equilibrium from equal incomes* (CEEI) [34], which also admits an approximate version for indivisible goods [11]. For indivisible goods, the MNW solution satisfies envy-freeness up to one good, Pareto optimality, and approximations to other fairness guarantees. One line of research aims to approximate the optimum Nash welfare [16, 25], although it is unclear if this achieves any of the appealing fairness guarantees of the MNW solution.

Our model is closely related to that of voting in combinatorial domains (see [24] for an overview). However, this literature focuses on the case where there is dependency between decisions on different issues. In contrast, our model remains interesting even though the issues are independent, and incorporating dependency is an interesting future direction. Although there is a range of work in the voting literature that focuses on fairness [2, 6, 15, 27], especially in the context of *representation* in multi-winner elections, it focuses on ordinal, rather than cardinal, preferences.[1]

[1]That said, there is a recent line of work on *implicit utilitarian voting* that attempts to maximize an objective with respect to the cardinal utilities underlying the ordinal preferences [7, 29], and is therefore closer to our work.

Another difference is that fairness concepts in voting apply most naturally when $n >> m$, whereas our notions of fairness are most interesting when $m \geqslant n$.

Our work is also reminiscent of the *participatory budgeting* problem [12], in which there are multiple public projects with different costs, and a set of projects need to be chosen based on preferences of the participants over the projects, subject to a budget constraint. Recently, researchers in computational social choice have addressed this problem from an axiomatic viewpoint [20], including fairness considerations [17], and from the viewpoint of *implicit utilitarian voting* [5]. However, they assume access only to ordinal preferences (that may stem from underlying cardinal utilities), while we assume a direct access to cardinal utilities, as is common in the fair division literature. Also, we do not have a budget constraint that binds the outcomes on different issues.

2 MODEL

For $k \in \mathbb{N}$, define $[k] \triangleq \{1, \ldots, k\}$. Before we introduce the problem we study in this paper, let us review the standard fair division setting with private goods.

Private goods division. A private goods division problem consists of a set of *players* $N = [n]$ and a set of m *goods* M. Each player $i \in N$ is endowed with a utility function $u_i : M \to \mathbb{R}_+$ such that $u_i(g)$ denotes the value player i derives from good $g \in M$. A standard assumption in the literature is that of additive valuations, i.e., (slightly abusing the notation) $u_i(S) = \sum_{g \in S} u_i(g)$ for $S \subseteq M$. An *allocation* $\mathbf{A}$ is a partition of the set of goods among the set of players, where A_i denotes the bundle of goods received by player i. Importantly, players only derive utility from the goods they receive, i.e., the goods private to them. The utility of player i under allocation $\mathbf{A}$ is $u_i(\mathbf{A}) = u_i(A_i)$.

Public decision making. A *public decision making* problem also has a set of players $N = [n]$, but instead of private goods, it has a set of *issues* $T = [m]$. Each issue $t \in T$ has an associated set of alternatives $A^t = \{a_1^t, \ldots, a_{k_t}^t\}$, exactly one of which must be chosen. Each player i is endowed with a utility function $u_i^t : A^t \to \mathbb{R}_+$ for each issue t, and derives utility $u_i^t(a_j^t)$ if alternative a_j^t is chosen for issue t. In contrast to private goods division, a single alternative can provide positive utility to multiple players.

An outcome $\mathbf{c} = (c_1, \ldots, c_m)$ of a public decision making problem is a choice of an alternative for every issue, i.e., it consists of an outcome $c_t \in A^t$ for each issue $t \in T$. Let C denote the space of possible outcomes. Slightly abusing the notation, let $u_i^t(\mathbf{c}) = u_i^t(c_t)$ be the utility player i derives from the outcome of issue t. We also assume additive valuations: let $u_i(\mathbf{c}) = \sum_{t \in T} u_i^t(\mathbf{c})$ be the utility player i derives from outcome $\mathbf{c}$.

In this work, we study deterministic outcomes, and in Section 5, discuss the implications when randomized outcomes are allowed. Further, we study the *offline* problem in which we are presented with the entire problem up front, and need to choose the outcomes on all issues simultaneously. One can also define an online version of the problem [19], in which we must commit to the outcome of issue t before observing issues t' with $t' > t$ for all t, but we do not consider that version here.

Private goods versus public decisions. To see why public decision making generalizes private goods division, take an instance of private goods division, and create an instance of public decision making as follows. Create an issue t_g for each good g. Let there be n alternatives in A^{t_g}, where alternative $a_i^{t_g}$ gives player i utility $u_i(g)$ while giving zero utility to all other players. It is easy to see that choosing alternative $a_i^{t_g}$ is equivalent to allocating good g to player i. Hence, the constructed public decision making problem effectively mimics the underlying private goods division problem.

2.1 Efficiency and Fairness

In this paper, we not only adapt classical notions of efficiency and fairness defined for private goods division to our public decision making problem, but also introduce three fairness axioms that are novel for both public decision making and private goods division. First, we need additional notation that we will use throughout the paper.

Let $p \triangleq \lfloor m/n \rfloor$. For issue $t \in T$ and player $i \in N$, let $a^t_{max}(i) \in \arg\max_{a \in A^t}\{u^t_i(a)\}$ and $u^t_{max}(i) = u^t_i(a^t_{max}(i))$. That is, $a^t_{max}(i)$ is an alternative that gives player i the most utility for issue t, and $u^t_{max}(i)$ is the utility player i derives from $a^t_{max}(i)$. Let the sequence $\langle u^{(1)}_{max}(i), \ldots, u^{(m)}_{max}(i)\rangle$ represent the maximum utilities player i can derive from different issues, sorted in a non-ascending order. Hence, $\{u^{(k)}_{max}(i)\}_{k \in [m]} = \{u^t_{max}(i)\}_{t \in T}$ and $u^{(k)}_{max}(i) \geqslant u^{(k+1)}_{max}(i)$ for $k \in [m-1]$.

Efficiency. In this paper, we focus on a popular notion of economic efficiency. We say that an outcome $\mathbf{c}$ is *Pareto optimal* (PO) if there does not exist another outcome $\mathbf{c}'$ that can provide at least as much utility as $\mathbf{c}$ to every player, i.e., $u_i(\mathbf{c}') \geqslant u_i(\mathbf{c})$ for all $i \in N$, and strictly more utility than $\mathbf{c}$ to some player, i.e., $u_{i^*}(\mathbf{c}') > u_{i^*}(\mathbf{c})$ for some $i^* \in N$.

Fairness. For private goods division, perhaps the most prominent notion of fairness is envy-freeness [18]. An allocation $\mathbf{A}$ is called *envy-free* (EF) if every player values her bundle at least as much as she values any other player's bundle, i.e., $u_i(A_i) \geqslant u_i(A_j)$ for all $i, j \in N$. Because envy-freeness cannot in general be guaranteed, prior work also focuses on its relaxations. For instance, an allocation $\mathbf{A}$ is called *envy-free up to one good* (EF1) if no player envies another player after removing at most one good from the latter player's bundle, i.e., for all $i, j \in N$, either $u_i(A_i) \geqslant u_i(A_j)$ or $\exists g_j \in A_j$ such that $u_i(A_i) \geqslant u_i(A_j \setminus \{g_j\})$.

Unfortunately, as argued in Section 1, the notion of envy is not well defined for public decisions. Hence, for public decision making, we focus on another fairness axiom, Proportionality, and its relaxations. For private goods division, proportionality is implied by envy-freeness.[2]

Proportionality (Prop). At a high level, proportionality requires that each player must receive at least her "proportional share", which is a $1/n$ fraction of the utility she would derive if she could act as the dictator. For a public decision making problem, the *proportional share* of player i (Prop_i) is $1/n$ times the sum of the maximum utilities the player can derive across all issues, i.e.,

$$\text{Prop}_i = \frac{1}{n}\sum_{t \in T} u^t_{max}(i).$$

For $\alpha \in (0, 1]$, we say that an outcome $\mathbf{c}$ satisfies *α-proportionality* (α-Prop) if $u_i(\mathbf{c}) \geqslant \alpha \cdot \text{Prop}_i$ for all players $i \in N$. We refer to 1-Prop simply as Prop.

Proportionality up to one issue (Prop1). We introduce a novel relaxation of proportionality (more generally, of α-proportionality) in the same spirit as envy-freeness up to one good, which is a relaxation of envy-freeness. For $\alpha \in (0, 1]$, we say that an outcome $\mathbf{c}$ satisfies *α-proportionality up to one issue* (α-Prop1) if for every player $i \in N$, there exists an issue $t \in T$ such that, ceteris paribus, changing the outcome of t from c_t to $a^t_{max}(i)$ ensures that player i achieves an α fraction of her proportional share, i.e., if

$$\forall i \in N \;\; \exists t \in T \;\text{ s.t. }\; u_i(\mathbf{c}) - u^t_i(\mathbf{c}) + u^t_{max}(i) \geqslant \alpha \cdot \text{Prop}_i.$$

We refer to 1-Prop1 simply as Prop1.

Round robin share (RRS). Next, we introduce another novel fairness axiom that is motivated from the classic round robin method that, for private goods, lets players take turns and in each turn, pick a single most favorite item left unclaimed. For public decision making, we instead let

[2]This assumes non-wastefulness, i.e., that all goods are allocated. We make this assumption throughout the paper.

players make a decision on a single issue in each turn. The utility guaranteed to the players by this approach is captured by the following fairness axiom.

Recall that the sequence $\langle u_{max}^{(1)}(i), \ldots, u_{max}^{(m)}(i) \rangle$ represents the maximum utility player i can derive from different issues, sorted in a non-ascending order. Then, we define the *round robin share* of player i (RRS_i) as

$$\text{RRS}_i = \sum_{k=1}^{p} u_{max}^{(k \cdot n)}(i).$$

This is player i's utility from the round robin method, if she is last in the ordering and all issues she does not control give her utility 0. For $\alpha \in (0, 1]$, we say that an outcome $\mathbf{c}$ satisfies *α-round robin share* (α-RRS) if $u_i(\mathbf{c}) \geqslant \alpha \cdot \text{RRS}_i$ for all players $i \in N$. Again, we refer to 1-RRS simply as RRS.

Pessimistic proportional share (PPS). We introduce another novel fairness axiom that is a further relaxation of round robin share. Note that the round robin method, by letting players make a decision on a single issue per turn, allows each player to make decisions on at least $p = \lfloor m/n \rfloor$ issues. The following axiom captures the utility players would be guaranteed if each player still made decisions on a "proportional share" of p issues, but if these issues were chosen pessimistically.

We define the *pessimistic proportional share* of player i (PPS_i) to be the sum of the maximum utilities the player can derive from a set of p issues, chosen adversarially to minimize this sum:

$$\text{PPS}_i = \sum_{k=m-p+1}^{m} u_{max}^{(k)}(i).$$

For $\alpha \in (0, 1]$, we say that an outcome $\mathbf{c}$ satisfies *α-pessimistic proportional share* (α-PPS) if $u_i(\mathbf{c}) \geqslant \alpha \cdot \text{PPS}_i$ for all players $i \in N$. Again, we refer to 1-PPS simply as PPS.

Connections among fairness properties. Trivially, proportionality (Prop) implies proportionality up to one issue (Prop1). In addition, it can also be checked that the following sequence of logical implications holds: Prop $\Longrightarrow$ MMS $\Longrightarrow$ RRS $\Longrightarrow$ PPS.

Here, MMS is the *maximin share guarantee* [11, 30]. Adapting the definition naturally from private goods division to public decision making, the maximin share of a player is the utility the player can guarantee herself by dividing the set of issues into n bundles, if she gets to make the decisions best for her on the issues in an adversarially chosen bundle. The maximin share (MMS) guarantee requires that each player must receive utility that is at least her maximin share. We do not focus on the maximin share guarantee in this paper.

2.2 Mechanisms

A mechanism for a public decision making problem (resp. a private goods division problem) maps each input instance of the problem to an outcome (resp. an allocation). We say that a mechanism satisfies a fairness or efficiency property if it always returns an outcome satisfying the property. There are three prominent mechanisms that play a key role in this paper.

Round robin method. As mentioned earlier, the round robin method first fixes an ordering of the players. Then the players take turns choosing their most preferred alternative on a single issue of their choice whose outcome has not yet been determined.

The leximin mechanism. The leximin mechanism chooses an outcome which maximizes the utility of the worst off player, i.e., $\min_{i \in N} u_i(\mathbf{c})$. Subject to this constraint, it maximizes the utility of the second least well off player, and so on. Note that the leximin mechanism is trivially Pareto optimal because if it were possible to improve some player's utility without reducing that of any other, it would improve the objective that the leximin mechanism optimizes.

Maximum Nash welfare (MNW). The *Nash welfare* of an outcome $\mathbf{c}$ is the product of utilities to all players under $\mathbf{c}$: $NW(\mathbf{c}) = \prod_{i \in N} u_i(\mathbf{c})$. When there exists an outcome $\mathbf{c}$ with $NW(\mathbf{c}) > 0$, then the MNW solution chooses an arbitrary outcome $\mathbf{c}$ that maximizes the Nash welfare. When all outcomes have zero Nash welfare, it finds a largest cardinality set S of players that can be given non-zero utility, and selects an outcome maximizing the product of their utilities, i.e., $\prod_{i \in S} u_i(\mathbf{c})$.

2.3 Examples

We illustrate the fairness properties through two examples.

Example 2.1. Consider a public decision making problem with two players ($N = [2]$) and two issues ($T = [2]$). Each issue has two alternatives ($|A^1| = |A^2| = 2$). The utilities of the two players for the two alternatives in both issues are as follows.

	a_1^t	a_2^t
u_1^t	1	0
u_2^t	0	1

for $t \in [2]$.

The various fair shares of the two players are $\text{Prop}_1 = \text{RRS}_1 = \text{PPS}_1 = \text{Prop}_2 = \text{RRS}_2 = \text{PPS}_2 = 1$. Now, outcome $\mathbf{c} = (a_1^1, a_1^2)$ gives utilities $u_1(\mathbf{c}) = 2$ and $u_2(\mathbf{c}) = 0$, and therefore violates Prop, RRS, and PPS. It satisfies Prop1 because switching the decision on either issue in favor of player 2 makes her achieve her proportional share. On the other hand, outcome $\mathbf{c} = (a_1^1, a_2^2)$ gives utility 1 to both players, and thus satisfies Prop (as well as Prop1, RRS, and PPS, which are relaxations of Prop).

Example 2.2. Consider a public decision making problem with two players ($N = [2]$) and eight issues ($T = [8]$). Once again, each issue has two alternatives, for which the utilities of the two players are as follows.

	a_1^t	a_2^t
u_1^t	1	0
u_2^t	0	1

for $t \in \{1, 2, 3, 4\}$, and

	a_1^t	a_2^t
u_1^t	1	0
u_2^t	0	0

for $t \in \{5, 6, 7, 8\}$.

In this case, we have $\text{Prop}_1 = \text{RRS}_1 = \text{PPS}_1 = 4$, whereas $\text{Prop}_2 = \text{RRS}_2 = 2$ and $\text{PPS}_2 = 0$. Consider outcome $\mathbf{c} = (a_1^1, a_1^2, a_1^3, a_1^4, a_1^5, a_1^6, a_1^7, a_1^8)$. Then, we have $u_1(\mathbf{c}) = 8$ while $u_2(\mathbf{c}) = 0$, which satisfies PPS but violates RRS. Further, $\mathbf{c}$ also violates Prop1 because switching the outcome of any single issue can only give player 2 utility at most 1, which is less than $\text{Prop}_2 = 2$. On the other hand, outcome $\mathbf{c} = (a_2^1, a_2^2, a_2^3, a_2^4, a_1^5, a_1^6, a_1^7, a_1^8)$ achieves $u_1(\mathbf{c}) = u_2(\mathbf{c}) = 4$, and satisfies Prop (and thus its relaxations Prop1, RRS, and PPS).

3 (APPROXIMATE) SATISFIABILITY OF AXIOMS

If we are willing to sacrifice Pareto optimality, then we can easily achieve both RRS (and therefore PPS) and Prop1 simultaneously with the round robin mechanism. This is not a surprising result. RRS is defined based on the guarantee provided by the round robin mechanism, and PPS is a relaxation of RRS. The round robin mechanism is also known to satisfy EF1 for private goods division, which is similar in spirit to Prop1.

Theorem 3.1. *The round robin mechanism satisfies RRS (and therefore PPS) and Prop1, and runs in polynomial time.*

Proof. The round robin mechanism clearly runs in polynomial time (note that it is easy for a player to choose the next issue on which to determine the outcome). To see why it satisfies RRS, note that the mechanism allows every player to make a decision on one issue once every n turns. Thus, for each $k \in [p]$, every player gets to make decisions on at least k of her "top" $k \cdot n$ issues, when issues are sorted in the descending order of the utility her favorite alternative in the issue gives her. It is easy to see that this implies every player i gets utility at least RRS_i. Because RRS implies PPS, the mechanism also satisfies PPS. It remains to show that it satisfies Prop1 as well.

Fix a player i and let $\mathbf{c}$ be the outcome produced by the round robin mechanism for some choosing order of the players. Because the round robin mechanism satisfies RRS, player i gets utility at least

$$u_i(\mathbf{c}) \geqslant \sum_{k=1}^{p} u_{max}^{(k \cdot n)}(i).$$

For $k \in [m]$, let the kth favorite issue of player i be the issue t for which $u_{max}^t(i)$ is the kth highest. Let $\ell \in \mathbb{N} \cup \{0\}$ be the largest index such that for every $k \in [\ell]$, outcome $\mathbf{c}$ chooses player i's most preferred alternative on her k^{th} favorite issue. Let t^* be her $(\ell+1)^{\text{th}}$ favorite issue. To show that $\mathbf{c}$ satisfies Prop1, we construct outcome $\mathbf{c}'$ from $\mathbf{c}$ by only changing the outcome of issue t^* to $a_{max}^{t^*}(i)$, and show that $u_i(\mathbf{c}') \geqslant \text{Prop}_i$. Note that if $\ell \geqslant p$, then

$$u_i(\mathbf{c}') \geqslant \sum_{k=1}^{\ell+1} u_{max}^{(k)}(i) \geqslant \sum_{k=1}^{p+1} u_{max}^{(k)}(i) \geqslant \frac{1}{n} \sum_{k=1}^{m} u_{max}^{(k)}(i) = \text{Prop}_i.$$

Let $\ell < p$. Then, using the fact that the round robin mechanism lets player i choose her most preferred alternative for at least k of her favorite $k \cdot n$ issues for every $k \leqslant p$ (and her $(\ell+1)^{\text{th}}$ favorite issue was not one of these), we have

$$u_i(\mathbf{c}') \geqslant \sum_{k=1}^{\ell+1} u_{max}^{(k)}(i) + \sum_{k=\ell+1}^{p} u_{max}^{(k \cdot n)}(i) \geqslant \frac{1}{n} \sum_{k=1}^{(\ell+1) \cdot n} u_{max}^{(k)}(i) + \frac{1}{n} \sum_{k=(\ell+1)n+1}^{m} u_{max}^{(k)}(i) = \text{Prop}_i.$$

Therefore, the round robin mechanism satisfies Prop1. ■

While this result seems to reflect favorably upon the round robin mechanism, recall that it violates Pareto optimality even for private goods division. For public decision making, a simple reason for this is that the round robin mechanism, for each issue, chooses an alternative that is some player's favorite, while it could be unanimously better to choose compromise solutions that make many players happy. Imagine there are two players and two issues, each with two alternatives. The "extreme" alternative in each issue $i \in \{1, 2\}$ gives utility 1 to player i but 0 to the other, while the "compromise" alternative in each issue $i \in \{1, 2\}$ gives utility 2/3 to both players. It is clear that both players prefer choosing the compromise alternative in both issues to choosing the extreme alternative in both issues. Because such "Pareto improvements" which make some players happier without making any player worse off are unanimously preferred by the players, the round robin outcome becomes highly undesirable. We therefore seek mechanisms that provide fairness guarantees while satisfying Pareto optimality.

A natural question is whether there exists a mechanism that satisfies RRS, Prop1, and PO. An obvious approach is to start from an outcome that already satisfies RRS and Prop1 (e.g., the round robin outcome), and make Pareto improvements until no such improvements are possible. While Pareto improvements preserve RRS as the utilities to the players do not decrease, Prop1 can be lost as it depends on the exact alternatives chosen and not only on the utilities to the players. We leave it as an important open question to determine if RRS, Prop1, and PO can be satisfied simultaneously.

We therefore consider satisfying each fairness guarantee individually with PO. One can easily find an outcome satisfying RRS and PO by following the aforementioned approach of starting with an outcome satisfying RRS, and making Pareto improvements while possible. There is also a more direct approach to satisfying RRS and PO. Recall that the leximin mechanism chooses the outcome which maximizes the minimum utility to any player, subject to that maximizes the second minimum utility, and so on. It is easy to see that this mechanism is always Pareto optimal. Now, let us normalize the utilities of all players such that $\text{RRS}_i = 1$ for every player $i \in N$.[3] Because the round robin mechanism gives every player i utility at least $\text{RRS}_i = 1$, it must be the case that the leximin mechanism operating on these normalized utilities must also give every player utility at least 1, and thus produce an outcome that is both RRS and PO.

Theorem 3.2. *The leximin mechanism satisfies RRS, PO, and (1/2)-Prop1.*

That leximin satisfies (1/2)-Prop1 follows directly from the following lemma, and noting that leximin satisfies RRS.

Lemma 3.3. *RRS implies (1/2)-Prop1.*

Proof. Note that $\text{RRS}_i = \sum_{k=1}^{p} u_{max}^{(k \cdot n)}(i) \geqslant \frac{1}{n} \sum_{t=n+1}^{m} u_{max}^{(t)}(i)$ and $u_{max}^{(1)}(i) \geqslant \frac{1}{n} \sum_{t=1}^{n} u_{max}^{(t)}(i)$. Summing the two equations, we get

$$\text{RRS}_i + u_{max}^{(1)}(i) \geqslant \frac{1}{n} \sum_{t=1}^{m} u_{max}^{(t)}(i) = \text{Prop}_i.$$

Therefore, $\max\{\text{RRS}_i, u_{max}^{(1)}(i)\} \geqslant \frac{1}{2}\text{Prop}_i$.

Suppose that $u_i(\mathbf{c}) \geqslant \text{RRS}_i$ for some outcome $\mathbf{c}$. Then either i already receives her most valued item, in which case she receives utility at least $\max\{\text{RRS}_i, u_{max}^{(1)}(i)\} \geqslant \frac{1}{2}\text{Prop}_i$, or she does not receive her most valued item. If she does not, then after giving it to her, she receives utility at least $\frac{1}{2}\text{Prop}_i$. Therefore, $\mathbf{c}$ satisfies (1/2)-Prop1. ∎

Next, we study whether we can achieve Prop1 and PO simultaneously. Neither of the previous approaches seems to work: we already argued that following Pareto improvements could lose Prop1, and the normalization trick is difficult to apply because Prop1 is not defined in terms of any fixed share of utility.

One starting point to achieving Prop1 and PO is the maximum Nash welfare (MNW) solution, which, for private goods division, is known to satisfy the similar guarantee of EF1 and PO [14]. It turns out that the MNW solution is precisely what we need.

Theorem 3.4. *The MNW solution satisfies proportionality up to one issue (Prop1) and Pareto optimality (PO).*

Before we prove this, we need a folklore result, which essentially states that if the sum of n terms is to be reduced by a fixed quantity δ that is less than each term, then their product reduces the most when δ is taken out of the lowest term. The following lemma proves this result when all initial terms are 1, which is sufficient for our purpose. The proof of the lemma appears in the full version of the paper.[4]

Lemma 3.5. *Let $\{x_1, \ldots, x_n\}$ be a set of n non-negative real numbers such that $\sum_{i=1}^{n} \max\{0, 1-x_i\} \leqslant \delta$, where $0 < \delta < 1$. Then, $\prod_{i=1}^{n} x_i \geqslant 1 - \delta$.*

Proof of Theorem 3.4. Fix an instance of the public decision making problem. Let $S \subseteq N$ be the set of players that the MNW outcome $\mathbf{c}$ gives positive utility to. Then, by the definition of the MNW outcome, S must be a largest set of players that can simultaneously be given positive utility, and $\mathbf{c}$ must maximize the product of utilities of players in S.

First, we show that $\mathbf{c}$ is PO. Note that a Pareto improvement over $\mathbf{c}$ must either give a positive utility to a player in $N \setminus S$ or give more utility to a player in S, without reducing the utility to any

[3] Players with zero round robin share can be incorporated via a simple extension to the argument.

[4] The full version is available at the authors' websites.

player in S. This is a contradiction because it violates either optimality of the size of S or optimality of the product of utilities of players in S. Hence, MNW satisfies PO.

We now show that MNW also satisfies Prop1. Suppose for contradiction that Prop1 is violated for player i under $\mathbf{c}$. First, note that we must have $\text{Prop}_i > 0$. Further, it must be the case that $u^t_{max}(i) > 0$ for at least $n + 1$ issues. Were this not the case, Prop1 would be trivially satisfied for player i since we can give her utility

$$u^{(1)}_{max}(i) \geqslant \frac{1}{n} \sum_{t=1}^{n} u^{(t)}_{max}(i) = \frac{1}{n} \sum_{t=1}^{m} u^{(t)}_{max}(i) = \text{Prop}_i$$

by changing the outcome on a single issue.

We now show that $u_i(\mathbf{c}) > 0$ (i.e., $i \in S$). For contradiction, suppose otherwise. For each of the (at least) $n + 1$ issues with $u^t_{max}(i) > 0$, there must exist another player $j \neq i$ that gets positive utility *only* from that issue under $\mathbf{c}$ (otherwise we could use that issue to give positive utility to i while not reducing any other agents' utility to zero, contradicting the maximality of S). But this is impossible, since there are at least $n + 1$ issues and only $n - 1$ agents (other than i).

Because MNW outcomes and the Prop1 property are invariant to individual scaling of utilities, let us scale the utilities such that $\text{Prop}_i = 1$ and $u_j(\mathbf{c}) = 1$ for all $j \in S \setminus \{i\}$. Select issue $t^* \in T$ as

$$t^* \in \arg\min_{t \in T} \frac{\sum_{j \in N \setminus \{i\}} u^t_j(\mathbf{c})}{u^t_{max}(i) - u^t_i(\mathbf{c})}.$$

Note that t^* is well defined because $u^t_{max}(i) > u^t_i(\mathbf{c})$ for at least one $t \in T$, otherwise Prop1 would not be violated for player i.

We now show that outcome $\mathbf{c}'$ such that $c'_{t^*} = a^{t^*}_{max}(i)$ and $c'_t = c_t$ for all $t \in T \setminus \{t^*\}$ achieves strictly greater product of utilities of players in S than outcome $\mathbf{c}$ does, which is a contradiction as $\mathbf{c}$ is an MNW outcome. First, note that

$$\frac{\sum_{j \in N \setminus \{i\}} u^{t^*}_j(\mathbf{c})}{u^{t^*}_{max}(i) - u^{t^*}_i(\mathbf{c})} \leqslant \frac{\sum_{t \in T} \sum_{j \in N \setminus \{i\}} u^t_j(\mathbf{c})}{\sum_{t \in T} (u^t_{max}(i) - u^t_i(\mathbf{c}))} = \frac{\sum_{j \in N \setminus \{i\}} u_j(\mathbf{c})}{n\text{Prop}_i - u_i(\mathbf{c})} \leqslant \frac{(n-1)}{(n-1)\text{Prop}_i} = 1, \tag{1}$$

where the penultimate transition follows because we normalized utilities to achieve $u_j(\mathbf{c}) = 1$ for every $j \in S \setminus \{i\}$, every $j \in N \setminus S$ satisfies $u_j(\mathbf{c}) = 0$, and player i does not receive her proportional share. The final transition holds due to our normalization $\text{Prop}_i = 1$.

Let $\delta = \sum_{j \in S \setminus \{i\}} u^{t^*}_j(\mathbf{c})$. Then, Equation (1) implies $u_i(\mathbf{c}') - u_i(\mathbf{c}) = u^{t^*}_{max}(i) - u^{t^*}_i(\mathbf{c}) \geqslant \delta$. Thus,

$$u_i(\mathbf{c}) + \delta \leqslant u_i(\mathbf{c}') < 1, \tag{2}$$

where the last inequality follows because the original outcome $\mathbf{c}$ violated Prop1 for player i. In particular, this implies $\delta < 1$. Our goal is to show that $\prod_{j \in S} u_j(\mathbf{c}') > u_i(\mathbf{c}) = \prod_{j \in S} u_j(\mathbf{c})$, where the last equality holds due to our normalization $u_j(\mathbf{c}) = 1$ for $j \in S \setminus \{i\}$ and because $i \in S$. This would be a contradiction because $\mathbf{c}$ maximizes the product of utilities of players in S. Now,

$$\sum_{j \in S \setminus \{i\}} \max\{0, 1 - u_j(\mathbf{c}')\} = \sum_{j \in S \setminus \{i\}} \max\{0, u^{t^*}_j(\mathbf{c}) - u^{t^*}_j(\mathbf{c}')\} \leqslant \sum_{j \in S \setminus \{i\}} u^{t^*}_j(\mathbf{c}) = \delta,$$

where the first transition follows from setting $1 = u_j(\mathbf{c})$ (by our normalization) and noting that $\mathbf{c}$ and $\mathbf{c}'$ are identical for all issues except t^*, and the second because all utilities are non-negative.

Hence, Lemma 3.5 implies that $\prod_{j \in S \setminus \{i\}} u_j(\mathbf{c}') \geqslant 1 - \delta$. Thus,

$$\prod_{j \in S} u_j(\mathbf{c}') \geqslant (1 - \delta) \cdot (u_i(\mathbf{c}) + \delta) = u_i(\mathbf{c}) + \delta \cdot (1 - u_i(\mathbf{c})) - \delta^2 > u_i(\mathbf{c}) + \delta^2 - \delta^2 = u_i(\mathbf{c}),$$

where the inequality holds because $u_i(\mathbf{c}) + \delta < 1$ from Equation (2). ■

For private goods division, this result can be derived in a simpler fashion. Caragiannis et al. [14] already show that MNW satisfies PO. In addition, they also show that MNW satisfies EF1, which implies Prop1 due to our next result. To be consistent with the goods division literature, we use proportionality up to one good (rather than one issue) in the private goods division context.

Lemma 3.6. *For private goods division, envy-freeness up to one good (EF1) implies proportionality up to one good (Prop1).*

Proof. Take an instance of private goods division with a set of players N and a set of goods M. Let $\mathbf{A}$ be an allocation satisfying EF1. Fix a player $i \in N$.

Due to the definition of EF1, there must exist[5] a set of goods $X = \{g_j\}_{j \in N \setminus \{i\}}$ such that $u_i(A_i) \geqslant u_i(A_j) - u_i(g_j)$ for every $j \in N \setminus \{i\}$. Summing over all $j \in N \setminus \{i\}$, we get

$$(n-1) \cdot u_i(A_i) \geqslant \left(\sum_{j \in N \setminus \{i\}} u_i(A_j) \right) - u_i(X) \implies n \cdot u_i(A_i) \geqslant u_i(M) - u_i(X)$$

$$\implies u_i(A_i) + \frac{u_i(X)}{n} \geqslant \frac{u_i(M)}{n}. \tag{3}$$

Note that X has less than n goods. Suppose player i receives good $g^* \in \arg\max_{g \in X} u_i(g)$. Note that $g^* \notin A_i$. Then, we have $u_i(A_i \cup \{g^*\}) \geqslant u_i(M)/n = \text{Prop}_i$, which implies that Prop1 is satisfied with respect to player i. Because player i was chosen arbitrarily, we have that EF1 implies Prop1. ∎

Equation 3 in the proof of Lemma 3.6 directly implies the following lemma because the set X in the equation contains at most $n-1$ goods.

Lemma 3.7. *Let $\mathbf{A}$ be an allocation of private goods that satisfies EF1. Then, for every player i,*

$$u_i(A_i) \geqslant Prop_i - \frac{1}{n} \sum_{t=1}^{n-1} u_{max}^{(t)}(i),$$

where $u_{max}^{(t)}(i)$ is the utility player i derives from her t^{th} most valued good.

Next, we turn our attention to RRS and PPS. While MNW does not satisfy either of them, it approximates both.

Theorem 3.8. *The MNW solution satisfies $1/n$-RRS (and therefore $1/n$-PPS). The approximation is tight for both RRS and PPS up to a factor of $O(\log n)$.*

Proof. We first show the lower bound. Fix an instance of public decision making, and let $\mathbf{c}$ denote an MNW outcome. Let $S \subseteq N$ denote the set of players that achieve positive utility under $\mathbf{c}$.

Without loss of generality, let us normalize the utilities such that $u_j(\mathbf{c}) = 1$ for every $j \in S$. Suppose for contradiction that for some player i, $u_i(\mathbf{c}) < (1/n) \cdot \text{RRS}_i$. First, this implies that $\text{RRS}_i > 0$, which in turn implies that player i must be able to derive a positive utility from at least n different issues. By an argument identical to that used to argue that $u_i(\mathbf{c}) > 0$ in the proof of Theorem 3.4, it can be shown that we must also have $u_i(\mathbf{c}) > 0$ in this case (i.e., $i \in S$).

Now, recall that the sequence $\langle u_{max}^{(1)}(i), \ldots, u_{max}^{(m)}(i) \rangle$ contains the maximum utility player i can derive from different issues, sorted in a non-ascending order. For every $q \in [p]$, let

$$t_q = \operatorname*{arg\,min}_{(q-1)n+1 \leqslant t \leqslant qn} \sum_{j \in S \setminus \{i\}} u_j^t(\mathbf{c}).$$

[5] If $A_j = \emptyset$, we can add a dummy good g_j that every player has utility 0 for, and make $A_j = \{g_j\}$.

That is, we divide the public decision making into sets of n issues, grouped by player i's maximum utility for them, and for each set of issues, we let t_q be the one that the remaining players derive the lowest total utility from. Note that $t_q \leqslant qn$ for each $q \in [p]$, and therefore $u_{max}^{(t_q)}(i) \geqslant u_{max}^{(qn)}(i)$.

We will show that outcome $\mathbf{c}'$, where $c'_{t_q} = a_{max}^{t_q}(i)$ for all $q \in [p]$ and $c'_t = c_t$ for all other issues t, achieves a higher product of utilities to players in S than $\mathbf{c}$ does, which is a contradiction because $\mathbf{c}$ is an MNW outcome. First, note that

$$u_i(\mathbf{c}') \geqslant \sum_{q=1}^{p} u_{max}^{(t_q)}(i) \geqslant \sum_{k=1}^{p} u_{max}^{(k \cdot n)}(i) = \text{RRS}_i > n.$$

Further, we have

$$\begin{aligned}\sum_{j \in S \setminus \{i\}} \max\{0, 1 - u_j(\mathbf{c}')\} &= \sum_{j \in S \setminus \{i\}} \max\{0, u_j(\mathbf{c}) - u_j(\mathbf{c}')\} \\ &= \sum_{j \in S \setminus \{i\}} \sum_{q=1}^{p} \max\{0, u_j^{t_q}(\mathbf{c}) - u_j^{t_q}(\mathbf{c}')\} \leqslant \sum_{j \in S \setminus \{i\}} \sum_{q=1}^{p} u_j^{t_q}(\mathbf{c}),\end{aligned}$$

where the first equality follows from our normalization, the second because $\mathbf{c}$ and $\mathbf{c}'$ only differ on issues $\{t_q\}_{q \in [p]}$, and the last because all utilities are non-negative.

Reversing the order of the summation and further manipulating the expression, we have

$$\sum_{q=1}^{p} \sum_{j \in S \setminus \{i\}} u_j^{t_q}(\mathbf{c}) \leqslant \sum_{q=1}^{p} \frac{1}{n} \sum_{t=(q-1)n+1}^{qn} \sum_{j \in S \setminus \{i\}} u_j^t(\mathbf{c}) = \frac{1}{n} \sum_{t=1}^{pn} \sum_{j \in S \setminus \{i\}} u_j^t(\mathbf{c}) \leqslant \frac{n-1}{n},$$

where the first transition follows from the definition of t_q. By Lemma 3.5, we have

$$\prod_{j \in S} u_j(\mathbf{c}') = u_i(\mathbf{c}') \prod_{j \in S \setminus \{i\}} u_j(\mathbf{c}') > n \cdot \left(1 - \frac{n-1}{n}\right) = 1 = \prod_{j=1}^{n} u_j(\mathbf{c}),$$

where the inequality holds because $u_i(\mathbf{c}') \geqslant \text{RRS}_i > n \cdot u_i(\mathbf{c}) = n$, as player i receives her round robin share under $\mathbf{c}'$ but did not even receive a $1/n$ fraction of it under $\mathbf{c}$. Hence, outcome $\mathbf{c}'$ achieves a higher product of utilities to players in S than $\mathbf{c}$ does, which is a contradiction.

Due to space considerations, the proof of the upper bound appears in the full version. ∎

For private goods, we can show that the MNW solution provides much better approximations to both RRS and PPS, as a result of its strong fairness guarantee of EF1.

Lemma 3.9. *For private goods division, envy-freeness up to one good (EF1) implies PPS and $n/(2n-1)$-RRS, but does not imply $n/(2n-2)$-RRS.*

Proof. Let $\mathbf{A}$ be an allocation of private goods that satisfies EF1. First, we show that $\mathbf{A}$ must also satisfy PPS. Suppose for contradiction that it violates PPS. Then, there exists a player i such that $u_i(A_i) < \text{PPS}_i$, which in turn implies that $|A_i| < p$. Because the average number of goods per player is $\frac{m}{n} \geqslant p$, there must exist a player j such that $|A_j| > p$. Hence, for any good $g \in A_j$, player j has at least p goods even after removing g from A_j, which implies $u_i(A_j \setminus \{g\}) \geqslant \text{PPS}_i > u_i(A_i)$. However, this contradicts the fact that $\mathbf{A}$ is EF1.

We now show that $\mathbf{A}$ also satisfies 1/2-RRS. By Lemma 3.7, we have

$$u_i(A_i) \geqslant \frac{1}{n} \sum_{t=n}^{m} u_{max}^{(t)}(i) \geqslant \frac{1}{n} u_{max}^{(n)}(i) + \sum_{k=2}^{p} u_{max}^{(k \cdot n)}(i). \tag{4}$$

Further, since **A** satisfies EF1, it must be the case that

$$u_i(A_i) \geqslant u_{max}^{(n)}(i). \tag{5}$$

To see this, suppose for contradiction that $u_i(A_i) < u_{max}^{(n)}(i)$, which implies that player i is not allocated any of her n most valued goods. Therefore, by the pigeonhole principle, there must exist a player $j \in N \setminus \{i\}$ that is allocated at least two of these goods. Hence, for any $g \in A_j$, we have $u_i(A_j \setminus \{g\}) \geqslant u_{max}^{(n)}(i) > u_i(A_i)$, which violates EF1. Finally, adding n times Equation (4) with $n-1$ times Equation (5), we obtain

$$(2n-1) \cdot u_i(A_i) \geqslant n \cdot u_{max}^{(n)}(i) + n \cdot \sum_{k=2}^{p} u_{max}^{(k \cdot n)}(i) = n \cdot \text{RRS}_i,$$

which implies the desired $n/(2n-1)$-RRS guarantee.

For the upper bound, consider an instance with n players and n^2 goods, and define player 1's utility function to be

$$u_1(g_j) = \begin{cases} 1 & 1 \leqslant j \leqslant n, \\ \frac{1}{n-1} & n+1 \leqslant j \leqslant n^2. \end{cases}$$

Note that $\text{RRS}_1 = 1 + (n-1)\frac{1}{n-1} = 2$. Consider the allocation **A** with $A_1 = \{g_{n+1}, \ldots, g_{2n}\}$, $A_2 = \{g_1, g_2\}$, and $A_i = \{g_i, g_{(i-1)n+1}, \ldots, g_{i \cdot n}\}$ for all players $i > 2$. Let the utilities of players 2 through n be positive for the goods they receive and zero for the remaining goods. Hence, they clearly do not envy any players. For player 1, we have $u_1(A_1) = \frac{n}{n-1}$, $u_1(A_2 \setminus \{g_2\}) = 1$, and $u_1(A_i \setminus \{g_i\}) = \frac{n}{n-1}$ for all $i > 2$. That is, player 1 does not envy any other player up to one good. Hence, **A** satisfies EF1, and player 1 obtains a $\frac{n}{2n-2}$ fraction of her RRS share, as required. ∎

As a corollary of Lemma 3.9, EF1 implies 1/2-RRS, and this approximation is asymptotically tight. Further, because the MNW solution satisfies EF1, Lemma 3.9 immediately provides guarantees (lower bounds) for the MNW solution. However, the upper bound in the proof of Lemma 3.9 does not work for the MNW solution. Next, we establish a much weaker lower bound, leaving open the possibility that the MNW solution may achieve a constant approximation better than 1/2 to RRS.

Theorem 3.10. *For private goods division, the MNW solution satisfies PPS and $n/(2n-1)$-RRS. For every $\varepsilon > 0$, the MNW solution does not satisfy $(2/3+\varepsilon)$-RRS.*

Proof. The lower bounds follow directly from Lemma 3.9 and the fact that the MNW solution satisfies EF1. For the upper bound, consider an instance with two players and four goods. Player 1 has utilities $(1-\delta, 1-\delta, 1/2, 1/2)$ and player 2 has utilities $(1, 1, 0, 0)$ for goods (g_1, g_2, g_3, g_4), respectively. Note that $\text{RRS}_1 = 3/2 - \delta$. The MNW allocation **A** is given by $A_1 = \{g_3, g_4\}$ and $A_2 = \{g_1, g_2\}$. Thus, $\frac{u_1(A_1)}{\text{RRS}_1} = \frac{2}{3-2\delta}$. The upper bound follows by setting δ sufficiently small. ∎

4 COMPUTATIONAL COMPLEXITY

In Section 3, we showed that without requiring Pareto optimality, we can achieve both RRS (thus PPS) and Prop1 in polynomial time using the round robin method (Theorem 3.1). In contrast, when we require PO, the leximin mechanism (with an appropriate normalization of utilities) provides RRS (thus PPS) and PO, while the MNW solution provides Prop1 and PO. However, both these solutions are $\mathcal{NP}$-hard to compute [4, 31]. This raises a natural question whether we can efficiently find outcomes satisfying our fairness guarantees along with PO. For PPS, the answer is negative.

Theorem 4.1. *It is $\mathcal{NP}$-hard to find an outcome satisfying PPS and PO.*

Note that it is the *search problem* of finding an outcome (any outcome) satisfying PPS and PO for which we prove computational hardness; the *decision problem* of testing the existence of such an outcome is trivial as we know it always exists. Before we prove this result, we need to introduce a new (to our knowledge) decision problem and show that it is $\mathcal{NP}$-complete.

Exact Triple-Cover by 3-sets (X33C):. An instance $(Y, \mathcal{T})$ of X33C is given by a set Y of r vertices and a set $\mathcal{T} = \{T_1, T_2, \ldots, T_m\}$, where each T_i is a set of three vertices. The decision problem is to determine whether it is possible to choose r sets, with repetition allowed, such that every vertex v is contained in exactly three of the chosen sets (an exact triple-cover).

Let us contrast this with the definition of the popular NP-complete problem, Exact Cover by 3-sets (X3C): An instance $(X, \mathcal{S})$ of X3C is given by a set X of $3q$ vertices and a set $\mathcal{S} = \{S_1, \ldots, S_n\}$, where each S_i is a set of three vertices. The decision problem is to determine if there exists a subset of $\mathcal{S}$ of size q that covers every vertex $x \in X$ exactly once (an exact cover).

Lemma 4.2. *X3CC is NP-complete.*

The proof of Lemma 4.2 proceeds via a reduction from X3C, and is presented in the full version. Using this lemma, we can now show that finding an outcome satisfying PPS and PO is $\mathcal{NP}$-hard through a reduction from X33C.

Proof of Theorem 4.1. Let $(Y, \mathcal{T})$ be an instance of X33C, with $|Y| = r$. Let $\varepsilon \in (0, 1/(3r))$. We define a public decision making problem as follows. There are r players, one corresponding to each vertex $v \in Y$, and r issues. For each issue, there are $|Y| + |\mathcal{T}|$ alternatives. For each issue t and each player i, there is an alternative $a_{t,i}$ which is valued at $1 - \varepsilon$ by player i, and 0 by all other players. The remaining $|\mathcal{T}|$ alternatives correspond to the 3-sets from the X33C instance. For a set $T_j \in \mathcal{T}$, the corresponding alternative is valued at $\frac{1}{3}$ by players $i \in T_j$, and valued at 0 by all other players. Note that $\text{PPS}_i = 1 - \varepsilon$ for each player i, because there are exactly as many issues as players, and each player values its most preferred alternative for each issue at $1 - \varepsilon$.

We now show that there exists an exact triple-cover by 3-sets if and only if all outcomes to the public decision making problem that satisfy PPS and PO have $u_i(\mathbf{c}) = 1$ for all i. First, suppose that there exists an exact triple-cover by 3-sets. We need to show that all outcomes satisfying PPS and PO have $u_i(\mathbf{c}) = 1$ for all i. So suppose otherwise – that there exists an outcome satisfying PPS and PO with $u_i(\mathbf{c}) \neq 1$ for some player i. In particular, some player must have $u_i(\mathbf{c}) > 1$, otherwise $\mathbf{c}$ is not PO (because it is possible to choose an outcome corresponding exactly to an exact triple-cover, which gives each player utility 1). But players only derive utility in discrete amounts of $1 - \varepsilon$ or $\frac{1}{3}$, which means that any player with $u_i(\mathbf{c}) > 1$ has $u_i(\mathbf{c}) \geqslant \frac{4}{3} - \varepsilon$. Since $\mathbf{c}$ satisfies PPS, the social welfare must satisfy

$$\sum_{i=1}^{r} u_i(\mathbf{c}) \geqslant \frac{4}{3} - \varepsilon + \sum_{i=1}^{r-1} (1 - \varepsilon) = \frac{1}{3} + r - r\varepsilon > r,$$

where the last inequality holds because $\varepsilon < 1/(3r)$. However, this is a contradiction because each alternative in each of the r issues contributes at most 1 to the social welfare. Therefore, every outcome satisfying PPS and PO has $u_i(\mathbf{c}) = 1$ for all i.

Next, suppose that there does not exist an exact triple-cover by 3-sets. So if we choose an alternative corresponding to a 3-set for every issue, it is not possible for every player to derive utility 1. Therefore, some player must derive utility $\frac{2}{3}$ (or lower), which violates PPS. Thus, every outcome that satisfies PPS must include at least one issue where the chosen alternative is one that corresponds to a player, not to a 3-set. Such an alternative only contributes $1 - \varepsilon$ to social welfare. Therefore, the social welfare is strictly less than r, which means that some player gets utility strictly less than 1. Therefore, there is no outcome satisfying PPS (either with or without PO) such that $u_i(\mathbf{c}) = 1$ for all i. Since the set of outcomes satisfying PPS is always non-empty, it is therefore not the case that all outcomes satisfying PPS and PO have $u_i(\mathbf{c}) = 1$ for all i. ■

Because every outcome satisfying RRS also satisfies PPS, we have the following corollary.

Corollary 4.3. *It is $\mathcal{NP}$-hard to find an outcome satisfying RRS and PO.*

For private goods division, we show, in stark contrast to Theorem 4.1, that we can find an allocation satisfying PPS and PO in polynomial time. This is achieved using Algorithm 1. Interestingly, it produces not an arbitrary allocation satisfying PPS and PO, but an allocation that assigns at least $p = \lfloor m/n \rfloor$ goods to every player — implying PPS, and maximizes weighted (utilitarian) social welfare according to some weight vector — implying PO.

ALGORITHM 1: Polynomial time algorithm to achieve PPS and PO for private goods

Input: The set of players N, the set of private goods M, and players' utility functions $\{u_i\}_{i \in N}$
Output: A deterministic allocation $\mathbf{A}$ satisfying PPS and PO

1 $\mathbf{w} \leftarrow (1/n, \ldots, 1/n) \in \mathbb{R}^n$;
2 $\mathbf{A} \leftarrow \arg\max_{\mathbf{A}'} \sum_{i \in N} w_i \cdot u_i(\mathbf{A}')$;
3 **while** $\exists i \in N, |A_i| < p$ **do** /* Until every player receives at least $p = \lfloor m/n \rfloor$ goods */
4     $GT \leftarrow \{i \in N : |A_i| > p\}$; /* Partition players by the number of goods they receive */
5     $EQ \leftarrow \{i \in N : |A_i| = p\}$;
6     $LS \leftarrow \{i \in N : |A_i| < p\}$;
7     $DEC = GT$; /* Players whose weights we will decrease */
8   **while** $DEC \cap LS = \emptyset$ **do**
        /* Minimally reduce weights of players in DEC so a player in DEC loses a good */
9         $(i^*, j^*, g^*) \leftarrow \arg\min_{i \in DEC, j \in N \setminus DEC, g \in A_i} (w_i \cdot v_{i,g})/(w_j \cdot v_{j,g})$;
10         $r \leftarrow (w_{i^*} \cdot v_{i^*,g^*})/(w_{j^*} \cdot v_{j^*,g^*})$;
11         $\forall i \in DEC,\ w_i \leftarrow w_i/r$;
12         $DEC \leftarrow DEC \cup \{j^*\}$;
13         $D(j^*) \leftarrow (i^*, g^*)$; /* Bookkeeping: j^* can receive g^* from i^* */
14   **end**
15     $j^* \leftarrow DEC \cap LS$; /* Player from LS who receives a good */
16   **while** $j^* \notin GT$ **do**
17         $(i^*, g^*) \leftarrow D(j^*)$;
18         $A_{i^*} \leftarrow A_{i^*} \setminus \{g^*\}$;
19         $A_{j^*} \leftarrow A_{j^*} \cup \{g^*\}$;
20         $j^* \leftarrow i^*$;
21   **end**
22 **end**
23 **return** $\mathbf{A}$;

At a high level, the algorithm works as follows. It begins with an arbitrary weight vector $\mathbf{w}$, and an allocation $\mathbf{A}$ maximizing the corresponding weighted (utilitarian) social welfare. Then, it executes a loop (Lines 3-22) while there exists a player receiving less than p goods, and each iteration of the loop alters the allocation in a way that one of the players who received more than p goods loses a good, one of the players who received less than p goods gains a good, and every other player retains the same number of goods as before.

Each iteration of the loop maintains a set *DEC* of players whose weight it reduces. Initially, *DEC* consists of players who have more than p goods (Line 7). When the weights are reduced enough so that a player in *DEC* is about to lose a good to a player, necessarily outside *DEC* (Lines 9-11), the latter player is added to *DEC* (Line 12) before proceeding further. When a player who has less than p goods is added to *DEC*, this process stops and the algorithm leverages the set of ties it created along the way to make the aforementioned alteration to the allocation (Lines 16-21).

We now formally state that this produces an allocation satisfying PPS and PO, and that it runs in polynomial time; the proof appears in the full version.

THEOREM 4.4. *For private goods division, PPS and PO can be satisfied in polynomial time.*

The complexity of finding an allocation (of private goods) satisfying the stronger guarantee RRS along with PO in polynomial time remains open, as does the complexity of finding an allocation satisfying Prop1 and PO.

We note that the convenient approach of weighted welfare maximization we use in Theorem 4.4 cannot be used for finding an outcome satisfying RRS and PO, as the following example shows. This leads us to conjecture that it may be $\mathcal{NP}$-hard to find such an outcome.

Example 4.5. Consider a private goods division problem with two players and four goods. Player 1 has utilities $(4, 4, 1, 1)$ and player 2 has utilities $(3, 3, 2, 2)$ for goods (g_1, g_2, g_3, g_4), respectively. Note that $\text{RRS}_1 = \text{RRS}_2 = 5$. Consider assigning weights w_1 and w_2 to players 1 and 2, respectively. If $4w_1 > 3w_2$, i.e., $w_1 > 3w_2/4$ then player 1 receives both g_1 and g_2, which means that player 2 receives utility less than her RRS share. On the other hand, if $3w_2 > 4w_1$, i.e., $w_1 < 3w_2/4$ then player 2 receives both g_1 and g_2, which means that player 1 receives utility less than her RRS share.

The only remaining possibility is that $w_1 = 3w_2/4$, but in that case, player 2 receives both g_3 and g_4. Regardless of how we divide goods g_1 and g_2, one of the two players still receives utility less than her RRS share.

In contrast, a simple modification of Algorithm 1 seems to quickly find an allocation satisfying Prop1 and PO in hundreds of thousands of randomized simulations. At each iteration of this version, the set *DEC* initially consists of players who attain their proportional share (it is easy to show using the Pigeonhole principle that this set is non-empty for any weighted welfare maximizing allocation), and ends when a player is added to *DEC* that is not currently achieving Prop1. Thus, at every loop, a player that was receiving her proportional share may lose a good (but will still achieve at least Prop1), the player added to *DEC* that was not achieving Prop1 gains a good, and some players that were achieving Prop1 but not their proportional share may lose a good, but only if they gain one too. These three classes of players are therefore analogous to players with more than p goods, less than p goods, and exactly p goods in Algorithm 1. Unfortunately, we are unable to prove termination of this algorithm because it is possible that a player who achieves Prop1 but not her proportional share loses a high-valued good while gaining a low-valued good, thus potentially sacrificing Prop1. Thus we do not get a property parallel to the key property of Algorithm 1, that no player's utility ever drops below her PPS share, after she attains it. However, our algorithm always seems to terminate quickly and finds an allocation satisfying Prop1 and PO in our randomized simulations, which leads us to conjecture that it may be possible to find an allocation satisfying Prop1 and PO in polynomial time, either from our algorithm directly or via some other utilization of weighted welfare maximization.

5 DISCUSSION

We introduced several novel fairness notions for public decision making and considered their relationships to existing mechanisms and fairness notions. Throughout the paper, we highlighted various open questions including the existence (and complexity) of a mechanism satisfying RRS, Prop1, and PO, the complexity of finding an outcome satisfying Prop1 and PO (for public decisions and private goods), the complexity of finding an outcome satisfying RRS and PO (for private goods), and whether MNW provides a constant approximation to RRS better than 1/2.

So far we only considered deterministic outcomes. If randomized outcomes are allowed (an alternative interpretation in the private goods case is that the goods are infinitely divisible), then the MNW solution satisfies Prop as a direct consequence of it satisfying Prop1 for deterministic outcomes (Theorem 3.4).[6] To see this, consider replicating each issue K times and dividing utilities by K. The relative effect of granting a single player control of a single issue becomes negligible. Thus, as K approaches infinity, the utility of each player i in an MNW outcome approaches a value that is at least their proportional share Prop_i. The fraction of copies of issue t in which outcome a_j^t is selected can be interpreted as the weight placed on a_j^t in the randomized outcome. Because RRS, PPS, and Prop1 are relaxations of Prop, the randomized MNW outcome also satisfies all of them.

For private goods division, this can be seen as a corollary of the fact that the randomized MNW outcome satisfies envy-freeness, which is strictly stronger than proportionality. This hints at a very interesting question: Is there a stronger fairness notion than proportionality in the public decision making framework that generalizes envy-freeness in private goods division? Although such a notion would not be satisfiable by deterministic mechanisms, it may be satisfied by randomized mechanisms, or it could have novel relaxations that may be of independent interest.

At a high level, our work provides a framework bringing together two long-studied branches of social choice theory — fair division theory and voting theory. Both have at their heart the aim to aggregate individual preferences into a collective outcome that is fair and agreeable, but approach the problem in different ways. Fair division theory typically deals with multiple private goods, assumes access to cardinal utilities, and focuses on notions of fairness such as envy-freeness and proportionality. Voting theory, in contrast, typically deals with a single public decision (with the exception of combinatorial voting mentioned earlier), assumes access only to less expressive ordinal preferences, has the "one voter, one vote" fairness built inherently into the voting rules, and focuses on different axiomatic desiderata such as Condorcet consistency and monotonicity.

Of course, one can use a voting approach to fair division, since we can have players express preferences over complete outcomes, and this approach has been used successfully to import mechanisms from voting to fair division and vice versa [1, 3]. However, not only does this approach result in an exponential blowup in the number of alternatives, it also does not provide a convenient way to express fair-division-like axioms. Continuing to explore connections between the two fields remains a compelling direction for future work.

ACKNOWLEDGMENTS

Conitzer and Freeman are supported by NSF under awards IIS-1527434 and CCF-1337215, ARO under grants W911NF-12-1-0550 and W911NF-11-1-0332, and a Guggenheim Fellowship.

REFERENCES

[1] H. Aziz, F. Brandt, and P. Stursberg. 2013. On popular random assignments. In *Proceedings of the 6th International Symposium on Algorithmic Game Theory (SAGT)*. 183–194.

[2] H. Aziz, M. Brill, V. Conitzer, E. Elkind, R. Freeman, and T. Walsh. 2017. Justified representation in approval-based committee voting. *Social Choice and Welfare* 48, 2 (2017), 461–485.

[3] H. Aziz and P. Stursberg. 2014. A Generalization of Probabilistic Serial to Randomized Social Choice.. In *Proceedings of the 28th AAAI Conference on Artificial Intelligence (AAAI)*. 559–565.

[6]Of course, the *realization* may fail to satisfy Prop (and other desiderata), but the *lottery* is fair if we consider expected utilities.

[4] N. Bansal and M. Sviridenko. 2006. The Santa Claus problem. In *Proceedings of the 38th Annual ACM Symposium on Theory of Computing (STOC)*. 31–40.

[5] G. Benade, A. D. Procaccia, S. Nath, and N. Shah. 2017. Preference Elicitation for Participatory Budgeting. In *Proceedings of the 31st AAAI Conference on Artificial Intelligence (AAAI)*. Forthcoming.

[6] A. Bogomolnaia, H. Moulin, and R. Stong. 2005. Collective choice under dichotomous preferences. *Journal of Economic Theory* 122, 2 (2005), 165–184.

[7] C. Boutilier, I. Caragiannis, S. Haber, T. Lu, A. D. Procaccia, and O. Sheffet. 2015. Optimal Social Choice Functions: A Utilitarian View. *Artificial Intelligence* 227 (2015), 190–213.

[8] S. Bouveret and J. Lang. 2008. Efficiency and envy-freeness in fair division of indivisible goods: logical representation and complexity. *Journal of Artificial Intelligence Research* 32 (2008), 525–564.

[9] S. J. Brams, M. Kilgour, and C. Klamler. 2012. The undercut procedure: An algorithm for the envy-free division of indivisible items. *Social Choice and Welfare* 39, 2–3 (2012), 615–631.

[10] F. Brandt, V. Conitzer, U. Endress, J. Lang, and A. D. Procaccia (Eds.). 2016. *Handbook of Computational Social Choice*. Cambridge University Press.

[11] E. Budish. 2011. The combinatorial assignment problem: Approximate competitive equilibrium from equal incomes. *Journal of Political Economy* 119, 6 (2011), 1061–1103.

[12] Y. Cabannes. 2004. Participatory budgeting: A significant contribution to participatory democracy. *Environment and Urbanization* 16, 1 (2004), 27–46.

[13] I. Caragiannis, C. Kaklamanis, P. Kanellopoulos, and M. Kyropoulou. 2012. The efficiency of fair division. *Theory of Computing Systems* 50, 4 (2012), 589–610.

[14] I. Caragiannis, D. Kurokawa, H. Moulin, A. D. Procaccia, N. Shah, and J. Wang. 2016. The Unreasonable Fairness of Maximum Nash Welfare. In *Proceedings of the 17th ACM Conference on Economics and Computation (EC)*. 305–322.

[15] J. R. Chamberlin and P. N. Courant. 1983. Representative Deliberations and Representative Decisions: Proportional Representation and the Borda Rule. *American Political Science Review* 77, 3 (1983), 718–733.

[16] R. Cole and V. Gkatzelis. 2015. Approximating the Nash Social Welfare with Indivisible Items. In *Proceedings of the 47th Annual ACM Symposium on Theory of Computing (STOC)*. 371–380.

[17] B. Fain, A. Goel, and K. Munagala. 2016. The Core of the Participatory Budgeting Problem. In *Proceedings of the 12th Conference on Web and Internet Economics (WINE)*. 384–399.

[18] D. Foley. 1967. Resource allocation and the public sector. *Yale Economics Essays* 7 (1967), 45–98.

[19] R. Freeman, S.M. Zahedi, and V. Conitzer. 2017. Fair Social Choice in Dynamic Settings. In *Proceedings of the 26th International Joint Conference on Artificial Intelligence (IJCAI)*. Forthcoming.

[20] A. Goel, A. K. Krishnaswamy, S. Sakshuwong, and T. Aitamurto. 2016. Knapsack Voting: Voting mechanisms for Participatory Budgeting. Manuscript. (2016).

[21] C.-J. Haake, M. G. Raith, and F. E. Su. 2002. Bidding for envy-freeness: A procedural approach to n-player fair-division problems. *Social Choice and Welfare* 19 (2002), 723–749.

[22] F. Klijn. 2000. An algorithm for envy-free allocations in an economy with indivisible objects and money. *Social Choice and Welfare* 17 (2000), 201–215.

[23] D. Kurokawa, A. D. Procaccia, and N. Shah. 2015. Leximin Allocations in the Real World. In *Proceedings of the 16th ACM Conference on Economics and Computation (EC)*. 345–362.

[24] J. Lang and L. Xia. 2016. Voting in combinatorial domains. In *Handbook of Computational Social Choice*, F. Brandt, V. Conitzer, U. Endress, J. Lang, and A. D. Procaccia (Eds.). Cambridge University Press, Chapter 8.

[25] E. Lee. 2015. APX-Hardness of Maximizing Nash Social Welfare with Indivisible Items. arXiv:1507.01159. (2015).

[26] R. J. Lipton, E. Markakis, E. Mossel, and A. Saberi. 2004. On approximately fair allocations of indivisible goods. In *Proceedings of the 6th ACM Conference on Economics and Computation (EC)*. 125–131.

[27] B. L. Monroe. 1995. Fully Proportional Representation. *American Political Science Review* 89, 4 (1995), 925–940.

[28] J. Nash. 1950. The bargaining problem. *Econometrica* 18, 2 (1950), 155–162.

[29] A. D. Procaccia and J. S. Rosenschein. 2006. The Distortion of Cardinal Preferences in Voting. In *Proceedings of the 10th International Workshop on Cooperative Information Agents (CIA)*. 317–331.

[30] A. D. Procaccia and J. Wang. 2014. Fair Enough: Guaranteeing Approximate Maximin Shares. In *Proceedings of the 14th ACM Conference on Economics and Computation (EC)*. 675–692.

[31] S. Ramezani and U. Endriss. 2010. Nash social welfare in multiagent resource allocation. In *Proceedings of the 12th International Workshop on Agent-Mediated Electronic Commerce (AMEC)*. 117–131.

[32] J.H. Reijnierse and J. A. M. Potters. 1998. On finding an envy-free Pareto-optimal division. *Mathematical Programming* 83 (1998), 291–311.

[33] H. Steinhaus. 1948. The problem of fair division. *Econometrica* 16 (1948), 101–104.

[34] H. Varian. 1974. Equity, envy and efficiency. *Journal of Economic Theory* 9 (1974), 63–91.

Approximation Algorithms for Maximin Fair Division

SIDDHARTH BARMAN, Indian Institute of Science
SANATH KUMAR KRISHNA MURTHY, Chennai Mathematical Institute

We consider the problem of dividing indivisible goods *fairly* among n agents who have additive and submodular valuations for the goods. Our fairness guarantees are in terms of the maximin share, that is defined to be the maximum value that an agent can ensure for herself, if she were to partition the goods into n bundles, and then receive a minimum valued bundle. Since maximin fair allocations (i.e., allocations in which each agent gets at least her maximin share) do not always exist, prior work has focussed on approximation results that aim to find allocations in which the value of the bundle allocated to each agent is (multiplicatively) as close to her maximin share as possible. In particular, Procaccia and Wang (2014) along with Amanatidis et al. (2015) have shown that under additive valuations a 2/3-approximate maximin fair allocation always exists and can be found in polynomial time. We complement these results by developing a simple and efficient algorithm that achieves the same approximation guarantee.

Furthermore, we initiate the study of approximate maximin fair division under submodular valuations. Specifically, we show that when the valuations of the agents are nonnegative, monotone, and submodular, then a 1/10-approximate maximin fair allocation is guaranteed to exist. In fact, we show that such an allocation can be efficiently found by using a simple round-robin algorithm. A technical contribution of the paper is to analyze the performance of this combinatorial algorithm by employing the concept of *multilinear extensions*.

Additional Key Words and Phrases: Fair Division; Maximin Shares; Submodular Valuations; Multilinear Extensions

ACM Reference format:
Siddharth Barman and Sanath Kumar Krishna Murthy. 2017. Approximation Algorithms for Maximin Fair Division. *ACM Transactions on Economics and Computation* 1, 1, Article 1 (January 2017), 18 pages.
DOI: http://dx.doi.org/10.1145/3033274.3085136

1 INTRODUCTION

This problem of allocating goods among agents in a "fair" manner has been extensively studied in the economics and mathematics literature for over fifty years; the first formal treatment of fair division appears in the work of Steinhaus, Banach, and Knaster [33]. Such problems naturally arise in many real-world settings—e.g., in government auctions, border disputes, and divorce settlements—and a vast literature has been developed to address fair division under various modeling assumptions. Multiple solution concepts, such as *envy-freeness*, *proportionality*, and *equitability*, have been proposed to formally capture fairness; see [10] and [29] for excellent expositions.

A full version of this paper is available at: https://arxiv.org/abs/1703.01851
The first author was supported in part by a Ramanujan Fellowship (SERB - SB/S2/RJN-128/2015).
Author's addresses: S. Barman, Indian Institute of Science, Bangalore, India and S.K. Krishna Murthy, Chennai Mathematical Institute, Chennai, India.

ACM ISBN 978-1-4503-4527-9/17/06...$15.00. http://dx.doi.org/10.1145/3033274.3085136

Even though there is a significant body of work aimed at understanding the division of *divisible* goods,[1] questions related to the fair division of *indivisible* goods are relatively underexplored. In particular, it is known that fair allocations of divisible goods necessarily exist (with respect to all the previously mentioned solution concepts), however, such guarantees do not hold for indivisible goods; for example, if we have two agents and a single indivisible good, then, under any allocation, the agent that does not get the good will *envy* the other. Furthermore, classical fairness notions like envy-freeness and proportionality cannot even be approximately satisfied in the case of indivisible goods.[2]

Motivated by these observations and the fact that many practical scenarios (such as course allocation at educational institutions [11] and division of inheritance consisting of, say, cars and houses) inherently entail division of discrete goods, recent results have focussed on the problem of fair division of indivisible goods; see, e.g., [1, 7, 11, 32] and references therein. Specifically, this thread of research has considered notions of fairness[3] which are applicable to indivisible goods, and established existence and computational results for these solution concepts.

One such fairness notion is the *maximin share*, which is defined in the notable work of Budish [11] (see also [28]). Conceptually, maximin share can be interpreted through a discrete (indivisible) generalization of the standard *cut-and-choose* protocol. In particular, this protocol is used to fairly divide a cake (i.e., a divisible good) between two agents: the first agent cuts the cake and then the second agent gets to select her favorite piece. Note that a risk-averse agent would cut the cake into two pieces that have equal value for her. In other words, the first agent will cut (partition) the cake to maximize the minimum value over the pieces in the cut (partition). The protocol leads to a fair allocation in terms of *envy-freeness*, i.e., it results in an allocation wherein each agent prefers her piece of the cake over the other agent's piece.

Analogously, while dividing indivisible goods among n agents, we can (hypothetically) ask an agent i to partition the goods into n bundles, and then the other agents get to pick a bundle before i. This could possibly lead to agent i getting her least desired bundle in the partition. Hence, as in the cut and choose protocol, a risk-averse agent would partition the goods so as to maximize the value of the least desirable bundle (according to her) in the partition. The value that agent i can guarantee for herself by partitioning in this manner is defined to be agent i's maximin share. An allocation is said to be maximin fair if, for every agent, the value of her bundle is at least as high as her maximin share.

Overall, the maximin share provides an intuitive threshold, and using it, we can deem an allocation to be fair if this threshold is met for every agent. Recent results in the computer science literature have considered whether maximin fair allocations exist and can they be efficiently computed. It turns out that the existence of a maximin fair allocation is not guaranteed [24, 32]. But, this concept lends well to approximation guarantees: Procaccia and Wang [32] have shown that when the agents have additive valuations, one can find an allocation wherein each agent gets a bundle of value greater than 2/3 times her maximin share, i.e., a 2/3-approximate maximin fair allocation always exists. The proof of existence by Procaccia and Wang is constructive, but it leads to a polynomial time algorithm only when the number of agents is constant. Extending this result, Amanatidis et al. [1] have developed an algorithm that finds a 2/3-approximate maximin fair allocation and runs in time polynomial in the number of agents. It is relevant to note that the approximation guarantees obtained in these results and the current paper are absolute, i.e., they guarantee that

[1]The metaphor of divisible goods is useful in settings such as land division.

[2]This is true, for example, when we have two agents and a single indivisible good.

[3]For example, EF1 [11], EFX [14], and maximin shares [11].

there always exists an allocation wherein each agent receives a value at least a constant times her maximin share. The guarantees are not relative to the "best-possible" allocation.

In the context of indivisible goods, the above mentioned results affirm the relevance of maximin shares as a measure of fairness, but they are confined to additive valuations. In this paper, we extend this line of work and establish maximin fairness guarantees for both *additive* and *submodular* valuations. Given that submodular functions are extensively used in economics and computer science to model preferences, our fairness guarantee for submodular valuations is a compelling generalization of prior work.

Our Results and Techniques: Our first result (Theorem 2.1) considers fair division of indivisible goods between agents with additive valuations for the goods. In particular, we show that the approximation guarantee obtained in [32] and [1] can be achieved by a simple,[4] combinatorial algorithm.[5] That is, we present a polynomial-time algorithm that finds a 2/3-approximate maximin fair allocation. To obtain this result we rely on a careful modification of an algorithm by Lipton et al. [27], which, in particular, finds an allocation which is envy free up to one good (EF1); formal definitions appear in Section 1.1. An arbitrary EF1 allocation might not provide any non-trivial approximation guarantee in terms of the maximin share; see the full version of the paper for an example. Hence, in and of itself, the algorithm of [27] is not guaranteed to find an allocation that satisfies the desired maximin fairness guarantee. Nonetheless, we show that any given additive instance can be reduced (using a result of [7]) to one with a specific structure and, then, an instantiation of the algorithm by Lipton et al. [27] (in a particular manner) finds an allocation with the desired fairness guarantee. Our contribution lies in a careful application and analysis of this algorithm.

In addition, we initiate the study of approximate maximin fair division under submodular valuations. Specifically, we show that when the valuations of the agents are nonnegative, monotone, and submodular, then a 1/10-approximate maximin fair allocation is guaranteed to exist and, in fact, such an allocation can be efficiently found by using a simple round-robin algorithm (Theorem 3.1).

A technical contribution of the paper is to analyze the performance of this simple algorithm by employing the concept of *multilinear extensions*. This concept has been used in recent results for constrained submodular maximization and, at a high level, it can be thought of as a continuous surrogate (a continuous extension) for a submodular function; see Section 3.2 for a definition. It is observed in [34] that the multilinear extension—of an agent's valuation function—achieves a high value if the agent is allocated a bundle uniformly at random. We use this observation to show that for each agent, in expectation, a bundle picked uniformly at random approximately satisfies the maximin requirement. Intuitively, this fact asserts that a uniformly random allocation is fair, in expectation. But, to obtain the desired approximation guarantee from this fact we cannot directly apply standard techniques (such as pipeage rounding or randomized rounding), since we need to satisfy the maximin requirement for multiple submodular functions simultaneously.[6] Instead, we show that in most rounds (of the round-robin algorithm), the gain in the value of an agent's bundle is comparable to the loss she incurs in the multilinear extension. We do so by defining the notion of

[4]Simple in the sense that our algorithm just entails sorting values and finding cycles in directed graphs. In contrast, the algorithm in [1] uses as a subroutine a PTAS (of Woeginger [36]) which is based on solving integer linear programs of constant dimension, using Lenstra's algorithm [26].

[5]In fact, we are able to compute a $\frac{2n}{3n-1}$ approximate maximin fair allocation in polynomial time. This is slightly better than the $(\frac{2}{3} - \epsilon)$ approximation guarantee of Amanatidis et al. [1].

[6]Note that, a direct application of randomized rounding leads to a logarithmic approximation guarantee. In particular, the concentration bounds for submodular functions [16] only establish the existence of a $\frac{1}{O(\log n)}$-approximate maximin fair allocation.

expected ordered marginals and using them to express the multilinear extension values; this notion might be of independent interest. Overall, this shows that using the round-robin algorithm we can efficiently find a 1/10-approximate maximin fair allocation.

In the full version of this paper, we also show that a 4/3-approximate maximin fair allocation can be efficiently computed when agents have additive valuations for chores (i.e., negatively valued goods). This improves upon the previously best known 2-approximation of Aziz et al. [4].[7]

Related Work: As mentioned previously, fair division is a well-studied problem in multiple disciplines [10, 29, 31]. In this paper we focus on allocating indivisible goods and, in particular, study the concept of maximin shares. This concept was defined by [11] as a natural relaxation of *fair-share guarantees* [30]. In particular, Budish [11] applied this solution concept to the problem of allocating courses to students, and showed that maximin shares for n agents can be guaranteed if some goods are over allocated and the share of each agent is computed with respect to $n + 1$ agents, instead of n. Note that these allocation errors cannot be ignored when, say, there is only copy of each good, and such a bi-criteria approximation guarantee does not provide any nontrivial multiplicative approximation bounds.

The work of Bouveret and Lemaitre [7] focuses on fair division of indivisible goods with additive valuations. Along with other results, they show that if an allocation is fair with respect to other solution concepts (such as envy freeness and proportionality), then it is maximin fair as well. They also show that maximin fair allocations are guaranteed to exist for binary, additive valuations. The empirical results presented in [7] suggest that maximin shares invariably exist when the additive valuations are drawn from particular distributions.

Procaccia and Wang [32] also study maximin shares under additive valuations. They prove that maximin fair allocations do not always exist, but allocations wherein each agent gets a bundle of value greater than 2/3 times her maximin share always exist. The proof of existence in [32] is constructive, but it leads to a polynomial time algorithm only when the number of agents is constant. Amanatidis et al. [1] extend this result by showing that a 2/3-approximate maximin fair allocation can be computed in polynomial time. Kurokawa et al. [24] strengthen the negative result of Procaccia and Wang [32]: they present smaller fair division instances which do not admit maximin fair allocations. In addition, they also show that when the valuations are randomly drawn then maximin fair allocations exist with high probability.

Aziz et al. [4] consider maximin fair allocations for chores (i.e., negatively valued goods). They show that, even in the case of chores, exact maximin fair allocations do not always exist and they complement this result by developing an efficient algorithm which finds a 2-approximate maximin fair allocation.

Maximin fair division is seemingly related to the well-studied Santa Claus problem [2, 3, 5, 6, 15, 19], where the goal is to find an allocation that maximizes the minimum value over all agents.[8] But, note that the Santa Claus problem is an optimization problem—the objective function is the egalitarian social welfare—whereas, in the maximin fair division problem the goal is to find an allocation that satisfies a property (that every agent gets her maximin share). The two problems behave differently with respect to scaling. In particular, a maximin fair allocation continues to be fair if a single agent scales her valuations, this is not the case with the Santa Claus problem. These problems differ significantly in terms of approximability as well: In the additive valuation case, the best known algorithm for the Santa Claus problem achieves a $\tilde{O}(n^{\varepsilon})$-approximation and runs in time $O(n^{\frac{1}{\varepsilon}})$ [15]; here n is the number of agents and $\varepsilon > 0$. For the submodular valuation case, a

[7] In the case of chores the approximation factor is greater than or equal to one.

[8] The Santa Claus problem is also called the max-min fair allocation problem.

$O(n^{1/4}m^{1/2})$-approximation algorithm was developed for the Santa Claus problem by Goemans et al. [21]; here m is the number of goods. On the other hand, as we show in this paper, constant-factor approximation guarantees can be achieved for the maximin fair division problem, even when the valuations are submodular.

In notable cases, fair division algorithms have been implemented: (i) Course Match [12] is used for course allocation at Wharton School at the University of Pennsylvania, (ii) the website Spliddit [22] provides free access to fair division methods, and (iii) the Adjusted Winner Website[9] implements an algorithm of Brams and Taylor [10] to fairly divide goods between two players. These practical applications enforce the idea that simple/easily implementable fair division algorithms—like the ones developed in this paper—have potential for impact.

1.1 Notation and Preliminaries

We let $[n] := \{1, 2, \ldots, n\}$ denote the set of agents and $[m] := \{1, 2, \ldots, m\}$ denote the set of indivisible goods. The valuation of an agent i for a subset of goods $S \subseteq [m]$ is denote by $v_i(S)$. For ease of presentation, we will use $v_i(j)$—instead of $v_i(\{j\})$—to denote the valuation of $j \in [m]$.

Agents are said to have *additive* valuations when, for any subset of goods $S \subseteq [m]$, the valuation of agent i satisfies $v_i(S) := \sum_{j \in S} v_i(j)$. For ease of presentation, in the case of additive valuations, we will also use v_{ij} to denote $v_i(j)$. Throughout, we will work with nonnegative valuations, $v_{ij} \geq 0$ for all $i \in [n]$ and $j \in [m]$.

Agents are said to have nonnegative, monotone, submodular valuations (with $v(\emptyset) = 0$) when for any $A \subseteq B \subset [m]$ and $g \in [m] \setminus B$, the valuation of agent i satisfies:

$$v_i(\emptyset) = 0$$
$$v_i(A) \leq v_i(B) \qquad \text{(Monotonicity)}$$
$$v_i(B \cup \{g\}) - v_i(B) \leq v_i(A \cup \{g\}) - v_i(A) \qquad \text{(Submodularity)}$$

Given a subset $H \subseteq [m]$, we will consider marginal values with respect to H and, in particular, define the marginal function f_H as follows: $f_H(S) := f(H \cup S) - f(H)$ for all $S \subseteq [m]$. Note that, for any $H \subseteq [m]$, if f is submodular then so is f_H.

Write $\Pi_n(S)$ to denote the set of all n-partitions of set $S \subseteq [m]$. With a slight abuse of notation, we will write $\Pi_n(m)$ to denote $\Pi_n([m])$. Throughout, we will use the word *allocation* to denote an n-partition $(A_1, \ldots, A_n)$ where set A_i is allocated to agent i. In addition, an allocation of a strict subset of the goods will be referred to as a *partial allocation*. We will use the term *bundles* to denote subsets, A_is, in an (partial) allocation.

Our fairness guarantee is in terms of maximin shares. Formally,

Definition 1.1 (Maximin Share). For an agent $i \in [n]$ and a subset of goods $S \subseteq [m]$, the n-maximin share is defined to be

$$\mu_i^n(S) := \max_{(M_1, M_2, \ldots, M_n) \in \Pi_n(S)} \min_{k \in [n]} v_i(M_k).$$

For ease of presentation, we will use μ_i to denote $\mu_i^n([m])$ and use maximin share for n-maximin share, whenever n is clear from context. Ideally, we would like to ensure fairness by partitioning the goods such that each agent gets her maximin share, i.e., partition the goods into subsets $(A_1, A_2, \ldots, A_n) \in \Pi_n(m)$ such that $v_i(A_i) \geq \mu_i$ for all $i \in [n]$.

Since such partitions do not always exist (see the full version of the paper for an example), a natural goal is to study approximation guarantees. In particular, our objective is to develop efficient algorithms that determine a partition $(A_1, \ldots, A_n) \in \Pi_n(m)$ wherein each agent, i, gets a bundle,

[9] http://www.nyu.edu/projects/adjustedwinner/

A_i, of value (under v_i) at least α times her maximin share, with $\alpha \in (0, 1]$ being as large as possible. We call such partitions as α-approximate maximin fair allocations. When $\alpha = 1$, we say that the allocation is maximin fair.

In this work we develop simple and efficient algorithms that achieve this objective with $\alpha = \frac{2}{3}$ for additive valuations and $\alpha = \frac{1}{10}$ for submodular valuations.

Our analysis of the algorithm (for additive valuations) that achieves this result relies, in particular, on understanding the fairness of an allocation in terms of *envy*. Formally, for an allocation $\mathcal{B} = (B_1, \ldots, B_n)$, we say that agent i *envies* agent j iff i prefers j's bundle to her own, i.e., $v_i(B_i) < v_i(B_j)$. An allocation is defined to be *envy free* iff no agent envies any other. Since envy-free allocations are not guaranteed to exist with indivisible goods,[10] a natural relaxation (which has been studied in literature; see, e.g., [11]) is *envy free up to one good* (EF1): an allocation $\mathcal{A}$ is said to be EF1 iff for each $i, j \in [n]$ there exists a good $g \in A_j$ such that $v_i(A_i) \geq v_i(A_j \setminus \{g\})$. In fact, we will show that—for a relevant class of problem instances—our algorithm finds an allocation with is envy free up to the least valued good (EFX) (defined in [14]).

Definition 1.2 (Envy free up to the least valued good (EFX)). An allocation $\mathcal{A}$ is said to be envy free up to the least valued good (EFX) iff for every $i, j \in [n]$ and each good $g \in A_j$ we have $v_i(A_i) \geq v_i(A_j \setminus \{g\})$.

2 ADDITIVE VALUATIONS

In this section we present an algorithm that efficiently finds a $\frac{2}{3}$-approximate maximin fair allocation under additive valuations.

Theorem 2.1 (Main Result for Additive Valuations). *Given a set of n agents with additive valuations, $\{v_i\}_{i \in [n]}$, for a set of m indivisible goods, we can find a partition $(A_1, \ldots, A_n) \in \Pi_n(m)$ in polynomial time that satisfies*

$$v_i(A_i) \geq \frac{2n}{3n-1}\, \mu_i \qquad \text{for all } i \in [n].$$

Here μ_i is the maximin share of agent i.

The proof of the theorem proceeds in two parts: (i) First, we show that the problem of finding an approximate maximin fair allocation can be reduced to a restricted setting where the agents value the goods in the same order. That is, the m goods can be ordered (indexed), say $g_1, g_2, \ldots, g_m$, such that the valuation of every agent i respects this ordering: for each $a < b$ we have $v_i(g_a) \geq v_i(g_b)$. (ii) Then, we develop a 2/3-approximation algorithm for this restricted setting.

2.1 The Reduction of Bouveret and Lemaître

Intuitively, the greater the conflict of interest among agents, the harder it is to ensure a fairness guarantee. For additive valuations, Bouveret and Lemaître [7] show that it is hardest to guarantee the agents their maximin share when all agents have the same order of preference over the goods. Formally, we say an instance is an *ordered instance* iff there exists a total ordering ($\prec$) over the set of goods $[m]$ such that for all $i \in [n]$ and $j, j' \in [m]$, such that $j \prec j'$, we have $v_{i,j} \geq v_{i,j'}$. Therefore, without loss of generality, we can say that an instance is ordered iff for all agents $i \in [n]$ and goods $j, j' \in [m]$, such that $j < j'$, we have $v_{i,j} \geq v_{i,j'}$, i.e., $v_{i,1} \geq v_{i,2} \geq \cdots \geq v_{i,m}$.

Given a fair division instance $I = ([n], [m], v)$ we will construct an ordered instance as follows. First, note that for every agent $i \in [n]$, there exists a permutation $\sigma_i : [m] \to [m]$ such that for all $j, j' \in [m]$ with $j < j'$ we have $v_{i,\sigma_i(j)} \geq v_{i,\sigma_i(j')}$. Using these permutations, we define a new

[10] Consider a setting with two players, and one indivisible good that has a nonzero value for both the players.

valuation function, v', for every agent i by setting $v'_{i,j} = v_{i,\sigma_i(j)}$ for all $j \in [m]$. That is, for agent i, the value of the jth good in the new instance is equal to the jth largest valuation of i in the original instance. We refer to $I' = ([n], [m], v')$ as the ordered instance of I. Note that we can find the ordered instance of I in $O(nm \log m)$ time.

Bouveret and Lemaître [7] show that if there is an allocation $\mathcal{A}'$ which guarantees every agent her maximin share in I', then there is an allocation $\mathcal{A}$ that guarantees every agent her maximin share in I. Moreover, given a maximin fair allocation $\mathcal{A}'$ (for I'), a maximin fair allocation $\mathcal{A}$ for the original instance I can be found in polynomial time. In fact, we directly use their proof to show the following slightly stronger statement that such a reduction is possible with respect to any set of scalars, α_is, and not just with respect to the maximin shares.

ALGORITHM 1: ALGBL: Algorithm of Bouveret and Lemaître

Input : Instance $I = ([n], [m], v)$ with an allocation $\mathcal{A}'$ for the ordered instance $I' = ([n], [m], v')$ such that $v'_i(A'_i) \geq \alpha_i$ for all $i \in [n]$.
Output: An allocation $\mathcal{A} = (A_1, \dots, A_n)$ such that, $v_i(A_i) \geq \alpha_i$ for all $i \in [n]$.

1: For all $i \in [n]$ and $j \in A'_i$ set $p_j := i$. {This defines a sequence of agents, $P := p_1, p_2, \dots, p_m$.}
2: Initialize allocation $\mathcal{A} = (A_1, A_2, \dots, A_n)$ with $A_i = \emptyset$, for all $i \in [n]$, and $R \leftarrow [m]$.
3: **for** $j = 1$ to m **do**
4:     Pick $k \in \arg\max_{g \in R}\{v_{p_j}(g)\}$.
5:     Update $A_{p_j} \leftarrow A_{p_j} \cup \{k\}$ and $R \leftarrow R \setminus \{k\}$.
6: **end for**
7: Return $\mathcal{A}$.

Theorem 2.2. *Given a maximin fair division instance $I = ([n], [m], v)$ and scalars $\{\alpha_i \in \mathbb{R}\}_{i=1}^n$, let $I' = ([n], [m], v')$ be the ordered instance of I. If there exists an allocation $\mathcal{A}' = (A'_1, A'_2, \dots, A'_n)$ that satisfies $v'_i(A'_i) \geq \alpha_i$ for all $i \in [n]$, then there exists an allocation $\mathcal{A} = (A_1, \dots, A_n)$ in which $v_i(A_i) \geq \alpha_i$, for all $i \in [n]$. Moreover, given I and $\mathcal{A}'$, ALGBL computes the allocation $\mathcal{A}$ in polynomial time.*

Proof. Clearly, ALGBL runs in polynomial time. Now, we will show that ALGBL computes the required allocation $\mathcal{A}$. Let k_j denote the good allocated in the jth iteration of the second for-loop (Steps 3 to 6) in ALGBL. Now consider agent i, suppose $j \in A'_i$ then $k_j \in A_i$. Note that, for any $j \neq j'$, we have $k_j \neq k_{j'}$; since, a good is removed from the set R after it is allocated. Before the jth iteration of the second for-loop in ALGBL, exactly $j - 1$ goods had been allocated. Therefore k_j is among the top j goods for agent i. Hence, for all $j \in A'_i$, $v_i(k_j) \geq v'_i(j)$. This implies that, $\sum_{j \in A'_i} v_i(k_j) \geq \sum_{j \in A'_i} v'_i(j)$, i.e., $v_i(A_i) \geq v'_i(A'_i)$. Hence the condition that $v'_i(A'_i) \geq \alpha_i$ gives us $v_i(A_i) \geq \alpha_i$ for all i. This completes the proof. □

Note that the maximin share depends on the values of the goods but not on the order, hence the maximin share of an agent i in an instance I is equal to her maximin share in the ordered instance I'. Therefore, instantiating Theorem 2.2, we have the following corollary.

Corollary 2.3. *Given a maximin fair division instance $I = ([n], [m], v)$ and $\alpha \in \mathbb{R}$ write I' to denote the ordered instance of I and μ_i (respectively μ'_i) to denote the maximin share of agent i in I (respectively I'). If there exists an allocation $\mathcal{A}' = (A'_1, A'_2, \dots, A'_n)$ that satisfies $v'_i(A'_i) \geq \alpha\mu'_i$, for all $i \in [n]$, then there exists is an allocation $\mathcal{A} = (A_1, A_2, \dots, A_n)$ in which $v_i(A_i) \geq \alpha\mu_i$, for all $i \in [n]$. Moreover, given I and $\mathcal{A}'$, the allocation $\mathcal{A}$ can be computed in polynomial time.*

2.2 Envy Graph Algorithm

As shown in Corollary 2.3, we only need address the setting in which the agents value the goods in the same order. Hence, in the remainder of this section, we solely focus on ordered instances. That is, we will establish the desired approximation for instances wherein the goods are indexed, say $g_1, g_2, \ldots, g_m$, such that for every agent i, we have $v_i(g_a) \geq v_i(g_b)$, for all indices $a < b$. The approximation algorithm given in this section iteratively allocates the goods in decreasing order of value (i.e., in increasing order of their index) and maintains a partial allocation, $\mathcal{A} = (A_1, \ldots, A_n)$, of the goods assigned so far. In order to assign a good, the algorithm selects a bundle, A_i, by considering a directed graph, $G(\mathcal{A})$, that captures the envy between agents. The nodes in this envy graph represent the agents and it contains a directed edge from i to j iff i envies j, i.e., $v_i(A_i) < v_i(A_j)$.

The following lemma was established in [27] and it shows that we can always "resolve" a partial allocation and obtain an acyclic envy graph. The proof of the lemma is direct, we provide it in the full version of the paper for completeness.

Lemma 2.4 ([27]). *Given a partial allocation $\mathcal{A} = (A_1, \ldots, A_n)$ of a subset of goods $S \subseteq [m]$, we can find another partial allocation $\mathcal{B} = (B_1, \ldots, B_n)$ of S in polynomial time such that*

(i) *The valuations of agents for their bundles do not decrease: $v_i(B_i) \geq v_i(A_i)$ for all $i \in [n]$.*
(ii) *The envy graph $G(\mathcal{B})$ is acyclic.*

Our algorithm uses Lemma 2.4 and is detailed below. Lemma 2.5 states that Alg returns an EFX allocation and is proved in the full version of the paper.

ALGORITHM 2: Envy Graph Algorithm Alg

Input: An ordered instance (i.e., an instance wherein the agents value the goods in the same order) with n agents, m items, and valuations v_{ij} for each $i \in [n]$ and $j \in [m]$.
Output: An allocation that provides approximate maximin shares guarantee

```
Order the goods, g_1, ..., g_m, s.t. for every agent i ∈ [n] and a < b we have v_{ig_a} ≥ v_{ig_b}.
Initialize allocation A = (A_1, A_2, ..., A_n) with A_i = ∅ for all i ∈ [n].
for j = 1 to m do
    Pick a vertex i that has no incoming edges in G(A), i.e., i is a source vertex in G(A).
    {The algorithm maintains the invariant that G(A) is acyclic. Hence, such a vertex is guaranteed to
    exist.}
    Update A_i ← A_i ∪ {g_j}.
    if the current envy graph G(A) contains a cycle then
        Use Lemma 2.4 to update A and, hence, obtain an acyclic envy graph.
    end if
end for
Return A.
```

Lemma 2.5. *For any ordered maximin fair division instance, the partial allocation found by Alg is envy free up to the least valued good (EFX).*

Next we introduce the concept of majorization and prove a technical proposition which will be useful in establishing the desired approximation ratio. We say that a multiset $X = \{x_i \in \mathbb{R} \mid 1 \leq$

$i \le n\}$ majorizes another multiset $Y = \{y_i \in \mathbb{R} \mid 1 \le i \le n\}$ iff

$$\sum_{i=1}^{k} x_{(i)} \ge \sum_{i=1}^{k} y_{(i)} \qquad \forall\, 1 \le k < n, \quad \text{and}$$

$$\sum_{i=1}^{n} x_{(i)} = \sum_{i=1}^{n} y_{(i)}.$$

Here $x_{(i)}$ ($y_{(i)}$) is the ith largest element of X (Y).[11]

A proof of Proposition 2.6 can be found in [37]. We provide a proof in the full version of the paper as well.

Proposition 2.6. *Let $v, v' \in \mathbb{R}$ be two elements of a multiset A of real numbers. In addition, say $u, u' \in \mathbb{R}$ satisfy $u + u' = v + v'$ and $|u - u'| < |v - v'|$. Then A majorizes $(A \setminus \{v, v'\}) \cup \{u, u'\}$.*

2.3 Proof of Theorem 2.1

To establish the stated claim, in the remainder of the proof we will show that $v_1(A_1) \ge \frac{2n}{3n-1}\mu_1$; an analogous argument establishes the desired bound, $v_i(A_i) \ge \frac{2n}{3n-1}\mu_i$, for all agents $i \in [n]$.

Write $\mathcal{A} = (A_1, \ldots, A_n)$ to denote the allocation returned by the algorithm Alg. Consider the set of goods that have value more than $\frac{1}{2}v_1(A_1)$; specifically, define $\tau := \arg\min\{j \mid v_1(g_j) \le \frac{1}{2}v_1(A_1)\}$ and let H denote the set of high valued goods $H := \{g_1, g_2, \ldots, g_{\tau-1}\}$. In addition, write $\mathcal{P} = (P_1, P_2, \ldots, P_n)$ to denote the partial allocation that Alg computes for H.[12]

Also, let t denote the smallest iteration count at which Alg assigns a good (in particular, good g_t) to a bundle of size two. Hence, every bundle in the partial allocation of the first $t-1$ goods is of size at most two.

Note that Alg keeps updating the partial allocations by adding goods to existing bundles.[13] This observation implies that the cardinalities of the bundles in successive partial allocations keep on increasing. This monotonic growth of the bundles also ensures that for each set A_i (in the final allocation $\mathcal{A}$), there exists a unique set P_j (in the partial allocation $\mathcal{P}$) such that $P_j \subseteq A_i$. Moreover, Lemma 2.4 guarantees that as Alg progresses the valuation of the agents also does not decrease; in particular, $v_1(A_1) \ge v_1(P_1)$.

Let $Q = (Q_1, Q_2, \ldots, Q_n)$ be the partial allocation considered by Alg at the beginning of the tth iteration. The definition of t ensures that $|Q_i| \le 2$ for all $i \in [n]$. Below we will show that $\tau \le t$ and, therefore, using the observation that the cardinalities of the bundles are nondecreasing, we get the following bound: $|P_i| \le 2$ for all $i \in [n]$. This, in turn, leads to the inequality $\tau \le 2n$.

Recall that good g_t was the first good that was assigned to a set of cardinality two. Write $Q_b = \{g_x, g_y\}$ to denote this set. Since g_t is included in Q_b, b must have been a source of the acyclic envy graph $G(Q)$. In other words, agent 1 does not envy b's current bundle, $v_1(Q_1) \ge v_1(Q_b) = v_1(g_x) + v_1(g_y)$. Moreover, since Alg assigns goods in decreasing order of value, g_t's value is no more than that of g_x and g_y: $v_1(g_x) \ge v_1(g_t)$ and $v_1(g_y) \ge v_1(g_t)$. Therefore, $v_1(Q_1) \ge 2v_1(g_t)$. Since the valuation of agent 1 does not decrease during the execution of Alg, we get $v_1(A_1) \ge 2v_1(g_t)$. By definition, g_τ is the smallest indexed good that satisfies this inequality and, hence, the inequality $\tau \le t$ holds.

We will first address the bundles that contain a good with index greater than $\tau - 1$. In particular, we establish the following claim.

[11]Ties for the ith largest position are broken arbitrarily.

[12]Without loss of generality, we can assume that $G(\mathcal{P})$ is acyclic, since an application of Lemma 2.4 in Alg simply reassigns the bundles between agents and the constituent bundles in $\mathcal{P}$ do not change.

[13]Though, the bundle assigned to an agent might change during an application of Lemma 2.4.

Claim 1. *In the partial allocation retuned by the* Alg, $\mathcal{A} = (A_1, \ldots, A_n)$, *the following inequality holds for all bundles the* A_i *that satisfy* $A_i \cap \{g_\tau, g_{\tau+1}, \ldots, g_m\} \neq \emptyset$

$$v_1(A_1) \geq \frac{2}{3} v_1(A_i) \tag{1}$$

Proof. Consider a bundle A_i which contains a good g_a with index $a \geq \tau$. Lemma 2.5 implies that $v_1(A_1) \geq v_1(A_i) - v_1(g_a)$. Also, note that $v_1(A_1) \geq 2v_1(g_\tau) \geq 2v_1(g_a)$; here, the second inequality follows from the fact that the values of the goods are ordered. Therefore, the claim holds. □

We now need to argue about bundles in $\mathcal{A}$ that do not contain any good with index greater than $\tau - 1$. For each such bundle, A_i, we have a unique set P_j in the partial allocation $\mathcal{P}$ such that $A_i = P_j$. This follows from the fact that after the $(\tau - 1)$th iteration no good is allocated to any of these bundles. Therefore, to get a handle on bundles in $\mathcal{A}$ that do not contain any good with index greater than $\tau - 1$ we will consider the partial allocation $\mathcal{P}$. By definition, $\mathcal{P}$ is a partial allocation of $H = \{g_1, \ldots, g_{\tau-1}\}$, i.e., $\cup_{i=1}^n P_i = H$. As mentioned above the cardinality of H (i.e., $\tau - 1$) is at most $2n$. Write $h := \max\{0, \tau - 1 - n\}$. We will consider the case in which $\tau \geq n + 1$—and, hence $\tau - 1 = n + h$—the other case wherein $\tau < n + 1$ is simpler and follows analogously. Proof of the following claim can be found in the full version of the paper.

Claim 2. *The partial allocation* $\mathcal{P}$ *consists of (up to reordering) the following bundles:*

$$\{g_1\}, \{g_2\}, \ldots, \{g_{n-h}\}, \{g_{n-h+1}, g_{n+h}\}, \{g_{n-h+2}, g_{n+h-1}\}, \ldots, \{g_{n-1}, g_{n+2}\}, \{g_n, g_{n+1}\}. \tag{2}$$

In the remainder of the proof we say that a partial allocation $\mathcal{R} = (R_1, \ldots, R_n)$ majorizes another partial allocation $\mathcal{R}' = (R'_1, \ldots, R'_n)$ iff $\{v_1(R_i)\}_i$ majorizes $\{v_1(R'_i)\}_i$. Specifically, we have the following claim for $\mathcal{P}$. The proof of Claim 3 is similar to the proof of Lemma 4 in [37] and appears in the full version of the paper.

Claim 3. *Every partial allocation of* H *(i.e., every* $\mathcal{R} \in \Pi_n(H)$*) majorizes* $\mathcal{P}$.

We will now complete the proof of Theorem 2.1. Let ℓ be the number of bundles in $\{A_2, A_3, \ldots, A_n\}$ that do not contain any good with index greater than $\tau - 1$. As mentioned above, for every such bundle, A_i there exists a unique bundle P_j in $\mathcal{P}$ such that $A_i = P_j$. Say, by reindexing, that $P_{n-\ell+1}, P_{n-\ell+2}, \ldots, P_n$ are these ℓ bundles in $\mathcal{A}$ that do not satisfy the condition in Claim 1.

Write $(M_1, M_2, \ldots, M_n)$ denote a partition of the $[m]$ goods that achieves the maximin share for player 1, i.e., $\min_{j \in [n]} v_1(M_j) = \mu_1$ (see Definition 1.1). Consider the partial allocation $(M_1 \cap H, M_2 \cap H, \ldots, M_n \cap H)$ and index the sets M_is such that $v_1(M_1 \cap H) \leq v_1(M_2 \cap H) \leq \ldots \leq v_1(M_n \cap H)$. Claim 3 implies that $(M_1 \cap H, M_2 \cap H, \ldots, M_n \cap H)$ majorizes $\mathcal{P}$. Hence, $\sum_{i=n-\ell+1}^n v_1(M_i \cap H) \geq \sum_{i=n-\ell+1}^n v_1(P_i)$. This inequality along with the fact that the valuations are monotone lead to the following useful bound

$$\sum_{i=n-\ell+1}^{n} v_1(M_i) \geq \sum_{i=n-\ell+1}^{n} v_1(P_i). \tag{3}$$

Recall that $P_{n-\ell+1}, P_{n-\ell+2}, \ldots, P_n$ are bundles in $\mathcal{A}$, and the remaining $(n-\ell)$ bundles of $\mathcal{A}$—say, $A_1, A_2, \ldots, A_{n-\ell}$—satisfy the inequality (1). Since v_1 is additive, we have $\sum_{i=1}^n v_1(M_i) = \sum_{i=1}^n v_1(A_i)$. Therefore, inequality (3) provides the following bound

$$\begin{aligned}\sum_{i=1}^{n-\ell} v_i(M_i) &\leq \sum_{i=1}^{n-\ell} v_1(A_i) \\ &\leq v_1(A_1) + (n - \ell - 1)\frac{3}{2} v_1(A_1) \qquad \text{(via Claim 1)}\end{aligned} \tag{4}$$

Overall, inequality (4) implies that $v_1(A_1)$ is at least $\frac{2(n-\ell)}{3(n-\ell)-1}$ times the average of the $(n-\ell)$ sets $M_{\ell+1}, M_{\ell+2}, \ldots, M_n$. Hence, $v_1(A_1) \geq \frac{2n}{3n-1} \min_{j \in [n]} v_1(M_j) = \frac{2n}{3n-1}\mu_1$. This completes the proof.

3 SUBMODULAR VALUATIONS

In this section we show that when the agents have submodular valuations, then a $\frac{1}{10}$-approximate maximin fair allocation is guaranteed to exist and, moreover, it can be found in polynomial time.[14]

3.1 Finding an Approximate Maximin Fair Allocation

We compute an approximate maximin fair allocation by employing Algorithm 3 (RoundRobin) as a subroutine. Algorithm 3 is quite direct: it takes as input thresholds, τ_is, for each agent i, allocates high-valued (with respect to τ_i) goods as singleton bundles, and then partitions the remaining goods in a round-robin fashion. The technical contribution here it to show that, for each agent i, as long as τ_i is no more than the maximin share μ_i, the bundle P_i allocated to i by Algorithm 3 satisfies $v_i(P_i) \geq \frac{1}{10}\tau_i$. It is relevant to note that this guarantee holds independently for each agent i (as long as $\tau_i \leq \mu_i$) and will not be violated even if $\tau_j > \mu_j$ for $j \neq i$. Formally, we establish this guarantee in Lemma 3.2 and use use its contrapositive version (i.e., if Algorithm 3 returns a P_i such that $v_i(P_i) < \frac{1}{10}\tau_i$, then it must be the case that $\tau_i > \mu_i$) to establish the main result of this section (Theorem 3.1).

In particular, AlgSub starts by setting thresholds τ_is, which are guaranteed to be more than the maximin shares. Then, it (geometrically) decreases the threshold for agent i, if the partition returned by RoundRobin does not satisfy $v_i(P_i) \geq \frac{1}{10}\tau_i$. In such a case, as stated previously, τ_i must have been greater than μ_i and, hence, decreasing the threshold is justified. Overall, in Section 3.4 we show that AlgSub efficiently finds thresholds, for each agent, which are comparable to their maximin share, and establish the following theorem.

Theorem 3.1 (Main Result for Submodular Valuations). *Given a maximin fair division instance with m goods and n agents that have nonnegative, monotone, submodular valuations $v_i : 2^{[m]} \to \mathbb{R}_+$ for $i \in [n]$. AlgSub, in polynomial time, finds an allocation $\mathcal{P} = (P_1, P_2, \ldots, P_n)$ which satisfies $v_i(P_i) \geq \frac{1}{10}\mu_i$, for all $i \in [n]$. Here μ_i is the maximin share of agent i.*

We begin by stating RoundRobin and establishing its key property, Lemma 3.2.[15]

Lemma 3.2. *Given a maximin fair division instance with m goods and n agents, whose valuations, $v_i : 2^{[m]} \to \mathbb{R}_+$, are nonnegative, monotone and submodular. Let $\mathcal{P} = (P_1, P_2, \ldots, P_n)$ be the allocation returned by RoundRobin for this instance, with thresholds $\tau_i \in \mathbb{R}_+$ for $i \in [n]$. Then, for each agent i whose input threshold satisfies $\tau_i \leq \mu_i$, we have*

$$v_i(P_i) \geq \frac{1}{10}\tau_i.$$

Here, μ_i is the n-maximin share of agent i.

Remark 1. *In the full version of the paper, we provide a polynomial-time 1/9-approximation algorithm for computing the maximin share of an agent whose valuation is nonnegative, monotone, and submodular. Hence, we can find also find an approximate maximin fair division by a single application of RoundRobin (specifically, by setting the thresholds τ_is to be 1/9 approximations of the actual maximin shares μ_is). The approximation guarantee obtained by this method, though constant, is worse than AlgSub, which invokes RoundRobin polynomially many times.*

[14] Our results only need oracle access to the submodular functions.

[15] Note that this lemma does not rule out the possibility that RoundRobin finds a bundle P_i which satisfies $v_i(P_i) \geq \frac{1}{10}\tau_i$, even if $\tau_i > \mu_i$.

ALGORITHM 3: RoundRobin: Computation of allocations with respect to thresholds

Input: An instance over m goods and n agents, whose valuations, $v_i : 2^{[m]} \to \mathbb{R}_+$, are nonnegative, monotone and submodular, along with thresholds τ_is for each $i \in [n]$.
Output: An allocation $\mathcal{P} = (P_1, P_2, \dots, P_n)$ such that $v_i(P_i) \geq \frac{1}{10}\tau_i$, for each agent $i \in [n]$ whose threshold satisfies $\tau_i \leq \mu_i$. Here μ_i is the n-maximin share of agent i.

Initialize set of agents $A = [n]$ and set of goods $G = [m]$.
while there exist agent $i \in A$ and good $j \in G$ such that $v_i(j) \geq \frac{1}{10}\tau_i$ **do**
  Allocate $P_i \leftarrow \{j\}$, and update $A \leftarrow A \setminus \{i\}$ and $G \leftarrow G \setminus \{j\}$.
end while
Assume, via reindexing, that the set of remaining agents $A = \{1, 2, \dots, |A|\}$.
while $G \neq \emptyset$ **do**
  for $i = 1$ to $|A|$ **do**
    Pick $g \in \arg\max_{j \in G}\{v_i(P_i \cup \{j\}) - v_i(P_i)\}$.
    $P_i \leftarrow P_i \cup \{g\}$, $G \leftarrow G \setminus \{g\}$
  end for
end while
return partition $\mathcal{P} = (P_1, P_2, \dots, P_n)$.

3.2 Multilinear Extensions and Expected Marginals

Our analysis of RoundRobin rests on studying the *multilinear extension* of the valuation functions. This concept has been used in recent results for constrained submodular maximization; see, e.g. [13, 17, 18, 23, 25, 34, 35]. Formally,

Definition 3.3 (Multilinear Extension). For a function $f : 2^{[m]} \to \mathbb{R}$, the multilinear extension $F : [0,1]^{[m]} \to \mathbb{R}$ is defined as follows:

$$F(x) := \mathbb{E}_{R \sim x}[f(R)] = \sum_{R \subseteq [m]} f(R) \left(\prod_{i \in R} x_i \prod_{i \in ([m] \setminus R)} (1 - x_i) \right).$$

Here sampling from $x \in [0,1]^m$ corresponds to selecting a random subset $R \subseteq [m]$ in which each $j \in [m]$ appears independently with probability x_j.

We say an n-tuple $\chi := (x^1, x^2, \dots, x^n)$ with $x^i \in [0,1]^m$ is a *fractional allocation* iff $\sum_{i=1}^n x^i_j \leq 1$ $\forall\, j \in [m]$. A binary fractional allocation corresponds to a (partial) allocation. Also, note that the set of all fractional allocations forms a partition matroid polytope over the set $[m]$. Next we state and prove a useful property of the *uniform* fractional allocation, a proof of which appears in the full version of the paper.

Lemma 3.4 (Proportionality). *Let $v_i : 2^{[m]} \to \mathbb{R}_+$ denote nonnegative, monotone, submodular valuations of agents $i \in [n]$ over m goods. Then, the fractional allocation $\omega = (u^1, u^2, \dots, u^n)$—in which $u^i := (\frac{1}{n}, \frac{1}{n}, \dots, \frac{1}{n}) \in [0,1]^m$ for all $i \in [n]$—satisfies $V_i(u^i) \geq \left(1 - \frac{1}{e}\right)\mu_i$ for all $i \in [n]$. Here $V_i : [0,1]^m \to \mathbb{R}_+$ is the multilinear extension of v_i and μ_i is the maximin share of agent i.*

Recall that f_H denotes the marginal function with respect to subset $H \subseteq [m]$, $f_H(S) := f(H \cup S) - f(H)$ for all $S \subseteq [m]$. Write F_H to denote the multilinear extension of f_H.
We define x^S to be the projection of a vector $x \in [0,1]^m$ onto $S \subseteq [m]$.

$$x^S_j := \begin{cases} x_j & \text{if } j \in S \\ 0 & \text{otherwise} \end{cases}$$

In addition, we will say that a vector y is supported over a set S iff the set of nonzero components of y is equal to S. Hence, for $u := (\frac{1}{n}, \frac{1}{n}, \ldots, \frac{1}{n}) \in [0,1]^m$ and $S \subseteq [m]$, the projection vector $u^S \in [0,1]^m$ is supported over S. In addition, the probability of drawing a subset R from u^S is nonzero iff $R \subseteq S$.

The following property of multilinear extensions will be used in the proof of Theorem 3.1. See the full version of the paper for a proof of this proposition.

Proposition 3.5. *Given a monotone, submodular function $f : 2^{[m]} \to \mathbb{R}_+$ along with subset $P \subseteq [m]$, good $g \in [m]$, and vector $x \in [0,1]^m$, the multilinear extensions of the marginal functions satisfy $F_{P \cup \{g\}}(x) \geq F_P(x) - f_P(g)$.*

For the analysis of the algorithm, we will define the notion of *expected ordered marginals* γ_js. This notion represents the (expected) marginal of a good $j \in J \subseteq [m]$ with respect to the goods in J that have a lower index than j, i.e., the marginal of j with respect to the set $S = \{j' \in J \mid j' < j\}$. The point is that we take expectation with respect to random draws of S. These marginals can be used to "locally" express the multilinear extension in a linear form; see Proposition 3.6.

Formally, given sets $J, H \subseteq [m]$, good $j \in [m]$ and $x \in [0,1]^m$, write

$$\gamma_j^{H,J}(x) := \mathbb{E}_{R \sim x}\left[f_{(H \,\cup\, (R \cap \{j' \in J \mid j' < j\}))}(j) \right]. \tag{5}$$

The multilinear extension of a function can be expressed in terms of these marginals as follows.

Proposition 3.6. *Given subsets $J, H \subseteq [m]$ and a vector $x \in [0,1]^m$ supported over J, the multilinear extension, F_H, of the submodular function f_H satisfies*

$$F_H(x) = \sum_{j \in J} \gamma_j^{H,J}(x)\, x_j$$

Proof. Consider the goods in set $J = \{j_1, j_2, \ldots, j_k\}$ such that $j_1 < j_2 < \cdots < j_k$, and let J_i denote the set of goods in J that have a lower index than j_i, i.e., $J_i := J \cap [j_i - 1] = \{j_1, j_2, \ldots, j_{i-1}\}$. Also, let J_0 denote the empty set.

For any subset $R \subseteq J$, the definition of the marginal function implies that

$$\begin{aligned} f_H(R) &= f(H \cup R) - f(H) \\ &= \sum_{i=1}^{k} f(H \cup (R \cap J_i)) - f(H \cup (R \cap J_{i-1})) \qquad \text{(telescoping sum)} \\ &= \sum_{i=1}^{k} f_{(H \,\cup\, (R \cap J_{i-1}))}(j_i)\ \mathbb{1}(j_i \in R). \end{aligned}$$

Here $\mathbb{1}(j \in R)$ is the indicator function of R. Note that x is supported over J and the above equality holds for all $R \subseteq J$, hence, taking expectation we get

$$\begin{aligned} F_H(x) &= \mathbb{E}_{R \sim x}\left[f_H(R)\right] \\ &= \sum_{i=1}^{k} \mathbb{E}_{R \sim x}\left[f_{(H \cup [R \cap J_{i-1}])}(j_i)\ \mathbb{1}(j_i \in R)\right] \\ &= \sum_{i=1}^{k} \mathbb{E}_{R \sim x}\left[f_{(H \cup [R \cap J_{i-1}])}(j_i)\right] \mathbb{E}_{R \sim x}[\mathbb{1}(j_i \in R)] \qquad \text{(x is a product distribution)} \\ &= \sum_{j \in J} \gamma_j^{H,J}(x)\, x_j \end{aligned}$$

□

Next we state a useful property of the expected ordered marginals. The proof of the following proposition appears in the full version of the paper.

Proposition 3.7. *Let $H \subseteq [m]$ and $x \in [0,1]^m$. Then, for subsets $J' \subseteq J \subseteq [m]$ and $j \in J'$, the expected ordered marginals are monotonic*

$$\gamma_j^{H,J'}(x^{J'}) \geq \gamma_j^{H,J}(x^J)$$

3.3 Proof of Lemma 3.2

In the proof we will fix an agent i and—under the assumption that $\tau_i \leq \mu_i$—establish the stated claim, $v_i(P_i) \geq \frac{1}{10}\tau_i$, for i; an analogous argument establishes the claim for all other agents.

If agent i was assigned a good in the first while-loop of RoundRobin (Algorithm 3), then we have the desired inequality $v_i(P_i) \geq \frac{1}{10}\tau_i$. Else, the first while-loop of Algorithm 3 terminates with, say, the good set $G = \{1, 2, \ldots, |G|\}$ (denoting the set of unallocated goods) and agent set $A = \{1, 2, \ldots, |A|\}$ (denoting the set of agents who have not been allocated a single good yet).

Let $\widehat{\mu}_i$ be agent i's maximin share in this reduced instance, $\widehat{\mu}_i := \max_{(B_1,\ldots,B_{|A|})\in\Pi_{|A|}(G)} \min_{j\in[|A|]} v_i(B_j)$. Next we will show that $\widehat{\mu}_i \geq \mu_i$ and $v_i(P_i) \geq \frac{1}{10}\widehat{\mu}_i$. Since we are working under the assumption that $\tau_i \leq \mu_i$, establishing an approximation guarantee in terms of $\widehat{\mu}_i$ (i.e., finding a $|A|$-partition $(P_1, \ldots, P_{|A|})$ of G such that $v_i(P_i) \geq 1/10\widehat{\mu}_i$ for all $i \in A$) will prove the lemma. Let $\mathcal{M}^* = (M_1^*, \ldots, M_n^*)$ denote a partition that achieves the maximin share with respect to v_i in the original instance: $\mathcal{M}^* \in \arg\max_{(B_1,\ldots,B_n)\in\Pi_n(m)} \min_{j\in[n]} v_i(B_j)$. Since $|[m] \setminus G| = n - |A|$, there are at most $n - |A|$ subsets M_j^*s which intersect with $[m] \setminus G$. In other words, there are at least $|A|$ bundles in $\mathcal{M}^*$ that are completely contained in G. Recall that $v_i(M_j^*) \geq \mu_i$ for all $j \in [n]$ and v_i is monotone. Hence, we can partition G into $|A|$ sets, say $(M_1, \ldots, M_{|A|})$, such that $v_i(M_j) \geq \mu_i$ for all $j \in [|A|]$. This proves that $\widehat{\mu}_i \geq \mu_i$. Therefore, in the rest of the proof we focus only on the reduced instance and, with slight abuse of notation, set $n = |A|$ and $m = |G|$.

We will now analyze the second while-loop of Algorithm 3, which allocates the goods in G to agents in A. A complete execution of the inner for-loop (Steps 8-11) will be called a *round.* So, in every round, each agent i is allocated exactly one good.[16]

In the remainder of the proof, f will be used to denote v_i and F to denote the multilinear relaxation of f. Write μ to denote $\widehat{\mu}_i$ and $u \in [0,1]^m$ to denote the uniform vector $\left(\frac{1}{n}, \frac{1}{n}, \ldots, \frac{1}{n}\right)$. For a particular round r (i.e., for the rth iteration of the inner for-loop): we will use P to denote goods allocated to the agent i before round r, G to denote the unallocated goods before round r, g to denote the good allocated to agent i in the round r, and L to denote the set of goods allocated during r.[17]

Also, define the maximum (expected ordered) marginal lost by the agent in round r as

$$\ell_r := \max_{j\in L} \gamma_j^{P,G}(u^G).$$

Recall that u^G corresponds to the projection of u onto the set G. We begin by establishing the following inequality for all rounds r:

$$F_P(u^{G\setminus L}) \geq F_P(u^G) - \ell_r \tag{6}$$

[16]Without loss of generality, we can assume that the number of goods in G is a multiple of $|A|$. We can do this by adding dummy goods of value 0.

[17]The set of unallocated goods after round r is equal to $G \setminus L$ and after the round the bundle allocated to the agent gets updated to $P \cup \{g\}$. Also, note that, by definition, $g \in L$.

Specifically, Propostion 3.6 (and the fact that $u^{G\setminus L}$ is supported over $G \setminus L$) gives us

$$\begin{aligned} F_P(u^{G\setminus L}) &= \sum_{j\in G\setminus L} \gamma_j^{P,G\setminus L}(u^{G\setminus L})\frac{1}{n} \\ &\geq \sum_{j\in G\setminus L} \gamma_j^{P,G}(u^{G})\frac{1}{n} \qquad \text{(via Proposition 3.7; } G\setminus L \subseteq G) \\ &= \sum_{j\in G} \gamma_j^{P,G}(u^{G})\frac{1}{n} - \sum_{j\in L} \gamma_j^{P,G}(u^{G})\frac{1}{n} \\ &\geq F_P(u^G) - \ell_r \qquad \text{(using Proposition 3.6 and the definition of } \ell_r) \end{aligned}$$

With a fixed constant $\alpha > 1$, define potential ϕ_r, for round r, as $\phi_r := \max\{\alpha f_P(g), \ell_r\}$. The following lemma shows that the "loss" incurred in the multilinear relaxation (due to the allocation of the set L) can be balanced by the potential ϕ_r.

Lemma 3.8. *For any round r,*

$$F_{P\cup\{g\}}(u^{G\setminus L}) + \left(1 + \frac{1}{\alpha}\right)\phi_r \geq F_P(u^G)$$

Proof. The definition of ϕ_r implies that

$$\begin{aligned} F_{P\cup\{g\}}(u^{G\setminus L}) + \left(1 + \frac{1}{\alpha}\right)\phi_r &\geq F_{P\cup\{g\}}(u^{G\setminus L}) + f_P(g) + \ell_r \\ &\geq F_P(u^{G\setminus L}) + \ell_r \qquad \text{(via Proposition 3.5; setting } x = u^{G\setminus L}) \\ &\geq F_P(u^G) \qquad \text{(using inequality (6))} \end{aligned}$$

□

Using this potential, we partition all the rounds into two sets: write $\mathcal{D}$ to denote the set of "decrementing" rounds, $\mathcal{D} := \{r \mid \phi_r = \ell_r\}$, and $\mathcal{I}$ to denote the set of "incrementing" rounds as $\mathcal{I} = \{r \mid \phi_r > \ell_r\}$. Proposition 3.9 bounds the loss incurred in decrementing rounds, see the full version of this paper for a proof.

Proposition 3.9. *The total loss incurred in decrementing rounds is upper bounded as follows*

$$\sum_{r\in\mathcal{D}} \ell_r \leq \frac{0.1}{1-\frac{1}{\alpha}}\mu.$$

We can now prove Lemma 3.2. Using Lemma 3.8 we get the following lower bound on the sum of the potentials

$$\begin{aligned} \left(1 + \frac{1}{\alpha}\right)\sum_r \phi_r &\geq \sum_r F_P(u^G) - F_{P\cup\{g\}}(u^{G\setminus L}) \\ &\geq F(u) \qquad \text{(telescoping sum)} \\ &\geq \left(1 - \frac{1}{e}\right)\mu \qquad \text{(via Lemma 3.4).} \end{aligned}$$

Since a round is either incrementing or decrementing, we can write $\sum_r \phi_r = \sum_{r\in\mathcal{D}} \phi_r + \sum_{r\in\mathcal{I}} \phi_r$. Therefore,

$$\left(1 + \frac{1}{\alpha}\right)\sum_{r\in\mathcal{I}} \phi_r \geq \left(1 - \frac{1}{e}\right)\mu - \left(1 + \frac{1}{\alpha}\right)\sum_{r\in\mathcal{D}} \phi_r.$$

Recall that $\phi_r = \ell_r$ for all $r \in \mathcal{D}$. Hence, Proposition 3.9 gives us

$$\sum_{r \in I} \phi_r \geq \left(\frac{1 - e^{-1}}{1 + \alpha^{-1}} \right) \mu - \left(\frac{0.1}{1 - \alpha^{-1}} \right) \mu.$$

Let $\widehat{P}$ be the final set of goods allocated to agent i. The fact that for all incrementing rounds the potential ϕ_r is equal to α times the marginal gain of the agent, i.e., $\phi_r = \alpha f_P(g)$ for all $r \in \mathcal{I}$, gives the upper bound $\alpha f(\widehat{P}) \geq \sum_{r \in I} \phi_r$. Therefore, the final bundle allocated to the agent satisfies $f(\widehat{P}) \geq \frac{1}{\alpha} \left(\frac{1-e^{-1}}{1+\alpha^{-1}} - \frac{0.1}{1-\alpha^{-1}} \right) \mu$.

To recap, we have proved that when agent i is assigned a good in the first while-loop of RoundRobin, then agent i gets a high valued good; i.e., $f(\widehat{P}) \geq 0.1\tau_i$.

When agent i is not assigned a good in the first while-loop of RoundRobin, then RoundRobin terminates with $f(\widehat{P}) \geq \frac{1}{\alpha} \left(\frac{1-e^{-1}}{1+\alpha^{-1}} - \frac{0.1}{1-\alpha^{-1}} \right) \mu$. Therefore, setting $\alpha = 1 + \sqrt{2}$ we get $f(\widehat{P}) \geq 0.1\mu$. Overall, the condition that $\tau_i \leq \mu$ implies the desired inequality—$f(\widehat{P}) \geq 0.1\tau_i$—in this case as well.

ALGORITHM 4: Computation of an approximate maximin fair allocations AlgSub

---

Input: An instance with m goods and n agents, whose valuations, $v_i : 2^{[m]} \to \mathbb{R}_+$, are nonnegative, monotone and submodular.
Output: An allocation $\mathcal{P} = (P_1, P_2, \dots, P_n)$ such that, $v_i(P_i) \geq \frac{1}{10(1+\delta)} \mu_i$ for all $i \in [n]$. Here μ_i is the n-maximin share of agent i and $\delta \in (0, 1)$ is an arbitrarily small constant.

For all $i \in [n]$, initialize $\tau_i = v_i([m])$ and $P_i = \emptyset$. {We assume that $\mu_i > 0$ for each agent i; agents that do not satisfy this assumption can be simply detected and removed from consideration.}
Initialize $V = \{i \mid v_i(P_i) < \frac{1}{10}\tau_i\}$, i.e., $V = [n]$.
while $V \neq \emptyset$ **do**
    For all $i \in V$, update $\tau_i \leftarrow \frac{1}{(1+\delta)} \tau_i$.
    Update the partition by executing RoundRobin with the current threshold values: $(P_1, P_2, \dots, P_n) \leftarrow$ RoundRobin$(\tau_1, \dots, \tau_n)$.
    Update $V \leftarrow \{i \mid v_i(P_i) < \frac{1}{10}\tau_i\}$
end while
return Partition $\mathcal{P} = (P_1, P_2, \dots, P_n)$

3.4 Proof of Theorem 3.1

In AlgSub the initial value of τ_i ($= v_i([m])$) is guaranteed to be at least μ_i. Furthermore, Lemma 3.2 ensures that, for each agent i, AlgSub never decrements τ_i below $\frac{1}{1+\delta}\mu_i$. Therefore, when AlgSub terminates, for every agent i, the final threshold value τ_i satisfies $\tau_i \geq \frac{1}{1+\delta}\mu_i$ and $v_i(P_i) \geq \frac{1}{10}\tau_i$ (since $V = \emptyset$ at termination). In other words, AlgSub returns $(P_1, P_2, \dots, P_n)$ which satisfies $v_i(P_i) \geq \frac{1}{10(1+\delta)}\mu_i$ for all $i \in [n]$ and, hence, satisfies the desired approximate fairness guarantee. Note that we can tighten the analysis of Lemma 3.2 to obtain an approximation factor slightly better than $\frac{1}{10}$.[18] Hence, with an appropriately small constant $\delta \in (0, 1)$, we can obtain the approximation guarantee of 1/10 (as stated in Theorem 3.1), instead of the slightly worse bound $\frac{1}{10(1+\delta)}$.

Finally, we can bound the running time of AlgSub by observing that initially $\tau_i = v_i([m])$ and, hence, the maximum number of times that agent i is contained in set V is $\log_{(1+\delta)} \left(\frac{v_i([m])}{\mu_i} \right)$.[19] Overall, this bound ensures that the algorithm runs in polynomial time.

[18] We did not optimize the parameters for ease of presentation.

[19] As stated in the algorithm, agents whose maximin share is zero can be removed from consideration.

4 CONCLUSIONS

The algorithms developed in this paper find allocations that are not only (approximately) fair but also *sequenceable*. Sequenceable allocations are allocations that can be obtained by ordering the agents and then letting them select their most valued unallocated good one after the other; see [9] for a formal definition. Bouveret and Lemaître [8] have studied this notion as an efficiency measure and shown that every Pareto-optimal allocation is also sequenceable. This observation leads to the open, interesting question of whether we can efficiently compute allocations which are both (approximately) fair and Pareto optimal.

In a recent preprint Ghodsi et al. [20] have also obtained constant-factor approximation guarantees for maximin fair division under additive and submodular valuations. In addition, they consider more general valuation functions; specifically, they obtain a constant-factor approximation for *XOS* valuations and a logarithmic approximation for *subadditive* valuations. Understanding if the ideas developed in this paper—along with [20], [32], and [1]—can be used to address fair division of indivisible goods among strategic agents remains an interesting direction for future work.

REFERENCES

[1] G. Amanatidis, E. Markakis, A. Nikzad, and A. Saberi. 2015. Approximation Algorithms for Computing Maximin Share Allocations. *Proceedings of the 42nd International Colloquium on Automata, Languages and Programming (ICALP)* (2015).

[2] Chidambaram Annamalai, Christos Kalaitzis, and Ola Svensson. 2014. Combinatorial algorithm for restricted max-min fair allocation. In *Proceedings of the Twenty-Sixth Annual ACM-SIAM Symposium on Discrete Algorithms*. SIAM, 1357–1372.

[3] Arash Asadpour and Amin Saberi. 2010. An approximation algorithm for max-min fair allocation of indivisible goods. *SIAM J. Comput.* 39, 7 (2010), 2970–2989.

[4] H. Aziz, Rauchecker, G., Schryen, G., and T. Walsh. 2017. Approximation Algorithms for Max-Min Share Allocations of Indivisible Chores and Goods. *Proceedings of the Thirty-First AAAI Conference on Artificial Intelligence* (2017).

[5] Nikhil Bansal and Maxim Sviridenko. 2006. The Santa Claus problem. In *Proceedings of the thirty-eighth annual ACM symposium on Theory of computing*. ACM, 31–40.

[6] Ivona Bezáková and Varsha Dani. 2005. Allocating indivisible goods. *ACM SIGecom Exchanges* 5, 3 (2005), 11–18.

[7] Sylvain Bouveret and Michel Lemaître. 2016. Characterizing conflicts in fair division of indivisible goods using a scale of criteria. *Autonomous Agents and Multi-Agent Systems* 30, 2 (2016), 259–290.

[8] Sylvain Bouveret and Michel Lematre. 2016. Efficiency and Sequenceability in Fair Division of Indivisible Goods with Additive Preferences. In *Proceedings of the Sixth International Workshop on Computational Social Choice (COMSOC'16)*.

[9] Steven J Brams and Daniel L King. 2005. Efficient fair division: help the worst off or avoid envy? *Rationality and Society* 17, 4 (2005), 387–421.

[10] Steven J Brams and Alan D Taylor. 1996. *Fair Division: From cake-cutting to dispute resolution*. Cambridge University Press.

[11] Eric Budish. 2011. The combinatorial assignment problem: Approximate competitive equilibrium from equal incomes. *Journal of Political Economy* 119, 6 (2011), 1061–1103.

[12] Eric Budish, Gérard P Cachon, Judd B Kessler, and Abraham Othman. 2016. Course match: A large-scale implementation of approximate competitive equilibrium from equal incomes for combinatorial allocation. *Operations Research* (2016).

[13] Gruia Calinescu, Chandra Chekuri, Martin Pál, and Jan Vondrák. 2011. Maximizing a monotone submodular function subject to a matroid constraint. *SIAM J. Comput.* (2011).

[14] Ioannis Caragiannis, David Kurokawa, Hervé Moulin, Ariel D Procaccia, Nisarg Shah, and Junxing Wang. 2016. The unreasonable fairness of maximum Nash welfare. In *Proceedings of the 2016 ACM Conference on Economics and Computation*. ACM, 305–322.

[15] Deeparnab Chakrabarty, Julia Chuzhoy, and Sanjeev Khanna. 2009. On allocating goods to maximize fairness. In *Foundations of Computer Science, 2009. FOCS'09. 50th Annual IEEE Symposium on*. IEEE, 107–116.

[16] Chandra Chekuri and Jan Vondrák. 2009. Randomized pipage rounding for matroid polytopes and applications. *CoRR, abs/0909.4348* (2009).

[17] Chandra Chekuri, Jan Vondrák, and Rico Zenklusen. 2010. Dependent randomized rounding via exchange properties of combinatorial structures. In *Foundations of Computer Science (FOCS), 2010 51st Annual IEEE Symposium on*. IEEE, 575–584.

[18] Chandra Chekuri, Jan Vondrák, and Rico Zenklusen. 2014. Submodular function maximization via the multilinear relaxation and contention resolution schemes. *SIAM J. Comput.* 43, 6 (2014), 1831–1879.

[19] Uriel Feige. 2008. On allocations that maximize fairness. In *Proceedings of the nineteenth annual ACM-SIAM symposium on Discrete algorithms*. Society for Industrial and Applied Mathematics, 287–293.

[20] Mohammad Ghodsi, MohammadTaghi HajiAghayi, Masoud Seddighin, Saeed Seddighin, and Hadi Yami. 2017. Fair Allocation of Indivisible Goods: Improvement and Generalization. *arXiv preprint arXiv:1704.00222* (2017).

[21] Michel X Goemans, Nicholas JA Harvey, Satoru Iwata, and Vahab Mirrokni. 2009. Approximating submodular functions everywhere. In *Proceedings of the twentieth annual ACM-SIAM symposium on Discrete algorithms*. Society for Industrial and Applied Mathematics, 535–544.

[22] J. Goldman, and A. D. Procaccia. 2014. Spliddit: Unleashing fair division algorithms. *SIGecom Exchanges* (2014).

[23] Ariel Kulik, Hadas Shachnai, and Tami Tamir. 2009. Maximizing submodular set functions subject to multiple linear constraints. In *Proceedings of the twentieth Annual ACM-SIAM Symposium on Discrete Algorithms*. Society for Industrial and Applied Mathematics, 545–554.

[24] David Kurokawa, Ariel D Procaccia, and Junxing Wang. 2016. When can the maximin share guarantee be guaranteed?. In *Proceedings of the Thirtieth AAAI Conference on Artificial Intelligence*. AAAI Press, 523–529.

[25] Jon Lee, Vahab S Mirrokni, Viswanath Nagarajan, and Maxim Sviridenko. 2010. Maximizing nonmonotone submodular functions under matroid or knapsack constraints. *SIAM Journal on Discrete Mathematics* 23, 4 (2010), 2053–2078.

[26] Hendrik W Lenstra Jr. 1983. Integer programming with a fixed number of variables. *Mathematics of operations research* 8, 4 (1983), 538–548.

[27] Richard J Lipton, Evangelos Markakis, Elchanan Mossel, and Amin Saberi. 2004. On approximately fair allocations of indivisible goods. In *Proceedings of the 5th ACM conference on Electronic commerce*. ACM, 125–131.

[28] Hervé Moulin. 1990. Uniform externalities: Two axioms for fair allocation. *Journal of Public Economics* 43, 3 (1990), 305–326.

[29] Hervé Moulin. 2004. *Fair division and collective welfare*. MIT press.

[30] Hervé Moulin. 2014. *Cooperative microeconomics: a game-theoretic introduction*. Princeton University Press.

[31] Hervé Moulin, Felix Brandt, Vincent Conitzer, Ulle Endriss, Ariel D Procaccia, and Jérôme Lang. 2016. *Handbook of Computational Social Choice*. Cambridge University Press.

[32] Ariel D Procaccia and Junxing Wang. 2014. Fair enough: Guaranteeing approximate maximin shares. (2014), 675–692.

[33] Hugo Steinhaus. 1948. The problem of fair division. *Econometrica* 16, 1 (1948).

[34] Jan Vondrák. 2008. Optimal approximation for the submodular welfare problem in the value oracle model. In *Proceedings of the fortieth annual ACM symposium on Theory of computing*. ACM, 67–74.

[35] Jan Vondrák. 2013. Symmetry and approximability of submodular maximization problems. *SIAM J. Comput.* 42, 1 (2013), 265–304.

[36] Gerhard J Woeginger. 1997. A polynomial-time approximation scheme for maximizing the minimum machine completion time. *Operations Research Letters* 20, 4 (1997), 149–154.

[37] Bang Ye Wu. 2005. An analysis of the LPT algorithm for the max–min and the min–ratio partition problems. *Theoretical computer science* 349, 3 (2005), 407–419.

Graphons: A Nonparametric Method to Model, Estimate, and Design Algorithms for Massive Networks*

CHRISTIAN BORGS, Microsoft Research
JENNIFER CHAYES, Microsoft Research

Many social and economic systems are naturally represented as networks, from off-line and on-line social networks, to bipartite networks, like Netflix and Amazon, between consumers and products. Graphons, developed as limits of graphs, form a natural, nonparametric method to describe and estimate large networks like Facebook and LinkedIn. Here we describe the development of the theory of graphons, for both dense and sparse networks, over the last decade. We also review theorems showing that we can consistently estimate graphons from massive networks in a wide variety of models. Finally, we show how to use graphons to estimate missing links in a sparse network, which has applications from estimating social and information networks in development economics, to rigorously and efficiently doing collaborative filtering with applications to movie recommendations in Netflix and product suggestions in Amazon.

Additional Key Words and Phrases: Networks; graphons; graph convergence; nonparametric estimation; collaborative filtering; network completion

Networks are the natural framework to describe social and economic systems with pairwise interactions. This includes not only social networks among individuals, like Facebook and LinkedIn, but also bipartite networks between different types of entities, like the Netflix movie-user network and the Amazon consumer-product network. Graphons, developed as limits of sequences of graphs, form a natural, non-parametric method to model and estimate large networks. Here we informally describe some of the development of the theory of graphons over the last dozen years, and provide an application of graphons to the completion of noisily, sparsely sampled massive networks.

1 GRAPH LIMITS

The theory of limits of sequences of dense graphs (i.e., graphs in which the number of edges scale as the square of the number of vertices) was developed over roughly a decade starting around 2006 [19–21, 37]. Of course, it is always possible to a define a limit of a graph sequence – if we make the notion too weak, then every sequence trivially converges to the same point; if we make it too strong, each sequence could converge to a different point. The key was to find a notion that was "just right." This was done in a series of papers with Lovász, Sos and Vestergombi [20, 21].

In [19] we define a metric to allow us to compare graphs of different sizes. For this, we rescale two graphs to be of the same size by creating copies of each vertex so that the two graphs then have

*This extended abstract summarizes the content of an invited keynote talk delivered by Jennifer Chayes at the eighteenth ACM Conference on Economics and Computation (ACM EC'17).

EC'17, June 26–30, 2017, Cambridge, MA, USA.

ACM ISBN 978-1-4503-4527-9/17/06..$15.00
http://dx.doi.org/10.1145/3033274.3084097

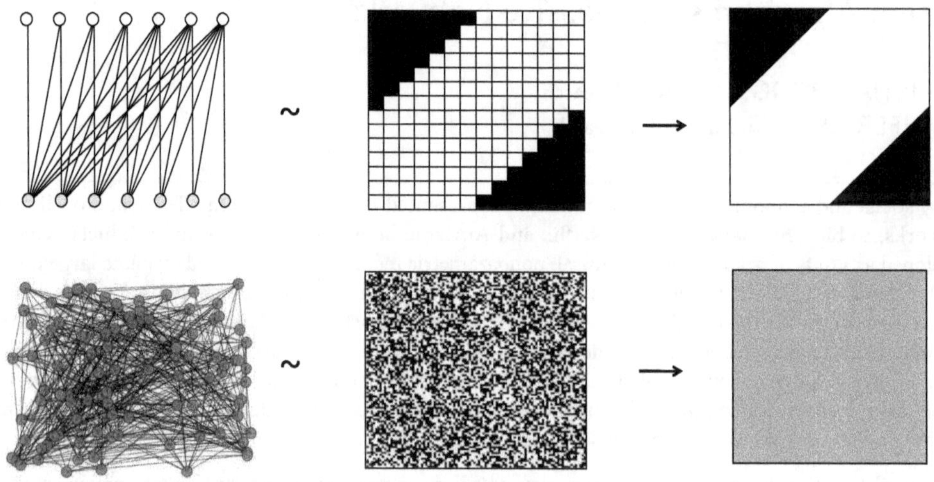

Fig. 1. The half-graph and a random graph, their empirical graphons, and their limits.

the same number of vertices. Specifically, if the two graphs have n_1 and n_2 vertices, and k_1 and k_2 are the smallest numbers such that $k_1n_1 = k_2n_2$, we "blow up" each vertex in the first graph by k_1, and each one in the second by k_2. We then replace each edge in the original graphs by complete bipartite graphs between the blown-up vertices. We look at the Frieze-Kannan cut distance [29] of the difference between the two blown-up graphs, where the cut distance is basically the value of the cut between a set and its complement, taking the sup over all sets. Finally, since vertex labels should not matter, we take the minimum over all relabelings of the vertices. The resulting metric is called the cut metric.

Our first notion of convergence [19, 20] is what we call metric convergence, which means simply that the sequence of graphs is Cauchy in the cut metric. The fact that a limit exists was established by Lovász and Szegedy [37] using a weak version of the Szemerédi Regularity Lemma [29] and a martingale argument. The limit is a two-variable symmetric function, called a graphon, often denoted by $W(x, y)$, which is basically a continuous version of the adjacency matrix of a graph on $[0, 1]^2$. In [12], we show that the limit is unique up to measure-preserving transformations of the underlying feature space.

Note that a graph on n vertices can be represented as a piecewise constant graphon by dividing the unit square $[0, 1]^2$ into n^2 small squares of side length $1/n$, and representing the presence of an edge between vertices i and j by a 1 on the squares ij and ji, and its absence by a 0. This representation is called the empirical graphon of the graph. If we visualize a 0 in the empirical graphon as a small white square, and a 1 as a small black square, graph convergence can be seen as convergence of the these black and white empirical graphons to a gray-scale limiting graphon. See Figure 1 for an illustration for the half-graph and an Erdös-Renyí random graph.

There is a natural local notion of convergence in dense graphs. We can ask that all induced finite subgraph densities (e.g., the edge density, triangle density, Peterson graph density, ...) converge simultaneously. We prove that a sequence of dense graphs converges in metric if and only if it is subgraph convergent [20].

We also introduce several "global" notions of convergence [10, 21]. We have one notion which corresponds to convergence of all finite two-body statistical physics models in the microcanonical ensemble (the ensemble in which each species of vertex represents a fixed percentage of all vertices). We have another notion which corresponds to all multi-way cuts and bisections converging. We show that a sequence of dense graphs converges according to these and a few other global notions if and only if it converges in metric [21]. More recently, a notion of large deviations convergence was defined [10], which is also equivalent with the other global and local notions for dense graphs.

Sparse graphs of bounded degree are much more fragile. Here we have no notion of metric convergence. The natural notion of local convergence is convergence of a graph rooted at a random point, known as Benjamini-Schramm convergence [5]. Benjamini-Schramm convergence is equivalent to subgraph convergence [11], but global notions of convergence are stronger [10].

The most interesting case is that of sparse graphs of unbounded average degree, like the power-law networks in Facebook and LinkedIn. These cases were much more complicated due to the fact that much of the necessary graph theory (e.g., the relevant case of the weak Regularity Lemma) had not yet been developed. Over the past five years, we have developed two ways to generalize the theory.

The first way is by rescaling the empirical graphon function, dividing it by the edge density ρ of the graph sequence (which is tending to zero in the case of sparse graphs). This was done by Bollobás and Riordan in the case when the graphs had no "dense spots," corresponding to the graphon being a bounded function [8]. In collaboration with Cohn and Zhao [15, 16], we develop a theory of "uniformly upper regular" sparse graphs of unbounded average degree; we show that these converge to graphons in L^p spaces, corresponding to growing sequences with power-law tails. In the process of doing this, we formulate and prove a weak form of the Regularity Lemma for sparse graphs corresponding to graphons of unbounded degree.

The second way to get graph limits for graphs of unbounded average degree, again graphs with very long tails, is by "stretching" the empirical graphon (and its domain) by $1/\sqrt{\rho}$ so that the integral of the graphon is again unity. This leads to a limit defined on the positive quadrant rather than the unit square, and hence these graphons provide a good description of networks where the underlying features cannot be restricted to bounded domains. See Figure 2 for a comparison of this with the rescaling approach. In work with Cohn and Holden [17], we develop a theory of sparse graphs of unbounded degree with "uniformly regular tails," show how to construct limits for sequences obeying this regularity condition, and prove many properties of the these graphons. Finally, we show that any graph sequence which satisfies both the conditions of uniform upper regularity and uniformly regular tails must be dense; so dense graphs are the only overlap of our two theories of sparse graphs of unbounded degree.

2 MODELING LARGE NETWORKS

The classic way to model large networks uses the so-called stochastic block model [32], which is a generalization of the Erdös-Renyí random graph to k species of vertices, with fixed densities of each species of vertex, and fixed probabilities that any two species connect to each other, including a fixed probability of intra-species connection, which is in general different within each species.

As graphs get larger and larger, reasonable descriptions have the number of species scale with the number of vertices: $k = k(n)$, which tends to lead to overfitting. Instead, starting over a decade ago [31], researchers began to model large networks non-parametrically by choosing n points randomly from some feature space, $x_1, x_2, \cdots, x_n \in \Omega$, and a two-variable, bounded symmetric function $W(x_i, x_j) : \Omega \times \Omega \to [0, 1]$. A random graph consistent with this function is then generated by saying that i is connected to j with probability $W(x_i, x_j)$.

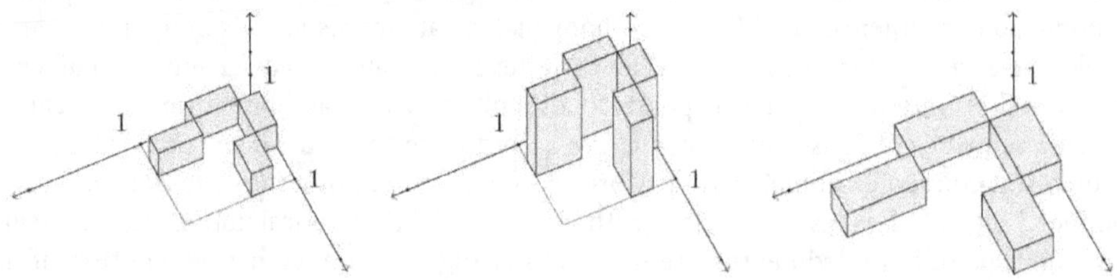

Fig. 2. Three graphons associated with the same simple graph G on five vertices: the emprical graphon used in theory of dense graph convergence, the rescaled a version used in the uniformly upper regular theory of sparse graph convergence, and the stretched version used in the theory for sparse graphs with uniformly regular tails.

The graphs generated in this way can easily be seen to be dense, whereas real life networks tend to be sparse. But our two methods for constructing graph limits for sequences of random sparse graphs of unbounded degree naturally yield random models of massive sparse networks.

Our first method [15] chooses features $x_1, x_2, \cdots, x_n$ from some compact feature space, and generates random graphs with long tails corresponding to unbounded graphons W, connecting vertices with features x_i and x_j with probability $\min\{1, \rho W(x_i, x_j)\}$, where ρ is the desired target density of our graph.

Our second method [17] is more complex: It chooses features $x_1, x_2, \cdots$ from an unbounded feature space according to a Poisson process with an intensity which scales linearly with time. At time t, the process connects vertices i and j born up to time t with probability $W(x_i, x_j)$. The resulting graph at time t retains only those vertices which have been connected to at least one other vertex by that time, leading to a graph with a finite number of vertices at any finite time. We show that this kind of model is quite natural by proving a generalization of the celebrated Aldous-Hoover Theorem [3, 33] to sparse graphs. In our setting, it says that under suitable regularity conditions, any family of graphs with vertices labeled by their birth time that is invariant under measure-preserving transformations of time must be of the above form. Our model generalizes the work of Caron and Fox [22], and is very similar to a model introduced simultaneously by Veitch and Roy [41].

3 LEARNING SPARSE GRAPHS

How does one learn a network from a single sample, e.g., allowing us to predict how the network might look when it's twice its current size? The traditional approach is to assume that the network is a stochastic block model with k types of vertices, cluster the vertices according to type, and then use this clustering to estimate the parameters of the model (the densities of each of the k types, plus the $k(k+1)/2$ connection probabilities within and between types) and then use that estimated stochastic block model to make predictions about the network [4, 9, 24, 26–28, 32, 34, 38, 40, 42, 43]. See [1, 2] for recent work with rigorous consistency guarantees for sparse graphs.

As we discussed above, for very large networks, it is often better to take a non-parametric approach [6, 7, 25, 35, 39]. Here the idea is to get an estimate, $\widehat{W}$ for the graphon W representing the network, and then generate realizations from that estimation. For bounded graphons, it had been shown that this leads to consistent estimation for both dense and sparse graphs, see, e.g., [23, 30, 36, 44], to name a few of the more recent papers on the subject. In collaboration with

Cohn and Ganguly [14], we showed that this leads to consistent estimation for sparse massive networks if, e.g., $W \in L^2$, provided that the average degree diverges. Hence one can use graphons for statistically consistent estimation for power-law graphs. In collaboration with Smith [13], we showed that, for sparse graphs corresponding to bounded W, it is possible to consistently estimate while maintaining edge differential privacy.

4 NETWORK COMPLETION AND COLLABORATIVE FILTERING ON SPARSE GRAPHS

An area of some interest in economics is how to "complete" sparsely, noisily sampled networks. For example, in development economics, one sometimes has measurements representing sparsely and noisily sampled connections among individuals. How sparsely can we sample and still get an accurate estimate of the missing links? Similarly, in bipartite networks like the Netflix user-movie network or the Amazon consumer-product network, can we show that we can complete the network even if it is very sparsely sampled with some general noise? Here we follow a collaborative filtering approach, which however must be modified to account for the sparsity of the sample. What if the sampling is so sparse that two people for whom we are trying to estimate the probability of a connection have no connections in common? Or what if there are no sets of movies in common between a given individual and another on the Netflix network? In collaboration with Lee and Shah [18], we used the "expanded neighborhood" approach of Abbe and Sandon [1, 2], who study estimation for stochastic block models. The idea is to look not just at individuals who share a common connection, but instead expand the neighborhood until a common connection is found. Similarly, we expand the bipartite user-movie-user-movie-$\cdots$ neighborhood until there an overlap. Here we treat graphons as operators in the expansion and need to do estimates to control the variance. Assume there are n individuals on the network, each described by features in a d-dimensional space. We show that, if the underlying graphon describing this network is Lipshitz, then the mean square error of our estimated graphon tends to zero provided that we sample the network with density $p = \omega(d^2 n^{-1})$. For high-dimensional latent spaces, which tend to be the appropriate descriptions for most real-world networks, this is a significant improvement over the best previous result, that of Chatterjee [23], who showed that the mean square error of the estimated graphon tends to zero provided that the network is sampled with density $p = \omega(n^{-2/(d+2)})$.

SPEAKER BIO

Jennifer Tour Chayes is Distinguished Scientist, Managing Director and Cofounder of Microsoft Research New England and Microsoft Research New York City. Before joining Microsoft in 1997, Chayes was for many years Professor of Mathematics at UCLA. Chayes is the author of over 140 academic papers and the inventor of over 30 patents. Her research areas include phase transitions in discrete mathematics and computer science, structural and dynamical properties of self-engineered networks, graph theory, graph algorithms, algorithmic game theory, and computational biology. Chayes is one of the inventors of the field of graphons, which are now widely used in the machine learning of massive networks.

Chayes holds a BA in biology and physics from Wesleyan, where she graduated first in her class, and a PhD in mathematical physics from Princeton. She did postdoctoral work in the Mathematics and Physics Departments at Harvard and Cornell. She is the recipient of the NSF Postdoctoral Fellowship, the Sloan Fellowship, the UCLA Distinguished Teaching Award, and the Anita Borg Institute Women of Leadership Vision Award, among many other leadership awards. She has twice been a member of the IAS in Princeton. Chayes is a Fellow of the American Association for the Advancement of Science, the Fields Institute, the Association for Computing Machinery, and the American Mathematical Society, and an Elected Member of the American Academy of Arts and Sciences. She is the winner of the 2015 John von Neumann Lecture Award, the highest honor of the Society of Industrial and Applied Mathematics. In 2016, Chayes received an Honorary Doctorate from Leiden University.

REFERENCES

[1] E. Abbe and C. Sandon. 2015. Community detection in general stochastic block models: fundamental limits and efficient recovery algorithms. In *Proceedings of the* 56th *Annual Symposium on Foundations of Computer Science (FOCS'15)*. 670–688.

[2] E. Abbe and C. Sandon. 2015. Recovering communities in the general stochastic block model without knowing the parameters. In *Advances in Neural Information Processing Systems 28 (NIPS'15)*. 676–684.

[3] D. Aldous. 1981. Representations for partially exchangeable arrays of random variables. *J. Multivar. Anal.* 11 (1981), 581–598.

[4] A. Anandkumar, R. Ge, D. Hsu, and S. M. Kakade. 2014. A tensor approach to learning mixed membership community models. *Journal of Machine Learning Research* 15 (2014), 2239–2312.

[5] I Benjamini and O Schramm. 2001. Recurrence of distributional limits of finite planar graphs. *Electronic Journal of Probability* 23 (2001), 1–13.

[6] P. J. Bickel and A. Chen. 2009. A nonparametric view of network models and Newman-Girvan and other modularities. *Proceedings of the National Academy of Sciences of the United States of America* 106 (2009), 21068–21073.

[7] P. J. Bickel, A. Chen, and E. Levina. 2011. The method of moments and degree distributions for network models. *Annals of Statistics* 39 (2011), 2280–2301.

[8] B. Bollobás and O. Riordan. 2009. Metrics for sparse graphs. In *Surveys in combinatorics 2009 (eds. S. Huczynska, J. D. Mitchell, and C. M. Roney-Dougal), London Math. Soc. Lecture Note Ser.* ***365****, Cambridge University Press*. London Math. Soc. Lecture Note Ser. **365**, Cambridge University Press, 211–287.

[9] R. B. Boppana. 1987. Eigenvalues and graph bisection: an average-case analysis. In *28th Annual Symposium on Foundations of Computer Science*. 280–285.

[10] C. Borgs, J. Chayes, and D Gamarnik. 2013. Convergent sequences of sparse graphs: A large deviations approach. *preprint, arXiv:1302.4615. To appear in Random Structures Algorithms* (2013).

[11] C. Borgs, J. Chayes, J Kahn, and L. Lovász. 2013. Left and right convergence of graphs with bounded degree. *Random Structures Algorithms* 42 (2013), 1–28.

[12] C. Borgs, J. Chayes, and L. Lovász. 2010. Moments of two-variable functions and the uniqueness of graph limits. *Geometric And Functional Analysis* 19, 6 (2010), 1597–1619.

[13] C. Borgs, J.T. Chayes, and A. Smith. 2015. Private graphon estimation for sparse graphs. In *Advances in Neural Information Processing Systems 28*. 1369–1377.

[14] C Borgs, J. T. Chayes, H Cohn, and S Ganguly. 2015. Consistent nonparametric estimation for heavy-tailed sparse graphs. *preprint, arXiv:1508.6675* (2015).

[15] C. Borgs, J. T. Chayes, H. Cohn, and Y. Zhao. 2014. An L^p theory of sparse graph convergence I: limits, sparse random graph models, and power law distributions. *preprint, arXiv:1401.2906* (2014).

[16] C. Borgs, J. T. Chayes, H. Cohn, and Y. Zhao. 2014. An L^p theory of sparse graph convergence II: LD convergence, quotients, and right convergence. *preprint, arXiv:1408.0744* (2014).

[17] C Borgs, J. T. Chayes, and N Cohn, H andd Holden. 2016. Sparse exchangeable graphs and their limits via graphon processes. *preprint, arXiv:1601.07134. To appear in Journal of Machine Learning Research* (2016).

[18] C Borgs, J. T. Chayes, C. E Lee, and D. Shah. 2017. Sparse graphon Estimation via Neighbor Method. *preprint* (2017).

[19] C. Borgs, J. T. Chayes, L. Lovász, V. Sós, and K. Vesztergombi. 2006. Counting graph homomorphisms. In *Topics in discrete mathematics (eds. M. Klazar, J. Kratochvíl, M. Loebl, J. Matoušek, R. Thomas, and P. Valtr), Springer*. Springer, 315–371.

[20] C. Borgs, J. T. Chayes, L. Lovász, V. Sós, and K. Vesztergombi. 2008. Convergent graph sequences I: subgraph frequencies, metric properties, and testing. *Advances in Math.* 219 (2008), 1801–1851.

[21] C. Borgs, J. T. Chayes, L. Lovász, V. Sós, and K. Vesztergombi. 2012. Convergent graph sequences II: multiway cuts and statistical physics. *Ann. of Math.* 176 (2012), 151–219.

[22] F. Caron and E. B Fox. 2014. Sparse graphs using exchangeable random measures. *preprint, arXiv:1401.1137* (2014).

[23] S. Chatterjee. 2015. Matrix estimation by universal singular value thresholding. *Annals of Statistics* 43, 1 (2015), 177–214.

[24] Kamalika Chaudhuri, Fan Chung, and Alexander Tsiatas. 2012. Spectral clustering of graphs with general degrees in the extended planted partition model. In *Proceedings of the 25th Annual Conference on Learning Theory (JMLR Workshop and Conference Proceedings Volume 23)*. 35.1–35.23. http://www.jmlr.org/proceedings/papers/v23/chaudhuri12/chaudhuri12.pdf

[25] D. S. Choi, P. J. Wolfe, and E. M. Airoldi. 2012. Stochastic blockmodels with a growing number of classes. *Biometrika* 99 (2012), 273–284.

[26] A. Coja-Oghlan. 2010. Graph partitioning via adaptive spectral techniques. *Combin. Probab. Comput.* 19 (2010), 227–284.

[27] A. Dasgupta, J. Hopcroft, R. Kannan, and P. Mitra. 2006. Spectral clustering by recursive partitioning. In *Algorithms – ESA 2006 (Lecture Notes in Computer Science)*, Y. Azar and T. Erlebach (Eds.), Vol. 4168. Springer, 256–267. http://dx.doi.org/10.1007/11841036_25

[28] S.E. Fienberg, M.M. Meyer, and S.S. Wasserman. 1985. Statistical analysis of multiple sociometric relations. *Journal of the American Statistical Association* 80 (1985), 51–67.

[29] A. Frieze and R. Kannan. 1999. Quick approximation to matrices and applications. *Combinatorica* 19 (1999), 175–220.

[30] C. Gao, Y. Lu, and H. H. Zhou. 2015. Rate-optimal graphon estimation. *Annals of Statististics* 43 (2015), 2624–2652.

[31] P. D. Hoff, A. E. Raftery, and M. S. Handcock. 2002. Latent space approaches to social network analysis. *J. Amer. Statist. Assoc.* 97, 460 (2002), 1090–1098.

[32] P.W. Holland, K.B. Laskey, and S. Leinhardt. 1983. Stochastic blockmodels: first steps. *Social Networks* 5 (1983), 109–137.

[33] D. Hoover. 1979. Relations on probability spaces and arrays of random variables. *preprint, Institute for Advanced Study, Princeton, NJ* (1979).

[34] Mark Jerrum and Gregory B. Sorkin. 1998. The Metropolis algorithm for graph bisection. *Discrete Appl. Math.* 82 (1998), 155–175.

[35] O. Kallenberg. 1999. Multivariate sampling and the estimation problem for exchangeable arrays. *Journal of Theoretical Probability* 12 (1999), 859–883.

[36] Olga Klopp, Alexandre B. Tsybakov, and Nicolas Verzelen. 2017. Oracle inequalities for network models and sparse graphon estimation. *Ann. Statist.* 45 (2017), 316–354.

[37] L. Lovász and B. Szegedy. 2006. Limits of dense graph sequences. *Journal of Combinatorial Theory, Series B* 96 (2006), 933–957.

[38] F. McSherry. 2001. Spectral partitioning of random graphs. In *Proceedings of the 42nd Annual IEEE Symposium on Foundations of Computer Science*. 529–537.

[39] K. Rohe, S. Chatterjee, and B. Yu. 2011. Spectral clustering and the high-dimensional stochastic blockmodel. *Ann. Statist.* 39 (2011), 1878–1915.

[40] T. A. B. Snijders and K. Nowicki. 1997. Estimation and prediction for stochastic blockmodels for graphs with latent block structure. *Journal of Classification* 14 (1997), 75–100.

[41] V. Veitch and D. M Roy. 2015. The class of random graphs arising from exchangeable random measures. *preprint, arXiv:1512.03099* (2015).

[42] Yuchung J. Wang and George Y. Wong. 1987. Stochastic blockmodels for directed graphs. *Journal of the American Statistical Association* 82 (1987), 8–19.

[43] H.C. White, S.A. Boorman, and R.L. Breiger. 1976. Social structure from multiple networks. I. Blockmodels of roles and positions. *American Journal of Sociology* 80 (1976), 730fi?!780.

[44] P. J. Wolfe and S. C. Olhede. 2013. Nonparametric graphon estimation. *preprint, arXiv:1309.5936* (2013).

Stability, Strategy-Proofness, and Cumulative Offer Mechanisms

JOHN WILLIAM HATFIELD, University of Texas at Austin
SCOTT DUKE KOMINERS, Harvard University
ALEXANDER WESTKAMP, University of Cologne

In many-to-one matching with contracts, agents on one side of the market, e.g., workers, can fulfill at most one contract, while agents on the other side of the market, e.g., firms, may desire multiple contracts. Hatfield and Milgrom [6] showed that when firms' preferences are *substitutable* and *size monotonic*, the worker-proposing cumulative offer mechanism is stable and strategy-proof (for workers).[1]

Recently, stable and strategy-proof matching has been shown to be possible in a number of real-world settings in which preferences are not necessarily substitutable (see, e.g., Sönmez and Switzer [13], Sönmez [12], Kamada and Kojima [7], and Aygün and Turhan [1]); this has motivated a search for weakened substitutability conditions that guarantee the existence of stable and strategy-proof mechanisms. Hatfield and Kojima [3] introduced *unilateral substitutability* and showed that when all firms' preferences are unilaterally substitutable (and size monotonic), the cumulative offer mechanism is stable and strategy-proof. Kominers and Sönmez [9] identified a novel class of preferences, called *slot-specific priorities*, and showed that if each firm's preferences are in this class, then the cumulative offer mechanism is again stable and strategy-proof. Subsequently, Hatfield and Kominers [4] developed a concept of *substitutable completion* and showed that when each firm's preferences admit a size monotonic substitutable completion, the cumulative offer mechanism is once more stable and strategy-proof.

In this paper, we introduce three novel conditions—*observable substitutability, observable size monotonicity,* and *non-manipulability via contractual terms*—and show that when these conditions are satisfied, the cumulative offer mechanism is the unique mechanism that is stable and strategy-proof. Moreover, when the choice function of any firm fails one of our three conditions, we can construct unit-demand choice functions for the other firms such that no stable and strategy-proof mechanism exists.

[1]Stable and strategy-proof matching has proven essential for many real-world matching applications (see, e.g., the work of Roth [11], Pathak and Sönmez [10], and Hassidim et al. [2]).

The authors appreciate the helpful comments of Ran Eilat, Ravi Jagadeesan, Fuhito Kojima, Shengwu Li, Paul Milgrom, Alvin E. Roth, Larry Samuelson, Jan Christoph Schlegel, Bertan Turhan, and seminar audiences at the American Economic Association Meetings, MATCH-UP, the Society for Economic Design, Caltech, Innsbruck, North Carolina State, Paris Dauphine, Sabancı, Stanford, and Texas A&M. Kominers gratefully acknowledges the support of National Science Foundation grants CCF-1216095 and SES-1459912, the Harvard Milton Fund, and the Ng Fund of the Harvard Center of Mathematical Sciences and Applications. Westkamp gratefully acknowledges funding from the People Programme (Marie Curie Intra-European Fellowship) of the European Union's Seventh Framework Programme (FP7/2007-2013) under REA grant agreement 628276.
Authors' addresses: J. W. Hatfield, McCombs School of Business, University of Texas at Austin, 2110 Speedway, Austin, TX 78172, john.hatfield@utexas.edu; S. D. Kominers, Society of Fellows, Department of Economics, Center of Mathematical Sciences and Applications, and Center for Research on Computation and Society, Harvard University, and Harvard Business School, Arthur Rock Center for Entrepreneurship, Soldiers Field, Boston, MA 02163, kominers@fas.harvard.edu; A. Westkamp, Department of Management, Economics, and Social Sciences, University of Cologne, Albertus-Magnus-Platz, 50923 Cologne, Germany, acwestk@gmail.com.

ACM ISBN 978-1-4503-4527-9/17/06. DOI: http://dx.doi.org/10.1145/3033274.3084085

Our results give the first characterization of sufficient and necessary conditions for the guaranteed existence of stable and strategy-proof mechanisms for many-to-one matching with contracts. Our conditions are strictly weaker than the previously known sufficient conditions for the existence of stable and strategy-proof mechanisms; this enables new applications, as well as a new interpretation of prior models of matching with distributional constraints (Hatfield et al. [5]; see also Kamada and Kojima [7, 8]). Additionally, our work gives a foundation for the use of cumulative offer mechanisms in many-to-one matching markets with contracts: Whenever a stable and strategy-proof matching mechanism exists, either it must coincide with a cumulative offer mechanism, or its stability and/or strategy-proofness depends crucially on some specific interdependence of preferences across hospitals that rules out certain unit-demand choice functions.

Full Paper: http://www.scottkom.com/articles/Hatfield_Kominers_Westkamp_Stability_Strategy-Proofness.pdf

CCS Concepts: •**Applied computing → Electronic commerce; Economics;**

Additional Key Words and Phrases: Matching with contracts; Stability; Strategy-proofness; Substitutability; Size monotonicity; Cumulative offer mechanisms

---

REFERENCES

[1] Orhan Aygün and Bertan Turhan. Forthcoming, 2017. Large Scale Affirmative Action in School Choice: Admissions to IITs and its Matching-Theoretical Problems. *American Economic Review Papers & Proceedings* (Forthcoming, 2017).

[2] Avinatan Hassidim, Assaf Romm, and Ran I. Shorrer. Forthcoming, 2017. Redesigning the Israeli Psychology Master's Match. *American Economic Review Papers & Proceedings* (Forthcoming, 2017).

[3] John William Hatfield and Fuhito Kojima. 2010. Substitutes and Stability for Matching with Contracts. *Journal of Economic Theory* 145, 5 (2010), 1704–1723.

[4] John William Hatfield and Scott Duke Kominers. 2016. Hidden Substitutes. (2016). Working paper.

[5] John William Hatfield, Scott Duke Kominers, and Alexander Westkamp. Forthcoming, 2017. Stable and Strategy-Proof Matching with Flexible Allotments. *American Economic Review Papers & Proceedings* (Forthcoming, 2017).

[6] John William Hatfield and Paul Milgrom. 2005. Matching with Contracts. *American Economic Review* 95, 4 (2005), 913–935.

[7] Yuichiro Kamada and Fuhito Kojima. 2015. Efficient Matching under Distributional Constraints: Theory and Applications. *American Economic Review* 105, 1 (2015), 67–99.

[8] Yuichiro Kamada and Fuhito Kojima. Forthcoming, 2017. Recent Developments in Matching with Constraints. *American Economic Review Papers & Proceedings* (Forthcoming, 2017).

[9] Scott Duke Kominers and Tayfun Sönmez. 2016. Matching with Slot-Specific Priorities: Theory. *Theoretical Economics* 11, 2 (2016), 683–710.

[10] Parag A. Pathak and Tayfun Sönmez. 2008. Leveling the Playing Field: Sincere and Sophisticated Players in the Boston Mechanism. *American Economic Review* 98, 4 (2008), 1636–1652.

[11] Alvin E. Roth. 2008. Deferred Acceptance Algorithms: History, Theory, Practice, and Open Questions. *International Journal of Game Theory* 36, 3-4 (2008), 537–569.

[12] Tayfun Sönmez. 2013. Bidding for Army Career Specialties: Improving the ROTC Branching Mechanism. *Journal of Political Economy* 121, 1 (2013), 186–219.

[13] Tayfun Sönmez and Tobias B. Switzer. 2013. Matching with (Branch-of-Choice) Contracts at United States Military Academy. *Econometrica* 81, 2 (2013), 451–488.

Stable Matching with Proportionality Constraints

THÀNH NGUYEN, Krannert School of Management, Purdue University
RAKESH VOHRA, University of Pennsylvania

The problem of finding stable matches that meet distributional concerns is usually formulated by imposing various side constraints. Prior work has focused on constraints whose "right hand sides" are absolute numbers specified before the preferences or number of agents on the "proposing" side are known. In many cases it is more natural to express the relevant constraints as proportions. We treat such constraints as soft, but provide ex-post guarantees on how well the constraints are satisfied while preserving stability. We violate the proportions by an amount proportional to the reciprocal of the number of students assigned to the school. For example, if a school is assigned 100 students, then the actual proportion will differ from the desired proportion by at most 2%. Our technique requires an extension of Scarf's lemma, which is of independent interest.

Additional Key Words and Phrases: Matching Market, Market Design, Scarf's lemma

A full version of this paper is available at http://web.ics.purdue.edu/~nguye161/proportional.pdf.

Authors' email addresses: First: nguye161@purdue.edu; Second: rvohra@seas.upenn.edu.

This research was supported in part by NSF under grant AST-1443965 and AST-1343381.

ACM ISBN 978-1-4503-4527-9/17/06. DOI: http://dx.doi.org/10.1145/3033274.3084091

Making it Safe to Use Centralized Markets: ε - Dominant Individual Rationality and Applications to Market Design

BENJAMIN N. ROTH, MIT
RAN I. SHORRER, Penn State University

A critical, yet underappreciated feature of market design is that centralized markets operate within a broader economic context; often market designers cannot force participants to join a centralized market. As such, well-designed centralized markets must induce participants to join voluntarily, in spite of pre-existing decentralized institutions they may already be using. Utilizing the general framework of Monderer and Tennenholtz (2009)[1], we take the view that centralizing a market is akin to designing a mediator to which people may sign away their decision rights. The mediator is voluntary in the sense that it cannot condition the actions of those who participate on the actions of those who do not.

Within this setting we propose a new desideratum for market design: Dominant Individual Rationality (D-IR). A mediator is D-IR if every decentralized strategy is weakly dominated by some centralized strategy. While such a criterion does not offer a prediction about how people will behave within the centralized market, it does provide a strong guarantee that all players will use centralized strategies rather than opting out of the centralized market.

We show that suitable modification of the Boston mechanism satisfies D-IR and a similar modification of any stable matching mechanism satisfies an approximation of D-IR. In both cases the modification relies on allowing the receiving end of the market to accept offers in either the centralized or decentralized part of the market. This design closely resembles the suggestion of Niederle et al. (2006) [2] about centralizing the market for gastroenterologists. Relative to their analysis, ours highlights why this design feature coupled with some, but not all, matching algorithms is effective in inducing participation of the proposing side of the market. Further, by highlighting its role in attaining (approximate) D-IR our analysis provides a new non-cooperative justification for stability. In other applications we demonstrate that, suitably modified, Top Trading Cycles satisfies D-IR, and double auctions satisfy approximate D-IR.

Additional Key Words and Phrases: Mechanism Design, Market Design, Mediators, Dominant Individual Rationality, Stable Matching

REFERENCES

[1] Dov Monderer and Moshe Tennenholtz. 2009. Strong Mediated Equilibrium. *Artificial Intelligence* 173, 1 (2009), 180–195.
[2] Muriel Niederle, Deborah D Proctor, and Alvin E Roth. 2006. What will be needed for the new gastroenterology fellowship match to succeed? *Gastroenterology* 130, 1 (2006), 218–224.

A full version of this paper is available at https://economics.mit.edu/files/12384.

Authors' email addresses: Roth: benroth@mit.edu; Shorrer: rshorrer@gmail.com.

EC'17, June 26–30, 2017, Cambridge, MA, USA.

ACM ISBN 978-1-4503-4527-9/17/06
http://dx.doi.org/10.1145/3033274.3085124

How (Not) to Allocate Affordable Housing

NICK ARNOSTI, Columbia University
PENG SHI, Microsoft Research

We consider a setting in which agents and items match dynamically over time. We show that repeated independent lotteries with unlimited entry (which are commonly used in practice) encourage agents to enter many lotteries, and may result in low match value.

We consider three alternate mechanisms: allowing agents to save unused tickets, limiting agents to entering at most one lottery, and allocating developments using a waiting list. We show that these three mechanisms are **equivalent**: for each agent, the probability of matching and expected value conditioned on matching are identical.

Compared to a repeated lottery, these mechanisms result in higher-quality matches for matched agents. However, in some cases, a repeated lottery is more likely to match agents with the worst outside options, and thus may outperform the other mechanisms in terms of utilitarian welfare. We discuss the implications of these findings for two systems in New York City that currently use a repeated lottery: the allocation of affordable housing and of discounted tickets to broadway shows.

Paper Available at https://ssrn.com/abstract=2963178

Received February 2017; accepted April 2017

 EC'17, June 26–30, 2017, Cambridge, MA, USA. ACM ISBN 978-1-4503-4527-9/17/06.

DOI: http://dx.doi.org/10.1145/3033274.3085157

Simple Approximate Equilibria in Games with Many Players

ITAI ARIELI, Technion, Industrial Engineering and Management, iarieli@technion.ac.il.
YAKOV BABICHENKO, Technion, Industrial Engineering and Management, yakovbab@technion.ac.il.

We consider ϵ-equilibria notions for a constant value of ϵ in n-player m-action games, where m is a constant. We focus on the following question: What is the largest grid size over the mixed strategies such that ϵ-equilibrium is guaranteed to exist over this grid.

For Nash equilibrium, we prove that constant grid size (that depends on ϵ and m, but not on n) is sufficient to guarantee the existence of a weak approximate equilibrium. This result implies a polynomial (in the input) algorithm for a weak approximate equilibrium.

For approximate Nash equilibrium we introduce a closely related question and prove its *equivalence* to the well-known Beck-Fiala conjecture from discrepancy theory. To the best of our knowledge, this is the first result that introduces a connection between game theory and discrepancy theory.

For a correlated equilibrium, we prove a $O(\frac{1}{\log n})$ lower-bound on the grid size, which matches the known upper bound of $\Omega(\frac{1}{\log n})$. Our result implies an $\Omega(\log n)$ lower bound on the rate of convergence of *any dynamic* to approximate correlated (and coarse correlated) equilibrium. Again, this lower bound matches the $O(\log n)$ upper bound that is achieved by regret minimizing algorithms.

1 INTRODUCTION

The algorithmic aspect of equilibria has been studied extensively from the moment the concept of Nash equilibrium was introduced [11], and mainly in the past three decades [7, 9, 14, 15]. A naive approach for the computation of an approximate Nash equilibrium in normal form games is the following:

- Set a "dense enough grid" of the strategy profiles, such that an approximate Nash equilibrium is guaranteed to exist on this grid.
- Exhaustively search over all grid points as to whether they form an approximate Nash equilibrium.

Despite the extensive study of equilibrium computation and the naivety of the above algorithm, no better algorithm is known (except for special classes of games, e.g. [8]). Surprisingly, the above algorithm is known to be *optimal* for games with a constant number of players (under the exponential time hypothesis for the PPAD class), see [15]. We show an additional case where this algorithm is optimal (see Corollary 3.2).

This motivates the study of the question: How dense should the grid of the strategy profiles be in order to guarantee the existence of an approximate equilibrium over the grid. A standard notion that captures the grid's density is the following.

Definition 1.1. A probability distribution $\mu \in \Delta(B)$ is called *k-uniform* if it is uniformly distributed over a multi-set of B of size k, or equivalently, if for every $b \in B$ we have $\mu(b) = \frac{c}{k}$ for some $c \in \mathbb{Z}$.

EC'17, June 26–30, 2017, Cambridge, Massachusetts, USA. ACM ISBN 978-1-4503-4527-9/17/06...$15.00.

DOI: http://dx.doi.org/10.1145/3033274.3085110

The class of grids (over the mixed strategies) that is considered in the present paper is the class of k-uniform distributions, and its density is determined by k. The larger the k is, the denser the grid.

The main question of the present paper can be formulated as follows:

Question 1: Given an ϵ-equilibrium solution concept, for which values of $k = k(\epsilon, n, m)$ is the existence of k-uniform ϵ-equilibrium guaranteed for every n-player m-action game? More concretely, we will be interested in understanding the asymptotic behaviour of $\lim_{n\to\infty} k(\epsilon, n, m)$ when we set m and ϵ as fixed constants.

The dependence of $k = k(\epsilon, n, m)$ on the number of actions m has a neat characterization of $k = \Theta(\log m)$ [1, 12]. However, the dependence on the number of players n is less understood: It is known that the dependence is at most $O(\log n)$ (see [2]), but no lower bounds were known (neither for Nash equilibria nor for correlated equilibria). The present paper aims to close these gaps. The established results have implications to equilibria computation, and to the rate of convergence of learning dynamics.

1.1 Weak equilibria

Unlike standard notions of equilibria that require rationality from *all* players, in *weak* equilibria, rationality is required for *large fraction* (close to 1) of the players. This solution concept has been shown to be useful for proving lower bounds for the standard notion of(approximate) Nash equilibrium (see [3, 15]). The concept of weak equilibria arises naturallyin evolutionary systems with mutations. In such a system, if we refer to each gene as a player, it is unreasonable to require that all players will react optimally to the environment,simply because at each point in time the system contains mutants whose action might be suboptimal. In this setting, the notion of weak equilibria which allows to a small fraction of mutants to act suboptimally is more appropriate. In fact, for any dynamical system where players have a positive probability of error (either due to mutations, trembling hand principle, or due to any other reason) the more suitable notion of equilibrium is that of a weak equilibrium.

Our positive results, as described below, show that the required grid size is small for notions of weak approximate equilibria.

1.2 Main results

1.2.1 Approximate Nash equilibria. Here, by a k-uniform approximate Nash equilibrium we refer to an action profile where every player uses a k-uniform strategy. The best known upper bound for ϵ-Nash equilibrium is $k = O(\log n)$, see [2]. The question as to whether $k = O(1)$ suffices is an interesting open question and we address it here. In Theorem 3.1 we prove that for a weak approximate Nash equilibrium, which is a strategy profile where *most of* the players are approximately best-replying (see Definition 2.2 and also [3]), indeed $k = O(1)$ suffices. This result implies a polynomial (in the input) algorithm for computing a weak approximate Nash equilibrium. To the best of our knowledge, no previous results have demonstrated the existence of a polynomial algorithm for any approximate notion of a Nash equilibrium in normal form games. It is interesting to note that the query complexity of a weak approximate Nash equilibrium is polynomial (in the input), [15]. Thus, a sub-polynomial algorithm for a weak approximate equilibrium is impossible. Hence, again, as in the two-player case, the naive exhaustive search algorithm is proved to be optimal.

Unfortunately, we did not manage to prove or disprove whether $k = O(1)$ suffices for the standard notion of ϵ-Nash equilibrium (or for the notion of ϵ-well supported Nash equilibrium). However, we do gain some insights into a closely-related question: Does there exist an approximate Nash equilibrium on the grid that is "close to" an exact Nash equilibrium?

A natural approach to prove the existence of an approximate equilibrium is to search for one that lies nearby an exact Nash equilibrium. More concretely, consider a binary-action game ($m = 2$) with an exact Nash equilibrium $x = (x_i)_{i\in[n]} \in [0,1]^n$, where x_i is the probability of playing the first action. Say that $y = (y_i)_{i\in[n]}$ is a $\frac{1}{k}$-rounding of x if for every $1 \le i \le n$ the following conditions hold: $y_i = \frac{c_i}{k}$ for some integer $0 \le c_i \le k$ and $|y_i - x_i| \le \frac{1}{k}$.

Question 2: For which values of k is it guaranteed that for every game there exists an exact equilibrium x such that some $\frac{1}{k}$-rounding of x constitute an ϵ-Nash equilibrium?

In Proposition 4.1 we show that for $k = O(\sqrt{\log n})$ there exists a binary action game with a unique Nash equilibrium x such that all of the $\frac{1}{k}$-rounding of x are not approximate Nash equilibria. Moreover, all approximate Nash equilibria in the grid (although they exist) are located "very far" from the equilibrium: There exist players who play a certain pure strategy in the exact equilibrium and the opposite strategy in any approximate well supported Nash equilibrium on the grid.

Proposition 4.1 demonstrates that finding a close approximate equilibrium for $k = O(1)$ is impossible in general. For particular classes of games such as degree d graphical games, it is easy to see that *every* rounding of exact equilibrium to the $\frac{1}{k}$-grid forms an ϵ-Nash equilibrium for $k = \frac{\epsilon}{d} = O(1)$. We can therefore ask whether ϵ-equilibrium which is $\frac{1}{k}$-rounding of an exact equilibrium exists in some particular classes of games.

An interesting observation is that for some classes of games the answer to the above question is (probably) mathematically very challenging. We introduce a class of games for which this question is *equivalent*[1] to the well known Beck-Fiala conjecture (since 1981) in discrepancy theory [4, 6, 13], see Theorem 4.5. To the best of our knowledge Theorem 4.5 is the first result that establishes a connection between game theory and discrepancy theory.

1.2.2 Approximate correlated equilibria. Since a correlated equilibrium is a distribution over the action profiles, here a k-uniform distribution means a uniform distribution over k action profiles.

A $k = O(\log n)$ upper bound was proved to be sufficient for the existence of ϵ-correlated equilibrium, see [2]. In fact, regret minimizing algorithms converge to an ϵ-correlated equilibrium in a rate of $O(\log n)$ [5, 10]. This provides an alternative proof for the existence of such a k-uniform approximate correlated equilibrium. In Theorem 5.1 we prove a lower bound of $k = \Omega(\log n)$. Our result shows that no dynamic can converge to an approximate correlated equilibrium faster than in $\Omega(\log n)$ steps, which shows the optimality in the rate of convergence of the regret minimizing dynamics. We note that it was known that regret minimizing dynamics cannot converge faster than in $\Omega(\log n)$ steps. Our result shows that no dynamic at all can converge faster.

In Proposition 5.3 we note that if we restrict attention to the notion of *weak* approximate correlated equilibrium: i.e., a distribution over the profiles such that *most of* the players have low regret (see Definition 2.5), then there exists a k-uniform weak approximate correlated equilibrium for $k = O(1)$. This observation demonstrates that, similarly to the product distribution solutions (Nash equilibrium), also in correlated solutions (correlated equilibrium) once we restrict attention to *weak* approximate solutions, the solution becomes simple with respect to the grid size; i.e., grid size of $\Omega(1)$ suffices.

[1] In fact, we prove the equivalence for some concrete instances of the Beck-Fiala conjecture of approximately-(up to a constant factor)-balanced matrices, see Section 4.1. By considering a closely-related question to Beck-Fiala conjecture where the answer is known, it is reasonable to believe that these concrete instances are "the hardest". So far, no one has proved or disproved the Beck-Fiala conjecture for these instances.

2 PRELIMINARIES

An n-player m-action game consists of a set of players $[n]$, with an action set $[m]$, and a payoff function $u_i : [m]^n \to [0,1]$ for every player i. Let $\Delta(B)$ denote the set of all probability distributions over the set B. The set of mixed strategies of player i is denoted by $\Delta([m])$. The set of correlated strategies is $\Delta([m]^n)$. The utility function of player i can be naturally extended to mixed strategy profiles $u_i : (\Delta([m]))^n \to [0,1]$ and to correlated strategies $u_i : \Delta([m]^n) \to [0,1]$ as the expected payoff under the given distributions. Given a profile of (mixed) actions $x = (x_i)$ we denote by x_{-i} the profile of actions of player i's opponents, namely $x_{-i} = (x_1, ..., x_{i-1}, x_{i+1}, ..., x_n)$.

Definition 2.1. **Approximate Nash equilibrium.** A profile of mixed actions $(x_i)_{i\in[n]}$ where $x_i \in \Delta([m])$ is an ϵ-*Nash equilibrium* if no player can gain more than ϵ by a unilateral deviation. Namely, $u_i(x_i, x_{-i}) \geq u_i(a_i, x_{-i}) - \epsilon$ for every player i and every action $a_i \in [m]$.

Definition 2.2. **Weak approximate Nash equilibrium.** A profile of mixed actions $(x_i)_{i\in[n]}$ where $x_i \in \Delta([m])$ is an (ϵ, δ)-*weak approximate Nash equilibrium* if at least $(1-\delta)$-fraction of the players cannot gain more than ϵ by a unilateral deviation.

Definition 2.3. **(Approximately) Individually rational payoffs.** The *individually rational level* of player i is the maximal number v_i that he can guarantee (using mixed strategies) against any action of the opponents. Namely,

$$v_i = \max_{x_i \in \Delta([m])} \min_{a_{-i} \in [m]^{n-1}} u_i(x_i, a_{-i}).$$

A correlated distribution $x \in \Delta([m]^n)$ is ϵ-*individually rational* if $u_i(x) \geq v_i - \epsilon$.

There are several notions of correlated equilibria and approximate correlated equilibria. Arguably the strongest notion of an approximate correlated equilibrium is the following.

Definition 2.4. **Approximate correlated equilibrium.** A correlated distribution $x \in \Delta([m]^n)$ is an ϵ-*correlated equilibrium* if

$$\mathbb{E}_{a\sim x}[u_i(a)] \geq \mathbb{E}_{a\sim x}[u_i(f(a_i), a_{-i})] - \epsilon$$

for every player i and every switching function $f : [m] \to [m]$.

The intuition behind this notion comes from the idea that a correlated strategy x can be implemented by a mediator who draws an action profile $a = (a_i)_{i\in[n]}$ according to x and recommends every player i to use a_i. If no player can gain more than ϵ by deviating from mediator's recommendation (namely to play action $f(j)$ every time mediator recommends j) then the distribution x is an ϵ-correlated equilibrium.

Approximate correlated equilibrium also has a weak analogue of the solution.

Definition 2.5. **Weak approximate correlated equilibrium.** A correlated distribution $x \in \Delta([m]^n)$ is an (ϵ, δ)-*weak approximate correlated equilibrium* if

$$\mathbb{E}_{a\sim x}[u_i(a)] \geq \mathbb{E}_{a\sim x}[u_i(f(a_i), a_{-i})] - \epsilon$$

for every switching function $f : [m] \to [m]$ for at least $(1-\delta)$-fraction of the players.

We would like to note that ϵ-individual rationality is the weakest possible notion for solutions that require rationality from all players (unlike the weak approximate correlated equilibrium for instance). In particular the set of approximately individually rational distributions contains the set of approximate correlated equilibria and approximate coarse correlated equilibria.

3 WEAK APPROXIMATE NASH EQUILIBRIUM

Our main positive result is the following.

THEOREM 3.1. *Every n-player m-action game admits a k-uniform (ϵ, δ)-weak approximate Nash equilibrium for every* $k \geq \frac{32(\ln 8+\ln m-\ln \epsilon-\ln \delta)}{\epsilon^2}$.

The important property of the bound on k is the fact that it *does not* depend on n. A straightforward corollary from Theorem 3.1 is the existence of a polynomial algorithm for a weak approximate equilibrium.

COROLLARY 3.2. *For every $\epsilon, \delta > 0$ and every $m \in \mathbb{N}$ there exists a poly(N) algorithm that computes an (ϵ, δ)-weak approximate Nash equilibrium in every n-player m-action game, where $N = n \cdot m^n$ is the input size (the size of the game).*

PROOF OF COROLLARY 3.2. The algorithm exhaustively searches for an (ϵ, δ)-weak approximate Nash equilibrium over all the k-uniform profiles, for $k = \frac{32(\ln 8+\ln m-\ln \epsilon-\ln \delta)}{\epsilon^2}$. The number of k-uniform mixed actions of a single player is bounded by k^m. Thus, the number of k-uniform action profiles is bounded by

$$(k^m)^n = (m^n)^{\frac{m \log k}{\log m}} \leq N^{\frac{m \log k}{\log m}} = poly(N).$$

Note that the algorithm is guaranteed to find an (ϵ, δ)-weak approximate Nash equilibrium by Theorem 3.1. □

The proof of Theorem 3.1 uses a similar technique to the one developed in [2]. We prove that after a *constant* number of samples from an exact Nash equilibrium distribution, with positive probability, the sampled mixed action profile forms an (ϵ, δ)-weak approximate Nash equilibrium. We rely on the following concentration inequality for product distributions that was derived in [2].

Given a discrete probability space (Ω, μ) we denote by $\mu^{(k)} \in \Delta(\Omega)$ the random distribution that is obtained by taking the average of k i.i.d. samples from μ. Namely, $\mu^{(k)}(\omega) = \frac{1}{k} \sum_i \mathbf{1}_{x_i=\omega}$ when $x_1, ..., x_k \sim \mu$ are i.i.d. random variables.

THEOREM 3.3 ([2]). *Let $(\Omega_1, \mu_1), ..., (\Omega_n, \mu_n)$ be discrete probability spaces. Consider the product space $(\Omega = \Pi_i \Omega_i, \mu = \Pi_i \mu_i)$. For every $\hat{\epsilon} > 0$, $k \in \mathbb{N}$, and $f : \Omega \to [0, 1]$ we have*

$$\mathbb{P}(|\mathbb{E}_{\Pi_i \mu_i^{(k)}}[f] - \mathbb{E}_\mu[f]| > \hat{\epsilon}) \leq \frac{4e^{-(\hat{\epsilon}^2/8)k}}{\hat{\epsilon}}.$$

PROOF OF THEOREM 3.1. Let $x = (x_i)_{i \in [n]}$ be a Nash equilibrium of the game. We denote $s_i^k = x_i^{(k)}$ the mixed action of player i that is obtained by sampling k i.i.d. draws from x_i.

Setting $f = u_i$ and $\hat{\epsilon} = \frac{\epsilon}{2}$ in Theorem 3.3 implies that

$$\mathbb{P}(|u_i(a_i, s_{-i}^k) - u_i(a_i, x_{-i})| \geq \epsilon) \leq \frac{8e^{-(\epsilon^2/32)k}}{\epsilon}$$

for every player $i \in [n]$ and every action $a_i \in [m]$. The choice of k guarantees that

$$\frac{8e^{-(\epsilon^2/32)k}}{\epsilon} < \frac{\delta}{m}.$$

Using the union bound, we get that for every player i with probability greater than $1 - \delta$ we have $|u_i(a_i, s_{-i}^k) - u_i(a_i, x_{-i})| \leq \frac{\epsilon}{2}$ for *all* actions $a_i \in [m]$. We denote the above event by g_i. Note that the event g_i is a sufficient condition for player i to ϵ-best reply at the profile $(s_i^k)_i$, because

$$u_i(a_i, s_{-i}^k) \leq u_i(a_i, x_{-i}) + \frac{\epsilon}{2} \leq \sum_{a_i' \in A_i} s_i^k(a_i') u_i(a_i', x_{-i}) + \frac{\epsilon}{2}$$
$$\leq \sum_{a_i' \in A_i} s_i^k(a_i') u_i(a_i', s_{-i}^k) + \epsilon = u_i(s_i^k, s_{-i}^k) + \epsilon.$$

Since each one of the events g_i happens with probability of at least $1 - \delta$ there exists a realization $(s_i^k)_i$ such that at least $(1 - \delta)$-fraction of the events g_i happen. Such a realization $(s_i^k)_i$ is an (ϵ, δ)-weak approximate Nash equilibrium. □

4 APPROXIMATE NASH EQUILIBRIUM

We consider games with binary actions where each player's mixed strategy is a real number $x_i \in [0, 1]$. For clarity of presentation, we assume that k is odd, and therefore the mixed strategy $\frac{1}{2}$ is $\frac{1}{2k}$-away from both closest points on the grid: $\frac{k-1}{2k}$ and $\frac{k+1}{2k}$. This assumption is for clarity of presentation only: For even values of k we can slightly change the payoffs in the constructed games such that the exact equilibrium will appear at the point $\frac{k+1}{2k}$. Here, again, we have a situation where the two closest points on the grid, $\frac{1}{2}$ and $\frac{k+2}{2k}$, are $\frac{1}{2k}$ away from the exact equilibrium.

We recall that given an equilibrium x and an integer k we define a $\frac{1}{k}$-rounding of x to be any point y in the k-grid of the simplex of mixed strategies for which $|x_i - y_i| \leq \frac{1}{k}$ for every player i.

Proposition 4.1. *There exists an n-player binary-action game with a unique exact Nash equilibrium x, such that for $k < \frac{\sqrt{\log n}}{8}$ there is no 0.1-Nash equilibrium that is $\frac{1}{k}$-rounding of x.*

Proof. Consider the following game with $2b + \binom{2b}{b}$ players. b pairs of players are playing matching-pennies with each other; we denote these players by $1, 2, \ldots, 2b$ and call them the *matching-pennies players*. Each one of the remaining $\binom{2b}{b}$ players is characterized by a set $S \subset [2b]$, and we call them the *observing players*. Player S has to guess whether the number of players that will play 1 in S is close to $\frac{b}{2}$. More formally, player S has two strategies 0 and 1. His utility is given by

$$u(0, a_S) = 0.5 \text{ (independently of } a_S\text{)},$$
$$u(1, a_S) = \begin{cases} 1 \text{ if } \frac{b}{2} - 2\sqrt{b} \leq \sum_{i \in S} a_i \leq \frac{b}{2} + 2\sqrt{b} \\ 0 \text{ otherwise.} \end{cases}$$

The unique exact equilibrium of this game is where all matching-pennies players are playing $(\frac{1}{2}, \frac{1}{2})$ and all the observing players are playing 1. The latter follows from the fact that the number of 1's is distributed according to a binomial distribution $Bin(b, \frac{1}{2}) \approx \mathcal{N}(\frac{b}{2}, \frac{b}{4})$. The probability that this amount will be in the segment $[\frac{b}{2} - \sqrt{b}, \frac{b}{2} + \sqrt{b}]$ is $1 - 2\Phi(-2) > 0.94$.

Consider now the case where the matching-pennies players are restricted to actions on an odd grid of size $k = \frac{\sqrt{b}}{4}$. More importantly, every player is playing a mixed strategy that is $\frac{2}{\sqrt{b}}$-away from $\frac{1}{2}$. There exists a set S such that either every player $i \in S$ plays a mixed strategy $x_i > \frac{1}{2}$ or every player $i \in S$ plays $x_i < \frac{1}{2}$. W.l.o.g., assume that the latter happens. Note that the amount of 1's for this specific set S is a distribution with expectation of at least $\mu \geq b(\frac{1}{2} + \frac{4}{\sqrt{b}}) = \frac{b}{2} + 2\sqrt{b}$, and a variance of at most $\sigma^2 \leq \frac{b}{4}$. By the Central Limit Theorem[2], the probability that the amount of

[2]Here and in the proof of Theorem 4.5 we rely on the powerful Central Limit Theorem. Similar arguments can be made by using the less powerful Chebishev's inequality.

1's are in the segment $(-\infty, \frac{b}{2} + \sqrt{b}]$ is at most $\Phi(-2) < 0.03$. Therefore player S must play 1 with probability of at most $\frac{0.1}{0.47} < 0.22$ in a 0.1-Nash equilibrium, which is far from his pure strategy 1 in the exact equilibrium.

To conclude, the total number of players in the game is $n = 2b + \binom{2b}{b} \leq 2^{2b}$, and for an odd grid of size $k < \frac{\sqrt{\log(n)}}{8}$ all approximate equilibria on the grid are far from the unique exact equilibrium. □

4.1 The connection to discrepancy theory

The basic question that is considered in discrepancy theory is the following: Given a 0, 1 matrix M of size $n \times m$, how close to 0 can one make the sum of (all) rows by multiplying every column by either 1 or -1.[3] More formally, define

$$disc(M) = \min_{\chi \in \{1,-1\}^m} ||M\chi||_\infty.$$

The classical "Six standard deviations suffice" Theorem by Spencer [16] states that for $m \geq n$ and for every matrix M we have $disc(M) \leq 6\sqrt{n}$. For the case where the matrix is *sparse* namely each column contains at most t 1's Back and Fiala [4] conjectured that $disc(M) = O(\sqrt{t})$ (independently of n and m) [4].

A particular case of the Back-Fiala conjecture is the case of balanced matrices (up to a constant factor).

Given a matrix $M \in \{0,1\}^{n \times m}$ we denote $r_i = \sum_{j \in [m]} M_{i,j}$ for every $i \in [n]$ and $c_j = \sum_{i \in [n]} M_{i,j}$ for every $j \in [m]$ the number of 1's in each row and column.

Definition 4.2. A matrix $M \in \{0,1\}^{n \times m}$ is called *α-balanced* if $\frac{1}{\alpha} \leq \frac{c_i}{c_j} \leq \alpha$, $\frac{1}{\alpha} \leq \frac{r_i}{r_j} \leq \alpha$, and $\frac{1}{\alpha} \leq \frac{r_i}{c_j} \leq \alpha$ for every pair of rows/ columns.

CONJECTURE 4.3. ***α-balanced Beck-Fiala conjecture.*** *For every α-balanced matrix M holds $disc(M) = O(\sqrt{t})$ where $t = r_1$ (or alternatively the sum of any other row or column).*

There is ample evidence showing that the α-balanced conjecture is not significantly simpler than the original conjecture, because for similar problems where tight lower bounds are known (for instance Spencer's Theorem [16]) the lower bounds satisfy balanceness.

The class of games that is considered, and that has close connection to discrepancy problems is *majority matching-pennies games.* A majority matching-pennies game is characterized by a matrix $M \in \{0,1\}^{n \times m}$, and it consists of $n + m$ players. Each row/column player has two actions $\{1, -1\}$, and he should decide whether to multiply all the elements in his row/column by -1. The utility of every row player is given by:

- 1 if the sum of numbers in his row is positive (after we take into account his action and the actions of his column opponents).
- 0 if the sum of numbers in his row is 0.
- -1 if the sum of numbers in his row is negative.

The utilities of every column player is the opposite of the row players:

- -1 if the sum of numbers in his row is positive.
- 0 if the sum of numbers in his row is 0.
- 1 if the sum of numbers in his row is negative.

We call these games majority matching-pennies since they are equivalent to a bipartite polymatrix game where row player i interacts with column player j in a matching-pennies game iff $M_{i,j} = 1$.

[3]The same question has an elegant equivalent formulation using the two-coloring problem of subsets.

Unlike standard polymatrix games where players receive the sum of payoffs, here players receive the sign of the sum of payoffs.

Note that the profile of actions where every player is playing $(\frac{1}{2}, \frac{1}{2})$ is an exact equilibrium in every majority matching-pennies game.

A subclass of majority matching-pennies games is *α-balanced majority matching-pennies games* where the matrix M is α-balanced.

Conjecture 4.4. ***Existence of close approximate equilibrium, for α-balanced games.*** *There exists a global constant $k = k(\alpha)$ such that one of the 2^{n+m} profiles of the form $(\frac{k\pm1}{2k})^{n+m}$ is a 0.4-Nash equilibrium.*

Now we are ready to state the equivalence of approximate equilibria and the discrepancy result.

Theorem 4.5. *For every constant α, Conjecture 4.3 is equivalent to Conjecture 4.4.*

Although Theorem 4.5 demonstrates a connection between the Back-Fiala conjecture and a very specific question on the approximation of equilibrium, we believe that the Theorem provides interesting insights for the following reasons. First, as mentioned in the Introduction, it connects the two seemingly unrelated topics of game theory and discrepancy theory. Second, it suggests that the question of the existence of a k-uniform ϵ-Nash equilibrium for $k = O(1)$ is probably quite involved. Third, if one comes up with a proof of sufficiency of $k = O(1)$ for the existence of a k-uniform ϵ-Nash equilibrium in binary-action games, then it would be interesting to understand where this approximate Nash equilibrium in majority matching-pennies games is located. Informally, note that majority matching-pennies games have conflicts of interest between the row players and the column players: row players want the matrix to increase the number of 1's whereas column players want to increase the number of (-1)'s. Thus it is reasonable to believe that the approximate Nash equilibrium will indeed be located "close to" (at least in the relative l_1 metric) the exact equilibrium $(\frac{1}{2})^{n+m}$.

Proof of Theorem 4.5. First we prove that Conjecture 4.3 implies Conjecture 4.4.

The Beck-Fiala conjecture implies that for every matrix M there exists $\chi \in \{-1, 1\}^m$ such that $||M\chi||_\infty \leq C\sqrt{t}$. Note that M^T is also an α-balanced matrix; thus there exists also $\chi' \in \{-1, 1\}^n$ such that $||M^T\chi'||_\infty \leq C\sqrt{t}$.

We set $k = 3\alpha C$, and we argue that the profile of actions where every column player j is playing $\frac{k+\chi_j}{2k}$, and every row player i is playing $\frac{k+\chi'_j}{2k}$ is a 0.4-Nash equilibrium.

We prove that the first row player cannot gain more than $\frac{1}{3}$ by deviation. For other players the same arguments hold. Given that the first row player is playing 1, we analyse the distribution S of the sum of elements in the first row (given the mixed strategy of the column players). S is a sum of t' Bernoulli ±1 variables for $\frac{1}{\alpha}t < t' < \alpha t$. The expectation of S is exactly $\mu = \mathbb{E}[S] = \sum_j \frac{\chi_j}{k} M_{1,j}$. In addition $\sigma^2 \geq \frac{1}{4}\frac{t}{\alpha}$. By the Central Limit Theorem the distribution S can be approximated by $S \sim N(\mu, \sigma^2)$. Note that by the Beck-Fiala conjecture we have $|\mu| \leq \frac{C\sqrt{t}}{k}$. Wlog, assume that $\mu \geq 0$. Then we have that $Pr(S < 0) \approx \Phi(-\frac{\mu}{\sigma}) \geq \Phi(-\frac{2C\alpha}{k}) \geq 0.4$. So by playing 1 the first row player receives a payoff of at most 0.2 and at least 0. Therefore by playing -1 the first row player receives a payoff of at least -0.2 and at most 0. So every mixed strategy is at least 0.4-best reply.

Now we prove the opposite direction, that Conjecture 4.4 implies Conjecture 4.3.

Given a matrix M, we consider the mixed action profile $(\frac{k\pm1}{2k})^{n+m}$ that forms a 0.4-Nash equilibrium in the majority matching-pennies game that is defined by M. We set $\chi_i = \pm1$ for $i \in [m]$ according to the mixed strategy of the ith column player at the 0.4-Nash equilibrium. Namely, if the ith column player is playing $\frac{k+1}{2k}$ we set $\chi_i = 1$; otherwise, if he plays $\frac{k-1}{2k}$, we set $\chi_i = -1$. We show that the first row sums up to $O(\sqrt{t})$. For every other row the same arguments hold. Note that the first row player plays a mixed strategy in $[0.4, 0.6]$. Therefore, in a 0.4-Nash equilibrium he must be 1-indifferent between the two actions 1 and -1. As before, denote by S the sum of elements in the first row in the 0.4-Nash equilibrium profile, given that the first row player is playing 1; 1-indifference implies that $0.25 \geq Pr(S \geq 0)$ and $0.25 \geq Pr(S \geq 0)$. The variance of S is at most $\sigma^2 \leq \alpha t$. If $\mu > \sqrt{\alpha t}$, then by the Central Limit Theorem we get that $Pr(S \leq 0) \leq 0.16$ which is a contradiction. Similarly it is impossible that $\mu < -\sqrt{\alpha t}$. Therefore, $|\mu| < \sqrt{\alpha t}$ which implies that $|\sum_j \frac{\chi_j}{k} M_{1,j}| \leq \sqrt{\alpha t}$. Namely $|\sum_j \chi_j M_{1,j}| \leq k\sqrt{\alpha t} = O(\sqrt{t})$. □

5 CORRELATED DISTRIBUTIONS

We turn to our main negative result concerning correlated equilibria.

Theorem 5.1. *There exists an n-player binary-action game where every distribution with support $k < \frac{1}{4}\log n$ is not $\frac{1}{4}$-individually rational.*

Since every ϵ-correlated/coarse correlated equilibrium distribution is, in particular, ϵ-individually rational, the above lower bound holds for correlated and coarse correlated equilibria.

We recall that a dynamic is *converging to an approximate correlated/coarse correlated equilibrium* in t steps if the empirical distribution of play forms an approximate correlated/coarse correlated equilibrium (with high probability).

Corollary 5.2. *No dynamic converges to an approximate correlated/coarse correlated equilibrium faster than in $\Omega(\log n)$.*

The corollary simply follows from the fact that no empirical distribution of size smaller than $\Omega(\log n)$ can form an approximate correlated/coarse correlated equilibrium in the game that is described in Theorem 5.1. On the other hand, it is known that regret minimizing dynamics converge to approximate correlated/coarse correlated equilibrium in $O(\log n)$ steps, see [5, 10]. Thus, $\Theta(\log n)$ is the fastest possible rate of convergence of dynamics to approximate correlated correlated/ coarse correlated equilibrium and regret minimizing dynamics achieve this bound.

Proof of Theorem 5.1. For two vectors $x, y \in \{0,1\}^k$ we denote $x \oplus y = (x + y) \mod 2 \in \{0,1\}^k$.

For every $k \in \mathbb{N}$ we consider a game with $n = (2^k - 1)2^{(2^{k-1})}$ players. Players are denoted by (s, p) where $0 \neq s \in \{0,1\}^k$ and $p \in \{0,1\}^{(2^{k-1})}$. We identify a player with a pair (s, V) where $V \subset \{0,1\}^k$ is a subset of size $|V| = \frac{1}{2}2^k$ as follows: note that s defines a matching over $\{0,1\}^k$ where x is matched with $x(x \oplus s)$. The matching has 2^{k-1} matched pairs. The vector p indicates which one of the two vectors (x or $(x \oplus s)$) belongs to the subset V.

Each player has a binary action set $\{0,1\}$. We define a mapping $f : \{0,1\}^n \to \{0,1\}^k$ which assigns a k-dimensional binary vector for each action profile in the game:

$$f(a) = \bigoplus_{(s,p):a_{(s,p)}=1} s.$$

Now we define the utility of player (s, p), or equivalently player (s, V) to be

$$u_{(s,p)}(a) = \begin{cases} 1 \text{ if } f(a) \in V \\ 0 \text{ otherwise.} \end{cases}$$

Note that any unilateral divination of a single player at any action profile switches his utility from 0 to 1, or from 1 to 0. Formally, for every player (s', p') (or equivalently (s', V')) and every action profile of the opponents $a_{-(s',p')}$ holds

$$(u_{(s',p')}(0, a_{-(s',p')}), u_{(s',p')}(1, a_{-(s',p')})) \in \{(0,1),(1,0)\},$$

because

$$u_{(s',p')}(0, a_{-(s',p')}) = 0 \Rightarrow \bigoplus_{(s,p):a_{(s,p)}=1} s \notin V' \Rightarrow \bigoplus_{(s,p):a_{(s,p)}=1} s \oplus s' \in V' \Rightarrow u_{(s',p')}(1, a_{-(s',p')}) = 1.$$

Similarly, $u_{(s',p')}(0, a_{-(s',p')}) = 1$ implies that $u_{(s',p')}(1, a_{-(s',p')}) = 0$.

Therefore, each player can guarantee a payoff of $\frac{1}{2}$ by playing $(\frac{1}{2}, \frac{1}{2})$, which shows that the individually rational level of every player is at least $\frac{1}{2}$.

We should show that for every distribution $\mu \in \Delta(\{0,1\}^n)$ with support of at most $\frac{1}{4}2^k \geq \frac{1}{4}\log n$, there exists a player who receives a payoff of at most $\frac{1}{4}$ (which is $\frac{1}{4}$-far from his individually rational level).

The distribution $\mu \in \Delta(\{0,1\}^n)$ induces a distribution $\nu = f(\mu) \in \Delta(\{0,1\}^k)$. The support of ν remains to be at most $\frac{1}{4}2^k$. We apply the probabilistic method to find a player with low payoff. We choose a vector x at random according to ν, and we choose a vector s (independently) uniformly at random from $\{0,1\}^k$. Note that for every fixed vector x, the vector $x \oplus s$ is distributed uniformly at random; therefore $Pr_{x,s}(x \oplus s \notin support(\nu)) \geq \frac{3}{4}$. Thus, there exists a vector s' such that $Pr_{x\sim\nu}(x \oplus s' \notin support(\nu)) \geq \frac{3}{4}$. Consider the matching of $\{0,1\}^k$ that is obtained by the vector s'. We set the vector p' as follows: For a matched pair $x \leftrightarrow x \oplus s'$ where $x \in support(\nu)$ and $x \oplus s' \notin support(\nu)$ we set $x \oplus s' \in V'$ (and thus $x \notin V'$). For all other pairs we set the choice of p' arbitrarily. By definition, the payoff of player (s', p') can be expressed as $u_i(\mu) = Pr_{x\sim\nu}(x \in V')$, but we have set V' in a way that guarantees $Pr_{x\sim\nu}(x \in V') \leq \frac{1}{4}$.

□

In contrast to an approximate correlated equilibrium which requires the support of size $k = \Omega(\log n)$, for the weaker notion of a weak approximate correlated equilibrium where we allow a small constant fraction of players to have an arbitrary regret, existence of a k-uniform weak approximate equilibrium is guaranteed for $k = O(1)$.

Proposition 5.3. *Every n-player m-actions game admits a k-uniform (ϵ, δ)-weak approximate correlated equilibrium for*[4] $k = 2\frac{m \ln m - \ln \delta}{\epsilon^2}$.

The proof is similar to the proof of Theorem 5 in [2]. Theorem 5 in [2] shows that after $k = O(\log n)$ samples from an exact correlated equilibrium *all* players will have low regret (w.h.p). Here we observe that after $k = O(1)$ samples *most* of the players will have low regret (w.h.p).

Sketch of the proof. We draw k samples from an exact correlated equilibrium, and we consider the regret of a single player i for not using the switching rule $f : [m] \to [m]$ (namely, every time player i was recommended to play action j he switches to $f(j)$). The probability that this regret will exceed ϵ is $e^{-\Theta(\frac{k}{\epsilon^2})}$. Denote by g_i the event where for player i the regret is below ϵ for all switching rules. By the union bound $Pr(g_i) \geq 1 - m^m e^{-\Theta(\frac{k}{\epsilon^2})}$. Therefore, there exists a realization for which at least $1 - m^m e^{-\Theta(\frac{k}{\epsilon^2})}$ fraction of the events g_i occur. By the choice of k we have $1 - m^m e^{-\Theta(\frac{k}{\epsilon^2})} > 1 - \delta$. Namely, this realization of the sampling forms an (ϵ, δ)-weak approximate equilibrium. □

[4] In fact, a polylogarithmic dependence on m can also be obtained, using slightly more involved arguments, as in Theorem 6 in [2].

ACKNOWLEDGMENTS

The authors gratefully acknowledge the support of the Israel Science Foundation under Grants No. ISF-2018889 (Itai Arieli) and ISF-2021296 (Yakov Babichenko).

REFERENCES

[1] Ingo Althöfer. 1994. On sparse approximations to randomized strategies and convex combinations. *Linear Algebra Appl.* 199 (1994), 339–355.

[2] Yakov Babichenko, Siddharth Barman, and Ron Peretz. 2016. Empirical Distribution of Equilibrium Play and Its Testing Application. *Mathematics of Operations Research* (2016).

[3] Yakov Babichenko, Christos Papadimitriou, and Aviad Rubinstein. 2016. Can Almost Everybody be Almost Happy?. In *Proceedings of the 2016 ACM Conference on Innovations in Theoretical Computer Science*. ACM, 1–9.

[4] József Beck and Tibor Fiala. 1981. fiInteger-makingfi theorems. *Discrete Applied Mathematics* 3, 1 (1981), 1–8.

[5] Nicolo Cesa-Bianchi and Gábor Lugosi. 2006. *Prediction, learning, and games.* Cambridge university press.

[6] Bernard Chazelle. 2000. *The discrepancy method: randomness and complexity.* Cambridge University Press.

[7] Constantinos Daskalakis, Paul W Goldberg, and Christos H Papadimitriou. 2009. The complexity of computing a Nash equilibrium. *SIAM J. Comput.* 39, 1 (2009), 195–259.

[8] Constantinos Daskalakis and Christos H Papadimitriou. 2015. Approximate Nash equilibria in anonymous games. *Journal of Economic Theory* 156 (2015), 207–245.

[9] Itzhak Gilboa and Eitan Zemel. 1989. Nash and correlated equilibria: Some complexity considerations. *Games and Economic Behavior* 1, 1 (1989), 80–93.

[10] Paul W Goldberg and Aaron Roth. 2016. Bounds for the query complexity of approximate equilibria. *ACM Transactions on Economics and Computation (TEAC)* 4, 4 (2016), 24.

[11] Carlton E Lemke and Joseph T Howson, Jr. 1964. Equilibrium points of bimatrix games. *J. Soc. Indust. Appl. Math.* 12, 2 (1964), 413–423.

[12] Richard J Lipton, Evangelos Markakis, and Aranyak Mehta. 2003. Playing large games using simple strategies. In *Proceedings of the 4th ACM conference on Electronic commerce*. ACM, 36–41.

[13] Jiri Matoušek. 1998. An L_p Version of the Beck–Fiala Conjecture. *European Journal of Combinatorics* 19, 2 (1998), 175–182.

[14] Christos H Papadimitriou. 1994. On the complexity of the parity argument and other inefficient proofs of existence. *Journal of Computer and system Sciences* 48, 3 (1994), 498–532.

[15] Aviad Rubinstein. 2016. Settling the complexity of computing approximate two-player Nash equilibria. In *Foundations of Computer Science (FOCS), 2016 IEEE 57th Annual Symposium on*. IEEE, 258–265.

[16] Joel Spencer. 1985. Six standard deviations suffice. *Transactions of the American mathematical society* 289, 2 (1985), 679–706.

Theoretical and Practical Advances on Smoothing for Extensive-Form Games

CHRISTIAN KROER, Carnegie Mellon University Computer Science Department
KEVIN WAUGH, University of Alberta Computer Science Department
FATMA KILINÇ-KARZAN, Carnegie Mellon University Tepper School of Business
TUOMAS SANDHOLM, Carnegie Mellon University Computer Science Department

Sparse iterative methods, in particular first-order methods, are known to be among the most effective in solving large-scale two-player zero-sum extensive-form games. The convergence rates of these methods depend heavily on the properties of the distance-generating function that they are based on. We investigate the acceleration of first-order methods for solving extensive-form games through better design of the dilated entropy function—a class of distance-generating functions related to the domains associated with the extensive-form games. By introducing a new weighting scheme for the dilated entropy function, we develop the first distance-generating function for the strategy spaces of sequential games that only a logarithmic dependence on the branching factor of the player. This result improves the convergence rate of several first-order methods by a factor of $\Omega(b^d d)$, where b is the branching factor of the player, and d is the depth of the game tree.

Thus far, counterfactual regret minimization methods have been faster in practice, and more popular, than first-order methods despite their theoretically inferior convergence rates. Using our new weighting scheme and practical tuning we show that, for the first time, the excessive gap technique can be made faster than the fastest counterfactual regret minimization algorithm, CFR+, in practice.

Additional Key Words and Phrases: Extensive-form game; equilibrium computation; saddle-point problem; convex analysis

A full version of this paper is available at https://arxiv.org/abs/1702.04849.

Author's email addresses: C. Kroer, ckroer@cs.cmu.edu, Kevin Waugh, kevin.waugh@gmail.com, F. Kılınç-Karzan, fkilinc@andrew.cmu.edu, Tuomas Sandholm, sandholm@cs.cmu.edu.

The first and fourth authors are supported by the National Science Foundation under grants IIS-1617590, IIS-1320620, and IIS-1546752 and the ARO under awards and W911NF-16-1-0061 and W911NF-17-1-0082.
The first author is supported by the Facebook Fellowship in Economics and Computation.
The third author is supported by the National Science Foundation grant CMMI 1454548.

ACM ISBN 978-1-4503-4527-9/17/06. DOI: http://dx.doi.org/10.1145/3033274.3085131

A Network Game of Dynamic Traffic

ZHIGANG CAO, Chinese Academy of Sciences
BO CHEN, University of Warwick
XUJIN CHEN, Chinese Academy of Sciences
CHANGJUN WANG, Beijing University of Technology

Selfish routing is one of the fundamental models in the study of network traffic systems. While most literature assumes essentially *static flows*, game theoretical models of *dynamic flows* began to draw attention recently [1–5].

We study a new dynamic flow game with atomic agents. The game is played over an acyclic directed network, with two special vertices called the origin o and the destination d, respectively, such that each edge is on at least one o-d path. Each edge of this network is associated with an integer capacity and a positive integer free-flow transit cost. Time horizon is infinite and discretized as $1, 2, \ldots$. At each time point, a set of selfish agents enter the network from the origin, trying to reach the destination as quickly as possible. When an agent uses an edge, two costs are incurred to him: the fixed transit cost of the edge and a variable waiting cost dependent on the volume of the traffic flow on that edge and the edge capacity as well as the agent's position in the queue of agents waiting at that edge. The total cost to each agent, the latency he experiences in the network, is the sum of the two costs on all edges he uses (which form an o-d path in the network).

The waiting time of each agent is determined in a way called *deterministic queuing*. At each time step, there is a (possibly empty) queue of agents waiting at the tail of each edge, and at most a capacity number of agents who have the highest priority (according to the queuing order) start to move along this edge. After the fixed period of transit time, each of these agents reaches the head of the edge, and enters the next edge (waiting at its tail for traveling along it) unless the destination d has been reached. The queue at each edge is updated according to the local First-In-First-Out rule (restricted to each edge) and pre-specified Edge Priorities – if two agents enter an edge simultaneously, their queue priorities are determined by the priorities of the preceding edges they just come from. To break ties when agents enter an edge simultaneously from the same edge, we divide each edge into the capacity number of lanes each with a unit capacity, and assign priorities among these lanes. Initially, the agents who enter the network at the same time are associated with original priorities *among them*, which are *temporarily valid* when they enter the network. This is a crucial difference between our model and those in [2, 4], where pre-specified priorities *among all agents* are permanent, working globally throughout the game.

The essence of our model is that each agent makes a routing decision at *every* nonterminal vertex he reaches. This is the second crucial (and fundamental) difference of our model from almost all in the literature [2, 4, 5], in which agents are assumed to make their routing decisions *only* at the origin o as to which o-d path to take. In addition, it is usually assumed that agents' decisions upon

---

A full version of this paper is available at http://arxiv.org/abs/1705.01784.

Authors' email addresses: First: zhigangcao@amss.ac.cn; Second: bo.chen@wbs.ac.uk; Third: xchen@amss.ac.cn; Fourth: wcj@bjut.edu.cn.

This work is supported by the National Natural Science Foundation of China (NSFC), under grant numbers 11601022, 11531014 and 11471326.

EC'17, June 26–30, 2017, Cambridge, MA, USA.
 ACM ISBN 978-1-4503-4527-9/17/06
http://dx.doi.org/10.1145/3033274.3085101

entering the system are independent of the decisions of the agents who are currently in the system. In game-theoretic terminology, while the dynamic traffic problem is usually modeled as a game of normal form (or a simultaneous-move game), we model it as a game of extensive form, which allows for agents' *online* adjustments and error corrections.

Let Γ denote our *extensive-form* game of dynamic traffic, for which we apply the solution concept of (pure strategy) *Subgame Perfect Equilibrium* (SPE). We demonstrate *in a constructive way* that Γ always possesses a very special SPE. To the best of our knowledge, this is the first SPE existence result in this field.

Then we study a very natural subset of SPEs of Γ, which is shown to possess desirable properties that are intuitively reasonable but technically hard to verify. This subset corresponds to the simplified setting, denoted as Γ^n, where agents choose their one-off *o-d* paths simultaneously at the very start of the game. The SPE existence of Γ implies that Γ^n admits at least one (pure strategy) Nash Equilibrium (NE). We show that the set of NEs of game Γ^n forms a proper subset of the realized path profiles of the SPEs of game Γ. Furthermore, we prove that in Γ^n every NE is also a strong NE and hence weakly Pareto optimal, and establish many other nice properties of all NE flows, including global (valid throughout the network) First-In-First-Out, hierarchal independence, and so on. These properties remain valid even if the network has *multiple origins* and a single destination. This is one of the key reasons that we are able to prove the existence of an SPE for Γ and the relationship between Γ and Γ^n (note that the off-equilibrium scenarios in Γ are essentially new problems with multiple origins).

Since there may be infinitely many agents in models like ours, a natural question is whether the queue length at each edge at equilibria can be bounded by a constant that depends *only* on the input *finite* network, when the inflow size never exceeds the minimum capacity of *o-d* cuts in the network. This interesting yet theoretically challenging issue has been listed as one of the important open problems in the literature [1, 4]. We prove that equilibrium queue lengths are indeed bounded in our games on two classes of networks: Γ^n on series-parallel networks, and Γ on networks in which the in-degree does not exceed the out-degree at any nonterminal vertex.

Additional Key Words and Phrases: Atomic selfish routing, dynamic network flows, deterministic queuing, subgame perfect equilibrium, Nash Equilibrium, bounded queue

REFERENCES

[1] COMINETTI, R., CORREA, J., AND LARRÉ, O. 2015. Dynamic equilibria in fluid queueing networks. *Operations Research 63,* 1, 21–34.

[2] HOEFER, M., MIRROKNI, V. S., RÖGLIN, H., AND TENG, S.-H. 2011. Competitive routing over time. *Theoretical Computer Science 412,* 39, 5420–5432.

[3] KOCH, R. AND SKUTELLA, M. 2011. Nash equilibria and the price of anarchy for flows over time. *Theory of Computing Systems 49,* 1, 71–97.

[4] SCARSINI, M., SCHRÖDER, M., AND TOMALA, T. 2016. Dynamic atomic congestion games with seasonal flows. *HEC Paris Research Paper No. ECO/SCD-2013-1016. Available at SSRN: https://ssrn.com/abstract=2278203 or http://dx.doi.org/10.2139/ssrn.2278203.*

[5] WERTH, T., HOLZHAUSER, M., AND KRUMKE, S. 2014. Atomic routing in a deterministic queuing model. *Operations Research Perspectives 1,* 1, 18–41.

A Polynomial Time Algorithm for Spatio-Temporal Security Games

SOHEIL BEHNEZHAD, University of Maryland
MAHSA DERAKHSHAN, University of Maryland
MOHAMMADTAGHI HAJIAGHAYI, University of Maryland
ALEKSANDRS SLIVKINS, Microsoft Research

An ever-important issue is protecting infrastructure and other valuable targets from a range of threats from vandalism to theft to piracy to terrorism. The "defender" can rarely afford the needed resources for a 100% protection. Thus, the key question is, *how to provide the best protection using the limited available resources.*

We study a practically important class of security games that is played out in space and time, with targets and "patrols" moving on a real line. A central open question here is whether the Nash equilibrium (i.e., the minimax strategy of the defender) can be computed in polynomial time. We resolve this question in the affirmative. Our algorithm runs in time polynomial in the input size, and only polylogarithmic in the number of possible patrol locations (M). Further, we provide a *continuous* extension in which patrol locations can take arbitrary real values. Prior work obtained polynomial-time algorithms only under a substantial assumption, e.g., a constant number of rounds. Further, all these algorithms have running times polynomial in M, which can be very large.

1 INTRODUCTION

Protecting infrastructure and other valuable targets from a range of threats from vandalism to theft to piracy to terrorism is an ever-important issue around the world, aggravated recently by increased threats of piracy and terrorism. Providing 100% protection usually requires more money or other resources than the "defender" can commit. Thus, the key question is, *how to provide the best protection using the limited resources that are available.*

A successful recent approach casts this issue in game-theoretic terms, modeling it as a *security game*: a zero-sum game between the *defender* who has some targets to protect, and the *attacker* who strives to inflict damage on these targets. Usually the defender needs to commit to a particular allocation of resources, such as the schedule of patrols, whereas the attacker can strike at will; this corresponds to a classic game-theoretic model called a *Stackelberg game*. The defender can (and should) randomize, e.g. so as to prevent the attacker

Supported in part by NSF CAREER award CCF-1053605, NSF BIGDATA grant IIS-1546108, NSF AF:Medium grant CCF-1161365, DARPA GRAPHS/AFOSR grant FA9550-12-1-0423, and another DARPA SIMPLEX grant. Authors' emails: {soheil,mahsaa,hajiagha}@cs.umd.edu, slivkins@microsoft.com.

EC'17, June 26–30, 2017, Cambridge, Massachusetts, USA. ACM ISBN 978-1-4503-4527-9/17/06...$15.00.

DOI: http://dx.doi.org/10.1145/3033274.3085133

from exploiting a particular gap in the patrol schedule. The attacker can be strategic and optimize his attack according to his beliefs about the defender's strategy. The literature has mostly adopted a pessimistic view, in which the attack is the exact best response to the defender's actual strategy. Thus, the defender's goal is to use an optimal (minimax) strategy.

This approach has resulted in a flurry of research activity, including several awards and nominations. Further, it has been adopted in a number of real-world deployments, ranging from patrol boats to airport checkpoints to US air marshals to an urban transit system to wildlife protection. (Many of them have been recognized with commendations and awards.) Other potential applications include protecting aid convoys in unstable regions, and protecting ships from piracy.

Most applications of security games are *spatio-temporal* in the sense that the patrols move from one location to another with a limited speed, and only protect targets that are sufficiently close. Then the defender's strategy is a rather complicated object: a pure strategy should specify a trajectory for every patrol, possibly choosing from a very large number of possible locations. Further, in many applications targets have their own trajectories that need to be taken into consideration.

The first-order question in spatio-temporal security games is computing the equilibrium, i.e., the minimax strategy for the defender. More specifically, we focus on exact equilibrium computation in polynomial time. The prior work (e.g., [5, 8, 20]), as well as the present paper, considers a one-dimensional space (that is, patrol and target locations are on the real line), and discretizes it uniformly into the possible patrol locations. The relevant parameters are: the number of patrols (K), the number of targets (A), the number of rounds of scheduling (T), and the number of possible patrol locations (M). The input specifies trajectories of targets and their values; the trajectories may be arbitrary, and the values may change over time. Thus, the input size is $O(T \cdot A + \log(K \cdot M))$. What makes the problem particularly challenging is that the number of pure strategies — tuples of patrol trajectories — is as large as $(M)^{KT}$.

A central open question here is whether the Nash equilibrium (i.e., the minimax strategy of the defender) can be computed in polynomial time. We resolve this question in the affirmative: our main result is an algorithm that computes the exact equilibrium in time polynomial in the input size. In particular, the running time scales only *polylogarithmically* in the number of possible patrol locations. Moreover, we provide a *continuous* extension in which patrol locations can take arbitrary real values, under a mild technical assumption that the target locations are rational. The dependence on the number of patrols is argued away: while a pure strategy of the defender must specify a trajectory for each patrol, we prove that $\texttt{poly}(TA)$ patrols suffices to protect all targets. The output is a distribution over $\texttt{poly}(TA)$-many pure strategies.

We improve over the state-of-art prior work [8, 20] in several ways. First, the running time in [8] is exponential in the number of patrols (K) and becomes impractical even for $K = 3$ [20]. Second, [20] achieves a polynomial running time only under a substantial assumption: either a constant number of rounds, or that all targets have a unit value at all times, or that the "protection ranges" of the patrols are so small that they cannot overlap for any two adjacent patrol locations. Third, the running times in [8, 20] depend polynomially on the the number of patrol locations (M). Finally, the polynomial running time in [20] relies on the Ellipsoid Algorithm for solving linear programs, which is notoriously slow in practice.

Our techniques. Our main algorithm works on the *discretized version* of the problem, in which the possible locations for patrols are integers from 1 to M (there is no such restriction on the location of targets). The algorithm consists of three parts: partitioning the spatial domain, formulating patrol placements in a single time point, and combining them to find the optimal strategy for all time points. Below we describe these three parts one by one.

First, we partition the spatial domain into a relatively small number of intervals so that the patrol locations inside each interval are "equivalent" to one another as far as our problem is concerned. Then we use these intervals as "atomic" patrol locations, thereby replacing the dependence on M with the dependence on the number of intervals. The partitioning algorithm starts from the last round T and goes backwards in time: for each round t it constructs a collection of intervals based on the target locations at time t and the intervals constructed for time $t+1$, so as to ensure the desired "equivalence" property. We bound the number of intervals by $\mathcal{O}(T^3 A)$.

Second, for each time point t we construct a graph G_t which models any possible *snapshot* of the patrol placements at this time. More specifically, every patrol placement at time t can be mapped to a specific path in G_t, and every *randomized* patrol placement can be mapped to a specific unit flow in G_t. Furthermore, we define the cost of a path/flow in G_t such that it equals the maximum utility of the attacker under the corresponding (randomized) patrol placement at time t, and can be computed via a linear program.

Third, we create a linear program that "unifies" the graphs G_t, and use this LP to construct the minimax strategy for the defender. The LP ensures that the (randomized) patrol placements computed in each G_t are consistent with one another, in the sense that there is a valid transition from one round to the next, without violating the speed restriction. To accomplish this, the LP finds min-cost flows in each G_t, and includes additional linear constraints that guarantee consistency. We post-process the solution of this LP and remove the crossing edges in the flows. Finally, we incrementally construct a mixed strategy of the defender based on the post-processed solution and prove that it is indeed the optimal strategy.

In the *continuous* version of the problem, patrol locations can take arbitrary real values, and the target locations are rational. We first re-scale all target locations to integers, and prove that this re-scaled problem instance admits a discrete solution. Then we use the algorithm from the discretized version. It is essential that the running time of the latter is polylogarithmic in M.

Related work. Security games have been studied extensively in the past decade, see the book [18] as well as more recent work, e.g. [5, 8, 12, 19, 20]. The research concerned both theoretical foundations as well as applications. Publicized real-world deployments include: US Coast Guard patrol boats [8], canine-patrol and vehicle-checkpoints scheduling in Los Angeles airport (LAX) [16], scheduling flights for air marshals by US Federal Air Marshal Service [10], airport passenger screening by US Transportation Security Administration [6], fare inspection in Los Angeles transit system [21], and wildlife protection in Malaysia [9].

Most relevant to the present work are papers on computing minimax strategy in zero-sum spatio-temporal security games. While the initial work assumed static targets [18], some of the later work addressed moving targets [5, 8, 20] (as discussed above). On a related note, if the patrols are allowed to *accelerate*, with an upper bound on the acceleration, then computing the defender's minimax strategy becomes NP-hard [19, 20]. Other work concerned solving security games that are not (necessarily) spatio-temporal or zero-sum, e.g. [7, 11, 20] A notable line of work in security games assumes that the defender does not fully know attackers' values for the targets, but can learn more about them over multiple rounds of interaction with the said attackers (see [15] for a recent survey of a subset of this work, as well as [2, 4, 13, 14]).

In a broader game-theoretic context, our work is related to Stackelberg games and equilibrium computation. Originally introduced to model competing firms, Stackelberg games is a classic concept in game theory which appears in many textbooks and countless papers.

Computing Nash Equilibria is a central problem in algorithmic economics. While this problem is known to be PPAD-hard in general, polynomial-time algorithms exist for many natural classes of games, particularly for zero-sum games (for background, see a survey [17] and references therein). Yet, these algorithmic results are insufficient for games in which the number of pure strategies can be exponential in the input size (see [1, 3] for examples of such games).

Further directions. Many ideas in this paper may be useful for solving other spatio-temporal security games. In particular, the overall algorithmic framework of locally solving each "time layer" under some compatibility constraints and then merging the "time layers" to compute the global optimum solution appears broadly applicable.

We believe our techniques can be extended to achieve a polynomial time algorithm for several extensions of the model. In particular, we can incorporate additional constraints on the patrols, such as obstacles that the patrols cannot cross over, or speed limits that depend on a particular location. We can also handle scenarios when the spatial domain or the timeline are not evenly discretized. (For ease of presentaton, we do not include these extensions in the present paper).

A general way to model such extensions is to assume that the range of valid movements for each location is given in the input. Whenever we still have a property that the patrols do not need to cross each other in an optimal solution (which indeed is a very natural property for homogeneous patrols), our techniques achieve a polynomial-time algorithm in the input size. However, the input size for this extended model gets large, and no longer scales polylogarithmically in M.

That said, some important special cases allow for succinct input. For example, a small number of obstacles can be specified directly, rather than given implicitly via the ranges of valid movements. Designing a polynomial-time algorithm for such cases requires a problem-specific pre-processing step for partitioning the locations (which could potentially be very different from the partitioning step in this paper). However, the rest of the algorithm could be essentially the same.

It is very tempting to extend our model to a two-dimensional space. We believe some of our techniques can be useful for this extension, most importantly the compatibility constraint technique from Section 3.3. The main challenge in extending our approach is an appropriate generalization of the "day graphs".

2 PRELIMINARIES

Our goal is to find an optimal patrol scheduling strategy for the defender to protect a set of A mobile targets in a one-dimensional space. Figure 1 illustrates the problem in a 2-D diagram; the x-axis denotes the evenly discretized temporal domain containing $T+1$ time points, and the y-axis denotes the one-dimensional space of length M. We say a spatial position i is above j, if $i > j$ and similarly define a spatial position i to be under j, if $i < j$.

The defender has K homogeneous patrols to protect a set of moving targets from a potential attack. Patrols have a maximum speed of Δ. This means, a move from a position

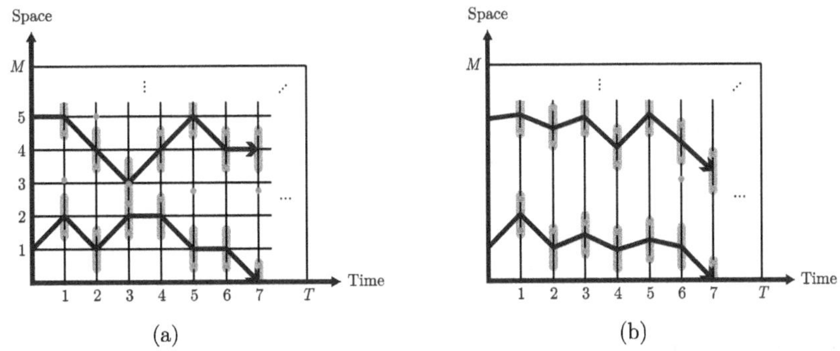

Fig. 1. An illustration of how targets and patrols move in discrete (a) and continuous (b) models of the problem.

m_t at time t to m_{t+1} at time $t+1$ is invalid if $|m_{t+1} - m_t| > \Delta$. We consider two models of the problem: *discretized model*, denoted by $\mathcal{DSG}$ (Figure 1-a), and *continuous model*, denoted by $\mathcal{CSG}$ (Figure 1-b). In the discretized model, the position of any patrol at any time point is an integer between 0 and M, but in the continuous model, the patrol locations are not restricted to be integers (note that the temporal domain is still discretized). Furthermore, for any target a, $h_{a,t}$ and $w_{a,t}$ respectively denote its position and weight at time t. Note that in both models, there is no restriction on the position and the speed of targets and the weight of the targets could change from time to time (e.g., ferries may not carry the same number of people at different times). The patrols protect any target within their protection radius R (a fixed number for all patrols). That is, a patrol k at position m_t at time t, protects a target a, if $|h_{a,t} - m_t| \leq R$. In Figure 1, the grey ranges around patrols denote the area they protect. We denote the set of targets, the set of spatial positions, the set of patrols and the set of all time points by $[A]$, $[M]$, $[K]$ and $[T]$ respectively.

A *patrol path*, is a sequence of T positions $(m_1, m_2, \ldots, m_T)$, such that for any $t \in [T]$, a move from m_t to m_{t+1} does not violate the speed limit (the black paths in Figure 1 denote patrol paths). A pure strategy of the defender is a set of K patrol paths denoted by $\{v_k\}_{k\in[K]}$. A mixed strategy of the defender, is a probability distribution over her pure strategies. A pure strategy of the attacker is a single target-time pair (a, t) which means the attacker attacks target a at time t. Let $\{v_k\}_{k\in[K]}$ be the pure strategy of the defender and (a, t) be the pure strategy of the attacker, attacker's utility is 0 if target a is protected by at least one patrol at time t and it is $w_{a,t}$ if it is not protected by any patrols. We assume the game is zero-sum and find minmax strategies.

Without loss of generality, we can assume $K \leq TA$. This observation comes from the fact that with only TA patrols, the defender can provide a 100% protection without needing any more patrols. To do this, for any target-time pair (a, t), the defender can put a still patrol at the location of target a at time t.

3 DISCRETE MODEL

The main goal of this section is to prove the following theorem:

THEOREM 3.1. *There is a polynomial time (in input size) algorithm to solve $\mathcal{DSG}$.*

Algorithm 1 Partitions the given positions into intervals

```
function GetIntervals
    for t = T to 1 do
        if t < T then P_t ← GetIntervalPoints(t, P_{t+1})
        else P_t ← GetIntervalPoints(t, ∅)
        I_t ← Array()
        for any two consecutive items p_i and p_{i+1} in P_t do
            I_t .Insert([p_i, p_{i+1}))
    return ⟨I_1, ..., I_T⟩
function GetIntervalPoints(t, P_{t+1})
    P_t ← SortedArray()
    P_t.Insert(0), P_t.Insert(M)
    ε ← a sufficiently small number in ℝ+
    for each target a ∈ [A_t] do
        if h_{a,t} − R > 0 then P_t.Insert(h_{a,t} − R)
        if h_{a,t} + R < M then P_t.Insert(h_{a,t} + R + ε)
    for p in P_{t+1} do
        if p − Δ > 0 then P_t.Insert(p − Δ)
        if p + Δ < M then P_t.Insert(p + Δ)
    for any item p_i in P_t do
        if interval [p_i, p_{i+1}) does not contain any patrol position then
            P_t.Remove(p_i)
    return P_t
```

3.1 Partitioning The Positions

The number of pure strategies in a single time point, even with only one patrol, is not polynomial in the input size, since the number of possible locations, M, could be exponentially larger than the input size. To overcome this difficulty, we partition the spatial positions into polynomially many sets of consecutive positions which we call *intervals* and we only keep track of these intervals instead of maintaining the exact position of a patrol within the intervals. For example, assume there is only one target, one patrol and $T = 1$, then it only matters whether the patrol's protection range contains the location of the target or not and the exact position of the patrol does not matter.

We use Algorithm 1 to partition the positions into meaningful intervals. For any given time point t, the function GetIntervalPoints, generates a sorted array $P_t = \langle p_1, \ldots, p_{n_t} \rangle$ of numbers that we call *interval points* and GetIntervals uses these generated interval points to partition the spatial positions of any time point t to intervals:

$$\mathcal{I}_t = \langle [p_1, p_2), [p_2, p_3), \ldots, [p_{n_t-1}, p_{n_t}) \rangle.$$

The intervals are assumed to be left-closed and right-open to simplify the calculations. We use $\mathcal{I}_t[i]$ to denote the i-th interval in $\mathcal{I}_t$ and use $\mathcal{I}_t[i : j]$ to denote the set of consecutive intervals $\{\mathcal{I}_t[i], \mathcal{I}_t[i+1], \ldots, \mathcal{I}_t[j]\}$.

The following lemma proves the total number of intervals is polynomial in the input size and as a corollary of that, Algorithm 1 runs in polynomial time in the input size.

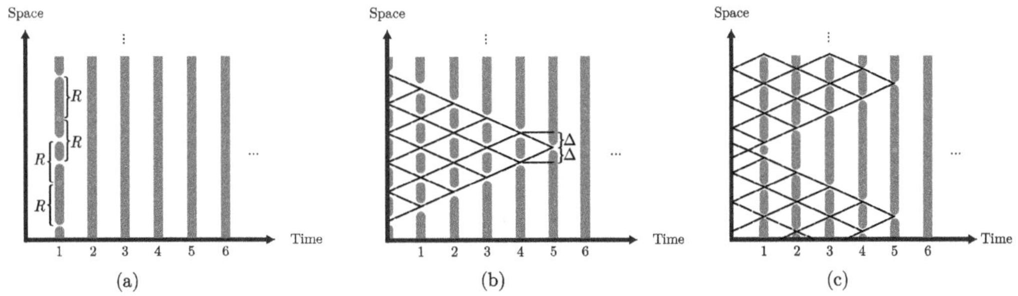

Fig. 2. Interval points are added to the partitioning sets in two ways: (a) around any target there are two interval points, and (b) any interval point propagates to the previous time points. A combination of both is shown in (c).

LEMMA 3.2. *The total number of intervals created by Algorithm 1 is $\mathcal{O}(T^3A)$.*

Proof. To prove this, we charge any interval point to a target/time pair and show no target/time pair will be charged more than $\mathcal{O}(T^2)$ times and since there are at most $\mathcal{O}(AT)$ target/time pairs, there will not be more than $\mathcal{O}(T^3A)$ interval points. Note that there are two ways for interval points to be added to a partitioning set P_t (Figure 2):

(1) For any target a at time point t, two interval points $h_{a,t} - R$ and $h_{a,t} + R + \epsilon$ are added to P_t. We charge these two interval points to (a, t).
(2) For any interval point p in P_{t+1} two interval points $p - \Delta$ and $p + \Delta$ are added to P_t. We recursively charge these two intervals to the target/time pair that the interval point p is charged to.

This means an interval point p could be charged to a target/time pair (a, t), only if $h_{a,t} = p \pm i\Delta + R + \epsilon$ or $h_{a,t} = p \pm i\Delta - R$ for any integer i where $i \leq t$. Although this condition is only necessary and not sufficient, but it implies at most $\mathcal{O}(T^2)$ interval positions could be charged to an arbitrary target/time pair and therefore the total number of partition points is $\mathcal{O}(T^3A)$. □

Note that since by Lemma 3.2, the total number of interval points at any time point t is polynomial in the input size, function GETINTERVALPOINTS(t, P_{t+1}), which is simply a loop over P_{t+1} and the targets, runs in polynomial time.

COROLLARY 3.3. *Algorithm 1 halts in polynomial time in the input size.*

The following lemmas prove two important properties of the partitions generated by Algorithm 1. These properties basically imply all patrol locations within the same interval are equivalent as far as the problem is concerned.

LEMMA 3.4. *Let k and k' be two patrols in the same interval at any time t. The set of targets that k and k' protect at time t are equal.*

LEMMA 3.5. *Let $[s_i, f_i)$ and $[s_j, f_j)$ be two arbitrary intervals in $\mathcal{I}_t$ and $\mathcal{I}_{t+1}$ respectively. If there exists a feasible move from an arbitrary position in $[s_i, f_i)$ to a position in $[s_j, f_j)$, for any position in $[s_i, f_i)$, there exists a feasible move to a position in $[s_j, f_j)$.*

We can now define the feasible set of a set of consecutive intervals:

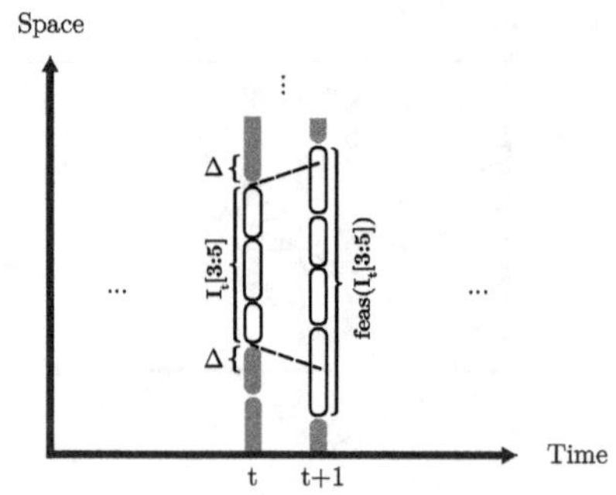

Fig. 3. The white intervals at time $t+1$, are in the feasible set of the white intervals at time t

Definition 3.6 (feasible sets). We define the feasible set of $\mathcal{I}_t[i:j]$, denoted by $\text{feas}_t(\mathcal{I}_t[i:j])$, to be a subset of $\mathcal{I}_{t+1}$, containing an interval $\mathcal{I}_{t+1}[i']$ iff there exists a feasible move from a position in some interval in $\mathcal{I}_t[i:j]$ to $\mathcal{I}_{t+1}[i']$. We may occasionally abuse this notation and use the simpler form of $\text{feas}_t(\mathcal{I}_t[i])$ instead of $\text{feas}_t(\mathcal{I}_t[i:i])$ (Figure 3).

It is easy to see the following corollary of Definition 3.6:

COROLLARY 3.7. *For any $\mathcal{I}_t[i:j]$ there exists a consecutive interval set $\mathcal{I}_{t+1}[i':j']$ such that*

$$\text{feas}_t(\mathcal{I}_t[i:j]) = \mathcal{I}_{t+1}[i':j'].$$

Definition 3.8 (interval path). We define an *interval path* to be a sequence of T intervals $\langle \mathcal{I}_i[x_i]\rangle_T$, such that for any time point $t \in [T]$, $\mathcal{I}_{t+1}[x_{t+1}] \in \text{feas}_t(\mathcal{I}_t[x_t])$. Moreover, for any interval path $\xi = \langle \mathcal{I}_i[x_i]\rangle_T$, we define $S(\xi)$ to be the set of all patrol paths that are within ξ. More formally, a patrol path $\langle m_i\rangle_T$ is within $S(\xi)$ if and only if for any time point $t \in [T]$, m_t is in interval $\mathcal{I}_t[x_t]$.

Note that any patrol path is within exactly one interval path, since intervals do not overlap and they cover all locations. It could also be obtained from the following lemma that $S(\xi)$ is never empty for an interval path ξ. The proof is to choose any position in $\mathcal{I}_1[x_1]$ and following the valid movements until we reach a position in $\mathcal{I}_T[x_T]$.

LEMMA 3.9. *For any interval path $\xi = \langle \mathcal{I}_i[x_i]\rangle_T$, there is at least one patrol path in $S(\xi)$.*

Note that by Lemma 3.4, two patrols that are in the same interval, protect the same set of targets at that specific time. This implies that the patrol paths that are within the same interval path, protect the same set of targets at all times and could be replaced with one another in any strategy, without changing the utilities. This means the amount of information encoded in an interval path is sufficient to describe the important characteristics of strategies and find the optimal one.

3.2 Strategies In a Single Time Point

In this section we explain how to locally find the best strategy for a single time point ignoring the speed limitations. Note that although we proved the number of intervals is polynomial in the input size, there are still exponentially many different ways to place our K patrols in them. This section describes how we can resolve this problem and find the best strategy.

We use the term *snapshot* to denote a patrol placement at a single time point and formally define it as follows:

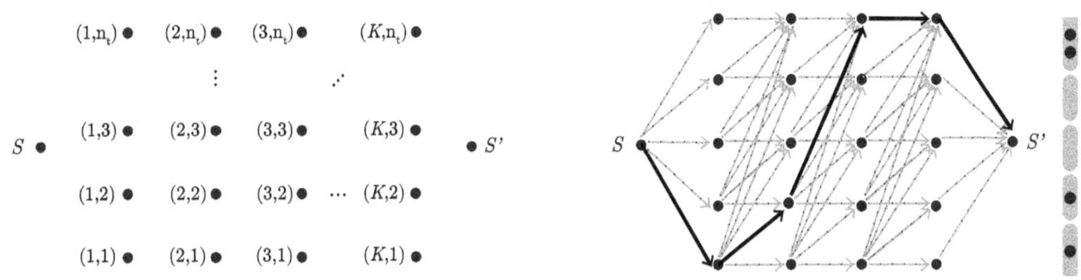

(a) (b)

Fig. 4. Figure (a) shows the vertices of a day graph and figure (b) shows a sample day graph. The highlighted path in figure (b) shows a canonical path and its equivalent patrol placement is shown in the vertical bar next to it, each grey piece denotes an intervals and the black dots denote the location of patrols in them.

Definition 3.10 (snapshots). A pure snapshot at time point t, is an assignment of patrols to intervals of time t. We denote it by a sorted sequence of K intervals $\langle \mathcal{I}_t[y_i] \rangle_K$ such that for any $i \in [K]$, $y_i \leq y_{i+1}$. A mixed snapshot, denoted by $\{(d_i, p_i)\}_n$ is a probability distribution over n pure snapshots where p_i denotes the probability of choosing pure snapshot d_i and $\Sigma_{i=1}^{n} p_i = 1$.

For any time point t, we construct a weighted directed graph G_t (called a *day graph*) and give a one-to-one mapping between pure snapshots at time t and paths from S_t (source vertex) to S'_t (sink vertex), where S_t and S'_t are two specific vertices of G_t. Moreover, we map any mixed snapshot at time point t, to a network flow of 1 unit from S_t to S'_t. This mapping is not necessarily one-to-one and many mixed snapshots may be mapped to the same network flow; however, the maximum utility of the attacker in all such mixed snapshots, will be the same.

In Definition 3.11 we formally explain how G_t is constructed. An informal explanation of it is as follows: the vertex set of G_t, as shown in Figure 4-a, includes a vertex S_t, a vertex S'_t and a grid of $K \times n_t$ vertices (recall that n_t is the number of intervals at time t) each denoted by $V_t[x, y]$. There is an edge from S_t to any vertex in the first column of the grid $V_t[1, y]$, and there is an edge from any vertex in the last column of the grid $V_t[K, y]$ to S'_t. Also for any x, y, and y', there is an edge from $V_t[x, y]$ to $V_t[x+1, y']$ if $y \leq y'$. Furthermore, we define a *canonical path* to be any path from S_t to S'_t and define a *canonical flow* to be any flow of unit 1 from S_t to S'_t (Definition 3.12). We give a one-to-one mapping between canonical paths in G_t and pure snapshots at time point t in Definition 3.13 and map any mixed snapshot to a canonical flow in Definition 3.14. Figure 4-b shows a sample day graph, a canonical path in it and its equivalent pure snapshot. Moreover, we assign weights to the edges of G_t such that the maximum payoff of the attacker for a pure (mixed) snapshot equals the cost of its corresponding canonical path (flow). The cost of a canonical path and a canonical flow is defined in Definition 3.12.

For any target a and any intervals i and i' at time t, we define the binary value $C_t(i, i'; a)$ to be 1 if the following two conditions hold: (1) target a is located in a position between i and i' (non-inclusive) at time t, and, (2) a could not be protected by any patrol at any arbitrary position in i or i'; otherwise we set $\mathcal{C}_t(i,i';a)$ to be 0. We similarly define two binary variables $\mathcal{C}_t(\varnothing,i;a)$ and $\mathcal{C}_t(i,\varnothing;a)$ for the border cases. We set $\mathcal{C}_t(\varnothing,i;a)$ to be 1 iff target a is in a position below i where no patrol in i can protect it and set $\mathcal{C}_t(i,\varnothing;a)$ to be 1 iff target a is in a position above i where no patrol in i can protect it. Assume a patrol placement p does not protect a target a at time t. Let i and i' be the closest intervals to target a, that contain at least one patrol and are below and above a respectively (set them to be $\varnothing$ if no such interval exits), then by definition $\mathcal{C}_t(i,i';a)=1$. Using this definition, we can now formally define a day graph and canonical path/flow.

Definition 3.11 (day graph). Given a time point t, we construct graph G_t as follows:

(1) Graph G_t contains a vertex S_t (source), a vertex S'_t (sink) and $K\times n_t$ other vertices, each denoted by $V_t[x,y]$ for $1\le x\le K$ and $1\le y\le n_t$.
(2) For any y such that $1\le y\le n_t$, there is an edge from S_t to $V_t[1,y]$. If e denotes an edge of this kind, for any target a, we define $c_{e,a}$ to be $\mathcal{C}_t(\varnothing,\mathcal{I}_t[y];a)$.
(3) For any y such that $1\le y\le n_t$, there is an edge from $V_t[K,y]$ to S'_t. If e denotes an edge of this kind, for any target a, we define $c_{e,a}$ to be $\mathcal{C}_t(\mathcal{I}_t[y],\varnothing;a)$.
(4) For any two vertices $V_t[x,y]$ and $V_t[x+1,y']$, if $y\le y'$, there is an edge from $V_t[x,y]$ to $V_t[x+1,y']$. If e denotes this edge, for any target a, we define $c_{e,a}=\mathcal{C}_t(\mathcal{I}_t[y],\mathcal{I}_t[y'];a)$.

Definition 3.12 (canonical path/flow). In a day graph G_t any path from S_t to S'_t is a canonical path. Let $E=\{e_1,e_2,\dots,e_{K+1}\}$ be the set of edges in a canonical path, and a be an arbitrary target. We define the cost of this canonical path for target a to be:

$$\sum_{e\in E} c_{e,a}.w_{t,a} \tag{1}$$

Also, any flow of unit 1 from S_t to S'_t is a canonical flow. We denote any canonical flow with a function $f: E(G_t)\to[0,1]$, where $f(e)$ denotes the flow passing through an edge e. The cost of an arbitrary canonical flow f, for day graph G_t is:

$$\max \sum_{e\in E(G_t)} f(e).c_{e,a}.w_{t,a} \qquad \forall a;\ \text{where } a\in[A.] \tag{2}$$

Intuitively speaking, $c_{e,a}$ is 1 if and only if having edge e in a canonical path p implies that in the "equivalent" pure snapshot of p, target a is not covered by any patrol. The formal mapping of canonical paths and flows to snapshots is as follows.

Definition 3.13 (pure snapshot mapping). Let $s_t=\langle\mathcal{I}_t[y_i]\rangle_K$ be a pure snapshot (recall that $y_i\le y_{i+1}$ for any $i\in[K]$). We map s_t to the following canonical path:

$$p_t=\langle S_t,V_t[1,y_1],V_t[2,y_2],\dots,V_t[K,y_K],S'_t\rangle$$

and similarly map p_t to s_t and say s_t and p_t are equivalent.

Definition 3.14 (mixed snapshot mapping). Let $m=\{(d_i,p_i)\}_n$ be a mixed snapshot at time t. Also let f_i denote a flow of unit p_i from S_t to S'_t through the edges of the equivalent canonical path of d_i. We construct flow f as follows: for any edge e of G_t, $f(e)=\Sigma_{i=1}^n f_i(e)$. Note that since by definition of a mixed snapshot, $\Sigma_{i=1}^n p_i=1$, f is a flow of unit 1 from S_t to S'_t, and hence is a canonical flow. We map m to f.

In Lemma 3.15 we prove that the payoff of the attacker if he attacks target a at time t while the placement of patrols is represented by the pure strategy s, equals to the cost of the target a in the canonical path equivalent to s. Then in Lemma 3.16 we prove that the maximum payoff of the attacker at time t while the strategy of defender is represented by the mixed snapshot m is equal to the cost of canonical flow equivalent to m. These two lemmas can be directly obtained by the given definitions, however, for space limitations, their formal proofs are left to the appendix.

LEMMA 3.15. *Let s be a pure snapshot at time t, and a be an arbitrary target. The payoff of the attacker with respect to s, if he attacks the target a at time t, equals the cost of the target a in the canonical path equivalent (Definition 3.13) to s.*

LEMMA 3.16. *Let r be a mixed snapshot at time t and let f denote the canonical flow that r is mapped to. The maximum expected payoff of the attacker at time t with respect to r, equals the cost of f.*

3.3 Best Strategy For All Time Points

Lemma 3.16 implies if our goal is to minimize the maximum payoff of the attacker at a single time point t, it suffices to find a canonical flow in G_t with minimum cost. Although this works for the special case when $T = 1$, but it does not consider the movement of patrols and their speed limits. More precisely, a pure strategy for the defender could be shown as a sequence of pure snapshots $\langle s_1, s_2, \dots, s_T\rangle$. However there is one important condition: for any $i \in [T]$, there must be a feasible transition from s_i to s_{i+1}. This is also the case for mixed snapshots and two consecutive ones may not be necessarily compatible. In this section we resolve this issue and prove Theorem 3.1.

Our algorithm to find the optimal strategy of the defender consists of three main steps. In the first step, which is explained in more details in Section 3.3.1, we run an LP that returns a canonical flow for each day graph $G_1, \dots, G_T$. Apart from the constraints to ensure we get valid canonical flows with minimum overall cost, our LP contains an extra constraint for compatibility of these canonical flows. In the second step (Section 3.3.2), while keeping the overall characteristics of these canonical flows unchanged, we adjust them in a way to make sure no two crossing edges in any of the day graphs have a positive flow. Finally, in the third step (Section 3.3.3), we construct a mixed strategy for the defender based on the adjusted canonical flows.

Let s_t and s_{t+1} denote two pure snapshots representing the placement of patrols in a valid pure strategy p at two consecutive times. In the following lemma we prove that there exists a feasible move from i-th interval of s_t to the i-th interval of s_{t+1} (recall that intervals in pure snapshots are sorted based on their position). We prove this lemma by induction on the number of patrols. At each step we prove that there exists a feasible move from the top most interval in s_t to the top most interval in s_{t+1} and we prove if we match these two together and remove them, we can construct another pure strategy that contains the remaining intervals.

LEMMA 3.17. *If $\langle \mathcal{I}_t[y_i^t]\rangle_K$ and $\langle \mathcal{I}_{t+1}[y_i^t]\rangle_K$ are two pure snapshots at time t and $t+1$ in at least one valid pure strategy p, then for any $j \in [K]$ we have $\mathcal{I}_{t+1}[y_j^{t+1}] \in \text{feas}_t(\mathcal{I}_t[y_j^t])$.*

In the following definition, we define what it means for a patrol path to be *intervally above*, *below* or *equal* to another patrol path:

Definition 3.18. Let $v = \langle m_0, m_1, \dots, m_r\rangle$ and $v' = \langle m'_0, m'_1, ..., m'_T\rangle$ be two patrol paths. We say v and v' are intervally equal if for any $t \in [T]$, m_t and m'_t are in the same interval. We also define v to be intervally under v', if for any $t \in [T]$, either $m_t < m'_t$ or m_t and m'_t are in the same interval. Similarly, we define v to be intervally above v', if v' is intervally under v.

Next, in Lemma 3.19 we prove that there exists an optimal strategy of the defender that for any pure strategy p in its support, there is an ordering of interval paths in p such that, i-th interval path is always intervally under j-th interval path if $1 \leq i < j \leq K$. To prove this we use Lemma 3.17 that indicates there exists a possible move from the k-th interval in pure snapshot s_1 to the k-th interval in pure snapshot s_2 if s_1 and s_2 represent the patrols' placement of a pure strategy in two consecutive times and $1 \leq k \leq K$. For any patrol $k \in [K]$, we construct an interval path that contains the k-th interval of all the pure snapshots in p, and we assign patrol k to this interval path. It is easy to see that if we order the patrols from 1 to K the interval path assigned to patrol k_1 is under the interval path assigned to patrol k_2 if $1 \leq k_1 \leq k_2 \leq K$. This lemma is very similar to Lemma 3 of [20] but adopted to intervals paths.

LEMMA 3.19. *There exists an optimal mixed strategy of the defender, such that for every pure strategy p in its support there is an ordering of interval paths $\langle \xi_1, \ldots, \xi_K \rangle$ such that the following condition holds for this ordering: for any two interval paths ξ_i and ξ_j, in the pure strategy p, ξ_i is intervally under ξ_j if $i \leq j$.*

Again, for space limitations, the full proof is left to the appendix. However, intuitively, starting from any given optimal solution one can swap the remaining path of any two patrols that cross each other without losing anything. This eventually resolves all crosses and gives a desired optimal solution.

Let s denote an optimal strategy of the defender that satisfies the condition mentioned in Lemma 3.19, and let $\langle \xi_{p,1}, \xi_{p,2} \ldots, \xi_{p,K} \rangle$ denote the ordering of interval paths in pure strategy p in support of s such that $\xi_{p,i}$ is intervally under $\xi_{p,j}$ if $1 \leq i \leq j \leq K$. Without loss of generality we assume for any $i \in [K]$ the same patrol is assigned to interval path $\xi_{p,i}$ for all p in support of s, and it is denoted by k_i. Therefore, if $\langle \mathcal{I}_t[y_1], \mathcal{I}_t[y_2], \ldots, \mathcal{I}_t[y_K] \rangle$ denotes a pure snapshot that represents the patrols' placement in an arbitrary time point $t \in [T]$ in pure strategy p in support of s, $\mathcal{I}_t[y_i]$ is the position of patrol k_i in pure strategy p at this time. Moreover, let m denote the mixed snapshot of strategy s at time t. The flow passing through the vertex $V_t[i, j]$, denotes the probability with which patrol k_i is placed in the j-th interval at time t. So, all the data related to position of patrol k_i at time t is in the column i of the day graph of time t. We use this later in the paper.

3.3.1 Linear Programming. In this section we explain how the first step of our algorithm, the LP, works.

Note that a flow of 1 unit in G_t with minimum weight, minimizes the attacker's payoff at time t. To minimize the attacker's payoff at all time points, we need to minimize the cost of the canonical flow with the maximum cost. To do this, for any edge e in any day graph G_t we define an LP variable $f_t(e)$ which specifies the amount of flow passing through e. Moreover for any time point t, we include the following constraints in our LP:

(1) For each vertex v of G_t (except for the source vertex S_t and the sink vertex S'_t) the amount of ingoing flow to v is equal to the amount of outgoing flow from v.
(2) The amount of outgoing flow from S_t is 1.
(3) The amount of ingoing flow to S'_t is 1.
(4) The amount of flow passing through any edge e is not negative.
(5) The cost of flow through any edge e and for any target a in G_t, specified by $w_{e,a} \times f_t(e)$ is not more than u.

And we set the objective function of our LP to minimize u, which is the overall cost of canonical flows. However, as we said earlier the canonical flows we find must be compatible;

$$\min \quad u \tag{3}$$

$$f_t^-(v) = f_t^+(v) \qquad \forall t, v : t \in [T], v \in V(G_t) - \{S_t, S_t'\} \tag{4}$$

$$f_t^+(S_t) = 1 \qquad \forall t : t \in [T] \tag{5}$$

$$f_t^-(S_t') = 1 \qquad \forall t : t \in [T] \tag{6}$$

$$f(e) \geq 0 \qquad \forall e, t : t \in [T], e \in G_t \tag{7}$$

$$\sum_{e \in E(G_t)} f(e).c_{e,a}.w_{t,a} \leq u \qquad \forall t, a : t \in [T], a \in [A_t] \tag{8}$$

$$\sum_{v \in V_t[k;i:j]} f_t^+(v) \leq \sum_{v' \in \text{feas}_t(V_t[k;i:j])} f_{t+1}^+(v') \quad \forall t, k, i, j : t \in [T], k \in [K], 1 \leq i \leq j \leq n_t \tag{9}$$

Linear Program 1. Variable $f_t(e)$, which is defined for any edge e in the day graph G_t where t could be any time point in $[T]$, denotes the amount of flow passing through e. By $f_t^-(v)$ we mean the total flow coming into vertex v (i.e., $f_t^-(v) = \Sigma f_t(e)$ where e is any edge ending at v). Also $f_t^+(v)$ denotes the total flow coming out of vertex v (i.e., $f_t^-(v) = \Sigma f_t(e)$ where e is any edge starting from v).

therefore apart from the aforementioned constraints, we define a compatibility constraint. Recall that $\text{feas}_t(\mathcal{I}_t[i:j])$ denotes a collection of intervals at time $t+1$ and contains an interval i', iff there is a valid move from an interval in $\mathcal{I}_t[i:j]$ to i'. We define a very similar concept for day graphs:

Definition 3.20. Let $V_t[x;i:j]$ denote the set of consecutive grid vertices $\{V_t[x,i], V_t[x,i+1], \ldots, V_t[x,j]\}$ in G_t. Recall that by definition of $\mathcal{I}_t[i:j]$, any vertices in $V_t[x;i:j]$ is equivalent to an interval in $\mathcal{I}_t[i:j]$. We define $\text{feas}_t(V_t[x;i:j])$ as follows: $\text{feas}_t(V_t[x;i:j])$ is a subset of grid vertices of G_{t+1} containing a vertex $V_{t+1}[x,i']$ if and only if $V_{t+1}[x,i']$ is equivalent to an interval in $\text{feas}_t(\mathcal{I}_t[i:j])$.

The compatibility constraint we use in our LP is as follows: for any set of consecutive vertices $V_t[x;i:j]$, the amount of flow passing through the vertices in $V_t[x;i:j]$ is not more than the amount of flow passing through the vertices in $\text{feas}_t(V_t[x;i:j])$. Intuitively, this constraint indicates that for any set of consecutive intervals $\mathcal{I}_t[i:j]$, the probability that there exists a patrol in it, should not be more than the probability of having a patrol in its feasible set ($\text{feas}_t(\mathcal{I}_t[i:j])$) in the next time point. Note that by definition, $\text{feas}_t(\mathcal{I}_t[i:j])$ contains all of the valid intervals that a patrol in $\mathcal{I}_t[i:j]$ can move to; therefore it is obvious why this constraint is necessary. The sufficiency of this constraint to prove compatibility of snapshots, however, comes later when we explain how we construct an optimal strategy based on the adjusted LP solution. The formal definition of the LP is given in Linear Program 1.

By the end of Section 3.3, we prove the solution of LP 1 is equal to the utility of the attacker if both players play their optimal strategies. Lemma 3.21 proves a weaker claim:

LEMMA 3.21. *The solution of Linear Program 1 gives a lower bound for the utility of the attacker when both players play their optimal strategies.*

To prove Lemma 3.21, we start from an optimal strategy of the defender satisfying the condition of Lemma 3.19 that the interval paths do not cross each other. Based on this strategy, we construct a feasible solution for LP 1 in which the value of u is equal to the maximum possible utility of the attacker. Note that this only proves LP 1 gives a lower bound

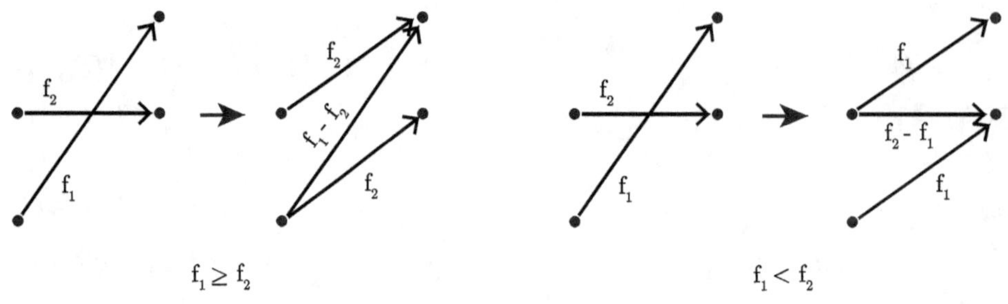

Fig. 5. The whole idea of how to locally resolve the issue of having a crossing flow. The details are formally explained in the text.

for the utility of the attacker when both players play their minimax strategies since the feasible solution we considered is not necessarily the optimum solution of the LP (although as we said before, we will later prove that they are exactly the same).

3.3.2 Adjusting The LP Solution. In this section we give an algorithm that adjusts any optimal solution of LP 1 to resolve their "crossing flows". We later use the adjusted solution to construct the defender's optimal strategy.

We start by defining what we mean by *crossing edges* and *crossing flows*:

Definition 3.22 (crossing edges and crossing flow). Let $e = (V_t[x, y_1], V_t[x+1, y_2])$ and $e' = (V_t[x, y'_1], V_t[x+1, y'_2])$ be two arbitrary edges of day graph G_t where $y_1 < y'_1$. We say e and e' cross, if and only if $y_2 > y'_2$. Moreover, if f is a canonical flow of G_t, the crossing edge pair (e, e') is a crossing flow in f, if $f(e) > 0$ and $f(e') > 0$.

In the following definition, we give a total ordering on the crossing flows in a canonical flow, which we later use in the algorithm we provide to resolve them.

Definition 3.23 (crossing flows' ordering). Let (e_1, e_2) and (e_3, e_4) be two crossing flows of a canonical flow. Also let $e_1 = (V_t[x, y_1], V_t[x+1, y'_1])$, $e_2 = (V_t[x, y_2], V_t[x+1, y'_2])$, $e_3 = (V_t[x', y_3], V_t[x'+1, y'_3])$, and $e_4 = (V_t[x', y_4], V_t[x'+1, y'_4])$ be the vertices of these edges. We say $(e_1, e_2) < (e_3, e_4)$ if and only if one of the following conditions hold:

(1) $x < x'$
(2) $x = x'$ and $y_1 < y_3$.
(3) $x = x'$ and $y_1 = y_3$ and $y'_1 < y'_3$.
(4) $x = x'$ and $y_1 = y_3$ and $y'_1 = y'_3$ and $y'_2 < y'_4$.
(5) $x = x'$ and $y_1 = y_3$ and $y'_1 = y'_3$ and $y'_2 = y'_4$ and $y_2 < y_4$.

Algorithm 2 is the formal pseudo-code of how we resolve all crossing flows. At each step, the algorithm resolves the minimum crossing flow (minimum based on the total ordering defined in Definition 3.23) and continues this process until there is no other one. Figure 5 illustrates how a single crossing flow is resolved.

LEMMA 3.24. *Function* RESOLVECROSSES *of Algorithm 2 does not increase the total cost of the input canonical flow.*

To prove Lemma 3.24, we consider all different locations of targets for which changing the flows might affect the utility of players and prove in none of these cases the total cost is increased. The complete proof is left to the appendix.

Algorithm 2 Resolves crossing flows

```
function ResolveCrosses(f_1, G_1, f_2, G_2, ..., f_T, G_t)
    for each timepoint t ∈ [T] do
        while f_t contains any crossing flow do
            {(V_t[x, y_1], V_t[x+1, y_2]), (V_t[x, y'_1], V_t[x+1, y'_2])} = FindNextCross(G_t, f_t)
            e ← (V_t[x, y_1], V_t[x+1, y_2])
            e' ← (V_t[x, y'_1], V_t[x+1, y'_2])
            ResolveCross(e, e')
function FindNextCross(G_t, f_t)
    (e, e') ← find the minimum crossing flow in f_t
    return (e, e')
function ResolveCross(e, e')
    f_m ← min(f_t(e), f_t(e'))
    f_t(e') ← f_t(e') − f_m
    f_t(e) ← f_t(e) − f_m
    (V_t[x, y_1], V_t[x+1, y_2]) ← e
    (V_t[x, y'_1], V_t[x+1, y'_2]) ← e'
    f_t((V_t[x, y_1], V_t[x+1, y'_2])) ← f_m
    f_t((V_t[x, y'_1], V_t[x+1, y_2])) ← f_m
```

LEMMA 3.25. *The running time of the function* RESOLVECROSSES *in the Algorithm 2 is polynomial.*

The proof scheme of Lemma 3.25 is to show the minimum crossing flow at step i is strictly less than the minimum crossing flow at step $i+1$ (after the previously minimum crossing flow is resolved). Consequently, since the total number of possible crossing edges of a day graph is polynomial, the number of steps until the algorithm halts is polynomial. Again, we left the formal proof of this lemma to the appendix for space limitations.

Note that another property of Algorithm 2 is that the flow passing through a vertex will not change and it is only the amount of flow passing through the edges that changes (Figure 5). This proves most of the constraints of LP 1 will still hold. The only two constraints that consider the flow passing through the edges, and not the vertices, are number 7 and number 8. The former will be true since the process does not produce any negative flow and the latter is true since by Lemma 3.24 the total cost does not change.

Consequently, the following statement is true since we can first solve LP 1 by any polynomial time LP-solver and the run Algorithm 2 on its solution.

COROLLARY 3.26. *There exists a polynomial time algorithm that finds $f\langle f_1, \ldots, f_T\rangle$, a collection of canonical flows, that is a solution of LP 1, and for any $t \in [T]$, f_t does not contain any crossing flow.*

3.3.3 Constructing A Strategy. Assuming f is a non-crossing solution of LP 1, this section gives an algorithm to find a mixed strategy of the defender that equivalent to the set of canonical flows in f and finally proves Theorem 3.1. We first define what we mean by the top most flow path of a non-crossing canonical flow:

Definition 3.27 (Top-Most Flow Path). Let f_t be a canonical flow of G_t without any crossing flows. We say a canonical path $p = \langle e_1, e_2, \ldots, e_{K+1}\rangle$ of G_t is a flow path of f_t if for any k ($1 \leq k \leq K+1$), $f_t(e_k) > 0$. The top-most flow path of f_t is the flow path of f_t that is above all other flow paths of f_t (that is well-defined because f_t does not have any crossing flow). The size of the flow path p of f_t, denoted by $|p|$, is m if for any k, $f_t(e_k) \geq m$ and there exists an edge e_i of p such that $f_t(e_i) = m$.

LEMMA 3.28. *Let $f = \langle f_1, \dots, f_T \rangle$ be a collection of non-crossing canonical flows that satisfies the compatibility constraint (constraint number 9) of LP 1. For any t that $\{t, t+1\} \subset [T]$, the top-most flow paths of f_t and f_{t+1} are compatible.*

Proof. Let $\langle S_t, V_t[1, y_1], \dots, V_t[K, y_K], S'_t \rangle$ and $\langle S_{t+1}, V_{t+1}[1, y'_1], \dots, V_{t+1}[K, y'_K], S'_{t+1} \rangle$ respectively denote the top-most flow paths of f_t and f_{t+1}. It suffices to prove for any $k \in [K]$, there is a valid movement from the corresponding interval of $V_t[k, y_k]$ to the corresponding interval of $V_{t+1}[k, y'_k]$. To do so, we assume this is not the case and obtain a contradiction. Let $V_{t+1}[k, y'_k] \notin \text{feas}_t(V_t[k, y_k])$ for some $k \in [K]$, then one of the following conditions should hold:

(1) $V_{t+1}[k, y'_k]$ is below the feasible range $\text{feas}_t(V_t[k, y_k])$.
(2) $V_{t+1}[k, y'_k]$ is above the feasible range $\text{feas}_t(V_t[k, y_k])$.

If the first condition is true, the contradiction is that $V_{t+1}[k, y'_k]$ cannot be in the top-most flow path of f_{t+1}. To see this, note that we know by constraint 9 of LP 1 that the total flow passing through the vertices of $\text{feas}_t(V_t[k, y_k])$ is not less than the flow passing through $V_t[k, y_k]$, therefore there is a vertex in $\text{feas}_t(V_t[k, y_k])$ (and above $V_{t+1}[k, y'_k]$) with a non-negative flow and thus $V_{t+1}[k, y'_k]$ cannot be in the top-most flow path of f_{t+1}.

If the second condition is true, the contradiction is that constraint 9 cannot be satisfied. To see this, note that since $V_t[k, y_k]$ is in the top-most flow path of f_t, no flow passes through the vertices above it and therefore $\sum_{v \in V_t[k;1:y]} f_t^+(v) = 1$. However, since $V_{t+1}[k, y'_k]$ is above the feasible range $\text{feas}_t(V_t[k, y_k])$, $\sum_{v' \in \text{feas}_t(V_t[k;1:y])} f_{t+1}^+(v') < 1$ which means constraint 9 that indicates the value of the latter summation should not be less than the former one, cannot be satisfied. □

THEOREM 3.29. *Let $f = \langle f_1, \dots, f_T \rangle$ be a solution of LP 1 without any crossing flows. There exists a polynomial time algorithm to find a mixed strategy of the defender that is equivalent to f.*

To prove Theorem 3.29, we show the following iterative algorithm constructs the desired mixed strategy in polynomial time:

(1) Find the top-most flow paths $p_1, \dots, p_T$ of $f_1, \dots, f_T$.
(2) Construct the pure strategy p, corresponding to $p_1, \dots, p_T$.
(3) Add p to s with probability $q = \min |p_i|$.
(4) For any edge e of any p_i, decrease $f_i(e)$ to $f_i(e) - q$.
(5) If there is any flow left in $f_1, \dots, f_T$, repeat all the steps.

Note that by Lemma 3.28, if the compatibility constraint of LP 1 is satisfied, the top-most flow paths are compatible. Since at the first round of the algorithm, we have an actual solution of the LP, the compatibility constraint is obviously satisfied. To completely prove the correctness of this algorithm, we also need to show after each iteration, changing the flows does not violate the compatibility constraint. For space limitations, we left this part of the proof to the appendix. Furthermore, the running time of this algorithm is polynomial in the input size since in each iteration, the flow passing through at least one edge decreases to zero and the total number of edges is polynomial.

We can now prove the main theorem of Section 3.

THEOREM (3.1). *There is a polynomial time (in input size) algorithm to solve $\mathcal{DSG}$.*

Proof. Recall that by Lemma 3.21, the optimal solution of LP 1 is a lower bound for the utility of the attacker when both players play their optimal (minimax) strategies. Also note that by Lemma 3.26 and Theorem 3.29, we can construct a mixed strategy s of the defender that is equivalent to the optimal solution of LP 1 in polynomial time. This means the maximum utility of the attacker when the defender plays s, is equal to its lower bound and therefore s minimizes the maximum expected utility of the attacker: i.e., it is a minimax strategy of the defender. □

4 CONTINUOUS MODEL

In this section we prove the following theorem for the continuous model:

THEOREM 4.1. *There exists a polynomial time algorithm to find an optimal solution for $\mathcal{CSG}$.*

The given proof is based on a technical assumption that all numbers in the input are rational.

Proof of Theorem 4.1: The main idea of this proof is to reduce any instance of $\mathcal{CSG}$ to an instance of $\mathcal{DSG}$, for which we know there exists a polynomial time algorithm.

Recall that any rational number can be represented by a fraction $\frac{a}{b}$ such that both a and b are integers. Let B be the set of denominators in this fractional representation of all numbers in the input. We define m to be the product of all numbers in B. Note that the number of digits needed to represent m is polynomial in the input size since every number in B appears in the input. To create an instance of $\mathcal{DSG}$, we multiply all target positions, Δ, R and M, given in the instance of $\mathcal{CSG}$ to m.

To use the algorithm for $\mathcal{DSG}$, it suffices to prove in the scaled solutions, there exists an optimal solution that places patrols only in the integer locations. To do this, we prove that for any given patrol path $p_1 = \langle m_i \rangle_T$ in the scaled version, there exists a patrol path $p_2 = \langle m'_i \rangle_T$ that covers the same set of targets and for any $t \in [T]$, m'_t is an integer position. It suffices to set m'_t to be $\lfloor m_t \rfloor$. Note that since the position of all targets and the protecting ranges of the patrols in the scaled version are all integers, this patrol path protects exactly the same set of targets. Now we can use the algorithm of Theorem 3.1 to find the optimal solution of this scaled input and then scale it back to the original size by dividing the patrols' locations by m. □

REFERENCES

[1] AmirMahdi Ahmadinejad, Sina Dehghani, MohammadTaghi Hajiaghayi, Brendan Lucier, Hamid Mahini, and Saeed Seddighin. 2016. From duels to battefields: Computing equilibria of blotto and other games. In *Proceedings of the Thirtieth AAAI Conference on Artificial Intelligence.*

[2] Maria-Florina Balcan, Avrim Blum, Nika Haghtalab, and Ariel D. Procaccia. 2015. Commitment Without Regrets: Online Learning in Stackelberg Security Games. In *Proceedings of the Sixteenth ACM Conference on Economics and Computation, EC.* 61–78.

[3] Soheil Behnezhad, Sina Dehghani, Mahsa Derakhshan, MohammadTaghi HajiAghayi, and Saeed Seddighin. 2017. Faster and Simpler Algorithm for Optimal Strategies of Blotto Game. In *Proceedings of the Thirty-First AAAI Conference on Artificial Intelligence.*

[4] Avrim Blum, Nika Haghtalab, and Ariel D. Procaccia. 2014. Learning Optimal Commitment to Overcome Insecurity. In *Annual Conference on Neural Information Processing Systems (NIPS).* 1826–1834.

[5] Branislav Bošanský, Viliam Lisý, Michal Jakob, and Michal Pěchouček. 2011. Computing time-dependent policies for patrolling games with mobile targets. In *The 10th International Conference on Autonomous Agents and Multiagent Systems-Volume 3*. International Foundation for Autonomous Agents and Multiagent Systems, 989–996.

[6] Matthew Brown, Arunesh Sinha, Aaron Schlenker, and Milind Tambe. 2016. One Size Does Not Fit All: A Game-Theoretic Approach for Dynamically and Effectively Screening for Threats. In *Proceedings of the Thirtieth AAAI Conference on Artificial Intelligence*. 425–431.

[7] Vincent Conitzer and Tuomas Sandholm. 2006. Computing the optimal strategy to commit to. In *Proceedings 7th ACM Conference on Electronic Commerce (EC-2006)*. 82–90.

[8] Fei Fang, Albert Xin Jiang, and Milind Tambe. 2013. Optimal patrol strategy for protecting moving targets with multiple mobile resources. In *Proceedings of the 2013 international conference on Autonomous agents and multi-agent systems*. International Foundation for Autonomous Agents and Multiagent Systems, 957–964.

[9] Fei Fang, Thanh Hong Nguyen, Rob Pickles, Wai Y. Lam, Gopalasamy R. Clements, Bo An, Amandeep Singh, Milind Tambe, and Andrew Lemieux. 2016. Deploying PAWS: Field Optimization of the Protection Assistant for Wildlife Security. In *Proceedings of the Thirtieth AAAI Conference on Artificial Intelligence*. 3966–3973.

[10] Christopher Kiekintveld, Manish Jain, Jason Tsai, James Pita, Fernando Ordóñez, and Milind Tambe. 2009. Computing optimal randomized resource allocations for massive security games. In *Proceedings of The 8th International Conference on Autonomous Agents and Multiagent Systems-Volume 1*. International Foundation for Autonomous Agents and Multiagent Systems, 689–696.

[11] Dmytro Korzhyk, Vincent Conitzer, and Ronald Parr. 2010. Complexity of Computing Optimal Stackelberg Strategies in Security Resource Allocation Games.. In *AAAI*.

[12] Joshua Letchford and Vincent Conitzer. 2013. Solving Security Games on Graphs via Marginal Probabilities. In *Proceedings of the Twenty-Seventh AAAI Conference on Artificial Intelligence*.

[13] Joshua Letchford, Vincent Conitzer, and Kamesh Munagala. 2009. Learning and Approximating the Optimal Strategy to Commit To. In *Algorithmic Game Theory, Second International Symposium, SAGT*. 250–262.

[14] Janusz Marecki, Gerald Tesauro, and Richard Segal. 2012. Playing repeated Stackelberg games with unknown opponents. In *International Conference on Autonomous Agents and Multiagent Systems, AAMAS*. 821–828.

[15] Giuseppe De Nittis and Francesco Trovò. 2016. Machine Learning Techniques for Stackelberg Security Games: a Survey. *Technical report on* `arxiv.org` abs/1609.09341 (2016).

[16] James Pita, Manish Jain, Janusz Marecki, Fernando Ordóñez, Christopher Portway, Milind Tambe, Craig Western, Praveen Paruchuri, and Sarit Kraus. 2008. Deployed ARMOR protection: the application of a game theoretic model for security at the Los Angeles International Airport. In *Proceedings of the 7th international joint conference on Autonomous agents and multiagent systems: industrial track*. International Foundation for Autonomous Agents and Multiagent Systems, 125–132.

[17] Tim Roughgarden. 2010. Computing Equilibria: A Computational Complexity Perspective. *Economic Theory* 42, 1 (2010), 193–236.

[18] Milind Tambe. 2011. *Security and game theory: algorithms, deployed systems, lessons learned*. Cambridge University Press.

[19] Haifeng Xu. 2016. The Mysteries of Security Games: Equilibrium Computation Becomes Combinatorial Algorithm Design. In *Proceedings of the 2016 ACM Conference on Economics and Computation, EC*. 497–514.

[20] Haifeng Xu, Fei Fang, Albert Xin Jiang, Vincent Conitzer, Shaddin Dughmi, and Milind Tambe. 2014. Solving Zero-Sum Security Games in Discretized Spatio-Temporal Domains.. In *AAAI*. Citeseer, 1500–1506.

[21] Zhengyu Yin, Albert Xin Jiang, Milind Tambe, Christopher Kiekintveld, Kevin Leyton-Brown, Tuomas Sandholm, and John P Sullivan. 2012. TRUSTS: Scheduling randomized patrols for fare inspection in transit systems using game theory. *AI Magazine* 33, 4 (2012), 59.

Author Index

NOTES

www.ingramcontent.com/pod-product-compliance
Lightning Source LLC
LaVergne TN
LVHW080109011026
849160LV00013B/1058
* 9 7 8 1 4 5 0 3 5 5 9 9 5 *